R.A.F. LYNEHAM
OFFICERS MESS LIBRARY

GERALD DURRELL

GERALD DURRELL

MY FAMILY AND OTHER ANIMALS

THE BAFUT BEAGLES

THE DRUNKEN FOREST

ENCOUNTERS WITH ANIMALS

A ZOO IN MY LUGGAGE

THE WHISPERING LAND

MENAGERIE MANOR

Heinemann/Octopus

My Family and Other Animals first published in Great Britain in 1956 by Rupert Hart-Davis Ltd
The Bafut Beagles first published in Great Britain in 1954 by Rupert Hart-Davis Ltd
The Drunken Forest first published in Great Britain in 1956 by Rupert Hart-Davis Ltd
Encounters with Animals first published in Great Britain in 1958 by Rupert Hart-Davis Ltd
The Whispering Land first published in Great Britain in 1961 by Rupert Hart-Davis Ltd
Menagerie Manor first published in Great Britain in 1964 by Rupert Hart-Davis Ltd
A Zoo in My Luggage first published in Great Britain in 1960 by Rupert Hart-Davis Ltd

This edition first published in Great Britain in 1981 jointly by

William Heinemann Limited
10 Upper Grosvenor Street
London W1

Martin Secker & Warburg Limited
54 Poland Street
London W1

and

Octopus Books Limited
59 Grosvenor Street
London W1

ISBN 0 905712 56 0

My Family and Other Animals © 1956 by Gerald Durrell
The Bafut Beagles © 1954 by Gerald Durrell
The Drunken Forest © Gerald Durrell 1956
Encounters with Animals © Gerald Durrell 1958
The Whispering Land © Gerald Durrell 1961
Menagerie Manor © Gerald Durrell 1964
A Zoo in My Luggage © Gerald Durrell 1960

Printed in the United States of America

CONTENTS

MY FAMILY AND OTHER ANIMALS
9

THE BAFUT BEAGLES
189

THE DRUNKEN FOREST
307

ENCOUNTERS WITH ANIMALS
429

A ZOO IN MY LUGGAGE
517

THE WHISPERING LAND
615

MENAGERIE MANOR
731

My Family and Other Animals

GERALD DURRELL

My Family and Other Animals

TO MY MOTHER

It is a melancholy of mine own, compound of many simples, extracted from many objects, and indeed the sundry contemplation of my travels, which, by often rumination, wraps me in a most humorous sadness.
As You Like It

The Speech for the Defence

'Why, sometimes I've believed as many as six impossible things before breakfast.'

The White Queen - *Alice Through the Looking-glass.*

This is the story of a five-year sojourn that I and my family made on the Greek island of Corfu. It was originally intended to be a mildly nostalgic account of the natural history of the island, but I made a grave mistake by introducing my family into the book in the first few pages. Having got themselves on paper, they then proceeded to establish themselves and invite various friends to share the chapters. It was only with the greatest difficulty, and by exercising considerable cunning, that I managed to retain a few pages here and there which I could devote exclusively to animals.

I have attempted to draw an accurate and unexaggerated picture of my family in the following pages; they appear as I saw them. To explain some of their more curious ways, however, I feel that I should state that the time we were in Corfu the family were all quite young: Larry, the eldest, was twenty-three; Leslie was nineteen; Margo eighteen; while I was the youngest, being of the tender and impressionable age of ten. We have never been very certain of my mother's age, for the simple reason that she can never remember her date of birth; all I can say is that she was old enough to have four children. My mother also insists that I explain that she is a widow, for, as she so penetratingly observed, you never know what people might think.

In order to compress five years of incident, observation and pleasant living into something a little less lengthy than the *Encyclopaedia Britannica,* I have been forced to telescope, prune and graft, so that there is little left of the original continuity of events. Also I have been forced to leave out many happenings and characters that I would have liked to describe.

It is doubtful if this would have been written without the help and enthusiasm of the following people. I mention this so that blame can be laid in the right quarter.

My grateful thanks, then, to:

Dr. Theodore Stephanides. With typical generosity, he allowed me to make use of material from his unpublished work on Corfu, and supplied me with a number of dreadful puns, some of which I have used.

My family. They, after all, unconsciously provided a lot of the material, and helped me considerably during the writing of the book by arguing ferociously and rarely agreeing about any incident on which I consulted them.

My wife, who pleased me by laughing uproariously when reading the manuscript, only to inform me that it was my spelling that amused her.

Sophie, my secretary, who was responsible for the introduction of commas and the ruthless eradication of the split infinitive.

I should like to pay a special tribute to my mother, to whom this book is dedicated. Like a gentle, enthusiastic and understanding Noah, she has steered her vessel full of strange progeny through the stormy seas of life with great skill, always faced with the possibility of mutiny, always surrounded by the dangerous shoals of overdraft and extravagance, never being sure that her navigation would be approved by the crew, but certain that she would be blamed for anything that went wrong. That she survived the voyage is a miracle, but survive it she did, and, moreover, with her reason more or less intact. As my brother Larry rightly points out, we can be proud of the way we have brought her up; she is a credit to us. That she has reached that happy Nirvana where nothing shocks or startles is exemplified by the fact that one week-end recently, when all alone in the house, she was treated to the sudden arrival of a series of crates containing two pelicans, a scarlet ibis, a vulture and eight monkeys. A lesser mortal might have quailed at such a contingency, but not Mother. On Monday morning I found her in the garage being pursued round and round by an irate pelican which she was trying to feed with sardines from a tin.

'I'm glad you've come, dear,' she panted; 'this pelican is a *little* difficult to handle.'

When I asked her how she *knew* the animals belonged to me, she replied: 'Well, of course I knew they were yours, dear; who else would send pelicans to me?'

Which goes to show how well she knows at least one of her family.

Lastly, I would like to make a point of stressing that all the anecdotes about the island and the islanders are absolutely true. Living in Corfu was rather like living in one of the more flamboyant and slapstick comic operas. The whole atmosphere and charm of the place was, I think, summed up neatly on an Admiralty map we had, which showed the island and the adjacent coastline in great detail. At the bottom was a little inset which read:

CAUTION: As the buoys marking the shoals are often out of position, mariners are cautioned to be on their guard when navigating these shores.

There is a pleasure sure
In being mad, which none but madmen know.
DRYDEN. *The Spanish Friar, II, i.*

The Migration

July had been blown out like a candle by a biting wind that ushered in a leaden August sky. A sharp, stinging drizzle fell, billowing into opaque grey sheets when the wind caught it. Along the Bournemouth sea-front the beach-huts turned blank wooden faces towards a greeny-grey, froth-chained sea that leapt eagerly at the cement bulwark of the shore. The gulls had been tumbled inland over the town, and they now drifted above the house-tops on taut wings, whining peevishly. It was the sort of weather calculated to try anyone's endurance.

Considered as a group my family was not a very prepossessing sight that afternoon, for the weather had brought with it the usual selection of ills to which we were prone. For me, lying on the floor, labelling my collection of shells, it had brought catarrh, pouring it into my skull like cement, so that I was forced to breath stertorously through open mouth. For my brother Leslie, hunched dark and glowering by the fire, it had inflamed the convolutions of his ears so that they bled delicately but persistently. To my sister Margo it had delivered a fresh dappling of acne spots to a face that was already blotched like a red veil. For my mother there was a rich, bubbling cold, and a twinge of rheumatism to season it. Only my eldest brother, Larry, was untouched, but it was sufficient that he was irritated by our failings.

It was Larry, of course, who started it. The rest of us felt too apathetic to think of anything except our own ills, but Larry was designed by Providence to go through life like a small, blond firework, exploding ideas in other people's minds, and then curling up with cat-like unctuousness and refusing to take any blame for the consequences. He had become increasingly irritable as the afternoon wore on. At length, glancing moodily round the room, he decided to attack Mother, as being the obvious cause of the trouble.

'Why do we stand this bloody climate?' he asked suddenly, making a gesture towards the rain-distorted window. 'Look at it! And, if it comes to that, look at us . . . Margo swollen up like a plate of scarlet porridge . . . Leslie wandering around with fourteen fathoms of cotton wool in each ear . . . Gerry sounds as though he's had a cleft palate from birth . . . And look at you: you're looking more decrepit and hagridden every day.'

Mother peered over the top of a large volume entitled *Easy Recipes from Rajputana*.

'Indeed I'm not,' she said indignantly.

'You *are*,' Larry insisted; 'you're beginning to look like an Irish washerwoman . . . and your family looks like a series of illustrations from a medical encyclopaedia.'

Mother could think of no really crushing reply to this, so she contented herself with a glare before retreating once more behind her book.

'What we need is sunshine,' Larry continued; 'don't you agree, Les? . . . Les . . . *Les!*'

Leslie unravelled a large quantity of cotton-wool from one ear.

'What d'you say?' he asked.

'There you are!' said Larry, turning triumphantly to Mother, 'it's become a major operation to hold a conversation with him. I ask you, what a position to be in! One brother can't hear what you say, and the other one can't be understood. Really, it's time something was done. I can't be expected to produce deathless prose in an atmosphere of gloom and eucalyptus.'

'Yes, dear,' said Mother vaguely.

'What we all need,' said Larry, getting into his stride again, 'is sunshine . . . a country where we can *grow*.'

'Yes, dear, that would be nice,' agreed Mother, not really listening.

'I had a letter from George this morning – he says Corfu's wonderful. Why don't we pack up and go to Greece?'

'Very well, dear, if you like,' said Mother unguardedly.

Where Larry was concerned she was generally very careful not to commit herself.

'When?' asked Larry, rather surprised at this co-operation.

Mother, perceiving that she had made a tactical error, cautiously lowered *Easy Recipes from Rajputana*.

'Well, I think it would be a sensible idea if you were to go on ahead, dear, and arrange things. Then you can write and tell me if it's nice, and we all can follow,' she said cleverly.

Larry gave her a withering look.

'You said *that* when I suggested going to Spain.' he reminded her, 'and I sat for two interminable months in Seville, waiting for you to come out, while you did nothing except write me massive letters about drains and drinking-water, as though I was the Town Clerk or something. No, if we're going to Greece, let's all go together.'

'You do *exaggerate*, Larry,' said Mother plaintively; 'anyway, I can't go just like that. I have to arrange something about this house.'

'Arrange? Arrange what, for heaven's sake? Sell it.'

'I can't do that, dear,' said Mother, shocked.

'Why not?'

'But I've only just bought it.'

'Sell it while it's still untarnished, then.'
'Don't be ridiculous, dear,' said Mother firmly; 'that's quite out of the question. It would be madness.'
So we sold the house and fled from the gloom of the English summer, like a flock of migrating swallows.

We all travelled light, taking with us only what we considered to be the bare essentials of life. When we opened our luggage for Customs inspection, the contents of our bags were a fair indication of character and interests. Thus Margo's luggage contained a multitude of diaphanous garments, three books on slimming and a regiment of small bottles each containing some elixir guaranteed to cure acne. Leslie's case held a couple of roll-top pullovers and a pair of trousers which were wrapped round two revolvers, an air-pistol, a book called *Be Your Own Gunsmith* and a large bottle of oil that leaked. Larry was accompanied by two trunks of books and a brief-case containing his clothes. Mother's luggage was sensibly divided between clothes and various volumes on cooking and gardening. I travelled with only those items that I thought necessary to relieve the tedium of a long journey: four books on natural history, a butterfly net, a dog and a jam-jar full of caterpillars all in imminent danger of turning into chrysalids. Thus, by our standards fully equipped, we left the clammy shores of England.

France rain-washed and sorrowful, Switzerland like a Christmas cake, Italy exuberant, noisy and smelly, were passed, leaving only confused memories. The tiny ship throbbed away from the heel of Italy out into the twilit sea, and as we slept in our stuffy cabins, somewhere in that tract of moon-polished water we passed the invisible dividing-line and entered the bright, looking-glass world of Greece. Slowly this sense of change seeped down to us, and so, at dawn, we awoke restless and went on deck.

The sea lifted smooth blue muscles of wave as it stirred in the dawnlight, and the foam of our wake spread gently behind us like a white peacock's tail, glinting with bubbles. The sky was pale and stained with yellow on the eastern horizon. Ahead lay a chocolate-brown smudge of land, huddled in mist, with a frill of foam at its base. This was Corfu, and we strained our eyes to make out the exact shapes of the mountains, to discover valleys, peaks, ravines and beaches, but it remained a silhouette. Then suddenly the sun lifted over the horizon, and the sky turned the smooth enamelled blue of a jay's eye. The endless, meticulous curves of the sea flamed for an instant and then changed to a deep royal purple flecked with green. The mist lifted in quick, lithe ribbons, and before us lay the island, the mountains as though sleeping beneath a crumpled blanket of brown, the folds stained with the green of olive-groves. Along the shore curved beaches as white as tusks among tottering cities of brilliant gold, red and white rocks. We rounded the northern cape, a smooth shoulder of rust-red cliff carved into a series of giant caves. The dark waves lifted our wake and carried it gently towards them, and then, at their very mouths, it crumpled and hissed thirstily among the rocks. Rounding the cape, we left the mountains, and the island sloped gently down, blurred with the silver and green iridescence of olives, with here and there an admonishing finger of black cypress against the sky. The shallow sea in the bays was butterfly blue, and even above the sound of the ship's engines we could hear, faintly ringing from the shore like a chorus of tiny voices, the shrill, triumphant cries of the cicadas.

Chapter One

The Unsuspected Isle

We threaded our way out of the noise and confusion of the Customs shed into the brilliant sunshine on the quay. Around us the town rose steeply, tiers of multi-coloured houses piled haphazardly, green shutters folded back from their windows, like the wings of a thousand moths. Behind us lay the bay, smooth as a plate, smouldering with that unbelievable blue.

Larry walked swiftly, with head thrown back and an expression of such regal disdain on his face that one did not notice his diminutive size, keeping a wary eye on the porters who struggled with his trunks. Behind him strolled Leslie, short, stocky, with an air of quiet belligerence, and then Margo, trailing yards of muslin and scent. Mother, looking like a tiny, harassed missionary in an uprising, was dragged unwillingly to the nearest lamp-post by an exuberant Roger, and was forced to stand there, staring into space, while he relieved the pent-up feelings that had accumulated in his kennel. Larry chose two magnificently dilapidated horse-drawn cabs, had the luggage installed in one and seated himself in the second. Then he looked round irritably.

'Well?' he asked. 'What are we waiting for?'

'We're waiting for Mother,' explained Leslie. 'Roger's found a lamp-post.'

'Dear God!' said Larry, and then hoisted himself upright in the cab and bellowed, 'Come *on,* Mother, come on. Can't the dog wait?'

'Coming, dear,' called Mother passively and untruthfully, for Roger showed no signs of quitting the post.

'That dog's been a damned nuisance all the way,' said Larry.

'Don't be so impatient,' said Margo indignantly; 'the dog can't help it ... and anyway, we had to wait an hour in Naples for *you.*'

'My stomach was out of order,' explained Larry coldly.

'Well, probably *his* stomach's out of order,' said Margo triumphantly. 'It's six of one and a dozen of the other.'

'You mean half a dozen of the other.'

'Whatever I mean, it's the same thing.'

At this moment Mother arrived, slightly dishevelled, and we had to turn

My Family and Other Animals

our attentions to the task of getting Roger into the cab. He had never been in such a vehicle, and treated it with suspicion. Eventually we had to lift him bodily and hurl him inside, yelping frantically, and then pile in breathlessly after him and hold him down. The horse, frightened by this activity, broke into a shambling trot, and we ended in a tangled heap on the floor of the cab with Roger moaning loudly underneath us.

'What an entry,' said Larry bitterly. 'I had hoped to give an impression of gracious majesty, and this is what happens ... we arrive in town like a troupe of mediaeval tumblers.'

'Don't keep *on*, dear,' Mother said soothingly, straightening her hat; 'we'll soon be at the hotel.'

So our cab clopped and jingled its way into the town, while we sat on the horsehair seats and tried to muster the appearance of gracious majesty Larry required. Roger, wrapped in Leslie's powerful grasp, lolled his head over the side of the vehicle and rolled his eyes as though at his last gasp. Then we rattled past an alley-way in which four scruffy mongrels were lying in the sun. Roger stiffened, glared at them and let forth a torrent of deep barks. The mongrels were immediately galvanized into activity, and they sped after the cab, yapping vociferously. Our pose was irretrievably shattered, for it took two people to restrain the raving Roger, while the rest of us leaned out of the cab and made wild gestures with magazines and books at the pursuing horde. This only had the effect of exciting them still further, and at each alley-way we passed their numbers increased, until by the time we were rolling down the main thoroughfare of the town there were some twenty-four dogs swirling about our wheels, almost hysterical with anger.

'Why doesn't somebody *do* something?' asked Larry, raising his voice above the uproar. 'This is like a scene from *Uncle Tom's Cabin*.'

'Why don't *you* do something; instead of criticizing?' snapped Leslie, who was locked in combat with Roger.

Larry promptly rose to his feet, snatched the whip from our astonished driver's hand, made a wild swipe at the herd of dogs, missed them and caught Leslie across the back of the neck.

'What the hell d'you think you're playing at?' Leslie snarled, twisting a scarlet and angry face towards Larry.

'Accident,' explained Larry airily. 'I'm out of practice ... it's so long since I used a horse-whip.'

'Well, watch what you're bloody well doing,' said Leslie loudly and belligerently.

'Now, now, dear, it was an accident,' said Mother.

Larry took another swipe at the dogs and knocked off Mother's hat.

'You're more trouble than the dogs,' said Margo.

'Do be careful, dear,' said Mother, clutching her hat; 'you might hurt someone. I should put the whip down.'

At that moment the cab shambled to a halt outside a doorway over which hung a board with Pension Suisse inscribed on it. The dogs, feeling that they were at last going to get to grips with this effeminate black canine who rode in cabs, surrounded us in a solid, panting wedge. The door of the hotel opened and an ancient bewhiskered porter appeared and stood staring glassily at the turmoil in the street. The difficulties of getting Roger out of the cab and into the hotel were considerable, for he was a heavy dog and it took the combined efforts of the family to lift, carry and restrain him. Larry had by now forgotten his majestic pose and was rather enjoying himself. He leapt down and danced about the pavement with the whip, cleaving a path through the dogs, along which Leslie, Margo, Mother and I hurried, bearing the struggling, snarling Roger. We staggered into the hall, and the porter slammed the front door and leant against it, his moustache quivering. The manager came forward, eyeing us with a mixture of apprehension and curiosity. Mother faced him, hat on one side of her head, clutching in one hand my jam-jar of caterpillars.

'Ah!' she said, smiling sweetly, as though our arrival had been the most normal thing in the world. 'Our name's Durrell. I believe you've got some rooms booked for us?'

'Yes, madame,' said the manager, edging round the still grumbling Roger; 'they are on the first floor ... four rooms and a balcony.'

'How nice,' beamed Mother; 'then I think we'll go straight up and have a little rest before lunch.'

And with considerable majestic graciousness she led her family upstairs.

Later we descended to lunch in a large and gloomy room full of dusty potted palms and contorted statuary. We were served by the bewhiskered porter, who had become the head waiter simply by donning tails and a celluloid dicky that creaked like a convention of crickets. The meal, however, was ample and well cooked, and we ate hungrily. As coffee was served, Larry sat back in his chair with a sigh.

'That was a passable meal,' he said generously. 'What do you think of this place, Mother?'

'Well, the *food*'s all right, dear,' said Mother, refusing to commit herself.

'They seem a helpful crowd,' Larry went on. 'The manager himself shifted my bed nearer the window.'

'He wasn't very helpful when I asked for paper,' said Leslie.

'Paper?' asked Mother. 'What did you want paper for?'

'For the lavatory ... there wasn't any in there,' explained Leslie.

'Shhh! Not at the table,' whispered Mother.

'You obviously don't look,' said Margo in a clear and penetrating voice; 'they've got a little box full by the pan.'

'Margo, dear!' exclaimed Mother, horrified.

'What's the matter? Didn't you see the little box?'

Larry gave a snort of laughter.

'Owing to the somewhat eccentric plumbing system of the town,' he explained to Margo kindly, 'that little box is provided for the ... er ... debris, as it were, when you have finished communing with nature.'

Margo's face turned scarlet with a mixture of embarrassment and disgust.

'You mean ... you mean ... that was ... My God! I might have caught some foul disease,' she wailed, and, bursting into tears, fled from the dining-room.

'Most insanitary,' said Mother severely; 'it really is a *disgusting* way to do things. Quite apart from the mistakes one can make, I should think there's a danger of getting typhoid.'

'Mistakes wouldn't happen if they'd organize things properly,' Leslie pointed out, returning to his original complaint.

'Yes, dear; but I don't think we ought to discuss it now. The best thing we can do is to find a house as soon as possible, before we all go down with something.'

Upstairs Margo was in a state of semi-nudity, splashing disinfectant over herself in quantities, and Mother spent an exhausting afternoon being forced to examine her at intervals for the symptoms of the diseases which Margo felt sure she was hatching. It was unfortunate for Mother's peace of mind that the Pension Suisse happened to be situated in the road leading to the local cemetery. As we sat on our small balcony overhanging the street an apparently endless succession of funerals passed beneath us. The inhabitants of Corfu obviously believed that the best part of a bereavement was the funeral, for each seemed more ornate than the last. Cabs decorated with yards of purple and black crêpe were drawn by horses so enveloped in plumes and canopies that it was a wonder they could move. Six or seven of these cabs, containing the mourners in full and uninhibited grief, preceded the corpse itself. This came on another cart-like vehicle, and was ensconced in a coffin so large and lush that it looked more like an enormous birthday cake. Some were white, with purple, black-and-scarlet and deep blue decorations; others were gleaming black with complicated filigrees of gold and silver twining abundantly over them, and glittering brass handles. I had never seen anything so colourful and attractive. This, I decided, was really the way to die, with shrouded horses, acres of flowers and a horde of most satisfactorily grief-stricken relatives. I hung over the balcony rail watching the coffins pass beneath, absorbed and fascinated.

As each funeral passed, and the sounds of mourning and the clopping of hooves died away in the distance, Mother became more and more agitated.

'I'm sure it's an epidemic,' she exclaimed at last, peering down nervously into the street.

'Nonsense, Mother; don't fuss,' said Larry airily.

'But, dear, so *many* of them . . . it's unnatural.'

'There's nothing unnatural about dying . . . people do it all the time.'

'Yes, but they don't die like flies unless there's something wrong.'

'Perhaps they save 'em up and bury 'em in a bunch,' suggested Leslie callously.

'Don't be silly,' said Mother. 'I'm sure it's something to do with the drains. It can't be healthy for people to have *those* sort of arrangements.'

'My God!' said Margo sepulchrally, 'then I suppose I'll get it.'

'No, no, dear; it doesn't follow,' said Mother vaguely; 'it might be something that's not catching.'

'I don't see how you can have an epidemic unless it's something catching,' Leslie remarked logically.

'Anyway,' said Mother, refusing to be drawn into any medical arguments, 'I think we ought to find out. Can't you ring up the health authorities, Larry?'

'There probably aren't any health authorities here,' Larry pointed out, 'and even if there were, I doubt if they'd tell me.'

'Well,' Mother said with determination, 'there's nothing for it. We'll have to move. We must get out of the town. We must find a house in the country *at once*.'

The next morning we started on our house-hunt, accompanied by Mr Beeler, the hotel guide. He was a fat little man with cringing eyes and sweat-polished jowls. He was quite sprightly when we set off, but then he did not know what was in store for him. No one who has not been house-hunting with my mother can possibly imagine it. We drove around the island in a cloud of dust while Mr Beeler showed us villa after villa in a bewildering selection of sizes, colours and situations, and Mother shook her head firmly at them all. At last we had contemplated the tenth and final villa on Mr Beeler's list, and Mother had shaken her head once again. Brokenly Mr Beeler seated himself on the stairs and mopped his face with his handkerchief.

'Madame Durrell,' he said at last, 'I have shown you every villa I know, yet you do not want any. Madame, what is it you require? What is the matter with these villas?'

Mother regarded him with astonishment.

'Didn't you *notice*?' she asked. 'None of them had a bathroom.'

Mr Beeler stared at Mother with bulging eyes.

'But Madame,' he wailed in genuine anguish, 'what for you want a bathroom? . . . Have you not got the sea?'

We returned in silence to the hotel.

By the following morning Mother had decided that we would hire a car and go out house-hunting on our own. She was convinced that somewhere on the island there lurked a villa with a bathroom. We did not share Mother's belief, and so it was a slightly irritable and argumentative group that she herded down to the taxi-rank in the main square. The taxi-drivers, perceiving our innocent appearance, scrambled from inside their cars and flocked round us like vultures, each trying to out-shout his compatriots. Their voices grew louder and louder, their eyes flashed, they clutched each other's arms and ground their teeth at one another, and then they laid hold of us as though they would tear us apart. Actually, we were being treated to the mildest of mild altercations, but we were not used to the Greek temperament, and to us it looked as though we were in danger of our lives.

'Can't you *do* something, Larry?' Mother squeaked, disentangling herself with difficulty from the grasp of a large driver.

'Tell them you'll report them to the British Consul,' suggested Larry, raising his voice above the noise.

'Don't be silly, dear,' said Mother breathlessly. 'Just explain that we don't understand.'

Margo, simpering, stepped into the breach.

'We English,' she yelled at the gesticulating drivers; 'we no understand Greek.'

'If that man pushes me again I'll poke him in the eye,' said Leslie, his face flushed red.

'Now, now, dear,' panted Mother, still struggling with the driver who was propelling her vigorously towards his car; 'I don't think they mean any harm.'

At that moment everyone was startled into silence by a voice that rumbled out above the uproar, a deep, rich, vibrant voice, the sort of voice you would expect a volcano to have.

'Hoy!' roared the voice, 'whys donts yous have someones who can talks your own language?'

Turning, we saw an ancient Dodge parked by the kerb, and behind the wheel sat a short, barrel-bodied individual, with ham-like hands and a great, leathery, scowling face surmounted by a jauntily-tilted peaked cap. He opened the door of the car, surged out on to the pavement and waddled across to us. Then he stopped, scowling even more ferociously, and surveyed the group of silent cab-drivers.

'Thems been worrying yous?' he asked Mother.

'No, no,' said Mother untruthfully; 'it was just that we had difficulty in understanding them.'

'Yous wants someones who can talks your own language,' repeated the new arrival; 'thems bastards ... if yous will excuses the words ... would swindles their own mothers. Excuses me a minute and I'll fix thems.'

He turned on the drivers a blast of Greek that almost swept them off their feet. Aggrieved, gesticulating, angry, they were herded back to their cars by this extraordinary man. Having given them a final and, it appeared, derogatory blast of Greek, he turned to us again.

'Wheres yous wants to gos?' he asked, almost truculently.

'Can you take us to look for a villa?' asked Larry.

'Sure. I'll takes yous anywheres. Just yous says.'

'We are looking,' said Mother firmly, 'for a villa with a bathroom. Do you know of one?'

The man brooded like a great, sun-tanned gargoyle, his black eyebrows twisted into a knot of thoughtfulness.

'Bathrooms?' he said. 'Yous wants a bathrooms?'

'None of the ones we have seen so far had them,' said Mother.

'Oh, I knows a villa with a bathrooms,' said the man. 'I was wondering if its was goings to be bigs enough for yous.'

'Will you take us to look at it, please?' asked Mother.

'Sure, I'll takes yous. Gets into the cars.'

We climbed into the spacious car, and our driver hoisted his bulk behind the steering-wheel and engaged his gears with a terrifying sound. We shot through the twisted streets on the outskirts of the town, swerving in and out among the loaded donkeys, the carts, the groups of peasant women and innumerable dogs, our horn honking a deafening warning. During this our driver seized the opportunity to engage us in conversation. Each time he addressed us he would crane his massive head round to see our reactions, and the car would swoop back and forth across the road like a drunken swallow.

'Yous English? Thought so.... English always wants bathrooms.... I gets a bathroom in my house.... Spiro's my name, Spiro Hakiaopulos ... they alls calls me Spiro Americano on accounts of I lives in America.... Yes, spent eight years in Chicago.... That's where I learnt my goods English.... Wents there to makes moneys.... Then after eight years I says: "Spiros," I says, "yous mades enough..." sos I comes backs to Greece ... brings this car ... best ons the islands ... no one else gets a car like this.

'... All the English tourists knows me, theys all asks for me when theys comes here.... Theys knows theys wonts be swindled.... I likes the English ... best kinds of peoples. ... Honest to Gods, ifs I wasn't Greek I'd likes to be English.'

We sped down a white road covered in a thick layer of silky dust that rose in a boiling cloud behind us, a road lined with prickly pears like a fence of green plates each cleverly balanced on another's edges, and splashed with knobs of scarlet fruit. We passed vineyards where the tiny, stunted vines were laced in green leaves, olive-groves where the pitted trunks made a hundred astonished faces at us out of the gloom of their own shadow, and great clumps of zebra-striped cane that fluttered their leaves like a multitude of green flags. At last we roared to the top of a hill, and Spiro crammed on his brakes and brought the car to a dust-misted halt.

'Theres you ares,' he said, pointing with a great stubby forefinger; 'thats the villa with the bathrooms, likes yous wanted.'

Mother, who had kept her eyes firmly shut throughout the drive, now opened them cautiously and looked. Spiro was pointing at a gentle curve of hillside that rose from the glittering sea. The hill and the valleys around it were an eiderdown of olive-groves that shone with a fish-like gleam where the breeze touched the leaves. Half way up the slope, guarded by a group of tall, slim cypress-trees, nestled a small stawberry-pink villa, like some exotic fruit lying in the greenery. The cypress-trees undulated gently in the breeze, as if they were busily painting the sky a still brighter blue for our arrival.

Chapter Two

The Strawberry-pink Villa

The villa was small and square, standing in its tiny garden with an air of pink-faced determination. Its shutters had been faded by the sun to a delicate creamy-green, cracked and bubbled in places. The garden, surrounded by tall fuchsia hedges, had the flower-beds worked in complicated geometrical patterns, marked with smooth white stones. The white cobbled paths, scarcely as wide as a rake's head, wound laboriously round beds hardly larger than a big straw hat, beds in the shape of stars, half-moons, triangles and circles, all overgrown with a shaggy tangle of flowers run wild. Roses dropped petals that seemed as big and smooth as saucers, flame-red, moon-white, glossy and unwrinkled; marigolds like broods of shaggy suns stood watching their parent's progress through the sky. In the low growth the pansies pushed their velvety, innocent faces through the leaves, and the violets drooped sorrowfully under their heart-shaped leaves. The bougainvillaea that sprawled luxuriously over the tiny front balcony was hung, as though for a carnival, with its lantern-shaped magenta flowers. In the darkness of the fuchsia-hedge a thousand ballerina-like blooms quivered expectantly. The warm air was thick with the scent of a hundred dying flowers, and full of the gentle, soothing whisper and murmur of insects. As soon as we saw it, we wanted to live there – it was as though the villa had been standing there waiting for our arrival. We felt we had come home.

Having lumbered so unexpectedly into our lives, Spiro now took over complete control of our affairs. It was better, he explained, for him to do things, as everyone knew him, and he would make sure we were not swindled.

'Donts you worrys yourselfs about anythings, Mrs Durrells,' he had scowled; 'leaves everythings to me.'

So he would take us shopping, and after an hour's sweating and roaring he would get the price of an article reduced by perhaps two drachmas. This was approximately a penny; it was not the cash, but the principle of the thing, he explained. The fact that he was Greek and adored bargaining was, of course, another reason. It was Spiro who, on discovering that our money had not yet arrived from England, subsidized us, and took it upon himself to go and speak severely to the bank manager about his lack of organization. That it was not the poor manager's fault did not deter him in the least. It was Spiro who paid our hotel bill, who organized a cart to carry our luggage to the villa, and who drove us out there himself, his car piled high with groceries that he had purchased for us.

That he knew everyone on the island, and that they all knew him, we soon discovered was no idle boast. Wherever his car stopped, half a dozen voices would shout out his name, and hands would beckon him to sit at the little tables under the trees and drink coffee. Policemen, peasants and priests waved and smiled as he passed; fishermen, grocers and café-owners greeted him like a brother. 'Ah, Spiro!' they would say, and smile at him affectionately as though he was a naughty but lovable child. They respected his honesty, his belligerence and above all they adored his typically Greek scorn and fearlessness when dealing with any form of Governmental red tape. On arrival, two of our cases containing linen and other things had been confiscated by the Customs on the curious grounds that they were merchandise. So, when we moved out to the strawberry-pink villa and the problem of bed-linen arose, Mother told Spiro about our cases languishing in the Customs, and asked his advice.

'Gollys, Mrs Durrells,' he bellowed, his huge face flushing red with wrath; 'whys you never tells me befores? Thems bastards in the Customs. I'll take you down theres tomorrows and fix thems: I knows thems alls, and they knows *me*. Leaves everythings to me – I'll fix thems.'

The following morning he drove Mother down to the Customs-shed. We all accompanied them, for we did not want to miss the fun. Spiro rolled into the Customs-house like an angry bear.

'Wheres these peoples things?' he inquired of the plump little Customs man.

'You mean their boxes of merchandise?' asked the Customs official in his best English.

'Whats you thinks I means?'

'They are here,' admitted the official cautiously.

'We've comes to takes thems,' scowled Spiro; 'gets them ready.'

He turned and stalked out of the shed to find someone to help carry the luggage, and when he returned he saw that the Customs man had taken the keys from Mother and was just lifting the lid of one of the cases. Spiro, with a grunt of wrath, surged forward and slammed the lid down on the unfortunate man's fingers.

'Whats fors you open it, you sonofabitch?' he asked, glaring.

The Customs official, waving his pinched hand about, protested wildly that it was his duty to examine the contents.

'Dutys?' said Spiro with fine scorn. 'Whats you means, dutys? Is it your dutys to attacks innocent foreigners, eh? Treats thems like smugglers, eh? Thats whats yous calls dutys?'

Spiro paused for a moment, breathing deeply, then he picked up a large suitcase in each great hand and walked towards the door. He paused and turned to fire his parting shot.

'I knows you, Christaki, sos don'ts you go talkings about dutys to me. I remembers when you was fined twelve thousand drachmas for dynamitings fish. I won't have any criminal talkings to *me* abouts dutys.'

We rode back from the Customs in triumph, all our luggage intact and unexamined.

'Thems bastards thinks they owns the islands,' was Spiro's comment. He seemed quite unaware of the fact that he was acting as though he did.

Once Spiro had taken charge he stuck to us like a burr. Within a few hours he had changed from a taxi-driver to our champion, and within a week he was our guide, philosopher and friend. He became so much a member of the family that very soon there was scarcely a thing we did, or planned to do, in which he was not involved in some way. He was always there, bull-voiced and scowling, arranging things we wanted done, telling us how much to pay for things, keeping a watchful eye on us all and reporting to Mother anything he thought she should know. Like a great, brown, ugly angel he watched over us as tenderly as though we were slightly weak-minded children. Mother he frankly adored, and he would sing her praises in a loud voice wherever we happened to be, to her acute embarrassment.

'You oughts to be carefuls whats you do,' he would tell us, screwing up his face earnestly; 'we donts wants to worrys your mothers.'

'Whatever for, Spiro?' Larry would protest in well-simulated astonishment. 'She's never done anything for us ... why should we consider her?'

'Gollys, Master Lorrys, donts *jokes* like that,' Spiro would say in anguish.

'He's quite right, Spiro,' Leslie would say very seriously; 'she's really not much good as a mother, you know.'

'Donts says that, *donts says that*,' Spiro would roar. 'Honest to Gods, if I hads a mother likes yours I'd gos down every mornings and kisses her feets.'

So we were installed in the villa, and we each settled down and adapted ourselves to our surroundings in our respective ways. Margo, merely by donning a microscopic swim-suit and sun-bathing in the olive-groves, had collected an ardent band of handsome peasant youths who appeared like magic from an apparently deserted landscape whenever a bee flew too near her or her deck-chair needed moving. Mother felt forced to point out that she thought this sun-bathing was rather *unwise*.

'After all, dear, that costume doesn't cover an awful lot, does it?' she pointed out.

'Oh, Mother, don't be so old-fashioned,' Margo said impatiently. 'After all, you only die once.'

This remark was as baffling as it was true, and successfully silenced Mother.

It had taken three husky peasant boys half an hour's sweating and panting to get Larry's trunks into the villa, while Larry bustled round them, directing operations. One of the trunks was so big it had to be hoisted in through the window. Once they were installed, Larry spent a happy day unpacking them, and the room was so full of books that it was almost impossible to get in or out. Having constructed battlements of books round the outer perimeter, Larry would spend the whole day in there with his typewriter, only emerging dreamily for meals. On the second morning he appeared in a highly irritable frame of mind, for a peasant had tethered his donkey just over the hedge. At regular intervals the beast would throw out its head and let forth a prolonged and lugubrious bray.

'I ask you! Isn't it laughable that future generations should be deprived of my work simply because some horny-handed idiot has tied that stinking beast of burden near my window?' Larry asked.

'Yes, dear,' said Mother; 'why don't you move it if it disturbs you?'

'My dear Mother, I can't be expected to spend my time chasing donkeys about the olive-groves. I threw a pamphlet on Christian Science at it; what more do you expect me to do?'

'The poor thing's tied up. You can't expect it to untie itself,' said Margo.

'There should be a law against parking those loathsome beasts anywhere near a house. Can't one of you go and move it?'

'Why should we? It's not disturbing us,' said Leslie.

'That's the trouble with this family,' said Larry bitterly: 'no give and take, no consideration for others.'

'*You* don't have much consideration for others,' said Margo.

'It's all your fault, Mother,' said Larry austerely; 'you shouldn't have brought us up to be so selfish.'

'I like that!' exclaimed Mother. 'I never did anything of the sort!'

'Well, we didn't get as selfish as this without *some* guidance,' said Larry.

In the end, Mother and I unhitched the donkey and moved it farther down the hill.

Leslie meanwhile had unpacked his revolvers and startled us all with an apparently endless series of explosions while he fired at an old tin can from his bedroom window. After a particularly deafening morning, Larry erupted from his room and said he could not be expected to work if the villa was going to be rocked to its foundations every five minutes. Leslie, aggrieved, said that he had to practise. Larry said it didn't sound like practice, but more like the Indian Mutiny. Mother, whose nerves had also been somewhat frayed by the reports, suggested that Leslie practise with an empty revolver. Leslie spent half an hour explaining why this was impossible. At length he reluctantly took his tin farther away from the house where the noise was slightly muffled but just as unexpected.

In between keeping a watchful eye on us all, Mother was settling down in her own way. The house was redolent with the scent of herbs and the sharp tang of garlic and onions, and the kitchen was full of a bubbling selection of pots, among which she moved, spectacles askew, muttering to herself. On the table was a tottering pile of books which she consulted from time to time. When she could drag herself away from the kitchen, she would drift happily about the garden, reluctantly pruning and cutting, enthusiastically weeding and planting.

For myself, the garden held sufficient interest; together Roger and I learnt some surprising things. Roger, for example, found that it was unwise to smell hornets, that the peasant dogs ran screaming if he glanced at them through the gate, and that the chickens that leapt suddenly from the fuchsia hedge, squawking wildly as they fled, were unlawful prey, however desirable.

This doll's-house garden was a magic land, a forest of flowers through which roamed creatures I had never seen before. Among the thick, silky petals of each rose-bloom lived tiny, crab-like spiders that scuttled sideways when disturbed. Their small, translucent bodies were coloured to match the flowers they inhabited: pink, ivory, wine-red or buttery-yellow. On the rose-stems, encrusted with green flies, lady-birds moved like newly painted toys; lady-birds pale red with large black spots; lady-birds apple-red with brown spots; lady-birds orange with grey-and-black freckles. Rotund and amiable, they prowled and fed among the anaemic flocks of greenfly. Carpenter bees, like furry, electric-blue bears, zigzagged among the flowers, growling fatly and busily. Humming-bird hawk-moths, sleek and neat, whipped up and down the paths with a fussy efficiency, pausing occasionally on speed-misty wings to lower a long, slender proboscis into a bloom. Among the white cobbles large black ants staggered and gesticulated in groups round strange trophies: a dead caterpillar, a piece of rose-petal or a dried grass-head fat with seeds. As an accompaniment to all this activity there came from the olive-groves outside the fuchsia hedge the incessant shimmering cries of the cicadas. If the curious, blurring heat-haze produced a sound, it would be exactly the strange, chiming cries of these insects.

At first I was so bewildered by this profusion of life on our very doorstep that I could only move about the garden in a daze, watching now this creature, now that, constantly having my attention distracted by the flights of brilliant butterflies that drifted over the hedge. Gradually, as I became more used to the bustle of insect life among the flowers, I found I could concentrate more. I would spend hours squatting on my heels or lying on my stomach watching the private lives of the creatures around me, while Roger sat nearby, a look of resignation on his face. In this way I learnt a lot of fascinating things.

I found that the little crab-spiders could change colour just as successfully as any chameleon. Take a spider from a wine-red rose, where he had been sitting like a bead of coral, and place him in the depths of a cool white rose. If he stayed there – and most of them did – you would see his colour gradually ebb away, as though the change had given him anaemia, until, some two days later, he would be crouching among the white petals like a pearl.

I discovered that in the dry leaves under the fuchsia hedge lived another type of spider, a fierce little huntsman with the cunning and ferocity of a tiger. He would stalk about his continent of leaves, eyes glistening in the sun, pausing now and then to raise himself up on his hairy legs to peer about. If he saw a fly settle to enjoy a sun-bath he would freeze; then, as slowly as a leaf growing, he would move forward, imperceptibly, edging nearer and nearer, pausing occasionally to fasten his life-line of silk to the surface of the leaves. Then, when close enough, the huntsman would pause, his legs shift minutely as he got a good purchase, and then he would leap, legs spread out in a hairy embrace, straight on to the dreaming fly. Never did I see one of these little spiders miss its kill, once it had manoeuvred into the right position.

All these discoveries filled me with a tremendous delight, so that they had to be shared, and I would burst suddenly into the house and startle the family with the news that the strange, spiky black caterpillars on the roses were not caterpillars at all, but the young of lady-birds, or with the equally astonishing news that lacewing-flies laid eggs on stilts. This last miracle I was lucky enough to witness. I found a lacewing-fly on the roses and watched her as she climbed about the leaves, admiring her beautiful, fragile wings like green glass, and her enormous liquid golden eyes. Presently she stopped on the surface of a rose-leaf and lowered the tip of her abdomen. She remained like that for a moment and then raised her tail, and from it, to my astonishment, rose a slender thread, like a pale hair. Then, on the very tip of this stalk, appeared the egg. The female had a rest, and then repeated the performance until the surface of the rose-leaf looked as though it was covered with a forest of tiny club moss. The laying over, the female rippled her antennae briefly and flew off in a mist of green gauze wings.

Perhaps the most exciting discovery I made in this multi-coloured Lilliput to which I had access was an earwig's nest. I had long wanted to find one and had searched everywhere without success, so the joy of stumbling upon one unexpectedly was overwhelming, like suddenly being given a wonderful present. I moved a piece of bark and there beneath it was the nursery, a small hollow in the earth that the insect must have burrowed out for herself. She squatted in the middle of it, shielding underneath her a few white eggs. She crouched over them like a hen, and did not move when the flood of sunlight struck her as I lifted the bark. I could not count the eggs, but there did not seem to be many, so I presumed that she had not yet laid her full complement. Tenderly I replaced her lid of bark.

From that moment I guarded the nest jealously. I erected a protecting wall of rocks round it, and as an additional precaution I wrote out a notice in red ink and stuck it on a pole nearby as a warning to the family. The notice read: 'BEWAR – EARWIG NEST – QUIAT PLESE.' It was only remarkable in that the two correctly spelt words were biological ones. Every hour or so I would subject the mother earwig to ten minutes' close scrutiny. I did not dare examine her more often for fear she might desert her nest. Eventually the pile of eggs beneath her grew, and she seemed to have become accustomed to my lifting off her bark roof. I even decided that she had begun to recognize me, from the friendly way she waggled her antennae.

To my acute disappointment, after all my efforts and constant sentry duty, the babies hatched out during the night. I felt that, after all I had done, the female might have held up the hatching until I was there to witness it. However, there they were, a fine brood of young earwigs, minute, frail, looking as though they had been carved out of ivory. They moved gently under their mother's body, walking between her legs, the more venturesome even climbing on to her pincers. It was a heart-warming sight. The next day the nursery was empty: my wonderful family had scattered over the garden. I saw one of the babies some time later: he was bigger, of course, browner and stronger, but I recognized him immediately. He was curled up in a maze of rosepetals, having a sleep, and when I disturbed him he merely raised his pincers irritably over his back. I would have liked to think that it was a salute, a cheerful greeting, but honesty compelled me to admit that it was nothing more than an earwig's warning to a potential enemy. Still, I excused him. After all, he had been very young when I last saw him.

I came to know the plump peasant girls who passed the garden every morning and evening. Riding side-saddle on their slouching, drooping-eared donkeys, they were shrill and colourful as parrots, and their chatter and laughter echoed among the olive-trees. In the mornings they would smile and shout greetings as their donkeys pattered past, and in the evenings they would lean over the fuchsia hedge, balancing precariously on their steeds' backs, and smiling, hold out gifts for me – a bunch of amber grapes still sun-warmed, some figs black as tar striped with pink where they had burst their seams with ripeness, or a giant water-melon with an inside like pink ice. As the days passed, I came gradually to understand them. What had at first been a confused babble became a series of recognizable separate sounds. Then, suddenly, these took on meaning, and slowly and haltingly I started to use them myself; then I took my newly acquired words and strung them into ungrammatical and stumbling sentences. Our neighbours were delighted, as though I had conferred some delicate compliment by trying to learn their language. They would lean over the hedge, their faces screwed up with concentration, as I groped my way through a greeting or a simple remark, and when I had successfully concluded they would beam at me, nodding and smiling, and clap their hands. By degrees I learnt their names, who was related to whom, which were married and which hoped to be, and other details. I learnt where their little cottages were among the olive-groves, and should Roger and I chance to pass that way the entire family, vociferous and pleased, would tumble out to greet us, to bring a chair, so that I might sit under their vine and eat some fruit with them.

Gradually the magic of the island settled over us as gently and clingingly as pollen. Each day had a tranquillity, a timelessness, about it, so that you wished it would never end. But then the dark skin of night would peel off and there would be a fresh day waiting for us, glossy and colourful as a child's transfer and with the same tinge of unreality.

Chapter Three

The Rose-beetle Man

In the morning, when I woke, the bedroom shutters were luminous and barred with gold from the rising sun. The morning air was full of the scent of charcoal from the kitchen fire, full of eager cock-crows, the distant yap of dogs and the unsteady, melancholy tune of the goat-bells as the flocks were driven out to pasture.

We ate breakfast out in the garden, under the small tangerine-trees. The sky was fresh and shining, not yet the fierce blue of noon, but a clear milky opal. The flowers were half-asleep, roses dew-crumpled, marigolds still tightly shut. Breakfast was, on the whole, a leisurely and silent meal, for no member of the family was very talkative at that hour. By the end of the meal the influence of the coffee, toast and eggs made itself felt, and we started to revive, to tell each other what we intended to do, why we intended to do it, and then argue earnestly as to whether each had made a wise decision. I never joined in these discussions, for I knew perfectly well what I intended to do, and would concentrate on finishing my food as rapidly as possible.

'*Must* you gulp and slush your food like that?' Larry would inquire in a pained voice, delicately picking his teeth with a match-stick.

'Eat it slowly, dear,' Mother would murmur; 'there's no hurry.'

No hurry? With Roger waiting at the garden gate, an alert black shape, watching for me with eager brown eyes? No hurry, with the first sleepy cicadas starting to fiddle experimentally among the olives? No hurry, with the island waiting, morning cool, bright as a star, to be explored? I could hardly expect the family to understand this point of view, however, so I would slow down until I felt that their attention had been attracted elsewhere, and then stuff my mouth again.

Finishing at last, I would slip from the table and saunter towards the gate, where Roger sat gazing at me with a questioning air. Together we would peer through the wrought-iron gates into the olive-groves beyond. I would suggest to Roger that perhaps it wasn't worth going out today. He would wag his stump in hasty denial, and his nose would butt at my hand. No, I would say, I really didn't think we ought to go out. It looked as though it was going to rain, and I would peer up into the clear, burnished sky with a worried expression. Roger, ears cocked, would peer into the sky too, and then look at me imploringly. Anyway, I would go on, if it didn't look like rain now it was almost certain to rain later, and so it would be much safer just to sit in the garden with a book. Roger, in desperation, would place a large black paw on the gate, and then look at me, lifting one side of his upper lip, displaying his white teeth in a lop-sided, ingratiating grin, his stump working itself into a blur of excitement. This was his trump card, for he knew I could never resist his ridiculous grin. So I would stop teasing him, fetch my matchboxes and my butterfly net, the garden gate would creak open and clang shut, and Roger would be off through the olive-groves swiftly as a cloud-shadow, his deep bark welcoming the new day.

In those early days of exploration Roger was my constant companion. Together we ventured farther and farther afield, discovering quiet, remote olive-groves which had to be investigated and remembered, working our way through a maze of blackbird-haunted myrtles, venturing into narrow valleys where the cypress-trees cast a cloak of mysterious, inky shadow. He was the perfect companion for an adventure, affectionate without exuberance, brave without being belligerent, intelligent and full of good-humoured tolerance for my eccentricities. If I slipped when climbing a dew-shiny bank, Roger appeared suddenly, gave a snort that sounded like suppressed laughter, a quick look over, a rapid lick of commiseration, shook himself, sneezed and gave me his lop-sided grin. If I found something that interested me – an ant's nest, a caterpillar on a leaf, a spider wrapping up a fly in swaddling clothes of silk – Roger sat down and waited until I had finished examining it. If he thought I was taking too long, he shifted nearer, gave a gentle, whiny yawn, and then sighed deeply and started to wag his tail. If the matter was of no great importance, we would move on, but if it was something absorbing that had to be pored over, I had only to frown at Roger and he would realize it was going to be a long job. His ears would droop, his tail slow down and stop, and he would slouch off to the nearest bush, fling himself down in the shade, giving me a martyred look as he did so.

During these trips Roger and I came to know and be known by a great number of people in various parts of the surrounding countryside. There was, for example, a strange, mentally defective youth with a round face as expressionless as a puffball. He was always dressed in tattered shirt, shiny blue serge trousers that were rolled up to the knee, and on his head the elderly remains of a bowler hat without a brim. Whenever he saw us he came hurrying through the olives, raised his absurd hat politely and wished us good day in a voice as childish and sweet as a flute. He would stand, watching us without expression, nodding at any remark I happened to make, for ten minutes or so. Then, raising his hat politely, he would go off through the trees. Then there was the immensely fat and cheerful Agathi, who lived in a tiny tumbledown cottage high up the hill. She was always sitting outside her house with a spindle of sheep's wool, twining and pulling it into coarse thread. She must have been well over seventy, but her hair was still black and lustrous, plaited carefully and wound round a pair of polished cow's horns, an ornament that some of the older peasant women adopted. As she sat in the sun, like a great black toad with a scarlet head-dress draped over the cow's horns, the bobbin of wool would rise and fall, twisting like a top, her fingers busy unravelling and plucking, and her drooping mouth with its hedge of broken and discoloured teeth wide open as she sang, loudly and harshly, but with great vigour.

It was from Agathi that I learnt some of the most beautiful and haunting of the peasant songs. Sitting on an old tin in the sun, eating grapes or pomegranates from her garden, I would sing with her, and she would break off now and then to correct my pronunciation. We sang (verse by verse) the gay, rousing song of the river, *Vangelió*, and of how it dropped from the mountains, making the gardens rich, the fields fertile and the trees heavy with fruit. We sang, rolling our eyes at each other in exaggerated coquetry, the funny little love-song called 'False-hood.' 'Lies, lies,' we warbled, shaking our heads, 'all lies, but it is my fault for teaching you to go round the countryside telling people I love you.' Then we would strike a mournful note and sing, perhaps, the slow, lilting song called 'Why are you leaving me?' We were almost overcome by this one, and would wail out the long, soulful lyrics, our voices quavering. When we came to the last bit, the most heart-rending of all, Agathi would clasp her hands to her great breasts, her black eyes would become misty and sad, and her chins would tremble with emotion. As the last discordant notes of our duet faded away, she would turn to me, wipe her nose on the corner of her headdress.

'What fools we are, eh? What fools, sitting here in the sun, singing. And of love, too! I am too old for it and you are too young, and yet we waste our time singing about it. Ah, well, let's have a glass of wine, eh?'

Apart from Agathi, the person I liked best was the old shepherd Yani, a tall, slouching man with a great hooked nose like an eagle, and incredible moustaches. I first met him one hot afternoon when Roger and I had spent an exhausting hour trying to dig a large green lizard out of its hole in a stone wall. At length, unsuccessful, sweaty and tired, we had flung ourselves down beneath five little cypress-trees that cast a neat square of shadow on the sun-bleached grass. Lying there, I heard the gentle, drowsy tinkling of a goat-bell, and presently the herds wandered past us, pausing to stare with vacant yellow eyes, bleat sneeringly and then move on. The soft sound of the bells, and of their mouths ripping and tearing at the undergrowth, had a soothing effect on me, and by the time they had drifted slowly past and the shepherd appeared I was nearly asleep. He stopped and looked at me, leaning heavily on his brown olive-wood stick, his little black eyes fierce under his shaggy brows, his big boots planted firmly in the heather.

'Good afternoon,' he greeted me gruffly; 'you are the foreigner ... the little English lord?'

By then I was used to the curious peasant idea that all English people were lords, and I admitted that that's who I was. He turned and roared at a goat which had reared on to its hind legs and was tearing at a young olive, and then turned back.

'I will tell you something, little lord,' he said; 'it is dangerous for you to lie here, beneath these trees.'

I glanced up at the cypresses, but they seemed safe enough to me, and so I asked why he thought they were dangerous.

'Ah, you may *sit* under them, yes. They cast a good shadow, cold as well-water; but that's the trouble, they tempt you to sleep. And you must never, for any reason, sleep beneath a cypress.'

He paused, stroked his moustache, waited for me to ask why, and then went on:

'Why? Why? Because if you did you would be changed when you woke. Yes, the black cypresses, they are dangerous. While you sleep, their roots grow into your brains and steal them, and when you wake up you are mad, head as empty as a whistle.'

I asked whether it was only the cypress that could do this, or did it apply to other trees.

'No, only the cypress,' said the old man, peering up fiercely at the trees above me as though to see whether they were listening; 'only the cypress is the thief of intelligence. So be warned, little lord, and don't sleep here.'

He nodded briefly, gave another fierce glance at the dark blades of the cypress, as if daring them to make some comment, and then picked his way carefully through the myrtle-bushes to where his goats grazed scattered about the hill, their great udders swinging like bagpipes beneath their bellies.

I got to know Yani very well, for I was always meeting him during my explorations, and occasionally I visited him in his little house, when he would ply me with fruit, and give me advice and warnings to keep me safe on my walks.

Perhaps one of the most weird and fascinating characters I met during my travels was the Rose-beetle Man. He had a fairy-tale air about him that was impossible to resist, and I used to look forward eagerly to my infrequent meetings with him. I first saw him on a high, lonely road leading to one of the remote mountain villages. I could hear him long before I could see him, for he was playing a rippling tune on a shepherd's pipe, breaking off now and then to sing a few words in a curious, nasal voice. As he rounded the corner both Roger and I stopped and stared at him in amazement.

He had a sharp, fox-like face with large, slanting eyes of such a dark brown that they appeared black. They had a weird, vacant look about them, and a sort of bloom such as one finds on a plum, a pearly covering almost like a cataract. He was short and slight, with a thinness about his wrists and neck that argued a lack of food. His dress was fantastic, and on his head was a shapeless hat with a very wide, floppy brim. It had once been bottle-green, but was now speckled and smeared with dust, wine-stains and cigarette-burns. In the band were stuck a fluttering forest of feathers: cock-feathers, hoopoe-feathers, owl-feathers, the wing of a kingfisher, the claw of a hawk, and a large dirty white feather that may have come from a swan. His shirt was worn and frayed, grey with sweat, and round the neck dangled an enormous cravat of the most startling blue satin. His coat was dark and shapeless, with patches of different hues here and there; on the sleeve a bit of white cloth with a design of rosebuds; on the shoulder a triangular patch of wine-red and white spots. The pockets of this garment bulged, the contents almost spilling out: combs, balloons, little highly coloured pictures of the saints, olive-wood carvings of snakes, camels, dogs and horses, cheap mirrors, a riot of handkerchiefs, and long twisted rolls of bread decorated with seeds. His trousers, patched like his coat, drooped over a pair of scarlet *charouhias*, leather shoes with upturned toes decorated with a large black-and-white pompon. This extraordinary character carried on his back bamboo cages full of pigeons and young chickens, several mysterious sacks and a large bunch of fresh green leeks. With one hand he held his pipe to his mouth, and in the other a number of lengths of cotton, to each of which was tied an almond-size rose-beetle, glittering golden green in the sun, all of them flying round his hat with desperate, deep buzzings, trying to escape from the thread tied firmly round their waists. Occasionally, tired of circling round and round without success, one of the beetles would settle for a moment on his hat, before launching itself off once more on its endless merry-go-round.

When he saw us the Rose-beetle Man stopped, gave a very exaggerated start, doffed his ridiculous hat and swept us a low bow. Roger was so overcome by this unlooked-for attention that he let out a volley of surprised barks. The man smiled at us, put on his hat again, raised his hands and waggled his long, bony fingers at me. Amused and rather startled by this apparition, I politely bade him good day. He gave another courtly bow. I asked him if he had been to some fiesta. He nodded his head vigorously, raised his pipe to his lips and played a lilting little tune on it, pranced a few steps in the dust of the road, and then stopped and jerked his thumb over his shoulder, pointing back the way he had come. He smiled, patted his pockets and rubbed his forefinger and thumb together in the Greek way of expressing money. I suddenly realized that he must be dumb. So, standing in the middle of the road, I carried on a conversation with him and he replied with a varied and very clever pantomime. I asked what the rose-beetles were for, and why he had them tied with pieces of cotton. He held his hand out to denote small boys, took one of the lengths of cotton from which a beetle hung, and whirled it rapidly round his head. Immediately the insect came to life and started on its planet-like circling of his hat, and he beamed at me. Pointing up at the sky, he stretched his arms out and gave a deep nasal buzzing, while he banked and swooped across the road. Aeroplane, any fool could see that. Then he pointed to the beetles, held out his hand to denote children and whirled his stock of beetles round his head so that they all started to buzz peevishly.

Exhausted by his explanation, he sat down by the edge of the road, played a short tune on his flute, breaking off to sing in his curious nasal voice. They were not articulate words he used, but a series of strange gruntings and tenor squeaks, that appeared to be formed at the back of his throat and expelled through his nose. He produced them, however, with such verve and such wonderful facial expressions that you were convinced the curious sounds really meant something. Presently he stuffed his flute into his bulging pocket, gazed at me reflectively for a moment and then swung a small sack off his shoulder, undid it and, to my delight and astonishment, tumbled half a dozen tortoises into the dusty road. Their shells had been polished with oil until they shone, and by some means or other he had managed to decorate their front legs with little red bows. Slowly and ponderously they unpacked their heads and legs from their gleaming shells and set off down the road, doggedly and without enthusiasm. I watched them, fascinated; the one that particularly took my fancy was quite a small one with a shell about the size of a tea-cup. It seemed more sprightly than the others, and its shell was a paler colour – chestnut, caramel and amber. Its eyes were bright and its walk was as alert as any tortoise's could be. I sat contemplating it for a long time. I convinced myself that the family would greet its arrival at the villa with tremendous enthusiasm, even, perhaps, congratulating me on finding such an elegant specimen. The fact that I had no money on me did not worry me in the slightest, for I would simply tell the man to call at the villa for payment the next day. It never occurred to me that he might not trust me. The fact that I was English was sufficient, for the islanders had a love and respect for the Englishman out of all proportion to his worth. They would trust an Englishman where they would not trust each other. I asked the Rose-beetle man the price of the little tortoise. He held up both hands, fingers spread out. However, I hadn't watched the peasants transacting business for nothing. I shook my head firmly and held up two fingers, unconsciously imitating the man. He closed his eyes in horror at the thought, and held up nine fingers; I held up three; he shook his head, and after some thought held up six fingers; I, in return, shook my head and held up five. The Rose-beetle Man shook his head, and sighed deeply and sorrowfully, so we sat in silence and stared at the tortoises crawling heavily and uncertainly about the road, with the curious graceless determination of babies. Presently the Rose-beetle Man indicated the little tortoise and held up six fingers again. I shook my head and held up five. Roger yawned loudly; he was thoroughly bored by this silent bargaining. The Rose-beetle Man picked up the reptile and showed me in pantomime how smooth and lovely its shell was, how erect its head, how pointed its nails. I remained implacable. He shrugged, handed me the tortoise and held up five fingers.

Then I told him I had no money, and that he would have to come the next day to the villa, and he nodded as if it were the most natural thing in the world. Excited by owning this new pet, I wanted to get back home as quickly as possible in order to show it to everyone, so I said good-bye, thanked him and hurried off along the road. When I reached the place where I had to cut down through the olive-groves, I stopped and examined my acquisition carefully. He was undoubtedly the finest tortoise I had ever seen, and worth, in my opinion, at least twice what I had paid for him. I patted his scaly head with my finger and placed him carefully in my pocket. Before diving down the hillside I glanced back. The Rose-beetle Man was still in the same place on the road, but he was doing a little jig, prancing and swaying, his flute warbling, while in the road at his feet the tortoises ambled to and fro, dimly and heavily.

The new arrival was duly christened Achilles, and turned out to be a most intelligent and lovable beast, possessed of a peculiar sense of humour. At first he was tethered by a leg in the garden, but as he grew tamer we let him go where he pleased. He learned his name in a very short time, and we had only to call out once or twice and then wait patiently for a while and he would appear, lumbering along the narrow cobbled paths on tip-toe, his head and neck stretched out eagerly. He loved being fed, and would squat regally in the sun while we held out bits of lettuce, dandelions or grapes for him. He loved grapes as much as Roger did, so there was always great rivalry. Achilles would sit mumbling the grapes in his mouth, the juice running down his chin, and Roger would lie nearby, watching him with agonized eyes, his mouth drooling saliva. Roger always had his fair share of the fruit, but even so he seemed to think it a waste to give such delicacies to a tortoise. When the feeding was over, if I didn't keep an eye on him, Roger would creep up to Achilles and lick his front vigorously in an attempt to get the grape-juice that the reptile had dribbled down himself. Achilles, affronted at such a liberty, would snap at Roger's nose, and then, when the licks became too overpowering and moist, he would retreat into his shell with an indignant wheeze, and refuse to come out until we had removed Roger from the scene.

But the fruit that Achilles liked best were wild strawberries. He would become positively hysterical at the mere sight of them, lumbering to and fro, craning his head to see if you were going to give him any, gazing at you pleadingly with his tiny boot-button eyes. The very small strawberries he could devour at a gulp, for they were only the size of a fat pea. But if you gave him a big one, say the size of a hazel nut, he behaved in a way that I have never seen another tortoise emulate. He would grab the fruit and, holding it firmly in his mouth, would stumble off at top speed until he reached a safe and secluded spot among the flower-beds, where he would drop the fruit and then eat it at leisure, returning for another one when he had finished.

As well as developing a passion for strawberries, Achilles also developed a passion for human company. Let anyone come into the garden to sit and sun-bathe, to read or for any other reason, and before long there would be a rustling among the sweet williams, and Achilles's wrinkled and earnest face would be poked through. If you were sitting in a chair, he contented himself with getting as close to your feet as possible, and there he would sink into a deep and peaceful sleep, his head drooping out of his shell, his nose resting on the ground. If, however, you were lying on a rug, sun-bathing, Achilles would be convinced that you were lying on the ground simply in order to provide him with amusement. He would surge down the path and on to the rug with an expression of bemused good humour on his face. He would pause, survey you thoughtfully and then choose a portion of your anatomy on which to practise mountaineering. Suddenly to have the sharp claws of a determined tortoise embedded in your thigh as he tries to lever himself up on to your stomach is not conducive to relaxation. If you shook him off and moved the rug it would only give you temporary respite, for Achilles would circle the garden grimly until he found you again. This habit became so tiresome that, after many complaints and threats from the family, I had to lock him up whenever we lay in the garden. Then one day the garden gate was left open and Achilles was nowhere to be found. Search-parties were immediately organized, and the family, who up till then had spent most of their time openly making threats against the reptile's life, wandered about the olive-groves, shouting, 'Achilles ... strawberries, Achilles ... Achilles ... strawberries. ...' At length we found him. Ambling along in his usual detached manner, he had fallen into a disused well, the wall of which had long since disintegrated, and the mouth of which was almost covered by ferns. He was, to our regret, quite dead. Even Leslie's attempts at artificial respiration, and Margo's suggestion of forcing straw-berries down his throat (to give him, as she explained, something to live for), failed to get any response. So, mournfully and solemnly, his corpse was buried in the garden under a small strawberry plant (Mother's suggestion). A short funeral address, written and read in a trembling voice by Larry, made the occasion a memorable one. It was only marred by Roger, who, in spite of all my protests, insisted on wagging his tail throughout the burial service.

Not long after Achilles had been taken from us I obtained another pet from the Rose-beetle Man. This time it was a pigeon. He was still very young and had to be force-fed on bread-and-milk and soaked corn. He was the most revolting bird to look at, with his feathers pushing through the wrinkled scarlet skin, mixed with the horrible yellow down that covers baby pigeons and makes them look as though they have been peroxiding their hair. Owing to his repulsive and obese appearance, Larry suggested we called him Quasimodo, and liking the name without realizing the implications, I agreed. For a long time after he could feed himself, and when all his feathers had grown, Quasimodo retained a sprig of yellow down on his head which gave him the appearance of a rather pompous judge wearing a wig several sizes too small.

Owing to his unorthodox upbringing, and the fact that he had no parents to teach him the facts of life, Quasimodo became convinced that he was not a bird at all, and refused to fly. Instead he walked everywhere. If he wanted to get on to a table, or a chair, he stood below it, ducking his head and cooing in a rich contralto until someone lifted him up. He was always eager to join us in anything we did, and would even try to come for walks with us. This, however, we had to stop, for either you carried him on your shoulder, which was risking an accident to your clothes, or else you let him walk behind. If you let him walk, then you had to slow down your own pace to suit his, for should you get too far ahead you would hear the most frantic and imploring coos and turn round to find Quasimodo running desperately after you, his tail wagging seductively, his iridescent chest pouted out with indignation at your cruelty.

Quasimodo insisted on sleeping in the house; no amount of coaxing or scolding would get him to inhabit the pigeon-loft I had constructed for him. He preferred to sleep on the end of Margo's bed. Eventually, however, he was banished to the drawing-room sofa, for if Margo turned over in bed at night Quasimodo would wake, hobble up the bed and perch on her face, cooing loudly and lovingly.

It was Larry who discovered that Quasimodo was a musical pigeon. Not only did he like music, but he actually seemed to recognize two different varieties, the waltz and the military march. For ordinary music he would waddle as close to the gramophone as possible and sit there with pouting chest, eyes half closed, purring softly to himself. But if the tune was a waltz he would move round and round the machine, bowing, twisting and cooing tremulously. For a march, on the other hand – Sousa for preference – he drew himself up to his full height, inflated his chest and stamped up and down the room, while his coo became so rich and throaty that he seemed in danger of strangling himself. He never attempted to perform these actions for any other kind of music except marches and waltzes. Occasionally, however, if he had not heard any music for some time, he would (in his enthusiasm at hearing the gramophone) do a march for a waltz, or vice versa, but he invariably stopped and corrected himself half-way through.

One sad day we found, on waking Quasimodo, that he had duped us all, for there among the cushions lay a glossy white egg. He never quite recovered from this. He became embittered, sullen, and started to peck irritably if you attempted to pick him up. Then he laid another egg, and his nature changed completely. He, or rather she, became wilder and wilder, treating us as though we were her worst enemies, slinking up to the kitchen door for food as if she feared for her life. Not even the gramophone would tempt her back into the house. The last time I saw her she was sitting in an olive-tree, cooing in the most pretentious and coy manner, while further along the branch a large and very masculine-looking pigeon twisted and cooed in a perfect ecstasy of admiration.

For some time the Rose-beetle Man would turn up at the villa fairly regularly with some new addition to my menagerie: a frog, perhaps, or a sparrow with a broken wing. One afternoon Mother and I, in a fit of extravagant sentimentalism, bought up his entire stock of rose-beetles and, when he had left, let them all go in the garden. For days the villa was full of rose-beetles, crawling on the beds, lurking in the bathroom, banging against the lights at night and falling like emeralds into our laps.

The last time I saw the Rose-beetle Man was one evening when I was sitting on a hill-top overlooking the road. He had obviously been to some fiesta and had been plied with much wine, for he swayed to and fro across the road, piping a melancholy tune on his flute. I shouted a greeting, and he waved extravagantly without looking back. As he rounded the corner he was silhouetted for a moment against the pale lavender evening sky. I could see his battered hat with the fluttering feathers, the bulging pockets of his coat, the bamboo cages full of sleepy pigeons on his back, and above his head, circling drowsily round and round, I could see the dim specks that were the rose-beetles. Then he rounded the curve of the road and there was only the pale sky with a new moon floating in it like a silver feather, and the soft twittering of his flute dying away in the dusk.

Chapter Four

A Bushel of Learning

Scarcely had we settled into the Strawberry-pink Villa before Mother decided that I was running wild, and that it was necessary for me to have some sort of education. But where to find this on a remote Greek island? As usual when a problem arose, the entire family flung itself with enthusiasm into the task of solving it. Each member had his or her own idea of what was best for me, and each argued with such fervour that any discussion about my future generally resulted in an uproar.

'Plenty of time for him to learn,' said Leslie; 'after all, he can read, can't he? I can teach him to shoot, and if we bought a boat I could teach him to sail.'

'But, dear, that wouldn't *really* be much use to him later on,' Mother pointed out, adding vaguely, 'unless he was going into the Merchant Navy or something.'

'I think it's essential that he learns to dance,' said Margo, 'or else he'll grow up into one of these awful tongue-tied hobbledehoys.'

'Yes, dear; but that sort of thing can come *later*. He should be getting some sort of grounding in things like mathematics and French ... and his spelling's appalling.'

'Literature,' said Larry, with conviction, 'that's what he wants, a good solid grounding in literature. The rest will follow naturally. I've been encouraging him to read some good stuff.'

'But don't you think Rabelais is a little *old* for him?' asked Mother doubtfully.

'Good, clean fun,' said Larry airily; 'it's important that he gets sex in its right perspective now.'

'You've got a mania about sex,' said Margo primly; 'it doesn't matter what we're discussing, you always have to drag it in.'

'What he wants is a healthy, outdoor life; if he learnt to shoot and sail ...' began Leslie.

'Oh, stop talking like a bishop ... you'll be advocating cold baths next.'

'The trouble with you is you get in one of these damned supercilious moods where you think you know best, and you won't even listen to anyone else's point of view.'

'With a point of view as limited as yours, you can hardly expect me to listen to it.'

'Now, now, there's no sense in fighting,' said Mother.

'Well, Larry's so bloody unreasonable.'

'I like that!' said Larry indignantly; 'I'm far and away the most reasonable member of the family.'

'Yes, dear, but fighting doesn't solve the problem. What we want is someone who can teach Gerry and who'll encourage him in his interests.'

'He appears to have only one interest,' said Larry bitterly, 'and that's this awful urge to fill things with animal life. I don't think he ought to be encouraged in *that*. Life is fraught with danger as it is.... I went to light a cigarette only this morning and a damn' great bumble-bee flew out of the box.'

'It was a grasshopper with me,' said Leslie gloomily.

'Yes, I think that sort of thing ought to be stopped,' said Margo. 'I found the *most revolting* jar of wriggling things on the dressing-table, of all places.'

'He doesn't mean any harm, poor little chap,' said Mother pacifically; 'he's so interested in all these things.'

'I wouldn't mind being attacked by bumble-bees, if it *led* anywhere,' Larry pointed out. 'But it's just a phase ... he'll grow out of it by the time he's fourteen.'

'He's been in this phase from the age of two,' said Mother, 'and he's showing no signs of growing out of it.'

'Well, if you insist on stuffing him full of useless information, I suppose George would have a shot at teaching him,' said Larry.

'*That's* a brain-wave,' said Mother delightedly. 'Will you go over and see him? I think the sooner he starts the better.'

Sitting under the open window in the twilight, with my arm round Roger's shaggy neck, I had listened with interest, not unmixed with indignation, to the family discussion on my fate. Now it was settled, I wondered vaguely who George was, and why it was so necessary for me to have lessons. But the dusk was thick with flower-scents, and the olive-groves were dark, mysterious and fascinating. I forgot about the imminent danger of being educated, and went off with Roger to hunt for glow-worms in the sprawling brambles.

I discovered that George was an old friend of Larry's, who had come to Corfu to write. There was nothing very unusual about this, for all Larry's acquaintances in those days were either authors, poets or painters. It was George, moreover, who was really responsible for our presence in Corfu, for he had written such eulogistic letters about the place that Larry had become convinced we could live nowhere else. Now George was to pay the penalty for his rashness. He came over to the villa to discuss my education with Mother, and we were introduced. We regarded each other with suspicion. George was a very tall and extremely thin man who moved with the odd disjointed grace of a puppet. His lean, skull-like face was partially concealed by a finely pointed brown beard and a pair of large tortoise-shell spectacles. He had a deep, melancholy voice, a dry and sarcastic sense of humour. Having made a joke, he would smile in his beard with a sort of vulpine pleasure which was quite unaffected by anyone else's reactions.

Gravely George set about the task of teaching me. He was undeterred by the fact that there were no school-books available on the island; he simply ransacked his own library and appeared on the appointed day armed with a most unorthodox selection of tomes. Sombrely and patiently he taught me the rudiments of geography from the maps in the back of an ancient copy of *Pears Cyclopaedia*, English from books that ranged from Wilde to Gibbon, French from a fat and exciting book called *Le Petit Larousse*, and mathematics from memory. From my point of view, however, the most important thing was that we devoted some of our time to natural history, and George meticulously and carefully taught me how to observe and how to note down observations in a diary. At once my enthusiastic but haphazard interest in nature became focused, for I found that by writing things down I could learn and remember much more. The only mornings that I was ever on time for my lessons were those which were given up to natural history.

Every morning at nine George would come stalking through the olive-trees, clad in shorts, sandals and an enormous straw hat with a frayed brim, clutching a wedge of books under one arm, swinging a walking-stick vigorously.

'Good morning. The disciple awaits the master agog with anticipation, I trust?' he would greet me, with a saturnine smile.

In the little dining-room of the villa the shutters would be closed against the sun, and in the green twilight George would loom over the table, methodically arranging the books. Flies, heat-drugged, would crawl slowly on the walls or fly drunkenly about the room, buzzing sleepily. Outside the cicadas were greeting the new day with shrill enthusiasm.

'Let me see, let me see,' George would murmur, running a long forefinger down our carefully prepared time-table; 'yes, yes, mathematics. If I remember rightly, we were involved in the Herculean task of discovering how long it would take six men to build a wall if three of them took a week. I seem to recall that we have spent almost as much time on this problem as the men spent on the wall. Ah, well, let us gird our loins and do battle once again. Perhaps it's the *shape* of the problem that worries you, eh? Let us see if we can make it more exciting.'

He would droop over the exercise-book pensively, pulling at his beard. Then in his large, clear writing he would set the problem out in a fresh way.

'If it took two caterpillars a week to eat eight leaves, how long would four caterpillars take to eat the same number? Now, apply yourself to that.'

While I struggled with the apparently insoluble problem of the caterpillars' appetites, George would be otherwise occupied. He was an expert fencer, and was at that time engaged in learning some of the local peasant dances, for which he had a passion. So, while waiting for me to finish the sum, he would drift about in the gloom of the room, practising fencing stances or complicated dancing-steps, a habit that I found disconcerting, to say the least, and to which I shall always attribute my inability to do mathematics. Place any simple sum before me, even now, and it immediately conjures up a vision of George's lanky body swaying and jerking round the dimly lit dining-room. He would accompany the dancing sequences with a deep and tuneless humming, like a hive of distraught bees.

'Tum-ti-tum-ti-tum . . . tiddle tiddle tumty *dee* . . . left leg over . . . three steps right . . . tum-ti-tum-ti-tum-ti-*dum* . . . back, round, down and up . . . tiddle iddle umpty *dee* . . . ,' he would drone, as he paced and pirouetted like a dismal crane. Then, suddenly, the humming would stop, a steely look would creep into his eyes and he would throw himself into an attitude of defence, pointing an imaginary foil at an imaginary enemy. His eyes narrowed, his spectacles a-glitter, he would drive his adversary back across the room, skilfully avoiding the furniture. When his enemy was backed into the corner, George would dodge and twist round him with the agility of a wasp, stabbing, thrusting, guarding. I could almost see the gleam of steel. Then came the final moment, the upward and outward flick that would catch his opponent's weapon and twist it harmlessly to one side, the swift withdrawal, followed by the long, straight lunge that drove the point of his foil right through the adversary's heart. Through all this I would be watching him, fascinated, the exercise-book lying forgotten in front of me. Mathematics was not one of our more successful subjects.

In geography we made better progress, for George was able to give a more zoological tinge to the lesson. We would draw giant maps, wrinkled with mountains, and then fill in the various places of interest, together with drawings of the more exciting fauna to be found there. Thus for me the chief products of Ceylon were tapirs and tea; of India tigers and rice; of Australia kangaroos and sheep, while the blue curves of currents we drew across the oceans carried whales, albatross, penguins and walrus, as well as hurricanes, trade winds, fair weather and foul. Our maps were works of art. The principal volcanoes belched such flames and sparks one feared they would set the paper continents alight; the mountain ranges of the world were so blue and white with ice and snow that it made one chilly to look at them. Our brown, sun-drenched deserts were lumpy with camel-humps and pyramids, and our tropical forests so tangled and luxuriant that it was only with difficulty that the slouching jaguars, lithe snakes and morose gorillas managed to get through them, while on their outskirts emaciated natives hacked wearily at the painted trees, forming little clearings apparently for the purpose of writing 'coffee' or perhaps 'cereals' across them in unsteady capitals. Our rivers were wide, and blue as forget-me-nots, freckled with canoes and crocodiles. Our oceans were anything but empty, for where they had not frothed themselves into a fury of storms or drawn themselves up into an awe-inspiring tidal wave that hung over some remote, palm-shaggy island, they were full of life. Good-natured whales allowed unseaworthy galleons, armed with a forest of harpoons, to pursue them relentlessly; bland and innocent-looking octopi tenderly engulfed small boats in their arms; Chinese junks, with jaundiced crews, were followed by shoals of well-dentured sharks, while fur-clad Eskimos pursued obese herds of walrus through ice-fields thickly populated by polar bears and penguins. They were maps that lived, maps that one could study, frown over and add to; maps, in short, that really *meant* something.

Our attempts at history were not, at first, conspicuously successful, until George discovered that by seasoning a series of unpalatable facts with a sprig of zoology and a sprinkle of completely irrelevant detail, he could get me interested. Thus I became conversant with some historical data which, to the best of my knowledge, have never been recorded before. Breathlessly, history lesson by history lesson, I followed Hannibal's progress over the Alps. His reason for attempting such a feat, and what he intended to do on the other side were details that scarcely worried me. No, my interest in what I considered to be a very badly planned expedition lay in the fact that *I knew the name of each and every elephant*. I also knew that Hannibal had appointed a special man not only to feed and look after the elephants, *but to give them hot-water bottles when the weather got cold.* This interesting fact seems to have escaped most serious historians. Another thing that most history books never seem to mention is that Columbus's first words on setting foot ashore in America were: 'Great heavens, look . . . a jaguar!' With such an introduction, how could one fail to take an interest in the continent's subsequent history? So George, hampered by inadequate books and a reluctant pupil, would strive to make his teaching interesting, so that the lessons did not drag.

Roger, of course, thought that I was simply wasting my mornings. However, he did not desert me, but lay under the table asleep while I wrestled with my work. Occasionally, if I had to fetch a book, he would wake, get up, shake himself, yawn loudly and wag his tail. Then, when he saw me returning to the table, his ears would droop, and he would walk heavily back to his private corner and flop down with a sigh of resignation. George did not mind Roger being in the room, for he behaved himself well, and did not distract my attention. Occasionally, if he was sleeping very heavily and heard a peasant dog barking, Roger would wake up with a start and utter a raucous roar of rage before realizing where he was. Then he would give an embarrassed look at our disapproving faces, his tail would twitch and he would glance round the room sheepishly.

For a short time Quasimodo also joined us for lessons, and behaved very well as long as he was allowed to sit in my lap. He would drowse there, cooing to himself, the entire morning. It was I who banished him, in fact, for one day he upset a bottle of green ink in the exact centre of a large and very beautiful map that we had just completed. I realized, of course, that this vandalism was not intentional, but even so I was annoyed. Quasimodo tried for a week to get back into favour by sitting outside the door and cooing seductively through the crack, but each time I weakened I would catch a glimpse of his tail-feathers, a bright and horrible green, and harden my heart again.

Achilles also attended one lesson, but he did not approve of being inside the house. He spent the morning wandering about the room and scratching at the skirting-boards and door. Then he kept getting wedged under bits of furniture and scrabbling frantically until we lifted the object and rescued him. The room being small, it meant that in order to move one bit of furniture we had to move practically everything else. After a third upheaval George said that as he had never worked with Carter Paterson and was unused to such exertions, he thought Achilles would be happier in the garden.

So there was only Roger left to keep me company. It was comforting, it's true, to be able to rest my feet on his woolly bulk while I grappled with a problem, but even then it was hard to concentrate, for the sun would pour through the shutters, tiger-striping the table and floor, reminding me of all the things I might be doing.

There around me were the vast, empty olive-groves echoing with cicadas; the moss-grown stone walls that made the vineyards into steps where the painted lizards ran; the thickets of myrtle alive with insects, and the rough headland where the flocks of garish goldfinches fluttered with excited pipings from thistle-head to thistle-head.

Realizing this, George wisely instituted the novel system of outdoor lessons. Some mornings he arrived, carrying a large furry towel, and together we would make our way down through the olive-groves and along the road that was like a carpet of white velvet under its layer of dust. Then we branched off on to a goat-track that ran along the top of miniature cliffs, until it led us to a bay, secluded and small, with a crescent-shaped fringe of white sand running round it. A grove of stunted olives grew there, providing a pleasant shade. From the top of the little cliff the water in the bay looked so still and transparent that it was hard to believe there was any at all. Fishes seemed to drift over the wave-wrinkled sand as though suspended in mid-air; while through six feet of clear water you could see rocks on which anemones lifted frail, coloured arms, and hermit crabs moved, dragging their top-shaped homes.

We would strip beneath the olives and walk out into the warm, bright water, to drift, face down, over the rocks and clumps of seaweed, occasionally diving to bring up something that caught our eye: a shell more brightly coloured than the rest; or a hermit crab of massive proportions, wearing an anemone on his shell, like a bonnet with a pink flower on it. Here and there on the sandy bottom grew rib-shaped beds of black ribbon-weed, and it was among these beds that the sea-slugs lived. Treading water and peering down, we could see below the shining, narrow fronds of green and black weeds growing close and tangled, over which we hung like hawks suspended in air above a strange woodland. In the clearing among the weed-bed lay the sea-slugs, perhaps the ugliest of the sea fauna. Some six inches long, they looked exactly like overgrown sausages made out of thick, brown, carunculated leather; dim, primitive beasts that just lie in one spot, rolling gently with the sea's swing, sucking in sea-water at one end of their bodies and passing it out at the other. The minute vegetable and animal life in the water is filtered off somewhere inside the sausage, and passed to the simple mechanism of the sea-slug's stomach. No one could say that the sea-slugs led interesting lives. Dully they rolled on the sand, sucking in the sea with monotonous regularity. It was hard to believe that these obese creatures could defend themselves in any way, or that they would ever need to, but in fact they had an unusual method of showing their displeasure. Pick them up out of the water, and they would squirt a jet of sea-water out of either end of their bodies, apparently without any muscular effort. It was this water-pistol habit of theirs that led us to invent a game. Each armed with a sea-slug we would make our weapon squirt, noting how and where the water struck the sea. Then we moved over to that spot, and the one who discovered the greatest amount of sea fauna in his area won a point. Occasionally, as in any game, feeling would run high, indignant accusations of cheating would be made and denied. It was then we found our sea-slugs useful for turning on our opponent. Whenever we had made use of the sea-slugs' services we always swam out and returned them to their forest of weed. Next time we came down they would still be there, probably in exactly the same position as we had left them, rolling quietly to and fro.

Having exhausted the possibilities of the slugs, we would hunt for new shells for my collection, or hold long discussions on the other fauna we had found; George would suddenly realize that all this, though most enjoyable, could hardly be described as education in the strictest sense of the word, so we would drift back to the shallows and lie there. The lesson then proceeded, while the shoals of little fish would gather about us and nibble gently at our legs.

'So the French and British Fleets were slowly drawing together for what was to be the decisive sea battle of the war. When the enemy was sighted, Nelson was on the bridge bird-watching through his telescope ... he had already been warned of the Frenchmen's approach by a friendly gull ... eh? ... oh, a greater black-backed gull I think it was ... well, the ships manoeuvred round each other ... of course they couldn't move so fast in those days, for they did everything by sail ... no engines ... no, not even outboard engines.... The British sailors were a bit worried because the French seemed so strong, but when they saw that Nelson was so little affected by the whole thing that he was sitting on the bridge labelling his birds'-egg collection, they decided that there was really nothing to be scared about....'

The sea was like a warm, silky coverlet that moved my body gently to and fro. There were no waves, only this gentle underwater movement, the pulse of the sea, rocking me softly. Around my legs the coloured fish flicked and trembled, and stood on their heads while they mumbled at me with toothless gums. In the drooping clusters of olives a cicada whispered gently to itself.

'... and so they carried Nelson down below as quickly as possible, so that none of the crew would know he had been hit.... He was mortally wounded, and lying below decks with the battle still raging above, he murmured his last words: 'Kiss me, Hardy,' and then he died. . . . What? Oh yes. Well, he had already told Hardy that if anything happened to him he could have his birds' eggs . . . so, though England had lost her finest seaman, the battle had been won, and it had far-reaching effects in Europe. . . .'

Across the mouth of the bay a sun-bleached boat would pass, rowed by a brown fisherman in tattered trousers, standing in the stern and twisting an oar in the water like a fish's tail. He would raise one hand in lazy salute, and across the still, blue water you could hear the plaintive squeak of the oar as it twisted, and the soft clop as it dug into the sea.

Chapter Five

A Treasure of Spiders

One hot, dreamy afternoon, when everything except the shouting cicadas seemed to be asleep, Roger and I set out to see how far we could climb over the hills before dark. We made our way up through the olive-groves, striped and dappled with white sunlight, where the air was hot and still, and eventually we clambered above the trees and out on to a bare, rocky peak, where we sat down for a rest. The island dozed below us, shimmering like a water-picture in the heat-haze: grey-green olives; black cypresses; multi-coloured rocks of the sea-coast; and the sea smooth and opalescent, kingfisher-blue, jade-green, with here and there a pleat or two in its sleek surface where it curved round a rocky, olive-tangled promontory. Directly below us was a small bay with a crescent-shaped rim of white sand, a bay so shallow, and with a floor of such dazzling sand, that the water was a pale blue, almost white. I was sweaty after the ascent, and Roger sat with flopping tongue and froth-flecked whiskers. We decided that we would not climb the hills after all; we would go for a bathe instead. So we hurried down the hillside until we reached the little bay, empty, silent, asleep under the brilliant shower of sunlight. We sat in the warm, shallow waters, drowsily, and I delved in the sand around me. Occasionally I found a smooth pebble, or a piece of bottle which had been rubbed and licked by the sea until it was like an astonishing jewel, green and translucent. These finds I handed to Roger, who sat watching me. He, not certain what I expected him to do but not wishing to offend me, took them delicately in his mouth. Then, when he thought I was not looking, he would drop them back into the water and sigh deeply.

Later, I lay on a rock to dry, while Roger sneezed and clopped his way along the shallows in an attempt to catch one of the blue-finned blennies, with their pouting, vacant faces, which flipped from rock to rock with the speed of swallows. Breathing heavily and staring down into the clear water, Roger followed them, a look of intense concentration on his face. When I was dry, I put on my shorts and shirt and called to Roger. He came reluctantly, with many a backward glance at the blennies which still flicked across the sandy, sun-ringed floor of the bay. Coming as close to me as possible, he shook himself vigorously, showering me with water from his curly coat.

After the swim, my body felt heavy and relaxed, and my skin as though it was covered with a silky crust of salt. Slowly and dreamily we made our way on to the road. Discovering that I was hungry, I wondered which was the nearest cottage where I could get something to eat. I stood kicking up puffs of fine white dust from the road as I considered this problem. If I went to see Leonora, who undoubtedly lived the nearest, she would give me figs and bread, but she would also insist on giving me the latest bulletin on her daughter's state of health. Her daughter was a husky-voiced virago with a cast in one eye, whom I cordially disliked, so I had no interest in her health. I decided not to go to Leonora; it was a pity, for she had the best fig-trees for miles around, but there was a limit to what I could endure for the sake of black figs. If I went to see Taki, the fisherman, he would be having his siesta, and would merely shout, 'Go away, little corn-top,' from the depths of his tightly shuttered house. Christaki and his family would probably be about, but in return for food they would expect me to answer a lot of tedious questions: Was England bigger than Corfu? How many people lived there? Were they all lords? What was a train like? Did trees grow in England? and so on, interminably. If it had been morning I could have cut through the fields and vineyards, and before reaching home I would have fed well on contributions from various of my friends on the way: olives, bread, grapes, figs, ending perhaps with a short detour that would take me through Philomena's fields, where I could be sure of ending my snack with a crisp, pink slice of water-melon, cold as ice. But now it was siesta time, and most of the peasants were asleep in their houses behind tightly closed doors and shutters. It was a difficult problem, and while I thought about it the pangs of hunger grew, and I kicked more energetically at the dusty road, until Roger sneezed protestingly and gave me an injured look.

Suddenly I had an idea. Just over the hill lived Yani, the old shepherd, and his wife, in a minute, sparkling white cottage. Yani, I knew, had his siesta in front of his house, in the shade of his grape-vine, and if I made enough noise approaching the house he would wake up. Once awake, it was certain that he would offer me hospitality. There was not a single peasant house you could visit and come empty away. Cheered by this thought, I set off up the stony, meandering pathway created by the pattering hooves of Yani's goats, over the brow of the hill and into the valley, where the red roof of the shepherd's house gleamed among the giant olive-trunks. When I judged I was close enough, I stopped and threw a stone for Roger to retrieve. This was one of Roger's favourite pastimes, but once having started it you had to continue, or else he would stand in front of you and bark hideously until you repeated the performance in sheer desperation. He retrieved the stone, dropped it at my feet and backed away expectantly, ears cocked, eyes gleaming, muscles taut and ready for action. I ignored both him and the stone. He looked faintly surprised; he examined the stone carefully, and then looked at me again. I whistled a short tune and looked up into the sky.

Roger gave an experimental yap; then, seeing I still took no notice, he followed it up with a volley of deep, rich barks that echoed among the olives. I let him bark for about five minutes. By this time I felt sure Yani must be aware of our arrival. Then I threw the stone for Roger, and as he fled after it joyfully, I made my way round to the front of the house.

The old shepherd, as I expected, was in the tattered shade of the vine that sprawled on its iron trellis-work above my head, but to my intense annoyance he had not woken up. He was sprawling in a plain deal chair, which was tilted back against the wall at a dangerous angle. His arms dangled limply, his legs were spread out, and his magnificent moustache, orange and white with nicotine and age, lifted and trembled with his snores, like some strange seaweed that is raised and lowered by a gentle swell. The thick fingers of his stumpy hands twitched as he slept, and I could see the thick-ribbed yellow nails, like flakes cut from a tallow candle. His brown face, wrinkled and furrowed as the bark of a pine, was expressionless, the eyes tightly shut. I stared at him, trying to will him to wake up, but with no result. It was not etiquette for me to wake him, and I was debating whether it would be worth while waiting until he awoke naturally, or whether it would be better to go and be bored by Leonora, when Roger came in search of me, bustling round the side of the house, ears pricked, tongue drooping. He saw me, wagged his tail in brief greeting, and glanced round with the air of a visitor who knows he is welcome. Suddenly he froze, his moustache bristled, and he started to walk forward slowly, stiff-legged and quivering. He had seen something that I had failed to observe: curled up under Yani's tilted chair sat a large, lanky grey cat, who was watching us with insolent green eyes. Before I could reach out and grab him, Roger had pounced. The cat, in a lithe movement that argued long practice, fled like a skimming stone to where the gnarled grape-vine twisted drunkenly round the trellis, and shot up it with a scutter of sharp claws. Crouched among the bunches of white grapes, she stared down at Roger and spat delicately. Roger, frustrated and angry, threw back his head and barked threats and insults. Yani's eyes flew open, his chair rocked and his arms flailed violently in an effort to keep his balance. The chair teetered uncertainly, and then settled on to all four legs with a thud.

'Saint Spiridion save me!' he implored loudly. 'God have mercy!'

He glared round, his moustache quivering, to find the cause of the uproar, and saw me sitting demurely on the wall. I greeted him sweetly and politely, as though nothing had happened, and asked if he had slept well. He rose to his feet, grinning, and scratched his stomach vigorously.

'Ah, it's you making enough noise to split my head. Your health, your health. Sit down, little lord,' he said, dusting off his chair and placing it for me; 'it is good to see you. You will eat with me, and have a drink, perhaps? It is a very hot afternoon, very hot – hot enough to melt a bottle.'

He stretched and, yawning loudly, displayed gums as innocent of teeth as a baby's. Then, turning towards the house, he roared:

'Aphrodite ... *Aphrodite* ... wake, woman ... foreigners have come ... the little lord is sitting with me. ... Bring food ... d'you hear?'

'I heard, I heard,' came a muffled voice from behind the shutters.

Yani grunted, wiped his moustache and made his way to the nearest olive-tree and retired discreetly behind it. He reappeared, doing up his trousers and yawning, and came over to sit on the wall near me.

'Today I should have taken my goats to Gastouri. But it was too hot, much too hot. In the hills the rocks will be so hot you could light a cigarette from them. So I went instead and tasted Taki's new white wine. Spiridion! what a wine . . . like the blood of a dragon and as smooth as a fish. . . . What a wine! When I came back the air was full of sleep, so here I am.'

He sighed deeply but impenitently, and fumbled in his pocket for his battered tin of tobacco and thin grey cigarette papers. His brown, calloused hand cupped to catch the little pile of golden leaf, and the fingers of his other hand tugged and pulled at it gently. He rolled the cigarette swiftly, nipped off the tobacco that dangled from the ends and replaced it in the tin, and then lit his smoke with the aid of a huge tin lighter from which a wick curled like an angry snake. He puffed reflectively for a moment, pulled a shred of tobacco off his moustache, and reached into his pocket again.

'Here, you are interested in the little ones of God; look at this that I caught this morning, crouching under a rock like the devil,' he said, pulling from his pocket a tiny bottle, firmly corked and filled with golden olive oil; 'a fine one this, a fighter. The only fighter I know who can do damage with his backside.'

The bottle, filled to the brim with oil, looked as though it were made of pale amber, and enshrined in the centre, held suspended by the thickness of the oil, was a small chocolate-brown scorpion, his tail curved like a scimitar over his back. He was quite dead, suffocated by the glutinous grave. Around his corpse was a faint wisp of discoloration, like a mist in the golden oil.

'See that?' said Yani. 'That's the poison. He was full, that one.'

I asked, curiously, why it was necessary to put the scorpion in oil.

Yani chuckled richly, and wiped his moustache.

'You do not know, little lord, though you spend all your time on your stomach catching these things, eh?' he said, greatly amused. 'Well, I will tell you. You never know, it may be of use to you. First catch the scorpion, catch him alive and catch him as gently as a falling feather. Then you put him, alive – mark you, alive – in a bottle of oil. Let him simmer, let him die in it, let the sweet oil soak up the poison. Then, should you ever be stung by one of his brothers (and Saint Spiridion protect you from that), you must rub the place with that oil. That will cure the sting for you so that it is of no more discomfort than the prick of a thorn.'

While I digested this curious information, Aphrodite appeared from the house, her wrinkled face as red as a pomegranate seed, bearing a tin tray on which was a bottle of wine, a jug of water and a plate with bread, olives and figs on it. Yani and I drank the wine, watered to a delicate pale pink, and ate the food in silence. In spite of his toothless gums, Yani tore large pieces of the bread off and champed them hungrily, swallowing great lumps that made his wrinkled throat swell. When we had finished, he sat back, wiped his moustache carefully and took up the conversation again, as if there had been no pause.

'I knew a man once, a shepherd like myself, who had been to a fiesta in a distant village. On the way back, as his stomach was warm with wine, he decided to have a sleep, so he found a spot beneath some myrtles. But while he slept a scorpion crept out from under the leaves and crawled into his ear, and when he awoke it stung him.'

Yani paused at this psychological moment to spit over the wall and roll himself another cigarette.

'Yes,' he sighed at last, 'it was very sad ... one so young. The tiny scorpion stung him in the ear ... phut! ... like that. The poor fellow flung himself about in his agony. He ran screaming through the olives, tearing at his head. ... Ah! it was dreadful. There was no one to hear his cries and help him ... no one at all. In terrible pain he started to run for the village, but he never reached it. He fell down dead, down there in the valley, not far from the road. We found him the next morning when we were going to the fields. What a sight! What a sight! With that one little bite his head had swollen up as though his brains were pregnant, and he was dead, quite dead.'

Yani sighed deeply and lugubriously, twirling the little bottle of oil in his fingers.

'That is why,' he went on, 'I never go up into the hills and sleep. And, in case I should perhaps share some wine with a friend and forget the danger, I always carry a scorpion bottle with me.'

The talk drifted to other and equally absorbing topics, and after an hour or so I rose, dusted the crumbs off my lap, thanked the old man and his wife for their hospitality, accepted a bunch of grapes as a parting present and set off towards home. Roger walked close to me, his eyes fixed on my pocket, for he had noticed the grapes. At length, finding an olive-grove, dark and cool with the long shadows of evening, we sat down by a mossy bank and shared the fruit. Roger ate his whole, pips and all. I spat out my pips into a circle around me, and imagined with satisfaction the flourishing vineyard that would grow up on the spot. When the grapes were finished I rolled over on to my stomach and, with my chin in my hands, examined the bank behind me.

A tiny green grasshopper with a long, melancholy face sat twitching his hind legs nervously. A fragile snail sat on a moss sprig, meditating and waiting for the evening dew. A plump scarlet mite, the size of a match-head, struggled like a tubby huntsman through the forest of moss. It was a microscopic world, full of fascinating life. As I watched the mite making his slow progress I noticed a curious thing. Here and there on the green plush surface of the moss were scattered faint circular marks, each the size of a shilling. So faint were they that it was only from certain angles they were noticeable at all. They reminded me of a full moon seen behind thick clouds, a faint circle that seemed to shift and change. I wondered idly what could have made them. They were too irregular, too scattered to be the prints of some beast, and what was it that would walk up an almost vertical bank in such a haphazard manner? Besides, they were not like imprints. I prodded the edge of one of these circles with a piece of grass. It remained unmoved. I began to think the mark was caused by some curious way in which the moss grew. I probed again, more vigorously, and suddenly my stomach gave a clutch of tremendous excitement. It was as though my grass-stalk had found a hidden spring, for the whole circle lifted up like a trapdoor. As I stared, I saw to my amazement that it *was* in fact a trapdoor, lined with silk, and with a neatly bevelled edge that fitted snugly into the mouth of the silk-lined shaft it concealed. The edge of the door was fastened to the lip of the tunnel by a small flap of silk that acted as a hinge. I gazed at this magnificent piece of workmanship and wondered what on earth could have made it. Peering down the silken tunnel, I could see nothing; I poked my grass-stalk down, but there was no response. For a long time I sat staring at this fantastic home, trying to decide what sort of beast had made it. I thought that it might be a wasp of some sort, but had never heard of a wasp that fitted its nest with secret doors. I felt that I must get to the bottom of this problem immediately. I would go down and ask George if he knew what this mysterious beast was. Calling Roger, who was busily trying to uproot an olive-tree, I set off at a brisk trot.

I arrived at George's villa out of breath, bursting with suppressed excitement, gave a perfunctory knock at the door and dashed in. Only then did I realize he had company. Seated in a chair near him was a figure which, at first glance, I decided must be George's brother, for he also wore a beard. He was, however, in contrast to George, immaculately dressed in a grey flannel suit with waistcoat, a spotless white shirt, a tasteful but sombre tie, and large, solid, highly polished boots. I paused on the threshold, embarrassed, while George surveyed me sardonically.

'Good evening,' he greeted me. 'From the joyful speed of your entry I take it that you have not come for a little extra tuition.'

I apologized for the intrusion, and then told George about the curious nests I had found.

'Thank heavens you're here, Theodore,' he said to his bearded companion. 'I shall now be able to hand the problem over to expert hands.'

'Hardly an expert . . .' mumbled the man called Theodore, deprecatingly.

'Gerry, this is Doctor Theodore Stephanides,' said George. 'He is an expert on practically everything you care to mention. And what you don't mention, he does. He, like you, is an eccentric nature-lover. Theodore, this is Gerry Durrell.'

I said how do you do, politely, but to my surprise the bearded man rose to his feet, stepped briskly across the room and held out a large white hand.

'Very pleased to meet you,' he said, apparently addressing his beard, and gave me a quick, shy glance from twinkling blue eyes.

I shook his hand and said I was very pleased to meet him, too. Then we stood in awkward silence, while George watched us, grinning.

'Well, Theodore,' he said at last, 'and what d'you think produced these strange secret passages?'

Theodore clasped his hands behind his back, lifted himself on to his toes several times, his boots squeaking protestingly, and gravely considered the floor.

'Well . . . er . . .' he said, his words coming slowly and meticulously, 'it sounds to me as though they might be the burrows of the trapdoor spider . . . er . . . it is a species which is quite common here in Corfu . . . that is to say, when I say common, I suppose I have found some thirty or . . .er . . .forty specimens during the time I have been here.'

'Ah,' said George, 'trapdoor spiders, eh?'

'Yes,' said Theodore. 'I feel that it's more than probable that that is what they are. However, I may be mistaken.'

He rose and fell on his toes, squeaking gently, and then he shot me a keen glance.

'Perhaps, if they are not too far away, we could go and verify it,' he suggested tentatively. 'I mean to say, if you have nothing better to do, and it's not too far . . .'

His voice trailed away on a faintly interrogative note. I said that they were only just up the hill, not really far.

'Um,' said Theodore.

'Don't let him drag you about all over the place, Theodore,' said George. 'You don't want to be galloped about the countryside.'

'No, no, not at all,' said Theodore; 'I was just about to leave, and I can easily walk that way back. It is quite a simple matter for me to . . . er . . .cut down through the olive-groves and reach Canoni.'

He picked up a neat grey homburg and placed it squarely on his head. At the door he held out his hand and shook George's briefly.

'Thank you for a delightful tea,' he said, and stumped gravely off along the path by my side.

As we walked along I studied him covertly. He had a straight, well-shaped nose; a humorous mouth lurking in the ash-blond beard; straight, rather bushy eyebrows under which his eyes, keen but with a twinkle in them and laughter-wrinkles at the corners, surveyed the world. He strode along energetically, humming to himself. When we came to a ditch full of stagnant water he stopped for a moment and stared down into it, his beard bristling.

'Um,' he said conversationally, *'daphnia magna.'*

He rasped at his beard with his thumb, and then set off down the path again.

'Unfortunately,' he said to me, 'I was coming out to see some people . . . er . . . *friends* of mine, and so I did not bring my collecting bag with me. It is a pity, for that ditch might have contained something.'

When we branched off the fairly smooth path we had been travelling along and started up the stony goat-track, I expected some sort of protest, but Theodore strode behind me with unabated vigour, still humming. At length we came to the gloomy olive-grove, and I led Theodore to the bank and pointed out the mysterious trapdoor.

He peered down at it, his eyes narrowed.

'Ah ha,' he said, 'yes . . . um . . . yes.'

He produced from his waistcoat pocket a tiny penknife, opened it, inserted the point of the blade delicately under the little door and flipped it back.

'Um, yes,' he repeated; *'cteniza.'*

He peered down the tunnel, blew down it and then let the trapdoor fall into place again.

'Yes, they are the burrows of the trapdoor spiders,' he said, 'but this one does not appear to be inhabited. Generally, the creature will hold on to the . . . er . . .*trapdoor* . . . with her legs, or rather, her *claws*, and she holds on with such tenacity that you have to be careful or you will damage the door, trying to force it open. Um . . . yes . . . these are the burrows of the females, of course. The male makes a similar burrow, but it is only about half the size.'

I remarked that it was the most curious structure I had seen.

'Ah ha! yes,' said Theodore, 'they are certainly very curious. A thing that always puzzles me is how the female knows when the male is approaching.'

I must have looked blank, for he teetered on his toes, shot me a quick look and went on:

'The spider, of course, waits inside its burrow until some insect – a fly or a grasshopper, or something similar – chances to walk past. They can judge, it seems, whether the insect is close enough to be caught. If it is, the spider ... er ... pops out of its hole and catches the creature. Now when the male comes in search of the female he must walk over the moss to the trapdoor, and I have often wondered why it is that he is not ... er ... devoured by the female in mistake. It is possible, of course, that his footsteps sound different. Or he may make some sort of ... you know ...some sort of *sound* which the female recognizes.'

We walked down the hill in silence. When we reached the place where the paths forked I said that I must leave him.

'Ah, well, I'll say good-bye,' he said, staring at his boots. 'I have enjoyed meeting you.'

We stood in silence for a moment. Theodore was afflicted with the acute embarrassment that always seemed to overwhelm him when greeting or saying good-bye to someone. He stared hard at his boots for a moment longer, and then he held out his hand and shook mine gravely.

'Good-bye,' he said. 'I ... er ... I expect we shall meet again.'

He turned and stumped off down the hill, swinging his stick, staring about him with observant eyes. I watched him out of sight and then walked slowly in the direction of the villa. I was at once confused and amazed by Theodore. First, since he was obviously a scientist of considerable repute (and I could have told this by his beard), he was to me a person of great importance. In fact he was the only person I had met until now who seemed to share my enthusiasm for zoology. Secondly, I was extremely flattered to find that he treated me and talked to me exactly as though I was his own age. I liked him for this, as I was not talked down to by my family, and I took rather a poor view of any outsider trying to do so. But Theodore not only talked to me as though I was grown up, but also as though I was as knowledgeable as he.

The facts he told me about the trapdoor spider haunted me: the idea of the creature crouching in its silken tunnel, holding the door closed with its hooked claws, listening to the movement of the insects on the moss above. What, I wondered, did things sound like to a trapdoor spider? I could imagine that a snail would trail over the door with a noise like sticking-plaster being slowly torn off. A centipede would sound like a troop of cavalry. A fly would patter in brisk spurts, followed by a pause while it washed its hands – a dull rasping sound like a knife-grinder at work. The larger beetles, I decided, would sound like steam-rollers, while the smaller ones, the lady-birds and others, would probably purr over the moss like clockwork motor-cars. Fascinated by this thought, I made my way back home through the darkening fields, to tell the family of my new discovery and of my meeting with Theodore. I hoped to see him again, for there were many things I wanted to ask him, but I felt it would be unlikely that he would have very much time to spare for me. I was mistaken, however, for two days later Leslie came back from an excursion into the town, and handed me a small parcel.

'Met that bearded johnny,' he said laconically; 'you know, that scientist bloke. Said this was for you.'

Incredulously I stared at the parcel. Surely it couldn't be for me? There must be some mistake, for a great scientist would hardly bother to send me parcels. I turned it over, and there, written on it in neat, spidery writing, was my name. I tore off the paper as quickly as I could. Inside was a small box and a letter.

My dear Gerry Durrell,

I wondered, after our conversation the other day, if it might not assist your investigations of the local natural history to have some form of magnifying instrument. I am therefore sending you this pocket microscope, in the hope that it will be of some use to you. It is, of course, not of very high magnification, but you will find it sufficient for *field* work.

With best wishes,
Yours sincerely,
Theo. Stephanides

P.S. If you have nothing better to do on Thursday, perhaps you would care to come to tea, and I could then show you some of my microscope slides.

Chapter Six

The Sweet Spring

During the last days of the dying summer, and throughout the warm, wet winter that followed, tea with Theodore became a weekly affair. Every Thursday I would set out, my pockets bulging with matchboxes and test-tubes full of specimens, to be driven into the town by Spiro. It was an appointment that I would not have missed for anything.

Theodore would welcome me in his study, a room that met with my full approval. It was, in my opinion, just what a room should be. The walls were lined with tall bookshelves filled with volumes on freshwater biology, botany, astronomy, medicine, folk-lore and similar fascinating and sensible subjects. Interspersed with these were selections of ghost and crime stories.

Thus Sherlock Holmes rubbed shoulders with Darwin, and Le Fanu with Fabre, in what I considered to be a thoroughly well-balanced library. At one window of the room stood Theodore's telescope, its nose to the sky like a howling dog, while the sills of every window bore a parade of jars and bottles containing minute freshwater fauna, whirling and twitching among the delicate fronds of green weed. On one side of the room was a massive desk, piled high with scrapbooks, micro-photographs, X-ray plates, diaries and note-books. On the opposite side of the room was the microscope table, with its powerful lamp on the jointed stem leaning like a lily over the flat boxes that housed Theodore's collection of slides. The microscopes themselves, gleaming like magpies, were housed under a series of beehive-like domes of glass.

'How are you?' Theodore would inquire, as if I were a complete stranger, and give me his characteristic handshake – a sharp downward tug, like a man testing a knot in a rope. The formalities being over, we could then turn our minds to more important topics.

'I was ... er ... you know ... looking through my slides just before your arrival, and I came across one which may interest you. It is a slide of the mouth-parts of the rat flea ... *ceratophyllus fasciatus,* you know. Now, I'll just adjust the microscope ... There! ... you see? Very curious. I mean to say, you could almost imagine it was a human face, couldn't you? Now I had another ... er ... slide here. ... That's funny. Ah! got it. Now this one is of the spinnerets of the garden or cross spider ... er ... *epeira fasciata.* ...'

So, absorbed and happy, we would pore over the microscope. Filled with enthusiasm, we would tack from subject to subject, and if Theodore could not answer my ceaseless flow of questions himself, he had books that could. Gaps would appear in the bookcase as volume after volume was extracted to be consulted, and by our side would be an ever-growing pile of volumes.

'Now this one is a cyclops ... *cyclops viridis* ... which I caught out near Govino the other day. It is a female with egg-sacs. ... Now, I'll just adjust ... you'll be able to see the eggs quite clearly. ... I'll just put her in the live box ... er ... hum ... there are several species of cyclops found here in Corfu. ...'

In the brilliant circle of white light a weird creature would appear, a pear-shaped body, long antennae that twitched indignantly, a tail like sprigs of heather, and on each side of it (slung like sacks of onions on a donkey) the two large sacs bulging with pink beads.

'... called cyclops because, as you can see, it has a single eye situated in the centre of its forehead. That's to say, in the centre of what *would* be its forehead if a cyclops had one. In Ancient Greek mythology, as you know, a cyclops was one of a group of giants ... er ... each of whom had one eye. Their task was to forge iron for Hephaestus.'

Outside, the warm wind would shoulder the shutters, making them creak, and the rain-drops would chase each other down the windowpane like transparent tadpoles.

'Ah ha! It is curious that you should mention that. The peasants in Salonika have a very similar ... er ... superstition. ... No, no, merely a superstition. I have a book here that gives a most *interesting* account of vampires in ... um ... Bosnia. It seems that the local people there ...'

Tea would arrive, the cakes squatting on cushions of cream, toast in a melting shawl of butter, cups agleam and a faint wisp of steam rising from the teapot spout.

'... but, on the other hand, it is impossible to say that there is *no* life on Mars. It is, in my opinion, quite possible that some form of life will be found ... er ... *discovered* there, should we ever succeed in *getting* there. But there is no reason to suppose that any form of life found there would be identical. ...'

Sitting there, neat and correct in his tweed suit, Theodore would chew his toast slowly and methodically, his beard bristling, his eyes kindling with enthusiasm at each new subject that swam into our conversation. To me his knowledge seemed inexhaustible. He was a rich vein of information, and I mined him assiduously. No matter what the subject, Theodore could contribute something interesting to it. At last I would hear Spiro honking his horn in the street below, and I would rise reluctantly to go.

'Good-bye,' Theodore would say, tugging my hand. 'It's been a pleasure having you ... er ... no, no, not at all. See you next Thursday. When the weather gets better ... er ... less damp ... in the *spring*, you know ... perhaps we might go for some walks together ... see what we can obtain. There are some most interesting ditches in the Val de Ropa ... um, yes. ... Well, good-bye. ... Not at all.'

Driving back along the dark, rain-washed roads, Spiro humming richly as he squatted behind the wheel, I would dream of the spring to come, and of all the wonderful creatures that Theodore and I would capture.

Eventually the warm wind and the rain of winter seemed to polish the sky, so that when January arrived it shone a clear, tender blue ... the same blue as that of the tiny flames that devoured the olive-logs in the charcoal pits. The nights were still and cool, with a moon so fragile it barely freckled the sea with silver points. The dawns were pale and translucent until the sun rose, mist-wrapped, like a gigantic silkworm cocoon, and washed the island with a delicate bloom of gold dust.

With March came the spring, and the island was flower-filled, scented, and a-flutter with new leaves. The cypress-trees that had tossed and hissed during the winds of winter now stood straight and sleek against the sky, covered with a misty coat of greenish-white cones. Waxy yellow crocuses appeared in great clusters, bubbling out among the tree-roots and tumbling down the banks. Under the myrtles, the grape-hyacinths lifted buds like magenta sugar-drops, and the gloom of the oak-thickets was filled with the dim smoke of a thousand blue day-irises. Anemones, delicate and easily wind-bruised, lifted ivory flowers the petals of which seemed to have been dipped in wine. Vetch, marigold, asphodel and a hundred others flooded the fields and woods. Even the ancient olives, bent and hollowed by a thousand springs, decked themselves in clusters of minute creamy flowers, modest and yet decorative, as became their great age. It was no half-hearted spring, this: the whole island vibrated with it as though a great, ringing chord had been struck. Everyone and everything heard it and responded. It was apparent in the gleam of flower-petals, the flash of bird wings and the sparkle in the dark, liquid eyes of the peasant girls. In the water-filled ditches the frogs that looked newly enamelled snored a rapturous chorus in the lush weeds.

In the village coffee-shops the wine seemed redder and, somehow, more potent. Blunt, work-calloused fingers plucked at guitar strings with strange gentleness, and rich voices rose in lilting, haunting song.

Spring affected the family in a variety of ways. Larry bought himself a guitar and a large barrel of strong red wine. He interspersed his bouts of work by playing haphazardly on the instrument and singing Elizabethan love-songs in a meek tenor voice, with frequent pauses for refreshment. This would soon induce a mood of melancholy, and the love-songs would become more doleful, while between each Larry would pause to inform whichever member of the family happened to be present that spring, for him, did not mean the beginning of a new year, but the death of the old one. The grave, he would proclaim, making the guitar rumble ominously, yawned a little wider with each season.

One evening the rest of us had gone out and left Mother and Larry alone together. Larry had spent the evening singing more and more dismally, until he had succeeded in working them both into a fit of acute depression. They attempted to alleviate this state with the aid of wine, but unfortunately this had the reverse effect, for they were not used to the heavy wines of Greece. When we returned we were somewhat startled to be greeted by Mother, standing at the door of the villa with a hurricane lantern. She informed us with lady-like precision and dignity that she wished to be buried under the rose-bushes. The novelty of this lay in the fact that she had chosen such an accessible place for the disposal of her remains. Mother spent a lot of her spare time choosing places to be buried in, but they were generally situated in the most remote areas, and one had visions of the funeral *cortège* dropping exhausted by the wayside long before it had reached the grave.

When left undisturbed by Larry, however, spring for Mother meant an endless array of fresh vegetables with which to experiment, and a riot of new flowers to delight her in the garden. There streamed from the kitchen a tremendous number of new dishes, soups, stews, savouries and curries, each richer, more fragrant and more exotic than the last. Larry began to suffer from dyspepsia. Scorning the simple remedy of eating less, he procured an immense tin of bicarbonate of soda, and would solemnly take a dose after every meal.

'Why do you *eat* so much if it upsets you, dear?' Mother asked.

'It would be an insult to your cooking to eat less,' Larry replied unctuously.

'You're getting terribly fat,' said Margo; 'it's very bad for you.'

'Nonsense!' said Larry in alarm. 'I'm not getting fat, Mother, am I?'

'You look as though you've put on a little weight,' Mother admitted, surveying him critically.

'It's your fault,' Larry said unreasonably. 'You will keep tempting me with these aromatic delicacies. You're driving me to ulcers. I shall have to go on a diet. What's a good diet, Margo?'

'Well,' said Margo, launching herself with enthusiasm into her favourite topic, 'you could try the orange-juice and salad one; that's awfully good. There's the milk and raw vegetable one . . . that's good too, but it takes a little time. Or there's the boiled fish and brown bread one. I don't know what that's like, I haven't tried it yet.'

'Dear God!' exclaimed Larry, genuinely shocked, 'are those diets?'

'Yes, and they're all very good ones,' said Margo earnestly. 'I've been trying the orange-juice one and it's done wonders for my acne.'

'No,' said Larry firmly. 'I'm not going to do it if it means that I have to champ my way like a damned ungulate through bushels of raw fruit and vegetables. You will all have to resign yourselves to the fact that I shall be taken from you at an early age, suffering from fatty degeneration of the heart.'

At the next meal he took the precaution of having a large dose of bicarbonate beforehand, and then protested bitterly that the food tasted queer.

Margo was always badly affected by the spring. Her personal appearance, always of absorbing interest to her, now became almost an obsession. Piles of freshly laundered clothes filled her bedroom, while the washing-line sagged under the weight of clothes newly washed. Singing shrilly and untunefully she would drift about the villa, carrying piles of flimsy underwear or bottles of scent. She would seize every opportunity to dive into the bathroom, in a swirl of white towels, and once in there she was as hard to dislodge as a limpet from a rock. The family in turn would bellow and batter on the door, getting no more satisfaction than an assurance that she was nearly finished, an assurance which we had learnt by bitter experience not to have any faith in. Eventually she would emerge, glowing and immaculate, and drift from the house, humming, to sun-bathe in the olive-groves or go down to the sea and swim. It was during one of these excursions to the sea that she met an over-good-looking young Turk. With unusual modesty she did not inform anyone of her frequent bathing assignations with this paragon, feeling, as she told us later, that we would not be interested. It was, of course, Spiro who discovered it. He watched over Margo's welfare with the earnest concern of a St Bernard, and there was precious little she could do without Spiro knowing about it. He cornered Mother in the kitchen one morning, glanced surreptitiously round to make sure they were not overheard, sighed deeply and broke the news to her.

'I'm very sorrys to haves to tells you this, Mrs Durrells,' he rumbled, 'buts I thinks you oughts to knows.'

Mother had by now become quite used to Spiro's conspiratorial air when he came to deliver some item of information about the family, and it no longer worried her.

"What's the matter now, Spiro?' she asked.

'It's Missy Margo,' said Spiro sorrowfully.

'What about her?'

Spiro glanced round uneasily.

'Dos you knows shes meetings a *mans*?' he inquired in a vibrant whisper.

'A man? Oh ... er ... yes, I did know,' said Mother, lying valiantly.

Spiro hitched up his trousers over his belly and leant forward.

'But dids you knows he's a *Turk*?' he questioned in tones of blood-curdling ferocity.

'A Turk?' said Mother vaguely. 'No, I didn't know he was a Turk. What's wrong with that?'

Spiro looked horrified.

'Gollys, Mrs Durrells, whats wrongs with it? He's a *Turk*. I wouldn'ts trust a sonofabitch Turk with any girls. He'll cuts her throats, thats what he'll do. Honest to Gods, Mrs Durrells, its not safe, Missy Margo swimmings with hims.'

'All right, Spiro,' said Mother soothingly, 'I'll speak to Margo about it.'

'I just thoughts you oughts to knows, thats all. Buts donts you worrys ... if he dids anythings to Missy Margo I'd fix the bastard,' Spiro assured her earnestly.

Acting on the information received, Mother mentioned the matter to Margo, in a slightly less bloodcurdling manner than Spiro's, and suggested that the young Turk be brought up to tea. Delighted, Margo went off to fetch him, while Mother hastily made a cake and some scones, and warned the rest of us to be on our best behaviour. The Turk, when he arrived, turned out to be a tall young man, with meticulously waved hair and a flashy smile that managed to convey the minimum of humour with the maximum of condescension. He had all the sleek, smug self-possession of a cat in season. He pressed Mother's hand to his lips as though he was conferring an honour on her, and scattered the largesse of his smile for the rest of us. Mother, feeling the hackles of the family rising, threw herself desperately into the breach.

'Lovely having you ... wanted so often ... never seems time, you know ... days simply *fly* past ... Margo's told us so much about you ... do have a scone ...' she said breathlessly, smiling with dazzling charm and handing him a piece of cake.

'So kind,' murmured the Turk, leaving us in some doubt as to whether he was referring to us or himself. There was a pause.

'He's on holiday here,' announced Margo suddenly, as though it was something quite unique.

'Really?' said Larry waspishly. 'On holiday? Amazing!'

'I had a holiday once,' said Leslie indistinctly through a mouthful of cake; 'remember it clearly.'

Mother rattled the tea-things nervously, and glared at them.

'Sugar?' she inquired fruitily. 'Sugar in your tea?'

'Thank you, yes.'

There was another short silence, during which we all sat and watched Mother pouring out the tea and searching her mind desperately for a topic of conversation. At length the Turk turned to Larry.

'You write, I believe?' he said with complete lack of interest.

Larry's eyes glittered. Mother, seeing the danger signs, rushed in quickly before he could reply.

'Yes, yes,' she smiled, 'he writes away, day after day. Always tapping at the typewriter.'

'I always feel that I could write superbly if I tried,' remarked the Turk.

'Really?' said Mother. 'Yes, well, it's a gift, I suppose, like so many things.'

'He swims well,' remarked Margo, 'and he goes out terribly far.'

'I have no fear,' said the Turk modestly. 'I am a superb swimmer, so I have no fear. When I ride the horse, I have no fear, for I ride superbly. I can sail the boat magnificently in the typhoon without fear.'

He sipped his tea delicately, regarding our awestruck faces with approval.

'You see,' he went on, in case we had missed the point, 'you see, I am not a fearful man.'

The result of the tea-party was that the next day Margo received a note from the Turk asking her if she would accompany him to the cinema that evening.

'Do you think I ought to go?' she asked Mother.

'If you want to, dear,' Mother answered, adding firmly, 'but tell him I'm coming too.'

'That should be a jolly evening for you,' remarked Larry.

'Oh, Mother, you can't,' protested Margo; 'he'll think it so queer.'

'Nonsense, dear,' said Mother vaguely. 'Turks are quite used to chaperones and things . . . look at their harems.'

So that evening Mother and Margo, dressed becomingly, made their way down the hill to meet the Turk. The only cinema was an open-air one in the town, and we calculated that the show should be over by ten at the latest. Larry, Leslie and I waited eagerly for their return. At half-past one in the morning Margo and Mother, in the last stages of exhaustion, crept into the villa and sank into chairs.

'Oh, so you've come back?' said Larry; 'we thought you'd flown with him. We imagined you galloping about Constantinople on camels, your yashmaks rippling seductively in the breeze.'

'We've had the most awful evening,' said Mother, easing her shoes off, 'really awful.'

'What happened?' asked Leslie.

'Well, to begin with he stank of the most frightful perfume,' said Margo, 'and that put me off straight away.'

'We went in the cheapest seats, so close to the screen that I got a headache,' said Mother, 'and simply crammed together like sardines. It was *so* oppressive I couldn't breathe. And then, to crown it all, I got a flea. It was nothing to laugh at, Larry; really I didn't know what to do. The blessed thing got inside my corsets and I could feel it running about. I couldn't very well scratch, it would have looked so peculiar. I had to keep pressing myself against the seat. I think he noticed, though . . . he kept giving me funny looks from the corner of his eye. Then in the interval he went out and came back with some of that horrible, sickly Turkish Delight, and before long we were all covered with white sugar, and I had a dreadful thirst. In the second interval he went out and came back with flowers. I ask you, dear, flowers in the middle of the cinema. That's Margo's bouquet, on the table.'

Mother pointed to a massive bunch of spring flowers, tied up in a tangle of coloured ribbons. She delved into her bag and produced a minute bunch of violets that looked at though they had been trodden on by an exceptionally hefty horse.

'This,' she said, 'was for me.'

'But the worst part was coming home,' said Margo.

'A dreadful journey!' Mother agreed. 'When we came out of the cinema I thought we were going to get a car, but no, he hustled us into a cab, and a very smelly one at that. Really, I think he must be mental to try and come all that way in a cab. Anyway, it took us hours and *hours*, because the poor horse was tired, and I was sitting there trying to be polite, dying to scratch myself, and longing for a drink. All the fool could do was to sit there grinning at Margo and singing Turkish love-songs. I could have cheerfully hit him. I thought we were *never* going to get back. We couldn't even get rid of him at the bottom of the hill. He insisted on coming up with us, armed with a huge stick, because he said the forests were full of serpents at this time of the year. I was *so* glad to see the back of him. I'm afraid you'll just *have* to choose your boy friends more carefully in future, Margo. I can't go through that sort of thing again. I was terrified he'd come right up to the door and we'd have to ask him in. I thought we'd *never* get away.'

'You obviously didn't make yourself fearful enough.' said Larry.

For Leslie the coming of spring meant the soft pipe of wings as the turtle-doves and wood-pigeons arrived, and the sudden flash and scuttle of a hare among the myrtles. So, after visiting numerous gun-shops and after much technical argument, he returned to the villa one day proudly carrying a double-barrelled shotgun. His first action was to take it to his room, strip it down and clean it, while I stood and watched, fascinated by the gleaming barrels and stock, sniffing rapturously at the rich heavy scent of the gun-oil.

'Isn't she a beauty?' he crooned, more to himself than to me, his vivid blue eyes shining. 'Isn't she a honey?'

Tenderly he ran his hands over the silken shape of the weapon. Then he whipped it suddenly to his shoulder and followed an imaginary flock of birds across the ceiling of the room.

'Pow! . . . pow!' he intoned, jerking the gun against his shoulder. 'A left and a right, and down they come.'

He gave the gun a final rub with the oily rag and set it carefully in the corner of the room by his bed.

'We'll have a try for some turtle-doves tomorrow, shall we?' he continued, splitting open a packet and spilling the scarlet shells on to the bed. 'They start coming over about six. That little hill across the valley is a good place.'

So at dawn he and I hurried through the hunched and misty olive-groves, up the valley where the myrtles were wet and squeaky with dew, and on to the top of the little hill. We stood waist-deep among the vines, waiting for the light to strengthen and for the birds to start flighting. Suddenly the pale morning sky was flecked with dark specks, moving as swiftly as arrows, and we could hear the quick wheep of wings. Leslie waited, standing stockily with legs apart, gun-stock resting on his hip, his eyes, intense and gleaming, following the birds. Nearer and nearer they flew, until it seemed that they must fly past us and be lost in the silvery, trembling olive-tops behind. At the very last moment the gun leapt smoothly to his shoulder, the beetle-shiny barrels lifted their mouths to the sky, the gun jerked as the report echoed briefly, like the crack of a great branch in a still forest. The turtle-dove, one minute so swift and intent in its flight, now fell languidly to earth, followed by a swirl of soft, cinnamon-coloured feathers. When five doves hung from his belt, limp, bloodstained, with demurely closed eyes, he lit a cigarette, pulled his hat-brim down over his eyes and cuddled the gun under his arm.

'Come on,' he said; 'we've got enough. Let's give the poor devils a rest.'

We returned through the sun-striped olive-groves where the chaffinches were pinking like a hundred tiny coins among the leaves. Yani, the shepherd, was driving his herd of goats out to graze. His brown face, with its great sweep of nicotine-stained moustache, wrinkled into a smile; a gnarled hand appeared from the heavy folds of his sheepskin cloak and was raised in salute.

'*Chairete*,' he called in his deep voice, the beautiful Greek greeting, '*chairete, kyrioi* ... be happy.'

The goats poured among the olives, uttering stammering cries to each other, the leader's bell clonking rhythmically. The chaffinches tinkled excitedly. A robin puffed out his chest like a tangerine among the myrtles and gave a trickle of song. The island was drenched with dew, radiant with early morning sun, full of stirring life. Be happy. How could one be anything else in such a season?

Conversation

As soon as we had settled down and started to enjoy the island, Larry, with characteristic generosity, wrote to all his friends and asked them to come out and stay. The fact that the villa was only just big enough to house the family apparently had not occurred to him.

'I've asked a few people out for a week or so,' he said casually to Mother one morning.

'That will be nice, dear,' said Mother unthinkingly.

'I thought it would do us good to have some intelligent and stimulating company around. We don't want to stagnate.'

'I hope they're not too *highbrow*, dear,' said Mother.

'Good Lord, Mother, of course they're *not*; just extremely charming, ordinary people. I don't know why you've got this phobia about people being highbrow.'

'I don't like the highbrow ones,' said Mother plaintively. 'I'm not highbrow, and I can't talk about poetry and things. But they always seem to imagine, just because I'm your mother, that I should be able to discuss literature at great length with them. And they always come and ask me silly questions just when I'm in the middle of cooking.'

'I don't ask you to discuss art with them,' said Larry testily, 'but I think you might try and conceal your revolting taste in literature. Here I fill the house with good books and I find your bedside table simply groaning under the weight of cookery books, gardening books and the most lurid-looking mystery stories. I can't think where you get hold of these things.'

'They're very good detective stories,' said Mother defensively. 'I borrowed them from Theodore.'

Larry gave a short, exasperated sigh and picked up his book again.

'You'd better let the Pension Suisse know when they're coming,' Mother remarked.

'What for?' asked Larry, surprised.

'So they can reserve the rooms,' said Mother, equally surprised.

'But I've invited them to stay here,' Larry pointed out.

"Larry! You haven't! Really, you are most *thoughtless*. How can they possibly stay here?'

'I really don't see what you're making a fuss about,' said Larry coldly.

'But where are they going to *sleep*?' said Mother, distraught. 'There's hardly enough room for us, as it is.'

'Nonsense, Mother, there's plenty of room if the place is organized properly. If Margo and Les sleep out on the veranda, that gives you two rooms; you and Gerry could move into the drawing-room, and that would leave those rooms free.'

'Don't be silly, dear. We can't all camp out all over the place like gypsies. Besides, it's chilly at night, and I don't think Margo and Les ought to sleep outside. There simply isn't room to entertain in this villa. You'll just have to write to these people and put them off.'

'I can't put them off,' said Larry, 'they're on their way.'

'Really, Larry, you are the most annoying creature. Why on earth didn't you tell me before? You wait until they're nearly here, and then you tell me.'

'I didn't know you were going to treat the arrival of a few friends as if it was a major catastrophe,' Larry explained.

'But, dear, it's so silly to invite people when you know there's no room in the villa.'

'I do wish you'd stop fussing,' said Larry irritably; 'there's quite a simple solution to the whole business.'

'What?' asked Mother suspiciously.

'Well, since the villa isn't big enough, let's, move to one that is.'

'Don't be ridiculous. Whoever heard of moving into a larger house because you've invited some friends to stay?'

'What's the matter with the idea? It seems a perfectly sensible solution to me; after all, if you say there's no room here, the obvious thing to do is to move.'

'The obvious thing to do is not to invite people,' said Mother severely.

'I don't think it's good for us to live like hermits,' said Larry. 'I only really invited them for you. They're a charming crowd. I thought you'd like to have them. Liven things up a bit for you.'

'I'm quite lively enough, thank you,' said Mother with dignity.

'Well, I don't know what we're going to do.'

'I really don't see why they can't stay in the Pension Suisse, dear.'

'You can't ask people out to stay with you and then make them live in a third-rate hotel.'

'How many have you invited?' asked Mother.

'Oh, just a few ... two or three. ... They won't all be coming at once. I expect they'll turn up in batches.'

'I think at least you might be able to tell me how many you've invited,' said Mother.

'Well, I can't remember now. Some of them didn't reply, but that doesn't mean anything... they're probably on their way and thought it was hardly worth letting us know. Anyway, if you budget for seven or eight people I should think that would cover it.'

'You mean, including ourselves?'

'No, no, I mean seven or eight people as well as the family.'

'But it's absurd, Larry; we can't possibly fit thirteen people into this villa, with all the good will in the world.'

'Well, let's *move*, then. I've offered you a perfectly sensible solution. I don't know what you're arguing about.'

'But don't be ridiculous, dear. Even if we did move into a villa large enough to house thirteen people, what are we going to do with the extra space when they've gone?'

'Invite some more people,' said Larry, astonished that Mother should not have thought of this simple answer for herself.

Mother glared at him, her spectacles askew.

'Really, Larry, you do make me cross,' she said at last.

'I think it's rather unfair that you should blame me because your organization breaks down with the arrival of a few guests,' said Larry austerely.

'A few guests!' squeaked Mother. 'I'm glad you think eight people are a few guests!'

'I think you're adopting a most unreasonable attitude.'

'I suppose there's nothing unreasonable in inviting people and not letting me know?'

Larry gave her an injured look, and picked up his book.

'Well, I've done all I can,' he said; 'I can't do any more.'

There was a long silence, during which Larry placidly read his book and Mother piled bunches of roses into vases and placed them haphazardly round the room, muttering to herself.

'I wish you wouldn't just *lie* there,' she said at last. 'After all, they're your friends. It's up to you to do something.'

Larry, with a long-suffering air, put down his book.

'I really don't know what you expect me to do,' he said. 'Every suggestion I've made you've disagreed with.'

'If you made sensible suggestions I wouldn't disagree.'

'I don't see anything ludicrous in anything I suggested.'

'But, Larry dear, do be reasonable. We can't just rush to a new villa because some people are coming. I doubt whether we'd find one in time, anyway. And there's Gerry's lessons.'

'All that could easily be sorted out if you put your mind to it.'

'We are *not* moving to another villa,' said Mother firmly; 'I've made up my mind about that.'

She straightened her spectacles, gave Larry a defiant glare, and strutted off towards the kitchen, registering determination in every inch.

BOOK TWO

Be not forgetful to entertain strangers:
for thereby some have entertained angels unawares.

Hebrews xiii. 2.

Chapter Seven

The Daffodil-yellow Villa

The new villa was enormous, a tall, square Venetian mansion, with faded daffodil-yellow walls, green shutters and a fox-red roof. It stood on a hill overlooking the sea, surrounded by unkempt olive-groves and silent orchards of lemon- and orange-trees. The whole place had an atmosphere of ancient melancholy about it: the house with its cracked and peeling walls, its tremendous echoing rooms, its verandas piled high with drifts of last year's leaves and so overgrown with creepers and vines that the lower rooms were in a perpetual green twilight; the little walled and sunken garden that ran along one side of the house, its wrought-iron gates scabby with rust, had roses, anemones and geraniums sprawling across the weed-grown paths, and the shaggy, untended tangerine-trees were so thick with flowers that the scent was almost overpowering; beyond the garden the orchards were still and silent, except for the hum of bees and an occasional splutter of birds among the leaves. The house and land were gently, sadly decaying, lying forgotten on the hillside overlooking the shining sea and the dark, eroded hills of Albania. It was as though villa and landscape were half asleep, lying there drugged in the spring sunshine, giving themselves up to the moss, the ferns and the crowds of tiny toadstools.

It was Spiro, of course, who had found the place, and who organized our move with the minimum of fuss and the maximum of efficiency. Within three days of seeing the villa for the first time the long wooden carts were trailing in a dusty procession along the roads, piled high with our possessions, and on the fourth day we were installed.

At the edge of the estate was a small cottage inhabited by the gardener and his wife, an elderly, rather decrepit pair who seemed to have decayed with the estate. His job was to fill the water-tanks, pick the fruit, crush the olives and get severely stung once a year extracting honey from the seventeen bee-hives that simmered beneath the lemon-trees. In a moment of misguided enthusiasm Mother engaged the gardener's wife to work for us in the villa. Her name was Lugaretzia, and she was a thin, lugubrious individual, whose hair was forever coming adrift from the ramparts of pins and combs with which she kept it attached to her skull. She was extremely sensitive, as Mother soon discovered, and the slightest criticism of her work, however tactfully phrased, would make her brown eyes swim with tears in an embarrassing display of grief. It was such a heart-rending sight to watch that Mother very soon gave up criticising her altogether.

There was only one thing in life that could bring a smile to Lugaretzia's gloomy countenance, a glint to her spaniel eyes, and that was a discussion of her ailments. Where most people are hypochondriacs as a hobby, Lugaretzia had turned it into a full-time occupation. When we took up residence it was her stomach that was worrying her. Bulletins on the state of her stomach would start at seven in the morning when she brought up the tea. She would move from room to room with the trays, giving each one of us a blow-by-blow account of her nightly bout with her inside. She was a master of the art of graphic description; groaning, gasping, doubling up in agony, stamping about the rooms, she would give us such a realistic picture of her suffering that we would find our own stomachs aching in sympathy.

'Can't you *do* something about that woman?' Larry asked Mother one morning, after Lugaretzia's stomach had been through a particularly bad night.

'What do you expect me to do?' she asked. 'I gave her some of your bicarbonate of soda.'

'That probably accounts for her bad night.'

'I'm sure she doesn't *eat* properly,' said Margo. 'What she probably wants is a good diet.'

'Nothing short of a bayonet would do her stomach any good,' said Larry caustically, 'and I know . . . during the last week I have become distressingly familiar with every tiny convolution of her larger intestine.'

'I know she's a bit trying,' said Mother, 'but, after all, the poor woman is obviously suffering.'

'Nonsense,' said Leslie; 'she enjoys every minute of it. Like Larry does when he's ill.'

'Well, anyway,' said Mother hurriedly, 'we'll just have to put up with her; there's no one else we can get locally. I'll get Theodore to look her over next time he comes out.'

'If all she told me this morning was true,' said Larry, 'you'll have to provide him with a pick and a miner's lamp.'

'Larry, don't be disgusting,' said Mother severely.

Shortly afterwards, to our relief, Lugaretzia's stomach got better, but almost immediately her feet gave out, and she would hobble pitifully round the house, groaning loudly and frequently. Larry said that Mother hadn't hired a maid, but a ghoul, and suggested buying her a ball and chain. He pointed out that this would at least let us know when she was coming, and allow us time to escape, for Lugaretzia had developed the habit of creeping up behind one and groaning loudly and unexpectedly in one's ear. Larry started having breakfast in his bedroom after the morning when Lugaretzia took off her shoes in the dining-room in order to show us exactly which toes were hurting.

But, apart from Lugaretzia's ailments, there were other snags in the house. The furniture (which we had rented with the villa) was a fantastic collection of Victorian relics that had been locked in the rooms for the past twenty years. They crouched everywhere, ugly, ungainly, unpractical, creaking hideously to each other and shedding bits of themselves with loud cracks like musket-shots, accompanied by clouds of dust if you walked past them too heavily. The first evening the leg came off the dining-room table, cascading the food on to the floor. Some days later Larry sat down on an immense and solid-looking chair, only to have the back disappear in a cloud of acrid dust. When Mother went to open a wardrobe the size of a cottage and the entire door came away in her hand, she decided that something must be done.

'We simply can't have people to stay in a house where everything comes to bits if you look at it,' she said. 'There's nothing for it, we'll have to buy some new furniture. Really, these guests are going to be the most expensive we've ever had.'

The next morning Spiro drove Mother, Margo and myself into the town to buy furniture. We noticed that the town was more crowded, more boisterous, than usual, but it never occurred to us that anything special was happening until we had finished bargaining with the dealer and made our way out of his shop into the narrow, twisted streets. We were jostled and pushed as we struggled to get back to the place where we had left the car. The crowd grew thicker and thicker, and the people were so tightly wedged together that we were carried forward against our will.

'I think there must be something going on,' said Margo observantly. 'Maybe it's a fiesta or something interesting.'

'I don't care *what* it is, as long as we get back to the car,' said Mother.

But we were swept along, in the opposite direction to the car, and eventually pushed out to join a vast crowd assembled in the main square of the town. I asked an elderly peasant woman near me what was happening, and she turned to me, her face lit up with pride.

'It is Saint Spiridion, *kyria*,' she explained. 'Today we may enter the church and kiss his feet.'

Saint Spiridion was the patron saint of the island. His mummified body was enshrined in a silver coffin in the church, and once a year he was carried in procession round the town. He was very powerful, and could grant requests, cure illness and do a number of other wonderful things for you if he happened to be in the right mood when asked. The islanders worshipped him, and every second male on the island was called Spiro in his honour. Today was a special day; apparently they would open the coffin and allow the faithful to kiss the slippered feet of the mummy, and make any request they cared to. The composition of the crowd showed how well loved the saint was by the Corfiots: there were elderly peasant women in their best black clothes, and their husbands, hunched as olive-trees, with sweeping white moustaches; there were fishermen, bronzed and muscular, with the dark stains of octopus ink on their shirts; there were the sick too, the mentally defective, the consumptive, the crippled, old people who could hardly walk and babies wrapped and bound like cocoons, their pale, waxy little faces crumpled up as they coughed and coughed. There were even a few tall, wild-looking Albanian shepherds, moustached and with shaven heads, wearing great sheepskin cloaks. This great multi-coloured wedge of humanity moved slowly towards the dark door of the church, and we were swept along with it, wedged like pebbles in a larva-flow. By now Margo had been pushed well ahead of me, while Mother was equally far behind. I was caught firmly between five fat peasant women, who pressed on me like cushions and exuded sweat and garlic, while Mother was hopelessly entangled between two of the enormous Albanian shepherds. Steadily, firmly, we were pushed up the steps and into the church.

Inside, it was dark as a well, lit only by a bed of candles that bloomed like yellow crocuses along one wall. A bearded, tall-hatted priest clad in black robes flapped like a crow in the gloom, making the crowd form into a single line that filed down the church, past the great silver coffin and out through another door into the street. The coffin was standing upright, looking like a silver chrysalis, and at its lower end a portion had been removed so that the saint's feet, clad in the richly-embroidered slippers, peeped out. As each person reached the coffin he bent, kissed the feet and murmured a prayer, while at the top of the sarcophagus the saint's black and withered face peered out of a glass panel with an expression of acute distaste. It became evident that, whether we wanted to or not, we were going to kiss Saint Spiridion's feet. I looked back and saw Mother making frantic efforts to get to my side, but the Albanian bodyguard would not give an inch, and she struggled ineffectually. Presently she caught my eye and started to grimace and point at the coffin, shaking her head vigorously. I was greatly puzzled by this, and so were the two Albanians, who were watching her with undisguised suspicion. I think they came to the conclusion that Mother was about to have a fit, and with some justification, for she was scarlet in the face, and her grimaces were getting wilder and wilder. At last, in desperation, she threw caution to the winds and hissed at me over the heads of the crowd:

'Tell Margo ... *not* to kiss ... kiss the air ... kiss the *air*.'

I turned to deliver Mother's message to Margo, but it was too late; there she was, crouched over the slippered feet, kissing them with an enthusiasm that enchanted and greatly surprised the crowd. When it came to my turn I obeyed Mother's instructions, kissing loudly and with a considerable show of reverence a point some six inches above the mummy's left foot. Then I was pushed along and disgorged through the church door and out into the street, where the crowd was breaking up into little groups, laughing and chattering. Margo was waiting on the steps, looking extremely self-satisfied. The next moment Mother appeared, shot from the door by the brawny shoulders of her shepherds She staggered widly down the steps and joined us.

'Those *shepherds*,' she exclaimed faintly. 'So ill-mannered ... the smell nearly killed me ... a mixture of incense and garlic. ... How do they manage to smell like that?'

'Oh, well,' said Margo cheerfully. 'It'll have been worth it if Saint Spiridion answers my request.'

'A most *insanitary* procedure,' said Mother, 'more likely to spread disease than cure it. I dread to think what we would have caught if we'd *really* kissed his feet."

'But I kissed his feet,' said Margo, surprised.
'Margo! You didn't!'
'Well, everyone else was doing it.'
'And after I expressly told you *not* to.'
'You never told me not to. ...'

I interrupted and explained that I had been too late with Mother's warning.

'After all those people have been slobbering over those slippers you have to go and kiss them.'

'I was only doing what the others did.'

'I can't think what on earth possessed you to *do* such a thing.'

'Well, I thought he might cure my acne.'

'Acne!' said Mother scornfully. 'You'll be lucky if you don't catch something to go with the acne.'

The next day Margo went down with a severe attack of influenza, and Saint Spiridion's prestige with Mother reached rock bottom. Spiro was sent racing into the town for a doctor, and he returned bringing a little dumpy man with patent-leather hair, a faint wisp of moustache and boot-button eyes behind great horn-rimmed spectacles.

This was Doctor Androuchelli. He was a charming man, with a bedside manner that was quite unique.

'Po-po-po,' he said, strutting into the bedroom and regarding Margo with scorn, 'po-po-*po*! Remarkably unintelligent you have been, no? Kissing the Saint's feet! Po-po-po-po-po! Nearly you might have caught some bugs unpleasant. You are lucky; she is influenza. Now you will do as I tell you, or I will rinse my hands of you. And please do not increase my work with such stupidity. If you kiss another saint's feet in the future I will not come to cure you. . . . Po-po-po . . . such a thing to do.'

So while Margo languished in bed for three weeks, with Androuchelli po-po-ing over her every two or three days, the rest of us settled into the villa. Larry took possession of one enormous attic and engaged two carpenters to make bookshelves; Leslie converted the large covered veranda behind the house into a shooting-gallery, and hung an enormous red flag up outside whenever he was practising; Mother pottered absent-mindedly round the vast, subterranean, stone-flagged kitchen, preparing gallons of beef-tea and trying to listen to Lugaretzia's monologues and worry about Margo at the same time. For Roger and myself, of course, there were fifteen acres of garden to explore, a vast new paradise sloping down to the shallow, tepid sea. Being temporarily without a tutor (for George had left the island) I could spend the whole day out, only returning to the villa for hurried meals.

In this varied terrain so close at hand I found many creatures which I now regarded as old friends: the rose-beetles, the blue carpenter-bees, the lady-birds and the trapdoor spiders. But I also discovered many new beasts to occupy me. In the crumbling walls of the sunken garden lived dozens of little black scorpions, shining and polished as if they had been made out of bakelite; in the fig- and lemon-trees just below the garden were quantities of emerald-green tree-frogs, like delicious satiny sweets among the leaves; up on the hillside lived snakes of various sorts, brilliant lizards and tortoises. In the fruit orchards there were many kinds of birds: goldfinches, greenfinches, redstarts, wagtails, orioles and an occasional hoopoe, salmon-pink, black and white, probing the soft ground with long curved beaks, erecting their crests in astonishment when they saw me, and flying off.

Under the eaves of the villa itself the swallows had taken up residence. They had arrived a short time before we had, and their knobbly mud houses were only just completed, still dark brown and damp like rich plum cake. As these were drying to a lighter biscuit brown, the parent birds were busy lining them, foraging round the garden for rootlets, lambs' wool or feathers. Two of the swallows' nests were lower than the others, and it was on these that I concentrated my attention. Over a period of days I leant a long ladder against the wall, midway between the two nests, and then slowly, day by day, I climbed higher and higher, until I could sit on the top rung and look into the nests, now some four feet away from me. The parent birds seemed in no way disturbed by my presence, and continued their stern work of preparing for a family, while I crouched on top of the ladder, and Roger lay at the bottom.

I grew to know these swallow families very well, and watched their daily work with considerable interest. What I took to be the two females were very similar in behaviour, earnest, rather preoccupied, over-anxious and fussy. The two males, on the other hand, displayed totally different characters. One of them, during the work of lining the nest, brought excellent material, but he refused to treat it as a job of work. He would come swooping home, carrying a wisp of sheep's wool in his mouth, and would waste several minutes skating low over the flowers in the garden, drawing figures of eight, or else weaving in and out of the columns that held up the grape-vine. His wife would cling to the nest and chitter at him exasperatedly, but he refused to take life seriously. The other female also had trouble with her mate, but it was trouble of a different sort. He was, if anything, over-enthusiastic. He seemed determined to leave no stone unturned in his efforts to provide his young with the finest nest-lining in the colony. But, unfortunately, he was no mathematician, and, try as he would, he could not remember the size of his nest. He would come flying back, twittering in an excited if somewhat muffled manner, carrying a chicken or turkey feather as big as himself, and with such a thick quill it was impossible to bend it. It would generally take his wife several minutes to convince him that, no matter how they struggled and juggled, the feather would not fit into the nest. Acutely disappointed he would eventually drop the feather so that it whirlpooled down to join the ever-increasing pile on the ground beneath, and then fly off in search of something more suitable. In a little while he would be back, struggling under a load of sheep's wool so matted and hard with earth and dung that he would have difficulty in getting up to the eaves, let alone into the nest.

When at last the nests were lined, the freckled eggs laid and hatched, the two husbands' characters seemed to change. The one who had brought so much futile nest-lining now swooped and hawked about the hillsides in a carefree manner, and would come drifting back carelessly carrying a mouthful of insect life of just the right size and softness to appeal to his fuzzy, trembling brood. The other male now became terribly harassed and apparently a prey to the dreadful thought that his babies might starve. So he would wear himself to a shadow in the pursuit of food, and return carrying the most unsuitable items, such as large spiky beetles, all legs and wing-case, and immense, dry and completely indigestible dragon-flies. He would cling to the edge of the nest and make valiant but vain attempts to get these gigantic offerings rammed down the ever-open gullets of his young. I dread to think what would have happened if he had succeeded in wedging one of these spiky captures down their throats. Luckily, however, he never succeeded, and eventually, looking more harassed than ever, he would drop the insect on to the ground and fly off hurriedly in search of something else. I was very grateful to this swallow, for he provided me with three species of butterfly, six dragon-flies and two ant-lions which were new to my collection.

The females, once the young were hatched, behaved in much the same way as they had always done: they flew a little faster, there was an air of brisk efficiency about them, but that was all. It intrigued me to see for the first time the hygienic arrangements of a bird's nest. I had often wondered, when hand-rearing a young bird, why it hoisted its bottom skywards with much waggling when it wanted to excrete. Now I discovered the reason. The excreta of the baby swallows was produced in globules which were coated with mucus that formed what was almost a gelatine packet round the dropping. The young would stand on their heads, waggle their bottoms in a brief but enthusiastic rumba and deposit their little offering on the rim of the nest. When the females arrived they would cram the food they had collected down the gaping throats, and then delicately pick up the dropping in their beaks and fly off to deposit it somewhere over the olive-groves. It was an admirable arrangement, and I would watch the whole performance fascinated, from the bottom-waggle – which always made me giggle – to the final swoop of the parent over the tree-top, and the dropping of the little black-and-white bomb earthwards.

Owing to the male swallow's habit of collecting strange and unsuitable insects for his young, I always used to examine the area below the nest twice a day, in the hope of finding new specimens to add to my collection. It was here that, one morning, I found the most extraordinary-looking beetle crawling about. I did not think that even that mentally defective swallow could have brought back such a large creature, or even that he could have caught it, but it was certainly there, underneath the colony. It was a large, clumsy, blue-black beetle, with a large round head, long jointed antennae and a bulbous body. The weird thing about it was its wing-cases; it looked as though it had sent them to the laundry and they had shrunk, for they were very small and appeared to have been constructed for a beetle half the size. I toyed with the idea that it may have found itself without a pair of clean wingcases to put on that morning and had to borrow its younger brother's pair, but I eventually decided that this idea, however enchanting, could not be described as scientific. I noticed, after I had picked it up, that my fingers smelled faintly acrid and oily, though it had not appeared to have exuded any liquid that I could see. I gave it to Roger to smell, to see if he agreed with me, and he sneezed violently and backed away, so I concluded that it must be the beetle and not my hand. I preserved it carefully, so that Theodore could identify it when he came.

Now that the warm days of spring had arrived, Theodore would come out to the villa every Thursday for tea, arriving in a horse-drawn cab from the town, his immaculate suit, stiff collar and homburg hat making a strange contrast to the nets, bags and boxes full of test-tubes with which he was surrounded. Before tea we would examine any new specimens I had acquired and identify them. After tea we would wander about the grounds in search of creatures, or else make what Theodore would call an excursion to some neighbouring pond or ditch in search of new microscopic life for Theodore's collection. He identified my strange beetle, with its ill-fitting electra, without much trouble, and proceeded to tell me some extraordinary things about it.

'Ah ha! Yes,' he said, closely scrutinizing the beast, 'it's an oil-beetle ... *meloe proscaraboeus*. ... Yes ... they are certainly very curious-looking beetles. What d'you say? Ah, yes, the wing-cases. ... Well, you see they are flightless. There are several species of coleoptera that have lost the power of flight, for one reason or another. It is the life-history of this beetle that is very curious. This, of course, is a female. The male is considerably smaller – I should say approximately half the size. It appears that the female lays a number of small yellow eggs in the soil. When these hatch out into larvae they climb up any flowers nearby and wait inside the blooms. There is a certain type of solitary bee which they must wait for, and when it enters the flower, the larvae ... hitch-hike ... er ... get a good grip with their claws on the bee's fur. If they are lucky, the bee is a female who is collecting honey to put in the cells with her egg. Then as soon as the bee has completed the filling of the cell and lays her egg, the larva jumps off on to the egg, and the bee closes the cell. Then the larva eats the egg and develops inside the cell. The thing that always strikes me as curious is that there is only *one* species of bee that the larvae prey on. I should have thought that a great many of the larvae catch hold of the wrong species of bee, and so eventually *die*. Then, of course, even if it's the *right* kind of bee, there is no ... um ... guarantee that it's a female about to lay eggs.'

He paused for a moment, raised himself on his toes several times, and thoughtfully contemplated the floor. Then he looked up, his eyes twinkling.

'I mean to say,' he continued, 'it's rather like backing a horse in a race ... um ...with the odds heavily against you.'

He waggled the glass-topped box gently so that the beetle slid from one end to the other, waving its antennae in surprise. Then he put it carefully back on the shelf among my other specimens.

'Talking of horses,' said Theodore happily, placing his hands on his hips and rocking gently, 'did I ever tell you about the time when I led the triumphant entry into Smyrna on a white charger? Well, it was in the First World War, you know, and the commander of my battalion was determined that we should march into Smyrna in a ... er ... triumphal column, led, if possible, by a man on a white horse. Unfortunately, they gave me the doubtful privilege of leading the troops. Of course, I had learnt to ride, you know, but I would not consider myself ... um ... an expert horseman. Well, everything went very well, and the horse behaved with great decorum, until we got into the outskirts of the town. It is custom in parts of Greece, as you know, to throw scent, perfume, rose-water or something of the sort over the ... er ... conquering heroes. As I was riding along at the head of the column, an old woman darted out of a side street and started to hurl eau-de-Cologne about. The horse did not mind *that*, but most unfortunately a small quantity of the scent must have splashed into his *eye*. Well, he was quite used to parades and so forth, and cheering crowds and things, but he was not used to having his eye squirted full of eau-de-Cologne. He became ... er ... most upset about it and was acting more like a circus horse than a charger. I only managed to stay on because my feet had become wedged in the stirrups. The column had to break ranks to try to calm him down, but he was so upset that eventually the commander decided it would be unwise to let him take part in the rest of the triumphal entry. So while the column marched through the main streets with bands playing and people cheering and so forth, I was forced to slink through the back streets on my white horse, both of us, to add insult to injury, by now smelling very strongly of eau-de-Cologne. Um . . . I have never really *enjoyed* horse-riding since then.'

Chapter Eight

The Tortoise Hills

Behind the villa there were a series of small hills that raised shaggy crests above the surrounding olive-groves. They were hills covered with great beds of green myrtle, tall heather and a patchy feathering of cypress-trees. This was probably the most fascinating area of the whole garden, for it was overflowing with life. In the sandy paths the ant-lion larvae dug their little cone-shaped pits, and lay in wait to spatter any unwary ant that stepped over the edge with a bombardment of sand that would send it tumbling down to the bottom of the trap, to be seized in the ant-lion larva's terrible, pincer-like jaws. In the red sandbanks the hunting wasps were digging their tunnels, and hawking low in pursuit of spiders; they would stab with their sting, paralysing them and carrying them off to serve as food for their larvae. Among the heather-blooms the great, fat, furry caterpillars of emperor moths fed slowly, looking like animated fur collars. Among the myrtles in the warm, scented twilight of their leaves, the mantids prowled, heads turning this way and that as they watched for prey. Among the cypress branches the chaffinches had their neat nests, full of gawping, goggle-eyed babies; and on the lower branches the goldcrests weaved their tiny, fragile cups of moss and hair, or foraged for insects, hanging upside down on the ends of the branches, giving almost inaudible squeaks of joy at the discovery of a tiny spider or a gnat, their golden crests gleaming like little forage caps as they flipped daintily through the gloom of the tree.

It was not long after we arrived at the villa that I discovered these hills really belonged to the tortoises. One hot afternoon Roger and I were concealed behind a bush, waiting patiently for a large swallow-tail butterfly to return to its favourite sunning patch, so that we might capture it. It was the first really hot day we had had that year, and everything seemed to be lying drugged and asleep, soaking up the sun. The swallow-tail was in no hurry; he was down by the olive-groves doing a ballet dance by himself, twisting, diving, pirouetting in the sun. As we watched him, I saw, from the corner of my eye, a faint movement at one side of the bush we were sheltering behind. I glanced quickly to see what it was, but the brown earth was sun-drenched and empty of life. I was just about to turn my attention to the butterfly again when I saw something that I could hardly believe: the patch of earth I had been looking at suddenly heaved upwards, as though pushed by a hand from beneath; the soil cracked and a tiny seedling waved about wildly before its pale roots gave way and it fell on its side.

What, I wondered, could be the cause of this sudden eruption? An earthquake? Surely not so small and confined. A mole? Not in such dry and waterless terrain. As I was speculating, the earth gave another heave, clods of it cracked off and rolled away, and I was looking at a brown and yellow shell. More earth was swept out of the way as the shell bucked upwards, and then, slowly and cautiously, a wrinkled, scaly head appeared out of the hole, a long, skinny neck followed it. The bleary eyes blinked once or twice as the tortoise surveyed me; then, deciding I must be harmless, he hoisted himself with infinite care and effort out of his earthy cell, walked two or three steps and sank down in the sunshine, drowsing gently. After the long winter under the damp and chilly soil, that first sun-bath must have been like a drink of wine to the reptile. His legs were spread out from his shell, his neck extended as far as it could, his head resting on the ground; with eyes closed, the creature seemed to be absorbing sunshine through every bit of his body and shell. He remained lying there for about ten minutes, and then he rose, slowly and deliberately, and rolled off down the path to where a patch of dandelion and clover spread in the shade of a cypress. Here his legs seemed to give way and he collapsed on to the bottom of his shell with a thump. Then his head appeared from his shell, bent slowly down towards the rich green pile of the clover patch, his mouth opened wide, there was a moment's suspense, and then his mouth closed round the succulent leaves, his head jerked back to tear them off and he sat there munching happily, his mouth stained with the first food of the year.

This must have been the first tortoise of spring, and as if his appearance from the subterranean dormitory was a signal, the hills suddenly became covered with tortoises. I have never seen so many congregated in so small an area: big ones the size of a soup plate and little ones the size of a cup, chocolate-coloured great-grandfathers and pale, horn-coloured youngsters, all lumbering heavily along the sandy paths, in and out of the heather and myrtles, occasionally descending to the olive-groves where the vegetation was more succulent. Sitting in one spot for an hour or so you could count as many as ten tortoises pass you, and on one afternoon, as an experiment, I collected thirty-five specimens in two hours, just walking about the hillside and picking them up as they wandered about with an air of preoccupied determination, their club feet thumping on the ground.

No sooner had the shelled owners of the hills appeared from their winter quarters and had their first meal, than the males became romantically inclined. Stalking along on tip-toe with stumbling rapidity, their necks stretched out to the fullest extent, they would set out in search of a mate, pausing now and then to give a strange, yawping cry, the passionate love-song of a male tortoise. The females, ambling heavily through the heather and pausing now and then for a snack, would answer in an off-hand manner. Two or three males, travelling at what – for a tortoise – was a gallop, would generally converge on the same female. They would arrive, out of breath and inflamed with passion, and glare at each other, their throats gulping convulsively. Then they would prepare to do battle.

These battles were exciting and interesting to watch, resembling all-in wrestling more than boxing, for the combatants did not possess either speed or the physical grace to indulge in fancy footwork. The general idea was for one to charge his rival as rapidly as possible, and just before impact to duck his head into his shell. The best blow was considered to be the broadside, for this gave the opportunity – by wedging yourself against your rival's shell and pushing hard – of overturning him and leaving him flapping helplessly on his back. If they couldn't manage to get in a broadside, any other part of the rival's anatomy did just as well. Charging each other, straining and pushing, their shells clattering together, occasionally taking a slow-motion bite at each other's necks or retreating into their shells with a hiss, the males would do battle. Meanwhile the object of their frenzy would amble slowly onwards, pausing now and then for a bite to eat, apparently unconcerned by the scraping and cracking of shells behind her. On more than one occasion these battles became so furious that a male in a fit of misplaced enthusiasm would deliver a broadside to his lady-love by mistake. She would merely fold herself into her shell with an outraged sniff, and wait patiently until the battle had passed her by. These fights seemed to me the most ill-organized and unnecessary affairs, for it was not always the strongest tortoise that won; with good terrain in his favour a small specimen could easily overturn one twice his size. Nor, indeed, was it invariably one of the warriors that got the lady, for on several occasions I saw a female wander away from a pair of fighting males to be accosted by a complete stranger (who had not even chipped his shell on her behalf) and go off with him quite happily.

Roger and I would squat by the hour in the heather, watching the tortoise knights in their ill-fitting armour jousting for the ladies, and the contests never failed to entertain us. Sometimes we would lay bets with each other as to which one was going to win, and by the end of the summer Roger had backed so many losers that he owed me a considerable amount of money. Sometimes, when the battle was very fierce, Roger would get carried away by the spirit of the thing and want to join in, and I would have to restrain him.

When the lady had eventually made her choice, we would follow the happy couple on their honeymoon among the myrtles, and even watch (discreetly hidden behind the bushes) the final acts in the romantic drama. The wedding night – or rather day – of a tortoise is not exactly inspiring. To begin with, the female performs in a disgracefully coy manner, and becomes heavily skittish in evading her bridegroom's attentions. She irritates him in this way until he is forced to adopt cave-man tactics, and subdues her maidenly antics with a few short, sharp broadsides. The actual sexual act was the most awkward and fumbling thing I had ever seen. The incredibly heavy-handed and inexpert way the male would attempt to hoist himself on to the female's shell, slipping and slithering, clawing desperately for a foothold on the shiny shields, overbalancing and almost overturning, was extremely painful to watch; the urge to go and assist the poor creature was almost overwhelming, and I had the greatest difficulty in restraining myself from interference. Once a male was infinitely more bungling than usual, and fell down three times during the mounting, and generally behaved in such an imbecile manner I was beginning to wonder if he were going to take all summer about it. ... At last, more by luck than skill, he hoisted himself up, and I was just heaving a sigh of relief with the female, obviously bored by the male's inadequacy, moved a few steps towards a dandelion leaf. Her husband clawed wildly at her moving shell, but could get no foothold; he slipped off, teetered for a minute and then rolled ignominiously over on to his back. This final blow seemed to be too much for him, because, instead of trying to right himself, he simply folded himself up in his shell and lay there mournfully. The female, meanwhile, ate the dandelion leaf. At last, since his passion seemed to have died, I rolled the male over, and after a minute or so he wandered off, peering about him in a dazed fashion, and ignoring his erstwhile bride, who regarded him unemotionally, her mouth full of food. As a punishment for her callous behaviour I carried her up to the most barren and desiccated part of the hillside and left her there, so that she would have an extremely long walk to the nearest clover patch.

I came to know many of the tortoises by sight, so closely and enthusiastically did I watch their daily lives. Some I could recognize by their shape and colour, others by some physical defect – a chip from the edge of their shells, the loss of a toe-nail and so on. There was one large, honey-and-tar-coloured female who was unmistakable, for she had only one eye. I got on such intimate terms with her that I christened her Madame Cyclops. She came to know me quite well, and, realizing that I meant her no harm, she would not disappear into her shell at my approach, but stretch up her neck to see if I had brought her a tit-bit in the shape of a lettuce leaf or some tiny snails, of which she was inordinately fond. She would roll about her business quite happily, while Roger and I followed her, and occasionally, as a special treat, we would carry her down to the olive-groves for a picnic lunch on the clover. To my infinite regret I was not present at her wedding, but I was lucky enough to witness the outcome of the honeymoon.

I found her one day busily engaged in digging a hole in the soft soil at the base of a bank. She had dug to a fair depth when I arrived, and seemed quite glad to have a rest and a little refreshment in the shape of some clover flowers. Then she set to work once more, scraping the earth out with her fore-feet and barging it to one side with her shell. Not being quite certain what she was trying to achieve, I did not attempt to help her, but merely lay on my stomach in the heather and watched. After some time, when she had excavated quite a pile of earth, she carefully scrutinized the hole from all angles and was apparently satisfied. She turned round, lowered her hind end over the hole and sat there with a rapt look on her face while she absent-mindedly laid nine white eggs. I was most surprised and delighted, and congratulated her heartily on this achievement, while she gulped at me in a meditative sort of way. She then proceeded to scrape the soil back over the eggs and pat it down firmly by the simple method of standing over it and flopping down on her tummy several times. This task accomplished, she had a rest and accepted the remains of the clover blooms.

I found myself in an awkward position, for I dearly wanted one of the eggs to add to my collection; I did not like to take it while she was there, for fear that she might feel insulted and perhaps dig up the remaining eggs and eat them, or do something equally horrible. So I had to sit and wait patiently while she finished her snack, had a short doze and then ambled off among the bushes. I followed her for some distance to make sure she did not turn back, and then hurried to the nest and carefully unearthed one of the eggs. It was about the size of a pigeon's, oval in shape and with a rough, chalky shell. I patted the earth back over the nest so that she would never know it had been disturbed, and carried my trophy triumphantly back to the villa. I blew the sticky yolk out of it with great care, and enshrined the shell among my natural history collection in a small glass-topped box of its own. The label, which was a nice blend of scientific and sentimental, read: *Egg of Greek Tortoise (Testudo graeca). Laid by Madame Cyclops.*

Throughout the spring and early summer, while I was studying the courtship of the tortoises, the villa was filled with an apparently endless stream of Larry's friends. No sooner had we seen one lot off, and sighed with relief, than another steamer would arrive, and the line of taxis and horse-carriages would hoot and clatter their way up the drive, and the house would be filled once more. Sometimes the fresh load of guests would turn up before we had got rid of the previous group, and the chaos was indescribable; the house and garden would be dotted with poets, authors, artists and playwrights arguing, painting, drinking, typing and composing. Far from being the ordinary, charming people that Larry had promised, they all turned out to be the most extraordinary eccentrics who were so highbrow that they had difficulty in understanding one another.

One of the first to arrive was Zatopec, an Armenian poet, a short, stocky individual with a swooping eagle nose, a shoulder-length mane of silvery hair and hands bulbous and twisted by arthritis. He arrived wearing an immense, swirling black cloak and a broad-brimmed black hat, riding in a carriage piled high with wine. His voice shook the house like a sirocco as he swept into it, his cloak rippling, his arms full of bottles. He scarcely stopped talking the whole time he stayed. He talked from morning till night, drinking prodigious quantities of wine, snatching forty winks wherever he happened to be and rarely going to bed at all. In spite of his advanced years he had lost none of his enthusiasm for the opposite sex, and, while he treated Mother and Margo with a sort of creaking, antique courtesy, no peasant girl for miles was free from his attentions. He would hobble through the olive-groves after them, roaring with laughter, shouting endearments, his cloak flapping behind him, his pocket bulging with a bottle of wine. Even Lugaretzia was not safe, and had her bottom pinched while she was sweeping under the sofa. This proved something of a blessing, as it made her forget her ailments for a few days, and blush and giggle kittenishly whenever Zatopec appeared. Eventually Zatopec departed as he had arrived, lying back regally in a cab, his cloak wrapped round him, shouting endearments to us as it clopped off down the drive, promising to return soon from Bosnia and bring some more wine for us.

The next invasion consisted of three artists, Jonquil, Durant and Michael. Jonquil looked, and sounded, like a cockney owl with a fringe; Durant was lank and mournful and so nervous that he would almost jump out of his skin if you spoke to him suddenly; by contrast, Michael was a short, fat, somnambulistic little man who looked like a well-boiled prawn with a mop of dark, curly hair. These three had only one thing in common, and that was a desire to get some work done. Jonquil, on striding into the house for the first time, made this quite clear to a startled Mother.

'I didn't come for no bleeding 'oliday,' she said severely; 'I came to get some work done, so I'm not interested in picnics and such, see?'

'Oh ... er ... no, no, of course not,' said Mother guiltily, as though she had been planning vast banquets among the myrtle bushes for Jonquil's benefit.

'Jus' so long as you know,' said Jonquil. 'I didn't want to upset nothing, see? I jus' want to get some work done.'

So she promptly retired to the garden, clad in a bathing costume, and slept peacefully in the sun throughout her stay.

Durant, he informed us, wanted to work too, but first he had to get his nerve back. He was shattered, he told us, quite, quite shattered by his recent experience. Apparently, while in Italy he had suddenly been seized with the desire to paint a masterpiece. After much thought he decided that an almond orchard in full bloom should give a certain scope to his brush. He spent considerable time and money driving about the countryside in search of the right orchard. At long last he found the perfect one, the setting was magnificent, and the blooms were full and thick. Feverishly he set to work, and by the end of the first day he had got the basis down on canvas. Tired, but satisfied, he packed up his things and returned to the village. After a good night's sleep he awoke refreshed and invigorated, and rushed back to the orchard to complete his picture. On arrival there he was struck dumb with horror and amazement, for every tree was gaunt and bare, while the ground was thickly carpeted with pink and white petals. Apparently during the night a spring storm had playfully stripped all the orchards in the vicinity of their blossom, including Durant's special one.

'I vas stricken,' he told us, his voice quivering, his eyes filled with tears. 'I swore I vould never paint again ... never! But slowly I am recovering my nerves ... I am feeling less shattered. ... Some time I vill start to paint again.'

On inquiry, it turned out that this unfortunate experience had taken place two years previously, and Durant had still not recovered from it.

Michael got off to a bad start. He was captivated by the colouring of the island, and told us enthusiastically that he would begin work on an immense canvas that would capture the very essence of Corfu. He could hardly wait to start. It was most unfortunate that he happened to be a prey to asthma. It was equally unfortunate that Lugaretzia had placed on a chair in his room a blanket which I used for horse-riding, there being no saddles available. In the middle of the night we were awakened by a noise that sounded like a troop of bloodhounds being slowly strangled. Assembling sleepily in Michael's room we found him wheezing and gasping, the sweat running down his face. While Margo rushed to make some tea, Larry to get some brandy and Leslie opened the windows, Mother put Michael back to bed, and, since he was now clammy with sweat, tenderly covered him with the horse-blanket. To our surprise, in spite of all remedies, he got worse. While he could still speak, we questioned him interestedly about his complaint and its cause.

'Psychological, purely psychological,' said Larry. 'What does the wheezing sound remind you of?'

Michael shook his head mutely.

'I think he ought to sniff something up . . . something like ammonia or something,' said Margo. 'It's wonderful if you're going to faint.'

'Well, he's not going to faint,' said Leslie tersely, 'but he probably would if he sniffed ammonia.'

'Yes, dear, it is a bit strong,' said Mother. 'I wonder what could have brought it on. . . . Are you allergic to something, Michael?'

Between gasps Michael informed us that he was only allergic to three things: the pollen of the lilac flowers, cats and horses. We all peered out of the window, but there was not a lilac-tree for miles. We searched the room, but there was not cat hidden anywhere. I indignantly denied Larry's accusation that I had smuggled a horse into the house. It was only when Michael seemed on the verge of death that we noticed the horse-rug, which Mother had tucked carefully under his chin. This incident had such a bad effect on the poor man that he was quite unable to put a brush to canvas during his stay; he and Durant lay side by side in deck-chairs, recovering their nerve together.

While we were still coping with these three, another guest arrived in the shape of Melanie, Countess de Torro. She was tall, thin, with a face like an ancient horse, crow-black eyebrows and an enormous cushion of scarlet hair on her head. She had hardly been in the house five minutes before she complained of the heat, and to mother's consternation and my delight, she caught hold of her scarlet hair and removed it, revealing a head as bald as a mushroom top. Seeing Mother's startled gaze, the Countess explained in her harsh, croaking voice. 'I've just recovered from erysipelas,' she said; 'lost all my hair . . . couldn't find eyebrows and wig to match in Milan . . . might get something in Athens.'

It was unfortunate that, owing to a slight impediment due to ill-fitting false teeth, the Countess was inclined to mumble, so Mother was under the impression that the disease she had just recovered from was of a much more unlady-like character. At the first available opportunity she got Larry into a corner.

'Disgusting!' She said in a vibrant whisper. 'Did you *hear* what she's had? And you call her a friend.'

'Friend?' said Larry in surprise. 'Why, I hardly know her . . . can't stand the woman; but she's an interesting character and I wanted to study her at close hand.'

'I like that,' said Mother indignantly. 'So you invite that *creature* here and we all catch some revolting disease while you take notes. No, I'm sorry, Larry, but she'll have to go.'

'Don't be silly, Mother,' said Larry irritably; 'you can't catch it . . . not unless you intend to share a bed with her.'

'Don't be *revolting*,' said Mother, glaring. 'I won't stand that obscene person in this house.'

They argued in whispers for the rest of the day, but Mother was adamant. Eventually Larry suggested asking Theodore out and getting his opinion on the matter, and to this Mother agreed. So a note was despatched, asking

Theodore to come out and spend the day. His reply accepting the invitation was brought by a carriage in which reclined the cloak-swathed form of Zatopec, who, it turned out, had drunk a farewell of prodigious size to Corfu, got on the wrong boat and ended up in Athens. As by then he had missed his appointment in Bosnia, he had philosophically boarded the next vessel back to Corfu, bringing with him several crates of wine. Theodore turned up the next day, wearing, as a concession to summer, a panama instead of his usual homburg. Before Mother had a chance to warn him about our hairless guest, Larry had introduced them.

'A doctor?' said Melanie, Countess de Torro, her eyes gleaming. 'How interesting. Perhaps you can advise me. . . . I've just had erysipelas.'

'Ah ha! Really?' said Theodore, eyeing her keenly. 'Which . . . er . . . treatment did you have?'

They embarked on a long and technical discussion with enthusiasm, and it was only the most determined efforts on Mother's part that got them away from what she still considered to be an indelicate subject.

'Really, Theodore's as bad as that woman,' she said to Larry. 'I do *try* and be broad-minded, but there is a limit, and I don't think things like that should be discussed at tea.'

Later Mother got Theodore alone, and the subject of the Countess's disease was explained. Mother was then stricken with a guilty conscience at having misjudged the woman, and was immensely affable to her for the rest of the day, even telling her to take her wig off if she felt the heat.

The dinner that night was colourful and extraordinary, and I was so fascinated by the assembly of characters and the various conversations that I did not know which one to listen to with undivided attention. The lamps smoked gently and cast a warm, honey-coloured light over the table, making the china and glass glitter, and setting fire to the red wine as it splashed into the glasses.

'But, dear boy, you have missed the meaning of it . . . yes, yes, you have!' Zatopec's voice booming out, his nose curving over his wine glass. 'You cannot discuss poetry as if it were house painting. . . .'

'. . . so I says to 'im, "I'm not doing a bleeding drawing for less than a tenner a time, and that's dirt cheap," I says . . .'

'. . . and the next morning I vas paralysed . . . shocked beyond everything . . . thousands of blossoms, bruised and torn. . . . I say I vill never paint again . . . my nerves had been shattered . . . the whole orchard gone . . . phuit! like that . . . and there vas I . . .'

'. . . and then, of course, I had the sulphur baths.'

'Ah, yes . . . um . . . though, mind you, I think the bath treatment is . . . er . . . a little . . . er . . . you know . . . a little *over-rated*. I believe that ninety-two per cent of sufferers. . .'

The plates of food, piled like volcanoes, steaming gently; the early fruit in a polished pile in the centre dish; Lugaretzia hobbling round the table, groaning gently to herself; Theodore's beard twinkling in the lamplight; Leslie carefully manufacturing bread pellets to shoot at a moth that hovered round the lamps; Mother, ladling out the food, smiling vaguely at everyone and keeping a watchful eye on Lugaretzia; under the table Roger's cold nose pressed hard against my knee in mute appeal.

Margo and the still-wheezing Michael discussing art: '... but then I think that Lawrence does that sort of thing so much *better*. He has a certain rich bloom, as it were ... don't you agree? I mean, take Lady Chatterley, eh?'

'Oh, yes, quite. And then, of course, he did wonderful things in the desert, didn't he? ... and writing that wonderful book ... the ... er ... *The Seven Pillows of Wisdom*, or whatever it was called ...'

Larry and the Countess discussing art: '... but you must have the straightforward simplicity, the clarity of a child's eyes. ... Take the finest *fundamental* verse ... take Humpty Dumpty. ... Now, there's poetry for you ... the simplicity and freedom from clichés and outdated shibboleths ...'

'... but then it's useless prating about the simple approach to poetry if you're going to produce jingles which are about as straightforward and uncomplicated as a camel's stomach ...'

Mother and Durant: '... and you can imagine the effect it had on me ... I vas shattered.'

'Yes, you must have been. Such a shame, after all that trouble. Will you have a little more rice?'

Jonquil and Theodore: '... and the Latvian peasants ... well, I've never seen anything like it ...'

'Yes, here in Corfu and ... er ... I believe ... in some parts of Albania, the peasants have a very ... er ... similar custom ...'

Outside, the moon's face was peering through a filigree of vine-leaves, and the owls were giving their strange, chiming cries. Coffee and wine were served on the balcony, between the vine-shaggy pillars. Larry strummed on the guitar and sang an Elizabethan marching song. This reminded Theodore of one of his fantastic but true Corfu anecdotes, which he related to us with impish glee.

'As you know, here in Corfu nothing is ever done the correct way. Everyone starts out with the ... er ... *best intentions,* but something always seems to go wrong. When the Greek king visited the island some years ago the ... er ... climax of his tour was to be a ... er ... sort of stage show ... a play. The climax of the drama was the Battle of Thermopylae, and, as the curtain fell, the Greek army was supposed to drive ... um ... the Persian army triumphantly into the ... what d'you call them? Ah, yes, the *wings*. Well, it appears that the people playing the part of the Persians were a bit disgruntled at the thought of having to retreat in front of the king, and the fact that they had to play the part of Persians also ... you know ... rankled. It only required a little incident to set things off. Unfortunately, during the battle scene the leader of the Greek army ... um ... misjudged the distance and caught the leader of the Persian army quite a heavy blow with his wooden sword. This, of course, was an accident. I mean to say, the poor fellow didn't *mean* to do it. But nevertheless it was sufficient to ... er ... inflame the Persian army to such an extent that instead of ... er ... retreating, they *advanced*. The centre of the stage became a milling mob of helmeted soldiers locked in mortal combat. Two of them were thrown into the orchestra pit before someone had the sense to lower the curtain. The king remarked later that he had been greatly impressed by the ... um ... *realism* shown in the battle scene.'

The burst of laughter sent the pale geckos scuttling up the wall in alarm.
'Theodore!' Larry laughed mockingly. 'I'm sure you made that up.'
'No, no!' Theodore would protest; 'it's quite true . . . I saw it myself.'
'It sounds the most unlikely story.'
'Here in Corfu,' said Theodore, his eyes twinkling with pride, *'anything can happen.'*

The sea striped with moonlight gleamed through the olives. Down by the well the tree-frogs croaked excitedly to each other. Two owls were having a contest in the tree below the veranda. In the grape-vine above our heads the geckos crept along the gnarled branches, eagerly watching the drifts of insects that were drawn, like a tide, by the lamplight.

Chapter Nine

The World in a Wall

The crumbling wall that surrounded the sunken garden alongside the house was a rich hunting ground for me. It was an ancient brick wall that had been plastered over, but now this outer skin was green with moss, bulging and sagging with the damp of many winters. The whole surface was an intricate map of cracks, some several inches wide, others as fine as hairs. Here and there large pieces had dropped off and revealed the rows of rose-pink bricks lying beneath like ribs. There was a whole landscape on this wall if you peered closely enough to see it; the roofs of a hundred tiny toadstools, red, yellow and brown, showed in patches like villages on the damper portions; mountains of bottle-green moss grew in tuffets so symmetrical that they might have been planted and trimmed; forests of small ferns sprouted from cracks in the shady places, drooping languidly like little green fountains. The top of the wall was a desert land, too dry for anything except a few rust-red mosses to live in it, too hot for anything except sun-bathing by the dragon-flies. At the base of the wall grew a mass of plants, cyclamen, crocus, asphodel, thrusting their leaves among the piles of broken and chipped roof-tiles that lay there. This whole strip was guarded by a labyrinth of blackberry hung, in season, with fruit that was plump and juicy and black as ebony.

The inhabitants of the wall were a mixed lot, and they were divided into day and night workers, the hunters and the hunted. At night the hunters were the toads that lived among the brambles, and the geckos, pale, translucent with bulging eyes, that lived in the cracks higher up the wall. Their prey was the population of stupid, absent-minded crane-flies that zoomed and barged their way among the leaves; moths of all sizes and shapes, moths striped, tessellated, checked, spotted and blotched, that fluttered in soft clouds along the withered plaster; the beetles, rotund and neatly clad as business men, hurrying with portly efficiency about their night's work. When the last glow-worm had dragged his frosty emerald lantern to bed over the hills of moss, and the sun rose, the wall was taken over by the next set of inhabitants. Here it was more difficult to differentiate between the prey and the predators, for everything seemed to feed indiscriminately off everything else. Thus the hunting wasps searched out caterpillars and spiders; the spiders hunted for flies; the dragon-flies, big, brittle and hunting-pink, fed off the spiders and the flies; and the swift, lithe and multi-coloured wall lizards fed off everything.

But the shyest and most self-effacing of the wall community were the most dangerous; you hardly ever saw one unless you looked for it, and yet there must have been several hundred living in the cracks of the wall. Slide a knife-blade carefully under a piece of the loose plaster and lever it gently away from the brick, and there, crouching beneath it, would be a little black scorpion an inch long, looking as though he were made out of polished chocolate. They were weird-looking little things, with their flattened, oval bodies, their neat, crooked legs, the enormous crab-like claws, bulbous and neatly jointed as armour, and the tail like a string of beads ending in a sting like a rose-thorn. The scorpion would lie there quite quietly as you examined him, only raising his tail in an almost apologetic gesture of warning if you breathed too hard on him. If you kept him in the sun too long he would simply turn his back on you and walk away, and then slide slowly but firmly under another section of plaster.

I grew very fond of these scorpions. I found them to be pleasant, unassuming creatures with, on the whole, the most charming habits. Provided you did nothing silly or clumsy (like putting your hand on one) the scorpions treated you with respect, their one desire being to get away and hide as quickly as possible. They must have found me rather a trial, for I was always ripping sections of the plaster away so that I could watch them, or capturing them and make them walk about in jam-jars so that I could see the way their feet moved. By means of my sudden and unexpected assaults on the wall I discovered quite a bit about the scorpions. I found that they would eat bluebottles (though how they caught them was a mystery I never solved), grasshoppers, moths and lacewing flies. Several times I found them eating each other, a habit I found most distressing in a creature otherwise so impeccable.

By crouching under the wall at night with a torch, I managed to catch some brief glimpses of the scorpions' wonderful courtship dances. I saw them standing, claws clasped, the bodies raised to the skies, their tails lovingly entwined; I saw them waltzing slowly in circles among the moss cushions, claw in claw. But my view of these performances was all too short, for almost as soon as I switched on the torch the partners would stop, pause for a moment, and then, seeing that I was not going to extinguish the light, they would turn round and walk firmly away, claw in claw, side by side. They were definitely beasts that believed in keeping themselves *to* themselves. If I could have kept a colony in captivity I would probably have been able to see the whole of the courtship, but the family had forbidden scorpions in the house, despite my arguments in favour of them.

Then one day I found a fat female scorpion in the wall, wearing what at first glance appeared to be a pale fawn fur coat. Closer inspection proved that this strange garment was made up of a mass of tiny babies clinging to the mother's back. I was enraptured by this family, and I made up my mind to smuggle them into the house and up to my bedroom so that I might keep them and watch them grow up. With infinite care I manoeuvred the mother and family into a matchbox, and then hurried to the villa. It was rather unfortunate that just as I entered the door lunch should be served; however, I placed the matchbox carefully on the mantelpiece in the drawing-room, so that the scorpions should get plenty of air, and made my way to the dining-room and joined the family for the meal. Dawdling over my food, feeding Roger surreptitiously under the table and listening to the family arguing, I completely forgot about my exciting new captures. At last Larry, having finished, fetched the cigarettes from the drawing-room, and lying back in his chair he put one in his mouth and picked up the matchbox he had brought. Oblivious of my impending doom I watched him interestedly as, still talking glibly, he opened the matchbox.

Now I maintain to this day that the female scorpion meant no harm. She was agitated and a trifle annoyed at being shut up in a matchbox for so long, and so she seized the first opportunity to escape. She hoisted herself out of the box with great rapidity, her babies clinging on desperately, and scuttled on to the back of Larry's hand. There, not quite certain what to do next, she paused, her sting curved up at the ready. Larry, feeling the movement of her claws, glanced down to see what it was, and from that moment things got increasingly confused.

He uttered a roar of fright that made Lugaretzia drop a plate and brought Roger out from beneath the table, barking wildly. With a flick of his hand he sent the unfortunate scorpion flying down the table, and she landed midway between Margo and Leslie, scattering babies like confetti as she thumped on to the cloth. Thoroughly enraged at this treatment, the creature sped towards Leslie, her sting quivering with emotion. Leslie leapt to his feet, overturning his chair, and flicked out desperately with his napkin, sending the scorpion rolling across the cloth towards Margo, who promptly let out a scream that any railway engine would have been proud to produce. Mother, completely bewildered by this sudden and rapid change from peace to chaos, put on her glasses and peered down the table to see what was causing the pandemonium, and at that moment Margo, in a vain attempt to stop the scorpion's advance, hurled a glass of water at it. The shower missed the animal completely, but successfully drenched Mother, who, not being able to stand cold water, promptly lost her breath and sat gasping at the end of the table, unable even to protest. The scorpion had now gone to ground under Leslie's plate, while her babies swarmed wildly all over the table. Roger, mystified by the panic, but determined to do his share, ran round and round the room, barking hysterically.

'It's that bloody boy again . . .' bellowed Larry.

'Look out! Look out! They're coming!' screamed Margo.

'All we need is a book,' roared Leslie; 'don't panic, hit 'em with a book.'

'What on earth's the *matter* with you all?' Mother kept imploring, mopping her glasses.

'It's that bloody boy . . . he'll kill the lot of us. . . . Look at the table . . . knee-deep in scorpions. . . .'

'Quick ... quick ... do something. ... Look out, look out!'
'Stop screeching and get a book, for God's sake. ... You're worse than the dog. ... Shut *up*, Roger. ...'
'By the Grace of God I wasn't bitten. ...'
'Look out ... there's another one. ... Quick ... quick ...'
'Oh, shut up and get me a book or something. ...'
'But *how* did the scorpions get on the table, dear?'
'That bloody boy. ... Every matchbox in the house is a deathtrap. ...'
'Look out, it's coming towards me. ... Quick, quick, do something. ...'
'Hit it with your knife ... *your knife*. ... Go on, hit it ...'

Since no one had bothered to explain things to him, Roger was under the mistaken impression that the family were being attacked, and that it was his duty to defend them. As Lugaretzia was the only stranger in the room, he came to the logical conclusion that she must be the responsible party, so he bit her in the ankle. This did not help matters very much.

By the time a certain amount of order had been restored, all the baby scorpions had hidden themselves under various plates and bits of cutlery. Eventually, after impassioned pleas on my part, backed up by Mother, Leslie's suggestion that the whole lot be slaughtered was quashed. While the family, still simmering with rage and fright, retired to the drawing-room, I spent half an hour rounding up the babies, picking them up in a teaspoon and returning them to their mother's back. Then I carried them outside on a saucer and, with the utmost reluctance, released them on the garden wall. Roger and I went and spent the afternoon on the hillside, for I felt it would be prudent to allow the family to have a siesta before seeing them again.

The results of this incident were numerous. Larry developed a phobia about matchboxes and opened them with the utmost caution, a handkerchief wrapped round his hand. Lugaretzia limped round the house, her ankle enveloped in yards of bandage, for weeks after the bite had healed, and came round every morning, with the tea, to show us how the scabs were getting on. But, from my point of view, the worst repercussion of the whole affair was that Mother decided I was running wild again, and that it was high time I received a little more education. While the problem of finding a full-time tutor was being solved, she was determined that my French, at least, should be kept in trim. So arrangements were made, and every morning Spiro would drive me into the town for my French lesson with the Belgian consul.

The consul's house was situated in the maze of narrow, smelly alleyways that made up the Jewish quarter of the town. It was a fascinating area, the cobbled streets crammed with stalls that were piled high with gaily-coloured bales of cloth, mountains of shining sweetmeats, ornaments of beaten silver, fruit and vegetables. The streets were so narrow that you had to stand back against the wall to allow the donkeys to stagger past with their loads of merchandise. It was a rich and colourful part of the town, full of noise and bustle, the screech of bargaining women, the cluck of hens, the barking of dogs and the wailing cry of the men carrying great trays of fresh hot loaves on their heads. Right in the very centre, in the top flat of a tall, rickety building that leant tiredly over a tiny square, lived the Belgian consul.

He was a sweet little man, whose most striking attribute was a magnificent three-pointed beard and carefully waxed moustache. He took his job rather seriously, and was always dressed as though he were on the verge of rushing off to some important official function, in a black cut-away coat, striped trousers, fawn spats over brightly polished shoes, an immense cravat like a silk waterfall, held in place by a plain gold pin, and a tall and gleaming top hat that completed the ensemble. One could see him at any hour of the day, clad like this, picking his way down the dirty, narrow alleys, stepping daintily among the puddles, drawing himself back against the wall with a magnificently courteous gesture to allow a donkey to pass, and tapping it coyly on the rump with his malacca cane. The people of the town did not find his garb at all unusual. They thought that he was an Englishman, and as all Englishmen were lords it was not only right but necessary that they should wear the correct uniform.

The first morning I arrived, he welcomed me into a living-room whose walls were decorated with a mass of heavily-framed photographs of himself in various Napoleonic attitudes. The Victorian chairs, covered with red brocade, were patched with antimacassars by the score; the table on which we worked was draped in a wine-red cloth of velvet, with a fringe of bright green tassels round the edge. It was an intriguingly ugly room. In order to test the extent of my knowledge of French, the consul sat me down at the table, produced a fat and battered edition of *Le Petit Larousse*, and placed it in front of me, open at page one.

'You will please to read zis,' he said, his gold teeth glittering amicably in his beard.

He twisted the points of his moustache, pursed his lips, clasped his hands behind his back and paced slowly across to the window, while I started down the list of words beginning with A. I had hardly stumbled through the first three when the consul stiffened and uttered a suppressed exclamation. I thought at first he was shocked by my accent, but it was apparently nothing to do with me. He rushed across the room, muttering to himself, tore open a cupboard and pulled out a powerful-looking air rifle, while I watched him with increasing mystification and interest, not unmixed with a certain alarm for my own safety. He loaded the weapon, dropping pellets all over the carpet in his frantic haste. Then he crouched and crept back to the window, where, half concealed by the curtain, he peered out eagerly. Then he raised the gun, took careful aim at something and fired. When he turned round, slowly and sadly shaking his head, and laid the gun aside, I was surprised to see tears in his eyes. He drew a yard or so of silk handkerchief out of his breast pocket and blew his nose violently.

'Ah, ah, ah,' he intoned, shaking his head dolefully, 'ze poor lizzle fellow. Buz we musz work . . . please to continuez wiz your reading, *mon ami*.'

For the rest of the morning I toyed with the exciting idea that the consul had committed a murder before my very eyes, or, at least, that he was carrying out a blood feud with some neighbouring householder. But when, after the fourth morning, the consul was still firing periodically out of his window, I decided that my explanation could not be the right one, unless it was an exceptionally large family he was feuding with, and a family, moreover, who were apparently incapable of firing back. It was a week before I found out the reason for the consul's incessant fusillade, and the reason was cats. In the Jewish quarter, as in other parts of the town, the cats were allowed to breed unchecked. There were literally hundreds of them. They belonged to no one and were uncared for, so that most of them were in a frightful state, covered with sores, their fur coming out in great bald patches, their legs bent with rickets, and all of them so thin that it was a wonder they were alive at all. The consul was a great cat-lover, and he possessed three large and well-fed Persians to prove it. But the sight of all these starving, sore-ridden felines stalking about on the roof-tops opposite his window was too much for his sensitive nature.

'I cannot feed zem all,' he explained to me, 'so I like to make zem happiness by zooting zem. Zey are bezzer so, buz iz makes me feel so zad.'

He was, in fact, performing a very necessary and humane service, as anyone who had seen the cats would agree. So my lessons in French were being continuously interrupted while the consul leapt to the window to send yet another cat to a happier hunting ground. After the report of the gun there would be a moment's silence, in respect for the dead, and then the consul would blow his nose violently, sigh tragically, and we would plunge once more into the tangled labyrinth of French verbs.

For some inexplicable reason the consul was under the impression that Mother could speak French, and he would never lose an opportunity of engaging her in conversation. If she had the good fortune, while shopping in the town, to notice his top hat bobbing through the crowd towards her, she would hastily retreat into the nearest shop and buy a number of things she had no use for, until the danger was past. Occasionally, however, the consul would appear suddenly out of an alleyway and take her by surprise. He would advance, smiling broadly and twirling his cane, sweep off his top hat and bow almost double before her, while clasping her reluctantly offered hand and pressing it passionately into his beard. Then they would stand in the middle of the street, occasionally being forced apart by a passing donkey, while the consul swamped Mother under a flood of French, gesturing elegantly with his hat and stick, apparently unaware of the blank expression on Mother's face. Now and then he would punctuate his speech with a questioning '*n'est-ce pas, madame?*' and this was Mother's cue. Summoning up all her courage, she would display her complete mastery over the French tongue.

'*Oui, oui!*' she would exclaim, smiling nervously, and then add, in case it had sounded rather unenthusiastic, 'OUI, OUI.'

This procedure satisfied the consul, and I'm sure he never realized that this was the only French word that Mother knew. But these conversations were a nerve-racking ordeal for her, and we had only to hiss "Look out, Mother, the consul's coming,' to set her tearing off down the street at a lady-like walk that was dangerously near to a gallop.

In some ways these French lessons were good for me; I did not learn any French, it's true, but by the end of the morning I was so bored that my afternoon sorties into the surrounding country were made with double the normal enthusiasm. And then, of course, there was always Thursday to look forward to. Theodore would come out to the villa as soon after lunch as was decent, and stay until the moon was high over the Albanian mountains. Thursday was happily chosen, from his point of view, because it was on this day that the seaplane from Athens arrived and landed in the bay not far from the house. Theodore had a passion for watching seaplanes land. Unfortunately the only part of the house from which you could get a good view of the bay was the attic, and then it meant leaning perilously out of the window and craning your neck. The plane would invariably arrive in the middle of tea; a dim, drowsy hum could be heard, so faint one could not be sure it was not a bee. Theodore, in the middle of an anecdote or an explanation, would suddenly stop talking, his eyes would take on a fanatical gleam, his beard would bristle and he would cock his head on one side.

'Is that ... er ... you know ... is that the sound of a *plane*?' he would inquire.

Everyone would stop talking and listen; slowly the sound would grow louder and louder. Theodore would carefully place his half-eaten scone on his plate.

'Ah ha!' he would say, wiping his fingers carefully. 'Yes, that certainly *sounds* like a plane ... er ... um ... yes.'

The sound would grow louder and louder, while Theodore shifted uneasily in his seat. At length Mother would put him out of his misery.

'Would you like to go up and watch it land?' she would ask.

'Well ... er ... if you're sure ...' Theodore would mumble, vacating his seat with alacrity. "I ... er ... find the sight very attractive ... if you're sure you don't mind.'

The sound of the plane's engines would now be directly overhead; there was not a moment to lose.

"I have always been ... er ... you know ... attracted. ...'

'Hurry up, Theo, or you'll miss it,' we would chorus.

The entire family then vacated the table, and, gathering Theodore *en route*, we sped up the four flights of stairs, Roger racing ahead, barking joyfully. We burst into the attic, out of breath, laughing, our feet thumping like gun-fire on the uncarpeted floor, threw open the windows and leaned out, peering over the olive-tops to where the bay lay like a round blue eye among the trees, its surface as smooth as honey. The plane, like a cumbersome overweight goose, flew over the olive-groves, sinking lower and lower. Suddenly it would be over the water, racing its reflection over the blue surface. Slowly the plane dropped lower and lower. Theodore, eyes narrowed, beard bristling, watched it with bated breath. Lower and lower, and then suddenly it touched the surface briefly, left a widening petal of foam, flew on, and then settled on the surface and surged across the bay, leaving a spreading fan of white foam behind it. As it came slowly to rest, Theodore would rasp the side of his beard with his thumb, and ease himself back into the attic.

'Um ... yes,' he would say, dusting his hands, "it is certainly a ... very ... er ... *enjoyable* sight.'

The show was over. He would have to wait another week for the next plane. We would shut the attic windows and troop noisily downstairs to resume our interrupted tea. The next week exactly the same thing would happen all over again.

It was on Thursdays that Theodore and I went out together, sometimes confining ourselves to the garden, sometimes venturing further afield. Loaded down with collecting boxes and nets, we wended our way through the olives, Roger galloping ahead of us, nose to the ground. Everything that we came across was grist to our mill: flowers, insects, rocks or birds. Theodore had an apparently inexhaustible fund of knowledge about everything, but he imparted this knowledge with a sort of meticulous diffidence that made you feel he was not so much teaching you something new, as reminding you of something which you were already aware of, but which had, for some reason or other, slipped your mind. His conversation was sprinkled with hilarious anecdotes, incredibly bad puns and even worse jokes, which he would tell with great relish, his eyes twinkling, his nose wrinkled as he laughed silently in his beard, as much at himself as at his own humour.

Every water-filled ditch or pool was, to us, a teeming and unexplored jungle, with the minute cyclops and water-fleas, green and coral pink, suspended like birds among the underwater branches, while on the muddy bottom the tigers of the pool would prowl: the leeches and the dragon-fly larvae. Every hollow tree had to be closely scrutinised in case it should contain a tiny pool of water in which mosquito-larvae were living, every mossy wigged rock had to be overturned to find out what lay beneath it, and every rotten log had to be dissected. Standing straight and immaculate at the edge of a pool, Theodore would carefully sweep his little net through the water, lift it out and peer keenly into the tiny glass bottle that dangled at the end, into which all the minute water life had been sifted.

'Ah ha!' he might say, his voice ringing with excitement, his beard bristling, 'I believe it's *ceriodaphnia laticaudata.*'

He would whip a magnifying glass from his waistcoat pocket and peer more closely.

'Ah, um ... yes ... very curious ... it is *laticaudata.* Could you just ... er ... hand me a clean test-tube ... um ... thank you. ...'

He would suck the minute creature out of the bottle with a fountain-pen filler, enshrine it carefully in the tube, and then examine the rest of the catch.

'There doesn't seem to be anything else that's particularly exciting. ... Ah, yes, I didn't notice ... there is rather a curious caddis larva ... there, d'you see it? ... um ... it appears to have made its case of the shells of certain molluscs. ... It's cetainly very pretty.'

At the bottom of the little bottle was an elongated case, half an inch long, constructed out of what appeared to be silk, and thick with tiny flat snail-shells like buttons. From one end of this delightful home the owner peered, an unattractive maggot-like beast with a head like an ant's. Slowly it crawled across the glass, dragging its beautiful house with it.

'I tried an interesting experiment once,' Theodore said. 'I caught a number of these ... er ... larvae, and removed their shells. Naturally it doesn't *hurt* them. Then I put them in some jars which contained perfectly clear water and nothing in the way of ... er ... materials with which to build new cases. Then I gave each set of larvae different-coloured materials to build with: some I gave very tiny blue and green beads, and some I gave chips of brick, white sand, even some ... er ... fragments of coloured glass. They all built new cases out of these different things, and I must say the result was very curious and ... er ... colourful. They are certainly very clever *architects*.'

He emptied the contents of the bottle back into the pool, put his net over his shoulder and we walked on our way.

'Talking of *building*,' Theodore continued, his eyes sparkling, 'did I tell you what happened to ... a ... er ... a friend of mine? Um, yes. Well, he had a small house in the country, and, as his family ... um ... increased, he decided that it was not big enough. He decided to add another floor to the house. He was, I think, a little *over-confident* of his own architectural ... um ... prowess, and he insisted on designing the new floor himself. Um, ha, yes. Well, everything went well and in next to no time the new floor was ready, complete with bedrooms, bathrooms, and so forth. My friend had a party to celebrate the completion of the work, we all drank toasts to the ... um ... new piece of building, and with great ceremony the scaffolding was taken down ... um ... removed. No one noticed anything ... um ... anything *amiss*, until a late arrival at the celebration wanted to look round the new rooms. It was then discovered that there was no staircase. It appears that my friend had forgotten to put a staircase in his plans, you know, and during the actual ... er ... the actual *building* operations he and the workmen had got so used to climbing to the top floor by means of the scaffolding that no one apparently noticed the ... er ... the *defect*.'

So we would walk on through the hot afternoon, pausing by the pools and ditches and stream, wading through the heavily scented myrtle-bushes, over the hillsides crisp with heather, along white, dusty roads where we were occasionally passed by a drooping, plodding donkey carrying a sleepy peasant on its back.

Towards evening, our jars, bottles and tubes full of strange and exciting forms of life, we would turn for home. The sky would be fading to a pale gold as we marched through the olive-groves, already dim with shadow, and the air would be cooler and more richly scented. Roger would trot ahead of us, his tongue flapping out, occasionally glancing over his shoulder to make sure we were following him. Theodore and I, hot and dusty and tired, our bulging collecting bags making our shoulders ache pleasantly, would stride along singing a song that Theodore had taught me. It had a rousing tune that gave a new life to tired feet, and Theodore's baritone voice and my shrill treble would ring out gaily through the gloomy trees:

'There was an old man who lived in Jerusalem,
   Glory Halleluiah, Hi-ero-jerum.
He wore a top hat and he looked very sprucelum,
   Glory Halleluiah, Hi-ero-jerum.
Skinermer rinki doodle dum, skinermer rinki doodle dum,
   Glory Halleluiah, Hi-ero-jerum ...'

Chapter Ten
The Pageant of Fireflies

Spring merged slowly into the long, hot, sun-sharp days of summer sung in by cicadas, shrill and excited, making the island vibrate with their cries. In the fields the maize was starting to fill out, the silken tassels turning from brown to butter-blond; when you tore off the wrapping of leaves and bit into the rows of pearly seeds the juice would spurt into your mouth like milk. On the vines the grapes hung in tiny clusters, freckled and warm. The olives seemed weighed down under the weight of their fruit, smooth drops of green jade among which the choirs of cicadas zithered. In the orange-groves, among the dark and shiny leaves, the fruit was starting to glow redly, like a blush spreading up the green, pitted skins.

Up on the hills, among the dark cypress and the heather, shoals of butterflies danced and twisted like wind-blown confetti, pausing now and then on a leaf to lay a salvo of eggs. The grasshoppers and locusts whirred like clockwork under my feet, and flew drunkenly across the heather, their wings shining in the sun. Among the myrtles the mantids moved, lightly, carefully, swaying slightly, the quintessence of evil. They were lank and green, with chinless faces and monstrous globular eyes, frosty gold, with an expression of intense, predatory madness in them. The crooked arms, with their fringes of sharp teeth, would be raised in mock supplication to the insect world, so humble, so fervent, trembling slightly when a butterfly flew too close.

Towards evening, when it grew cooler, the cicadas stopped singing; their place being taken by the green tree-frogs, glued damply to the lemon-tree leaves down by the well. With bulging eyes staring as though hypnotised, their backs as shiny as the leaves they sat amongst, they swelled out their vocal sacs and croaked harshly and with such violence that they seemed in danger of splitting their damp bodies with the effort. When the sun sank there was a brief, apple-green twilight which faded and became mauve, and the air cooled and took on the scents of evening. The toads appeared, putty-coloured with strange, map-like blotches of bottle-green on their skins. They hopped furtively among the long grass clumps in the olive-groves, where the crane-flies' unsteady flight seemed to cover the ground with a drifting curtain of gauze. They sat there blinking, and then would suddenly snap at a passing crane-fly; sitting back, looking a trifle embarrassed, they stuffed the trailing ends of wing and leg into their great mouths with the aid of their thumbs. Above them, on the crumbling walls of the sunken garden, the little black scorpions walked solemnly, hand in hand, among the plump mounds of green moss and the groves of tiny toadstools.

The sea was smooth, warm and as dark as black velvet, not a ripple disturbing the surface. The distant coastline of Albania was dimly outlined by a faint reddish glow in the sky. Gradually, minute by minute, this glow deepened and grew brighter, spreading across the sky. Then suddenly the moon, enormous, wine-red, edged herself over the fretted battlement of mountains, and threw a straight, blood-red path across the dark sea. The owls appeared now, drifting from tree to tree as silently as flakes of soot, hooting in astonishment as the moon rose higher and higher, turning to pink, then gold, and finally riding in a nest of stars, like a silver bubble.

With the summer came Peter to tutor me, a tall, handsome young man, fresh from Oxford, with decided ideas on education which I found rather trying to begin with. But gradually the atmosphere of the island worked its way insidiously under his skin, and he relaxed and became quite human. At first the lessons were painful to an extreme: interminable wrestling with fractions and percentages, geological strata and warm currents, nouns, verbs and adverbs. But, as the sunshine worked its magic on Peter, the fractions and percentages no longer seemed to him an overwhelmingly important part of life and they were gradually pushed more and more into the background; he discovered that the intricacies of geological strata and the effects of warm currents could be explained much more easily while swimming along the coast, while the simplest way of teaching me English was to allow me to write something each day which he would correct. He had suggested a diary, but I was against this, pointing out that I already kept one on nature, in which was recorded everything of interest that happened each day. If I were to keep another diary, what was I to put in it? Peter could find no answer to this argument. I suggested that I might try something a little more ambitious and interesting than a diary. Diffidently, I suggested I wrote a book, and Peter, somewhat startled, but not being able to think of any reason why I should *not* write a book, agreed. So every morning I spent a happy hour or so adding another chapter to my epic, a stirring tale which involved a voyage round the world with the family, during which we captured every conceivable kind of fauna in the most unlikely traps. I modelled my style on the *Boy's Own Paper,* and so each chapter ended on a thrilling note, with Mother being attacked by a jaguar, or Larry struggling in the coils of an enormous python. Sometimes these climaxes were so complicated and fraught with danger that I had great difficulty in extricating the family intact on the following day. While I was at work on my masterpiece, breathing heavily, tongue protruding, breaking off for discussions with Roger on the finer points of the plot, Peter and Margo would take a stroll in the sunken garden to look at the flowers. To my surprise, they had both suddenly become very botanically minded. In this way the mornings passed very pleasantly for all concerned. Occasionally, in the early days, Peter suffered from sudden spasms of conscience, my epic would be relegated to a drawer, and we would pore over mathematical problems. But as the summer days grew longer, and Margo's interest in gardening became more sustained, these irritating periods became less frequent.

After the unfortunate affair of the scorpion, the family had given me a large room on the first floor in which to house my beasts, in the vague hope that this would confine them to one particular portion of the house. This room – which I called my study, and which the rest of the family called the

Bug House – smelt pleasantly of ether and methylated spirits. It was here that I kept my natural history books, my diary, microscope, dissecting instruments, nets, collecting bags and other important items. Large cardboard boxes housed my birds' egg, beetle, butterfly and dragon-fly collections, while on the shelves above were a fine range of bottles full of methylated spirits in which were preserved such interesting items as a four-legged chicken (a present from Lugaretzia's husband), various lizards and snakes, frog-spawn in different stages of growth, a baby octopus, three half-grown brown rats (a contribution from Roger) and a minute tortoise, newly hatched, that had been unable to survive the winter. The walls were sparsely, but tastefully, decorated with a slab slate containing the fossilized remains of a fish, a photograph of myself shaking hands with a chimpanzee, and a stuffed bat. I had prepared the bat myself, without assistance, and I was extremely proud of the result. Considering how limited my knowledge of taxidermy was, it looked, I thought, extremely *like* a bat, especially if you stood at the other side of the room. With wings outstretched it glowered down from the wall from its slab of cork. When summer came, however, the bat appeared to feel the heat: it sagged a little, its coat no longer glossy, and a new and mysterious smell started to make itself felt above the ether and methylated spirits. Poor Roger was wrongly accused at first, and it was only later, when the smell had penetrated even to Larry's bedroom, that a thorough investigation traced the odour to my bat. I was surprised and not a little annoyed. Under pressure I was forced to get rid of it. Peter explained that I had not cured it properly, and said that if I could obtain another specimen he would show me the correct procedure. I thanked him profusely, but tactfully suggested that we keep the whole thing a secret; I explained that I felt the family now looked with a suspicious eye on the art of taxidermy, and it would require a lot of tedious persuasion to get them into an agreeable frame of mind.

My efforts to secure another bat were unsuccessful. Armed with a long bamboo I waited for hours in the moon-splashed corridors between the olive-trees, but the bats flickered past like quicksilver and vanished before I could use my weapon. But, while waiting in vain for a chance to hit a bat, I saw a number of other night creatures which I would not otherwise have seen. I watched a young fox hopefully digging for beetles in the hillside, scrabbling with slim paws at the earth, and scrunching the insects up hungrily as he unearthed them. Once, five jackals appeared out of the myrtle bushes, paused in surprise at seeing me, and then melted away among the trees, like shadows. The nightjars on silent, silky wings would slide as smoothly as great black swallows along the rows of olives, sweeping across the grass in pursuit of the drunken, whirling crane-flies. One night a pair of squirrel dormice appeared in the tree above me, and chased each other in wild exuberance up and down the grove, leaping from branch to branch like acrobats, skittering up and down the tree-trunks, their bushy tails like puffs of grey smoke in the moonlight. I was so fascinated by these creatures that I was determined to try to catch one. The best time to search for them was, of course, during the day, when they would be asleep. So, I hunted laboriously through the olive-groves for their hideout, but it was a hopeless quest, for every gnarled and twisted trunk was hollow, and each contained half a dozen holes. However, my patience did not go entirely unrewarded, for one day I thrust my arm into a hole, and my fingers closed round something small and soft, something that wiggled as I pulled it out. At first glance my capture appeared to be an outsize bundle of dandelion seeds, furnished with a pair of enormous golden eyes; closer inspection proved it to be a young Scops owl, still clad in his baby down. We regarded each other for a moment, and then the bird, apparently indignant at my ill-mannered laughter at his appearance, dug his tiny claws deeply into my thumb, and I lost my grip on the branch, so that we fell out of the tree together.

I carried the indignant owlet back home in my pocket, and introduced him to the family with a certain trepidation. To my surprise, he was greeted with unqualified approval, and no objection was raised to my keeping him. He took up residence in a basket kept in my study and, after much argument, he was christened Ulysses. From the first he showed that he was a bird of great strength of character, and not to be trifled with. Although he would have fitted comfortably into a tea-cup, he showed no fear and would unhesitatingly attack anything and everyone, regardless of size. As we all had to share the room, I felt it would be a good idea if he and Roger got on intimate terms, so, as soon as the owl had settled down, I performed the introductions by placing Ulysses on the floor, and telling Roger to approach and make friends. Roger had become very philosophical about having to make friends with the various creatures that I adopted, and he took the appearance of an owl in his stride. Wagging his tail briskly, in an ingratiating manner, he approached Ulysses, who squatted on the floor with anything but a friendly expression on his face. He watched Roger's approach in an unwinking stare of ferocity. Roger's advance became less confident. Ulysses continued to glare as though trying to hypnotize the dog. Roger stopped, his ears drooped, his tail wagging only feebly, and he glanced at me for inspiration. I ordered him sternly to continue his overtures of friendship. Roger looked nervously at the owl, and then with great nonchalance walked round him, in an effort to approach him from the back. Ulysses, however, let his head revolve too, and kept his eyes still fixed on the dog. Roger, never having met a creature that could look behind itself without turning round, seemed a trifle nonplussed. After a moment's thought he decided to try the skittish, let's-all-have-a-jolly-game approach. He lay down on his stomach, put his head between his paws and crept slowly towards the bird, whining gently and wagging his tail with abandon. Ulysses continued to look as though he were stuffed. Roger, still progressing on his stomach, managed to get quite close, but then he made a fatal mistake. He pushed his woolly face forward and sniffed loudly and interestedly at the bird. Now Ulysses would stand a lot, but he was not going to be sniffed at by a mountainous dog covered with black curls. He decided that he would have to show this ungainly and wingless beast exactly where he got off. He lowered his eyelids, clicked his beak, hopped up into the air and landed squarely on the dog's muzzle, burying his razor-sharp claws in the black nose. Roger, with a stricken yelp, shook the bird off and retired beneath the table; no amount of coaxing would get him to come out until Ulysses was safely back in his basket.

When Ulysses grew older he lost his baby down and developed the fine ash-grey, rust-red and black plumage of his kind, with the pale breast handsomely marked with Maltese crosses in black. He also developed long ear-tufts, which he would raise in indignation when you attempted to take liberties with him. As he was now far too old to be kept in a basket, and strongly opposed to the idea of a cage, I was forced to give him the run of the study. He performed his flying lessons between the table and the door-handle, and, as soon as he had mastered the art, chose the pelmet above the window as his home, and would spend the day sleeping up there, eyes closed, looking exactly like an olive-stump. If you spoke to him he would open his eyes a fraction, raise his ear-tufts and elongate his whole body, so that he looked like some weird, emaciated Chinese idol. If he was feeling particularly affectionate he would click his beak at you, or, as a great concession, fly down and give you a hurried peck on the ear.

As the sun sank and the geckos started to scuttle about the shadowy walls of the house, Ulysses would wake up. He would yawn delicately, stretch his wings, clean his tail and then shiver violently so that all his feathers stood out like the petals of a wind-blown chrysanthemum. With great nonchalance he would regurgitate a pellet of undigested food on to the newspaper spread below for this, and other, purposes. Having prepared himself for the night's work, he would utter an experimental 'tywhoo?' to make sure his voice was in trim, and then launch himself on soft wings, to drift round the room as silently as a flake of ash and land on my shoulder. For a short time he would sit there, nibbling my ear, and then he would give himself another shake, put sentiment to one side and become business-like. He would fly on to the window-sill and give another questioning 'tywhoo?', staring at me with his honey-coloured eyes. This was the signal that he wanted the shutters opened. As soon as I threw them back he would float out through the window, to be silhouetted for a moment against the moon before diving into the dark olives. A moment later a loud challenging 'tywhoo! tywhoo!' would ring out, the warning that Ulysses was about to start his hunting.

The length of time Ulysses spent on his hunts varied; sometimes he would swoop back into the room after only an hour, and on other occasions he would be out all night. But, wherever he went, he never failed to come back to the house between nine and ten for his supper. If there was no light in my study, he would fly down and peer through the drawing-room window to see if I was there. If I was not there, he would fly up the side of the house again to land on my bedroom window-sill and tap briskly on the shutters, until I opened them and served him with his saucer of mince, or chopped chicken's heart, or whatever delicacy was on the menu that day. When the last gory morsel had been swallowed he would give a soft, hiccoughing chirrup, sit meditating for a moment and then fly off over the moon-bright tree-tops.

Since he had proved himself an able fighter, Ulysses became fairly friendly towards Roger, and if we were going down for a late evening swim I could sometimes prevail upon him to honour us with his company. He would ride on Roger's back, clinging tight to the black wool; if, as occasionally happened, Roger forgot his passenger and went too fast, or skittishly jumped over a stone, Ulysses's eye would blaze, his wings flap in a frantic effort to keep his balance and he would click his beak loudly and indignantly until I reprimanded Roger for his carelessness. On the shore Ulysses would perch on my shorts and shirt, while Roger and I gambolled in the warm, shallow water. Ulysses would watch our antics with round and faintly disapproving eyes, sitting up as straight as a guardsman. Now and then he would leave his post to skim out over us, click his beak and return to shore, but whether he did this in alarm for our safety or in order to join in our game, I could never decide. Sometimes, if we took too long over the swim, he would get bored, and fly up the hill to the garden, crying 'Tywhoo!' in farewell.

In the summer, when the moon was full, the family took to bathing at night, for during the day the sun was so fierce that the sea became too hot to be refreshing. As soon as the moon had risen we would make our way down through the trees to the creaking wooden jetty, and clamber into the *Sea Cow*. With Larry and Peter on one oar, Margo and Leslie on the other and Roger and myself in the bows to act as look-outs, we would drift down the coast for half a mile or so to where there was a small bay with a lip of white sand and a few carefully arranged boulders, smooth and still sun-warm, ideal for sitting on. We would anchor the *Sea Cow* in deep water and then dive over the side to gambol and plunge, and set the moonlight shaking across the waters of the bay. When tired, we swam languidly to the shore and lay on the warm rocks, gazing up into the star-freckled sky. Generally after half an hour or so I would get bored with the conversation, and slip back into the water and swim slowly out across the bay, to lie on my back, cushioned by the warm sea, gazing up at the moon. One night, while I was thus occupied, I discovered that our bay was used by other creatures as well.

Lying spread-eagled in the silky water, gazing into the sky, only moving my hands and feet slightly to keep afloat, I was looking at the Milky Way stretched like a chiffon scarf across the sky and wondering how many stars it contained. I could hear the voices of the others, laughing and talking on the beach, echoing over the water, and by lifting my head I could see their position on the shore by the pulsing lights of their cigarettes. Drifting there, relaxed and dreamy, I was suddenly startled to hear, quite close to me, a clop and gurgle of water, followed by a long, deep sigh, and a series of gentle ripples rocked me up and down. Hastily I righted myself and trod water, looking to see how far from the beach I had drifted. To my alarm I found that not only was I some considerable distance from the shore, but from the *Sea Cow* as well, and I was not at all sure what sort of creature it was swimming around in the dark waters beneath me. I could hear the others laughing on the shore at some joke or other, and I saw someone flip a cigarette-end high into the sky like a red star that curved over and extinguished itself at the rim of the sea. I was feeling more and more uncomfortable, and I was just about to call for assistance when, some twenty feet away from me, the sea seemed to part with a gentle swish and gurgle, a gleaming back appeared, gave a deep, satisfied sigh, and sank below the surface again. I had hardly time to recognize it as a porpoise before I found I was right in the midst of them. They rose all around me, sighing luxuriously, their black backs shining as they humped in the moonlight. There must have been about eight of them, and one rose so close that I could have swum forward three strokes and touched his ebony head. Heaving and sighing heavily, they played across the bay, and I swam with them, watching fascinated as they rose to the surface, crumpling the water, breathed deeply, and then dived beneath the surface again, leaving only an expanding hoop of foam to mark the spot. Presently, as if obeying a signal, they turned and headed out of the bay towards the distant coast of Albania, and I trod water and watched them go, swimming up the white chain of moonlight, backs agleam as they rose and plunged with heavy ecstasy in the water as warm as fresh milk. Behind them they left a trail of great bubbles that rocked and shone briefly like miniature moons before vanishing under the ripples.

After this we often met the porpoises when we went moonlight bathing, and one evening they put on an illuminated show for our benefit, aided by one of the most attractive insects that inhabited the island. We had discovered that in the hot months of the year the sea became full of phosphorescence. When there was moonlight this was not so noticeable – a faint greenish flicker round the bows of the boat, a brief flash as someone dived into the water. We found that the best time for the phosphorescence was when there was no moon at all. Another illuminated inhabitant of the summer months was the firefly. These slender brown beetles would fly as soon as it got dark, floating through the olive-groves by the score, their tails flashing on and off, giving a light that was greenish-white, not golden-green, as the sea was. Again, however, the fireflies were at their best when there was no bright moonlight to detract from their lights. Strangely enough, we would never have seen the porpoises, the fireflies and the phosphorescence acting together if it had not been for Mother's bathing-costume.

For some time Mother had greatly envied us our swimming, both in the daytime and at night, but, as she pointed out when we suggested she join us, she was far too old for that sort of thing. Eventually, however, under constant pressure from us, Mother paid a visit into town and returned to the villa coyly bearing a mysterious parcel. Opening this she astonished us all by holding up an extraordinary shapeless garment of black cloth, covered from top to bottom with hundreds of frills and pleats and tucks.

'Well, what d'you think of it?' Mother asked.

We stared at the odd garment and wondered what it was for.

'What is it?' asked Larry at length.

'It's a bathing-costume, of course,' said Mother. 'What on earth did you think it was?'

'It looks to me like a badly-skinned whale,' said Larry, peering at it closely.

'You can't *possibly* wear that, Mother,' said Margo, horrified, 'why, it looks as though it was made in nineteen-twenty.'

'What are all those frills and things for?' asked Larry with interest.

'Decoration, of course,' said Mother indignantly.

'What a jolly idea! Don't forget to shake the fish out of them when you come out of the water.'

'Well, *I* like it, anyway,' Mother said firmly, wrapping the monstrosity up again, 'and I'm going to wear it.'

'You'll have to be careful you don't get waterlogged, with all that cloth around you,' said Leslie seriously.

'Mother, it's *awful*; you can't wear it,' said Margo. 'Why on earth didn't you get something more up to date?'

'When you get to my age, dear, you can't go around in a two-piece bathing-suit . . . you don't have the figure for it.'

'I'd love to know what sort of figure that was designed for,' remarked Larry.

'You really are *hopeless,* Mother,' said Margo despairingly.

'But I *like* it . . . and I'm not asking you to wear it,' Mother pointed out belligerently.

'That's right, you do what you want to do,' agreed Larry; 'don't be put off. It'll probably suit you very well if you can grow another three or four legs to go with it.'

Mother snorted indignantly and swept upstairs to try on her costume. Presently she called to us to come and see the effect, and we all trooped up to the bedroom. Roger was the first to enter, and on being greeted by this strange apparition clad in its voluminous black costume rippling with frills, he retreated hurriedly through the door, backwards, barking ferociously. It was some time before we could persuade him that it really was Mother, and even then he kept giving her vaguely uncertain looks from the corner of his eye. However, in spite of all opposition, Mother stuck to her tent-like bathing-suit, and in the end we gave up.

In order to celebrate her first entry into the sea we decided to have a moonlight picnic down at the bay, and sent an invitation to Theodore, who was the only stranger that Mother would tolerate on such a great occasion. The day for the great immersion arrived, food and wine were prepared, the boat was cleaned out and filled with cushions, and everything was ready when Theodore turned up. On hearing that we had planned a moonlight picnic and swim he reminded us that on that particular night there was no moon. Everyone blamed everyone else for not having checked on the moon's progress, and the argument went on until dusk. Eventually we decided that we would go on the picnic in spite of everything, since all the arrangements were made, so we staggered down to the boat, loaded down with food, wine, towels and cigarettes, and set off down the coast. Theodore and I sat in the bows as look-outs, and the rest took it in turn to row while Mother steered. To begin with, her eyes not having become accustomed to the dark, Mother skilfully steered us in a tight circle, so that after ten minutes' strenuous rowing the jetty suddenly loomed up and we ran into it with a splintering crash. Unnerved by this, Mother went to the opposite extreme and steered out to sea, and we would eventually have made a landfall somewhere on the Albanian coastline if Leslie had not noticed in time. After this Margo took over the steering, and she did it quite well, except that she would, in a crisis, get flurried and forget that to turn right one had to put the tiller over to the left. The result was that we had to spend ten minutes straining and tugging at the boat which Margo had, in her excitement, steered on to, instead of away from, a rock. Taken all round it was an auspicious start to Mother's first bathe.

Eventually we reached the bay, spread out the rugs on the sand, arranged the food, placed the battalion of wine-bottles in a row in the shallows to keep cool, and the great moment had arrived. Amid much cheering Mother removed her housecoat and stood revealed in all her glory, clad in the bathing-costume which made her look, as Larry pointed out, like a sort of marine Albert Memorial. Roger behaved very well until he saw Mother wade into the shallow water in a slow and dignified manner. He then got terribly excited. He seemed to be under the impression that the bathing-costume was some sort of sea monster that had enveloped Mother and was now about to carry her out to sea. Barking wildly, he flung himself to the rescue, grabbed one of the frills dangling so plentifully round the edge of the costume and tugged with all his strength in order to pull Mother back to safety. Mother, who had just remarked that she thought the water a little cold, suddenly found herself being pulled backwards. With a squeak of dismay she lost her footing and sat down heavily in two feet of water, while Roger tugged so hard that a large section of the frill gave way. Elated by the fact that the enemy appeared to be disintegrating, Roger, growling encouragement to Mother, set to work to remove the rest of the offending monster from her person. We writhed on the sand, helpless with laughter, while Mother sat gasping in the shallows, making desperate attempts to regain her feet, beat Roger off and retain at least a portion of her costume. Unfortunately, owing to the extreme thickness of the material from which the costume was constructed, the air was trapped inside; the effect of the water made it inflate like a balloon, and trying to keep this airship of frills and tucks under control added to Mother's difficulties. In the end it was Theodore who shooed Roger away and helped Mother to her feet. Eventually, after we had partaken of a glass of wine to celebrate and recover from what Larry referred to as Perseus's rescue of Andromeda, we went in to swim, and Mother sat discreetly in the shallows, while Roger crouched nearby, growling ominously at the costume as it bulged and fluttered round Mother's waist.

The phosphorescence was particularly good that night. By plunging your hand into the water and dragging it along you could draw a wide golden-green ribbon of cold fire across the sea, and when you dived as you hit the surface it seemed as though you had plunged into a frosty furnace of glinting light. When we were tired we waded out of the sea the water running off our bodies so that we seemed to be on fire, and lay on the sand to eat. Then, as the wine was opened at the end of the meal, as if by arrangement, a few fireflies appeared in the olives behind us – a sort of overture to the show.

First of all there were just two or three green specks, sliding smoothly through the trees, winking regularly. But gradually more and more appeared, until parts of the olive-grove were lit with a weird green glow. Never had we seen so many fireflies congregated in one spot; they flicked through the trees in swarms, they crawled on the grass, the bushes and the olive-trunks, they drifted in swarms over our heads and landed on the rugs, like green embers. Glittering streams of them flew out over the bay, swirling over the water, and then, right on cue, the porpoises appeared, swimming in line into the bay, rocking rhythmically through the water, their backs as if painted with phosphorus. In the centre of the bay they swam round, diving and rolling, occasionally leaping high in the air and falling back into a conflagration of light. With the fireflies above and the illuminated porpoises below it was a fantastic sight. We could even see the luminous trails beneath the surface where the porpoises swam in fiery patterns across the sandy bottom, and when they leapt high in the air the drops of emerald glowing water flicked from them, and you could not tell if it was phosphorescence or fireflies you were looking at. For an hour or so we watched this pageant, and then slowly the fireflies drifted back inland and farther down the coast. Then the porpoises lined up and sped out to sea, leaving a flaming path behind them that flickered and glowed, and then died slowly, like a glowing branch laid across the bay.

Chapter Eleven

The Enchanted Archipelago

As the summer grew hotter and hotter we decided that it required too much effort to row the *Sea Cow* down the coast to our bathing bay, so we invested in an outboard engine. The acquisition of this machine opened up a vast area of coastland for us, for we could now venture much farther afield, making trips along the jagged coastline to remote and deserted beaches golden as corn, or lying like fallen moons among the contorted rocks. It was thus that I became aware of the fact that, stretching along the coast for miles, was a scattered archipelago of small islands, some fairly extensive, some that were really outsize rocks with a wig of greenery perched precariously on top. For some reason, which I could not discover, the sea faunae were greatly attracted by this archipelago, and round the edges of the islands, in rock-pools and sandy bays the size of a large table, there was a bewildering assortment of life. I managed to inveigle the family into several trips to these islets, but as these had few good bathing spots the family soon got bored with having to sit on sun-baked rocks while I fished interminably in the pools and unearthed at intervals strange and, to them, revolting sea-creatures. Also, the islands were strung out close to the coast, some of them being separated from the mainland only by a channel twenty feet wide, and there were plenty of reefs and rocks. So, guiding the *Sea Cow* through these hazards, and making sure the propeller did not strike and break, made any excursion to the islands a difficult navigational problem. Our trips there became less and less frequent, in spite of all arguments on my part, and I was tortured by the thought of all the wonderful animal life waiting in the limpid pools to be caught; but I was unable to do anything about it, simply because I had no boat. I suggested that I might be allowed to take the *Sea Cow* out myself, say once a week, but the family were, for a variety of reasons, against this. But then, just when I had almost given up hope, I was struck with a brilliant idea: my birthday was due fairly soon, and if I dealt with the family skilfully I felt sure I could not only get a boat, but a lot of other equipment as well. I therefore suggested to the family that, instead of letting them choose my birthday presents, I might tell them the things which I wanted most. In this way they could be sure of not disappointing me. The family, rather taken aback, agreed, and then, somewhat suspiciously, asked me what I wanted. Innocently, I said that I hadn't thought about it much, but that I would work out a list for each person, and they could then choose one or more items on it.

My list took a lot of time and thought to work out, and a considerable amount of applied psychology. Mother, for instance, I knew would buy me everything on her list, so I put down some of the most necessary and expensive equipment: five wooden cases, glass-topped, corked lined, to house my insect collection; two dozen test tubes; five pints of methylated spirits, five pints of formalin and a microscope. Margo's list was a little more difficult, for the items had to be chosen so that they would encourage her to go to her favourite shops. So from her I asked for ten yards of butter muslin, ten yards of white calico, six large packets of pins, two bundles of cotton wool, two pints of ether, a pair of forceps and two fountain-pen fillers. It was, I realized resignedly, quite useless to ask Larry for anything like formalin or pins, but if my list showed some sort of literary leaning I stood a good chance. Accordingly I made out a formidable sheet covered with the titles, authors' names, publishers and price of all the natural history books I felt in need of, and put an asterisk against those that would be most gratefully received. Since I had only one request left, I decided to tackle Leslie verbally instead of handing him a list, but I knew I should have to choose my moment with care. I had to wait some days for what I considered to be a propitious moment.

I had just helped him to the successful conclusion of some ballistic experiments he was making, which involved tying an ancient muzzle-loader to a tree and firing it by means of a long string attached to the trigger. At the fourth attempt we achieved what apparently Leslie considered to be success: the barrel burst and bits of metal whined in all directions. Leslie was delighted and made copious notes on the back of an envelope. Together we set about picking up the remains of the gun. While we were thus engaged I casually asked him what he would like to give me for my birthday.

'Hadn't thought about it,' he replied absently, examining with evident satisfaction a contorted piece of metal. 'I don't mind ... anything you like ... you choose.'

I said I wanted a boat. Leslie, realizing how he had been trapped, said indignantly that a boat was far too large a present for a birthday, and anyway he couldn't afford it. I said, equally indignantly, that he had *told* me to choose what I liked. Leslie said yes, he had, but he hadn't meant a boat, as they were terribly expensive. I said that when one said *anything* one meant anything, which included boats, and anyway I didn't expect him to buy me one. I had thought, since he knew so much about boats, he would be able to build me one. However, if he thought that would be too difficult ...

'Of course it's not difficult,' said Leslie, unguardedly, and then added hastily, 'Well ... not terribly difficult. But it's the *time*. It would take ages and ages to do. Look, wouldn't it be better if I took you out in the *Sea Cow* twice a week?'

But I was adamant; I wanted a boat and I was quite prepared to wait for it.

'Oh, all right, all right,' said Leslie exasperatedly, 'I'll build you a boat.

But I'm not having you hanging around while I do it, understand? You're to keep well away. You're not to see it until it's finished.'

Delightedly I agreed to these conditions, and so for the next two weeks Spiro kept turning up with car-loads of planks, and the sounds of sawing, hammering and blasphemy floated round from the back veranda. The house was littered with wood shavings, and everywhere he walked Leslie left a trail of sawdust. I found it fairly easy to restrain my impatience and curiosity, for I had, at that time, something else to occupy me. Some repairs had just been completed to the back of the house, and three large bags of beautiful pink cement had been left over. These I had appropriated, and I set to work to build a series of small ponds in which I could keep not only my freshwater fauna, but also all the wonderful sea creatures I hoped to catch in my new boat. Digging ponds, in midsummer, was harder work than I had anticipated, but eventually I had some reasonably square holes dug, and a couple of days splashing around in a sticky porridge of lovely coral-pink cement soon revived me. Leslie's trails of sawdust and shaving through the house were now interwoven with a striking pattern of pink footprints.

The day before my birthday the entire family made an expedition into the town. The reasons were three-fold. Firstly, they wanted to purchase my presents. Secondly, the larder had to be stocked up. We had agreed that we would not invite a lot of people to the party; we said we didn't like crowds, and so ten guests, carefully selected, were the most we were prepared to put up with. It would be a small but distinguished gathering of people we liked best. Having unanimously decided on this, each member of the family then proceeded to invite ten people. Unfortunately they didn't all invite the same ten, with the exception of Theodore, who received five separate invitations. The result was that Mother, on the eve of the party, suddenly discovered we were going to have not ten guests but forty-five. The third reason for going to town was to make sure that Lugaretzia attended the dentist. Recently her teeth had been her chief woe, and Doctor Androuchelli, having peered into her mouth, had uttered a series of popping noises indicative of horror, and said that she must have all her teeth out, since it was obvious that they were the cause of all her ailments. After a week's arguing, accompanied by floods of tears, we managed to get Lugaretzia to consent, but she had refused to go without moral support. So, bearing her, white and weeping, in our midst, we swept into town.

We returned in the evening, exhausted and irritable, the car piled high with food, and Lugaretzia lying across our laps like a corpse, moaning frightfully. It was perfectly obvious that she would be in no condition to assist with the cooking and other work on the morrow. Spiro, when asked to suggest a solution, gave his usual answer.

'Nevers you minds,' he scowled, 'leaves everything to me.'

The following morning was full of incident. Lugaretzia had recovered sufficiently to undertake light duties, and she followed us all round the house, displaying with pride the gory cavities in her gums, and describing in detail the agonies she had suffered with each individual tooth. My presents having been duly inspected and the family thanked, I then went round to the back veranda with Leslie, and there lay a mysterious shape covered with a tarpaulin. Leslie drew this aside with the air of a conjuror, and there lay my boat. I gazed at it rapturously; it was surely the most perfect boat that anyone had ever had. Gleaming in her coat of new paint she lay there, my steed to the enchanted archipelago.

The boat was some seven feet long, and almost circular in shape. Leslie explained hurriedly – in case I thought the shape was due to defective craftsmanship – that the reason for this was that the planks had been too short for the frame, an explanation I found perfectly satisfactory. After all, it was the sort of irritating thing that could have happened to anyone. I said stoutly that I thought it was a lovely shape for a boat, and indeed I thought it was. She was not sleek, slim and rather predatory looking, like most boats, but rotund, placid and somehow comforting in her circular solidarity. She reminded me of an earnest dungbeetle, an insect for which I had great affection. Leslie, pleased at my evident delight, said deprecatingly that he had been forced to make her flat-bottomed, since, for a variety of technical reasons this was the safest. I said that I liked flat-bottomed boats the best, because it was possible to put jars of specimens on the floor without so much risk of them upsetting. Leslie asked me if I liked the colour scheme, as he had not been too sure about it. Now, in my opinion, the colour scheme was the best thing about it, the final touch that completed the unique craft. Inside she was painted green and white, while her bulging sides were tastefully covered in white, black and brilliant orange stripes, a combination of colours that struck me as being both artistic and friendly. Leslie then showed me the long, smooth cypress pole he had cut for a mast, but explained that it could not be fitted into position until the boat was launched. Enthusiastically I suggested launching her at once. Leslie, who was a stickler for procedure, said you couldn't launch a ship without naming her, and had I thought of a name yet? This was a difficult problem, and the whole family were called out to help me solve it. They stood clustered round the boat, which looked like a gigantic flower in their midst, and racked their brains.

'Why not call it the *Jolly Roger*?' suggested Margo.

I rejected this scornfully; I explained that I wanted a sort of *fat* name that would go with the boat's appearance and personality.

'*Arbuckle*,' suggested Mother vaguely.

That was no use, either; the boat simply didn't look like an Arbuckle.

'Call it the *Ark*,' said Leslie, but I shook my head.

There was another silence while we all stared at the boat. Suddenly I had it, the perfect name: *Bootle*, that's what I'd call her.

'Very nice, dear,' approved Mother.

'I was just about to suggest the *Bumtrinket*,' said Larry.

'Larry, dear!' Mother reproved. 'Don't teach the boy things like that.'

I turned Larry's suggestion over in my mind; it was certainly an unusual name, but then so was *Bootle*. They both seemed to conjure up the shape and personality of the boat. After much thought I decided what to do. A pot of black paint was produced and laboriously, in rather trickly capitals, I traced her name along the side: THE BOOTLE-BUMTRINKET. There it was; not only an *unusual* name, but an aristocratically hyphenated one as well. In order to ease Mother's mind I had to promise that I would only refer to the boat as the *Bootle* in conversation with strangers. The matter of the name being settled, we set about the task of launching her. It took the combined efforts of Margo, Peter, Leslie and Larry to carry the boat down the hill to the jetty, while Mother and I followed behind with the mast and a small bottle of wine with which to do the launching properly. At the end of the jetty the boat-bearers stopped, swaying with exhaustion, and Mother and I struggled with the cork of the wine-bottle.

'What are you *doing*?' asked Larry irritably. 'For Heaven's sake hurry up; I'm not used to being a slipway.'

At last we got the cork from the bottle, and I announced in a clear voice that I christened this ship the *Bootle-Bumtrinket*. Then I slapped her rotund backside with the bottle, with the unhappy result that half a pint of white wine splashed over Larry's head.

'Look out, look out,' he remonstrated. 'Which one of us are you supposed to be launching?'

At last they cast the *Bootle-Bumtrinket* off the jetty with a mighty heave, and she landed on her flat bottom with a report like a cannon, showering sea-water in all directions, and then bobbed steadily and confidently on the ripples. She had the faintest suggestion of a list to starboard, but I generously attributed this to the wine and not to Leslie's workmanship.

'Now!' said Leslie, organizing things. 'Let's get the mast in ... Margo, you hold her nose ... that's it. . . . Now, Peter, if you'll get into the stern, Larry and I will hand you the mast ... all you have to do is stick it in that socket.'

So, while Margo lay on her tummy holding the nose of the boat, Peter leapt nimbly into the stern and settled himself, with legs apart, to receive the mast which Larry and Leslie were holding.

'This mast looks a bit long to me, Les,' said Larry, eyeing it critically.

'Nonsense! It'll be fine when it's in,' retorted Leslie. 'Now ... are you ready, Peter?'

Peter nodded, braced himself, clasped the mast firmly in both hands and plunged it into the socket. Then he stood back, dusted his hands, and the *Bootle-Bumtrinket*, with a speed remarkable for a craft of her circumference, turned turtle. Peter, clad in one decent suit which he had put on in honour of my birthday, disappeared with scarcely a splash. All that remained on the surface of the water was his hat, the mast and the *Bootle-Bumtrinket*'s bright orange bottom.

'He'll drown! He'll drown!' screamed Margo, who always tended to look on the dark side in a crisis.

'Nonsense! It's not deep enough,' said Leslie.

'I told you that mast was too long,' said Larry unctuously.

'It *isn't* too long,' Leslie snapped irritably; 'that fool didn't set it right.'

'Don't you dare call him a fool,' said Margo.

'You can't fit a twenty-foot mast on to a thing like a washtub and expect it to keep upright,' said Larry.

'If you're so damn clever why didn't *you* make the boat?'

'I wasn't asked to. . . . Besides, you're supposed to be the expert, though I doubt if they'd employ you on Clydeside.'

'Very funny. It's easy enough to criticize ... just because that fool ...'

'Don't you call him a fool. . . . How dare you?'

'Now, now, don't argue about it, dears,' said Mother peaceably.

'Well, Larry's so damn patronizing . . .'

'Thank God! He's come up,' said Margo in fervent tones as the bedraggled and spluttering Peter rose to the surface.

We hauled him out, and Margo hurried him up to the house to try to get his suit dry before the party. The rest of us followed, still arguing. Leslie, incensed at Larry's criticism, changed into trunks and, armed with a massive manual on yacht construction and a tape measure, went down to salvage the boat. For the rest of the morning he kept sawing bits off the mast until she eventually floated upright, but by then the mast was only about three feet high. Leslie was very puzzled, but he promised to fit a new mast as soon as he'd worked out the correct specification. So the *Bootle-Bumtrinket*, tied to the end of the jetty, floated there in all her glory, looking like a very vivid, overweight Manx cat.

Spiro arrived soon after lunch, bringing with him a tall, elderly man who had the air of an ambassador. This, Spiro explained, was the King of Greece's ex-butler, who had been prevailed upon to come out of retirement and help with the party. Spiro then turned everyone out of the kitchen and he and the butler closeted themselves in there together. When I went round and peered through the window, I saw the butler in his waistcoat, polishing glasses, while Spiro, scowling thoughtfully and humming to himself, was attacking a vast pile of vegetables. Occasionally he would waddle over and blow vigorously at the seven charcoal fires along the wall, making them glow like rubies.

The first guest to arrive was Theodore, sitting spick and span in a carriage, his best suit on, his boots polished, and, as a concession to the occasion, without any collecting gear. He clasped in one hand a walking-stick, and in the other a neatly tied parcel. 'Ah ha! Many . . . er . . . happy returns of the day,' he said, shaking my hand. 'I have brought you a . . . er . . . small . . . er . . . memento . . . a small gift, that is to say, *present* to er . . . commemorate the occasion . . . um.'

On opening the parcel I was delighted to find that it contained a fat volume entitled *Life in Ponds and Streams*.

'I think you will find it a useful . . . um . . . addition to your library,' said Theodore, rocking on his toes. 'It contains some very interesting information on . . . er . . . *general* freshwater life.'

Gradually the guests arrived, and the front of the villa was a surging mass of carriages and taxis. The great drawing-room and dining-room were full of people, talking and arguing and laughing, and the butler (who to Mother's dismay had donned a tail coat) moved swiftly through the throng like an elderly penguin, serving drinks and food with such a regal air that a lot of the guests were not at all sure if he was a real butler, or merely some eccentric relative we had staying with us. Down in the kitchen Spiro drank prodigious quantities of wine as he moved among the pots and pans, his scowling face glowing redly in the light from the fires, his deep voice roaring out in song. The air was full of the scent of garlic and herbs, and Lugaretzia was kept hobbling to and fro from kitchen to drawing-room at considerable speed. Occasionally she would succeed in backing some unfortunate guest into a corner and, holding a plate of food under his nose, would proceed to give him the details of her ordeal at the dentist, giving the most life-like and repulsive imitation of what a molar sounded like when it was torn from its socket, and opening her mouth wide to show her victims the ghastly havoc that had been wrought inside.

More and more guests arrived, and with them came presents. Most of these were, from my point of view, useless, as they could not be adapted for natural history work. The best of the presents were, in my opinion, two puppies brought by a peasant family I knew who lived not far away. One puppy was liver and white, with large ginger eyebrows, and the other was coal black with large ginger eyebrows. As they were presents, the family had, of course, to accept them. Roger viewed them with suspicion and interest, so in order that they should all get acquainted I locked them in the dining-room with a large plate of party delicacies between them. The results were not quite what I had anticipated, for when the flood of guests grew so large that we had to slide back the doors and let some of them into the dining-room, we found Roger seated gloomily on the floor, the two puppies gambolling round him, while the room was decorated in a fashion that left us in no doubt that the new additions had both eaten and drunk to their hearts' content. Larry's suggestion that they be called Widdle and Puke was greeted with disgust by Mother, but the names stuck and Widdle and Puke they remained.

Still the guests came, overflowing the drawing-room into the dining-room, and out of the french windows on to the veranda. Some of them had come thinking that they would be bored, and after an hour or so they enjoyed themselves so much that they called their carriages, went home and reappeared with the rest of their families. The wine flowed, the air was blue with cigarette smoke, and the geckos were too frightened to come out of the cracks in the ceiling because of the noise and laughter. In one corner of the room Theodore, having daringly removed his coat, was dancing the *Kalamatiano* with Leslie and several other of the more exhilarated guests, their feet crashing and shuddering on the floor as they leapt and stamped. The butler, having perhaps taken a little more wine than was good for him, was so carried away by the sight of the national dance that he put his tray down and joined in, leaping and stamping as vigorously as anyone in spite of his age, his coat tails flapping behind him. Mother, smiling in a rather forced and distraught manner, was wedged between the English padre, who was looking with increasing disapproval at the revelry, and the Belgian consul, who was chattering away in her ear and twirling his moustache. Spiro appeared from the kitchen to find out where the butler had got to, and promptly joined in the *Kalamatiano*. Balloons drifted across the room, bouncing against the dancers' legs, exploding suddenly with loud bangs; Larry, out on the veranda, was endeavouring to teach a group of Greeks some of the finer English limericks. Puke and Widdle had gone to sleep in someone's hat. Doctor Androuchelli arrived and apologized to Mother for being late.

'It was my wife, madame; she has just been delivered of a baby,' he said with pride.

'Oh, congratulations, doctor,' said Mother; 'we must drink to them.'

Spiro, exhausted by the dance, was sitting on the sofa nearby, fanning himself.

'Whats?' he roared at Androuchelli, scowling ferociously. 'You gets anothers babys?'

'Yes, Spiro, a boy,' said Androuchelli, beaming.

'How manys you gets now?' asked Spiro.

'Six, only six,' said the doctor in surprise. 'Why?'

'You oughts to be ashames of yourself,' said Spiro in disgust. 'Six ... Gollys! Carrying on like cats and dogses.'

'But I like children,' protested Androuchelli.

'When I gots married I asks my wifes how many she wants,' said Spiro in a loud voice, 'and she says twos, so I gives her twos and then I gets her sewed ups. Six childrens.... Honest to Gods, you makes me wants to throws ... cats and dogses.'

At this point the English padre decided that he would, most reluctantly, have to leave, as he had a long day ahead of him tomorrow. Mother and I saw him out, and when we returned Androuchelli and Spiro had joined the dancers.

The sea was dawn-calm, and the eastern horizon flushed with pink when we stood yawning at the front door and the last carriage clopped its way down the drive. As I lay in bed with Roger across my feet, a puppy on each side of me and Ulysses sitting fluffed out on the pelmet, I gazed through the window at the sky, watching the pink spread across the olive top, extinguishing the stars one by one, and thought that, taken all round, it had been an extremely good birthday party.

Very early next morning I packed my collecting gear and some food, and with Roger, Widdle and Puke as company set off on a voyage in the *Bootle-Bumtrinket*. The sea was calm, the sun was shining out of a gentian-blue sky, and there was just the faintest breeze; it was a perfect day. The *Bootle-Bumtrinket* wallowed up the coast in a slow and dignified manner, while Roger sat in the bows as look-out, and Widdle and Puke ran from one side of the boat to the other, fighting, trying to lean over the side and drink the sea, and generally behaving in a pathetically land-lubberish fashion.

The joy of having a boat of your own! The feeling of pleasant power as you pulled on the oars and felt the boat surge forward with a quick rustle of water, like someone cutting silk; the sun gently warming your back and making the sea surface flicker with a hundred different colours; the thrill of wending your way through the complex maze of weed-shaggy reefs that glowed just beneath the surface of the sea. It was even with pleasure that I contemplated the blisters that were rising on my palms, making my hands feel stiff and awkward.

Though I spent many days voyaging in the *Bootle-Bumtrinket*, and had many adventures, there was nothing to compare with that very first voyage. The sea seemed bluer, more limpid and transparent, the islands seemed more remote, sun-drenched and enchanting than ever before, and it seemed as though the life of the sea had congregated in the little bays and channels to greet me and my new boat. A hundred feet or so from an islet I shipped the oars and scrambled up to the bows, where I lay side by side with Roger, peering down through a fathom of crystal water at the sea bottom, while the *Bootle-Bumtrinket* floated towards the shore with the placid buoyancy of a celluloid duck. As the boat's turtle-shaped shadow edged across the sea-bed, the multi-coloured, ever-moving tapestry of sea life was unfolded.

In the patches of silver sand the clams were stuck upright in small clusters, their mouths gaping. Sometimes, perched between the shell's horny lips, here would be a tiny, pale ivory pea-crab, the frail, soft-shelled, degenerate creature that lived a parasitic life in the safety of the great shell's corrugated walls. It was interesting to set off the clam colony's burglar alarm. I drifted over a group of them until they lay below, gaping up at me, and then gently edged the handle of the butterfly net down and tapped on the shell. Immediately the shell snapped shut, the movement causing a small puff of white sand to swirl up like a tornado. As the currents of this shell's alarm slid through the water the rest of the colony felt them. In a moment clams were slamming their front doors shut left and right, and the water was full of little whirls of sand, drifting and swirling about the shells, falling back to the sea-bed like silver dust.

Interspersed with the clams were the serpulas, beautiful feathery petals, forever moving round and round, perched on the end of a long, thick, greyish tube. The moving petals, orange-gold and blue, looked curiously out of place on the end of these stubby stalks, like an orchid on a mushroom stem. Again the serpulas had a burglar-alarm system, but it was much more sensitive than the clams; the net handle would get within six inches of the whirlpool of shimmering petals, and they would suddenly all point skywards, bunch together and dive head-first down the stalk, so that all that was left was a series of what looked like bits of miniature hosepipe stuck in the sand.

On the reefs that were only a few inches below the water, and that were uncovered at low tide, you found the thickest congregation of life. In the holes were the pouting blennies, which stared at you with their thick lips, giving their faces an expression of negroid insolence as they fluttered their fins at you. In the shady clefts among the weeds the sea urchins would be gathered in clusters, like shiny brown horse-chestnut seed-cases, their spines moving gently like compass needles towards possible danger. Around them the anemones clung to the rocks, plump and lustrous, their arms waving in an abandoned and somehow Eastern-looking dance in an effort to catch the shrimps that flipped past, transparent as glass. Routing in the dark underwater caverns, I unearthed a baby octopus, who settled on the rocks like a Medusa head, blushed to a muddy brown and regarded me with rather sad eyes from beneath the bald dome of its head. A further movement on my part and it spat out a small storm-cloud of black ink that hung and rolled in the clear water, while the octopus skimmed off behind it, shooting through the water with its arms trailing behind it, looking like a streamer-decorated balloon. There were crabs too, fat, green, shiny ones on the tops of the reef, waving their claws in what appeared to be a friendly manner, and down below, on the weedy bed of the sea, the spider-crabs with their strange spiky-edged shells, their long, thin legs, each wearing a coat of weeds, sponges or occasionally, an anemone which they had carefully planted on their backs. Everywhere on the reefs, the weed patches, the sandy bottom, moved hundreds of top shells, neatly striped and speckled in blue, silver, grey and red, with the scarlet and rather indignant face of a hermit crab peering out from underneath. They were like small ungainly caravans moving about, bumping into each other, barging through the weeds, or rumbling swiftly across the sand among the towering clam-shells and sea-fans.

The sun sank lower, and the water in the bays and below the tottering castles of rock was washed with the slate grey of evening shadow. Slowly, the oars creaking softly to themselves, I rowed the *Bootle-Bumtrinket* homewards. Widdle and Puke lay asleep, exhausted by the sun and sea air, their paws twitching, their ginger eyebrows moving as they chased dream crabs across endless reefs. Roger sat surrounded by glass jars and tubes in which tiny fish hung suspended, anemones waved their arms and spider-crabs touched the sides of their glass prisons with delicate claws. He sat staring down into the jars, ears pricked, occasionally looking up at me and wagging his tail briefly, before becoming absorbed once again in his studies. Roger was a keen student of marine life. The sun gleamed like a coin behind the olive-trees, and the sea was striped with gold and silver when the *Bootle-Bumtrinket* brought her round behind bumping gently against the jetty. Hungry, thirsty, tired, with my head buzzing full of the colours and shapes I had seen, I carried my precious specimens slowly up the hill to the villa, while the three dogs, yawning and stretching, followed behind.

Chapter Twelve

The Woodcock Winter

As the summer drew to a close I found myself, to my delight, once more without a tutor. Mother had discovered that, as she so delicately put it, Margo and Peter were becoming '*too* fond of one another'. As the family was unanimous in its disapproval of Peter as a prospective relation by marriage, something obviously had to be done. Leslie's only contribution to the problem was to suggest shooting Peter, a plan that was, for some reason, greeted derisively. I thought it was a splendid idea, but I was in the minority. Larry's suggestion that the happy couple should be sent to live in Athens for a month, in order, as he explained, to get it out of their systems, was quashed by Mother on the grounds of immorality. Eventually Mother dispensed with Peter's services, he left hurriedly and furtively and we had to cope with a tragic, tearful and wildly indignant Margo, who, dressed in her most flowing and gloomy clothing for the event, played her part magnificently. Mother soothed and uttered gentle platitudes, Larry gave Margo lectures on free love, and Leslie, for reasons best known to himself, decided to play the part of the outraged brother and kept appearing at intervals, brandishing a revolver and threatening to shoot Peter down like a dog if he set foot in the house again. In the midst of all this Margo, tears trickling effectively down her face, made tragic gestures and told us her life was blighted. Spiro, who loved a good dramatic situation as well as anyone, spent his time weeping in sympathy with Margo, and posting various friends of his along the docks to make sure that Peter did not attempt to get back on to the island. We all enjoyed ourselves very much. Just as the thing seemed to be dying a natural death, and Margo was able to eat a whole meal without bursting into tears, she got a note from Peter saying he would return for her. Margo, rather panic-stricken by the idea, showed the note to Mother, and once more the family leapt with enthusiasm into the farce. Spiro doubled his guard on the docks, Leslie oiled his guns and practised on a large cardboard figure pinned to the front of the house, Larry went about alternately urging Margo to disguise herself as a peasant and fly to Peter's arms, or to stop behaving like Camille. Margo, insulted, locked herself in the attic and refused to see anyone except me, as I was the only member of the family who had not taken sides. She lay there, weeping copiously, and reading a volume of Tennyson; occasionally she would break off to consume a large meal – which I carried up on a tray – with undiminished appetite.

Margo stayed closeted in the attic for a week. She was eventually brought down from there by a situation which made a fitting climax to the whole affair. Leslie had discovered that several small items had been vanishing from the *Sea Cow*, and he suspected the fishermen who rowed past the jetty at night. He decided that he would give the thieves something to think about, so he attached to his bedroom window three long-barrelled shotguns aiming down the hill at the jetty. By an ingenious arrangement of strings he could fire one barrel after the other without even getting out of bed. The range was, of course, too far to do any damage, but the whistling of shot through the olive-leaves and the splashing as it pattered into the sea would, he felt, act as a fairly good deterrent. So carried away was he by his own brilliance that he omitted to mention to anyone that he had constructed his burglar trap.

We had all retired to our rooms and were variously occupied. The house was silent. Outside came the gentle whispering of crickets in the hot night air. Suddenly there came a rapid series of colossal explosions that rocked the house and set all the dogs barking downstairs. I rushed out on to the landing, where pandemonium reigned: the dogs had rushed upstairs in a body to join in the fun, and were leaping about, yelping excitedly. Mother, looking wild and distraught, had rushed out of her bedroom in her voluminous nightie, under the impression that Margo had committed suicide. Larry burst angrily from his room to find out what the row was about, and Margo, under the impression that Peter had returned to claim her and was being slaughtered by Leslie, was fumbling madly at the lock on the attic door and screaming at the top of her voice.

'She's done something silly ... she's done something silly ...' wailed Mother, making frantic endeavours to get herself free from Widdle and Puke, who, thinking this was all a jolly nocturnal romp, had seized the end of her nightie and were tugging at it, growling ferociously.

'It's the limit. ... You can't even sleep in peace. ... This family's driving me mad ...' bellowed Larry.

'Don't hurt him ... leave him alone ... you cowards,' came Margo's voice, shrill and tearful, as she scrabbled wildly in an attempt to get the attic door opened.

'Burglars.... Keep calm... it's only burglars,' yelled Leslie, opening his bedroom door.

'She's still alive... she's still alive.... Get these dogs away....'

'You brutes... how dare you shoot him?... Let me out, *let* me out....'

'Stop fussing; it's only burglars....'

'Animals and explosions all day, and then bloody great twelve gun salutes in the middle of the night.... It's carrying eccentricity too far....'

Eventually Mother struggled up to the attic, trailing Widdle and Puke from the hem of her night attire, and, white and shaking, threw open the door to find an equally white and shaking Margo. After a lot of confusion we discovered what had happened, and what each of us had thought. Mother, trembling with shock, reprimanded Leslie severely.

'You mustn't do things like that, dear,' she pointed out. 'It's really stupid. If you fire your guns off do at least let us *know*.'

'Yes,' said Larry bitterly, 'just give us a bit of warning, will you? Shout "Timber", or something of the sort.'

'I don't see how I can be expected to take burglars by surprise if I've got to shout out warnings to you all,' said Leslie aggrievedly.

'I'm damned if I see why we should be taken by surprise too,' said Larry.

'Well, ring a bell or something, dear. Only please don't do that again ... it's made me feel quite queer.'

But the episode got Margo out of the attic, which, as Mother said, was one mercy.

In spite of being on nodding acquaintance with the family once again, Margo still preferred to nurse her broken heart in private, so she took to disappearing for long periods with only the dogs for company. She waited until the sudden, fierce siroccos of autumn had started before deciding that the ideal place for her to be alone was a small island situated in the bay opposite the house, about half a mile out. One day, when her desire for solitude became overwhelming, she borrowed the *Bootle-Bumtrinket* (without my permission), piled the dogs into it and set off to the island to lie in the sun and meditate on Love.

It was not until tea-time, and with the aid of field-glasses, that I discovered where my boat and Margo had got to. Irately, and somewhat unwisely, I told Mother of Margo's whereabouts, and pointed out that she had no business to borrow my boat without permission. Who, I asked acidly, was going to build me a new boat if the *Bootle-Bumtrinket* was wrecked? By now the sirocco was howling round the house like a pack of wolves, and Mother, actuated by what I at first considered to be acute worry regarding the fate of the *Bootle-Bumtrinket,* panted upstairs and hung out of the bedroom window, scanning the bay with the fieldglasses. Lugaretzia, sobbing and ringing her hands, hobbled up as well, and the two of them, trembling and anxious, kept chasing from window to window peering out at the foam-flecked bay. Mother was all for sending someone out to rescue Margo, but there was no one available. So all she could do was squat at the window with the glasses glued to her eyes while Lugaretzia offered up prayers to Saint Spiridion and kept telling Mother a long and involved story about her uncle who had been drowned in just such a sirocco. Fortunately, Mother could only understand about one word in seven of Lugaretzia's tale.

Eventually it apparently dawned on Margo that she had better start for home before the sirocco got any worse, and we saw her come down through the trees to where the *Bootle-Bumtrinket* bobbed and jerked at her moorings. But Margo's progress was slow and, to say the least, curious; first she fell down twice, then she ended up on the shore about fifty yards away from the boat, and wandered about in circles for some time, apparently looking for it. Eventually, attracted by barks from Roger, she stumbled along the shore and found the boat. Then she had great difficulty in persuading Widdle and Puke to get into it. They did not mind boating when the weather was calm, but they had never been in a rough sea and they had no intention of starting now. As soon as Widdle was safely installed in the boat she would turn to catch Puke, and by the time she had caught him, Widdle had leapt ashore again. This went on for some time. At last she managed to get them both in together, leapt in after them and rowed strenuously for some time before realizing that she had not untied the boat.

Mother watched her progress across the bay with bated breath. The *Bootle-Bumtrinket,* being low in the water, was not always visible, and whenever it disappeared behind a particularly large wave Mother would stiffen anxiously, convinced that the boat had foundered with all hands. Then the brave orange-and-white blob would appear once more on the crest of a wave and Mother would breath again. The course Margo steered was peculiar, for the *Bootle-Bumtrinket* tacked to and fro across the bay in a haphazard fashion, occasionally even reappearing above the waves with her nose pointing towards Albania. Once or twice Margo rose unsteadily to her feet and peered around the horizon, shading her eyes with her hand; then she would sit down and start rowing once more. Eventually, when the boat had, more by accident than design, drifted within hailing distance, we all went down to the jetty and yelled instructions above the hiss and splash of the waves and the roar of the wind. Guided by our shouts Margo pulled valiantly for the shore, hitting the jetty with such violence that she almost knocked Mother off into the sea. The dogs scrambled out and fled up the hill, obviously scared that we might make them undertake another trip with the same captain. When we had helped Margo ashore we discovered the reason for her unorthodox navigation. Having reached the island, she had draped herself out in the sun and fallen into a deep sleep, to be woken by the noise of the wind. Having slept for the better part of three hours in the fierce sun, she found her eyes so puffy and swollen that she could hardly see out of them. The wind and spray had made them worse, and by the time she reached the jetty she could hardly see at all. She was red and raw with sunburn and her eyelids so puffed out that she looked like a particularly malevolent Mongolian pirate.

'Really, Margo, I sometimes wonder if you're quite *right*,' said Mother, as she bathed Margo's eyes with cold tea; 'you do the most stupid things.'

'Oh, rubbish, Mother. You do *fuss*,' said Margo. 'It could have happened to anyone.'

But this incident seemed to cure her broken heart, for she no longer took solitary walks, nor did she venture out in the boat again; she behaved once more as normally as it was possible for her to do.

Winter came to the island gently as a rule. The sky was still clear, the sea blue and calm and the sun warm. But there would be an uncertainty in the air. The gold and scarlet leaves that littered the countryside in great drifts whispered and chuckled among themselves, or took experimental runs from place to place, rolling like coloured hoops among the trees. It was as if they were practising something, preparing for something, and they would discuss it excitedly in rustly voices as they crowded round the tree-trunks. The birds, too, congregated in little groups, puffing out their feathers, twittering thoughtfully. The whole air was one of expectancy, like a vast audience waiting for the curtain to go up. Then one morning you threw back the shutters and looked down over the olive-trees, across the blue bay to the russet mountains of the mainland and became aware that winter had arrived, for each mountain peak would be wearing a tattered skull-cap of snow. Now the air of expectancy grew almost hourly.

In a few days small white clouds started their winter parade, trooping across the sky, soft and chubby, long, languorous and unkempt, or small and crisp as feathers, and driving them before it, like an ill-assorted flock of sheep, would come the wind. This was warm at first, and came in gentle gusts, rubbing through the olive-groves so that the leaves trembled and turned silver with excitement, rocking the cypresses so that they undulated gently, and stirring the dead leaves into gay, swirling little dances that died as suddenly as they began. Playfully it ruffled the feathers on the sparrows' backs, so that they shuddered and fluffed themselves; and it leapt without warning at the gulls, so that they were stopped in mid-air and had to curve their white wings against it. Shutters started to bang and doors chattered suddenly in their frames. But still the sun shone, the sea remained placid, and the mountains sat complacently, summer bronzed, wearing their splintered snow hats.

For a week or so the wind played with the island, patting it, stroking it, humming to itself among the bare branches. Then there was a lull, a few days' strange calm; suddenly, when you least expected it, the wind would be back. But it was a changed wind, a mad, hooting, bellowing wind that leapt down on the island and tried to blow it into the sea. The blue sky vanished as a cloak of fine grey cloud was thrown over the island. The sea turned a deep blue, almost black, and became crusted with foam. The cypress trees were whipped like dark pendulums against the sky, and the olives (so fossilised all summer, so still and witch-like) were infected with the madness of the wind and swayed creaking on their misshapen, sinewy trunks, their leaves hissing as they turned, like mother of pearl, from green to silver. This is what the dead leaves had whispered about, this is what they had practised for; exultantly they rose in the air and danced, whirligiging about, dipping swooping, falling exhausted when the wind tired of them and passed on. Rain followed the wind, but it was a warm rain that you could walk in and enjoy, great fat drops that rattled on the shutters, tapped on the vine leaves like drums, and gurgled musically in the gutters. The rivers up in the Albanian mountains became swollen and showed white teeth in a snarl as they rushed down to the sea, tearing at their banks, grabbing the summer debris of sticks, logs, grass tussocks and other things and disgorging them into the bay, so that the dark-blue waters became patterned with great coiling veins of mud and other flotsam. Gradually all these veins burst, and the sea changed from blue to yellow-brown; then the wind tore at the surface, piling the water into ponderous waves, like great tawny lions with white manes that stalked and leaped upon the shore.

This was the shooting season: on the mainland the great lake of Butrinto had a fringe of tinkling ice round its rim, and its surface was patterned with flocks of wild duck. On the brown hills, damp and crumbling with rain, the hares, roe deer and wild boar gathered in the thickets to stamp and gnaw at the frozen ground, unearthing the bulbs and roots beneath. On the island the swamps and pools had their wisps of snipe, probing the mushy earth with their long rubbery beaks, humming like arrows as they flipped up from under your feet. In the olive-groves, among the myrtles, the woodcock lurked, fat and ungainly, leaping away when disturbed with a tremendous purring of wings, looking like bundles of wind-blown autumn leaves.

Leslie, of course, was in his element at this time. With a band of fellow enthusiasts he made trips over to the mainland once a fortnight, returning with the great bristly carcase of wild boar, cloaks of bloodstained hares, and huge baskets brimming over with the iridescent carcases of ducks. Dirty, unshaven smelling strongly of gun-oil and blood, Leslie would give us the details of the hunt, his eyes gleaming as he strode about the room demonstrating where and how he had stood, where and how the boar had broken cover, the crash of the gun rolling and bouncing among the bare mountains, the thud of the bullet, and the skidding somersault that the boar took into the heather. He described it so vividly that we felt we had been present at the hunt. Now he was the boar, testing the wind, shifting uneasily in the cane thicket, glaring under its bristling eyebrows, listening to the sound of the beaters and dogs; now he was one of the beaters, moving cautiously through waisthigh undergrowth, looking from side to side, making the curious bubbling cry to drive the game from cover; now, as the boar broke cover and started down the hill, snorting, he flung the imaginary gun to his shoulder and fired, the gun kicked realistically and in the corner of the room the boar somersaulted and rolled to his death.

Mother thought little about Leslie's hunting trips until he brought the first wild boar back. Having surveyed the ponderous, muscular body and the sharp tusks that lifted the upper lip in a snarl, she gasped faintly.

'Goodness! I never realized they were so big,' she said. 'I do hope you'll be careful, dear.'

'Nothing to worry about,' said Leslie, 'unless they break cover right at your feet; then it's a bit of a job, because if you miss they're on you.'

'Most *dangerous*,' said Mother. 'I never realized they were so big ... you might easily be injured or killed by one of those brutes, dear.'

'No, no, Mother; it's perfectly safe unless they break right under your feet.'

'I don't see why it should be dangerous even then,' said Larry.

'Why not?' asked Leslie.

'Well, if they charge you, and you miss, why not just jump over them?'

'Don't be ridiculous,' said Leslie, grinning. 'The damn' things stand about three feet at the shoulder, and they're hellish fast. You haven't got time to jump over them.'

'I really don't see why not,' said Larry; 'after all, it would be no more difficult than jumping over a chair. Anyway, if you couldn't jump over them, why not vault over them?'

'You do talk nonsense, Larry; you've never seen these things move. It would be impossible to vault *or* jump.'

'The trouble with you hunting blokes is lack of imagination,' said Larry critically. 'I supply magnificent ideas – all you have to do is to try them out. But no, you condemn them out of hand.'

'Well, you come on the next trip and demonstrate how to do it,' suggested Leslie.

'I don't profess to being a hairy-chested man of action,' said Larry austerely. 'My place is in the realm of ideas – the brainwork, as it were. I put my brain at your disposal for the formation of schemes and stratagems, and then you, the muscular ones, carry them out.'

'Yes; well, I'm not carrying *that* one out,' said Leslie with conviction.

'It sounds most foolhardy,' said Mother. 'Don't you do anything silly, dear. And, Larry, stop putting dangerous ideas into his head.'

Larry was always full of ideas about things of which he had no experience. He advised me on the best way to study nature, Margo on clothes, Mother on how to manage the family and pay up her overdraft, and Leslie on shooting. He was perfectly safe, for he knew that none of us could retaliate by telling him the best way to write. Invariably, if any member of the family had a problem, Larry knew the best way to solve it; if anyone boasted of an achievement, Larry could never see what the fuss was about – the thing was perfectly easy to do, providing one used one's brain. It was due to this attitude of pomposity that he set the villa on fire.

Leslie had returned from a trip to the mainland, loaded with game, and puffed up with pride. He had, he explained to us, pulled off his first left and right. He had to explain in detail, however, before we grasped the full glory of his action. Apparently a left-and-a-right in hunting parlance meant to shoot and kill two birds or animals in quick succession, first with your left barrel and then with your right. Standing in the great stone-flagged kitchen, lit by the red glow of the charcoal fires, he explained how the flock of ducks had come over in the wintry dawn, spread out across the sky. With a shrill whistle of wings they had swept overhead, and Leslie had picked out the leader, fired, turned his gun on to the second bird and fired again with terrific speed, so that when he lowered his smoking barrels the two ducks splashed into the lake almost as one. Gathered in the kitchen, the family listened spellbound to his graphic description. The broad wooden table was piled high with game, Mother and Margo were plucking a brace of ducks for dinner, I was examining the various species and making notes on them in my diary (which was rapidly becoming more bloodstained and feather-covered), and Larry was sitting on a chair, a neat, dead mallard in his lap, stroking its crisp wings and watching, as Leslie, up to the waist in an imaginary swamp, for the third time showed us how he achieved his left-and-a-right.

'Very good, dear,' said Mother, when Leslie had described the scene for the fourth time. 'It must have been very difficult.'

'I don't see why,' said Larry.

Leslie, who was just about to describe the whole thing over again, broke off and glared at him.

'Oh, you don't?' he asked belligerently. 'And what d'you know about it? You couldn't hit an olive-tree at three paces, let alone a flying bird.'

'My dear fellow, I'm not belittling you,' said Larry in his most irritating and unctuous voice. 'I just don't see why it is considered so difficult to perform what seems to me a simple task.'

'*Simple?* If you'd had any experience of shooting you wouldn't call it simple.'

'I don't see that it's necessary to have had shooting experience. It seems to me to be merely a matter of keeping a cool head and aiming reasonably straight.'

'Don't be silly,' said Les disgustedly. 'You always think the things other people do are simple.'

'It's the penalty of being versatile,' sighed Larry. 'Generally they turn out to be ridiculously simple when I try them. That's why I can't see what you're making a fuss for, over a perfectly ordinary piece of marksmanship.'

'Ridiculously simple when *you* try them?' repeated Leslie incredulously. 'I've never seen you carry out one of your suggestions yet.'

'A gross slander,' said Larry, nettled. 'I'm always ready to prove my ideas are right.'

'All right, let's see you pull off a left-and-a-right, then.'

'Certainly. You supply the gun and the victims and I'll show you that it requires no ability whatsoever: it's a question of a mercurial mind that can weigh up the mathematics of the problem.'

'Right. We'll go after snipe down in the marsh tomorrow. You can get your mercurial mind to work on those.'

'It gives me no pleasure to slaughter birds that have every appearance of having been stunted from birth,' said Larry, 'but, since my honour is at stake, I suppose they must be sacrificed.'

'If you get *one* you'll be lucky,' said Leslie with satisfaction.

'Really, you children do argue about the stupidest things,' said Mother philosophically, wiping the feathers off her glasses.

'I agree with Les,' said Margo unexpectedly; 'Larry's too fond of telling people how to do things, and doing nothing himself. It'll do him good to be taught a lesson. *I* think it was jolly clever of Les to kill two birds with one stone, or whatever it's called.'

Leslie, under the impression that Margo had misunderstood his feat, started on a new and more detailed recital of the episode.

It had rained all night, so early next morning, when we set off to see Larry perform his feat, the ground was moist and squelchy underfoot, and smelt as rich and fragrant as plum cake. To honour the occasion Larry had placed a large turkey feather in his tweed hat, and he looked like a small, portly and immensely dignified Robin Hood. He complained vigorously all the way down to the swamp in the valley where the snipe congregated. It was cold, it was extremely slippery, he didn't see why Leslie couldn't take his word for it without this ridiculous farce, his gun was heavy, there probably wouldn't be any game at all, for he couldn't see anything except a mentally defective penguin being out on a day like this. Coldly and relentlessly we urged him down to the swamp, turning a deaf ear to all his arguments and protests.

The swamp was really the level floor of a small valley, some ten acres of flat land which were cultivated during the spring and summer months. In the winter it was allowed to run wild, and it became a forest of bamboos and grass, intersected by the brimming irrigation ditches. These ditches that criss-crossed about the swamp made hunting difficult, for most of them were too wide to jump, and you could not wade them, since they consisted of about six feet of liquid mud and four feet of dirty water. They were spanned, here and there, by narrow plank bridges, most of which were rickety and decayed, but which were the only means of getting about the swamp. Your time during a hunt was divided between looking for game and looking for the next bridge.

We had hardly crossed the first little bridge when three snipe purred up from under our feet and zoomed away, swinging from side to side as they flew. Larry flung the gun to his shoulder and pulled the triggers excitedly. The hammers fell, but there was no sound.

'It would be an idea to load it,' said Leslie with a certain quiet triumph.

'I thought *you'd* done that,' Larry said bitterly; 'you're acting as the blasted gunbearer, after all. I'd have got that pair if it hadn't been for your inefficiency.'

He loaded the gun and we moved slowly on through the bamboos. Ahead we could hear a pair of magpies cackling fiendishly whenever we moved. Larry muttered threats and curses on them for warning the game. They kept flying ahead of us, cackling loudly, until Larry was thoroughly exasperated. He stopped at the head of a tiny bridge that sagged over a wide expanse of placid water.

'Can't we do something about those birds?' he inquired heatedly. 'They'll scare everything for miles.'

'Not the snipe,' said Leslie; 'the snipe stick close until you almost walk on them.'

'It seems quite futile to continue,' said Larry. 'We might as well send a brass band ahead of us.'

He tucked the gun under his arm and stamped irritably on to the bridge. It was then that the accident occurred. He was in the middle of the groaning, shuddering plank when two snipe which had been lying concealed in the long grass at the other end of the bridge rocketed out of the grass and shot skywards. Larry, forgetting in his excitement his rather peculiar situation, shipped the gun to his shoulder and, balancing precariously on the swaying bridge, fired both barrels. The gun roared and kicked, the snipe flew away undamaged, and Larry with a yell of fright fell backwards into the irrigation ditch.

'Hold the gun above your head! ... Hold it above your head!' roared Leslie.

'Don't stand up or you'll sink,' screeched Margo. 'Sit still.'

But Larry, spreadeagled on his back, had only one idea, and that was to get out as quickly as possible. He sat up and then tried to get to his feet, using, to Leslie's anguish, the gun barrels as a support. He raised himself up, the liquid mud shuddered and boiled, the gun sank out of sight, and Larry disappeared up to his waist.

'Look what you've done to the gun,' yelled Leslie furiously; 'you've choked the bloody barrels.'

'What the hell do you expect me to do?' snarled Larry. 'Lie here and be sucked under? Give me a hand, for heaven's sake.'

'Get the gun out,' said Leslie angrily.

'I refuse to save the gun if you don't save me,' Larry yelled. 'Damn it, I'm not a seal . . . *get me out!*'

'If you give me the end of the gun I can pull you out, you idiot,' shouted Leslie. 'I can't reach you otherwise.'

Larry groped wildly under the surface for the gun, and sank several inches before he retrieved it, clotted with black and evil-smelling mud.

'Dear God! just *look* at it,' moaned Leslie, wiping the mud off it with his handkerchief, 'just look at it.'

'Will you stop carrying on over that beastly weapon and get me out of here?' asked Larry vitriolically. 'Or do you want me to sink beneath the mud like a sort of sportsmen's Shelley?'

Leslie handed him the ends of the barrels, and we all heaved mightily. It seemed to make no impression whatsoever, except that when we stopped, exhausted, Larry sank a little deeper.

'The idea is to *rescue* me,' he pointed out, panting, 'not deliver the *coup de grâce.*'

'Oh, stop yapping and try to heave yourself out,' said Leslie.

'What d'you think I've been doing, for heaven's sake? I've ruptured myself in three places as it is.'

At last, after much effort, there came a prolonged belch from the mud and Larry shot to the surface and we hauled him up the bank. He stood there, covered with the black and stinking slush, looking like a chocolate statue that has come in contact with a blast furnace; he appeared to be melting as we watched.

'Are you all right?' asked Margo.

Larry glared at her.

'I'm fine,' he said sarcastically, 'simply fine. Never enjoyed myself more. Apart from a slight touch of pneumonia, a ricked back, and the fact that one of my shoes lies full fathoms five, I'm having a wonderful time.'

As he limped homewards he poured scorn and wrath on our heads, and by the time we reached home he was convinced that the whole thing had been a plot. As he entered the house, leaving a trail like a ploughed field, Mother uttered a gasp of horror.

'What *have* you been doing, dear?' she asked.

'Doing? What do you think I've been doing? I've been shooting.'

'But how did you get like that, dear? You're *sopping.* Did you fall in?'

'Really, Mother, you and Margo have such remarkable perspicacity I sometimes wonder how you survive.'

'I only *asked*, dear,' said Mother.

'Well, of course I fell in; what did you think I'd been doing?'

'You must change, dear, or you'll catch cold.'

'I can manage,' said Larry with dignity; 'I've had quite enough attempts on my life for one day.'

He refused all offers of assistance, collected a bottle of brandy from the larder and retired to his room, where, on his instructions, Lugaretzia built a huge fire. He sat muffled up in bed, sneezing and consuming brandy. By lunch-time he sent down for another bottle, and at tea-time we could hear him singing lustily, interspersed with gigantic sneezes. At supper-time Lugaretzia had paddled upstairs with the third bottle, and Mother began to get worried. She sent Margo up to see if Larry was all right. There was a long silence, followed by Larry's voice raised in wrath, and Margo's pleading plaintively. Mother, frowning, stumped upstairs to see what was happening, and Leslie and I followed her.

In Larry's room a fire roared in the grate, and Larry lay concealed under a towering pile of bedclothes. Margo, clasping a glass, stood despairingly by the bed.

'What's the matter with him?' asked Mother, advancing determinedly.

'He's drunk,' said Margo despairingly, 'and I can't get any sense out of him. I'm trying to get him to take this Epsom salts, otherwise he'll feel awful tomorrow, but he won't touch it. He keeps hiding under the bedclothes and saying I'm trying to poison him.'

Mother seized the glass from Margo's hand and strode to the bedside.

'Now come on, Larry, and stop being a fool,' she snapped briskly; 'drink this down *at once*.'

The bedclothes heaved and Larry's tousled head appeared from the depths. He peered blearily at Mother, and blinked thoughtfully to himself.

'You're a horrible old woman ... I'm sure I've seen you somewhere before,' he remarked, and before Mother had recovered from the shock of this observation he had sunk into a deep sleep.

'Well,' said Mother, aghast, 'he must have had a lot. Anyway, he's asleep now, so let's just build up the fire and leave him. He'll feel better in the morning.'

It was Margo who discovered, early the following morning, that a pile of glowing wood from the fire had slipped down between the boards of the room and set fire to the beam underneath. She came flying downstairs in her nightie, pale with emotion, and burst into Mother's room.

'The house is on fire. . . . Get out . . . get out . . .' she yelled dramatically.

Mother leapt out of bed with alacrity.

'Wake Gerry ... wake Gerry,' she shouted, struggling, for some reason best known to herself, to get her corsets on over her nightie.

'Wake up ... wake up. ... Fire ... fire!' screamed Margo at the top of her voice.

Leslie and I tumbled out on to the landing.

'What's going on?' demanded Leslie.

'Fire!' screamed Margo in his ear. 'Larry's on fire!'

Mother appeared, looking decidedly eccentric with her corsets done up crookedly over her nightie.

'Larry's on fire? Quick, save him,' she screamed, and rushed upstairs to the attic, closely followed by the rest of us. Larry's room was full of acrid smoke, which poured up from between the floor-boards. Larry himself lay sleeping peacefully. Mother dashed over to the bed and shook him vigorously.

'Wake *up*, Larry; for heaven's sake wake up.'

'What's the matter?' he asked, sitting up sleepily.

'The room's on fire.'

'I'm not surprised,' he said, lying down again. 'Ask Les to put it out.'

'Pour something on it,' shouted Les, 'get something to pour on it.'

Margo, acting on these instructions, seized a half-empty brandy bottle and scattered the contents over a wide area of floor. The flames leapt up and crackled merrily.

'You fool, not *brandy*!' yelled Leslie; 'water ... get some water.'

But Margo, overcome at her contribution to the holocaust, burst into tears. Les, muttering wrathfully, hauled the bedclothes off the recumbent Larry and used them to smother the flames. Larry sat up indignantly.

'What the hell's going on?' he demanded.

'The room's on fire, dear.'

'Well, I don't see why I should freeze to death ... why tear all the bedclothes off? Really, the fuss you all make. It's quite simple to put out a fire.'

'Oh, shut up,' snapped Leslie, jumping up and down on the bedclothes.

'I've never known people for panicking like you all do,' said Larry 'it's simply a matter of keeping your head. Les has the worst of it under control; now if Gerry fetches the hatchet, and you, Mother, and Margo fetch some water, we'll soon have it out.'

Eventually, while Larry lay in bed and directed operations, the rest of us managed to rip up the planks and put out the smouldering beam. It must have been smouldering throughout the night, for the beam, a twelve-inch-thick slab of olive wood, was charred half-way through. When, eventually, Lugaretzia appeared and started to clean up the mass of smouldering bedclothes, wood splinters, water and brandy, Larry lay back on the bed with a sigh.

'There you are,' he pointed out; 'all done without fuss and panic. It's just a matter of keeping your head. I would like someone to bring me a cup of tea, please; I've got the most splitting headache.'

'I'm not surprised; you were as tiddled as an owl last night,' said Leslie.

'If you can't tell the difference between a high fever due to exposure and a drunken orgy it's hardly fair to besmirch my character,' Larry pointed out.

'Well, the fever's left you with a good hangover, anyway,' said Margo.

'It's not a hangover,' said Larry with dignity, 'it's just the strain of being woken up at the crack of dawn by an hysterical pack of people and having to take control of a crisis.'

'Fat lot of controlling you did, lying in bed,' snorted Leslie.

'It's not the action that counts, it's the brainwork behind it, the quickness of wit, the ability to keep your head when all about you are losing their's. If it hadn't been for me you would probably all have been burnt in your beds.'

Conversation

Spring had arrived and the island was sparkling with flowers. Lambs with flapping tails gambolled under the olives, crushing the yellow crocuses under their tiny hooves. Baby donkeys with bulbous and uncertain legs munched among the asphodels. The ponds and streams and ditches were tangled in chains of spotted toads' spawn, the tortoises were heaving aside their winter bedclothes of leaves and earth, and the first butterflies, winter-faded and frayed, were flitting wanly among the flowers.

In this crisp, heady weather the family spent most of its time on the veranda, eating, sleeping, reading or just simply arguing. It was here, once a week, that we used to congregate to read our mail which Spiro had brought out to us. The bulk of it consisted of gun catalogues for Leslie, fashion magazines for Margo and animal journals for myself. Larry's post generally contained books and interminable letters from authors, artists and musicians, about authors, artists and musicians. Mother's contained a wedge of mail from various relatives, sprinkled with a few seed catalogues. As we browsed we would frequently pass remarks to one another, or read bits aloud. This was not done with any motive of sociability (for no other member of the family would listen, anyway), but merely because we seemed unable to extract the full flavour of our letters and magazines unless they were shared. Occasionally, however, an item of news would be sufficiently startling to rivet the family's attention on it, and this happened one day in spring when the sky was like blue glass, and we sat in the dappled shade of the vine, devouring our mail.

'Oh, this is nice. ... Look. ... organdie with puffed sleeves ... I think I would prefer it in *velvet,* though ... or maybe a brocade top with a *flared* skirt. Now, that's nice ... it would look good with long white gloves and one of those sort of summery hats, wouldn't it?'

A pause, the faint sound of Lugaretzia moaning in the dining-room, mingled with the rustle of paper. Roger yawned loudly, followed in succession by Puke and Widdle.

'God! What a beauty! ... Just *look* at her ... telescopic sight, bolt action. ... What a beaut! Um ... a hundred and fifty ... not really expensive, I suppose. ... Now *this* is good value. ... Let's see ... double-barrelled ... choke. ... Yes ... I suppose one really needs something a bit heavier for ducks.'

Roger scratched his ears in turn, twisting his head on one side, a look of bliss on his face, groaning gently with pleasure. Widdle lay down and closed his eyes. Puke vainly tried to catch a fly, his jaws clopping as he snapped at it.

'Ah! Antoine's had a poem accepted at last! Real talent there, if he can only dig down to it. Varlaine's starting a printing press in a stable. . . . Pah! limited editions of his own works. Oh, God, George Bullock's trying his hand at portraits . . . portraits, I ask you! He couldn't paint a candlestick. Good book here you should read, Mother: *The Elizabethan Dramatists* . . . a wonderful piece of work . . . some fine stuff in it. . . .'

Roger worked his way over his hind-quarters in search of a flea, using his front teeth like a pair of hair-clippers, snuffling noisily to himself. Widdle twitched his legs and tail minutely, his ginger eyebrows going up and down in astonishment at his own dream. Puke lay down and pretended to be asleep, keeping an eye cocked for the fly to settle.

'Aunt Mabel's moved to Sussex. . . . She says Henry's passed all his exams and is going into a bank . . . at least, I *think* it's a bank . . . her writing really is awful, in spite of that expensive education she's always boasting about. . . . Uncle Stephen's broken his leg, poor old dear . . . and done something to his *bladder?* . . . Oh, no, I see . . . really this writing . . . he broke his leg falling off a ladder. . . . You'd think he'd have more sense than to go up a ladder at his age . . . ridiculous. . . . Tom's married . . . one of the Garnet girls. . . .'

Mother always left until the last a fat letter, addressed in large, firm, well-rounded handwriting, which was the monthly instalment from Greataunt Hermione. Her letters invariably created an indignant uproar among the family, so we all put aside our mail and concentrated when Mother, with a sigh of resignation, unfurled the twenty odd pages, settled herself comfortably and began to read.

'She says that the doctors don't hold out much hope for her,' observed Mother.

'They haven't held out any hope for her for the last forty years and she's still as strong as an ox,' said Larry.

'She says she always thought it a little peculiar of us, rushing off to Greece like that, but they've just had a bad winter and she thinks that perhaps it was wise of us to choose such a salubrious climate.'

'Salubrious! What a word to use!'

'Oh, heavens! . . . oh, no . . . oh, Lord! . . .'

'What's the matter?'

'She says she wants to come and stay . . . the doctors have advised a warm climate!'

'No, I refuse! I couldn't bear it,' shouted Larry, leaping to his feet; 'it's bad enough being shown Lugaretzia's gums every morning, without having Great-aunt Hermione dying by inches all over the place. You'll have to put her off, Mother . . . tell her there's no room.'

'But I can't, dear; I told her in the last letter what a big villa we had.'

'She's probably forgotten,' said Leslie hopefully.

'She hasn't. She mentions it here . . . where is it? . . . oh, yes, here you are: "As you now seem able to afford such an extensive establishment, I am sure, Louie dear, that you would not begrudge a small corner to an old woman who has not much longer to live." There you are! What on earth can we *do?*'

'Write and tell her we've got an epidemic of smallpox raging out here, and send her a photograph of Margo's acne,' suggested Larry.

'Don't be silly, dear. Besides, I told her how healthy it is here.'

'Really, Mother, you are impossible!' exclaimed Larry angrily. 'I was looking forward to a nice quiet summer's work, with just a few select friends, and now we're going to be invaded by that evil old camel, smelling of mothballs and singing hymns in the lavatory.'

'Really, dear, you do *exaggerate*. And I don't know why you have to bring lavatories into it – I've never heard her sing hymns anywhere.'

'She does nothing else *but* sing hymns . . . "Lead, Kindly Light", while everyone queues on the landing.'

'Well, anyway, we've got to think of a good excuse. I can't write and tell her we don't want her because she sings hymns.'

'Why not?'

'Don't be unreasonable, dear; after all, she *is* a relation.'

'What on earth's that got to do with it? Why should we have to fawn all over the old hag because she's a relation, when the really sensible thing to do would be to burn her at the stake.'

'She's not as bad as that,' protested Mother half-heartedly.

'My dear mother, of all the foul relatives with which we are cluttered, she is definitely the worst. Why you keep in touch with her I cannot, for the life of me, imagine.'

'Well, I've got to answer her *letters*, haven't I?'

'Why? Just write "Gone Away" across them and send them back.'

'I couldn't do that, dear; they'd recognize my handwriting,' said Mother vaguely; 'besides, I've opened this now.'

'Can't one of us write and say you're ill?' suggested Margo.

'Yes, we'll say the doctors have given up hope,' said Leslie.

'*I'll* write the letter,' said Larry with relish. 'I'll get one of those lovely black-edged envelopes . . . that will add an air of verisimilitude to the whole thing.'

'You'll do nothing of the sort,' said Mother firmly. 'If you did that she'd come straight out to nurse me. You know what she is.'

'Why keep in touch with them; that's what I want to know,' asked Larry despairingly. 'What satisfaction does it give you? They're all either fossilized or mental.'

'Indeed, they're *not* mental,' said Mother indignantly.

'Nonsense, Mother. . . . Look at Aunt Bertha, keeping flocks of imaginary cats . . . and there's Great Uncle Patrick, who wanders about nude and tells complete strangers how he killed whales with a penknife. . . . They're *all* bats.'

'Well, they're *queer;* but they're all very old, and so they're bound to be. But they're not *mental*,' explained Mother; adding candidly, 'Anyway, not enough to be put away.'

'Well, if we're going to be invaded by relations, there's only one thing to do,' said Larry resignedly.

'What's that?' inquired Mother, peering over her spectacles expectantly.

'We must move, of course.'

'Move? Move where?' asked Mother, bewildered.

'Move to a smaller villa. Then you can write to all these zombies and tell them we haven't any room.'

'But don't be stupid, Larry. We can't *keep* moving. We moved here in order to cope with your friends.'

'Well, now we'll have to move to cope with the relations.'

'But we can't *keep* rushing to and fro about the island ... people will think we've gone mad.'

'They'll think we're even madder if that old harpy turns up. Honestly, Mother, I couldn't stand it if she came. I should probably borrow one of Leslie's guns and blow a hole in her corsets.'

'Larry! I do wish you *wouldn't* say things like that in front of Gerry.'

'I'm just warning you.'

There was a pause, while Mother polished her spectacles feverishly.

'But it seems so ... so ... *eccentric* to keep changing villas like that, dear,' she said at last.

'There's nothing eccentric about it,' said Larry, surprised; 'it's a perfectly logical thing to do.'

'Of course it is,' agreed Leslie; 'it's a sort of self-defence, anyway.'

'Do be sensible, Mother,' said Margo; 'after all, a change is as good as a feast.'

So, bearing that novel proverb in mind, we moved.

BOOK THREE

As long liveth the merry man (they say)
As doth the sorry man, and longer by a day.

UDALL. *Ralph Roister Doister.*

Chapter Thirteen

The Snow-white Villa

Perched on a hill-top among olive-trees, the new villa, white as snow, had a broad veranda running along one side, which was hung with a thick pelmet of grape-vine. In front of the house was a pocket-handkerchief-sized garden, neatly walled, which was a solid tangle of wild flowers. The whole garden was overshadowed by a large magnolia tree, the glossy dark green leaves of which cast a deep shadow. The rutted driveway wound away from the house, down the hillside through olive-groves, vineyards and orchards, before reaching the road. We had liked the villa the moment Spiro had shown it to us. It stood, decrepit but immensely elegant, among the drunken olives, and looked rather like an eighteenth-century exquisite reclining among a congregation of charladies. Its charms had been greatly enhanced, from my point of view, by the discovery of a bat in one of the rooms, clinging upside down to a shutter and chittering with dark malevolence. I had hoped that he would continue to spend the day in the house, but as soon as we moved in he decided that the place was getting overcrowded and departed to some peaceful olive-trunk. I regretted his decision, but having many other things to occupy me, I soon forgot about him.

It was at the white villa that I got on really intimate terms with the mantids; up till then I had seen them, occasionally, prowling through the myrtles, but I had never taken very much notice of them. Now they forced me to take notice of them, for the hill-top on which the villa stood contained hundreds, and most of them were much larger than any I had seen before. They squatted disdainfully on the olives, among the myrtles, on the smooth green magnolia leaves, and at night they would converge on the house, whirring into the lamplight with their green wings churning like the wheels of ancient paddle-steamers, to alight on the tables or chairs and stalk mincingly about, turning their heads from side to side in search of prey, regarding us fixedly from bulbous eyes in chinless faces. I had never realised before that mantids could grow so large, for some of the specimens that visited us were fully four and a half inches long; these monsters feared nothing, and would, without hesitation, attack something as big as or bigger than themselves. These insects seemed to consider that the house was their property, and the walls and ceilings their legitimate hunting grounds. But the geckos that lived in the cracks in the garden wall also considered the house their hunting ground, and so the mantids and the geckos waged a constant war against each other. Most of the battles were mere skirmishes between individual members of the two forms of animals, but as they were generally well matched the fights rarely came to much. Occasionally, however, there would be a battle really worth watching. I was lucky enough to have a grandstand view of such a fight, for it took place above, on and in my bed.

During the day most of the geckos lived under the loose plaster on the garden wall. As the sun sank and the cool shadow of the magnolia tree enveloped the house and garden they would appear, thrusting their small heads out of the cracks and staring interestedly around with their golden eyes. Gradually they slid out on to the wall, their flat bodies and stubby, almost conical tails looking ash-grey in the twilight. They would move cautiously across the moss-patched wall until they reached the safety of the vine over the veranda, and there wait patiently until the sky grew dark and the lamps were lit. Then they would choose their hunting areas and make their way to them across the wall of the house, some to the bedrooms, some to the kitchen, while others remained on the veranda among the vine leaves.

There was a particular gecko that had taken over my bedroom as his hunting ground, and I grew to know him quite well and christened him Geronimo, since his assaults on the insect life seemed to me as cunning and well-planned as anything that famous Red Indian had achieved. Geronimo seemed to be a cut above the other geckos. To begin with, he lived alone, under a large stone in the zinnia bed beneath my window, and he would not tolerate another gecko anywhere near his home; nor, for that matter, would he allow any strange gecko to enter my bedroom. He rose earlier than the others of his kind, coming out from beneath his stone while the wall and house were still suffused with pale sunset-light. He would scuttle up the flaky white plaster precipice until he reached my bedroom window, and poke his head over the sill, peering about curiously and nodding his head rapidly, two or three times, whether in greeting to me or in satisfaction at finding the room as he had left it, I could never make up my mind. He would sit on the windowsill, gulping to himself, until it got dark and a light was brought in; in the lamp's golden gleam he seemed to change colour, from ash-grey to a pale, translucent pinky-pearl that made his neat pattern of goosepimples stand out, and made his skin look so fine and thin that you felt it should be transparent so that you could see the viscera, coiled neatly as a butterfly's proboscis, in his fat tummy. His eyes glowing with enthusiasm, he would waddle up the wall to his favourite spot, the left-hand outside corner of the ceiling, and hang there upside down, waiting for his evening meal to appear.

The food was not long in arriving. The first shoal of gnats, mosquitoes and lady-birds, which Geronimo ignored, was very soon followed by the daddy-longlegs, the lacewing flies, the smaller moths and some of the more robust beetles. Watching Geronimo's stalking tactics was quite an education. A lacewing or a moth, having spun round the lamp until it was dizzy, would flutter up and settle on the ceiling in the white circle of lamplight printed there. Geronimo, hanging upside down in his corner, would stiffen. He would nod his head two or three times very rapidly, and then start to edge across the ceiling cautiously, millimetre by millimetre, his bright eyes on the insect in a fixed stare. Slowly he would slide over the plaster until he was six inches or so away from his prey, whereupon he stopped for a second and you could see his padded toes moving as he made his grip on the plaster more secure. His eyes would become more protuberant with excitement, what he imagined to be a look of blood-curdling ferocity would spread over his face, the tip of his tail would twitch minutely, and then he would skim across the ceiling as smoothly as a drop of water, there would be a faint snap, and he would turn round, an expression of smug happiness on his face, the lacewing inside his mouth with its legs and wings trailing over his lips like a strange, quivering walrus moustache. He would wag his tail vigorously, like an excited puppy, and then trot back to his resting-place to consume his meal in comfort. He had incredibly sharp eyesight, for I frequently saw him spot a minute moth from the other side of the room, and circle the ceiling in order to get near enough for the capture.

His attitude towards rivals who tried to usurp his territory was very straightforward. No sooner had they hauled themselves over the edge of the sill and settled down for a short rest after the long climb up the side of the villa, than there would be a scuffling noise, and Geronimo would flash across the ceiling and down the wall, to land on the window-sill with a faint thump. Before the newcomer could make a move, Geronimo would rush forward and leap on him. The curious thing was that, unlike the other geckos, he did not attack the head or body of his enemy. He made straight for his opponent's tail, and seizing it in his mouth, about half an inch from the tip, he would hang on like a bulldog and shake it from side to side. The newcomer, unnerved by this dastardly and unusual mode of attack, immediately took refuge in the time-honoured protective device of the lizards: he would drop his tail and scuttle over the edge of the sill and down the wall to the zinnia bed as fast as he could. Geronimo, panting a little from the exertion, would be left standing triumphantly on the sill, his opponent's tail hanging out of his mouth and thrashing to and fro like a snake. Having made sure his rival had departed, Geronimo would then settle down and proceed to eat the tail, a disgusting habit of which I strongly disapproved. However, it was apparently his way of celebrating a victory, and he was not really happy until the tail was safely inside his bulging stomach.

Most of the mantids that flew into my room were fairly small. Geronimo was always eager to tackle them, but they were too quick for him. Unlike the other insects the mantids seemed unaffected by the lamplight: instead of whirling round and round drunkenly, they would calmly settle in a convenient spot and proceed to devour the dancers whenever they settled to regain their strength. Their bulbous eyes seemed just as keen as the gecko's, and they would always spot him and move hurriedly, long before he had crept within fighting range. The night of the great fight, however, he met a mantis that not only refused to fly away, but actually went to meet him, and it was almost more than he could cope with.

I had for some time been intrigued by the breeding habits of the mantids. I had watched the unfortunate male crouching on the back of a female who, with complete equanimity, was browsing on him over her shoulder. Even after his head and thorax had disappeared into the female's neat mouth his hinder end continued to do its duty. Having watched their rather savage love life, I was now very anxious to see the laying and hatching of the eggs. My chance came one day when I was in the hills and I came face to face, as it were, with an exceptionally large female mantis who was stalking regally through the grass. Her belly was distended, and I felt sure that she was expecting a happy event. Having paused, swaying from side to side on her slender legs, and surveyed me coldly, she continued on her way, mincing through the grass-stalks. I decided that the best thing to do would be to capture her so that she could lay her eggs in a box where I could watch over them in comfort. As soon as she realized that I was attempting to capture her, she whirled round and stood up on end, her pale, jade-green wings outspread, her toothed arms curved upwards in a warning gesture of defiance. Amused at her belligerence towards a creature so much bigger than herself, I casually caught her round the thorax between finger and thumb. Instantly her long, sharp arms reached over her back and closed on my thumb, and it felt as though half a dozen needles had been driven through the skin. In my surprise I dropped her and sat back to suck my wound: I found that three of the little punctures had gone really deep, and that, by squeezing, tiny drops of blood appeared. My respect for her increased; she was obviously an insect to be reckoned with. At the next attempt I was more cautious and used two hands, grabbing her round the thorax with one and holding on to her dangerous front arms with the other. She wiggled ineffectually, and tried to bite me with her jaws, lowering her evil little pointed face and nibbling at my skin, but her jaws were too weak to have any effect. I carried her home and imprisoned her in a large gauze-covered cage in my bedroom, tastefully decorated with ferns, heather and rocks, among which she moved with light-footed grace. I christened her Cicely, for no obvious reason, and spent a lot of time catching butterflies for her, which she ate in large quantities and with apparently undiminishing appetite, while her stomach got bigger and bigger. Just when I was certain that at any moment she would lay her eggs, she somehow or other found a hole in her cage and escaped.

I was sitting in bed reading one night when, with a great whirring of wings, Cicely flew across the room and landed heavily on the wall, some ten feet away from where Geronimo was busily cleaning up the last bits of an exceptionally furry moth. He paused with bits of fluff adhering to his lips, and gazed in astonishment at Cicely. He had, I am sure, never seen such a large mantis before, for Cicely was a good half-inch longer than he was. Amazed by her size and taken aback by her effrontery at settling in his room, Geronimo could do nothing but stare at her for a few seconds. Meanwhile Cicely turned her head from side to side and looked about with an air of grim interest, like an angular spinster in an art gallery. Recovering from his surprise, Geronimo decided that this impertinent insect would have to be taught a lesson. He wiped his mouth on the ceiling, and then nodded his head rapidly and lashed his tail from side to side, obviously working himself up into a death-defying fury. Cicely took no notice at all, but continued to stare about her, swaying slightly on her long, slender legs. Geronimo slid slowly from the wall, gulping with fury, until about three feet away from the mantis he paused and shifted his feet in turn to make sure that his grip was good. Cicely, with well-simulated astonishment, appeared to notice him for the first time. Without changing her position she turned her head round and peered over her shoulder. Geronimo glared at her and gulped harder. Cicely, having surveyed him coolly with her bulging eyes, continued her inspection of the ceiling as if the gecko did not exist. Geronimo edged forward a few inches, scuffled his toes once more and the tip of his tail twitched. Then he launched himself forward, and a strange thing happened. Cicely, who up till then was apparently absorbed in the inspection of a crack in the plaster, leapt suddenly into the air, turned round and landed in the same spot, but with her wings spread out like a cloak, reared up on her hind legs and curved both serviceable forefeet at the ready. Geronimo had not been prepared for this spiky reception, and he skidded to a halt about three inches away and stared at her. She returned his stare with one of scornful belligerence. Geronimo seemed a little puzzled by the whole thing; according to his experience the mantis should have taken flight and zoomed away across the room at his approach, and yet here she was standing on end, arms ready to stab, her green cloak of wings rustling gently as she swayed from side to side. However, he could not back out now, having got so far, so he braced himself and leapt in for the kill.

His speed and weight told, for he crashed into the mantis and made her reel, and grabbed the underside of her thorax in his jaws. Cicely retaliated by snapping both her front legs shut on Geronimo's hind legs. They rustled and staggered across the ceiling and down the wall, each seeking to gain some advantage. Then there was a pause while the contestants had a rest and prepared for the second round, without either losing their grips. I wondered whether I ought to interfere; I did not want either of them to get killed, but at the same time the fight was so intriguing that I was loath to separate them. Before I could decide, they started once again.

For some reason or other Cicely was bent on trying to drag Geronimo down the wall to the floor, while he was equally determined that he should drag her up to the ceiling. They lurched to and fro for some time, first one and then the other gaining the upper hand, but nothing decisive really happening. Then Cicely made her fatal mistake: seizing the opportunity during one of their periodic pauses, she hurled herself into the air in what seemed to be an attempt to fly across the room with Geronimo dangling from her claws, like and eagle with a lamb. But she had not taken his weight into consideration. Her sudden leap took the gecko by surprise and tore the suction-pads on his toes free from their grip on the ceiling, but no sooner were they in mid-air than he became a dead weight, and a weight that not even Cicely could cope with. In an intricate tangle of tail and wings they fell on to the bed.

The fall surprised them both so much that they let go of each other, and sat on the blanket regarding each other with blazing eyes. Thinking this was a suitable opportunity to come between them and call it a draw, I was just about to grab the contestants when they launched themselves at each other once again. This time Geronimo was wiser and grasped one of Cicely's sharp forearms in his mouth. She retaliated by grabbing him round the neck with the other arm. Both were at an equal disadvantage on the blanket, for their toes and claws got caught in it and tripped them up. They struggled to and fro across the bed, and then started to work their way up towards the pillow. By now they were both looking very much the worse for wear: Cicely had a wing crushed and torn and one leg bent and useless, while Geronimo had a great number of bloody scratches across his back and neck caused by Cicely's front claws. I was now far too interested to see who was going to win to dream of stopping them, so I vacated the bed as they neared the pillow, for I had no desire to have one of Cicely's claws dug into my chest.

It looked as though the mantis was tiring, but as her feet made contact with the smooth surface of the sheet it seemed as if she was given a new lease of life. It was a pity that she applied her new-found strength towards the wrong objective. She released her grip on Geronimo's neck and seized his tail instead; whether she thought that by doing so she could hoist him into the air and thus immobilise him, I don't know, but it had the opposite effect. As soon as the claws dug into his tail Geronimo dropped it, but the furious wiggle he gave to accomplish this made his head wag rapidly from side to side, and the result was that he tore Cicely's forearm off in his mouth. So there was Cicely with Geronimo's lashing tail clasped in one claw, while Geronimo, tailless and bloody, had Cicely's left forearm twitching in his mouth. Cicely might still have saved the fight if she had grabbed Geronimo quickly, before he spat out his mouthful of arm; but she was too wrapped up in the thrashing tail, which I think she thought was a vital part of her adversary, and with her one claw she maintained a firm grip on it. Geronimo spat out the forearm and leapt forward, his mouth snapped, and Cicely's head and thorax disappeared into his mouth.

This was really the end of the fight; now it was merely a matter of Geronimo hanging on until Cicely was dead. Her legs twitched, her wings unfurled like green fans and rustled crisply as they flapped, her great abdomen pulsed, and the movements of her dying body toppled them both into a cleft in the rumpled bedclothes. For a long time I could not see them; all I could hear was the faint crackle of the mantis's wings, but presently even this ceased. There was a pause, and then a small, scratched and bloodstained head poked above the edge of the sheet, and a pair of golden eyes contemplated me triumphantly as Geronimo crawled tiredly into view. A large piece of skin had been torn from his shoulder, leaving a raw, red patch; his back was freckled with beads of blood where the claws had dug into him, and his gory tailstump left a red smear on the sheet when he moved. He was battered, limp and exhausted, but victorious. He sat there for some time, gulping to himself, and allowed me to mop his back with a ball of cotton wool on the end of a match-stick. Then, as a prize, I caught five fat flies and gave them to him, and he ate them with enjoyment. Having recovered his strength somewhat, he made his way slowly round the wall, over the window-sill and down the outside wall of the house to his home under the stone in the zinnia bed. Obviously he had decided that a good night's rest was needed after such a hectic brawl. The following night he was back in his usual corner, perky as ever, wagging his stump of a tail with pleasure as he eyed the feast of insects drifting about the lamp.

It was a couple of weeks after his great battle that Geronimo appeared one night over the window-sill and, to my astonishment, he had with him another gecko. The newcomer was quite tiny, only about half Geronimo's size, and a very delicate pearly pink with large and lustrous eyes. Geronimo took up his usual stand in one corner while the newcomer chose a spot in the centre of the ceiling. They set about the task of insect-hunting with immense concentration, completely ignoring each other. I thought at first that the newcomer, being so dainty, was Geronimo's bride, but investigation in the zinnia bed proved that he still maintained a bachelor establishment under his stone. The new gecko apparently slept elsewhere, appearing only at night to join Geronimo as he shinned up the wall to the bedroom. In view of his pugnacious attitude towards other geckos I found it difficult to understand his toleration of this newcomer. I toyed with the idea that it might be Geronimo's son or daughter, but I knew that geckos had no family life whatsoever, simply laying their eggs and leaving the young (when hatched) to fend for themselves, so this did not seem probable. I was still undecided as to what name I should bestow on this new inhabitant of my bedroom when it met with a dreadful fate.

To the left of the villa was a large valley like a bowl of greensward, thickly studded with the twisted columns of the olive-trunks. This valley was surrounded by clay and gravel cliffs about twenty feet high, along the base of which grew a thick bed of myrtles that covered a tumbled mass of rocks. This was a fertile hunting ground from my point of view, for a great quantity of various animals lived in and round this area. I was hunting among these boulders one day when I found a large, half-rotten olive-trunk lying under the bushes. Thinking there might be something of interest beneath it, I heaved valiantly until it rolled over and settled on its back soggily. In the trough left by its weight crouched two creatures that made me gasp with astonishment.

They were, as far as I could see, common toads, but they were the largest I had ever seen. Each one had a girth greater than the average saucer. They were greyish-green, heavily carunculated, and with curious white patches here and there on their bodies where the skin was shiny and lacking in pigment. They squatted there like two obese, leprous Buddhas, peering at me and gulping in the guilty way that toads have. Holding one in each hand, it was like handling two flaccid, leathery balloons, and the toads blinked their fine golden filigreed eyes at me, and settled themselves more comfortably on my fingers, gazing at me trustfully, their wide, thick-lipped mouths seeming to spread in embarrassed and uncertain grins. I was delighted with them, and so excited at their discovery that I felt I must immediately share them with someone or I would burst with suppressed joy. I tore back to the villa, clutching a toad in each hand, to show my new acquisitions to the family.

Mother and Spiro were in the larder checking the groceries when I burst in. I held the toads aloft and implored them to look at the wonderful amphibians. I was standing fairly close to Spiro so that when he turned round he found himself staring into a toad's face. Spiro's scowl faded, his eyes bulged and his skin took on a greenish hue; the resemblance between him and the toad was quite remarkable. Whipping out his handkerchief and holding it to his mouth, Spiro waddled uncertainly out on to the veranda and was violently sick.

'You shouldn't show Spiro things like that, dear,' Mother remonstrated 'You know he's got a weak stomach.'

I pointed out that although I was aware of Spiro's weak stomach I had not thought that the sight of such lovely creatures as the toads would affect him so violently. What was wrong with them? I asked, greatly puzzled.

'There's nothing wrong with them, dear; they're lovely,' said Mother, eyeing the toads suspiciously. 'It's just that *everyone* doesn't like them.'

Spiro waddled in again, looking pale, mopping his forehead with his handkerchief. I hastily hid the toads behind my back.

'Gollys, Master Gerrys,' he said dolefully, 'whys you shows me things like that? I'm sorrys I had to rush outs, Mrs Durrells, but honest to Gods when I sees one of them bastards I haves to throws, and I thought it was betters if I throws out theres than in heres. Donts you ever shows me them things again, Master Gerrys, please.'

To my disappointment the rest of the family reacted in much the same way as Spiro had done to the toad twins, and so, finding that I could not stir up any enthusiasm among the others, I sadly took the creatures up to my room and placed them carefully under my bed.

That evening, when the lamps were lit, I let the toads out for a walk about the room, and amused myself by knocking down insects that swirled round the lamp for them to eat. They flopped ponderously to and fro, gulping up these offerings, their wide mouths snapping shut with a faint clopping sound as their sticky tongues flipped the insect inside. Presently an exceptionally large and hysterical moth came barging into the room, and thinking what a fine titbit it would make, I pursued it relentlessly. Presently it settled on the ceiling, out of my reach, within a few inches of Geronimo's friend. Since the moth was at least twice its size, the gecko wisely ignored it. In an effort to knock it down for the toads I hurled a magazine at it, which was a stupid thing to do. The magazine missed the moth but caught the gecko amidships, just as it was staring at an approaching lacewing fly. The book flew into the corner of the room, and the gecko fell with a plop on to the carpet right in front of the larger of the two toads. Before the reptile had recovered its breath, and before I could do anything to save it, the toad leant forward with a benign expression on its face, the wide mouth fell open like a drawbridge, the tongue flicked out and in again, carrying the gecko with it, and the toad's mouth closed once more and assumed its expression of shy good humour. Geronimo, hanging upside down in his corner, seemed quite indifferent to the fate of his companion, but I was horrified by the whole incident and mortified to feel that it was my fault. I hastily gathered up the toads and locked them in their box, for fear that Geronimo himself might be the next victim of their ferocity.

I was very intrigued by these giant toads for a number of reasons. First, they appeared to be the common species, yet they were blotched with the curious white patches on body and legs. Also all the other common toads I has seen had been only a quarter of the size of these monsters. Another curious thing was that I had found them together under the log; to find one such monster would have been unusual, but to find a pair sitting side by side like that was, I felt sure, a unique discovery. I even wondered if they might turn out to be something quite new to science. Hopefully I kept them imprisoned under my bed until the following Thursday, when Theodore arrived. Then I rushed breathlessly up to the bedroom and brought them down for him to see.

'Ah ha!' Theodore observed, peering at them closely and prodding one with his forefinger; 'yes, they are certainly very large specimens.'

He lifted one out of the box and placed it on the floor, where it sat staring at him mournfully, bulging and sagging like a blob of mildewed dough.

'Um ... yes,' said Theodore; 'they seem to be ... er ... the common toad, though, as I say, they are exceptionally *fine* specimens. These curious marks are due to lack of pigmentation. I should think it's due to age, though of course I ... er ... I may be wrong. They must be a considerable age to have reached ... er ... to have attained such proportions.'

I was surprised, for I had never looked upon toads as being particularly long-lived creatures. I asked Theodore what the usual age was that they attained.

'Well, it's difficult to say ... um ... there are no statistics to go on,' he pointed out, his eyes twinkling, 'but I should imagine that ones as large as these might well be twelve or even twenty years old. They seem to have a great tenacity for life. I have read somewhere of toads being walled up in houses and so forth, and it appears that they must have been confined like that for a number of years. In one case I believe it was something like twenty-five years.'

He lifted the other toad out of the box and set it down beside its companion. They sat side by side, gulping and blinking, their flabby sides wobbling as they breathed. Theodore contemplated them fully for a moment, and then took a pair of forceps out of his waistcoat pocket. He strode into the garden and overturned several rocks until he found a large, moist and liver-coloured earthworm. He picked it up neatly with his forceps and strode back to the veranda. He stood over the toads and dropped the writhing earthworm on to the stone flags. It coiled itself into a knot, and then slowly started to unravel itself. The nearest toad lifted its head, blinked its eyes rapidly, and turned slightly so that it was facing the worm. The worm continued to writhe like a piece of wool on a hot coal. The toad bent forward, staring down at it with an expression of extreme interest on its broad face.

'Ah ha!' said Theodore, and smiled in his beard.

The worm performed a particularly convulsive figure of eight, and the toad lent further forward with excitement. Its great mouth opened, the pink tongue flicked out, and the forepart of the worm was carried into the gaping maw. The toad shut its mouth with a snap, and most of the worm, which hung outside, coiled about wildly. The toad sat back and with great care proceeded to stuff the tail end of the worm into its mouth, using its thumbs. As each section of thrashing worm was pushed in, the toad would gulp hard, closing its eyes with an expression as if of acute pain. Slowly but surely, bit by bit, the worm disappeared between the thick lips, until at last there was only a fraction of an inch dangling outside, twitching to and fro.

'Um,' said Theodore in an amused tone of voice. 'I always like watching them do that. It reminds me of those conjurers, you know, that pull yards and yards of tapes or coloured ribbons out of their mouths ... er ... only, of course, the other way *round*.'

The toad blinked, gulped desperately, its eyes screwed up, and the last bit of worm disappeared inside its mouth.

'I wonder,' said Theodore meditatively, his eyes twinkling – 'I wonder if one could teach toads to swallow *swords*? It would be interesting to try.'

He picked up the toads carefully and replaced them in their box.

'Not sharp swords, of course,' he said, straightening up and rocking on his toes, his eyes gleaming. 'If the swords were sharp you might get your toad *in a hole*.'

He chuckled quietly to himself, rasping the side of his beard with his thumb.

Chapter Fourteen

The Talking Flowers

It was not long before I received the unwelcome news that yet another tutor had been found for me. This time it was a certain individual named Kralefsky, a person descended from an intricate tangle of nationalities but predominantly English. The family informed me that he was a very nice man and one who was, moreover, interested in birds, so we should get on together. I was not, however, the least impressed by this last bit of information; I had met a number of people who professed to be interested in birds, and who had turned out (after careful questioning) to be charlatans who did not know what a hoopoe looked like, or could not tell the difference between a black redstart and an ordinary one. I felt certain that the family had invented this bird-loving tutor simply in an effort to make me feel happier about having to start work once again. I was sure that his reputation as an ornithologist would turn out to have grown from the fact that he once kept a canary when he was fourteen. Therefore I set off for town to my first lesson in the gloomiest possible frame of mind.

Kralefsky lived in the top two storeys of a square, mildewed old mansion that stood on the outskirts of the town. I climbed the wide staircase and, with disdainful bravado, rapped a sharp tattoo on the knocker that decorated the front door. I waited, glowering to myself and digging the heel of my shoe into the wine-red carpet with considerable violence; presently, just as I was about to knock again, there came the soft pad of footsteps, and the front door was flung wide to reveal my new tutor.

I decided immediately that Kralefsky was not a human being at all, but a gnome who had disguised himself as one by donning an antiquated but very dapper suit. He had a large, egg-shaped head with flattened sides that were tilted back against a smoothly rounded hump-back. This gave him the curious appearance of being permanently in the middle of shrugging his shoulders and peering up into the sky. A long, fine-bridged nose with widely flared nostrils curved out of his face, and his extremely large eyes were liquid and of a pale sherry colour. They had a fixed, far-away look in them, as though their owner were just waking up out of a trance. His wide, thin mouth managed to combine primness with humour, and now it was stretched across his face in a smile of welcome, showing even but discoloured teeth.

'Gerry Durrell?' he asked, bobbing like a courting sparrow, and flapping his large, bony hands at me. 'Gerry Durrell, is it not? Come in, my dear boy, do come in.'

He beckoned me with a long forefinger, and I walked past him into the dark hall, the floorboards creaking protestingly under their mangy skin of carpet.

'Through here; this is the room we shall work in,' fluted Kralefsky, throwing open a door and ushering me into a small, sparsely furnished room. I put my books on the table and sat down in the chair he indicated. he leaned over the table, balancing on the tips of his beautifully manicured fingers, and smiled at me in a vague way. I smiled back, not knowing quite what he expected.

'Friends!' he exclaimed rapturously. 'It is most *important* that we are friends. I am quite, quite certain we will become friends, aren't you?'

I nodded seriously, biting the inside of my cheeks to prevent myself from smiling.

'Friendship,' he murmured, shutting his eyes in ecstasy at the thought, 'friendship! That's the ticket!'

His lips moved silently, and I wondered if he was praying, and if so whether it was for me, himself or both of us. A fly circled his head and then settled confidently on his nose. Kralefsky started, brushed it away, opened his eyes and blinked at me.

'Yes, .yes, that's it,' he said firmly; 'I'm sure we shall be friends. Your mother tells me that you have a great love of natural history. This, you see, gives us something in common straight away ... a bond, as it were, eh?'

He inserted a forefinger and thumb into his waistcoat pocket, drew out a large gold watch and regarded it reproachfully. He sighed, replaced the watch, and then smoothed the bald patch on his head that gleamed like a brown pebble through his licheny hair.

'I am by way of being an aviculturist, albeit an amateur,' he volunteered modestly. 'I thought perhaps you might care to see my collection. Half an hour or so with the feathered creatures will, I venture to think, do us no harm before we start work. Besides, I was a *little* late this morning, and one or two of them need fresh water.'

He led the way up a creaking staircase to the top of the house, and paused in front of a green baize door. He produced an immense bunch of keys that jangled musically as he searched for the right one; he inserted it, twisted it round and drew open the heavy door. A dazzle of sunlight poured out of the room, blinding me, and with it came a deafening chorus of bird-song; it was as though Kralefsky had opened the gates of Paradise in the grubby corridor at the top of his house. The attic was vast, stretching away across almost the whole top of the house. It was uncarpeted, and the only piece of furniture was a large deal table in the centre of the room. But the walls were lined, from floor to ceiling, with row upon row of big, airy cages containing dozens of fluttering, chirruping birds. The floor of the room was covered with a fine layer of bird seed, so that as you walked your feet scrunched pleasantly, as though you were on a shingle beach. Fascinated by this mass of birds I edged slowly round the room, pausing to gaze into each cage, while Krelefsky (who appeared to have forgotten my existence) seized a large watering-can from the table and danced nimbly from cage to cage, filling water-pots.

My first impression, that the birds were all canaries, was quite wrong; to my delight I found there were goldfinches painted like clowns in vivid scarlet, yellow and black; greenfinches as green and yellow as lemon leaves in midsummer; linnets in their neat chocolate-and-white tweed suiting; bullfinches with bulging, rose-pink breasts, and a host of other birds. In one corner of the room I found small french windows that led me out on to a balcony. At each end a large aviary had been built, and in one lived a cock blackbird, black and velvety with a flaunting, banana-yellow beak; while in the other aviary opposite was a thrush-like bird which was clad in the most gorgeous blue feathering, a celestial combination of shades from navy to opal.

'Rock-thrush,' announced Kralefsky, poking his head round the door suddenly and pointing at this beautiful bird; 'I had it sent over as a nestling last year ... from Albania, you know. Unfortunately I have not, as yet, been able to obtain a lady for him.'

He waved the watering-can amiably at the thrush, and disappeared inside again. The thrush regarded me with a roguish eye, fluffed his breast out, and gave a series of little clucks that sounded like an amused chuckle. Having gazed long and greedily at him, I went back into the attic, where I found Kralefsky still filling water-pots.

'I wonder if you would care to assist?' he asked, staring at me with vacant eyes, the can drooping in his hand so that a fine stream of water dribbled on to the highly polished toe of one shoe. 'A task like this is so much easier if two pairs of hands work at it, I always think. Now, if you hold the watering-can ... so ... I will hold out the pots to be filled ... excellent! That's the ticket! We shall accomplish this in no time at all.'

So, while I filled the little earthenware pots with water, Kralefsky took them carefully between finger and thumb and inserted them deftly through the cage doors, as though he were popping sweets into a child's mouth. As he worked he talked to both me and the birds with complete impartiality, but as he did not vary his tone at all I was sometimes at a loss to know whether the remark was addressed to me or to some occupant of the cages.

'Yes, they're in fine fettle today; it's the sunshine, you know ... as soon as it gets to this side of the house they start to sing, don't you? You must lay more next time ... only two, my dear, only two. You couldn't call *that* a clutch, with all the goodwill in the world. Do you like this new seed? Do you keep any yourself, eh? There are a number of most interesting seed-eaters found here.... Don't do that in your clean water.... Breeding some of them is, of course, a task, but a most rewarding one, I find, especially the crosses. I have generally had great success with crosses ... except when you only lay two, of course ... rascal, *rascal*!'

Eventually the watering was done, and Kralefsky stood surveying his birds for a moment or so, smiling to himself and wiping his hands carefully on a small towel. Then he led me round the room, pausing before each cage to give me an account of the bird's history, its ancestors and what he hoped to do with it. We were examining – in a satisfied silence – a fat, flushed bullfinch, when suddenly a loud, tremulous ringing sound rose above the clamour of bird song. To my astonishment the noise appeared to emanate from somewhere inside Kralefsky's stomach.

'By Jove!' he exclaimed in horror, turning agonised eyes on me, 'by Jove!'

He inserted finger and thumb into his waistcoat and drew out his watch. He depressed a tiny lever and the ringing sound ceased. I was a little disappointed that the noise should have such a commonplace source; to have a tutor whose inside chimed at intervals would, I felt, have added greatly to the charm of the lessons. Kralefsky peered eagerly at the watch and then screwed up his face in disgust.

'By Jove!' he repeated faintly, 'twelve o'clock already ... winged time indeed.... Dear me, and you leave at half-past, don't you?'

He slipped the watch back into its pocket and smoothed his bald patch.

'Well,' he said at last, 'we cannot, I feel, achieve any scholastic advancement in half an hour. Therefore, if it would pass the time pleasantly for you, I suggest we go into the garden below and pick some groundsel for the birds. It's so good for them, you know, especially when they're laying.'

So we went into the garden and picked groundsel until Spiro's car honked its way down the street like a wounded duck.

'Your car, I believe,' observed Kralefsky politely. 'We have certainly managed to gather a good supply of green stuff in the time. Your assistance was invaluable. Now, tomorrow you will be here at nine o'clock sharp, won't you? That's the ticket! We may consider this morning was not wasted; it was a form of introduction, a measuring up of each other. And I hope a chord of friendship has been struck. By Jove, yes, that's very important! Well, *au revoir* until tomorrow, then.'

As I closed the creaking, wrought-iron gates he waved at me courteously and then wandered back towards the house, leaving a trail of golden-flowered groundsel behind him, his hump back bobbing among the rose-bushes.

When I got home the family asked me how I liked my new tutor. Without going into details, I said that I found him very nice, and that I was sure we should become firm friends. To the query as to what we had studied during our first morning I replied, with a certain amount of honesty, that the morning had been devoted to ornithology and botany. The family seemed satisfied. But I very soon found that Mr Kralefsky was a stickler for work, and he had made up his mind to educate me in spite of any ideas I might have on the subject. The lessons were boring to a degree, for he employed a method of teaching that must have been in fashion round about the middle of the eighteenth century. History was served in great, indigestible chunks, and the dates were learnt by heart. We would sit and repeat them in a monotonous, sing-song chorus, until they became like some incantation that we chanted automatically, our minds busy with other things. For geography I was confined, to my annoyance, to the British Isles, and innumerable maps had to be traced and filled in with the bevies of counties and the county towns. Then the counties and the towns had to be learnt by heart, together with the names of the important rivers, the main produce of places, the populations and much other dreary and completely useless information.

'Somerset?' he would trill, pointing at me accusingly.

I would frown in a desperate attempt to remember something about that county. Kralefsky's eyes would grow large with anxiety as he watched my mental struggle.

'Well,' he would say at length, when it became obvious that my knowledge of Somerset was non-existent – 'well, let us leave Somerset and try Warwickshire. Now then, Warwickshire: county town? Warwick! That's the ticket! Now, what do they produce in Warwick, eh?'

As far as I was concerned they did not produce anything in Warwick, but I would hazard a wild guess at coal. I had discovered that if one went on naming a product relentlessly (regardless of the county or town under discussion), sooner of later you would find the answer to be correct. Kralefsky's anguish at my mistakes was very real; the day I informed him that Essex produced stainless steel there were tears in his eyes. But these long periods of depression were more than made up for by his extreme pleasure and delight when, by some strange chance, I answered a question correctly.

Once a week we tortured ourselves by devoting a morning to French. Kralefsky spoke French beautifully, and to hear me massacring the language was almost more than he could bear. He very soon found that it was quite useless to try to teach me from normal text-books, so these were set aside in favour of a three-volume set of bird books; but even with these it was up-hill going. Occasionally, when we were reading the description of the robin's plumage for the twentieth time, a look of grim determination would settle on Kralefsky's face. He would slam the book shut, rush out into the hall, to reappear a minute later wearing a jaunty panama.

'I think it would freshen us up a little ... blow the cobwebs away ... if we went for a short *walk*," he would announce, giving a distasteful glance at *Les Petits Oiseaux de l'Europe*. 'I think we will make our way through the town and come back along the esplanade, eh? Excellent! Now, we must not waste time, must we? It will be a good opportunity for us to practise our *conversational* French, won't it? So no English, please – everything to be said in French. It is in this way that we become familiar with a language.'

So, in almost complete silence, we would wend our way through the town. The beauty of these walks was that, no matter which direction we set out in, we invariably found ourselves, somehow or other, in the bird market. We were rather like Alice in the Looking-glass garden: no matter how determinedly we strode off in the opposite direction, in no time at all we found ourselves in the little square where the stalls were piled high with wicker cages and the air rang with the song of birds. Here French would be forgotten; it would fade away into the limbo to join algebra, geometry, history dates, county towns and similar subjects. Our eyes sparkling, our faces flushed, we would move from stall to stall, examining the birds carefully and bargaining fiercely with the vendors, and gradually our arms would become laden with cages.

Then we would be brought suddenly back to earth by the watch in Kralefsky's waistcoat pocket, chiming daintily, and he would almost drop his tottering burden of cages in his efforts to extract the watch and stop it.

'By Jove! Twelve o'clock! Who would have thought it, eh? Just hold this linnet for me, will you, while I stop the watch. . . . Thank you. . . . We will have to be quick, eh? I doubt whether we can make it on foot, laden as we are. Dear me! I think we had better have a cab. An extravagance, of course, but needs must where the devil drives, eh?'

So we would hurry across the square, pile our twittering, fluttering purchases into a cab and be driven back to Kralefsky's house, the jingle of the harness and the thud of hooves mingling pleasantly with the cries of our bird cargo.

I had worked for some weeks with Kralefsky before I discovered that he did not live alone. At intervals during the morning he would pause suddenly, in the middle of a sum or a recitation of county towns, and cock his head on one side, as if listening.

'Excuse me a moment,' he would say. 'I must go and see Mother.'

At first this rather puzzled me, for I was convinced that Kralefsky was far too old to have a mother still living. After considerable thought, I came to the conclusion that this was merely his polite way of saying that he wished to retire to the lavatory, for I realized that not everyone shared my family's lack of embarrassment when discussing this topic. It never occurred to me that, if this was so, Kralefsky closeted himself more often than any other human being I had met. One morning I had consumed for breakfast a large quantity of loquats, and they had distressing effects on me when we were in the middle of a history lesson. Since Kralefsky was so finicky about the subject of lavatories I decided that I would have to phrase my request politely, so I thought it best to adopt his own curious term. I looked him firmly in the eye and said that I would like to pay a visit to his mother.

'My mother?' he repeated in astonishment. 'Visit my mother? Now?'

I could not see what the fuss was about, so I merely nodded.

'Well,' he said doubtfully, 'I'm sure she'll be delighted to see you, of course, but I'd better just go and see if it's convenient.'

He left the room, still looking a trifle puzzled, and returned after a few minutes.

'Mother would be delighted to see you,' he announced, 'but she says will you please excuse her being a little untidy?'

I thought it was carrying politeness to an extreme to talk about the lavatory as if it were a human being, but, since Kralefsky was obviously a bit eccentric on the subject, I felt I had better humour him. I said I did not mind a bit if his mother was in a mess, as ours frequently was as well.

'Ah ... er ... yes, yes, I expect so,' he murmured, giving me rather a startled glance. He led me down the corridor, opened a door and, to my complete surprise, ushered me into a large shadowy bedroom. The room was a forest of flowers; vases, bowls and pots were perched everywhere, and each contained a mass of beautiful blooms that shone in the gloom, like walls of jewels in a green-shadowed cave. At one end of the room was an enormous bed, and in it, propped up on a heap of pillows, lay a tiny figure not much bigger than a child. She must have been very old, I decided as we drew nearer, for her fine, delicate features were covered with a network of wrinkles that grooved a skin as soft and velvety-looking as a baby mushroom's. But the astonishing thing about her was her hair. It fell over her shoulders in a thick cascade, and then spread half way down the bed. It was the richest and most beautiful auburn colour imaginable, glinting and shining as though on fire, making me think of autumn leaves and the brilliant winter coat of a fox.

'Mother dear,' Kralefsky called softly, bobbing across the room and seating himself on a chair by the bed, 'Mother dear, here's Gerry come to see you.'

The minute figure on the bed lifted thin, pale lids and looked at me with great tawny eyes that were as bright and intelligent as a bird's. She lifted a slender, beautifully shaped hand, weighed down with rings, from the depths of the auburn tresses and held it out to me, smiling mischievously.

'I am so very flattered that you asked to see me,' she said in a soft, husky voice. 'So many people nowadays consider a person of my age a bore.'

Embarrassed, I muttered something, and the bright eyes looked at me, twinkling, and she gave a fluting blackbird laugh, and patted the bed with her hand.

'Do sit down,' she invited; 'do sit down and talk for a minute.'

Gingerly I picked up the mass of auburn hair and moved it to one side so that I could sit on the bed. The hair was soft, silky and heavy, like a flame-coloured wave swishing through my fingers. Mrs Kralefsky smiled at me, and lifted a strand of it in her fingers, twisting it gently so that it sparkled.

'My one remaining vanity,' she said; 'all that is left of my beauty.'

She gazed down at the flood of hair as though it were a pet, or some other creature that had nothing to do with her, and patted it affectionately.

'It's strange,' she said, 'very strange. I have a theory, you know, that some beautiful things fall in love with themselves, as Narcissus did. When they do that, they need no help in order to live; they become so absorbed in their own beauty that they live for that alone, feeding on themselves, as it were.

Thus, the more beautiful they become, the stronger they become; they live in a circle. That's what my hair has done. It is self-sufficient, it grows only for itself, and the fact that my old body has fallen to ruin does not affect it a bit. When I die they will be able to pack my coffin deep with it, and it will probably go on growing after my body is dust.'

'Now, now, Mother, you shouldn't talk like that,' Kralefsky chided her gently. 'I don't like these morbid thoughts of yours.'

She turned her head and regarded him affectionately, chuckling softly.

'But it's not morbid, John; it's only a theory I have,' she explained. 'Besides, think what a beautiful shroud it will make.'

She gazed down at her hair, smiling happily. In the silence Kralefsky's watch chimed eagerly, and he started, pulled it out of his pocket and stared at it.

'By Jove!' he said, jumping to his feet, 'those eggs should have hatched. Excuse me a minute, will you, Mother? I really must go and see.'

'Run along, run along,' she said. 'Gerry and I will chat until you come back ... don't worry about *us*.'

'That's the ticket!' exclaimed Kralefsky, and bobbed rapidly across the room between the banks of flowers, like a mole burrowing through a rainbow. The door sighed shut behind him, and Mrs Kralefsky turned her head and smiled at me.

'They say,' she announced – 'they *say* that when you get old, as I am, your body slows down. I don't believe it. No, I think that is quite wrong. I have a theory that you do *not* slow down at all, but that *life slows down for you*. You understand me? Everything becomes languid, as it were, and you can notice so much more when things are in slow motion. The things you see! The extraordinary things that happen all around you, that you never even suspected before! It is really a delightful adventure, quite delightful!'

She sighed with satisfaction, and glanced round the room.

'Take flowers,' she said, pointing at the blooms that filled the room. 'Have you heard flowers *talking*?'

Greatly intrigued, I shook my head; the idea of flowers talking was quite new to me.

'Well, I can assure you that they *do* talk,' she said. 'They hold long conversations with each other ... at least I presume them to be conversations, for I don't understand what they're saying, naturally. When you're as old as I am you'll probably be able to hear them as well; that is, if you retain an open mind about such matters. *Most* people say that as one gets older one believes nothing and is surprised at nothing; so that one becomes more receptive to ideas. Nonsense! All the old people I know have had their minds locked up like grey, scaly oysters since they were in their teens.'

She glanced at me sharply.

'D'you think I'm queer? Touched, eh? Talking about flowers holding conversations?'

Hastily and truthfully I denied this. I said that I thought it was more than likely that flowers conversed with each other. I pointed out that bats produced minute squeaks which I was able to hear, but which would be inaudible to an elderly person, since the sound was too high-pitched.

'That's it, that's it!' she exclaimed delightedly. 'It's a question of wavelength. I put it all down to this slowing-up process. Another thing that you don't notice when you're young is that flowers have personality. They are different from each other, just as people are. Look, I'll show you. D'you see that rose over there, in the bowl by itself?'

On a small table in the corner, enshrined in a small silver bowl, was a magnificent velvety rose, so deep a garnet red that it was almost black. It was a gorgeous flower, the petals curled to perfection, the bloom on them as soft and unblemished as the down on a newly-hatched butterfly's wing.

'Isn't he a beauty?' inquired Mrs Kralefsky. 'Isn't he wonderful? Now, I've had him two weeks. You'd hardly believe it, would you? And he was not a bud when he came. No, no, he was fully open. But, do you know, he was so sick that I did not think he would live? The person who plucked him was careless enough to put him in with a bunch of Michaelmas daisies. Fatal, absolutely fatal! You have no idea how cruel the daisy family is, on the whole. They are very rough-and-ready sort of flowers, very down to earth, and, of course, to put such an aristocrat as a rose amongst them is just *asking* for trouble. By the time he got here he had drooped and faded to such an extent that I did not even notice him among the daisies. But, luckily, I heard them at it. I was dozing here when they started, particularly, it seemed to me, the yellow ones, who always seem so belligerent. Well, of course, I didn't know what they were saying, but it sounded *horrible*. I couldn't think *who* they were talking to at first; I thought they were quarrelling among themselves. Then I got out of bed to have a look and I found that poor rose, crushed in the middle of them, being harried to death. I got him out and put him by himself and gave him half an aspirin. Aspirin is so good for roses. Drachma pieces for the chrysanthemums, aspirin for roses, brandy for sweet peas, and a squeeze of lemon-juice for the fleshy flowers, like begonias. Well, removed from the company of the daisies and given that pick-me-up, he revived in no time, and he seems so grateful; he's obviously making an effort to remain beautiful for as long as possible in order to thank me.'

She gazed at the rose affectionately, as it glowed in its silver bowl.

'Yes, there's a lot I have learnt about flowers. They're just like people. Put too many together and they get on each other's nerves and start to wilt. Mix some kinds and you get what appears to be a dreadful form of class distinction. And, of course, the water is so important. Do you know that some people think it's kind to change the water every day? Dreadful! You can *hear* the flowers dying if you do that. I change the water once a week, put a handful of earth in it, and they thrive.'

The door opened and Kralefsky came bobbing in, smiling triumphantly.

'They've all hatched!' he announced, 'all four of them. I'm so glad. I was quite worried, as it's her first clutch.'

'Good, dear; I'm so glad,' said Mrs Kralefsky delightedly. 'That is nice for you. Well, Gerry and I have been having a most interesting conversation. At least, I found it interesting, anyway.'

Getting to my feet, I said that I had found it most interesting as well.

'You must come and see me again, if it would not bore you,' she said. 'You will find my ideas a little eccentric, I think, but they are worth listening to.'

She smiled up at me, lying on the bed under her great cloak of hair, and lifted a hand in a courteous gesture of dismissal. I followed Kralefsky across the room, and at the door I looked back and smiled. She was lying quite still, submissive under the weight of her hair. She lifted her hand again and waved. It seemed to me, in the gloom, that the flowers had moved closer to her, had crowded eagerly about her bed, as though waiting for her to tell them something. A ravaged old queen, lying in state, surrounded by her whispering court of flowers.

Chapter Fifteen

The Cyclamen Woods

Half a mile or so from the villa rose a fairly large conical hill, covered with grass and heather, and crowned with three tiny olive-groves, separated from each other by wide beds of myrtle. I called these three little groves the Cyclamen Woods, for in the right season the ground beneath the olive-trees was flushed magenta and wine-red with the flowers of cyclamen that seemed to grow more thickly and more luxuriantly here than anywhere else in the countryside. The flashy, circular bulbs, with their flaky peeling skin, grew in beds like oysters, each with its cluster of deep green, white-veined leaves, a fountain of beautiful flowers that looked as though they had been made from magenta-stained snowflakes.

The Cyclamen Woods were an excellent place to spend an afternoon. Lying beneath the shade of the olive-trunks, you could look out over the valley, a mosaic of fields, vineyards and orchards, to where the sea shone between the olive-trunks, a thousand fiery sparkles running over it as it rubbed itself gently and languorously along the shore. The hill-top seemed to have its own breeze, albeit a baby one, for no matter how hot it was below in the valley, up in the three olive-groves the tiny wind played constantly, the leaves whispered and the drooping cyclamen flowers bowed to each other in endless greeting. It was an ideal spot in which to rest after a hectic lizard hunt, when your head was pounding with the heat, your clothes limp and discoloured with perspiration and the three dogs hung out their pink tongues and panted like ancient, miniature railway engines. It was while the dogs and I were resting after just such a hunt that I acquired two new pets, and, indirectly, started off a chain of coincidences that affected both Larry and Mr Kralefsky.

The dogs, tongues rippling, had flung themselves down among the cyclamens, and lay on their stomachs, hindlegs spread out, in order to get as much of the cool earth against their bodies as possible. Their eyes were half-closed and their jowls dark with saliva. I was leaning against an olive-trunk that had spent the past hundred years growing itself into the right shape for a perfect back-rest, and gazing out over the fields and trying to identify my peasant friends among the tiny coloured blobs that moved there. Far below, over a blond square of ripening maize, a small black and white shape appeared, like a piebald Maltese cross, skimming rapidly across the flat areas of cultivation, heading determinedly for the hill-top on which I sat. As it flew up towards me the magpie uttered three brief, harsh chucks, that sounded rather muffled, as though its beak were full of food. It dived as neatly as an arrow into the depths of an olive-tree some distance away; there was a pause, and then there arose a chorus of shrill wheezing shrieks from among the leaves, which swept to a crescendo and died slowly away. Again I heard the magpie chuck, softly and warningly, and it leapt out of the leaves and glided off down the hillside once more. I waited until the bird was a mere speck, like a dust-mote floating over the frilly triangle of vineyard on the horizon, and then got to my feet and cautiously circled the tree from which the curious sounds had come. High up among the branches, half hidden by the green and silver leaves, I could make out a large, oval bundle of twigs, like a huge, furry football wedged among the branches. Excitedly I started to scramble up the tree, while the dogs gathered at the bottom of the trunk and watched me with interest; when I was near to the nest I looked down and my stomach writhed, for the dogs' faces, peering up at me eagerly, were the size of pimpernel flowers. Carefully, my palms sweating, I edged my way out along the branches until I crouched side by side with the nest among the breeze-ruffled leaves. It was a massive structure, a great basket of carefully interwoven sticks, a deep cup of mud and rootlets in its heart. The entrance hole through the wall was small, and the twigs that surrounded it bristled with sharp thorns, as did the sides of the nest and the neatly domed, wickerwork roof. It was the sort of nest designed to discourage the most ardent ornithologist.

Trying to avoid looking down, I lay on my stomach along the branch and pushed my hand carefully inside the thorny bundle, groping in the mud cup. Under my fingers I could feel soft, quivering skin and fluff, while a shrill chorus of wheezes rose from inside the nest. Carefully I curved my fingers round one fat, warm baby and drew it out. Enthusiastic though I was, even I had to admit it was no beauty. Its squat beak, with a yellow fold at each corner, the bald head and the half-open and bleary eyes gave it a drunken and rather imbecile look. The skin hung in folds and wrinkles all over its body, apparently pinned loosely and haphazardly to its flesh by black feather-stubs. Between the lanky legs drooped a huge flaccid stomach, the skin of it so fine that you could dimly see the internal organs beneath. The baby squatted in my palm, its belly spreading out like a water-filled balloon, and wheezed hopefully. Groping about inside the nest I found that there were three other youngsters, each as revolting as the one I had in my hand. After some thought, and having examined each of them with care, I decided to take two and leave the other pair for the mother. This struck me as being quite fair, and I did not see how the mother could possibly object. I chose the largest (because he would grow up quickly) and the smallest (because he looked so pathetic), put them carefully inside my shirt, and climbed cautiously back to the waiting dogs. On being shown the new additions to the menagerie Widdle and Puke immediately decided that they must be edible, and tried to find out if their conclusion was correct. After I had reprimanded them, I showed the birds to Roger. He sniffed at them in his usual benign way, and then retreated hastily when the babies shot their heads up on long, scrawny necks, red mouths gaping wide, and wheezed lustily.

As I carried my new pets back homewards I tried to decide what to call them; I was still debating this problem when I reached the villa and found the family, who had just been on a shopping expedition into town, disgorging from the car. Holding out the babies in my cupped hands, I inquired if anyone could think of a suitable pair of names for them. The family took one look and all reacted in their individual ways.

'Aren't they *sweet*?' said Margo.

'What are you going to feed them on?' asked Mother.

'What revolting things!' said Leslie.

'Not *more* animals?' asked Larry with distaste.

'Gollys, Master Gerrys,' said Spiro, looking disgusted, 'whats thems?'

I replied, rather coldly, that they were baby magpies, that I hadn't asked anyone's opinion on them, but merely wanted some help in christening them. What should I call them?

But the family were not in a helpful mood.

'Fancy taking them away from their mother, poor little things,' said Margo.

'I hope they're old enough to eat, dear,' said Mother.

'Honest to gods! The things Master Gerrys *finds*,' said Spiro.

'You'll have to watch out they don't steal,' said Leslie.

'Steal?' said Larry in alarm. 'I thought that was jackdaws?'

'Magpies too,' said Leslie; 'awful thieves, magpies.'

Larry took a hundred drachma note from his pocket and waved it over the babies, and they immediately shot their heads skywards, necks wavering, mouths gaping, wheezing and bubbling frantically. Larry jumped back hastily.

'You're right, by God!' he exclaimed excitedly. 'Did you see that? They tried to attack me and get the money!'

'Don't be ridiculous, dear; they're only hungry,' said Mother.

'Nonsense, Mother . . . you saw them leap at me, didn't you? It's the money that did it . . . even at that age they have criminal instincts. He can't possibly keep them; it will be like living with Arsène Lupin. Go and put them back where you found them, Gerry.'

Innocently and untruthfully I explained that I couldn't do that, as the mother would desert them, and they would then starve to death. This, as I had anticipated, immediately got Mother and Margo on my side.

'We can't let the poor little things starve,' protested Margo.

'I don't see that it would do any harm to keep them,' said Mother.

'You'll regret it,' said Larry; 'it's asking for trouble. Every room in the house will be rifled. We'll have to bury all our valuables and post an armed guard over them. It's lunacy.'

'Don't be silly, dear,' said Mother soothingly. 'We can keep them in a cage and only let them out for exercise.'

'Exercise!' exclaimed Larry. 'I suppose you'll call it exercise when they're flapping round the house with hundred drachma notes in their filthy beaks.'

I promised faithfully that the magpies should not, in any circumstance, be allowed to steal. Larry gave me a withering look. I pointed out that the birds had still to be named, but nobody could think of anything suitable. We stood and stared at the quivering babies, but nothing suggested itself.

'Whats you goings to do with them bastards?' asked Spiro.

Somewhat acidly I said that I intended to keep them as pets, and that, furthermore, they were not bastards, but magpies.

'*Whats* you calls them?' asked Spiro, scowling.

'Magpies, Spiro, magpies,' said Mother, enunciating slowly and clearly.

Spiro turned this new addition to his English vocabulary over in his mind, repeating it to himself, getting it firmly embedded.

'Magenpies,' he said at last, 'magenpies, eh?'

'Magpies, Spiro,' corrected Margo.

'Thats what I says,' said Spiro indignantly, 'magenpies.'

So from that moment we gave up trying to find a name for them and they became known simply as the Magenpies.

By the time the Magenpies had gorged themselves to a size where they were fully fledged, Larry had become so used to seeing them around that he had forgotten their allegedly criminal habits. Fat, glossy and garrulous, squatting on top of their basket and flapping their wings vigorously, the Magenpies looked the very picture of innocence. All went well until they learnt to fly. The early stages consisted in leaping off the table on the veranda, flapping their wings frantically, and gliding down to crash on to the stone flags some fifteen feet away. Their courage grew with the strength of their wings, and before very long they accomplished their first real flight, a merry-go-round affair around the villa. They looked so lovely, their long tails glittering in the sun, their wings hissing as they swooped down to fly under the vine, that I called the family out to have a look at them. Aware of their audience, the Magenpies flew faster and faster, chasing each other, diving within inches of the wall before banking to one side, and doing acrobatics on the branches of the magnolia tree. Eventually one of them, made over-confident by our applause, misjudged his distance, crashed into the grape-vine and fell on to the veranda, no longer a bold, swerving ace of the air, but a woebegone bundle of feathers that opened its mouth and wheezed plaintively at me when I picked it up and soothed it. But, once having mastered their wings, the Magenpies quickly mapped out the villa and then they were all set for their banditry.

The kitchen, they knew, was an excellent place to visit, providing they stayed on the doorstep and did not venture inside; the drawing-room and dining-room they never entered if someone was there; of the bedrooms they knew that the only one in which they were assured of a warm welcome was mine. They would certainly fly into Mother's or Margo's, but they were constantly being told not to do things, and they found this boring. Leslie would allow them on to his window-sill but no farther, but they gave up visiting him after the day he let off a gun by accident. It unnerved them, and I think they had a vague idea that Leslie had made an attempt on their lives. But the bedroom that really intrigued and fascinated them was, of course, Larry's, and I think this was because they never managed to get a good look inside. Before they had even touched down on the window-sill they would be greeted with such roars of rage, followed by a rapidly discharged shower of missiles, that they would be forced to flap rapidly away to the safety of the magnolia tree. They could not understand Larry's attitude at all; they decided that – since he made such a fuss – it must be that he had something to hide, and that it was their duty to find out what it was. They chose their time carefully, waiting patiently until one afternoon Larry went off for a swim and left his window open.

I did not discover what the Magenpies had been up to until Larry came back; I had missed the birds, but thought they had flown down the hill to steal some grapes. They were obviously well aware that they were doing wrong, for though normally loquacious they carried out their raid in silence, and (according to Larry) took it in turns to do sentry duty on the window-sill. As he came up the hill he saw, to his horror, one of them sitting on the sill, and shouted wrathfully at it. The bird gave a chuck of alarm and the other one flew out of the room and joined it; they flapped off into the magnolia tree, chuckling hoarsely, like schoolboys caught raiding an orchard. Larry burst into the house, and swept up to his room, grabbing me *en route*. When he opened the door Larry uttered a moan like a soul in torment.

The Magenpies had been through the room as thoroughly as any Secret Service agent searching for missing plans. Piles of manuscript and typing paper lay scattered about the floor like drifts of autumn leaves, most of them with an attractive pattern of holes punched in them. The Magenpies never could resist paper. The typewriter stood stolidly on the table, looking like a disembowelled horse in a bull ring, its ribbon coiling out of its interior, its keys bespattered with droppings. The carpet, bed and table were a-glitter with a layer of paper clips like frost. The Magenpies, obviously suspecting Larry of being a dope smuggler, had fought valiantly with the tin of bicarbonate of soda, and had scattered its contents along a line of books, so that they looked like a snow-covered mountain range. The table, the floor, the manuscript, the bed and especially the pillow, were decorated with an artistic and unusual chain of footprints in green and red ink. It seemed almost as though each bird had overturned his favourite colour and walked in it. The bottle of blue ink, which would not have been so noticeable, was untouched.

'This is the last straw,' said Larry in a shaking voice, 'positively the last straw. Either you do something about those birds or I will personally wring their necks.'

I protested that he could hardly blame the Magenpies. They were interested in things, I explained; they couldn't help it, they were just made like that. All members of the crow tribe, I went on, warming to my defence work, were naturally curious. They didn't know they were doing wrong.

'I did not ask for a lecture on the crow tribe,' said Larry ominously, 'and I am not interested in the moral sense of magpies, either inherited or acquired. I am just telling you that you will have to either get rid of them or lock them up, otherwise I shall tear them wing from wing.'

The rest of the family, finding they could not siesta with the argument going on, assembled to find out the trouble.

'Good heavens! dear, what *have* you been doing?' asked Mother, peering round the wrecked room.

'Mother, I am in no mood to answer imbecile questions.'

'Must be the Magenpies,' said Leslie, with the relish of a prophet proved right. 'Anything missing?'

'No, nothing missing,' said Larry bitterly; 'they spared me that.'

'They've made an awful mess of your papers,' observed Margo.

Larry stared at her for a moment, breathing deeply.

'What a masterly understatement,' he said at last; 'you are always ready with the apt platitude to sum up a catastrophe. How I envy you your ability to be inarticulate in the face of Fate.'

'There's no need to be rude,' said Margo.

'Larry didn't mean it, dear,' explained Mother untruthfully; 'he's naturally upset.'

'Upset? *Upset*? Those scab-ridden vultures come flapping in here like a pair of critics and tear and be-spatter my manuscript before it's even finished, and you say I'm *upset*?'

'It's *very* annoying, dear,' said Mother, in an attempt to be vehement about the incident, 'but I'm sure they didn't mean it. After all, they don't understand . . . they're only birds.'

'Now don't you start,' said Larry fiercely. 'I've already been treated to a discourse on the sense of right and wrong in the crow tribe. It's disgusting the way this family carries on over animals; all this anthropomorphic slush that's drooled out as an excuse. Why don't you all become Magpie Worshippers, and erect a prison to pray in? The way *you* all carry on one would think that *I* was to blame, and that it's *my* fault that my room looks as though it's been plundered by Attila the Hun. Well, I'm telling you: if something isn't done about those birds right away, I shall deal with them myself.'

Larry looked so murderous that I decided it would probably be safer if the Magenpies were removed from danger, so I lured them into my bedroom with the aid of a raw egg and locked them up in their basket while I considered the best thing to do. It was obvious that they would have to go into a cage of sorts, but I wanted a really large one for them, and I did not feel that I could cope with the building of a really big aviary by myself. It was useless asking the family to help me, so I decided that I would have to inveigle Mr Kralefsky into the constructional work. He could come out and spend the day, and once the cage was finished he would have the opportunity of teaching me how to wrestle. I had waited a long time for a favourable opportunity of getting these wrestling lessons, and this seemed to me to be ideal. Mr Kralefsky's ability to wrestle was only one of his many hidden accomplishments, as I had found out.

Apart from his mother and his birds I had discovered that Kralefsky had one great interest in life, and that was an entirely imaginary world he had evoked in his mind, a world in which rich and strange adventures were always happening, adventures in which there were only two major characters: himself (as hero) and a member of the opposite sex who was generally known as a Lady. Finding that I appeared to believe the anecdotes he related to me, he got bolder and bolder, and day by day allowed me to enter a little further into his private paradise. It all started one morning when we were having a break for coffee and biscuits. The conversation somehow got on to dogs, and I confessed to an overwhelming desire to possess a bulldog – creatures that I found quite irresistibly ugly.

'By Jove, yes! Bulldogs!' said Kralefsky. 'Fine beasts, trustworthy and brave. One cannot say the same of *bull-terriers*, unfortunately.'

He sipped his coffee and glanced at me shyly; I sensed that I was expected to draw him out, so I asked why he thought bull-terriers particularly untrustworthy.

'Treacherous!' he explained, wiping his mouth. '*Most* treacherous.'

He leant back in his chair, closed his eyes and placed the tips of his fingers together, as if praying.

'I recall that once – many years ago when I was in England – I was instrumental in saving a lady's life when she was attacked by one of those brutes.'

He opened his eyes and peeped at me; seeing that I was all attention, he closed them again and continued:

'It was a fine morning in spring, and I was taking a constitutional in Hyde Park. Being so early, there was no one else about, and the park was silent except for the bird-songs. I had walked quite some distance when I suddenly became aware of a deep, powerful baying.'

His voice sank to a thrilling whisper and, with his eyes still closed, he cocked his head on one side as if listening. So realistic was it that I, too, felt I could hear the savage, regular barks echoing among the daffodils.

'I thought nothing of it at first. I supposed it to be some dog out enjoying itself chasing squirrels. Then, suddenly, I heard cries for help mingling with the ferocious baying.' He stiffened in his chair, frowned, and his nostrils quivered. 'I hurried through the trees, and suddenly came upon a terrible sight.'

He paused, and passed a hand over his brow, as though even now he could hardly bear to recall the scene.

'There, with her back to a tree, stood a Lady. Her skirt was torn and ripped, her legs bitten and bloody, and with a deckchair she was fending off a ravening bull-terrier. The brute, froth flecking its yawning mouth, leapt and snarled, waiting for an opening. It was obvious that the Lady's strength was ebbing. There was not a moment to be lost.'

Eyes still firmly closed, the better to see the vision, Kralefsky drew himself up in his chair, straightened his shoulders and fixed his features into an expression of sneering defiance, a devil-may-care expression – the expression of a man about to save a Lady from a bull-terrier.

'I raised my heavy walking-stick and leapt forward, giving a loud cry to encourage the Lady. The hound, attracted by my voice, immediately sprang at me, growling horribly, and I struck it such a blow on the head that my stick broke in half. The animal, though of course dazed, was still full of strength; I stood there, defenceless, as it gathered itself and launched itself at my throat with gaping jaws.'

Kralefsky's forehead had become quite moist during this recital, and he paused to take out his handkerchief and pat his brow with it. I asked eagerly what had happened then. Kralefsky reunited his finger-tips and went on.

'I did the only thing possible. It was a thousand-to-one chance, but I had to take it. As the beast leapt at my face I plunged my hand into his mouth, seized his tongue and twisted it as hard as I could. The teeth closed on my wrist, blood spurted out, but I hung on grimly, knowing my life was at stake. The dog lashed to and fro for what seemed like an age. I was exhausted. I felt I could not hold on any longer. Then, suddenly, the brute gave a convulsive heave and went limp. I had succeeded. The creature had been suffocated by its own tongue.'

I sighed rapturously. It was a wonderful story, and might well be true. Even if it wasn't true, it was the sort of thing that *should* happen, I felt; and I sympathized with Kralefsky if, finding that life had so far denied him a bull-terrier to strangle, he had supplied it himself. I said that I thought he had been very brave to tackle the dog in that way. Kralefsky opened his eyes, flushed with pleasure at my obvious enthusiasm and smiled deprecatingly.

'No, no, not really brave,' he corrected. 'The Lady was in distress, you see, and a gentleman could do nothing else. By Jove, no!'

Having found in me a willing and delighted listener, Kralefsky's confidence grew. He told me more and more of his adventures, and each became more thrilling than the last. I discovered that, by skilfully planting an idea in his mind one morning, I could be sure of an adventure dealing with it the following day, when his imagination had had a chance to weave a story. Enthralled, I heard how he, and a Lady, had been the sole survivors of a shipwreck on a voyage to Murmansk ('I had some business to attend to there'). For two weeks he and the Lady drifted on an iceberg, their clothes frozen, feeding on an occasional raw fish or sea-gull, until they were rescued. The ship that spotted them might easily have overlooked them if it had not been for Kralefsky's quick wit: he used the Lady's fur coat to light a signal fire.

I was enchanted with the story of the time he had been held up by bandits in the Syrian desert ('while taking a Lady to see some tombs'), and, when the ruffians threatened to carry his fair companion off and hold her to ransom, he offered to go in her place. But the bandits obviously thought the Lady would make a more attractive hostage, and refused. Kralefsky hated bloodshed, but, in the circumstances, what could a gentleman do? He killed all six of them with a knife he had concealed in his mosquito boot. During the first world war he had, naturally, been in the Secret Service. Disguised in a beard, he had been dropped behind the enemy lines to contact another English spy and obtain some plans. Not altogether to my surprise, the other spy turned out to be a Lady. Their escape (with the plans) from the firing squad was a masterpiece of ingenuity. Who but Kralefsky would have thought of breaking into the armoury, loading all the rifles with blanks, and then feigning death as the guns roared out?

I became so used to Kralefsky's extraordinary stories that on the rare occasions when he told me one that was faintly possible I generally believed it. This was his downfall. One day he told me a story of how, when he was a young man in Paris, he was walking along one evening and came across a great brute of a man ill-treating a Lady. Kralefsky, his gentlemanly instincts outraged, promptly hit the man on the head with his walking-stick. The man turned out to be the champion wrestler of France, and he immediately demanded that his honour be satisfied; Kralefsky agreed. The man suggested that they meet in the ring and wrestle it out; Kralefsky agreed. A date was fixed and Kralefsky started to go into training for the fight ('a vegetable diet and many exercises'), and when the great day came he had never felt fitter. Kralefsky's opponent – who, to judge from his description, bore a close resemblance, both in size and mentality, to Neanderthal Man – was surprised to find Kralefsky was a match for him. They struggled round the ring for an hour, neither succeeding in throwing the other. Then, suddenly, Kralefsky remembered a throw he had been taught by a Japanese friend of his. With a twist and a jerk he heaved his massive adversary up, twirled him round and hurled him right out of the ring. The unfortunate man was in hospital for three months, so badly was he hurt. As Kralefsky rightly pointed out, this was a just and fitting punishment for a cad who was so low as to raise his hand to a Lady.

Intrigued by this tale, I asked Kralefsky if he would teach me the rudiments of wrestling, as I felt it would be most useful to me should I ever come across a Lady in distress. Kralefsky seemed rather reluctant; perhaps at some later date, when we had plenty of room, he might show me a few throws, he said. He had forgotten the incident, but I had not, and so the day he came out to help me build the Magenpies their new home I determined to remind him of his promise. During tea I waited until there was a suitable pause in the conversation and then reminded Kralefsky of his famous fight with the French Champion Wrestler. Kralefsky was not at all pleased to be reminded of this exploit, it appeared. He turned pale, and shushed me hurriedly.

'One does not boast in public about such things,' he whispered hoarsely.

I was quite willing to respect his modesty, providing he gave me a wrestling lesson. I pointed out that all I wanted was to be shown a few of the more simple tricks.

'Well,' said Kralefsky, licking his lips, 'I suppose I can show you a few of the more *elementary* holds. But it takes a long time to become a proficient wrestler, you know.'

Delighted, I asked him if we should wrestle out on the veranda, where the family could watch us, or in the seclusion of the drawing-room? Kralefsky decided on the drawing-room. It was important not to be distracted, he said. So we went into the house and moved the furniture out of the way, and Kralefsky reluctantly took off his coat. He explained that the basic and most important principle of wrestling was to try to throw your opponent off balance. You could do this by seizing him round the waist and giving a quick sideways twitch. He demonstrated what he meant, catching me and throwing me gently on to the sofa.

'Now!' he said, holding up a finger, 'have you got the idea?'

I said yes, I thought I'd got the idea all right.

'That's the ticket!' said Kralefsky. 'Now you throw *me*.'

Determined to be a credit to my instructor, I threw him with great enthusiasm. I hurled myself across the room, seized him round the chest, squeezed as hard as I could to prevent his escape, and then flung him with a dextrous twist of my wrist towards the nearest chair. Unfortunately, I did not throw him hard enough, and he missed the chair altogether and crashed on to the floor, uttering a yell that brought the family rushing in from the veranda. We lifted the white-faced, groaning wrestling champion on to the couch, and Margo went to bring some brandy.

'What on earth did you *do* to him?' Mother asked.

I said that all I had done was to follow instructions. I'd been invited to throw him and I had thrown him. It was perfectly simple, and I didn't see that any blame could be attached to me.

'You don't know your own *strength*, dear,' said Mother; 'you should be more careful.'

'Damn silly thing to do,' said Leslie. 'Might have killed him.'

'I knew a man once who was crippled for life by a wrestling throw,' remarked Larry conversationally.

Kralefsky groaned more loudly.

'Really, Gerry, you do some very silly things,' said Mother, distraught, obviously with visions of Kralefsky being confined to a wheelchair for the rest of his days.

Irritated by what I considered to be quite unfair criticisms, I pointed out again that it was not my fault. I had been shown how to throw a person, and then invited to demonstrate. So I had thrown him.

'I'm sure he didn't mean you to lay him out like *that*,' said Larry; 'you might have damaged his spine. Like this fellow I knew, his spine was split like a banana. Very curious. He told me that bits of the bone were sticking out. . . .'

Kralefsky opened his eyes and gave Larry an anguished look.

'I wonder if I might have some water?' he said faintly.

At this moment Margo returned with the brandy, and we made Kralefsky take some. A little colour came into his cheeks again, and he lay back and closed his eyes once more.

'Well, you can sit up, and that's one good sign,' said Larry cheerfully; 'though I believe it's not really a trustworthy indication. I knew an artist who fell off a ladder and broke his back, and he was walking round for a week before they discovered it.'

'Good God, really?' asked Leslie, deeply interested. 'What happened to him?'

'He died,' said Larry.

Kralefsky raised himself into a sitting position and gave a wan smile.

'I think perhaps, if you would be kind enough to let Spiro drive me, it would be wiser if I went into town and consulted a doctor.'

'Yes, of course Spiro will take you,' said Mother. 'I should go along to Theodore's laboratory and get him to take an X-ray, just to put your mind at rest.'

So we wrapped Kralefsky, pale but composed, in quantities of rugs and placed him tenderly in the back of the car.

'Tell Theodore to send us a note with Spiro to let us know how you are,' said Mother. 'I do hope you'll soon be better. I'm really so sorry this had to happen; it was so very careless of Gerry.'

It was Kralefsky's big moment. He smiled a smile of pain-racked nonchalance and waved a hand feebly.

'Please, please don't distress yourself. Think nothing more about it,' he said. 'Don't blame the boy; it was not his fault. You see, I'm a *little* out of practice.'

Much later that evening Spiro returned from his errand of mercy, bearing a note from Theodore.

Dear Mrs Durrell,

    It appears from the X-ray photographs I have taken of Mr Kralefsky's *chest* that he has cracked two ribs: one of them, I'm sorry to say, quite severely. He was reticent as to the *cause* of the damage, but quite considerable force must have been employed. However, if he keeps them bound up for a week or so he should suffer no *permanent* injury.

With kindest regards to you all,
Yours,
Theodore.

P.S. I didn't by any chance leave a small black box at your house when I came out last Thursday, did I? It contains some very interesting Anopheles mosquitoes I had obtained, and it seems I must have mislaid it. Perhaps you would let me know?

Chapter Sixteen

The Lake of Lilies

The Magenpies were most indignant at their imprisonment, in spite of the large size of their quarters. Suffering from insatiable curiosity as they did, they found it most frustrating not to be able to investigate and comment on everything that happened. Their field of view was limited to the front of the house, and so if anything happened round the back they would go almost frantic, cackling and chucking indignantly as they flew round and round their cage, poking their heads through the wire in an effort to see what was going on. Confined as they were, they were able to devote a lot of time to their studies, which consisted of getting a solid grounding in the Greek and English language, and producing skilful imitations of natural sounds. Within a very short time they were able to call all members of the family by name, and they would, with extreme cunning, wait until Spiro had got into the car and coasted some distance down the hill, before rushing to the corner of their cage and screaming 'Spiro ... *Spiro* ... *Spiro* ...' making him cram on his brakes and return to the house to find out who was calling him. They would also derive a lot of innocent amusement by shouting 'Go away!' and 'Come here' in rapid succession, in both Greek and English, to the complete confusion of the dogs. Another trick, out of which they got endless pleasure, was deluding the poor unfortunate flock of chickens, which spent the day scratching hopefully round the olive-groves. Periodically the maid would come to the kitchen door and utter a series of piping noises, interspersed with strange hiccoughing cries, which the hens knew was a signal for food, and they would assemble at the backdoor like magic. As soon as the Magenpies had mastered the chicken-food call they worried the poor hens into a decline. They would wait until the most awkward time before using it; until the hens, with infinite effort and much squawking, had gone to roost in the smaller trees, or, in the heat of the day, when they had all settled down for a pleasant siesta in the shade of the myrtles. No sooner were they drowsing pleasantly than the Magenpies would start the food call, one doing the hiccoughs while the other did the piping. The hens would all glance nervously round, each waiting for one of the others to show signs of life. The Magenpies would call again, more seductively and urgently. Suddenly, one hen with less self-control than the rest would leap squawking to her feet and bounce towards the Magenpies' cage, and the rest, clucking and flapping, would follow her with all speed. They would rush up to the wire of the cage, barging and squawking, treading on each other's feet, pecking at each other, and then stand in a disorderly, panting crowd looking up into the cage where the Magenpies, sleek and elegant in their black and white suits, would stare down at them and chuckle, like a pair of city slickers that have successfully duped a crowd of bumbling and earnest villagers.

The Magenpies liked the dogs, although they seized every opportunity to tease them. They were particularly fond of Roger, and he would frequently go and call on them, lying down close to the wire netting, ears pricked, while the Magenpies sat on the ground inside the cage, three inches away from his nose, and talked to him in soft, wheezy chucks, with an occasional raucous guffaw, as though they were telling him dirty jokes. They never teased Roger as much as they teased the other two, and they never attempted to lure him close to the wire with soft blandishment so that they could flap down and pull his tail, as they frequently did with both Widdle and Puke. On the whole the Magenpies approved of dogs, but they liked them to look *and* behave like dogs; so, when Dodo made her appearance in our midst the Magenpies absolutely refused to believe that she was a dog, and treated her from the beginning with a sort of rowdy, jeering disdain.

Dodo was a breed known as a Dandy Dinmont. They look like long, fat, hair-covered balloons, with minute bow legs, enormous and protuberant eyes and long flopping ears. Strangely enough it was due to Mother that this curious misshapen breed of dog made its appearance among us. A friend of ours had a pair of these beasts which had suddenly (after years of barrenness) produced a litter of six puppies. The poor man was at his wits' end trying to find good homes for all these offspring, and so Mother, good-naturedly and unthinkingly, said she would have one. She set off one afternoon to choose her puppy and, rather unwisely, selected a female. At the time it did not strike her as imprudent to introduce a bitch into a household exclusively populated by very masculine dogs. So, clasping the puppy (like a dimly conscious sausage) under one arm, Mother climbed into the car and drove home in triumph to show the new addition to the family. The puppy, determined to make the occasion a memorable one, was violently and persistently sick from the moment she got in the car to the moment she got out. The family, assembled on the veranda, viewed Mother's prize as it waddled up the path towards them, eyes bulging, minute legs working frantically to keep the long, drooping body in motion, ears flapping wildly, pausing now and then to vomit into a flower-bed.

'Oh, isn't he *sweet*?' cried Margo.

'Good God! It looks like a sea-slug,' said Leslie.

'Mother! Really!' said Larry, contemplating Dodo with loathing, 'where did you dig up that canine Frankenstein?'

'Oh, but he's *sweet*,' repeated Margo. 'What's wrong with him?'

'It's not a him, it's a her,' said Mother, regarding her acquisition proudly; 'she's called Dodo.'

'Well, that's two things wrong with it for a start,' said Larry. 'It's a ghastly name for an animal, and to introduce a bitch into the house with those other three lechers about is asking for trouble. Apart from that, just look at it! Look at the shape! How did it get like that? Did it have an accident, or was it born like that?'

'Don't be silly, dear; it's the breed. They're *meant* to be like that.'

'Nonsense, mother; it's a monster. Who would want to deliberately produce a thing that shape?'

I pointed out that dachshunds were much the same shape, and they had been bred specially to enable them to get down holes after badgers. Probably the Dandy Dinmont had been bred for a similar reason.

'She looks as though she was bred to go down holes after sewage,' said Larry.

'Don't be disgusting, dear. They're very nice little dogs, and very faithful, apparently.'

'I should imagine they have to be faithful to anyone who shows interest in them: they can't possibly have many admirers in the world.'

'I think you're being very nasty about her, and, anyway, you're in no position to talk about beauty; it's only skin deep after all, and before you go throwing stones you should look for the beam in *your* eye,' said Margo triumphantly.

Larry looked puzzled.

'Is that a proverb, or a quotation from the *Builders' Gazette*?' he inquired.

'I think she means that it's an ill-wind that gathers no moss,' said Leslie.

'You make me sick,' said Margo, with dignified scorn.

'Well, join little Dodo in the flower-bed.'

'Now, now,' said Mother, 'don't argue about it. It's my dog and I like her, so that's all that matters.'

So Dodo settled in, and almost immediately showed faults in her make-up which caused us more trouble than all the other dogs put together. To begin with she had a weak hind-leg, and at any time during the day or night her hip joint was liable to come out of its socket, for no apparent reason. Dodo, who was no stoic, would greet this catastrophe with a series of piercing shrieks that worked up to a crescendo of such quivering intensity that it was unbearable. Strangely enough, her leg never seemed to worry her when she went for walks, or gambolled with elephantine enthusiasm after a ball on the veranda. But invariably in the evening when the family were all sitting quietly, absorbed in writing or reading or knitting, Dodo's leg would suddenly leap out of its socket, she would roll on her back and utter a scream that would make everybody jump and lose control of whatever they were doing. By the time we had massaged her leg back into place Dodo would have screamed herself to exhaustion, and immediately fall into a deep and peaceful sleep, while we would be so unnerved that we would be unable to concentrate on anything for the rest of the evening.

We soon discovered that Dodo had an extremely limited intelligence. There was only room for one idea at a time in her skull, and once it was there Dodo would retain it grimly in spite of all opposition. She decided quite early in her career that Mother belonged to her, but she was not over-possessive at first until one afternoon Mother went off to town to do some shopping and left Dodo behind. Convinced that she would never see Mother again, Dodo went into mourning and waddled, howling sorrowfully, round the house, occasionally being so overcome with grief that her leg would come out of joint. She greeted Mother's return with incredulous joy, but made up her mind from that moment she would not let Mother out of her sight, for fear she escaped again. So she attached herself to Mother with the tenacity of a limpet, never moving more than a couple of feet away at the most. If Mother sat down, Dodo would lie at her feet; if Mother had to get up and cross the room for a book or a cigarette, Dodo would accompany her, and then they would return together and sit down again, Dodo giving a deep sigh of satisfaction at the thought that once more she had foiled Mother's attempts at escape. She even insisted in being present when Mother had a bath, sitting dolefully by the tub and staring at Mother with embarrassing intensity. Any attempts to leave her outside the bathroom door resulted in Dodo howling madly and hurling herself at the door-panels, which almost invariably resulted in her hip slipping out of its socket. She seemed to be under the impression that it was not safe to let Mother go alone into the bathroom, even if she stood guard over the door. There was always the possibility, she seemed to think, that Mother might give her the slip by crawling down the plug-hole.

At first Dodo was regarded with tolerant scorn by Roger, Widdle and Puke; they did not think much of her, for she was too fat and too low slung to walk far, and if they made any attempts to play with her it seemed to bring on an attack of persecution mania, and Dodo would gallop back to the house, howling for protection. Taken all round they were inclined to consider her a boring and useless addition to the household, until they discovered that she had one superlative and overwhelmingly delightful characteristic: she came into season with monotonous regularity. Dodo herself displayed an innocence about the facts of life that was rather touching. She seemed not only puzzled but positively scared at her sudden bursts of popularity, when her admirers arrived in such numbers that Mother had to go about armed with a massive stick. It was owing to this Victorian innocence that Dodo fell an easy victim to the lure of Puke's magnificent ginger eyebrows, and so met a fate worse than death when Mother inadvertently locked them in the drawing-room together while she supervised the making of tea. The sudden and unexpected arrival of the English padre and his wife, ushering them into the room in which the happy couple were disporting themselves, and the subsequent efforts to maintain a normal conversation, left Mother feeling limp, and with a raging headache.

To everyone's surprise (including Dodo's) a puppy was born of this union, a strange, mewling blob of a creature with its mother's figure and its father's unusual liver-and-white markings. To suddenly become a mother like that, Dodo found, was very demoralizing, and she almost had a nervous breakdown, for she was torn between the desire to stay in one spot with her puppy and the urge to keep as close to Mother as possible. We were, however, unaware of this psychological turmoil. Eventually Dodo decided to compromise, so she followed Mother around and carried the puppy in her mouth. She had spent a whole morning doing this before we discovered what she was up to; the unfortunate baby hung from her mouth by its head, its body swinging to and fro as Dodo waddled along at Mother's heels. Scolding and pleading having no effect, Mother was forced to confine herself to the bedroom with Dodo and her puppy, and we carried their meals up on a tray. Even this was not altogether successful, for if Mother moved out of the chair, Dodo, ever alert, would seize her puppy and sit there regarding Mother with starting eyes, ready to give chase if necessary.

'If this goes on much longer that puppy'll grow into a giraffe,' observed Leslie.

'I know, poor little thing,' said Mother; 'but what can I *do*? She picks it up if she sees me lighting a cigarette.'

'Simplest thing would be to drown it,' said Larry. 'It's going to grow into the most horrifying animal, anyway. Look at its parents.'

'No, indeed you won't drown it!' exclaimed Mother indignantly.

'Don't be *horrible*,' said Margo; 'the poor little thing.'

'Well, I think it's a perfectly ridiculous situation, allowing yourself to be chained to a chair by a dog.'

'It's my dog, and if I want to sit here I *shall*,' said Mother firmly.

'But for how long? This might go on for months.'

'I shall think of something,' said Mother with dignity.

The solution to the problem that Mother eventually thought of was simple. She hired the maid's youngest daughter to carry the puppy for Dodo. This arrangement seemed to satisfy Dodo very well, and once more Mother was able to move about the house. She pottered from room to room like some Eastern potentate, Dodo pattering at her heels, and young Sophia bringing up the end of the line, tongue protruding and eyes squinting with the effort, bearing in her arms a large cushion on which reposed Dodo's strange offspring. When Mother was going to be in one spot for any length of time Sophia would place the cushion reverently on the ground, and Dodo would surge on to it and sigh deeply. As soon as Mother was ready to go to another part of the house, Dodo would get off her cushion, shake herself and take up her position in the cavalcade, while Sophia lifted the cushion aloft as though it carried a crown. Mother would peer over her spectacles to make sure the column was ready, give a little nod, and they would wind their way off to the next job.

Every morning Mother would go for a walk with the dogs, and the family would derive much amusement from watching her progress down the hill. Roger, as senior dog, would lead the procession, followed by Widdle and

Puke. Then came Mother, wearing an enormous straw hat, which made her look like an animated mushroom, clutching in one hand a large trowel with which to dig any interesting wild plants she found. Dodo would waddle behind, eyes protruding and tongue flapping, and Sophia would bring up the rear, pacing along solemnly, carrying the imperial puppy on its cushion. Mother's Circus, Larry called it, and would irritate her by bellowing out of the window:

'Oi! Lady, wot time does the big top go up, hay?'

He purchased a bottle of hair restorer for her so that, as he explained, she could conduct experiments on Sophia and try to turn her into a bearded lady.

'That's wot your show *needs*, lady,' he assured her in a hoarse voice – 'a bit of clarse, see? Nothing like a bearded lady for bringin' a bit o' clarse to a show.'

But in spite of all this Mother continued to lead her strange caravan off into the olive-groves at five o'clock every evening.

Up in the north of the island lay a large lake with the pleasant, jingling name of Antiniotissa, and this place was one of our favourite haunts. It was about a mile long, an elongated sheet of shallow water surrounded by a thick mane of cane and reed, and separated from the sea at one end by a wide, gently curving dune of fine white sand. Theodore always accompanied us when we paid our visits to the lake, for he and I would find a rich field of exploration in the ponds, ditches and marshy pot-holes that lay around the shore of the lake. Leslie invariably took a battery of guns with him, since the cane forest rustled with game, while Larry insisted on taking an enormous harpoon, and would stand for hours in the stream that marked the lake's entry into the sea, endeavouring to spear the large fish that swam there. Mother would be laden with baskets full of food, empty baskets for plants, and various gardening implements for digging up her finds. Margo was perhaps the most simply equipped, with a bathing-costume, a large towel and a bottle of sun-tan lotion. With all this equipment our trips to Antiniotissa were something in the nature of major expeditions.

There was, however, a certain time of the year when the lake was at its best, and that was the season of lilies. The smooth curve of the dune that ran between the bay and the lake was the only place on the island where these sand lilies grew, strange, misshapen bulbs buried in the sand, that once a year sent up thick green leaves and white flowers above the surface, so that the dune became a glacier of flowers. We always visited the lake at this time, for the experience was a memorable one. Not long after Dodo had become a mother, Theodore informed us that the time of the lilies was at hand, and we started to make preparations for our trip to Antiniotissa. We soon found that having a nursing mother in our midst was going to complicate matters considerably.

'We'll have to go by boat this time,' Mother said, frowning at a complicated, jigsaw-like jersey she was knitting.

'Why, by boat it takes twice as long,' said Larry.

'We can't go by car, dear, because Dodo will be sick, and anyway there wouldn't be room for all of us.'

'You're *not* going to take that animal, are you?' asked Larry in horror.

'But I have to, dear . . . purl two, cast off one. . . . I can't leave her behind . . . purl three . . . you know what she's like.'

'Well, hire a special car for her then. I'm damned if I'm going to drive about the countryside looking as though I've just burgled Battersea Dogs' Home.'

'She can't travel by car. That's what I'm explaining to you. You know she gets car-sick. . . . Now be quiet a minute, dear, I'm counting.'

'It's ridiculous . . .' began Larry exasperatedly.

'Seventeen, eighteen, *nineteen, twenty*,' said Mother loudly and fiercely.

'It's ridiculous that we should have to go the longest way round just because Dodo vomits every time she sees a car.'

'There!' said Mother irritably, 'you've made me lose count. I do wish you wouldn't argue with me when I'm knitting.'

'How d'you know she won't be sea-sick?' inquired Leslie interestedly.

'People who are car-sick are never sea-sick,' explained Mother.

'I don't believe it,' said Larry. 'That's an old wives' tale, isn't it, Theodore?'

'Well, I wouldn't like to say,' said Theodore judicially. 'I have heard it before, but whether there's any . . . um . . . you know . . . any *truth* in it, I can't say. All I know is that I have, so far, not felt sick in a car.'

Larry looked at him blankly. 'What does that prove?' he asked, bewildered.

'Well, I am always sick in a boat,' explained Theodore simply.

'That's wonderful!' said Larry. 'If we travel by car Dodo will be sick, and if we travel by boat Theodore will. Take your choice.'

'I didn't know you got sea-sick, Theodore,' said Mother.

'Oh, yes, unfortunately I do. I find it a great drawback.'

'Well, in weather like this the sea will be very calm, so I should think you'll be all right,' said Margo.

'Unfortunately,' said Theodore, rocking on his toes, 'that does not make any difference at all. I suffer from the . . . er . . . *slightest* motion. In fact on several occasions when I have been in the cinema and they have shown films of ships in rough seas I have been forced to . . . um . . . forced to leave my seat.'

'Simplest thing would be to divide up,' said Leslie; 'half go by boat and the other half go by car.'

'That's a brain-wave!' said Mother. 'The problem is solved.'

But it did not settle the problem at all, for we discovered that the road to Antiniotissa was blocked by a minor landslide, and so to get there by car was impossible. We would have to go by sea or not at all.

We set off in a warm pearly dawn that foretold a breathlessly warm day and a calm sea. In order to cope with the family, the dogs, Spiro and Sophia, we had to take the *Bootle-Bumtrinket* as well as the *Sea Cow*. Having to trail the *Bootle-Bumtrinket*'s rotund shape behind her cut down on the *Sea Cow*'s speed, but it was the only way to do it. At Larry's suggestion the dogs, Sophia, Mother and Theodore travelled in the *Bootle-Bumtrinket* while the rest of us piled into the *Sea Cow*. Unfortunately Larry had not taken into consideration one important factor: the wash caused by *Sea Cow*'s passage. The wave curved like a wall of blue glass from her stern and reached its maximum height just as it struck the broad breast of the *Bootle-Bumtrinket*, lifting her up into the air and dropping her down again with a thump. We did not notice the effect the wash was having for some considerable time, for the noise of the engine drowned the frantic cries for help from Mother. When we eventually stopped and let the *Bootle-Bumtrinket* bounce up to us, we found that not only were both Theodore and Dodo ill, but everyone else was as well, including such a hardened and experienced sailor as Roger. We had to get them all into the *Sea Cow* and lay them out in a row, and Spiro, Larry, Margo and myself took up their positions in the *Bootle-Bumtrinket*. By the time we were nearing Antiniotissa everyone was feeling better, with the exception of Theodore, who still kept as close to the side of the boat as possible, staring hard at his boots and answering questions monosyllabically. We rounded the last headland of red and gold rocks, lying in wavy layers like piles of gigantic fossilized newspapers, or the rusty and mould-covered wreckage of a colossus's library, and the *Sea Cow* and the *Bootle-Bumtrinket* turned into the wide blue bay that lay at the mouth of the lake. The curve of pearl-white sand was backed by the great lily-covered dune behind, a thousand white flowers in the sunshine like a multitude of ivory horns lifting their lips to the sky and producing, instead of music, a rich, heavy scent that was the distilled essence of summer, a warm sweetness that made you breathe deeply time and again in an effort to retain it within you. The engine died away in a final splutter that echoed briefly among the rocks, and then the two boats whispered their way shorewards, and the scent of the lilies came out over the water to greet us.

Having got the equipment ashore and installed it on the white sand, we each wandered off about our own business. Larry and Margo lay in the shallow water half asleep, being rocked by the faint, gentle ripples. Mother led her cavalcade off on a short walk, armed with a trowel and a basket. Spiro, clad only in his underpants and looking like some dark hairy prehistoric man, waddled into the stream that flowed from the lake to the sea and stood knee deep, scowling down into the transparent waters, a trident held at the ready as the shoals of fish flicked around his feet. Theodore and I drew lots with Leslie as to which side of the lake we should have, and then set off in opposite directions. The boundary marking the half-way mark on the lake-shore was a large and particularly misshapen olive. Once we reached there we would turn back and retrace our footsteps, and Leslie would do the same on his side. This cut out the possibility of his shooting us, by mistake, in some dense and confusing cane brake. So, while Theodore and I dipped and pottered among the pools and streamlets, like a pair of eager herons, Leslie strode stockily through the undergrowth on the other side of the lake, and an occasional explosion would echo across to us to mark his progress.

Lunch-time came and we assembled hungrily on the beach, Leslie with a bulging bag of game, hares damp with blood, partridge and quail, snipe and wood pigeons; Theodore and I with our test-tubes and bottles a-shimmer with small life. A fire blazed, the food was piled on the rugs, and the wine fetched from the sea's edge where it had been put to cool. Larry pulled his corner of the rug up the dune so that he could stretch full-length surrounded by the white trumpets of the lilies. Theodore sat upright and neat, his beard wagging as he chewed his food slowly and methodically. Margo sprawled elegantly in the sun, picking daintily at a pile of fruit and vegetables. Mother and Dodo were installed in the shade of a large umbrella. Leslie squatted on his haunches in the sand, his gun across his thighs, eating a huge hunk of cold meat with one hand and stroking the barrels of the weapon meditatively with the other. Nearby Spiro crouched by the fire, sweat running down his furrowed face and dropping in gleaming drops into the thick pelt of black hair of his chest, as he turned an improvised olive-wood spit, with seven fat snipe on it, over the flames.

'What a heavenly place!' mumbled Larry through a mouthful of food, lying back luxuriously among the shining flowers. 'I feel this place was designed for me. I should like to lie here forever, having food and wine pressed into my mouth by groups of naked and voluptuous dryads. Eventually, of course, over the centuries, by breathing deeply and evenly I should embalm myself with this scent, and then one day my faithful dryads would find me gone, and only the scent would remain. Will someone throw me one of those *delicious*-looking figs?'

'I read a most interesting book on embalming once,' said Theodore enthusiastically. 'They certainly seemed to go to a great deal of trouble to prepare the bodies in Egypt. I must say I thought the method of . . . er . . . extracting the brain through the nose was *most* ingenious.'

'Dragged them down through the nostrils with a sort of hook arrangement, didn't they?' inquired Larry.

'Larry, dear, not while we're *eating*.'

Lunch being over we drifted into the shade of the nearby olives and drowsed sleepily through the heat of the afternoon, while the sharp, soothing song of the cicadas poured over us. Occasionally one or other of us would rise, wander down to the sea and flop into the shallows for a minute before coming back, cooled, to resume his siesta. At four o'clock Spiro, who had been stretched out massive and limp, bubbling with snores, regained consciousness with a snort and waddled down the beach to relight the fire for tea. The rest of us awoke slowly, dreamily, stretching and sighing, and drifted down over the sand towards the steaming, chattering kettle. As we crouched with the cups in our hands, blinking and musing, still half asleep, a robin appeared among the lilies and hopped down towards us, his breast glowing, his eyes bright. He paused some ten feet away and surveyed us critically. Deciding that we needed some entertainment, he hopped to where a pair of lilies formed a beautiful arch, posed beneath them theatrically, puffed out his chest and piped a liquid, warbling song. When he had finished he suddenly ducked his head in what appeared to be a ludicrously conceited bow, and then flipped off through the lilies, frightened by our burst of laughter.

'They *are* dear little things, robins,' said Mother. 'There was one in England that used to spend hours by me when I was gardening. I love the way they puff up their little chests.'

'The way that one bobbed looked exactly as if he was bowing,' said Theodore. 'I must say when he . . er . . . puffed up his chest he looked very like a rather . . . you know . . . a rather *outsize* opera singer.'

'Yes, singing something rather frothy and light. . . . Strauss, I should think,' agreed Larry.

'Talking of operas,' said Theodore, his eyes gleaming, 'did I ever tell you about the last opera we had in Corfu?'

We said no, he hadn't told us, and settled ourselves comfortably, getting almost as much amusement from the sight of Theodore telling the story as from the story itself.

'It was ... um ... one of those travelling opera companies, you know. I think it came from Athens, but it may have been Italy. Anyway, their first performance was to be *Tosca*. The singer who took the part of the heroine was exceptionally ... er ... *well developed*, as they always seem to be. Well, as you know, in the final act of the opera the heroine casts herself to her doom from the battlements of a fortress – or, rather, a *castle*. On the first night the heroine climbed up on to the castle walls, sang her final song and then cast herself to her ... you know ... her *doom* on the rocks below. Unfortunately it seems that the stage hands had forgotten to put anything beneath the walls for her to *land* on. The result was that the crash of her landing and her subsequent ... er ... yells of pain detracted somewhat from the impression that she was a shattered corpse on the rocks far below. The singer who was just bewailing the fact that she was dead had to sing quite ... er ... quite *powerfully* in order to drown her cries. The heroine was, rather naturally, somewhat upset by the incident, and so the following night the stage hands threw themselves with enthusiasm into the job of giving her a pleasant landing. The heroine, somewhat battered, managed to hobble her way through the opera until she reached the ... er ... final scene. Then she again climbed on to the battlements, sang her last song and cast herself to her death. Unfortunately the stage hands, having made the landing *too* hard on the first occasion, had gone to the opposite extreme. The huge pile of mattresses and ... er ... you know, those springy bed things, was so *resilient* that the heroine hit them and then bounced up again. So while the cast was down at the ... er ... what d'you call them? ... ah, yes, the *footlights*, telling each other she was dead, the upper portions of the heroine reappeared two or three times above the battlements, to the mystification of the audience.'

The robin, who had hopped nearer during the telling of the story, took fright and flew off again at our burst of laughter.

'Really, Theodore, I'm sure you spend your spare time making up these stories,' protested Larry.

'No, no,' said Theodore, smiling happily in his beard; 'If it were anywhere else in the world I would have to, but here in Corfu they ... er ... anticipate art, as it were.'

Tea over, Theodore and I returned to the lake's edge once more and continued our investigation until it grew too shadowy to see properly; then we walked slowly back to the beach, where the fire Spiro had built pulsed and glowed like an enormous chrysanthemum among the ghostly white lilies. Spiro, having speared three large fish, was roasting them on a grid, absorbed and scowling, putting now a flake of garlic, now a squeeze of lemon-juice or a sprinkle of pepper on the delicate white flesh that showed through where the charred skin was starting to peel off. The moon rose above the mountains, turned the lilies to silver except where the flickering flames illuminated them with a flush of pink. The tiny ripples sped over the moonlit sea and breathed with relief as they reached the shore at last. Owls started to chime in the trees, and in the gloomy shadows fireflies gleamed as they flew, their jade-green, misty lights pulsing on and off.

Eventually, yawning and stretching, we carried out things down to the boats. We rowed out to the mouth of the bay, and then in the pause while Leslie fiddled with the engine, we looked back at Antiniotissa. The lilies were like a snow-field under the moon, and the dark backcloth of olives was pricked with the lights of fireflies. The fire we had built, stamped and ground underfoot before we left, glowed like a patch of garnets at the edge of the flowers.

'It is certainly a very ... er ... *beautiful* place,' said Theodore with immense satisfaction.

'It's a glorious place,' agreed Mother, and then gave it her highest accolade, 'I should like to be buried there.'

The engine stuttered uncertainly, then broke into a deep roar; the *Sea Cow* gathered speed and headed along the coastline, trailing the *Bootle-Bumtrinket* behind, and beyond that our wash fanned out, white and delicate as a spider's web on the dark water, flaming here and there with a momentary spark of phosphorescence.

Chapter Seventeen

The Chessboard Fields

Below the villa, between the line of hills on which it stood and the sea, were the Chessboard Fields. The sea curved into the coast in a great, almost landlocked bay, shallow and bright, and on the flat land along its edges lay the intricate pattern of narrow waterways that had once been salt pans in the Venetian days. Each neat little patch of earth, framed with canals, was richly cultivated and green with crops of maize, potatoes, figs and grapes. These fields, small coloured squares edged with shining waters, lay like a sprawling, multi-coloured chessboard on which the peasants' coloured figures moved from place to place.

This was one of my favourite areas for hunting in, for the tiny waterways and the lush undergrowth harboured a multitude of creatures. It was easy to get lost there, for if you were enthusiastically chasing a butterfly and crossed the wrong little wooden bridge from one island to the next you could find yourself wandering to and fro, trying to get your bearings in a bewildering maze of fig-trees, reeds and curtains of tall maize. Most of the fields belonged to friends of mine, peasant families who lived up in the hills, and so when I was walking there I was always sure of being able to rest and gossip over a bunch of grapes with some acquaintance, or to receive interesting items of news, such as the fact that there was a lark's nest under the melon-plants on Georgio's land. If you walked straight across the chessboard without being distracted by friends, side-tracked by terrapins sliding down the mud banks and plopping into the water, or the sudden crackling buzz of a dragon-fly swooping past, you eventually came to the spot where all the channels widened and vanished into a great flat acreage of sand, moulded into endless neat pleats by the previous night's tides. Here long winding chains of flotsam marked the sea's slow retreat, fascinating chains full of coloured seaweed, dead pipe-fish, fishing-net corks that looked good enough to eat – like lumps of rich fruit cake – bits of bottle-glass emeried and carved into translucent jewels by the tide and the sand, shells as spiky as hedgehogs, others smooth, oval and delicate pink, like the finger-nails of some drowned goddess. This was the sea-birds' country: snipe, oyster-catcher, dunlin and terns strewn in small pattering groups at the edge of the sea, where the long ripples ran towards the land and broke in long curving ruffs round the little humps of sand. Here, if you felt hungry, you could wade out into the shallows and catch fat, transparent shrimps that tasted as sweet as grapes when eaten raw, or you could dig down with your toes until you found the ribbed, nut-like cockles. Two of these, placed end to end, hinge to hinge, and then twisted sharply in opposite directions, opened each other neatly; the contents, though slightly rubbery, were milky and delicious to eat.

One afternoon, having nothing better to do, I decided to take the dogs and visit the fields. I would make yet another attempt to catch Old Plop, cut across to the sea for a feed of cockles and a swim, and make my way home via Petro's land so that I could sit and exchange gossip with him over a water-melon or a few plump pomegranates. Old Plop was a large and ancient terrapin that lived on one of the canals. I had been trying to capture him for a month or more, but in spite of his age he was very wily and quick, and no matter how cautiously I stalked him when he lay asleep on the muddy bank, he would always wake up at the crucial moment, his legs would flail frantically, and he would slide down the mud slope and plop into the water like a corpulent life-boat being launched. I had caught a great many terrapins, of course, both the black ones with the thick freckling of golden pin-head spots on them, and the slim grey ones with fawny-cream lines; but Old Plop was something I had set my heart on. He was bigger than any terrapin I had seen, and so old that his battered shell and wrinkled skin had become completely black, losing any markings they may have had in his distant youth. I was determined to possess him, and as I had left him alone for a whole week I thought it was high time to launch another attack.

With my bag of bottles and boxes, my net and a basket to put Old Plop in should I catch him, I set off down the hill with the dogs. The Magenpies called 'Gerry! ... Gerry! ... *Gerry* ...' after me in tones of agonized entreaty, and then, finding I did not turn, they fell to jeering and cackling and making rude noises. Their harsh voices faded as we entered the olive-groves, and were then obliterated by the choir of cicadas whose song made the air tremble. We made our way along the road, hot, white and as soft as a powder-puff underfoot. I paused at Yani's well for a drink, and then leant over the rough sty made from olive branches in which the two pigs lived, wallowing with sonorous content in a sea of glutinous mud. Having sniffed deeply and appreciatively at them, and slapped the largest on his grubby, quivering behind, I continued down the road. At the next bend I had a brisk argument with two fat peasant ladies, balancing baskets of fruit on their heads, who were wildly indignant at Widdle. He had crept up on them when they were engrossed in conversation and after sniffing at them had lived up to his name over their skirts and legs. The argument as to whose fault it was kept all of us happily occupied for ten minutes, and was then continued as I walked on down the road, until we were separated by such a distance that we could no longer hear and appreciate each other's insults.

Cutting across the first three fields, I paused for a moment in Taki's patch to sample his grapes. He wasn't there, but I knew he wouldn't mind. The grapes were the small fat variety, with a sweet, musky flavour. When you squeezed them the entire contents, soft and seedless, shot into your mouth, leaving the flaccid skin between your finger and thumb. The dogs and I ate four bunches and I put another two bunches in my collecting bag for future reference, after which we followed the edge of the canal towards the place where Old Plop had his favourite mud slide. As we were drawing near to this spot, I was just about to caution the dogs on the need for absolute silence, when a large green lizard flashed out of a corn-patch and scuttled away. The dogs, barking wildly, galloped in eager pursuit. By the time I reached Old Plop's mud slide there was only a series of gently expanding ripples on the water to tell me that he had been present. I sat down and waited for the dogs to rejoin me, running through in my mind the rich and colourful insults with which I would bombard them. But to my surprise they did not come back. Their yelping in the distance died away, there was a pause, and then they started to bark in a chorus – monotonous, evenly spaced barks that meant they had found something. Wondering what it could be I hurried after them.

They were clustered in a half-circle round a clump of grass at the water's edge, and came gambolling to meet me, tails thrashing, whining with excitement, Roger lifting his upper lip in a pleased grin that I had come to examine their find. At first I could not see what it was they were so excited over; then what I had taken to be a rootlet moved, and I was looking at a pair of fat brown water-snakes, coiled passionately together in the grass, regarding me with impersonal silvery eyes from their spade-shaped heads. This was a thrilling find, and one that almost compensated for the loss of Old Plop. I had long wanted to catch one of these snakes, but they were such fast and skilful swimmers that I had never succeeded in getting close enough to accomplish a capture. Now the dogs had found this fine pair, lying in the sun – there for the taking, as it were.

The dogs, having done their duty by finding these creatures and leading me to them, now retreated to a safe distance (for they did not trust reptiles) and sat watching me interestedly. Slowly I manoeuvred my butterfly net round until I could unscrew the handle; having done this, I had a stick with which to do the catching, but the problem was *how* to catch two snakes with one stick? While I was working this out, one of them decided the thing for me, uncoiling himself unhurriedly and sliding into the water as cleanly as a knife-blade. Thinking that I had lost him, I watched irritably as his undulating length merged with the water reflection. Then, to my delight, I saw a column of mud rise slowly through the water and expand like a rose on the surface; the reptile had buried himself at the bottom, and I knew he would stay there until he thought I had gone. I turned my attention to his mate, pressing her down in the lush grass with the stick; she twisted herself into a complicated knot, and opening her pink mouth, hissed at me. I grabbed her firmly round the neck between finger and thumb, and she hung limp in my hand while I stroked her handsome white belly, and the brown back where the scales were raised slightly like the surface of a fir-cone. I put her tenderly into the basket, and then prepared to capture the other one. I walked a little way down the bank and stuck the handle of the net into the canal to test the depth, and discovered that about two feet of water lay on a three-foot bed of soft, quivering mud. Since the water was opaque, and the snake was buried in the bottom slush, I thought the simplest method would be to feel for him with my toes (as I did when searching for cockles) and, having located him, to make a quick pounce.

I took off my sandles and lowered myself into the warm water, feeling the liquid mud squeeze up between my toes and stroke up my legs, as soft as ashes. Two great black clouds bloomed about my thighs and drifted across the channel. I made my way towards the spot where my quarry lay hidden, moving my feet slowly and carefully in the shifting curtain of mud. Suddenly, under my foot, I felt the slithering body, and I plunged my arms elbow-deep into the water and grabbed. My fingers closed only on mud which oozed between them and drifted away in turbulent, slow-motion clouds. I was just cursing my ill-luck when the snake shot to the surface a yard away from me, and started to swim sinuously along the surface. With a yell of triumph I flung myself full length on top of him.

There was a confused moment as I sank beneath the dark waters and the silt boiled up into my eyes, ears and mouth, but I could feel the reptile's body thrashing wildly to and fro, firmly clasped in my left hand, and I glowed with triumph. Gasping and spluttering under my layer of mud, I sat up in the canal and grabbed the snake round the neck before he could recover his wits and bite me; then I spat for a long time, to rid my teeth and lips of the fine, gritty layer which coated them. When I at last rose to my feet and turned to wade ashore I found to my surprise that my audience of dogs had been enlarged by the silent arrival of a man, who was squatting comfortably on his haunches and watching me with a mixture of interest and amusement.

He was a short, stocky individual whose brown face was topped by a thatch of close-cropped fair hair, the colour of tobacco. He had large, very blue eyes that had a pleasant humorous twinkle in them, and crow's feet in the fine skin at the corners. A short, hawk's-beak nose curved over a wide and humorous mouth. He was wearing a blue cotton shirt that was bleached and faded to the colour of a forget-me-not dried by the sun, and old grey flannel trousers. I did not recognize him, and supposed him to be a fisherman from some village farther down the coast. He regarded me gravely as I scrambled up the bank, and then smiled.

'Your health,' he said in a rich, deep voice.

I returned his greeting politely, and then busied myself with the job of trying to get the second snake into the basket without letting the first one escape. I expected him to deliver a lecture to me on the deadliness of the harmless water-snakes and the dangers I ran by handling them, but to my surprise he remained silent, watching with interest while I pushed the writhing reptile into the basket. This done, I washed my hands and produced the grapes I had filched from Taki's fields. The man accepted half the fruit and we sat without talking, sucking the pulp from the grapes with noisy enjoyment. When the last skin had plopped into the canal, the man produced tobacco and rolled a cigarette between his blunt, brown fingers.

'You are a stranger?' he asked, inhaling deeply and with immense satisfaction.

I said that I was English, and that I and my family lived in a villa up in the hills. Then I waited for the inevitable questions as to the sex, number and age of my family, their work and aspirations, followed by a skilful cross-examination as to why we lived in Corfu. This was the usual peasant way; it was not done unpleasantly, nor with any motive other than friendly interest. They would vouchsafe their own private business to you with great simplicity and frankness, and would be hurt if you did not do the same. But, to my surprise, the man seemed satisfied with my answer, and asked nothing further, but sat there blowing fine streamers of smoke into the sky and staring about him with dreamy blue eyes. With my finger-nail I scraped an attractive pattern in the hardening carapace of grey mud on my thigh, and decided that I would have to go down to the sea and wash both myself and my clothes before returning home. I got to my feet and shouldered my bag and nets; the dogs got to their feet, shook themselves and yawned. More out of politeness than anything, I asked the man where he was going. It was, after all, peasant etiquette to ask questions. It showed your interest in the person. So far I hadn't asked him anything at all.

'I'm going down to the sea,' he said, gesturing with his cigarette – 'down to my boat. . . . Where are you going?'

I said I was making for the sea too, first to wash and secondly to find some cockles to eat.

'I will walk with you,' he said, rising and stretching. 'I have a basketful of cockles in my boat; you may have some of those if you like.'

We walked through the fields in silence, and when we came out on to the sands he pointed at the distant shape of a rowing-boat, lying comfortably on her side, with a frilly skirt of ripples round her stern. As we walked towards her I asked if he was a fisherman, and if so, where he came from.

'I come from here . . . from the hills,' he replied – 'at least, my home is here, but I am at Vido.'

The reply puzzled me, for Vido was a tiny islet lying off the town of Corfu, and as far as I knew it had no one on it at all except convicts and warders, for it was the local prison island. I pointed this out to him.

'That's right,' he agreed, stooping to pat Roger as he ambled past, 'that's right. I'm a convict.'

I thought he was joking, and glanced at him sharply, but his expression was quite serious. I said I presumed he had just been let out.

'No, no, worse luck,' he smiled. 'I have another two years to do. But I'm a good prisoner, you see. Trustworthy and make no trouble. Any like me, those they feel they can trust, are allowed to make boats and sail home for the week-end, if it's not too far. I've got to be back there first thing Monday morning.'

Once the thing was explained, of course, it was simple. It never even occurred to me that the procedure was unusual. I knew one wasn't allowed home for week-ends from an English prison, but this was Corfu, and in Corfu anything could happen. I was bursting with curiosity to know what his crime had been, and I was just phrasing a tactful inquiry in my mind when we reached the boat, and inside it was something that drove all other thoughts from my head. In the stern, tethered to the seat by one yellow leg, sat an immense black-backed gull, who contemplated me with sneering yellow eyes. I stepped forward eagerly and stretched out my hand to the broad, dark back.

'Be careful . . . watch out; he is a bully, that one!' said the man urgently.

His warning came too late, for I had already placed my hand on the bird's back and was gently running my fingers over the silken feathering. The gull crouched, opened his beak slightly, and the dark iris of his eye contracted with surprise, but he was so taken aback by my audacity that he did nothing.

'Spiridion!' said the man in amazement, 'he must like you; he's never let anyone else touch him without biting.'

I buried my fingers in the crisp white feathers on the bird's neck, and as I scratched gently the gull's head drooped forwards and his yellow eyes became dreamy. I asked the man where he had managed to catch such a magnificent bird.

'I sailed over to Albania in the spring to try to get some hares, and I found him in a nest. He was small then, and fluffy as a lamb. Now he's like a great duck,' the man said, staring pensively at the gull, 'fat duck, ugly duck, biting duck, aren't you, eh?'

The gull at being thus addressed opened one eye and gave a short, harsh yarp, which may have been repudiation or agreement. The man leant down and pulled a big basket from under the seat; it was full to the brim with great fat cockles that chinked musically. We sat in the boat and ate the shellfish, and all the time I watched the bird, fascinated by the snow-white breast and head, his long hooked beak and fierce eyes, as yellow as spring crocuses, the broad back and powerful wings, sooty black. From the soles of his great webbed feet to the tip of his beak he was, in my opinion, quite admirable. I swallowed a final cockle, wiped my hands on the side of the boat and asked the man if he could get a baby gull for me the following spring.

'You want one?' he said in surprise; 'you like them?'

I felt this was understating my feelings. I would have sold my soul for such a gull.

'Well, have him if you want him,' said the man casually, jerking a thumb at the bird.

I could hardly believe my ears. For someone to possess such a wonderful creature and to offer him as a gift so carelessly was incredible. Didn't he *want* the bird, I asked?

'Yes, I like him,' said the man, looking at the bird meditatively, 'but he eats more than I can catch for him, and he is such a wicked one that he bites everybody; none of the other prisoners or the warders like him. I've tried letting him go, but he *won't* go – he keeps coming back. I was going to take him over to Albania one week-end and leave him there. So if you're sure you want him you can have him.'

Sure I wanted him? It was like being offered an angel. A slightly sardonic-looking angel, it's true, but one with the most magnificent wings. In my excitement I never even stopped to wonder how the family would greet the arrival of a bird the size of a goose with a beak like a razor. In case the man changed his mind I hastily took off my clothes, beat as much of the dried mud off them as possible, and had a quick swim in the shallows. I put on my clothes again, whistled the dogs, and prepared to carry my prize home. The man untied the string, lifted the gull up and handed him to me; I clasped it under one arm, surprised that such a huge bird should be so feather-light. I thanked the man profusely for his wonderful present.

'He knows his name,' he remarked, clasping the gull's beak between his fingers and waggling it gently. 'I call him Alecko. He'll come when you call.'

Alecko, on hearing his name, paddled his feet wildly and looked up into my face with questioning yellow eyes.

'You'll be wanting some fish for him,' remarked the man. 'I'm going out in the boat tomorrow, about eight. If you like to come we can catch a good lot for him.'

I said that would be fine, and Alecko gave a yarp of agreement. The man leant against the bows of the boat to push it out, and I suddenly remembered something. As casually as I could I asked him what his name was, and why he was in prison. He smiled charmingly over his shoulder.

'My name's Kosti,' he said, 'Kosti Panopoulos. I killed my wife.'

He leant against the bows of the boat and heaved; she slid whispering across the sand and into the water, and the little ripples leapt and licked at her stern, like excited puppies. Kosti scrambled into the boat and took up the oars.

'Your health,' he called. 'Until tomorrow.'

The oars creaked musically, and the boat skimmed rapidly over the limpid waters. I turned, clasping my precious bird under my arm, and started to trudge back over the sand, towards the chessboard fields.

The walk home took me some time. I decided that I had misjudged Alecko's weight, for he appeared to get heavier and heavier as we progressed. He was a dead weight that sagged lower and lower, until I was forced to jerk him up under my arm again, whereupon he would protest with a vigorous yarp. We were half way through the fields when I saw a convenient fig tree which would, I thought, provide both shade and sustenance, so I decided to take a rest. While I lay in the long grass and munched figs, Alecko sat nearby as still as though he were carved out of wood, watching the dogs with unblinking eyes. The only sign of life were his irises, which would expand and contract excitedly each time one of the dogs moved.

Presently, rested and refreshed, I suggested to my band that we tackle the last stage of the journey; the dogs rose obediently, but Alecko fluffed out his feathers so that they rustled like dry leaves, and shuddered all over at the thought. Apparently he disapproved of my hawking him around under my arm like an old sack, ruffling his feathers. Now that he had persuaded me to put him down in such a pleasant spot he had no intention of continuing what appeared to him to be a tedious and unnecessary journey. As I stooped to pick him up he snapped his beak, uttered a loud, harsh scream, and lifted his wings above his back in the posture usually adopted by tombstone angels. He glared at me. Why, his look seemed to imply, leave this spot? There was shade, soft grass to sit on, and water nearby; what point was there in leaving it to be humped about the countryside in a manner both uncomfortable and undignified? I pleaded with him for some time, and, as he appeared to have calmed down, I made another attempt to pick him up. This time he left me in no doubt as to his desire to stay where he was. His beak shot out so fast I could not avoid it, and it hit my approaching hand accurately. It was as though I had been slashed by an ice-pick. My knuckles were bruised and aching, and a two-inch gash welled blood in great profusion. Alecko looked so smug and satisfied with this attack that I lost my temper. Grabbing my butterfly net I brought it down skilfully and, to his surprise, enveloped him in its folds. I jumped on him before he could recover from the shock and grabbed his beak in one hand. Then I wrapped my handkerchief round and round his beak and tied it securely in place with a bit of string, after which I took off my shirt and wrapped it round him, so that his flailing wings were pinioned tightly to his body. He lay there, trussed up as though for market, glaring at me and uttering muffled screams of rage. Grimly I picked up my equipment, put him under my arm and stalked off towards home. Having got the gull, I wasn't going to stand any nonsense about getting him back to the villa. For the rest of the journey Alecko proceeded to produce, uninterruptedly, a series of wild, strangled cries of piercing quality, so by the time we reached the house I was thoroughly angry with him.

I stamped into the drawing-room, put Alecko on the floor and started to unwrap him, while he accompanied the operation raucously. The noise brought Mother and Margo hurrying in from the kitchen. Alecko, now freed from my shirt, stood in the middle of the room with the handkerchief still tied round his beak and trumpeted furiously.

'What on earth's that?' gasped Mother.

'What an *enormous* bird!' exclaimed Margo. 'What is it, an eagle?'

My family's lack of ornithological knowledge had always been a source of annoyance to me. I explained testily that it was not an eagle but a black-backed gull, and told them how I had got him.

'But, dear, how on earth are we going to *feed* him?' asked Mother. 'Does he eat fish?'

Alecko, I said hopefully, would eat anything. I tried to catch him to remove the handkerchief from his beak, but he was obviously under the impression that I was trying to attack him, so he screamed and trumpeted loudly and ferociously through the handkerchief. This fresh outburst brought Larry and Leslie down from their rooms.

'Who the hell's playing *bagpipes*?' demanded Larry as he swept in.

Alecko paused for a moment, surveyed his newcomer coldly, and, having summed him up, yarped loudly and scornfully.

'My God!' said Larry, backing hastily and bumping into Leslie. 'What the devil's *that*?'

'It's a new bird Gerry's got,' said Margo; 'doesn't it look *fierce*?'

'It's a gull,' said Leslie, peering over Larry's shoulder; 'what a whacking great thing!'

'Nonsense,' said Larry; 'it's an albatross.'

'No, it's a gull.'

'Don't be silly. Whoever saw a gull that size? I tell you it's a bloody great albatross.'

Alecko padded a few paces towards Larry and yarped at him again.

'Call him off,' Larry commanded. 'Gerry, get the damn thing under *control*; it's attacking me.'

'Just stand still. He won't hurt you,' advised Leslie.

'It's all very well for you; you're behind me. Gerry, catch that bird at once, before it does me irreparable damage.'

'Don't shout so, dear; you'll frighten it.'

'I like that! A thing like a Roc flapping about on the floor attacking everyone, and you tell me not to frighten it.'

I managed to creep up behind Alecko and grab him; then, amid his deafening protests, I removed the handkerchief from his beak. When I let him go again he shuddered indignantly, and snapped his beak two or three times with a sound like a whip-crack.

'Listen to it!' exclaimed Larry. 'Gnashing its teeth!'

'They haven't got teeth,' observed Leslie.

'Well, it's gnashing *something*. I hope you're not going to let him keep it, Mother? It's obviously a dangerous brute; look at its eyes. Besides, it's unlucky.'

'Why unlucky?' asked Mother, who had a deep interest in superstition.

'It's a well-known thing. Even if you have just the *feathers* in the house everyone goes down with plague, or goes mad or something.'

'That's peacocks you're thinking of, dear.'

'No, I tell you it's albatrosses. It's well known.'

'No, dear, it's peacocks that are unlucky.'

'Well, anyway, we can't have that thing in the house. It would be sheer lunacy. Look what happened to the Ancient Mariner. We'll all have to sleep with crossbows under our pillows.'

'Really, Larry, you do *complicate* things,' said Mother. 'It seems quite tame to me.'

'You wait until you wake up one morning and find you've had your eyes gouged out.'

'What nonsense you talk, dear. It looks quite harmless.'

At this moment Dodo, who always took a little while to catch up with rapidly moving events, noticed Alecko for the first time. Breathing heavily, her eyes protruding with interest, she waddled forward and sniffed at him. Aleck's beak flashed out, and if Dodo had not turned her head at that moment – in response to my cry of alarm – her nose would have been neatly sliced off; as it was she received a glancing blow on the side of the head that surprised her so much that her leg leapt out of joint. She threw back her head and let forth a piercing yell. Alecko, evidently under the impression that it was a sort of vocal contest, did his best to out-scream Dodo, and flapped his wings so vigorously that he blew out the nearest lamp.

'There you are,' said Larry in triumph. 'What did I say? Hasn't been in the house five minutes and it kills the dog.'

Mother and Margo massaged Dodo back to silence, and Alecko sat and watched the operation with interest. He clicked his beak sharply, as if astonished at the frailty of the dog tribe, decorated the floor lavishly and wagged his tail with the swagger of one who had done something clever.

'How nice!' said Larry. 'Now we're expected to wade about the house waist deep in guano.'

'Hadn't you better take him outside, dear?' suggested Mother. 'Where are you going to keep him?'

I said that I had thought of dividing the Magenpies' cage and keeping Alecko there. Mother said this was a very good idea. Until his cage was ready I tethered him on the veranda, warning each member of the family in turn as to his whereabouts.

'Well,' observed Larry as we sat over dinner, 'Don't blame *me* if the house is hit by a cyclone. I've warned you; I can do no more.'

'Why a cyclone, dear?'

'Albatrosses always bring bad weather with them.'

'It's the first time I've heard a cyclone described as bad weather,' observed Leslie.

'But it's *peacocks* that are unlucky, dear; I keep telling you,' Mother said plaintively. 'I know, because an aunt of mine had some of the tail-feathers in the house and the cook died.'

'My dear Mother, the albatross is world famous as a bird of ill-omen. Hardened old salts are known to go white and faint when they see one. I tell you, we'll find the chimney covered with Saint Elmo's fire one night, and before we know where we are we'll be drowned in our beds by a tidal wave.'

'You said it would be a cyclone,' Margo pointed out.

'A cyclone *and* a tidal wave,' said Larry, 'with probably a touch of earthquake and one or two volcanic eruptions thrown in. It's tempting Providence to keep that beast.'

'Where did you get him, anyway?' Leslie asked me.

I explained about my meeting with Kosti (omitting any mention of the water-snakes, for all snakes were taboo with Leslie) and how he had given me the bird.

'Nobody in their right senses would give somebody a present like that,' observed Larry. 'Who is this man, anyway?'

Without thinking, I said he was a convict.

'A *convict*?' quavered Mother. 'What d'you mean, a convict?'

I explained about Kosti being allowed home for the week-ends, because he was a trusted member of the Vido community. I added that he and I were going fishing the next morning.

'I don't know whether it's very wise, dear,' Mother said doubtfully. 'I don't like the idea of your going about with a convict. You never know what he's done.'

Indignantly, I said I knew perfectly well what he'd done. He killed his wife.

'A *murderer*?' said Mother, aghast. 'But what's he doing wandering round the countryside? Why didn't they hang him?'

'They don't have the death penalty here for anything except bandits,' explained Leslie; 'you get three years for murder and five years if you're caught dynamiting fish.'

'Ridiculous!' said Mother indignantly. 'I've never heard of anything so scandalous.'

'I think it shows a nice sense of the importance of things,' said Larry. 'Whitebait before women.'

'Anyway, I won't have you wandering around with a murderer,' said Mother to me. 'He might cut your throat or something.'

After an hour's arguing and pleading I finally got Mother to agree that I should go fishing with Kosti, providing that Leslie came down and had a look at him first. So the next morning I went fishing with Kosti, and when we returned with enough food to keep Alecko occupied for a couple of days, I asked my friend to come up to the villa, so that Mother could inspect him for herself.

Mother had, after considerable mental effort, managed to commit to memory two or three Greek words. This lack of vocabulary had a restrictive effect on her conversation at the best of times, but when she was faced with the ordeal of exchanging small talk with a murderer she promptly forgot all the Greek she knew. So she had to sit on the veranda, smiling nervously, while Kosti in his faded shirt and tattered pants drank a glass of beer, and while I translated his conversation.

'He seems such a *nice* man,' Mother said, when Kosti had taken his leave; 'he doesn't look a bit like a murderer.'

'What did you think a murderer looked like?' asked Larry – 'someone with a hare lip and a club foot, clutching a bottle marked POISON in one hand?'

'Don't be silly, dear; of course not. But I thought he'd look . . . well, you know, a little more *murderous*.'

'You simply can't judge by physical appearance,' Larry pointed out; 'you can only tell by a person's actions. I could have told you he was a murderer at once.'

'How, dear?' asked Mother, very intrigued.

'Elementary,' said Larry with a deprecating sigh. 'No one but a murderer would have thought of giving Gerry that albatross.'

Chapter Eighteen

An Entertainment with Animals

The house was humming with activity. Groups of peasants, loaded with baskets of produce and bunches of squawking hens, clustered round the back door. Spiro arrived twice, and sometimes three times, a day, the car piled high with crates of wine, chairs, trestle tables and boxes of foodstuffs. The Magenpies, infected with the excitement, flapped from one end of their cage to the other, poking their heads through the wire and uttering loud raucous comments on the bustle and activity. In the dining-room Margo lay on the floor, surrounded by huge sheets of brown paper on which she was drawing large and highly coloured murals in chalk; in the drawing-room Leslie was surrounded by huge piles of furniture, and was mathematically working out the number of chairs and tables the house could contain without becoming uninhabitable; in the kitchen Mother (assisted by two shrill peasant girls) moved in an atmosphere like the interior of a volcano, surrounded by clouds of steam, sparkling fires, and the soft bubbling and wheezing of pots; the dogs and I wandered from room to room helping where we could, giving advice and generally making ourselves useful; upstairs in his bedroom Larry slept peacefully. The family was preparing for a party.

As always, we had decided to give the party at a moment's notice, and for no other reason than that we suddenly felt like it. Overflowing with the milk of human kindness, the family had invited everyone they could think of, including people they cordially disliked. Everyone threw themselves into the preparations with enthusiasm. Since it was early September we decided to call it a Christmas party, and, in order that the whole thing should not be too straightforward, we invited our guests to lunch, as well as to tea and dinner. This meant the preparation of a vast quantity of food, and Mother (armed with a pile of dog-eared recipe books) disappeared into the kitchen and stayed there for hours at a time. Even when she did emerge, her spectacles misted with steam, it was almost impossible to conduct a conversation with her that was not confined exclusively to food.

As usual, on the rare occasions when the family were unanimous in their desire to entertain, they started organising so far in advance, and with such zest, that by the time the day of the festivities dawned they were generally exhausted and irritable. Our parties, needless to say, never went as we envisaged. No matter how we tried there was always some last-minute hitch that switched the points and sent our carefully arranged plans careering off on a completely different track from the one we had anticipated. We had, over the years, become used to this, which is just as well, for otherwise our Christmas party would have been doomed from the outset, for it was almost completely taken over by the animals. It all started, innocently enough, with goldfish.

I had recently captured, with the aid of Kosti, the ancient terrapin I called Old Plop. To have obtained such a regal and interesting addition to my collection of pets made me feel that I should do something to commemorate the event. The best thing would be, I decided, to reorganise my terrapin pond, which was merely an old tin wash-tub. I felt it was far too lowly a hovel for such a creature as Old Plop to inhabit, so I obtained a large, square stone tank (which had once been used as an olive oil store) and proceeded to furnish it artistically with rocks, waterplants, sand and shingle. When completed it looked most natural, and the terrapins and watersnakes seemed to approve. However, I was not quite satisfied. The whole thing, though undeniably a remarkable effort, seemed to lack something. After considerable thought I came to the conclusion that what it needed to add the final touch was goldfish. The problem was, where to get them? The nearest place to purchase such a thing would be Athens, but this would be a complicated business, and, moreover, take time. I wanted my pond to be complete for the day of the party. The family were, I knew, too occupied to be able to devote any time to the task of obtaining goldfish, so I took my problem to Spiro. He, after I had described in graphic detail what goldfish were, said that he thought my request was impossible; he had never come across any such fish in Corfu. Anyway, he said he would see what he could do. There was a long period of waiting, during which I thought he had forgotten, and then, the day before the party, he beckoned me into a quiet corner, and looked around to make sure we were not overheard.

'Master Gerrys, I thinks I can gets you them golden fishes,' he rumbled hoarsely. 'Donts says anythings to anyones. You comes into towns with me this evenings, whens I takes your Mothers in to haves her hairs done, and brings somethings to puts them in.'

Thrilled with this news, for Spiro's conspiratorial air lent a pleasant flavour of danger and intrigue to the acquisition of goldfish, I spent the afternoon preparing a can to bring them home in. That evening Spiro was late, and Mother and I had been waiting on the veranda some considerable time before his car came honking and roaring up the drive, and squealed to a halt in front of the villa.

'Gollys, Mrs Durrells, I'm sorrys I'm lates,' he apologised as he helped Mother into the car.

'That's all right, Spiro. We were only afraid that you might have had an accident.'

'Accidents?' said Spiro scornfully. 'I never has accidents. No, it was them piles again.'

'*Piles?*' said Mother, mystified.

'Yes, I always gets them piles at this times,' said Spiro moodily.

'Shouldn't you see a doctor if they're worrying you?' suggested Mother.

'Doctors?' repeated Spiro, puzzled. 'Whats fors?'

'Well, piles can be dangerous, you know,' Mother pointed out.

'*Dangerous?*'

'Yes, they can be if they're neglected.'

Spiro scowled thoughtfully for a minute.

'I mean them aeroplane piles,' he said at last.

'*Aeroplane* piles?'

'Yes. French I thinks theys are.'

'You mean aeroplane *pilots*.'

'Thats whats I says, piles,' Spiro pointed out indignantly.

It was dusk when we dropped Mother at the hairdressers, and Spiro drove me over to the other side of the town, parking outside some enormous wrought-iron gates. He surged out of the car, glanced around surreptitiously, then lumbered up to the gates and whistled. Presently an ancient and be-whiskered individual appeared out of the bushes, and the two of them held a whispered consultation. Spiro came back to the car.

'Gives me the cans, Master Gerrys, and yous stay heres,' he rumbled. 'I wonts be longs.'

The be-whiskered individual opened the gates, Spiro waddled in, and they both tip-toed off into the bushes. Half an hour later Spiro reappeared, clutching the tin to his massive chest, his shoes squelching, his trouser legs dripping water.

'Theres you ares, Master Gerrys,' he said, thrusting the tin at me. Inside swam five fat and gleaming goldfish.

Immensely pleased, I thanked Spiro profusely.

'That's all rights,' he said, starting the engine; 'only donts says a things to anyones, eh?'

I asked where it was he had got them; who did the garden belong to?

'Nevers you minds,' he scowled; 'jus' you keeps thems things hidden, and donts tells a soul about them.'

It was not until some weeks later that, in company with Theodore, I happened to pass the same wrought-iron gates, and I asked what the place was. He explained that it was the palace in which the Greek King (or any other visiting royalty) stayed when he descended on the island. My admiration for Spiro knew no bounds: to actually burgle a palace and steal goldfish from the King's pond struck me as being a remarkable achievement. It also considerably enhanced the prestige of the fish as far as I was concerned, and gave an added lustre to their fat forms as they drifted casually among the terrapins.

It was on the morning of the party that things really started to happen. To begin with, Mother discovered that Dodo had chosen this day, of all days, to come into season. One of the peasant girls had to be detailed to stand outside the backdoor with a broom to repel suitors so that Mother could cook uninterruptedly, but even with this precaution there were occasional moments of panic when one of the bolder Romeos found a way into the kitchen via the front of the house.

After breakfast I hurried out to see my goldfish and discovered, to my horror, that two of them had been killed and partially eaten. In my delight at getting the fish, I had forgotten that both terrapins and the water-snakes were partial to a plump fish occasionally. So I was forced to move all the reptiles into kerosene tins until I could think of a solution to the problem. By the time I had cleaned and fed the Magenpies and Alecko I had still thought of no way of being able to keep the fish and reptiles together, and it was nearing lunchtime. The arrival of the first guests was imminent. Moodily I wandered round to my carefully arranged pond, to discover, to my horror, that someone had moved the water-snakes' tin into the full glare of the sun. They lay on the surface of the water so limp and hot that for a moment I thought they were dead; it was obvious that only immediate first aid could save them, and picking up the tin I rushed into the house. Mother was in the kitchen, harassed and absent-minded, trying to divide her attention between the cooking and Dodo's followers.

I explained the plight of the snakes and said that the only thing that would save them was a long, cool immersion in the bath. Could I put them in the bath for an hour or so?

'Well, yes, dear; I suppose that would be all right. Make sure everyone's finished, though, and don't forget to disinfect it, will you?' she said.

I filled the bath with nice cool water and placed the snakes tenderly inside; in a few minutes they showed distinct signs of reviving. Feeling well satisfied, I left them for a good soak, while I went upstairs to change. On coming down again I sauntered out on to the veranda to have a look at the lunch table, which had been put out in the shade of the vine. In the centre of what had been a very attractive floral centrepiece perched the Magenpies, reeling gently from side to side. Cold with dismay I surveyed the table. The cutlery was flung about in a haphazard manner, a layer of butter had been spread over the side plates, and buttery footprints wandered to and fro across the cloth. Pepper and salt had been used to considerable effect to decorate the smeared remains of a bowl of chutney. The water-jug had been emptied over everything to give it that final, inimitable Magenpie touch.

There was something decidedly queer about the culprits, I decided; instead of flying away as quickly as possible they remained squatting among the tattered flowers, swaying rhythmically, their eyes bright, uttering tiny chucks of satisfaction to each other. Having gazed at me with rapt attention for a moment, one of them walked very unsteadily across the table, a flower in his beak, lost his balance on the edge of the cloth and fell heavily to the ground. The other one gave a hoarse cluck of amusement, put his head under his wing and went to sleep. I was mystified by this unusual behaviour. Then I noticed a smashed bottle of beer on the flagstones. It became obvious that the Magenpies had indulged in a party of their own, and were very drunk. I caught them both quite easily, though the one on the table tried to hide under a butter-bespattered napkin and pretend he was not there. I was just standing with them in my hands, wondering if I could slip them back in their cage and deny all knowledge of the outrage, when Mother appeared carrying a jug of sauce. Caught, as it were, red-handed I had no chance of being believed if I attributed the mess to a sudden gale, or to rats, or any one of the excuses that had occurred to me. The Magenpies and I had to take our medicine.

'Really, dear, you *must* be careful about their cage door. You know what they're like,' Mother said plaintively. 'Never mind, it was an accident. And I suppose they're not really responsible if they're *drunk*.'

On taking the bleary and incapable Magenpies back to their cage I discovered, as I had feared, that Alecko had seized the opportunity to escape as well. I put the Magenpies back in their compartment and gave them a good telling off; they had by now reached the belligerent stage, and attacked my shoe fiercely. Squabbling over who should have the honour of eating the lace, they then attacked each other. I left them flapping round in wild, disorderly circles, making ineffectual stabs with their beaks, and went in search of Alecko. I hunted through the garden and all over the house, but he was nowhere to be seen. I thought he must have flown down to the sea for a quick swim, and felt relieved that he was out of the way.

By this time the first of the guests had arrived, and were drinking on the veranda. I joined them, and was soon deep in a discussion with Theodore; while we were talking, I was surprised to see Leslie appear out of the olive-groves, his gun under his arm, carrying a string bag full of snipe, and a large hare. I had forgotten that he had gone out shooting in the hope of getting some early woodcock.

'Ah ha!' said Theodore with relish, as Leslie vaulted over the veranda rail and showed us his game bag. 'Is that your own hare or is it . . . um . . . a *wig?*'

'Theodore! You pinched that from Lamb!' said Larry accusingly.

'Yes ... er ... um ... I'm afraid I did. But it seemed such a good *opportunity*,' explained Theodore contritely.

Leslie disappeared into the house to change, and Theodore and I resumed our conversation. Mother appeared and seated herself on the wall, Dodo at her feet. Her gracious hostess act was somewhat marred by the fact that she kept breaking off her conversation to grimace fiercely and brandish a large stick at the panting group of dogs gathered in the front garden. Occasionally an irritable, snarling fight would flare up among Dodo's boy friends, and whenever this occurred the entire family would turn round and bellow 'Shut up' in menacing tones. This had the effect of making the more nervous of our guests spill their drinks. After every such interruption Mother would smile round brightly and endeavour to steer the conversation back to normal. She had just succeeded in doing this for the third time when all talk was abruptly frozen again by a bellow from inside the house. It sounded the sort of cry the minotaur would have produced if suffering from toothache.

'Whatever's the matter with Leslie?' asked Mother.

She was not left long in doubt, for he appeared on the veranda clad in nothing but a small towel.

'Gerry,' he roared, his face a deep red with rage. 'Where's that boy?'

'Now, *now*, dear,' said Mother soothingly, 'whatever's the matter?'

'Snakes,' snarled Leslie, making a wild gesture with his hands to indicate extreme length, and then hastily clutching at his slipping towel, 'snakes, that's what's the matter.'

The effect on the guests was interesting. The ones that knew us were following the whole scene with avid interest; the uninitiated wondered if perhaps Leslie was a little touched, and were not sure whether to ignore the whole incident and go on talking, or whether to leap on him before he attacked someone.

'What *are* you talking about, dear?'

'That bloody *boy's* filled the sodding *bath* full of bleeding *snakes*,' said Leslie, making things quite clear.

'Language, dear, language!' said Mother automatically, adding absently, 'I do wish you'd put some clothes on; you'll catch a chill like that.'

'Damn great things like *hosepipes*.... It's a wonder I wasn't bitten.'

'Never mind, dear, it's really my fault. I told him to put them there,' Mother apologised, and then added, feeling that the guests needed some explanation, 'they were suffering from sunstroke, poor things.'

'Really, Mother!' exclaimed Larry, 'I think that's carrying things too far.'

'Now don't *you* start, dear,' said Mother firmly; 'it was Leslie who was bathing with the snakes.'

'I don't know why Larry always has to interfere,' Margo remarked bitterly.

'Interfere? I'm not interfering. When Mother conspires with Gerry in filling the bath with snakes I think it's my duty to complain.'

'Oh, shut up,' said Leslie. 'What I want to know is, when's he going to remove the bloody things?'

'I think you're making a lot of fuss about nothing,' said Margo.

'If it has become necessary for us to perform our ablutions in a nest of hamadryads I shall be forced to move,' Larry warned.

'Am I going to get a bath or not?' asked Leslie throatily.
'Why can't you take them out yourself?'
'Only Saint Francis of Assisi would feel really at *home* here ...'
'Oh, for heaven's sake be quiet!'
'I've got just as much right to air my views ...'
'I want a *bath*, that's all. Surely it is not too much to ask ...'
'Now, now, dears, don't quarrel,' said Mother. 'Gerry, you'd better go and take the snakes out of the bath. Put them in the basin or somewhere for the moment.'
'No! They've got to go right outside!'
'All right, dear; don't shout.'

Eventually I borrowed a saucepan from the kitchen and put my water-snakes in that. They had, to my delight, recovered completely, and hissed vigorously when I removed them from the bath. On returning to the veranda I was in time to hear Larry holding forth at length to the assembled guests.

'I assure you the house is a death-trap. Every conceivable nook and cranny is stuffed with malignant faunae waiting to pounce. How I have escaped being maimed for life is beyond me. A simple, innocuous action like lighting a cigarette is fraught with danger. Even the sanctity of my bedroom is not respected. First, I was attacked by a scorpion, a hideous beast that dripped venom and babies all over the place. Then my room was torn asunder by magpies. Now we have snakes in the bath and huge flocks of albatrosses flapping round the house, making noises like defective plumbing.'

'Larry, dear, you do *exaggerate*,' said Mother, smiling vaguely at the guests.

"My dear Mother, if anything I am understating the case. What about the night Quasimodo decided to sleep in my room?'

'That wasn't very dreadful, dear.'

'Well,' said Larry with dignity, 'it may give *you* pleasure to be woken at half-past three in the morning by a pigeon who seems intent on pushing his rectum into your eye ...'

'Yes, well, we've talked quite enough about animals,' said Mother hurriedly. 'I think lunch is ready, so shall we all sit down?'

'Well, anyway,' said Larry as we moved down the veranda to the table, 'that boy's a menace ... he's got beasts in his belfry.'

The guests were shown their places, there was a loud scraping as chairs were drawn out, and then everyone sat down and smiled at each other. The next moment two of the guests uttered yells of agony and soared out of their seats, like rockets.

'Oh, dear, *now* what's happened?' asked Mother in agitation.

'It's probably scorpions again,' said Larry, vacating his seat hurriedly.

'Something bit me ... bit me in the leg!'

'There you are!' exclaimed Larry, looking round triumphantly. '*Exactly* what I said! You'll probably find a brace of bears under there.'

The only one not frozen with horror at the thought of some hidden menace lurking round his feet was Theodore, and he gravely bent down, lifted the cloth and poked his head under the table.

'Ah ha!' he said interestedly, his voice muffled.

'What is it?' asked Mother.

Theodore reappeared from under the cloth.

'It seems to be some sort of a ... er ... some sort of a *bird*. A large black and white one.'

'It's that albatross!' said Larry excitedly.

'No, no,' corrected Theodore; 'it's some species of *gull*, I think.'

'Don't move ... keep quite still, unless you want your legs taken off at the knee!' Larry informed the company.

As a statement calculated to quell alarm it left a lot to be desired. Everybody rose in a body and vacated the table.

From beneath the cloth Alecko gave a long, menacing yarp; whether in dismay at losing his victims or protest at the noise, it was difficult to say.

'Gerry, catch that bird up immediately!' commanded Larry from a safe distance.

'Yes, dear,' Mother agreed. 'You'd better put him back in his cage. He can't stay under there.'

I gently lifted the edge of the cloth, and Alecko, squatting regally under the table, surveyed me with angry yellow eyes. I stretched out a hand towards him, and he lifted his wings and clicked his beak savagely. He was obviously in no mood to be trifled with. I got a napkin and started to try to manoeuvre it towards his beak.

'Do you require any assistance, my dear boy?' inquired Kralefsky, obviously feeling that his reputation as an ornithologist required him to make some sort of offer.

To his obvious relief I refused his help. I explained that Alecko was in a bad mood and would take a little while to catch.

'Well, for heaven's sake hurry up; the soup's getting cold,' snapped Larry irritably. 'Can't you tempt the brute with something? What do they eat?'

'All the nice gulls love a sailor,' observed Theodore with immense satisfaction.

'Oh, Theodore, please!' protested Larry, pained; 'not in moments of crisis.'

'By Jove! It does look savage!' said Kralefsky as I struggled with Alecko.

'It's probably hungry,' said Theodore happily, 'and the sight of us sitting down to eat was gull and wormwood to it.'

'*Theodore!*'

I succeeded at last in getting a grip on Alecko's beak, and I hauled him screaming and flapping out from under the table. I was hot and dishevelled by the time I had pinioned his wings and carried him back to his cage. I left him there, screaming insults and threats at me, and went back to resume my interrupted lunch.

'I remember a very dear friend of mine being molested by a large gull, once,' remarked Kralefsky reminiscently, sipping his soup.

'Really?' said Larry. 'I didn't know they were such depraved birds.'

'He was walking along the cliffs with a lady,' Kralefsky went on without listening to Larry, 'when the bird swooped out of the sky and attacked them. My friend told me he had the greatest difficulty in beating it off with his umbrella. Not an enviable experience, by Jove, eh?'

'Extraordinary!' said Larry.

'What he *should* have done,' Theodore pointed out gravely, 'was to point his umbrella at it and shout – "Stand back or I'll fire".'

'Whatever for?' inquired Kralefsky, very puzzled.

'The gull would have believed him and flown away in terror,' explained Theodore blandly.

'But I don't quite understand . . .' began Kralefsky, frowning.

'You see, they're terribly *gullible* creatures,' said Theodore in triumph.

'Honestly, Theodore, you're like an ancient copy of *Punch*,' groaned Larry.

The glasses clinked, knives and forks clattered, and the wine-bottles glugged as we progressed through the meal. Delicacy after delicacy made its appearance, and after the guests had shown their unanimous approval of each dish Mother would smile deprecatingly. Naturally, the conversation revolved around animals.

'I remember when I was a child being sent to visit one of our numerous elderly and eccentric aunts. She had a bee fetish; she kept vast quantities of them; the garden was overflowing with hundreds of hives humming like telegraph poles. One afternoon she put on an enormous veil and a pair of gloves, locked us all in the cottage for safety and went out to try to get some honey out of one of the hives. Apparently she didn't stupefy them properly, or whatever it is you do, and when she took the lid off, a sort of waterspout of bees poured out and settled on her. We were watching all this through the window. We didn't know much about bees, so we thought this was the correct procedure, until we saw her flying round the garden making desperate attempts to evade the bees, getting her veil tangled up in the rose-bushes. Eventually she reached the cottage and flung herself at the door. We couldn't open it because she had the key. We kept trying to impress this on her, but her screams of agony and the humming of the bees drowned our voices. It was, I believe Leslie who had the brilliant idea of throwing a bucket of water over her from the bedroom window. Unfortunately in his enthusiasm he threw the bucket as well. To be drenched with cold water and then hit on the head with a large galvanised-iron bucket is irritating enough, but to have to fight off a mass of bees at the same time makes the whole thing extremely trying. When we eventually got her inside she was so swollen as to be almost unrecognisable.' Larry paused in his story and sighed sorrowfully.

'Dreadful by Jove,' exclaimed Kralefsky, his eyes wide. 'She might have been killed.'

'Yes, she might,' agreed Larry. 'As it was, it completely ruined my holiday.'

'Did she recover?' asked Kralefsky. It was obvious that he was planning a thrilling Infuriated Bee Adventure that he could have with his lady.

'Oh, yes, after a few weeks in hospital,' Larry replied carelessly. 'It didn't seem to put her off bees though. Shortly afterwards a whole flock of them swarmed in the chimney, and in trying to smoke them out she set fire to the cottage. By the time the fire brigade arrived the place was a mere charred shell, surrounded by bees.'

'Dreadful, *dreadful*,' murmured Kralefsky.

Theodore, meticulously buttering a piece of bread, gave a tiny grunt of amusement. He popped the bread into his mouth, chewed it stolidly for a minute or so, swallowed, and wiped his beard carefully on his napkin.

'Talking of fires,' he began, his eyes alight with impish humour, 'did I tell you about the time the Corfu Fire Brigade was modernised? It seems that the Chief of the fire service had been to Athens and had been greatly ... er ... *impressed* by the new fire-fighting equipment there. He felt it was high time that Corfu got rid of its horse-drawn fire engine and should obtain a new one ... um ... preferably a nice, shiny *red* one. There were several other improvements he had thought of as well. He came back here alight with ... um ... with *enthusiasm*. The first thing he did was to cut a round hole in the ceiling of the fire station, so that the firemen could slide down a pole in the correct manner. It appears that in his haste to become modernised he forgot the pole, and so the first time they had a *practice* two of the firemen broke their legs.'

'No, Theodore, I refuse to believe that. It couldn't be true.'

'No, no, I assure you it's perfectly true. They brought the men to my laboratory to be X-rayed. Apparently what had happened was that the Chief had not explained to the men about the pole, and they thought they had to *jump* down the hole. That was only the beginning. At quite considerable cost an extremely ... er ... large fire engine was purchased. The Chief insisted on the *biggest* and *best*. Unfortunately it was so big that there was only one way they could drive it through the town – you know how narrow most of the streets are. Quite often you would see it rushing along, its bell clanging like mad, in the *opposite* direction to the fire. Once outside the town, where the roads are somewhat ... er ... broader, they could cut round to the fire. The most curious thing, I thought, was the business about the very modern fire alarm the Chief had sent for: you know, it was one of those ones where you break the glass and there is a little sort of ... um ... telephone inside. Well, there was great argument as to where they should put this. The Chief told me that it was a very difficult thing to decide, as they were not sure *where* the fires were going to break out. So, in order to avoid any confusion, they fixed the fire alarm on the *door* of the fire station.'

Theodore paused, rasped his beard with his thumb and took a sip of wine.

'They had hardly got things organised before they had their first fire. Fortunately I happened to be in the vicinity and could watch the whole thing. The place was a garage, and the flames had got a pretty good hold before the owner had managed to run to the fire station and break the glass on the fire alarm. Then there were angry words exchanged, it seems, because the Chief was annoyed at having his fire alarm broken so *soon*. He told the man that he should have knocked on the door; the fire alarm was brand new, and it would take weeks to replace the glass. Eventually the fire engine was wheeled out into the street and the firemen assembled. The Chief made a short speech, urging each man to do his ... um ... duty. Then they took their places. There was a bit of a fuss about who should have the honour of ringing the bell, but eventually the Chief did the job himself. I must say that when the engine *did* arrive it looked very impressive. They all leapt off and bustled about, and looked very efficient. They uncoiled a very large hose, and then a fresh hitch became apparent. No one could find the key which was needed to unlock the back of the engine so that the hose could be attached. The Chief said he had given it to Yani, but it was Yani's night off, it seems. After a lot of argument someone was sent running to Yani's house, which was ... er ... *fortunately,* not too far away. While they were waiting, the firemen admired the blaze, which by now was quite considerable. The man came back and said that Yani was not at his house, but his wife said he had gone to the fire. A search through the crowd was made and to the Chief's indignation they found Yani among the onlookers, the key in his pocket. The Chief was very angry, and pointed out that it was *this* sort of thing that created a bad impression. They got the back of the engine open, attached the hose and turned on the water. By that time, of course, there was hardly any garage left to ... er ... *put out.*'

Lunch over, the guests were too bloated with food to do anything except siesta on the veranda, and Kralefsky's attempts to organise a cricket match were greeted with complete lack of enthusiasm. A few of the more energetic of us got Spiro to drive us down for a swim, and we lolled in the sea until it was time to return for tea, another of Mother's gastronomic triumphs. Tottering mounds of hot scones; crisp, paperthin biscuits; cakes like snow-drifts, oozing jam; cakes dark, rich and moist, crammed with fruit; brandy snaps brittle as coral and overflowing with honey. Conversation was almost at a standstill; all that could be heard was the gentle tinkle of cups, and the heartfelt sigh of some guest, already stuffed to capacity, accepting another slice of cake. Afterwards we lay about on the veranda in little groups, talking in a desultory, dreamy fashion as the tide of green twilight washed through the olive-groves and deepened the shade beneath the vine so that faces became obscured in the shadow.

Presently Spiro, who had been off in the car on some mysterious expedition of his own, came driving through the trees, his horn blaring to warn everything and everyone of his arrival.

'Why *does* Spiro have to shatter the evening calm with that ghastly noise?' inquired Larry in a pained voice.

'I agree, I agree,' murmured Kralefsky sleepily; 'one should have night-ingales at this time of day, not motor-car horns.'

'I remember being very puzzled,' remarked Theodore's voice out of the shadows, with an undertone of amusement, 'on the first occasion when I drove with Spiro. I can't recall exactly what the conversation was about, but he suddenly remarked to me, "Yes, Doctors, peoples are scarce when I drive through a village." I had a ... um ... curious mental picture of villages quite empty of people, and huge piles of corpses by the side of the road. Then Spiro went on , "Yes, when I goes through the village I blows my horns like Hells and scares them all to death".'

The car swept round to the front of the house, and the headlight raked along the veranda briefly, showing up the frilly ceiling of misty green vine leaves, the scattered groups of guests talking and laughing, the two peasant girls with their scarlet headscarves, padding softly to and fro, their bare feet scuffing on the flags, laying the table. The car stopped, the sound of the engine died away, and Spiro came waddling up the path, clutching an enormous and apparently heavy brown-paper parcel to his chest.

'Good God! Look!' exclaimed Larry dramatically, pointing a trembling finger. 'The publishers have returned my manuscript again.'

Spiro, on his way into the house, stopped and scowled over his shoulder.

'Golly, nos, Master Lorrys,' he explained seriously, 'this is thems three turkeys my wifes cooked for your mothers.'

'Ah, then there is still hope,' sighed Larry in exaggerated relief; 'the shock has made me feel quite faint. Let's all go inside and have a drink.'

Inside, the rooms glowed with lamplight, and Margo's brilliantly coloured murals moved gently on the walls as the evening breeze straightened them carefully. Glasses started to titter and chime, corks popped with a sound like stones dropping into a well, the siphons sighed like tired trains. The guests livened up; their eyes gleamed, the talk mounted into a crescendo.

Bored with the party, and being unable to attract Mother's attention, Dodo decided to pay a short visit to the garden by herself. She waddled out into the moonlight and chose a suitable patch beneath the magnolia tree to commune with nature. Suddenly, to her dismay, she was confronted by a pack of bristling, belligerent and rough-looking dogs who obviously had the worst possible designs on her. With a yell of fright she turned tail and fled back into the house as quickly as her short, fat little legs would permit. But the ardent suitors were not going to give up without a struggle. They had spent a hot and irritating afternoon trying to make Dodo's acquaintance, and they were not going to waste this apparently Heaven-sent opportunity to try to get their relationship with her on a more intimate footing. Dodo galloped into the crowded drawing-room, screaming for help, and hot on her heels came the panting, snarling, barging wave of dogs. Roger, Puke and Widdle, who had slipped off to the kitchen for a snack, returned with all speed and were horrified by the scene. If anyone was going to seduce Dodo, they felt, it was going to be one of them, not some scrawny village pariah. They hurled themselves with gusto upon Dodo's pursuers, and in a moment the room was a confused mass of fighting, snarling dogs and leaping hysterical guests trying to avoid being bitten.

'It's wolves! . . . It means we're in for a hard winter,' yelled Larry, leaping nimbly on to a chair.

'Keep calm, keep calm!' bellowed Leslie, as he seized a cushion and hurled it at the nearest knot of struggling dogs. The cushion landed, was immediately seized by five angry mouths and torn asunder. A great whirling cloud of feathers gushed up into the air and drifted over the scene.

'Where's Dodo?' quavered Mother. 'Find Dodo; they'll hurt her.'

'Stop them! Stop them! They're killing each other,' shrilled Margo, and seizing a soda syphon she proceeded to spray both guests and dogs with complete impartiality.

'I believe *pepper* is a good thing for dog-fights,' observed Theodore, the feathers settling on his beard like snow, 'though of course I have never tried it *myself.*'

'By Jove!' yelped Kralefsky, 'watch out . . . save the ladies!'

He followed this advice by helping the nearest female on to the sofa and climbing up beside her.

'Water also is considered to be good,' Theodore went on musingly, and as if to test this he poured his glass of wine with meticulous accuracy over a passing dog.

Acting on Theodore's advice, Spiro surged out to the kitchen and returned with a kerosene tin of water clasped in his ham-like hands. He paused in the doorway and raised it above his head.

'Watch outs,' he roared; 'I'll fixes the bastards.'

The guests fled in all directions, but they were not quick enough. The polished, glittering mass of water curved through the air and hit the floor, to burst up again and then curve and break like a tidal wave over the room. It had the most disastrous results as far as the nearest guests were concerned, but it had the most startling and instantaneous effect on the dogs. Frightened by the boom and swish of water, they let go of each other and fled out into the night, leaving behind them a scene of carnage that was breath-taking. The room looked like a hen-roost that had been hit by a cyclone; our friends milled about, damp and feather-encrusted; feathers had settled on the lamps and the acrid smell of burning filled the air. Mother, clasping Dodo in her arms, surveyed the room.

'Leslie, dear, go and get some towels so that we can dry ourselves. The room *is* in a mess. Never mind, let's all go out on to the veranda, shall we?' she said, and added sweetly, 'I'm so sorry this happened. It's Dodo, you see; she's very *interesting* to the dogs at the moment.'

Eventually the party was dried, the feathers plucked off them, their glasses were filled and they were installed on the veranda where the moon was stamping the flags with ink-black shadows of the vine leaves. Larry, his mouth full of food, strummed softly on his guitar and hummed indistinctly; through the french windows we could see Leslie and Spiro both scowling with concentration, skilfully dismembering the great brown turkeys; Mother drifted to and fro through the shadows, anxiously asking everyone if they were getting enough to eat; Kralefsky was perched on the veranda wall – his body crab-like in silhouette, the moon peering over his hump – telling Margo a long and involved story; Theodore was giving a lecture on the stars to Dr Androuchelli, pointing out the constellations with a half-eaten turkey leg.

Outside, the island was striped and patched in black and silver by moonlight. Far down in the dark cypress trees the owls called to each other comfortingly. The sky looked as black and soft as a mole-skin covered with a delicate dew of stars. The magnolia tree loomed vast over the house, its branches full of white blooms, like a hundred miniature reflections of the moon, and their thick, sweet scent hung over the veranda languorously, the scent that was an enchantment luring you out into the mysterious, moonlit countryside.

The Return

With a gentlemanly honesty which I found hard to forgive, Mr Kralefsky had informed Mother that he had taught me as much as he was able; the time had come, he thought, for me to go somewhere like England or Switzerland to finish my education. In desperation I argued against any such idea; I said I *liked* being half-educated; you were so much more *surprised* at everything when you were ignorant. But Mother was adamant. We were to return to England and spend a month or so there consolidating our position (which meant arguing with the bank) and then we would decide where I was to continue my studies. In order to quell the angry mutterings of rebellion in the family she told us that we should look upon it merely as a holiday, a pleasant trip. We should soon be back again in Corfu.

So our boxes, bags and trunks were packed, cages were made for birds and tortoises, and the dogs looked uncomfortable and slightly guilty in their new collars. The last walks were taken among the olives, the last tearful good-byes exchanged with our numerous peasant friends, and then the cars, piled high with our possessions, moved slowly down the drive in procession, looking as Larry pointed out, rather like the funeral of a successful rag-and-bone merchant.

Our mountain of possessions was arranged in the Customs shed, and Mother stood by it jangling an enormous bunch of keys. Outside in the brilliant white sunlight the rest of the family talked with Theodore and Kralefsky, who had come to see us off. The Customs officer made his appearance and wilted slightly at the sight of our mound of baggage, crowned with a cage from which the Magenpies peered malevolently. Mother smiled nervously and shook her keys, looking as guilty as a diamond smuggler. The Customs man surveyed Mother and the luggage, tightened his belt and frowned.

'Theese your?' he inquired, making quite sure.

'Yes, yes, all mine,' twittered Mother, playing a rapid solo on her keys. 'Did you want me to open anything?'

The Customs man considered, pursing his lips thoughtfully.

'Hoff yew any noo clooes?' he asked.

'I'm sorry?' said Mother.

'Hoff yew any noo clooes?'

Mother cast a desperate glance round for Spiro.

'I'm so sorry. I didn't quite catch . . .'

'Hoff yew any noo clooes . . . *any noo clooes?*'

Mother smiled with desperate charm.

'I'm sorry I can't quite . . .'

The Customs man fixed her with an angry eye.

'Madame,' he said ominously, leaning over the counter, 'do yew spik English?'

'Oh yes,' exclaimed Mother, delighted at having understood him, 'yes, a *little*.'

She was saved from the wrath of the man by the timely arrival of Spiro. He lumbered in, sweating profusely, soothed Mother, calmed the Customs man, explained that we had not had any new clothes for years, and had the luggage shifted outside on to the quay almost before anyone could draw breath. Then he borrowed the Customs man's piece of chalk and marked all the baggage himself, so there would be no further confusion.

'Well, I won't say good-bye but only *au revoir*,' mumbled Theodore, shaking hands precisely with each of us. 'I hope we shall have you back with us ... um ... *very soon*.'

'Good-bye, good-bye,' fluted Kralefsky, bobbing from one person to the other. 'We shall so look forward to your return. By Jove, yes! And have a good time, make the most of your stay in old England. Make it a *real* holiday, eh? That's the ticket!'

Spiro shook each of us silently by the hand, and then stood staring at us, his face screwed up into the familiar scowl, twisting his cap in his huge hands.

'Wells, I'll says good-byes,' he began and his voice wavered and broke, great fat tears squeezing themselves from his eyes and running down his furrowed cheeks. 'Honest to Gods, I didn't means to cry,' he sobbed, his vast stomach heaving, 'but it's just likes saying goods-bye to my own peoples. I feels you belongs to me.'

The tender had to wait patiently while we comforted him. Then, as its engine throbbed and it drew away across the dark blue water, our three friends stood out against the multi-coloured background, the tottering houses sprawled up the hillside, Theodore neat and erect, his stick raised in grave salute, his beard twinkling in the sun; Kralefsky bobbing and ducking and waving extravagantly; Spiro, barrel-bodied and scowling, alternately wiping his eyes with his handkerchief and waving it to us.

As the ship drew across the sea and Corfu sank shimmering into a pearly heat haze on the horizon a black depression settled on us, which lasted all the way back to England. The grimy train scuttled its way up from Brindisi towards Switzerland, and we sat in silence, not wishing to talk. Above our heads, on the rack, the finches sang in their cages, the Magenpies chucked and hammered with their beaks, and Alecko gave a mournful yarp at intervals. Around our feet the dogs lay snoring. At the Swiss frontier our passports were examined by a disgracefully efficient official. He handed them back to Mother, together with a small slip of paper, bowed unsmilingly and left us to our gloom. Some moments later Mother glanced at the form the official had filled in, and as she read it, she stiffened.

'Just look what he's put,' she exclaimed indignantly, '*impertinent* man.'

Larry stared at the little form and snorted.

'Well, that's the penalty you pay for leaving Corfu,' he pointed out.

On the little card, in the column headed *Description of Passengers* had been written, in neat capitals: One travelling Circus and Staff.

'What a thing to write,' said Mother, still simmering, 'really, some people are *peculiar*.'

The train rattled towards England.

The Bafut Beagles

GERALD DURRELL

The Bafut Beagles

For
KENNETH SMITH
In memory of
Fons, False Teeth, and Flying Mice

In Which We Done Come

The Cross River picks its way down from the mountains of the Cameroons, until it runs sprawling and glittering into the great bowl of forest land around Mamfe. After being all froth, waterfalls and eager chattering in the mountains, it settles down when it reaches this forest, and runs sedately in its rocky bed, the gently moving waters creating ribs of pure white sand across its width, and washing the mud away from the tree roots, so that they look as though they stand at the edge of the water on a tangled, writhing mass of octopus-like legs. It moves along majestically, its brown waters full of hippo and crocodile, and the warm air above it filled with hawking swallows, blue and orange and white.

Just above Mamfe the river increases its pace slightly, squeezing itself between two high rocky cliffs, cliffs that are worn smooth by the passing waters and wear a tattered antimacassar of undergrowth that hangs down from the forest above; emerging from the gorge it swirls out into a vast egg-shaped basin. A little further along, through an identical gorge, another river empties itself into this same basin, and the waters meet and mix in a skein of tiny currents, whirlpools and ripples, and then continue onwards as one waterway, leaving, as a result of their marriage, a huge glittering hummock of white sand in the centre of the river, sand that is pockmarked with the footprints of hippo and patterned with chains of bird-tracks. Near this island of sand the forest on the bank gives way to the small grassfield that surrounds the village of Mamfe, and it was here, on the edge of the forest, above the smooth brown river, that we chose to have our base camp.

It took two days of cutting and levelling to get the camp site ready, and on the third day Smith and I stood at the edge of the grassfield watching while thirty sweating, shouting Africans hauled and pulled at what appeared to be the vast, brown, wrinkled carcase of a whale that lay on the freshly turned red earth. Gradually, as this sea of canvas was pulled and pushed, it rose into the air, swelling like an unhealthy looking puffball. Then it seemed to spread out suddenly, leech-like, and turned itself into a marquee of impressive dimensions. When it had thus revealed its identity, there came a full-throated roar, a mixture of astonishment, amazement and delight, from the crowd of villagers who had come to watch our camp building.

Once the marquee was ready to house us, it took another week of hard work before we were ready to start collecting. Cages had to be erected, ponds dug, various chiefs from nearby villages interviewed and told of the animals we required, food supplies had to be laid on, and a hundred and one other things had to be done. Eventually, when the camp was functioning smoothly, we felt we could start collecting in earnest. We had decided that Smith should stay in Mamfe and keep the base camp going, gleaning what forest fauna he could with the help of the local inhabitants, while I was to travel further inland to the mountains, where the forest gave place to the great grasslands. In this mountain world, with its strange vegetation and cooler climate, a completely different fauna from that of the steamy forest region was to be found.

I was not certain which part of the grasslands would be the best for me to operate in, so I went to the District Officer for advice. I explained my dilemma, and he produced a map of the mountains and together we pored over it. Suddenly he dabbed his forefinger down and glanced at me.

'What about Bafut?' he asked.

'Is that a good place? What are the people like?'

'There is only one person you have to worry about in Bafut, and that's the Fon,' he said; 'get him on your side and the people will help you all they can.'

'Is he the chief?'

'He's the sort of Nero of this region,' said the D.O, marking a large circle on the map with his finger, 'and what he says goes. He's the most delightful old rogue, and the quickest and surest way to his heart is to prove to him that you can carry your liquor. He's got a wonderful great villa there, which he built in case he had any European visitors, and I'm sure if you wrote to him he would let you stay there. It's worth a visit, is Bafut, even if you don't stay.'

'Well, I'll drop him a note and see what he says.'

'See that your communication is ... er ... well lubricated,' said the D.O.

'I'll go down to the store and get a bottle of lubrication at once,' I assured him.

So that afternoon a messenger went off to the mountains, carrying with him my note and a bottle of gin. Four days later he returned, bearing a letter from the Fon, a masterly document that encouraged me tremendously.

                                  Fon's Office Bafut, Bafut Bemenda Division,
                                              5th March, 1949.

My good friend,

    Yours of 3rd March, 1949, came in hand with all contents well marked out.

    Yes, I accept your arrival to Bafut in course of two month stay about your animals and too, I shall be overjoyed to let you be in possession of a house in my compound if you will do well in arrangement of rentages.

                                                        Yours cordially,
                                                          Fon of Bafut.

I made arrangements to leave for Bafut at once.

Chapter One

Toads and Dancing Monkeys

Most West African lorries are not in what one would call the first flush of youth, and I had learnt by bitter experience not to expect anything very much of them. But the lorry that arrived to take me up to the mountains was worse than anything I had seen before: it tottered on the borders of senile decay. It stood there on buckled wheels, wheezing and gasping with exhaustion from having to climb up the gentle slope to the camp, and I consigned myself and my loads to it with some trepidation. The driver, who was a cheerful fellow, pointed out that he would require my assistance in two very necessary operations: first, I had to keep the hand-brake pressed down when travelling downhill, for unless it was held thus almost level with the floor it sullenly refused to function. Secondly, I had to keep a stern eye on the clutch, a wilful piece of mechanism, that seized every chance to leap out of its socket with a noise like a strangling leopard. As it was obvious that not even a West African lorry driver could be successful in driving while crouched under the dashboard in a pre-natal position, I had to take over control of these instruments if I valued my life. So, while I ducked at intervals to put on the brake, amid the rich smell of burning rubber, our noble lorry jerked its way towards the mountains at a steady twenty miles per hour; sometimes, when a downward slope favoured it, it threw caution to the winds and careered along in a madcap fashion at twenty-five.

For the first thirty miles the red earth road wound its way through the lowland forest, the giant trees standing in solid ranks alongside and their branches entwined in an archway of leaves above us. Flocks of hornbills flapped across the road, honking like the ghosts of ancient taxis, and on the banks, draped decoratively in the patches of sunlight, the agama lizards lay, blushing into sunset colouring with excitement and nodding their heads furiously. Slowly and almost imperceptibly the road started to climb upwards, looping its way in languid curves round the forested hills. In the back of the lorry the boys lifted up their voices in song:

>Home again, home again,
>When shall I see ma home?
>When shall I see ma mammy?
>I'll never forget ma home. . . .

The driver hummed the refrain softly to himself, glancing at me to see if I would object. To his surprise I joined in, and so while the lorry rolled onwards trailing a swirling tail of red dust behind it, the boys in the back maintained the chorus while the driver and I harmonized and sang complicated twiddly bits, and the driver played a staccato accompaniment on the horn.

Breaks in the forest became more frequent the higher we climbed, and presently a new type of undergrowth began to appear: massive tree-ferns standing in conspiratorial groups at the roadside on their thick, squat and hairy trunks, the fronds of leaves sprouting from the tops like delicate green fountains. These ferns were the guardians of a new world, for suddenly, as though the hills had shrugged themselves free of a cloak, the forest disappeared. It lay behind us in the valley, a thick pelt of green undulating away into the heat-shimmered distance, while above us the hillside rose majestically, covered in a coat of rippling, waist-high grass, bleached golden by the sun. The lorry crept higher and higher, the engine gasping and shuddering with this unaccustomed activity. I began to think that we should have to push the wretched thing up the last two or three hundred feet, but to everyone's surprise we made it, and the lorry crept on to the brow of the hill, trembling with fatigue, spouting steam from its radiator like a dying whale. We crawled to a standstill and the driver switched off the engine.

'We go wait small-time, engine get hot,' he explained, pointing to the forequarters of the lorry, which were by now completely invisible under a cloud of steam. Thankfully I descended from the red-hot inside of the cab and strolled down to where the road dipped into the next valley. From this vantage point I could see the country we had travelled through and the country we were about to enter.

Behind lay the vast green forest, looking from this distance as tight and impenetrable as lambs' wool; only on the hilltops was there any apparent break in the smooth surface of those millions of leaves, for against the sky the trees were silhouetted in a tattered fringe. Ahead of us lay a world so different that it seemed incredible that the two should be found side by side. There was no gradual merging: behind lay the forest of huge trees, each clad in its robe of polished leaves, glittering like green and gigantic pearly kings; ahead, to the furthermost dim blue horizon, lay range after range of hills, merging and folding into one another like great frozen waves, tilting their faces to the sun, covered from valley to crest with a rippling fur of golden-green grass that paled or darkened as the wind curved and smoothed it. Behind us the forest was decked out in the most vivid of greens and scarlets – harsh and intense colours. Before us, in this strange mountain world of grass, the colours were soft and delicate – fawns, pale greens, warm browns and golds. The smoothly crumpled hills covered with this pastel-tinted grass could have been an English scene: the downland country of the south on a larger scale. The illusion was spoilt, however, by the sun, which shone fiercely and steadily in a completely un-English manner.

From then onwards the road resembled a switchback, and we rattled and squeaked our way down into valleys, and coughed and grunted our way up the steep hillsides. We had paused on one hilltop to let the engine cool again, and I noticed in the valley ahead a village, looking at that distance like an irregular patch of black toadstools against the green. When the engine was switched off, the silence descended like a blanket; all we could hear was the soft hiss of the grass moved by the wind and, from the village far below us, the barking of a dog and the crowing of a cockerel, the sounds tiny and remote but clear as a bell. Through my field-glasses I could see that there was some activity going on in the village: crowds of people milled round the huts, and I could see the flash of machetes and spears, and the occasional glint of a gaudy sarong.

'Na whatee dat palaver for dat place?' I asked the driver.

He peered down the hill, screwing up his eyes, and then turned to me, grinning delightedly.

'Na market, sah,' he explained, and then, hopefully, 'Masa want to stop for dat place?'

'You tink sometime we go find beef for sale dere?'

'Yes, sah!'

'For true?'

'For true, sah!'

'You lie, bushman,' I said in mock anger. 'You want to stop for dis place so you go find corn beer. No be so?'

'Eh! Na so, sah,' admitted the driver, smiling, 'but sometimes Masa go find beef there also.'

'All right, we go stop small time.'

'Yes, sah,' said the driver eagerly, and sent the lorry hurtling down the slope towards the village.

The big huts, with their conical thatched roofs, were grouped neatly round a small square which was shaded with groups of young eucalyptus trees. In this square was the market; in the patchwork of light and shadow under the slim trees the traders had spread their wares on the ground, each on his own little patch, and around them thronged the villagers in a gesticulating, chattering, arguing wedge. The wares offered for sale were astonishing in their variety and, sometimes, in their incongruity. There were freshwater catfish, dried by wood smoke and spitted on short sticks. These are unpleasant-looking fish when alive, but when dried and shrivelled and blackened by the smoking they looked like some fiendish little juju dolls, twisted into strange contortions by a revolting dance. There were great bales of cloth, some of it the highly coloured prints so beloved of the African, imported from England; more tasteful was the locally woven cloth, thick and soft. Among these patches of highly coloured cloth were an odd assortment of eggs, chickens in bamboo baskets, green peppers, cabbages, potatoes, sugar-cane, great gory hunks of meat, giant Cane Rats, neatly gutted and hung on strings, earthenware pots and cane baskets, eroco-wood chairs, needles, gunpowder, corn beer, gin-traps, mangoes, pawpaws, enemas, lemons, native shoes, lovely raffia-work bags, nails, flints, carbide and cascara, spades and leopard skins, plimsolls, trilbys, calabashes full of palm wine, and old kerosene tins full of palm and groundnut oil.

The inhabitants of the market were as varied and as curious as the wares offered for sale: there were Hausa men clad in their brilliant white robes and little white skull-caps; local chieftains in multi-coloured robes and richly embroidered caps with tassels; there were the pagans from distant mountain villages, wearing nothing but a scrap of dirty leather round the loins, their teeth filed to points, their faces tattooed. For them this represented a teeming metropolis, and the market was perhaps the high spot of the year's amusements. They argued fiercely, waving their arms, pushing each other, their dark eyes shining with delight, over such things as cocoa yams or Cane Rats; or else they stood in little groups gazing with hopeless longing at the toppling piles of multicoloured cloth, milling round from one vantage point to another, in order to get the best views of these unobtainable luxuries.

My staff and the lorry driver disappeared into this pungent, swirling crowd like ants into a treacle tin, and I was left to wander round by myself. After a time I decided to try to take some photographs of the pagan tribesmen, so I set up the camera and started to focus it. Immediately, pandemonium broke loose; the tribesmen with one accord dropped their goods and chattels and fled for the nearest shelter, screaming wildly. Rather bewildered by this, for the average African is generally only too pleased to have his photograph taken, I turned to a Hausa standing close by and asked him what was the matter. The explanation was interesting: apparently the pagans knew what a camera was, and knew that it produced pictures of the people it was pointed at. But they were firmly convinced that with each photograph taken the photographer gained a small portion of his subject's soul, and if he took many photographs he would gain complete control over the person in question. This is a good example of witchcraft being brought up to date; in the old days if you obtained some of your victim's hair or toe-nails you had great power over him; nowadays if you get a photograph it apparently acts just as well. However, in spite of the reluctance on the part of my subjects, I did manage to get a few shots of them, by the simple method of standing sideways on, looking in the opposite direction, and taking the photographs from under my arm.

It was not long before I discovered something that drove all thoughts of photography and witchcraft out of my head. In one of the dark little stalls that lined the square I caught a flash of reddish fur, and, moving over to investigate, I found the most delightful monkey on the end of a long string, squatting in the dust and uttering loud and penetrating 'prroup' noises. She had light ginger-coloured fur, a white shirt-front and a mournful black face, and the strange noises she was making sounded like a cross between a bird cry and the friendly greetings of a cat. She sat and watched me very intently for a few seconds, and then she got up suddenly and started to dance. First she rose on her hind legs and jumped up and down vigorously, holding her long arms wide apart, as though she were going to clasp me to her bosom. Then she got down on all fours and started to bounce like a ball, all four feet leaving the ground, her jumps getting higher and higher the more excited she became. Then she stopped and had a short rest before starting on the next part of the dance; this consisted of standing on all fours, keeping her hindquarters quite still, while she flung her forequarters from side to side like a pendulum. Having demonstrated the outline, she then showed me what could be done by a really experienced dancing monkey, and she twirled and leapt and bounced until I felt quite dizzy. I had been attracted to her from the first, but this wild dervish dance was irresistible, and I felt that I simply had to buy her. I paid her owner twice what she was worth and carried her off triumphantly. I bought her a bunch of bananas at one of the stalls, and she was so overcome by my generosity that she repaid me by wetting all down the front of my shirt. I rounded up the staff and the driver, all breathing corn beer, and we climbed into the lorry and continued our journey. The monkey sat on my knee, stuffing her mouth with bananas and uttering little cries of excitement and pleasure as she watched the scenery out of the window. In view of her accomplishment, I decided to call her Pavlova, and Pavlova the Patas monkey she became forthwith.

We drove on for some hours, and by the time we were nearing our destination the valleys were washed with deep purple shadows and the sun was sinking leisurely into a thousand scarlet-and-green feathers of cloud behind the highest range of western hills.

We knew when we reached Bafut, for there the road ended. On our left lay an emormous dusty courtyard surrounded by a high red brick wall. Behind this was a great assembly of circular huts with high thatched roofs, clustered round a small, neat villa. But all these structures were dominated and dwarfed by an edifice that looked like an old-fashioned bee-hive, magnified a thousand times. It was a huge circular hut, with a massive domed roof of thatch, black and mysterious with age. On the opposite side of the road the ground rose steeply, and a wide flight of some seventy steps curved upwards to another large villa, shoe-box shaped, its upper and lower storeys completely surrounded by wide verandas, the pillars of which were hung with bougainvillaea and other creepers in great profusion. This, I realized, was to be my home for the next few months.

As I got stiffly out of the lorry, an arched doorway in the far wall of the large courtyard opened and a small procession made its way across to where I stood. It consisted of a group of men, most of them elderly, clad in flowing multi-coloured robes that swished as they moved; on their heads they wore little skull-caps which were thickly embroidered in a riot of coloured wools. In the midst of this group walked a tall, slim man with a lively and humorous face. He was dressed in a plain white robe, and his skull-cap was innocent of decoration, yet, in spite of this lack of colour, I at once singled him out as the only one of any importance in the little cavalcade, so regal was his manner. He was the Fon of Bafut, ruler of the great grassland kingdom we had been travelling through and its immense population of black subjects. He was enormously wealthy, and he ruled his kingdom, I knew, with an intelligent, if slightly despotic, cunning. He stopped in front of me, smiling gently, and extended a large and slender hand.

'Welcome,' he said.

It was not until later that I learnt he could speak pidgin English as well as any of his subjects, but for some reason he was shy of his accomplishment, so we talked through an interpreter who stood, bent deferentially, translating my speech of welcome through his cupped hands. The Fon listened politely while my speech was translated, and then he waved one huge hand at the villa on top of the slope above us.

'Foine!' he said, grinning.

We shook hands again, then he walked back across the courtyard with his councillors and disappeared through the arched doorway, leaving me to install myself in his 'foine' house.

Some two hours later, when I had bathed and eaten, a messenger arrived and informed me that the Fon would like to visit me for a chat, if I had sufficiently 'calmed' myself after my journey. I sent back a reply to the effect that I was quite calmed and that I would be delighted to receive a visit from the Fon; then I got out the whisky and awaited his coming. Presently he arrived, accompanied by his small retinue, and we sat on the veranda in the lamplight and talked. I drank his health in whisky and water, and he drank mine in neat whisky. We talked, at first, through an interpreter, but as the level of the whisky fell the Fon started to speak pidgin English. For two hours I was fully occupied in explaining my mission in his country: I brought out books and photographs of the animals I wanted, I drew them on bits of paper and made noises like them when all else failed, and all the time the Fon's glass was being replenished with frightening regularity.

He said that he thought I should be able to get most of the animals I had shown him, and he promised that the next day he would send some good hunters to work for me. But, he went on, the best thing for him to do was to spread the word among his people so that they would all try to 'catch beef' for me; the best opportunity for this, he explained, was in about ten days' time. Then there was to be a certain ceremony: apparently his subjects, on an appointed day, gathered large quantities of dry grass from the hills and valleys and brought it into Bafut so that the Fon could re-thatch the roof of the great juju house and the roofs of his innumerable wives' houses. When the grass had been brought in he provided the food and drink for a feast. There would be many hundreds of people at this ceremony, assembled from all over the surrounding countryside, and the Fon explained that this would be an ideal opportunity for him to make a speech and explain to his people what I wanted. I agreed heartily, thanked him profusely and refilled his empty glass. The level in the bottle fell lower and lower, until it was obviously innocent of even the most reluctant drops of liquid. The Fon rose majestically to his feet, stifled a hiccup and then held out a hand.

'I go!' he proclaimed, waving in the vague direction of his small villa.

'I'm sorry too much,' I said politely; 'you like I go walk for road with you?'

'Yes, my friend,' he beamed. 'Na foine!'

I called for a member of the staff, who came running at the double carrying a hurricane lantern. He preceded us as we walked down the veranda towards the steps. The Fon was still clasping my hand in his, while with the other he gestured at the veranda, the rooms and the moonlit garden some thirty feet below, muttering 'Foine, foine,' to himself in a self-satisfied way. When we reached the top of the long flight of steps he paused and stared at me pensively for a moment, then he pointed downwards with one long arm:

'Sheventy-foif step,' he beamed.

'Very fine,' I agreed, nodding.

'We go count um,' said the Fon, delighted at the idea. 'Sheventy-foif, we go count um.'

He draped a long arm around my shoulders, leant heavily upon me, and we descended to the road below, counting loudly. As he could not remember the English for any number higher than six we got somewhat confused half-way down, and on reaching the bottom we found that according to the Fon's reckoning there were three steps missing.

'Sheventy-two?' he asked himself; 'no, na, sheventy-foif. Which side dey done go?'

He glared fiercely at his cringing retinue, who were waiting in the road, as though he suspected them of having secreted the missing steps under their robes. Hastily I suggested that we should count them again. We climbed up to the veranda once more, counting wildly, and then, to make quite sure, we counted them all the way down again. The Fon kept counting up to six and then starting again, and I could see that unless something was done we should spend all night searching for the missing steps; so, when we reached the top, and again when we got to the bottom, I said 'Seventy-five!' in loud, triumphant tones, and beamed at my companion. He was a bit reluctant to accept my reckoning at first, for he had only got up to five, and felt that the missing seventy needed some explaining. However, I assured him that I had won innumerable prizes for mental arithmetic in my youth, and that my total was the correct one. He clasped me to his chest, clutched my hand and wrung it, muttering 'Foine, foine, my friend,' and then wended his way across the great courtyard to his own residence, leaving me to crawl up the seventy-five steps to bed.

The next day, in between coping with a headache brought on by my session with the Fon, I was kept busy building cages for the flood of specimens that I hoped would soon be rolling in. At noon four tall and impressive-looking young men turned up, clad in their best and brightest sarongs, and carrying flintlocks. These fearsome weapons were incredibly ancient, and their barrels were pitted and eroded with rust holes, as though each gun had suffered an acute attack of smallpox. I got them to stack these dangerous-looking weapons outside the gate before they came in and talked to me. They were the hunters the Fon had sent, and for half an hour I sat and showed them pictures of animals and explained how much I would pay for the various creatures. Then I told them to go away and spend the afternoon hunting, and to return in the evening with anything they caught. If they caught nothing they were to come again early the following morning. Then I distributed cigarettes, and they wandered off down the road, talking earnestly to each other, and pointing their guns in all directions with great abandon.

That evening one of the four young men turned up again carrying a small basket. He squatted down and gazed at me sorrowfully while he explained that he and his companions had not had very good luck with their hunting. They had been a considerable distance, he said, but had found none of the animals I had shown them. However, they had got *something*.

Here he leant forward and put the basket at my feet.

'I no savvy if Masa want dis kind of beef,' he said.

I removed the lid of the basket and peered inside. I thought that it might contain a squirrel, or possibly a rat, but there sat a pair of large and beautiful toads.

'Masa like dis kind of beef?' asked the hunter, watching my face anxiously.

'Yes, I like um too much,' I said, and he grinned.

I paid him the required sum of money, 'dashed' him some cigarettes, and he went off, promising to return the following morning with his companions. When he had gone I could turn my attention back to the toads. They were each about the circumference of a saucer, with enormous liquid eyes and short, fat legs that seemed to have some difficulty in supporting their heavy bodies. Their coloration was amazing: their backs were a rich cream, sprinkled with minute black vermiculations; the sides of the heads and bodies were a deep red, a colour that was a cross between mahogany and wine. On their bellies this was replaced by a vivid buttercup yellow.

Now I have always liked toads, for I have found them to be quiet, well-behaved creatures with a charm of their own; they have not the wildly excitable and rather oafish character of the frog, nor his gulping and moist appearance. But, until I met these two, I had always imagined that all toads were pretty much the same, and that having met one you had met them all as far as personality was concerned, though they might differ much in colour and appearance. But I very soon found out that these two amphibians had personalities so striking that they might almost have been mammals.

These creatures are called Brow-leaf Toads, because the curious cream-coloured marking on the back is, in shape and colour, exactly like a dead and withered leaf. If the toad crouches down on the floor of the forest it merges into its background perfectly. Hence its English title; its scientific title is 'Eyebrow Toad', which in Latin sounds even more apt: *Bufo superciliarus,* for the Brow-leaf, on first acquaintance, gives the impression of being overwhelmingly supercilious. Above its large eyes the skin is hitched up into two little points, so that the creature has its eyebrows raised at the world in a markedly sardonic manner. The immensely wide mouth adds to this impression of aristocratic conceit by drooping gently at the corners, thus giving the toad a faintly sneering expression that can only be achieved by one other animal that I know of, the camel. Add to this the slow, swaggering walk, and the fact that the creature squats down every two or three steps and gazes at you with a sort of pitying disdain, and you begin to feel that superciliousness could not go much farther.

My two Brow-leafs squatted side by side on a bed of fresh grass in the bottom of the basket and gazed up at me with expressions of withering scorn. I tipped the basket on its side, and they waddled out on to the floor with all the indignation and dignity of a couple of Lord Mayors who had been accidentally locked in a public lavatory. They walked about three feet across the floor and then, apparently exhausted by this effort, squatted down, gulping gently. They surveyed me very fixedly for some ten minutes with what appeared to be ever-increasing disgust. Then one of them wandered away and eventually crouched down by the leg of the table, evidently under the mistaken impression that it was the trunk of a tree. The other continued to stare at me, and after mature reflection he summed up his opinion of my worth by being sick, bringing up the semi-digested corpses of a grasshopper and two moths. Then he gave me a pained and reproachful look and joined his friend under the table.

As I had no suitable cage ready for them, the Brow-leafs spent the first few days locked in my bedroom, wandering slowly and meditatively about the floor, or squatting in a trance-like state under my bed, and affording me untold amusement by their actions. I discovered, after a few hours' acquaintance with my plump room-mates, that I had sadly misjudged them, for they were not the arrogant, conceited creatures they pretended to be. They were actually shy and easily embarrassed beasts, completely lacking in self-confidence; I suspect that they suffered from deep and ineradicable inferiority complexes, and that their insufferable air of superiority was merely a pose to hide from the world the hideous truth, that they had no faith in their fat selves. I discovered this quite by accident the night of their arrival. I was making notes on their coloration, while the toads squatted on the floor at my feet, looking as though they were composing their own entries for Burke's *Peerage*. Wanting to examine their hindquarters more closely, I bent down and picked up one of them between finger and thumb, holding him under the arm-pits, so that he dangled in the air in a most undignified manner. He uttered a loud indignant belch at this treatment and kicked out with his fat hind legs, but my grip was too strong for him and he just had to dangle there until I had finished my examination of his lower regions. Eventually, when I replaced him on the ground next to his companion, he was a different toad altogether. Gone was his aristocratic expression: he was a deflated and humble amphibian. He crouched down, blinking his great eyes nervously, while a sad and timid expression spread over his face. He looked almost as if he were going to cry. This transformation was so sudden and complete that it was astonishing, and I felt absurdly guilty at having been the cause of his ignominy. In order to even things up a bit, I picked up the other one and let him dangle for a while, and he, too, lost his self-confidence and became timid and embarrassed when I replaced him on the floor. They sat there looking so dejected and miserable that it was ludicrous, and my unmannerly laughter proved too much for their sensitive natures, for they waddled rapidly away and hid under the table for the next half-hour. But now that I had learnt their secret I could deflate them at will when they became too haughty: all I had to do was to rap them gently on the nose with my finger, and they would crouch down guiltily, looking as though they were about to blush, and gaze at me with pleading eyes.

I built a nice large cage for my Brow-leafs, and they settled down in it quite happily; however, to keep them healthy, I allowed them to have a walk in the garden every day. When the collection increased, I found that there was too much work to be done for me to be able to stand around patiently while my two blue-blooded aristocrats took the air; I had to cut down on their walks, much to their annoyance. Then, one day, I found a guardian for them in whose hands I could safely leave them while I got on with my work. This guardian was none other than Pavlova the Patas monkey.

Pavlova was extremely tame and gentle, and she took an intense interest in everything that went on around her. The first time I put the Brow-leafs out for a walk near her she was quite captivated by them and stood up on her hind legs, craning her neck to get a better view as they walked sedately across the compound. Going back ten minutes later to see how the toads were getting on, I found that they had both wandered close to the spot where Pavlova was tied. She was squatting between them, stroking them gently with her hands, and uttering loud purring cries of astonishment and pleasure. The toads had the most ridiculously self-satisfied expressions on their faces, and they were sitting there unmoving, apparently flattered and soothed by her caresses.

Every day after that I would put the toads out near to the place where Pavlova was tied, and she would watch them wandering about. She would give occasional cries of amazement at the sight of them, or else stroke them gently until they lay there in a semi-hypnotized condition. If ever they wandered too far away and were in danger of disappearing into the thick undergrowth at the edge of the compound, Pavlova would get very excited and call me with shrill screams to let me know that her charges were escaping, and I would hurry down and bring them back to her. One day she called me when the toads had wandered too far afield, but I did not hear her, and when I went down some time later Pavlova was dancing hysterically at the end of her string, screaming furiously, and the Brow-leafs were nowhere to be seen. I undid the monkey's leash, and she at once led me towards the thick bushes at the edge of the compound, and within a very short time she had found the runaways and had fallen on them with loud purring cries of joy.

Pavlova really got terribly fond of these fat toads, and it was quite touching to see how eagerly she greeted them in the morning, gently stroking and patting them, and how worried she got when they wandered too far away. A thing that she found very difficult to understand was why the toads were not clad in fur, as another monkey would be. She would touch their smooth skins with her fingers, endeavouring to part the non-existent fur, a worried expression on her little black face; occasionally she would bend down and lick their backs in a thoughtful sort of way. Eventually she ceased to worry over their baldness, and treated them with the same gentleness and affection she would have displayed towards offspring of her own. The toads, in their own curious way, seemed to become quite fond of her as well, though she sometimes upset their dignity, which annoyed them. I remember one morning I had just given them both a bath, which they thoroughly enjoyed, and on walking across the compound they got various bits of stick and dirt stuck to their wet tummies. This worried Pavlova, for she liked her protégés to be clean and neat. I found her sitting in the sunshine, her feet resting on the back of one Brow-leaf as though he were a footstool, while the other one dangled in the most undignified fashion from her hand. As he slowly revolved in mid-air, Pavlova solemnly picked all the bits of rubbish from his tummy, talking to him all the time in a series of squeaks and trills. When she had finished with him she put him on the ground, where he sat looking very crestfallen, while his partner was hoisted up into the air and forced to undergo the same indignity. The poor Brow-leafs had no chance of being superior and pompous when Pavlova was around.

Chapter Two

The Bafut Beagles

In order to hunt for the various members of the Bafut fauna, I employed, as well as the four hunters the Fon had supplied, a pack of six thin and ungainly mongrels, who, their owners assured me, were the finest hunting dogs in West Africa. I called this untidy ensemble of men and dogs the Bafut Beagles. Although the hunters did not understand the meaning of this title they grew extremely proud of it, and I once heard a hunter, when arguing with a neighbour, proclaim in shrill and indignant tones, 'You no go shout me like dat, ma friend. You no savvy dat I be Bafut Beagle?'

Our hunting method was as follows: we would walk out to some remote hillside or valley, and then choose a thick patch of grass and bushes. At a suitable point we would spread the nets in a half-moon shape; then, with the dogs, we would walk through the undergrowth, driving whatever creatures we found there into the nets. Each dog wore round its neck a little wooden bell, so that when the pack disappeared into the long grass we could still keep a track on their whereabouts by the loud clonking noise from these ornaments. The advantage of this method of hunting was that I was on the spot to handle the creatures from the very moment of capture, and they could be hastily transported back to Bafut and placed in decent cages with the minimum of delay. We transported our captures in bags with special air holes, ringed with brass, let into the sides; for the bigger and tougher creatures the bags were of canvas or hessian, and for the more delicate beasts they were made out of soft cloth. Once in the darkness of the bag the captives generally ceased to struggle, and lay quite quiet until we got them home again; the most frightening part of the process from the animals' point of view was disentangling them from the net, but after a bit of practice we got this down to a fine art, and an animal could be caught, removed from the net and placed in a bag within the space of two minutes.

The first day that I went out with the Bafut Beagles the hunters turned up so heavily armed one would have thought that we were going out to hunt a lion. Apart from the usual machetes, they were carrying spears and flintlocks. As I did not fancy receiving a backside full of rusty nails and gravel, I insisted, amid much lamentation, that the guns be left behind. The hunters were horrified at my decision.

'Masa,' said one of them plaintively, 'if we go meet bad beef how we go kill um if we go lef' our gun for dis place?'

'If we go meet bad beef we go catch um, no kill um,' I said firmly.

'Eh! Masa go catch bad beef?'

'Na so, my friend. If you fear, you no go come, you hear?'

'Masa, I no de fear,' he said indignantly; 'but if we go meet bad beef and it go kill Masa, de Fon get angry too much.'

'Hush your mouth, my friend,' I said, producing the shotgun. 'I go take my own gun. Den if beef go kill me it no be your palaver, you hear?'

'I hear, sah,' said the hunter.

It was very early morning, and the sun had not yet risen above the encircling mountain ranges. The sky was a very delicate shade of rose pink, trimmed here and there with a lacing of white cloud. The valleys and hills were still blurred and obscured with mist, and the long golden grass at the roadside was bent and heavy with dew. The hunters walked ahead in single file, the pack of dogs scampering in and out of the undergrowth, their bells making a pleasant clonking as they ran. Presently we turned off the road and followed a narrow twisting pathway that led over the hills. Here the mist was thicker, but low-lying. You could not see the lower half of your body, and you got the eerie impression that you were wading waist deep in a smooth and gently undulating lake of foam. The long grass, moist with dew, squeaked across my shoes, and all around me, under the surface of this opaque mist lake, tiny frogs were sharing an amphibian joke with each other in a series of explosive chuckles. Soon the sun rose like a frosted orange above the distant fringe of hills, and as its heat grew stronger the mist started to rise from the ground and coil up to the sky, until it seemed as though we were walking through a forest of pale white trees that twisted and bent, broke and re-formed with amoebic skill as they stretched and spiralled their way upwards. It took us two hours to reach our destination, the place that the hunters had chosen for our first hunt. It was a deep, wide valley lying between two ridges of hills, curving slightly, like a bow. Along the bottom of this valley a tiny stream made its way between black rocks and golden grass, glinting in the sun like a fine skein of spun glass. The undergrowth in the valley was thick and tangled, shaded here and there by small clumps of shrubs and bushes.

We made our way down into the valley, and there spread about a hundred yards of nets right across it. Then the hunters took the dogs and went to the head of the valley, while I waited near the nets. For half an hour there was silence as they moved slowly towards the net, a silence broken only by the faint sound of the dogs' bells and an occasional shrill expletive from the hunters when one of them trod on a thorn. I was just beginning to think that we had drawn a blank when the hunters started a great uproar and the dogs began barking furiously. They were still some distance away from the net, and hidden from my view by a small clump of trees.

'Na whatee?' I shouted above the noise.

'Na beef for dis place, Masa,' came the answer.

I waited patiently, and presently a panting hunter burst through the trees.

'Masa, you go give me dis small catch-net,' he said, pointing at the smaller nets neatly piled beside the bags.

'Na what kind of beef you done find?' I asked him.

'Na squirrel, sah. 'E done run for up stick.'

I picked up a thick canvas bag, and followed him through the undergrowth until we reached the clump of trees. Here the hunters were grouped, all chattering and arguing as to the best way of catching the quarry, while the dogs leapt and barked round the trunk of a small tree.

'Which side dis beef?' I asked.

' 'E dere dere for up, Masa.'

'Na fine beef dis, Masa.'

'We go catch um one time, Masa.'

I stepped to the base of the tree and peered up into the foliage; there, perched on a branch some twenty feet above us, was a large and handsome squirrel, of a brindled grey colour with a white stripe along his ribs, and orange paws. His tail was long and not bushy, banded faintly with grey and black. He squatted on the branch, occasionally flipping his tail at us and crying 'Chuck! ... chuck!' in a testy sort of manner, as though he was more irritated than alarmed. He watched us with a malevolent eye while we set up the nets in a circle, about ten feet away from the base of the tree. Then we tied up the dogs, and the smallest of the hunters was detailed to climb after the squirrel and drive him down. This latter part of the operation was the hunters' idea; I felt that to try and out-manoeuvre a squirrel in a tree would be impossible, but the hunters insisted that once someone climbed up, the squirrel would come down to the ground. As it turned out they were quite right: no sooner had the hunter reached the upper branches on one side of the tree, than the squirrel shot down the trunk on the other side. With incredible cunning he dashed at the one part of the net that had a tear in it, struggled through the hole and galloped off through the grass, the hunters and myself in hot pursuit, all of us shouting instructions to one another which were completely disregarded. We rounded a clump of bushes to see the squirrel scrambling up the trunk of another small tree.

Once again we spread the nets, and once again the hunter climbed up after the squirrel. This time, however, our quarry was more cunning, for he saw that we were guarding the hole in the net through which he had escaped last time. He ran down the tree-trunk on to the ground, gathered himself into a bunch and jumped. He sailed through the air and cleared the top of the net by about half an inch; the hunter nearest to him made a wild grab, but missed him, and the squirrel galloped off chuck-chucking indignantly to himself. This time he decided on new evasive tactics, and so instead of climbing up a tree, he dived into a hole at the base of one of them.

Once again we surrounded the tree with nets, and then started to poke long, slender sticks down into the network of tunnels in which he was hiding. This, however, had no effect whatsoever, except to make him chuck a bit faster, so we gave it up. Our next attempt was more successful: we stuffed a handful of smouldering grass into the largest hole, and as the pungent smoke was swept through the various tunnels we could hear the squirrel coughing and sneezing in an angry fashion. At last he could bear it no longer and dashed out of one of the holes, diving head-first into the nets. But even then he had not finished causing trouble, for he bit me and two of the hunters while we were disentangling him, and bit a third hunter while he was being forced into a canvas bag. I hung the bag on the branches of a small bush, and we all sat down to have a much-needed smoke while the squirrel peered at us through the brass-ringed air holes and chattered ferociously, daring us to open the bag and face him.

The Side-striped Ground Squirrels are common enough in the grasslands of West Africa, but I was pleased to have caught this one, as he was the first live specimen I had obtained. As their name implies, these squirrels are almost completely terrestrial in their habits, so it rather surprised me to see the one we had caught taking refuge up in the trees. I discovered later that all the grassland squirrels (most of which *are* terrestrial) made straight for the trees when pursued, and only chose holes in the ground, or hollow logs, as a last resort.

Presently, when we had bound up our wounds, smoked cigarettes and congratulated each other on our first capture, we moved the big net further down the valley, to an area where the grass was thick and tangled and almost six feet tall. This was a good place for a special kind of beef, the hunters informed me, though, with understandable caution, they refused to specify what kind. We set up the net, I placed myself at a suitable point half-way along it and inside the curve, so that I could disentangle anything that was caught, and the hunters took the dogs and made their way about a quarter of a mile up the valley. They gave a prolonged yodel to let me know they had started to beat through the long grass, and then silence descended. All I could hear was the whirr and tick of innumerable grasshoppers and locusts around me, and the faint sounds of the dogs' bells. Half an hour passed and nothing happened; I was hemmed in by tall, rustling grass, so thick and interwoven that it was impossible to see through it for more than a couple of feet.

The tiny clearing in which I was sitting shimmered with heat, and I began to feel extremely thirsty; looking round, I noticed something that I had forgotten: a thermos flask of tea which my thoughtful cook had stuck into one of the collecting bags. Thankfully, I got it out, and, squatting down at the edge of the long grass, poured myself a cup. As I was drinking, I noticed the mouth of a dark tunnel in the wall of grass opposite to where I was squatting; it was obviously some creature's private pathway through the forest of grass stalks, and I decided that when I had finished my drink I would investigate it.

I had just poured out my second cup of tea when a terrific uproar broke out to my right, and startlingly near at hand; the hunters were uttering shrills yelps to encourage the dogs, and the dogs were barking furiously. I was just wondering what it was all about when I heard a rustling noise in the grass; I moved closer to the tunnel to try to see what was causing the sound, when quite suddenly the grass parted and a large dark-brown shape hurled itself out of the hole and ran straight into me. I was at a distinct disadvantage: to begin with, I was not expecting the attack, and secondly, I was squatting on my heels, clasping a thermos flask in one hand and a cup of tea in the other. The animal, which, to my startled eyes, seemed to be twice the size of a beaver, landed amidships, and I went flat on my back, the creature on my stomach, and the thermos flask pouring a stream of scalding tea into my lap with deadly accuracy. Both the creature and I seemed equally astonished, and our shrill squeals of fright were almost identical. My hands were full, so I could do nothing more than make a wild grab at him with my arms, but he bounced off me like a rubber ball and scuttled away through the grass. A portion of the net started to jerk and quiver, and despairing squeals were wafted to me, so I presumed that he must have run straight into the net. Shouting for the hunters, I struggled through the long grass towards the spot where the net was moving.

Our quarry had entangled himself very thoroughly, and he lay hunched up in the net, quivering and snorting, and occasionally making ineffectual attempts to bite through the mesh. Peering at it, I could see we had caught a very large Cane Rat, a creature known to the Africans as a Cutting-grass, a name which describes its habits very well, for with its large and well-developed incisors the Cutting-grass goes through the grassfields – and the farmlands – like a mowing machine. It measured about two and a half feet in length, and was covered with a coarse brownish fur. It had a chubby, rather beaver-like face, small ears set close to the head, a thick naked tail and large naked feet. It seem so scared of my presence that I did not approach it until the hunters arrived, for fear it would break out of the net. It lay there quivering violently, and occasionally giving little jerks and leaps into the air, accompanying them with a despairing squeal. At the time, this action worried me quite a lot, for it looked at though the creature was in the last stages of a heart attack. It was only later, when I grew to know these animals better, that I discovered they greeted any unusual experience with this display of hysteria, in the hope, I suppose, of frightening or confusing the enemy. In reality, Cane Rats are not very timid animals, and would not hesitate to bury their large incisors in the back of your hand if you tried to take liberties with them. I kept a discreet distance until the hunters joined me; then we went forward and removed the rat from the net.

While we were manoeuvring him from the net into a stout bag, he suddenly jumped violently in my hands; to my surprise, as I tightened my grip on him, a large quantity of his fur came away in my fingers. When we had him safely in the bag, I sat down and examined the hair that my clutch had removed from his fat body; it was fairly long and quite thick, more like a coarse bristle; it is apparently planted so loosely in the skin that it comes away in handfuls at the slightest pull. Once it has come away, the hair takes a remarkably long time to grow again, and, as bald Cane Rats are not exactly beautiful, one had to handle them with extreme care.

After we had captured the Cane Rat we made our way slowly up the valley, spreading the net at intervals and beating likely looking patches of undergrowth. When it was obvious that the valley would yield no more specimens, we rolled up the nets and made our way towards a large hill about half a mile away. This hill was so beautifully formed that it might well have been a barrow, the grave of some giant who had prowled the grassland in days gone by; on the very top was a cluster of boulders, each the size of a house, rearing themselves up like a monument. Growing in the narrow crevices and gullies between these rocks were a number of tiny trees, their trunks twisted and crumpled by the winds, each bearing a small cluster of bright golden fruit. In the long grass round the base of the trunks grew several purple and yellow orchids, and in places the great rocks were covered with a thick mat of climbing plant, a kind of convolvulus, from which dangled the ivory-coloured, trumpet-shaped flowers. The great pile of rocks, the bright flowers and the shaggy and misshapen trees formed a wonderful picture against the smouldering blue of the afternoon sky.

We climbed up into the shade of these rocks and squatted in the long grass to have our meal. The mountain grassland spread away from us in all directions, its multitude of colours shimmering and changing with the wind. The hill-crests were pale gold changing to white, while the valleys were pale greeny-blue, darker in places where a pompous cumulus cloud swept over, trailing a purple shadow in its wake. Directly ahead of us lay a long range of delicately sculptured hills whose base was almost hidden in a litter of great boulders and small trees. The hills were so smoothly and beautifully formed, and clad in grass which showed such a bewildering variety of greens, golds, purples and whites, that they looked like a great rambling wave rearing up to break over the puny barrier of rocks and shrubs below. The peace and silence of these heights was remarkable; nearly all sounds were created by the wind, and it was busy moving here and there, making each object produce its own song. It combed the grass and brought forth a soft, lisping rustle; it squeezed and wriggled between the cracks and joints of the rocks above us and made owl-like moans and sudden hoots of mirth; it pushed and wrestled with the tough little trees, making them creak and groan, and making their leaves flutter and purr like kittens. Yet all these small sounds seemed to enhance rather than destroy the silence of the grassland.

Suddenly the silence was shattered by a terrific uproar that broke out behind the massive pile of rocks. Working my way round there, I found the hunters and dogs in a group at the base of a giant rock. Three of the hunters were arguing vigorously with each other, while the fourth was dancing about, yelping with pain and scattering large quantities of blood from a wound in his hand, with the excited dogs leaping and barking frenziedly around him.

'Na whatee dis palaver?' I asked.

All four hunters turned on me and offered their separate descriptions of the event, their voices becoming louder and louder as they tried to shout each other down.

'Why you all de shout? How I go hear if you all go talk together like women, eh?' I said.

Having thus produced silence, I pointed at the bloodstained hunter.

'Now, how you done get dis wound, ma friend?'

'Masa, beef done chop me.'

'Beef? What kind of beef?'

'Eh! Masa, I no savvay. 'E de bite *too much,* sah.'

I examined his hand and found that a chunk the size of a shilling had been neatly removed from the palm. I rendered primitive first-aid, and then went into the matter of the animal that had bitten him.

'Which side dis beef?'

' 'E dere dere for dat hole, sah,' said the wounded one, pointing at a cleft in the base of a large rock.

'You no savvay what kind of beef?'

'No, sah,' he said aggrievedly, 'I no see um. I go come for dis place an' I see dat hole. I tink sometime dere go be beef for inside, so I done put ma hand for dere. Den dis beef 'e done chop me.'

'Whah! Dis man no get fear,' I said, turning to the other hunters, 'he no go look de hole first. He done put his hand for inside and beef done chop him.'

The other hunters giggled. I turned to the wounded man again.

'Ma friend, you done put your hand for dis hole, eh? Now, sometimes you go find snake for dis kind of place, no be so? If snake done chop you what you go do?'

'I no savvay, Masa,' he said, grinning.

'I no want dead hunter man, ma friend, so you no go do dis sort of foolish ting again, you hear?'

'I hear, sah.'

'All right. Now we go look dis beef that done chop you.'

Taking a torch from the collecting bag I crouched down by the hole and peered up it. In the torch beam a pair of small eyes glowed ruby red, and then a little, pointed, ginger-coloured face appeared round them, uttered a shrill, snarling screech and disappeared into the gloom at the back of the hole.

'Ah!' said one of the hunters who had heard the noise, 'dis na bush dog. Dis beef 'e fierce too much, sah.'

Unfortunately, the pidgin English term 'bush dog' is used indiscriminately to describe a great variety of small mammals, few of which are even remotely related to dogs, so the hunter's remark left me none the wiser as to what sort of an animal it was. After some argument, we decided that the best way to get the beast to show itself was to light a fire outside the hole, and then blow smoke into it by fanning with a bunch of leaves. This we proceeded to do, having first hung a small net over the mouth of the hole. The first whiff of smoke had hardly drifted in amongst the rocks when the beast shot out of the hole and into the net with such force that it was torn from its moorings, and the animal rolled down the slope into the long grass, carrying the net with him. The dogs scrambled after him, barking uproariously with excitement, and we followed close on their heels, yelling threats as to what punishment they would receive if they harmed the quarry. However, the beast hardly needed our help, for he was perfectly capable of looking after himself, as we soon found out.

He shook himself free of the folds of netting, and stood up on his hind legs, revealing himself as a slim ginger mongoose, about the size of a stoat. He stood there, swaying slightly from side to side, his mouth wide open, uttering the shrillest and most ear-piercing shrieks I have ever heard from an animal of that size. The dogs pulled up short and surveyed him in consternation as he swayed and shrieked before them; one, slightly braver than the rest, moved forward gingerly and sniffed at this strange creature. This was obviously what the mongoose had been waiting for; he dropped flat in the grass and slid forward like a snake, disappearing among the long grass stalks, and then suddenly reappearing in between the feet of our noble pack, where he proceeded to whirl round like a top, biting at every paw and leg in sight, and keeping up an incessant yarring scream as he did so. The dogs did their best to avoid his jaws, but they were at a disadvantage, for the long grass hid his approach, and all they could do was leap wildly in the air. Then, suddenly, their courage failed them, and they all turned tail and fled up the hill again, leaving the mongoose standing on his hind legs in the field of battle, panting slightly, but still able to screech taunts at their retreating tails.

The pack having thus been vanquished, it was left to us to try to capture this fierce, if diminutive, adversary. This we accomplished more easily than I had thought possible: I attracted his attention, and then got him to attack a canvas collecting bag, and while he was busily engaged in biting this, one of the hunters crept round behind him and threw a net over him. During the time we were disentangling the mongoose from the net and getting him into a bag, he nearly deafened us with his screams of rage, and he kept up this ghastly noise all the way home, though mercifully it was slightly muffled by the thick canvas. He did not stop until, on reaching Bafut, I tipped him into a large cage and threw in a gory chicken's head. He settled down to eat this in a very philosophical manner, and soon finished it. After that he remained silent, except went he caught sight of anyone, and then he would rush to the bars and start to scream abuse at them. It became so nerve-racking in the end that I was forced to cover the front of his cage with a bit of sacking until he had become more used to human company. Three days later I heard those familiar screeches echoing down the road, and long before the native hunter appeared in sight I knew that another Dwarf Mongoose was being brought in. I was pleased to find that this second one was a young female, so I put her in with the one we had already captured. This was rather unwise of me, for they took to screaming in chorus, each trying to outdo the other, until the noise was as soothing as a knife drawn sideways across a plate, magnified several thousand times.

On arrival back at Bafut after my first day out with the Beagles, I received a note from the Fon asking me to go over to his house for a drink and to give him any hunting news there might be, so when I had eaten and changed I set off across the great courtyard and presently came to the Fon's little villa. He was seated on the veranda, holding a bottle of gin up to the light to see what the contents were.

'Ah, ma friend!' he said, 'you done come? You done have good hunting for bush?'

'Yes,' I said, taking the chair he offered, 'hunter man for Bafut savvay catch fine beef. We done catch three beef.'

'Foine, foine,' said the Fon, pouring out five fingers of gin into a glass and handing it to me. 'You go stay here small time you go get plenty plenty beef. I go tell all ma peoples.'

'Na so. I think Bafut people savvay catch beef pass all people for Cameroons.'

'Na true, na true,' said the Fon delightedly; 'you speak true, ma friend.'

We raised our glasses, chinked them together, beamed at one another and then drank deeply. The Fon filled up the glasses again, and then sent one of his numerous retinue in search of a fresh bottle. By the time we had worked our way through most of this bottle we had mellowed considerably, and the Fon turned to me:

'You like musica?' he inquired.

'Yes, too much,' I said, truthfully, for I had heard that the Fon possessed a band of more than usual skill.

'Good! We go have some musica,' he said, and issued a terse command to one of his servants.

Presently the band filed into the compound below the veranda, and to my surprise it consisted of about twenty of the Fon's wives, all naked except for meagre loin-cloths. They were armed with a tremendous variety of drums, ranging from one the size of a small saucepan to the great deep-bellied specimens that required two people to carry them; there were also wooden and bamboo flutes that had a curious sweetness of tone, and large bamboo boxes filled with dried maize that gave forth a wonderful rustling rattle when shaken. But the most curious instrument in the band was a wooden pipe about four feet long. This was held upright, one end resting on the ground, and blown into in a special way, producing a deep, vibrating noise that was quite astonishing, for it was the sort of sound you would expect to come only from a lavatory with exceptional acoustics.

The band began to play, and soon various members of the Fon's household started to dance in the compound. The dance consisted of a sort of cross between folk dancing and ballroom dancing. The couples, clasping each other, would gyrate slowly round and round, their feet performing tiny and complicated steps, while their bodies wiggled and swayed in a way that no Palais de Dance would have allowed. Occasionally, a couple would break apart and each twirl off on their own for a time, doing their own swaying steps to the music, completely absorbed. The flutes twittered and squeaked, the drums galloped and shuddered, the rattles crashed and rustled with the monotonous regularity of waves on a shingle beach, and steadily, behind this frenzy of sound, you could hear the tuba-like instrument's cry, a gigantic catharsis every few seconds with the constancy of a heartbeat.

'You like my musica?' shouted the Fon.

'Yes, na very fine,' I roared back.

'You get dis kind of musica for your country?'

'No,' I said with genuine regret, 'we no get um.'

The Fon filled my glass again.

'Soon, when my people bring grass, we go have plenty musica, plenty dancing, eh? We go have happy time, we go be happy too much, no be so?'

'Yes, na so. We go have happy time.'

Outside in the compound the band played on, and the steady roll and thud of the drums seemed to drift up into the dark sky and make even the stars shiver and dance to their rhythm.

Chapter Three

The Squirrel that Booms

There were two species of the grassland fauna that I was very anxious to obtain during my stay in Bafut; one was the Rock Hyrax, and the other was Stanger's squirrel. To get them I had to undertake two hunts in very different types of country, and they remain in my mind more vividly than almost all the other hunting experiences I had in the grasslands.

The first of these hunts was after the squirrel, and it was chiefly remarkable because for once I was able to plan a campaign in advance and carry it through successfully without any last-minute, unforeseen hitches. Stanger's squirrel is a reasonably common animal in the Cameroons, but previously I had hunted for it in the deep forest in the Mamfe basin. In this sort of country it spent its time in the top branches of the higher trees (feeding on the rich banquet of fruit growing in those sunny heights) and rarely coming down to ground level. This made its capture almost impossible. However, I had since learnt that in the grassland the squirrel frequented the small patches of forest on river-banks, and spent quite a large part of its time on the ground, foraging in the grass for food. This, I felt would give one a better chance of capturing it. When I had shown a picture of the squirrel to the Bafut Beagles, they identified it immediately, and vociferously maintained that they knew where it was to be found. Questioning them, I discovered that they knew the habits of the creature quite well, for they had hunted it often.

Apparently the squirrels lived in a small patch of mountain forest, but in the very early morning or in the evening they came down from the trees and ventured into the grassland to feed. Then, said the Bafut Beagles, was the time to catch them. What, I asked, did this beef do during the night?

'Ah! Masa, you no fit catch um for night time,' came the reply; 'dis beef 'e de sleep for up dat big stick where no man fit pass. But for evening time, or early-early morning time we fit catch um.'

'Right,' I said, 'we go catch um for early-early morning time.'

We left Bafut at one o'clock in the morning, and after a long and tedious walk over hills, through valleys and grassfields, we reached our destination an hour before dawn. It was a small plateau that lay half-way up a steep mountain-side. The area was comparatively flat, and across it tinkled a wide and shallow stream, along the sides of which grew a thick but narrow strip of forest. Crouching in the lee of a big rock, peering into the gloom and wiping the dew from our faces, we spied out the land and made our plans. The idea was to erect two or three strips of net in the long grass about five hundred yards away from the edge of the trees. This we had to do immediately, before it got so light that the squirrels could see us.

Erecting nets in long grass up to your waist, when it is sodden with dew, is not a soothing pastime, and we were glad when the last one had been tied in place. Then we cautiously approached the forest, and crawled into hiding beneath a large bush. Here we squatted, trying to keep our teeth from chattering, not able to smoke or talk or move, watching the eastern sky grow paler as the darkness of the night was drained out of it. Slowly it turned to a pale opalescent grey, then it flushed to pink, and then, as the sun rose above the horizon, it turned suddenly and blindingly to a brilliant kingfisher blue. This pure and delicate light showed the mountains around us covered in a low-lying mist; as the sun rose higher, the mist started to move and slide on the ridges and pour down the hillsides to fill the valleys. For one brief instant we had seen the grasslands quiet and asleep under the blanket of mist; now it seemed as though the mountains were awakening, yawning and stretching under the white coverlet, pushing it aside in some places, gathering it more tightly in others, hoisting itself, dew-misted and sleepy, from the depths of its white bed-clothes. On many occasions later I watched this awakening of the mountains, and I never wearied of the sight. Considering that the same thing has been happening each morning since the ancient mountains came into being, it is astonishing how fresh and new the sight appears each time you witness it. Never does it become dull and mechanical; it is always different: sometimes the mist in rising shaped itself into strange animal shapes – dragons, phoenix, wyvern and milk-white unicorns – sometimes it would form itself into strange, drifting strands of seaweed, trees or great tumbling bushes of white flowers; occasionally, if there was a breeze to help it, it would startle you by assuming the most severe and complicated geometrical shapes, while all the time, underneath it, in tantalizing glimpses as it shifted, you could see the mountains gleaming in a range of soft colours so delicate and ethereal that it was impossible to put a name to them.

I decided as I squatted there, peering between the branches of the bush we sheltered under, watching the mountains waken, that it was worth feeling tired, cold and hungry, worth being drenched with dew and suffering cramps, in order to see such a sight. My meditations were interrupted by a loud and aggressive 'Chuck . . . chuck!' from the trees above us, and one of the hunters gripped my arm and looked at me with glowing eyes. He leant forward slowly and whispered in my ear:

'Masa, dis na de beef Masa want. We go sit softly softly 'e go come down for ground small time.'

I wiped the dew from my face and peered out at the grassfield where we had set the nets. Presently we heard other chucking noises from deeper in the forest as more of the squirrels awoke and glanced at the day with suspicious eyes. We waited for what seemed a long time, and then I suddenly saw something moving in the grassfield between us and the nets; a curious object that at first sight looked like an elongated black-and-white-striped balloon, appearing now and then above the long grass. In that mist-blurred morning haze I could not make out what this strange object could be, so I attracted the hunter's attention and pointed to it silently.

'Dis na de beef, Masa,' said one.

' 'E done go for ground, 'e done go for ground,' said the other gleefully.

'Na whatee dat ting?' I whispered, for I could not reconcile that strange balloon-like object with any part of a squirrel's anatomy.

'Dis ting na 'e tail, sah,' explained a hunter, and, so that I should be left in no doubt, 'dat ting 'e get for 'e larse.'

Like all tricks, once it had been explained, it became obvious. I could see quite clearly that the black-and-white-striped object *was* a squirrel's tail, and I wondered why on earth I had thought that it resembled a balloon. Presently the one tail was joined by others, and as the mist lifted and cleared we could see the squirrels themselves.

There were eight of them hopping out into the grassfield. They were large and rather bulky animals, with heavy heads, but the largest and most flamboyant parts of their anatomies were their tails. They hopped cautiously from tussock to tussock, pausing to sit up on their hind legs and sniff carefully in the direction they were travelling. Then they would get down and hop forward a few more feet, flipping their tails as they moved. Sometimes they would crouch perfectly still for a few seconds, their tails laid carefully over their backs, the bushy ends hanging down and almost obscuring their faces. The ones in the grassfield were silent, but in the trees behind us we could still hear an occasional suspicious 'chuck' from those that had not yet plucked up the courage to descend. I decided that eight would be quite enough for us to try to catch, so I signalled the hunters and we rose from our hide-out. We spread out in a line through the trees, and then the hunters paused and waited for the signal to advance.

The squirrels were now about a hundred and fifty yards from the forest's edge, and I decided that this was far enough for our purposes. I waved my hand, and then we walked out from the shelter of the trees into the long grass. The squirrels in the forest gave loud chucks of alarm, and the squirrels in the grassfield sat up on their hind legs to see what was the matter. They saw us and all froze instantly; then, as we moved slowly forward, they hopped off into the grass, further and further from the trees. I do not think they could quite make out what we were, for we advanced very slowly and with the minimum of movement. They felt we were something hostile, but they were not certain; they would run a few yards and then stop and sit up to survey us, sniffing vigorously. This was really the most tricky part of the whole proceeding, for the animals were not yet within the half circle of the nets, and by breaking away to left or right they could easily escape into the grassfields. We drifted towards them cautiously, the only sounds being the swish of our feet in the grass and faint and frantic chucks from the forest behind us.

Quite suddenly one squirrel more quick-witted than the rest realized what was happening. He could not see the nets ahead, for they were hidden in the long grass and well camouflaged, but he saw that as we advanced we were driving him further and further away from the forest and the safety of the tall trees. He gave a loud chuck of alarm and dashed off through the grass, his long tail streaming out behind him, and then suddenly twisted to the left and galloped through the grass away from the nets. His one ambition was to get round us and back to the trees. The rest of the squirrels sat up and watched him nervously, and I realized that unless something was done they would all pluck up courage and follow his example. I had planned to wait until they were well within the circle of nets before charging down on them and causing a panic that would send them scuttling into the mesh, but it now became obvious that we should have to take a chance and stampede them. I raised my hand, and the hunters and I surged forward, yelling and hooting, waving our arms and trying to appear as fearsome as possible. For a split second the squirrels watched us without movement; then they fled.

Four of them followed the example of the first one and dashed off at right angles, thus avoiding both the hunters and the nets; the remaining three, however, ran straight for our trap, and as we dashed towards the scene we could see the top of the net jerking – a certain indication that they had got themselves entangled. Sure enough, we found them firmly entwined, glaring out at us and giving vent to the loudest and most awesome gurking noises I have heard from a squirrel. It was a completely different sound from the loud chuck that they had been making: it was fearsome and full of warning – a cross between a snore and a snarl. They kept this up while we were unwinding them, giving savage bites at our hands with their great orange incisors. When we had at last got them into canvas bags we had to hang the bags on the end of a stick to carry them, for, unlike the other grassland squirrels, who lay quietly when they were put in the gloom of a bag, these creatures seemed quite willing to continue the fight, and the slightest touch on the outside of the bag would be greeted by a furious attack and a rapid series of gurks.

The squirrels in the forest were thoroughly alarmed, and the trees echoed to the sound of frantic chuckings. Now that they had realized how dangerous we were it was useless to try to attempt another capture, so we had to be content with the three we had caught; we packed up our nets and other equipment and made our way back to Bafut. Once there I placed my precious squirrels in three solid, tin-lined cages, filled their plates with food, and left them severely alone until they should have recovered from the indignity of capture. As soon as they were left alone they ventured out of the darkness of their bedrooms and demolished the pile of succulent fruits with which I had provided them, upset their water-pots, tested the tin lining of the cages to see if they could be gnawed through and, finding that this was impossible, retired to their bedrooms again and slept. Seen at close quarters they were quite handsome beasts, with pale yellow bellies and cheeks, russet-red backs and great banded tails. The effect was somewhat spoilt by their heads, which were large and rather horse-like, with tiny ears set close to the skull, and protuberant teeth.

I had read somewhere that these squirrels climb to the top branches of the forest trees in the early morning and utter the most powerful and astonishing cries: deep rolling sounds that were like the last notes of a giant gong being struck. I was interested to hear this cry, but I thought it unlikely that they would produce it in captivity. However, the morning after the capture I was awakened at about five-thirty by a peculiar noise; the collection was on the veranda outside my window, and when I sat up in bed I decided that the noise was coming from one of the cages, but I could not tell from which. I put on my dressing-gown and crept out of the door. I waited patiently in the dim light, chilly and half awake, for a repetition of the sound. It came again in a few minutes, and I could defintely trace it to the squirrels' cage. The noise is extremely difficult to describe: it started like a groan, and as it got louder it took on a throbbing, vibrating note, the sort of thrumming you hear from telegraph poles – the sound seemed to blur and waver, like a gong hit very softly, rising to a crescendo and then dying away. The squirrels were obviously being rather half-hearted about their attempt; in the forest they would have put much more force into it, and then I should imagine it would be a weird and fascinating cry to hear, drifting through the misty branches.

That evening the Fon appeared, as usual, to find out what success the day had brought, and to present me with a calabash of fresh palm wine. With great pride I showed him the squirrels, and described the capture in detail for him. He was intrigued to know exactly where we had caught them, and as I did not really know the locality, I had to go and call one of the hunters – who was merry-making in the kitchen – to explain to him. He stood in front of the Fon, answering his questions through cupped hands. It took quite a long time for the hunter to do this, for the country we had been in was uninhabited, so he could only describe our route by reference to various landmarks in the shape of rocks, trees and curiously shaped hills. At last the Fon started to nod vigorously, and then sat for a few minutes in thought. Then he spoke to the hunter rapidly, making wide gestures with his long arms, while the hunter nodded and bowed. At length the Fon turned to me, smiling benignly, and carelessly, almost absent-mindedly, holding out his empty glass.

'I done tell dis man,' he explained, watching me fill the glass with an apparently uninterested eye, ''e go take you for some special place for mountain. For dis place you get some special kind of beef.'

'What kind of beef?' I asked.

'Beef,' said the Fon vaguely, gesturing with his half-empty glass, 'special kind of beef. You no get um yet.'

'Na bad beef dis?' I suggested.

The Fon put his glass on the table and spread out his enormous hands.

'Na so big,' he said, 'no be bad bad beef, but 'e bite too much. 'E go live for dat big big rock, 'e go go for under. Sometime 'e de hollar too much, 'e go Wheeeeeeeee!!!'

I sat and puzzled over the creature, while the Fon watched me hopefully.

''E look same same for Cutting-grass, but 'e no get tail for 'e larse,' he said at last, helpfully.

Light suddenly dawned, and I went in search of a book; I found the picture I wanted, and showed it to the Fon.

'Dis na de beef?' I asked.

'Ah! Na so,' said the Fon delightedly, stroking the portrait of the rock hyrax with his long fingers; 'dis na de beef. How you de call um?'

'Rock hyrax.'

'Rooke hyrix?'

'Yes. How you de call um for Bafut?'

'Here we call um N'eer.'

I wrote the name down on the list of local names I was compiling, and then refilled the Fon's glass. He was still gazing in a trance at the engraving of the hyrax, tracing its outline with one slender finger.

'Wha!' he said at length in a wistful voice, 'na fine chop dis beef. You go cook um with coco yam....'

His voice died away and he licked his lips reminiscently.

The hunter fixed me with his eye, and shuffled his feet as an indication that he wanted to speak.

'Yes, na whatee?'

'Masa want to go for dis place de Fon de talk?'

'Yes. We go go tomorrow for morning time.'

'Yes, sah. For catch dis beef Masa go need plenty people. Dis beef fit run too much, sah.'

'All right, you go tell all my boys dey go for bush tomorrow.'

'Yes, sah.'

He stood and shuffled his feet again.

'Whatee?'

'Masa go want me again?'

'No, my friend. Go back for kitchen and drink your wine.'

'Tank you, sah,' he said, grinning, and disappeared into the gloom of the veranda.

Presently the Fon rose to go, and I walked with him as far as the road. As we paused at the edge of the compound he turned and smiled down at me from his great height.

'I be ole man,' he said; 'I de tire too much. If I no be ole man I go come with you for bush tomorrow.'

'You lie, my friend. You no be ole man. You done get power too much. You get plenty power, power pass all dis picken hunter man.'

He chuckled, and then sighed.

'No, my friend, you no speak true. My time done pass. I de tire too much. I get plenty wife, and dey de tire me too much. I get palaver with dis man, and dat man, an' it de tire me too much. Bafut na big place, plenty people. If you get plenty people you get plenty palaver.'

'Na so, I savvay you get plenty work.'

'True,' he said, and then added, his eyes twinkling wickedly, 'sometimes I get palaver with the D.O., an' dat de tire me most of all.'

He shook my hand, and I could hear him chuckling as he walked off across the courtyard.

The next morning we set off on our hyrax hunt – myself, the four Bafut Beagles and five of the household staff. For the first two or three miles we walked through the cultivated areas and the small farms. On the gently sloping hills fields had been dug, and the rich red earth shone in the early morning sunshine. In some of the fields the crops were already planted and ripe, the feathery bushes of cassava or the row of maize, each golden head with its blond tassel of silken thread waving in the breeze. In other fields the women were working, stripped to the waist, wielding short-handled, broad-bladed hoes. Some of them had tiny babies strapped to their backs, and they seemed as unaware of these encumbrances as a hunchback would be of his hump. Most of the older ones were smoking long black pipes, and the rank grey smoke swirled up into their faces as they bent over the ground. It was mostly the younger women who were doing the harder work of hoeing, and their lithe, glistening bodies moved rhythmically in the sun as they raised the heavy and clumsy implements high above their heads and then brought them sweeping down. Each time the blade buried itself in the red earth the owner would give a loud grunt.

As we walked through the fields among them they talked with us in their shrill voices, made jokes and laughed uproariously, all without pausing in their work, and without losing its rhythm. The grunts that interspersed their remarks gave a curious sound to the conversation.

'Morning, Masa . . . ugh! . . . which side you go? . . . ugh!'
'Masa go go for bush . . . ugh! . . . no be so, Masa? . . . ugh!'
'Masa go catch plenty beef . . . ugh! . . . Masa get power . . . ugh!'
'Walker strong, Masa . . . ugh! . . . catch beef *plenty* . . . ugh!'

Long after we had left the fields and were scrambling up the golden slopes of the foothills we could hear them chattering and laughing and the steady thump of the hoes striking home.

When we reached the crest of the highest range of hills that surrounded Bafut the hunters pointed out our destination: a range of mountains, purple and misty, that seemed an enormous distance away. The household staff gave gasps and moans of dismay and astonishment that I should want them to walk so far, and Jacob, the cook, said that he did not think he would be able to manage it, as he had unfortunately picked up a thorn in his foot. Examination proved that there was no thorn in his foot, but a small stone in his shoe. The discovery and removal of the stone left him moody and disgruntled, and he lagged behind, talking to himself in a ferocious undertone. To my surprise, the distance was deceptive and within three hours we were walking through a long winding valley at the end of which the mountains reared up in a wall of glittering gold and green. As we toiled up the slope through the waist-high grass, the hunters explained to me what the plan of campaign was to be. Apparently we had to round one of the smooth buttresses of the mountain range, and in between this projection and the next lay a long valley that thrust its way into the heart of the mountains. The sides of this valley were composed of almost sheer cliffs, at the base of which were the rocks where hyrax lived.

We scrambled round the great elbow of mountain, and there lay the valley before us, quiet and remote and filled with sparkling sunlight that lit the gaunt cliffs on each side – two long, crumpled curtains of rock flushed to pink and grey, patched with golden sunlight and soft blue shadows. Piled at the base of these cliffs were the legacies of many past cliff falls and landslides, a jumble of boulders of all shapes and sizes, some scattered about the curving floor of the valley, some piled up into tall, tottering chimneys. Over and around these rocks grew a rippling green rug of short undergrowth, long grass, hunched and crafty looking trees, small orchids and tall lilies, and a thick, strangling web of convolvulus with yellow, cream and pink flowers. Scattered along the cliff faces were a series of cave mouths, dark and mysterious, some mere narrow clefts in the rock, others the size of a cathedral door. Down the centre of the valley ran a boisterous baby stream that wiggled joyfully in and out of the rocks, and leapt impatiently in lacy waterfalls from one level to the next as it hurried down the slope.

We paused at the head of the valley for a rest and a smoke, and I examined the rocks ahead with my field glasses for any signs of life. But the valley seemed lifeless and deserted; the only sounds were the self-important and rather ridiculous tinkle of the diminutive stream, and the wind and the grass moving together with a stealthy sibilant whisper. High overhead a small hawk appeared against the delicate blue sky, paused for an instant and swept out of view behind the jagged edge of the cliff. Jacob stood and surveyed the valley with a sour and gloomy expression on his pudgy countenance.

'Na whatee, Jacob?' I asked innocently; 'you see beef?'

'No, sah,' he said, glowering at his feet.

'You no like dis place?'

'No, sah, I no like um.'

'Why?'

'Na bad place dis, sah.'

'Why na bad place?'

'Eh! Sometime for dis kind of place you get bad juju, Masa.'

I looked at the Bafut Beagles, who were lying in the grass.

'You get juju for dis place?' I asked them.

'No, sah, attall,' they said unanimously.

'You see,' I said to Jacob, 'dere no be juju for here, so you no go fear, you hear?'

'Yes, sah,' said Jacob with complete lack of conviction.

'And if you go catch dis beef for me I go give you fine dash,' I went on.

Jacob brightened visibly. 'Masa go give us dash same same for hunter man?' he asked hopefully.

'Na so.'

He sighed and scratched his stomach thoughtfully.

'You still think dere be juju for dis place?'

'Eh!' he said, shrugging, 'sometimes I done make mistake.'

'Ah, Jacob! If Masa go give you dash you go kill your own Mammy,' said one of the Bafut Beagles, chuckling, for Jacob's preoccupation with money was well known in Bafut.

'Wha',' said Jacob angrily, 'an' you no love money, eh? Why you go come for bush with Masa if you no love money, eh?'

'Na my job,' said the hunter, and added by way of explanation, 'I be Beagle.'

Before Jacob could think up a suitable retort to this, one of the other hunters held up his hand.

'Listen, Masa!' he said excitedly.

We all fell silent, and then from the valley ahead a strange cry drifted down to us; it started as a series of short, tremulous whistles, delivered at intervals, and then suddenly turned into a prolonged hoot which echoed weirdly from the rocky walls of the valley.

'Na N'eer dis, Masa,' the Beagles whispered. ' 'E de hollar for dat big rock dere.'

I trained my field-glasses on the big huddle of rocks they indicated, but it was some seconds before I saw the hyrax. He was squatting on a ledge of rock, surveying the valley with a haughty expression on his face. He was about the size of a large rabbit, but with short, thick legs and a rather blunt, lion-like face. His ears were small and neat, and he appeared to have no tail at all. Presently, as I watched, he turned on the narrow ledge and ran to the top of the rock, paused for a moment to judge the distance, and then leapt lightly to the next pile of boulders and disappeared into a tangle of convolvulus that obviously masked a hole of some sort. I lowered the glasses and looked at the Bafut Beagles.

'Well?' I asked, 'how we go catch dis beef?'

They had a rapid exchange of ideas in their own language, then one of them turned to me.

'Masa,' he said, screwing up his face and scratching his head, 'dis beef 'e cleaver too much. We no fit catch him with net, and 'e fit run pass man.'

'Well, my friend, how we go do?'

'We go find hole for rock, sah, and we go make fire with plenty smoke; we go put net for de hole, an' when de beef run, so we go catch um.'

'All right,' I said; 'come, we go start.'

We started off up the valley, Jacob leading the way with a look of grim determination on his face. We struggled through the thick web of short undergrowth until we reached the first tottering pile of boulders, and there we spread out like terriers, and scrambled and crawled our way round, peering into every crevice to see if it was inhabited. It was Jacob, strangely enough, who first struck lucky; he raised a sweaty and glowing face from the tangle of undergrowth and called to me.

'Masa, I done find hole. 'E get beef for inside,' he said excitedly.

We crowded round the hole and listened. Sure enough, we could hear something stirring inside: faint scrabbling sounds were wafted to us. Rapidly we laid a fire of dried grass in the entrance to the hole, and when it was well alight we covered it with green leaves, which produced a column of thick and pungent smoke. We hung a net over the hole, and then fanned the smoke into the depths of the rock with the aid of large bunches of leaves. Blown by our vigorous fanning, the smoke rolled and rumbled up the tunnel into the darkness, and then suddenly things began to happen with bewildering rapidity. Two baby hyrax, each the size of a large guinea-pig, shot out into the net with such force that they tore it down, and rolled into the bushes with it tangled round them. Close on their heels came the mother, a corpulent beast in a towering rage. She raced out of the hole and leapt at the nearest person, who happened to be one of the Beagles; she moved so rapidly that he had no time to get out of her way, and she fastened her teeth in his ankle and hung on like a bulldog, giving loud and terrifying 'Weeeeeeeee!' noises through her nose. The Beagle fell backwards into a great blanket of convolvulus, kicking out wildly with his legs and uttering loud cries of pain.

The other Beagles were busy trying to disentangle the baby hyrax from the net and were finding it a whole-time job. The household staff had fled at the appearance of the irate mother, so it was left to Jacob and me to go to the rescue of the Beagle who was lashing about in the undergrowth, screaming at the top of his voice. Before I could do anything sensible, however, Jacob came into his own. For once his brain actually caught up with the rapidity of events. His action was not, I fear, the result of any sympathetic consideration for the sufferings of his black brother, but prompted rather by the thought that unless something was done quickly the female hyrax might escape, in which case he would get no money for her. He leapt past me, with extraordinary speed for one normally so somnolent, clutching in his hand one of the larger canvas bags. Before I could stop him he had grabbed the unfortunate Beagle's leg and stuffed it into the bag, together with the hyrax. Then he drew the mouth of the bag tight with a smile of satisfaction and turned to me.

'Masa!' he said, raising his voice above the indignant screams of his countryman, 'I done catch um!'

His triumph, however, was short-lived, for the Beagle had come to the end of his tether, and he rose out of the undergrowth and hit Jacob hard on the back of his woolly head. Jacob gave a roar of anguish and rolled backwards down the slope, while the Beagle rose to his feet and made desperate efforts to rid his foot of the hyrax-infested bag. I regret to admit that I could do nothing more sensible than sit down on a rock and laugh until the tears ran down my face. Jacob also rose to his feet, uttering loud threats, and saw the Beagle trying to remove the bag.

'Arrrr!' he yelled, leaping up the slope; 'stupid man, de beef go run.'

He clasped the Beagle in his arms and they both fell backwards into the undergrowth. By now the other Beagles had successfully bagged the baby hyrax, so they could come to their companion's rescue; they dragged Jacob away and helped their fellow hunter to remove the bag from his foot. Luckily the hyrax had released her hold on his foot when she was crammed into the bag, and had obviously become too frightened to bite him again, but even so it must have been an unpleasant experience.

Still shaken with gusts of laughter, which I did my best to conceal, I soothed the wounded Beagle and gave Jacob a good talking to, informing him that he would get only half the price of the capture, owing to his stupidity, and the other half would go to the hunter whose foot he had been so anxious to sacrifice. This decision was greeted with nods and grunts of satisfaction from everyone, including, strangely enough, Jacob himself. Most Africans, I have found, have a remarkably well-developed sense of justice, and will agree heartily with a fair verdict even if it is against themselves.

With order thus restored and first aid rendered to the wounded, we went further up the valley. After smoking out several caves and holes, with no results, we at last cornered and captured, without bloodshed on either side, a large male hyrax. Having thus got four of the animals, I felt I had had more than my fair share of luck, and that it would be a good idea to return home. We made our way out of the valley, along the edge of the mountain, and then down the gentle slopes of rolling golden grass towards Bafut. When we reached more or less level country we stopped for a smoke and a rest, and as we squatted in the warm grass I glanced back towards the mountains, my attention attracted by a low rumble of thunder. Unnoticed by us, a dark and heavy cloud had drifted across the sky, the shape of a great Persian cat, and had sprawled itself along the crest of the mountains. Its shadow changed them from green and gold to a deep and ugly purple, with harsh black stripes where the valleys lay. The cloud seemed to move, shifting and coiling within itself, and appeared to be padding and kneading the mountain crests like a cat on the arm of a gigantic chair. Occasionally a rent would appear in this nebulous shape, and then it would be pierced by an arrow of sunlight which would illuminate an area of the mountain below with a pure golden light, turning the grass to jade-green patches on the purple flanks of the mountains.

With amazing rapidity the cloud grew darker and darker, and seemed to swell as though gathering itself for a spring. Then the lightning began falling like jagged silver icicles, and the mountains shuddered with the vibrations of the thunder that followed.

'Masa, we go walka quick,' said one of the Beagles; 'sometime dat storm go reach us.'

We continued on our way as fast as we could, but we were not fast enough, for the cloud spilled over the mountain top and spread over the sky behind us in a slow-motion leap. A cold and agitated wind came hurrying ahead, and close on its heels came the rain, in an almost solid silver curtain that drenched us within the first few seconds. The red earth turned dark and slippery, and the hiss of the rain in the grass made conversation almost impossible. By the time we had gained the outskirts of Bafut our teeth were chattering with cold and our sodden garments were sticking icily to us as we moved. We reached the last stretch of road and the rain dwindled to a fine, drifting spray, and then ceased altogether, while a white mist rose from the sodden earth and broke round our legs like the backwash of an enormous wave.

Chapter Four

The King and the Conga

The great day of the grass-gathering ceremony arrived at last. Before dawn, when the stars had only just started to fade and dwindle, before even the youngest and most enthusiastic village cockerel had tried his voice, I was awakened by the gentle throb of small drums, laughter and chatter of shrill voices, and the soft scuff of bare feet on the dusty road below the house. I lay and listened to these sounds until the sky outside the window was faintly tinged with the green of the coming day, then I went out on to the veranda to see what was happening.

The mountains that clustered around Bafut were mauve and grey in the dim morning light, striped and patterned with deep purple and black in the valleys, where it was still night. The sky was magnificent, black in the West where the last stars quivered, jade green above me, fading to the palest kingfisher blue at the eastern rim of hills. I leant on the wall of the veranda where a great web of bougainvillaea had grown, like a carelessly flung cloak of brick-red flowers, and looked down the long flight of steps to the road below, and beyond it to the Fon's courtyard. Down the road, from both directions, came a steady stream of people, laughing and talking and beating on small drums when the mood took them. Over their shoulders were long wooden poles, and tied to these with creepers were big conical bundles of dried grass. The children trotted along carrying smaller bundles on thin saplings. They made their way down past the arched opening into the Fon's courtyard and deposited their grass in heaps under the trees by the side of the road. Then they went through the arch into the courtyard, and there they stood about in chattering groups; occasionally a flute and a drum would strike up a brief melody, and then some of the crowd would break into a shuffling dance, amid handclaps and cries of delight from the onlookers. They were a happy, excited and eager throng.

By the time I had finished breakfast the piles of grass bundles by the roadside were towering skywards, and threatening to overbalance as each new lot was added; the courtyard was now black with people, and they overflowed through the arched door and out into the road. The air was full of noise as the first arrivals greeted the late-comers and chaffed them for their laziness. Children chased each other in and out of the crowd, shrieking with laughter, and hordes of thin and scruffy dogs galloped joyfully at their heels, yelping enthusiastically. I walked down the seventy-five steps to the road to join the crowd, and I was pleased and flattered to find that they did not seem to resent my presence among them, but greeted me with quick, welcoming smiles that swiftly turned to broad grins of delight when I exchanged salutations in pidgin English. I eventually took up a suitable position by the roadside, in the shade of a huge hibiscus bush, scarlet with flowers and filled with the drone of insects. I soon had round me an absorbed circle of youths and children, who watched me silently as I sat and smoked and gazed at the gay crowd that surged past us. Eventually I was run to earth by a panting Ben, who pointed out reproachfully that it was long past lunchtime, and that the delicacy the cook had prepared would undoubtedly be ruined. Reluctantly I left my circle of disciples (who all stood up politely and shook my hand) and followed the grumbling Ben back to the house.

Having eaten, I descended once more to my vantage point beneath the hibiscus, and continued my anthropological survey of the Bafut people as they streamed steadily past. Apparently during the morning I had been witnessing the arrival of the common or working man. He was, as a rule, dressed in a gaudy sarong twisted tightly round the hips; the women wore the same, though some of the very old ones wore nothing but a dirty scrap of leather at the loins. This, I gathered, was the old style of costume: the bright sarong was a modern idea. Most of the older women smoked pipes – not the short, stubby pipes of the lowland tribes, but ones with long, slender stems, like old-fashioned clay pipes; and they were black with use. This was how the lower orders of Bafut dressed. In the afternoon the council members, the petty chiefs, and other men of substance and importance started to arrive, and there was no mistaking them for just ordinary creatures of the soil. They all wore long, loose-fitting robes of splendid colours, which swished and sparkled as they walked, and on their heads were perched the little flat skull-caps I had noticed before, each embroidered with an intricate and colourful design. Some of them carried long, slender staves of dark brown wood, covered with a surprisingly delicate tracery of carving. They were all middle-aged or elderly, obviously very conscious of their high office, and each greeted me with great solemnity, shaking me by the hand and saying 'Welcome' several times very earnestly. There were many of these aristocrats and they added a wonderful touch of colour to the proceedings. When I went back to the house for tea I paused at the top of the steps and looked down at the great courtyard: it was a solid block of humanity, packed so tightly together that the red earth was invisible, except in places where some happy dancers cleared a small circle by their antics. Dotted among the crowd I could see the colourful robes of the elders like flowers scattered across a bed of black earth.

Towards evening I was in the midst of the thickest part of the throng, endeavouring to take photographs before the light got too bad, when a resplendent figure made his appearance at my side. His robes glowed with magenta, gold and green, and in one hand he held a long leather switch. He was the Fon's messenger, he informed me, and, if I was quite ready, he would take me to the Fon for the grass ceremony. Hastily cramming another film into the camera, I followed him through the crowd, watching with admiration as he cut a way through the thickest part by the simple but effective method of slicing with his switch across the bare buttocks that presented themselves so plentifully on all sides. To my surprise the crowd did not seem to take exception to this treatment but yelped and screamed in mock fear, and pushed and stumbled out of our way, all laughing with delight. The messenger led me across the great courtyard, through the arched doorway, along a narrow passage, and then through another arched doorway that brought us out into a honeycomb of tiny courtyards and passages. It was as complicated as a maze, but the messenger knew his way about, and ducked and twisted along passages, through courtyards, and up and down small flights of steps until at length we went through a crumbling brick archway and came out into an oblong courtyard about a quarter of an acre in extent, surrounded by a high red brick wall. At one end of this courtyard grew a large mango tree, and around its smooth trunk had been built a circular raised dais; on this was a big heavily carved chair, and in it sat the Fon of Bafut.

His clothing was so gloriously bright that, for the moment, I did not recognize him. His robe was a beautiful shade of sky blue, with a wonderful design embroidered on it in red, yellow and white. On his head was a conical red felt hat, to which had been stitched vast numbers of hairs from elephants' tails. From a distance it made him look as though he were wearing a cone-shaped haystack on his head. In one hand he held a fly-whisk, the handle of delicately carved wood and the switch made from the long, black-and-white tail of a colobus monkey – a thick silky plume of hair. The whole very impressive effect was somewhat marred by the Fon's feet: they were resting on a huge elephant tusk – freckled yellow and black with age – that lay before him, and they were clad in a pair of very pointed piebald shoes, topped off by jade-green socks.

After he had shaken me by the hand and asked earnestly after my health, a chair was brought for me and I sat down beside him. The courtyard was lined with various councillors, petty chiefs and their half-naked wives, all of them squatting along the walls on their haunches, drinking out of carved cow-horn flasks. The men's multicoloured robes made a wonderful tapestry along the red stone wall. To the left of the Fon's throne was a great pile of black calabashes, their necks stuffed with bunches of green leaves, containing mimbo or palm wine, the most common drink in the Cameroons. One of the Fon's wives brought a glass for me, and then lifted a calabash, removed the plug of leaves, and poured a drop of mimbo into the Fon's extended hand. He rolled the liquid round his mouth thoughtfully, and then spat it out and shook his head. Another flask was broached with the same result, and then two more. At last a calabash was found that contained mimbo the Fon considered fine enough to share with me, and the girl filled my glass. Mimbo looks like well-watered milk, and has a mild, faintly sour, lemonade taste which is most deceptive. A really good mimbo tastes innocuous, and thus lures you on to drink more and more, until suddenly you discover that it is not so harmless as you had thought. I tasted my glass of wine, smacked my lips, and complimented the Fon on the vintage. I noticed that all the councillors and petty chiefs were drinking out of flasks made from cows' horn, whereas the Fon imbibed his mimbo from a beautifully carved and polished buffalo horn. We sat until it was almost dark, talking and gradually emptying the calabashes of mimbo.

Eventually the Fon decided that the great moment for feeding the masses had arrived. We rose and walked down the courtyard between the double ranks of bowing subjects, the men clapping their hands rhythmically, while the women held their hands over their mouths, patting their lips and hooting, producing a noise that I, in my ignorance, had thought to be the prerogative of the Red Indian. We made our way through the doors, passages and tiny courtyards, the concourse filing behind, still clapping and hooting. As we came out of the archway into the main courtyard there arose from the multitude a deafening roar of approval, accompanied by clapping and drumming. Amid this tumultuous reception the Fon and I walked along the wall to where the Fon's throne had been placed on a leopard skin. We took our seats, the Fon waved his hand, and the feast began.

Through the archway came an apparently endless stream of young men, naked except for small loin-cloths, carrying on their shining and muscular shoulders the various foods for the people. There were calabashes of palm wine and corn beer, huge bunches of plantain and bananas, both green and golden yellow; there was meat in the shape of giant Cane Rats, mongooses, bats and antelope, monkeys and great hunks of python, all carefully smoked and spitted on bamboo poles. Then there were dried fish, dried shrimps and fresh crabs, scarlet and green peppers, mangoes, oranges, pawpaws, pineapples, coconuts, cassava and sweet potatoes. While this enormous quantity of food was being distributed, the Fon greeted all the headmen, councillors and chiefs. They would each approach him, then bend double before him and clap their hands three times. The Fon would give a brief and regal nod, and the man would retire backwards. If anyone wanted to address the Fon they had to do so through their cupped hands.

I had by now absorbed quite a quantity of mimbo and was feeling more than ordinarily benign; it seemed to have much the same effect on the Fon. He barked a sudden order, and, to my horror, a table was produced on which reposed two glasses and a bottle of gin, a French brand that I had never heard of, and whose acquaintance I am not eager to renew. The Fon poured out about three inches of gin into a glass and handed it to me; I smiled and tried to look as though gin, neat and in large quantities, was just what I had been wanting. I smelt it gingerly, and found that it was not unlike one of the finer brands of paraffin. Deciding that I really could not face such a large amount undiluted, I asked for some water. The Fon barked out another order, and one of his wives came running, clutching a bottle of Angostura bitters in her hand.

'Beeters!' said the Fon proudly, shaking about two teaspoonfuls into my gin; 'you like gin wit beeters?'

'Yes,' I said with a sickly smile, 'I love gin with bitters.'

The first sip of the liquid nearly burnt my throat out: it was quite the most filthy raw spirits I have ever tasted. Even the Fon, who did not appear to worry unduly about such things, blinked a bit after his first gulp. He coughed vigorously and turned to me, wiping his streaming eyes.

'Very strong,' he pointed out.

Presently, when all the food had been brought out and arranged in huge piles in front of us, the Fon called for silence and made a short speech to the assembled Bafutians, telling them who I was, why I was there and what I wanted. He ended by explaining to them that they had to procure plenty of animals for me. The crowd listened to the speech in complete silence, and when it had ended a chorus of loud 'Arhhh's!' broke loose, and much handclapping. The Fon sat down looking rather pleased with himself, and, carried away by his enthusiasm, he took a long swig at his gin. The result was an anxious five minutes for us all as he coughed and writhed on his throne, tears streaming down his face. He recovered eventually and sat there glaring at the gin in his glass with red and angry eyes. He took another very small sip of it, and rolled it round his mouth, musing. Then he leant over to confide in me.

'Dis gin strong too much,' he said in a hoarse whisper; 'we go give dis strong drink to all dis small-small men, den we go for my house and we drink, eh?'

I agreed that the idea of distributing the gin among the petty chiefs and councillors – the small-small men as the Fon called them – was an excellent one.

The Fon looked cautiously around to make sure we were not overheard; as there were only some five thousand people wedged around us he felt that he could tell me a secret in complete safety. He leant over and lowered his voice to a whisper once more.

'Soon we go for my house,' he said, gleefully; 'we go drink White Horshe.'

He sat back to watch the effect of his words on me. I rolled my eyes and tried to appear overcome with joy at the thought of this treat, while wondering what effect whisky would have on top of mimbo and gin. The Fon, however, seemed satisfied, and presently he called over the small-small men, one by one, and poured the remains of the gin into their cow-horn drinking cups, which were already half-filled with mimbo. Never have I given up a drink so gladly. I wondered at the cast-iron stomachs that could face with equanimity, and even pleasure, a cocktail composed of that gin and mimbo. I felt quite sick at the mere thought of it.

Having distributed his rather doubtful largesse among his following, the Fon rose to his feet, amid handclaps, drumbeats and Red Indian hootings, and led the way back through the intricate web of passages and courts, until we came to his own small village, almost hidden among the wives' many grass huts, like a matchbox in an apiary. We went inside, and I found myself in a large, low room furnished with easy-chairs and a big table, the wooden floor covered with fine leopard skins and highly coloured, locally made grass mats. The Fon, having done his duty to his people, relaxed in a long chair, and the White Horse was produced; my host smacked his lips as the virginal bottle was uncorked, and gave me to understand that, now the boring duties of state were over, we could start to drink in earnest. For the next two hours we drank steadily, and discussed at great length and in the most complicated detail such fascinating topics as the best type of gun to use on an elephant, what White Horse was made of, why I didn't attend dinners at Buckingham Palace, the Russian question, and so on. After this neither the Fon's questions nor my answers had the skill and delicate construction that we would have liked, so the Fon called for his band, being under the misguided impression that the ravages of strong drink could be dissipated by sweet music. The band came into the courtyard outside and played and danced for a long time, while the Fon insisted that another bottle of White Horse be broached to celebrate the arrival of the musicians. Presently the band formed a half-circle, and a woman did a swaying, shuffling dance and sang a song in a shrill and doleful voice. I could not understand the words, but the song was strangely mournful, and both the Fon and I were deeply affected by it. Eventually the Fon, wiping his eyes, sharply informed the band that they had better play something else. They had a long discussion among themselves and finally broke into a tune which was the most perfect Conga rhythm imaginable. It was so bright and gay that it quickly revived our spirits, and very soon I was tapping the rhythm out with my feet, while the Fon conducted the band with a glass of White Horse clutched in one hand. Flushed with the Fon's hospitality, and carried away by the tune, an idea came to me.

'The other night you done show me native dance, no be so?' I asked the Fon.

'Na so,' he agreed, stifling a hiccup.

'All right. Tonight you like I go teach you European dance?'

'Ah! my friend,' said the Fon, beaming and embracing me; 'yes, yes, foine, you go teach me. Come, we go for dancing house.'

We rose unsteadily to our feet and made our way to the dance-hall. When we reached it, however, I found that the effort of walking fifty yards had told on my companion; he sank on to his ornate throne with a gasp.

'You go teach all dis small-small men first,' he said, gesturing wildly at the throng of chiefs and councillors, 'den I go dance.'

I surveyed the shuffling, embarrassed crowd of council members that I was supposed to teach, and decided that the more intricate parts of the Conga – which was the jig I proposed to tutor them in – would be beyond them. Indeed, I was beginning to feel that they might even be beyond me. So I decided that I would content myself with showing them the latter part of the dance only, the part where everyone joins into a line and does a sort of follow-my-leader around the place. The whole dance-hall was hushed as I beckoned the two-and-twenty council members to join me on the floor, and in the silence you could hear their robes swishing as they walked. I made them tag on behind me, each holding on to his predecessor's waist; then I gave a nod to the band, who, with great gusto, threw themselves into the

Conga rhythm, and we were off. I had carefully instructed the pupils to follow my every movement, and this they did. I soon discovered, however, that everything I knew about the Conga had been swamped by the Fon cellars: all I could remember was that somewhere, some time, one gave a kick. So off we went, with the band playing frenziedly, round and round the dance-hall: one, two, three, kick; one, two, three, kick. My pupils had no difficulty in following this simple movement, and we went round the floor in great style, all their robes swishing in unison. I was counting the beats and shouting 'Kick' at the appropriate moment, in order to make the thing simpler for them to follow; apparently they took this to be part of the dance, a sort of religious chant that went with it, for they all started shouting in unison. The effect on our very considerable audience was terrific: screeching with delight, various other members of the Fon's retinue, about forty of his wives, and several of his older offspring, all rushed to join on to the column of dancing councillors, and as each new dancer joined on to the tail he or she also joined the chant.

'One, two, three, keek!' yelled the councillors.

'One, two, three, YARR!' yelled the wives.

'Oh, doo, ree, YARR!' screeched the children.

The Fon was not going to be left out of this dance. He struggled up from his throne and, supported by a man on each side, he tagged on behind; his kicks did not altogether coincide with the rhythmic movement of the rest of us, but he enjoyed himself none the less. I led them round and round the dance-hall until I grew giddy and the whole structure seemed to vibrate with the kicks and yells. Then, feeling that a little fresh air was indicated, I led them out of the door and into the open. Off we went in a tremendous, swaying line, up and down steps, in and out of courtyards, through strange huts – in fact everywhere that offered a free passage. The band, not to be outdone, followed us as we danced, running behind, sweating profusely, but never for one moment losing the tune. At last, more by luck than a sense of direction, I led my followers back into the dance-hall, where we collapsed in a panting, laughing heap. The Fon, who had fallen down two or three times during our tour, was escorted back to his chair, beaming and gasping.

'Na foine dance, dis,' he proclaimed; 'foine, foine!'

'You like?' I asked, gulping for air.

'I like too much,' said the Fon firmly; 'you get plenty power; I never see European dance like dis.'

I was not surprised; few Europeans in West Africa spend their spare time teaching the Conga to native chieftains and their courts. I have no doubt that, if they could have seen me doing that dance, they would have informed me that I had done more damage to the White Man's prestige in half an hour than anyone else had done in the whole history of the West Coast. However, my Conga appeared to have increased my prestige with the Fon and his court. 'One, two, three, keek!' murmured the Fon reminiscently; 'na fine song dis.'

'Na very special song,' said I.

'Na so?' said the Fon, nodding his head; 'na foine one.'

He sat on his throne and brooded for a while; the band struck up again and the dancers took the floor; I regained my breath and was beginning to feel rather proud of myself, when my companion woke up suddenly and gave an order. A young girl of about fifteen left the dancers and approached the dais where we sat. She was plump and shining with oil, and clad in a minute loin-cloth which left few of her charms to the imagination. She sidled up to us, smiling shyly, and the Fon leant forward and seized her by the wrist. With a quick pull and a twist he catapulted her into my lap, where she sat convulsed with giggles.

'Na for you, dis woman,' said the Fon, with a lordly wave of one enormous hand, 'na fine one. Na my daughter. You go marry her.'

To say that I was startled means nothing; I was horror-stricken. My host was by now in that happy state that precedes belligerency, and I knew that my refusal would have to be most tactfully put so that I should not undo the good work of the evening. I glanced around helplessly and noticed for the first time what a very large number of the crowd had spears with them. By now the band had stopped playing, and everyone was watching me expectantly. My host was regarding me glassy-eyed. I had no means of telling whether he was really offering me the girl as a wife, or whether this term was used as an euphemism for a more indelicate suggestion. Whichever it was, I had to refuse: quite apart from anything else, the girl was not my type. I licked my lips, cleared my throat, and did the best I could. First, I thanked the Fon graciously for the kind offer of his well-oiled daughter, whose eleven odd stone were at that moment making my knees ache. However, I knew that he was well versed in the stupid customs of my countrymen, and that being so, he knew it was impossible (however desirable) for a man in England to have more than one wife. The Fon nodded wisely at this. Therefore, I went on, I would be forced to refuse his extremely generous offer, for I already had one wife in England, and it would be unlawful, as well as unsafe, to take a second one back with me. If I had not already been married, I went on fluently, there would have been nothing I could have liked better than to accept his gift, marry the girl and settle down in Bafut for the rest of my life.

To my great relief a loud round of applause greeted my speech, and the Fon wept a bit that this lovely dream could never be realized. During the uproar I eased my dusky girl friend off my lap, gave her a slap on the rump and sent her giggling back to the dance-floor. Feeling that I had undergone quite enough for one night in the cause of diplomatic relations, I suggested that the party break up. The Fon and his retinue accompanied me to the great courtyard and here he insisted on clasping me round the waist and doing the Durrell Conga once more. The crowd fell in behind and we danced across the square, kicking and yelling, frightening the Fruit Bats out of the mango trees, and setting all the dogs barking for miles around. At the bottom of the steps the Fon and I bade each other a maudlin farewell, and I watched them doing an erratic Conga back across the courtyard. Then I climbed up the seventy-five steps, thinking longingly of bed. I was met at the top by a disapproving Ben with a hurricane lamp.

'Sah, some hunter-man done come,' he said.

'What, at this hour?' I asked, surprised, for it was after three.

'Yes, sah. You want I tell um to go?'

'They done bring beef?' I asked hopefully, with visions of some rare specimen.

'No, sah. They want palaver with Masa.'

'All right. Bring um,' I said, sinking into a chair.

Presently Ben ushered in five embarrassed young hunters, all clutching spears. They bowed and said good evening politely. Apparently they had been at the feast that night, and had heard the Fon's speech; as they lived at a village some distance away, they thought they had better see me before they returned home, in order to find out exactly what kind of animals I wanted. I commended their zeal, distributed cigarettes and brought out books and photographs. We pored over them for a long time, while I told them which creatures I particularly wanted and how much I was willing to pay. Just as they were about to go one young man noticed a drawing lying on my bed that I had not shown them.

'Masa want dis kind of beef?' he asked, pointing.

I peered at the drawing, and then looked at the young man: he seemed to be quite serious about it.

'Yes,' I said emphatically, 'I want dis kind of beef *too much*. Why, you savvay dis beef?'

'Yes, sah, I savvay um,' said the hunter.

I held out the picture to the men.

'Look um fine,' I said.

They all stared at the bit of paper.

'Now, for true, you savvay dis beef?' I asked again, trying to stifle my excitement.

'Yes, sah,' they said, 'we savvay um fine.'

I sat and gazed at them as though they had been beings from another world. Their casual identification of the picture, coming so unexpectedly, had quite startled me, for the drawing depicted a creature that I had long wanted to get hold of, perhaps the most remarkable amphibian in the world, known to scientists as *Trichobatrachus robustus*, and to anyone else as the Hairy Frog.

A word of explanation is called for at this point. On a previous visit to the Cameroons I had set my heart on capturing some of these weird creatures, but without success. I had been operating then in the lowland forests, and all the hunters there to whom I had shown the picture stoutly denied that any such beast existed. They had looked at me pityingly when I insisted, taking it as just another example of the curiously unbalanced outlook of the white man, for did not everyone know that no frog had hair? Animals had hairs, birds had feathers, but frogs had skin and nothing more. Since it was patently obvious to them that the creature did not exist, they did not bother to search for it, in spite of the huge rewards I offered for its capture. What was the use of looking for a mythical monster, a frog with hairs? I had spent many exhausting nights in the forest, wading up and down streams in search of the elusive amphibian, but with no result, and I had come to believe that, in spite of the textbooks, the hunters were right: the creature was not to be found in the lowland forests. I had been so disillusioned by the scorn and derision which any mention of the Hairy Frog had provoked among the lowland tribes, that on my second trip I had omitted to show the drawing, feeling that the highland hunters would be of the same opinion as their relatives in the great forests. Hence my excitement and astonishment when the young hunter, unprompted, had identified the fabulous beast, and moreover wanted to know if I would like some.

I questioned the hunters closely, quivering like an expectant bloodhound. Yes, for the third time, they did know the beast; yes, it did have hair; yes, it was easy to catch. When I asked where it was found they made sweeping gestures, indicating that the woods were full of them. With glittering eyes I asked if they knew of any particular spot where the frogs were to be found. Yes, they knew of a 'small water' some two miles away where there were generally a few to be seen at night. That was enough for me. I rushed out on to the veranda and uttered a roar. The staff came tumbling out of their hut, bleary-eyed, half asleep, and assembled on the veranda.

'Dis hunter man savvay which side I go and dis frog 'e get beer-beer for 'e l'arse,' I explained, 'so we go catch um one time.'

'*Now*, sah?' asked Ben, horrified.

'Yes, now, now, all you go get bag and torch. Quickly, quickly.'

'For night-time?' asked Ben faintly, for he loved his bed.

'Yes, NOW. Don't just stand there yawning, *go and get torches and bags*.'

The staff, reluctant, puffy-eyed and yawning, shuffled off to obey. Jacob, the cook stopped for a moment to explain to me that he was a cook and not a hunter, and that he did not see why he should be expected to change his vocation at four o'clock in the morning.

'My friend,' I said firmly, 'if you no get bag and torch in five minutes, tomorrow you no be hunter man *or* cook, savvay?'

Hastily he followed the rest of the staff in search of his frog-hunting equipment. Within half an hour my sleepy band was assembled, and we set off down the dewy road on the hunt for the Hairy Frogs.

Chapter Five

Hunt for the Hairy Frogs

In the dim starlight we made our way down the dusty road, the grass on either side glistening and heavy with dew. There was no moon, which was most fortunate: when you are hunting at night by torchlight a moon is a hindrance and not a help, for it casts strange shadows in which your quarry can disappear, and it enfeebles your torch beam.

The little group of hunters walked ahead, wide awake and eager, while my well-paid staff trailed behind, dragging their toes in the dust and yawning prodigiously. Only Jacob, having decided that, as the hunt was inevitable, he had better make the best of it, walked beside me. Occasionally he would glance over his shoulder with a snort of derision, as a more than usually powerful yawn made itself heard from behind.

'Dis people no get power,' he said scornfully.

'I tink sometime dey done forget I go pay five shillings for dis frog we go hunt,' I explained loudly and clearly. My voice carried well in the still night air, and immediately the yawning and the dragging footsteps ceased as the rear column became very much awake. Five shillings was a large sum to pay for a frog.

'I no forget,' said Jacob, slyly grinning up at me.

'That I do not doubt,' I said severely; 'you're a thoroughly unprincipled West African Shylock.'

'Yes, sah,' Jacob agreed unemotionally. It was impossible to crush him: if he did not understand you he simply played safe and agreed with all you said.

We walked down the road for perhaps a mile and a half, then the hunters turned off on to a narrow path through the long grass, a path that was slippery with dew and that led in an erratic series of zig-zags up the side of a hill. All around us in the damp tangle of long grass the tiny frogs and crickets were calling, like a million Lilliputian metronomes; once a large, pale moth rose, spiralling vaguely from the side of the path, and as it fluttered upwards a nightjar came out of the shadows, swiftly and smoothly as an arrow, and I heard the click of its beak as the moth disappeared. The bird turned and skimmed off down the hillside as silently as it had come. When we reached the crest of the hill the hunters informed me that the small stream they had referred to lay in the valley ahead of us. It was a deep, narrow, shadow-filled cleft that ran between the two smooth, buttock-shaped hills, and the curving line of the stream was marked by a dark fringe of small trees and bushes. As we descended into the gloom of the valley the sound of water came to us, gurgling and clopping among the boulders of its bed, and the surface of the path turned to glutinous clay that made unpleasant sucking noises round our feet as we picked our way down, slipping and sliding.

The stream fled down the valley, slithering down a series of wide, shallow, boulder-strewn steps; at the edge of each step was a diminutive waterfall, perhaps eight feet high, and here the stream gathered itself into a polished column of water and plunged down into a circular pool gouged out among the rocks, where it swirled round and round in a nest of silver bubbles before diving on among the litter of rocks towards the next fall. The long grass curved over the edge of the stream in an uncombed mane of golden hair, and among the glistening boulders grew delicate ferns and tiny plants embedded in thick moss that spread everywhere like a layer of green velvet. On the bank, walking delicately on tip-toe, were numbers of small pink and chocolate crabs, and as our torch-beams picked them out they raised their claws menacingly and backed, with infinite caution, down the holes in the red clay that they had dug for themselves. Dozens of minute white moths rose from the long grass as we walked through it, and drifted out across the stream like a cloud of snowflakes. We squatted on the bank to have a smoke and discuss our plan of campaign. The hunters explained that the best place to search for frogs was in the pools at the base of the small waterfalls, but that you also found them under flat rocks in the shallower parts of the stream. I decided that we had better spread out in a line across the stream, and wade up it turning over every movable stone and searching every nook and cranny that might harbour a Hairy Frog. This we did, and for an hour we worked our way steadily uphill towards the source of the stream, splashing through the shallow icy water, slipping on the wet rocks, shining our torches into every hiding-place and turning over the loose rocks with infinite care.

There were plenty of crabs, scuttling and clicking among the stones, bullet-shaped frogs of bright grass green that leapt into the water with loud plops and startled us; there was a wavering curtain of small moths fluttering everywhere, small bats that flicked in and out of our torch-beams, but no Hairy Frogs. We walked, for the most part, in silence; there were the hundred different voices of the stream as it moved in its bed, the zinging of crickets in the long grass, the occasional cry of a startled bird disturbed by our torch-beams, or the sucking gurgle, followed by a splash, as one of us turned a stone over in deep water. Once when we were negotiating a small cliff over which, like a pulsating lace curtain, hung a waterfall, we were startled by a loud scream and a splash. Directing our battery of lights down to the base of the fall we found that Jacob, who had been last to scale the cliff, had put his foot on a water-snake which lay coiled up in a hollow. In his fright he had attempted to leap in the air, but without much success, for he was clinging precariously to the cliff face some five feet from the ground. He fell into the pool at the base of the falls, and emerged unhurt – but soaking wet and with his teeth chattering from his immersion in the freezing waters.

The eastern skies were turning slowly from black to pale green with the coming of dawn, and still we had not found our elusive amphibian. The hunters, who were acutely depressed by our failure, explained that it was useless continuing the search once it was light, for then the frog would not show itself. This meant that we had some two hours left in which to track down the beast and capture it, and, though we continued on our way up the stream, I was convinced that our luck was out and that we would not be successful. At last, damp, cold and dispirited, we came to a broad, flat valley filled with great boulders through which the stream picked its way like a snake. At certain points it had formed deep, quiet pools among the rocks, and, as the ground was flat, the movement of the waters was slow and even, and the stream had doubled its width. The boulders were strewn haphazardly about, all tilted at peculiar angles like giant, archaic gravestones, black under the starry sky. Each one was tapestried with moss, and hung with the sprawling plants of wild begonias.

We had moved about half-way up this valley when I decided to break off for a cigarette. I came to a small pool that lay like a black mirror ringed round with tall rocks, and choosing a smooth dry stone to sit on I switched off my torch and sat down to enjoy my smoke. The torch-beams of my retinue twinkled and flashed among the rocks as they continued up the valley, and the splashing of their feet in the water was soon lost among the many night sounds around me. When I had finished my cigarette, I flipped the butt into the air so that it swooped like a glowing firefly and fell into the pool, where it extinguished itself with a hiss. Almost immediately afterwards something jumped into the pool with a loud plop, and the smooth black waters were netted with a thousand silver ripples. I switched on my torch quickly and shone it on the surface of the water, but there was nothing to be seen. Then I flashed the beam along the moss-covered rocks which formed the lip of the pool. There, not a yard from where I was sitting, squatting on the extreme edge of a rock, sat a great, gleaming, chocolate-coloured frog, his fat thighs and the side of his body covered with a tangled pelt of something that looked like hair.

I sat there hardly daring to breathe, for the frog was perched on the extreme edge of the rock, overhanging the pool; he was alert and suspicious, his legs bunched ready to jump. If he was frightened, he would leap straight off the rock and into the dark waters, and then there would be no hope of catching him. For perhaps five minutes I remained as immobile as the rocks around me, and gradually, as he got used to the light, the Hairy Frog relaxed. Once he shifted his position slightly, blinking his moist eyes, and I was filled with panic thinking that he was going to jump. But he settled down again and I sighed with relief. As I sat there I was busy working out a plan: first, I had to switch the torch from my right to my left hand without disturbing him; then I had to lean forward until my hand was near enough to his fat body to risk grabbing at him. Shifting the torch caused me acute anguish, for he watched the manoeuvre with an alert and suspicious eye; when I had achieved the change I sat quietly for a few minutes to allow him to settle down again, then, with great caution, I moved my cupped hand slowly towards him. Inch by inch I moved until my hand was hanging just above him; then I took a deep breath and grabbed. As my hand swooped downwards the frog jumped, but he was not quite quick enough and my grasping fingers caught him by one slippery hind leg. But he was not going to give up his liberty without a fight, and he uttered a loud screaming gurk, and kicked out frantically with his free hind leg, scraping his toes across the back of my hand. As he did so, I felt as though it had been scratched with several needles, and on the skin of the back of my hand appeared several deep grooves which turned red with the welling blood. I was so astonished at this unexpected attack from a creature which I had thought to be completely harmless, that I must have relaxed my hold slightly. The frog gave an extra hard kick and a wriggle, his moist leg slid through my fingers, there was a plop as he hit the water and the ripples danced. My Hairy Frog had escaped.

My heart, if I can so describe it, was too full for words. An extensive collection of lurid descriptive phrases which I had accumulated over the years seemed anaemic and inadequate to describe this catastrophe. I tried one or two, but they were a very weak indication of how I felt. After all this time I had come face to face with a Hairy Frog, after being told that it did not exist; after many hours of fruitless search, I had actually had the beast in my grasp, and then, through my own stupidity, had let it get away. I clambered on to a tall rock to see where my hunters had got to; I could see their lights flashing a quarter of a mile away down the valley, and I uttered the prolonged yodelling call that the hunters use to communicate with each other. When they answered me, I shouted that they were to hurry back, as I had found the beef we were looking for. Then I climbed down and examined the pool carefully. It was perhaps ten feet long and about five feet across at the widest point. It was fed and emptied through two very narrow channels among the rocks, and I decided that if we blocked these, and the frog was still in the pool, we stood a fair chance of recapturing him. When my panting hunters arrived I explained what had happened, and they clicked their fingers and groaned with annoyance upon learning that the frog had escaped. However, we set to work, and soon we had blocked the entrance and exit channels of the pool with piles of flat stones. Then two of the hunters stood on the rocks and shone our battery of torches into the pool so that we could see what we were doing. First, I tested the depth of the water with the long handle of the butterfly net, and found that it was about two feet deep; the bottom of the pool was of coarse gravel and small stones, a terrain that provided ample hiding-places for the frog. Jacob, myself and two hunters then removed all the garments we had on and slid into the icy water: Jacob and I at one end of the pool, and the two hunters at the other. Slowly we moved down towards each other, bent double, feeling with our fingers and toes in every crack, turning over every stone. Presently, when we had worked to the centre of the pool, one of the hunters gave a yelp of delight and grabbed wildly at something under the water, almost losing his balance and falling on his face.

'Na whatee, na whatee?' we all asked excitedly.

'Na flog,' spluttered the hunter, 'but 'e done run.'

'You no get hand?' inquired Jacob wrathfully through chattering teeth.

' 'E done run for Masa,' said the hunter, pointing in my direction.

As he spoke, I felt something moving near my bare foot, and I bent down and groped frantically under the water. At the same moment, Jacob uttered a shrill scream and dived under the water, and one of the hunters was frantically grabbing at something between his legs. My hand felt a smooth, fat body burrowing in the gravel near my toes, and I grabbed at it; at the same moment, Jacob reappeared above the water, spitting and gasping and waving one arm triumphantly, his hand clasped firmly round a fat frog. He splashed through the water towards me to show me his capture, and as he reached me I straightened up with my own prize caught in my cupped hands. I glanced hurriedly between my fingers and had a quick glimpse of the frog's thick thighs covered with a mat of the hair-like substance; it was a Hairy Frog. Then I looked at Jacob's capture, and found that he had caught one also. After congratulating each other, we cautiously placed our frogs in a deep, soft cloth bag, and tied up the mouth of it carefully. Just as we had done this, the hunter who had been groping wildly between his legs straightened up with a roar of delight, swinging yet another Hairy Frog by the leg.

Warmed and encouraged by our success, we plunged back into the pool once again and searched it carefully, but we found no more frogs. By now the rim of the eastern horizon was a pale powder blue, flecked with gold, and in the sky above us the remaining stars were flickering and dying as stripes of jade green spread across the sky. It was obviously too late to continue with our hunt, but I was well pleased with the results. As the Africans crouched on the rocks, laughing and chattering, smoking the cigarettes I had distributed, I dried myself, rather inadequately, with my handkerchief and put on my dew-soaked clothes. My head was aching savagely, partly, I think, because of the excitement of the capture, but principally owing to the party I had had with the Fon. However, with the glow of triumph enveloping me I cared not for the cold dampness of my clothes, nor for my aching head. The bag with the Hairy Frogs inside I dipped into the pool until it was sodden and cool, then I wrapped it in wet grass and placed it in the bottom of the basket.

As we reached the top of the hill, the sun rose above the distant mountains and flooded the world with a brittle, golden light. The long grass was bent and heavy with dampness, and a thousand tiny spiders had spun their nets among the stalks, and the nets had dredged up from the night a rich haul of dewdrops that shone white and ice blue in the sun. Dozens of great locusts leapt up from under our feet and sped over the grass in a whirring glitter of magenta wings; and some fat bumble bees, electric blue and as furry as bears, formed a humming choir over a group of pale yellow orchids growing in the shelter of a large rock. The air was fresh and cool, full of the scent of flowers, grass, earth and dew. The hunters, happy in the knowledge that the night's activities had been successful, broke into song as they picked their way down the path in single file; a lilting Bafutian melody that they rendered with great verve; the staff joined in, and Jacob beat a gentle tattoo on a collecting tin by way of accompaniment. Thus we marched back to Bafut, singing loudly, Jacob working out more and more complicated rhythms on his improvised drum.

My first job, when we at last reached home, was to prepare a deep tin to house the frogs; this I filled with fresh water, and placed a number of stones at the bottom to act as cover for them. I put two of them into this tin, but the third I placed in a large jam jar. While I had my breakfast, the jam jar rested on the table, and between mouthfuls I contemplated my capture with adoring eyes.

My Hairy Frog was, as frogs go, quite large: with his legs tucked neatly in he would have fitted on to a saucer without very much room left over. His head was broad and rather flat, with very protuberant eyes and a mouth with an extraordinarily wide gape. The ground colour of the upper parts was a deep chocolate brown, mottled dimly in places with darker brown, almost black, markings; the underside was white, flushed with pink on the lower belly and the inside of the thighs. The eyes were very large, jet black netted with a fine filigree of golden marks. The most astonishing thing about the creature – the hair – was confined to the sides of the body and the thighs, where it grew thick and black, about a quarter of an inch long. This adornment is not really hair at all, but consists of fine, elongated filaments of skin, which on close examination resemble the tentacles of a sea anemone. Until you examine the creature closely, however, the illusion that its hindquarters are clothed in a thick layer of fur is complete. In the water the hair stands out, floating like weed, and so is seen to the best advantage; when the frog is out of water the hair takes on a tangled, jelly-like look.

There has been much controversy, ever since the frog was first discovered, over the exact use of this curious hirsute decoration, but it is now believed that the filaments act as an aid to respiration. All frogs breathe, to a certain extent, through their skins: that is to say, the skin absorbs oxygen from the moisture on the creature's body. In this way a frog has, so to speak, two breathing apparatuses – the skin and the lungs. Thus, by breathing through the skin a frog can stay submerged in the water for quite considerable periods. In the case of the Hairy Frog, the great number of filaments give it a much increased skin area, and so must aid its respiration a good deal.

There was considerable doubt originally as to the precise function of the Hairy Frog's hairs, owing to the fact that only the male is hairy; the female is smooth-skinned like any ordinary frog. Thus it appeared as though the hairs were purely ornamental rather than useful, for it seemed ridiculous to suppose that the male was so short-winded that he needed hair to enable him to breathe properly, while the female pursued a hairless and well-aerated existence. This unusual discrepancy was, however, soon explained: it was found that the male spent his life submerged in water, whereas the female led a purely terrestrial existence for the greater part of the year, only going to water during the mating season. So was the mystery explained – the female on land, using her lungs to breathe with for the most part; whereas her husband in his watery lair found the hairs a very useful addition, for much of his time was spent beneath the water.

Next to its hairiness, the most curious thing about this frog is that it possesses, in the fleshy toes of each hind foot, a set of long, semi-transparent white claws; these claws, like those of a cat, are retractile, and when not in use disappear back into the sheaths in the toes. That these claws are sharp and useful had been proved to me by the scratches on my hand. I should imagine that the use of these weapons is twofold: first as a means of defence, and secondly as a useful tool which enables the amphibian to cling to the slippery rocks in the fast-running streams which it inhabits. Whenever the frogs were picked up they would kick out frantically with their hind legs, and the claws would appear from their sheaths; they would at the same time utter their curious screaming grunts, a cross between the cries of a contented pig and tortured mouse, a sound astonishingly loud and inclined to be very startling when you were not expecting it.

My Hairy Frogs settled down very nicely in their large tin, and after numerous night hunts, I added to their number until I had seven of them, all males with the most luxuriant backsides. For many weeks I searched high and low to try to find some females to go with them, but without success. Then, one day, a dear old lady who looked about ninety-five appeared on the veranda, carrying two calabashes: in one was a pair of shrews, and in the other was a large female Hairy Frog. This was the only female of the species that I ever obtained, and she was accordingly given special care and attention. She was similar to the males in appearance, except that her skin was drier and slightly rougher, and her colouring was a bright brick-red with chocolate flecks. She settled down quite happily with her seven suitors, and even adopted their habits. During the day they all lay in the water, almost completely submerged, ready to dive to the bottom of the tin should anyone approach; at night, however, they grew braver, and climbed out on to the rocks I had put in there for them, where they would sit gulping at each other with vacant expressions. During all the time I had them in Africa, and on the long voyage back to England, the frogs stubbornly refused to eat any of the tempting delicacies I put before them. But as they were extremely fat, this long fast did not unduly worry me, for most reptiles can go for long periods without food and be none the worse for it.

When the time came for me to leave Bafut and travel down to the base camp, and then on to the coast, I packed the frogs in a shallow wooden box filled with wet banana leaves. The box had to be shallow, for otherwise the frogs when scared would jump wildly into the air and bang their delicate noses on the wooden top; in a shallow box, however, they got no chance of doing this. They caused me considerable trouble on the way down from Bafut, and many anxious moments: in the highlands the climate is cool and pleasant, but as you descend into the forested lowlands it is like entering a Turkish bath, and the frogs did not like this change at all. When I opened the box, during one of our halts on the way down, I was horrified to find all my Hairy Frogs in the bottom, limp and apparently lifeless. I rushed frantically down into a nearby ravine and plunged the box into a stream. The cool waters gradually revived four of the frogs, but three were too far gone and soon died. This left me with three males and the female. I had to stop the lorry every two or three miles for the rest of the journey while I ducked the frog box into a stream to revive its inmates; and it was only in this fashion that I managed to get them to base camp alive. On arrival, however, I discovered another problem: the Hairy Frogs had not been able to jump and damage their noses, but they had tried to burrow into the corners of the box, and had thus managed to rub all the skin off their noses and upper lips. This was most serious, for once the delicate skin on a frog's nose is damaged it very soon develops a nasty sore on the spot, which spreads like a rodent ulcer, and can eventually eat away the whole nose and lip. Hastily, I had to create a new box for the frogs to live in; this one was also shallow, but it was completely padded inside, top, bottom and sides, with soft cloth stuffed with cotton wool. The box resembled a small padded cell. In this the Hairy Frogs did very well, since whether they jumped or burrowed, they could not injure themselves on the soft surface. By keeping them drier than usual I managed to heal up their scraped noses, but they always had faint white scars on the skin afterwards.

When we finally left the base camp and travelled down to the coast to catch the ship, the journey was a nightmare. It was incredibly hot, and the Hairy Frogs' box dried up very rapidly. I tried keeping it in a tin full of water, but the roads were so bad that most of the water sloshed out inside the first half-mile. The only alternative to this was to stop the lorry at a stream every half-hour or so and give the box a thorough soaking. Yet in spite of this one of the males succumbed, so that only three Hairy Frogs arrived on board ship. The cool sea-breeze soon revived them, and they seemed fit enough, though very thin, due to their self-imposed fast. This fast continued until they reached England, and for some time after they were installed in the Reptile House at London Zoo. The Curator, as I had done, tried to tempt them with all sorts of delicious tit-bits, but they still refused to eat. Then one day, more or less as a last resort, he put some pink newly born white mice into the cage with them, and to his surprise the frogs fell on them and devoured the lot as though baby mice were their favourite food. From then onwards they lived entirely on this mammalian diet, refusing all the usual froggy foods like locusts and mealworms. It seemed highly improbable that they live exclusively on baby mice in the wild state, so it must be that the mice resembled the food that they were used to eating, though what that might be remains shrouded in mystery.

Chapter Six

Snakes and Shillings

The Fon's speech at the grass-gathering ceremony produced the most astonishing and immediate results. The next afternoon I was endeavouring to dissipate the effects of the Fon's party, and the subsequent frog hunt, by lying down for a couple of hours and catching up on some sleep. When I awoke, I decided that some tea would help to restore me to a more amiable frame of mind, so I staggered off the bed and made my way to the door, intending to shout my instructions down to the kitchen from the veranda. I opened the door and then stopped dead, wondering if I was dreaming, for the whole veranda was literally covered with a weird assortment of sacks, palm-leaf baskets and calabashes, all of which shook and quivered gently, while leaning up against the wall were four or five long bamboos to the ends of which were tied writhing and infuriated snakes. The veranda looked more like a native market than anything else. At the top of the steps squatted Jacob, scowling at me disapprovingly.

'Masa wake up?' he said mournfully, 'why Masa wake up?'

'What's all this?' I asked, waving my hand at the collection of bags and baskets.

'Beef,' said Jacob succinctly.

I examined the snakes' bonds to make sure they were secure.

'Which man done bring dis beef?' I asked, feeling rather stunned by the profusion of arrivals.

'Dis men done bring um,' said Jacob laconically, gesturing down the steps behind him. I stepped over to where he sat and saw that the seventy-five steps up to the villa, and a good deal of the road beyond, was jammed with a great variety of Bafutians of all ages and both sexes. There must have been about a hundred and fifty of them, and they gazed up at me, unmoving and strangely quiet. As a rule a small group of four or five Africans can make more noise than any other race on earth, yet this great crowd might have been composed of deaf mutes for all the sound it was making. The silence was uncanny.

'What's the matter with them?' I asked Jacob.

'Sah?'

'Why dey no make noise, eh?'

'Ah!' said Jacob, light dawning, 'I done tell um Masa 'e sleep.'

This was the first of many examples I was to have of the courtesy and good manners of the Bafut people. For nearly two hours, I discovered, they had sat there in the hot sun, curbing their natural exuberance so that my slumbers might not be disturbed.

'Why you no wake me before?' I said to Jacob; 'you no savvay na bad ting for dis beef to wait, eh?'

'Yes, sah. Sorry, sah.'

'All right, let's get on with it and see what they've brought.'

I picked up the first basket and peered into it: it contained five mice with pale ginger fur, white tummies and long tails. I handed the basket to Jacob, who carried it to the top of the steps and held it aloft.

'Who done bring dis beef?' he shouted.

'I done bring um,' called an old woman shrilly. She fought her way up on to the veranda, bargained with me breathlessly for five minutes, and then fought her way down the steps again, clutching her money.

The next basket contained two delightful little owls. They were speckled grey and black, and the area round the eyes was pure white with a black rim, so that they looked as though they were wearing large horn-rimmed glasses. They clicked their beaks at me, and lowered their long eyelashes over their fierce golden eyes when they saw me, and as I tried to pick them up they rolled over on to their backs, presenting their large talons, and uttering loud screams. They were quite young, and in places were still clad in the cottonwool-like down of infancy, so that they looked as if they had both been caught in a snowstorm. I can never resist owls at the best of times, but these two babies were quite adorable. They were White-faced Scops Owls, and something quite new to my collection, so I had an excellent reason for buying them.

The next item was a squirrel who created a considerable diversion. He was confined in a palm-leaf bag, and as soon as I opened it he shot out like a jack-in-the-box, bit my hand, and then galloped off across the veranda. Jacob gave chase, and as he drew near, the squirrel suddenly darted to one side and then ran down the steps, weaving his way skilfully through the dozens of black legs that stood there. The panic he created was tremendous: those on the first step leapt into the air as he rushed at their feet, lost their balance and fell backwards against those on the next step. They, in turn, fell against the ones below them, who went down like grass before a scythe. In a matter of seconds the steps were covered with a tangled mass of struggling bodies, with arms and legs sticking out at the oddest angles. I quite thought that the unfortunate squirrel would be crushed to death under this human avalanche, but to my surprise he appeared at the bottom of the steps apparently unhurt, flipped his tail a couple of times and set off down the road at a brisk trot, leaving behind him a scene which looked like a negro version of the Odessa steps massacre. At the top of the steps I was fuming impotently and struggling to push my way through the tangle of Africans, for the squirrel was a rarity, and I was determined that he should not escape. Half-way down someone clutched my ankle and I collapsed abruptly on top of a large body which, judging from the bits I could see, was female. I glanced desperately down at the road as I endeavoured to regain my feet, and to my joy I saw a band of some twenty young men approaching. Seeing the squirrel, they stopped short, whereupon the creature sat up and sniffed at them suspiciously.

'You!' I roared, 'you dere for de road . . . catch dat beef.'

The young men put down their bundles and advanced determinedly upon the squirrel, who took one look at them and then turned and fled. They set off in hot pursuit, each resolved that he should be the one to recapture the rodent. The squirrel ran well, but he was no match for the long legs of his pursuers. They drew level with him in a tight bunch, their faces grim and set. Then, to my horror, they launched themselves at my precious specimen in a body, and for the second time the squirrel disappeared under a huge pile of struggling Africans. This time, I thought, the poor beast really *would* be crushed, but that squirrel seemed indestructible. When the heap in the road had sorted itself out a bit, one of the young men stood up holding the chattering and panting squirrel by the scruff of its neck.

'Masa!' he called, beaming up at me, 'I done catch um!'

I threw down a bag for him to put the animal in, and then it was passed up the steps to me. Hastily I got the beast into a cage so that I could examine him to make sure he was not damaged in any way, but he seemed all right except that he was in an extremely bad temper. He was a Black-eared Squirrel, perhaps one of the most beautiful of the Cameroon squirrels. His upper parts were a deep olive green, while his belly was a rich yellow-orange. Along his sides were a series of white spots, set in a line from shoulder to buttocks, and there was a rim of black fur marking the edge of each ear, making him look at though he had never washed behind them. But the most beautiful part of his furry anatomy was his tail. This was long and tremendously bushy: the upper parts were a brindled greeny-brown, while the underparts were the most vivid flame-orange imaginable. Placed in a cage he flipped this dazzling tail at me once or twice, and then squatted down to the stern task of devouring a mango which I had put in there for him. I watched him fondly, thinking what a lucky escape he had had, and how pleased I was to have got him. If I had known what trouble he was going to cause in the future I might have viewed his arrival with considerably less excitement.

I turned my attention back to the various containers that littered the veranda, and picked up a large calabash at random. As usual, its neck was stuffed with a tightly packed plug of green leaves; I removed these and peered into the depths, but the calabash was so capacious and so dark that I could not see what was inside. I carried it to the head of the steps and held it up.

'Which side de man who done bring dis calabash?' I asked.

'Na me, sah, na me!' shouted a man half-way down the steps.

It was always a source of astonishment to me how the Africans could distinguish their own calabashes among hundreds of others. Except for a difference in size I could never tell one from the other, but the Africans knew at a glance which was theirs and which belonged to some other hunter.

'What beef 'e dere-dere for inside?' I asked, negligently swinging the calabash by its cord.

'Snake, sah.' said the man, and I hastily replaced the plug of green leaves.

'What kind of snake, my friend?'

'Na Gera, sah.'

I consulted my list of local names and found this meant a Green-leaf

Viper. These were common and beautiful snakes in Bafut, and I already had quite a number of them. They were about eighteen inches long, a startlingly bright grass green in colour, with canary-yellow bellies and broad diagonal white stripes along their sides. I carried the calabash over to empty the new arrival into the shallow, gauze-topped box in which I kept vipers. Now, emptying a snake from a calabash into a cage is one of the simplest of operations, providing you observe one or two rudimentary rules. First, make sure that any inmates of the cage are far away from the door. This I did. Secondly, make sure how many snakes you have in the calabash before starting to shake them out. This I omitted to do.

I opened the door of the cage, unplugged the mouth of the calabash and began to shake gently. Sometimes it requires quite a lot of shaking to get a snake out of a calabash, for he will coil himself round inside, and press himself against the sides, making it difficult to dislodge him. Jacob stood behind me, breathing heavily down my neck, and behind him stood a solid wall of Africans, watching open-mouthed. I shook the calabash, gently, and nothing happened. I shook it a bit harder, with the same result. I had never known a viper cling with such tenacity to the interior of a receptacle. Becoming irritated, I gave the calabash a really vigorous shaking, and it promptly broke in half. An intricately tangled knot of Green-leaf Vipers, composed of about half a dozen large, vigorous and angry snakes, fell out on to the cage with what can only be described as a sickening thud.

They were plaited together in such a large and solid ball that instead of falling through the door and into the cage, they got jammed half-way, so that I could not slam the door on them. Then, with a fluid grace which I had no time to admire, they disentangled themselves and wriggled determinedly over the edge of the door and on to the floor. Here they spread out fanwise with an almost military precision, and came towards us. Jacob and the Africans who had been jammed behind him disappeared with the startling suddenness of a conjuring trick. I could hardly blame them, for none of them was wearing shoes. But I was not clad to galavant with a tribe of vipers either, for I was wearing shorts and a pair of sandals. My only armament, moreover, consisted of the two halves of the broken calabash, which is not the most useful thing to have when tackling a snake. Leaving the snakes in sole charge of the veranda, I shot into my bedroom. Here I found a stick, and then went cautiously out on to the veranda again. The snakes had scattered widely, so they were quite easy to corner, pin down with the stick and then pick up. One by one I dropped them into the cage, and then shut and locked the door with a sigh of relief. The Africans reappeared just as suddenly as they had disappeared, all chattering and laughing and clicking their fingers as they described to each other the great danger they had been in. I fixed the snake-bringer with a very cold eye.

'You!' I said, 'why you no tell me dere be plenty snake for inside dat calabash, eh?'

'Wah!' he said, looking surprised, 'I done tell Masa dere be snake for inside.'

'Snake, yes. *One* snake. You no tell me dere be six for inside.'

'I done tell Masa dere be snake for inside,' he said indignantly.

'I done ask you what beef you done bring,' I explained patiently, 'and you say, "snake". You no say dere be six snake. How you tink I go savvay how many snake you bring, eh? You tink sometime I get juju for my eye and I go savvay how many snake you done catch?'

'Stupid man,' said Jacob, joining in the fray. 'Sometime dis snake bite Masa, and Masa go die. Den how you go do, eh?'

I turned on Jacob.

'I noticed that you were conspicuous by your absence, my noble and heroic creature.'

'Yes, sah!' said Jacob, beaming.

It was not until quite late that evening that the last hunter had been paid, and I was left with such a weird assortment of live creatures on my hands that it took me until three o'clock the following morning to cage them. Even so, there were five large rats left over, and no box from which to make a cage. I was forced to release them in my bedroom, where they spent the entire night trying to gnaw through the leg of the table.

The next morning when I arose and cleaned out and fed my now considerable collection, I thought that probably nothing more would turn up that day. I was wrong. The Bafutians had obviously thrown themselves wholeheartedly into the task of providing me with specimens, and by ten o'clock the roadway and the seventy-five steps were black with people, and in desperation I had to bargain for the creatures. By lunch-time it was obvious that the supply of animals had far exceeded my store of wood and boxes to make cages for them, so I was forced to employ a team of small boys to tour Bafut, buying up any and every box or plank of wood they could find. The prices I had to pay for boxes were exorbitant, for to the African any sort of receptacle, be it a bottle, an old tin or a box, was worth its weight in gold.

By four o'clock that evening both the staff and I were exhausted, and we had been bitten so many times and in so many places by such a variety of creatures that any additional bites went almost unnoticed. The whole villa was overflowing with animals, and they squeaked and chirruped, rattled and bumped in their calabashes, baskets and sacks while we worked furiously to make the cages for them. It was one of those twenty-four hours that one prefers to forget. By midnight we were all so tired we could hardly keep awake, and there were still some ten cages to be made; a large pot of tea, heavily laced with whisky, gave us a sort of spurious enthusiasm for our task that carried us on, and at two-thirty the last nail was driven in and the last animal released into its new quarters. As I crawled into bed, I was horribly aware of the fact that I should have to be up at six the next morning if I wanted to have everything cleaned and fed by the time the next influx of specimens began.

The next day was, if anything, slightly worse than the preceding one, for the Bafutians started to arrive before I had finished attending to the collection. There is nothing quite so nerve-racking as struggling to clean and feed several dozen creatures when twenty or thirty more have arrived in airless and insanitary containers and are crying out for attention. As I watched out of the corner of my eye the pile of calabashes and baskets growing on the veranda, so the number of cages that I had still to clean and attend to seemed to multiply, until I felt rather as Hercules must have felt when he got his first glimpse of the Augean stables.

When I had finished the work, before buying any fresh specimens I made a speech to the assembled Bafutians from the top of the steps. I pointed out that in the last couple of days they had brought me a vast quantity of beef of all shapes, sizes and descriptions. This proved that the Bafutians were by far the best hunters I had come across, and I was very grateful to them. However, I went on, as they would realize, there was a limit to the amount of beef I could purchase and house in any one day. So I would be glad if they would desist from hunting for the space of three days, in order that my caging and food supply might catch up with them. There was no sense, I pointed out, in my buying beef from them if it was going to die for lack of adequate housing; that was just simply a waste of money. The African is nothing if not a business man, and at this remark the nodding of heads sent a ripple over the crowd, and a chorus of 'Arrrrr!' arose. Having thus driven the point home, and, I hoped, given myself three days' respite, I purchased the animals they had brought and once more set about the task of cage-building.

At four o'clock the caging was under control, and I was having a break for a cup of tea. As I leant on the veranda rail I saw the arched doorway in the red brick wall fly open and the Fon appeared. He strode across the great courtyard with enormous strides, his robes fluttering and hissing as he moved. He was scowling worriedly and muttering to himself. As it was obvious that he was on his way to pay me a visit, I went down the steps to meet him.

'Iseeya, my friend,' I said politely as he reached me.

'My friend!' he said, enveloping my hand in his and peering earnestly into my face, 'some man done tell me you no go buy beef again. Na so?'

'No be so,' I said.

'Ah! Good, good!' he said in a relieved voice. 'Sometime I fear you done get enough beef an' you go lef' dis place.'

'No, no be so,' I explained. 'People for Bafut savvay hunting too much, and dey done bring me so many beef I no get box for put um. So I done tell all dis people dey no go hunt for three days, so I get chance for make box for put all dis beef.'

'Ah! I savvay,' said the Fon, smiling at me affectionately. 'I tink sometime you go lef' us.'

'No, I no go lef' Bafut.'

The Fon peered anxiously round in a conspiratorial fashion, and then, draping one arm lovingly round my shoulders, he drew me down the road.

'Ma friend,' he said in a hoarse whisper, 'I done find beef for you. Na fine beef, na beef you never get.'

'What kind of beef?' I asked curiously.

'Beef,' said the Fon explicitly, 'you go like *too much*. We go catch um now, eh?'

'You never catch um yet?'

'No, my friend, but I savvay which side dey de hide.'

'All right. We go look um now, eh?'

Eagerly he led me across the great courtyard, through a maze of narrow passages, until we reached a small hut.

'Wait here small time, my friend, I go come,' he said, and then disappeared hurriedly into the gloom of the hut. I waited outside, wondering where he had gone to and what kind of beef it was that he had discovered. He had an air of mystery about him which made the whole thing rather intriguing.

When he eventually reappeared, for a moment I did not recognize him. He had removed his robes, his skull-cap and his sandals, and was now naked except for a small and spotlessly white loin-cloth. In one hand he held a long and slender spear. His thin, muscular body gleamed with oil, and his feet were bare. He approached me, twirling his spear professionally, beaming with delight at my obvious surprise.

'You done get new hunter man,' he said, chuckling; 'now you fit call me Bafut Beagle, no be so?'

'I tink dis hunter man be best for all,' I said, grinning at him.

'I savvay hunting fine,' he said, nodding. 'Sometime my people tink I get ole too much for go bush. My friend, if some man get hunting for 'e eye, for 'e nose, and' for 'e blood, 'e *never* get ole too much for go bush, no be so?'

'You speak true my friend,' I said.

He led me out of the environs of his compound, along the road for perhaps half a mile, and then branched off through some maize-fields. He walked at a great pace, twirling his spear and humming to himself, occasionally turning to grin at me with a mischievous delight illuminating his features. Presently we left the fields, passed through a small thicket of mimbo palms, dark and mysterious and full of the rustling of the fronds, and then started to climb up the golden hillside. When we reached the top, the Fon paused, stuck his spear into the ground, folded his arms and surveyed the view. I had stopped a little way down the hillside to collect some delicately coloured snails; when I had arrived at the top, the Fon appeared to have gone into a trance. Presently he sighed deeply, and, turning towards me, smiled and swept his arms wide.

Na my country dis,' he said, 'na foine, dis country.'

I nodded in agreement, and we stood there in silence for a few minutes and looked at the view. Below us lay a mosaic of small fields, green and silver and fawn, broken up by mimbo palm thickets and an occasional patch of rust red where the earth of a field had been newly hoed. This small area of cultivation was like a coloured handkerchief laid on the earth and forgotten, surrounded on all sides by the great ocean of mountains, their crests gilded and their valleys smudged with shadow by the falling sun. The Fon gazed slowly round, and expression on his face that was a mixture of affection and child-like pleasure. He sighed again, a sigh of satisfaction.

'Foine!' he murmured. Then he plucked his spear from the earth and led the way down into the next valley, humming tunefully to himself.

The valley was shallow and flat, thickly overgrown with a wood of small stunted trees, some only about ten feet high. Many of them were completely invisible under immense cloaks of convolvulus, squat towers of trembling leaves and ivory-coloured flowers. The valley had captured the sunshine of the day, and the warm air was heavy and sweet with the scent of flowers and leaves. A sleepy throbbing drone came from a thousand bees that hovered round the flowers; a tiny anonymous bird let a melodious trickle of song fill the valley, and then stopped suddenly, so that the only sound was the blurred singing of the bees again, as they hovered round the trees or waddled up the smooth tunnel of the convolvulus flowers. The Fon surveyed the trees for a moment, and then moved quietly through the grass to a better vantage point, where our view into the wood was not so clogged with convolvulus.

'Na for here we go see beef,' he whispered, pointing at the trees; 'we sit down an' wait small time.'

He squatted down on his haunches and waited in relaxed immobility; I squatted down beside him and found my attention equally divided between watching him and watching the trees. As the trees remained devoid of life, I concentrated on my companion. He sat there, clutching his spear upright in his large hands, and on his face was a look of eager expectancy, like that of a child at a pantomime before the curtain goes up. When he had appeared out of that dark little hut in Bafut, it seemed as though he had not only left behind his robes and trappings of state, but that he had also shed that regal air which had seemed so much part of his character. Here, crouching in this quiet, warm valley with his spear, he appeared to be just another hunter, his bright dark eyes fixed on the trees, waiting for the quarry he knew would come. But, as I looked at him, I realized that he was not just another hunter; there was something different about him which I could not place. It came to me what it was: any ordinary hunter would have crouched there, patient, a trifle bored, for he would have done the same thing so many times before. But the Fon waited, his eyes gleaming, a half-smile on his wide mouth, and I realized that he was thoroughly enjoying himself. I wondered how many times in the past he had become tired of his deferential councillors and his worshipping subjects, and felt his magnificent robes to be hot and cumbersome and his pointed shoes cramping and hard. Then perhaps the urge had come to him to feel the soft red earth under his bare feet and the wind on his naked body, so that he would steal off to his hut, put on the clothes of a hunter and stride away over the hills, twirling his spear and humming, pausing on the hilltops to admire the beautiful country over which he ruled. I remembered the words he had spoken to me only a short time before, 'If a man has hunting for his eye, his nose and his blood, he never gets too old to go to bush.' The Fon, I decided, was definitely one of that sort of men. My meditations on the Fon's character were interrupted: he leant forward and gripped my arm, pointing a long finger at the trees.

'Dey done come,' he whispered, his face wreathed in smiles.

I followed the pointing of his finger, and for a moment I could see nothing but a confused net of branches. Then something moved, and I saw the animal that we had been awaiting.

It came drifting through the tangled branches with all the gentle, airy grace of a piece of thistledown. When it got nearer, I discovered that it looked exactly like my idea of a leprechaun: it was clad in a little fur coat of greenish-grey, and it had a long, slender, furry tail. Its hands, which were pink, were large for its size, and its fingers tremendously long and attenuated. Its ears were large and the skin so fine that it was semi-transparent; these ears seemed to have a life of their own, for they twisted and turned independently, sometimes crumpling and folding flat to the head as if they were a fan, at others standing up pricked and straight like anaemic arum lilies. The face of the little creature was dominated by a pair of tremendous dark eyes, eyes that would have put any self-respecting owl to shame. Moreover, the creature could twist its head round and look over its back in much the same way that an owl does. It ran to the tip of a slender branch that scarcely dipped beneath its weight, and there it sat, clutching the bark with its long, slender fingers, peering about with its great eyes and chirruping dimly to itself. It was, I knew, a galago, but it looked much more like something out of a fairy tale.

It sat on the branch, twittering vaguely to itself, for about a minute; then an astonishing thing happened. Quite suddenly the trees were full of galagos, galagos of every age and size, ranging from those little bigger than a walnut to adults that could have fitted themselves quite comfortably into an ordinary drinking-glass. They jumped from branch to branch, grasping the leaves and twigs with their large, thin hands, twittering softly to each other and gazing round them with the wide-eyed innocence of a troupe of cherubim. The baby ones, who seemed to be composed almost entirely of eyes, kept fairly close to their parents; occasionally they would sit up on their hind legs and hold up their tiny pink hands, fingers spread wide, as though in horror at the depravity they were seeing in the world of leaves around them.

One of these babies discovered, while I watched, that he was sitting on the same branch as a large and succulent locust. It was evening time, and the insect was drowsy and slow to realize its danger. Before it could do anything, the baby galago had flitted down the branch and grabbed it firmly round the middle. The locust woke up abruptly and decided that something must be done. It was a large insect, and was, in fact, almost as big as the baby galago; also it possessed a pair of long and muscular hind legs, and it started to kick out vigorously with them. It was a fascinating fight to watch: the galago clasped the locust desperately in his long fingers, and tried to bite it. Each time he tried to bite, the locust would give a terrific kick with its hind legs and knock its adversary off balance, so he would fall off the branch and hang beneath, suspended by his feet. When this had happened several times, I decided that the galago must have adhesive soles. And even when hanging upside down and being kicked in the stomach by a large locust, he maintained his expression of wide-eyed innocence.

The end of the fight was unexpected: when they were hanging upside down, the locust gave an extra hefty kick, and the galago's feet lost their grip, so that they fell through the leaves clasped together. As they tumbled earthwards, the galago loosened one hand from his grip round the locust's waist and grabbed a passing branch with the effortless ease of a trained acrobat. He hauled himself on to the branch and bit the locust's head off before the insect could recover sufficiently to continue the fight. Holding the decapitated but still kicking body in one hand, the galago stuffed the insect's head into his mouth and chewed it with evident enjoyment. Then he sat, clasping the twitching body in one hand, and contemplated it with his head on one side, giving vent to shrill and excited screams of delight. When the corpse had ceased to move and the big hind legs had stiffened in death, the galago tore them off, one by one, and ate them. He looked ridiculously like a diminutive elderly gourmet, clasping in one hand the drumstick of some gigantic chicken.

Soon the valley was filled with shadow and it became difficult to see the galagos among the leaves, though we could hear their soft chittering. We rose from our cramped positions and made our way back up the hillside. At the top the Fon paused and gazed down at the woods below, smiling delightedly.

'Dat beef!' he chuckled, 'I like um too much. All time 'e make funny for me, an' I go laugh.'

'Na fine beef,' I said. 'How you call um?'

'For Bafut,' said the Fon, 'we call um Shilling.'

'You think sometimes my hunter men fit catch some?'

'Tomorrow you go have some,' promised the Fon, but he would not tell me how they were to be captured, nor who was to do the capturing. We reached Bafut in the dusk, and when the Fon was respectably clothed once more he came and had a drink. As I said good night to him I reminded him of his promise to get me some of the galagos.

'Yes, my friend, I no go forget,' he said. 'I go get you some Shilling.'

Four days passed, and I began to think that either the Fon had forgotten, or else the creatures were proving more difficult to capture than he had imagined. Then, on the fifth morning, my tea was brought in, and reposing on the tray was a small, highly-coloured raffia basket. I pulled off the lid and looked sleepily inside, and four pairs of enormous, liquid, innocent eyes peered up at me with expressions of gentle inquiry.

It was a basketful of Shillings from the Fon.

Chapter Seven

The Que-fong-goo

The grassland country was populated by a rich variety of reptile life, and most of it seemed easily caught. In the lowland forests you very rarely saw a snake of any description, even if you searched for them. There *were* snakes there, of course, but I think that they were more widely dispersed, and probably most of the species were tree-dwellers, which made them much more difficult to see and to capture. In the mountains, however, the grass was alive with small rodents and frogs, and the patches of mountain forest filled with birds, so it was a paradise for snakes. There were great black spitting cobras, green mambas, slim tree-snakes with enormous, innocent-looking eyes, the multi-coloured Gaboon viper, with a forked rhino-like horn on its nose, and a host of others. As well as snakes, there were plenty of frogs and toads; the frogs ranged in size from the Hairy Frog down to the tiny tree-frogs the size of an acorn, some spotted and streaked with such a dazzling array of colours that they looked more like delicious sweets than amphibians. The toads, on the whole, were fairly drab, but they made up for this by being decorated with strange clusters of warts and protuberances on their bodies, and an astonishing variety of colouring in their eyes.

But the commonest of the reptiles were the lizards, which could be found everywhere; in the long herbage at the roadside scuttled fat skinks with stubby legs, fawn and silver and black in colour, and on the walls of the huts, in the road and on the rocks the rainbow-coloured agamas pranced and nodded. Under the bark of trees or beneath stones you could find small geckos with great golden eyes, their bodies neatly and handsomely marked in chocolate and cream, and in the houses at night the ordinary house geckos, translucent and ghostly as pink pearls, paraded across the ceiling.

All these reptiles were brought in to me at one time or another by the local population. Sometimes it would be a snake tied insecurely to the end of a stick, or a calabash full of gulping frogs. Sometimes the capture would be carefully wrapped in the hunter's hat or shirt, or dangling on the end of a fine string. By these haphazard and dangerous methods such things as cobras, mambas and Gaboon vipers would be brought to me, and although their captors knew their deadliness they handled them with an offhand carelessness that amazed me. As a rule, the African is no fool over snakes and prefers to regard every species as poisonous, just to be on the safe side, so to find the Bafutians treating them with such casualness was surprising, to say the least. I found it even more surprising when I discovered that the one reptile they all feared intensely was completely harmless.

I was out with the Bafut Beagles one day, and during the course of the hunt we came to a wide grassy valley about half a mile from the village. The Beagles had wandered off to set the nets, and while waiting for them I sat down in the grass to enjoy a cigarette. Suddenly my attention was attracted by a slight movement to my left, and on looking down I saw a reptile whose appearance made me gasp; hitherto I had been under the impression that the most colourful lizard in the grasslands was the agama, but, in comparison with the one that had crawled into view among the grass stems, the agama was as dull and colourless as a lump of putty. I sat there hardly daring to move, in case this wonderful creature dashed off into the herbage; as I remained quite still, it eventually decided that I was harmless, so slowly and luxuriously it slithered out into the sun and lay there contemplating me with its golden-flecked eyes. I could see that it was a skink of sorts, but one of the largest and most colourful skinks I had ever seen. It lay there quite still, basking in the early morning sun, so I had plenty of time to examine it.

Including its tail, it was about a foot in length and some two inches across the widest part of its body. It had a short, broad head and small but powerful legs. Its colouring and pattern were so dazzling and so intricate that it is almost impossible to describe. To begin with, the scales were large and very slightly raised, so that the whole creature looked as though it had been cleverly constructed out of mosaic. The throat was banded lengthwise with black and white, the top of the head was reddish-rust colour, while the cheeks, upper lip and chin were bright brick red. The main body colour was a deep glossy black, against which the other colours showed up extremely well. Running from the angle of the jaw to the front legs were stripes of bright cherry red separated from each other by narrower bands composed of black-and-white scales. The tail and the outsides of the legs were spotted with white, the spots being fine and small on the legs, but so thickly distributed on the tail that in places they formed vertical bands. Its back was striped lengthwise in alternate stripes of black and canary yellow. As if that was not enough, the yellow stripes were broken in places by a series of pinkish scales. The whole reptile was bright and glossy, looking as though it had just been varnished and was still sticky.

As the skink and I sat there and watched each other I was busy trying to work out a plan for its capture. The butterfly net was some twenty feet away, but it might just as well have been in England for all the use it was, for I knew the skink would not lie there and allow me to trot over and fetch it. Behind him stretched a limitless jungle of long grass, and once he ran into that I knew he would disappear for good. Just then, to my dismay, I heard the Beagles returning. I knew I should have to do something quickly, as their approach would frighten the reptile. Slowly I rose to my feet, and the skink raised his head in alarm; as the first of the Beagles trotted through the grass, I flung myself desperately towards the skink. I had him at a slight disadvantage, for, having contemplated me in a motionless condition for a quarter of an hour, he had not expected me to launch myself through the air like a hawk. But my advantage was only temporary, for he recovered from his surprise quickly enough, and as I landed in the grass with a thump he scuttled to one side with great agility. I rolled over and made a wild grab at his rapidly retreating form, and as I did so the Beagle entered the clearing and saw what I was doing. Instead of leaping to my rescue, as I had expected, he uttered a prolonged shriek, jumped forward and proceeded to drag me away from my quarry. The skink scuttled off into the dense tangle of grass and was lost; I shook off the Beagle's clutch on my arm and turned on him savagely.

'Bushman!' I snarled angrily. 'Na what foolish ting you do?'

'Masa,' said the Beagle, clicking his fingers in agitation, 'na bad, bad beef, dat ting. If 'e go bite Masa, Masa go die one time.'

With an effort I controlled my irritation. I had long ago found that, in spite of all arguments, the Africans clung tenaciously to their belief that some harmless species of reptile were deadly poisonous. So I resisted the temptation of telling the Beagle that he was an unmitigated idiot, and tried another line of argument instead.

'How do you de call dis beef?' I asked.

'We call um Que-fong-goo, sah.'

'You say he get poison too much, eh?'

'Time no dere, Masa. Na bad beef.'

'All right, stupid man, you done forget that European get special medicine for dis kind of beef, eh? You done forget if dis beef go bite me I no go die, eh?'

'Eh! Masa, I done forget dis ting.'

'So you go run like woman, you de hollar and you de hold me so I go lose dis fine beef because you forget, eh?'

'Sorry, sah,' said the Beagle contritely.

I tapped his woolly skull with my finger.

'Next time, my friend,' I said sternly, 'you go tink with your brain before you go do dis kind of ting, you hear?'

'I hear, sah.'

When the other Beagles arrived on the scene, the incident was described to them, and there was much gasping and clicking of fingers.

'Wah!' said one of them admiringly. 'Masa no get fear. 'E done try for catch Que-fong-goo.'

'An' Uano done catch Masa,' said another, and they all laughed uproariously.

'Ay, Uano, you get lucky today. Sometime Masa go kill you for do dis stupid ting,' said another, and they all went off into fresh paroxysms of laughter at the thought of the Beagle having the temerity to stop me catching a specimen.

When they had recovered from the humour of the situation, I questioned them closely about the reptile. To my relief they assured me that it was fairly common in the grasslands and I should have plenty of opportunities of obtaining more specimens. They were all agreed, however, on the deadly properties of the skink. It was so poisonous, they assured me, that even if you so much as touched its body you immediately fell to the ground writhing in agony, and died within a few minutes. Then they asked me about the medicine I had to counteract this deadly creature, but I was suitably mysterious. I said if they found me a Que-fong-goo I would catch it and prove to them that I did not die writhing in agony. Cheered and intrigued by the thought of this grisly experiment (for none of them really believed in my medicine), they promised to do this. One of the Beagles said that he knew of a place where a great many such reptiles were to be found; he insisted that it was not very far distant, so we packed up the equipment and set off, the hunters chattering away to each other, presumably laying bets as to whether or not I could survive an encounter with a Que-fong-goo.

The Beagle eventually led us to a hillside about a mile away. The heavy mountain rains had stripped most of the red earth from the slope and left great sheets of grey rock exposed in its place. Occasional clefts in the rock had allowed a pocket of earth to form, and in these grew such plants as could draw nourishment from so small an area of soil. The sheets of rock were hemmed in by tall golden grass and a curious thistle-like plant with a pale buttercup-yellow head. The rock, lying exposed to the sun, was almost too hot to touch; the thin rubber soles of my shoes stuck to the surface as I walked across, so that I felt as though I was walking over a fly-paper. I began to wonder if this baking rock-face would not prove too much for even the most sun-loving of reptiles. Suddenly a flying streak of colour shot out of a clump of low growth across the shimmering rock, and disappeared into the sanctuary of the long grass and thistles.

'Que-fong-goo!' said the Bafut Beagles, stopping short and clutching their spears more tightly. Thinking that they would probably be more hindrance than help in any capture I might have to make, I told them to stay where they were and went ahead by myself. I had armed myself with a butterfly net, and as I cautiously approached the clumps of herbage that grew in the rock crevices I prodded them gently with the handle of the net to make sure there were no Que-fong-goos lurking inside. It was quite astonishing what even a small clump of grass would contain, and I disturbed innumerable large locusts, clouds of moths and gnats, a mass a brilliant butterflies, some beetles and a few dragon-flies. I began to understand the attractions that this scorched and barren place might have for lizards.

Presently I struck lucky: on inserting the net handle into a clump of grass and wiggling it gently, I disturbed a Que-fong-goo. He slithered out of hiding and skimmed across the rough surface of the rock as smoothly as a stone on ice. I gave chase, but discovered almost immediately that a skink's idea of suitable country for sprinting was not mine. I caught my toe in a crack and fell flat on my face, and by the time I had picked myself up and recovered the net my quarry had disappeared. By now I was dripping with sweat, and the heat from the rock slabs was so great that any exertion made the blood pound in my head like a drum. The Beagles were standing at the edge of the long grass in a silent and fascinated group watching my progress. I wiped my face, clutched the net in one sticky hand and approached the next clump of grass doggedly. Here I was more careful; I edged the handle in among the grass-stalks and moved it to and fro very gently and slowly once or twice, and then withdrew it to see what would happen. I was rewarded by the sight of a Que-fong-goo, who stuck his head out of the undergrowth in a cautious manner to see what had caused the upheaval. Quickly I kicked the clump of grass behind him, and swept the net down as he ran out. The next moment I lifted the net triumphantly with the Que-fong-goo lashing furiously about in its folds. I pushed my hand inside the net and grabbed the reptile round the middle, and he retaliated by fastening his jaws on my thumb. Though his jaws were powerful, his teeth were minute, so his bite was quite painless and harmless. In order to keep him occupied, I let him chew away on my thumb, while I lifted him from the net. I held his dazzlingly beautiful body up aloft and waved it like a banner.

'Lookum!' I shouted to the Beagles, who were watching me open-mouthed. 'I done catch Que-fong-goo!'

As the Beagles were carrying the soft cloth bags I used to transport reptiles in, I left the net lying on the rocks and walked towards them, still clutching the skink in my hand. As one man, the Bafut Beagles dropped their spears and fled into the long grass like a herd of startled antelopes.

'What you de fear, eh?' I shouted. 'I go hold um tight for my hand, I no go let um run.'

'Masa, we de fear too much,' they replied in chorus, keeping a safe distance away in the long grass.

'Bring me bag for put dis beef,' I ordered sternly, mopping my brow.

'Masa we de fear . . . na bad beef dat,' came the cry again.

It became apparent that I should have to think of a fairly stiff argument, or else I should have to pursue my tribe of hunters all over the grasslands in my efforts to get a bag to put the skink in. I sat down at the edge of the long grass and glared at them.

'If someone no go bring me bag for put dis beef *one time*,' I proclaimed loudly and angrily, 'tomorrow I go get new hunter man. And, if de Fon go ask me why I go do dis ting, I go tell him I want hunter man who no get fear, I no want women.'

A silence descended upon the long grass while the Bafut Beagles decided whether it was better to face a Que-fong-goo in the hand, or a Fon at Bafut. After a short time the Que-fong-goo won, and they approached me slowly and reluctantly. One of them, still keeping a safe distance, threw me a bag to put my capture in, but before I put the skink inside it I thought a little demonstration would be a good thing.

'Lookum,' I said, holding the struggling lizard up for them to see. 'Now, you go watch fine and you see dis beef no get power for poison me.'

Holding the skink in one hand, I slowly brought the forefinger of my other hand close to his nose; the reptile immediately gaped in a fearsome manner, and, amid cries of horror from the Beagles, I stuffed as much of my finger as I could into his mouth and let him chew on it. The Bafut Beagles stood rooted to the spot, watching with expressions of incredulous stupefaction as the reptile gnawed away at my finger; their eyes were wide, they held their breath and leant slightly forward with open mouths as they watched to see if the creature's bite would have any effect. After a few seconds the Que-fong-goo tired of biting ineffectually at my finger, and let go. I dropped him neatly into the bag and tied up the neck before turning to the hunters.

'You see?' I inquired. 'Dis beef done bit me, no be so?'

'Na so, sah,' came an awed whisper from the Beagles.

'All right: he done give me poison, eh? You tink sometime I go die, eh?'

'No, sah. If dat beef done bit Masa and Masa no die one time, den Masa no go die atall.'

'No, dis special medicine I done get,' I lied, shrugging with becoming modesty.

'Whah!' Na so; Masa get fine medicine,' said the Beagle.

I had not gone through all this merely as a demonstration of the white man's superiority over the black; the true reason for this little charade was that I dearly wanted a great many Que-fong-goos and I knew that I should not obtain them unless I had the help and co-operation of the Beagles. In order to get this, I had to overcome their fear, and the only way I could do this was by showing them that my mythical medicine was more than a match for the deadly bite of the Que-fong-goo. At some future date, I thought, I would provide them with a quantity of innocuous liquid disguised as the medicine in question, and, armed with this elixir, they would sally forth and return with sackfuls of glittering Que-fong-goos.

On the way back to Bafut I strutted along, proudly carrying my precious skink and feeling very pleased with myself for having devised such a cunning scheme for obtaining more of the lovely reptiles. Behind me the Beagles trotted in silence, still gazing at me with awed expressions. Each time we passed someone on the path they would give a rapid *résumé* of my powers, and I would hear gasps of surprise and horror as the tale was told, slightly embellished with each repetition, I have no doubt. When we reached the villa, and I had my skink nicely housed in a large box, I gathered the Beagles together and made them a little speech. I pointed out that, as they had seen with their own eyes, my medicine was sufficient protection against the bites of Que-fong-goos. They all nodded vigorously. Therefore, I went on, as I wanted a great many specimens of the reptile, I proposed to supply them with the magic potion the next day, and thus armed they would be able to go out and hunt Que-fong-goos for me. Then I beamed at them complacently, waiting for the cries of delight I expected. None came; instead the Beagles stood there looking extremely glum and twiddling their toes in the dust.

'Well,' I inquired after a long pause, 'you no agree?'

'No, Masa,' they mumbled.

'Why you no agree? You no savvay dat I go give you dis special medicine, eh?' Why you de fear?'

They scratched their heads, shuffled their feet, glanced helplessly at each other, and then one of them eventually plucked up the courage to speak.

'Masa,' he said, having cleared his throat several times, 'dis medicine you done get na fine one. We savvy dis ting. We done see dis beef bite Masa time no dere, and Masa no die.'

'Well?'

'Dis medicine, Masa, na juju for white man. No be juju for black man. For Masa na good ting dis medicine, but for we no be good ting.'

For half an hour I argued, pleaded and cajoled them. They were polite but firm; the medicine was fine for whites, but it would not work with black people. That was their belief and they were sticking to it. I tried every argument I could think of to make them change their minds, but it was no use. At last, thoroughly irritated by the failure of my little scheme, I dismissed the Beagles and stalked off to have my meal.

Later that evening the Fon turned up, accompanied by five council members and a bottle of gin. We sat on the moonlit veranda for half an hour or so, discussing various subjects in a desultory fashion, and then the Fon hitched his chair closer to mine and leant forward, giving me his wide and engaging grin that lit up his whole face.

'Some man done tell me dat you done catch Que-fong-goo,' he said. 'Dis man speak true?'

'Na so,' I nodded, 'na fine beef dat.'

'Dis man done say you catch dis beef with your hand,' said the Fon. 'I tink sometime dis man tell me lie, eh? Dis na bad beef, dis Que-fong-goo; you no fit catch um with your hand eh? 'E go kill you one time, no be so?'

'No,' I said firmly, 'dis man no tell lie. I done catch dis beef with my hand.'

The council members let out their breath with a hiss at this information, and the Fon sat back and regarded me wide-eyed.

'An when you done catch um what 'e done do?' asked the Fon at last.

'He done bite me.'

'Whaaaaa!' said the Fon and the council members in unison.

'He done bite me here,' I said, holding out my hand, and the Fon shied away as though I had pointed a gun at him. He and the council members examined my finger from a safe distance, chattering eagerly to each other.

'Why you no die?' asked the Fon presently.

'Die?' I asked, frowning. 'Why I go die?'

'Na bad beef dis ting,' said the Fon excitedly. ' 'E de bite too much. If black man go hold him 'e go die one time. Why you never die, my friend?'

'Oh, I get special medicine for dis ting,' I said airily. A chorus of 'Ahhs!' came from my audience.

'Na European medicine dis?' asked the Fon.

'Yes. You like I go show you?'

'Yes, yes, na foine!' he said eagerly.

They sat there silent and expectant while I went and fetched my small medicine chest; from it I extracted a packet of boracic powder, and spread a little on the palm of my hand. They all craned eagerly forward to see it. I filled a glass of water, mixed in the powder and then rubbed the result on my hands.

'There!' I said, spreading my hands out like a conjurer. 'Now Que-fong-goo no fit kill me.'

I walked over to the skink box, opened it, and turned round holding the beast in my hands. There was a fluttering of robes and the council members fled to the other end of the veranda in a disorderly stampede. The Fon remained rooted to his chair, a look of disgust and fright on his face as I walked towards him. I stopped in front of him and held out the reptile, who was busily trying to amputate my finger.

'Look . . . you see?' I said; 'dis beef no fit kill me.'

The Fon's breath escaped in a prolonged 'Aieeeeeee!' of astonishment as he watched the lizard. Presently he tore his fascinated eyes away from it and looked up at me.

'Dis medicine,' he said hoarsely, ' 'e good for black man?'

'Na fine for black man.'

'Black man no go die?'

'Atall, my friend.'

The Fon sat back and gazed at me in wonder.

'Wha!' he said at last, 'na fine ting dis.'

'You like you go try dis medicine?' I asked casually.

'Er . . . er . . . yes, yes, na foine,' said the Fon nervously.

Before he could change his mind, I put the skink back in the box, and then prepared some more of the boracic mixture. I showed the Fon how to rub it on his enormous hands, and he massaged away for a long time. Then I brought the box, pulled out the skink and held it out for him.

It was a tense moment; the ring of council members watched with bated breath and screwed-up countenances while the Fon licked his lips, put out his hand towards the skink, drew it back nervously, and then reached out again. There was a moment's suspense as his hand hovered over the highly-coloured reptile, then he drew a deep breath and grabbed the beast firmly round the waist.

'Ahhh!' hissed the council members.

'Wheee! I done hold um,' yelped the Fon, clutching the unfortunate skink so tightly that I feared for its life.

'Hold um softly,' I begged. 'You go kill um if you hold um tight.'

But the Fon, paralysed by a mixture of fright and pleasure at his own daring, could only sit there glaring at the skink in his hand and muttering, 'I done hold um . . . I done hold um . . .' until I was forced to prise the unfortunate skink loose and return it to its box.

The Fon examined his hands, and then looked up at me with an expression of child-like delight on his face. The council members were chattering away to each other. The Fon waved his hands at me and started to laugh. He laughed and laughed and laughed, slapping his thighs, doubling up in his chair, coughing and spluttering, while the tears ran down his face. It was so infectious that I started to laugh as well, and soon the councillors joined in. We sat there stamping our feet, laughing as though we would never stop until some of the councillors rolled on the floor and fought for breath, and the Fon lay back weakly in his chair shaken by huge gusts of mirth.

'Why you de laugh?' I spluttered at last.

'Na funny ting,' said the Fon, shaken with fresh laughter, 'for long time, ever since I be picken, I done fear dis beef. Wah! I done fear um too much. Now you give me medicine and I no de fear any more.'

He leant back in his chair and sobbed with mirth at the thought.

'Que-fong-goo, your time done pass; I no go fear you again,' he gurgled.

Later, still aching from our laughter, we finished our drinks, and the Fon went back to his own villa, carefully clutching a small packet of boracic powder. I had warned him that, although the medicine could be used with success against Que-fong-goos, agamas and geckos, it could not, in any circumstances, be used to guard against the bite of snakes. As I had hoped, the story that the Fon had picked up a Que-fong-goo after having been immunized by my medicine, and that he had survived the encounter, was common gossip the next day. In the afternoon the Bafut Beagles turned up, and stood grinning at me disarmingly.

'Whatee?' I asked coldly.

'Masa,' said the Beagles, 'give us dat medicine you done give for Fon, and we go hunt Que-fong-goos for Masa.'

That evening I had two boxes full of the beautiful grassland skinks, and the Bafut Beagles were drinking corn beer, surrounded by an admiring crowd of Bafutians, while they recounted the story of the day's hunt, with, I have no doubt, suitable embellishments. While I listened to them, I sat on the veranda and wrote a note to the nearest U.A.C. stores, asking them to send me another packet of boracic. I felt that it might come in useful.

Chapter Eight

The Typhlops in Disguise

After a few weeks the number of people who brought me specimens dwindled to a steady daily trickle. This was because I had, by this time, obtained enough of the commoner species of animals, and I was refusing to buy any more of them. The veranda outside my bedroom was piled high with a strange variety of cages, containing the most fantastically assorted collection of mammals, birds and reptiles, and my mornings and the better part of my evenings were devoted to their care. My days were full, but never dull; apart from cleaning and feeding the collection, there was endless enjoyment to be got from watching the habits of my specimens and their reaction to captivity and to myself. Then there was the life of Bafut. Working on the veranda I was in an elevated vantage point that commanded an excellent view of the road and the Fon's courtyard and houses. Peering through the tattered fringe of bougainvillaea, I could watch the movements of the Fon's numerous wives, offspring and councillors, and the constant comings and going of the Bafut population on the road. From the veranda I observed many a scene enacted below me, and by reaching out a hand for my field-glasses I could bring the actors so close that every slight change of expression on their faces could be noticed.

One evening I saw a slim, good-looking girl walk down the road; she was meandering, dragging her feet, as though waiting for someone to catch up with her. I was just about to call a greeting to her as she passed beneath the house when I saw a powerful young man come trotting up behind her, his face distorted into a ferocious scowl. He called out sharply, and the girl paused, then turned round with an expression of sulky insolence on her handsome face, which the young man obviously found very irritating. He halted in front of her and started to talk in a loud and angry voice, gesturing fiercely with his arms, his eyes and teeth flashing in his dark face. The girl stood without movement, a faint, rather sneering smile on her lips. Then a third actor joined the scene: an old woman came scuttling down the road, screaming at the top of her voice and waving a long bamboo. The man took no notice of the newcomer, but continued his rather one-sided argument with the girl. The old woman danced round the two of them, brandishing her bamboo, screeching shrilly, her flat and wrinkled dugs flapping up and down on her chest as she moved. The more she screeched the louder the man shouted, and the more he shouted the more sullen became the girl's expression. Suddenly the old woman whirled round on one leg like a dervish and struck the man across the shoulders with her bamboo. The only notice he took of this assault was to reach out a long, muscular arm, twitch the stick from the old woman's hand and fling it high into the air so that it fell over the red brick wall into the great courtyard. The old woman stood nonplussed for a moment, then she danced up behind the young man and kicked him hard in the behind. He took no notice whatsoever, but continued to shout at the girl, his gestures getting wilder and wilder. All at once the girl snarled some reply at him and spat accurately on to his feet.

The young man up till then had obviously been adopting a non-belligerent attitude, and he had, I felt, been getting the worst of things; the women, I decided, were taking an unfair advantage of him. However, having his feet spat upon was apparently the last straw; he stood for a moment openmouthed at such a treacherous attack, and then with a roar of rage he leapt forward, grasped the girl round the throat with one hand while boxing her ears soundly with the other, and finally gave her a push so that she fell to the ground. The old woman was quite overcome by this action, falling flat on her back into the ditch and indulging in the finest fit of hysterics I have ever seen. Rolling from side to side and patting her mouth, she gave vent to prolonged Red Indian hoots of the most bloodcurdling quality. Occasionally, she would break off these noises to scream. The girl lay in the red dust, sobbing bitterly; the man took no notice of the old lady, but squatted down beside the girl and appeared to be pleading with her. After a while the girl looked up and gave a watery smile, whereupon the young man sprang to his feet, grabbed her by the wrist and they set off down the road, leaving the old woman still rolling and hooting in the ditch.

I was, quite frankly, puzzled by the whole affair. What had it all been about? Was the girl the man's wife, and had she been unfaithful to him, and had he found out? But what then was the reason for the old woman's presence? Perhaps the girl has stolen something from the man? Or, more likely, the girl and the old woman has been practising juju on him, and he had found out? Juju, I thought; that must be the explanation. The girl, tiring of her young husband, had tried to poison him by mixing chopped-up leopard whiskers with his food – leopard whiskers which she had obtained from the old woman, who was, of course, a well-known local witch. But the husband had become suspicious, and the girl had fled to the witch for protection. The husband had followed the girl, and the witch (who felt some sort of obligation towards her customers) had followed them both to try to to sort things out. I had just worked this theory out into a form that would have been acceptable to the *Wide World Magazine*, when I looked over the edge of the veranda and saw Jacob below peering through the hedge at the old woman, who was still rolling in the ditch and making noises reminiscent of Clapham Junction.

'Jacob,' I called, 'na whatee all dat palaver?'

Jacob looked up and gave a throaty chuckle.

'Dis ole woman, sah, she be mammy for dat picken woman. Dat picken woman be wife for dat man. Dat man 'e done go for bush all day, an' when 'e done come back 'e find 'e wife never make him food, 'E belly de cry out, an' de man angry too much, so he like beat 'e wife. De wife 'e run, de man 'e run, for beat 'e wife, an' de ole woman 'e run for beat dis man.'

I was bitterly disappointed; I felt that Africa, the dark and mysterious continent, had let me down. Instead of my juicy intrigue, my witches and magic potions full of leopard whiskers, I had been witnessing an ordinary domestic upheaval with the usual ingredients of an erring wife, a hungry husband, an uncooked dinner and an interfering mother-in-law. I turned my attention back to the collection, feeling distinctly cheated. It was the mother-in-law, I think, that rankled most.

Not long after this there was another upheaval on and around the veranda, in which I played the chief part, but it was not until long afterwards that I was able to appreciate its humour. It was a beautiful evening, and in the west shoals of narrow, puffy clouds were assembling for what was obviously going to be a glorious sunset.

I had just finished a well-earned cup of tea, and was sitting on the top step in the late sunlight trying to teach an incredibly stupid baby squirrel how to suck milk from a lob of cotton wool on the end of a matchstick. Pausing for a moment in this nerve-racking work, I saw a fat and elderly woman waddling down the road. She was wearing the briefest of loin-cloths, and was smoking a long, slender black pipe. On top of her grey, cropped hair was perched a tiny calabash. When she reached the bottom step, she knocked out her pipe and hung it carefully from the cord round her ample waist, before starting to climb towards the veranda.

'Iseeya, mammy,' I called.

She stopped and grinned up at me.

'Iseeya, Masa,' she replied, and then continued to heave her body from step to step, panting and wheezing with the exertion. When she reached me, she placed the calabash at my feet, and then leant her bulk against the wall, gasping for breath.

'You done tire, Mammy?' I asked.

'Wah! Masa, I get fat too much,' she explained.

'Fat!' I said in shocked tones; 'you no get fat, Mammy. You no get fat pass me.'

She chuckled richly, and her gigantic body quivered.

'No, Masa, you go fun with me.'

'No, Mammy, I speak true, you be small woman.'

She fell back against the wall, convulsed with laughter at the thought of being called a small woman, her vast stomach and breasts heaving. Presently, when she had recovered from the joke, she gestured at the calabash.

'I done bring beef for you, Masa.'

'Na what kind of beef?'

'Na snake, Masa.'

I unplugged the calabash and peered inside. Coiled up in the bottom was a thin, brown snake about eight inches long. I recognised it as a typhlops, a species of blind snake which spends its life burrowing underground. It resembles the English slow-worm in appearance, and is quite harmless. I already had a box full of these reptiles, but I liked my fat girl friend so much that I did not want to disappoint her by refusing it.

'How much you want for dis beef, Mammy?' I asked.

'Eh, Masa go pay me how 'e tink.'

'Snake no get wound?'

'Na, Masa, atall.'

I turned the calabash upside down and the snake fell out on to the smooth concrete. The woman moved to the other end of the veranda with a speed that was amazing for one so huge.

' 'E go bite you Masa,' she called warningly.

Jacob, who had appeared to see what was going on, gave the woman a withering look at this remark.

'You no savvay Masa no get fear for dis ting?' he asked. 'Masa get special juju so dis kind of snake no go chop 'e.'

'Ah, na so?' said the woman.

I leant forward and picked up the typhlops in my hand, so that I could examine it closely to make sure it was unhurt. I gripped its body gently between my thumb and forefinger, and it twisted itself round my finger. As I looked at it, I noticed a curious thing: it possessed a pair of large and glittering eyes, a thing which no typhlops ever possessed. Foolishly, rather startled by my discovery, I still held the reptile loosely in my hand, and spoke to Jacob.

'Jacob, look, dis snake 'e get eye,' I said.

As I spoke, I suddenly realized that I was holding loosely in my hand not a harmless typhlops but some unidentified snake of unknown potentialities. Before I could open my hand and drop it, the snake twisted round smoothly and buried a fang in the ball of my thumb.

Off-hand I can never remember receiving quite such a shock. The bite itself was nothing – like the prick of a pin, followed by a slight burning sensation, rather similar to a wasp sting. I dropped the snake with alacrity, and squeezed my thumb as hard as I could, so that the blood oozed out of the wound, and as I squeezed I remembered three things. First, there was no snake-bite serum in the Cameroons; secondly, the nearest doctor was some thirty miles away; thirdly, I had no means of getting to him. These thoughts did not make me feel any happier, and I sucked vigorously at the bite, still holding the base of my thumb as tightly as I could. Looking about, I found that Jacob had vanished, and I was just about to utter a roar of rage, when he came scurrying back on to the veranda, carrying in one hand a razor blade, and in the other a couple of ties. Under my frenzied directions, he tied the latter round my wrist and forearm as tightly as he could, and then, with a courteous gesture, he handed me the razor blade.

I had never realized before quite how much determination it requires to slash yourself with a razor blade, nor had I realized quite how sharp a razor blade could be. After an awful moment's hesitation, I slashed at my hand, and then found I had given myself a nasty and unnecessary cut about half an inch away from the bite, in a place where it could be of no possible use.

I tried again, with much the same result, and I thought gloomily that if I did not die of the bite, I would probably bleed to death as a result of my own first aid. I thought vindictively of all those books I had read that gave tips on how to deal with snake-bite. All of them, without exception, told you how to make an incision across the bite to the full depth of the fang punctures. It's easy enough to write that sort of thing, but it is quite a different matter to put it into practice successfully when the thumb you are slitting open is your own. There was only one thing to be done, unless I wanted to go on hacking my hand about in the hope of hitting the bite sooner or later. I placed the blade carefully on the ball of my thumb and, gritting my teeth, I pressed and pulled as hard as I could. This was successful, and the blood flowed freely in all directions. The next thing to do, I remembered, was to use permanganate of potash, so I sprinkled some crystals into the gaping wound, and wrapped my hand in a clean handkerchief. By now my hand, wrist and the glands in my armpit were considerably swollen, and I was getting shooting pains in my thumb, though whether this was due to the bite or to my surgery, I could not tell.

'Masa go for doctor?' asked Jacob, staring at my hand.

'How I go for doctor,' I asked irritably; 'we no get car for dis place. You tink sometimes I go walk?'

'Masa go ask de Fon for 'e kitcar,' suggested Jacob.

'Kitcar?' I repeated, hope dawning, 'de Fon get kitcar?'

'Yes, sah.'

'Go ask him den ... one time.'

Jacob galloped down the steps and across the great courtyard, while I paced up and down on the balcony. Suddenly I remembered that in my bedroom reposed a large and untouched bottle of French brandy, and I sped inside in search of it. I had just managed to pull out the cork when I recalled that all the books on snake-bite were adamant when it came to the point of spirits. On no account, they all stated, must spirits be taken by anyone suffering from snake-bite; apparently they accelerated the heart action and did all sorts of other strange things to you. For a moment I paused, the bottle clutched in one hand; then I decided that if I were going to die I might as well die happy, and I raised the bottle and drank. Warmed and encouraged, I trotted out on to the veranda again, carrying the bottle with me.

A large crowd of people, headed by Jacob and the Fon, were hurrying across the courtyard. They went over to a big hut, and the Fon threw open the door and the crowd poured inside, to reappear almost immediately pushing in front of them an ancient and battered kitcar. They trundled this out through the archway and into the road, and there the Fon left them and hurried up the steps followed by Jacob.

'My friend,' gasped the Fon, 'na bad palaver dis!'

'Na so,' I admitted.

'Your boy done tell me you no get European medicine for dis kind of bite. Na so?'

'Yes, na so. Sometime doctor done get medicine, I no savvay.'

'By God power 'e go give you medicine,' said the Fon piously.

'You go drink with me?' I asked, waving the bottle of brandy.

'Yes, yes,' said the Fon, brightening, 'we go drink. Drink na good medicine for dis kind of ting.'

Jacob brought glasses and I poured out a liberal measure for us both. Then we went to the top of the steps to see what progress was being made with the preparation of the ambulance.

The kitcar had reposed inside the hut for such a great length of time that its innards seemed to have seized up. Under the driver's gentle ministrations the engine coughed vigorously several times and then ceased. The large crowd round the vehicle clustered closer, all shouting instructions to him, while he leant out of the window and abused them roundly. This went on for some time, and then the driver climbed out and tried to crank her up. This was even less successful, and when he had exhausted himself, he handed the crank to a councillor and went and sat on the running-board for a rest. The councillor hitched up his robes and struggled manfully with the crank, but was unable to rouse the engine to life.

The crowd, which now numbered about fifty people, all clamoured for a turn, so the councillor handed the job over to them and joined the driver on the running-board. A disgraceful fight broke out among the crowd as to who should have first turn, and everyone was shouting and pushing and snatching the crank from one another. The uproar attracted the attention of the Fon, and he drained his glass and stalked over to the veranda rail, scowling angrily. He leant over and glared down at the road.

'Wah!' he roared suddenly. 'Start dat motor!'

The crowd fell silent, and all turned to look up at the veranda, while the driver and council member jumped off the running-board and rushed round to the front of the car with an amazing display of enthusiasm. This was somewhat spoilt by the fact that when they did arrive there, the crank was missing. Uproar started again, with everyone accusing everyone else of having lost it. It was found eventually, and the two of them made several more ineffectual attempts to get the engine started.

By now I was beginning to feel rather ill and not at all brave. My hand and fore-arm had swollen considerably, and were inflamed and painful. I was also getting shooting pains across my shoulders, and my hand felt as though it was grasping a red-hot coal.

It would take me about an hour to reach the doctor, I thought, and if the kitcar did not start soon, there would be little point in going at all. The driver, having nearly ruptured himself in his efforts to crank, was suddenly struck by a brilliant idea. They would push the car. He explained his idea to the crowd, and it was greeted with exclamations of delight and acclamation. The driver got in and the crowd swarmed round behind the kitcar and began to push. Grunting rhythmically, they pushed the kitcar slowly down the road, round the corner and out of sight.

'Soon 'e go start,' smiled the Fon encouragingly, pouring me some more brandy, 'den you go reach doctor one time.'

'You tink 'e go start?' I asked sceptically.

'Yes, yes, ma friend,' said the Fon, looking hurt; 'na my kitcar dis, na foine one. 'E go start small time, no go fear.'

Presently we heard the grunting again, and, on looking over the veranda rail, we saw the kitcar appear round the corner, still being propelled by what seemed to be the entire population of Bafut. It crept towards us like a snail, and then, just as it reached the bottom step, the engine gave a couple of preliminary hiccoughs and then roared into life. The crowd screamed with delight and began to caper about in the road.

' 'E done start,' explained the Fon proudly, in case I had missed the point of the celebrations.

The driver manoeuvred the car through the archway into the courtyard, turned her round, and swept out on to the road again, impatiently tootling his horn and narrowly missing his erstwhile helpers. The Fon and I drained our glasses and then marched down the seventy-five steps. At the bottom the Fon clasped me to his bosom and gazed earnestly into my face. It was obvious that he wanted to say something that would encourage and sustain me on my journey. He thought deeply for a moment.

'My friend,' he said at last, 'if you go die I get sorry too much.'

Not daring to trust my voice, I clasped his hand in what I hoped was a suitably affected manner, climbed into the kitcar and we were off, bouncing and jerking down the road, leaving the Fon and his subjects enveloped in a large cloud of red dust.

Three-quarters of an hour later we drew up outside the doctor's house with an impressive squealing of brakes. The doctor was standing outside gloomily surveying a flower-bed. He looked at me in surprise when I appeared, and then, coming forward to greet me, he peered closely into my face.

'What have you been bitten by?' he inquired.

'How did you know I'd been bitten?' I asked, rather startled by this rapid diagnosis.

'Your pupils are tremendously distended,' explained the doctor with professional relish. 'What was it?'

'A snake. I don't know what kind, but it hurts like hell. I don't suppose there was really much use in my coming in to you. There's no serum to be had, is there?'

'Well!' he said in a pleased tone of voice. 'Isn't that a strange thing? Last time I was on leave I got some serum. Thought it might come in useful. It's been sitting in the fridge for the last six months.'

'Well, thank heaven for that.'

'Come into the house, my dear fellow. I shall be most interested to see if it works.'

'So shall I,' I admitted.

We went into the house, and I sat down in a chair while the doctor and his wife busied themselves with methylated spirits, hypodermic needles and the other accoutrements necessary for the operation. Then the doctor gave me three injections in the thumb, as near to the bite as was possible, and a couple more in my arm. These hurt me considerably more than the original bite had done.

'Made you feel a bit rocky?' inquired the doctor cheerfully, feeling my pulse.

'They've made me feel bloody,' I said bitterly.

'What you need is a good stiff whisky.'

'I thought one wasn't allowed spirits?'

'Oh, yes. It won't hurt you,' he said, and poured me out a liberal glassful. I can never remember a drink tasting so good.

'And now,' the doctor went on, 'you're to spend the night in the spare room. I want you in bed in five minutes. You can have a bath if you feel like it.'

'Can't I go back to Bafut?' I asked. 'I've got all my animals there, and there's no one really competent to look after them.'

'You're in no state to go back to Bafut, or to look after animals,' he said firmly. 'Now no arguments, into bed. You can go back in the morning, if I think you're well enough.'

To my surprise, I slept soundly, and when I awoke the next day I felt extremely well, though my arm was still swollen and mildly painful. I had breakfast in bed, and then the doctor came to have a look at me.

'How d'you feel?' he asked.

'Fine. I'm feeling so well that I'm beginning to think the snake must have been harmless.'

'No, it was poisonous all right. You said it only got you with one fang, and you probably dropped it so quickly that it didn't have time to inject the full shot of venom. If it had, it might have been another story.'

'Can I go back to Bafut?'

'Well, yes, if you feel up to it, but I shouldn't think that arm will be up to much for a day or two. Anyway, if it worries you, come in and see me.'

Spurred on by the thought of my precious collection waiting at Bafut, uncleaned and unfed, I goaded the unfortunate driver so that he got us back in record time. As we drew up in the road below the villa, I saw a figure seated on the bottom step. It was my fat girl friend of the day before.

'Iseeya, Mammy,' I said, as I stepped down into the road.

'Iseeya, Masa,' she replied, hoisting herself to her feet and waddling towards me.

'Na what you de want?' I asked, for I was impatient to get up to my animals.

'Masa done forget?' she inquired, surprised.

'Forget what, Mammy?'

'Eh, Masa!' she said accusingly, 'Masa never pay me for dat fine snake I done bring.'

Chapter Nine

The Fon and the Golden Cat

My stay in Bafut eventually drew to a close. I had collected a vast quantity of animal life, and it was time to take it all back to the base camp, where it could be re-caged and got ready for the voyage. Reluctantly I informed all the hunters that I would be leaving in a week, so that they would not bring in any specimens after I had left. I ordered the lorry, and sent a note to Smith, telling him to expect me. The Fon, when he heard the news, came flying over, clasping a bottle of gin, and did his best to persuade me to stay. But, as I explained to him, I could not stay any longer, much as I would like to do so; our return passages were booked, and that meant the whole collection had to be ready to move down country on the prescribed date. If there was any hitch we would miss the ship, and we might not be able to get another one for a couple of months, a delay which the trip's budget was not designed to cope with.

'Ah! my friend, I sorry too much you go,' said the Fon, pouring gin into my glass with the gay abandon of a fountain.

'I sorry too much as well,' I said with truth; 'but I no get chance for stay Bafut any more.'

'You go remember Bafut,' said the Fon, pointing a long finger at me; 'you go remember Bafut fine. Na for Bafut you done get plenty fine beef, not be so?'

'Na so,' I said, pointing at my vast piles of cages; 'I done get beef too much for Bafut.'

The Fon nodded benignly. Then he leant forward and clasped my hand.

'When you go for your country, sometime you go tell your people de Fon of Bafut na your friend, an' 'e done get you all dis fine beef, eh?'

'I go tell um all,' I promised, 'and I go tell um dat de Fon be fine hunter man, better pass all hunter for Cameroons.'

'Foine, foine!' said the Fon delightedly.

'Na one beef I never get for here,' I said; 'I sorry too much.'

'Na whatee, my friend?' he asked, leaning forward anxiously.

'Na dat big bush cat dat get skin like gold and mark-mark for 'e belly. I done show you photograph, you remember?'

'Ah! Dat beef!' he said; 'you speak true. Dat beef you never get yet.'

He relapsed into a gloomy silence and scowled at the gin bottle. I wondered if perhaps reminding him of this gap in my collection had not been a little tactless. The animal to which I was referring was the Golden Cat, one of the smaller, but one of the most beautiful, members of the cat family to be found in that part of Africa. I knew that it was reasonably common around Bafut, but the hunters treated it with more respect than they showed for the Serval and the Leopard, both of which were considerably bigger. Whenever I had shown pictures of the beast to the hunters they had chuckled and shaken their heads over it, and assured me that it was extremely difficult to catch, that it was 'fierce too much' and that it 'get plenty clever'. In vain I had offered large rewards, not only for the animal's capture, but even for news of its whereabouts. With slightly less than a week to go before I left, I had resigned myself to not being able to add a Golden Cat to the collection.

The Fon sat back in his chair with a twinkle in his eye, and grinned at me infectiously.

'I go get you dat beef,' he said, nodding portentously.

'But, my friend, in five days I go leave Bafut. How you go catch dis beef in five days?'

'I go catch um,' said the Fon firmly. 'Wait small time you go see. I go get you dat beef.'

He refused to tell me by what methods he was going to bring about this miracle, but he was so sure of himself that I began to wonder if he really would be able to get me one of these creatures. When, however, the day before my departure dawned and there was still no sign of any Golden Cat, I gave up all hope. In his enthusiasm, the Fon had made a promise which he could not fulfil.

It was a sombre, overcast day, for up there in the mountains the rainy season started earlier than in the lowlands. The low, fast-moving clouds, grey as slate, the thin drizzle of rain, and the occasional shudder of thunder in the distant mountain ranges, none of these things helped to make me feel any the less depressed at the thought of leaving Bafut. I had grown very fond of this silent grassland world, and of the people who lived there. The Fon I had come to admire and like, and I felt genuinely sorry at the thought of saying good-bye to him, for he had been an amusing and charming companion.

About four o'clock the fine drizzle turned into a steady downpour that blurred the landscape, drummed and rattled on the roof of the villa and the fronds of the palm trees nearby, turned the red earth of the great courtyard into a shimmering sea of blood-red clay freckled with pockmarks of the falling rain. I had finished my cleaning and feeding of the collection, and I wandered moodily up and down the veranda, watching the rain beat and bruise the scarlet bougainvillaea flowers against the brickwork. My luggage was packed, the cages were stacked and ready for loading into the lorry. I could think of nothing to do, and I did not fancy venturing out into the icy downpour.

Glancing down at the road, I saw a man appear at a trot, slipping and sliding in the mud, carrying on his back a large sack. Hoping that he was bringing me some rare specimen to lighten my gloom, I watched his approach eagerly, but to my annoyance he turned off under the archway and splashed his way across the great courtyard and disappeared through the arched door leading to the Fon's quarters. Shortly after he had vanished, a loud uproar broke out near the Fon's small villa, but it died down after some minutes and all I could hear was the rain. I went and drank my tea in solitary state, and then finished feeding all the nocturnal creatures; they all looked a trifle surprised, for I did not feed them as early as that as a rule, but as the Fon was coming over to spend the evening I wanted to have everything done before he arrived. By the time I had finished my work the rain had died away to a fine, mist-like drizzle, and there were breaks appearing in the low-flying grey clouds through which the sky shone a pale and limpid blue. Within an hour the clouds had dispersed altogether, and the sky was smooth and clear and full of evening sunlight. A small drum started to beat over near the Fon's house, and the sound gradually grew louder. The door into the courtyard opened and a small procession marched through. First came the Fon, dressed in the most magnificent scarlet-and-white robes, striding delicately through the shining puddles. Following him came the strange man I had seen in the rain, still with the sack on his back. Behind him were four council members, and at the end of the procession trotted a small boy in white robes and minute skull-cap, beating importantly on a little drum. The Fon was obviously coming to pay me his last visit in some style. I went down the steps to meet him. He halted in front of me and put his hands on my shoulders, staring into my face with a most impressive sternness.

'My friend,' he said slowly and solemnly, 'I done get something for you.'
'Na whatee?' I asked.
The Fon flung back his trailing sleeves with a regal gesture, and pointed at the man with the sack.
'Bushcat!' he said.
For a moment I was puzzled, and then suddenly I remembered the creature he had promised to get for me.
'Bushcat? Dat kind I de want too much?' I asked, hardly daring to believe it.
The Fon nodded with the quiet satisfaction of one who had done a job well.
'Let me look um,' I said excitedly; 'quick, open dat bag.'
The man placed the sack on the ground in front of me, and I, forgetful of the clean trousers I had put on in the Fon's honour, went down on my knees in the mud and struggled with the tough cord that bound the neck of the sack. The Fon stood by, beaming down at me like a benevolent Santa Claus. The cord was wet and tight, and as I tugged and pulled at it there arose from the interior of the sack a weird and ferocious cry: it started as a rumbling moan, and as it became louder it developed into a yarring scream with such a malevolent undertone that it sent a chill up my spine. The hunter, the councillors and the boy with the drum all retreated several paces.
'Careful, Masa,' the hunter warned; 'na bad beef dat. 'E get power too much.'
'You done get rope for 'e foot?' I asked, and he nodded.
I unwound the last bit of cord, and then slowly opened the sack and peered inside.
Glaring up at me was a face of such beauty that I gasped. The fur was short, smooth and the rich golden-brown of wild honey. The pointed ears were flattened close to the skull, and the upper lip was drawn back in a series of fine ripples from milk-white teeth and pink gums. But it was the

eyes I noticed more than anything else: large, and set at a slight slant in the golden face, they stared up at me with a look of such cold fury that I was thankful the animal's feet were tied. They were green, the green of leaves under ice, and they glittered like mica in the evening sun. For a second we stared at each other, then the Golden Cat drew back her lips even further away from her gums, opened her mouth and gave another of those loud and frightening cries. Hastily I tied the sack up again, for I did not know if her bonds were really strong or not, and, judging by her eyes, she would not deal with me very kindly if she got free.

'You like?' asked the Fon.

'Wah! I like dis beef *too much*,' I replied.

We carried the precious sack up on to the veranda, and I hastily turned a specimen out of the largest and strongest cage I had. Then we emptied the Golden Cat gently out of the sack and rolled her inside, shutting and bolting the door. She lay on her side, hissing and snarling, but unable to move, for her front and back legs were neatly tied together with strong raffia-like cord. By fixing a knife to the end of a stick I managed to saw through these cords, and as they fell away she got to her feet in one smooth movement, leapt at the bars, stuck a fat golden paw through and took a swipe at my face. I drew back only just in time.

'Aha!' said the Fon, chuckling, 'dis beef get angry too much.'

' 'E fit chop man time no dere,' said the hunter.

' 'E get power,' agreed the Fon, nodding, ' 'e get plenty power for 'e foot. You go watch um, my friend, less 'e go wound you.'

I sent down to the kitchen for a small chicken, and this, freshly killed and warm, I dangled near the bars of the cage. A golden paw again shot out between the bars, white claws buried themselves in the fowl and it was jerked up against the bars. Leaning forward, the cat got a grip on the neck of the bird, and with one quick heave the entire fowl vanished into the cage, and clouds of feathers started to pour out from between the bars as the Golden Cat began to feed. Reverently I covered the front of the cage with a sack and we left her in peace to enjoy her meal.

'How you done catch dis beef?' I asked the hunter. He gave a grin and wiggled his toes with embarrassment.

'You no de hear?' asked the Fon, 'you no get mouth? Speak now!'

'Masa,' began the man, scratching his stomach, 'de Fon done tell me Masa want dis kind of beef too much, an' so three days I done go for bush, I look um. I done walka, walka, I done tire too much, but I never see dis beef. Yesterday, for evening time, dis bushcat 'e done come softly for my farm, an' 'e done chop three chicken. Dis morning I see 'e foot for de mud, an' I done follow for bush. Far too much I done follow um, Masa, an' den, for some big hill, I done see um.'

The Fon shifted in his chair and fixed the man with a glittering eye.

'You speak true?' he asked sternly.

'Yes, Masa,' protested the hunter, 'I speak true.'

'Good,' said the Fon.

'I done see dis bushcat,' the man went on; ' 'e done walka for dis big hill. Den 'e done go for some place dere be rock too much. 'E done go for hole in de ground. I look dis hole, but man no fit pass, 'e tight too much. I done go back for my house an' I done bring fine dog an' catchnet, den I go back for dis place. I done put catchnet for de hole, an' den I done make small fire an' put smoke for de hole.'

He paused and hopped on one leg, clicking his fingers.

'Wah! Dat beef fierce too much! When 'e done smell de smoke 'e de hollar an' 'e de hollar, time no dere. My dog dey de fear an' dey all done run. I de fear bushcat go catch me an' I done run also. Small time I hear de beef 'e hollar an' hollar, an' so I done go softly softly for look um. Wah! Masa, dat beef 'e run run for inside catchnet, an' de catchnet done hold um fine. When I see um for catchnet I no get fear again, an' so I done go an' I tie 'e foot with rope, an' I done bring um one time for Masa.'

The man ended his story and stood watching us anxiously, twisting his short spear in both hands.

'My friend,' I told him, 'I tink you be fine hunter man, an' I go pay you good money for dis beef.'

'Na so, na so,' agreed the Fon waving a lordly hand, 'dis man done make find hunting for you.'

I paid him a handsome sum of money, and made him a present of several packets of cigarettes, and he went off grinning and ejaculating, 'Tank you Masa, tank you,' all the way down the steps and along the road until he was out of earshot. Then I turned to the Fon, who was sitting back watching me with a smug expression on his face.

'My friend, I tank you too much for dis ting you done do,' I said.

The Fon waved his hands deprecatingly.

'No, no, my friend, na small ting dis. It no be good ting if you go leave Bafut and you never get all de beef you want. I sorry too much you do go leave. But, when you look dis fine beef you go tink of Bafut, no be so?'

'Na true,' I said, 'and now, my friend, you go drink with me?'

'Foine, foine,' said the Fon.

As if to compensate for the dreariness of the early part of the day, the sunset was one of the finest I have ever seen. The sun sank down behind a grid of pale, elongated clouds, and as it sank, the clouds turned from white to pearly pink, and then flushed to crimson edged with gold. The sky itself was washed with the palest of blues and greens, smudged here and there with a touch of gold, with pale, trembling stars gaining strength as the world darkened. Presently the moon came up, blood-red at first, changing to yellow and then silver as she rose, turning the world a frosty silver, with shadows as black as charcoal.

The Fon and I sat drinking in the misty moonlight until it was late. Then he turned to me, pointing towards his villa.

'I tink sometime you like to dance,' he said, 'so I done tell um to make musica. You like we go dance before you leave, eh?'

'Yes, I like to dance,' I said.

The Fon lurched to his feet, and, leaning perilously over the veranda rail, he shouted an order to someone waiting below. In a short time a cluster of lights moved across the great courtyard, and the Fon's all-female band assembled in the road below and started to play. Soon they were joined by numerous others, including most of the council members. The Fon listened to the music for a bit, waving his hands and smiling, and then he got up and held out his hand to me.

'Come!' he said, 'we go dance, eh?'

'Foine, foine!' I mimicked him, and he crowed with glee.

We made our way across the moon-misty veranda to the head of the steps; the Fon draped a long arm over my shoulders, partly out of affection and partly for support, and we started to descend. Half-way down, my companion stopped to execute a short dance to the music. His foot got tangled up in his impressive robes, and, but for his firm grip round my neck, he would have rolled down the steps into the road. As it was, we struggled there for a moment, swaying violently, as we tried to regain our balance; the crowd of wives, offspring and councillors gave a great gasp of horror and consternation at the sight of their lord in such peril, and the band stopped playing.

'Musica, musica!' roared the Fon, as we reeled together on the steps; 'why you done stop, eh?'

The band started up again, we regained our equilibrium and walked down the rest of the way without mishap. The Fon was in fine fettle, and he insisted on holding my hand and dancing across the courtyard, splashing through the puddles, while the band trotted behind, playing a trifle short-windedly. When we reached the dancing-hut he sat down on his throne for a rest, while his court took the floor. Presently, when there was a slight lull in the dancing, I asked the Fon if he would call the band over, so that I could examine the instruments more closely. They trouped over and stood in front of the dais on which we sat, while I tried each instrument in turn and was shown the correct way of playing it. To everyone's surprise, including my own, I succeeded in playing the first few bars of 'The Campbells are Coming' on a bamboo flute. The Fon was so delighted with this that he made me repeat it several times while he accompanied me on a big drum, and one of the council members on the strange foghorn-like instrument. The effect was not altogether musical, but we rendered it with great verve and feeling. Then he had to repeat it all over again, so that the Fon could hear how it sounded with a full band accompaniment. Actually, it sounded rather good, as most of my flat notes were drowned by the drums.

When we had exhausted the musical possibilities of the tune, the Fon sent for another bottle, and we settled down to watch the dancers. The inactivity soon told on my companion, and after an hour or so he started to shift on his throne and to scowl at the band. He filled up our glasses, and then leant back and glared at the dancers.

'Dis dance no be good,' he confided at last.

'Na fine,' I said; 'why you no like?'

' 'E slow too much,' he pointed out, and then he leant over and smiled at me disarmingly, 'You like we go dance your special dance?'

'Special dance?' I queried, slightly fuddled; 'what dance?'

'One, two, three, keek; one, two, three, keek,' yodelled the Fon.

'Ah, dat dance you de talk. Yes, we go dance um if you like.'

'I like too much,' said the Fon firmly.

He led the way on to the dance-floor, and clutched my waist in a firm grip, while everyone else, all chattering and grinning with delight, joined on behind. In order to add a little variety to the affair I borrowed a flute, and piped noisily and inaccurately on it as I led them on a wild dance round the dance-hall and out among the huts of the Fon's wives. The night was warm, and half an hour of this exercise made me stream with sweat and gasp for breath. We stopped for a rest and some liquid refreshment. It was obvious, however, that my Conga had got into the Fon's blood. He sat on his throne, his eyes gleaming, feet tapping, humming reminiscently to himself, and obviously waiting with ill-concealed impatience until I had recovered my breath before suggesting that we repeat the whole performance. I decided that I would have to lead him off in some way, for I found the Conga too enervating for such a close night, and I had barked my shin quite painfully on a door-post during our last round. I cast around in my mind for another dance I could teach him which would be less strenuous to perform, and yet whose tune could be easily mastered by the band. I made my choice, and then called once more for a flute, and practised on it for a few minutes. Then I turned to the Fon, who had been watching me with great interest.

'If you go tell de band 'e go learn dis special music I go teach you other European dance,' I said.

'Ah! Foine, foine,' he said, his eyes gleaming, and he turned and roared the band to silence, and then marshalled them round the dais while I played the tune to them. In a surprisingly short time they had picked it up, and were even adding little variations of their own. The Fon stamped his feet delightedly.

'Na fine music dis,' he said; 'now you go show me dis dance, eh?'

I looked round and singled out a young damsel who, I had noticed, seemed exceptionally bright, and, clasping her as closely as propriety would permit (for her clothing was non-existent), I set off across the dance-floor in a dashing polka. My partner after only a momentary hesitation picked up the step perfectly, and we bobbed and hopped round in great style. To show his appreciation of this new dance, the Fon started to clap, and immediately the rest of the court followed suit; it started off as normal, ragged applause; but, being Africans, our audience kept clapping and worked it into the rhythm of the dance. The girl and I circled round the large floor five times, and then we were forced to stop for a rest. When I reached the dais, the Fon held out a brimming glass of whisky for me and clapped me on the back as I sat down.

'Na foine dance!' he said.

I nodded and gulped down my drink. As soon as I had put my glass down, the Fon seized me by the hand and pulled me on to the floor again.

'Come,' he said persuasively, 'you go show me dis dance.'

Clasped in each other's arms, we polkaed round the room, but it was not a great success, chiefly because my partner's robes became entangled with my feet and jerked us both to a halt. We would then have to stand patiently while a crowd of council members unwound us, after which away we would go again: one, two, three, hop, only to end up in the opposite corner entwined together like a couple of maypoles.

Eventually I glanced at my watch and discovered to my dismay that it was three o'clock. Reluctantly I had to take my leave of the Fon and retire to bed. He and the court followed me out into the great courtyard, and there I left them. As I climbed up the steps to the villa I looked back at them. In among the twinkling hurricane lanterns they were all dancing the polka. In the centre of them the Fon was jigging and hopping by himself, waving one long arm and shouting 'Good night, my friend, good night!' I waved back, and then went and crawled thankfully into my bed.

By eight-thirty the next morning the lorry had arrived and the collection had been stacked on to it. An incredible number of Bafutians had come to say good-bye and to see me off; they had been arriving since early that morning, and now lined the roadside, chattering together, waiting for me to depart. The last load was hoisted on to the lorry, and the sound of drums, flutes and rattles heralded the arrival of the Fon to take his leave of me. He was dressed as I had seen him on the day of my arrival, in a plain white robe and a wine-red skull-cap. He was accompanied by his retinue of highly coloured councillors. He strode up and embraced me, and then, holding me by the hand, addressed the assembled Bafutians in a few rapid sentences. When he stopped, the crowd broke into loud 'arrr's' and started to clap rhythmically. The Fon turned to me and raised his voice.

'My people 'e sorry too much you go leave Bafut. All dis people dey go remember you, and you no go forget Bafut, eh?'

'I never go forget Bafut,' I said truthfully, making myself heard with difficulty above the loud and steady clapping of those hundreds of black hands.

'Good,' he said with satisfaction; then he clasped my hand firmly in his and wrung it. 'My friend always I go get you for my eye. I no go forget dis happy time we done get. By God power you go reach your own country safe. Walka good, my friend, walka good.'

As the lorry started off down the road the clapping got faster and faster, until it sounded like rain on a tin roof. We jolted our way slowly along until we reached the corner; looking back I saw the road lined with naked black humanity, their hands fluttering as they clapped, and at the end of this avenue of moving hands and flashing teeth stood a tall figure in dazzling white. It raised a long arm, and a huge hand waved a last farewell as the lorry rounded the corner and started up the red earth road that wound over the golden, glittering hills.

Chapter Ten

Zoo Under Canvas

One of the most frustrating things for the collector is that he can rarely get to know any of his animals until towards the end of a trip. During the first four months or so they are just specimens to him, for he has not the time to observe them closely enough for them to assume characters of their own. He sees that they are adequately housed, feeds and cleans them; but beyond that he cannot go, for all his spare time is spent in trying to add to his menagerie.

Towards the end of a trip, however, his collection has grown to such proportions that he cannot wander far afield, for he has too much to do. Then is the time when he had to rely entirely on the native hunters to bring in new specimens, and he, being confined to camp all day, has the opportunity of getting to know the creatures he has already assembled. Our collection had reached such a point when I returned from Bafut. Not only had we the grassland animals, but during my stay in the mountains Smith had been steadily increasing the collection with the local forest fauna. Under the great canvas roof of our marquee we had a large and varied enough collection of creatures to start a small zoo.

So, on my return to our hot and humid base camp on the banks of the Cross River, I began to appreciate some of my grassland captures for the first time. For example, take the case of the hyrax. Until I got them down to base camp I had considered them to be rather dull creatures, whose only claim to fame was their relatives. At first glance one would be pardoned for mistaking a hyrax for an ordinary member of the great group of rodents, and as you watched them nibbling away at leaves or gnawing at some juicy bark, you would probably hazard a guess that they were related to the rabbits. In this you would be quite wrong, for a hyrax is an ungulate, an order which includes cattle, deer, swine and horses; and the nearest relative to the hyrax is not the rabbit but the elephant, of all unlikely things. In the bone formation of the feet, and in other anatomical details, the hyrax is classified as coming closer to the elephant and the rhino than anything else. This is the sort of information that makes people wonder whether zoologists are quite sane, for a hyrax resembles an elephant about as closely as an elephant does a humming-bird. However, the relationship is clearer if one goes into the more complicated details of anatomy and dentition. This, frankly, was all the information I had about the hyrax.

When I reached base camp, the old female hyrax, which had savaged the Beagle's foot, and her two fat babies were transferred from the small cage they had been confined in to a much bigger affair that gave them plenty of space to move about in and had a private bedroom to which to retire if they felt in any way anti-social. In this cage I noticed several things about them which I had not observed before. To begin with, they had what are called 'lavatory habits'; that is to say, they always deposited their dirt in one spot in the cage. Until then I had not realized what a godsend an animal with these habits could be to a hard-working collector. As soon as I had grasped the meaning of the neat little pile of dung I found in the corner of the cage each morning, I set about making the cleaning of the hyrax cage a much simpler operation. I simply provided them with a round, shallow tin as a latrine. To my annoyance, the next morning I found that they had spurned my offer; they had simply pushed the tin out of the way and deposited their dirt in the usual place in the normal fashion. So that night I put the tin in again, but this time I placed a few of their droppings in the bottom. The following day, to my delight, the tin was piled high with dirt, and the floor of the cage was spotless. After that cleaning of the cage took approximately five minutes: you simply emptied the tin, washed and replaced it in the corner. It became a real pleasure to clean out the hyrax.

As a contrast in habits there were the Pouched Rats: these rodents, each as large as a small kitten, lived in the cage next door to the hyrax family. These belonged to that irritating group of beasts that won't – or can't – evacuate their bowels unless it is done into water, and preferably running water. In the wild state they would probably use a stream for this purpose, and the current would carry the dirt away to fertilize some plant further downstream. In a cage, however, I could not provide the Pouched Rats with a stream, so they used the next best thing, which was their water-pot. There is nothing quite so frustrating as putting a nice clean water-pot, brimming with clear liquid, into a cage, and, on looking at it five minutes later, finding that it resembles a pot full of liquid manure. It was very worrying, for in the heat the animals needed a constant supply of fresh drinking-water, and yet here were the rats dirtying their water before drinking it. After many futile attempts to get them to abandon this habit, I used to supply them with a large pot of water as a lavatory, and plenty of juicy fruit to eat, in the hope that this would quench their thirst.

But to return to the hyrax: in Bafut I had decided that they were dull, unfriendly animals who spent their whole lives sitting on their haunches chewing leaves with a glazed look in their eyes. At base camp I discovered that I was quite mistaken, for a hyrax can be as lively as a lamb when it puts its mind to it. In the evening, when their cage was flooded with sunlight, the old female would lie there looking as imposing as a Trafalgar Square lion, munching methodically at a bunch of tender spinach, or a cluster of cassava leaves, while her babies played with each other. These were wild and exhilarating romps they used to have: they would chase one another round and round the cage, sometimes astonishing me by running straight up the smooth wooden back of the cage until they reached the roof before dropping off on to the floor. When they tired of these Wall-of-Death stunts they would use their mother's portly and recumbent body as a castle. One would climb up on to her back, while the other would attack and try to knock him off. Occasionally they would both be on their mother's back together, locked in mortal combat, while their parent lay there unmoved, chewing steadily, a trance-like look on her face. These games were delightful to watch, but there was one annoying thing about them, and this was that the babies would sometimes carry on far into the night, especially if there was a moon. It is extremely difficult to get to sleep when a pair of baby hyrax are dashing about their cage, producing a noise like a couple of stallions fighting in a loose-box. Sitting up in bed and shouting 'SHUT UP' in fearsome tones had the effect of stopping them for about half an hour; if you had not drifted into sleep by then, you would be brought back to life once again by the thumping of wood, twanging of wire and the melodious crash of food-pots being kicked over. The hyraxes were certainly anything but dull.

Another creature that started to blossom into his true colours when we arrived at base camp was the Black-eared Squirrel, the beast that had created such havoc on the steps of the villa in Bafut. This episode of the steps was, if I had only known it at the time, but a slight indication of what he could do when he put his mind to it, for his one delight in life seemed to consist in escaping and being chased by a crowd of people. He was, as I have already mentioned, quite a baby, and within a very short time after his arrival he had become extraordinarily tame and would allow me to pick him up and place him on my shoulder, where he would sit up on his hind legs and investigate my ear, in the hope that I had been sensible enough to secrete a palm-nut or some other delicacy there. As long as there were not more than four people about, he would behave with the utmost decorum; a crowd, however, filled him with the unholy desire to be chased. At first I thought that a crowd of people worried and frightened him and that he ran away to try to escape from them. I soon discovered that it was nothing of the sort, for if he found his pursuers lagging behind, he would stop, sit up on his hind legs and wait for them to catch up. There was a certain humour in the fact that we had christened the little brute Sweeti-pie (because of his docility and nice nature) before we discovered his vice. The first race organized by Sweeti-pie took place three days after we had arrived at the marquee.

Our water supply for the camp was kept in two great petrol drums which stood near the kitchen. These were filled every day by the convicts from the local prison. They were a cheerful group of men, clad in spotless white smocks and shorts, who toiled up the hill to camp every morning carrying brimming kerosene tins of water on their shaven heads. Behind them would walk a warder in an impressive fawn uniform, his brass buttons flashing in the sun, swinging a short truncheon with a capable air. The convicts, whose crimes ranged from petty theft to manslaughter, went about their tedious task with great good humour, and when you greeted them they would all beam with pleasure. Once a week I distributed a couple of packets of cigarettes among them, and they would be allowed by their warder (who was having a glass of beer with me) to wander round the camp and look at our collection of animals. They thoroughly enjoyed this break in routine, and they would cluster round the monkeys and double up with laughter at their antics, or else peer into the snake-box and give themselves thrills.

On this particular morning when the convicts arrived I was on my way to feed Sweeti-pie. The convicts filed past me, their faces gleaming with sweat, grinning amicably and greeting me with, 'Morning, Masa. We done come ... we done bring water for Masa ... Iseeya, Masa ...', and so on. The warder gave me a frightfully military salute, and then grinned like a small boy. While they were emptying the contents of their tins into the petrol drums, I got Sweeti-pie out of his cage, sat him on the palm of my hand and gave him a lump of sugar to eat. He seized the sugar in his mouth and then, glancing round, he saw the group of convicts near the kitchen, exchanging gossip and saucy badinage with the staff. Having made sure that there were enough people there to give him a good run for his money, he took a firmer grip on his sugar, leapt lightly off my hand and galloped off across the camp clearing, his tail streaming out behind him like a flame in a draught. I set off in pursuit, but before I had gone more than a few paces Sweeti-pie had gained the thick bushes at the edge of the clearing and dived out of sight. Thinking that it would be the last I should see of him, I uttered such a wail of anguish that everyone dropped what they were doing and ran towards me.

'Dat beef done run,' I yelled to the convicts; 'I go pay five shillings to man who catch um.'

The results of my offer were quite startling: the convicts dropped their kerosene tins and rushed off into the bushes, closely followed by their warder, who discarded both truncheon and hat in case they hampered his movements. The entire staff also joined in the hunt, and the whole crowd of them went crashing through the bushes and short undergrowth in search of Sweeti-pie. They combed the area thoroughly without finding any signs of the animal, and then it was discovered that the little brute had been sitting in the branches of a small bush, watching the search sweep to and fro around him, quietly finishing off his sugar-lump. When he saw that he was spotted, he leapt to the ground, ran through the camp clearing and out on to the path leading away over the hill, hotly pursued by a panting mob consisting of warder, convicts and staff. They all disappeared from view over the skyline and peace descended on the camp. But not for long, for in a few minutes Sweeti-pie appeared again over the brow of the hill, galloped down into camp, shot through the marquee and scrambled into his cage, where he innocently started to eat a piece of sugar-cane. Half an hour later the warder, the convicts and the staff straggled back to camp, all hot and perspiring, to report that the animal had escaped them and was now doubtless deep in the bush. When I showed them Sweeti-pie (who had now finished his meal and was quietly sleeping) and told them how he had returned, they gaped at me for a minute in amazement. And then, being Africans, the humour of the situation struck them and they reeled around the camp yelling with laughter, slapping their thighs, the tears streaming down their faces. The warder was so overcome that he collapsed on the neck of one of the convicts and sobbed with mirth.

Every day after that the warder and the convicts would bring some offering to the beef that had made them run so fast and 'fooled them too much': sometimes it was a bit of sugar-cane, or a handful of groundnuts, sometimes a bit of cassava or a piece of bread. Whatever it was, Sweeti-pie would sit up at the wire and receive the offering with squeaks of pleasure, while the convicts would gather round and relate to each other, or to any new member of their group, the story of how they had chased the squirrel. Then there would be much laughter, and Sweeti-pie would be praised for his skilful evasive tactics. This was only the first of many occasions when Sweeti-pie caused havoc in the camp.

Of the many different creatures that were brought to us while we were at base camp, about a fifth were babies, and, although they were charming little things for the most part, they caused a great deal of extra work for us, for very young animals require just as much care and attention as a human baby. All these young creatures endeared themselves to us, but one of the most charming and, at the same time, irritating trio of beasts we acquired were three little fellows that we called the Bandits. These animals were Kusimanses, a kind of mongoose which is fairly common in the forest. When adult, they are about the size of a large guinea-pig, clad in thick, coarse chocolate fur, a bushy tail, and a long pointed face with a rubbery pink nose and circular, protuberant boot-button eyes. The Bandits, when they arrived, were about the size of small rats and had only just got their eyes open. Their fur was a bright gingery colour, and it stuck up in tufts and sprigs all over their bodies, making them look rather like hedgehogs. Their noses were the most prominent part of their anatomy, long and bright pink, and so flexible that they could be whiffled from side to side like a miniature elephant's trunk. At first they had to be fed on milk mixed with calcium and cod-liver oil, and this was no easy task; they drank more milk than any other baby animal I have ever met, and the whole business was made more difficult because they were far too small to suck it out of the feeding-bottle I used for the others. So they had to be fed by wrapping a lump of cotton wool round a stick, dipping it in the milk and then letting them suck it. This worked admirably at first, but as soon as their sharp little teeth began to appear through the gums, they started to be troublesome. They were so greedy that they would take hold of the cotton wool and hang on to it like bulldogs, refusing to let go and allow me to dip it into the milk again. On many occasions they would grip so hard that the cotton wool would come off the end of the stick, and then they would try to swallow it; only by sticking my finger down their throats and capturing the cotton wool as it was disappearing could I save them from being choked to death. Sticking a finger down their throats always made them sick, and, of course, as soon as they had been sick they would feel hungry again, so the whole performance would have to be repeated. Anyone who prides himself on his patience should try hand-rearing some baby Kusimanses.

When their teeth had come through and they had learnt to walk really well they became most inquisitive and were always trying to push their pink noses into someone else's business. They lived in what we called the nursery – a collection of baskets that housed all the baby animals – and were placed between our two beds, where they were within easy reach for any bottle feeds that had to be given at night. The top of the basket which the Bandits inhabited was not too secure, and it was not long before they learnt how to push it off; then they would scramble out and go on a tour of inspection round the camp. This was extremely worrying, for the Bandits seemed to be completely lacking in fear and would stick their noses into monkey cages or snake-boxes with equal freedom. Their lives were devoted to a search for food, and everything they came across they would bite in the hope that it would turn out to be tasty. At that time we had a fully grown female Colobus monkey, a creature which possessed a wonderfully long, thick coat of silky black and white hair, and a long, plume-like tail, also black and white, of which she seemed very proud, for she was always most particular about keeping it clean and glossy. One day the Bandits escaped from the nursery and wandered round by the monkey cages to see what they could pick up. The Colobus was reclining on the bottom of her cage having a sun bath, and her long and beautiful tail was sticking out between the bars and lying on the ground. One of the Bandits discovered this curious object and, since it did not appear to belong to anyone, he rushed at it and sank his sharp little teeth into it to see whether it was edible. The other two, seeing what he had found, immediately joined him and laid hold of the tail as well. The unfortunate monkey, screaming loudly with rage and fright, scrambled up to the top of her cage, but this did not shake off the Bandits; they clung on like a vice, and the higher the Colobus climbed in her cage, the higher her tail lifted the Bandits off the ground. When I arrived on the scene they were suspended about a foot in the air, and were hanging there, revolving slowly, all growling through clenched teeth. It took me several minutes to induce them to let go, and then they did so only because I blew cigarette smoke into their faces and made them cough.

When the Bandits became old enough to have a special cage of their own, complete with bedroom, feeding them was a job fraught with great difficulty and danger. They grew so excited at meal-times that they would fasten their teeth into anything that looked even remotely like food, so that you had to watch your hands. Instead of waiting until the food dish was put inside their cage, like any sensible animal, they would leap through the door to meet it, knock the dish out of your hand, and then fall to the ground in a tangled heap, all screaming loudly with frustrated rage. Eventually I became rather tired of having the Bandits shoot out like ginger rockets every time I went to feed them, so I evolved a plan. Two of us would approach the cage at meal-times, and the Bandits would hurl themselves at the bar, screaming loudly, their eyes popping with emotion. Then one of us would rattle the bedroom door, and they, thinking that the food was being put in there, would throw themselves into the sleeping quarters, fighting and scrambling to get there first. While they were thus engaged you had exactly two seconds' grace before they found out the deception: during that time you had to open the cage door, put the food inside and withdraw your hand and lock the door again. If you were not quick, or made some slight noise to attract their attention, the Bandits would tumble out of the bedroom, screeching and chittering, upset the plate and bite indiscriminately at the food and your hand. It was all very trying.

About this time we had another pair of babies brought to us, who proved to be full of charm and personality. They were a pair of baby Red River Hogs and, as with the Kusimanses, they looked totally unlike the adult. A fully grown Red River Hog is probably the most attractive member of the pig family, and certainly the most highly coloured. They have bright rusty-orange fur with deeper, almost chocolate markings round the snout. Their large ears end in two extraordinary pencil-like tufts of pure white hair, and a mane of this white hair runs along their backs. The two babies were, like all young pigs, striped: the ground colour was a deep brown, almost black, and from snout to tail they were banded with wide lines of bright mustard-yellow fur, a colour scheme that had the effect of making them look more like fat wasps than baby pigs.

The little male was the first to arrive, sitting forlornly in a basket carried on the head of a brawny hunter. He was obviously in need of a good feed of warm milk, and as soon as I had paid for him I prepared a bottle and then lifted him out on to my knee. He was about the size of a pekinese, and had very sharp little hooves and tusks, as I soon found out. He had never seen a feeding-bottle and treated it with the gravest suspicion from the start. When I lifted him on to my knee and tried to get the teat into his mouth, he kicked and squealed, ripping my trousers with his hooves and trying to bite with his tiny tusks. At the end of five minutes we both looked as though we had bathed in milk, but not a drop of it had gone down his throat. In the end I had to hold him firmly between my knees, wedge his mouth open with one hand while squirting milk in with the other. As soon as the first few drops trickled down his throat he stopped struggling and screaming, and within a few minutes he was sucking away at the bottle as hard as he could go. After this he was no more trouble, and within two days had lost all his fear of me, and would come running to the bars of his pen when I appeared, squeaking and grunting with delight, rolling over on to his back to have his bulging stomach scratched.

The female piglet arrived a week later, and she was brought in protesting so loudly that we could hear her long before she and the hunter came in sight. She was almost twice the size of the male, so I decided that they must have separate cages to start with, as I was afraid that she might hurt him. But when I put her in the pen next door to him, their obvious delight at seeing each other, and the way they rushed to the intervening bars, squeaking and rubbing noses, made me decide that they should share a cage straight away. When I put them together the tiny male ran forward, sniffing loudly, and then butted the female gently in the ribs; she snorted and skipped away across the cage. He chased her, and together they ran round and round the cage, twisting and turning and doubling back with astonishing agility for such portly beasts. When they had worked off their high spirits, they burrowed deep into the pile of dry banana leaves I had provided for them and fell asleep, snoring like a beehive on a summer night.

The female, being so much older, very soon learnt to supplement her bottle-feed with a dish of chopped fruit and vegetables. After giving both of them their bottle I would put a broad, shallow pan full of this mixture into the cage, and she would spend the morning standing there with her nose buried in it, making slushy, squelching piggy noises and sighing dreamily at intervals. The little male could not understand this, and he used to become very incensed at being ignored; he would go and prod her with his snout, or nibble at her legs, until she would suddenly turn on him with squeals of rage and drive him away. He tried several times to see what it was in the dish that was attracting her, but could not discover anything very exciting about a lot of chopped fruit, so he would wander off moodily and sit in a corner by himself until she had finished. One day, however, he decided that he, too, could get an extra meal, by the simple expedient of sucking the female's long tail. He became convinced that if he sucked it long enough and hard enough he would get milk from it. So she used to stand there with her nose buried in the dish of food, while behind her stood the male with her tail held hopefully in his mouth. This did not seem to worry her unduly, but he sucked so enthusiastically that her tail became quite bald, and in order to let the hair grow again I had to keep them in separate cages, only allowing them to be with one another for a game twice a day.

Life in the marquee with half a hundred animals to look after was anything but dull. We were surrounded on all sides by animals of all shapes, sizes and kinds, from tree-frogs to owls, and from pythons to monkeys. At all hours of the day and night a steady mutter of strange noises filled the air – noises that ranged from the maniacal screams and giggles of the chimpanzees to the steady rasping sound of a Pouched Rat who was convinced that, by sticking to it in spite of all opposition, he could gnaw his way through a metal feeding-pot. At any time of the day you could find something to do, or something new to note or observe. The following extracts from a week's entries in my diary give some indication of the wealth of small but exciting or interesting incidents that were worth noting:

The young female Stanger's Squirrel's eyes have now changed from that beautiful shade of sky blue to steel grey; when you disturb her at night she makes a noise like a clockwork train when it is lifted off the rails ... one of the Palm Vipers has given birth to eleven young: about five inches long, ground colour pale slate grey with cross bands of dark ash grey, making wonderful contrast to vivid green and white mother; they all struck viciously at a stick when only a couple of hours old ... large green tree frogs make a noise like a clock slowly ticking, just before rain, but will stop if you go near their cage, and won't perform again until next cloudburst ... discovered that the galagos like the flowers of a species of marigold that grows around here; they hold flower head in one hand and pluck off petals with the other, cramming them into their mouths; then they play with the remains as though it were a shuttlecock, looking quite ridiculous, with their great eyes staring. ...

Feeding notes: Golden Cat adores brain and liver chopped up and mixed with raw egg – exotic tastes some of these beasts have! Pangolins [Scaly Anteaters] won't eat their egg and milk mixture if it's sweetened, but simply overturn dish – extremely annoying! Fruit Bats prefer their bananas to be given with the skins on; they eat the whole lot, and the skin seems to prevent their bowels from becoming too loose. Over-ripe fruit causes havoc among the monkey bowels (especially chimps – messy!), yet the bats will eat and enjoy without ill-effects fruit that is fermenting, providing there is roughage with it. Too much goat meat causes rupture of the anus in the March Mongooses, for some peculiar reason; warm cod-liver oil and *very gentle* pressure will get it back into place; animal will become very exhausted and then one drop whisky in tablespoon of water helps them.

These were the little things that made up life in base camp, but they were of absorbing interest to us, and the days seemed so full of colour and incident that they sped past unnoticed. So it is not surprising that I was rather terse with a pleasant but stupid young man who said, after being shown round the collection, 'Don't you ever go out and have a pot at a monkey or something? Should have thought you would have died of boredom, stuck down here all day with this lot.'

Chapter Eleven

The Forest of Flying Mice

When I returned from the mountains to our Cross River base camp there was only one gap of importance in our collection. The gap was noticeable to me, for it was caused by the absence of a tiny animal which I wanted to catch more than practically any other creature in the Cameroons. The English name for this beast is the Pigmy Scaly-tail, while zoologists, in their usual flippant and familiar manner, call it *Idiurus kivuensis*. When in England I had pored over drawings and museum skins of the beast, and since our arrival in Africa I had talked about it incessantly, until even the staff knew that *Idiurus kivuensis* was the name of a beef that I prized beyond all measure.

I knew that *Idiurus* was a stricly nocturnal animal; it was, moreover, only the size of a small mouse, which made it unlikely that any of the hunters would know it. I was right, for they did not recognize the drawing I had. From the small amount of literature dealing with the species I had managed to glean the fact that they lived in colonies in hollow trees, preferring the less accessible portions of the forest. I explained this to the hunters, in the faint hope that it would spur them on to search for specimens, but it was no use; the African will not hunt for an animal he has never seen, for he considers it likely that it may not exist – to hunt for it would be a waste of time. I had had precisely the same trouble over the Hairy Frogs, so I realized that my tales of small-small rats that flew like birds from tree to tree were doomed from the start. One thing was very clear: if I wanted *Idiurus* I would have to go out and hunt for it myself, and I should have to do so quickly, for our time was short. I decided to make the village of Eshobi my headquarters for the *Idiurus* hunt; it was a day's march from base camp, in the depths of the forest, and I knew the inhabitants well, for I had stayed there on a previous visit to the Cameroons. Hunting for a creature the size of a mouse in the deep rain-forest that stretches for several hundred miles in all directions may sound like an improved version of the needle-in-the-haystack routine, but it is this sort of thing that makes collecting so interesting. My chances of success were one in a thousand, but I set off cheerfully into the forest.

The Eshobi road can only be appreciated by someone with a saint-like predilection for mortifying the flesh. Most of it resembles an old dried watercourse, though it follows a route that no self-respecting river would take. It runs in a series of erratic zig-zags through the trees, occasionally tumbling down a steep slope into a valley, crossing a small stream and climbing up the opposite side. On the downward slope the rocks and stones which made up its surface were always loose, so that on occasions your descent was quicker than you anticipated. As the road started to climb up the opposite side of the valley, however, you would find that the rocks had increased considerably in size and were placed like a series of steps. This was a snare and a delusion, for each rock had been so cunningly placed that it was quite impossible to step from it to the next one. They were all thickly covered with a cloak of green moss, wild begonias and ferns, so you could not tell, before jumping, exactly what shape your landing ground was going to be.

The track went on like this for some three miles, then we toiled up from the bottom of a deep valley and found that the forest floor was level and the path almost as smooth as a motor road. It wound and twisted its way through the giant trees, and here and there along its length there was a rent in the foliage above, which let through a shaft of sunlight. In these patches of sun, warming themselves after the night's dew, sat a host of butterflies. They rose and flew round us as we walked, dipping and fluttering and wheeling in a sun-drunken condition. There were tiny white ones like fragile chips of snow, great clumsy ones whose wings shone like burnished copper, and others decked out in blacks, greens, reds and yellows. Once we had passed, they settled again on the sunlit path and sat there gaily, occasionally opening and closing their wings. This ballet of butterflies was always to be seen on the Eshobi path, and is moreover the only life you are likely to see, for the deep forest does not teem with dangerous game, as some books would have you believe.

We followed this path for about three hours, stopping at times so that the sweating carriers could lower their loads to the ground and have a rest. Presently the path curved, and as we rounded a corner the forest ended and we found ourselves walking up the main and only street of Eshobi. Dogs barked, chickens scuttled and squawked out of our way, and a small toddler rose from the dust where he had been playing and fled into the nearest hut, screaming his lungs out. Suddenly, as if from nowhere, we were surrounded by a milling crowd of humanity: men and boys, women of all ages, all grinning and clapping, pushing forward to shake me by the hand.

'Welcome, Masa, welcome!'
'You done come, Masa!'
'Iseeya, Masa, welcome!'
'Eh ... eahh! Masa, you done come back to Eshobi!'

I was escorted down the village street by this welcoming, chattering mob of humanity as though I were royalty. Someone rushed for a chair and I was seated in state with the entire village standing admiringly around me, beaming and ejaculating 'Welcome' at intervals, now and again clapping their hands, or cracking their knuckles, in an excess of delight.

I was still greeting old friends and inquiring after people's relatives and offspring when my carriers and the cook appeared. Then a long argument arose as to where I should stay, and at last the villagers decided that the only place fit for such a distinguished visitor was their newly built dance-hall. This was a very large, circular hut, the floor of which had been worn to the smoothness of planed wood through the trampling and shuffling of hundreds of feet. The band of drums, flutes and rattles was hastily removed, the floor was swept, and I was installed.

After I had eaten and drunk, the village gathered round once again to hear what I had come for this time. I explained at great length that I had only come for a short visit, and that I wanted only one kind of creature, and I went on to describe *Idiurus*. I showed them a drawing of the animal, and it was passed from hand to hand, and everyone shook their heads over it and said sorrowfully that they had never seen it. My heart sank. Then I picked out three hunters with whom I had worked before. I told them that they were to go to the forest immediately and to hunt for all the hollow trees they could find, and then to mark them. On the following day they would come and tell me what success they had met with, and guide me to the trees they had found. Then I asked if there was anyone present who could climb trees. A dozen or so hands went up. The volunteers were a very mixed crowd, and I eyed them doubtfully.

'You fit climb stick?' I asked.

'Yes sah, we fit,' came the instant and untruthful chorus.

I pointed to an enormous tree that grew at the edge of the village.

'You fit climb dat big stick?' I inquired.

Immediately the number of volunteers dwindled, until at last only one man still had his hand up.

'You fit climb dat big stick?' I repeated, thinking he had not heard.

'Yes, sah,' he said.

'For true?'

'Yes, sah, I fit climb um. I fit climb stick big pass dat one.'

'All right, then you go come for bush with me tomorrow, you hear.'

'Yes, sah,' said the man, grinning.

'Na what they de call you?'

'Peter, sah.'

'Right, you go come tomorrow for early-early morning time.'

The hunters and the other village inhabitants dispersed, and I unpacked my equipment and made ready for the next day. The entire village returned that evening, silently and cautiously, and watched me having my bath. This they were able to do in comparative comfort, for the walls of the dance-hall had many windows and cracks in them. There must have been some fifty people watching me as I covered myself with soap, and sang lustily, but I did not become aware of the fact for quite some time. It did not worry me, for I am not unduly modest, and as long as my audience (half of which consisted of women) were silent and made no ribald remarks I was content that they should watch. However, Jacob arrived at that moment, and was shocked beyond belief at the disgusting inquisitiveness of the villagers. Seizing a stick, he dashed at them and drove them away in a rushing, screaming mob. He returned panting and full of righteous indignation. Soon afterwards I discovered that he had overlooked two of the crowd, for their earnest black faces were wedged in one of the windows. I called Jacob.

'Jacob,' I said, waving a soapy hand at the window, 'they done come back.'

He examined the faces at the window.

'No, sah,' he said seriously, 'dis one na my friends.'

Apparently I was not to be defiled by being watched by an indiscriminate mass of villagers, but any personal friends of Jacob's were in a different category. It was not until later that I learned that Jacob was something of a business man: after driving away the crowd, he had announced that those who would pay him a penny for the privilege of watching me bath would be allowed to return. He did quite a brisk trade among the smaller members of the village, many of whom had never seen a European, and who wanted to settle various bets among each other as to whether or not I was white all over.

Very early the next morning my hunters and my tree-climber appeared. The hunters, it transpired, had found and marked some thirty hollow trees in different parts of the forest. These were, however, dispersed over such a wide area that it would prove impossible to visit them all in one day, so I decided that we would visit the furthest ones first, and gradually work back towards the village.

The path we followed was a typical bush path, about eighteen inches wide, that coiled and twisted among the trees like a dying snake. At first it led up an extremely steep hillside, through massive boulders, each topped with a patch of ferns and moss and starred with the flowers of a tiny pink primrose-like plant. Here and there the great lianas coiled down from the trees, and lay across our path in strange shapes, curving and twisting like giant pythons. At the top of this steep incline the path flattened out, and ran across the level forest floor between the giant tree-trunks. The interior of the forest is cool, and the light is dim; it flickers through the dense fretwork of leaves, which gives it a curious underwater quality. The forest is not the tangled mass of undergrowth that you read about: it is composed of the enormous pillar-like trunks of the trees, set well apart, and interspersed with the thin undergrowth, the young saplings and low-growing plants that lurk in the half-light. We travelled onwards, following the faint trail, for some four miles, and then one of the hunters stopped and stuck his cutlass into the trunk of a great tree with a ringing 'chunk'.

'Dis na tree dat get hole for inside, sah,' he proclaimed.

At the base of the trunk was a slit, some two feet wide and three feet high; I bent and stuck my head inside, and then twisted round so that I could look up the tree. But if there was a top opening, it was hidden from me by some bend in the trunk, for no light filtered down from above. I sniffed vigorously, but all I could smell was rotting wood. The base of the tree yielded nothing but a few bat droppings and the dried husks of various insects. It did not look a particularly good tree, but I thought we might as well try smoking it out and see what it contained.

Smoking out a big forest tree, when it is only done occasionally, is a thrilling procedure. During my search for *Idiurus* the thrill rather wore off, but this was because we were forced to smoke so many trees a day, and a great proportion of them proved to have nothing inside. Smoking a tree is quite an art, and requires a certain amount of practice before you can perfect it. First, having found your tree and made sure that it is really hollow all the way up, you have to discover whether there are any exit holes further up the trunk, and if there are you have to send a man up to cover them with nets. Then you drape a net over the main hole at the base of the tree in such a way that it does not interfere with the smoking, and yet prevents anything from getting away. The important thing is to make sure that this net is secure: there is nothing quite so exasperating as to have it fall down and envelop you in its folds just as the creatures inside the tree are starting to come out.

With all your nets in position you have to deal with the problem of the fire: this, contrary to all proverbial expectations, has to be all smoke and no fire, unless you want your specimens roasted. First, a small pile of dry twigs is laid in the opening, soaked with kerosene and set alight. As soon as it is ablaze you lay a handful of green leaves on top, and keep replenishing them. The burning of these green leaves produces scarcely any flame, but vast quantities of pungent smoke, which is immediately sucked up into the hollow of the tree. Your next problem is to make sure that there is not too *much* smoke; for if you are not careful you can quite easily asphyxiate your specimens before they can rush out of the tree. The idea is to strike a happy medium between roasting and suffocation of your quarry. Once the fire has been lit and piled with green leaves, it generally takes about three minutes (depending on the size of the tree) before the smoke percolates to every part and the animals start to break cover.

We smoked our first tree, and all we got out of it was a large and indignant moth. We took down the nets, put out the fire, and continued on our way. The next tree that the hunters had marked was half a mile away, and when we reached it we went through the same procedure. This time it was slightly more exciting, for, although there were no *Idiurus* in the trunk, there was some life: the first thing to break cover was a small gecko, beautifully banded in chocolate and ash-grey. These little lizards are quite plentiful in the deep forest, and you generally find two or three in any hollow tree you smoke. Following hard on the gecko's tail came three creatures which looked, as they crawled hastily out of the smoke, like large brown sausages with a fringe of undulating legs along each side: they were giant millipedes, large, stupid and completely harmless beasts that are very common all over the forest. The inside of hollow trees is their favourite abode, for their diet is rotten wood. This, it seemed, was the entire contents of the tree. We took down the nets, put out the fire and went on. The next tree was completely empty, as were the three that followed it. The seventh tree produced a small colony of bats, all of which flew frantically out of a hole at the top as soon as Peter tried to climb the tree.

This laborious process of setting up the nets, smoking the tree, taking down the nets and moving on to the next tree was repeated fifteen times that day, and towards evening we were sore and smarting from a thousand cuts and bruises, and our throats were rough from breathing in lungfuls of smoke. We were all in the deepest depths of depression, for not only had we caught no *Idiurus*, but we had caught nothing else of any value either. By the time we reached the last tree that we would have time to smoke before it got dark I was so tired that I really felt I did not care whether there were any *Idiurus* in its trunk or not. I squatted on the ground, smoking a cigarette and watching the hunters as they made the preparations. The tree was smoked and nothing whatsoever appeared from inside. The hunters looked at me.

'Take down the nets; we go back for Eshobi,' I said wearily.

Jacob was busily disentangling the net from the trunk, when he paused and peered at something that lay inside the tree. He bent, picked it up and came towards me.

'Masa want dis kind of beef?' he inquired diffidently.

I glanced up, and received a considerable shock, for there, dangling from his fingers by its long feathery tail, its eyes closed and its sides heaving, was an *Idiurus*. He deposited the mouse-sized creature in my cupped hands, and I peered at it: it was quite unconscious, apparently almost asphyxiated by the smoke.

'Quick, quick, Jacob!' I yelped, in an agony of fear, 'bring me small box for put um. . . . No, no, *not that one,* a good one. . . . Now put small leaf for inside . . . *small leaf,* you moron, not half a tree. . . . There, that's right.' I placed the *Idiurus* reverently inside the box, and took another look at him. He lay there quite limp and unconscious, his chest heaving and his tiny pink paws twitching. He looked to me to be on the verge of death; frantically seizing a huge bunch of leaves I fanned him vigorously. A quarter of an hour of this peculiar form of artificial respiration and, to my delight, he started to recover. His eyes opened in a bleary fashion, he rolled on to his stomach and lay there looking miserable. I fanned him for a while longer, and then carefully closed the lid of the box.

While I had been trying to revive the *Idiurus*, the hunters had been grouped round me in a silent and sorrowful circle; now that they saw the creature regain its faculties, they gave broad grins of delight. We hastily searched the inside of the tree to see if there were any more lying about, but we found nothing. This puzzled me considerably, for *Idiurus* was supposed to live in large colonies. To find a solitary one, therefore, would be unusual. I sincerely hoped that the textbooks were not wrong; to catch some specimens from a colony of animals is infinitely easier than trying to track down and capture individuals. However, I could not stop to worry about it then; I wanted to get the precious creature back to the village and out of the small travelling box he was in. We packed up the nets and set off through the twilit forest as speedily as we could. I carried the box containing *Idiurus* in my cupped hands as delicately as if it contained eggs, and at intervals I would fan the creature through the wire gauze top.

When I was safely back in the village dance-hall, I prepared a larger cage for the precious beast, and then moved him into it. This was not so easy, for he had fully recovered from the smoke by now, and scuttled about with considerable speed. At last, without letting him escape, or getting myself bitten, I succeeded in manoeuvring him into the new cage, and then I placed my strongest light next to it in order to have a good look at him.

He was about the size of a common House Mouse, and very similar to it in general shape. The first thing that caught your attention was his tail: it was very long (almost twice as long as his body), and down each side of it grew a fringe of long, wavy hairs, so the whole tail looked like a bedraggled feather. His head was large, and rather domed, with small, pixie-pointed ears. His eyes were pitch black, small and rather prominent. His rodent teeth, a pair of great bright orange incisors, protruded from his mouth in a gentle curve, so that from the side it gave him a most extraordinarily supercilious expression. Perhaps the most curious part about him was the 'flying' membrane, which stretched along each side of his body. This was a long, fine flap of skin, which was attached to his ankles, and to a long, slightly curved, cartilaginous shaft that grew out from his arm, just behind the elbow. When at rest, this membrane was curled and rucked along the side of his body like a curtain pelmet; when he launched himself into the air, however, the legs were stretched out straight, and the membrane thus drawn taut, so that it acted like the wings of a glider. Later I was to discover just how skilful *Idiurus* could be in the air with this primitive gliding apparatus.

When I had gone to bed that night and switched off the light, I could hear my new specimen rustling and scuttling round his cage, and I imagined what a feast he was making on the variety of foods I had put in there for him. But when dawn came and I crawled sleepily out of bed to have a look, I discovered that he had not eaten anything. I was not unduly worried by this, for some creatures when newly caught refuse to eat until they have settled down in captivity. The length of time this takes varies not only with the species, but with the individual animal. I felt that some time during the day *Idiurus* would come down from the top of the cage, where he was clinging, and eat his fill.

When the hunters arrived we set out through the mist-whitened forest to a fresh series of trees. Refreshed by a night's sleep, and by our capture of an *Idiurus* the day before, we went about the laborious smoking process with a great deal more enthusiasm. But by midday we had investigated ten trees and found nothing. We had by this time reached a section of the forest where the trees were of enormous size, even for the West African forest. They stood well apart from each other, but even so their massive branches interlocked above. The trunks of these trees were, in most cases, at least fifteen feet in diameter. They had great buttress roots – growing out from the base of the trunks like supporting walls of a cathedral, each well over ten feet high where it joined the trunk, and with a space of a good-sized room between each flange. Some of them had wound round them massive, muscular-looking creepers as thick as my body. We made our way through the giant trunks, and came presently to a dip in the level forest floor, a small dell in which stood one of these enormous trees, more or less by itself. At the edge of the dell the hunters paused and pointed.

'Na dis big stick get hole too much, sah,' they said.

We approached the trunk of the tree, and I saw that there was a great arched rent in the wood, between two of the flanges; this hole was about the same size and shape as a small church door. I paused at the entrance to the hole and looked up: the tree-trunk towered above me, shooting up towards the sky smooth and branchless for about two hundred feet. Not a stump, not a branch broke the smooth surface of that column of wood. I began to hope that there would be nothing inside the tree, for I could not see for the life of me how anyone was going to climb up to the top and put nets over the exit holes, if any. I walked into the hollow of the tree as I would walk into a room, and found there was plenty of space; the sunlight filtered gently in through the entrance, and gradually my eyes became accustomed to the dim light. I peered upwards, but a slight bend in the trunk prevented me seeing very far. I tested the sides of the tree and found them composed of rotten wood, soft and spongy. By kicking with my toes I found it was quite easy to make footholds, and I laboriously climbed up the inside of the trunk until I was high enough to crane round the corner. The trunk stretched up as hollow as a factory chimney, and just as big. At the very summit of the tree there was a large exit hole, and through it a shaft of sunlight poured. Then, suddenly, I nearly released my rather precarious hold with excitement, for I saw that the top part of the trunk was literally a moving carpet of *Idiurus*. They slid about on the rotten wood as swiftly and silently as shadows, and when they were still they disappeared completely from sight, so perfectly did they match the background. I slithered to the ground and made my way out into the open. The hunters looked at me expectantly.

'Na beef for inside, Masa?' asked one.

'Yes. Na plenty beef for inside. You go look.'

Chattering excitedly, they pushed and scrambled their way into the inside of the tree; some idea of its size may be gained from the fact that the three hunters, Peter, the tree-climber and Jacob could all fit comfortably into its spacious interior. I could hear their ejaculations of astonishment as they saw the *Idiurus*, and sharp words being exchanged when someone (I suspected Jacob) trod on somebody else's face in his excitement. I walked slowly round the tree, searching the trunk for any foot or handholds on the bark which would enable Peter to climb to the top, but the bark was as smooth as a billiard ball. As far as I could see, the tree was unclimbable, and I damped the hunters' gaiety by pointing this out to them when they came out of the trunk. While we all sat on the ground and smoked and discussed the matter, Jacob prowled around the dell, scowling ferociously at the trees, and presently he came over to us and said that he thought he had found a way in which Peter could get to the top. We followed him across the dell to its extreme edge, and there he pointed to a tall, thin sapling whose top just reached one of the great branches of the main tree. Jacob suggested that Peter should shin up the sapling, get on to the branch and then work his way along it until he reached the top of the hollow trunk. Peter examined the sapling, suspiciously, and then said he would try. He spat on his hands, seized the trunk of the sapling and swarmed aloft, using his almost prehensile toes to get an extra grip upon the bark. When he reached the half-way mark, however, some seventy feet from the ground, his weight started to bend the sapling over like a bow, and before he had gone much further the trunk was giving ominous creakings. It was obvious that the tree was too slender to support the weight of my corpulent tree-climber, and he was forced to return to earth. Jacob, grinning with excitement, came strutting across to where I stood.

'Masa, I fit climb dat stick,' he said. 'I no be fat man like Peter.'

'Fat!' said Peter indignantly; 'who you de call fat, eh? I no be fat; dat stick no get power for hold man, dat's all.'

'You be fat,' said Jacob scornfully; 'all time you fill your belly with food, an' now Masa want you to climb stick you no fit.'

'All right, all right,' I said hastily, 'you go try and climb, Jacob. But take care you no go fall, eh?'

'Yes, sah,' he said, and running to the sapling he flung himself on to the trunk and swarmed up it like a caterpillar.

Now Jacob weighed about half of what Peter weighed, so he was soon clinging to the very tip of the sapling, and the tree was still upright, though it swayed round and round in a gentle curve. Each time it passed the branch of the big tree, Jacob made a wild grab, but each time he missed. Presently he looked down.

'Masa, I no fit catch um,' he called.

'All right, come down,' I shouted back.

He descended rapidly to the ground, and I gave him the end of a long length of strong cord.

'You go tie dis for top, eh? Den, when you ready, we go dis small stick so it come for dis big one. Understand?'

'Yes, sah,' said Jacob gleefully, and scuttled up the sapling again.

When he reached the top, he fastened the rope round the sapling and shouted down that he was ready. We laid hold of the rope and pulled lustily; as we backed slowly across the clearing, digging our toes into the soft leaf-mould to gain a grip, the sapling bent slowly over until its tip touched the great branch. Quickly as a squirrel, Jacob had reached out, got a grip on the branch and hauled himself across. We still held on to the sapling until he had pulled a piece of rope from out of his loincloth and tied the top of it to the branch on which he was now lying. When the sapling was tied, we released our hold on the rope gently. Jacob was now standing upright on the branch, holding on to the smaller growth that sprouted from it, and he slowly groped his way along towards the main trunk, walking warily, for the branch he was using as a road was thickly overgrown with orchids, creepers and tree-ferns, an ideal habitat for a tree-snake. When he reached the place where the branch joined the tree, he squatted astride it, and lowered a long piece of string to us; to the end of this we tied a bundle of nets and some small boxes in which to put any specimens he caught at the top. With these safely tied to his waist he moved round the tree to the hole, which was situated in the crutch where the great branches spread away from the trunk. Squatting down, he spread the net over the hole, arranged the boxes within easy reach, and then grinned down at us mischievously.

'All right, Masa, your hunter man 'e ready now,' he shouted.

'Hunter man!' muttered Peter indignantly; 'dis cook call himself hunter man . . . eh . . .aehh!'

We collected a mass of dry twigs and green leaves, and laid the fire in the huge chimney-like opening of the tree. We lit it and piled the green leaves on, after draping a net over the arched opening. The fire smouldered sullenly for a few minutes, and then the frail wisp of smoke grew stronger, and soon a great stream of grey smoke was pouring up the hollow shell of the tree. As the smoke rose up the trunk I became aware that there were other holes which we had not spotted, for at various points in the bark, some thirty feet above the ground, frail wisps of smoke started to appear, coiling out and fading into the air.

Jacob, perched precariously, was peering down into the inside of the trunk when the thick column of grey smoke swept up and enveloped him. We could hear him coughing and choking, and could see him moving round gingerly in the smoke, in an effort to find a more suitable spot to sit. It seemed to me, waiting excitedly, that the *Idiurus* took a tremendously long time to be affected by the smoke.

I was just wondering if perhaps they had all been knocked immediately unconscious before they could attempt to escape, when the first one broke cover. It scuttled out of the opening in the base of the tree, tried to launch itself into the air, and became immediately entangled in the nets. One of the hunters rushed forward to disentangle it, but before I could go and help him, the entire colony decided to vacate the tree in a body. Some twenty *Idiurus* appeared at the main opening, and leapt into the net. Up on the top of the tree, now hidden by billows of smoke, I could hear Jacob squeaking with excitement, and occasionally giving a roar of anguish as one of the *Idiurus* bit him. I discovered to my annoyance that there were two or three cracks in the trunk which we had overlooked, some thirty feet above the ground, and through these minute openings the *Idiurus* were swarming out into the open air. They scuttled about the bark, and seemed quite unperturbed by either the strong sunlight or our presence, for some of them came down to within six feet of the ground. They moved with remarkable rapidity over the surface of the wood, seeming to glide rather than run. Then an extra large and pungent cloud of smoke burst upwards and spread over them, and they decided to take to the air.

I have seen some extraordinary sights at one time and another, but the flight of the flying mice I shall remember until my dying day. The great tree was bound round with shifting columns of grey smoke that turned to the most ethereal blue where the great bars of sunlight stabbed through it. Into this the *Idiurus* launched themselves. They left the trunk of the tree without any apparent effort at jumping; one minute they were clinging spread-eagled to the bark, the next they were in the air. Their tiny legs were stretched out, and the membranes along their sides were taut. They swooped and drifted through the tumbling clouds of smoke with all the assurance and skill of hawking swallows, twisting and banking with incredible skill and apparently little or no movement of the body. This was pure gliding, and what they achieved was astonishing. I saw one leave the trunk of the tree at a height of about thirty feet. He glided across the dell in a straight and steady swoop, and landed on a tree about a hundred and fifty feet away, losing little, if any, height in the process. Others left the trunk of the smoke-enveloped tree and glided round it in a series of diminishing spirals, to land on a portion of the trunk lower down. Some patrolled the tree in a series of S-shaped patterns, doubling back on their tracks with great smoothness and efficiency. Their wonderful ability in the air amazed me, for there was no breeze in the forest to set up the air currents I should have thought essential for such intricate manoeuvring.

I noticed that although a number of them had flown off into the forest the majority stayed on the main trunk, contenting themselves with taking short flights around it when the smoke got too dense. This gave me an idea; I put out the fire, and as the smoke gradually drifted and dispersed, the *Idiurus* that were on the tree all scuttled back inside. We gave them a few minutes to settle down, while I examined the ones we had caught. At the base of the tree we had captured eight females and four males; Jacob lowered his catch down from the smoke-filled heavens, which consisted of two more males and one female. With them were two of the most extraordinary bats I had ever seen, with golden-brown backs and bright lemon-yellow shirt-fronts, faces like pigs and long, pig-like ears twisted down over their noses.

When the *Idiurus* had all returned to the tree we re-lit the fire, and once again they all rushed out. This time, however, they had grown wiser, and the majority refused to come anywhere near the nets at the main opening. Jacob, however, had better luck at the top of the tree, and soon lowered down a bag of twenty specimens, which I thought was quite enough to be getting on with. We put out the fire, removed the nets, got Jacob down from his tree-top perch (not without some difficulty, for he was very eager to try to catch the rest of the colony), and then we set off through the forest to walk the four odd miles that separated us from the village. I carried the precious bag of squeaking and scrambling *Idiurus* carefully in my hands, occasionally stopping to undo the top and fan them, for I was not at all sure they were getting sufficient air through the sides of the fine linen bag.

We reached the village, tired and dirty, just after dark. I put the *Idiurus* in the largest cage I had, but I found, to my annoyance, that it was far too small for such a great number. Stupidly, I had only banked on getting two or three *Idiurus*, if I got any at all, so had not brought a really large cage with me. I feared that if I left them in that confined space overnight the casualties in the morning would be heavy; there was only one thing to do, and that was to get the precious beasts back to the base camp as quickly as possible. I wrote a brief note to Smith, telling him that I had been successful and that I would be arriving some time about midnight with the animals, and would he please have a large cage ready for them. I sent this off at once, then I had a bath and some food. I reckoned that my letter would arrive at the camp about an hour before I did, which should give Smith plenty of time to improvise a cage.

About ten o'clock my little party started off along the Eshobi road. First walked Jacob carrying the lantern. Following him came a carrier with the box of *Idiurus* balanced on his woolly head. I was next in the row, and behind me was another carrier with my bed on his head. The Eshobi path is bad enough in broad daylight, but by night it is a death-trap. As a source of illumination the lantern was about as much use as an anaemic glow-worm; the light it gave was just sufficient to distort everything and to shroud rocks in deep shadow. Thus our progress was necessarily slow. Normally that walk would have taken us about two hours; that night it took us five. Most of the way I was on the edge of a nervous breakdown, for the carrier with the *Idiurus* hopped and jumped among the rocks like a mountain goat, and every minute I expected to see him slip and my precious box of specimens go hurtling into a ravine. He became more and more daring as the path got worse, until I felt that it was only a matter of time before he fell.

'My friend,' I called, 'if you go drop my beef, we no go reach Mamfe together. I go bury you here.'

He took the hint and slowed his progress considerably.

Half-way across a small stream my shadow got in the way of the carrier behind me, he missed his footing and stumbled and deposited my bed and bedding into the water with a loud splash. He was very upset about it, although I pointed out that it was mainly my fault. We continued on our way, the carrier with the dripping load on his head ejaculating at intervals 'Eh! Sorry, sah,' in a loud and doleful voice.

The forest around us was full of tiny sounds: the faint cracking of twigs, an occasional call from a frightened bird, the steady throbbing cry of the cicadas on the tree-trunks, and now and again a shrill piping from a tree-frog. The streams we crossed were ice-cold and transparent, and they whispered and licked at the big boulders in a conspiratorial fashion. At one point Jacob, up ahead, let out a loud yelp and started to dance around wildly, swinging the lamp so that the shadows writhed and twisted among the tree-trunks.

'Na whatee, na whatee?' called the carriers.

'Na ant,' said Jacob, still twirling round, 'blurry ant too much.'

Not looking where he was going, he had trodden straight in a column of Driver ants crossing the path, a black stream of them two inches wide that poured from the undergrowth on one side of the path and into that on the other side like a steady, silent river of tar. As his foot came down on them, the whole line seemed to boil up suddenly and silently, and within a second the ants were swarming over the ground in a horde, spreading further and further round the scene of the attack, like an inkstain on the brown leaves. The carriers and I had to make a detour into the forest to avoid their ferocious attentions.

As we left the shelter of the forest and walked out into the first moon-silvered grassfield, it started to rain. At first it was a fine drifting drizzle, more like mist; then, without warning, the sky let down a seemingly solid deluge of water, that bent the grass flat and turned the path into a treacherous slide of red mud. Fearing that my precious box of specimens would get drenched, and the *Idiurus* die in consequence, I took off my coat and draped it over the cage on the carrier's head. It was not much protection, but it helped. We struggled on, up to our ankles in mud, until we came to the river which we had to ford. Crossing this took us, I suppose, roughly three minutes, but it was quite long enough, for the carrier with the *Idiurus* on his head stumbled and staggered over the rocky bed, while the current plucked and pushed at him, waiting an opportunity to catch him off balance. But we arrived intact on the opposite bank, and soon we saw the lights of the camp gleaming through the trees. Just as we got to the marquee the rain stopped.

The cage that Smith had prepared for the *Idiurus* was not really large enough, but I felt that the main thing was to get the creatures out of the box they were in as soon as possible, for it was dripping like a newly submerged submarine. Carefully we undid the door and stood watching with bated breath as the tiny animals scuttled into their new home. None appeared to have got wet, which relieved me, though one or two of them looked a bit the worse for wear after the journey.

'What do they eat?' inquired Smith, when we had gloated over them for five minutes.

'I haven't the faintest idea. The one I caught yesterday didn't eat anything, though God knows I gave him enough choice.'

'Um, I expect they'll eat when they settle down a bit.'

'Oh, yes, I think they will,' I said cheerfully, and I really believed it.

We filled the cage with every form of food and drink there was to be had in camp, until it looked like a native market. Then we hung a sack over the front of the cage and left the *Idiurus* to eat. My bed having absorbed rain and river water like a sponge, I was forced to spend a most uncomfortable night dozing in an upright camp chair. I slept fitfully until dawn, when I got up and hobbled over to the *Idiurus* cage, lifted the sacking and peered inside.

On the floor, among the completely untouched food and drink, lay a dead *Idiurus*. The others clung to the top of the cage like a flock of bats and twittered suspiciously at me. I retrieved the dead specimen and carried it over to the table, where I subjected it to a careful dissection. The stomach, to my complete surprise, was crammed with the partially digested red husk of the palm-nut. This was the very last thing I expected to find, for the palm-nut is, in the Cameroons at any rate, a cultivated product, and does not grow wild in the forest. If the rest of the colony had been eating palm-nuts on the night before they were captured by us, it meant that they must have travelled some four miles to the nearest native farm, and then come down to within a few feet of the ground to feed. This was all very puzzling, but at any rate it gave me something to work on, so the next night the *Idiurus* cage was festooned like a Christmas tree with bunches of red palm-nuts, in addition to the other foods. We put the food in at dusk, and for the next three hours Smith and I carried on long conversations that had nothing to do with *Idiurus*, and with an effort we pretended not to hear the squeaks and rustlings that came from their cage. After we had eaten, however, the strain became too great, and we crept up to the cage and gently lifted a corner of the sacking.

The entire colony of *Idiurus* was down on the floor of the cage, and all of them were busily engaged in eating palm-nuts. They squatted on their haunches and held the nuts in their minute pink forepaws like squirrels, turning the nuts quickly as their teeth shredded off the scarlet rind. They stopped eating as we lifted the sacking and peered at us; one or two of the more timid ones dropped their nuts and fled to the top of the cage, but the majority decided that we were harmless and continued to eat. We lowered the sacking into place and executed a war dance round the marquee, uttering loud cries to indicate our pleasure, cries that awoke the monkeys and set them chattering a protest and brought the staff tumbling out of the kitchen to see what was the matter. When they heard the good news that the new beef was chopping at last, they grinned and cracked their knuckles with pleasure, for they took our work very much to heart. All day gloom had pervaded the camp because the new beef would not chop, but now everything was all right, so the staff returned to the kitchen, chattering and laughing.

But our joy was short-lived, for on going to the cage next morning we found two *Idiurus* dead. From then on our little colony diminished steadily, week by week. They would eat only palm-nuts, and, apparently, this was not enough for them. It was quite astonishing the variety of food we put in the cage, and which they refused – astonishing because even with the most finicky animal you will generally strike something it likes, if you offer it a wide enough choice of food. It appeared that the *Idiurus* were not going to be easy to get back to England.

Chapter Twelve

A Wilderness of Monkeys

Perhaps the most noisy, the most irritating and the most lovable creatures that shared our marquee were the monkeys. There were forty of them altogether, and life under the same roof with forty monkeys is anything but quiet. The adult animals were not so bad; it was the baby monkeys that caused so much trouble and extra work for us: they would scream loudly if left alone, demand bottles full of warm milk at the most ungodly hours of night and morning; they would get stricken with all sorts of baby complaints and frighten us to death; they would escape from the nursery and get near the Golden Cat's cage, or fall into kerosene tins full of water, and generally drive us to the edge of a nervous breakdown. We were forced to think up the most Machiavellian schemes for dealing with these babies, and some of them were quite extraordinary. Take the case of the baby Drills: these baboons are extremely common in the forests of the Cameroons, and we were always being brought babies of all ages. The Drill is that rather ugly-looking creature you can see in most zoos, who has a bright pink behind and does not hesitate to share its glory with you. Very young Drills are among the most pathetic and ridiculous-looking creatures in the world: they are covered with a very fine silvery grey fur, and their heads, hands and feet look at least three times too big for their bodies. The hands, feet and face are a shade that we used to describe as boiled baby pink, and their minute bottoms were the same colour. The skin on their bodies was white, spotted in places with large areas, exactly like big birthmarks, of bright china blue. Like all baby monkeys, they have staring eyes, and their arms and legs are long and attenuated and tremble like the limbs of a very old person. This should give you some idea of a baby Drill.

    The early days of a Drill's life are spent clinging with its muscular hands and feet to the thick fur of its mother. So our baby Drills, when they had transferred their affections to us and decided that we were their parents, demanded loudly and vociferously that they should be allowed to cling to us. Next to vast quantities of food, the most important thing in a young Drill's life is to feel that it has a good grip on the provider of the food. As it is almost impossible to work when you have four or five baby Drills clinging to you like miniature, cackling Old Men of the Sea, we had to devise some plan to keep them happy. We found two old coats and slung these over the backs of chairs in the centre of the marquee; then we introduced the babies to them. They were used to seeing us in these coats, and I expect the garments retained a certain characteristic odour, so they apparently decided that the coats were a sort of skin that we had discarded. They clung to the empty sleeves, the lapels and the tails of these two coats as though they had been glued on, and while we went on with our work around the camp they would hang there, half asleep, occasionally waking up to carry on a cackling conversation with us.

The great numbers of people who used to visit our camp-site and look round the collection always seemed most affected by our group of baby monkeys. A baby monkey, in all its ways, is very like a human baby, only infinitely more pathetic. The women in these parties would gaze at our young monkeys with melting eyes, making inarticulate crooning noises and generally brimming over with mother love. There was one young lady who visited us several times and was so affected by the pathetic expressions of the young monkeys that she unwisely took it upon herself to deliver a lecture to me about the extreme cruelty of taking these poor little creatures from their mothers and incarcerating them in cages. She waxed quite poetical on the joys of freedom, and contrasted the carefree, happy existence these babies would have in the tree-tops with the ghastly imprisonment for which I was responsible. That morning a baby monkey had been brought in by a native hunter, and since the young lady seemed to be such an expert on monkey life in the tree-tops, I suggested that she might like to help me perform a little task that had to be gone through with each new monkey that arrived. She agreed eagerly, seeing herself in the role of a sort of simian Florence Nightingale.

The little task consisted, quite simply, in searching the new baby for internal and external parasites. I explained this, and the young lady looked surprised: she said that she did not know that monkeys had parasites – beyond fleas, of course. I produced the little basket that the monkey was brought in, and removing some of its excreta I spread it out on a clean piece of paper and showed her the numbers of threadlike worms it contained. My helper remained strangely silent. Then I brought out the baby: he was a Putty-nose Guenon, an adorable little fellow clad in black fur, with a white shirtfront and a gleaming, heart-shaped patch of white fur on his nose. I examined his tiny hands and feet and his long slender fingers and toes and found no fewer than six jiggers comfortably ensconced. These minute creatures burrow their way into the skin of the feet and hands, particularly under the nails, where the skin is soft, and there they eat and swell and grow, until they reach the size of a match-head. Then they lay their eggs and die; in due course the eggs hatch and the baby jiggers continue the good work that their parent had begun. If a jigger infection is not dealt with in the early stages it can lead to the loss of the joint of a toe or finger, and in extreme cases it can destroy all the toes or fingers, for the jiggers go on burrowing and breeding until they have hollowed the part out to a bag of skin filled with pus. I have had jiggers in my foot on several occasions, and can vouch for the fact that they can be extremely painful. All this I explained to my helper in graphic detail. Then I got the tube of local anaesthetic, froze the fingers and toes of the little Guenon, and with a sterilized needle proceeded to remove the jiggers and disinfect the wounds they left. I found this local anaesthetic a boon, for the operation is painful and the baby monkeys would not sit still otherwise.

When this was over I ran my fingers down the monkey's tail and felt two sausage-shaped swellings, each as long as the first joint of my little finger and about the same circumference. I showed these to my companion, and then parted the hair so that she could see the circular, porthole-like opening at the end of each swelling. Looking through this porthole into the interior of the swelling, you could see something white and loathsome moving. I explained, with my best Harley Street air, that a certain forest fly lays its eggs on the fur of various animals, and when the maggot hatches it burrows down into the flesh of its host and lives there, fattening like a pig in a sty, getting air through the porthole, and, when it finally leaves to turn into a fly, the host has a hole the circumference of a cigarette in its flesh, which generally becomes a suppurating sore. I showed my helper, who was by now quite pale, that it was impossible to hook these maggots out. I got the needle and, parting the hair, showed her the creature lying in its burrow like a miniature barrage balloon; as soon as the tip of the needle touched it, however, it just compressed itself into a wrinkled blob, folding up like a concertina, and slid back into the depths of the monkey's tail. Then I showed her how to get them out – a method I had invented: pushing the nozzle of the anaesthetic tube into the porthole, I squirted the liquid inside until I had frozen the maggot into immobility; then, with a scalpel, I enlarged the porthole slightly, stabbed the maggot with the end of the needle and withdrew it from its lair. As I pulled the wrinkled white horror out of the bloodstained hole, my helper left me suddenly and precipitately. I removed the second maggot, disinfected the gaping holes they had left and then joined her at the other side of the camp clearing. She explained that she was late for a lunch date, thanked me for a most interesting morning, and took her leave, never to visit us again. I always think it rather a pity that people don't learn more about the drawbacks of life in the jungle before prating about the cruelty of captivity.

One of the most delightful monkeys we had was a baby moustached Guenon, whom Smith procured on a trip up-country. He was the smallest monkey I had ever seen, and, except for his long slender tail, he could fit comfortably into a tea-cup. He was a greenish-grey in colour, with buttercup-yellow cheek-patches and a white shirt-front. But the most remarkable thing about him was his face, for across his upper lip was a broad, curving band of white hair that made him look as though he had an impressive moustache. For his size, his mouth was enormous, and could quite easily accommodate the teat of the feeding-bottle. It was a most amusing sight to see this tiny, moustached animal hurl himself on to the bottle when it arrived, uttering shrill squeaks of joy, wrap his arms and legs round it tightly, and lie there with his eyes closed, sucking away frantically. It looked rather as though he was being suckled by a large white airship, for the bottle was three times his size. He was very quick to learn, and it was not long before we had taught him to drink his milk out of a saucer. He would be put on the camp table to be fed, and the moment he saw the saucer approaching he would get quite hysterical with excitement, trembling and twitching, and screaming at the top of his voice. As soon as the saucer was placed before him he would, without any hesitation, dive head first into it. He would push his face completely under the milk, and only come up for air when he could hold out no longer. Sometimes, in his greed, he would wait too long, and a shower of bubbles would break the surface, and he would follow them, coughing and sneezing and spattering himself and the table with a fountain of milk. There were times during his meal when he would become convinced that you were hanging around waiting an opportunity to take his saucer away from him, and, giving a quavering scream of rage, he would frustrate your plan by the simple expedient of leaping into the air and landing in the centre of the saucer with a splash, where he would sit glaring at you triumphantly. At meal-times he would get his head and face so covered with milk that it was only with difficulty you could tell where his moustache began and ended, and the table would look as though someone had milked a large and healthy cow over it.

The two most forceful characters in our monkey collection were, of course, the chimpanzees Mary and Charlie. Charlie had been the pet of a planter before he came to us, so he was fairly domesticated. He had a small, wrinkled, sorrowful face and melting brown eyes; he looked as though the world had treated him harshly but that he was too much of a saint to complain. This wounded, dejected air was a lot of moonshine, for in reality Charlie, far from being an ill-treated, misunderstood ape, was a disgraceful little street urchin, full of low cunning and deceit. Every day we used to let him out of his cage for exercise, and he would roam about the camp looking radiantly innocent until he thought he had lulled you into believing in his integrity. Then he would wander nonchalantly towards the food-table, give a quick glance round to see if he was observed, grab the largest bunch of bananas within reach and dash madly away towards the nearest tree. If you gave chase he would drop the fruit and skid to a standstill. Then he would sit in the dust while you scolded him, gazing up at you sorrowfully, the picture of injured innocence, the expression on his face showing quite plainly that he was being wrongfully accused of a monstrous crime, but that he was far too noble to point that out to you if you were too obtuse to realize it. Wave the bunch of stolen fruit under his nose and he would regard it with faint surprise, mingled with disgust. Why should you imagine that he had stolen the fruit? his expression seemed to say. Were you not aware of the fact that he disliked bananas? Never in his whole life (devoted to philanthropy and self-denial) had he felt the slightest inclination to even sample the loathsome fruit, much less steal any. The scolding over, Charlie would rise, give a deep sigh, throw you a look of compassion tinged with disgust, and lope off to the kitchen to see what he could steal there. He was quite incorrigible, and his face was so expressive that he could carry on a long conversation with you without any need of speech.

Charlie's greatest triumph came when we received a visit from the High Commissioner for the Cameroons, who was passing through on one of his periodical visits of inspection. He came down to our camp accompanied by a vast army of secretaries and other supporters, and was greatly interested in our large array of beasts. But the animal that attracted him most was Charlie. While we explained to H.E. what a disgusting hypocrite the ape was, Charlie was sitting in his cage, holding the great man's hand through the bars, and gazing up at him with woebegone expression and pleading eyes, begging that His Excellency would not listen to the foul slander we were uttering. When His Excellency left, he invited Smith and myself to his At Home, which was to take place the following evening. The next morning a most impressive messenger, glittering with golden buttons, delivered an envelope from the District Office. Inside was a large card which informed us, in magnificent twirly writing, that His Excellency, the High Commissioner for the Cameroons, requested the pleasure of Charlie's presence during his At Home, between the hours of six and eight. When we showed it to Charlie he was sitting in his cage meditating, and he gave it a brief glance and then ignored it. His attitude told us he was quite used to being showered with such invitations, but that these things were too worldly to be of any interest to him. He was, he implied, far too busy with his saint-like meditations to get excited about invitations to drinking-orgies with mere High Commissioners. As he had been into the kitchen that morning and stolen six eggs, a loaf of bread and a leg of cold chicken, we did not believe him.

Mary was a chimp of completely different character. She was older than Charlie, and much bigger, being about the size of a two-year-old human. Before we bought her she had been in the hands of a Hausa trader, and I am afraid she must have been teased and ill-treated, for at first she was sullen and vicious, and we feared we would never be able to gain her confidence as she had developed a deep-rooted mistrust of anything human, black or white. But after a few months of good food and kind handling she delighted us by blossoming forth into a chimp with much charm, a sunny disposition and a terrific sense of humour. She had a pale pink, rather oafish face, and a large pot belly. She reminded me rather of a fat barmaid, who was always ready to laugh uproariously at some bawdy jest. After she got to know and trust us, she developed a trick which she thought was frightfully funny. She would lie back in her cage, balanced precariously on her perch, and present an unmentionable part of her anatomy to the bars. You were then expected to lean forward and blow hard whereupon Mary would utter a screech of laughter and modestly cover herself up with her hands. Then she would give you a coy look from over the mound of her stomach, and uncover herself again, and you were expected to repeat this mirth-provoking action. This became known to both us and the staff as Blowing Mary's Wicked Parts, and no matter how many times a day you repeated it, Mary still found it exceedingly funny; she would throw back her head and open her mouth wide, showing vast areas of pink gum and white teeth, hooting and tittering with hysterical laughter.

Although Mary treated us and the staff with great gentleness, she never forgot that she had a grudge against Africans in general, and she used to pick on any strange ones that came to camp. She would grin at them ingratiatingly and slap her chest, or turn somersaults – anything to gain their attention. By her antics she would lure them closer and closer to the cage, looking the picture of cheerful good humour, while her shrewd eyes judged the distance carefully. Suddenly the long and powerful arm would shoot out through the bars, there would be a loud ripping noise, a yelp of fright from the African, and Mary would be dancing round her cage triumphantly waving a torn shirt or singlet that she had pulled off her admirer's back. Her strength was extraordinary, and it cost me a small fortune in replacements until I put her cage in such a position that she could not commit these outrages.

The monkey collection kept up a continuous noise all through the day, but in the afternoon, at about four-thirty, this rose to a crescendo of sound that would tax the strongest nerves, for it was at this time that the monkeys had their milk. About four they would start to get impatient, leaping and jumping about their cages, turning somersaults, or sitting with their faces pressed to the bars making mournful squeaks. As soon as the line of clean pots was laid out, however, and the great kerosene tin full of warm milk, malt and cod-liver oil, sugar and calcium came in sight, a wave of excitement would sweep the cages and the uproar would be deafening. The chimps would be giving prolonged hoots through pursed lips and thumping on the sides of their cages with their fists, the Drills would be uttering their loud and penetrating 'Ar-ar-ar-ar-ar-erererer!' cries, like miniature machine-guns, the Guenons would be giving faint, bird-like whistles and trills, the Patas monkeys would be dancing up and down like mad ballerinas, shouting 'Proup . . . proup' plaintively, and the beautiful Colobus, with her swaying shawl of white and black hair, would be calling 'Arroup! arroup! arroup! ye-ye-ye-ye!' in a commanding tone of voice. As we moved along the cages, pushing the pots of milk through the doors, the noises would gradually cease, until all that could be heard was a low snorting, sucking sound, interspersed by an occasional cough as some milk went down the wrong way. Then, the pots empty, the monkeys would climb up on to their perches and sit there, their bellies bulging, uttering loud and satisfied belches at regular intervals. After a while they would all climb down again on to the floor to examine their pots and make quite sure there was no milk left in them, even picking them up and looking underneath. Then they would curl up on their perches in the evening sun and fall into a bloated stupor, while peace came to the camp.

One of the things that I find particularly endearing about monkeys is the fact that they are completely uninhibited, and will perform any action they feel like with an entire lack of embarrassment. They will urinate copiously, or bend down and watch their own faeces appear with expressions of absorbed interest; they will mate or masturbate with great freedom, regardless of any audience. I have heard embarrassed human beings call monkeys dirty, filthy creatures when they have watched them innocently perform these actions in public, and it is an attitude of mind that I always find difficult to understand. After all, it is we, with our superior intelligence, who have decided that the perfectly natural functions of our bodies are something unclean; monkeys do not share our view.

Similarly, one of the things I liked about the Africans was this same innocent attitude towards the functions of the body. In this respect they were extremely like the monkeys. I had a wonderful example of this one day when a couple of rather stuffy missionaries came to look round the camp.

I showed them our various animals and birds, and they made a lot of unctuous comments about them. Then we came to the monkeys, and the missionaries were delighted with them. Presently, however, we reached a cage where a monkey was sitting on the perch in a curious hunched-up attitude.

'Oh! What's *he* doing?' cried the lady gaily, and before I could prevent her she had bent down to get a better look. She shot up again, her face a deep, rich scarlet, for the monkey had been whiling away the hours to meal time by sitting there and sucking himself.

We hurried through the rest of the monkey collection in record time, and I was much amused by the expression of frozen disgust that had replaced the look of benevolent delight on the lady missionary's face. They might be God's creatures, her expression implied, but she wished He would do something about their habits. However, as we rounded the corner of the marquee we were greeted by another of God's creatures in the shape of a lanky African hunter. He was a man who had brought in specimens regularly each week, but for the past fortnight he had not come near us.

'Iseeya, Samuel!' I greeted him.

'Iseeya, Masa,' he said, coming towards us.

'Which side you done go all dis time?' I asked; 'why you never bring me beef for two weeks, eh?'

'Eh! Masa, I done get sickness,' he explained.

'Sickness? Eh, sorry, my friend. Na what sickness you get?'

'Na my ghonereah, Masa,' he explained innocently, 'my ghonereah de worry me *too much*.'

The missionaries were among the people who never called twice at the camp site.

In Which We Walka Good

The last few days before you and the collection join the ship that is to take you back to England are always the most hectic of the whole trip. There are a thousand things that have to be done: lorries to hire, cages to strengthen, vast quantities of food to be purchased and crated up, and all this on top of the normal routine work of maintaining the collection.

One of the things that worried us most were the *Idiurus*. Our colony had by now diminished to four specimens, and we were determined to try to get them safely back to England. We had, after superhuman efforts, got them to eat avocado pears as well as palm-nuts, and on this diet they seemed to do quite well. I decided that if we took three dozen avocados with us, in varying stages from ripe to green, there would be enough to last the voyage and with some left over to use in England while the *Idiurus* were settling down. Accordingly, I called Jacob and informed him that he must procure three dozen avocados without delay. To my surprise, he looked at me as though I had taken leave of my senses.

'Avocado pear, sah?' he asked.

'Yes, avocado pear,' I said.

'I no fit get 'um, sah,' he said mournfully.

'You no fit get 'um? Why not?'

'Avocado pear done finish,' said Jacob helplessly.

'Finish? What you mean, finish? I want you go for market and get 'um, not from kitchen.'

'Done finish for market, sah,' said Jacob patiently.

Suddenly it dawned on me what he was trying to explain: the season for avocado pears had finished, and he could not get me any. I would have to face the voyage with no supply of the fruit for the precious *Idiurus*.

It was just like the *Idiurus*, I reflected bitterly, to start eating something when it was going out of season. However, avocados I had to have, so in the few days at our disposal I marshalled the staff and made them scour the countryside for the fruit. By the time we were ready to move down country we had obtained a few small, shrivelled avocados, and that was all. These almost mummified remains had to last my precious *Idiurus* until we reached England.

We had to travel some two hundred miles down to the coast from our base camp, and it required three lorries and a small van to carry our collection. We travelled by night, for it was cooler for the animals, and the journey took us two days. It was one of the worst journeys I can ever remember. We had to stop the lorries every three hours, take out all the frog-boxes and sprinkle them with cold water to prevent them drying up. Twice during each night we had to make prolonged stops to bottlefeed the young animals on warm milk which we carried ready mixed in thermos flasks. Then, when dawn came, we had to pull the lorries into the side of the road under the shade of the great trees, unload every single cage on to the grass and clean and feed every specimen. On the morning of the third day we arrived at the small rest-house on the coast which had been put at our disposal; here everything had to be unpacked once again and cleaned and fed before we could crawl into the house, eat a meal, and collapse on our beds to sleep. That evening parties of people from the local banana plantations came round to see the animals and, half dead with sleep, we were forced to conduct tours, answer questions and be polite.

'Are you travelling on this ship that's in?' inquired someone.

'Yes,' I said, stifling a yawn; 'sailing tomorrow.'

'Good Lord! I pity you, then,' they said cheerfully.

'Oh. Why is that?'

'Captain's a bloody Tartar, old boy, and he hates animals. It's a fact. Old Robinson wanted to take his pet baboon back with him on this ship when he went on leave last time. Captain chucked it off. Wouldn't have it on board. Said he didn't want his ship filled with stinking monkeys. Frightful uproar about it, so I heard.'

Smith and I exchanged anxious looks, for of all the evils that can befall a collector, an unsympathetic captain is perhaps the worst. Later, when the last party of sightseers had gone, we discussed this disturbing bit of news. We decided that we should have to go out of our way to be polite to the Captain; and we would take extra care to make sure there were no untoward incidents among the monkeys to earn his wrath.

Our collection was placed on the forward deck under the supervision of the Chief Officer, a most charming and helpful man. The Captain we did not see that night, and the next morning, when we arose early to clean out the cages, we could see him pacing on the bridge, a hunched and terrifying figure. We had been told that he would be down to breakfast, and we were looking forward to meeting him with some trepidation.

'Remember,' said Smith as we cleaned out the monkeys, 'we must keep on the right side of him.' He filled a basket full of sawdust, trotted to the rail and cast it into the sea.

'We must be careful not to do anything that will annoy him,' he went on when he had returned.

Just at that moment a figure in spotless white uniform came running breathlessly down from the bridge.

'Excuse me, sir,' he said, 'but the Captain's compliments, sir, and will you please make sure which way the wind's blowing before you chuck that sawdust overboard?'

Horror-stricken, we looked up towards the bridge: the air was full of swirling fragments of sawdust, and the Captain, scowling angrily, was brushing his bespattered uniform.

'Please apologize to the Captain for us,' I said, conquering a frightful desire to laugh. When the officer had gone, I turned to Smith.

'Keep on the right side of him!' I said bitterly; 'don't do anything to annoy him! Only fling about three hundredweight of sawdust all over him and his precious bridge. Trust you to know the right way to a captain's heart.'

When the gong sounded we hurried down to our cabin, washed, and took our seats in the dining-saloon. We found, to our dismay, that we were seated at the Captain's table. The Captain sat with his back to the bulkhead, in which there were three portholes, and Smith and I sat on the opposite side of the circular table. The portholes behind the Captain's chair looked out into the well-deck in which our collection was stacked. Half-way through the meal the Captain had thawed out a little and was even starting to make tolerant little jokes about sawdust.

'As long as you don't let anything escape, I don't mind,' he said jovially, disembowelling a fried egg.

'Oh, we won't let that happen,' I said, and the words were hardly out of my mouth when something moved in the porthole, and, glancing up, there was Sweeti-pie, the Black-eared Squirrel, perched in the opening, examining the inside of the saloon with a kindly eye.

The Captain, of course, could not see the squirrel sitting on a level with his shoulder and about three feet away, and he went on eating and talking unconcernedly, while behind him Sweeti-pie sat on his hind legs and cleaned his whiskers. For a few seconds I was so startled that my brain refused to function, and I could only sit there gaping at the porthole. Luckily the Captain was too intent on his breakfast to notice. Sweeti-pie finished his wash and brush-up, and began to look round the saloon again. He decided that the place would be worth investigating, and glanced around to see which was the best way to get down from his perch. He decided that the quickest method would be to jump from the porthole on to the Captain's shoulder. I could see this plan taking shape in the little brute's head, and the thought of his landing on the Captain's shoulder galvanized me into action. Muttering a hasty 'Excuse me,' I pushed back my chair and walked out of the saloon; as soon as I was out of sight of the Captain I ran as fast as I could out on to the deck. To my relief, Sweeti-pie had not jumped, and his long bushy tail was still hanging outside the porthole. I flung myself across the hatch-cover and grabbed him by his tail just as he bunched himself up to spring. I bundled him, chattering indignantly, into his cage, and then returned, flushed but triumphant, to the saloon. The Captain was still talking and, if he had noticed my abrupt departure at all, must have attributed it to the pangs of nature, for he made no mention of it.

On the third day of the voyage two of the *Idiurus* were dead. I was examining their corpses sorrowfully when a member of the crew appeared. He asked why the little animals had died, and I explained at great length the tragic tale of the non-existent avocado pears.

'What's an avocado pear?' he inquired.

I showed him one of the shrivelled wrecks.

'Oh, *those* things,' he said. 'Do you want some?'

I gazed at him speechlessly for a minute.

'Have you got some?' I said at last.

'Well,' he said, 'I haven't exactly got any, but I think I can get you some.'

That evening he reappeared with his pockets bulging.

'Here,' he said, stuffing some beautifully ripe avocados into my hand; 'give me three of those ones of yours, and don't say a word to anyone.'

I gave him three of my dried-up fruits and hastily fed the *Idiurus* with the ripe ones he had procured, and they enjoyed them thoroughly. My spirits rose, and I began to have hopes once more of landing them in England.

My sailor friend brought me plump, ripe avocados whenever I informed him that my stock was running low, and always he took some of my desiccated stock in exchange. It was very curious, but I felt the best thing I could do was not to inquire too deeply into the matter. However, in spite of the fresh fruit, another *Idiurus* died, so by the time we were rolling through the Bay of Biscay I had only one specimen left. It was now, I realized, a fight against time: if I could keep this solitary specimen alive until we reached England, I would have a tremendous variety of food to offer it, and I felt sure that I could find something it would eat. As we drew closer and closer to England I watched the little chap carefully. He seemed fit, and in the best of spirits. As an additional precaution, I smuggled his cage into my cabin each night, so that he would not catch a chill. The day before we docked he was in fine fettle, and I became almost convinced that I would land him. That night, quite suddenly and for no apparent reason, he died. So, after travelling four thousand miles, the last *Idiurus* died twenty-four hours out of Liverpool. I was bitterly disappointed, and black depression settled on me.

Even the sight of the collection being taken ashore did not fill me with the usual mixture of relief and pride. The Hairy Frogs had come through, as had the Brow-leaf Toads; Charlie and Mary were hooting in their cages as they were swung overboard. Sweeti-pie was eating a sugar-lump and eyeing the crowd on the docks with hopeful eyes, while the Moustached Monkey peered from his cage, his whiskers gleaming, looking like a juvenile Santa Claus. But even the sight of all these creatures being landed safely after so long and so dangerous a trip did not altogether compensate me for the loss of my little *Idiurus*, and Smith and I were just going to leave the ship when my sailor friend appeared. He had heard the news about *Idiurus*, and was extremely upset to think that our combined efforts had been in vain.

'By the way,' I said, just as I was leaving him, 'I am very curious to know where you got those avocado pears from in mid-ocean.'

He glanced round to make sure we were not overheard.

'I'll tell you, mate; only keep it under your hat,' he said in a hoarse whisper. 'The Captain's very partial to an avocado, see, and he had a big box of them in the fridge. He always brings home a box, see? I just got some of them for you.'

'Do you mean to say those were the Captain's avocados?' I asked faintly.

'Sure. But he won't miss 'em,' my friend assured me cheerfully; 'you see, every time I took some of *his* out I put the same number of *yours* back in the box.'

The Customs men could not understand why I kept shaking with laughter as I was showing them our crates, and they kept darting suspicious looks at me. But it was not, unfortunately, the sort of joke you could share.

The Drunken Forest

GERALD DURRELL

The Drunken Forest

For my wife
JACQUIE
in memory of Prairie Pigs
and other Bichos

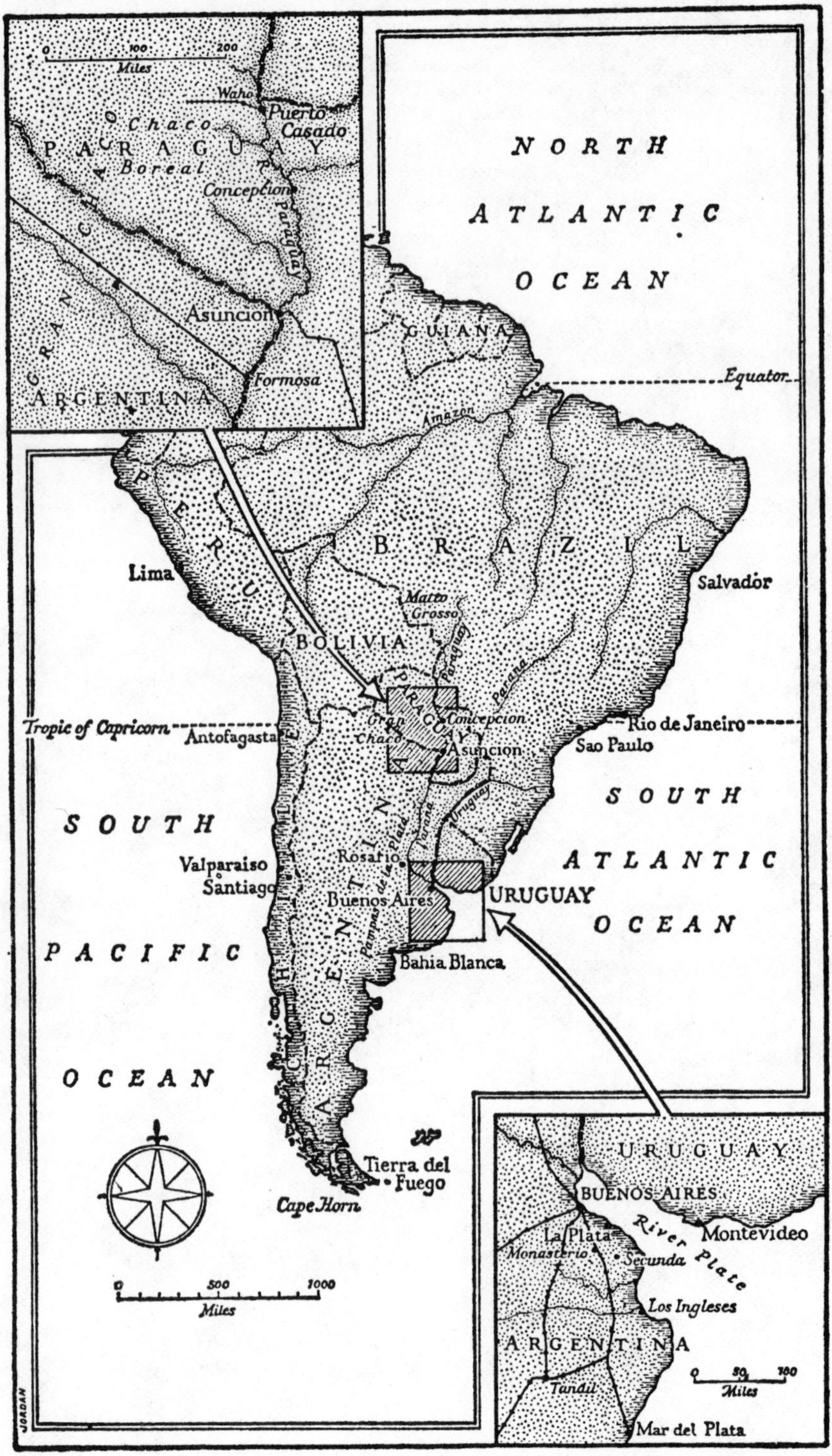

0 100 200
Miles
Waho
Puerto Casado
Chaco
PARAGUAY
Boreal
Concepcion
Paraguay
GRAN CHACO
Asuncion
Formosa
ARGENTINA
NORTH ATLANTIC OCEAN
GUIANA
Equator
Amazon
PERU
BRAZIL
Lima
Salvador
Matto Grosso
BOLIVIA
Paraguay
Parana
PARAGUAY
Gran Chaco
Concepcion
Asuncion
Tropic of Capricorn
Antofagasta
Rio de Janeiro
Sao Paulo
SOUTH ATLANTIC OCEAN
SOUTH PACIFIC OCEAN
Uruguay
Parana
Rosario
Valparaiso
Santiago
Pampas de la Plata
Buenos Aires
URUGUAY
ARGENTINA
CHILE
Bahia Blanca
Tierra del Fuego
Cape Horn
0 500 1000
Miles
URUGUAY
BUENOS AIRES
River Plate
Montevideo
La Plata
Monasterio
Secunda
Los Ingleses
ARGENTINA
0 50 100
Miles
Tandil
Mar del Plata
JORDAN

Explanation

This is an account of a six months' trip that my wife and I made to South America in 1954. Our plan was to make a collection of the strange animals and birds found in this part of the world and bring them back alive for zoos in this country. From our point of view the trip was a failure, for, owing to a number of unforeseen circumstances, all our plans were upset. Our trip was to be divided into two parts. First, we were to make our way down to the southernmost tip of the Continent, Tierra del Fuego, to collect ducks and geese for the Severn Wildfowl Trust. On arrival in Buenos Aires we found that it was the holiday season, and all the planes flying south to the Argentine lakes and thence to Tierra del Fuego were booked for months in advance. Shipping was equally difficult. It was impossible for us to reach our destination in time to capture the nestlings, as we had hoped to do, so very reluctantly we called that part of the trip off. Our second plan was to go to Paraguay, spend some weeks collecting there, and then work our way back to Buenos Aires in easy stages by the Parana and Paraguay Rivers. This plan was also thwarted, though in this case the reasons were political. So we returned from South America with only a handful of specimens in place of the large collection we had hoped for. However, even a failure has its lighter side, and this I have tried to portray in this book.

The failure of our trip was in no way due to lack of sympathy or support from people both here and in Argentina, and we owe a very great debt of gratitude to a vast number of individuals. Our thanks will be found in the acknowledgments at the end of the book.

Saludos

As the ship nosed its way into port we leant on the rail and gazed at the panorama of Buenos Aires gradually curving around us. The sky-scrapers reared up under a vivid blue sky like multi-coloured stalagmites, their surfaces pitted with a million flashing windows. We were still staring raptly when the ship had tied up alongside the tree-lined docks, and the enormous buildings loomed over us, sending their shivering, Venetian-blind reflections across the rippling black water. Our meditations on modern architecture were interrupted by a man who looked so extraordinarily like Adolphe Menjou that for a moment I wondered if we had come to the right end of the American continent. Picking his way disdainfully through the gesticulating, yelling, garlic-breathing mob of immigrants that thronged the deck, he arrived in front of us, calm, unhurried and looking so immaculate that one could hardly believe the temperature was ninety in the shade.

'I am Gibbs from the Embassy,' he announced, smiling. 'I've been looking all over First Class for you; no one told me you were travelling down here.'

'We didn't know we'd be travelling down here until we got on board,' I explained, 'but by then it was too late.'

'It must have been a rather ... er ... unusual voyage for you,' said Mr Gibbs, glaring at a large Spanish peasant who had expectorated with enthusiasm within an inch of his foot, 'and rather on the moist side, I should have thought.'

I began to like Mr Gibbs tremendously.

'This is nothing,' I said airily; 'you should have been here when the weather was rough; it was positively damp then.'

Mr Gibbs shuddered delicately.

'I should imagine you will be rather glad to get ashore,' he said. 'Everything's in order, and we should have you through the Customs in next to no time.'

My liking for Mr Gibbs was reinforced with considerable respect when he sauntered carelessly into the Customs' shed, smiling and exchanging a word or two here and there with the officials, suave and unruffled. From his pockets he produced gigantic forms covered in a rash of red seals that whisked our eccentric luggage through the shed and out the other side into a brace of taxis within ten minutes. Then we were whirled through streets that appeared to be as broad as the Amazon, lined with sky-scrapers, trees and beautifully laid out parks. Within an hour of our arrival we were installed, six floors up, in a lovely flat overlooking the harbour. Mr Gibbs had drifted off to the Embassy, presumably to perform a few more miracles before lunch, and we were left to recover from our voyage. After half an hour's training in the intricate art of using the Argentine telephone, we spent a merry hour ringing up all the people we had introductions to and telling them that we had arrived. There were quite a number of these, for my brother had spent some time in Argentina and, displaying a rather cold-blooded indifference to the fate of his friends, had supplied me with their names and addresses. A few days before we had left England a postcard had arrived from him on which was scribbled the cryptic message: 'In B.A. don't forget to contact Bebita Ferreyra, Calle Posadas 1503, our best friend in Argentina. She is a sweetie.' I frequently receive this sort of information from my brother. So, acting on instructions, we phoned Bebita Ferreyra. When she came on the line my first impression was that she had a voice like the coo of a wood-pigeon. Then I decided it was something much more attractive than this: it was the coo of a wood-pigeon with a sense of humour.

'Mrs Ferreyra? My name is Gerald Durrell.'

'Ah, you are Larry's b-b-brother? B-b-but where are you? Twice I phoned the Customs to find if you had arrived. Can you come to lunch?'

'We'd love to. . . . Can we get to your place by taxi?'

'But naturally. Come about one. Goodbye.'

'She sounds an extraordinary sort of woman,' I said to Jacquie as I put down the phone. I had no idea then that I was making the understatement of the century.

At one o'clock we were ushered into a large flat in a quiet street. On the tables were strewn a multitude of books on a variety of subjects – painting, music, ballet – and among them novels and magazines in three languages. The piano was similarly decorated with music ranging from opera to Chopin, and the radiogram was surrounded by records which included Beethoven, Nat King Cole, Sibelius and Spike Jones. Even Sherlock Holmes, I felt, would have been unable to make a lightning diagnosis of character from these clues. On one wall hung a portrait of an exceptionally lovely woman in a large hat. On the beautiful face was an expression which was at once humorous and calm. It was, in fact, the sort of face that exactly fitted the voice I had heard on the telephone.

'D'you think that's her?' asked Jacquie.

'Very likely. But I expect that was painted years ago. I shouldn't think she looks a bit like that now.'

At that moment there were quick, firm footsteps in the hall, and Bebita entered. I took one look at her and decided that, in comparison to the portrait, the portrait definitely came a very poor second. She was the nearest approach to a Greek goddess that I have ever seen.

'I am B-B-Bebita Ferreyra,' she said, and appeared to understand our astonishment, for the amused expression in her blue eyes deepened.

'I hope you didn't mind us phoning you?' I said; 'only Larry told me I must contact you.'

'B-b-but naturally. I should have b-b-been insulted if you had not.'

'Larry said to give you his love.'

'And how is Larry? Ahh, he is an angel, that man; you have no idea what an angel he is,' she said.

It was only later that I discovered Bebita described everyone thus, however charming or malignant. At the time I found it a trifle astonishing to hear this term used to describe my brother. Of all the descriptions I could have thought of, this one seemed the least appropriate. We fell under Bebita's unique spell during that first meeting, and from then on we practically lived at her flat, eating tremendous and beautifully constructed meals, listening to music, talking nonsense and enjoying ourselves. Very soon we came to rely on her for nearly everything. The most fantastic requests never ruffled her, and she always managed to accomplish something.

The first blow to our plans for the trip fell within three days of arriving in Buenos Aires. We discovered that the chances of our being able to get down to Tierra del Fuego were, to say the least, remote. The airline company were polite but depressing. If we cared to wait ten days or so it was possible that they might have a cancellation, but they could not promise. Gloomily we said that we would wait and see. It was Ian who suggested that, instead of mooching round Buenos Aires for ten days in a depressed and irritated frame of mind, we make a trip into the countryside near the city. Ian is an old friend of mine whom I had met in England during the war. In a moment of rash enthusiasm he said that I should really come out to Argentina on a collecting trip. If I did, he would do all he could to help; now he was stuck with us. He went to see his cousins, the Boote family, who owned a large *estancia* near the coast, some hundred odd miles from the capital. They, with a generosity that is typical of Argentina and all who live there, said they would be delighted to have us.

So early one morning the Bootes' car collected us. Ian hoisted his lugubrious and lanky frame from the depths and introduced us to a beautiful blonde sitting in the front seat, who turned out to be Elizabeth Boote, daughter of the house. Apart from her loveliness, we soon discovered that she had a remarkable ability to sleep; anywhere, at any time, you would find her sleeping peacefully and deeply, ignoring any minor uproar that happened to be taking place around her. This remarkable gift made us nickname her Dormouse, a name that she took grave exception to, but which nevertheless stuck.

Chapter One

Oven-birds and Burrowing Owls

Argentina is one of the few countries in the world where you can go on a journey, and when half-way there see both your starting point and your destination. Flat as a billiard table, the pampa stretches around you, continuing, apparently, to the very edge of the earth. Here and there it is blurred with purple where the thistle grows, and here and there lies a dark rib of trees, but otherwise nothing breaks the smooth expanse of grass.

After we had left the outskirts of Buenos Aires behind, the blond and ivory sky-scrapers dwindling and shimmering in the haze like some curious crystal formation on the horizon, the road lay straight as a lance through the grassland. In places the roadside was crowded with rather fragile-looking bushes covered with pale green leaves and minute golden flowers. These flowers were so tiny, but grew in such profusion, that from a distance they could not be seen as individual blooms, giving instead a curious golden radiance to the bushes, as though each plant were wearing a misty halo around it. From among these bushes flew scissor-tails as we passed, small black-and-white birds with immensely elongated tail-feathers. They have a curious dipping flight, and with each dip the tail-feathers would open and close like the blades of a pair of scissors. Occasionally a chimango hawk would fly across the road on heavy, blunt wings, looking clean and portly in its chocolate-brown-and-caramel plumage.

After an hour or so of driving, we turned off the main road on to a country track, deeply rutted and dusty, its edge lined with neat fencing. I noticed on each fence-pole strange lumps of what appeared to be dried mud; they reminded me of the termites' nests I had seen in Africa, but I thought it unlikely that termites would be found this far south in the world. I was puzzling over these curious protuberances when suddenly a bird flew out of one, a bird resembling the English robin in shape, with a plump breast and a pert tail. It was about the size of a thrush, with a pale fawn breast and rich rusty red upper parts. It was an oven-bird, and immediately I saw it I realized that all those peculiar hummocks of mud decorating the fence-posts were the extraordinary nests of which this bird was the architect and chief mason. Later I found that the oven-bird is one of the commonest, as well as one of the most endearing, of the Argentine birds, and its nests are as much a feature of the landscape as the giant thistles.

Now that our route curved towards the sea, we entered the swampy lands, and the edges of the roads were lined with wide, water-filled ditches, while vivid green patches on the golden grass of the pampa denoted the presence of wider stretches of water, thickly fringed with reed. The place of the oven-birds, scissor-tails and chimangos was taken by waders and waterfowl.

Screamers – great ash-grey birds the size of turkeys – rose from the roadside in strong but ungainly flight, giving their broken flute-like cries of 'Wheeup ... wheeup ... wheeup' as they circled round. On the still, gleaming expanses of water, flocks of ducks swam, looking like plump, sleek business men hurrying to catch a train. There were grey teal, tiny and neat with their steel-blue beaks and black caps; red shovellers, heavy birds with vacant expressions behind the long, spade-shaped beaks; rosybills, immaculate in their gleaming black-and-grey plumage, their beaks looking as though they had been freshly dipped in blood; drab little black-headed ducks, that swam among the others in a self-effacing way that was almost hypocritical, for this bird has emulated the habits of the cuckoo, laying its eggs in others' nests, so that they are adopted and the hard work of hatching and rearing is done by some other and easily hoodwinked species. On the mud flats were a scattering of herons; great jostling crowds of glossy ibis, whose long, curved beaks and deep mourning plumage contrasted strangely with their exuberant spirits as they pecked each other, pirouetted and flapped in the shallows. Here and there among them were smaller groups of scarlet ibis, vivid as shreds of a sunset against the darker plumage of their cousins. On the more open and extensive patches of water swam royal squadrons of black-necked swans, beautiful and unhurried, their foam-white plumage contrasting with the deep black of the head and delicately arched neck. Like courtiers among the proud flocks of black-necks were swimming a few coscoroba swans, dumpy, plain white and definitely barnyard looking. Also on these larger sheets of water were small skeins of flamingos, feeding in the shallows against the tall reeds. From a distance they were like moving heaps of pink and scarlet roses against the green. Each paced slowly and methodically in the dark waters, head down, neck curved in the shape of a large pink S, each bird attached by its sealing-wax pink legs to a blurred, shimmering reflection of itself. Drugged with such a gorgeous banquet of bird life, I sat in the car in a sort of ornithological stupor, noticing nothing but the glittering of feathered bodies, the splash and wrinkle of smooth water and the flash of wing.

The car swerved suddenly off the track, bounced down a narrow lane shining with puddles, through a copse of giant eucalyptus trees, and drew up outside a long, low, white building that might have been an English farmhouse. In the front seat Dormouse Boote awoke from a sleep that had lasted unbroken since we left the capital, and surveyed us with dreamy blue eyes.

'Welcome to Los Ingleses,' she said, and yawned delicately.

The house inside had a delightfully Victorian flavour, with its dark and massive furniture, its animal heads and faded prints on the walls, its stone-flagged passages, and everywhere the faint and pleasantly astringent smell of paraffin from the tall, gleaming, mosque-like lamps. The room Jacquie and I occupied, though large, was dwarfed by an immense feather bed which was obviously straight out of Hans Andersen's story of 'The Princess and the Pea'. It was a bed to end all beds, almost as big as a tennis-court and as thick as a bale of hay. It enveloped you, when you lay on it, in a voluptuous embrace; you sank fathoms deep into its thistledown-soft depths, and were lulled immediately into a sleep so complete and so relaxed that your rage on being awoken was almost homicidal. The window of the room, looking out on to the smooth lawn and rows of diminutive fruit trees, was fringed with eyelashes of blue-flowered creeper. Hung among the flowers, in such a position that I could see it from where I lay in bed, was a humming-bird's nest, a tiny cup the size of half a walnut shell, containing two pea-size white eggs. The morning after our arrival, as I lay in the warm depths of the gargantuan bed, sipping my tea, I watched the female humming-bird sitting quietly on her eggs, while her mate hovered and flipped among the blue flowers, like a microscopic, glittering comet. Bird-watching in these circumstances had a very great deal to be said for it, but at length Jacquie refused to believe that, under those conditions, I was adding greatly to ornithological knowledge of the family *trochilidae*, so I was dragged reluctantly from the octopus-like embrace of the bed and forced to dress. Having done so, I was revolted at the thought that Ian might still be asleep, and strode across the passage to his room, determined to rout him out. I found him clad in pyjamas and a *poncho*, that useful Argentine garment that resembles a blanket with a hole in the middle through which you stick your head. He was squatting on the floor, sucking at a slender, silver pipe that was immersed in a small, round, silver pot which contained a dark and rather revolting-looking liquid with what appeared to be bits of grass floating on the top.

'Hullo, Gerry! You up?' he said, faintly surprised, and sucked vigorously at the little pipe, which responded with a musical gurgle like a miniature bath emptying.

'What are you doing?' I asked austerely.

'Having my morning *mate*,' he answered, giving another liquid gurgle on the pipe. 'Like to try it?'

'Isn't that the herb tea?' I inquired.

'Yes. Drink it out here as frequently, if not more frequently, than tea in England. Try some; you might like it,' he suggested, and handed me the little silver pot and pipe.

I sniffed suspiciously at the dark brown liquid with its crust of floating herbage. The scent was rich and pleasant, like a hay-field under a hot sun. I put my lips to the little pipe and sucked. There was a fruity wheeze, and a stream of boiling liquid gushed into my mouth and scalded my tongue. Wiping my streaming eyes, I handed the pot back to Ian.

'Thanks,' I said. 'I've no doubt it's an acquired taste to drink it at that temperature, but I'm afraid my taste-buds wouldn't stand it.'

'Well, you can drink it cooler than this,' said Ian doubtfully, 'but I think it loses its flavour.'

Later I tried drinking *mate* at a more humane temperature, and I found it pleasantly soothing, with its aroma of new-mown hay and faintly bitter, astringent taste that was quite refreshing. But I could never cultivate the ability to drink it at the heat of molten metal, as I presume a connoisseur would like it.

We meandered through an excellent breakfast, and then wandered out into the brilliant day to examine the surrounding countryside. Hardly had we left the copse of eucalyptus that ringed the *estancia* like a giant fence, when we came upon a tree-stump in the long grass, and perched on top of it was an oven-bird's nest. I was amazed, when I examined it closely, that a bird of this size could produce such a large and complicated structure. The nest was globe-shaped, roughly twice the size of a football, strongly made of mud combined with roots and fibres, so that it formed a sort of avian reinforced concrete. Looked at from the front, where there was an arched entrance, the whole thing resembled a miniature version of an old-fashioned bread-oven. I was interested to see what the inside of the nest was like, so, being assured by Ian that it was an old one, I prised it off the tree-stump and cut carefully through the brick-like top of the dome with a sharp knife. When the top was removed, the whole thing looked like the inside of a snail shell: a passage-way ran in to the left for some six inches from the arched door, following the curve of the outside wall, but bent in at the right of the door so as to form the passage-way. Where the passage ended, the natural shape of the nest formed a circular room, which was neatly lined with grass and a few feathers. While the outside of the whole structure was rough and uneven, the inside of the little room and the passage-way was smooth and almost polished. The more I examined the nest, the more astonished I became that a bird, using only its beak as a tool, could have achieved such a building triumph. No wonder the people of Argentina look with affection upon this sprightly bird that paces so pompously about their gardens and makes the air shiver with its cheerful, ringing cries. Hudson relates a charming story about a pair which had built a nest on the roof of a ranch-house. One day the female unfortunately got caught in a rat trap, which broke both her legs. Struggling free, she managed to fly up into her nest, and there eventually died. Her mate flew about for several days, calling incessantly, and finally disappeared. Within two days he was back again, accompanied by another hen. The two birds promptly set to work and plastered up the entrance of the old nest, containing the first wife's remains. This done, they constructed a second nest on top of this crypt, and here they successfully reared their brood.

Certainly, as birds go, the oven-bird appears to have more than his fair share of personality and charm, for he has a strange power over even the most hardened cynics. Later on during our stay an elderly peon, who had no sentimentality in his make-up and suffered no qualms at killing anything from men to insects, solemnly told me that he would never harm an *hornero*. Once, he said, when out riding in the pampa, he came upon an oven-bird's nest on a stump. The nest was half completed and the mud still damp. Dangling from one side of it was the owner, caught round the feet by a long thread of grass it had obviously been using as reinforcement. The bird must have been hanging there for some time, fluttering vainly in an attempt to free itself, and it was nearly exhausted. Moved by a sudden impulse, the peon rode up to the nest, took out his knife and carefully cut away the entangling grass and placed the exhausted bird carefully on top of its nest to recover. Then an extraordinary thing happened.

'I swear that this is true, señor,' said the peon. 'There was I, not more than a couple of feet away from the bird, and yet it showed no fear. Weak as it was, it struggled to its feet, and then put its beak up and started to sing. For nearly two minutes it sang to me, señor – a beautiful song – and I sat on my horse listening. Then it flew off across the grass. That bird was thanking me for saving its life. A bird that can show gratitude in that manner, señor, deserves respect from a man.'

A hundred yards or so from the oven-bird's nest, Jacquie, who was some distance away to my right, started to make inarticulate crooning noises and to beckon me frantically. Joining her, I found she was gazing rapturously at the mouth of a small burrow, half hidden among the grass tussocks. At the mouth of the burrow squatted a small owl, stiff as a guardsman, watching us with round eyes. Suddenly he bowed up and down two or three times, very rapidly, and then froze once more into his military stance. This was such a ludicrous performance that both Jacquie and I giggled, and the owl, after giving us a withering glare, launched himself on silent wings and glided away across the wind-rippled grass.

'We must catch some of those,' said Jacquie firmly. 'I think they're delightful.'

I agreed, for owls of any sort have always appealed to me, and I have never been able to make any collection without a sprinkling of these attractive birds finding their way into it. I turned towards where Ian was pacing through the grass, like a solitary and depressed-looking crane.

'Ian,' I shouted, 'come over here. I think we've found a burrowing owl's nest.'

He came loping over, and together we examined the entrance of the hole where the owl had been sitting. There was a patch of bare earth from the excavations, and this was liberally sprinkled with the gleaming chitinous shells of various beetles and round castings composed of tiny bones, fluff and feathers. It certainly looked as though the burrow was used for more than just roosting in. Ian gazed down, pulling his nose reflectively.

'D'you think there's anything in there?' I asked.

'Hard to say,' he replied. 'It's the right season, of course – in fact the youngsters should be fully fledged by now. Trouble is these owls make several burrows, and they only use one for nesting in. The peons say that the male uses the others as sort of bachelor apartments, but I don't know. It means we may have to dig out any number of these holes before we strike lucky; but, if you don't mind a good many disappointments, we can have a try.'

'You can disappoint me as much as you like, as long as we get some owls in the end,' I said firmly.

'Right. Well, we'll need spades, and a stick of some sort to see which way the tunnels lie.'

So we retraced our steps to the *estancia*, and there Mrs Boote, delighted that we were hot on the trail of specimens so soon after our arrival, unearthed a fascinating array of gardening tools, and told a peon to stop whatever he was doing and to go with us in case we needed help. As we trailed across the garden, looking like a gravediggers' convention, we stumbled upon Dormouse Boote, slumbering peacefully on a rug. She awoke as we passed and asked sleepily where we were off to. On being informed that we were off to capture burrowing owls, her blue eyes opened wide and she suggested that she should drive us out in the car to the owl's nest.

'But you can't drive the car across the pampa ... it's not a jeep,' I protested.

'And your father's just had the springs renewed,' Ian reminded her.

She gave us a ravishing smile.

'I'll drive very slowly,' she promised, and then, seeing that we were still doubtful, she cunningly added, 'and think how much more ground you'll be able to cover in a car.'

So we lurched out across the pampa to the first owl-hole, the springs of the car twanging melodiously, and causing everyone except Dormouse twinges of conscience.

The hole we had found turned out to be some eight feet in length, curving slightly like the letter C, and about two feet at the greatest depths below the surface. We discovered all this by probing gently with a long and slender bamboo. Having marked out with sticks a rough plan of how the burrow lay, we proceeded to dig down, sinking a shaft into the tunnel at intervals of about two feet. Then each section of tunnel between the shafts was carefully searched to make sure nothing was hiding in it, and blocked off with clods of earth. At length we came to the final shaft, which, if our primitive reckoning was correct, should lead us down into the nesting chamber. We worked in excited silence, gently chipping away the hard-baked soil. At intervals during our excavations we had pressed our ears to the turf, but there had been no sound from inside, and I was half convinced that the burrow would prove empty. Then the last crust of the earth gave way, and cascaded into the nesting chamber, and glaring up out of the gloomy hole were two little ash-grey faces, with great dandelion-golden eyes. We all gave a whoop of triumph, and the owls blinked very rapidly and clicked their beaks like castanets. They looked so fluffy and adorable that I completely forgot all about owls' habits, and reached into the ruins of the nest-chamber and tried to pick one up. Immediately they transformed themselves from bewildered bundles consisting of soft plumage and great eyes, to swollen, belligerent furies. Puffing out their feathers on their backs, so that they looked twice their real size, they opened their wings on each side of their bodies like feathered shields, and, with clutching talons and snapping beaks, swooped at my hand. I sat back and sucked my bloodstained fingers.

'Have we got a thick cloth of some sort?' I asked – 'something thicker than a handkerchief, with which to handle these innocent little dears?'

Dormouse sped off to the car and returned with an ancient and oil-stained towel. I doubled this over my hand and made a fresh attempt. This time I succeeded in grabbing one of the babies round the body, and although the towel kept off the attacks of his beak, I was still pricked by his clutching talons. Having got a good grip on the towel, he then refused to let go, and it took some time to disentangle his feet and pop him into a bag. His brother, now facing the enemy alone, seemed to lose a lot of his nerve, and he was much less trouble to catch and put in a bag. Hot, earth-stained, but feeling very pleased with ourselves, we re-entered the car. For the rest of the day we zig-zagged across the pampa, waiting for pairs of burrowing owls to fly out of the grass. Then we would wander about the spot until we had located the hole and proceed to dig it out. We met with more disappointments than successes, as Ian had predicted we would, but at the end of the day (having dug up what appeared to be several miles of tunnel), we returned to the *estancia* with a very satisfying bag of eight baby burrowing owls, who prompty proceeded to consume meat and beetles in such vast quantities that we began to wonder if their harassed parents would really miss them, or whether they would look upon the capture of their offspring as a merciful release.

Having now got our first specimens from Los Ingleses, others followed rapidly. The day after the capture of the burrowing owls, a peon came to the house holding a box which contained two fledgling guira cuckoos. These birds are quite common in Argentina, and even more so in Paraguay. In shape and size they look like an English starling, but there the resemblance ends, for guira cuckoos are clad in pale fawny-cream plumage, streaked with greenish black, with a tattered gingery crest on the head, and long, magpie-like tails. They travel together through the bushes and woods in little companies of between ten and twenty, and they look very handsome as they glide from bush to bush *en masse*, like flights of brown-paper darts. Apart from admiring these flocks of cuckoos in flight, I had not really given the species any serious thought, until we received these two babies. I discovered immediately I undid the box in which they were confined that guira cuckoos are not like other birds at all. To begin with, I am convinced that they are mentally defective from the moment of hatching, and nothing will make me alter my opinion. As I lifted the lid from the box, it disclosed the two guiras squatting straddle-legged in the bottom of the box, long tails spread out, and ginger crests erect. They surveyed me calmly with pale yellow eyes that had a glazed, dreamy, far-away expression in them, as though they were listening to distant and heavenly music too faint for mere mammals like myself to hear. Then, like a perfectly trained harmony team, they raised their uneven crests still further, opened their yellow beaks and let forth a loud, hysterical series of sounds like a machine-gun. This done, they lowered their crests and flew heavily out of the box, one landing on my wrist and one on my head. The one on my wrist uttered a pleased, chuckling sound and sidled up to the buttons on my coat sleeve, which he proceeded to attack with raised crest and every symptom of ferocity. The one on my head grasped a large quantity of hair in his beak, straddled his legs and proceeded to pull at it with all his might.

'How long has this man had them?' I asked Ian, astonished at the birds' impudence and tameness.

Ian and the peon had a rapid exchange of Spanish, and then Ian turned to me.

'He says he caught them half an hour ago,' said Ian.

'But that's impossible,' I protested, 'these birds are tame. They must be someone's pets who've escaped.'

'Oh, no,' said Ian; 'guiras are always like that.'

'What, as tame as this?'

'Yes. They seem to have no fear at all when they're young. They're not quite so silly when they are adult, but almost.'

The one on my head, discovering that the idea of scalping me was impossible, now descended to my shoulder and tried to see how much of his beak would fit into my ear without getting stuck. I removed him hurriedly and placed him on my wrist with his brother. They both immediately carried on as though they had not seen each other for years, raising their crests, gazing lovingly into each other's eyes, and trilling with the speed of a couple of road drills. When I opened the door of a cage and placed my wrist near it, both birds hopped inside and up on to the perch as if they had been born in captivity. Intrigued by this display of avian nonchalance, I went in search of Jacquie.

'Come and see the new arrivals,' I said, when I found her, '—the answer to a collector's dream.'

'What are they?'

'A pair of those guira cuckoos.'

'Oh, you mean those gingery things,' she said disparagingly. 'I don't call them very exciting.'

'Well, come and see them,' I urged; 'they're certainly the weirdest pair of birds I've come across.'

The cuckoos were sitting on the perch, preening themselves. They paused briefly in their toilet to fix us with a glittering eye and rattle a brief greeting before continuing.

'They're a bit more attractive when you seen them close to,' Jacquie admitted; 'but I don't see what you're making a fuss about.'

'Don't you notice anything about them . . . anything unusual?'

'No,' she said, surveying them critically. 'It's a good thing they're tame. Saves a lot of trouble.'

'But they're not tame,' I said triumphantly; 'they were only caught half an hour ago.'

'Nonsense!' said Jacquie firmly. 'Why, just look at them. You can see they're quite used to being in a cage.'

'No, they're not. According to Ian, at this age they're quite stupid, and they're very easy to catch, and as tame as anything. When they get older they develop a little more sense, but apparently not very much.'

'I must say they are rather peculiar-looking birds,' said Jacquie, peering at them closely.

'They look mentally defective to me,' I said.

Jacquie inserted a finger through the wire and waggled it at the nearest cuckoo. Without hesitation he sidled up to the bars and lowered his head to be scratched. His brother, enthusiasm gleaming in his eyes, immediately climbed on his brother's back to receive his share of the treat. Quite unconcernedly they sat like that, one perched precariously on the other, both swaying to and fro on the perch, while Jacquie scratched their necks. Gradually, soothed by the massage, their crests came up, their heads tilted until their beaks pointed heavenwards, their eyes closed in ecstasy, and the feathers on the neck stood out straight, while the neck itself was stretched upwards and outwards until they looked more like feathered giraffes than birds.

'Quite definitely mental,' I repeated, as the top cuckoo stretched his neck too far, overbalanced and fell to the bottom of the cage, where he sat blinking and chuckling testily to himself.

Later we got more of these fatuous birds, and they all proved equally simple. One pair was caught later on, in Paraguay, by our companion in the most amazing fashion. Walking along a path, he passed within a yard of a pair of guiras feeding in the grass. Thinking it strange that they had not flown away at his approach, he retraced his steps and again passed them. They just sat and stared at him foolishly. The third time he jumped at them and returned triumphantly to camp, carrying one in each hand. Owing to the ease with which even an unprepared person could capture these birds, it was not long before we had several pairs, and they afforded us endless amusement. In each of their cages there was an inch gap left for cleaning purposes. The cuckoos could have asked for nothing better, as by squatting on the floor and sticking their heads out, they could keep an eye on everything that went on in camp, and discuss it together in loud trills and chuckles. When they peered out of their cages like this, tattered crests erect, eyes bright with curiosity, their shrill voices screeching comments, they reminded me of groups of frowsty old charladies peering out of some attic window at a street-fight below.

The guiras had a passion for sun-bathing that was almost an obsession. The slightest gleam of sunshine in their cage would excite them beyond all measure. Trilling happily, they would crowd on to the perch and prepare for their sun bath, which they considered a serious matter and one not to be undertaken lightly. To begin with, it was very important that the posture should be exactly right. They had to be seated comfortably on the perch, balanced so skilfully that they could remain sitting there even if they released their grip on the wood. Then they would puff out their feathers and shake them vigorously, like an old feather duster. After this they would puff out the feathers of their breasts, raise the feathers on the rump, lower their long tails, close their eyes and gradually sink down until their breast-bones rested against the perch, breast-feathers drooping one side, the tail drooping the other. Then, very slowly and carefully, they would unclench their feet, and sit there, swaying delicately. When sun-bathing like this, with their feathers stuck out at odd and completely unbird-like angles, they looked as though they were completely egg-bound; in that unprotected condition they also looked as if they had been severely attacked by clothes-moth. But, in spite of their crazy ways, the cuckoos were endearing birds, and even if we had only left them for half an hour they would greet our return with such joyful trills of greeting that you could not help feeling affectionate towards them.

The first pair we got – the ones from Los Ingleses – always remained our favourites, and underwent a lot of spoiling from Jacquie. At the end of the trip, when we had handed them over to London Zoo, we were not able to go and see them for nearly two months. Thinking that such brainless birds would by now have completely forgotten us, we approached their cage in the bird-house with mixed feelings. It was a week-end, and there were a number of other visitors clustered round the guiras' cage. But no sooner had we joined the spectators than the cuckoos, who a moment before had been preening themselves on their perch, stared at us with bright, mad eyes, erected their crests in astonishment, and flew down to the wire with loud rattles of excitement and pleasure. As we scratched their necks and watched them stretch out like rubber, we decided that perhaps they were not quite so unintelligent as we had supposed them to be.

Chapter Two

Eggbert and the Terrible Twins

The great screamers were one of the commonest birds round Los Ingleses; within a radius of a mile or so one could see ten or twelve pairs of these stately creatures, pacing side by side through the grass, or wheeling through the sky on wide wings, making the air ring with their melodious trumpet-calls. How to catch the eight I wanted was a problem, for, as well as being the commonest of the pampa birds, they were also the most wary. Their goose-like habit of grazing in huge flocks, completely devastating enormous fields of alfalfa in the winter, has earned the wrath of the Argentine farmers, and they are hunted and killed whenever possible. So, while you could approach fairly close to most of the bird-life on the pampa, you were extremely lucky if you got within a hundred and fifty yards of a pair of screamers. We knew they were nesting all about us, but the nests were well concealed; and though we realized that several times we had been close to finding one, by the way the parents flew low over us with loud cries, we had never been successful.

One evening we were out at a small lake, thickly fringed with reed, setting up flight-nets to try to obtain some ducks. Having fixed my side of the net, I hauled myself out of the brackish water and wandered through the reed-beds. I stopped to examine a small nest, rather like a reed-warbler's, which was cunningly suspended between two leaves, and which proved to be empty, when my attention was attracted to a pile of grey clay which winked at me. Just as I was becoming convinced that there must be something wrong with me, the pile of clay winked again. Then, as the patch of ground at which I had been staring came into focus, I saw that I was not looking at a patch of clay, but at an almost fully grown baby screamer, crouched among the reeds, still as a stone, with only the lids flicking over its dark eyes to give it away. I went forward slowly and squatted down near it. Still it did not move. I reached forward and touched its head, but it lay quite quietly, ignoring me. I picked it up and put it under my arm like a domestic fowl, carrying it back to the car. It made no effort to struggle and displayed no symptoms of panic. Just as I reached the car, however, a pair of adult screamers flew over quite low, and, on seeing us, gave a series of wild cries. Immediately the bird in my arms turned from a placid and well-behaved creature into a flapping, panic-stricken beast that took me all my time to subdue and place in a box.

When we returned to the *estancia*, Dormouse's brother John came out to see how we had fared. With considerable pride I showed him my screamer.

'One of those damn things,' he said in disgust. 'I didn't know you wanted them.'

'Of course I do,' I said indignantly; 'they're a most attractive show in any zoo.'

'How many do you want?' asked John.

'Well, I need eight, really, though judging by the difficulty we had in getting this one I doubt whether I'll get that many,' I said gloomily.

'Oh, don't worry about that; I'll get eight for you,' said John airily. 'When d'you want them? . . . Tomorrow?'

'I don't want to be greedy,' I said sarcastically, 'so suppose you just bring me four tomorrow, and four the next day?'

'O.K.,' said John laconically, and wandered off.

Beyond reflecting that John had a peculiar sense of humour if he could joke about such a sacred subject as screamer-catching, I thought no more about it until the following morning I saw him mounting his horse. A peon, already mounted, waited nearby.

'Oh, Gerry,' he called, as his horse waltzed round and round impatiently, 'did you say eight or a dozen?'

'Eight or a dozen what?'

'*Chajás*, of course,' he said in mild surprise.

I glared at him.

'I want eight,' I said, 'and then you can get me a dozen or so tomorrow.'

'O.K.,' said John, and, turning his horse, cantered off through the eucalyptus trees.

At lunch-time I was in the small hut in which we housed the animals, attempting to make a cage. Three pieces of wood had split, and I had hit myself twice on the hand with the hammer, and nearly taken the top off my thumb with the saw. Altogether I was not in the most jovial of moods, and Jacquie and Ian had long since left me to my own devices. I was making another frenzied assault on the cage, when there was the clop of hooves, and John's voice hailed me cheerfully from outside.

'Hola, Gerry,' he called. 'Here are your *chajás*.'

This was the last straw. Clutching a hammer murderously, I strode out to explain to John, in no uncertain terms, that I was in no mood for practical jokes. He was leaning against the sweating flanks of his horse, a smile on his face. But what brought me up short and made my irritation evaporate was the sight of two large sacks lying at his feet, sacks that bulged, sacks that heaved and quivered. The peon was getting off another horse and also lowering a couple of sacks to the ground, sacks that seemed heavy, and that gave forth a rustling sound.

'Are you serious?' I asked faintly. 'Are those sacks really full of screamers?'

'But of course,' said John, surprised. 'What did you think?'

'I thought you were joking,' I said meekly. 'How many have you got?'

'Eight, like you asked for,' said John.

'Eight?' I squawked hoarsely.

'Yes, only eight. I'm sorry I couldn't get a dozen, but I'll try and get you eight more tomorrow.'

'No, no, don't . . . Let me get these established first.'

'But you said . . .' began John, bewildered.

'Never mind what I said,' I interjected hastily; 'just don't get me any more until I tell you.'

'Right,' he said cheerfully; 'you know best. By the way, there's a very young one in one of the sacks. I had to put him in there. I hope he's all right. You'd better have a look.'

Feeling that the age of miracles was not past, I staggered into the hut with the heavy, heaving sacks, and then went in search of Jacquie and Ian to tell them the good news and get them to help me unpack the birds. Most of the screamers that we hauled out, tousled and indignant, from inside the sacks, were about the same size as the one I had caught the day before. But right at the very bottom of the last sack we emptied we discovered the young one that John had mentioned. He was quite the most pathetic, the most ridiculous-looking and the most charming baby bird I had ever seen.

He could not have been much more than a week old. His body was about the size of a coconut, and completely circular. At the end of a long neck was a high, domed head, with a tiny beak and a pair of friendly brown eyes. His legs and feet, which were greyish-pink, appeared to be four times too big for him, and not completely under control. On his back were two small, flaccid bits of skin, like a couple of cast-off glove fingers which had become attached there by accident, which did duty as wings. He was clad entirely in what appeared to be a badly knitted bright yellow suit of cotton wool. He rolled out of the sack, fell on his back, struggled manfully on to his enormous flat feet, and stood there, his ridiculous wings slightly raised, surveying us with interest. Then he opened his beak and shyly said 'Wheep'. As we were too enchanted to respond to this greeting, he very slowly and carefully picked up one huge foot, swayed forward, put it down and then brought the other one up alongside it. He stood and beamed at us with evident delight at having accomplished such a complicated manoeuvre. He had a short rest, said 'wheep' again, and then proceeded to take another step, in order to show us that the first one had been no fluke, but a solid achievement. Unfortunately, when he had taken the first step, he had not watched what he was doing, and so his left foot was resting on the toes of his right foot. The results were disastrous. He struggled wildly to extricate his right foot from underneath his left, swaying dangerously. Then, with a mighty heave, he succeeded in lifting both feet from the ground, and promptly fell flat on his face. At our burst of laughter, he looked up into our faces from his recumbent posture, and gave another deprecating 'wheep'.

At first, owing to his shape and the colouring of his suit, we called this baby, Egg. But later, as he grew older, it was changed to a more sedate Eggbert. Now, I have met a lot of amusing birds at one time and another, but they generally appeared funny because their appearance was ridiculous, and so even the most commonplace action took on some element of humour. But I have never met a bird like Eggbert, who not only *looked* funny without doing anything, but also acted in a riotously comical manner whenever he moved. I have never met a bird, before or since, that could make me literally laugh until I cried. Very few human comedians can do that to me. Yet Eggbert had only to stand there on his outsize feet, cock his head on one side and say 'wheep!' in a slyly interrogative way, and I would feel unconquerable laughter bubbling up inside me. Every afternoon we would take Eggbert out of his cage and allow him an hour's constitutional on the lawn. We looked forward to these walks as eagerly as he did, but an hour was enough. At the end of that time we would be forced to return him to his cage, in sheer self-defence.

Eggbert's feet were the bane of his life. There was so much of them, and they would get tangled together when he walked. Then there was the danger that he would tread on his own toes and fall down and make an exhibition of himself, as he had done on the first day. So he kept a very close watch on his feet for any signs of insubordination. He would sometimes stand for as long as ten minutes with bent head, gravely staring at his toes as they wiggled gently in the grass, spread out like the arms of a starfish. Eggbert's whole desire, obviously, was to be dissociated from these outsize feet. He felt irritated by them. Without them, he was sure, he could gambol about the lawn with the airy grace of a dried thistle-head. Occasionally, having watched his feet for some time, he would decide that he had lulled them into a sense of false security. Then, when they least suspected it, he would launch his body forward in an effort to speed across the lawn and leave these hateful extremities behind. But although he tried this trick many times, it never succeeded. The feet were always too quick for him, and as soon as he moved they would deliberately and maliciously twist themselves into a knot, and Eggbert would fall head first into the daisies.

His feet were continually letting him down, in more ways than one. Eggbert had a deep ambition to capture a butterfly. Why this was we could not find out, for Eggbert could not tell us. All we knew was that screamers were supposed to be entirely vegetarian, but whenever a butterfly hovered within six feet of Eggbert his whole being seemed to be filled with blood-lust, his eyes would take on a fanatical and most unvegetarian-like gleam, and he would endeavour to stalk it. However, in order to stalk a butterfly with any hope of success one has to keep one's eyes firmly fixed on it. This Eggbert knew, but the trouble was that as soon as he watched the butterfly with quivering concentration, his feet, left to their own devices, would start to play up, treading on each other's toes, crossing over each other, and sometimes even trying to walk in the wrong direction. As soon as Eggbert dragged his eyes away from the quarry, his feet would start to behave, but by the time he looked back again the butterfly would have disappeared. Then came the never-to-be-forgotten day when Eggbert was standing in the sun, feet turned out, dreaming to himself, and a large, ill-mannered and obviously working-class butterfly of the worst type flew rapidly across the lawn, flapped down and settled on Eggbert's beak, made what can only be described as a rude gesture with its antennae, and soared up into the air again. Eggbert, quivering with justifiable rage, pecked at it as it swooped over his domed forehead. Unfortunately, he leaned too far back, and for one awful moment he swayed and then he crashed on to his back, his feet waving helplessly in the air. As he lay there, demoralized and helpless, the cowardly butterfly took the opportunity to land on his protuberant, fluff-covered tummy, and have a quick wash-and-brush-up before flying off again. This painful episode naturally only made Eggbert feel even more belligerently inclined towards the lepidoptera, but in spite of all his efforts he never caught one.

At first, Eggbert gave us some concern over his food. He rejected with disdain such commonplace vegetation as cabbage, lettuce, clover and alfalfa.

We tried him on biscuit with hard-boiled egg, and he regarded us with horror for trying to force him into cannibalism. Fruit, bran, maize and a variety of other things were inspected briefly and then ignored. In desperation I suggested that the only thing to do was to let him out in the kitchen garden in the faint hope that he would, young as he was, give us some indication of the sort of menu he desired. By this time Eggbert's food problem was worrying practically the whole *estancia*, so there was quite a crowd of anxious people assembled in the kitchen garden when we carried Eggbert out for the experiment. He greeted the assembled company with a friendly 'wheep', stood on his own foot and fell down, regained his equilibrium with an effort, and started off on his tour, while we followed in a hushed and expectant group. He passed through the rows of cabbages without a glance, and seemed mainly concerned with gaining control over his feet. At the tomatoes he started to look about him with interest, but just as it seemed he was coming to some sort of decision, his attention was distracted by a large locust. Among the potatoes he was overcome with fatigue, so he had a short nap while we stood patiently and waited. He awoke, apparently much refreshed, greeted us with surprise, yawned, and then ambled drunkenly on his journey. The carrots were passed with scorn. Among the peas he obviously felt that a little relaxation would be in order, and he tried to inveigle us into playing hide-and-seek among the plants. He reluctantly gave up this idea and moved on to the beans when he discovered that we refused to be sidetracked from the matter in hand. The bean-flowers seemed to fascinate him, but the interest was apparently aesthetic rather than gastronomic. Among the parsley and mint he was seized with a tickling sensation in the sole of his left foot, and his attempts to stand on one leg to search for the cause of the irritation made him fall back heavily into a pool of rainwater. When he had been picked up, dried and comforted, he staggered off and entered the neat rows of spinach. Here he came to a sudden halt and examined the plants minutely and suspiciously. Then he edged forward and glared at them from close range with his head on one side. The suspense was terrific. Just as he leant forward to peck at a leaf, he tripped and fell head first into a large spinach plant. He extricated himself with difficulty and tried again. This time he managed to seize the tip of a leaf in his beak. He tugged at it, but the leaf was a tough one and would not give way. He leant back, legs wide apart, and tugged frantically. The end of the leaf broke, and Eggbert was once more on his back, but this time looking distinctly triumphant with a tiny fragment of spinach in his beak. Amid much applause, he was carried back to his cage, and a large plate of chopped spinach was prepared for him. But then a new difficulty made its appearance. Even finely chopped spinach was too coarse for him, for having gulped it down he would straight away proceed to be sick.

'It's far too coarse, even when we chop it up finely,' I said; 'I'm afraid we'll have to prepare it in much the same way as his mother used to.'

'How's that?' asked Jacquie with interest.

'Well, they regurgitate a mass of semi-digested leaf for the young, so that it's soft and pulp-like.'

'Are you suggesting that we should try *that*?' inquired Jacquie suspiciously.

'No, no. Only I think that the nearest we can get to it is to offer him *chewed* spinach.'

'Oh, well, rather you than me,' said my wife gaily.

'But that's just the trouble,' I explained; 'I smoke, and I don't think he'd care to have a mixture of spinach and nicotine.'

'In other words, as I don't smoke, I suppose you want me to chew it?'

'That's the general idea.'

'If anyone had told me,' said Jacquie plaintively, 'that when I married you I should have to spend my spare time chewing spinach for birds, I would never have believed them.'

'It's for the good of the cause,' I pointed out.

'In fact,' she continued darkly, ignoring my remark, 'if anyone *had* told me that, and I'd *believed* them, I don't think I would have married you.'

She picked up a large plate of spinach, gave me a cold look, and took it off to a quiet corner to chew. During the time we had Eggbert he got through a lot of spinach, all of which Jacquie chewed for him with the monotonous persistence of one of the larger ungulates. At the end she calculated she had masticated something in the region of a hundredweight or so of leaves. Even today, spinach is not among her favourite vegetables.

Shortly after the arrival of Eggbert and his brethren we received a pair of animals which soon became known as the Terrible Twins. They were a pair of large and very corpulent hairy armadillos. Both of them were nearly identical in size and girth and, we soon discovered, in habits. As they were both female, one could quite easily have supposed that they were sisters from the same litter, except for the fact that while one was caught a stone's throw away from Los Ingleses, the other was sent over from a neighbouring *estancia* several miles away. The Twins were housed in a cage with a special sleeping compartment. It had originally been designed to accommodate one large armadillo, but owing to a housing shortage when they arrived, we were forced to put them both in the one cage. As it happened, since they were not quite fully grown, they fitted in very snugly. Their two pleasures in life were food and sleep, neither of which they could apparently get enough of. In their sleeping compartment they would lie on their backs, head to tail, their great pink and wrinkled tummies bulging and deflating as they breathed stertorously, their paws twitching and quivering. Once they were asleep, it seemed that nothing on earth would wake them. You could bang on the box, shout through the bars, open the bedroom door and, holding your breath (for the Twins had a powerful scent all their own), poke their obese stomachs, pinch their paws or flick their tails, but still they slumbered as though they were both in a deep hypnotic trance. Then, under the impression that nothing short of a world catastrophe would shake them into consciousness, you would fill a tin tray high with the revolting mixture they liked, and proceed to insert it into the outside portion of the cage. However delicately you performed this operation, however careful you were to make sure the silence was not broken by the slightest sound, no sooner had you got the dish and your hand inside the door than from the bedroom would come a noise like a sea-serpent demolishing a woodshed with its tail. This was the Twins tumbling and struggling to get upright – to get to action stations, as it were. That was the warning to drop the plate and remove your hand with all speed, for within a split second the armadillos would burst from their bedroom door, like cannonballs, skid wildly across the cage, shoulder to shoulder, in the manner of a couple of Rugby players fighting for the ball, grunting with the effort. They would hit the tin (and your hand if it was still there) amidships, and the armadillos and tin would end in the far corner in a tangled heap, and a tidal wave of chopped banana, milk, raw egg and minced meat would splash against the wall, and then rebound to settle like a glutinous shawl over the Twins' grey backs. They would stand there, giving satisfied squeaks and grunts, licking the food as it trickled down their shells, occasionally going into a scrum in the corner over some choice bit of fruit or meat which had just given up the unequal contest with gravity and descended suddenly from the ceiling. Watching them standing knee-deep in that tide of food, you might think that it was impossible for two animals to get through such a quantity of vitamin and protein. Yet within half an hour the cage would be spotless, licked clean even to the least splashes on the ceiling, which they had to stand on their hind legs to reach. And the Twins themselves would be in their odoriferous boudoir, on their backs, head to tail, deeply and noisily asleep. Eventually, owing to this health-giving diet, the Twins increased their girth to such an extent that they could only just manage to get through the bedroom door, leaving about a milli-metre's clearance all round. I was contemplating some drastic structural alterations when I found that one of the Twins had discovered the way to utilize this middle-age spread to her advantage. Instead of sleeping lengthwise in the bedroom, as she used to do, she now started to sleep across it, the right way up, with her head pointing towards the door. As soon as the first faint sound or smell of food reached her, she would shoot across the intervening space, before her companion could even get the right way up, and then, when halfway through the door, she would hunch her back and become wedged there as firmly as a cork in a bottle. Then, taking her time, she would reach out a claw, hook the food-pan into position, and proceed to browse dreamily, if not altogether quietly, in the depths, while in the bedroom her frantic relative squealed and snorted and scrabbled ineffectually at the well-corseted and impervious behind.

The hairy armadillo is the vulture of the Argentine pampa. Low-slung, armoured against most forms of attack, he trots through the moonlit grass like a miniature tank, and nearly everything is grist to his mill. He will eat fruit and vegetables, but failing those he is quite happy with a bird's nest containing eggs or young; a light snack of young mice; or even a snake, should he happen to meet one. But what attracts the armadillo, as a magnet attracts steel filings, is a nice juicy rotten carcase. In Argentina, where distances and herds are so great, it often happens that a sick or elderly cow will die, and its body will lie out in the grasslands unnoticed, the sun ripening it until its scent is wafted far and wide, and the humming of flies sounds like a swarm of bees. When this smell reaches the nose of a foraging armadillo it is an invitation to a banquet. Leaving his burrow, he scuttles along until he reaches the delectable feast: the vast, maggot-ridden dish lying in the grass. Then, having filled himself on a mixture of rotten meat and maggots, he cannot bring himself to leave the carcase when there is still so much nourishment left on it, so he proceeds to burrow under it. Here he ponders and sleeps his first course off until the pangs of hunger assail him once again. Then all he has to do is to scramble to the top of his burrow, stick out his head and there he is, so to speak, right in the middle of dinner. An armadillo will very rarely leave a carcase until the last shreds of meat have been stripped from the already bleaching bones. Then, sighing the happy sigh of an animal that is replete, he will return home, to wait hopefully for the next fatality among the cattle or sheep. Yet, despite its depraved tastes, the armadillo is considered excellent eating, the flesh tasting midway between veal and sucking pig. He is frequently caught by the peons on the *estancia* and kept in a barrelful of mud, being fattened up until he is ready for the pot. Now, it may be considered rather disgusting that anyone should eat a creature with such a low taste in carrion, but, on the other hand, pigs have some pretty revolting feeding habits, while the feeding habits of plaice and dabs would, I've no doubt, leave most ghouls feeling queasy.

There was another inhabitant of the pampa, with habits as charming as the armadillos' were revolting, but I was never privileged to meet it. This was the viscacha, a rodent about the size of a cairn terrier, and with the same sort of low-slung body. They have rather rabbit-like faces, decorated with a band of black fur running from the nose along the cheek under the eyes. Beneath this band is another one, in greyish-white, and beneath this again is another black one, so the viscacha gives the impression that he had once decided to disguise himself as a zebra, but had tired of the idea when half-way through the alterations. They live in colonies of up to forty, in vast subterranean warrens known as *vizcacheras*.

Viscachas are the Bohemian artists of the pampa. They are very free and easy in their ways, and their massive underground community warrens are generally filled with an assortment of friends who have moved in. Burrowing owls dig small flatlets in the side of the viscacha's hallway. Snakes sometimes take up residence in the disused portions of the nest – presumably the viscacha's equivalent of the attic. If the viscachas enlarge their residence and several tunnels fall into disuse, a species of swallow immediately moves in. So many a *vizcachera* contains an odder assortment of types than most Bloomsbury boarding-houses. Providing these lodgers behave themselves, the viscachas do not seem to worry in the slightest how crowded the warren gets. The viscachas' artistic inclinations are, I feel sure, more than slightly influenced by surrealism. The area immediately around the mouth of the warren is cleared of every vestige of green stuff, so the front doors of the colony are surrounded by a ballroom-like expanse of earth, packed hard by the passing of many small feet. This bald patch in the middle of the pampa acts as their studio, for it is here that the viscachas arrange their artistic displays. The long, dry, hollow stems of the thistles are piled carefully into heaps, interspersed with stones, twigs and roots. Anything else that catches the viscacha's eye is added to this still-life to make it more attractive. Outside one *vizcachera* I examined the usual pile of twigs, stones and thistle stems which was tastefully intermixed with several oil tin cans, three bits of silver paper, eight scarlet cigarette packets and a cow's horn. Somehow this whimsical display, arranged so carefully and lovingly out in the vast and empty pampa, made me feel a tremendous desire to meet a viscacha on his own ground. I could imagine the portly little animal, with its sad, striped face, squatting in the moonlight at the mouth of its burrow, absorbed in the task of arranging its exhibition of dried plants and other inanimate objects. At one time the viscacha used to be one of the commonest of the pampa animals, but his vegetarian habits and his insistence on clearing large areas of grass for holding his artistic displays got him into trouble with the agriculturists. So the farmers went to war, and the viscacha has been harried and slaughtered and driven away from most of his old haunts.

We never caught a viscacha, nor, as I say, even saw one. It was one member of the Argentine fauna that I most regretted not having met.

Interlude

We had been assured by the air company that once we had got our specimens to Buenos Aires we would be able to send them off to London within twenty-four hours. So, when our lorry reached the outskirts of the capital, I phoned the freight department to tell them we had arrived, and to ask them which was the best place at the airfield in which to house the animals for the night. With exquisite courtesy, they informed me that we would not be able to send the animals off for a week, and that there was nowhere on the airport to keep them. To be stranded in the middle of Buenos Aires with a lorry-load of animals and nowhere to keep them was, to say the least, a trifle disconcerting.

Appreciating our predicament, the kindly lorry driver said that we might leave the animals in the lorry overnight, but that they would have to be removed first thing in the morning, as he had a job. Gratefully we accepted this offer, and, having parked our vehicle in the yard near his house, we set about the job of feeding the animals. Half-way through this operation Jacquie had an idea.

'I know!' she exclaimed triumphantly; 'let's phone the Embassy.'

'You can't phone an Embassy and ask them to put up your animals for a week,' I pointed out. 'Embassies aren't provided for that sort of thing.'

'If you phone Mr Gibbs he might be able to help,' she persisted. 'I think it's worth trying, anyway.'

Reluctantly, and much against my better judgment, I phoned the Embassy.

'Hullo! You back?' said Mr Gibbs jovially. 'Did you have a good time?'

'Yes, we had a wonderful time, thanks.'

'Good. Did you catch much of the local fauna?'

'Well, a fair amount. As a matter of fact that's why I phoned you; I was wondering if you could help us.'

'Certainly. What's the trouble?' asked Mr Gibbs unsuspectingly.

'We want a place to put our animals in for a week.'

There was a short silence at the other end, during which I presumed that

Mr Gibbs was fighting a wild desire to slam down his receiver. But I had under-estimated his self-control, for when he answered, his voice was suave and even, unruffled by the slightest trace of hysteria.

'That's a bit of a problem. You mean you want a garden or something like that?'

'Yes, preferably with a garage. Do you know of one?'

'I don't, off-hand. I'm not often asked to find ... er ... hotel accommodation for livestock, so my experience is limited,' he pointed out. 'However, if you come round and see me in the morning I may have thought of something.'

'Thanks very much,' I said gratefully. 'What time d'you get to the Embassy?'

'Don't come as early as that,' said Mr Gibbs hastily. 'Come round about ten-thirty. It'll give me a chance to contact a few people.'

I went back and related the conversation to Jacquie and Ian.

'Ten-thirty is no good,' said Jacquie. 'The lorry driver's just told us that his first job's at six.'

We sat in gloomy silence for some time, racking our brains.

'I know!' said Jacquie suddenly.

'No,' I said firmly. 'I am *not* going to phone the Ambassador.'

'No, let's phone Bebita.'

'Good Lord, yes! Why didn't we think of it before?'

'She's sure to be able to find a place,' said Jacquie, who seemed to be under the impression that everyone in Buenos Aires was adept at finding accommodation for wild animals at a moment's notice. For the third time I went to the phone. The conversation that ensued was Bebita at her best.

'Hullo, Bebita. How are you?'

'Gerry? Ah, child, I was just talking about you. Where are you?'

'Somewhere in the wilder outskirts of the city, that's all I know.'

'Well, find out where you are and come and have dinner.'

'We'd love to, if we may.'

'B-b-but of course you may.'

'Bebita, I really phoned to ask you if you could help us.'

'Of course, child. What is it?'

'Well, we're stranded here with all our animals. Could you find somewhere for us to put them for a week?'

Bebita chuckled.

'Ahh!' she sighed, in mock resignation, 'what a man! You phone me at this hour to ask for shelter for your animals. Do you never think of anything else b-b-but animals?'

'I know it's an awful hour,' I said contritely, 'but we'll be in a devil of a mess if we don't find somewhere soon.'

'Don't despair, child. I will find somewhere for you. Ring me b-b-back in half an hour.'

'Wonderful!' I said, my spirits rising. 'I'm sorry to worry you with all this, but there's no one else I can ask.'

'Silly, silly, silly,' said Bebita; 'b-b-but naturally you must ask me. Goodbye.'

Half an hour crept by, and then I phoned again.

'Gerry? Well, I have found you a place. A friend of mine will let you keep them in his garden. He has a sort of garage.'

'Bebita, you're marvellous!' I said enthusiastically.

'B-b-but naturally,' she said, chuckling. 'Now, write down the address, take your animals round there, and then come here for dinner.'

In high spirits we rattled through the twilit streets to the address Bebita had given us. Ten minutes later the lorry stopped, and peering out of the back I saw a pair of wrought-iron gates some twenty feet high, and behind them a wide gravel pathway stretched up to a house that looked like an offspring of Windsor Castle. I was just about to inform the lorry driver that he had brought us to the wrong house, when the gates were flung open by a beaming porter, who bowed our dilapidated vehicle in as though it had been a Rolls. Along one side of the house was a sort of covered veranda which, the porter informed us, was where we were to put our things. Feeling slightly dazed, we unloaded the animals. I still had a strong suspicion that it might prove to be the wrong house, but at least the animals were accommodated, so we hurried down the gravel path and out through the wrought-iron gates as quickly as possible, before the owner could turn up and start protesting. At her flat Bebita greeted us, calm, beautiful and looking slightly amused.

'Ah, children, did you arrange your animals comfortably?'

'Yes, they're all fixed up. It's a wonderful place for them. It's very generous of your friend, Bebita.'

'Ahh!' she sighed, 'b-b-but he is like that ... so sweet ... so generous ... and such charm ... ahh! you've no idea what charm that man has.'

'How long did it take you to persuade him?' I asked sceptically.

'B-b-but he offered; I did not persuade,' said Bebita innocently. 'I rang him up and told him that we wanted to put a few small animals in his garden, and he agreed straight away. He is my friend, so naturally he will say yes.'

She smiled at us brilliantly.

'I don't see how he could have refused,' I said; 'but seriously, we're terribly grateful to you. You're rapidly becoming our Fairy Godmother.'

'Silly, silly, silly,' said Bebita. 'Come and have dinner.'

Though we appreciated Bebita's legerdemain in producing a place for our animals, we did not realize quite what an extraordinary piece of magic it was until the following day, when we called on Mr Gibbs.

'I'm sorry,' he said apologetically, as we entered his office. 'I've tried several places, but I haven't had any success.'

'Oh, don't worry about that. A friend of ours found us a place,' I said.

'I am glad,' said Mr Gibbs; 'it must have been very worrying for you. Where have you got them?'

'In a house in Avenida Alvear.'

'*Where?*'

'A house in Avenida Alvear.'

'Avenida Alvear?' asked Mr Gibbs faintly.

'Yes; what's wrong with that?'

'Nothing ... nothing at all,' said Mr Gibbs, staring at us blankly – 'except that Avenida Alvear is to Buenos Aires what Park Lane is to London.'

Some time later, when our captures had eventually gone off by air, we found that we definitely could not go South. The problem was, where to go? Then, one day, Bebita phoned.

'Listen, child,' she commanded. 'Would you like to go to Paraguay for a trip?'

'I should love to go to Paraguay,' I said fervently.

'Well, I think I can arrange it. You will have to fly to Asunción, and then my friend's plane will pick you up there and fly you to this place . . . it is called Puerto Casada.'

'I suppose you arranged all this with one of your friends?'

'B-b-but naturally. With who else would I arrange it, silly?'

'The only snag I can see is our primitive Spanish.'

'I have also thought of that. You remember Rafael?'

'Yes, I remember him.'

'Well, he is on holiday from school, and he would like to go with you as interpreter. His mother thinks that the trip would do him good, on condition that you do not let him catch any snakes.'

'What an extraordinarily intelligent mother. I think the idea's excellent, and I love you and all your friends.'

'Silly, silly, silly,' said Bebita, and rang off.

So it was that Jacquie and I flew up to Asunción, the capital of Paraguay, and with us travelled Rafael de Soto Acebal, bubbling over with such enthusiasm for the whole trip that by the end of the flight he was making me feel like a cynical and jaded old globe-trotter.

Chapter Three

Fields of Flying Flowers

The sky was pale blue and full of morning light when the lorry bumped on to the small airfield outside Asunción. Still half-drugged with sleep, we descended stiffly and unloaded our equipment. Then we stood around, yawning and stretching, while the lorry driver and the pilot disappeared into a dilapidated hangar that stood on the edge of the field. Presently, to the accompaniment of loud grunts of exertion, they reappeared, pushing a small four-seater monoplane tastefully painted in silver and red. As the two men edged it out of the hangar into the sunlight, they looked extraordinarily like a pair of corpulent brown ants manoeuvring an extremely small moth. Rafael had seated himself on a suitcase, his head drooping languidly, his eyes half closed.

'Look, Rafael,' I said cheerfully; 'our aeroplane.'

He jerked upright and looked at the tiny plane being pushed towards us. His eyes widened behind his spectacles.

'No!' he exclaimed incredulously. '*This* our plane?'

'Yes, I'm afraid so.'

'Oh, migosh!'

'What's the matter with it?' inquired Jacquie; 'it's a dear little plane.'

'Yes,' said Rafael, 'that is what the matter . . . it is *little*.'

'It looks strong enough,' I said soothingly, and at that moment one of the wheels went over a small tussock of grass and the whole structure wobbled and twanged melodiously.

'Oh, migosh, no!' came from Rafael, aghast. 'Gerry, *ce n'est pas* possible we fly in this . . . she is too small . . .'

'It's quite all right, Rafael, really,' said Jacquie, with the cheerful optimism of one who had never travelled in a small plane; 'this kind is very good.'

'Sure?' asked our friend, his spectacles glittering anxiously.

'Yes, quite sure . . . they use this kind a lot in America.'

'Yes, but, Jacquie, America is not this Chaco. . . . See, she has only one wing, *n'est-ce pas*? That wing break, we go . . . brr . . . bang . . . into the forest,' and he sat back and surveyed us like a dejected owl.

Meanwhile the plane had been wheeled into position, and the pilot approached us, his gold teeth flashing in a smile.

'*Bueno, vamos*,' he said, and started to pick up the luggage.

Rafael got to his feet and picked up his suitcase.

'Gerry, I no like this,' he said plaintively, as he started towards our aerial transport.

When all our equipment was loaded, we found there was very little room left for us, but we managed to squeeze in, I and the pilot in the front, Rafael and Jacquie behind. I climbed in last and slammed the incredibly fragile-looking door, and it immediately flew open again. The pilot leaned across me and glared at the door.

'*No bueno*,' he explained, grabbing it with one powerful hand and slamming it so hard that the whole plane rocked.

'Oh, migosh!' came from Rafael faintly.

The pilot fiddled with the controls, whistling merrily between his teeth, the engine roared, and the plane began to shudder and vibrate. Then we lurched forward, the plane bouncing over the uneven ground, the green grass became a blur and we were airborne. As we circled round, we could see the countryside below, rich tropical green, with the red-earth roads running like veins across it. We flew over Asunción, its pink houses gleaming in the sunlight, and then, in front of the blunt nose and the glittering circle of propeller, I could see the River Paraguay ahead.

Flying at that height, we could see that the river formed a fiery, flickering barrier between two types of country: below us was the rich red earth, the green forests and farmlands that surrounded Asunción and made up the eastern half of Paraguay; across the sprawling river lay the Chaco, a vast level plain stretching away to the horizon. Slightly blurred by the morning mist, this plain seemed to be covered with silver-bronze grass, marked here and there with vivid green patches of undergrowth. It looked as though a pair of shears had been taken to it and it had been clipped like the flank of an enormous poodle, leaving the green patches of wool decorating the tawny skin of grass. It was a curious, lifeless landscape, the only moving thing being the river, which glittered and twinkled as it moved over the plain, split now into three or four channels, now into fifty or sixty, each coiling and interweaving in an intricate pattern like the shining viscera of some monstrous silver dragon disembowelled across the plain.

When we crossed the river and flew lower, I could see that what I had first thought to be a dry plain of grass was in reality marshland, for now and then the water gleamed, as the sun's reflection caught it. The poodle wool turned out to be thorn-scrub, tightly packed, with occasional palm trees bursting up through it. In places the palms grew in serried ranks, almost as if planted: green feather dusters stuck in the bronze grass. Everywhere you could see the sudden, brilliant sparkle of water: an explosion of white light as the sun caught it; yet everywhere the undergrowth looked dusty and parched, its roots in water, but its leaves withered by the sun. It was weird, desolate, but strangely fascinating country. After a while, though, the landscape became monotonous, for there were no shadows except those of the shock-headed palms.

From somewhere under his seat the pilot produced a bottle, uncorked it with the aid of his teeth and handed it to me. It was iced coffee, bitter but refreshing. I drank, handed it to Jacquie and Rafael and returned the remains to the pilot. As he stuck the neck of the bottle between his teeth and tipped back his head to drink, the nose of the plane dipped sickeningly towards the silver curve of the river, two thousand feet below. Having drunk, he wiped his mouth with the back of his hand, and then leant over and shouted in my ear:

'Puerto Casado,' and pointed ahead.

Dimly through the heat-haze I could see that we were flying towards the black shape of a hill that had appeared suddenly and surprisingly in the flatness below.

'*Una hora, más o menos*,' yelled the pilot, pointing and holding up one finger – '*una hora* . . . Puerto Casado . . . *comprende?*'

For an hour I dozed intermittently, while the dark bulk of the hill grew closer and closer. The nose of the plane dipped as we glided down towards the earth, and the warm upward currents of air caught the tiny machine and shook and buffeted it until it swayed and dipped drunkenly like a flake of wood-ash over a bonfire. Then we banked sharply, and for one miraculous second the Chaco tilted up like a wall, the river hung over one wing and the horizon appeared above us. We straightened out and dropped steadily down to a strip of grassfield which would have been indistinguishable from any other part of the scenery if it had not been for a yellow wind-sock hanging limply on a pole. We bumped on to the grass and taxied to a standstill. The pilot grinned at me, switched off the engine and waved his hand in an all-embracing gesture.

'Chaco!' he explained.

As we opened the door of the plane and got out, the heat hit us with an almost physical blow, and it felt as though the air had suddenly been sucked out of our lungs. The golden grass underfoot was as crisp and dry as wood shavings, patched here and there with clumps of yellow and flame-coloured flowers. We had just got the last of the equipment out of the plane when a lorry appeared in the distance, bumping over the grass towards us. It was driven by a short, fat Paraguayan with a twinkling smile, who seemed vastly amused at our arrival. He helped us pile the stuff into the back of the truck, and then we jolted off across the air-strip and along a dusty, deeply rutted road through the forest. There was so much dust from our progress, and we were so busily engaged in holding on to the bucking sides of the vehicle, that I did not have a chance to see much of the passing countryside, and within ten minutes we roared into the village of Casado. It was the usual conglomeration of tumble-down shacks, separated by earth roads worn into furrows. We swept past a large mango tree which was obviously the centre of the village, for everyone seemed to be congregated in its shade, either sleeping, gossiping or bargaining for the odd assortment of pumpkins, sugar-cane, eggs, bananas and other produce lying there in the dust.

The little house in which we were to live was at one end of the village, and it was half hidden behind a screen of grapefruit and orange trees and shaggy bushes of hibiscus splashed with enormous scarlet flowers. The house and its cloak of foliage was surrounded by a network of narrow, shallow irrigation ditches, half choked with grass and water-plants. Round these a choir of mosquitoes hummed melodiously, and they were joined at night by a great variety of tree-frogs, toads and cicadas. The tree-frogs would pipe and trill excitedly, the toads would belch in a ponderous and thoughtful sort of manner and the cicadas would produce at intervals a sound like that of a soprano electric saw cutting through a sheet of tin. The house was adequate, without being luxurious. It consisted of three rooms, all inter-communicating in the Spanish fashion, and all of which leaked. Some distance away was the kitchen and the bathroom connected to the house by a covered way. Ten minutes after our arrival I discovered we were expected to share our bathroom with quite a varied assortment of the local fauna: there were several hundred mosquitoes in there, together with a number of large, glittering and agile cockroaches and several depressed-looking spiders that occupied the floor. The lavatory cistern had been taken over by some wide-eyed and anaemic-looking tree-frogs and a small vampire bat, which hung there chittering ferociously, and looking, as all bats do, rather like an umbrella that has seen better days.

It was rather unfortunate that I should have kept these zoological discoveries to myself, for Jacquie was the next one to enter the bathroom, and she reappeared at startling speed leaving a trail of soap, towels and tooth-brushes behind her. Apparently, when she had entered, the bat had decided he was getting a bit bored with these constant interruptions, and he had swooped down from the cistern and hung, fluttering, in front of her face. She pointed out, rather acidly, that she had not hitherto considered bats essential to clean living. Eventually I managed to persuade her that the creature was harmless, in spite of his anti-social attitude; but afterwards, whenever she used the bathroom, she kept a very wary eye on the bat as he hung aloft, regarding her with an inimical stare.

We had just finished unpacking our things when we were greeted by another member of the local fauna, in the shape of our housekeeper, a dark-skinned, dark-eyed Paraguayan woman, whose name, she assured us, was Paula. At one time she must have been a handsome woman, but now she had run slightly to seed. Her body bulged in all directions, but, even so, she still possessed an extraordinary grace and lightness of movement. She would drift through the house like a chocolate cumulus-cloud on its way to a storm, humming some lovesong to herself, her eyes misty, indulging in her own peculiar brand of dusting, which consisted of sweeping everything off tables and chairs on to the floor, and then bending down with great grunts of exertion to pick up the remains. It was not long before we discovered that Paula occupied a high and honoured position in the local community: she was nothing less than the local Madam, and she had all the young unmarried females of the village in her care. As their manager, trainer and protector she took her job seriously. Once a fortnight, when the river-steamer arrived, she would take her girls down to the river-bank and keep a motherly eye on them while they argued and bargained with the steamer's crew and passengers. The steamer always hooted when it was about three-quarters of a mile down the river, to give warning of its arrival, and this was Paula's signal to rush into her hut and dress. She would force her enormous breasts into a minute brassière, leaving out those portions which it could not accommodate, clad herself in a dress, the design of which was almost as startling as its colour scheme, push her feet into shoes with six-inch heels, pour about a cupful of asphyxiating scent over the ensemble and then set off down the road to the jetty, driving a chattering and giggling selection of her wares before her. She looked rather like an amiable and elderly schoolmistress, as she herded them along in this untidy, shrill crocodile. Owing to the importance of Paula's position, she had everyone, including the local constabulary, eating out of her hand. No task was too difficult for her. Ask her for something – whether it was some smuggled Brazilian cigarettes or a bowl of delicious *Dulce de Leche* – and she would immediately marshal her girls and set them to scour the village for it. Woe betide the man who refused to help Paula. His position in the village (biologically speaking) became impossible. She was definitely an ally worth having, as we soon found out.

Although I was eager to get out and see something of the country, I had to restrain my impatience. The rest of the day was spent in unpacking and checking our equipment and getting the house more or less organized. Rafael, at my instigation, questioned Paula about methods of getting into the interior. She said there were three ways of doing this: on horseback, by ox-cart or on an *autovía*. Further questioning revealed the fact that the *autovía* was the form of transport which we came to call the Chaco railway, although the term railway was really a euphemism. It consisted of very narrow-gauge rails, on which were mounted dilapidated Ford 8s. This railway went some two hundred kilometres into the Chaco, and so from our point of view seemed a godsend. Paula said that if we went through the village to the line, we would find the *autovías* parked there, and a driver was sure to be around who could tell us when the next one was due to leave. So Rafael and I trotted off to investigate the possibilities of the Chaco railway.

Sure enough, on the other side of the village we came on the line, though it took a bit of finding, for it was so overgrown with weeds it was almost indistinguishable from the surrounding terrain. The line itself was so fantastic that I could only stare at it in mute, horror-stricken silence. It was approximately two and a half feet wide, each rail worn down and glossy with use, so buckled that they looked like a couple of silver snakes wriggling away through the grass. How any vehicle managed to stay on them was more than I would understand. Later, when I discovered the speed at which the *autovías* were driven along these lines, it seemed to me a miracle that we managed to survive our trips on them at all.

Some distance away we discovered a siding in which were parked several battered and inscrutable *autovías*, and under a tree nearby we found an equally battered and inscrutable driver, asleep in the long grass. On being awoken, he admitted that there was an *autovía* travelling some twenty kilometres up the line on the following morning, and, if we wished, we could travel in it. Endeavouring to forget the buckled lines, I said that this was what we would do; it would give us some sort of picture of the country, and we could find out what kind of bird-life was the commonest. We thanked the driver, who mumbled, '*Nada, nada* . . . it's nothing,' before falling back and dropping into a deep sleep again. Rafael and I went back to the house and told Jacquie the good news, carefully omitting any reference to the state of the railway.

The next morning, just before dawn, we were awakened by Paula, who undulated into the room, carrying tea, and beamed at us with grisly cheerfulness that some people seem to reserve for the very early morning. She waddled into Rafael's room, and we heard him groan unintelligible replies to her sprightly questions. Outside, it was still dark, but the whine of the cicadas was punctuated by an occasional sleepy cockcrow. Rafael appeared, clad in a pair of underpants and his glasses.

'That woman,' he complained; 'she so glad when she wake me . . . I no like.'

'It's good for you to get up early,' I said; 'you spend half your life in a somnambulistic condition, like a hibernating bear.'

'Early morning rising makes you fit,' said Jacquie unctuously, stifling a yawn.

'Are you coming like that?' I asked our puzzled interpreter, 'or are you going to put some clothes on?'

Rafael's brow was furrowed as he tried to work out these remarks.

'I should come like that,' I continued facetiously; 'it's a very fetching outfit . . . and if you leave your glasses behind, you won't be able to see the mosquitoes.'

'I no understand, Gerry,' said Rafael at length. His English was not at its best in the early morning.

'Never mind. Get some clothes on . . . the *autovía* won't wait, you know.'

Half an hour later we clattered down the line in the *autovía*, through the banks of river-mist, opalescent in the early morning light. As we left the outskirts of the village, and the last village dog dropped panting behind, the sun rose with sudden brilliance from behind the trees and washed all the colour from the rim of the eastern horizon, and we rocked and swayed along the line, deeper and deeper into the Chaco forests.

The trees were not tall, but they grew so closely together that their branches interlinked; beneath them the ground was waterlogged and overgrown with a profusion of plants, thorny bushes and, incredibly enough, cacti. There were cacti that looked like a series of green plates stuck together by their edges, and covered with bunches of yellow spikes and pale mauve flowers; others were like octopuses, their long arms spread out across the ground, or curling round the tree-trunks in a spiky embrace; others again looked like plump green busbies covered with a haze of black spines. Some of these cacti were growing and flowering with their fleshy bodies half covered in water. In between the *autovia* lines there grew a small plant in great profusion; it was only a few inches high, and topped with a delicate cup-shaped flower of magenta red. So thickly had it spread in places along the track that I had the impression of travelling along an endless flower-bed.

Occasionally the forest would be broken by a great grass-field, studded with tall, flame-coloured flowers that covered several acres, and neatly bisected by rows of palms, their curving fronds making them look like green rockets bursting against the sky. These grass-fields were sprinkled with dozens of widow tyrants – birds about the size of a sparrow but with jet-black upper parts and their breasts and throats as white as ermine. They perched on convenient sticks and dead trees, and now and again one would flip off, catch a passing insect and return to its perch, its breast gleaming and twinkling against the grass like a shooting star. They were known locally as *flor blanca* – the white flower – a beautiful name for them. Here, then, was a whole field of flying flowers, fluttering and swooping, their breasts shining with the pure whiteness of the sun's reflection on water.

Probably the most astonishing tree in this landscape was one with a trunk which bulged out suddenly at the base, making it look like a wine-jar; it had short, twisted branches decorated half-heartedly with small pale-green leaves. These trees stood around in small groups, looking as though they had sucked up so much from the ground that their trunks had swollen in obesity.

'What are those trees called, Rafael?' I called above the clatter of the *autovia's* wheels.

'*Palo borracho*,' he answered; 'you see how they are, Gerry – very fat, no? They say they have drunk too much, so they call them the stick that is drunk.'

'The drunken stick . . . that's a lovely name for them. Most appropriate place for them to live, too . . . the whole forest looks drunken.'

And, indeed, the whole landscape did look as though nature had organized an enormous bottle party, inviting the weird mixture of temperate, sub-tropical and tropical plants to it. Everywhere the palms leaned tiredly, the professional bar loungers with their too long heads of hair; the thorn-bushes grappled in an inebriated brawl; the well-dressed flowers and the unshaven cacti side by side; and everywhere, the *palo borrachos* stood with their bulging, beer-drinkers' stomachs, tilted at unbalanced angles; and everywhere among this floral throng hurried the widow tyrants, like small, slick waiters with incredibly immaculate shirt-fronts.

One of the disadvantages of this countryside was made very apparent when we rounded a bend and saw before us a beautiful stretch of marsh, ringed with palms, in which were feeding four enormous jabiru storks. They moved through the grassy areas and the lanes of bright water with a slow and stately step, reminding me irresistibly of a procession I had once seen of negro preachers in white surplices. Their bodies were spotless white, and the heads and beaks, sunk meditatively into the hunched shoulders, were coal black; they moved slowly and thoughtfully through the water, pausing occasionally to stand on one leg and shrug their wings gently. Wanting to watch them for a few minutes, I called out to the driver to stop, and he, looking rather surprised, brought the *autovía* to a screeching halt on the line, some fifty feet away from the storks, who took not the slightest notice. I had just settled comfortably back on the wooden seat and reached for the binoculars when a zebra-striped mosquito of incredible dimensions rose from the marsh, zoomed into the *autovía* and settled on my arm. I swatted him carelessly, and raised the binoculars to my eyes, only to lower them almost immediately to swat at my legs, on which another four mosquitoes had materialized. Looking about, I saw to my horror that what I had taken to be a slight mist drifting over the grass was in reality a cloud of these insects which was descending on the *autovía* with shrill whines of excitement. Within seconds, the cloud had enveloped us: mosquitoes clung to our faces, necks and arms, and even settled on our trouser legs and proceeded to bite right through the cloth with undiminished ability. Slapping and cursing, I told the driver to start up, for bird-watching under those conditions was impossible, however enthusiastic one might be. As the *autovía* rattled off, most of the mosquitoes were left behind, but a few of the tougher ones managed to keep up with us for half a mile or so down the track. Being attacked every time you stopped rather detracted from the ride, for it was really quite impossible to halt in a place for more than ten minutes at a time without being driven nearly mad by the mosquitoes. This made any hunting, and particularly filming, a painful and irritating job; when fiddling about with lens and exposure meters I found it essential to have someone stand over me with a hat, to keep at least some of the insects at bay, otherwise it was impossible to concentrate and my temper frayed rapidly. By the time we had reached Puerto Casado again that afternoon I had exposed about twenty feet of film, and all three of us were scarlet and swollen with bites. But that first ride, however unpleasant, had given me some idea of the type of country we had to operate in, and the snags that were likely to be encountered. Now we had to settle down to the real job of extracting the fauna from the mosquito-infested depths of the Drunken Forests.

Chapter Four

The Orange Armadillos

The first specimen caught by the local inhabitants of Puerto Casado turned up at our house forty-eight hours after our arrival. I was awakened at some dark and deadly hour in the morning, when the cicadas and tree-frogs were vying with the local cockerels for vocal supremacy, by a scream so loud and indignant that it completely drowned all other sounds. I sat bolt upright in bed and stared at Jacquie, who peered back at me, equally astonished. Before we had time to speak there came another ear-splitting cry, which I placed this time as emanating from the kitchen; it was followed by a shrill and incomprehensible burst of Guarani.

'Good heavens!' said Jacquie; 'that sounds like Paula ... whatever *is* happening out there?'

I crawled out of bed and felt for my slippers.

'It sounds as though she's being raped,' I said.

'It can't be that,' said my wife sleepily; 'she wouldn't scream about *that*.'

I eyed her disapprovingly and made my way out on to the mist-shrouded back-veranda. I was just in time to witness an extraordinary scene in the kitchen. The door stood wide open, and framed against the rosy glow of the fire stood our housekeeper, arms akimbo, her magnificent chest heaving with the effort of having produced that flood of Guarani. In front of her stood a short, thin little Indian, clad in tattered vest and pants, clutching in one hand a very battered straw hat, and in the other what appeared to be a football. As I watched, he spoke softly and soothingly to Paula, and then held out his hand with the football in it; Paula recoiled, and let out another scream of indignation so powerful that a large toad, who had been sitting near the kitchen door, leapt wildly into the dark safety of the hibiscus bushes. The Indian, who was made of sterner stuff, put his straw hat on the floor, placed the football in it, and proceeded to wave his arms and chatter; Paula drew a deep breath and started to wither him with a blast of invective. Two people, at five o'clock in the morning, preparing to shout each other down in the series of catarrhal honks which constitute the Guarani language, was more than I could stand.

'Oi!' I yelled loudly, *'buenos días.'*

The effect was immediate. The Indian scooped up his hat containing the football, and, clutching it to his gaping shirt-front, bowed and backed into the shadows. Paula hitched up her bosom, gave a minute but graceful curtsy, and then drifted towards me, quivering with emotion. *'Ah, señor,'* she said, panting a little and clasping her hands together fervently. *'Ah, señor, qué hombre ... buenos días, señor, ... yo lo siento ... '*

I frowned at her, and broke into my most fluent Spanish.

'Hombre,' I said, pointing at the Indian, who was giving a wonderful display of adaptive coloration in the shadows, *'hombre ... por qué usted argumentos?'*

Paula rushed into the shadows and dragged the unwilling Indian out. She pushed him in front of me, where he stood with hanging head, and then stood back and with a magnificent gesture pointed a fat brown finger at him.

'Hombre,' she said, her voice vibrating with passion, *'mal hombre.'*

'Why?' I asked. I was rather sorry for the Indian.

Paula gazed at me as though I was mad.

'Por qué,' she repeated. *'Por qué?'*

'Por qué,' I nodded, beginning to feel like something out of a Gilbert and Sullivan chorus.

'Mire, señor,' she said, 'look!' and she seized the hat that the Indian had crushed to his breast and displayed the football nestling inside. Now it was at close quarters, but in the shadow, I could see that the offending object was smaller than a football, but much the same shape. We all three gazed at it in silence for a minute; then Paula refilled her lungs and paralysed me

with a machine-gun fire of rapid Spanish, the only word of which I could understand was the oft-repeated one of *hombre*. I began to feel in need of some assistance.

'*Momento!*' I said, holding up my hand, and then I turned and stalked back into the house.

'What on earth's going on out there?' asked Jacquie, as I reappeared.

'I haven't the faintest idea. Paula seems to be mortally wounded by the fact that an Indian is trying to sell her a plum pudding.'

'A plum pudding?'

'Well, a plum pudding or a football. It looks like a hybrid of the two. I'm just going to get Rafael to find out what it's all about.'

'It can't be a plum pudding.'

'Aha!' I said, 'this is the Chaco . . . anything can happen in the Chaco.'

In Rafael's room I found him, as usual, curled into a tight knot underneath a pile of bed-clothes, vibrating gently with snores. I stripped the clothes off him and slapped his rump. He groaned loudly. I slapped him again, and he sat up and peered at me, his mouth drooping open.

'Rafael, wake up. I want you to come and translate.'

'Oh, no, Gerry, not now,' he wailed, peering myopically at his watch. 'Look, she is only five-thirty . . . I cannot.'

'Come on,' I said relentlessly, 'out of bed. You're supposed to be the translator of this party.'

Rafael put on his glasses and glared at me with tousled dignity.

'I am translate, yes,' he said, 'but I am not translate at five in the morning.'

'Look, stop talking and get some clothes on. Paula's got an Indian out there and they're arguing over something that looks like a football. . . . I can't understand what it's all about, so you've got to come out and translate.'

'How I love this Chaco,' said Rafael bitterly, as he pulled on his shoes and followed me, groaning and yawning, to the kitchen. Paula and the Indian were still standing there, and the football still reposed in the Indian's hat.

'*Buenos días*,' said Rafael, blinking sleepily at them, '*qué pasa?*'

Paula's bosom swelled, as she proceeded to tell the whole story to Rafael, dancing about the veranda in a wonderful, flesh-undulating pantomime, breaking off now and then to point at the silent culprit with his plum pudding. Eventually she came to a breathless halt, and leaned exhausted against the wall, holding a fat hand to her heaving torso.

'Well?' I asked Rafael, who was looking bewildered, 'what's it all about?'

Rafael scratched his head.

'I no understand very well, Gerry,' he said. 'She say this man bring a bad thing . . . er . . . how you say? a dirty thing, no? Then he tell her lie and say you buy this.'

'Well, what is the blasted thing, for Heaven's sake?'

Rafael rapped a question at the plum-pudding owner, who looked up and smiled shyly.

'*Bicho*,' said the Indian, holding out the hat.

Now, the first and, to my mind, most important word I had learned on arriving in South America was '*bicho*'. It meant, literally, an animal. Any and every living creature was classified under this all-embracing term, and so it was naturally one of the first that I had committed to memory. So, hearing the Indian use the magic word, I suddenly realized that what I had mistaken for a plum pudding was a living creature. With a cry of delight I pushed past Rafael and pulled the straw hat from the little Indian's grasp and rushed into the kitchen, so that I could see its contents by the light of the oil lamp. Inside the hat, curled into a tight ball, lay a creature I had long wanted to meet. It was a three-banded armadillo.

'Rafael,' I called excitedly, 'just come and look at this.'

He came into the kitchen and stared at the creature in my cupped hands.

'What it is, Gerry?' he asked curiously.

'It's an armadillo ... you know, a *peludo*, the small kind that rolls into a ball ... I showed you pictures of it.'

'Ah, yes,' said Rafael, light dawning, 'here she is called the *tatu naranja*.'

'What does *naranja* mean?' I asked curiously.

'*Naranja* mean orange, Gerry – you know, the fruit.'

'Oh, yes, of course. It does look rather like a big orange rolled up.'

'You want this?' Rafael inquired, prodding it with a cautious finger.

'Good Lord, yes; I want lots of them. Look, Rafael, ask him where he caught it, how much he wants for it, and can he get me some more.'

Rafael turned to the Indian, who was standing beaming in the doorway, and asked him.

The little man nodded his head vigorously, and then broke into halting Spanish.

Rafael listened and then turned to me.

'He say he can get you plenty, Gerry. *Il y a* plenty in the forest. He want to know how many you want.'

'Well, I want at least six. ... But what price does he want?'

For ten minutes Rafael and the Indian bargained, and then Rafael turned to me.

'It is a good for five *guaraní*?' he asked.

'Yes, that's a reasonable price. I'll pay him that. Look, Rafael, ask him if he can show me the place where these things live, will you?'

Again Rafael and the Indian conferred.

'Yes, he say he can show you ... but it is in the forest, Gerry. ... We must go on horse, you know.'

'Fine,' I said delightedly. 'Tell him to come back this afternoon and we'll go out and look for some.'

Rafael relayed my suggestion, and the Indian nodded his head and gave me a wide, friendly smile.

'*Bueno ... muy bueno*,' I said, smiling at him; 'now I'll go and get his money.'

As I sped away into the house, the armadillo still lovingly clasped in my hands, I heard Paula give a despairing yelp of horror, but I was in no mood to consider her outraged feelings. I found Jacquie still sitting up in bed, moodily contemplating the mosquito bites on her arms.

'Look what I've got,' I said gleefully, and rolled the creature on to her bed.

In my delight at receiving such an unusual specimen I had forgotten that my wife was, as yet, not quite used to the delights of collecting. She emerged from her cocoon of bed-clothes and landed on the opposite side of the room with a leap that any ballerina might have envied. From this safe vantage point she glared at my offering.

'What is it?' she inquired.

'Good Lord, darling, what are you leaping about like that for? It's an armadillo . . . it's perfectly harmless.'

'And how was I supposed to know?' she inquired; 'you rush in here and hurl the thing at me like that. And do you mind taking it off my bed?'

'But it won't hurt you,' I explained. 'It's quite harmless, honestly.'

'Yes, I'm sure it is, darling, but I don't want to romp about in bed with it at five in the morning. Why can't you put it on your bed?'

I placed the offending animal tenderly on my bed, and then went out to pay the Indian. Rafael and I returned to the house to find Jacquie sitting in her bed, wearing a martyred expression. I glanced at my bed, and to my horror, saw that the armadillo had disappeared.

'Don't worry,' said Jacquie sweetly; 'the dear little thing's only buried itself.'

I dug down among the bed-clothes and felt the armadillo scrabbling frantically in a tangle of sheets. I hauled him out, and he immediately rolled into a tight ball again. Sitting down on the bed, I examined him. Rolled up, he was about the size and shape of a small melon; on one side of the ball were the three bands from which he got his name, horny strips which were separated from each other by a thin line of pinkish-grey skin that acted as a hinge; on the other side of the ball you could see how his head and tail fitted into the general scheme of armour-plating. Both these extremities were guarded on top by a section of armour-plate, very gnarled and carunculated, shaped like an acute isosceles triangle. When the head and tail were folded into the ball, these two pieces of armour lay side by side, base to point, together forming a broad triangle which effectively blocked the vulnerable entrance that led to the armadillo's soft undersides. Seen in the light, this armour-plating was a pale amber colour, and appeared as though it had been constructed from a delicate mosaic work. When I had pointed out to my audience the marvels of the creature's external anatomy, I put him on the floor, and we sat in silence, waiting for him to unroll. For some minutes the ball lay immobile; then it started to twitch and jerk slightly. I saw a crack appear between the triangle of head and tail and, as it widened, a small pig-like snout was pushed out. Then, with speed and vigour, the armadillo proceeded to unroll himself. He just split open like some weird bud unfolding, and we had a quick glimpse of a pink, wrinkled tummy covered with dirty white hair, small pink legs, and a sad little face like a miniature pig's, with circular protuberant black eyes. Then he rolled over again and righted himself, and all that was visible beneath the shell were the tips of his feet and a few wisps of hair. From the back of his humped shell his tail protruded like one of those ancient war-clubs, covered with spikes and lumps. At the other end his head stuck out, decorated with its triangular cap of knobbed plating, on either side of which had blossomed two tiny, mule-like ears. Beneath this cap of horn I could see the bare cheeks, pink nose and the small, suspicious eyes gleaming like drops of tar. His hind-feet were circular, with short blunt nails, and looked rather like the feet of a miniature rhinoceros. His forefeet were so completely different that they might have belonged to another species of animal: they were armed with three curved nails, the centre one of which was the largest, and resembled the curving talon of some bird of prey. The weight of his hindquarters rested on his flat hind-feet, but that of his fore-quarters rested on this large nail, so the sole of the foot was raised off the ground, making it seem as though he were standing on tip-toe.

For a moment or so he stood motionless, his nose and ears twitching nervously; then he decided to move. His little legs leapt into motion, moving so fast that they were only a blur beneath his shell, and his claws hit the cement with a steady clickity-clickity-click sound. The complete absence of body movement, combined with the rhythmic clicking of his nails, made him appear more like some weird clockwork toy than an animal, a resemblance which was even more marked when he ran straight into the wall, which he apparently had not noticed. Our burst of laughter made him pause for a moment and hunch himself defensively, in readiness to roll up; then, when we were silent again, he sniffed at the wall and spent a fruitless five minutes scrabbling at it with his claws in an effort to dig his way through. Finding this an impossibility, he swung round and clickity-clicked his way busily across the room disappearing beneath my bed.

'He looks just like a gigantic wood-louse,' whispered Jacquie.

'I like this *bicho*, Gerry,' said Rafael, in a stage whisper, beaming through his spectacles; 'he walks just like a tank, no?'

The armadillo, having clicked about under my bed for some time, suddenly reappeared and scuttled off in the direction of the door. It was unfortunate that Paula chose that precise moment to waft massively into the room, bearing a tray on which was our morning tea. Her entrance, with bare feet, was silent, and so the armadillo (whose sight apparently left much to be desired) was unaware of her presence. Paula, her vision of the floor impeded by a combination of bosom and tray, paused in the doorway to beam at us.

'*Buenos días*,' she said to Jacquie, '*el té, señora.*'

The armadillo bustled up to Paula's feet, stopped and sniffed at this new obstacle, and then decided, since it appeared to be soft, that he would dig his way through. Before any of us could do anything, he stuck an experimental claw into Paula's big toe.

'*Madre de Dios!*' screamed Paula, surpassing in that short exclamation all her previous vocal efforts of the morning.

She sprang backwards through the door, miraculously keeping hold of the tray, but as she disappeared into the darkened living-room the tray tilted and a jug crashed to the floor, spreading a great pool of milk in front of the animal. He sniffed at it suspiciously, sneezed, sniffed again, and then started to lap it up quickly. Rafael and I, weak with laughter, hurried into the living-room to soothe our palpitating housekeeper and relieve her of the tray. When I carried the tray into the bedroom I found that the armadillo, uneasy at the noise, had pattered off and sought refuge behind a pile of suitcases. Some idea of his strength may be gathered from the fact that the pile of cases was filled with film, batteries and other equipment, and they were so heavy that it took me all my time to lift one of them. Yet the little creature, having decided that sanctuary lay behind them, stuck his nose into the crack between the cases and the wall and proceeded to push them to one side as easily as though they had been cardboard boxes. He disappeared from view, scrabbling wildly, and then lay still. I decided to leave him there until we had finished tea. Rafael reappeared, mopping his spectacles and tittering.

'That woman,' he said, 'she makes much noise.'

'Is she bringing some more milk?'

'Yes, I tell her. You know, Gerry, she not understand why you want *bichos*. No one tell her we come here for *bichos*.'

'Well, did you explain?'

'Oh, yes, I tell her that we come to the Chaco special for *bichos* for *zoológicos*.'

'And what did she say to that?'

'She said that all gringos were mad and hoped God would protect her,' said Rafael, grinning.

After breakfast, served by a still-trembling Paula, we set to work and made a cage for the armadillo, optimistically making it big enough to contain several others, should we be lucky enough to get them. Then I went and dug the little beast from his sanctuary behind the suitcases; it was quite a job, for he was wedged between the cases and the wall as snugly as a nail in wood. As soon as I had extracted him, he half rolled himself, and uttered a few faint hissing sounds; each time I touched his nose or tail he would hunch himself and give a tiny irritable snort. I yelled for Jacquie to bring the recording machine, and when it was placed in position, and the microphone was hovering only a few inches from the animal, I touched him gently on the nose. He promptly and silently rolled himself into a tight ball and lay there immobile; no amount of cajoling, tapping or scratching would induce him to repeat the sound. Eventually, in disgust, we pushed him into his cage and left him to his own devices; it was not until the next day that we managed to record his Lilliputian snorts of annoyance.

That afternoon the Indian reappeared, leading three depressed-looking horses, and, arming ourselves with bags, string and other impedimenta of the collector, we set out on the hunt for more orange armadillos. We rode through the village, and for some two miles followed a track that ran alongside the railway line; then our guide's horse plunged down the side of the embankment, and made its way along a narrow, twisting path through the dense, thorny scrub and sprawling cacti. A humming-bird, glittering green-gold through a misty blur of wings, hung feeding from a white convolvulus flower some three feet above my head; I reached up my hand as we passed beneath it, there was a sudden purring sound and the bird vanished, leaving the trumpet-shaped flower dipping in the breeze caused by its wings. The heat at this hour of the afternoon was intense: a dry, prickly sort of heat that seemed to suck the moisture out of you; even under the broad brim of my hat I had to screw up my eyes against the ferocious glare. All around, the cicadas sun-worshipped with such a penetrating shrillness that it seemed as though the noise did not come from outside, but was manufactured in the echoing recesses of your own skull.

Presently the dense, thorny growth ended abruptly, and we rode out into a great grass-field decorated with row after row of enormous palms, shock-headed and still in the sun, the shadows of their trunks tiger-striping the golden grass. A pair of black-faced ibis, with neat black moustaches and cinnamon, grey-and-black bodies, paced through the grass, probing the water-filled earth below with their long, sickle-shaped beaks. When they saw us, they flapped up between the palm trunks, crying 'Cronk ... cronk ... arcronk' in deep, harsh voices. Half-way across the grass-field we found that it was divided in two by a wide, meandering strip of wonderful misty blue flowers which stretched away in either direction like a stream; as we got close to it I discovered that it was really a stream, but a stream so thickly overgrown with these blue water-plants that the water was invisible. There was the haze of blue flowers and, underneath, the glint of glossy green leaves growing interlocked. The blue was so clear and delicate that it looked as though a tattered piece of the sky had floated down and settled between the ranks of brown palm-trunks. We took our horses across the river, and their hooves crushed the plants and flowers and left a narrow lane of glittering water. Black-and-scarlet dragon-flies droned smoothly around us, their transparent wings winking in the sun. When we reached the other side and entered the shade of the palm-forest again, I turned in my saddle and looked back at the magnificent lane of blue flowers, across which was marked our path in a stripe of flickering water, like a lightning flash across a summer sky.

We passed through the hot shadow of the palms and re-entered the thorny scrub, startling a solitary toucan. With its monstrous marigold-yellow beak, the blue patch round the eye and the neat black plumage and white shirt-front, it looked like a clown who, having put on a dress-suit, has forgotten to remove his make-up. It watched our approach, turning its head from side to side, uttering soft wheezing and churring noises, reminding me of an ancient, unoiled clock about to strike. One of the horses gave a loud snort, the toucan took fright and, clicking its great beak and giving strange yelping cries of alarm, it dived into the tangle of branches.

Gradually the thorn scrub became less and less thick, and soon it was broken up into clumps and patches, interspersed with areas of whitish, sandy soil, dotted with clumps of grass and cacti. The grass was bleached almost white by the sun, and the soil had a hard crust baked over it, through which the horses' hooves broke with a soft scrunch. Only the cacti were green in that area of sun-white grass and sand, for they, with the curious alchemy of their family, could capture the dews and infrequent rain, store it in the flesh of their prickly limbs and live on it, as a hibernating animal lives in the winter off the autumn's accumulated layer of fat. This region was not flooded and soggy as the other parts of the country had been, for it was raised a few inches above the surrounding area; the contour was almost imperceptible, but sufficient to make it a dry island in the swampy lands around. Any piece of land that raised itself six inches above the surrounding territory could almost be classified as a mountain in the vast uniform flatness of the Chaco. Rafael and our guide had a rapid conversation, and then Rafael pushed his horse alongside mine.

'Here we find the *tatu*, Gerry,' he explained, his eyes gleaming through his spectacles in anticipation; 'we no ride close together, eh? We make a line, no? When you see the *tatu*, make your horse go fast, and the *tatu* she will make a ball.'

'You mean it won't run away?'
'No, the Indian he say she stop and make a ball.'
'That sounds very unlikely to me,' I said sceptically.
'No, it is true, Gerry.'
'Well, it must be a damn stupid animal, then.'
'Yes, the Indian he say it is *muy estúpido*.'

We rode in silence, fifty yards apart, manoeuvring our horses in and out of the clumps of thorn-bushes. The only sounds were the brain-probing cries of the cicadas, the soft scrunch of the horses' hooves and the gentle creak and clink of leather and metal. My eyes ached with searching the heat-shimmering undergrowth ahead. A flock of ten guira cuckoos burst from a thorn-bush and flew off, cackling harshly, looking like small fawn-and-brown magpies, with their long and handsome tails.

Suddenly, fifty yards to my right, I saw the hunched shape of an armadillo, clock-working his way between the clumps of grass. With a yell of triumph, I dug my heels into my mount's sides, and he responded with such vigour that I only saved myself from a fall among the cacti by an undignified clutch at the saddle; the horse broke into a lumbering canter, the white sand spurting spray-like beneath his hooves as we bore down upon the quarry. We were within about fifty feet of him when the creature heard us; he swivelled round, sniffed briefly and then with astonishing rapidity rolled himself into a ball and lay there. I was rather disappointed that the beast had lived up to his reputation for stupidity, for I felt he should have had the sense to try to make a dash for a clump of thorns. I stopped within twenty-five feet of him, dismounted, tied my horse to a clump of grass and then walked forward to collect my prize. To my surprise, I discovered the grass, which had appeared quite short when I was up on my horse, was really quite high, and I could not see the armadillo at all; however, I knew he was not far and in which direction he lay, so I walked forward. Presently I stopped walking and looked around: my horse was now a good distance away – certainly more than twenty-five feet. I decided that I must have walked in the wrong direction, and, cursing myself for my carelessness, I retraced my steps, zig-zagging through the undergrowth and reaching my horse without seeing the armadillo. I felt rather crestfallen and annoyed, for I decided that the little animal must have made a dash for it when I walked past him. Muttering angrily to myself, I remounted and sat there transfixed with surprise, for in the same position, about twenty-five feet away, lay the armadillo. I dismounted again and walked forward, stopping every now and then to look carefully around me. When I reached the area in which I knew he must lie, I paced slowly backwards and forwards, and even then I passed him twice before I noticed him. As I picked up the creature, heavy and warm from the sun, I mentally apologized to him for having thought that his tactics were stupid. I rode after Rafael and the Indian, and for the next two hours we worked our way carefully over the island of dry soil, and by the same simple means we managed to catch three more of them. Then, as it was getting late, we set off homewards, through the shadowy trees. Crossing the river of blue flowers, the mosquitoes rose in a shrill cloud and settled on us and the horses, gorging themselves so that their transparent abdomens, swollen with our blood, looked like scarlet Japanese lanterns. It was dark when we reached the village and our horses clopped their way tiredly down the muddy road, past bushes alive with the green lights of fireflies, and the bats flicked across our path, uttering their microscopic squeaks of amusement.

In our house we found Jacquie sitting at the table, writing, while our first armadillo trotted importantly round and round the room. It turned out that he had spent an exhilarating afternoon tearing the wire front from his cage and was just disappearing into the hibiscus bushes when Jacquie discovered him. Having recaptured him, she had let him loose in the living-room to await our return. While we had our evening meal, we turned all the armadillos out on to the floor, where they clattered and clicked their way about like a flock of castanets. Rafael and I spent the rest of the evening stripping the wire from the cage-front and replacing it with wooden bars. Then we left the cage in the living-room all night, just to make sure that it could hold the animals. In the morning the bars looked a bit battered, but they still held firm, and the armadillos were all curled up asleep in their bedroom.

Having solved the caging problem, I felt that the three-banded armadillos ought to be plain sailing, for, normally, armadillos are the easiest of creatures to keep in captivity. They will live happily on a diet of meat and fruit, and they are not particular about the freshness of the offerings, for in the wild state they will eat meat that is suppurating and maggot-ridden. According to the textbooks, the three-banded armadillo, in the wild state, lives on a diet of insects and grubs; I thought that if we first offered our specimens their natural diet we could then get them on to some substitute food. So we spent hours collecting a revolting assortment of the local insect life and presenting it to the armadillos. Instead of falling on it with joy, as we had expected, the beasts seemed positively afraid of the worms, caterpillars and beetles that we had taken such pains to collect. In fact, they backed away from them hurriedly, displaying every symptom of disgust and revulsion. After this failure, I tried them on the usual armadillo's diet in captivity: minced meat mixed with milk, but though they drank some of the milk, they refused the meat. They carried on in this irritating manner for three days, until I was sure that they would become so weak with lack of food that I should have to release them. Our lives were a misery, for on and off throughout the day one or other of us would have an idea and rush with some fresh offering to the cage, to try to tempt the armadillos, only to have them treat it with disgust. At last, more by chance than anything else, I invented a mixture that met with their approval. It consisted of mashed banana, milk, minced meat and raw egg mixed up with raw brain. The result looked like a particularly revolting street accident, but the armadillos adored it. They would rush for the plate at feeding time and stand round the edge, jostling each other, their noses buried deep in the slush, snorting and snuffling, and occasionally sneezing violently and spraying each other with the mixture.

Having got the little creatures on to a substitute diet, I felt that this had been the final obstacle, and that by all the laws of collecting we should have no more trouble with them. For a time all went well. During the day they would sleep in their bedroom, either curled up into a ball, or else lying on their sides, half unrolled, one armadillo fitting into the other. At three-thirty they would wake up and come out of their bedroom to tip-toe round the cage, like ballerinas, occasionally tick-tacking up to the bars and sticking their heads through to test the breeze with their pink noses to find out if the food was on its way. Very occasionally, the males would have a fight. This consisted of one armadillo barging another into a corner, and then endeavouring to get his head under the edge of his opponent's shell, in order to turn him over; once he was on his side, the victor also turned on his side and scrabbled frantically in an effort to disembowel him. As soon as I noticed these tournaments, I kept a close watch on them. Though they never seemed to do each other any harm, I saw that the big ones were fighting the smaller ones at feeding time, and, by their superior size and weight, keeping the smaller and lighter ones from the food. I decided the best thing would be to keep them in pairs, male and female of approximately the same size. So I built a cage that Jacquie used to call Sing-Sing: it was a series of 'flats', one on top of the other, each with its own bedroom. By this time we had acquired ten of these little armadillos, consisting of four pairs and two odd males. It was a curious thing that the females seemed to be in the minority, for any number of males were brought to us, but only very occasionally did a female get caught. The married couples settled down very well in the Sing-Sing apartments, and there were no more tournaments at feeding time.

One day Jacquie had just finished giving them their food, and she appeared holding one of the large males in her hand. By this time they had become so used to handling that they no longer curled into a tight ball when touched. Jacquie looked worried, but the armadillo lay blissfully on his back in her cupped hands, while she stroked his pink, furry tummy.

'Just look at this one's feet,' she said, holding out the beast for my inspection.

'What's the matter with them?' I inquired, taking the semi-hypnotized beast and looking at it.

'Look . . . the soles of his hind-feet are all raw.'

'Good Lord! so they are. I wonder what he's been doing?'

'It strikes me,' said Jacquie, 'that these animals are going to be more trouble than they're worth . . . they've already caused us more worry than the rest of the collection put together.'

'Are the others all right?'

'I didn't look. I wouldn't have noticed this one, only he came rushing to the door and fell out when I put the plate in; when I picked him up I noticed his feet.'

We went and examined the others, and discovered to our consternation that all of them had these circular, sixpenny size raw patches on their hind-feet. The only reason for this that I could think of was that the wooden floors of their cages were too hard for them, and, trotting about as much as they did, they had worn the delicate skin off the soles of their hind-feet. So every day all the armadillos had to be taken out of Sing-Sing and laid on the ground, like a row of pumpkins, while we anointed their hind-feet with penicillin ointment. Then something had to be done about the floor of their cages, and I tried covering them with a thick layer of soft earth. This was quite useless, for at feeding time the armadillos splashed their food about with wild abandon, and then trod the sticky mixture of mud and brain into a paste that set as hard as cement, not only on the floor of the cage, but on the soles of their hind-feet as well. After some experiment, I discovered that the best flooring consisted of a deep layer of sawdust, covered by another layer of dry leaves and grass. This acted very well, and within a few weeks their feet had healed up nicely, and we had no recurrence of the trouble.

To the average person it would no doubt seem as though we had taken a lot of unnecessary trouble over a small and unimportant beast, but to us it represented a major triumph. To find and capture a difficult and delicate creature, to house it properly, teach it to eat a substitute food, cope successfully with its illnesses and other problems – these are some of the most irritating, heart-breaking and worrying of a collector's jobs, but the accomplishment of them is by far the most exciting and satisfying. A creature which settles down well in captivity, never becomes ill, and eats whatever it is given, is regarded with affection by the collector; but the tricky, stubborn and delicate animal is regarded as a challenge which, though it may be exhausting, is much more satisfying when one achieves success in the end.

Chapter Five

Bevy of Bichos

Our own efforts, combined with the help of the local male population (under orders from Paula), soon produced a flood of local fauna; and Jacquie, Rafael and I were kept hard at work all day, cage-building, cage-cleaning, feeding and watering, recording and photographing. Even with the three of us working, we were still hard put to it to cope with all the work. Reluctantly, I decided that we would have to employ a carpenter to deal with the caging. I say reluctantly, because I have had a good deal of experience of these craftsmen in various parts of the world. Carpenters, as a breed, I have discovered have one-track minds: employ them to make a door or a table, and, however unskilfully, they will produce the article required. But engage a carpenter and tell him that he must make a variety of cages for animals, and he immediately goes all to pieces. By the time you have taught him the rudiments of cage-making, it is generally time for you to leave. So it was with certain misgivings that I asked Rafael to get Paula to obtain a carpenter for us. The following day he turned up, a short, plump little man with a face so devoid of expression that he might have been a goldfish. In a hoarse voice he confided to us that his name was Anastacius. We spent an exhausting half-hour explaining to him what we wanted, and then gave him a box and told him to convert it into a bird-cage. We very soon discovered that Anastacius had two most irritating habits: first, he whistled loudly and tunelessly while he worked, and, secondly, he seemed to be under the impression that nails had a life of their own, or were possessed of malignant spirits. He would hammer a nail into the wood with a series of tremendous blows that continued to rain down long after the head was flush with the board. Then he would pause and survey the nail narrowly out of the corner of his eye, presumably waiting for it to start creeping out of the wood. Usually the nail remained immobile, but occasionally Anastacius would notice some slight movement, and he would leap forward and bring the hammer down with devastating violence until he was sure that the nail had succumbed. As soon as he had successfully killed a nail, he would break into a loud, tuneless whistle of triumph. So he toiled for two hours over the first cage, and then, when we all had splitting headaches, he produced the result for my inspection.

Now, a bird's cage is one of the simplest things to construct: all it needs is a wire front, with a half-inch gap at the bottom for cleaning purposes; two perches; and a door just big enough to admit one's hand. Anastacius' effort was a materpiece: the woodwork was a mortuary of dead nails, mostly twisted and crushed, and the wire front had several large dents in it where the creator had swung too wildly in his pursuit of a nail. The door was so contrived that, once shut, it was almost impossible to open, and, once open, it was impossible for me to get my hand inside. The gap he had left for cleaning out was so ample that anything, except a very fat vulture, could have flown through it with ease. We contemplated it in gloomy silence.

'I think it better we do ourselves, Gerry, no?' said Rafael at last.

'No, Rafael, we've got too much to do – we'll just have to put up with this butcher and hope he'll improve.'

'It couldn't be difficult to improve on *that*,' said Jacquie. 'What on earth are we going to put in it? It'll have to be something tame, so that if it escapes we can catch it again easily.'

For a week the Butcher, as we called him, produced a series of cages each worse than the last. The climax came when I asked him to make me a cage for a creature which needed its housing lined with tin. He had attached the tin to the inside of the cage by the novel method of drawing huge nails through from the outside. The result was that the inside of the cage was full of jagged bits of tin and a forest of nail-points. The whole construction looked rather like some strange medieval device for torture.

'It's no good, Rafael, he'll have to go – I can't stand any more of this – the man's obviously mental. Just look at this effort; one would think we wanted to kill the animals, instead of keeping them alive,' I said. 'Tell him he's sacked, and tell Paula we want someone else – someone who at least has some rudiments of intelligence.'

So the Butcher returned to whatever work of demolition he'd been engaged on in the village, and the next morning Paula appeared leading a thin, shy young man wearing a peaked cap. Paula introduced him as the new carpenter, and held forth at great length of his prowess, personality and intelligence. Rafael showed him the cages that we had made, and the man examined them carefully, and then said he thought he would be able to construct similar ones.

'Good,' I said, when all this had been translated to me. 'What's his name, Rafael?'

'*Como se llama?*' asked Rafael.

'Julius Caesar Centurian,' said the man, giving a nervous giggle.

So Julius Caesar Centurian came into our midst, and a charming, resourceful and likeable character he turned out to be. What was more important, he was an excellent carpenter as well. As soon as he took over the caging, we found we had far more time to concentrate on the animal work.

In any collection of animals there are bound to be two or three which endear themselves to you particularly; they need not necessarily be very rare or exotic, nor overburdened with intelligence. But the moment you see them you realize they are possessed of those rare and indefinable qualities, charm and personality, and that they are destined to become characters in camp. To begin with, we had three such beasts in the Chaco; later this trio was joined by a fourth who outshone them all – but more of her anon. The three beasts were as unlike one another as possible, yet they all possessed the basic qualification to turn them into characters rather than just specimens.

The first of these was Cai, the douroucouli monkey. She was brought in one day by a rather repulsive-looking Indian who wore a very battered straw hat with a blue ribbon dangling from it. I was very pleased to get her; apart from liking monkeys, I was particularly interested in douroucoulis, since they are the only nocturnal monkey in the world. Cai was about the size of a small cat and clad in lichen-grey fur. On her chest the fur was a pale orange shade fading to cream on her tummy. Her small ears were so deeply embedded in the hair of her head that they were almost invisible. She had enormous owl-like eyes of pale amber and they were surrounded by an area of white fur edged with black. This marking, together with her big eyes and her apparent lack of ears, gave her a most remarkable resemblance to an owl. She was very shabby and unkempt and terribly thin. For the first three days she was intensely nervous, and we could do nothing with her. We kept her tied to a stake with a big box to retreat into, and at first she spent her whole time cowering out of sight. If we made any overtures of friendship she would cringe back, gazing at us with wide-eyed horror, her little hands trembling with fright. She was, of course, half-starved, and ate greedily of the food we gave her. But, however hungry she was, she would never come out of her box to feed until we had retreated some distance. Then, one day, I succeeded in catching a lizard for her. I killed it and, approaching Cai's box, I squatted down and held out the still-writhing reptile on the palm of my hand. Cai took one look at the delicacy, and delight overcame her caution. She leapt out of her box, gave a faint ghost-like scream, and, grabbing the lizard firmly, she squatted down in front of me. Suddenly she realized that I was much closer than she normally allowed me, and she was just proposing to retreat into her box when the lizard's tail gave a convulsive wriggle. Immediately she forgot me, and with a look of intense concentration she bit the tail off and sat there holding it in one hand, munching happily, as though it was a stick of celery. I sat perfectly still until she had finished her meal, and she gazed at me while she ate, with a watchful expression in her enormous liquid eyes. When the last bit of lizard had been chewed, taken out and gazed at, chewed again and finally swallowed, she examined her hands carefully, and the ground around her, to make sure no bits were left. Then she stretched out her hind-leg, scratched her thigh vigorously, got up and sauntered off to her box. From that day onwards her confidence increased.

We soon discovered that Cai did not care for being tied up in the open. I think it gave her a naked, unprotected feeling. So I set to work and built her a cage. This was a tall, narrow structure, with a little bedroom at the top, into which she could retire when she felt like it. She adored this bedroom and would spend her whole day sitting in there, just her head and front paws poking out of the door. In this position she would go off to sleep. Her eyes would droop half shut, and then suddenly open again; a few seconds later they would droop once more, her head would start to nod, until eventually, after many fits and starts and sudden awakenings, her head would sink down and rest peacefully on her paws. But let anything interesting or unusual happen, and her great eyes would fly open and she would crane out of her bedroom to see what was going on, sometimes, in her excitement, twisting her head round so that it was completely upside down and you feared that another half an inch and it would drop off. She could also turn her head round and look over her back, with an almost owl-like ability. She was intensely curious and could not bear to stop watching something, even if it frightened her. Sometimes she would witness the arrival of a new snake and, uttering a series of her faint, squeaky sighs, would come down and peer at it through the wire, wide-eyed with horror, glancing continually over her shoulder to make sure her line of retreat was secure. If she thought the snake was too close, she would leap on to the branch near her bedroom and sit facing the door, and then screw her head round and continue to watch the snake over her shoulder. Thus her body was facing the exact way for a rapid retreat to safety, and she could still keep an eye on the reptile. For a nocturnal creature she spent an awful lot of the day awake, and scarcely anything happened in camp that her big eyes did not notice or her faint voice remark on.

One day when I was hacking up a rotten log for the woodpecker, I discovered some large and juicy cockroaches hiding under the bark. Thinking I would give Cai a treat, I captured them and carried them to her. She was spread-eagled on the floor of the cage, having a sun-bath, eyes closed, mouth half open in ecstasy. She woke up when I called her, and sat blinking in a bemused fashion. I opened the door of her cage and dropped in the largest and most agile cockroach, thinking that it would amuse her to catch it for herself. But Cai, half-awake, only saw that I had put something in her cage which was alive, and she was not going to hang about and see what it was. She disappeared into her bedroom in a flash, while the cockroach stalked about the floor of the cage, waving its antennae in a vague sort of way. Presently Cai poked her head cautiously out of her bedroom door to see what my offering was. She gazed down at the cockroach with suspicion, her face, as always when she was nervous or excited, seeming to be all eyes. After due consideration, she decided that the insect was harmless, and possibly edible, and so she climbed down and sat contemplating it closely for a while. The cockroach ambled about for a bit and then stopped for a quick wash and brush-up. Cai sat, hands folded over her stomach, watching it with absorbed interest. Then she stretched out a cautious hand and very delicately, with one finger, tapped the cockroach on the back. The insect immediately scuttled frantically across the floor, and Cai leapt backwards in fright and wiped her hand hurriedly on her chest. The cockroach, legs and feelers working overtime, reached the front of the cage and started to squeeze through the wire. With a shrill twitter, Cai leapt forward and grabbed at it, but she was too late. I caught the insect and reintroduced it into the cage, and this time Cai followed it about, tapping it on the back and then smelling her fingers. Finally she decided that, however revolting its appearance, it must be edible, and so, closing her eyes tightly and screwing up her face into an expression of determination tinged with disgust, she grabbed at it with both hands and stuffed it into her mouth, so that the wriggling legs stuck out like a walrus moustache. Ever after that I used to kill her cockroaches before giving them to her, otherwise she would take so long plucking up the courage to catch them that they always escaped through the wire.

As soon as she knew she had her bedroom to retire to in moments of stress, Cai became very tame and trusting, even allowing us to stroke her. Jacquie would hold a piece of banana or a grape in her clenched hand, and offer it to Cai. She would come down from her bedroom and sit there solemnly opening Jacquie's hand, finger by finger, until she could get at the delicacy. With plenty of fruit and insect life, and two bowls of milk with raw egg and vitamins beaten in it a day, she soon put on weight, and her fur became glossy and thick as a powder-puff. You would not have recognized her as the frightened, faded scrap of fur she had been when we first got her. The credit for her well-being was Jacquie's, for Cai liked her better than she liked me, and so Jacquie had the task of cleaning and feeding her, tempting her appetite with delicacies, and playing with her so that she did not become bored. I can honestly say (without vanity, since it was not my handiwork) that when we landed Cai in England I have never seen a douroucouli like her in any zoo.

For some time Cai reigned supreme as Queen of the Camp, and then one day there arrived another creature to share her throne. On being tipped out of the basket, this new addition resembled a very small, very fluffy chow puppy, with a black-and-white ringed tail, and wearing, for reasons best known to himself, a mask of black fur across his face, from which two wistful, rather sad brown eyes contemplated us. He stood there on immensely large and very flat feet, looking like a dismal highwayman who has lost his pistol. The soles of his paws, we noticed, were pink, and his fingers and toes long and slender, of the type that is generally known as artistic. He was a baby crab-eating raccoon, and we soon decided to call him Pooh, for he closely resembled the famous bear of that name, and it was generally the first thing we said when we went to clean out his cage in the morning.

I put Pooh into a nice roomy cage with wooden bars and a neat door with a latch, gave him a couple of buckets of sawdust to sit in and left him to settle down. He behaved, to begin with, with the utmost decorum, squatting on his ample behind and gazing through the bars, looking like Dick Turpin awaiting trial. When we came back after lunch, however, we found Pooh had been busy. He was sitting with an air of depressed innocence, surrounded by our day's egg supply, or, to be more accurate, he was surrounded by the shells, while his paws, face and coat were sticky with yolk or white. He gazed at us, when we scolded him, with the expression of one who has always found life harsh and is beyond expecting sympathy or understanding. I decided that his burglar-like method of getting out of his cage deserved further study, for I could not see how he had managed it. I put him back inside the cage, securely latched the door and then kept a wary eye on him from a distance. After a long pause, a black nose appeared through the bars and whiffled to and fro; having decided the coast was clear, this was withdrawn and its place taken by a long, slender set of fingers and a pink paw which groped in the most human fashion round the bars in the direction of the latch. Having located it, one of the artistic fingers was inserted under the hook, and with an expert flick it knocked the latch up. The door was pushed open guiltily and Pooh's face appeared slowly and thoughtfully round the edge. The next quarter of an hour I spent fixing a bolt to the door, as well as the latch, and it took him three days to learn the intricacies of this and escape again. By the end of the week the door of his cage bristled with an assortment of bolts, latches and hooks that would have made Houdini think a bit, but the only result was that we took longer to open the door than Pooh did. In the end, I had to fix a padlock on the door, and that did the trick. But Pooh would sit for hours with his paws stuck through the bars, fondling the padlock with his sensitive, pink paws, occasionally sticking a finger into the keyhole in a hopeful sort of way.

Now a sentimentalist might argue that Pooh was trying desperately to escape from his wooden prison to the gay, abandoned freedom of the forest. This, however, would be exaggerating. Whenever Pooh escaped, he had only two objectives: firstly, the food-table, and, if this was empty, the bird-cages. If food was available, Pooh would be found in the midst of it. If there was no food, he would send the birds into a hysterical twitter by peering through the wire at them and licking his lips. It might be argued that, if Pooh was not interested in regaining his lost freedom, he was merely escaping in order to secure a square meal which we denied him. To counter this, I should like it to go on record that Pooh, for his size, ate more than any other animal I have ever come across. This walking stomach had a daily ration consisting of two raw eggs, vitamins and cod-liver oil, beaten up in half a pint of milk, a quarter of a pound of minced steak or heart, and fruit in the shape of bananas, guavas or pawpaws. Having consumed all this in the space of an hour, he would, after a slight doze, be ready for more.

When Pooh discovered that the padlock would not yield its secrets to him, he did not give up hope, but devoted half an hour a day to it, and the rest of the time he devoted to other good works. Among these were his spring-cleaning activities. Every day, having indulged in the herculean task of cleaning his cage, we would spread a layer of clean sawdust in the bottom of it. Pooh would then be seized with what appeared to be a housewifely desire for tidiness. The fact that the sawdust was spread all over the cage would get on his nerves. Starting in one corner, he would begin to work backwards, sweeping the sawdust with his front paws and shooting it out between his hind legs to be bulldozed along by his ample bottom. He would solemnly work his way over the cage like this until the floor was not marred by one speck of sawdust, while in one corner his bottom had amassed a huge conical pile of the stuff; needless to say, the corner with the sawdust in it was the one he did not use for those functions of nature for which this commodity had been provided. Instead, he used it as a couch, a sort of sawdust chaise-longue, against which, during the heat of the afternoon, he would recline, on his back, plucking meditatively with his long fingers at the hair on the enormous mound of his stomach. He like nothing better, while wrapped in these Buddhist meditations, than to have a piece of fat to play with. Holding one end in his mouth and the other end between his hind-paws, he would pull alternately with his teeth or toes, thus producing a gentle rocking-chair-like motion which was apparently very conducive to slumber.

In order to give Pooh more exercise, I thought it would be a good idea to put him out on a lead for a few hours every day, so I drove a stake into the ground, fashioned a collar out of plaited string, and a lead out of rope. Within half an hour Pooh had gnawed his way through the rope, visited the food-table and had eaten twenty bananas. I tried a variety of different materials as leads, and the one that took him longest to get through was a thong of rawhide, but even this gave up the unequal struggle eventually. In the end I procured a length of chain which had, originally, been intended for other purposes, and this, though short, at least resisted all Pooh's efforts to bite through it. In spite of Pooh's flat-footed, slow, shuffling walk and his air of benign obesity, he was really a most active creature, rarely still and always on the look-out for something to stick his paws into. Being so active, he was easily bored, and sometimes we had to exercise the utmost ingenuity in finding things to occupy him. A length of old ciné-film kept him amused for days: he would stroll back and forth with yards of celluloid trailing from his mouth, or else lie on his back, holding the film in his paws and peering at it short-sightedly, looking like a plump and rather melancholy film mogul contemplating his latest epic.

The day I found the husk of an old coconut was a red-letter one for Pooh. At first he was a bit suspicious of it and approached it with a curious sideways shuffle, ready to run for it should the coconut attack him. Then he touched it delicately with one paw and discovered to his pleasure that the coconut would roll about. He spent a happy half-hour chasing it to and fro; and several times he grew over-excited and knocked it outside the limit of his chain, so he had to give his loud yarring screams until Jacquie or I retrieved it for him. Then Jacquie had an idea and suggested I should bore a hole in the husk. This simple action transformed the coconut from being a passing fancy to being Pooh's favourite toy. Now he would sit for hours with it clasped between his hind legs, one arm and paw delving deep inside it and occasionally surfacing with some microscopic fragment of shell. The first time, he delved so enthusiastically that he got stuck, and, having extricated him, I had to enlarge the hole. So Pooh would spend the day with his coconut, playing football with it, plunging his hand into it like a child with a bran-tub, and eventually, when he was tired, falling asleep draped over it.

Our third animal character was known by the rather unimaginative name of Foxey. He was a small, delicately made, grey pampas fox, with slender legs and enormous brush and eager brown eyes. Foxey had been procured by a Paraguayan at a very tender age, and when he came to us he must have been some three or four months old. He was about the size of a wire-haired terrier, and he had obviously given up all ideas of behaving like a fox. In fact, I think that privately he was convinced he wasn't a fox, but a dog, and he had certainly developed some most unfox-like habits. We kept Foxey on a collar and chain, which was, in turn, attached to a ring. Through the ring was threaded a wire stretched between two posts. In this way he would have a greater area to run about in and yet his leash was short enough to ensure he did not get tangled up in it. At night he slept in a large, grass-filled cage. Every morning when he caught sight of us he would greet us with loud and prolonged yowls of joy, and as soon as his cage was opened he would wag his great tail frantically from side to side, lift his upper lip and display his baby teeth in the most endearing grin of delight. His final moment of ecstasy came as he was lifted out of his cage, and then you had to be careful how you held him, for he would be so overcome with joy at seeing you again that he could no longer contain himself, and the resulting stream could drench you if you were not careful.

Shortly after he arrived we discovered he had two passions in life: one was chickens, and the second was cigarette butts. Chickens, or for that matter any birds, fascinated him. Occasionally one or two members of Paula's fowl-run would invade the collection and wander near to where Foxey was tethered. He would crouch down, head on his paws, ears pricked and his tail moving gently from side to side. The hens would approach, pecking and uttering hiccupping, slightly inebriated, chucks, and the closer they got, the brighter grew Foxey's eyes. The hens' vacant meanderings always took some time, and Foxey could not contain himself. Long before they were within range, he would gather himself together and charge to the limit of his leash, yapping excitedly. The hens would scuttle off, squawking hysterically, and Foxey would squat down and beam over his shoulder at us, creating a miniature dust-storm with the frantic wagging of his tail.

His interest in cigarette butts amounted to almost an obsession. Whenever he found one he would pounce on it and devour it, with an expression of utmost loathing on his face. Then he would spend an uncomfortable half an hour coughing violently, have a long drink of water and be ready for the next butt-end. One awful day, however, Foxey learnt his lesson. Carelessly I had left a nearly full packet of cigarettes within his reach, and before I had discovered it Foxey had eaten the lot. To say that he was sick would be a vast understatement. His stomach performed the emesis of all time, and every last shred of paper and tobacco was returned to the light of day, tastefully mixed with Foxey's breakfast. He was so exhausted by this effort that he just lay and let a chicken walk right past him, and never even twitched an ear. By evening he had recovered enough to eat a couple of pounds of meat and two raw eggs, but the offer of a cigarette caused him to back away, sneezing indignantly. Never again did he sample tobacco in any shape or form.

Chapter Six

Fawns, Frogs and Fer-de-lance

One day we learnt that on the following morning an *autovía* was travelling some twenty-five kilometres up the line to a place that delighted in the name of Waho. Apart from the name, which attracted me, Waho seemed worth a visit, for I had been told that it was the best area for jaguar, and I wanted to see the overseer about setting some traps. Also, being a cattle-station, Waho had quite a substantial population – at least fifty people, which is substantial by Chaco standards – and I thought that they might have some pets which they would be willing to part with.

We had been told that the *autovía* would start at four in the morning and could not, on any account, wait for us if we were late. With a considerable effort we managed to get Rafael out of bed and semi-conscious by this hour, and we stumbled down the road to the railway line, past the canals where the frogs and toads were still holding their nightly jazz club, and through the dark and lifeless village, shrouded in mist from the river. We found the *autovía* squatting on the line, and climbed in and sat dozing on the hard seats for half an hour, waiting for the driver. He appeared at last, yawning prodigiously, and informed us that we could not start until five, as they had forgotten to give him the mails for Waho, and he had had to send someone to collect them. We sat in an irritated silence, listening to the village cockerels starting up, and presently a small boy appeared out of the mist, bearing the sack of mails. The driver flung the sack into the back of the *autovía*, engaged his gears with a retching sound that any of the cockerels would have envied, and we clattered off down the buckled lines into the mist.

Gradually, as the line curved inland and away from the river, the mist grew thinner, and eventually disappeared altogether, except for small eiderdown patches of it that hung over the pools and streams we passed. The sky ahead turned steel grey, and against it the tangled crest of the forest was etched with microscopic exactness. Gradually the grey faded, to be replaced by a purplish-red which spread across the horizon like a bruise. This, in its turn, rapidly faded to pale pink, and then to blue, as the sun rose over the rim of the forest. In the first slanting rays the whole landscape gained perspective and became alive. The forest was no longer a flat black silhouette, but a solid, interlaced crochet work of branches, vines and thorns, its leaves glossy with mist. Flocks of guira cuckoos sat preening the moisture from their feathers, or crouched with drooped wings in the first heat of the day. We passed a small lake, the edge of which was trembling with the movement of birds: ibis strolling in groups, probing the mud eagerly with their curved beaks; an openbill stork, lank and dark, standing in rapt contemplation of his own reflection; two jacanas bathing, their underwings flashing buttercup yellow as they threw up a glittering spray of water over their heads and bodies. A small grey fox, returning from his night's hunting, scuttled on to the line and then galloped ahead of us for about fifty yards before swerving off into the undergrowth. We chugged on, and very soon we passed a small grass-field that was an incredible sight. It was some two acres in extent, neatly fenced in with tall palms, and in it the great chaco spiders had been at work. These spiders have a body the size of a hazel nut, spotted with pink and white, and mounted on long, slender legs covering the area of a saucer. The silk they spin is thick, elastic and the colour of gold. In this small grass field they had covered every available bush and grass tussock with their great golden webs, each one the size of a cartwheel. In the centre of each web a spider was spread-eagled, and around it each delicate thread and spoke of their kingdom was decorated with dew, like diamonds on cloth of gold. The decorative effect was breathtakingly beautiful as they shimmered and glittered in the early sunlight.

We reached Waho at about seven-thirty. The line swept out of the forest into an immense field, glinting here and there with water. In the grass at the edge of the line flocks of black-headed conures were feeding. These small parrots had the most vivid grass-green plumage with coal-black heads and necks. They flew up and wheeled, glittering, through the sky as we passed, screaming shrilly. The line ended here, in an area of churned mud; it was the usual sort of Chaco out-station, with a long, low, whitewashed house for the overseer, and a collection of dilapidated palm-log huts that housed the workers. The *autovía* drew up with an important chuffing and rattle, and Fernandez, the overseer, appeared, striding over the sea of mud to greet us. He was a tall, powerful man with a handsome, rather Mongolian face and very fine teeth. He had the most charming manners, and greeted us as though we were royalty, ushering us into the living-room of his house and sending his small, dark wife bustling round to prepare us some *mate* with milk. While we drank this thick, sweet and rather sickly drink, I spread out my books and drawings on the table, and with Rafael acting as interpreter, I went into the subject of the local fauna with Fernandez. He recognized all the creatures that I particularly wanted, and promised to do his best to try to obtain some for me. Jaguar and ocelot were very common, he told us, some cows having been killed by a jaguar only a week before; however, they were wary and not easily caught. He promised to set traps in all the likely places, and should he be successful in catching anything he would send me a message at once. When I questioned him about the smaller creatures – the frogs, toads, snakes and lizards – he gave a disarming grin and said that we had better go over to an area of the out-station where they were clearing a section of the forest; here, he told us, they were finding any number of small *bichos*. While we hastily gulped down our drinks, Fernandez called two Indians, and we set off to look for small *bichos*.

We followed a narrow, muddy path that zig-zagged through the long grass from which the mosquitoes rose in clouds. We passed by the cattle-slaughtering pen, a large corral some seventy feet square, with walls made of palm logs. The top of the walls was decorated with a frieze of black vultures, sitting in their usual hunch-backed, rather menacing way, waiting for the next killing. They were so bold that we walked within six feet of them and they did not take wing, but merely surveyed us appraisingly, looking like a convention of elderly undertakers. Fernandez led us down the path for about half a mile, until it left the grass field and entered the forest. Here we found a group of Indians hacking away at the thorny undergrowth with machetes, chattering and laughing, their huge straw hats bobbing about like animated mushrooms in the tangle of scrub. Fernandez called them together and explained what we wanted, and the Indians glanced shyly at us and grinned at each other; then one of them addressed Fernandez and pointed to a large log lying half-hidden in the undergrowth. Fernandez relayed the information to Rafael, who, in turn, translated for me.

'The Indian say they find a snake, Gerry, but she run very fast and she is sitting under that tree.'

'Well, ask Señor Fernandez if the Indians can help us shift it, and then I can have a shot at catching it.'

Once again there was a pause while my request was translated, and then Fernandez gave an order, and the group of Indians sped towards the log, giggling and pushing each other like school-children, and started to hack the undergrowth away from its length. When a sufficient space around the log had been cleared, I cut myself a suitable stick and prepared for action. To Rafael's extreme irritation, I would not let him help, for, as I explained, I had promised his mother that, whatever else I let him do, I would not let him mess about with snakes. After some argument, during which Rafael almost came to the point of rebellion, I persuaded him to retreat to a safe distance. Then I nodded to the Indians, they stuck their machetes under the curve of the log and with a quick heave turned it over and took to their heels.

As the log rolled over, a thick, brown snake about four feet long wriggled elegantly out of the depression, travelled for about six feet, when it suddenly saw me approaching, and stopped. As I leant forward to pin it down with my stick, it did something which shook me considerably: it raised its blunt, rather heavy-looking head, and some six inches of its body, from the ground, and proceeded to inflate the skin of its neck. Slowly the skin expanded until I was looking at what appeared to be a cobra with its hood up. Now, there is more that one species of snake in the world that can inflate the skin of its neck like a cobra, but this generally results in a slight balloon-like expansion which could not compare with the beautifully flattened hood of that reptile. Yet here, in the middle of the Chaco, in a Continent which does not contain cobras, I was confronted by a snake that looked so like one that even an Asiatic snake-charmer might have been forgiven for getting out his flute. I lowered my stick gently to try to pin it to the ground, but the snake was well aware of my motives. It lowered its hood and proceeded to glide towards the nearest bit of forest with considerable agility. I made one or two ineffectual attempts to pin it down, and then, in desperation when it neared the undergrowth, I slid the stick under the gliding body, lifted it up and flipped it back into the clearing again. This obviously irritated my quarry, for it paused for a moment and glared at me with open mouth before once more setting off determinedly in the direction of the nearest bush. Once more I pursued it, slid my stick under it and lifted it into the air, preparatory to giving it the backward flick that would keep it away from the undergrowth, but this time the snake had its own ideas on the subject. It gave a violent wiggle as it felt itself lifted, and, while still in mid-air, expanded its hood to the fullest extent and flung itself sideways at me with open mouth. Luckily, I realized what was happening and scuttled backwards, and the snake missed my trouser leg by a fraction. It fell to the ground and lay there quite quietly; presumably, having tried out all its tricks and failed, it decided to give up the unequal struggle. I picked it up by the back of the neck and put it into a bag without any further trouble. Jacquie came forward and gave me a bitter look.

'If you insist on doing things like that,' she said, 'I'd be glad if you did them when I wasn't around.'

'Nearly she bite you,' said Rafael, his eyes large behind his spectacles.

'What sort of snake was it, anyway?' asked Jacquie.

'I don't know. I can't place that hood, although I have a feeling that I've read about the thing somewhere. I'll look it up when we get back.'

'She have poison?' asked Rafael, seating himself on the log.

'No, I don't think it's poisonous . . . only mildly so, anyway.'

'I seem to remember that a snake you identified as being non-poisonous in Africa turned out to be exactly the opposite, after it had bitten you,' said Jacquie.

'Oh, that was different,' I explained – 'that one looked just like a non-poisonous kind, and I picked it up.'

'Yes, and this one looks just like a cobra, and you picked it up,' retorted my wife, crushingly.

'Don't sit on that log, Rafael,' I said, changing the subject; 'it might have scorpions under the bark.'

Rafael shifted rapidly, and, borrowing a machete from one of the Indians, I approached the log and began to hack away at the rotten bark. The first blow of the blade brought forth a shower of beetle larvae and a large centipede; the second, more beetle larvae, two beetles and a depressed-looking tree-frog. I worked slowly down the length of the trunk, sticking the point of the machete in and then levering the bark up and ripping it off with a soft scrunch. There seemed to be nothing except this wonderful array of insect life. Then I stripped the piece of bark away near the place where Rafael had been sitting, and a snake some six inches long and as thick as a cigarette fell out. It was gaily banded with black, cream, grey and fire-engine red, and was very handsome.

'Oh, migosh!' said Rafael, as I picked it up, 'I sit there, no?'

'Yes,' I said severely. 'You should be careful where you're sitting. You might have killed it.'

'What is it?' asked Jacquie.

'A baby coral snake . . . we seem to be having a rather snaky day today.'

'But they're deadly, aren't they?'

'Yes, but not so deadly that they could kill Rafael through half an inch of bark,' I said.

Putting the snake into a bag, I investigated the rest of the log, but found nothing more of interest. Fernandez, who had been watching fascinated from a safe distance, now suggested that we should make our way back to the out-station and make a tour of the huts to see if they contained any pets. As we wandered back along the path, I caught the glint of water through the trees, and insisted we should all go and investigate. We found a large pond, its water stained by decaying leaves to the colour of rum, from which rose the intoxicating smell of rotting leaves. I started to potter happily round the edge in search of frogs, and was still doing this some ten minutes later when I was brought to earth by an uproar that broke out at the far end of the pond. Looking up, I saw Fernandez, Rafael and the two Indians dancing round Jacquie, shouting, while she was calling me loudly. Above the uproar a strange sound was wafted to me: it sounded like someone blowing prolonged blasts on a toy trumpet. I hurried round the pool to see what was happening. I found Jacquie clutching something in her hands which was producing the trumpet-like sound, while Fernandez and the Indians kept shouting '*Venenosa, muy venenosa, señora*,' in a sort of despairing chorus.

Rafael approached me, looking very startled.

'Gerry, some bad *bicho* Jacquie catch. They say she is very bad,' he explained.

'It's only a frog,' said Jacquie, raising her voice above the jabbering of the Indians and the irritated blasts from her capture.

'Let's have a look at it.'

She opened her hands and displayed the most extraordinary amphibian imaginable. It was black with a pale yellowish-white belly, and was almost completely circular in shape. Its golden eyes were perched up on the top of its broad, flat head, like those of a miniature hippo. But it was the mouth of the beast that startled me: it had thick, yellow lips which stretched from side to side of the frog's head in a great, grinning curve, exactly like the Tenniel illustration of Humpty Dumpty. As I watched it, it suddenly blew up its body like a balloon, stood up on its short, stubby legs, opened its mouth wide (showing that the inside was a bright primrose yellow) and proceeded to give another series of yarring trumpet-blasts. When I took it in my hand, it struggled wildly, so I put it on the ground. It stood up on its small legs, opened wide its mouth, and took little jumps towards me, snapping its mouth fiercely and giving trumpet-blasts of rage. It was an enchanting beast.

'Where did you catch it?' I asked Jacquie.

'Just there. It was sitting in the water with just its eye showing, rather like a hippo, so I grabbed it. What is it?'

'I haven't the faintest idea. It looks like a horned toad in some ways, but it's not the ordinary sort. Whatever it is, it's jolly interesting . . . might even turn out to be something quite new.'

Filled with enthusiasm, we searched the little pond and managed to capture three more of these peculiar frogs, which elated me considerably. At the time I thought they might well turn out to be a new species, related to the horned toads which, in some respects, they resembled closely. However, on return to England, they were identified as being a Budgett's frog, a name which I think is singularly appropriate to their portly form and demeanour. But, although they had already been scientifically described, they were considered very rare, and the Natural History Museum had only one specimen.

As we approached the cluster of dilapidated huts we could see that the cattle-men had returned for their midday meal and siesta. The horses were tethered near the houses, and close by was a cluster of the heavy, sheepskin-covered saddles. The men, their straw hats tilted on to the backs of their heads, leaned against the walls of the houses, sipping their *mate* out of the little pots. They were dressed in tattered shirts, grey with sweat, and the thick leather chaps over their *bombachas* were ripped and scarred by the thorns they had ridden through. In the lean-to kitchens their wives crouched over smoky fires, cooking the meal, while around them sprawled broods of dirty-faced, dark-eyed children and mangy dogs. As we approached the first of the houses, Jacquie imparted some advice.

'Now, if they have got any pets, for goodness' sake don't leap at them with cries of delight. They double the price straight away,' she said.

'No, no, I won't,' I promised.

'Well, you did it the other day with that bird. If you hadn't looked so delighted with it, we'd have got it for half the price. Just pretend you're not really interested in whatever it is they've got.'

'I shouldn't think they'll have much here, anyway,' I said, surveying the decaying group of shanties.

We moved slowly from house to house, and Fernandez explained to the men what we wanted. They laughed and chattered among themselves, promising to try to catch specimens for us, but no pets were forthcoming. Outside one hut we were talking to the owner, a villainous, unshaven man, who was holding forth at great length about jaguar, when something appeared in the doorway of the house and trotted out into the open. At first, seeing it out of the corner of my eye, I thought it was a dog. The next thing I knew, Jacquie had uttered a shrill cry, and, turning, I found her embracing a small spotted fawn, who was regarding her suspiciously from large dark eyes.

'Just look at this . . . isn't it sweet?' she cried, regardless of the fact that the fawn's owner was standing within two feet of her. 'Isn't it adorable? Just look at its eyes. . . . We must have it. D'you think they'll sell it?'

I looked at the creature's owner, noted the gleam in his eye, and sighed.

'After watching your display of indifference to the beast's charms, I should think he's only too willing to sell,' I said bitterly. 'Rafael, ask him how much he wants for it, will you?'

The man, after devoting ten minutes to telling us how attached he was to the little deer, and how heartbroken he would be to part with it, named a price that made us all wilt. Half an hour later the price had dropped considerably, but was still much more than the animal was really worth. Jacquie gazed at me mutely.

'Look,' I said desperately, 'he wants twice what the little wretch is worth. We'd have got it for a quarter the price if you hadn't started to drool over it the minute it appeared.'

'I didn't drool,' said Jacquie indignantly; 'I was just drawing your attention to it.'

This monstrous understatement struck me speechless; silently I paid the man, and we made our way back towards the railway line, Jacquie clutching the fawn in her arms and whispering endearments into its silky ears. As we

The Drunken Forest

got into the *autovía*, the driver leant forward and stroked the little deer's head, beaming at it.

'*Lindo*,' he said, '*muy lindo bicho.*'

'*Lindo* means beautiful, doesn't it?' asked Jacquie.

'Yes, that is right,' said Rafael. 'Why, Jacquie?'

'I think it would be a good name for her, don't you?'

So, Lindo, the beautiful, she became forthwith. She behaved with the utmost decorum, sniffing interestedly round inside the *autovía*, and then going to Jacquie and nuzzling her with a moist, black nose. But with the first jerk of the *autovía* starting she decided that she did not approve of this form of travel, and made a wild leap for the tailboard of the vehicle. She sprawled over it, and was just about to crash on to the line when I managed to grab her hind legs and haul her back. She fought like a demon, lashing out with her sharp little hooves and uttering prolonged and piercing 'barrrs'. Fawns are extremely difficult things to handle when they become frightened; their hind legs must be held, or they kick violently and are liable to rip you to bits with their sharp hooves. On the other hand their legs are so fragile that there is always the danger that you might break one if you hold them too tightly. After a hectic five minutes we managed to subdue Lindo, and then I took off my shirt and wrapped her in it, so that even if she did struggle she could not damage herself or us. The driver was so tickled with the sight of a fawn wearing a shirt that he narrowly missed overturning the *autovía* at a sharp corner.

As we walked down the road towards our little house we were surprised to see a group of some thirty people standing outside the gate, forming a circle round a man with a large wooden box. This man, and the crowd around him, were all waving their arms and chattering. On the veranda of our house stood the mountainous form of Paula, clutching in her hands a rusty shot-gun with which she was menacing the crowd. We pushed through the people and made our way on to the veranda, to find out what was going on. Paula greeted us with evident relief, and proceeded to spout Spanish at us, rolling her eyes, clutching her brow and pointing the shot-gun at each of us in turn with complete impartiality. I removed the weapon from her reluctant hands, while Rafael listened to her story. That morning the señor had asked her to procure a shot-gun, in order to shoot some small birds for the *lechuchita*, the little owl, no? Well, she had gone to the village and procured this fine gun for the señor. On her return she had found that creature (here she pointed a trembling finger at the man with the box), sitting on the veranda. He said that he had brought a *bicho* for the señor. She, being curious, had asked him what sort of *bicho*, and he had removed the lid of the box and displayed to her horrified gaze a large and obviously angry *yarará*. Now, of all the dangerous creatures found in the Chaco, the *yarará* is the most feared, for a *yarará* is a fer-de-lance, one of the most poisonous and bad-tempered of South American snakes. Paula had not hesitated for a minute. She had ordered the man to remove his offering to a safe distance from the house. As it was very hot outside, and the veranda was shady, the man refused to do this, whereupon Paula had loaded the shot-gun and driven him off by force. The man, who turned out to be a trifle weak-minded, was not unnaturally rather upset at this reception. After having been brave enough to capture a *yarará*, he felt that he ought to be received with due solemnity and congratulation, not driven away by an irate outsize female with a shot-gun. Standing outside the gate, he had howled abuse at Paula, while she mounted guard over the front door with her gun. Our arrival luckily put an end to the whole business; we despatched Paula to the kitchen to make us some tea, and called the man inside.

The fer-de-lance, having been bumped about in the hot sun all afternoon, was not in the best of tempers, and as soon as I lifted the lid of the box to take a look at him he leapt at the opening and struck at me viciously. He was quite a small specimen, being only about two and a half feet long, but what he lacked in length he made up for in pugnacity, and it was a long time before I could get a noose round him and grab him behind the head. He was a very handsome reptile, the whole of his body being ashy grey, patterned with a series of diamond-shaped charcoal-black patches, bordered with creamy-white, that extended from head to tail. His head was flattened and arrow-shaped, with fierce, golden-flecked eyes. I managed to get him into a shallow snake-box with a gauze top, and he lay among the twigs and dead leaves, hissing loudly and vibrating his tail so rapidly that it struck among the leaves and rattled like a rattlesnake. If the slightest shadow fell across the box, he would strike up at the wire gauze, his fangs coming right through the mesh. I would never have believed this unless I had seen it, for normally a snake cannot make any impression on a completely flat surface. His gape was tremendous, and he would throw his head right back as he struck, to get the maximum force behind his long, curved fangs. Within half an hour there were several spots of golden venom on the wire gauze, and he was still striking wildly. I was forced, in the end, to put another layer of gauze half an inch above the first, to prevent accidents.

That evening, as Paula surged round the table, serving the meal, she treated us to a long discourse on *yarará* and their habits. It appeared that nearly every member of her family had, at one time or other during their lives, been within inches of death from a *yarará*. One received the impression that the entire fer-de-lance population of the Chaco spent its time stalking Paula's relatives. As they all escaped with monotonous regularity, the snakes must have led the most frustrating lives. Our meal over, Paula came in to say good night. She cast a black look at the fer-de-lance box in the corner of the room and observed that she would not spend the night in a house with a *yarará*, even if she were paid to do so, added a prayer that she would find us all still alive in the morning, and swept off in the direction of her home in the village. As it turned out, it was not snakes that disturbed us that evening.

Rafael was strumming on the guitar, singing a Gaucho ditty, in which alliteration appeared to be nicely blended with vulgarity; Jacquie had retired to bed with a month-old copy of the *Buenos Aires Herald*, which she had unearthed from somewhere; and I was examining the gun which Paula had procured for me. It was a Spanish make which I had not come across before, but it seemed in reasonable condition. As far as I could see, there appeared to be only one thing wrong with it.

'Rafael,' I said, 'this gun's got no safety-catch.'

He came across the room and peered at it.

'Yes, Gerry . . . see, that is the safety.'

'What, this little lever?'

'Yes, that is safety,' he said.

'It isn't, you know. I've tried it in both positions and the hammer still falls.'

'No, no, Gerry . . . she go click, yes. But she no go bang.'

I looked at him sceptically.

'Well, it seems very queer to me. A safety-catch is a safety-catch, and when it's on you should be able to pull the trigger without anything at all happening,' I pointed out.

'No, Gerry, you no understand . . . she is Spanish gun. . . . I show you how she work,' he said.

He loaded the gun, pressed the small lever down, pointed it out of the window and pulled the trigger. There was a shattering roar, all the dogs in the village started barking, and Jacquie appeared suddenly out of the bedroom, under the impression that the *yarará* had escaped from its box. Rafael straightened his spectacles and stared at the gun.

'Well,' he said philosophically, 'this way must be safety.'

He pressed the lever up, reloaded, aimed out of the window and pulled the trigger again. For the second time the gun went off with a roar, and the village dogs became almost hysterical.

'You can tell it's a Spanish gun,' I pointed out to Jacquie, 'because you can shoot yourself just as easily with the safety-catch on or off.'

'No, Gerry, she is good gun,' said Rafael indignantly, 'but I think she is broke inside.'

'I'm sure she is broke inside,' I agreed.

We were still arguing about this some ten minutes later when there came a thunderous knocking on the front door. Mystified, for it was quite late, Rafael and I went to see who our visitors were. On the veranda we found two rather scared Paraguayans, dressed in tattered green uniforms, peaked caps and clutching in their hands a brace of antiquated and rusty rifles. As they saluted in unison, we recognized them as two members of the local constabulary. Having said good evening, they asked us if we had fired a gun, and if so, who was dead. Rafael, rather taken aback, said the gun had gone off by accident and that no one was dead. The policemen shuffled their bare feet in the dust and looked at each other for inspiration. Then they explained, rather hesitatingly, that they had been sent out by the chief of police to arrest us and bring in the corpse of our victim. As there was no corpse, they were not quite sure what to do next. They would, they explained earnestly, earn the wrath of their chief if they returned without us, even though we had killed no one. They looked so woe-begone and puzzled by the whole matter that Rafael and I took pity on them, and offered to accompany them to the police-station and explain to the chief of police ourselves. They were pathetically grateful for this, and saluted a great number of times, smiling and saying, '*Gracias, señor, gracias.*'

We made our way down the moonlit village street, our captors trotting ahead, occasionally stopping to steer us carefully round a puddle or a patch of mud. At the other end of the village we came to the police-station, a two-room, white-washed shack, shaded by a large, golliwog-headed palm tree.

Our escort led us into a bare little room where, behind an ancient table piled high with an impressive array of documents, sat the chief of police. He was a lank and scowling man, whose polished boots and belt proclaimed his importance; he had only recently taken over this post, and it was obvious that he intended to prove to the inhabitants that crime did not pay. Our escort saluted, stood more or less to attention, and proceeded, in a chorus, to give an account of the incident. Their chief heard them out, scowling impressively, and when they reached the end of the story he gave us a searching look through narrowed eyes; then, with a magnificent gesture, he pulled a cigarette butt from behind his ear and lit it.

'So,' he hissed melodramatically, blowing smoke through his nose, 'you are responsible for the outrage, eh?'

'*Si, señor*,' said Rafael meekly, his lips twitching, 'we are responsible.'

'Ah! So you admit it?' said the chief of police, pleased at having trapped us into a confession.

'*Si, señor*,' said Rafael.

'So,' said the chief of police, sticking his thumbs in his belt and leaning precariously back in his chair, 'so, you confess, eh? You come here to the Chaco and you think you can commit these outrages with impunity, eh? You think that here it is *incivilizado*, and that you can get away with this sort of thing, eh?'

'*Si, señor*,' said Rafael.

There is nothing so irritating as having a purely rhetorical question answered, and the chief of police glared at him.

'But you didn't realize that there were laws here, the same as anywhere else, did you? You did not realize that you had a police force to contend with, did you, eh?'

The police force had, meanwhile, relaxed, content to let their chief handle the matter. One of them was picking his teeth very thoroughly, while the other was sticking his finger down the barrel of his rifle, and then pulling it out and examining it with a worried expression: presumably the gun was due for its annual clean.

'Look, señor,' said Rafael patiently, 'we haven't committed any crime. All we did was let off a gun by accident.'

'That's not the point,' said the chief of police cleverly; 'you *might* have been committing a crime.'

In the face of such astute reasoning, Rafael was struck dumb.

'As it is,' the chief went on magnanimously, 'I will not arrest you at once. I will consider the matter. But you must report here first thing tomorrow morning with your police permits. D'you understand?'

It was useless to argue, so we just nodded. The chief of police rose to his feet, bowed to us, and then clicked his heels together with such vigour that one of the constables dropped his rifle, and had to salute hurriedly to cover up his clumsiness. Rafael and I managed to get out of earshot of the police-station before dissolving into helpless mirth over our interview. When we got back to the house, Rafael gave a wonderful imitation of the chief of police for Jacquie's benefit, and was so amused by his own act that the tears of laughter ran out from under his spectacles.

The next morning, while we had breakfast, we related the whole incident to Paula. Instead of being amused, as we thought she would be, she was shocked and revolted by the whole thing. She described the chief of police in terms no lady should use, and told us that he was far too full of his own importance; once before she had been forced to have words with him, when he had tried to stop her girls going on board the river steamer. But this treatment we had received was the last straw. This time he had gone too far, and she herself was going to come down to the police-station and tell him where he got off. So after breakfast she draped her massive shoulders in a purple-and-green shawl, pinned a large straw hat covered with scarlet poppies to her head, and accompanied us, breathlessly indignant, down the road to the village.

When we reached the police-station we saw outside it an enormous double bed placed in the shade of a palm tree, and in it, snoring blissfully, lay the chief of police himself. His unshaven face wore a seraphic expression, and a couple of empty bottles by the bed argued that he had celebrated our arrest in a lavish fashion. Paula, at the sight of him, uttered a grunt of derision, and then, waddling rapidly forward, she drew back her hand and slapped vigorously at the heap of bed-clothes that presumably covered the chief of police's rear end. It was a fine, powerful blow, delivered with the full weight of Paula's massive body behind it, and the chief sat bolt upright in bed and stared wildly around; then he recognized Paula, and modestly drew the bedclothes up to his chin while giving her good morning. But Paula was in no mood for niceties, and she swept aside his greeting and launched her attack. Bosom heaving, eyes flashing, she hung over the bed and proceeded to tell him what she thought of him in a voice so shrill and so clear that half the village could hear. I began to feel rather sorry for the poor man; pinned down as he was, in his own bed and in full view of the village, he was forced to lie there while Paula loomed over him like a great avalanche of brown flesh, pouring scorn, ridicule, slander and threats over him in a remorseless stream that flowed so steadily he had no chance to get a word in. His sallow face turned from indignant pink to white, and then, when Paula got on to the more intimate details of his love life, it turned a delicate shade of green. All the inhabitants of the nearby houses had gathered in their doorways to watch the fun and shout encouragement to Paula, and it became apparent that the chief of police was not a popular member of the community. At length the poor man could stand it no longer; he flung back the blankets, leapt out of bed and scuttled into the police-station, clad only in his vest and a pair of natty, striped underpants, to the raucous delight of the assembled villagers. Paula, panting but triumphant, sat down for a short rest on the vacated bed, and was then able to accompany us homewards, stopping at various houses *en route* to receive the congratulations of her admirers.

The sequel to this episode came that evening, when one of the constables turned up at the house, looking distinctly embarrassed, clutching in one hand his trusty rifle and in the other a large and disorderly bunch of canna lilies. He explained that the chief of police had sent this floral offering for the señora, and Jacquie accepted them with suitable expressions of gratitude. After that, whenever we met the chief striding importantly about the village, he would come to attention and salute smartly, and then sweep off his peaked cap and beam at us. But he never did get around to seeing our police permits.

Chapter Seven

Terrible Toads and a Bushel of Birds

By the time we had been in the Chaco two months our collection had reached such proportions that it took us all our time to cope with it. Our day would begin just before dawn, when Paula would surge into the bedroom with the tea. The reason we arose at such an ungodly hour was not, I regret to state, because we liked early rising, but simply that we found it paid to get the heavier work done before the sun got too high and the temperature shot up.

Our first job was the cleaning out – a long, tedious and messy business that generally took us a couple of hours. The length of time taken over a cage depended entirely on the occupant: if it was bad-tempered, a longer time was needed in order to avoid being bitten or pecked; and if it was playful, a lot of time was wasted trying to persuade it that the cleaning out was not a game designed for its benefit. Most of the specimens very soon learnt the routine and would stand patiently to one side while half the cage was cleaned out, and then they would skip over into the clean section while the other half was dealt with. After the cleaning out was done and all cages had received a fresh bed of dry leaves or sawdust, we could start preparing the food. First of all came the fruit, which had to be peeled or cut up. Now, this sounds a fairly straightforward job, and it would have been so if we could have prepared the fruit in exactly the same way for every member of the collection, but, unfortunately, it was not quite as easy as that. Some birds, for example, liked their banana split lengthwise, put on a hook and hung on the wire front of their cage; others like their bananas cut up into small pieces, just the right size to swallow. Some would not touch their mango unless it was mixed into a slush with bread and milk, while others demanded (before they would touch anything else) that they should have a slice of over-ripe pawpaw with the seeds left in. Remove the seeds and they would not touch it, although they did not eat the seeds but merely plucked them out of the soft orange flesh and scattered them about the cage. So preparing the fruit was a long job that required a good memory for the animals' likes and dislikes.

After the fruit, the next big task was the meat. We used fourteen pounds a day: a sort of gigantic mixed grill that was composed of heart, liver, brain and steak, all of which had to be chopped or minced into an acceptable form. Preparing fourteen pounds of meat when the temperature is over a hundred in the shade is no joke, and, in order to try to facilitate this operation, I had purchased in Asunción a gigantic mincing machine. On its base was proudly embossed 'Primero classe', but in spite of its rash boast this ponderous piece of mechanism was the bane of our lives. Bits dropped off it at the slightest provocation, and no matter how small the pieces of meat we inserted into its maw, they always managed to stick, which meant that the whole thing had to be dismantled. Even when working properly, it shuddered and groaned, emitting at intervals a piercing shriek calculated to try the sternest nerves.

The meat prepared, the next job was to wash all the food- and water-pots. Anyone who thinks that by taking up collecting they will be rid of such domestic chores as washing up are sadly mistaken. Towards the end of our trip we had some fifty cages, and all of these had at least two pots in them, while some had three and even four. Every one of these had to be scrupulously scrubbed and rinsed before feeding could begin. In that heat any small bits of food left in the pots would soon start to decay, infect the fresh food and probably kill the specimens.

To someone who has never been collecting, it may seem as though we gave ourselves a lot of unnecessary trouble by pampering our animals. The answer is, of course, that unless you pamper them you will get precious few back alive. In every collection there is a nucleus of creatures of such phlegmatic disposition that they will put up with almost any sort of treatment, but for every one animal like this there will be twenty which are just the opposite.

Having got through the routine work, we could then devote ourselves to the more unusual and sometimes complicated jobs, such as bottle-feeding baby animals, doctoring any sick specimens and dealing with any new arrivals. These would turn up at any time of the day or night, and most of them caused trouble before we had them settled. Most specimens are fairly straightforward and are not much trouble once they are used to the routine, but occasionally we would get a creature which appeared to go out of its way to cause extra work. In a lot of instances this would be an animal which, by normal collecting standards, should be the easiest thing on earth to keep in captivity.

There is found in certain parts of South America a toad which must be one of the most bizarre looking of the batrachians. It is called the horned toad, and, as toads as a general rule are easy enough to keep, I thought the horned toad would be simple. For some reason, I had an overwhelming desire to obtain some of these toads while we were in the Chaco. I knew that they were found there, that the local name for them was *escuerzo*, but there, so to speak, the matter ended. It is one of the strange things about collecting that a creature you are most anxious to capture, no matter how common it was before, immediately becomes non-existent as soon as you ask about it. So it was with the horned toad; I showed everyone pictures of it, I offered fabulous rewards for its capture, and I nearly drove Jacquie and Rafael mad by forcing them out of bed at two o'clock in the morning to investigate marshes with me in the hope of catching some, but with no success. If I had known the trouble that the horned toads were to cause me, I would not have made such efforts to try to obtain them.

One lunch-time I found a battered tin can, the mouth plugged with leaves, waiting for me on the veranda. Paula could give me no more information than that it was a *bicho*, which was fairly obvious, and that it had been brought by an elderly Indian. I removed the plug of leaves circumspectly with a stick. Peering into the rusty inside, I saw, to my surprise, a gigantic horned toad squatting placidly on the backs of two smaller ones.

'What is it?' inquired Jacquie, who had kept a discreet distance with Paula.

'Horned toads ... three beauties,' I answered delightedly.

I tipped the tin over, and out spilled the toads on to the veranda in a tangled heap. Paula let out a whoop and disappeared into the house; from behind the safety of a window she looked out, palpitating.

'Señor, señor, look out,' she wailed; '*es un bicho muy malo, señor, muy venenoso.*'

'Rubbish,' I said. '*No es venenoso ... no es yarará ... es escuerzo, bicho muy lindo.*'

'*Madre de Dois,*' said Paula, rolling her eyes to Heaven at the idea of a horned toad being called beautiful.

'Are they poisonous?' inquired Jacquie.

'No, of course not ... they just look as though they ought to be, that's all.'

By now the toads had sorted themselves out, and the largest was squatting there, regarding us with an angry eye. He was about the circumference of a saucer, and three-quarters of his bulk seemed to consist of head. He had short, thick legs, a paunchy body, and this enormous head in which were set two large eyes filigreed with a pattern of gold and silver. Above each of these the skin was raised into an isosceles triangle, like the horns of a baby goat. His mouth was incredible, for it was so large it almost appeared to split him in two. The toad, with his rubbery lips, horned head and sulkily drooping mouth, managed to achieve an expression that was a combination of extreme malevolence with the arrogant bearing of an obese monarch. His whole air of evil was enhanced by the fact that he was a pale mustard-yellow in colour, covered with rust-red and sage-green patches that looked as though someone, lacking in artistic and geographical knowledge, had tried to draw a map of the world all over him.

While Paula was evoking the aid of the saints and assuring Jacquie that she would be a widow within half an hour, I bent down to get a closer look at our protégé. Immediately he gulped convulsively, blew himself up to twice his previous size, and then exhaled the air in a series of indignant wheezing screams, at the same time taking little jumps towards me and snapping his great mouth. This was a most effective and startling display, for the inside of his lips was a bright primrose-yellow.

At the sound of the toad's war-cry, Paula clasped her hands and rocked to and fro in the window. I thought this would be a most suitable opportunity to teach her some elementary natural history and, at the same time, enhance my prestige. I picked up the toad, who kicked violently and wheezed asthmatically, and approached the window where Paula was posturing like an outsize puppet. '*Bueno, Paula, mira ... no es venenoso ... nada, nada,*' I said.

As the toad opened his colossal mouth for another bagpipe-like cry, I stuffed my thumb into it. The creature was so surprised that his mouth remained open for a second, and I smiled soothingly at Paula, who appeared to be on the verge of a swoon.

'*No es venenoso,*' I repeated. '*No es ...*'

At that precise moment the toad recovered from his surprise and snapped his mouth shut. My first impression was that someone had amputated the entire first joint of my thumb with an extremely blunt hatchet. With an effort, I stifled the cry of agony that rose to my lips. Paula was regarding me pop-eyed, and, for the first time, without a sound. I gave a lop-sided sneer, which I hoped she would mistake for a debonair grin, while the toad amused himself by clenching his jaws as hard as he could at half-second intervals, so that the effect was as if my thumb was lying in the path of an extremely long goods train with more than the normal complement of wheels.

'*Santa Maria*,' said Paula, '*qué extraordinario . . . no tiene veneno, señor?*'

'*No, nada de veneno*,' I said hoarsely, still wearing my fixed smile.

'What's the matter?' asked Jacquie curiously.

'For Heaven's sake, get the woman away. This damn thing's nearly taken my thumb off.'

Jacquie hastily distracted Paula's attention with a discreet inquiry about the lunch, and she floated off to the kitchen, still ejaculating '*extraordinario*' at intervals. When she had vanished, we turned our attention to saving the remnants of my thumb. This was not so easy, for the toad had an immensely powerful grip but very fragile jaw-bones, and all our attempts at prising open his mouth with a stick caused them to bend alarmingly. Then, every time we removed the stick, he would give my thumb a triumphant squeeze. At last, in desperation, I laid my hand and the toad down on the concrete, hoping that this would persuade him to let go, but he just squatted there like a nightmare bulldog, and glared up at me with defiance.

'Perhaps it's the wrong sort of place,' suggested Jacquie helpfully.

'Well, what do you expect me to do?' I inquired irritably. 'Go and sit in a swamp with him?'

'No, but if you stuck your hand into that hibiscus bush, he might feel he could escape if he let go.'

'If he won't let go here, I don't see that crawling about in an hibiscus bush is going to help.'

'Have it your own way. What are you going to do, spend the rest of your life wearing a horned toad on your thumb?'

Eventually I saw that the only alternative to the hibiscus-bush experiment was to risk damaging the toad's mouth in prising it open, so I crawled into the shade of the bush and plunged my hand into the thickest tangle of the undergrowth. Immediately the toad sprang backwards, at the same time spitting out my thumb with every indication of disgust. I recaptured and put him back in the tin, without much opposition beyond a few half-hearted wheezes. My thumb had a scarlet line round it where his jaws had clamped together, and within an hour an ugly bruise had spread across the nail. It was three days before I could use my thumb without pain, and a month before the bruise faded.

It was the last time I attempted to demonstrate to the inhabitants of the Chaco the harmlessness of the horned toad.

The Chaco being such a paradise for bird-life, naturally the specimens in the avian section of our collection outnumbered the others by about two to one. The largest of our birds were the Brazilian seriemas. Their bodies were about the size of a chicken and were mounted on long, powerful legs;

their necks were also long and their heads large. Their beaks were slightly curved at the end, and this, with the big, pale silver eyes, made them somewhat like hawks. Their plumage was a soft greyish-brown on the neck and back, with cream underparts. On their heads, just over the nostrils, they had curious tufts of feathers that stuck up in the air. When they walked with their necks curved and the head thrown back, wearing their usual haughty expressions, they reminded me of immensely superior feathered camels. The two we had were perfectly tame, and so we used to let them out each day to wander round the camp.

When they were released from their cage in the morning, they would first walk all round the camp on a tour of inspection. They would stalk along for a few yards, pacing slowly and solemnly on long legs, and then all of a sudden they would stop with one leg in mid-air and freeze in that position, their tattered tiara of feathers quivering, expressions of outraged, aristocratic indignation on their faces. After a moment or so they would unfreeze, the suspended leg would come down and they would continue their constitutional with measured steps before once again becoming immobile a few yards further on. From their demeanour you would imagine them to be a couple of dowager duchesses who, whilst strolling in the park, had been whistled at by a tipsy soldier.

Occasionally the duchesses would drop their aloof pose and indulge in wild and fantastic dances. One of them would discover a twig, or tuft of grass, and, picking it up in her beak, she would rush towards her companion with great bouncing strides and then toss the offering on to the ground. They would both stare at it for a minute and then start to pirouette around it on their long, ungainly legs, bowing courteously to each other and fluttering their wings, now and again picking up the twig or grass and tossing it into the air with gay abandon. Then, as suddenly as it had begun, the dance would stop; they would freeze, glare at each other with what seemed like glacial rage, and then stalk off in opposite directions.

The seriemas developed a passion for nails, which they were convinced (rather as Anastacius, the butcher, had been) were live creatures. They would carefully pick a nail out of the packet and proceed to bang it on the ground until it was 'dead'. Then they would drop it and pick up another. In a short time the packet would be empty and the seriemas would be standing proudly in a sea of 'dead' nails. Fortunately, they never attempted to swallow them, but the habit grew irritating, for every time I wanted to construct something I had to spend a considerable time grovelling about in the dust, collecting the slaughtered nails which the seriemas had spent a happy morning scattering about the camp.

Apart from the seriemas, the bird that probably amused us most was a rail: a small marsh bird with piercing eyes of rich wine-red, a long, sharply pointed beak, and enormously large feet. This bird had the honour to be the one and only specimen that Paula obtained for us during our sojourn in the Chaco and, needless to say, no one was more surprised than Paula herself. It happened like this.

One day Jacquie woke up with a slight temperature and shivering fits which indicated a mild dose of sandfly fever, and so I made her stay in bed. After a hurried breakfast, I told Paula that the Señora was ill and would be staying in bed, and then left to get on with the animal work. When I returned at lunch-time I was amazed to see Jacquie's bed, with her still in it, out on the veranda, while from inside the house rose a confused cacophony of sounds, among which Paula's steamship-like hoot was predominant.

'What's going on?' I inquired of my wife.

'Thank goodness you've come back,' she said wearily. 'I've had the most exhilarating morning. For the first two hours Paula kept tiptoeing in and out of the room with the most ghastly selection of herb-teas and jellies, but when she found I only wanted to sleep she gave that up and started to clean the house. Apparently she gives the whole place a thorough going over once a week, and this happens to be the day.'

It sounded as if a troop of Cossacks was galloping round and round the house, pursued by several soprano Red Indians. There was a crash and a tinkle of glass, and a broom-handle appeared through a window-pane.

'But what the hell's going on in there?' I demanded.

'Wait a minute and I'll tell you,' said Jacquie. 'Well, just as I was dropping off to sleep, Paula came in and said she wanted to clean out the bedroom. I said that I didn't want to get out of bed and she'd have to leave it until next week. She seemed very shocked at the idea, rushed out here and screamed for her girls. About ten of them came over, and before I knew what was happening they'd lifted the whole bed up and carried it out here. Then they set to work to clean out the bedroom . . . the whole crowd.'

There came another crash from inside the house, followed by shrill squeals and the patter of running feet.

'Is that what they're doing now? It seems a novel way of cleaning out a bedroom.'

'No, no; they've finished the bedroom. They all trooped out here to carry me back inside, when Paula gave one of those screams of hers and nearly took the top of my head off, and said she could see a *bicho* in the garden. I couldn't see anything, but all the girls apparently could. Before I could ask them what sort of *bicho* it was, they'd all dashed down to the end of the garden and were crashing about in the bushes with Paula directing operations. Whatever the thing was, it took to its heels and for some peculiar reason it dashed straight into the house through the door . . . they all followed it inside and they've been chasing if from room to room ever since. Heaven alone knows what they've broken in there, but they've been galloping around for the past half-hour. I've shouted at them till I'm hoarse, but they won't answer. It's a wonder the beast hasn't died of heart failure, the row they've been making.'

'Well, there's one thing certain: it must be a harmless kind of *bicho*, or they wouldn't have chased it in the first place. Anyway, I'll go and have a look.'

Cautiously I poked my head round the front door. The living-room was a shambles of overturned chairs and broken plates. Distant crashes and yelps indicated that the hunt had ended in the second bedroom. I edged open the bedroom door, and was almost deafened by the chorus from inside; pushing the door open further, I peered round it. A broom-handle appeared from nowhere and swiped viciously downwards, missing my head by inches. I retreated and closed the door a trifle.

'Hey, Paula, *qué pasa?*' I bellowed through the crack.

There was silence for a moment, and then the door was flung open and Paula stood on the threshold, quivering like a half-inflated barrage balloon.

'*Señor!*' she proclaimed, pointing a fat finger at the bed, '*un bicho, señor, un pájaro muy lindo.*'

I entered the room and closed the door. Paula's gang of girls surveyed me with glittering smiles of satisfaction from among the ruins of the room. Their hair was disarranged, they panted with exhaustion, and one of them had lost a large portion of the front of her dress, which left little of her more obvious charms to the imagination. This seemed to cause her more gratification than anything else, and I noticed that she panted more vigorously than the others. The smell of eleven different varieties of scent in such a small space made my senses reel, but I approached the bed and got down on all fours to look under it. The girls and Paula clustered round me in a giggling, asphyxiating scrum as I looked for the *bicho*. Under the bed, covered with bits of fluff and dust, stood a panting, irritated, but still extremely belligerent rail. An exciting five minutes followed: the girls and Paula went round one side of the bed to chivvy the bird out, while I crawled under the bed with a towel and tried to grab him. My first attempt was thwarted because when I came to hurl the towel at him I discovered that Paula was innocently standing on one end. My second attempt was also a failure, for one of the girls in her excitement trod heavily on my hand. The third time, however, I was lucky and scrambled out from underneath the bed with the rail wrapped up in the towel and screaming at the top of his voice. I carried him out to show Jacquie, while Paula marshalled her girls and set them to repairing some of the chaos the rail hunt had produced.

'D'you mean to say that all that row was over *that?*' asked Jacquie in disgust, looking at the dust-covered head of the rail sticking out from the depths of the towel.

'Yes. Ten of them chasing him, and they couldn't get him. Amazing, isn't it?'

'He doesn't look worth getting to me,' said Jacquie; 'in fact he looks a horribly dull brute.'

But there, as it happened, she was quite wrong, for the rail turned out to be a bird which, though exceedingly irascible and short-tempered, had a distinct personality, and he very soon became one of our favourite bird characters.

We soon discovered that he moved about in almost as unusual and comical a way as the seriemas. Like a lanky school-master, he would stop and lower his head and peer myopically, neck stretched out, as though glaring through a keyhole, in the hope of catching his class misbehaving. Then, apparently satisfied, he would straighten up, give three or four quick flips of his short, pointed tail, and mince off to the next imaginary keyhole. This habit of flipping his tail up and down earned him the apt but regrettable name of Flap-arse. His spear-like beak he never hesitated to employ, lunging wildly at the hand of whoever was cleaning out his cage; this job became one of the bloodier and more painful tasks. I remember, on the day of his capture, putting in a large Players' cigarette tin filled with water. As soon as it appeared through the door, Flap-arse leapt forward and stabbed at it; to our surprise, his beak went straight through the tin, like a needle through cloth. He danced about the cage, wearing the tin on his beak, and it was some time before I was able to catch him and remove it. Flap-arse was kept in a cage with wooden bars, through which he was forever peering hopefully, occasionally uttering a rasping 'Arrrk', in an admonishing tone of voice.

In the cage on top of Flap-arse's lived a bird, one of Jacquie's favourites, whom, to her annoyance, I christened Dracula almost as soon as he arrived. He was a bare-faced ibis, a bird the size of a pigeon, and had stubby, flesh-coloured legs and a long, curved beak of the same shade. His whole body was covered in funereal-black plumage, with the exception of an area round the eyes and base of his beak, which was bare and a pale tallow yellow. From his bald area a pair of small, circular and sad little eyes peered forth mistily. Dracula was a very dainty feeder, and seemed quite incapable of eating his meat unless it was shredded to a microscopic minuteness and saturated with water. If a little raw brain was mixed into this slush, his happiness was complete and he would dip and patter his beak in the food, giving tiny, wheezing titters of pleasure. Although he was a sweet-tempered and very likeable little bird, there was something rather eerie about the way he would chuckle to himself as he probed the bloody slush of brain and meat, with the enthusiasm of a ghoul that has found a fresh grave.

Another bird that enjoyed brain was a black-faced ibis, known to us simply as B.F.I. He throve on a pure meat diet for some time, until one day, thinking he would like a treat, I mixed some brain with it. B.F.I. could have had no opportunity of sampling this delicacy in the wild state, but he fell on it as though it was his favourite food. Unfortunately, he then decided that meat was too coarse and lowly a fare for him, and vociferously demanded brain at every meal. Whereas Dracula was a dainty feeder, B.F.I. had no pretensions to manners. His idea of feeding was to stand as close to his food-pan as possible (preferably *in* it) and then toss bits of brain all over himself and the cage with the gay abandon of someone throwing confetti, and crying 'Arrr-onk!' loudly and triumphantly with his beak full.

Once a week Flap-arse, Dracula and B.F.I. had a fish-feed to keep them in condition. This had been difficult to organize, for no one ever dreams of eating fish in the Chaco, so it could not be bought in the local market. Armed with lengths of thick string and fearsome barbed fish-hooks that appeared to have been designed for catching sharks, we would make our way down to the river-bank in the morning. Half a mile below the village was an old landing-stage, now disused, its worm-eaten timbers infested with spiders and other creatures, and almost hidden under a great eiderdown of glossy convolvulus leaves brocaded with pink, trumpet-shaped flowers. By picking our way from beam to beam, moving cautiously, so as not to disturb the great electric-blue wasps that had their nests in the wood, we would eventually arrive at the remains of the small jetty that jutted out into the dark waters, its fragile piles decorated with ruffs of lily leaves. Perched on the end, we would bait our hooks and cast them into the brown waters. It could scarcely be called fishing, for the river was infested with piranhas, and a bloody scrap of meat as bait would soon create a churning, snapping merry-go-round of fish below us, all fighting to be caught. It could not, therefore, be classified as sport, for there was no element of doubt about the outcome, but these fishing expeditions gave us an excuse to sit on the jetty's edge which commanded a wonderful view of the river as it wound away westwards. The sunsets were so magnificent that not even the haze of mosquitoes around us lessened our pleasure. After two months, Rafael had to leave us in the Chaco and return to Buenos Aires. The night before he left, we went fishing, and were rewarded with one of the most spectacular and impressive sunsets I have ever seen.

Somewhere to the north, in the great Brazilian forests, there had been rain, and so the river was swollen and swift with the extra water. The sky was a pale blue, smooth and unclouded as a polished turquoise. As the sun sank lower and lower, it changed from yellow to a deep red that was almost wine colour, and the black river-waters took on the appearance of a bale of shot silk being unwound between the banks. As the sun reached the horizon, it seemed to pause in its descent, and from somewhere out of the vast empty sky appeared three small clouds which looked as though they were composed of a small crowd of black soap-bubbles edged with blood red. The clouds arranged themselves with artistic precision, curtain-like, and the sun sank discreetly behind them. Then, round the bend of the river, appeared the vanguard of the camelotes. The flood-water had brought them down from higher levels, these islands of lilies, convolvulus and grass entwined round water-softened logs from the great forests. The sun had sunk and the river was moon-white in the brief twilight; and the camelotes in their hundreds swept past us silently and swiftly on their eager journey to the sea, some only as big as a hat, others a solid tangled mat as big as a room, each carrying their cargo of seeds, shoots, bulbs, leeches, frogs, snakes and snails. We watched this strange armada sliding past us, until it was too dark to distinguish anything, only now and then becoming aware of the passing of the great fleet of camelotes, for one would brush against the piles of the jetty with a quiet, soothing whisper of soft leaves and grass. Soon, mosquito-bitten and stiff, we made our way silently back to the village, and all night long the endless string of camelotes hurried on, but in the morning the river was as smooth and empty as a mirror.

Chapter Eight

The Four-eyed Bird and the Anaconda

One morning we received an addition to the collection, which we could hear arriving when it was still a good half-mile down the road. I saw an Indian trotting rapidly towards the camp clearing, endeavouring with moderate success to keep his large straw hat on with one hand while with the other he tried to prevent something from climbing out of a rather frayed wicker basket. The thing, whatever it was, kept complaining about its confinement in a series of rich, base honks which sounded like someone trying to play a complicated Bach fugue on an old bulb motor-horn. The Indian dashed up to me, laid the basket at my feet, then stood back, doffing his big hat and grinning broadly.

'*Buenos días, señor,*' he said, '*es un bicho, señor, un pájaro muy lindo.*'

I wondered what species of bird could possibly produce that complicated series of organ-like brays. The basket lay on the ground, shuddering, and more of the wild cries broke out. Looking down, I found myself staring into a cold, fish-like eye of pale bronze colour that glared through the wickerwork at me. I bent down, undid the lid of the basket and lifted it a trifle, so that I could see the occupant; I caught a brief glimpse of a tumble of tawny feathers, and then a long, green, dagger-shaped beak shot out through the crack, buried itself half an inch in the fleshy part of my thumb, and was immediately whipped back into the basket again. Drawn by my yelp of pain and resulting flood of bad language, Jacquie appeared on the scene and asked resignedly what had bitten me this time.

'A bittern,' I said, indistinctly, sucking my wound.

'I know, darling, but *what* bit you?'

'I was bitten by a bittern,' I explained.

Jacquie stared at me blankly for a moment.

'Are you being funny?' she inquired at length.

'No, I tell you I was bitten by this blasted bird . . . or rather I was pecked by it . . . It's a tiger bittern.'

'Not a jaguar bittern?' she asked sweetly.

'This is no time for silly jokes,' I said severely; 'help me get it out of the basket . . . I want to have a look at it.'

Jacquie squatted down and eased the lid off the basket, and once more the green beak shot out, but this time I was ready for it and grabbed it adroitly between finger and thumb. The bird protested deafeningly, and kicked and struggled violently in the basket, but I managed to get my other hand inside and to grab him firmly by the wings and lift him out.

I don't know what Jacquie was expecting, but the sight of him made her gasp, for a tiger bittern is definitely one of the more spectacular of the wading birds. Imagine a small, rather hump-backed heron, with sage-green legs and beak, and clad entirely in plumage of pale-green colour spotted and striped with a wonderful, flamboyant pattern of black and tiger-orange so that the whole bird seems to glow like a miniature feathered bonfire.

'Isn't he lovely?' said Jacquie. 'What gorgeous colouring!'

'Here,' I said, 'just hang on to his feet a second – I want to look at this wing. It seems to be hanging in a rather peculiar fashion.'

While Jacquie held on to his green legs, I ran my hand down the underside of his left wing, and half-way down the main bone I found the ominous swelling of the muscles that generally denotes a break. I probed the swelling with my fingers, and manipulated the wing gently: sure enough, there was a break about three-quarters of the way down, but to my relief it was a clean break, and not a complicated mess of splintered bone.

'Anything wrong with it?' asked Jacquie.

'Yes, it's broken fairly high up. Quite a clean break.'

'What a shame! He's such a lovely bird. Isn't there anything we can do about it?'

'Well, I can have a shot at setting it. But you know how damn stupid these creatures are about bandages and things.'

'Let's try, anyway. I think it's worth it.'

'O.K. You go and get the money, and I'll try to explain to Daniel Boone, here.'

Jacquie disappeared into the house, while I explained slowly and tortuously to the Indian that the bird's wing was broken. He felt it and agreed, shaking his head and looking very sad. I went on to explain that I would pay him half the value of the bird then, and the other half should it still be alive in a week's time. This was a fairly complicated explanation that taxed my primitive Spanish to the extreme. Also, I find it helpful, when attempting to speak a language other than my own, to use my hands lavishly, for a gesture can explain something when a limited vocabulary would let me down. Clutching the infuriated bittern to my bosom, I could not indulge in gestures to help me out, for one hand held the bird round the body, while the other clasped his beak; in consequence I had to repeat everything two or three times before the Indian got the hang of it. At length he grasped my meaning and nodded vigorously, and we both smiled at each other and gave little bows and murmured '*Gracias, gracias.*' Then a thought struck the Indian, and he asked me how much I was going to pay; this simple question was my undoing. Without thinking, I let go of the bittern's beak, and lifted my hand to show him the requisite number of fingers. It was the opportunity the bird had been waiting for, and he did what all members of his family do in a fight. He looked upwards and launched his beak in a murderous lunge at my eyes. By sheer luck I managed to jerk back my head in time, so that he missed my eyes, but I did not jerk it back far enough; his beak shot squarely up my left nostril, and the point imbedded itself briefly somewhere near my sinus.

Those who have never been pecked in the nose by a tiger bittern can have little idea of the exquisite agony it produces, nor of the force of the blow. I felt rather as though I had been kicked in the face by a horse, and reeled back, momentarily blinded by the pain and stunned by the force of the thrust. I managed to keep my head well back to avoid a second stab from the beak, while my nose gushed blood like a fountain that splashed all over me, the bittern, and the Indian, who had rushed forward to help me. I handed the bird over to him and went to the house in search of first-aid; Jacquie busied herself with wet towels, cotton wool and boracic, scolding and commiserating as she did so.

'What would have happened if he'd got you in the eye?' she asked, scrubbing at the crust of dried blood on my lips and cheeks.

'I dread to think. His beak's at least six inches long, and if he'd got a straight peck, with that force behind it, he'd have gone right through into my brain, I should imagine.'

'Well, perhaps that will teach you to be more careful in future,' she said unsympathetically. 'Here, hold this cotton wool to your nose; it's still bleeding a bit.'

I went outside again, looking rather like one of those lurid anti-vivisection posters, and concluded my bargain with the Indian. Then I put the bittern into a temporary cage and went to collect the necessary medical appliances for the operation on his wing. First, I had to carve two splints out of soft white wood and pad them carefully with a layer of cotton wool held in place by lint. Then we prepared a large box as an operating table, and laid out bandages, scissors, razor-blade. I put on a thick gauntlet glove and went to fetch the patient. As I opened the door of his cage he lunged at me, and I caught him by the beak and pulled him out, squawking protestingly. We bound his feet with a bandage, and dealt in the same way with his beak. Then he was laid on the table, and, while Jacquie held his feet and beak, I set to work. I had to clip off all the feathers on the wing; this was not only in order to make it easier to fix the splint, but also to take as much weight off the wing as possible. When the wing was almost as bare as a plucked chicken, I manoeuvred one of the flat splints under the wing, so that the break lay in the centre of it; then came the delicate and tricky job of feeling until I located the two broken ends of bone, and then twisting and pulling them gently until they lay together in a normal position. Holding them in this position on the splint with my thumb, I slid the other splint on top, and held the break firmly, trapped between the two slats of padded wool. Then the whole thing had to be bound round and round with yards of bandages, and the finished product tied firmly against the body with a sort of sling, so that the weight of the bandages and splints did not drag the wing down and pull the broken ends of bone out of place. This done, our patient was put back in his cage, and supplied with a plate of chopped meat and some fresh water.

For the rest of the day he behaved very well, eating all his food, standing in one position, not attempting to interfere with his wing, and generally behaving as though he had been in captivity for years. Most wild creatures have the strongest possible views about bandages, splints and other medical accoutrements, and no sooner do you put them on, than their one ambition in life is to get them off again as quickly as possible. I had had a number of irritating experiences in the past with both birds and mammals over this vexed question of first-aid, and so I was surprised and pleased when the tiger bittern seemed to take the whole thing calmly and philosophically. I felt that at last I had found a bird who was sensible and who realized that we were strapping him up for the best possible reasons. However, I was a bit premature in my judgment, for next morning, when we were checking round the collection, Jacquie peered into the bittern's cage, and then uttered an anguished groan.

'Just come and look at this stupid bird,' she called.

'What's he done?'

'He's got all his bandage off. . . . I thought you were being a little too optimistic about him last night.'

The tiger bittern was standing gloomily in the corner of his cage, glaring at us with his sardonic bronze eyes. He had obviously spent an energetic evening stripping the bandages from his wing, and he had made a good job of it. But he had not reckoned with one thing: the inside edge of his beak was minutely serrated, like a fretsaw, the teeth of which were directed backwards, towards the bird's throat. When he caught fish, these little 'teeth' helped him to hold on to the slippery body, and made sure that it only slid one way. This is a very fine thing when you are catching fish, but when you are unwinding bandages you find this type of beak a grave disadvantage, for the bandages get hooked on to the serrated edge. So the tiger bittern stood there with some twelve feet of bandage, firmly hooked to his beak, and dangling down in a magnificent festoon. He looked like an attenuated, morose Father Christmas whose beard had come askew after a hot half-hour distributing presents. He glared at us when we laughed, and gave an indignant and slightly muffled honk through the bandages.

We had to get him out of his cage and spend half an hour with a pair of tweezers stripping the tattered bandages from his beak. To my surprise and pleasure, I found that he had not succeeded in removing the splints, so the wing-bones were still held in the same position. We bound him up once more, and he looked so contrite that I felt he had learnt his lesson. The next morning, though, all the bandages were off and trailing from his beak, and we had to go through the whole laborious re-bandaging again. But it was no use, for every morning we would be treated to the sight of him standing in his cage, heavily disguised under a patriarchal cascade of white beard.

'I'm getting sick of bandaging this bloody bird,' I said as Jacquie and I cleaned his beak for the eighth morning running.

'I am, too. But what can we do? We're using up an awful lot of bandage; I wish we'd thought of bringing some sticking-plaster.'

'Or even some plaster bandage ... that would have fooled him. What worries me, though, is that all this messing about isn't going to do the wing any good. For all I know, the bones may have shifted under the splint, and his wing will heal with a damn great bend in it, like a croquet hoop.'

'Well,' said Jacquie philosophically, 'all we can do is to wait and see. We can't do any more than we're doing.'

So, every morning for three interminable weeks, we unpicked, unravelled and re-bandaged the bittern. Then the great day came when the bones should have healed, and the bandage was removed from his beak for the last time. I seized the scissors and started to cut away the splints.

'I wonder what it'll be like,' said Jacquie.

'Probably look like a corkscrew,' I said gloomily.

But as the splints fell away, they revealed the bittern's wing lying there as straight as a die. I could hardly believe my eyes; it was impossible to see where the break had been, and even when I felt the bone with my fingers I could not have located the break if it had not been for a slight ridge of protecting bone which had appeared at the point where the two broken ends had grown together. The wing-muscles had, of course, grown weak through lack of use, and so the wing dropped considerably, but after a week or so of use he soon regained the power in it, and the wing went back to its normal position. For some time it remained bald, but eventually the feathers grew again, and when he attacked his food-pan with beak snapping and wing flapping, you could not have told that there had ever been anything wrong with him at all. We were very proud of him, not only because he was a good advertisement for our surgery, but also because he was a good example of how worth while it is to persevere with even the most hopeless-looking cases. Of course, we never received any gratitude from the bird himself – unless a savage attack every feeding time could be interpreted as gratitude – but we were repaid in another way, for indirectly the tiger bittern was the cause of our meeting the Four-eyed Bird and the anaconda.

The Indian who had brought us the bittern did not turn up to collect the other half of his money on the appointed date – a most unusual occurrence. But he did appear some ten days later, and seemed genuinely pleased at the good job we had done on the bird. He explained that the reason he had delayed in coming was that he had been trying to catch us a snake of monstrous proportions, 'muy, muy grande,' as he put it, and of incredibly evil disposition. This grandfather of all reptiles lived in a swamp behind his house, and twice in the past three months it had paid a visit to him and stolen one of his chickens. Each time he had followed it into the swamp, but had failed to find it. Now, the night before, the snake had made a third raid on his chickens, but this time he was fairly sure he knew the area in which it was lying up to digest its meal. Would the señor, he inquired diffidently, care to accompany him to catch it? The señor said that nothing would give him greater pleasure, and the Indian promised to come back early the next morning to guide us to the serpent's lair.

I felt that this hunt for – and I hoped capture of – the anaconda (for that was obviously what the snake was) would make an ideal subject for our ciné-camera, so I made arrangements for an ox-cart to come the next morning, in which Jacquie and the camera could travel. These ox-carts are fitted with gigantic wheels, some seven feet in diameter, which enable them to get through swamp-land that would bog down any other form of vehicle. They are pulled by any number of oxen, according to the load, and though they are slow and uncomfortable, they enable you to get right into the swampy areas that would otherwise be inaccessible. So early the next morning we set off, the Indian and I on horse-back, and Jacquie squatting in a cart drawn by a couple of dreamy-eyed and stoical oxen.

Our destination proved to be further than I had thought. I had hoped that we would reach the swamp before the sun had risen too high in the sky, but by ten o'clock the heat was intense and we were still wending our way through the thorn-scrub. The speed of our little caravan was governed entirely by the oxen; they kept going at a steady slouching walk, but, as it was only half the speed of the horses, it slowed down our progress considerably. The country we were travelling through was dry and dusty, and we were forced to ride alongside the cart; for if we rode behind we were suffocated by the clouds of dust kicked up by the oxen, and if we rode in front our horses enveloped the cart in *their* dust. The landscape was alive with birds, all filled with that early-morning liveliness and bustle which seems common to birds the world over. Flocks of guira cuckoos fed in the short growth by the side of the path, churring and giggling to each other. They would wait until the lumbering cart was within six feet of them, and then they would take wing and stream off like a flock of brown-paper darts, chattering excitedly, to land twenty yards further on. In a group of tall *palo borracho* five toucans leapt and scuttled among the branches from which the Spanish moss hung like the faint silvery spray of a fountain. The toucans watched us knowingly over their great, gleaming beaks, uttering high-pitched, Pomeranian-like yelps to each other. On every tree-stump or other vantage point sat a little white flower, a widow tyrant, its breast shining like a star. Every now and then they would slip off their perch, dive through the air like determined snowflakes, snip a passing insect neatly in their beaks and swoop back to their perch again with a flutter of neat black wings. A seriema swept across the path, paused with one leg in the air to give us an aristocratically sneering glance, dismissed us as being of no importance and hurried on as though late for some civic function.

Presently the forest became more broken and open, and on every side was the gleam and reflection of water. Ibis, storks and herons strolled two by two in the luxuriant herbage, with all the dignity of monks in a cloister. In the distance ahead of us we could see the small shack that was our destination, but to reach it we had to cross a level area like a small plain, which was in reality several acres of water overgrown with plants. We entered it, and within a few yards the horses and oxen were up to their bellies in water. The oxen, with their short, stubby and very strong legs, came off better here, for the entangling underwater roots did not hamper them at all. They simply ploughed forward steadily at the same speed they had used on dry land, the thick herbage being crushed and pushed out of the way. The horses, on the other hand, were constantly getting a long lily-root entwined round their legs and stumbling. We reached the other side, and the horses hauled themselves free of the web of plants with obvious relief, while the oxen marched ashore wearing decorative swathes of lily-roots and leaves round their legs.

When we reached the hut, the Indian's wife insisted on our having a short rest and the inevitable cup of *mate*, and after the hot ride we were glad enough to sit in the shade for ten minutes. Jacquie and I were offered cups to drink from, but the rest of them shared the pot and the pipe. A small girl stood near the group, solemnly handing it from person to person as each sucked up a mouthful of the *mate* through the pipe. Presently, feeling rested and refreshed, we thanked our guide's wife for her hospitality and continued on our hunt. If we had thought that the worst of the ride was over we were sadly disappointed, for the next hour or so was sheer hell. We made our way across a large swamp surrounded on all sides by forest, so that not a breath of wind came to relieve the fierce heat of the sun. The water was deep – up to the axles of the cart-wheels – and was so overgrown with weeds and lilies that even the oxen found it heavy going. This patch of water must have been a sort of gigantic hatching ground for mosquitoes of all shapes and sizes. They rose in front of us so thickly that it was like looking through a gauzy curtain of shimmering wings; they fell on us with shrill whines of joy, and clung to us in great scab-like crusts, half drowned by our sweat but hanging on grimly, sucking with ferocious eagerness at our blood. After a few minutes of wild irritated swiping, you sank into a sort of hypnotic trance and let them drink their fill, for if we killed a hundred with one slap there were five million others to take their places. After a while, through the shifting veil of mosquitoes, I saw that we were approaching an island in the swamp, a hillock about two hundred feet square that raised itself above the flat carpet of plants and water. It was thickly wooded and shady, and it looked a wonderful place for a rest.

Apparently, our guide was of the same mind, for he turned in his saddle, wiping the insects away from his face with a careless hand, and pointed at the island.

'Señor, bueno, eh?'

'Si, si, muy lindo,' I agreed, and turning my horse I floundered back to where the cart was following, trailing a wide train of uprooted plants from its wheels. Jacquie was squatting in the back, an enormous straw hat perched on her head and her face invisible under a tightly wound scarf.

'Feel like a rest?' I asked.

One eye regarded me balefully from the depths of the scarf. Then she unwrapped it, displaying a face that was red and swollen with mosquito bites.

'I would like a rest,' she said bitterly, 'I would also like a cold shower, an iced drink and about four hundred tons of D.D.T., but I don't expect for a minute I'll get them.'

'Well, you'll get the rest, anyway. There's a little island ahead and we can sit there for a bit.'

'Where is this blasted snake?'

'I don't know, but our guide seems quite confident.'

'I suppose one of us has to be.'

Our caravan hauled itself wearily out of the swamp and into the blessed shade of the trees, and while Jacquie and I sat and scratched moodily, our two Indians had a long conversation. Then the guide approached and explained that the snake should, according to his reckoning, be somewhere about here, but it had obviously gone further than he had thought. He suggested that we should wait there for him while he rode ahead and reconnoitred. I commended the idea, gave him a cigarette, and watched him splash off into the swamp again, wearing a cloud of mosquitoes round his head and shoulders. After a doze and a cigarette I felt my spirits revive, and started to potter about among the thorn-bushes to see if I could find any reptile life. Presently I was roused by a loud cry of anguish from Jacquie.

'What's the matter?' I inquired.

'Come here quickly and get it off,' she called.

'Get what off?' I asked, hurrying through the bushes towards her.

I found her with the leg of her trousers rolled up, and there on her skin was hanging an enormous leech, like an elongated fig, its body swollen with blood.

'Good Lord!' I said; 'it's a leech.'

'I know it's a leech. . . . Get it off.'

'It looks like a sort of horse-leech,' I said, kneeling down and peering at it.

'I don't want to know what damn species it is; get it off,' said Jacquie furiously; 'get if off my leg – you know I can't stand them.'

I lit a cigarette and drew on it until the end was glowing red; then I applied it to the creature's swollen posterior. It curved itself into the most violent contortions for a minute, and then released its hold and dropped to the ground, where I put my foot on it. It burst like a balloon, and a splash of scarlet blood stained the ground. Jacquie shuddered.

'Have a look and see if there are any more on me.'

But careful examination revealed no more leeches on her anatomy.

'I can't think where you got it from,' I said – 'none of us got any.'

'I don't know ... perhaps it came from the trees,' she said, and gazed up into the branches above as though expecting to see an enormous flock of leeches perched on the branches, waiting to leap on us. Then suddenly she froze.

'Gerry, look up there, quickly.'

I peered up and saw that our little scene with the leech had been witnessed by another inhabitant of the island. Half-way up the trunk of the tree we had been sitting under there was a small hole, and from its dark depths was glaring a tiny feathered face the size of a half-crown in which were two huge golden eyes. It observed us in shocked silence for a minute and then disappeared.

'What on earth was it?' asked Jacquie.

'It's one of those pigmy owls. Quick, go and get the driver's machete ... only for heaven's sake be quick and quiet about it.'

While Jacquie crept away, I circled round the tree to see if there was an exit hole, but I could see none. Then Jacquie returned with the machete; I hastily cut a long slender sapling, and then took off my shirt.

'What on earth are you doing?'

'We've got to block that hole somehow until I climb up there,' I explained, hastily tying my shirt in a bundle at the end of the stick. I approached the tree carefully with my improvised plug, and when I had manoeuvred the stick into position I suddenly jammed the shirt over the mouth of the hole.

'Hold this in place while I climb up,' I said, and, when Jacquie had taken over the stick, I shinned my way up the bark of the tree until I was perched precariously on a branch stump near the place where my shirt was decorating the trunk. Very carefully I edged my hand under it and into the hole behind. To my relief, I found that the cavity was quite shallow, and groping round I soon felt the flutter of soft wings against my fingers; I grabbed quickly and got the owl's body in my hand, but it felt so small that I wondered for the moment if I had caught the right bird. Then a small curved beak dug itself painfully into my thumb, and I knew I was not mistaken. I pulled my hand out of the hole with the ruffled and indignant little creature glaring at me over my fingers.

'I've got him,' I called triumphantly, and at that moment the stump I was standing on snapped and the owl and I fell to the ground. Luckily, I fell on my back, with my hand holding the bird in the air, so the owl had the best of the fall. Jacquie helped me up, and then I showed her our capture.

'Is it a baby?' she asked, staring at it fascinated.

'No, it's a pigmy.'

'You mean it's fully grown?' she asked incredulously, staring at the sparrow-sized bundle of ferocity, blinking its eyes and clicking its beak at us in Lilliputian rage.

'Yes, he's fully grown. They're one of the smallest owls in the world. Let's get a box out of the cart to put him in.'

Placed in a box with a wire front, the owl drew himself up to his full height of four and a half inches and uttered a faint, wheezy, chittering noise before starting to preen his disarranged plumage. His back and head were a rich, dark chocolate colour, minutely speckled with grey, and his shirt-front was creamy grey streaked with black markings. The driver of the ox-cart was as captivated with the little bird as we were, and went to great lengths to explain to me that they were called Four-eyes. I found this a rather puzzling name, until the driver tapped on the edge of the box and the owl turned his head towards the noise. On the feathers just above the nape of his neck were two circular patches of grey, showing up well against the chocolate-coloured feathers, and making it look as though he really had eyes in the back of his head.

While we were still gloating over the owl, our guide reappeared in a great flurry of water and mosquitoes, to tell us, excitedly, that he had found the snake. It was apparently about half a mile away, lying on the mat of water-plants on the surface of the swamp, quite close to the edge. He explained that we should have to take it by surprise, for it was so close to the trees that it might take cover there, and once in the thorny thickets it would be difficult, if not impossible, to find. We set off, and when we reached a spot that the guide said was close to the reptile we sent the cart off to a suitable vantage-point on the right, while we ploughed steadily forward. The water here at the edge of the swamp was fairly shallow, and not nearly so overgrown, but the bottom was uneven, and the horses kept stumbling. I realized that if the snake ran for it I could not follow on horse-back: to try to make one's horse canter in that swamp was suicidal. I should have to follow it on foot, and I began to wonder for the first time if the snake was perhaps as big as our guide had described.

Unfortunately, the snake saw us before we saw him. The guide suddenly uttered a sharp exclamation and pointed ahead. About fifty feet away, in a clear patch of water between two great rafts of weeds, I could see a V-shaped ripple heading rapidly towards the forest edge. Uttering a brief prayer that the snake would be of a suitable size for one person to handle I flung the reins of my horse to the guide, grabbed a sack and leapt down into the lukewarm water. Running in water up to your knees is an exhausting pastime on any occasion, but to do it when the temperatures are in the hundreds is the sort of stupid action only a collector would contemplate. I struggled on, the sweat pouring down my face in such quantities that even the mosquitoes had no chance to settle, while ahead I could see the arrow-head of ripples rapidly approaching dry land. I was some thirty feet away when the anaconda hauled his glossy yellow and black body out of the water and started to glide into the tall grass. As I rushed forward in a desperate spurt, I tripped and fell flat on my face in the water. When I got to my feet the anaconda had vanished. I waded ashore, cursing bitterly, and walked into the tall grass where he had disappeared, to see if I could follow his trail. I had only walked about six feet when a blunt head with open mouth struck at me from a small bush, making me leap like a startled rocket. Under the bush lay the anaconda, his gleaming coils with their pattern merging into the speckled shadows so beautifully that I had not noticed him. Apparently, being full of chicken, he had found progress through the swamp just as exhausting as I had, and on reaching the tall grass had decided to rest. As I had stumbled upon him, he felt he must fight for it.

In nearly every book written about South America the author at some point or other (in some books once every other chapter) stumbles upon an anaconda. These generally measure anything from forty to a hundred and fifty feet, according to the description, in spite of the fact that the largest anaconda ever officially measured was a mere thirty feet. Inevitably, the monster attacks, and for three or four pages the author wrestles in its mighty coils until either he manages to shoot it with his trusty revolver, or it is speared by one of his trusty Indians. Now, at the risk of being described either as a charlatan or a man of immense modesty, I must describe my own joust with the anaconda.

The reptile struck at me in a very half-hearted manner, to begin with. He was not really interested in giving me good copy for a fight to the death. He merely lunged forward with open mouth, in the faint hope that I would become scared and leave him in peace, so that his digestive juices could resume their work on his chicken. Having made the gesture, and upheld his tribe's reputation for ferocity and unprovoked attack, he curled up into a tight knot under his bush and lay there, hissing gently and rather plaintively to himself. I realized that a stick of some sort would have been very useful, but the nearest clump of bushes was some distance away, and I did not dare leave him. I flipped my sack at him several times, in the hope that he would bite at it and get his teeth caught in the cloth, a method which I have found useful on more than one occasion. However, he merely ducked his head under his coils and hissed a bit louder. I decided that I would have to have some assistance to distract the beast's attention, so, turning round, I waved frantically to our guide, who was ensconced with the horses in the middle of the swamp. At first, being reluctant to come any closer, he just waved back amicably, but when he saw I was getting annoyed, he urged the horse forward and splashed through the water towards me. I turned round and was just in time to see the tail of the vicious, awe-inspiring and deadly anaconda disappearing hurriedly among the grass-stalks. There was only one thing to do. I stepped forward, grabbed the end of his tail and hauled him back into the open again.

Now what the anaconda should have done was to immediately envelop me in coil after coil of his muscular body. What he actually did was to curl up into a knot again and give a faint, frustrated hiss. I dropped the sack over his head quickly and then grabbed him behind the neck. And that, really, was that. He lay quite still, giving an occasional twitch to his tail and a faint hiss, until the guide arrived. In fact I had more trouble with the human than the reptile, for the guide was not at all keen to help me, and one is hampered in an argument when forced to embrace large quantities of snake. At last I managed to persuade the guide that I would not let the snake harm him, and he very gingerly held the sack open while I hoisted the reptile up and put it inside.

'Did you get some good shots?' I asked Jacquie when we got back to the cart.

'I think so,' she said, 'although it was all filmed through a haze of mosquitoes. Did the snake give much trouble?'

'No; he behaved better than our guide did.'

'How big is it? It looked enormous in the view-finder. I began to wonder if you could handle it.'

'He's not terribly big. A fairly average size. I should say about eight feet, but he may not be as long as that.'

The cart and horse lurched tiredly through the swamp, where the leaves of the water-plants were touched with a pink glow from the sunset. Overhead, immense flocks of black-headed conures filled the sky, infected with the hysteria that always seems to appear in parrots towards roosting time. In great tattered formations they swept to and fro over us, chattering and screaming, while the sun sank into a lemon-coloured blur among the backs of cloud. Tired, itchy, and glowing from the sun, we reached our house at eight o'clock. After a shower and a meal we felt more human. The pigmy owl ate four fat frogs, pouncing on them with his curious tiny cry of delight, like the gentle stridulation of a baby cricket. The anaconda, now in a sort of digestive stupor, made no objection to being measured. Stretched out, he came to exactly nine feet three inches.

Chapter Nine

Sarah Huggersack

Next to the parrakeets in the collection – who were shrill little friends – probably the noisiest and most cheeky of our birds were the two pileated jays. These birds are similar to the English jay in shape, though smaller and of a slighter build. Here, however, the resemblance ends, for pileated jays have long, magpie-like tails of black and white, dark velvet backs and pale primrose-yellow shirt-fronts. The colouring on the head is extraordinary. To begin with, the feathers on the forehead were black, short and plushy, and stuck up straight, so the bird looked as though it has just had a crew cut. Behind this, on the nape, the feathers were smooth, and formed a sort of bluish-white marking which resembled a bald patch. Above each bright and roguish bronze eye was a thick 'eyebrow' of feathers of the brightest delphinium-blue. The effect of this peculiar decoration was to give the birds a permanent appearance of surprise.

The jays were inveterate hoarders. Their motto was obviously 'waste not, want not'. Any other bird given more minced meat than it could eat would have wastefully scattered it about the cage, but not so the jays; all those bits which they could not manage were carefully collected and stored in, of all places, their water-pot. For some reason they had decided the water-pot was the best place in which to keep their supply of food, and nothing we could do would make them alter their opinion. I tried giving them two water-pots, so that they could store their meat in one and drink out of the other. The jays were delighted with the idea and promptly divided up their meat and stored it in both water-pots. They would also store peanuts, of which they were inordinately fond. There were several cracks and holes in their cage, which were admirably suited for nut-storing, except that the nuts were too big to fit in; so the jays would pick up the nuts one at a time and hop on to their perches, then by some remarkably clever juggling they would insert the peanut under the toes of their feet and proceed to deal it several hefty blows with their beaks until it was split up. Then they would pick up the pieces and try them for size; if they were too big, the same performance would be repeated. They did the same thing when eating the peanuts, except that when the nut was broken up they would put all the pieces carefully in one of their water-pots for ten minutes or so, so that they were softened and easier to eat.

One of the nicest things about the jays was their incessant chattering, for it was always subdued in tone. They would spend hours on their perches, facing each other with raised eyebrows, carrying on the most involved conversations in a series of squawks, wheezes, trills, chuckles and yaps, managing to get the most astonishing variety of expression into these sounds. They were great mimics, and in a few days had added the barking of the village dogs to their repertoire, together with the squawk of triumph of a laying hen, cockerels crowing, Pooh the crab-eating raccoon's yarring cries, and even the metallic tapping of Julius Caesar Centurian's hammer. Just after the jays had finished their breakfast and settled down to a good gossip, the variety of sounds that came from their cage was amazing, and you would have thought the cage contained an assortment of twenty or thirty different species of birds, instead of the solitary pair. Before we had kept them long, they had mastered the cries of nearly every creature in the collection and were becoming very cocky about it. But with the arrival of Sarah Huggersack a new noise was added to the camp chorus, and it was one that the jays found impossible to master.

Paula appeared in the living-room one day bearing the luncheon tray in her brawny arms at double her normal speed. Almost inundating me with hot soup, she asked if I would please go out to the kitchen, as an Indian had brought a *bicho*, an animal of enormous stature and indescribable ferocity. No, she didn't know what sort of *bicho* it was – it was inside a sack and she hadn't seen it, but it was tearing the sack to pieces and she feared for her life. Outside the back door I found a young Indian boy squatting on his haunches, chewing a straw and watching a small sack which was busily shuffling round in vague circles and snuffling at intervals. My only clue to the contents of the sack was a very large, curved claw sticking through at one place, but even this did not help me, for I could not, offhand, think of an animal small enough to fit in the sack, and yet at the same time big enough to possess such a claw. I surveyed the youth, who grinned back at me and bobbed his head, so that his long, straight, soot-black hair rippled.

'*Buenos días, señor.*'

'*Buenos días. Tiene un bicho?*' I asked, pointing at the waltzing sack.

'*Si, si, señor, un bicho muy lindo,*' he replied earnestly.

I decided the best thing to do was to open the sack and see the creature, but first I wanted to know what it was. I did not want to take any chances with such a claw.

'*Es bravo?*' I asked.

'No, no, señor,' said the Indian, smiling, '*es manso – es chiquitito – muy manso.*'

I didn't feel my command of Spanish was sufficient for me to point out that because a creature was young it need not necessarily be very tame. Some of the most impressive scars I possess are legacies from baby animals that didn't look capable of killing a cockroach. Hoping for the best, and trying to remember where the penicillin ointment was, I grabbed the gyrating sack and undid the mouth. There was a pause, and then from between the folds of sacking appeared a long, curved, icicle-shaped head and snout, with small, neat, furry ears and, embedded in the ash-grey fur, two bleary little eyes that looked like soaked currants. There was another pause and then the tiny, prim mouth at the extreme end of the snout opened, and about eight inches of slender greyish-pink tongue curved out gracefully. It slid back inside again, the mouth opened a bit wider and from it came a sound that defies description. It was midway between the growl of a dog and the raucous bellow of a calf, with just the faintest suggestion of a ship's foghorn suffering from laryngitis. The sound was so powerful that Jacquie came out on to the veranda, looking startled. By this time the head had retired into the sack, except for the end of the snout. Jacquie frowned at it.

'What in the world's *that* thing?' she asked.

'That,' I said happily, 'is the end of a baby giant ant-eater's snout.'

'Is it responsible for that ghastly noise?'

'Yes, it was just greeting me in ant-eater fashion.'

Jacquie sighed lugubriously. 'It isn't enough to have the jays and parrots deafening us all day long, now we've got to add a sort of bassoon to it,' she said.

'Oh, it will be quiet enough when it's settled down,' I said airily, and the creature thrust its head out of the sack, as if in response to my remark, and let forth another bassoon solo.

I opened the sack further and peered down into it. I was astonished that such a small creature could produce such a volume of sound, for from the tip of its curved snout to the end of its tail the ant-eater measured two and a half feet.

'Why, she's minute,' I said in amazement; 'she couldn't be more than a week or so old.'

Jacquie moved over, looked into the sack and was lost.

'Oh, isn't she adorable?' she crooned, taking it for granted that it was a female. 'Poor little thing.... Here, you pay, and I'll take her inside.'

She picked up the sack and carried it gently into the house, leaving me to argue with the Indian.

When I re-entered the house, I tried to get the creature out of the sack, but this was not an easy task, for the long, curved claws on the front paws clung to the sacking with a vice-like grip. In the end it took the combined efforts of Jacquie and myself to remove her. She was the first really young giant ant-eater I had seen, and I was surprised to find that she was, in almost every way, a miniature replica of the adult. The chief difference was that her fur was short, and she had no mane of long hair on her back, but merely a ridge of bristles. Her tail, too, gave no indication of the enormous shaggy plume it was to become; it looked just like the blade of a canoe-paddle covered with hair. To my consternation, I found that the central great claw on her left foot had been ripped away and was hanging by a thread.

We had to cut this away carefully and put disinfectant on the raw toe, an operation which seemed to cause her no discomfort, for she lay across my lap, clasping a large section of my trouser leg with one claw, while we doctored the other. I thought she was doomed to go through life with only one large claw, but I was mistaken, for it eventually grew again.

In the sack and on my knee she had behaved with great self-assurance and aplomb, but as soon as she was placed on the floor, she staggered round in vague circles, bellowing wildly, until she discovered Jacquie's leg, and with an inarticulate bray of delight clutched it and endeavoured to shin up it. As the trousers Jacquie was wearing were thin, the effect of the little animal's claws was considerable, and it took us some time to unhook her. During this process she attached herself to my arm, like a leech, and before I could stop her she had shinned up and arranged herself across my shoulders like a fox fur, digging her claws into my neck and back to prevent herself slipping, her long snout on one side of my face and her tail on the other. Any attempt to remove her from this perch was received with indignant snorts and a fiercer tightening of her grip, and this was so painful that I was forced to leave her where she was while we ate our lunch. She dozed intermittently while I drank my lukewarm soup, and I found that my gestures had to be very slow and deliberate, or she would suddenly awake in a panic and dig her grappling irons in, almost decapitating me. Things were complicated by Paula, who refused to come into the room. I was in no position to argue, for any incautious movement of my head put my jugular vein in grave danger. Fortified by food, we made another attempt to remove the ant-eater from my shoulders, but after my shirt had been ripped in five places and my neck in three, we abandoned the project. The difficulty was that as soon as Jacquie had prised one set of claws loose and turned to the next lot the first set would regain the ground they had lost. I began to feel like Sinbad during his association with the Old Man of the Sea. Eventually an idea struck me:

'Get a sack full of grass, darling, and when you've got one paw loose, let her take hold of the sack.'

This simple stratagem worked perfectly, and we lowered the stuffed sack to the floor, with the ant-eater clasping it desperately, a blissful expression on her face.

'What are we going to call her?' asked Jacquie, as she dealt with my honourable wounds.

'How about Sarah?' I suggested; 'she looks like a Sarah, somehow. . . . I know – let's call her Sarah Huggersack.'

So, Sarah Huggersack entered our lives, and a more charming and lovable personality I have rarely encountered. Up to the time I had met Sarah, I had had a fair amount of experience with giant ant-eaters, for I had captured some adults on another collecting trip to British Guiana, but I had never considered them to be beasts that were overburdened with intelligence or scintillating qualities. Sarah, however, converted me.

To begin with, she was tremendously vocal, and would not hesitate to blare her head off if she could not get her own way, whereas adult ant-eaters rarely make any sound louder than a hiss. Keep her waiting for her food, or refuse to cuddle her when she demanded affection, and Sarah battered you into submission by sheer lung-power. Although I could not have resisted buying her, I had qualms about it, for ant-eaters, having such a restricted diet in the wild state, are not the easiest things to establish on a substitute diet in captivity, even when adult. To take on the job of hand-rearing a week-old baby, therefore, was a very doubtful proposition, to say the least. Right from the start we had trouble over her bottle: the teats we had were too large for Sarah to hold comfortably in her tiny mouth. Paula made a frantic search which resulted in a very battered teat being found in some village house. This was the same size as ours, but had been used, and so was soft, and Sarah approved of it. She grew so attached to this teat, in fact, that even when we once again had a variety to offer her, she refused to drink from them and clung obstinately to the old one, sucking it so vigorously that it changed from scarlet to pink, and then to white; it became so limp that it was difficult to get it to stay on the bottle, and the hole enlarged to such an extent that, instead of a gentle stream, a positive flood of milk used to pour down Sarah's eager throat.

It was fascinating to have caught Sarah so young, for I could watch her develop day by day, and she taught me a great deal about her family. The use of her claws was an example. The front feet of an ant-eater are so designed that the animal walks on its knuckles, the two large claws thus pointing inwards and upwards. The claws, of course, are primarily used for breaking open the tough ant nests, to obtain food. I have also seen the adults using their claws as a comb for their fur. In Sarah's case, in her early stages, her claws were used solely to grip with, for the female ant-eater carries her young perched on her back. An adult, with its claw bent back against the palms like the blade of a penknife, can of course get a tremendous grip in this way, and so I was not surprised to find that Sarah, once she had fastened on to something, was extremely difficult to dislodge. As I have said, the slightest movement on the part of the thing to which she was clinging would cause her to tighten her grip convulsively. Thus, carrying her baby on her back must be an extremely painful undertaking for the female ant-eater.

Sarah also used her claws when feeding. She liked to grip a finger with one claw and keep the other raised in a sort of salute as she sucked at her bottle. Periodically, about once every fifteen seconds, she would use this claw to squeeze the teat. The teat suffered in consequence, and I was always expecting her claw to go right through it; but I couldn't break her of the habit. The female ant-eater has, therefore, to put up with the grip on the back when carrying her young, and then submit to what must be a painful assault at feeding time. Some indication of Sarah's grip can be gathered from the fact that I once placed an empty matchbox in the palm of her front paw, and when she tightened her grip – but not to the full extent – her claw went straight through the box. Then she put on full pressure and the box was flattened. The extraordinary thing was that I had placed the box *edgewise* on, and not flat, so there was quite considerable resistance.

The most worrying time with any baby wild animal is the first week, for, although it may be feeding well, you cannot tell if the milk you are giving it agrees with it. So for the first seven days or so its bowel motions become of absorbing interest to you, and you have to check them, to see that they are neither too hard nor too soft, and that the consistency is more or less normal.

Diarrhoea or constipation indicates that the food is too rich or perhaps does not contain enough nourishment, and you have to vary the food accordingly. Sarah, during her first week, nearly drove us mad. To begin with, her motions were small and of a putty-like consistency, but what was more worrying still was that she only relieved herself once in two days. Thinking that she was not perhaps getting enough nourishment from her milk, I increased the vitamin content, but this made no difference at all. I thought it might help to feed her more often, and so we increased the number of feeds per day, but she still stuck rigidly to her forty-eight-hour routine. The constipation might be due to insufficient exercising, though a young ant-eater carried on its mother's back would receive little in the way of direct exercise, but might obtain a certain amount when the mother moved around. So, for half an hour every day Jacquie and I would walk slowly to and fro, while Sarah, honking indignantly, would shuffle behind, trying to climb up our legs. But this enforced exercise made no difference, and she so obviously and heartily disapproved of it that we gave it up. So she would spend all day lying in her box, clutching her sackful of straw and dozing, while her stomach grew more and more bloated. Then would come the great moment, she would relieve herself, her stomach would assume normal proportions, and for a few hours – until the next feed – she would have a slim and sylph-like figure. As this rather curious biological functioning appeared to do her no harm, I eventually ceased to worry about it. I came to the conclusion that all baby ant-eaters, when they are young, do this. I believe this must be so, for when Sarah was a little older and started to sleep without her sack, her bowels started working normally.

Sarah's one delight in life was to be hugged, and to hug in return. If I held her to my chest and supported her with one arm, I found that she clung with less painful tenacity; but her favourite perch was always across my shoulders, and no matter where she started off, she slowly crept upwards, a few inches at a time, hoping that I would not notice, until she was lying across my shoulders. At first she could not bear to be put on the ground and would bellow forlornly. When you picked her up, you could feel her heart beating like a trip hammer, and she would clutch you frantically. She did not object to being on the ground providing she could hang on to some part of you, even your foot, for it gave her a feeling of security.

When she was about a month old, she grew less scared of being on the ground, but she liked to feel that Jacquie or I was near. Her sight, like that of all ant-eaters, was very bad and if you moved more than five feet away from her, she could not see you, even if you moved. Only by smell, or by hearing you call, could she locate you. Stand still and silent, and Sarah would revolve like a top, her long snout pointing frantically in all directions, trying to find you.

The older she grew, the more skittish she became. Gone now were the days when you lifted her out of the cage, lying like some Roman potentate on her sack, to give her food. The moment the door of her cage was opened she would rush out like a tornado, breathing deeply with excitement, and clutch at her bottle so eagerly you would have thought it was the first food she had seen for weeks. She was always most lively in the evenings, and it was after her pint of supper that she felt most energetic. Her stomach bulging like a hairy balloon, you would have to work her into the mood for one of her boxing matches by pulling her tail gently. She would peer at you short-sightedly over her shoulder, and one hefty fore-paw would be brought slowly up until it was raised above her head; then, with amazing speed, she would whirl round and try to clout you. If you showed no further interest in her, she would shuffle past you several times with a preoccupied air, trailing her tail temptingly near. Grab it, and pull a second time, and Sarah would change her tactics: this time she would whirl round, stand on her hind legs, with arms raised above her head as though about to dive, and then fall flat on her face, in the hope that your hand would be underneath her. These exchanges would continue for some time until Sarah had worked off all her surplus energy, and then another stage in the game would be reached. You were supposed to lay her on her back and tickle her ribs, while she, in ecstasy, would pluck at her tummy with her long claws. When we were exhausted, we would proclaim her the winner, by picking her up and holding her under the arms, whereupon she would put both paws straight up in the air and interlock the claws over her head in the usual champ manner. She grew to like these evening romps so much that if for some reason we were forced to forego them one evening, Sarah would sulk all next day.

The other animals, Cai, Foxey and Pooh, were inclined to look upon Sarah with jealous eyes, for we made such a fuss of her. One day, pottering aimlessly about the camp, she wandered towards the spot where Pooh was tied. Cai and Foxey watched Sarah blundering along to what they thought was going to be the fright of her life. Pooh sat stolidly on his haunches, like a Buddha, patting his stomach with pink paws and watching Sarah's approach with a thoughtful eye. Being full of low cunning, he waited until she had ambled past, and then, leaning forward, he grabbed a large section of her trailing tail and tried to bite it. Now Sarah looks slow and stupid, but I knew from our nightly games that she could move with great speed when she wanted to. She whirled round, reared up and bashed Pooh on the head with great force and precision; Pooh, grunting with astonishment, scuttled off and hid in his box. Sarah, however, had tasted blood, and was not going to let her enemy off that easily; fur bristling, she wheeled about, nose in the air, trying to find out where Pooh had gone. Catching a dim glimpse of the box, she proceeded to give it a severe beating, while Pooh cowered inside. Foxey saw her heading in his direction and hastily retreated behind a bush. Cai sat smugly on top of her post, chattering softly to herself. Sarah, as she passed, caught sight of the post and, still being in a bad temper, decided to teach it a lesson. She leapt at it and delivered several upper-cuts, and, while the pole swayed wildly, Cai clung to the top, screaming for help. Not until the post was leaning over drunkenly, and Cai was almost hysterical, did Sarah decide that she was the victor and wander off in search of someone to hug. It was the last time any of them tried tricks with Sarah.

The birds were quite unanimous in their dislike of the little ant-eater. I think that her long, slender snout had a faint resemblance to a snake, and this they disapproved of. I once heard the most terrible commotion in the bird section, and on going to investigate, I discovered that Sarah had somehow escaped from her cage and had her nose stuck through the wire of the seriemas' cage, to whom she had taken a fancy; the seriemas did not share her friendly attitude, and were screaming shrilly for assistance. As soon as she heard me call, however, she lost interest in the seriemas and came galloping lopsidedly towards me and shinned up my legs as far as my waist, where she settled down with a happy sigh.

Sarah had been with us some weeks when the first rains of the Chaco winter started. Now was the time when we should have to start thinking about travelling back the thousand odd miles to Buenos Aires to catch our ship. There was still one big job to accomplish before we left, and that was to make our film. I had decided that we would refrain from filming the animals in the collection until the very last moment, for then we should have a larger cast of stars. I had therefore reserved the last three weeks of our stay in the Chaco purely for filming. When this was completed, we would travel down the river to Asunción. That was our plan, but then the blow fell.

Paula brought in the tea one morning in a state of great excitement, and was so incoherent that it was some time before I could make out what she was talking about. When I at last understood, I laughed long and heartily.

Jacquie, in a semi-conscious early-morning condition, wanted to know what was amusing me.

'Paula says that there's a revolution in Asunción,' I said, chuckling.

'No, really?' said Jacquie, joining in my mirth; 'well, I must say Paraguay's living up to its reputation.'

'It's a wonder to me they know who's in power half the time, they liquidate them so rapidly,' I said, with the jovial and unctuous manner of one whose country is too cold-blooded to waste bullets or blood on politics.

'I suppose it won't affect us in any way, will it?' suggested Jacquie, sipping her tea thoughtfully.

'Good Lord, no! It'll probably all be over in a few hours – you know what it is. Instead of football, they have revolutions as the national game here – a few shots fired and everyone's happy,' I said. 'Anyway, I shall go down and find out if the radio station has any news.'

Puerta Casado boasted the astonishing luxury of a minute radio station which was in contact with the capital. By this means, lists of supplies were broadcast to Asunción and sent up on the next river steamer.

'I'll go down after breakfast,' I said, 'but I shouldn't be surprised to find it all over by now.'

I only wish I had been right.

Chapter Ten
Rattlesnakes and Revolution

When I arrived at the radio station after breakfast I asked the radio operator if he had heard which side had scored the winning goal in the revolution. Eyes flashing, arms waving he gave me the latest information, and I suddenly realized that the situation was far from funny. To begin with, Asunción appeared to be in a complete uproar, with indiscriminate street-fighting all over the place. The main centre of the battle was near the police headquarters and the military college, where the Government forces were being besieged by the rebels. Far more serious was the fact that the rebels had also gained control of the airfield, and had put all the planes out of action by removing various vital parts. But, from our point of view, the worst piece of news was that the rebels had commandeered the river shipping, and so there would be no more river steamers of any description until after the revolution was over. This item of news really shook me, for the only way we could get our collection out of the country and down to Buenos Aires was by river transport. The radio operator went on to say that the last time he had tried to contact Asunción there had been no reply, so he presumed that either everyone was in hiding, or else dead.

I returned to our little house in a much more sober frame of mind and told Jacquie the news. It was a situation with which we were totally unprepared to cope. Quite apart from anything else, our passports and most of our money were down in the capital, and we could do little without them. We sat drinking tea and discussing our plight, while Paula hovered round us commiseratingly, occasionally interjecting a remark which, though obviously kindly meant, generally had a depressing effect on us. When I tried to look on the bright side and suggested that within a few days either the Government forces or the rebels would have won, thus making things easier, Paula proudly informed us that Paraguay had never had such a short revolution; the last one had taken six months to die down. This time perhaps, she suggested kindly, we would have to spend six months in the Chaco. It would, she pointed out, give us plenty of opportunity to increase our collection. Ignoring this, I said that, providing the fighting was over fairly soon, everything would resume its normal course, and we could then get a river steamer down to Buenos Aires. Interrupting this flight of fancy, Paula remarked that she thought this unlikely, as during the last revolution the rebels had, for some obscure tactical reason of their own, promptly sunk all the river craft, thereby disorganizing not only the Government forces but their own as well.

In desperation I adopted Paula's attitude of looking on the darkest possible side of the picture, saying that if the worst came to the worst we could make our way across the river into Brazil, and thence overland to the coast. This idea was immediately quashed by both Jacquie and Paula: Jacquie pointed out that we were hardly in a position to undertake a thousand-mile journey through Brazil without passports or money, while Paula said that, during the *last* revolution, Brazil had armed guards posted on the river-banks, in order to repel any of the rebel forces who attempted to flee from justice. It was quite likely, she added gloomily, that if we attempted to get across the river the Brazilians might mistake us for leaders of the revolution trying to escape. I pointed out, rather acidly, that the leader of a revolution would hardly attempt to flee from justice together with his wife, a baby ant-eater, several dozen species of birds, snakes and mammals, and equipment ranging from recording machines to ciné-cameras, but Paula insisted that, on the whole, the Brazilians were not '*simpáticos*' and that this aspect would probably not occur to the guards.

After this brisk exchange, we sat in mournful silence for a bit. Then, suddenly, Jacquie had a bright idea. There was an American, a laconic, long-limbed individual, who bore a strong resemblance to Gary Cooper and owned a ranch some forty odd miles higher up the river. He had dropped in one day and had told us that if at any time we required any assistance we were not to hesitate to get in touch with him by radio. As he had spent a good many years in Paraguay, Jacquie suggested that we contact him, explain our predicament and ask for his advice. Once again I hurried down to the radio station and persuaded the operator to put in a call to the American's ranch.

Presently his soft drawl came over the loudspeaker, slightly distorted by the roars, crackles and wheeps of the atmospherics. Hastily I explained why I was worrying him, and asked his advice. His advice was simple and straightforward: get out of the country at the first available opportunity.

'But how can we?' I protested; 'there aren't any river steamers to take the animals on.'

'Son, you'll just have to leave your animals behind.'

'Well, supposing we did that?' I asked, a sinking feeling in the pit of my stomach, 'how do we get out then?'

'I've got a plane . . . only a small one, a four-seater. . . . Soon as there's a suitable break I'll send her over, and then you can beat it. They generally have a parley some time during these revolutions, and it's my guess they'll be having one any day now. So be ready; I'll try and give you some warning, but I may not be able to.'

'Thanks . . . thanks a lot,' I said, my thoughts whirling.

'That's O.K. Happy landings,' said the voice, and then with a series of loud crackles the loudspeaker went dead.

I thanked the radio operator absent-mindedly, and walked back to the house in the grip of one of the blackest moods of depression I can ever remember. To have worked so hard for so many months and to have assembled such a lovely collection, and then to be told at the end of it that you had to let the whole lot go, simply because some obscure Paraguayan wanted to become President by force, is not the sort of thing calculated to make you feel on top of the world. Jacquie, on being told the news, shared my view, and together we spent half an hour dealing with the ancestry, physical deformation and purely personal habits of the leaders of the rebels – a sheer waste of time, not helping our position in any way, but it certainly relieved our feelings.

'Well,' said Jacquie when we had run out of adjectives, 'which ones are we going to let go?'

'He said to let all of them go,' I pointed out.

'But we can't,' Jacquie protested, ' – we can't let them *all* go. Some of them wouldn't last two minutes in the wilds. We'll have to take some with us, even if it means leaving most of our clothing behind.'

'Look, even if we travel naked we can't take more than three or four of the smaller things.'

'Well, that's better than nothing.'

I sighed.

'All right, have it your own way. But that brings us back to the question: which ones do we let go and which ones do we keep?'

We sat and thought about it for a bit.

'We must take Sarah, anyway,' said Jacquie at length. 'After all, she's only a baby, and she couldn't possibly fend for herself.'

'Yes, we must take her . . . but she's damned heavy, remember.'

'Then there's Cai,' continued Jacquie, warming to her rescue work; 'we can't leave her behind . . . and Pooh, poor little chap. If we let them go, they're so tame they'd go up to the first person they met, and probably get their heads blown off.'

'I must take a pair of orange armadillos, they're too rare to leave,' I said brightening, 'oh, yes, and the horned toads and those curious black ones.'

'And then there are the cuckoos,' agreed Jacquie, 'and the jays. . . . They're far too tame to let go.'

'Wait a minute,' I said, coming suddenly down to earth, 'if we go on like this we'll be taking the whole damn collection, and there won't be room for us on the plane.'

'I'm sure just those few wouldn't weigh much,' said Jacquie convincingly, 'and you could make them some light travelling cages, couldn't you?'

'Yes, I think I could. I might be able to construct something entirely out of wire.'

Greatly heartened by the thought that we would be able at least to save a few specimens from our collection, we set to work to prepare for our escape. Jacquie packed busily, dividing our belongings into two groups – those things that we simply had to take with us, such as recording machine, films and so on, and those things that could conveniently be left behind, such as clothing, towels, nets, traps and so forth. Meanwhile, armed with a pair of shears, a coil of wire and a roll of small-mesh wire-netting I set to work to try and make some very light yet strong travelling cages that would hold the creatures until we reached Buenos Aires. It was no easy job, for the netting had to be bent into shape, 'sewn' up with wire, and then any sharp points had to be felt for and bent over. At the end of two hours I had made one cage large enough to hold Sarah, and my fingers and hands were scratched and torn.

'How are you getting on?' asked Jacquie, appearing with a most welcome cup of tea.

'Fine,' I said, surveying my bleeding fingers. 'I feel as though I'm doing a life sentence in Dartmoor. But I bet picking oakum is child's play to this.'

So while I continued to lacerate my hands, Jacquie took each cage as it was finished and covered it with a 'skin' of sacking sewn on with a large darning-needle. So, by ten o'clock that night we had enough cages to house those animals we intended to take with us. The cages were feather light, being only sacking and wire-netting, warm and fairly strong. They were, of course, not roomy, but for twenty-four hours the animals would come to no harm in them. The heaviest of the lot was Pooh's cage, for, knowing his burglar-like ability to break in or out of a cage, I had been forced to use wood in the construction. Tired and depressed, we crawled into bed.

'I'll start letting the other stuff go tomorrow,' I said as I switched off the light, and knew, as I said it, that it was not going to be a job I relished.

The next morning I put off the liberation duty for as long as I could, but eventually I could think of no more excuses for delaying it. The tiger bittern was the first one to be released; his wing had healed perfectly by now, and this, combined with his bad temper, gave me no qualms as to his ability to look after himself. I hauled him, protesting loudly, from his cage, carried him over to the edge of the small swamp that bordered our domain and perched him in a convenient tree. He sat on the branch, swaying drunkenly to and fro, and uttering loud and rather surprised honks. Dracula, the bare-faced ibis, was next on the list. As I carried him over to the swamp he twittered excitedly, but as soon as I placed him in the long grass and walked away he gave a squeak of alarm and scuttled after me. I picked him up and returned him to the swamp and hurried away, while he uttered hysterical squeaks for help.

I next turned my attention to the parrots and parrakeets, and had the greatest difficulty in persuading them to leave their cages. When I eventually got them out, they perched in a tree nearby and refused to move, screaming loudly at intervals. Just at that moment I heard a shrill and triumphant titter and, turning round, I saw Dracula running into the camp clearing, having found his way back. I caught him and again carried him to the swamp, only to discover that the tiger bittern was rapidly approaching camp, flying heavily from tree to tree with a determined expression on his face. Having shooed them both back to the swamp, I set about letting the black-faced ibis and the seriemas go. In my melancholy mood I committed a *faux pas* by letting both species of seriemas go at once, and before I knew what was happening I was surrounded by a whirling merry-go-round of feathers, and the air was quivering with indignant screams as each seriema tried to prove its superiority over the others. I managed to separate them with the aid of a broom, and hustled them off into the undergrowth in different directions. Feeling hot, flustered and not a little indignant that I was receiving so little co-operation from the specimens in my distasteful task, I suddenly discovered that the parrots had seized the opportunity to descend from their trees, and were now sitting in a row on top of their cages, regarding me with pensive eyes; obviously waiting for the doors to be opened so that they could return.

I felt that I had better ignore the birds for the moment, so I started on the mammals and reptiles. Keeping only the pair we were going to take with us, I rolled all the other armadillos off into the undergrowth. The other species I arranged in a circle round the camp, their noses pointing out in the direction of the great open spaces, and hoped that they would be all right. The reptiles, to my relief, behaved perfectly and showed no inclination to stay, wriggling off into the swamp with gratifying rapidity. Feeling that I had done a good morning's work (considered from the animals' point of view alone), I went in to have some food.

Lunch was a gloomy affair, and as soon as it was over we went outside to attend to the rest of our charges. The sight that met our eyes would have been extremely funny if it had not been so depressing.

In one corner of the camp Dracula, the tiger bittern and the black-faced ibis were squabbling over a piece of fat that Pooh had discarded. Round the pile of unwashed pots the three-banded armadillos foraged, like a troupe of animated cannonballs. The seriemas paced like sentries round the empty cages, and Flap-arse was pacing to and fro in an agitated manner, looking like a schoolmaster whose entire class has played truant. The parrots and parrakeets still sat in a hopeful row on top of their cages, with the exception of two who, obviously tired of waiting for me to let them in again, had taken the law into their own hands, gnawed through the wire-netting front and gained access to the cage that way. They sat on their perch glowering at us hungrily and giving those curious asthmatic grunts that some Amazon parrots use to show their indignation. Jacquie and I sat down on a box and surveyed them hopelessly.

'What are we going to *do* with them?' she asked at length.

'I haven't the faintest idea. We can't leave them wandering around here, or they'll all be killed the moment our backs are turned.'

'Have you tried shooing them away?'

'I've tried everything short of hitting them over the head with a stick. They just won't go.'

Dracula had now left the contest over the piece of fat to the bittern and the ibis, and was busily trying to get back into his cage by trying to climb through the wire mesh which would have been a tight fit for a humming-bird.

'I wish,' I said viciously, 'we had one of those twee individuals here to see this.'

'What twee individuals?'

'Those knowledgeable sentimentalists who are forever telling me that it's cruel to lock up the poor wild creatures in little wooden boxes. I'd just like them to see how eagerly our furred and feathered brothers rush back to the wilds as soon as they're given the opportunity.'

One of the seriemas approached us and started to peck hopefully at my shoe-lace, evidently hoping it would turn out to be a worm of gigantic proportions. Dracula had eventually given up the attempt to get back into his own cage, and had compromised by squeezing through the bars of the ibis cage. He now sat inside it, peering at us with misty eyes, twittering delightedly.

'Well,' I said at length, 'I suppose if we just ignore them they'll get so hungry that they'll go off in search of food, and that will solve the problem. By tomorrow they should have disappeared.'

The rest of that day was a nightmare. Feeling that the animals should not be fed in any circumstance, we went about the task of feeding the ones we were keeping while the hungry horde of birds and animals hooted, whistled, tittered and honked at us hungrily, rushing to cluster round our feet when ever they saw us carrying a dish, perching in rows on the food-table and watching us hopefully. The impulse to feed them was almost irresistible, but we had to harden our hearts and ignore them. The only thing that kept us going was the knowledge that by the next day hunger would have driven them back into the wilds.

But the next morning when we went out to feed our charges we found the animals and birds still assembled around the camp, looking slightly more irritable and dejected than the day before. They greeted us with such manifestations of delight that we almost broke down and fed them. But we hardened our hearts and pretended to ignore them, even when they clustered round our feet and we were in grave danger of stepping on them. In the middle of this uproar an Indian stalked into camp carrying an old soap-box, and placed it reverently in the middle of the camp site. Then he stepped back, tripped over a seriema who happened to be walking past, recovered himself and doffed his straw hat.

'*Buenos días, señor,*' he said, 'a fine *bicho* for you.'

'Oh, Lord,' groaned Jacquie; 'this *would* happen.'

'You're too late, my friend,' I said sadly. 'I do not want any more *bichos.*'

The Indian regarded me, frowning.

'But, señor, you said you would buy *bichos*,' he said.

'I know, but that was before the revolution. Now I cannot buy, for I cannot take my *bichos* with me. . . . There are no boats.' I pointed to the mass of fauna wandering round the camp site; 'you see, I have had to let all these other *bichos* go.'

The Indian looked around him, bewildered.

'But they have not gone,' he pointed out.

'I realize that. But they will go. I am very sorry, but I cannot buy any more.'

The Indian regarded me fixedly. He seemed to be fully aware that I was dying to look inside the soap-box and see what the *bicho* was.

'It is a good *bicho*,' he said at last in a cajoling tone, 'a very fine *bicho* . . . *muy bravo, muy venenoso* . . . I had much trouble to catch it.'

'What sort of *bicho* is it?' I asked, weakening.

He became animated.

'A *bicho* of great rarity, señor, and *muy, muy venenoso,*' he said, his black eyes sparkling, a '*cascabel*, señor, of proportions so immense that it is impossible to describe. When he is angry he makes a noise like a thousand horses.'

I touched the box cautiously with the toe of my shoe, and immediately from inside rose the weird sound with which a rattlesnake informs the world of his presence, bad temper and evil intentions. It is certainly one of the most extraordinary sounds made by any reptile, this curious rustling crackle that starts like a whisper and ends like the crackle of toy musketry. It is far more frightening than the ordinary hissing of a snake, for it seems to have a sort of vibrating malevolence about it, a bubbling viciousness like the simmering of a witch's brew.

'Nevertheless,' I said sadly, 'I cannot buy it, my friend.'

The Indian looked crestfallen.

'Not even for ten *guaranies*?' he asked.

I shook my head.

'Eight *guaranies*, señor?'

'No, I'm sorry, but I cannot buy it.'

The Indian sighed, knowing that I meant what I said.

'Well, señor, I will leave it with you, for it is of no use to me,' he said, and, accepting the packet of cigarettes I gave him, he picked his way through the motley crew of birds and departed, leaving us with a rattlesnake on our hands.

'And what are we going to do with that?' asked Jacquie.

'We'll record his rattle and then let him go,' I said; 'he's got a very fine rattle. I should think he's quite a big one.'

For a variety of reasons we could not get around to recording the rattlesnake that day. The next morning our released collection was still with us, but an hour's chasing eventually convinced at least some of them that we were not going to feed them, and they started to drift away. Then we got the recording machine and rigged it up near the rattlesnake's box, placed the microphone in an advantageous position, and tapped on the box hopefully. There was not a sound from within. I tapped again. Silence. I thumped on the box vigorously, with no result.

'D'you think he's dead?' asked Jacquie.

'No, it's the usual thing. These damned animals make a hell of a row until you get a recording machine anywhere near them, and then they make as much noise as a dead giraffe.'

I tipped the box gently, and felt the weight of the snake slide from one end to the other. This had the desired effect, he rattled viciously, and the green needle on the recorder swung and quivered, registering an astonishing volume of sound. Three times I tipped the box, and three times the snake responded with increasing fury. At last we had enough tape, but by this time the snake was so annoyed that he was producing a steady rattle like a machine-gun.

'Now to let him go,' I said, seizing a machete.

'You aren't going to let him go here, are you?' inquired Jacquie in alarm.

'Yes, he'll be all right. I'll give him a prod and he'll whisk off into the swamp.'

'He sounds very bad-tempered. Make sure he *does* whisk off into the swamp.'

'Now stop fussing and go and stand over there,' I said, with doubtless irritating unctuousness.

Jacquie retreated to a safe place, and I proceeded to try and remove the lid of the rattlesnake's prison. This was not so easy, for the Indian had nailed it on with large and rusty nails in incredible quantities. At last I managed to force the tip of my machete blade into the crack and with a stupendous heave a large section of the lid flew off. I gave a sigh of relief and then did a very foolish thing: I bent down and peered into the box to see if the snake was all right. To say that he was furious would be an understatement. He was positively bubbling with rage, and as my face appeared in the sky above him he lunged upwards with open mouth.

Now I had always been under the impression that a rattlesnake could not lunge *upwards* at his victim, but that he had to lunge forward like any other snake. So it was with fright not unmixed with surprise that I saw the blunt head, carunculated like a pineapple, flying upwards to meet my descending face. The mouth was wide open, pink and moist, and the fangs hung down at the ready and appeared, to my startled gaze, to be about the size of a tiger's claws. I flung myself backwards in a leap that could only have been emulated but not bettered by a wallaby in the prime of life and in full control of its faculties. Unfortunately, I rather spoilt the athletic effect by tripping over my machete and sitting down heavily. The snake crawled out of the box and coiled himself up like a watch-spring, with head raised and his rattle vibrating so rapidly that it was a mere blur hanging round the end of his tail.

'Just give him a prod and he will whisk off into the swamp,' said Jacquie sarcastically.

I was in no mood to exchange saucy badinage. I went and cut myself a long stick and again approached the rattlesnake, in the hope of being able to pin him down and pick him up. However, the reptile had other ideas on the subject. He struck twice at the descending stick and then wriggled towards me rapidly with such obvious menace that I had once again to repeat my ballerina-like leap. The snake by now was in the worst possible temper and, what was more annoying, stubbornly refused to be frightened or cajoled into leaving the camp site. We tried throwing clods of earth at him, but he just coiled up and rattled. Then I threw a bucket of water over him. This worsened his obviously already high blood-pressure, and he uncoiled and wriggled towards me. The irritating part of the whole business was that we could not just leave him there to make off in his own time. There was work to be done, and one's work is rather apt to suffer by continually having to look over one's shoulder to make sure a four-foot rattlesnake isn't there to be stepped on. Also Pooh and Cai were out on their leads, and I was worried in case the reptile went up and perhaps bit one of them. Very reluctantly, I decided that the only thing to be done was to despatch the infuriated snake as quickly and as painlessly as possible, so, while Jacquie attracted his attention with the aid of the stick, I approached him cautiously from behind, manoeuvred into position and sliced off his head with the machete. His jaws kept on snapping for a full minute after his head had been severed from his body, and half an hour later you could still see slight muscular contraction if you touched his ribs with the stick. The extraordinary thing about this snake was that rattlesnakes normally cannot strike unless they are coiled up – so as a rule, however angry one gets, they will always stay coiled up in one position ready to bite – this one, on the other hand, seemed to have no hesitation in uncoiling and coming straight for you. Whether he could have bitten us successfully with his body stretched out was rather a moot point, but it was not the sort of experiment that I cared to make.

By the following day a great number of our specimens had disappeared, though there were still one or two hanging around the camp. At midday a messenger arrived from the radio station, to say that the American had got through to inform them that there was a lull in the fighting in Asunción, and that he was sending the plane over for us in the afternoon. Frantically we bustled about packing the rest of our things and endeavouring to console Paula, who followed us from room to room, giving long, shuddering, heart-strangled sobs at the thought of our imminent departure. Having packed, we made a hurried lunch, and then set about the job of putting the animals into their travelling boxes. All of them went in without demur except Pooh, who seemed to imagine that it was some new and refined form of torture that we had invented. First we tried to lure him by throwing bananas into the cage, but with the aid of his long, artistic fingers he managed to hook them out and eat them complacently without venturing inside. Eventually, as time was growing short, I had to grab him by the scruff of his neck and the loose skin of his large behind, and bundle him head-first into his box, while he screamed like a soul in torment and clutched madly at everything with all four feet. Once inside, we gave him an egg, and he settled down quite philosophically to suck it and gave no further trouble.

Paula had now been joined by her girls and they all stood around in forlorn groups, looking rather like mourners at a funeral. The tears trickled steadily and in ever-increasing quantities down Paula's face, making havoc with her make-up, but as she appeared to derive much satisfaction from her grief, I presumed that this did not matter. Suddenly she startled us all by uttering a loud groan that would have done credit to Hamlet's father's ghost, and then crying in a sepulchral voice: 'It has come!' before plunging into another Niagara of grief. Very faintly echoing through the blue sky we could hear the pulsating throb of an aeroplane engine, and at that moment the lorry drew up outside the house. While I loaded the luggage and animals on to it, Jacquie was embraced by each of Paula's girls and then eventually clutched to Paula's moist and magnificently palpitating bosom. When my turn came, I was relieved to find Paula's girls had no intention of embracing me, but merely shook my hand and gave a little dipping curtsy, making me feel like some obscure species of royalty. Paula clasped my hand in both hers and clutched it to her stomach, then she raised her tear-stained face to me.

'*Adiós, señor,*' she said, large fat tears trickling out of her black eyes. 'Good journey to you and your señora. If God wills it, you will return to the Chaco.'

Then the lorry was bouncing down the dusty rutted road and we were waving from the window to Paula and her girls, who looked like a cluster of brilliant tropical birds as they stood waving frantically, their shrill voices shouting '*Adiós*'.

We arrived at the airfield just as the plane, like a glittering silver dragon-fly, swooped down. It made an extremely bad landing and then taxied towards us.

'Ah,' said the driver of the lorry, 'you have got the mad one.'

'Mad one,' I said, puzzled; 'what mad one?'

'This pilot,' he said scornfully, jerking his thumb at the approaching plane. 'They say he is mad. Certainly he never seems to land the plane without making it jump like a deer.'

The pilot, when he scrambled down out of the machine, turned out to be a short, stocky Pole with silvery hair and the vague, gentle expression of the White Knight in *Alice through the Looking Glass*. With the aid of a small hand-weighing machine we weighed our luggage and discovered to our consternation that we were several kilos over the maximum weight that the plane was allowed to take.

'Never mind,' said the pilot, beaming at us. 'I think she will do it.'

So we proceeded to wedge our suitcases into the plane, and then we scrambled in ourselves, while the lorry driver piled my lap head-high with the assortment of animal life that we were taking with us. Sarah, who had refused her bottle half an hour before, now decided that she was hungry and honked dismally at the front of her cage until I was forced to take her out and put her on Jacquie's lap to keep her quiet.

The pilot fiddled with the controls, then gave a smile of child-like pleasure when the engine roared into life. 'Very difficult,' he said, and laughed merrily. We taxied about in all directions for some five minutes before we found a dry enough patch to allow us to take off. The pilot let her out and the plane roared across the grass, jumping and lurching. We left the ground at the last possible moment and, zooming some six inches over the tops of the trees that bordered the airfield, the pilot wiped his forehead.

'Now she is up,' he yelled at me. 'All we have to worry about now is to get her down again.'

Below us the great flat plain stretched, blurred with heat-haze. The plane banked and then straightened out, and we were flying over the great molten curves of the river that coiled and wound away into the shimmering obscurity of the horizon towards Asunción.

Interlude

I have never liked cities particularly, and I never thought that I should be glad to see one. But the relief and pleasure we felt were extraordinary when we looked out of the plane and saw Buenos Aires beneath the wing, like a vast geometrical pattern of sequins glittering in the dusk. At the airport I made my inevitable pilgrimage to the nearest phone booth and dialled Bebita's number.

'Ah, child, I am so glad you are safe. Ah, you have no idea how we worried about you. Where are you now? At the airport? Well, come to dinner.'

'It's the animals again,' I said gloomily. 'We've got to find somewhere to put them. It's bitterly cold here, and they'll get pneumonia if we don't get them into the warm soon.'

'Ah, of course, the animals,' said Bebita. 'I have fixed a little house for them B-B-Belgrano.'

'A *house*?'

'Yes, only a little one, of course. It has, I think, two rooms. It has running water, but I do not think it is heated. B-b-but that does not matter – you can call here and I will lend you a stove.'

'I can only suppose that this house belongs to a friend of yours?'

'B-b-but naturally. You will have to return the stove soon, though, b-b-because it b-b-belongs to Monono, and he will simply die without it.'

Bebita's 'little house' turned out to be two good-sized rooms leading out into a little courtyard surrounded by a high wall. Leading off this was another small building which contained a large sink. With the aid of the stove, surreptitiously removed from Bebita's husband's room, we got the temperature nice and high, and all the animals started to look better. A phone call to Rafael had brought him scurrying round, spectacles gleaming, armed with fruit, meat and bread removed from his mother's larder. When I protested that his mother would probably take exception to this, he pointed out that the only alternative was for the animals to go hungry, for all the shops were shut. My indignation at this rape of his mother's larder was then forgotten, and we gave ourselves up to the pleasure of stuffing our animals with delicacies which they had never had before – such things as grapes, pears, apples and cherries. Then, leaving them warm and full, we went to Bebita's, where we sat down to the first civilized meal we had eaten in months. At last, as replete as our animals, we sank into chairs and sipped our coffee.

'And what will you do now?' asked Bebita.

'Well, we've got a few days left before the ship sails. We'll just have to try and get as much stuff in that time as we can.'

'You will want to go out into the *campo*?' she asked.

'If it's possible.'

'I will ask Maria Mercedes if she will let you go down to her *estancia*.'

'D'you think she would?'

'But naturally,' began Bebita, 'she's . . .'

'I know . . . she's a friend of yours.'

So it was arranged that we take the train from Buenos Aires out to Monasterio, some forty miles away. Near here lay Secunda, the *estancia* of the De Sotos. Here Rafael and his brother Carlos would be waiting to help us.

Chapter Eleven

The Rhea Hunt

The village of Monasterio lay some forty miles from Buenos Aires, and we travelled there by train. Once we had left the last straggling houses of the capital behind, the pampa stretched on either side of the track, limitless and frosted with dew. Along the edge of the track grew a wide swathe of convolvulus, the flowers a brilliant electric blue, growing so thickly that they all but obscured the heart-shaped leaves.

Monasterio turned out to be a small village that looked like a Hollywood film-set for a Western film. A straggle of square houses lined a street that was muddy, deeply lined with wheel-ruts and the marks of horses' hooves. On the corner stood the village store and tavern, its shelves lined with an incredible quantity of merchandise, from cigarettes to gin, from rat-traps to khaki drill. Outside this store several horses were tethered to a fence, while inside their owners drank and gossiped. They were on the whole short, rather stocky men with brown faces, sun-crinkled, eyes as black as jet, and large rather Victorian moustaches stained with nicotine. They were wearing the typical peon's outfit: wrinkled, black half-boots with small spurs; *bombachas*, the baggy trousers that hang down over the top of the boot like plus-fours; blouse-like shirts with a brightly coloured handkerchief knotted round the throat, and perched on their heads were the small, black pork-pie hats with narrow brims turned up in front, held on to the head by an elastic band round the back of the head. Their broad leather belts were studded with silver crowns, stars and other decorations, and from each hung a short but serviceable knife.

As we entered the store they turned to stare at us, not rudely, but with interest. In reply to our greeting in bad Spanish, they grinned broadly and replied courteously. I bought some cigarettes, and we hung around the store, waiting for Carlos and Rafael to appear. Presently there was a jingling of harness, the clop of hooves and the scrunch of wheels, and a small dog-cart came lurching down the road; and in it was our erstwhile interpreter and his brother Carlos. Rafael greeted us with overwhelming enthusiasm, his spectacles flashing like a lighthouse, and introduced us to his brother. Carlos was taller than Rafael, and gave the erroneous impression of being portly. His pale, calm face had a faintly Asiatic look about it, with small dark eyes and glossy black hair. While Rafael hopped about like an excited crow, talking fast and almost incomprehensibly, Carlos quietly and methodically loaded our bags into the cart and then sat patiently waiting for us to climb in. When we were installed he slapped the horses' rumps with the reins, clucked at them affectionately, and the cart trundled down the road. We drove for about half an hour, the road lying as straight as a wand across the vast expanse of grass. Here and there a herd of some hundred head of cattle grazed slowly, knee-deep in the pasture, and over them wheeled the spur-winged plovers on black-and-white wings. In the ditches at the roadside, filled with water and lush plants, ducks fed in small flocks, and rose with a clap of wings as we passed. Presently, Carlos pointed ahead to where a wood of dark trees lay – a black reef across the green of the pampa.

'That is Secunda,' he said, smiling at us, 'ten minutes we'll arrive there.'

'I hope we'll like it,' I said jokingly.

Rafael turned to me, his eyes wide with shocked expression behind his glasses.

'Migosh!' he said, aghast at such a thought, 'of course you will like, Gerry. Secunda is *our estancia.*'

Secunda was a long, low, whitewashed house squatting elegantly between the huge lake on one hand and a thick wood of eucalyptus and cedar of Lebanon on the other. From the back windows you looked out over the placid grey waters of the lake with its faint green rim of pampa; and from the front you looked out at a formal Victorian garden, the clipped box hedges lining the wood-grown path, the small well, its mouth nearly choked with ferns and moss. In odd corners, among the geometrical flower-beds littered with a glowing mass of fallen oranges, the pale statues glimmered in the shade of the cedars. On the lake the black-necked swans swam in droves, like drifting ice-packs on the steel-grey surface, and groups of spoonbills fed among the reed-beds, like heaps of roses among the green. In the cool garden humming-birds hung purring over the well, and among the orange trees and on the path strutted the oven-birds, with inflated chests; and on the flower-beds minute grey doves with mauve eyes fed hurriedly and secretively. There was a silence and peace here of a lost and forgotten world, a silence broken only by the staccato cry of the oven-birds, or the soft stammer of wings as the tiny doves flew up into the eucalyptus.

After we had settled in and unpacked our things, we assembled in the living-room for a conference about our plan of campaign. The first thing I wanted to do was to try to film the rhea, the South American equivalent of the African ostrich. Secunda was one of the few *estancias* within easy reach of Buenos Aires which still had wild flocks of these great birds. I had mentioned this to Rafael in Buenos Aires, and now I asked him what chance there was of locating a flock and filming it.

'Do not worry,' said Rafael complacently. 'Carlos and I have fix everything.'

'Yes,' said Carlos, 'we go look for the ñandu this afternoon.'

'Also, I think maybe you like to film the way the peons catch the ñandu, no?' asked Rafael.

'How do they catch them?'

'The old way, with the *boleadoras* ... you know, the three balls on a string.'

'Good Lord! yes,' I said enthusiastically. 'I'd love to film that.'

'It is all arrange,' said Carlos. 'This afternoon we go in the cart, the peons go on horses. We find ñandu, the peons catch them, you film them. It is good?'

'Wonderful,' I said; 'and if we don't get them today, can we try tomorrow?'

'Of course,' said Rafael.

'We will try and try until we find them,' said Cárlos, and the two brothers beamed at each other.

After lunch the small cart appeared, its wheels scrunching softly on the damp gravel. Carlos was driving, slapping the grey horses' buttocks gently with the reins. He pulled up opposite the veranda, jumped to the ground and walked towards me; the big, fat greys stood with drooping heads, champing thoughtfully on their bits.

'You ready, Gerry?' inquired Carlos.

'Yes, I'm ready. Have the others gone on?'

'Yes, they and Rafael have taken horses . . . I get six peons. Is that good?'

'Fine. . . . All we want now is my wife,' I said, gazing round hopefully.

Carlos sat down on the wall and lit a cigarette.

'Always we wait for womans,' he said philosophically.

A large yellow butterfly drifted over the greys' heads, pausing by their ears as if struck with the thought that they might turn out to be a variety of hairy arum. The greys nodded their heads vigorously, and the butterfly flew off in its drunken, zig-zag way. A humming-bird sped past the dark cedars, stopped suddenly in its own length, flew backwards for six inches, turned and dived at a low swinging cedar branch, where it captured a spider with a minute squeak of triumph, and then shot off between the orange trees. Jacquie appeared on the veranda.

'Hullo!' she said brightly. 'Are you ready?'

'Yes,' said Carlos and I in unison.

'Now, are you sure you've got everything? The ciné, the Rollei, film, exposure metre, lens hood, tripod?'

'Yes, everything,' I said smugly; 'nothing left out, nothing forgotten.'

'What about the umbrella?' she inquired.

'Damn, no. I forgot the umbrella.' I turned to Carlos, 'You haven't got an umbrella I could borrow, have you?'

'Umbrella?' echoed Carlos, mystified.

'Yes, an umbrella.'

'What is this umbrella?' asked Carlos.

It's extremely difficult to think of a good description of an umbrella at a moment's notice.

'It's one of those things you use when it's raining,' I said.

'It folds up,' said Jacquie.

'You open it out again when it rains.'

'It's like a mushroom.'

'Ah!' said Carlos, his face clearing; 'I know.'

'Have you got one?'

Carlos gave me a reproachful look.

'Of course. . . . I tell you we have everything.'

He disappeared into the house, and returned carrying a Japanese paper parasol decked out in gay colours, with a circumference about half that of a bicycle wheel.

'It is good?' he asked, twirling it proudly so that the colours ran together.

'You haven't got anything bigger, have you?'

'Bigger? No, no bigger. What you want this for, Gerry?'

'To cover the camera, so that the sun doesn't make the film too hot.'
'Ah!' said Carlos. 'Well, this will be good. I will hold it.'

We climbed into the little cart, and Carlos slapped the massive grey rumps with the flat of the reins and chirruped. The greys sighed deeply and sorrowfully and lurched forward. The drive was lined with giant eucalyptus trees, with their bark peeling off in huge twisted strips, showing the gleaming white trunk beneath. In the branches were massive structures, huge matted haystack-like collections of twigs, the tenement nests of the Quaker parrakeets. These slender grass-green birds flew chittering and screaming through the branches as we passed below, and swooped, glittering in the sunshine, into the entrance holes of their enormous communal nests. 'Eeee-hup! eeee-hup!' sang Carlos falsetto, and the greys broke into a shambling trot, snorting affrontedly. We reached the end of the long, tree-lined drive, and there before us lay the pampa, glistening and golden in the morning sun. The greys pulled the cart over the dew-soaked grass, weaving in and out among the giant thistles, each standing stiffly, as tall as a man on horseback, like spiky and weird candelabra with the bright purple flame of the flower on each branch. A burrowing owl, like a little grey ghost, did a dance above the mouth of its burrow as we passed: two steps one way, two steps the other; pause, to stare with golden eyes; shake the head from side to side, bob up and down rapidly; then a leap off the ground and a swift circling flight on wings as soft and silent as a cloud.

The cart rumbled and staggered on and, ahead, the pampa stretched to the horizon, a flat, placid sea of golden grass, shadowed in places where the thistles grew more thickly. Here and there, like a small dark wave on that smooth expanse, a small copse of wind-tangled trees gave shade to the cattle. The sky was early morning blue, and great puffy cumulous-clouds moved across it with the speed and dignity of albino snails on a pale window-pane. The thistles grew thicker, and the horses had to weave more and more, to avoid bumping into them and retaining a bellyful of spikes. The wheels crushed the brittle plants down with a noise like miniature musketry. A hare leapt from under the greys' thudding hooves and loped off in a curving run before freezing again and melting into the brownish haze of thistles. Far ahead we could see tiny dark shapes spotted with bright colours ... the peons on horseback on the horizon.

They were waiting for me, bunched together in the long grass. Their horses moved restlessly, heads tossing and feet mincing. The peons laughed and chattered together, their brown faces alight with excitement, and, as they swayed and turned on their waltzing horses, the silver medallions that studded their broad leather belts glittered in the sun. Carlos drove our cart into their midst and the greys stopped, heads drooping, emitting loud sighs as of exhaustion. Carlos and the peons worked out our plan of campaign: the peons would split up into two groups, riding spread out into a long line, with the cart at the centre. As soon as the rheas broke cover, they would try to encircle the birds and drive them back to the cart, so that I could get the ciné-camera working.

When the babel had died down a bit: 'D'you think we'll find some *ñandu*, Carlos?'

Carlos shrugged. 'I think so. Rafael say he see them here yesterday. If they not here they will be in the next *potrero*.'

He chirruped to the horses, and they roused themselves from their trance and the cart moved on through the crackling thistle plants. We had not travelled more than fifty feet when one of the outriders let out a long-drawn whoop and waved excitedly at us, pointing ahead at a particularly thick patch of thistles into which the cart was just about to plunge. Carlos pulled the greys up sharply, and we stood on the seat to peer over the thistles, a mist of purple flowers. For a minute we could see nothing, and then Carlos grasped my arm and pointed.

'There, Gerry, see? *ñandu*. . . .'

In the maze of thistles with their grey-and-white stalks I could distinguish a bulky form dodging and twisting. The peons had started to close in, when suddenly one of them stood up in his stirrups and waved his hand and shouted.

'What's he saying, Carlos?' I asked.

'He says it *ñandu* with babies,' said Carlos, and, pulling the greys round, he slapped them into a canter, so that the cart bounced and rattled along the side of the thistle-patch. Where the thistles ended and the grass began he pulled up.

'Watch, Gerry, watch; they will come this way,' he said.

We sat watching the tall wall of thistles, listening to the scrunching as the peons' horses forced their way through. Then, suddenly, a tall thistle swayed, cracked and fell to the ground, and over its prickly carcase a rhea leapt out on to the green grass, with the grace and lightness of a ballet-dancer making an entrance. It was a large male, and he paused for one brief moment after his appearance, so that we could see him. He looked like a small, grey ostrich, with black markings on his face and throat. But his neck and head were not bald and ugly, like the ostrich's, but neatly feathered; his eyes had not the oafish expression of the ostrich, but were large, liquid and intelligent. He paused for that one brief moment, getting his bearings, and then he saw us. He twirled like a top and was off across the pampa, taking great strides, with his head and neck stretched out in front of him and his great feet almost touching his chin with every step. He seemed to bounce more than run, as though his legs were giant springs causing him to rebound from the earth. Standing upright, he had been some five and a half feet high, but now, running with the speed of a galloping horse, his whole being – body, legs and neck – was stretched out and streamlined. As he ran, one of the peons crashed through the barrier of thistles and cantered out on to the grass within twenty feet of the flying bird, and we were treated to the sight of a rhea's evasive tactics. As soon as he saw the horse and rider, his head came up, and he seemed to stop dead in the middle of one of his prodigious bounds, twist round in mid-air and set off in the opposite direction, without any appreciable loss of speed. This time he ran in a zig-zag pattern, each bound taking him six feet to the right, and then six feet to the left, so that from the rear he looked like a gigantic feathered frog.

Just as Carlos was about to urge the greys forward again, the second rhea broke cover. It was a smaller bird, and of a lighter shade of grey, and it bounded through the gap in the thistles that the first one had created, and then skidded to a halt on the grass.

'This one is womans,' whispered Carlos. 'See, she is small.'

The female rhea could see us, but she did not sprint off as the male had done: instead, she stood there, shifting uneasily from one leg to the other, and watching us with large, timid eyes. Suddenly we realized the reason for her delayed flight, for through the thistles scuttled her brood – eleven baby rheas that could not have been much more than a few days old. Their round, fluffy bodies were about half the size of a football, mounted on thick, stumpy legs ending in great splay feet. Their baby down was a light creamy fawn, with neat slate-grey stripes, and they stood about a foot high. They waddled out of the forest of thistles and gathered round their mother's enormous feet, their eyes bright and unafraid, squeaking shrilly to each other. The mother glanced down at them, but it was obviously impossible for her to know by looking at the milling, wasp-striped swarm whether they were all there or not, so she turned and set off across the grass. She ran, as it were, in slow motion, her head up, her big feet thumping the turf with each stride. The babies followed, running as their mother ran, but strung out in a line behind her: the effect was rather ludicrous, for the mother looked like an elderly, rather arty, spinster running for a bus with all the dignity she could muster, trailing behind her a striped feather boa that bobbed and twisted through the grass.

When the rhea family had vanished from view, and Jacquie had finished uttering crooning noises over the appearance of the babies, Carlos started the cart once more and we crackled onwards through the thistles.

'Soon we will see more, the big ones,' said Carlos, and the words were hardly out of his mouth when we saw Rafael galloping towards us, waving his hat, his scarlet scarf trailing out behind. He crashed through the thistles and pulled up alongside the cart, spouting a flood of Spanish and gesturing wildly. Carlos turned to us, his eyes gleaming.

'Rafael say that many ñandues are sitting over there. He says we take this cart and go over there, then Rafael and the other mens will make the ñandues run near us.'

Rafael galloped off the instruct the other horsemen in their part in the plan, while Carlos urged the reluctant greys through the prickly thistles at a gallop. We burst out on to the pampa and thundered across it, the cart swaying so much that I thought it would overturn at any minute. Carlos crouched on the seat, slapping the swaying bottoms of the horses with the reins and uttering shrill nasal cries of encouragement. A pair of spur-wing plover, black and white as two dominos against the green, watched our lurching approach and then ran six feet and leapt lightly into the air, where they flew around on their pibald wings, screaming 'Tero ... tero ... tero ...' as they swooped over us, warning the creatures of the pampa of our approach. Leaning precariously out of the swaying cart, I caught a glimpse of the horsemen about half a mile away, strung out in a line, waiting for us to reach the right position. The heat from the sun was now terrific, and the greys' flanks were striped darkly with sweat: the horizon was blurred and heat-shimmered, as though you looked at it through a misted glass. Carlos suddenly pulled on the reins and brought the cart to a standstill.

'Here is good, Gerry. We will take the camera over there,' he said, pointing. 'The *ñandu* will run this way.'

We scrambled down from the cart, I carrying the camera and tripod, while Carlos strode ahead armed with the tiny paper parasol. Jacquie remained in the cart, field-glasses glued to her eyes, ready to warn us when the rheas broke cover. Carlos and I walked some fifty yards away from the cart to a spot where we could command a clear view of a wide 'avenue' of grass between two great thistle patches, and there I set up the camera, took light readings and focused, while Carlos held the ridiculous parasol over me to keep the camera cool.

'All right,' I said at last, wiping the sweat from my face.

Carlos raised the vivid parasol and waved it from side to side, and in the distance we could faintly hear the shrill cries of the peons as they urged their horses into the thistle jungle. Then there was silence. Since we remained without movement, the two plovers circled round several times and then landed near us, where they took sudden darting runs from side to side, and paused while they bobbed up and down suspiciously. Jacquie sat immobile in the cart, her hat pushed on to the back of her head, the glasses to her eyes. The greys stood with drooping heads, occasionally shifting their weight from one haunch to the other, like elderly barmaids towards closing time. I could feel the sweat trickling down my face and back, and my shirt stuck unpleasantly to me. Suddenly Jacquie raised her hat and waved it wildly from side to side, at the same time emitting ear-splitting and incomprehensible instructions to us. At the same moment the two plovers leapt from the ground and circled round wildly, screaming loudly, and we could hear the distant cracking of the thistles, the thunder of the horses' hooves and the excited cries of the peons. Then from the thistle-bed appeared the rheas.

I never would have believed that a ground bird could move with the speed and grace of a bird in flight, but I learnt otherwise that morning. There were eight rheas, spread out in roughly a V-formation, and they seemed to be running as fast as they could. Their long legs were moving with such speed that they were blurred, being only clearly defined on the downward stroke when the foot touched the ground and lifted the bird forward. Their necks were stretched out almost straight, and the wings were held away from their bodies and hanging down slightly. Clearly above the noisy screams of the plovers we could hear the rapid and rhythmic thudding of their feet on the iron-hard ground. If it had not been for this, you could have imagined they were on wheels, so swift and effortless was their movement. As I say, they appeared to be running as fast as they were able, but suddenly two peons galloped out of the thistles, uttering shrill whoops, and an amazing thing happened. Each rhea tucked his tail in as though fearing a slap on the rump, and they all accelerated to twice their previous speed in what appeared to be three enormous, splay-footed leaps. Certainly they dwindled into the distance with astonishing rapidity. The peons galloped after them, and I could see one of them loosening the boleadoras that hung from his belt.

'Surely they're not going to catch them right over there, Carlos; I can't possibly film them at that distance?'

'No, no,' said Carlos soothingly; 'they will go round them and bring them back. Let us go back to the cart . . . there is most shade there.'

'How long will they be rounding them up?'

'Oh, five minutes, maybe.'

We walked back to the cart, where Jacquie in her grandstand seat was bouncing up and down, field-glasses to her eyes, giving onomatopoeic cries of encouragement to the distant hunt. I set the camera up in the small patch of shade cast by the cart, and climbed up beside her.

'What's happening?' I asked, for by now the peons and the quarry were distant specks on the horizon.

'Isn't this exciting?' she cried, retaining a firm hold on the glasses as I tried to take them from her; 'it's terribly exciting. Did you see them run? I didn't know they could run so fast.'

'Let's have a look.'

'All right, all right, in a minute. I just want to see . . . Oh, oh, no, no, look out . . .'

'What's happened?'

'They tried to break back, but Rafael saw them in time. . . . Oh, just look at that one running. . . . Did you ever see anything like it?'

'No,' I said truthfully; 'so what about letting me have a look?'

I prised the glasses from her reluctant grasp and trained them on the distant scene. I could see the rheas dodging and twisting among the thistles with an ease and grace that would have been the envy and despair of a professional footballer. The peons were galloping hither and thither, endeavouring to keep the birds in a fairly tight bunch and drive them back. All the peons now had their boleadoras out, and I could see the balls gleaming on the ends of the long strings as they whirled them round and round their heads. The rheas turned in a bunch and ran towards us, and with cries of triumph the peons wheeled their horses and followed. I handed the glasses back to Jacquie and scrambled down to set up the camera. I had scarcely focused when the rheas appeared, running in a tight bunch, straight towards us. At about seventy yards they saw us, and all swerved at right angles at the same moment and with such precision that the move might have been carefully rehearsed. Hot on their heels came the peons, the horses' hooves kicking up lumps of black earth, the boleadoras whirling round their heads in a blurred glinting pattern emitting a shrill whistling sound. The shrill cries, the vibrating thud of the hooves, the whine of the boleadoras, and then they were all past, and the noises faded in the distance. Only the plovers flew round and round above us, hysterically calling. Jacquie kept up a running commentry from the cart above.

'Rafael's going to the right with Eduardo . . . they're still running . . . ah! . . . one's broken away to the right and Eduardo after it . . . oh, now the whole bunch have scattered . . . they're all over the place . . . they'll never round them up now . . . one of them's going to throw his boleadoras . . . oh, he's missed . . . you should have seen that rhea's swerve . . . what on earth's that one doing? . . . it's turned right round . . . it's coming back . . . Rafael's after it . . . it's coming back . . . it's coming back . . .'

I had just lit a cigarette, but had to throw it down and leap for the camera as the rhea came crashing through the thistles. I had thought that there would be a pause of at least a quarter of an hour before the peons succeeded in rounding up the birds, and so, although the camera was wound up, it was not focused, nor had I taken a light reading. But there was no time to remedy the defect, for the bird was bearing down upon us at a speed of twenty miles an hour. I slewed the camera round on the tripod, got the rhea framed in the view-finder and pressed the button, wondering, as I did so, whether anything would come out at all. The rhea was about a hundred and fifty feet away when I started to film, with Rafael fairly close behind. His proximity obviously worried the bird, for it did not seem to notice either the cart or the camera, through which I could see it running straight towards me. It came nearer and nearer, gradually filling the view-finder; I could hear muffled squeaks from Jacquie above me. The rhea kept on coming towards me until the whole of the view-finder was filled. I began to get worried, for the bird did not seem to notice either me or the camera, and I had no particular desire to be hit amidships by a couple of hundred pounds of speeding rhea; uttering a brief prayer, I kept my finger down on the button. The rhea suddenly seemed to notice me for the first time, a ludicrously horrified look came into its eyes and its muscles contracted as it made a sudden wild swerve to the left and disappeared from my vision. I stood up and wiped my forehead. Jacquie and Carlos were regarding me owlishly from the safety of the cart.

'How close did it get?' I asked, for it was difficult to tell whilst filming.

'It swerved when it got to that tuft of grass there,' said Jacquie.

I paced from the tripod to the tuft of grass. It was just under six feet.

The rhea's wild swerve was its undoing, for Rafael was so close behind that even that slight deviation lost it several yards of its lead. Rafael, urging his sweat-stained horse to a terrific effort, overhauled the flying bird and turned it back towards the camera. The rhea came scudding back, and this time I was ready. I could hear the whine of the boleadoras reach a crescendo ending in a sort of long-drawn 'wheep'. The cord and the balls flew flailing through the air, wound themselves with octopus-like skill round the legs and neck of the flying bird. It ran for two more steps, then the cord tightened and it fell to the ground, legs and wings thrashing. Rafael, uttering a long-drawn cry of triumph, pulled up alongside it and was down in a second, grasping the kicking legs that could easily have disembowelled him if his grip had loosened. The rhea struggled briefly and then lay still. Carlos, dancing triumphantly on the seat of the cart, whooped long and loud to tell the other peons we had been successful, and when they galloped up we all gathered round our quarry.

It was a large bird, with great muscular thighs like a ballerina's. In contrast, the wing-bones were fragile and soft, for they could be bent like a green twig. The eyes were enormous, almost covering the side of the skull, fringed with thick, film-star-like eyelashes. The large feet with their four toes were thick and powerful. The centre toe was the longest, and it was armed with a long, curved claw. Whether the bird kicked from the back or the front, this claw met its adversary first, and acted with the slashing, tearing qualities of a sharp knife. The feathers, which were quite long, looked more like elongated fronds of grey fern. When I had examined the bird, and taken some close-ups of it, we unwound the boleadoras from its legs and neck. It lay for a moment in the grass, and then suddenly its strong legs shot it to its feet, and it bounced off through the thistles, gathering speed as it ran.

We turned the cart round and started back towards Secunda and a meal. The peons, laughing and chattering, rode close around us, their belts glittering in the sun, their bits and bridles jangling musically. The horses were black with sweat, but though they must obviously have been tired, their step was jaunty and light, and they bickered and snapped skittishly at each other. The greys, who had done little but stand between the shafts all afternoon, plodded onwards as though at the end of their strength. Behind us the pampa stretched, limitless, golden and quiet. In the distance two black-and-white specks rose above the grass briefly, and very faintly I could hear the voice of the pampa, the shrill warning to all the living creatures that lived there, the cry of the ever-watchful plovers: 'Tero . . . tero . . . tero . . . teroterotero. . . .'

Adios!

It was nearing the day of departure. With the utmost reluctance we had to leave the *estancia* Secunda, taking with us the animals we had caught: armadillos, opossums, and a handful of nice birds. We travelled back to Buenos Aires in the train, the animals accompanying us in the luggage van. With these new additions our collection began to look *more* like a collection and less like the remnants from a pet-shop sale. But we still had very few birds, and, as I knew that Argentina contains some extremely interesting species, this gap in our collection irritated me.

Then, the day before we sailed, I remembered something that Bebita had told me, so I phoned her up.

'Bebita, didn't you say you knew of a bird shop somewhere in Buenos Aires.'

'A b-b-bird shop? Ahhh, yes, there is one I have seen. It is somewhere near the station.'

'Will you take me and show me?'

'B-b-but naturally. Come to lunch, and we will go afterwards.'

After a prolonged lunch, Bebita, Jacquie and I climbed into a taxi and sped through the wide streets in search of the bird shop. We ran it to earth, eventually, on one side of an enormous square which was lined with hundreds of tiny stalls, selling meat, vegetables and other produce. The shop was large, and, to our delight, contained an extensive and varied stock. Slowly we walked round staring avidly into cages that pulsated with birds of all shapes, sizes and colours. The proprietor, who looked like an unsuccessful all-in-wrestler, followed us around with a predatory gleam in his black eyes.

'Have you decided what you want?' inquired Bebita.

'Yes, I know what I want, but it's a question of price. The owner does not look as though he's going to be reasonable.'

Bebita, tall, elegantly clad, turned her amused gaze on to the squat owner of the store. Taking off her gloves, she placed them carefully on a sack of bird seed, and then smiled dazzlingly at the man. He blushed and ducked his head in salute. Bebita turned to me.

'He looks so *sweet*,' she said, and really meant it.

Still unused to Bebita's ability to see something divine in people who looked to me as though they would cheerfully deliver their own mothers to the knackers' yard for half a crown, I just gaped at the villainous pet-shop owner.

'Well,' I said at last, 'he doesn't look sweet to *me*.'

'B-b-but I'm sure he is an angel,' said Bebita firmly; 'now, you just show me the b-b-birds you want and I will talk with him.'

Feeling that this was quite the wrong way to start a bargain, I led her round the cages again and pointed out the specimens, some of which were so unusual that they made my mouth water just to look at them. Bebita then asked me how much I was prepared to pay for them, and I named a price which I thought was fair without being exorbitant. Bebita floated over to the owner, turned him scarlet again with another smile, and in a gentle voice – the sort of voice which you use for talking with angels – she started to discuss the purchase of the birds. As her voice went on, punctuated now and then by an eager, '*Si, si, señora*' from the owner, Jacquie and I wandered round the darker and less accessible parts of the shop. Eventually, some twenty minutes later, we drifted back. Bebita still stood among the dirty cages like a visiting goddess, while the proprietor had seated himself on a sack of seed and was mopping his face. His '*Si, si, señora*,' which still accompanied Bebita's discourse, had lost its first enthusiasm, and was now more doubtful. Suddenly he shrugged, threw out his hands and smiled up at her. Bebita looked at him fondly as though he had been her only son.

'*B-b-bueno*,' she said, '*muchísimas gracias, señor.*'

'*De nada, señora*,' he replied.

Bebita turned to me.

'I have b-b-bought them for you,' she said.

'Good. What's the damage?'

Bebita then named a price which was a quarter of what I said I was willing to pay.

'But, Bebita, that's highway robbery,' I said incredulously.

'No, no, child,' she said earnestly; 'all these b-b-birds are very common here, so it's silly for you to pay too much. B-b-besides, the man is, as I said, an angel, and he likes reducing his price for me.'

'I give up,' I said resignedly. 'Would you like to come on my next trip with me? You'd save me pounds.'

'Silly, silly, silly,' said Bebita, chuckling, 'I didn't save you pounds; it was this man that you said looked so awful.'

I glared at her, and then made a dignified retreat to choose my birds and cage them. When this was done, a mountainous pile of cages done up in brown paper stood on the counter. Having paid the man, amid the usual exchange of '*gracias*,' I then asked him, through Bebita, whether he ever had any waterfowl for sale.

Not waterfowl, he replied, but he had some other, similar birds, which the señor might be interested in. He led us through a door at the back of the shop out to a tiny lavatory. Throwing open the door, he pointed, and I only just managed to stifle the exclamation of delight that rose to my lips, for there, crouched on either side of the lavatory, were two dirty, exhausted but still beautiful black-necked swans. Trying to appear unconcerned, I examined them. They were both very thin, and seemed to have reached the stage of weakness which is characterized by complete apathy and lack of fear. In any other circumstances I would not have dreamt of buying such decrepit birds, but I knew that this was my last chance to obtain any of these swans. Apart from this, I felt that if they were going to die, at least they should die in comfort; to leave those lovely birds languishing by the side of a lavatory pan was more than I was able to do. Bebita therefore went into battle again, and after some stiff bargaining the swans were mine. Then came a problem, for the owner had no cages big enough to transport them. At length we unearthed two sacks, and the swans were encased in them, with their heads sticking out. Then, collecting up our purchases, we were bowed out of the shop by the owner. Once outside, a sudden thought came to me.

'And how are we going to get to Belgrano?' I asked.

'We will get a taxi,' said Bebita.

I had a swan under each arm, and felt rather as Alice must have felt when she took part in the famous croquet match with the flamingoes.

'We won't get in a taxi with this lot,' I said; 'they're not allowed to carry livestock. . . . We've had this trouble before.'

'Wait here and I will find a taxi,' said Bebita, and she floated across the road to the rank, picked out the car with the most unsympathetic and unsavoury-looking driver, and brought him round to where we were standing.

For one startled moment he stared at the sacks under my arm, from which the swans' heads protruded like albino pythons, then he turned to Bebita.

'These are *bichos*,' he said; 'we are forbidden to carry *bichos*.'

Bebita smiled at him.

'But if you did not *know* we had b-b-bichos you would not be to b-b-blame,' she explained.

The taxi-driver reeled under the smile, but was not quite convinced.

'But one can see they are *bichos*,' he protested.

'Only these,' said Bebita, pointing at the swans, 'and if they were in the b-b-boot you would not see them.'

The taxi-man grunted sceptically.

'All right, but I haven't seen anything, remember. If they stop us I shall deny all knowledge.'

So, with the swans in the boot and the front seat piled high with cages from which came a chorus of flutterings and twitterings which the taxi-man endeavoured to ignore, we drove towards Belgrano.

'How d'you manage to get these taxi-men to do what you want?' I asked. 'I can't even get them to carry *me* sometimes, let alone a menagerie.'

'But they are so sweet,' said Bebita, regarding with affection the fat neck of our driver; 'they will always try and help.'

I sighed; Bebita had a magic touch which no one else could attempt to emulate. The irritating part was that, when she made the obviously ludicrous statement that some person who looked like a fugitive from a chain gang was an angel, he then proceeded to act just like one. It was all very puzzling.

This load of last-minute specimens created several difficulties for us. Before we could get on the ship the following afternoon, we had to have them all caged properly, and this was no easy job. A frantic phone call brought Carlos and Rafael scurrying to Belgrano, bringing with them their cousin Enrique. We rushed out in a body to the local wood-yard, and while I drew designs of the sort of cages I wanted, the carpenter worked his circular saw frantically, cutting out pieces of ply-wood to the correct dimensions. Then, staggering under the weight, we carried the wood back to the house in Belgrano and set about nailing it into cages. By half-past eleven that night we had succeeded in caging a quarter of the birds. Seeing that it was going to be an all-night job, we sent Jacquie back to the hotel, so that in the morning, when we would feel terrible, she would feel rested and refreshed and able to cope with feeding the animals. Carlos made a rapid pilgrimage to a nearby café and returned with hot coffee, rolls and a bottle of gin. Consuming these supplies, we carried on with our cage-making. At ten to twelve there came a knock on the outside door.

'This,' I said to Carlos, 'is the first outraged neighbour wanting to know what the hell we're hammering at this hour of night. . . . You'd better go; that gin hasn't done my Spanish any good.'

Carlos returned soon, and with him was a thin, bespectacled man with a marked American accent who introduced himself as Mr Hahn, the Buenos Aires correspondent of the *Daily Mirror* – of all things.

'I heard that you all escaped from the Paraguayan revolution by the skin of your teeth, and I wondered if you'd care to give me the story,' he explained.

'Certainly,' I said, hospitably pulling up a cage for him to sit on, and pouring him a cupful of gin. 'What would you like to know?'

He smelt the gin suspiciously, glanced into the cage before seating himself, and took out a notebook.

'Everything,' he said firmly.

So I started to relate the story of our Paraguayan journey, my highly coloured account being interrupted by bursts of hammering, sawing and even louder bursts of Spanish oaths from Carlos, Rafael and Enrique. At length, Mr Hahn put his notebook away.

'I think,' he said, taking off his coat and rolling up his shirt sleeves – '*I think* I could concentrate better on your story if I had some more gin and joined in this woodcutters' ball.'

So throughout the night, fortified by gin, coffee, rolls and bursts of song, Carlos, Rafael, Enrique, myself and the Buenos Aires correspondent of the *Daily Mirror* laboured to finish the cages. By the time the first coffee-shops opened at five-thirty we had finished. After a quick coffee, I crawled back to the hotel and flung myself on the bed to try to get some rest before starting for the docks.

Our lorry, with Carlos and Rafael perched on top and Jacquie and I in the cab, rolled on to the docks alongside the ship at two-thirty. By four o'clock nearly everyone in the place, including several interested by standers, had examined our export permits. At four-thirty they told us we could carry the stuff on board. It was then that something occurred which might not only have put paid to the trip entirely, but finished me off as well. They were loading enormous bales of skins, which, for some obscure reason, were being swung on to the ship over the gangway up which we had to carry our animals. I descended from the lorry, took the cage containing Cai, the monkey, in my arms, and was just about to tell Carlos to carry Sarah himself, when something that felt like a howitzer shell caught me across the back and thighs, lifted me into the air and hurled me flat on my face some twenty feet from where I had been standing. The shock of this was indescribable. As I soared through the air, I could not even imagine what it was that had delivered such a blow. Then I hit the ground and rolled over. My back was numb, my left thigh was aching savagely, so that I was sure it was broken, and I was shaking so much with the shock that I could not even stand when a horrified Carlos tried to get me to my feet. It was five minutes before I could stand upright and discover to my relief that my leg was not broken. Even then my hands were shaking so much that I could not hold a cigarette, and Carlos had to do it for me. While I sat and tried to control my nerves, Carlos explained what had happened. A crane-driver had swung a bale of skins off the dock, but had kept them too low. Instead of clearing the heavy wooden gangway, they had struck it amidships, and then the bale of skins and the gangway had swept along the docks and hit me. Luckily, this murderous missile had almost reached the end of its swing when it struck me, or else I should have been split in half like a soft banana.

'I must say,' I pointed out shakily to Carlos, 'it's not the sort of farewell I expected of Argentina.'

Eventually the animals were safely stowed on deck, with tarpaulins over them, and we could go down to the smoking-room, where all our friends were gathered. We drank and talked with them in the usual bright and rather inane way that one does when one knows that parting is imminent. Then, at last, the time came when they had to go ashore. We stood by the rail and watched our string of friends go down the gangway and then assemble in a crowd on the docks. We could just see them in the fast-gathering dusk: Carlos's moon face and the flash of his wife's dark hair; Rafael and Enrique with their gaucho hats tilted on the backs of their heads; Marie and Rene Mercedes waving handkerchiefs; Marie Mercedes looking more like a Dresden shepherdess than ever in the dim light; and Bebita, tall, beautiful and calm. Her voice came to us clearly as the ship drew away.

'Good journey, children; b-b-but don't forget to come back.'

We waved and nodded and then, as our friends started to disappear into the fast-gathering dusk, the air was full of the most mournful sound in the world: the deep, lugubrious roar of the siren, the sound of a ship saying goodbye.

Acknowledgments

Britain

Our trip would have had little hope of maturing had it not been for the enthusiasm and kindness of Dr Derisi, the former Argentine Ambassador in London, who gave the whole plan his official blessing and helped in a variety of ways. Mr Peter Newborn, of the Argentine Embassy, was most helpful and gave us much valuable advice on complicated matters of currency and customs permits.

At the Foreign office, Mr Hiller gave us much valuable help and advice.

Mr Peter Scott and the Severn Wildfowl Trust also gave us much assistance and provided us with numerous introductions.

At the B.B.C. the following people gave us help and advice on sound-recording equipment, and also supplied us with letters of introduction: Mrs Nesta Pain, Mr Laurence Gilliam, Mr Leonard Cottrell and Mr W. O. Galbraith.

Miss Rosemary Clifford of the Latin-American Department of the Central Office of Information did a great deal towards smoothing our path on arrival in Buenos Aires.

Mr Norman Zimmern gave us many valuable introductions in South America.

Messrs A. P. Manners Ltd. of Bournemouth were most courteous and helpful in advising us on photographic equipment and in developing our films.

To Joseph Gundry & Co. of Bridport go our thanks for making a number of flight-nets in record time, all of which were excellent.

Argentina

We should like to express our gratitude to Señor Apold and Señor Vasquez of the Ministry of Information.

At the Ministry of Agriculture the following people gave us help without which we could have achieved very little: Señor Hogan, the Minister of Agriculture; Dr Lago, Secretary General, and Dr Godoy, who was in charge of the Department of Animal Conservation, and who was so efficient and helpful over our collecting permits.

We met with nothing but courtesy and efficiency from all officials during our stay in Argentina, and we should like to thank all those members of the Airport, Docks and Customs with whom we came in contact.

The Head of the Aduana was extremely kind in granting us import and export licences for our weird assortment of equipment.

At the British Embassy our thanks go to the former Ambassador, Sir

Henry Bradshaw Mack, K.C.M.G.; Mr Allan, First Secretary; Mr Stephen Lockhart, Head of Chancery; Mr King, the Consul-General; Mr Leadbitter, First Secretary of Information. Our very special thanks go to Mr George Gibbs, assuredly the most long-suffering Assistant Secretary for Information that any Embassy has ever had. He managed to cope successfully with problems so far removed from his job as the best way to bottle feed an anteater while on an aerodrome, and the cheapest place to buy wire-netting. He was throughout our stay a tower of strength, and we are forever in his debt. Also of the Embassy we should like to thank Mr Kelly, Mr Roquet, who sorted out our photographic problems, and Mr O'Brien, who arranged all our baggage difficulties.

We should also like to thank the Blue Star Line for allowing us to bring our animals back on one of their ships. Mr Wilson, the Manager, and Mr Fraser, the Passenger Manager, at their Buenos Aires office did everything they could to help us. Captain Horne and the whole crew of the *Uruguay Star* went out of their way to make our return voyage as pleasant as possible.

In Argentina we had so much help and kindness shown to us that the list is necessarily a long one. We should like to thank the following:

Mrs Lassie Greenslet, who so kindly put her delightful Buenos Aires flat at our disposal, in which we stayed for so long she must have wondered if she was ever going to get rid of us. Her sister, Mrs Puleston, was most kind to us, and we are indebted to their niece, Miss Ada Osborn, for some nice specimens she collected for us.

Mr Ian Gibson for acting as our guide and assistant. Mr and Mrs Boote and their family for allowing us to stay on their delightful *estancia* and for displaying such enthusiasm in helping us with our work. Mr Donald McIver, who gave us a lot of very valuable assistance in collecting and putting transport at our disposal. Mr William Partridge of the Natural History Museum, who supplied us with much information on bird distribution and who put at our disposal the magnificent series of skins he had collected from various parts of Argentina. Mr Carr-Vernon of Western Union, who gave us many facilities.

Marie Mercedes De Soto Acebal, her husband and family showed us such kindness during our stay in Argentina that it is impossible for us to thank them adequately. The youngest son, Rafael, accompanied us to Paraguay, and without his help we would have achieved very little. When in Buenos Aires, and also when staying on their *estancia*, the rest of the family readily devoted their time and energies to help us with our work, and we could not have wished for more delightful assistants and friends.

Bebita Fanny de Llambi de Campbell de Ferreyra, her husband and their family were wonderful to us during our stay. We practically lived at their flat, and Bebita herself did more than any other one person towards making our stay in Argentina such a happy one. I have repaid her very uncharitably by portraying her in the foregoing pages. Her brother, Boy de Llambi de Campbell, and his wife, Bebe, were also charming to us, and without their assistance on our Paraguayan venture we would not have obtained some of our best specimens.

The President and the ladies of the Twentieth Century Club of Buenos

Aires showed us lavish hospitality and much courage in inviting me to address them.

I should like to make a special point of thanking all those peons and other workers on the *estancias*: Los Ingleses and Secunda, for the generous way in which they gave up their spare time to helping us.

Paraguay

In Paraguay we should like to thank Captain Sarmaniego and Señor Axxolini, who both showed us much kindness and assisted us in many ways.

We should also like to thank Braniff Airways, who took over so competently the last stage of our retreat from Paraguay.

Last but not least I should like to thank Sophie, my secretary, who did so much of the donkey work in the preparation of the manuscript without being able to share in the pleasures of the trip.

Encounters with Animals

GERALD DURRELL

Encounters with Animals

For
EILEEN MOLONY
In memory of late scripts, deep sighs
and over-long announcements

Introduction

During the past nine years, between leading expeditions to various parts of the world, catching a multitude of curious creatures, getting married, having malaria and writing several books, I made a number of broadcasts on different animal subjects for the B.B.C. As a result of these I had many letters from people asking if they could have copies of the scripts. The simplest way of dealing with this problem was to amass all the various talks in the form of a book, and this I have now done.

That the original talks were at all popular is entirely due to the producers I have had, and in particular Miss Eileen Molony, to whom this book is dedicated. I shall always remember her tact and patience during rehearsals. In a bilious green studio, with the microphone leering at you from the table like a Martian monster, I am never completely at ease. So it was Eileen's unenviable task to counteract the faults in delivery that these nerves produced. I remember with pleasure her voice coming over the intercom. with such remarks as: 'Very good, Gerald, but at the rate you're reading it will be a five-minute talk, not a fifteen-minute one.' Or, 'Try to get a little enthusiasm into your voice there, will you? It sounds as if you hated the animal . . . and try not to sigh when you say your opening sentence . . . you nearly blew the microphone away, and you've no idea how lugubrious it sounded.' Poor Eileen suffered much attempting to teach me the elements of broadcasting, and any success I have achieved in this direction has been entirely due to her guidance. In view of this, it seems rather uncharitable of me to burden her with the dedication of this book, but I know of no other way of thanking her publicly for her help. And anyway, I don't expect her to read it.

BOOK ONE

Background for Animals

I am constantly being surprised by the number of people, in different parts of the world, who seem to be quite oblivious to the animal life around them. To them the tropical forests or the savannah or the mountains in which they live, are apparently devoid of life. All they see is a sterile landscape. This was brought home most forcibly to me when I was in Argentina. In Buenos Aires I met a man, an Englishman who had spent his whole life in Argentina, and when he learnt that my wife and I intended to go out into the pampa to look for animals he stared at us in genuine astonishment.

'But, my dear chap, you won't find anything *there*,' he exclaimed.

'Why not?' I enquired, rather puzzled, for he seemed an intelligent person.

'But the pampa is just a lot of grass,' he explained, waving his arms wildly in an attempt to show the extent of the grass, 'nothing, my dear fellow, absolutely nothing but grass punctuated by cows.'

Now, as a rough description of the pampa this is not so very wide of the mark except that life on this vast plain does not consist entirely of cows and gauchos. Standing in the pampa you can turn slowly round and on all sides of you, stretching away to the horizon, the grass lies flat as a billiard-table, broken here and there by the clumps of giant thistles, six or seven feet high, like some extraordinary surrealist candelabra. Under the hot blue sky it does seem to be a dead landscape, but under the shimmering cloak of grass, and in the small forests of dry, brittle thistle-stalks the amount of life is extraordinary. During the hot part of the day, riding on horseback across the thick carpet of grass, or pushing through a giant thistle-forest so that the brittle stems cracked and rattled like fireworks, there was little to be seen except the birds. Every forty or fifty yards there would be burrowing owls, perched straight as guardsmen on a tussock of grass near their holes, regarding you with astonished frosty-cold eyes, and, when you got too close, doing a little bobbing dance of anxiety before taking off and wheeling over the grass on silent wings.

Inevitably your progress would be observed and reported on by the watchdogs of the pampa, the black-and-white spur-winged plovers, who would run furtively to and fro, ducking their heads and watching you carefully, eventually taking off and swooping round and round you on piebald wings, screaming 'Tero-tero-tero . . . tero . . . tero,' the alarm cry that warned everything for miles around of your presence. Once this strident warning had been given, other plovers in the distance would take it up, until it seemed as though the whole pampa rang with their cries. Every living thing was now alert and suspicious. Ahead, from the skeleton of a dead tree, what appeared to be two dead branches would suddenly take wing and soar up into the hot blue sky: chimango hawks with handsome rust-and-white plumage and long slender legs. What you had thought was merely an extra-large tussock of sun-dried grass would suddenly hoist itself up on to long stout legs and speed away across the grass in great loping strides, neck stretched out, dodging and twisting between the thistles, and you realized that your grass tussock had been a rhea, crouching low in the hope that you would pass it by. So, while the plovers were a nuisance in advertising your advance, they helped to panic the other inhabitants of the pampa into showing themselves.

Occasionally you would come across a 'laguana,' a small shallow lake fringed with reeds and a few stunted trees. Here there were fat green frogs, but frogs which, if molested, jumped *at* you with open mouth, uttering fearsome gurking noises. In pursuit of the frogs were slender snakes marked in grey, black and vermilion red, like old school ties, slithering through the grass. In the rushes you would be almost sure to find the nest of a screamer, a bird like a great grey turkey: the youngster crouching in the slight depression in the sun-baked ground, yellow as a buttercup, but keeping absolutely still even when your horse's legs straddled it, while its parents paced frantically about, giving plaintive trumpeting cries of anxiety, intermixed with softer instructions to their chick.

This was the pampa during the day. In the evening, as you rode homeward, the sun was setting in a blaze of coloured clouds, and on the laguanas various ducks were flighting in, arrowing the smooth water with ripples as they landed. Small flocks of spoonbills drifted down like pink clouds to feed in the shallows among snowdrifts of black-necked swans.

As you rode among the thistles and it grew darker you might meet armadillos, hunched and intent, trotting like strange mechanical toys on their nightly scavenging; or perhaps a skunk who would stand, gleaming vividly black and white in the twilight, holding his tail stiffly erect while he stamped his front feet in petulant warning.

This, then, was what I saw of the pampa in the first few days. My friend had lived in Argentina all his life and had never realized that this small world of birds and animals existed. To him the pampa was 'nothing but grass punctuated by cows.' I felt sorry for him.

The Black Bush

Africa is an unfortunate continent in many ways. In Victorian times it acquired the reputation of being the Dark Continent, and even today, when it contains modern cities, railways, macadam roads, cocktail bars and other necessary adjuncts of civilization, it is still looked upon in the same way.

Reputations, whether true or false, die hard, and for some reason a bad reputation dies hardest of all.

Perhaps the most maligned area of the whole continent is the West Coast, so vividly described as the White Man's Grave. It has been depicted in so many stories – quite inaccurately – as a vast, unbroken stretch of impenetrable jungle. If you ever manage to penetrate the twining creepers, the thorns and undergrowth (and it is quite surprising how frequently the impenetrable jungle is penetrated in stories), you find that every bush shakes and quivers with a mass of wild life waiting its chance to leap out at you: leopards with glowing eyes, snakes hissing petulantly, crocodiles in the streams straining every nerve to look more like a log of wood than a log of wood does. If you should escape these dangers there are always the savage native tribes to give the unfortunate traveller the *coup de grâce*. The natives are of two kinds, cannibal and non-cannibal: if they are cannibal, they are always armed with spears; if non-cannibal, they are armed with arrows whose tips drip deadly poison of a kind generally unknown to science.

Now, no one minds giving an author a bit of poetic licence, provided it is recognizable as such. But unfortunately the West Coast of Africa has been libelled to such an extent that anyone who tries to contradict the accepted ideas is branded as a liar who has never been there. It seems to me a great pity that an area of the world where you find nature at its most bizarre, flamboyant and beautiful should be so abused, though I realize that I am a voice crying rather plaintively in the wilderness.

My work has enabled me, one way and another, to see quite a lot of tropical forest, for when you collect live wild animals for a living you have to go out into the so-called impenetrable jungle and look for them. They do not, unfortunately, come to you. It has been brought home to me that in the average tropical forest there is an extraordinary *lack of* wild life: you can walk all day and see nothing more exciting than an odd bird or butterfly. The animals are there, of course, and in rich profusion, but they very wisely avoid you, and in order to see or capture them you have to know exactly where to look. I remember once, after a six months' collecting trip in the forests of the Cameroons, that I showed my collection of about one hundred and fifty different mammals, birds and reptiles to a gentleman who had spent some twenty-five years in that area, and he was astonished that such a variety should have been living, as it were, on his doorstep, in the forest he had considered uninteresting and almost devoid of life.

In the pidgin-English dialect spoken in West Africa, the forest is called the Bush. There are two kinds of Bush: the area that surrounds a village or a town and which is fairly well trodden by hunters and in some places encroached on by farmland. Here the animals are wary and difficult to see. The other type is called the Black Bush, areas miles away from the nearest village, visited by an odd hunter only now and then; and it is here, if you are patient and quiet, that you will see the wild life.

To catch animals, it is no use just scattering your traps wildly about the forest, for, although at first the movements of the animals seem haphazard, you very soon realize that the majority of them have rooted habits, following the same paths year in and year out, appearing in certain districts at certain times when the food supply is abundant, disappearing again when the food fails, always visiting the same places for water. Some of them even have special lavatories which may be some distance away from the place where they spend most of their lives. You may set a trap in the forest and catch nothing in it, then shift that trap three yards to the left or right on to a roadway habitually used by some creature; and thus make your capture at once. Therefore, before you can start on your trapping, you must patiently and carefully investigate the area around you, watching to see which routes are used through the tree-tops or on the forest floor; where supplies of wild fruit are ripening; and which holes are used as bedrooms during the daytime by the nocturnal animals. When I was in West Africa I spent many hours in the Black Bush, watching the forest creatures, studying their habits, so that I would find it more easy to catch and keep them.

I watched one such area over a period of about three weeks. In the Cameroon forests you occasionally find a place where the soil is too shallow to support the roots of the giant trees, and here their place has been taken by the lower growth of shrubs and bushes and long grass which manages to exist on the thin layer of earth covering a grey carapace of rock beneath. I soon found that the edge of one of these natural grassfields, which was about three miles from my camp, was an ideal place to see animal life, for here there were three distinct zones of vegetation: first, the grass itself, five acres in extent, bleached almost white by the sun; then surrounding it a narrow strip of shrubs and bushes thickly entwined with parasitic creepers and hung with the vivid flowers of the wild convolvulus; and finally, behind this zone of low growth spread the forest proper, the giant tree-trunks a hundred and fifty feet high like massive columns supporting the endless roof of green leaves. By choosing your vantage-point carefully you could get a glimpse of a small section of each of these types of vegetation.

I would leave the camp very early in the morning; even at that hour the sun was fierce. Leaving the camp clearing, I then plunged into the coolness of the forest, into a dim green light that filtered through the multitude of leaves above. Picking my way through the gigantic tree-trunks, I moved across the forest floor, so thickly covered with layer upon layer of dead leaves that it was as soft and springy as a Persian carpet. The only sounds were the incessant zithering of the millions of cicadas, beautiful green-and-silver insects that clung to the bark of the trees, making the air vibrate with their cries, and when you approached too closely zooming away through the forest like miniature aeroplanes, their transparent wings glittering as they flew. Then there would be an occasional plaintive 'whowee' of some small bird which I never managed to identify, but which always accompanied me through the forest, asking questions in its soft liquid tones.

In places there would be a great gap in the roof of leaves above, where some massive branch had perhaps been undermined by insects and damp until it had eventually broken loose and crashed hundreds of feet to the forest floor below, leaving this rent in the forest canopy through which the sunlight sent its golden shafts. In these patches of brilliant light you would find butterflies congregating: large ones with long, narrow, orange-red wings that shone against the darkness of the forest like dozens of candle flames; delicate little white ones like snowflakes would rise in clouds about my feet, then drift slowly back on to the dark leaf-mould, pirouetting as they went.

Eventually I reached the banks of a tiny stream which whispered its way through the water-worn boulders, each wearing a cap of green moss and tiny plants. This stream flowed through the forest, through the rim of short growth and out into the grassfield. Just before it reached the edge of the forest, however, the ground sloped and the water flowed over a series of miniature waterfalls, each decorated with clumps of wild begonias whose flowers were a brilliant waxy yellow. Here, at the edge of the forest, the heavy rains had gradually washed the soil from under the massive roots of one of the giant trees which had crashed down and now lay half in the forest and half in the grassfield, a great hollow, gently rotting shell, thickly overgrown with convolvulus, moss, and with battalions of tiny toadstools marching over its peeling bark. This was my hideout, for in one part of the trunk the bark had given way and the hollow interior lay revealed, like a canoe, in which I could sit well hidden by the low growth. When I had made sure that the trunk had no other occupant I would conceal myself and settle down to wait.

For the first hour or so there would be nothing – only the cries of cicadas, an occasional trill from a tree-frog on the banks of the stream, and sometimes a passing butterfly. Within a short time the forest would have forgotten and absorbed you, and within the hour, if you kept still, you would be accepted just as another, if rather ungainly, part of the scenery.

Generally, the first arrivals were the giant plantain-eaters who came to feed on the wild figs which grew round the edge of the grassfield. These huge birds, with long, dangling magpie-like tails, would give notice of their arrival when they were half a mile or so away in the forest, by a series of loud, ringing and joyful cries . . . caroo, coo, coo, coo. They would appear, flying swiftly from the forest with a curious dipping flight and land in the fig trees, shouting delightedly to each other, flipping their long tails so that their golden-green plumage gleamed iridescently. They would run along the branches in a totally unbirdlike way and leap from one branch to another with great kangaroo jumps, plucking off the wild figs and gulping them down. The next arrivals to the feast would be a troop of Mona monkeys, with their russet-red fur, grey legs and the two strange, vivid white patches like giant thumbprints on each side of the base of the tail. To hear the monkeys approaching sounded like a sudden wind roaring and rustling through the forest, but if you listened carefully you would hear in the background a peculiar sort of whoop-whoop noise followed by loud and rather drunken honkings, like a fleet of ancient taxi-cabs caught in a traffic jam. This was the sound of the hornbills, birds who always followed the monkey troops around, feeding not only on the fruit that the monkeys discovered but also on the lizards, tree-frogs and insects that the movements of the monkeys through the tree-tops disturbed.

On reaching the edge of the forest, the leader of the monkeys would climb to a vantage-point and, uttering suspicious grunts, survey the grassfield in front of him with the greatest care. Behind him the troop, numbering perhaps fifty individuals, would be silent except for the wheezy cry now and again from some tiny baby. Presently, when he was satisfied that the clearing contained nothing, the old male would stalk along a branch slowly and gravely, his tail curled up over his back like a question-mark, and then give a prodigious leap that sent him crashing into the fig-tree leaves. Here he paused again and once more examined the grassfield; then he plucked the first fruit and uttered a series of loud imperative calls: oink, oink, oink. Immediately, the still forest behind him was alive with movement, branches swishing and roaring like giant waves on a beach as the monkeys leapt out of cover and landed in the fig-trees, grunting and squeaking to each other as they plummeted through the air. Many of the female monkeys carried tiny babies which clung under their bellies, and as their mothers jumped you could hear the infant squeaking shrilly, though whether from fear or excitement it was difficult to judge.

The monkeys settled down on the branches to feed on the ripe figs, and presently with loud swishings and honks of delight the hornbills discovered their whereabouts and came crashing among the branches in the wild disorderly way in which hornbills always land. Their great round eyes, thickly fringed with heavy eyelashes, stared roguishly and slightly idiotically at the monkeys, while with their enormous and apparently cumbersome beaks they delicately and with great precision plucked the fruit and tossed it carelessly into the air, so that it fell back into their gaping mouths and disappeared. The hornbills were by no means such wasteful feeders as the monkeys, for they would invariably eat each fruit they plucked, whereas the monkeys would take only one bite from a fruit before dropping it to the ground below and moving along the branch to the next delicacy.

The arrival of such rowdy feeding companions was evidently distasteful to the giant plantain-eaters, for they moved off as soon as the monkeys and hornbills arrived. After half an hour or so the gound beneath the fig-trees was littered with half-eaten fruit, and the monkeys then made their way back into the forest, calling oink-oink to each other in a self-satisfied kind of way. The hornbills paused to have just one more fig and then flew excitedly after the monkeys, and as the sound of their wings faded away the next customers for the fig-tree arrived on the scene. They were so small and appeared so suddenly and silently out of the long grass that unless you had field-glasses and kept a careful watch they would come and go without giving a sign of their presence. They were the little striped mice whose homes were amongst the tussocks of grass, the tree-roots and the boulders along the edge of the forest. Each about the size of a house mouse, with a long and delicately tapering tail, they were clad in sleek, fawny-grey fur which was boldly marked with creamy white stripes from nose to rump. They would drift out from among the grass stalks, moving in little fits and starts, with many long pauses when they sat on their haunches, their tiny pink paws clenched into fists, their noses and whiskers quivering as they tested the wind for enemies. When they froze thus into immobility against the grass stalks, their striped coats, which when they were moving seemed so bright and decorative, acted like an invisible cloak and made them almost disappear.

Having assured themselves that the hornbills had really left (for a hornbill is occasionally partial to a mouse), they set about the serious task of eating the fruit that the monkeys had so lavishly scattered on the ground. Unlike a lot of the other forest mice and rats, these little creatures were of a quarrelsome disposition and would argue over the food, sitting up on their hind legs and abusing each other in thin, reedy squeaks of annoyance.

Sometimes two of them would come upon the same fruit and both lay hold of it, one at either end, digging their little pink paws into the leaf mould and tugging frantically in an effort to break the other's grip. If the fig were exceptionally ripe, it generally gave way in the middle so that both mice fell over backwards, each clutching his share of the trophy. They then sat quite peacefully within six inches of one another, each eating his portion. At times, if some sudden noise alarmed them, they all leapt vertically into the air six inches or even more as though suddenly plucked upwards by strings, and on landing they sat quivering and alert until they were sure the danger had passed, when they once more started bickering and fighting over the food.

Once I saw a tragedy enacted among these striped mice as they squabbled amongst the monkeys' left-overs. Suddenly a genet appeared out of the forest. This is perhaps one of the most lithe and beautiful animals to be seen in the forest, with its long sinuously weasel-shaped body and cat-like face, handsome golden fur heavily blotched with a pattern of black spots and long tail banded in black and white. It is not an animal you generally see in the early morning, for its favourite hunting time is in the evenings or at night. I presume this particular one must have had a fruitless night's hunting, and so when morning arrived he was still searching for something to fill his stomach. When he appeared at the edge of the grassfield and saw the striped mice, he flattened close to the ground and then launched himself as smoothly as a skimming stone across the intervening space, and was in amongst the rodents before they knew what was happening. As usual, they all leapt perpendicularly into the air and then fled, looking like portly little business men in their striped suits, rushing through the grass stems; but the genet had been too quick and he walked off into the forest, carrying in his mouth two limp little bodies which had so recently been abusing each other as to the sole ownership of a fig and had consequently left it too late to retreat.

Towards midday the whole country fell quiet under the hot rays of the sun, and even the incessant cries of the cicadas seemed to take on a sleepy note. This was siesta time, and very few creatures were to be seen. In the grassfield only the skinks, who loved the sun, emerged to bask on the rocks or to stalk the grasshoppers and locusts. These brilliant lizards, shining and polished as though freshly painted, had skins like mosaic work, made up of hundreds of tiny scales coloured cherry-red, cream and black. They would run swiftly through the grass stalks, their bodies glinting in the sun, so that they looked like some weird firework. Apart from these reptiles, there was practically nothing to be seen until the sun dipped and the day became a trifle cooler, so it was during this period of inactivity that I used to eat the food I had brought with me and smoke a much-needed cigarette.

Once during my lunch break I witnessed an extraordinary comedy that was performed almost, I felt, for my special benefit. On the tree-trunk where I was sitting, not six feet away, out of a tangle of thick undergrowth, up over the bark of the trunk, there glided slowly and laboriously and very regally a giant land-snail, the size of an apple. I watched it as I ate, fascinated by the way the snail's body glided over the bark, apparently without any muscular effort whatever, and the way its horns with the round, rather surprised eyes on top, twisted this way and that as it picked its route through the miniature landscape of toadstools and moss. Suddenly I realized that as the snail was making its slow and rather vague progress along the trunk it was leaving behind it the usual glistening trail, and this trail was being followed by one of the most ferocious and bloodthirsty animals, for its size, to be found in the West African forest.

The twining convolvulus was thrust aside, and out on to the log strutted a tiny creature only as long as a cigarette, clad in jet-black fur and with a long slender nose that it kept glued to the snail's track, like a miniature black hound. It was one of the forest's shrews, whose courage is incredible and whose appetite is prodigious and insatiable. If anything lives to eat, this forest shrew does. They will even in a moment of peckishness think nothing of eating one another. Chittering to himself, the shrew trotted rapidly after the snail and very soon overtook it. Uttering a high-pitched squeak, it flung itself on that portion of the snail which protruded from the rear of the shell and sank its teeth into it. The snail, finding itself so suddenly and unceremoniously attacked from the rear, did the only possible thing and drew its body rapidly back inside its shell. This movement was performed so swiftly and the muscular contraction of the snail was so strong, that as the tail disappeared inside the shell the shrew's face was banged against it and his grip was broken. The shell, having now nothing to balance it, fell on its side, and the shrew, screaming with frustration, rushed forward and plunged his head into the interior, in an effort to retrieve the retreating mollusc. However, the snail was prepared for this attack and as soon as the shrew's head was pushed into the opening of the shell it was greeted by a sudden fountain of greenish-white froth that bubbled out and enveloped nose and head. The shrew leapt back with surprise, knocking against the shell as it did so. The snail teetered for a moment and then rolled sideways and dropped into the undergrowth beneath the log. The shrew meanwhile was sitting on its hind legs, almost incoherent with rage, sneezing violently and trying to wipe the froth from its face with its paws. The whole thing was so ludicrous that I started to laugh, and the shrew, casting a hasty and frightened glance in my direction, leapt down into the undergrowth and hurried away. It was not often during the forest's siesta-time that I could enjoy such a scene as this.

At mid-afternoon, when the heat had lessened, the life of the forest would start again. There were new visitors to the fig-trees, in particular the squirrels. There was one pair who obviously believed in combining business with pleasure, for they ran and leapt among the fig-tree branches, playing hide-and-seek and leap-frog, courting each other in this way, and occasionally breaking off their wild and exuberant activities to sit very quietly and solemnly, their tails draped over their backs, eating figs. As the shadows grew longer, you might, if you were lucky, see a duiker coming down to drink at the stream. These small antelopes, clad in shining russet coats, with their long, pencil-slim legs, would pick their way slowly and suspiciously through the forest trees, pausing frequently while their large liquid eyes searched the path ahead, and their ears twitched backwards and forwards, picking up the sounds of the forest. As they drifted their way without a sound through the lush plants bordering the stream, they would generally disturb some of the curious aquatic mice who were feeding there. These little grey rodents have long, rather stupid-looking faces, big semi-transparent ears shaped like a mule's, and long hind legs on which they would at times hop like miniature kangaroos. At this hour of the evening it was their habit to wade through the shallow water, combing the water-weed with their slender front paws and picking out tiny water-insects, baby crabs and water-snails. At this time rats of another type would also come out, and these were probably the most fussy, pompous and endearing of the rodents. They were clad all over in greenish fur, with the exception of their noses and their behinds which were, rather incongruously, a bright foxy red, and made them look rather as though they were wearing red running shorts and masks. Their favourite hunting-ground was in the soft leaf-mould between the towering buttress roots of the great trees. Here they would waddle about, squeaking to each other, turning over leaves and bits of rock and twigs for the insects which were concealed underneath. Occasionally they would stop and hold conversations, sitting on their hind legs, facing each other, their whiskers trembling as they chittered and squeaked very rapidly and in a complaining sort of tone as though commiserating with one another on the lack of food in that particular part of the forest. There were times when, sniffing about in certain patches, they became terribly excited, squeaking loudly and digging, like terriers, down into the soft leaf-mould. Eventually they would triumphantly unearth a big chocolate-coloured beetle, almost as large as themselves. These insects were horny and very strong, and it took the rats a good deal of effort to subdue them. They would turn them on to their backs and then rapidly nip off the spiky, kicking legs. Once they had immobilized their prey, a couple of quick bites and the beetle was dead. Then the little rat would sit up on its hind legs, clasping the body of the beetle in both hands and proceed to eat it, as though it were a stick of rock, with loud scrunchings and occasional muffled squeaks of delight.

By now, although still light in the grassfield, it was gloomy and difficult to see in the forest itself. You might, if you were fortunate, catch a glimpse of some of the nocturnal animals venturing out on their hunting: perhaps a brush-tailed porcupine would trot past, portly and serious, his spines rustling through the leaves as he hurried on his way. Now the fig-trees would once again become the focal-point, as these nocturnal animals appeared. The galagos, or bush-babies, would materialize magically, like fairies, and sit among the branches, peering about them with their great saucer-shaped eyes, and their little incredibly human-looking hands held up in horror, like a flock of pixies who had just discovered that the world was a sinful place. They would feed on the figs and sometimes take prodigious leaps through the branches in pursuit of a passing moth, while overhead, across a sky already flushed with sunset colours, pairs of grey parrots flew into the forest to roost, whistling and cooing to each other, shrilly, so that the forest echoed. Far away in the distance a chorus of hoots suddenly rose, screams and wild bursts of maniacal laughter, the hair-raising noise of a troop of chimpanzees going to bed. The galagos would now have disappeared as quickly and as silently as they had come, and through the darkening sky the fruit-bats would appear in great tattered clouds, flapping down, giving their ringing cries, diving into the trees to fight and flutter round the remains of the fruit, so that the sound of their wings was like a hundred wet umbrellas being shaken amongst the trees. There would be one more shrill and hysterical outburst from the chimpanzees, and then the forest was completely dark, but still alive and vibrating with a million little rustles, squeaks, patters and grunts, as the night creatures took over.

I rose to my feet, cramped and stiff, and stumbled off through the forest, the glow of my torch seeming pathetically frail and tiny among the great silent tree-trunks. This, then, was the tropical forest that I had read about as savage, dangerous and unpleasant. To me it seemed a beautiful and incredible world made up of a million tiny lives, plants and animals, each different and yet dependent on the other, like the many parts of a gigantic jigsaw puzzle. It seemed to me such a pity that people should still cling to their old ideas of the unpleasantness of the jungle when here was a world of magical beauty waiting to be explored, observed and understood.

Lily-trotter Lake

British Guiana, lying in the northern part of South America, is probably one of the most beautiful places in the world, with its thick tropical forest, its rolling savannah land, its jagged mountain ranges and giant foaming waterfalls. To me, however, one of the most lovely parts of Guiana is the creek lands. This is a strip of coastal territory that runs from Georgetown to the Venezuelan border; here a thousand forest rivers and streams have made their way down towards the sea, and on reaching the flat land have spread out into a million creeks and tiny waterways that glimmer and glitter like a flood of quicksilver. The lushness and variety of the vegetation is extraordinary, and its beauty has turned the place into an incredible fairyland. In 1950 I was in British Guiana collecting wild animals for zoos in England, and during my six months there I visited the savannah lands to the north, the tropical forest and, of course, the creek lands, in pursuit of the strange creatures living there.

I had chosen a tiny Amerindian village near a place called Santa Rosa as my headquarters in the creek lands, and to reach it required a two-day journey. First, by launch down the Essequibo River and then through the wider creeks until we reached the place where the launch could go no farther, for the water was too shallow and too choked with vegetation. Here we took to dug-out canoes, paddled by the quiet and charming Indians who were our hosts, and leaving the broad main creek we plunged into a maze of tiny waterways on one of the most beautiful journeys I can remember.

Some of the creeks along which we travelled were only about ten feet wide, and the surface of the water was completely hidden under a thick layer of great creamy water-lilies, their petals delicately tinted pink, and a small fern-like water-plant that raised, just above the surface of the water, on a slender stem, a tiny magenta flower. The banks of the creek were thickly covered with undergrowth and great trees, gnarled and bent, leant over the waters to form a tunnel; their branches were festooned with long streamers of greenish-grey Spanish moss and clumps of bright pink-and-yellow orchids. With the water so thickly covered with vegetation, you had the impression when sitting in the bows of the canoe that you were travelling smoothly and silently over a flower-studded green lawn that undulated gently in the wake of your craft. Great black woodpeckers, with scarlet crests and whitish beaks, cackled loudly as they flipped from tree to tree, hammering away at the rotten bark, and from the reeds and plants along the edges of the creek there would be a sudden explosion of colour as we disturbed a marsh bird which flew vertically into the air, with its hunting-pink breast flashing like a sudden light in the sky.

The village, I discovered, was situated on an area of high ground which was virtually an island, for it was completely surrounded by a chess-board of creeks. The little native hut that was to be my headquarters was some distance away from the village and placed in the most lovely surroundings. On the edge of a tiny valley an acre or so in extent, it was perched amongst some great trees which stood round it like a group of very old men, with long grey beards of Spanish moss. During the winter rains the surrounding creeks had overflowed so that the valley was now drowned under some six feet of water out of which stuck a number of large trees, their reflections shimmering in the sherry-coloured water. The rim of the valley had grown a fringe of reeds and great patches of lilies. Sitting in the doorway of the hut, one had a perfect view of this miniature lake and its surroundings, and it was sitting here quietly in the early morning or evening that I discovered what a wealth of animal life inhabited this tiny patch of water and its surrounding frame of undergrowth.

In the evening, for example, a crab-eating raccoon would come down to drink. They are strange-looking animals, about the size of a small dog, with bushy tails ringed in black and white, large, flat, pink paws, the grey of their body-fur relieved only by a mask of black across the eyes, which gives the creature a rather ludicrous appearance. These animals walk in a curious humpbacked manner with their feet turned out, shuffling along in this awkward fashion like someone afflicted with chilblains. The raccoon came down to the water's edge and, having stared at his reflection dismally for a minute or so, drank a little and then with a pessimistic air shuffled slowly round the outer rim of the valley in search of food. In patches of shallow water he would wade in a little way and, squatting on his haunches, feel about in the dark water with the long fingers of his front paws, patting and touching and running them through the mud, and he would suddenly extract something with a look of pleased surprise and carry it to the bank to be eaten. The trophy was always carried clasped delicately between his front paws and dealt with when he arrived on dry land. If it was a frog, he would hold it down and with one quick snap decapitate it. If, however, as was often the case, it was one of the large freshwater crabs, he would hurry shorewards as quickly as possible, and on reaching land flick the crab away from him. The crab would recover its poise and menace him with open pincers, and the raccoon would then deal with it in a very novel and practical way. A crab is very easily discomfited, and if you keep tapping at it and it finds that every grab it makes at you with its pincers misses the mark, it will eventually fold itself up and sulk, refusing to participate any more in such a one-sided contest. So the raccoon simply followed the crab around, tapping him on his carapace with his long fingers and whipping them out of the way every time the pincers came within grabbing distance. After five minutes or so of this the frustrated crab would fold up and just squat. The raccoon, who till then had resembled a dear old lady playing with a Pekinese, would straighten up and become businesslike, and, leaning forward, with one quick snap would cut the unfortunate crab almost in two.

Along one side of the valley some previous Indian owner of the hut had planted a few mango and guava trees, and while I was there the fruit ripened and attracted a great number of creatures. The tree-porcupines were generally the first on the scene. They lumbered out of the undergrowth, looking like portly and slightly inebriated old men, their great bulbous noses whiffling to and fro, while their tiny and rather sad little eyes, that always seemed full of unshed tears, peered about them hopefully. They climbed up into the mango-trees very skilfully, winding their long, prehensile tails round the branches to prevent themselves from falling, their black-and-white spines rattling among the leaves. They then made their way along to a comfortable spot on a branch, anchored themselves firmly with a couple of twists of the tail, then sat up on their hind legs, and plucked off a fruit. Holding it in their front paws, they turned it round and round while their large buck teeth got to work on the flesh. When they had finished a mango they sometimes began playing a rather odd game with the big seed. Sitting there they looked round in a vague and rather helpless manner while juggling the seed from paw to paw as though not quite certain what to do with it, and occasionally pretending to drop it and recovering it at the last moment. After above five minutes of this they tossed the seed down to the ground below and shuffled about the tree in search of more fruit.

Sometimes when one porcupine met another face to face on a branch, they both anchored themselves with their tails, sat up on their hind legs and indulged in the most ridiculous boxing-match, ducking, and slapping with their front paws, feinting and lunging, giving left hooks, uppercuts and body blows, but never once making contact. Throughout this performance (which lasted perhaps for a quarter of an hour) their expression never changed from one of bewildered and benign interest. Then, as though prompted by an invisible signal, they went down on all fours and scrambled away to different parts of the tree. I could never discover the purpose of these boxing bouts nor identify the winner, but they afforded me an immense amount of amusement.

Another fascinating creature that used to come to the fruit trees was the douroucouli. These curious little monkeys, with long tails, delicate, almost squirrel-like bodies and enormous owl-like eyes, are the only nocturnal species of monkey in the world. They arrived in small troops of seven or eight and, though they made no noise as they jumped into the fruit trees, you could soon tell they were there by the long and complicated conversation they held while they fed. They had the biggest range of noises I have ever heard from a monkey, or for that matter from any animal of similar size. First they could produce a loud purring bark, a very powerful vibrating cry which they used as a warning; when they delivered it their throats would swell up to the size of a small apple with the effort. Then, to converse with one another, they would use shrill squeaks, grunts, a mewing noise not unlike a cat's and a series of liquid, bubbling sounds quite different from anything else I have ever heard. Sometimes one of them in an excess of affection would drape his arm over a companion's shoulder and they would sit side by side, arms round each other, bubbling away, peering earnestly into each other's faces. They were the only monkeys I know that would on the slightest provocation give one another the most passionate human kisses, mouth to mouth, arms round each other, tails entwined.

Naturally these animals made only sporadic appearances; there were, however, two creatures which were in constant evidence in the waters of the drowned valley. One was a young cayman, the South American alligator, about four feet long. He was a very handsome reptile with black-and-white skin as knobbly and convoluted as a walnut, a dragon's fringe on his tail, and large eyes of golden-green flecked with amber. He was the only cayman to live in this little stretch of water. I could never understand why no others had joined him, for the creeks and waterways, only a hundred feet or so away, were alive with them. None the less this little cayman lived in solitary state in the pool outside my hut and spent the day swimming round and round with a rather proprietory air. The other creature always to be seen was a jacana, probably one of the strangest birds in South America. In size and appearance it is not unlike the English moorhen, but its neat body is perched on long slender legs which end in a bunch of enormously elongated toes. It is with the aid of these long toes and the even distribution of weight they give that the jacana manages to walk across water, using the water-lily leaves and other water-plants as its pathways. It has thus earned its name of lily-trotter.

The jacana disliked the cayman, while the cayman had formed the impression that Nature had placed the jacana in his pool to add a little variety to his diet. He was, however, a young and inexperienced reptile, and at first his attempts to stalk and capture the bird were ridiculously obvious. The jacana would come mincing out of the undergrowth, where it used to spend much of its time, and walk out across the water, stepping delicately from one lily leaf to the next, its long toes spreading out like spiders and the leaves dipping gently under its weight. The cayman, on spotting it, immediately submerged until only his eyes showed above water. No ripple disturbed the surface, yet his head seemed to glide along until he got nearer and nearer to the bird. The jacana, always pecking busily among the water-plants in search of worms and snails and tiny fish, rarely noticed the cayman's approach and would probably have fallen an easy victim if it had not been for one thing. As soon as the cayman was within ten or twelve feet he would become so excited that instead of submerging and taking the bird from underneath he would suddenly start to wag his tail vigorously and shoot along the surface of the water like a speedboat, making such large splashes that not even the most dim-witted bird could have been taken unawares; and the jacana would fly up into the air with a shrill cry of alarm, wildly flapping its buttercup-yellow wings.

For a long time it did not occur to me to wonder why the bird should spend a greater part of the day in the reed-bed at one end of the lake. But on investigating this patch of reed I soon discovered the reason, for there on the boggy ground I found a mat neatly made of weed on which lay four round creamy eggs heavily blotched with chocolate and silver. The bird must have been sitting for some time, for only a couple of days later I found the nest empty and a few hours after that saw the jacana leading out her brood for its first walk into the world.

She emerged from the reed-bed, trotted out on the lily leaves, then paused and looked back. Out of the reeds her four babies appeared, with the look of outsize bumble-bees, in their golden-and-black fluff, while their long slender legs and toes seemed as fragile as spider-webs. They walked in single file behind their mother, always a lily leaf behind, and they waited patiently for their mother to test everything before moving forward. They could all cluster on one of the great plate-like leaves, and they were so tiny and light that it scarcely dipped beneath their weight. Once the cayman had seen them, of course, he redoubled his efforts, but the jacana was a very careful mother. She kept her brood near the edge of the lake, and if the cayman showed any signs of approaching, the babies immediately dived off the lily leaves and vanished into the water, to reappear mysteriously on dry land a moment later.

The cayman tried every method he knew, drifting as close as possible without giving a sign, concealing himself by plunging under a mat of water-weeds and then surfacing so that the weeds almost covered eyes and nose. There he lay patiently, sometimes even moving very close inshore, presumably in the hope of catching the jacanas before they ventured out too far. For a week he tried each of these methods in turn, and only once did he come anywhere near success. On this particular day he had spent the hot noon hours lying, fully visible, in the very centre of the lake, revolving slowly round and round so that he could keep an eye on what was happening on the shore. In the late afternoon he drifted over to the fringe of lilies and weeds and managed to catch a small frog that had been sunning itself in the centre of a lily. Fortified by this, he swam over to a floating raft of green weeds, studded with tiny flowers, and dived right under it. It was only after half an hour of fruitless search in other parts of the little lake that I realized he must be concealed under the weeds. I trained my field-glasses on them, and although the entire patch was no larger than a door, it took me at least ten minutes to spot him. He was almost exactly in the centre and as he had risen to the surface a frond of weed had become draped between his eyes; on the top of this was a small cluster of pink flowers. He looked somewhat roguish with this weed on his head, as though he were wearing a vivid Easter bonnet, but it served to conceal him remarkably well. Another half an hour passed before the jacanas appeared and the drama began.

The mother, as usual, emerged suddenly from the reed-bed, and stepping daintily on to the lily leaves paused and called her brood, who pattered out after her like a row of quaint clockwork toys and then stood patiently clustered on a lily leaf, awaiting instructions. Slowly the mother led them out into the lake, feeding as they went. She would poise herself on one leaf and, bending over, catch another in her beak, which she would pull and twist until it was sufficiently out of the water to expose the underside. A host of tiny worms and leeches, snails and small crustaceans, generally clung to it. The babies clustered round and pecked vigorously, picking off all this small fry until the underside of the leaf was clean, whereupon they all moved off to another.

Quite early in the proceedings I realized that the female was leading her brood straight towards the patch of weeds beneath which the cayman was hiding, and I remembered then that this particular area was one of her favourite hunting-grounds. I had watched her standing on the lily pads, pulling out the delicate, fern-like weed in large tangled pieces and draping it across a convenient lily flower so that her babies could work over it for the mass of microscopic life it contained. I felt sure that, having successfully managed to evade the cayman so far, she would notice him on this occasion, but although she paused frequently to look about her, she continued to lead her brood towards the reptile's hiding-place.

I was now in a predicament. I was determined that the cayman was not going to eat either the female jacana or her brood if I could help it, but I was not quite sure what to do. The bird was quite used to human noises and took no notice of them whatever, so there was no point in clapping my hands. Nor was there any way of getting close to her, for this scene was being enacted on the other side of the lake, and it would have taken me ten minutes to work my way round, by which time it would be too late, for already she was within twenty feet of the cayman. It was useless to shout, too far to throw stones, so I could only sit there with my eyes glued to my field-glasses, swearing that if the cayman so much as touched a feather of my jacana family I would hunt him out and slaughter him. And then I suddenly remembered the shotgun.

It was, of course, too far for me to shoot at the cayman: the shot would have spread out so much by the time it reached the other side of the lake that only a few pellets would hit him, whereas I might easily kill the birds I was trying to protect. It occurred to me, however, that as far as I knew the jacana had never heard a gun, and a shot fired into the air might therefore frighten her into taking her brood to safety. I dashed into the hut and found the gun, and then spent an agonizing minute or two trying to remember where I had put the cartridges. At last I had it loaded and hurried out to my vantage-point again. Holding the gun under my arm, its barrels pointing into the soft earth at my feet, I held the field-glasses up in my other hand and peered across the lake to see if I was in time.

The jacana had just reached the edge of the lilies nearest the weed patch. Her babies were clustered on a leaf just behind and to one side of her. As I looked she bent forward, grabbed a large trailing section of weed and pulled it on to the lily leaves, and at that moment the cayman, only about four feet away, rose suddenly from his nest of flowers and weeds and, still wearing his ridiculous bonnet, charged forward. At the same moment I let off both barrels of the shotgun, and the roar echoed round the lake.

Whether it was my action that saved the jacana or her own quick-wittedness I do not know, but she rose from the leaf with extraordinary speed just as the cayman's jaws closed and cut the leaf in half. She swooped over his head, he leapt half out of the water in an effort to grab her (I could hear the clop of his jaws) and she flew off unhurt but screaming wildly.

The attack had been so sudden that she had apparently given no orders to her brood, who had meanwhile been crouching on the lily leaf. Now, hearing her call, they were galvanized into action, and as they dived overboard the cayman swept towards them. By the time he reached the spot, they were under water, so he dived too and gradually the ripples died away and the surface of the water became calm. I watched anxiously while the female jacana, calling in agitation, flew round and round the lake. Presently she disappeared into the reed-bed and I saw her no more that day. Nor did I see the cayman for that matter. I had a horrible feeling that he had succeeded in catching all those tiny bundles of fluff as they swam desperately under water, and I spent the evening planning revenge.

The next morning I went round to the reed-bed, and there to my delight I found the jacana, and with her three rather subdued-looking babies. I searched for the fourth one, but as he was nowhere to be seen it was obvious that the cayman had been at any rate partially successful. To my consternation the jacana, instead of being frightened off by her experience of the previous day, proceeded once more to lead her brood out to the water-lilies, and for the rest of the day I watched her with my heart in my mouth. Though there was no sign of the cayman, I spent several nerve-wracking hours, and by evening I decided I could stand it no longer. I went to the village and borrowed a tiny canoe which two Indians kindly carried down to the little lake for me. As soon as it was dark I armed myself with a powerful torch and a long stick with a slip-knot of rope on the end, and set off on my search for the cayman. Though the lake was so small, an hour had passed before I spotted him, lying on the surface near some lilies. As the torch-beam caught him, his great eyes gleamed like rubies. With infinite caution I edged closer and closer until I could gently lower the noose and pull it carefully over his head, while he lay there quietly, blinded or mesmerized by the light. Then I jerked the noose tight and hauled his thrashing and wriggling body on board, his jaws snapping and his throat swelling as he gave vent to loud harsh barks of rage. I tied him up in a sack and the next day took him five miles deep into the creeks and let him go. He never managed to find his way back, and for the rest of my stay in the little hut by the drowned valley I could sit and enjoy the sight of my lily-trotter family pottering happily over the lake in search of food, without suffering any anxiety every time a breeze ruffled the surface of the rich tawny water.

BOOK TWO

Animals in General

The way animals behave, the way they cope with the problems of existence, has always been a source of fascination to me. In the following talks I tried to show some of the astonishing methods they use to obtain a mate, to defend themselves or to build their homes.

An ugly or horrifying animal – like an ugly or horrifying human being – is never completely devoid of certain attractive qualities. And one of the most disarming things about the animal world is the sudden encounter with what appeared to be a very dull and nasty beast behaving in a charming and captivating way: an earwig squatting like a hen over her nest of eggs, and carefully gathering them all together again if you are unkind enough to scatter them; a spider who, having tickled his lady-love into a trance, takes the precaution of tying her down with silk threads so that she will not suddenly wake up and devour him after the mating; the sea-otter that carefully ties itself to a bed of seaweed so that it may sleep without fear of being carried too far away by the tides and currents.

I remember once, when I was quite young, sitting on the banks of a small sluggish stream in Greece. Suddenly, out of the water crawled an insect that looked as if it had just arrived from outer space. It made its laborious way up the stalk of a bullrush. It had great bulbous eyes, a carunculated body supported on spidery legs, and slung across its chest was a curious contraption, carefully folded, that looked as though it might be some sort of Martian aqualung. The insect made its way carefully up the bullrush while the hot sun dried the water off its ugly body. Then it paused and appeared to go into a trance. I was fascinated and yet interested by its repulsive appearance, for in those days my interest in natural history was only equalled by my lack of knowledge, and I did not recognize it for what it was. Suddenly I noticed that the creature, now thoroughly sun-dried and as brown as a nut, had split right down its back and, as I watched, it seemed as though the animal inside was struggling to get out. As the minutes passed, the struggles grew stronger and the split grew larger, and presently the creature inside hauled itself free of its ugly skin and crawled feebly on to the rush stalk, and I saw it was a dragonfly. Its wings were still wet and crumpled from this strange birth, and its body soft, but, as I watched, the sun did its work and the wings dried stiff and straight, as fragile as snowflakes and as intricate as a cathedral window. The body also stiffened, and changed to a brilliant sky-blue. The dragonfly whirred its wings a couple of times, making them shimmer in the sun, and then flew unsteadily away, leaving behind, still clinging to the stem, the unpleasant shell of its former self.

I had never seen such a transformation before, and as I gazed with amazement at the unattractive husk which had housed the beautiful shining insect, I made a vow that never again would I judge an animal by its appearance.

Animal Courtships

Most animals take their courtship very seriously, and through the ages some of them have evolved fascinating ways of attracting the female of their choice. They have grown a bewildering mass of feathers, horns, spikes and dewlaps, and have developed an astonishing variety of colours, patterns and scents, all for the purpose of obtaining a mate. Not content with this, they will sometimes bring the female a gift, or construct a flower show for her, or intrigue her with an acrobatic display, or a dance, or a song. When the animals are courting they put their heart and soul into it, and are even, if necessary, ready to die.

The Elizabethan lovers of the animal world are, of course, the birds: they dress themselves magnificently, they dance and posture and they are prepared at a moment's notice to sing a madrigal or fight a duel to the death.

The most famous are the birds of paradise, for not only do they possess some of the most gorgeous courting dresses in the world but they show them off so well.

Take, for example, the king bird of paradise. I was once lucky enough to see one of these birds displaying in a Brazilian zoo. Here, in a huge outdoor aviary full of tropical plants and trees, three king birds of paradise were living – two females and a male. The male is about the size of a blackbird, with a velvety orange head contrasting vividly with a snow-white breast and a brilliant scarlet back, the feathers having such a sheen on them that they seem polished. The beak is yellow and the legs are a beautiful cobalt blue. The feathers along the side of its body – since it was the breeding season – were long, and the middle pair of tail feathers were produced in long slender stalks about ten inches in length. The feather was tightly coiled like a watch spring, so that at the end of each of these wire-like feathers shone a disc of emerald green. In the sunlight he gleamed and glittered with every movement, and the slender tail-wire trembled and the green disc shook and scintillated in the sun. He was sitting on a long bare branch, and the two females were squatting in a bush close by, watching him. Suddenly he puffed himself out a little and gave a curious cry midway between a whine and a yap. He was silent for a minute as if watching the effect of this sound on the females; but they continued to sit there, observing him unemotionally. He bobbed once or twice on the branch, to fix their attention perhaps, then raised his wings above his back and flapped them wildly, just as if he were about to take off on a triumphant flight. He spread them out wide and ducked forward, so that his head was hidden by the feathers. Then he raised them again, flapped vigorously once more, and wheeled round so that the two females should be dazzled by his beautiful snow-white breast. He gave a lovely liquid warbling cry, while the long side-plumes on his body suddenly burst out, like a beautiful fountain of ash-grey, buff and emerald-green that quivered delicately in time to his song. He raised his short tail and pressed it closely to his back, so that the two long tail-wires curved over his head and on each side of his yellow beak hung the two emerald-green discs. He swayed his body gently to and fro; the discs swung like pendulums and gave the odd impression that he was juggling with them. He lifted and lowered his head, singing with all his might, while the green discs gyrated to and fro.

The females seemed completely oblivious. They sat there regarding him with the mild interest of a couple of housewives at an expensive mannequin parade, who, though they admired the gowns, realized they have no hope of purchasing them. Then the male, as if in a last desperate effort to work his audience into some show of enthusiasm, suddenly swung right round on the perch and showed his beautiful scarlet back to them, lowered himself to a crouch and opened wide his beak, revealing the interior of his mouth which was a rich apple-green in colour and as glossy as though it had just been painted. He stood like this, singing with open mouth, and then gradually, as his song died away, his gorgeous plumes ceased to twitch and tremble and fell against his body. He stood upright on the branch for a moment and regarded the females. They stared back at him with the expectant air of people who, having watched a conjurer performing one good trick, are waiting for the next. The male gave a few slight chirrups and then burst into song again and suddenly let himself drop, so that he hung beneath the branch. Still singing, he spread his wings wide and then walked to and fro upside down. This acrobatic display seemed to intrigue one of the females for the first time, for she cocked her head on one side in a gesture of enquiry. I could not for the life of me see how they could remain so unimpressed, for I was dazzled and captivated by the male's song and colouring. Having walked backwards and forwards for a minute or so, he closed his wings tightly and let his body dangle straight down, swaying softly from side to side, singing passionately all the while. He looked like some weird crimson fruit attached to the bough by the blue stalks of his legs, stirring gently in a breeze.

At this point, one of the females grew bored and flew off to another part of the aviary. The remaining one, however, with head cocked to one side, was peering closely at the male. With a quick flap of his wings he regained his upright position on the perch, looking a trifle smug I thought, as well he might. Now I waited excitedly to see what would happen next. The male was standing stock-still, letting his feathers shimmer in the sunlight, and the female was becoming decidedly excited. I felt sure that she had succumbed to his fantastic courtship which was as sudden and as beautiful as a burst of highly coloured fireworks. Sure enough, the female took wing. Now, I thought, she was going up to congratulate him on his performance and they would start married life together at once, but to my astonishment she merely flew on to the branch where the male sat, picked up a small beetle, which was wandering aimlessly across the bark, and with a satisfied chuck flew off to the other end of the aviary with it. The male puffed himself out and started to preen in a resigned sort of fashion, and I decided that the females must be especially hard-hearted, or especially inartistic, to have been able to resist such an exhibition. I felt very sorry for the male that his magnificent courtship should go unrewarded. However my sympathy was wasted, for with a squeak of triumph he had discovered another beetle, which he was happily banging on the branch. He obviously did not mind in the least being turned down.

Not all birds are such good dancers as the birds of paradise, nor are they so well dressed, but they have compensated for this by the charming originality of their approach to the opposite sex. Take, for example, the bower-birds. They have, in my opinion, one of the most delightful courtship methods in the world. The satin bower-bird, for instance, is not particularly impressive to look at: about the size of a thrush, he is clad in dark blue feathers that have a metallic glint when the light catches them. He looks, quite frankly, as if he is wearing an old and shiny suit of blue serge, and you would think that his chances of inducing the female to overlook the poverty of his wardrobe were non-existent. But he contrives it by an extremely cunning device: he builds a bower.

Once again it was in a zoo that I was lucky enough to see a satin bower-bird building his temple of love. He had chosen two large tussocks of grass in the middle of his aviary and had carefully cleared a large circular patch all round and a channel between them. Then he had carried twigs, pieces of string and straw, and had woven them into the grass, so that the finished building was like a tunnel. It was at this stage that I first noticed what he was doing, and by then, having built his little week-end cottage, he was in the process of decorating it. Two empty snail-shells were the first items, and they were followed by the silver paper from a packet of cigarettes, a piece of wool that he had picked up, six coloured pebbles and a bit of string with a blob of sealing wax on it. Feeling that he might like some more decoration, I brought him some strands of coloured wool, a few multi-coloured sea-shells and some bus-tickets.

He was delighted; he came down to the wire to take them carefully from my fingers, and then hopped back to his bower to arrange them. He would stand staring at the decorations for a minute and then hop forward and move a bus-ticket or a strand of wool into what he considered a more artistic position. When the bower was finished it really looked very charming and decorative, and he stood in front of it preening himself and stretched out one wing at a time as if indicating his handiwork with pride. Then he dodged to and fro through his little tunnel, rearranged a couple of sea-shells, and started posturing again with one wing outspread. He had really worked hard on his bower, and I felt sorry for him, for the whole effort was in vain: his mate had apparently died some time previously and he now shared the aviary with a few squawking common finches that took no interest whatsoever in his architectural abilities or in his display of household treasures.

In the wild state, the satin bower-bird is one of the few birds that uses a tool, for he will sometimes paint the twigs used in the construction of his bower with highly coloured berries and moist charcoal, using a piece of some fibrous material as a brush. Unfortunately, by the time I had remembered this and had made plans to provide my bower-bird with a pot of blue paint and a piece of old rope – the bower-birds are particularly fond of blue – he had lost interest in his bower and not even the presentation of a complete set of cigarette cards, depicting soldiers' uniforms through the ages, could arouse his enthusiasm again.

Another species of bower-bird builds an even more impressive structure, four to six feet high, by piling sticks round two trees and then roofing it over with creepers. The inside is carefully laid with moss, and the outside, for this bower-bird is plainly a man of the world with expensive tastes, is decorated with orchids. In front of the bower he constructs a little bed of green moss on which he places all the brightly coloured flowers and berries he can find; being a fastidious bird, he renews these every day, taking the withered decorations and piling them carefully out of sight behind the bower.

Among the mammals, of course, you do not come across quite such displays as among the birds. On the whole, mammals seem to have a more down-to-earth, even modern attitude, towards their love problems.

I was able to watch the courtship of two tigers when I worked at Whipsnade Zoo. The female was a timid, servile creature, cringing at the slightest snarl from her mate until the day she came into season. Then she changed suddenly into a slinking, dangerous creature, fully aware of her attraction but biding her time. By the end of the morning the male was following her round, belly-crawling and abject, while on his nose were several deep, bloody grooves caused by slashing backhands from her mate. Every time he forgot himself and approached too closely he got one of these backhand swipes across the nose. If he seemed at all offended by this treatment and lay down under a bush, the female would approach him, purring loudly, and rub herself against him until he got up and followed her again, moving closer and closer until he received another blow on the nose for his pains.

Eventually the female led him down into a little dell where the grass was long, and there she lay down and purred to herself, with her green eyes half-closed. The tip of her tail, like a big black-and-white bumble-bee, twitched to and fro in the grass, and the poor besotted male chased it from side to side, like a kitten, slapping it gently with his great paws. At last the female tired of her vamping; she crouched lower in the grass and gave a curious purring cry. The male, rumbling in his throat, moved towards her. She cried again, and raised her head, while the male gently bit along the line of her arched neck, a gentle nibble with his great teeth. Then the female cried again, a self-satisfied purr, and the two great striped bodies seemed to melt together in the green grass.

Not all mammals are so decorative and highly coloured as the tiger, but they generally compensate by being brawny. They therefore have to rely on cave-man tactics for obtaining their mates. Take, for example, the hippopotamus. To see one of these great chubby beasts lying in the water, staring at you with a sort of benign innocence out of bulbous eyes, sighing occasionally in a smug and lethargic manner, would scarcely lead you to believe that they could be roused to bursts of terrible savagery when it came to choosing a mate. If you have ever seen a hippo yawning, displaying on each side of its mouth four great curved razor-sharp tusks (hidden among which, two more point outwards like a couple of ivory spikes) you will realize what damage they could do.

When I was collecting animals in West Africa we once camped on the banks of a river in which lived a hippo herd of moderate size. They seemed a placid and happy group, and every time we went up or down the stream by canoe they would follow us a short distance, swimming nearer and nearer, wiggling their ears and occasionally snorting up clouds of spray, as they watched us with interest. As far as I could make out, the herd consisted of four females, a large elderly male and a young male. One of the females had a medium-sized baby with her which, though already large and fat, was still occasionally carried on her back. They seemed, as I say, a very happy family group. But one night, just as it was growing dark, they launched into a series of roars and brays which sounded like a choir of demented donkeys. These were interspersed with moments of silence broken only by a snort or a splash, but as it grew darker the noise became worse, until, eventually realizing I would be unlikely to get any sleep, I decided to go down and see what was happening. Taking a canoe, I paddled down to the curve of the river a couple of hundred yards away, where the brown water had carved a deep pool out of the bank and thrown up a great half-moon of glittering white sand. I knew the hippos liked to spend the day here, and it was from this direction that all the noise was coming. I knew something was wrong, for usually by this time each evening they had hauled their fat bodies out of the water and trekked along the bank to raid some unfortunate native's plantation, but here they were in the pool, long past the beginning of their feeding-time. I landed on the sandbank and walked along to a spot which gave me a good view. There was no reason for me to worry about noise: the terrible roars and bellows and splashes coming from the pool were quite sufficient to cover the scrunch of my footsteps.

At first I could see nothing but an occasional flash of white where the hippos' bodies thrashed in the water and churned it into foam, but presently the moon rose, and in its brilliant light I could see the females and the baby gathered at one end of the pool in a tight bunch, their heads gleaming above the surface of the water, their ears flicking to and fro. Now and again they would open their mouths and bray, rather in the manner of a Greek chorus. They were watching with interest both the old male and the young who were in the shallows at the centre of the pool. The water reached up only to their tummies, and their great barrel-shaped bodies and the rolls of fat under their chins gleamed as though they had been oiled. They were facing each other with lowered heads, snorting like a couple of steam-engines. Suddenly the young male lifted his great head, opened his mouth so that his teeth flashed in the moonlight, gave a prolonged and blood-curdling bray, and, just as he was finishing, the old male rushed at him with open mouth and with incredible speed for such a bulky animal. The young male, equally quick, twisted to one side. The old male splashed in a welter of foam like some misshapen battleship, and was now going so fast that he could not stop. As he passed, the young male, with a terrible sideways chop of his huge jaws, bit him in the shoulder. The old male swerved round and charged again, and just as he reached his opponent the moon went behind a cloud. When it came out again, they were standing as I had first seen them, facing each other with lowered heads, snorting.

I sat on that sandbank for two hours, watching these great roly-poly creatures churning up the water and sand as they duelled in the shallows.

As far as I could see, the old male was getting the worst of it, and I felt sorry for him. Like some once-great pugilist who had now grown flabby and stiff, he seemed to be fighting a battle which he knew was already lost. The young male, lighter and more agile, seemed to dodge him every time, and his teeth always managed to find their mark in the shoulder or neck of the old male. In the background the females watched with semaphoring ears, occasionally breaking into a loud lugubrious chorus which may have been sorrow for the plight of the old male, or delight at the success of the young one, but was probably merely the excitement of watching the fight. Eventually, since the fight did not seem as if it would end for several more hours, I paddled home to the village and went to bed.

I awoke just as the horizon was paling into dawn, and the hippos were quiet. Apparently the fight was over. I hoped that the old male had won, but I very much doubted it. The answer was given to me later that morning by one of my hunters; the corpse of the old male, he said, was about two miles downstream, lying where the current of the river had carried it into the curving arms of a sandbank. I went down to examine it and was horrified at the havoc the young male's teeth had wrought on the massive body. The shoulders, the neck, the great dewlaps that hung under the chin, the flanks and the belly: all were ripped and tattered, and the shallows around the carcase were still tinged with blood. The entire village had accompanied me, for such an enormous windfall of meat was a red-letter day for them. They stood silent and interested while I examined the old male's carcase, and when I had finished and walked away they poured over it like ants, screaming and pushing with excitement, vigorously wielding their knives and machetes. It seemed to me, watching the huge hippo's carcase disintegrate under the pile of hungry humans, that it was a heavy price to pay for love.

A notably romantic member of the human race is described as hot-blooded; yet in the animal world it is among the cold-blooded creatures that you find some of the best courtship displays. The average crocodile looks as though he would prove a pretty cold-blooded lover as he lies on the bank, watching with his perpetual, sardonic grin and unwinking eyes the passing pageant of river life. Yet when the time and the place and the lady are right, he will fling himself into battle for her hand; and the two males, snapping and thrashing, will roll over and over in the water. At last the winner, flushed with victory, proceeds to do a strange dance on the surface of the water, whirling round and round with his head and tail thrust into the air, bellowing like a foghorn in what is apparently the reptilian equivalent of an old-fashioned waltz.

It is among the terrapins or water-tortoises that we find an example of the 'treat 'em rough and they'll love you' school of thought. In one of these little reptiles the claws on the front flippers are greatly elongated. Swimming along, the male sees a suitable female and starts to head her off. He then beats her over the head with his long fingernails, an action so quickly performed that his claws are a mere blur. This does not seem to make the female suffer in any way; it may even give her pleasure. But at any rate, even a female terrapin cannot succumb at the very first sign of interest on the part of the male. She must play hard to get, even if only for a short time, and she therefore breaks away and continues swimming in the stream. The male, now roused to a frenzy, swims after her, heads her off again, backs her up to the bank and proceeds to give her another beating. And this may happen several times before the female agrees to take up housekeeping with him. Whatever one may say against this reptile, he is certainly no hypocrite; he starts as he means to go on. And the female does not appear to mind these somewhat hectic advances. In fact, she seems to find them a pleasant and rather original form of approach. But there is no accounting for tastes – even among human beings.

However, for bewildering variety and ingenuity in the management of their love affairs, I think one must give pride of place to the insects.

Take the praying mantis – mind you, one look at their faces and nothing would surprise you about their private lives. The small head, the large bulbous eyes dominating a tiny, pointed face that ends in a little quivering moustache; and the eyes themselves, a pale watery straw colour with black cat-like pupils that give them a wild and maniacal look. Under the chest a pair of powerful, savagely barbed arms are bent in a permanent and hypocritical attitude of prayer, being ready at a moment's notice to leap out and crush the victim in an embrace as though he had been caught in a pair of serrated scissors. Another unpleasant habit of the mantis is the way it looks at things, for it can turn its head to and fro in the most human manner and, if puzzled, will cock its little chinless face on one side, staring at you with wild eyes. Or, if you walk behind it, it will peer at you over its shoulder with an unpleasant air of expectancy. Only a male mantis, I feel, could see anything remotely attractive in the female, and you would think he would be sensible enough not to trust a bride with a face like that. But no, I have seen one, his heart overflowing with love, clasp a female passionately, and while they were actually consummating their marriage his spouse leaned tenderly over her shoulder and proceeded to eat him, browsing with the air of a gourmet over his corpse still clasped to her back, while her whiskers quivered and twitched as each delicate, glistening morsel was savoured to the full.

Female spiders, of course, have this same rather anti-social habit of eating their husbands; and the male's approach to the web of the female is thus fraught with danger. If she happens to be hungry, he will hardly have a chance to get the first words of his proposal out, as it were, before he finds himself a neatly trussed bundle being sucked of his vital juices by the lady. In one such species of the spider, the male has worked out a method to make certain he can get close enough to the female to tickle and massage her into a receptive frame of mind, without being eaten. He brings her a little gift – may be a bluebottle or something of the sort – neatly wrapped up in silk. While she is busily devouring this, he creeps up behind her and strokes her into a sort of trance with his legs. Sometimes, when the nuptials are over, he manages to get away, but in most cases he is eaten at the end of the honeymoon, for it appears that the only true way to a female spider's heart is through her stomach.

In another species of spider the male has evolved an even more brilliant device for subduing his tigerish wife. Having approached her, he then starts to massage her gently with his legs until, as is usual with female spiders, she enters a sort of hypnotic state. Then the male, as swiftly as he can, proceeds to bind her to the ground with a length of silken cord, so that, when she awakes from her trance in the marriage bed, she finds herself unable to turn her husband into a wedding breakfast until she has set about the tedious business of untying herself. This generally saves the husband's life.

But if you want a really exotic romance you need not go to the tropical jungle to find it: just go into you own back-garden and creep up on the common snail. Here you have a situation as complex as the plot of any modern novel, for snails are hermaphrodite, and so each one can enjoy the pleasure of both the male and female side of courtship and mating. But apart from this dual sex, the snail possesses something even more extraordinary, a small sack-like container in its body in which is manufactured a tiny leaf-shaped splinter of carbonate of lime, known as the love-dart. Thus when one snail – who, as I say, is both male and female – crawls alongside another snail, also male and female, the two of them indulge in the most curious courtship action. They proceed to stab each other with their love-darts, which penetrate deeply and are quite quickly dissolved in the body. It seems that this curious duel is not as painful as it appears; in fact, the dart sinking into its side seems to give the snail a pleasant feeling, perhaps an exotic tickling sensation. But, whatever it is, it puts both snails into an enthusiastic frame of mind for the stern business of mating. I am no gardener, but if I were I would probably have a soft spot for any snails in my garden, even if they did eat my plants. Any creature who has dispensed with Cupid, who carries his own quiverful of arrows around with him is, in my opinion, worth any number of dull and sexless cabbages. It is an honour to have him in the garden.

Animal Architects

Some time ago I received a small parcel from a friend of mine in India. Inside the box I found a note which read: 'I bet you don't know what this is.' Greatly intrigued, I lifted off the top layer of wrapping paper, and underneath I found what appeared to be two large leaves which had been rather inexpertly sewn together.

My friend would have lost his bet. As soon as I saw the large and rather amateur stitches, I knew what it was: the nest of a tailor-bird, a thing I had always wanted to see. The two leaves were about six inches long, shaped rather like laurel leaves, and only the edges had been sewn together, so that it formed a sort of pointed bag. Inside the bag was a neat nest of grass and moss, and inside that were two small eggs. The tailor-bird is quite small, about the size of a tit, but with a rather long beak. This is its needle. Having found the two leaves it likes, hanging close together, it then proceeds to sew them together, using fine cotton as thread. The curious thing about it is not so much that the tailor-bird stitches the leaves together as that nobody seems to know where he finds the cotton material with which to do the sewing. Some experts insist that he weaves it himself, others that he has some source of supply that has never been discovered. As I say, the stitches were rather large and inartistic, but then how many people could make a success of sewing up two leaves, using only a beak as a needle?

Architecture in the animal world differs a great deal. Some animals, of course, have only the haziest idea of constructing a suitable dwelling, while others produce most complicated and delightful homes. It is strange that even among closely related animals there should be such a wide variety of taste in the style, situation and size of the home and the choice of materials used in its construction.

In the bird world, of course, one finds homes of every shape and size. They range from the tailor-bird's cradle of leaves to the emperor penguin, who, with nothing but snow for his building, has dispensed with the idea of a nest altogether. The egg is simply carried on the top of the large flat foot, and the skin and feathers of the stomach form a sort of pouch to cover it. Then you have the edible swift who makes a fragile, cup-shaped nest of saliva and bits of twigs and sticks it to the wall of a cave. Among the weaver-birds of Africa, too, the variety of nests is bewildering. One species lives in a community which builds a nest half the size of a haystack, rather like a block of flats, in which each bird has its own nesting-hole. In these gigantic nests you sometimes get an odd variety of creatures living as well as the rightful occupants. Snakes are very fond of them; so are bush-babies and squirrels. One of these nests, if taken to pieces, might display an extraordinary assortment of inmates. No wonder that trees have been known to collapse under the weight of these colossal nests. The common weaver-bird of West Africa builds a neat round nest, like a small basket woven from palm fibres. They also live in communities and hang their nests on every available branch of a tree, until it seems festooned with some extraordinary form of fruit. In the most human way the brilliant and shrill-voiced owners go about the business of courting, hatching the eggs, feeding their young, and bickering with their neighbours, so that the whole thing rather resembles an odd sort of council estate.

To construct their nests, the weaver-birds have become adept not only at weaving but at tying knots, for the nest is strapped very firmly to the branch and requires considerable force to remove it. I once watched a weaver-bird starting its nest, a fascinating performance. He had decided that the nest should hang from the end of a delicate twig half-way up a tree, and he arrived on the spot carrying a long strand of palm fibre in his beak. He alighted on the branch, which at once swung to and fro so that he had to flap his wings to keep his balance. When he was fairly steady he juggled with the palm fibre until he got to the centre of it. Then he tried to drape it over the branch, so that the two ends hung one side and the loop hung the other. The branch still swayed about, and twice he dropped the fibre and had to fly down to retrieve it, but at last he got it slung over the branch to his satisfaction. He then placed one foot on it to keep it in position and leaning forward precariously he pulled the two dangling ends from one side of the branch through the loop on the other and tugged it tight. After this he flew off for some more fibre and repeated the performance. He went on in this way for the whole day, until by evening he had twenty or thirty pieces of fibre lashed to the branch, the ends dangling down like a beard.

Unfortunately I missed the following stages in the construction of this nest, and I next saw it empty, for the bird had presumably reared its young and moved off. The nest was flask-shaped – a small round entrance, guarded by a small porch of plaited fibre. I tried to pull the nest off the branch, but it was impossible, and in the end I had to break the whole branch off. Then I tried to tear the nest in half so that I could examine the inside. But so intricately interlaced and knotted were the palm fibres that it took me a long time and all my strength before I could do so. It was really an incredible construction, when you consider the bird had only its beak and its feet for tools.

When I went to Argentina four years ago I noticed that nearly every tree-stump or rail-post in the pampa was decorated with a strange earthenware construction about the size and shape of a football. At first, I believed they were termite nests, for they were very similar to a common feature of the landscape in West Africa. It was not until I saw, perched on top of one of them, a small tubby bird about the size of a robin with a rusty-red back and grey shirt-front that I realized they were the nests of the oven-bird.

As soon as I found an unoccupied nest, I carefully cut it in half and was amazed at the skill with which it had been built. Wet mud had been mixed with tiny fragments of dried grass, roots and hair to act as reinforcement. The sides of the nest were approximately an inch and a half thick. The outside had been left rough – unrendered, as it were – but the inside had been smoothed to a glass-like finish. The entrance to the nest was a small arched hole, rather like a church door, which led into a narrow passage-way that curved round the outer edge of the nest and eventually led into the circular nesting-chamber lined with a pad of soft roots and feathers. The whole thing rather resembled a snail shell.

Although I searched a large area, I was never lucky enough to find a nest that had been newly started, for it was fairly well into the breeding season. But I did find one half-completed. Oven-birds are very common in Argentina, and in the way they move and cock their heads on one side and regard you with their shining dark eyes, they reminded me very much of the English robin. The pair building this nest took no notice of me whatever, provided I remained at a distance of about twelve feet, though occasionally they would fly over to take a closer look at me, and after inspecting me with their heads on one side, they would flap their wings as though shrugging, and return to their building work. The nest, as I say, was half-finished: the base was firmly cemented on to a fence-post and the outer walls and inner wall of the passage-way were already some four or five inches high. All that remined now was for the whole thing to be covered with the domed roof.

The nearest place for wet mud was about half a mile away at the edge of a shallow lagoon. They would hop round the edge of the water in a fussy, rather pompous manner, testing the mud every few feet. It had to be of exactly the right consistency. Having found a suitable patch, they would hop about excitedly, picking up tiny rootlets and bits of grass until their beaks were full and they looked as though they had suddenly sprouted large walrus moustaches. They would carry these beakfuls of reinforcement down to the mud patch, and then by skilful juggling, without dropping the material, pick up a large amount of mud as well. By a curious movement of the beak they matted the two materials together until their walrus moustaches looked distinctly bedraggled and mudstained. Then, with a muffled squeak of triumph, they flew off to the nest. Here the bundle was placed in the right position and pecked and trampled on and pushed until it had firmly adhered to the original wall. Then they entered the nest and smoothed off the new patch, using their beaks, their breasts and even the sides of their wings to get the required shining finish.

When only a small patch on the very top of the roof needed to be finished, I took some bright scarlet threads of wool down to the edge of the lagoon and scattered them around the place where the oven-birds gathered their material. On my next trip down there, to my delight, they had picked them up, and the result, a small russet bird apparently wearing a bright scarlet moustache, was quite startling. They incorporated the wool into the last piece of building on the nest, and it was, I feel sure, the only Argentinian oven-bird's nest on the pampa flying what appeared to be a small red flag at half-mast.

If the oven-bird is a master-builder, whose nest is so solid that it takes several blows of a hammer to demolish it, members of the pigeon family go to the opposite extreme. They have absolutely no idea of proper nest-making. Four or five twigs laid across a branch: that is the average pigeon's idea of a highly complicated structure. On this frail platform the eggs, generally two, are laid. Every time the tree sways in the wind this silly nest trembles and shakes and the eggs almost fall out. How any pigeon ever reaches maturity is a mystery to me.

I knew that pigeons were stupid and inefficient builders, but I never thought that their nests might prove an irritating menace to a naturalist. When I was in Argentina I learned differently. On the banks of a river outside Buenos Aires I found a small wood. The trees, only about thirty feet high, were occupied by what might almost be called a pigeon colony. Every tree had about thirty or forty nests in it. Walking underneath the branches you could see the fat bellies of the young, or the gleam of the eggs, through the carelessly arranged twigs. The nests looked so insecure that I felt like walking on tip-toe for fear that my footsteps would destroy the delicate balance.

In the centre of the wood I found a tree full of pigeons' nests but for some odd reason devoid of pigeons. At the very top of the tree I noticed a great bundle of twigs and leaves which was obviously a nest of some sort and equally obviously not a pigeon's nest. I wondered if it was the occupant of this rather untidy bundle of stuff that had made the pigeon's desert all the nests in the tree. I decided to climb and see if the owner was at home. Unfortunately, it was only when I had started to climb that I realized my mistake, for nearly every pigeon's nest in the tree contained eggs, and as I made my way slowly up the branches my movements created a sort of waterfall of pigeon eggs which bounced and broke against me, smearing my coat and trousers with yolk and bits of shell. I would not have minded this so much, but every single egg was well and truly addled, and by the time

I had reached the top of the tree, hot and sweating, I smelt like a cross between a tannery and a sewage farm. To add insult to injury, I found that the occupant of the nest I had climbed up to was out, so I had gained nothing by my climb except a thick coating of egg and a scent that would have made a skunk envious. Laboriously I climbed down the tree again, looking forward to the moment when I would reach ground and could light a cigarette, to take the strong smell of rotten egg out of my nostrils. The ground under the tree was littered with broken eggs tastefully interspersed with the bodies of a few baby pigeons in a decomposed condition. I made my way out into the open as quickly as possible. With a sigh of relief, I sat down and reached into my pocket for my cigarettes. I drew them out dripping with egg-yolk. At some point during my climb, by some curious chance, an egg had fallen into my pocket and broken. My cigarettes were ruined. I had to walk two miles home without a smoke, breathing in a strong aroma of egg and looking as though I had rather unsuccessfully taken part in an omelette-making competition. I have never really liked pigeons since then.

Mammals, on the whole, are not such good builders as the birds, though, of course, a few of them are experts. The badger, for example, builds the most complicated burrow, which is sometimes added to by successive generations until the whole thing resembles an intricate underground system with passages, culs-de-sac, bedrooms, nurseries and feeding-quarters. The beaver, too, is another master-builder, constructing his lodge half in and half out of the water: thick walls of mud and logs with an underground entrance, so that he can get in and out even when the surface of the lake is iced over. Beavers also build canals, so that when they have to fell a tree some distance inland for food or repair work on their dam, they can float it down the canal to the main body of water. Their dams are, of course, masterpieces – massive constructions of mud and logs, welded together, stretching sometimes many hundreds of yards. The slightest breach in these is frantically repaired by the beavers, for fear that the water would drain away and leave their lodge with its door no longer covered by water, an easy prey to any passing enemy. What with their home, their canals and their dams, one has the impression that the beaver must be a remarkably intelligent and astute animal. Unfortunately, however, this is not the case. It appears that the desire to build a dam is an urge which no self-respecting beaver can repress even when there is no need for the construction, and when kept in a large cement pool they will solemnly and methodically run a dam across it to keep the water in.

But, of course, the real master-architects of the animal world are, without a doubt, the insects. You need only look at the beautiful mathematical precision with which a common or garden honeycomb is built. Insects seem capable of building the most astonishing homes from a vast array of materials – wood, paper, wax, mud, silk and sand – and they differ just as widely in their design. In Greece, when I was a boy, I used to spend hours searching mossy banks for the nests of the trap-door-spiders. These are one of the most beautiful and astonishing pieces of animal architecture in the world. The spider itself, with its legs spread out, would just about cover a two-shilling piece and looks as though it has been made out of highly polished chocolate. It has a squat fat body and rather short legs, and does not look at all the sort of creature you would associate with delicate construction work. Yet these rather clumsy-looking spiders sink a shaft into the earth of a bank about six inches deep and about the diameter of a shilling. This is carefully lined, so that when finished it is like a tube of silk. Then comes the most important part, the trapdoor. This is circular and with a neatly bevelled edge, so that it fits securely into the mouth of the tunnel. It is then fixed with a silken hinge, and the outside of it camouflaged with sprigs of moss or lichen; it is almost indistinguishable from the surrounding earth when closed. If the owner is not at home and you flip back the door, you will see on its silken underside a series of neat little black pinpricks. These are the handles, so to speak, in which the spider latches her claws to hold the door firmly shut against intruders. The only person, I think, who would not be amazed at the beauty of a trapdoor-spider's nest is the male trapdoor-spider himself, for once he has lifted the trapdoor and entered the silken shaft, it is for him both a tunnel of love and death. Once having gone down into the dark interior and mated with the female, he is promptly killed and eaten by her.

One of my first experiences with animal architects was when I was about ten years old. At that time I was extremely interested in freshwater biology and used to spend most of my spare time dredging about in ponds and streams, catching the minute fauna that lived there and keeping them in large jam-jars in my bedroom. Among other things, I had one jam-jar full of caddis larvae. These curious caterpillar-like creatures encase themselves in a sort of silken cocoon with one end open, and then decorate the outside of the cocoon with whatever materials they think will produce the best camouflage. The caddis I had were rather dull, for I had caught them in a very stagnant pool. They had merely decorated the outside of their cocoons with little bits of dead water-plant.

I had been told, however, that if you remove a caddis larva from its cocoon and place it in a jar of clean water, it would spin itself a new cocoon and decorate the outside with whatever materials you cared to supply. I was a bit sceptical about this, but decided to experiment. I took four of my caddis larvae and very carefully removed them, wriggling indignantly, from their cocoons. Then I placed them in a jar of clean water and lined the bottom of the jar with a handful of tiny bleached seashells. To my astonishment and delight the creatures did exactly what my friend said they would do, and by the time the larvae had finished the new cocoons were like a filigree of seashells.

I was so enthusiastic about this that I gave the poor creatures a rather hectic time of it. Every now and then I would force them to manufacture new cocoons decorated with more and more improbable substances. The climax came with my discovery that by moving the larvae to a new jar with a new substance at the bottom when they were half-way through building operations, you could get them to build a parti-coloured cocoon. Some of the results I got were very odd. There was one, for example, who had half his cocoon magnificently arrayed in seashells and the other half in bits of charcoal. My greatest triumph, however, lay in forcing three of them to decorate their cocoons with fragments of blue glass, red brick and white seashells. Moreover, the materials were put on in stripes – rather uneven stripes, I grant you, but stripes nevertheless.

Since then I have had a lot of animals of which I have been proud, but

I never remember feeling quite the same sort of satisfaction as I did when I used to show off my red, white and blue caddis larvae to my friends. I think the poor creatures were really rather relieved when they could hatch out and fly away and forget about the problems of cocoon-building.

Animal Warfare

I remember once lying on a sun-drenched hillside in Greece – a hillside covered with twisted olive-trees and myrtle bushes – and watching a protracted and bloody war being waged within inches of my feet. I was extremely lucky to be, as it were, war correspondent for this battle. It was the only one of its kind I have ever seen and I would not have missed it for the world.

The two armies involved were ants. The attacking force was a shining, fierce red, while the defending army was as black as coal. I might quite easily have missed this if one day I had not noticed what struck me as an extremely peculiar ants' nest. It contained two species of ants, one red and one black, living together on the most amicable terms. Never having seen two species of ants living in the same nest before, I took the trouble to check up on them, and discovered that the red ones, who were the true owners of the nest, were known by the resounding title of the blood-red slave-makers, and the black ones were in fact their slaves who had been captured and placed in their service while they were still eggs. After reading about the habits of the slave-makers, I kept a cautious eye on the nest in the hope of seeing them indulge in one of their slave raids. Several months passed and I began to think that either these slave-makers were too lazy or else they had enough slaves to keep them happy.

The slave-makers' fortress lay near the roots of an olive-tree, and some thirty feet farther down the hillside was a nest of black ants. Passing this nest one morning, I noticed several of the slave-makers wandering about within a yard or so of it, and I stopped to watch. There were perhaps thirty or forty of them, spread over quite a large area. They did not appear to be foraging for food, as they were not moving with their normal brisk inquisitiveness. They kept wandering round in vague circles, occasionally climbing a grass blade and standing pensively on its tip, waving their antennae. Periodically, two of them would meet and stand there in what appeared to be animated conversation, their antennae twitching together. It was not until I had watched them for some time that I realized what they were doing. Their wanderings were not as aimless as they appeared, for they were quartering the ground very thoroughly like a pack of hunting-dogs, investigating every bit of the terrain over which their army would have to travel. The black ants seemed distinctly ill at ease. Occasionally one of them would meet one of the slave-makers and would turn tail and run back to the nest to join one of the many groups of his relatives who were gathered in little knots, apparently holding a council of war. This careful investigation of the ground by the scouts of the slave-makers' army continued for two days, and I had begun to think that they had decided the black ants' city was too difficult to attack. Then I arrived one morning to find that the war had started.

The scouts, accompanied by four or five small platoons, had now moved in closer to the black ants, and already several skirmishes were taking place within two or three feet of the nest. Black ants were hurling themselves on the red ones with almost hysterical fervour, while the red ones were advancing slowly but inexorably, now and then catching a black ant and with a swift, savage bite piercing it through the head or the thorax with their huge jaws.

Half-way up the hillside the main body of the slave-makers' army was marching down. In about an hour they had got within four or five feet of the black ants' city, and here, with a beautiful military precision which was quite amazing to watch, they split into three columns. While one column marched directly on the nest the other two spread out and proceeded to execute a flanking or pincer movement. It was fascinating to watch. I felt I was suspended in some miraculous way above the field of battle of some old military campaign – the battle of Waterloo or some similar historic battle. I could see at a glance the disposition of the attackers and the defenders; I could see the columns of reinforcements hurrying up through the jungle of grass; see the two outflanking columns of slave-makers moving nearer and nearer to the nest, while the black ants, unaware of their presence, were concentrating on fighting off the central column. It was quite obvious to me that unless the black ants very soon realized that they were being encircled, they had lost all hope of survival. I was torn between a desire to help the black ants in some way and a longing to leave things as they were and see how matters developed. I did pick up one of the black ants and place him near the encircling red-ant column, but he was set upon and killed rapidly, and I felt quite guilty.

Eventually, however, the black ants suddenly became aware of the fact that they were being neatly surrounded. Immediately they seemed to panic; numbers of them ran to and fro aimlessly, some of them in their fright running straight into the red invaders and being instantly killed. Others, however, seemed to keep their heads, and they rushed down into the depths of the fortress and started on the work of evacuating the eggs, which they brought up and stacked on the side of the nest farthest away from the invaders. Other members of the community then seized the eggs and started to rush them away to safety. But they had left it too late.

The encircling columns of slave-makers, so orderly and neat, now suddenly burst their ranks and spread over the whole area, like a scuttling red tide. Everywhere there were knots of struggling ants. Black ones, clasping eggs in their jaws, were pursued by the slave-makers, cornered and then forced to give up the eggs. If they showed fight, they were immediately killed; the more cowardly, however, saved their lives by dropping the eggs they were carrying as soon as a slave-maker hove in sight. The whole area on and around the nest was littered with dead and dying ants of both species, while between the corpses the black ants ran futilely hither and thither, and the slave-makers gathered the eggs and started on the journey back to their fortress on the hill. At that point, very reluctantly, I had to leave the scene of battle, for it was getting too dark to see properly.

Early next morning I arrived at the scene again, to find the war was over. The black ants' city was deserted, except for the dead and injured ants littered all over it. Neither the black nor the red army were anywhere to be seen. I hurried up to the red ants' nest and was just in time to see the last of the army arrive there, carrying their spoils of war, the eggs, carefully in their jaws. At the entrance to the nest their black slaves greeted them excitedly, touching the eggs with their antennae and scuttling eagerly around their masters, obviously full of enthusiasm for the successful raid on their own relations that the slave-makers had achieved. There was something unpleasantly human about the whole thing.

It is perhaps unfair to describe animals as indulging in warfare, because for the most part they are far too sensible to engage in warfare as we know it. The exceptions are, of course, the ants, and the slave-makers in particular. But for most other creatures warfare consists of either defending themselves against an enemy, or attacking something for food.

After watching the slave-makers wage war I had the greatest admiration for their military strategy, but it did not make me like them very much. In fact, I was delighted to find that there existed what might be described as an underground movement bent on their destruction; the ant-lions. An adult ant-lion is very like a dragonfly, and looks fairly innocent. But in its childhood, as it were, it is a voracious monster that has evolved an extremely cunning way of trapping its prey, most of which consists of ants.

The larva is round-bodied, with a large head armed with great pincer-like jaws. Picking a spot where the soil is loose and sandy, it buries itself in the earth and makes a circular depression like the cone of a volcano. At the bottom of this, concealed by sand, the larva waits for its prey. Sooner or later an ant comes hurrying along in that preoccupied way so typical of ants, and blunders over the edge of the ant-lion's cone. It immediately realizes its mistake and tries to climb out again, but it finds this difficult, for the sand is soft and gives way under its weight. As it struggles futilely at the rim of this volcano it dislodges grains of sand which trickle down inside the cone and awake the deadly occupant that lurks there. Immediately the ant-lion springs into action. Using its great head and jaws like a steam-shovel, it shoots a rapid spray of sand grains at the ant, still struggling desperately to climb over the lip of the volcano. The earth sliding away from under its claws, knocked off its balance by this stream of sand and unable to regain it, the ant rolls down to the bottom of the cone where the sand parts like a curtain and it is enfolded lovingly in the great curved jaws of the ant-lion. Slowly, kicking and struggling, it disappears, as though it were being sucked down by quicksand, and within a few seconds the cone is empty, while below the innocent-looking sand the ant-lion is sucking the vital juices out of its victim.

Another creature that uses this sort of machine-gunning to bring down its prey is the archer-fish. This is a rather handsome creature found in the streams of Asia. It has evolved a most ingenious method of obtaining its prey, which consists of flies, butterflies, moths and other insects. Swimming slowly along under the surface it waits until it sees an insect alight on a twig or leaf overhanging the water. Then the fish slows down and approaches cautiously. When it is within range it stops, takes aim, and then suddenly and startlingly spits a stream of tiny water droplets at its prey. These travel with deadly accuracy, and the startled insect is knocked off its perch and into the water below, and the next minute the fish swims up beneath it, there is a swirl of water and a gulp, and the insect has vanished for ever.

I once worked in a pet-shop in London, and one day with a consignment of other creatures we received an archer-fish. I was delighted with it, and with the permission of the manager I wrote out a notice describing the fish's curious habits, arranged the aquarium carefully, put the fish inside and placed it in the window as the main display. It proved very popular, except that people wanted to see the archer-fish actually taking his prey, and this was not easy to manage. Eventually I had a brainwave. A few doors down from us was a fish shop, and I saw no reason why we should not benefit from some of their surplus bluebottles. So I suspended a bit of very smelly meat over the archer-fish's aquarium and left the door of the shop open. I did this without the knowledge of the manager. I wanted it to be a surprise for him.

It was certainly a surprise.

By the time he arrived, there must have been several thousand bluebottles in the shop. The archer-fish was having the time of his life, watched by myself inside the shop and fifty or sixty people on the pavement outside. The manager arrived neck and neck with a very unzoological policeman, who wanted to know the meaning of the obstruction outside. To my surprise the manager, instead of being delighted with my ingenious window display, tended to side with the policeman. The climax came when the manager, leaning over the aquarium to unfasten the bit of meat that hung above it, was hit accurately in the face by a stream of water which the fish had just released in the hope of hitting a particularly succulent bluebottle. The manager never referred to the incident again, but the next day the archer-fish disappeared, and it was the last time I was allowed to dress the window.

Of course, one of the favourite tricks in animal warfare is for some harmless creature to persuade a potential enemy that it is really a hideous, ferocious beast, best left alone. One of the most amusing examples of this I have seen was given to me by a sun bittern when I was collecting live animals in British Guiana. This slender bird, with a delicate, pointed beak and slow stately movements, had been hand-reared by an Indian and was therefore perfectly tame. I used to let it wander freely round my camp during the day and lock it in a cage only at night. Sun bitterns are clad in lovely feathering that has all the tints of an autumn woodland, and sometimes when this bird stood unmoving against a background of dry leaves she seemed to disappear completely. As I say, she was a frail, dainty little bird who, one would have thought, had no defence of any sort against an enemy. But this was not the case.

Three large and belligerent hunting-dogs followed their master into camp one afternoon, and before long one of them spotted the sun bittern, standing lost in meditation on the edge of the clearing. He approached her, his ears pricked, growling softly. The other two quickly joined him, and the three of them bore down on the bird with a swaggering air. The bird let them get within about four feet of her before deigning to notice them. Then she turned her head, gave them a withering stare and turned round to face them. The dogs paused, not quite sure what to do about a bird that did not run squawking at their approach. They moved closer. Suddenly the bittern ducked her head and spread her wings, so that the dogs were presented with a fan of feathers. In the centre of each wing was a beautiful marking, not noticeable when the wings were closed, which looked exactly like the two eyes of an enormous owl glaring at you. The whole transformation was done so slickly, from a slim meek little bird to something that resembled an infuriated eagle owl at bay, that the dogs were taken completely by surprise. They stopped their advance, took one look at the shivering wings and then turned tail and fled. The sun bittern shuffled her wings back into place, preened a few of her breast feathers that had become disarranged and fell to meditating again. It was obvious that dogs did not trouble her in the slightest.

Some of the most ingenious methods of defence in the animal world are displayed by insects. They are masters of the art of disguise, of setting traps, and other methods of defence and attack. But, certainly, one of the most extraordinary is the bombardier beetle.

I was once the proud owner of a genuine wild black rat which I had caught when he was a half-grown youngster. He was an extremely handsome beast with his shining ebony fur and gleaming black eyes. He divided his time equally between cleaning himself and eating. His great passion was for insects of any shape or size: butterflies, praying mantis, stick-insects, cockroaches, they all went the same way as soon as they were put into his cage. Not even the largest praying mantis stood a chance against him, though they would occasionally manage to dig their hooked arms into his nose and draw a bead of blood before he scrunched them up. But one day I found an insect which got the better of him. It was a large, blackish beetle which had been sitting reflecting under a stone that I had inquisitively turned over; and, thinking it would make a nice titbit for my rat, I put it in a matchbox in my pocket. When I arrived home I pulled the rat out of his sleeping-box, opened the matchbox and shook the large succulent beetle on to the floor of his cage. Now the rat had two methods of dealing with insects, which varied according to their kind. If they were as fast-moving and as belligerent as a mantis, he would rush in and bite as quickly as possible in order to destroy it, but with anything harmless and slow, like a beetle, he would pick it up in his paws and sit scrunching it up as though it were a piece of toast.

Seeing this great fat delicacy wandering rather aimlessly around on the floor of his cage, he trotted forward, rapidly seized it with his little pink paws and then sat back on his haunches with the air of a gourmet about to sample the first truffle of the season. His whiskers twitched in anticipation as he lifted the beetle to his mouth, and then a curious thing happened. He uttered the most prodigious sniff, dropped the beetle and leaped backwards as though he had been stung, and sat rubbing his paws hastily over his nose and face. At first I thought he had merely been taken with a sneezing fit just as he was about to eat the beetle. Having wiped his face, he again approached it, slightly more cautiously this time, picked it up and lifted it to his mouth.

Then he uttered a strangled snort, dropped it as though it were red-hot and sat wiping his face indignantly. The second experience had obviously been enough for him, for he refused to go near the beetle after that; in fact he seemed positively scared of it. Every time it ambled round to the corner of the cage where he was sitting, he would back away hurriedly. I put the beetle back in the matchbox and took it inside to identify it and it was only then that I discovered that I had offered my unfortunate rat a bombardier beetle. Apparently the beetle, when attacked, squirts out a liquid which, on reaching the air, explodes with a tiny crack and forms a sort of pungent and unpleasant gas, sufficiently horrible to make any creature who has experienced it leave the bombardier beetle severely alone in future.

I felt rather sorry for my black rat. It was, I felt, an unfortunate experience to pick up what amounted to a particularly delicious dinner, only to have it suddenly turn into a gas attack in your paws. It gave him a complex about beetles, too, because for days afterwards he would dash into his sleeping-box at the sight of one, even a fat and harmless dung-beetle. However, he was a young rat, and I suppose he had to learn at some time or another that one cannot judge by appearances in this life.

Animal Inventors

I once travelled back from Africa on a ship with an Irish captain who did not like animals. This was unfortunate, because most of my luggage consisted of about two hundred-odd cages of assorted wild life, which were stacked on the forward well deck. The captain (more out of devilment than anything else, I think) never missed a chance of trying to provoke me into an argument by disparaging animals in general and my animals in particular. But fortunately I managed to avoid getting myself involved. To begin with, one should never argue with the captain of a ship, and to argue with a captain who was also an Irishman was simply asking for trouble. However, when the voyage was drawing to an end, I felt the captain needed a lesson and I was determined to teach him one if I could.

One evening when we were nearing the English Channel, the wind and rain had driven us all into the smoking-room, where we sat and listened to someone on the radio giving a talk on radar, which in those days was still sufficiently new to be of interest to the general public. The captain listened to the talk with a gleam in his eye, and when it had finished he turned to me.

'So much for your animals,' he said, 'they couldn't produce anything like that, in spite of the fact that, according to you, they're supposed to be so clever.'

By this simple statement the captain had played right into my hands, and I prepared to make him suffer.

'What will you bet,' I enquired, 'that I can't describe at least two great scientific inventions and prove to you that the principle was being used in the animal world long before man ever thought of it?'

'Make it four inventions instead of two and I'll bet you a bottle of whisky,' said the captain, obviously feeling he was on to a good thing. I agreed to this.

'Well,' said the captain smugly, 'off you go.'

'You'll have to give me a minute to think,' I protested.

'Ha,' said the captain triumphantly, 'you're stuck already.'

'Oh, no,' I explained, 'it's just that there are so many examples I'm not sure which to choose.'

The captain gave me a dirty look.

'Why not try radar, then?' he enquired sarcastically.

'Well, I could,' I said, 'but I really felt it was too easy. However, since you choose it, I suppose I'd better.'

It was fortunate for me that the captain was no naturalist; otherwise he would never have suggested radar. It was a gift, from my point of view, because I simply described the humble bat.

Many people must have been visited by a bat in their drawing-room or bedroom at one time or another, and if they have not been too scared of it, they will have been fascinated by its swift, skilful flight and the rapid twists and turns with which it avoids all obstacles, including objects like shoes and towels that are sometimes hurled at it. Now, despite the old saying, bats are not blind. They have perfectly good eyes, but these are so tiny that they are not easily detected in the thick fur. Their eyes, however, are certainly not good enough for them to perform some of the extraordinary flying stunts in which they indulge. It was an Italian naturalist called Spallanzani, in the eighteenth century, who first started to investigate the flight of bats, and by the unnecessarily cruel method of blinding several bats he found that they could still fly about unhampered, avoiding obstacles as though they were uninjured. But how they managed to do this he could not guess.

It was not until fairly recently that this problem was solved, at least partially. The discovery of radar, the sending out of sound-waves and judging the obstacles ahead by the returning echo, made some investigators wonder if this was not the system employed by bats. A series of experiments was conducted, and some fascinating things were discovered. First of all, some bats were blindfolded with tiny pieces of wax over their eyes, and as usual they had no difficulty in flying to and fro without hitting anything. Then it was found that if they were blindfolded and their ears were covered they were no longer able to avoid collisions, and in fact did not seem at all keen on flying in the first place. If only one ear was covered they could fly with only moderate success, and would frequently hit objects. This showed that bats could get information about the obstacles ahead by means of sound-waves reflected from them. Then the investigators covered the noses and mouths of their bats, but left the ears uncovered, and again the bats were unable to fly without collision. This proved that the nose, ears and mouth all played some part in the bat's radar system. Eventually, by the use of extremely delicate instruments, the facts were discovered. As the bat flies along, it emits a continuous succession of supersonic squeaks, far too high for the human ear to pick up. They give out, in fact, about thirty squeaks a second. The echoes from these squeaks, bouncing off the obstacles ahead, return to the bat's ears and, in some species, to the curious fleshy ridges round the creature's nose, and the bat can thus tell what lies ahead, and how far away it is. It is, in fact, in every detail the principle of radar. But one thing rather puzzled the investigators: when you are transmitting sound-waves on radar, you must shut off your receiver when you are actually sending out the sound, so that you receive only the echo. Otherwise the receiver would pick up both the sound transmitted and the echo back, and the result would be a confused jumble. This might be possible on electrical apparatus, but they could not imagine how the bats managed to do it. It was then discovered that there was a tiny muscle in the bat's ear that did the job. Just at the moment the bat squeaks, this muscle contracts and puts the ear out of action. The squeak over, the muscle relaxes and the ear is ready to receive the echo.

But the amazing thing about this is not that bats have this private radar system – for after a while very little surprises one in Nature – but that they should have had it so long before man did. Fossil bats have been found in early Eocene rocks, and they differed very little from their modern relatives. It is possible, therefore, that bats have been employing radar for something like fifty million years. Man has possessed the secret for about twenty.

It was quite obvious that my first example had made the captain think. He did not seem quite so sure of winning the bet. I said that my next choice would be electricity, and this apparently cheered him up a bit. He laughed in a disbelieving way, and said I would have a job to persuade him that animals had electric lights. I pointed out that I had said nothing about electric lights, but merely electricity, and there were several creatures that employed it. There is, for example, the electric-ray or torpedo-fish, a curious creature that looks rather like a frying-pan run over by a steam-roller. These fish are excessively well camouflaged: not only does their colouring imitate the sandy bottom but they have also the annoying habit of half-burying themselves in the sand, which renders them really invisible. I remember once seeing the effect of this fish's electric organs, which are large and situated on its back. I was in Greece at the time, and was watching a young peasant boy fishing in the shallow waters of a sandy bay. He was wading up to his knees in the clear waters, holding in his hand a three-pronged spear such as the fishermen used for night-fishing. As he made his way round the bay, he was having quite a successful time: he had speared several large fish and a young octopus which had been concealed in a small group of rocks. As he came opposite where I was sitting a curious and rather startling thing happened. One minute he was walking slowly forward, peering down intently into the water, his trident at the ready; the next minute he had straightened up as stiffly as a guardsman and projected himself out of the water like a rocket, uttering a yell that could have been heard half a mile away. He fell back into the water with a splash and immediately uttered another and louder scream and leapt up again. This time he fell back into the water and seemed unable to regain his feet, for he struggled out on to the sand, half-crawling, half-dragging himself. When I got down to where he lay, I found him white and shaking, panting as though he had just run half a mile. How much of this was due to shock and how much to the actual effect of the electricity I could not tell, but at any rate I never again went bathing in that particular bay.

Probably the most famous electricity-producing creature is the electric-eel which, strangely enough, is not an eel at all but a species of fish that looks like an eel. These long, black creatures live in the streams and rivers of South America, and can grow to eight feet in length and the thickness of a man's thigh. No doubt a lot of stories about them are grossly exaggerated, but it is possible for a big one to shock a horse fording a river strongly enough to knock down the animal.

When I was collecting animals in British Guiana I very much wanted to catch some electric-eels to bring back to this country. At one place where we were camped the river was full of them, but they lived in deep caves hollowed out in the rocky shores. Most of these caves communicated with the air by means of round pot-holes that had been worn by the flood waters, and in the cave beneath each pot-hole lived an electric-eel. If you made your way to a pot-hole and stamped heavily with your shoes it would annoy the eel into replying with a strange purring grunt, as though a large pig were entombed beneath your feet.

Try as I would I did not manage to catch one of these eels. Then one day my partner and I, accompanied by two Indians, went for a trip to a village a few miles away, where the inhabitants were great fishermen. We found several animals and birds in the village which we purchased from them, including a tame tree-porcupine. Then, to my delight, someone appeared with an electric-eel in a rather insecure fish-basket. Having bargained for and bought these creatures, including the eel, we piled them into the canoe and set out for home. The porcupine sat in the bow, apparently very interested in the scenery, and in front of him lay the eel in its basket. We were half-way home when the eel escaped.

We were first made aware of this by the porcupine. He was, I think, under the impression that the eel was a snake, for he galloped down from the bows and endeavoured to climb on to my head. Struggling to evade the porcupine's prickly embrace, I suddenly saw the eel wriggling determinedly towards me, and indulged in a feat which I would not have believed possible. I leapt into the air from a sitting position, clasping the porcupine to my bosom, and landed again when the eel had passed, without upsetting the canoe. I had a very vivid mental picture of what had happened to the young peasant who had trodden on the torpedo-fish, and I had no intention of indulging in a similar experience with an electric-eel. Luckily none of us received a shock from the eel, for while we were trying to juggle it back into its basket it wriggled over the side of the canoe and fell into the river. I cannot say any of us were really sorry to see it go.

I remember once feeding an electric-eel that lived in a large tank in a zoo, and it was quite fascinating to watch his method of dealing with his prey. He was about five feet long and could cope adequately with a fish of about eight or ten inches in length. These had to be fed to him alive, and as their death was instantaneous, I had no qualms about this. The eel seemed to know when it was feeding-time and he would be patrolling his tank with the monotonous regularity of a sentry outside Buckingham Palace. As soon as a fish was dropped into his tank he would freeze instantly and apparently watch it as it swam closer and closer. When it was within range, which was about a foot or so, he would suddenly appear to quiver all over as if a dynamo had started within his long dark length. The fish would be, as it were, frozen in its tracks; it was dead before you realized that anything was happening, and then very slowly it would tilt over and start floating belly uppermost. The eel would move a little closer, open his mouth and suck violently, and, as though he were an elongated vacuum-cleaner, the fish would disappear into him.

Having dispensed quite successfully, I thought, with electricity, I now turned my attention to another field: medicine. Anaesthetics, I said, would be my next example, and the captain looked if anything even more sceptical than before.

The hunting-wasp is the Harley Street specialist of the insect world, and he performs an operation which would give a skilled surgeon pause. There are many different species of hunting-wasp, but most of them have similar habits. For the reception of her young the female has to build a nursery out of clay. This is neatly divided into long cells about the circumference of a cigarette and about half its length. In these the wasp intends to lay her eggs. However, she has another duty to perform before she can seal them up, for her eggs will hatch into grubs, and they will then require food until such time as they are ready to undergo the last stage of their metamorphosis into the perfect wasp. The hunting-wasp could stock her nursery with dead food, but by the time the eggs had hatched this food would have gone bad, so she is forced to evolve another method. Her favourite prey is the spider. Flying like some fierce hawk, she descends upon her unsuspecting victim and proceeds to sting it deeply and skilfully. The effect of this sting is extraordinary, for the spider is completely paralysed. The hunting-wasp then seizes it and carries it off to her nursery where it is carefully tucked away in one of the cells and an egg laid on it. If the spiders are small, there may be anything up to seven or eight in a cell. Having satisfied herself that the food-supply is adequate for her youngsters, the wasp then seals up the cells and flies off. Inside this grisly nursery the spiders lie in an unmoving row, in some cases for as much as seven weeks. To all intents and purposes the spiders are dead, even when you handle them, and not even under a magnifying glass can you detect the faintest sign of life. Thus they wait, so to speak, in cold storage until the eggs hatch out and the tiny grubs of the hunting-wasp start browsing on their paralysed bodies.

I think even the captain was a little shaken by the idea of being completely paralysed while something consumed you bit by bit, so I hastily switched to something a shade more pleasant. It was, in fact, the most delightful little creature, and a most ingenious one – the water-spider. Only recently in his history has man been able to live under water for any length of time, and one of his first steps in this direction was the diving-bell. Thousands of years before this the water-spider had evolved his own method of penetrating this new world beneath the surface of the water. To begin with, he can quite happily swim below the surface of the water, wearing his equivalent of the aqualung in the shape of an air bubble which he traps beneath his stomach and between his legs, so that he may breathe under water. This alone is extraordinary, but the water-spider goes even further: he builds his home beneath the surface of the water, a web shaped like an inverted cup, firmly anchored to the water-weeds. He then proceeds to make several journeys to the surface, bringing with him air bubbles which he pushes into this dome-shaped web until it is full of them, and in this he can live and breathe as easily as if he were on land. In the breeding-season he picks out the house of a likely looking female and builds himself a cottage next door, and then, presumably being of a romantic turn of mind, he builds a sort of secret passage linking his house with that of his lady-love. Then he breaks down her wall, so that the air bubbles in each house intermix, and here in this strange underwater dwelling he courts the female, mates with her, and lives with her until the eggs are laid and hatched, and until their children, each carrying their little globule of air from their parent's home, swim out to start life on their own.

Even the captain seemed amused and intrigued by my story of the water-spider, and he was bound to admit, albeit reluctantly, that I had won my bet.

I suppose it must have been about a year later I was talking to a lady who had travelled on the same ship with the same captain.

'Wasn't he a delightful man?' she asked me. I agreed politely.

'He must have enjoyed having you on board,' she went on, 'because he was so keen on animals, you know. One night he kept us all spellbound for *at least* an hour, telling us about all these scientific discoveries – you know, things like radar – and how animals had been employing them for years and years before man discovered them. Really it was fascinating. I told him he ought to write it up into a talk and broadcast it on the B.B.C.'

Vanishing Animals

Some time ago I was watching what must be the strangest group of refugees in this country, strange because they did not come here for the usual reasons, driven by either religious or political persecution from their own country. They came here quite by chance, and in doing so they were saved from extermination. They are the last of their kind, for in their country of origin their relatives were long ago hunted down, killed and eaten. They were, in fact, a herd of Père David deer.

Their existence was first discovered by a French missionary, one Father David, during the course of his work in China in the early eighteen hundreds. In those days China was as little known, zoologically speaking, as the great forests of Africa, and so Father David, who was a keen naturalist, spent his spare time collecting specimens of the flora and fauna to send back to the museum in Paris. In 1865 his work took him to Peking, and while he was there he heard a rumour that there was a strange herd of deer kept in the Imperial Hunting Park, just south of the city. This park had been for centuries a sort of combined hunting- and pleasure-ground for the Emperors of China, a great tract of land completely surrounded by a high wall forty-five miles long. It was strictly guarded by Tartar soldiers, and no one was allowed to enter or approach it. The French missionary was intrigued by the stories he heard about these peculiar deer, and he was determined that, guards or no guards, he was going to look inside the walled park and try to see the animals for himself. One day he got his opportunity and was soon lying up on top of the wall, looking down into the forbidden park and watching the various game animals feeding among the trees below him. Among them was a large herd of deer, and Father David realized that he was looking at an animal he had never seen before, and one which was, very probably, new to science.

Father David soon found out that the deer were strictly protected, and for anyone caught harming or killing them the sentence was death. He knew that any official request he might put forward for a specimen would be politely refused by the Chinese authorities, so he had to use other, less legal methods to get what he wanted. He discovered that the Tartar guards occasionally improved their rather sparse rations by the addition of a little venison; they were well aware what the penalty for their poaching would be if they were caught, and so, in spite of the missionary's pleadings, they refused to sell him the skins and antlers of the deer they killed, or indeed anything that might be evidence of their crime. However, Father David did not give up hope, and after a considerable time he was successful. He met some guards who were either braver or perhaps poorer than the rest, and they obtained for him two deer skins, which he triumphantly shipped off to Paris. As he had expected, the deer turned out to be an entirely new species, and so it was named, in honour of its discoverer, the Père David deer – Father's David's deer.

Naturally, when zoos in Europe heard about this new kind of deer they wanted specimens for exhibition, and after protracted negotiations the Chinese authorities rather reluctantly allowed a few of the animals to be sent to the Continent. Although no one realized it at the time, it was this action that was to save the animals. In 1895, thirty years after the Père David deer first became known to the world, there were great floods around Peking; the Hun-Ho river overflowed its banks and caused havoc in the countryside, destroying the crops and bringing the population to near starvation. The waters also undermined the great wall round the Imperial Hunting Park. Parts of it collapsed, and through these gaps the herd of Père David deer escaped into the surrounding countryside, where they were quickly killed and eaten by the hungry peasants. So the deer perished in China, and the only ones left were the handful of live specimens in the various zoos in Europe.

Shortly before this disaster overtook the deer in China, a small herd of them had arrived in England. The present Duke of Bedford's father had, on his estate at Woburn in Bedfordshire, a wonderful collection of rare animals, and he had been most anxious to try to establish a herd of this new Chinese deer there. He bought as many specimens as he could from the Continental zoos, eighteen in all, and released them in his park. To the deer this must have seemed like home from home, for they settled down wonderfully, and soon started to breed. Today, the herd that started with eighteen now numbers over a hundred and fifty animals, the only herd of Père David deer in the world.

When I was working at Whipsnade Zoo four newly born Père David deer were sent over from Woburn for us to hand-rear. They were delightful little things, with long gangling limbs over which they had no control and strange slanted eyes that gave them a distinctly Oriental appearance. To begin with of course, they did not know what a feeding-bottle was for, and we had to hold them firmly between our knees and force them to drink. But they very soon got the hang of it, and within a few days we had to open the stable door with extreme caution if we did not want to be knocked flying by an avalanche of deer, pushing and shoving in an effort to get at the bottle first.

They had to be fed once during the night, at midnight, and again at dawn, and so we worked out a system of night duties, one week on, one week off, between four keepers. I must say that I rather enjoyed the night duties. To pick one's way through the moonlit park towards the stable where the baby deer were kept, you had to pass several of the cages and paddocks, and the occupants were always on the move. The bears, looking twice as big in the half-light, would be snorting to each other as they shambled heavily through the riot of brambles in their cage, and they could be persuaded to leave their quest for snails and other delicacies if one had a bribe of sugar-lumps. They would come and squat upright in the moonlight, like a row of shaggy, heavy-breathing Buddhas, their great paws resting on their knees. They would throw back their heads and catch the flying lumps of sugar and eat them with much scrunching and smacking of lips. Then, seeing that you had no more in your pockets, they would sigh in a long-suffering manner and shamble off into the brambles again.

At one point the path led past the wolf wood, two acres or so of pines, dark and mysterious, with the moonlight silvering the trunks and laying dark shadows along the ground through which the wolf pack danced on swift, silent feet, like a strange black tide, swirling and twisting among the trunks. As a rule they made no sound, but occasionally you would hear them panting gently, or the sudden snap of jaws and a snarl when one wolf barged against another.

Then you would reach the stable and light the lantern. The baby deer would hear you and start moving restlessly in their straw beds, bleating tremulously. As you opened the door they rushed forward, wobbling on their unsteady legs, sucking frantically at your fingers, the edge of your coat, and butting you suddenly in the legs with their heads, so that you were almost knocked down. Then came the exquisite moment when the teat was pushed into their mouths and they sucked frantically at the warm milk, their eyes staring, bubbles gathering like a moustache at the corners of their mouths. There is always a certain pleasure to be gained from bottle-feeding a baby animal, if only from its wholehearted enthusiasm and concentration on the job. But in the case of these deer there was something else as well. In the flickering light of the lantern, while the deer sucked and slobbered over the bottles, occasionally ducking their heads and butting at an imaginary udder with their heads, I was very conscious of the fact that they were the last of their kind.

At Whipsnade I had to look after another group of animals which belonged to a species now extinct in the wild state, and they were some of the most charming and comic animals I have ever had anything to do with. They were a small herd of white-tailed gnus.

The white-tailed gnu is a weird creature to look at: if you can imagine an animal with the body and legs of a finely built pony, a squat blunt face with very wide-spaced nostrils, a heavy mane of white hair on its thick neck, and a long white sweeping plume of a tail. The buffalo horns curve outward and upwards over the eyes, and the animal peers at you from under them with a perpetually indignant and suspicious expression. If the gnu behaved normally, this appearance would not be so noticeable, but the animal does not behave normally. Anything but, in fact. Its actions can only be described, very inadequately, as a cross between bebop and ballet, with a bit of yogi thrown in.

In the mornings, when I went to feed them, it always took me twice as long as it should have done because the gnus would start performing for me, and the sight was so ludicrous that I would lose all sense of time. They would prance and twist and buck, gallop, rear and pirouette, and while they did so they would throw their slim legs out at extraordinary and completely un-anatomical angles, and swish and curve their long tails as a circus ringmaster uses his whip. In the middle of the wild dance they would suddenly stop dead and glare at me, uttering loud, indignant belching snorts at my laughter. I watched them dancing their swift, wild dance across the paddock and they reminded me, in their antics and attitudes, of some strange heraldic creature from an ancient coat-of-arms, miraculously brought to life, prancing and posturing on a field of green turf.

It is difficult to imagine how anyone had the heart to kill these agile and amusing antelopes. However, the fact remains that the early settlers in South Africa found in the white-tailed gnu a valuable source of food, and so the great herds of high-spirited creatures were slaughtered unmercifully. The antelope contributed to its own downfall in an unusual way. They are incorrigibly curious creatures, and so when they saw the ox-drawn waggons of the early settlers moving across the veldt they simply had to go and investigate. They would dance and gallop round the waggons in circles, snorting and kicking their heels, and then suddenly stopping to stare. Naturally, with these habits of running away and then stopping to stare before they were out of range, they were used by enterprising 'sportsmen' for rifle practice. So they were killed, and their numbers decreased so rapidly that it is amazing that they did not become extinct. Today there are under a thousand of these charming animals left alive, and these are split up into small herds on various estates in South Africa. If they were to become extinct, South Africa would have lost one of the most amusing and talented of her native fauna, an antelope whose actions could enliven any landscape, however dull.

Unfortunately, the Père David deer and the white-tailed gnu are not the only creatures in the world that are nearly extinct. The list of creatures that have vanished altogether, and others that have almost vanished, is a long and melancholy one. As man has spread across the earth he has wrought the most terrible havoc among the wild life by shooting, trapping, cutting and burning the forest, and by the callous and stupid introduction of enemies where there were no enemies before.

Take the dodo, for example, the great ponderous waddling pigeon, the size of a goose, that inhabited the island of Mauritius. Secure in its island home, this bird had lost the power of flight since there were no enemies to fly from, and, since there were no enemies, it nested on the ground in complete safety. But, as well as losing the power of flight, it seems to have lost the power of recognizing an enemy when it saw one, for it was apparently an extremely tame and confiding creature. Then man discovered the dodos' paradise in about 1507, and with him came his evil familiars: dogs, cats, pigs, rats and goats. The dodo surveyed these new arrivals with an air of innocent interest. Then the slaughter began. The goats ate the undergrowth which provided the dodo with cover; dogs and cats hunted and harried the old birds; while pigs grunted their way round the island, eating the eggs and young, and the rats followed behind to finish the feast. By 1681 the fat, ungainly and harmless pigeon was extinct – as dead as the dodo.

All over the world the wild fauna has been whittled down steadily and remorselessly, and many lovely and interesting animals have been so reduced in numbers that, without protection and help, they can never re-establish themselves. If they cannot find sanctuary where they can live and breed undisturbed, their numbers will dwindle until they join the dodo, the quagga, and the great auk on the long list of extinct creatures.

Of course, in the last decade or so much has been done for the protection of wild life: sanctuaries and reserves have been started, and the reintroduction of a species into areas where it had become extinct is taking place. In Canada, for instance, beavers are now reintroduced into certain areas by means of aeroplane. The animal is put in a special box attached to a parachute, and when the plane flies over the area it drops the cage and its beaver passenger out. The cage floats down on the end of the parachute, and when it hits the ground it opens automatically and the beaver then makes its way to the nearest stream or lake.

But although much is being done, there is still a very great deal to do. Unfortunately, the majority of useful work in animal preservation has been done mainly for animals which are of some economic importance to man, and there are many obscure species of no economic importance which, although they are protected on paper, as it were, are in actual fact being allowed to die out because nobody, except a few interested zoologists, considers them important enough to spend money on.

As mankind increases year by year, and as he spreads farther over the globe burning and destroying, it is some small comfort to know that there are certain private individuals and some institutions who consider that the work of trying to save and give sanctuary to these harried animals is of some importance. It is important work for many reasons, but perhaps the best of them is this: man, for all his genius, cannot create a species, nor can he recreate one he has destroyed. There would be a dreadful outcry if anyone suggested obliterating, say, the Tower of London, and quite rightly so; yet a unique and wonderful species of animal which has taken hundreds of thousands of years to develop to the stage we see today, can be snuffed out like a candle without more than a handful of people raising a finger or a voice in protest. So, until we consider animal life to be worthy of the consideration and reverence we bestow upon old books and pictures and historic monuments, there will always be the animal refugee living a precarious life on the edge of extermination, dependent for existence on the charity of a few human beings.

BOOK THREE

Animals in Particular

Keeping wild animals as pets, whether on an expedition or in your own home, can be a tedious, irritating and frustrating business, but it can also give you a great deal of pleasure. Many people have asked me why I like animals, and I have always found it a difficult question to answer. You might just as well ask me why I like eating. But, apart from the obvious interest and pleasure that animals give me, there is another aspect as well. I think that their chief charm lies in the fact that they have all the basic qualities of a human being but with none of the hypocrisy which is now apparently such an essential in the world of man. With an animal you do know more or less where you are: if it does not like you it tells you so in no uncertain manner; if it likes you, again it leaves you in no doubt. But an animal who likes you is sometimes a mixed blessing. Recently I had a pied crow from West Africa who, after six months' deliberation, during which time he ignored me, suddenly decided that I was the only person in the world for him. If I went near the cage he would crouch on the floor trembling in ecstasy, or bring me an offering (a bit of newspaper or a feather) and hold it out for me to take, all the while talking hoarsely to himself in a series of hiccoughing cries and ejaculations. This was all right, but as soon as I let him out of his cage he would fly on to my head and perch there, first digging his claws firmly into my scalp, then decorating the back of my jacket with a nice moist dropping and finally proceeding to give me a series of love pecks on the head. As his beak was three inches long and extremely sharp, this was, to say the least, painful.

Of course, you have to know where to draw the line with animals. You can let pet-keeping develop into eccentricity if you are not careful. I drew the line last Christmas. For a present I decided to buy my wife a North American flying-squirrel, a creature which I had always wanted to possess myself, and which I was sure she would like. The animal duly arrived, and we were both captivated by it. As it seemed extremely nervous, we thought it would be a good idea to keep it in our bedroom for a week or two, so that we could talk to it at night when it came out, and let it grow used to us. This plan would have worked quite well but for one thing. The squirrel cunningly gnawed its way out of the cage and took up residence behind the wardrobe. At first this did not seem too bad. We could sit in bed at night and watch it doing acrobatics on the wardrobe, scuttling up and down the dressing-table, carrying off the nuts and apple we had left there for it. Then came New Year's Eve when we had been invited to a party for which I had to don my dinner-jacket. All was well until I opened a drawer in my dressing-table, when I discovered the answer to the question that had puzzled us for some time: where did the flying-squirrel store all the nuts, apple, bread and other bits of food? My brand-new cummerbund, which I had never even worn, looked like a piece of delicate Madeira lacework. The bits that had been chewed out of it had been very economically saved and used to build little nests, one on the front of each of my dress shirts. In these nests had been collected seventy-two hazel nuts, five walnuts, fourteen pieces of bread, six mealworms, fifty-two bits of apple and twenty grapes. The grapes and the apple had, of course, disintegrated somewhat with the passage of time and had left most interesting Picasso designs in juice across the front of my shirts.

I had to go to the party in a suit. The squirrel is now in Paignton Zoo.

The other day my wife said that she thought a baby otter would make a delightful pet, but I changed the subject hurriedly.

Animal Parents

I have the greatest respect for animal parents. When I was young I tried my hand at rearing a number of different creatures, and since then, on my animal-collecting trips for zoos to various parts of the world, I have had to mother quite a number of baby animals, and I have always found it a most nerve-racking task.

The first real attempt I made at being a foster-mother was to four baby hedgehogs. The female hedgehog is a very good mother. She constructs an underground nursery for the reception of her young; a circular chamber about a foot below ground-level, lined with a thick layer of dry leaves. Here she gives birth to her babies, which are blind and helpless. They are covered with a thick coating of spikes, but these are white and soft, as though made of rubber. They gradually harden and turn brown when the babies are a few weeks old. When they are old enough to leave the nursery the mother leads them out and shows them how to hunt for food; they walk in line, rather like a school crocodile, the tail of one held in the mouth of the baby behind. The baby at the head of the column holds tight to mother's tail with grim determination, and they wend their way through the twilit hedgerows like a strange prickly centipede.

To a mother hedgehog the rearing of her babies seems to present no problems. But when I was suddenly presented with four blind, white, rubbery-spiked babies to rear, I was not so sure. We were living in Greece at the time, and the nest, which was about the size of a football and made of oak leaves, had been dug up by a peasant working in his fields. The first job was to feed the babies, for the ordinary baby's feeding-bottle only took a teat far too large for their tiny mouths. Luckily, the young daughter of a friend of mine had a doll's feeding-bottle, and after much bribery I got her to part with it. After a time the hedgehogs took to this and thrived on a diet of diluted cow's milk.

I kept them at first in a shallow cardboard box where I had put the nest. But in record time the original nest was so unhygienic that I found myself having to change the leaves ten or twelve times a day. I began to wonder if the mother hedgehog spent her day rushing to and fro with piles of fresh leaves to keep her nest clean, and, if she did, how on earth she found time to satisfy the appetites of her babies. Mine were always ready for food at any hour of the day or night. You had only to touch the box and a chorus of shrill screams arose from four little pointed faces poking out of the leaves, each head decorated with a crew-cut of white spikes; and the little black noses would whiffle desperately from side to side in an effort to locate the bottle.

Most baby animals know when they have had enough, but in my experience this does not apply to baby hedgehogs. Like four survivors from a raft, they flung themselves on to the bottle and sucked and sucked and sucked as though they had not had a decent meal in weeks. If I had allowed it they would have drunk twice as much as was good for them. As it was, I think I tended to overfeed them, for their tiny legs could not support the weight of their fat bodies, and they would advance across the carpet with a curious swimming motion, their tummies dragging on the ground. However, they progressed very well: their legs grew stronger, their eyes opened, and they would even make daring excursions as much as six inches away from their box.

I was very proud of my prickly family, and looked forward to the day when I would be able to take them for walks in the evening and find them delicious titbits like snails or wild strawberries. Unfortunately this dream was never realized. It so happened that I had to leave home for a day, to return the following morning. It was impossible for me to take the babies with me, so I had to leave them in charge of my sister. Before I left, I emphasized the greediness of the hedgehogs and told her that on no account were they to have more than one bottle of milk each, however much they squeaked for it.

I should have known my sister better.

When I returned the following day and enquired how my hedgehogs were, she gave me a reproachful look. I had, she said, been slowly starving the poor little things to death. With a dreadful sense of foreboding, I asked her how much she had been giving them at each meal. Four bottles each, she replied, and you should just see how lovely and fat they are getting.

There was no denying they were fat. Their little tummies were so bloated their tiny feet could not even touch the ground. They looked like weird, prickly footballs to which someone by mistake had attached four legs and a nose. I did the best I could, but within twenty-four hours all four of them had died of acute enteritis. No one, of course, was more sorry than my sister, but I think she could tell by the frigid way I accepted her apologies that it was the last time she would be left in charge of any of my foster-children.

Not all animals are as good as the hedgehog at looking after their babies. Some, in fact, treat the whole business with a rather casual and modern attitude. One such is the kangaroo. Baby kangaroos are born in a very unfinished condition. They are actually embryos, for a big red kangaroo squatting on its haunches may measure five feet high and yet give birth to a baby only about half an inch long. This blind and naked blob of life has to find its way up over the mother's belly and into her pouch. In its primitive condition you would think this would be hard enough, but the whole thing is made doubly difficult by the fact that as yet the baby kangaroo can use only its front legs; the hind legs are neatly crossed over its tail. During this time the mother just squats there and gives her baby no help whatever, though occasionally she has been seen to lick a kind of trail through the fur, which may act as some sort of guide. Thus the tiny, premature offspring is forced to crawl through a jungle of fur until, as much by chance as good management, it reaches the pouch, climbs inside and clamps itself on to the teat. This is a feat that makes the ascent of Everest pale into insignificance.

I have never had the privilege of trying to hand-rear a baby kangaroo, but I have had some experience with a young wallaby, which is closely related to the species and looks just like a miniature kangaroo. I was working at Whipsnade Zoo as a keeper. The wallabies there are allowed to run free in the park, and one female, carrying a well-formed youngster, was chased by a group of young lads. In her fright she did what all the kangaroo family does in moments of stress: she tossed her youngster out of her pouch. I found it some time afterwards, lying in the long grass, twitching convulsively and making faint sucking squeaks with its mouth. It was, quite frankly, the most unprepossessing baby animal I had ever seen. About a foot long, it was blind, hairless and a bright sugar-pink. It seemed to possess no control over any part of its body except its immense hind feet, which it kicked vigorously at intervals. It had been badly bruised by its fall and I had grave doubts as to whether it would live. None the less I took it back to my lodgings and, after some argument with the landlady, kept it in my bedroom.

It fed eagerly from a bottle, but the chief difficulty lay in keeping it warm enough. I wrapped it in flannel and surrounded it with hot-water bottles, but these kept growing cold, and I was afraid it would catch a chill. The obvious thing to do was to carry it close to my body, so I put it inside my shirt. It was then that I realized for the first time what a mother wallaby must suffer. Apart from the nuzzling and sucking that went on, at regular intervals the baby would lash out its hind feet, well armed with claws, and kick me accurately in the pit of the stomach. After a few hours I began to feel as though I had been in the ring with Primo Carnera for a practice bout. It was obvious I would have to think of something else, or develop stomach ulcers. I tried putting him round the back of my shirt, but he would very soon scramble his way round to the front with his long claws in a series of convulsive kicks. Sleeping with him at night was purgatory, for apart from the all-in wrestling in which he indulged, he would sometimes kick so strongly that he shot out of bed altogether, and I was constantly forced to lean out of bed and pick him up from the floor. Unfortunately he died in two days, obviously from some sort of internal haemorrhage. I am afraid I viewed his demise with mixed feelings, although it was a pity to be deprived of the opportunity of mothering such an unusual baby.

If the kangaroo is rather dilatory about her child, the pigmy marmoset is a paragon of virtue, or rather the male is. About the size of a large mouse, clad in neat brindled green fur, and with a tiny face and bright hazel eyes, the pigmy marmoset looks like something out of a fairy tale, a small furry gnome or perhaps a kelpie. As soon as the courtship is over and the female gives birth, her diminutive spouse turns into the ideal husband. The babies, generally twins, he takes over from the moment they are born and carries them slung on his hips like a couple of saddle-bags. He keeps them clean by constant grooming, hugs them to him at night to keep them warm, and only hands them over to his rather disinterested wife at feeding-time. But he is so anxious to get them back that you have the impression he would feed them himself if only he could. The pigmy marmoset is definitely a husband worth having.

Strangely enough, monkeys are generally the stupidest babies, and it takes them a long time to learn to drink out of a bottle. Having successfully induced them to do this, you have to go through the whole tedious performance again, when they are a little bit older, in an attempt to teach them to drink out of a saucer. They always seem to feel that the only way of drinking out of a saucer is to duck the face beneath the surface of the milk and stay there until you either burst for want of air or drown in your own drink.

One of the most charming baby monkeys I have ever had was a little moustached guenon. His back and tail were moss-green and his belly and whiskers a beautiful shade of buttercup yellow. Across his upper lip spread a large banana-shaped area of white, like the magnificent moustaches of some retired brigadier. Like all baby monkeys, his head seemed too big for his body, and he had long gangling limbs. He fitted very comfortably into a tea-cup. When I first had him he refused to drink out of a bottle, plainly convinced that it was some sort of fiendish torture I had invented, but eventually, when he got the hang of it, he would go quite mad when he saw the bottle arrive, fasten his mouth on to the teat, clasp the bottle passionately in his arms and roll on his back. As the bottle was at least three times his size, he made one think of a desperate survivor clinging on to a large white airship.

When he learnt, after the normal grampus-like splutterings, to drink out of a saucer, the situation became fraught with difficulty. He would be placed on a table and then his saucer of milk produced. As soon as he saw it coming he would utter a piercing scream and start trembling all over, as if he were suffering with ague or St. Vitus dance, but it was really a form of excited rage: excitement at the sight of the milk, rage that it was never put on the table quickly enough for him. He screamed and trembled to such an extent that he bounced up in the air like a grasshopper. If you were unwise enough to put the saucer down without hanging on to his tail, he would utter one final shrill scream of triumph and dive headfirst into the centre of it, and when you had mopped the resulting tidal wave of milk from your face, you would find him sitting indignantly in the middle of an empty saucer, chattering with rage because there was nothing for him to drink.

One of the main problems when you are rearing baby animals is to keep them warm enough at night, and this, strangely enough, applies even in the tropics where the temperature drops considerably after dark. In the wild state, of course, the babies cling to the dense fur of the mother and obtain warmth and shelter in that way. Hot-water bottles, as a substitute, I have found of very little use. They grow cold so quickly and you have to get up several times during the night to refill them, an exhausting process when you have a lot of baby animals to look after, as well as a whole collection of adult ones. So in most cases the simplest way is to take the babies into bed with you. You soon learn to sleep in one position – half-waking up in the night, should you wish to move, so that you avoid crushing them as you turn over.

I have at one time or another shared my bed with a great variety of young creatures, and sometimes several different species at once. On one occasion my narrow camp-bed contained three mongooses, two baby monkeys, a squirrel and a young chimpanzee. There was just enough room left over for me. You might think that after taking all this trouble a little gratitude would come your way, but in many cases you get the opposite. One of my most impressive scars was inflicted by a young mongoose because I was five minutes late with his bottle. When people ask me about it now, I am forced to pretend it was given me by a charging jaguar. Nobody would believe me if I told them it was really a baby mongoose under the bedclothes.

The Bandits

My first introduction to the extraordinary little animals known as kusimanses took place at the London Zoo. I had gone into the Rodent House to examine at close range some rather lovely squirrels from West Africa. I was just about to set out on my first animal-collecting expedition, and I felt that the more familiar I was with the creatures I was likely to meet in the great rain-forest, the easier my job would be.

After watching the squirrels for a time, I walked round the house peering into the other cages. On one of them hung a rather impressive label which informed me that the cage contained a creature known as a Kusimanse (*Crossarchus obscurus*) and that it came from West Africa. All I could see in the cage was a pile of straw that heaved gently and rhythmically, while a faint sound of snoring was wafted out to me. As I felt that this animal was one I was sure to meet, I felt justified in waking it up and forcing it to appear.

Every zoo has a rule I always observe, and many others should observe it too: not to disturb a sleeping animal by poking it or throwing peanuts. They have precious little privacy as it is. However, I ignored my rule on this occasion and rattled my thumbnail to and fro along the bars. I did not really think this would have any effect. But as I did so a sort of explosion took place in the depths of the straw, and the next moment a long, rubbery tip-tilted nose appeared, to be followed by a rather rat-like face with small neat ears and bright inquisitive eyes. This little face appraised me for a minute; then, noticing the lump of sugar which I held tactfully near the bars, the animal uttered a faint, spinsterish squeak and struggled madly to release itself from the cocoon of straw wound round it.

When only the head had been visible, I had the impression it was only a small creature, about the size of the average ferret, but when it eventually broke loose from its covering and waddled into view, I was astonished at its relatively large body: it was, in fact, so fat as to be almost circular. Yet it shuffled over to the bars on its short legs and fell on the lump of sugar I offered, as though that was the first piece of decent food it had received in years.

It was, I decided, a species of mongoose, but its tip-tilted, whiffling nose and the glittering, almost fanatical eyes made it look totally unlike any mongoose I had ever seen. I was convinced now that its shape was due not to Nature but to overeating. It has very short legs and fine, rather slender paws, and when it trotted about the cage these legs moved so fast that they were little more than a blur beneath the bulky body. Each time I fed it a morsel of food it gave the same faint, breathless squeak: as much as to reproach me for tempting it away from its diet.

I was so captivated by this little animal that before I realized what I was doing I had fed it all the lump-sugar in my pocket. As soon as it knew that no more titbits were forthcoming, it uttered a long-suffering sigh and trotted away to dive into the straw. Within a couple of seconds it was sound asleep once more. I decided there and then that if kusimanses were to be obtained in the area I was visiting, I would strain every nerve to find one.

Three months later I was deep in the heart of the Cameroon rain-forests and here I found I had ample opportunity for getting to know the kusimanse. Indeed, they were about the commonest members of the mongoose family, and I often saw them when I was sitting concealed in the forest waiting for some completely different animal to make its appearance.

The first one I saw appeared suddenly out of the undergrowth on the banks of a small stream. He kept me amused for a long time with a display of his crab-catching methods: he waded into the shallow water and with the aid of his long, turned-up nose (presumably holding his breath when he did so) he turned over all the rocks he could find until he unearthed one of the large, black, freshwater crabs. Without a second's hesitation he grabbed it in his mouth and, with a quick flick of his head, tossed it on to the bank. He then chased after it, squeaking with delight and danced round it, snapping away until at last it was dead. When an exceptionally large crab succeeded in giving him a nip on the end of his *retroussé* nose, I am afraid my stifled amusement caused the kusimanse to depart hastily into the forest.

On another occasion I watched one of these little beasts using precisely the same methods to catch frogs, but this time without much success. I felt he must be young and inexperienced in the art of frog-catching. After much laborious hunting and snuffling, he would catch a frog and hurl it shorewards; but, long before he had waddled out to the bank after it, the frog would have recovered itself and leapt back into the water, and the kusimanse would be forced to start all over again.

One morning a native hunter walked into my camp carrying a small palm-leaf basket, and peering into it I saw three of the strangest little animals imaginable. They were about the size of new-born kittens, with tiny legs and somewhat moth-eaten tails. They were covered with bright gingery-red fur which stood up in spikes and tufts all over their bodies, making them look almost like some weird species of hedgehog. As I gazed down at them, trying to identify them, they lifted their little faces and peered up at me. The moment I saw the long, pink, rubbery noses I knew they were kusimanses, and very young ones at that, for their eyes were only just open and they had no teeth. I was very pleased to obtain these babies, but after I had paid the hunter and set to work on the task of trying to teach them to feed, I began to wonder if I had not got more than I bargained for. Among the numerous feeding-bottles I had brought with me I could not find a teat small enough to fit their mouths, so I was forced to try the old trick of wrapping some cotton-wool round the end of a matchstick, dipping it in milk and letting them suck it. At first they took the view that I was some sort of monster endeavouring to choke them. They struggled and squeaked, and every time I pushed the cotton-wool into their mouths they frantically spat it out again. Fortunately it was not long before they discovered that the cotton-wool contained milk, and then they were no more trouble, except that they were liable to suck so hard in their enthusiasm that the cotton-wool would part company with the end of the matchstick and disappear down their throats.

At first I kept them in a small basket by my bed. This was the most convenient spot, for I had to get up in the middle of the night to feed them. For the first week or so they really behaved very well, spending most of the day sprawled on their bed of dried leaves, their stomachs bulging and their paws twitching. Only at meal-times would they grow excited, scrambling round and round inside the basket, uttering loud squeaks and treading heavily on one another.

It was not long before the baby kusimanses developed their front teeth (which gave them a firmer and more disastrous grip on the cotton-wool), and as their legs got stronger they became more and more eager to see the world that lay outside their basket. They had the first feed of the day when I drank my morning tea; and I would lift them out of their basket and put them on my bed so that they could have a walk round. I had, however, to call an abrupt halt to this habit, for one morning, while I was quietly sipping my tea, one of the baby kusimanses discovered my bare foot sticking out from under the bedclothes, and decided that if he bit my toe hard enough it might produce milk. He laid hold with his needle-sharp teeth, and his brothers, thinking they were missing a feed, instantly joined him. When I had locked them up in their basket again and finished mopping tea off myself and the bed, I decided these morning romps would have to cease. They were too painful.

This was merely the first indication of the trouble in store for me. Very soon they had become such a nuisance that I was forced to christen them the Bandits. They grew fast, and as soon as their teeth had come through they started to eat egg and a little raw meat every day, as well as their milk. Their appetites seemed insatiable, and their lives turned into one long quest for food. They appeared to think that everything was edible unless proved otherwise. One of the things of which they made a light snack was the lid of their basket. Having demolished this they hauled themselves out and went on a tour of inspection round the camp. Unfortunately, and with unerring accuracy, they made their way to the one place where they could do the maximum damage in the minimum time: the place where the food and medical supplies were stored. Before I discovered them they had broken a dozen eggs and, to judge by the state of them, rolled in the contents. They had fought with a couple of bunches of bananas and apparently won, for the bananas looked distinctly the worse for wear. Having slaughtered the fruit, they had moved on and upset two bottles of vitamin product. Then, to their delight, they had found two large packets of boracic powder. These they had burst open and scattered far and wide, while large quantities of the white powder had stuck to their egg-soaked fur. By the time I found them they were on the point of having a quick drink from a highly pungent and poisonous bucket of disinfectant, and I grabbed them only just in time. Each of them looked like some weird Christmas-cake decoration, in a coat stiff with boracic and egg-yolk. It took me three-quarters of an hour to clean them up. Then I put them in a larger and stronger basket and hoped that this would settle them.

It took them two days to break out of *this* basket.

This time they had decided to pay a visit to all the other animals I had. They must have had a fine time round the cages, for there were always some scraps of food lying about.

Now at that time I had a large and very beautiful monkey, called Colly, in my collection. Colly was a colobus, perhaps one of the most handsome of African monkeys. Their fur is coal-black and snow-white, hanging in long silky strands round their bodies like a shawl. They have a very long plume-like tail, also black and white. Colly was a somewhat vain monkey and spent a lot of her time grooming her lovely coat and posing in various parts of the cage. On this particular afternoon she had decided to enjoy a siesta in the bottom of her box, while waiting for me to bring her some fruit. She lay there like a sunbather on a beach, her eyes closed, her hands folded neatly on her chest. Unfortunately, however, she had pushed her tail through the bars so that it lay on the ground outside like a feathery black-and-white scarf that someone had dropped. Just as Colly was drifting off into a deep sleep, the Bandits appeared on the scene.

The Bandits, as I pointed out, believed that everything in the world, no matter how curious it looked, might turn out to be edible. In their opinion it was always worth sampling everything, just in case. When he saw Colly's tail lying on the ground ahead, apparently not belonging to anyone, the eldest Bandit decided it must be a tasty morsel of something or other that Providence had placed in his path. So he rushed forward and sank his sharp little teeth into it. His two brothers, feeling that there was plenty of this meal for everyone, joined him immediately. Thus was Colly woken out of a deep and refreshing sleep by three sets of extremely sharp little teeth fastening themselves almost simultaneously in her tail. She gave a wild scream of fright and scrambled towards the top of her cage. But the Bandits were not going to be deprived of this tasty morsel without a struggle, and they hung on grimly. The higher Colly climbed in her cage, the higher she lifted the Bandits off the ground, and when eventually I got there in response to her yells, I found the Bandits, like some miniature trapeze-artists, hanging by their teeth three feet off the ground. It took me five minutes to make them let go, and then I managed it only by blowing cigarette-smoke in their faces and making them sneeze. By the time I had got them safely locked up again, poor Colly was a nervous wreck.

I decided the Bandits must have a proper cage if I did not want the rest of my animals driven hysterical by their attentions. I built them a very nice one, with every modern convenience. It had a large and spacious bedroom at one end, and an open playground and dining-room at the other. There were two doors, one to admit my hand to their bedroom, the other to put their food into their dining-room. The trouble lay in feeding them. As soon as they saw me approach with a plate they would cluster round the doorway, screaming excitedly, and the moment the door was opened they would shoot out, knock the plate from my hand and fall to the ground with it, a tangled mass of kusimanses, raw meat, raw egg and milk. Quite often when I went to pick them up they would bite me, not vindictively but simply because they would mistake my fingers for something edible. Yes, feeding the Bandits was not only a wasteful process but an extremely painful one as well. By the time I got them safely back to England they had bitten me twice as frequently as any animal I have ever kept. So it was with a real feeling of relief that I handed them over to a zoo.

The next day I went round to see how they were settling down. I found them in a huge cage, pattering about and looking, I felt, rather lost and bewildered by all the new sights and sounds. Poor little things, I thought, they have had the wind taken out of their sails. They looked so subdued and forlorn. I began to feel quite sorry to have parted with them. I stuck my finger through the wire and waggled it, calling to them. I thought it might comfort them to talk to someone they knew. I should have known better: the Bandits shot across the cage in a grim-faced bunch and fastened on to my finger like bulldogs. With a yelp of pain I at last managed to get my finger away, and as I left them, mopping the blood from my hand, I decided that perhaps, after all, I was not *so* sorry to see the back of them. Life without the Bandits might be considerably less exciting – but it would not hurt nearly so much.

Wilhelmina

Most people, when they learn for the first time that I collect wild animals for zoos, ask the same series of questions in the same order. First they ask if it is dangerous, to which the answer is no, it is not, providing you do not make any silly mistakes. Then they ask how I catch the animals – a more difficult question to answer, for there are many hundreds of ways of capturing wild animals: sometimes you have no set method, but have to improvise something on the spur of the moment. Their third question is, invariably: don't you become attached to your animals and find it difficult to part with them at the end of an expedition? The answer is, of course, that you do, and sometimes parting with a creature you have kept for eight months can be a heartbreaking process.

Occasionally you even find yourself getting attached to the strangest of beasts, some weird creature you would never in the normal way have thought you could like. One such beast as this, I remember, was Wilhelmina.

Wilhelmina was a whip-scorpion, and if anyone had told me that the day would come when I would feel even the remotest trace of affection for a whip-scorpion I would never have believed them. Of all the creatures on the face of this earth the whip-scorpion is one of the least prepossessing. To those who do not adore spiders (and I am one of those people) the whip-scorpion is a form of living nightmare. It resembles a spider with a body the size of a walnut that has been run over by a steamroller and flattened to a wafer-thin flake. To this flake are attached what appear to be an immense number of long, fine and crooked legs which spread out to the size of a soup-plate. To cap it all, on the front (if such a creature can be said to have a front), are two enormously long slender legs like whips, about twelve inches long in a robust specimen. It possesses the ability to skim about at incredible speed and with apparently no effort – up, down or sideways – and to squeeze its revolting body into a crack that would scarcely accommodate a piece of tissue-paper.

That is a whip-scorpion, and to anyone who distrusts spiders it is the personification of the devil. Fortunately they are harmless, unless you happen to have a weak heart.

I made my first acquaintance with Wilhelmina's family when I was on a collecting trip to the tropical forest of West Africa. For many different reasons, hunting in these forests is always difficult. To begin with, the trees are enormous, some as much as a hundred and fifty feet high, with trunks as fat as a factory chimney. Their head foliage is thick, luxuriant and twined with creepers and the branches are decorated with various parasitic plants like a curious hanging garden. All this may be eighty or a hundred feet above the forest floor, and the only way to reach it is to climb a trunk as smooth as a plank which has not a single branch for the first seventy feet of its length. This, the top layer of the forest, is by far the most thickly populated, for in the comparative safety of the tree-tops live a host of creatures which rarely, if ever, descends to ground-level. Setting traps in the forest canopy is a difficult and tedious operation. It may take a whole morning to find a way up a tree, climb it and set the trap in a suitable position. Then, just as you have safely regained the forest floor, your trap goes off with a triumphant clang, and the whole laborious process has to be endured once more. Thus, although trap-setting in the treetops is a painful necessity, you are always on the look-out for some slightly easier method of obtaining the animals you want. Probably one of the most successful and exciting of these methods is to smoke out the giant trees.

Some of the forest trees, although apparently sound and solid, are actually hollow for part or all of their length. These are the trees to look for, though they are not so easy to find. A day of searching in the forest might end with the discovery of six of them, perhaps one of which will yield good results when finally smoked out.

Smoking out a hollow tree is quite an art. To begin with, you must, if necessary, enlarge the opening at the base of the trunk and lay a small fire of dry twigs. Then two Africans are sent up the tree with nets to cover all the holes and cracks at the upper end of the trunk, and then station themselves at convenient points to catch any animals that emerge. When all is ready, you start the fire, and as soon as it is crackling you lay on top of the flames a large bundle of fresh green leaves. Immediately the flames die away and in their place rises a column of thick and pungent smoke. The great hollow interior of the tree acts like a gigantic chimney, and the smoke is whisked up inside. You never realize, until you light the fire, quite how many holes and cracks there are in the trunk of the tree. As you watch, you see a tiny tendril of smoke appear magically on the bark perhaps twenty feet from the ground, coiling out of an almost invisible hole; a short pause and ten feet higher three more little holes puff smoke like miniature cannon-mouths. Thus, guided by the tiny streamers of smoke appearing at intervals along the trunk, you can watch the progress of the smoking. If the tree is a good one, you have only time to watch the smoke get half-way up, for it is then that the animals start to break cover and you become very busy indeed.

When one of these hollow trees is inhabited, it is really like a block of flats. In the ground-floor apartments, for example, you find things like the giant land-snails, each the size of an apple, and they come gliding out of the base of the tree with all the speed a snail is capable of mustering, even in an emergency. They may be followed by other creatures who prefer the lower apartments or else are unable to climb: the big forest toads, for example, whose backs are cleverly marked out to resemble a dead leaf, and whose cheeks and sides are a beautiful mahogany red. They come waddling out from among the tree-roots with the most ludicrously indignant expressions on their faces, and on reaching the open air suddenly squat down and stare about them in a pathetic and helpless sort of way.

Having evicted all the ground-floor tenants, you then have to wait a short time before the occupants higher up have a chance to make their way down to the opening. Almost invariably giant millipedes are among the first to appear – charming creatures that look like long brown sausages, with a fringe of legs along the underside of their bodies. They are quite harmless and rather imbecile creatures for which I have a very soft spot. One of their most ridiculous antics, when placed on a table, is to set off walking, all their legs working furiously, and on coming to the edge they never seem to notice it and continue to walk out into space until the weight of their body bends them over. Then, half on and half off the table, they pause, consider, and eventually decide that something is wrong. And so, starting with the extreme hind pair of legs, they go into reverse and get themselves on to the table again – only to crawl to the other side and repeat the performance.

Immediately after the appearance of the giant millipedes all the other top-floor tenants of the tree break cover together, some making for the top of the tree, others for the bottom. Perhaps there are squirrels with black ears, green bodies and tails of the most beautiful flame colour; giant grey dormice who gallop out of the tree, trailing their bushy tails behind them like puffs of smoke; perhaps a pair of bush-babies, with their great innocent eyes and their slender attenuated and trembly hands, like those of very old men. And then, of course, there are the bats: great fat brown bats with curious flower-like decorations on the skin of their noses and large transparent ears; others bright ginger, with black ears twisted down over their heads and pig-like snouts. And as this pageant of wild life appears the whip-scorpions are all over the place, skimming up and down the tree with a speed and silence that is unnerving and uncanny, squeezing their revolting bodies into the thinnest crack as you make a swipe at them with the net, only to reappear suddenly ten feet lower down the tree, skimming towards you apparently with the intention of disappearing into your shirt. You step back hurriedly and the creature vanishes: only the tips of a pair of antennae, wiggling from the depths of a crevice in the bark that would hardly accommodate a visiting-card, tells you of its whereabouts. Of the many creatures in the West African forest the whip-scorpion has been responsible for more shocks to my system than any other. The day a particularly large and leggy specimen ran over my bare arm, as I leant against a tree, will always be one of my most vivid memories. It took at least a year off my life.

But to return to Wilhelmina. She was a well-brought-up little whip-scorpion, one of a family of ten, and I started my intimate acquaintance with her when I captured her mother. All this happened quite by chance.

I had for many days been smoking out trees in the forest in search of an elusive and rare little animal known as the pigmy scaly-tail. These little mammals, which look like mice with long feathery tails, have a curious membrane of skin stretched from ankle to wrist, with the aid of which they glide around the forest with the ease of swallows. The scaly-tails live in colonies in hollow trees, but the difficulty lay in finding a tree that contained a colony. When, after much fruitless hunting, I did discover a group of these prizes, and moreover actually managed to capture some, I felt considerably elated. I even started to take a benign interest in the numerous whip-scorpions that were scuttling about the tree. Then suddenly I noticed one which looked so extraordinary, and was behaving in such a peculiar manner, that my attention was at once arrested. To begin with, this whip-scorpion seemed to be wearing a green fur-coat that almost completely covered her chocolate body. Secondly, it was working its way slowly and carefully down the tree with none of the sudden fits and starts common to the normal whip-scorpion.

Wondering if the green fur-coat and the slow walk were symptoms of extreme age in the whip-scorpion world I moved closer to examine the creature. To my astonishment I found that the fur-coat was composed of baby whip-scorpions, each not much larger than my thumb-nail, which were obviously fairly recent additions to the family. They were, in extraordinary contrast to their dark-coloured mother, a bright and bilious green, the sort of green that confectioners are fond of using in cake decorations. The mother's slow and stately progress was due to her concern lest one of her babies lose its grip and drop off. I realized, rather ruefully, that I had never given the private life of the whip-scorpion much thought, and it had certainly never occurred to me that the female would be sufficiently maternal to carry her babies on her back. Overcome with remorse at my thoughtlessness, I decided that here was an ideal chance for me to catch up on my studies of these creatures. So I captured the female very carefully – to avoid dropping any of her progeny – and carried her back to camp.

I placed the mother and children in a large roomy box with plenty of cover in the way of bark and leaves. Every morning I had to look under these, rather gingerly I admit, to see if she was all right. At first, the moment I lifted the bark under which she was hiding, she would rush out and scuttle up the side of the box, a distressing habit which always made me jump and slam the lid down. I was very much afraid that one day I might do this and trap her legs or antennae, but fortunately after the first three days or so she settled down, and would even let me renew the leaves and bark in her box without taking any notice.

I had the female whip-scorpion and her babies for two months, and during that time the babies ceased to ride on their mother's back. They scattered and took up residence in various parts of the box, grew steadily and lost their green colouring in favour of brown. Whenever they grew too big for their skins they would split them down the back and step out of them, like spiders. Each time they did so they would emerge a little larger and a little browner. I discovered that while the mother would tackle anything from a small grasshopper to a large beetle, the babies were fussy and demanded small spiders, slugs and other easily digestible fare. They all appeared to be thriving, and I began to feel rather proud of them. Then one day I returned to camp after a few hours hunting in the forest to find that tragedy had struck.

A tame Patas monkey I kept tied up outside the tent had eaten through his rope and been on a tour of investigation. Before anyone had noticed it he had eaten a bunch of bananas, three mangos and four hard-boiled eggs, he had broken two bottles of disinfectant, and rounded the whole thing off by knocking my whip-scorpion box on to the floor. It promptly broke open and scattered the family on the ground, and the Patas monkey, a creature of depraved habits, had set to work and eaten them. When I got back he was safely tied up again, and suffering from an acute attack of hiccoughs.

I picked up my whip-scorpion nursery and peered mournfully into it, cursing myself for having left it in such an accessible place, and cursing the monkey for having such an appetite. But then, to my surprise and delight, I found, squatting in solitary state on a piece of bark, one of the baby whip-scorpions, the sole survivor of the massacre. Tenderly I moved it to a smaller and more burglar-proof cage, showered it with slugs and other delicacies and christened it, for no reason at all, Wilhelmina.

During the time I had Wilhelmina's mother, and Wilhelmina herself, I learnt quite a lot about whip-scorpions. I discovered that though quite willing to hunt by day if hungry, they were at their most lively during the night. During the day Wilhelmina was always a little dull-witted, but in the evening she woke up and, if I may use the expression, blossomed. She would stalk to and fro in her box, her pincers at the ready, her long antennae-like legs lashing out like whips ahead of her, seeking the best route. Although these tremendously elongated legs are supposed to be merely feelers, I got the impression that they could do more than this. I have seen them wave in the direction of an insect, pause and twitch, whereupon Wilhelmina would brace herself, almost as if she had smelt or heard her prey with the aid of her long legs. Sometimes she would stalk her food like this; at other times she would simply lie in wait until the unfortunate insect walked almost into her arms, and the powerful pincers would gather it lovingly into her mouth.

As she grew older I gave her bigger and bigger things to eat, and I found her courage extraordinary. She was rather like a pugnacious terrier who, the larger the opponent, the better he likes the fight. I was so fascinated by her skill and bravery in tackling insects as big or bigger than herself that one day, rather unwisely, I put a very large locust in with her. Without a moment's hesitation, she flew at him and grasped his bulky body in her pincers. To my alarm, however, the locust gave a hearty kick with his powerful hind legs and both he and Wilhelmina soared upwards and hit the wire-gauze roof of the cage with a resounding thump, then crashed back to the floor again. This rough treatment did not deter Wilhelmina at all, and she continued to hug the locust while he leapt wildly around the cage, thumping against the roof, until eventually he was exhausted. Then she settled down and made short work of him. But after this I was always careful to give her the smaller insects, for I had visions of a leg or one of her whips being broken off in such a rough contest.

By now I had become very fond and not a little proud of Wilhelmina. She was, as far as I knew, the only whip-scorpion to have been kept in captivity. What is more, she had become very tame. I had only to rap on the side of her box with my fingers and she would appear from under her piece of bark and wave her whips at me. Then, if I put my hand inside, she would climb on to my palm and sit there quietly while I fed her with slugs, creatures for which she still retained a passion.

When the time drew near for me to transport my large collection of animals back to England, I began to grow rather worried over Wilhelmina. It was a two-week voyage, and I could not take enough insect food for that length of time. I decided therefore to try making her eat raw meat. It took me a long time to achieve it, but once I had learnt the art of waggling the bit of meat seductively enough I found that Wilhelmina would grab it, and on this unlikely diet she seemed to thrive. On the journey down to the coast by lorry Wilhelmina behaved like a veteran traveller, sitting in her box and sucking a large chunk of raw meat almost throughout the trip. For the first day on board ship the strange surroundings made her a little sulky, but after that the sea air seemed to do her good and she became positively skittish. This was her undoing.

One evening when I went to feed her, she scuttled up as far as my elbow before I knew what was happening, dropped on to a hatch-cover and was just about to squeeze her way through a crack on a tour of investigation when I recovered from my astonishment and managed to grab her. For the next few days I fed her very cautiously, and she seemed to have quietened down and regained her former self-possession.

Then one evening she waggled her whips at me so plaintively that I lifted her out of her cage on the palm of my hand and started to feed her on the few remaining slugs I had brought for her in a tin. She ate two slugs, sitting quietly and decorously on my hand, and then suddenly she jumped. She could not have chosen a worse time, for as she was in mid-air a puff of wind swept round the bulkhead and whisked her away. I had a brief glimpse of her whips waving wildly, and then she was over the rail and gone, into the vast heaving landscape of the sea. I rushed to the rail and peered over, but it was impossible to spot so small a creature in the waves and froth below. Hurriedly I threw her box over, in the vain hope that she might find it and use it as a raft. A ridiculous hope, I know, but I did not like to think of her drowning without making some attempt to save her. I could have kicked myself for my stupidity in lifting her out of her box; I never thought I would have been so affected by the loss of such a creature. I had grown very fond of her; she in her turn had seemed to trust me. It was a tragic way for the relationship to end. But there was one slight consolation: after my association with Wilhelmina I shall never again look at a whip-scorpion with quite the same distaste.

Adopting an Anteater

Making a collection of two hundred birds, mammals and reptiles is rather like having two hundred delicate babies to look after. It needs a lot of hard work and patience. You have to make sure their diet suits them, that their cages are big enough, that they get neither too hot in the tropics nor too cold when you get near England. You have to de-worm, de-tick and de-flea them; you have to keep their cages and feeding-pots spotlessly clean.

But, above all, you have to make sure that your animals are *happy*. However well looked after, a wild animal will not live in captivity unless it is happy. I am talking, of course, of the adult, wild-caught creature. But occasionally you get a baby wild animal whose mother has perhaps met with an accident, and who has been found wandering in the forest. When you capture one of these, you must be prepared for a good deal of hard work and worry, and above all you must be ready to give the animal the affection and confidence it requires; for after a day or two you will have become the parent, and the baby will trust you and depend on you completely.

This can sometimes make life rather difficult. There have been periods when I have played the adopted parent to as many as six baby animals at once, and this is no joke. Quite apart from anything else, imagine rising at three o'clock in the morning, stumbling about, half-asleep, in an effort to prepare six different bottles of milk, trying to keep your eyes open enough to put the right amount of vitamin drops and sugar in, knowing all the time that you will have to be up again in three hours to repeat the performance.

Some time ago my wife and I were on a collecting trip in Paraguay, that country shaped like a boot-box which lies almost in the exact centre of South America. Here, in a remote part of the Chaco, we assembled a lovely collection of animals. Many things quite unconnected with animals happen on a collecting trip, things that frustrate your plans or irritate you in other ways. But politics, mercifully, had never before been among them. On this occasion, however, the Paraguayans decided to have a revolution, and as a direct result we had to release nearly the whole of our collection and escape to Argentina in a tiny four-seater plane.

Just before our retreat, an Indian had wandered into our camp carrying a sack from which had come the most extraordinary noises. It sounded like a cross between a cello in pain and a donkey with laryngitis. Opening the sack, the Indian tipped out one of the most delightful baby animals I had ever seen. She was a young giant anteater, and she could not have been more than a week old. She was about the size of a corgie, with black, ash-grey and white fur, a long slender snout and a pair of tiny, rather bleary eyes. The Indian said he had found her wandering about in the forest, honking forlornly. He thought her mother might have been killed by a jaguar.

The arrival of this baby put me in a predicament. I knew that we would be leaving soon and that the plane was so tiny that most of our equipment would have to be left behind to make room for the five or six creatures we were determined to take with us. To accept, at that stage, a baby anteater who weighed a considerable amount and who would have to be fussed over and bottle-fed, would be lunatic. Quite apart from anything else, no one as far as I knew, had ever tried to rear a baby anteater on a bottle. The whole thing was obviously out of the question. Just as I had made up my mind the baby, still blaring pathetically, suddenly discovered my leg, and with a honk of joy shinned up it, settled herself in my lap and went to sleep. Silently I paid the Indian the price he demanded, and thus became a father to one of the most charming children I have ever met.

The first difficulty cropped up almost at once. We had a baby's feeding-bottle, but we had exhausted our supply of teats. Luckily a frantic house-to-house search of the little village where we were living resulted in the discovery of one teat, of extreme age and unhygienic appearance. After one or two false starts the baby took to the bottle far better than I had dared hope, though feeding her was a painful performance.

Young anteaters, at that age, cling to their mother's back, and, since we had, so to speak, become her parents, she insisted on climbing on to one or the other of us nearly the whole time. Her claws were about three inches long, and she had a prodigious grip with them. During meals she clasped your leg affectionately with three paws, while with her remaining paw held your finger and squeezed it hard at intervals, for she was convinced that this would increase the flow of milk from the bottle. At the end of each feed you felt as though you had been mauled by a grizzly bear, while your fingers had been jammed in a door.

For the first few days I carried her about with me to give her confidence. She liked to lie across the back of my neck, her long nose hanging down one side of me and her long tail down the other, like a fur collar. Every time I moved she would tighten her grip in a panic, and this was painful. After the fourth shirt had been ruined I decided that she would have to cling to something else, so I filled a sack full of straw and introduced her to that. She accepted it without any fuss, and so between meals she would lie in her cage, clutching this substitute happily. We had already christened her 'Sarah,' and now that she developed this habit of sack-clutching we gave her a surname, so she became known as 'Sarah Huggersack.'

Sarah was a model baby. Between feeds she lay quietly on her sack, occasionally yawning and showing a sticky, pinky-grey tongue about twelve inches long. When feeding-time came round she would suck the teat on her bottle so vigorously that it had soon changed from red to pale pink, the hole at the end of it had become about the size of a matchstick, and the whole thing dropped dismally from the neck of the bottle.

When we had to leave Paraguay in our extremely unsafe-looking four-seater plane, Sarah slept peacefully throughout the flight, lying on my wife's lap and snoring gently, occasionally blowing a few bubbles of sticky saliva out of her nose.

On arriving in Buenos Aires our first thought was to give Sarah a treat. We would buy her a nice new shiny teat. We went to endless trouble selecting one exactly the right size, shape and colour, put it on the bottle and presented it to Sarah. She was scandalized. She honked wildly at the mere thought of a new teat, and sent the bottle flying with a well-directed clout from her paw. Nor did she calm down and start to feed until we had replaced the old withered teat on the bottle. She clung to it ever after; months after her arrival in England she still refused to be parted from it.

In Buenos Aires we housed our animals in an empty house on the outskirts of the city. From the centre, where we stayed, it took us half an hour in a taxi to reach it, and this journey we had to do twice and sometimes three times a day. We soon found that having a baby anteater made our social life difficult in the extreme. Have you ever tried to explain to a hostess that you must suddenly leave in the middle of dinner because you have to give a bottle to an anteater? In the end our friends gave up in despair. They used to telephone and ascertain the times of Sarah's feeds before inviting us.

By this time Sarah had become much more grown up and independent. After her evening feed she would go for a walk round the room by herself. This was a great advance, for up till then she had screamed blue murder if you moved more than a foot or so away from her. After her tour of inspection she liked to have a game. This consisted in walking past us, her nose in the air, her tail trailing temptingly. You were then supposed to grab the end of her tail and pull, whereupon she would swing round on three legs and give you a gentle clout with her paw. When this had been repeated twenty or thirty times she felt satisfied, and then you had to lay her on her back and tickle her tummy for ten minutes or so while she closed her eyes and blew bubbles of ecstasy at you. After this she would go to bed without any fuss. But try to put her to bed without giving her a game and she would kick and struggle and honk, and generally behave in a thoroughly spoilt manner.

When we eventually got on board ship, Sarah was not at all sure that she approved of sea-voyages. To begin with, the ship smelt queer; then there was a strong wind which nearly blew her over every time she went for a walk on deck; and lastly, which she hated most of all, the deck would not keep still. First it tilted one way, then it tilted another, and Sarah would go staggering about, honking plaintively, banging her nose on bulkheads and hatch-covers. When the weather improved, however, she seemed to enjoy the trip. Sometimes in the afternoon, when I had time, I would take her up to the promenade deck and we would sit in a deck-chair and sun-bathe. She even paid a visit to the bridge, by special request of the captain. I thought it was because he had fallen for her charm and personality, but he confessed that it was because (having seen her only from a distance) he wanted to make sure which end of her was the front.

I must say we felt very proud of Sarah when we arrived in London Docks and she posed for the Press photographers with all the unselfconscious ease of a born celebrity. She even went so far as to lick one of the reporters – a great honour. I hastily tried to point this out to him, while helping to remove a large patch of sticky saliva from his coat. It was not everyone she would lick, I told him. His expression told me that he did not appreciate the point.

Sarah went straight from the docks to a zoo in Devonshire, and we hated to see her go. However, we were kept informed about her progress and she seemed to be doing well. She had formed a deep attachment to her keeper.

Some weeks later I was giving a lecture at the Festival Hall, and the organizer thought it would be rather a good idea if I introduced some animal on stage at the end of my talk. I immediately thought of Sarah. Both the zoo authorities and the Festival Hall Management were willing, but, as it was now winter, I insisted that Sarah must have a dressing-room to wait in.

I met Sarah and her keeper at Paddington Station. Sarah was in a huge crate, for she had grown as big as a red setter, and she created quite a sensation on the platform. As soon as she heard my voice she flung herself at the bars of her cage and protruded twelve inches of sticky tongue in a moist and affectionate greeting. People standing near the cage leapt back hurriedly, thinking some curious form of snake was escaping and it took a lot of persuasion before we could find a porter brave enough to wheel the cage on a truck.

When we reached the Festival Hall we found that the rehearsal of a symphony concert had just come to an end. We wheeled Sarah's big box down long corridors to the dressing-room, and just as we reached the door it was flung open and Sir Thomas Beecham strode out, smoking a large cigar. We waited for him to pass and then, very humbly, we wheeled Sarah into the dressing-room he had just vacated.

While I was on the stage, my wife kept Sarah occupied by running round and round the dressing-room with her, to the consternation and horror of one of the porters, who, hearing the noise was convinced that Sarah had broken out of her cage and was attacking my wife. Eventually, however, the great moment arrived and amid tumultuous applause Sarah was carried on to the stage. She was very short-sighted, as all anteaters are, so to her the audience was non-existent. She looked round vaguely to see where the noise was coming from, but decided that it was not really worth worrying about. While I extolled her virtues, she wandered about the stage, oblivious, occasionally snuffling loudly in a corner, and repeatedly approaching the microphone and giving it a quick lick, which left it in a very sticky condition for the next performer. Just as I was telling the audience how well-behaved she was, she discovered the table in the middle of the stage, and with an immense sigh of satisfaction proceeded to scratch her bottom against one of the legs. She was a great success.

After the show, Sarah held court for a few select guests in her dressing-room, and became so skittish that she even galloped up and down outside in the corridor. Then we bundled her up warmly and put her on the night train for Devon with her keeper.

Apparently, on reaching the zoo again, Sarah was thoroughly spoilt. Her short spell as a celebrity had gone to her head. For three days she refused to be left alone, stamping about her cage and honking wildly, and refusing all food unless she was fed by hand.

A few months later I wanted Sarah to make an appearance on a television show I was doing, and so once again she tasted the glamour and glitter of show business. She behaved with the utmost decorum during rehearsals, except that she was dying to investigate the camera closely, and had to be restrained by force. When the show was over she resisted going back to her cage, and it took the united efforts of myself, my wife, Sarah's keeper and the studio manager to get her back into the box – for Sarah was then quite grown up, measuring six feet from nose to tail, standing three feet at the shoulder and with forearms as thick as my thigh.

We did not see Sarah again until quite recently, when we paid her a visit at her zoo. It had been six months since she had last seen us, and quite frankly I thought she would have forgotten us. Anteater fan though I am, I would be the first to admit that they are not creatures who are overburdened with brains, and six months is a long time. But the moment we called to her she came bounding out of her sleeping den and rushed to the wire to lick us. We even went into the cage and played with her, a sure sign that she really did recognize us, for no one else except her keeper dared enter.

Eventually we said good-bye to her, rather sadly, and left her sitting in the straw blowing bubbles after us. As my wife said: 'It was rather as though we were leaving our child at boarding school.' We are certainly her adopted parents, as far as Sarah is concerned.

Yesterday we had some good news. We heard that Sarah has got a mate. He is as yet too young to be put in with her, but soon he should be big enough. Who knows, by this time next year we may be grandparents to a fine bouncing baby anteater!

Portrait of Pavlo

It is a curious thing, but when you keep animals as pets you tend to look upon them so much as miniature human beings that you generally manage to impress some of your own characteristics on to them. This anthropomorphic attitude is awfully difficult to avoid. If you possess a golden hamster and are always watching the way he sits up and eats a nut, his little pink paws trembling with excitement, his pouches bulging as he saves in his cheeks what cannot be eaten immediately, you might one day come to the conclusion that he looks exactly like your own Uncle Amos sitting, full of port and nuts, in his favourite club. From that moment the damage is done. The hamster continues to behave like a hamster, but you regard him only as a miniature Uncle Amos, clad in a ginger fur-coat, for ever sitting in his club, his cheeks bulging with food. There are very few animals who have characters strong and distinct enough to overcome this treatment, who display such powerful personalities that you are forced to treat them as individuals and not as miniature human beings. Of the many hundreds of animals I have collected for zoos in this country, and of the many I have kept as pets, I can remember at the most about a dozen creatures who had this strength of personality that not only made them completely different from others of their kind, but enabled them to resist all attempts on my part to turn them into something they were not.

One of the smallest of these animals was Pavlo, a black-eared marmoset, and his story really started one evening when, on a collecting trip in British Guiana, I sat quietly in the bushes near a clearing, watching a hole in a bank which I had good reason to believe contained an animal of some description. The sun was setting and the sky was a glorious salmon pink, and outlined against it were the massive trees of the forest, their branches so entwined with creepers that each tree looked as though it had been caught in a giant spider's web. There is nothing quite so soothing as a tropical forest at this time of day. I sat there absorbing sights and colours, my mind in the blank and receptive state that the Buddhists tell us is the first step towards Nirvana. Suddenly my trance was shattered by a shrill and prolonged squeak of such intensity that it felt as though someone had driven a needle into my ear. Peering above me cautiously, I tried to see where the sound had come from: it seemed the wrong sort of note for a tree-frog or an insect, and far too sharp and tuneless to be a bird. There, on a great branch about thirty feet above me, I saw the source of the noise: a diminutive marmoset was trotting along a wide branch as if it were an arterial road, picking his way in and out of the forest of orchids and other parasitic plants that grew in clumps from the bark. As I watched, he stopped, sat up on his hind legs and uttered another of his piercing cries; this time he was answered from some distance away, and within a moment or two other marmosets had joined him. Trilling and squeaking to each other, they moved among the orchids, searching diligently, occasionally uttering shrill squeaks of joy as they unearthed a cockroach or a beetle among the leaves. One of them pursued something through an orchid plant for a long time, parting the leaves and peering between them with an intense expression on his tiny face. Every time he made a grab the leaves got in the way and the insect managed to escape round the other side of the plant. Eventually, more by good luck than skill, he dived his small hands in amongst the leaves and, with a twitter of triumph, emerged with a fat cockroach clutched firmly between his fingers. The insect was a large one and its wriggling was strenuous, so, presumably in case he dropped it, he stuffed the whole thing into his mouth. He sat there munching happily, and when he had swallowed the last morsel, he carefully examined both the palms and backs of his paws to make sure there was none left.

I was so entranced by this glimpse into the private life of the marmoset that it was not until the little party had moved off into the now-gloomy forest that I realized I had an acute crick in my neck and that one of my legs had gone to sleep.

A considerable time later my attention was once again drawn to marmosets. I went down to an animal dealer's shop in London, to enquire about something quite different, and the first thing I saw on entering the shop was a cage full of marmosets, a pathetic, scruffy group of ten, crouched in a dirty cage on a perch so small that they were continuously having to jostle and squabble for a place to sit. Most of them were adults, but there was one youngster who seemed to be getting rather a rough time of it. He was thin and unkempt, so small that whenever there was a reshuffling of positions on the perch he was always the one to get knocked off. As I watched this pathetic, shivering little group, I remembered the little family party I had seen in Guiana, grubbing happily for their dinner among the orchids, and I felt that I could not leave the shop without rescuing at least one of the tiny animals. So within five minutes I had paid the price of liberation, and the smallest occupant of the cage was dragged out, screaming with alarm, and bundled into a cardboard box.

When I got him home I christened him Pavlo and introduced him to the family, who viewed him with suspicion. However, as soon as Pavlo had settled down he set about the task of winning their confidence, and in a very short time he had all of us under his minute thumb. In spite of his size (he fitted comfortably into a large teacup), he had a terrific personality, a Napoleonic air about him which was difficult to resist. His head was only the size of a large walnut, but it soon became apparent that it contained a brain of considerable power and intelligence. At first we kept him in a large cage in the drawing-room, where he could have plenty of company, but he was so obviously miserable when confined that we started letting him out for an hour or two every day. This was our undoing. Very soon Pavlo had convinced us that the cage was unnecessary, so it was consigned to the rubbish-heap, and he had the run of the house all day and every day. He became accepted as a diminutive member of the family, and he treated the house as though he owned it and we were his guests.

At first sight Pavlo resembled a curious kind of squirrel, until you noticed his very human face and his bright, shrewd, brown eyes. His fur was soft, and presented a brindled appearance because the individual hairs were banded with orange, black and grey, in that order; his tail, however, was ringed with black and white. The fur on his head and neck was chocolate brown, and hung round his shoulders and chest in a tattered fringe. His large ears were hidden by long ear-tufts of the same chocolate colour. Across his forehead, above his eyes and the aristocratic bridge of his tiny nose, was a broad white patch.

Everyone who saw him, and who had any knowledge of animals, assured me that I would not keep him long: marmosets, they said, coming from the warm tropical forests of South America, never lived more than a year in this climate. It seemed that their cheerful prophecies were right when, after six months, Pavlo developed a form of paralysis and from the waist downwards lost all power of movement. We fought hard to save his life while those who had predicted this trouble said he ought to be destroyed. But he seemed in no pain, so we persevered. Four times a day we massaged his tiny legs, his back and tail with warm cod-liver oil, and he had more cod-liver oil in his special diet, which included such delicacies as grapes and pears. He lay pathetically on a cushion, wrapped in cotton-wool for warmth, while the family took it in turn to minister to his wants. Sunshine was what he needed most and plenty of it, but the English climate provided precious little. So the neighbours were treated to the sight of us carrying our Lilliputian invalid round the garden, carefully placing his cushion in every patch of sunlight that appeared. This went on for a month, and at the end of it Pavlo could move his feet slightly and twitch his tail; two weeks later he was hobbling round the house, almost his old self again. We were delighted, even though the house did reek of cod-liver oil for months afterwards.

Instead of making him more delicate, his illness seemed to make him tougher, and at times he appeared almost indestructible. We never pampered him, and the only concession we made was to give him a hot-water bottle in his bed during the winter. He liked this so much that he would refuse to go to bed without it, even in mid-summer. His bedroom was a drawer in a tall-boy in my mother's room, and his bed consisted of an old dressing-gown and a piece of fur-coat. Putting Pavlo to bed was quite a ritual: first the dressing-gown had to be spread in the drawer and the bottle wrapped in it so that he did not burn himself. Then the piece of fur-coat had to be made into a sort of furry cave, into which Pavlo would crawl, curl up into a ball and close his eyes blissfully. At first we used to push the drawer closed, except for a crack to allow for air, as this prevented Pavlo from getting up too early in the morning. But he very soon learned that by pushing his head into the crack he could widen it and escape.

About six in the morning he would wake up and find that his bottle had gone cold, so he would sally forth in search of alternative warmth. He would scuttle across the floor and up the leg of my mother's bed, landing on the eiderdown. Then he would make his way up the bed, uttering squeaks of welcome, and burrow under the pillow where he would stay, cosy and warm, until it was time for her to get up. When she eventually got out of bed and left him, Pavlo would be furious, and would stand on the pillow chattering and screaming with rage. When he saw, however, that she had no intention of getting back to bed to keep him warm, he would scuttle down the passage to my room and crawl in with me. Here he would remain, stretched luxuriously on my chest, until it was time for me to get up, and then he would stand on my pillow and abuse me, screwing his tiny face up into a ferocious and most human scowl. Having told me what he thought of me, he would dash off and get into bed with my brother, and when he was turned out of there would go and join my sister for a quick nap before breakfast. This migration from bed to bed was a regular morning performance.

Downstairs he had plenty of heating at his disposal. There was a tall standard-lamp in the drawing-room which belonged to him: in the winter he would crawl inside the shade and sit next to the bulb, basking in the heat. He also had a stool and a cushion by the fire, but he preferred the lamp, and so it had to be kept on all day for his benefit, and our electricity bill went up by leaps and bounds. In the first warm days of spring Pavlo would venture out into the garden, where his favourite haunt was the fence; he would sit in the sun, or potter up and down catching spiders and other delicacies for himself. Half-way along this fence was a sort of rustic arbour made out of poles thickly overgrown with creepers, and it was into this net of creepers that Pavlo would dash if danger threatened. For many years he carried on a feud with the big white cat from next door, for this beast was obviously under the impression that Pavlo was a strange type of rat which it was her duty to kill. She would spend many painful hours stalking him, but since she was an inconspicuous as a snowball against the green leaves she never managed to catch Pavlo unawares. He would wait until she was quite close, her yellow eye glaring, her tongue flicking her lips, and then he would trot off along the fence and dive in among the creepers. Sitting there in safety, he would scream and chitter like an urchin from between the flowers, while the frustrated cat prowled about trying to find a hole among the creepers big enough for her portly body to squeeze through.

Growing by the fence, between the house and Pavlo's creeper-covered hide-out, were two young fig-trees, and round the base of their trunks we had dug deep trenches which we kept full of water during the hot weather. Pavlo was pottering along the fence one day, chattering to himself and catching spiders, when he looked up and discovered that this arch-enemy the cat, huge and white, was sitting on the fence between him and his creeper-covered arbour. His only chance of escape was to go back along the fence and into the house, so Pavlo turned and bolted, squeaking for help as he ran. The fat white cat was not such an expert tight-rope walker as Pavlo, so her progress along the fence top was slow, but even so she was catching up on him. She was uncomfortably close behind him when he reached the fig-trees, and he became so nervous that he missed his footing and with a frantic scream of fright fell off the fence and straight into the water-filled trench below. He rose to the surface, spluttering and screaming, and splashing around in circles, while the cat watched him in amazement: she had obviously never seen an aquatic marmoset before. Luckily, before she had recovered from her astonishment and hooked him out of the water, I arrived on the scene and she fled. I rescued Pavlo, gibbering with rage, and he spent the rest of the afternoon in front of the fire, wrapped in a piece of blanket, muttering darkly to himself. This episode had a bad effect on his nerves, and for a whole week he refused to go out on the fence, and if he caught so much as a glimpse of the white cat he would scream until someone put him on their shoulder and comforted him.

Pavlo lived with us for eight years, and it was rather like having a leprechaun in the house: you never knew what was going to happen next. He did not adapt himself to our ways, we had to adapt ourselves to his. He insisted, for example, on having his meals with us, and his meals had to be the same as ours. He ate on the window-sill out of a saucer. For breakfast he would have porridge or cornflakes, and warm milk and sugar; at lunch he had green vegetables, potatoes and a spoonful of whatever pudding was going. At tea-time he had to be kept off the table by force, or he would dive into the jam-pot with shrill squeaks of delight; he was under the impression that the jam was put on the table for his benefit, and would get most annoyed if you differed with him on this point. We had to be ready to put him to bed at six o'clock sharp, and if we were late he would stalk furiously up and down outside his drawer, his fur standing on end with rage. We had to learn not to slam doors shut without first looking to see if Pavlo was sitting on top, because, for some reason, he like to sit on doors and meditate. But our worst crime, according to him, was when we went out and left him for an afternoon. When we returned he would leave us in no doubt as to his feelings on the subject; we would be in disgrace; he would turn his back on us in disgust when we tried to talk to him; he would go and sit in a corner and glower at us, his little face screwed up into a scowl. After half an hour or so he would, very reluctantly, forgive us and with regal condescension accept a lump of sugar and some warm milk before retiring to bed. Pavlo's moods were most human, for he would scowl and mutter at you when he felt bad-tempered, and, very probably, try to give you a nip. When he was feeling affectionate, however, he would approach you with a loving expression on his face, poking his tongue out and in very rapidly, and smacking his lips, climb on to your shoulder and give your ear a series of passionate nibbles.

His method of getting about the house was a source of astonishment to everyone, for he hated running on the ground, and would never descend to the floor if he could avoid it. In his native forest he would have made his way through the trees from branch to branch and from creeper to creeper, but there were no such refinements in a suburban house. So Pavlo used the picture-rails as his highways, and he would scuttle along them at incredible speeds, hanging on with one hand and one foot, humping himself along like a hairy caterpillar, until he was able to drop on to the window-sill. He could shin up the smooth edge of a door more quickly and easily than we could walk up a flight of stairs. Sometimes he would cadge a lift from the dog, leaping on to his back and clinging there like a miniature Old Man of the Sea. The dog, who had been taught that Pavlo's person was sacred, would give us mute and appealing looks until we removed the monkey from his back. He disliked Pavlo for two reasons: firstly, he did not see why such a rat-like object should be allowed the run of the house, and secondly, Pavlo used to go out of his way to be annoying. He would hang down from the arm of a chair when the dog passed and pull his eyebrows or whiskers and then leap back out of range. Or else he would wait until the dog was asleep and then make a swift attack on his unprotected tail. Occasionally, however, there would be a sort of armed truce, and the dog would lie in front of the fire while Pavlo, perched on his ribs, would diligently comb his shaggy coat.

When Pavlo died, he staged his deathbed scene in the best Victorian traditions. He had been unwell for a couple of days, and had spent his time on the window-sill of my sister's room, lying in the sun on his bit of furcoat. One morning he started to squeak frantically to my sister, who became alarmed and shouted out to the rest of us that she thought he was dying. The whole family at once dropped whatever they were doing and fled upstairs. We gathered round the window-sill and watched Pavlo carefully, but there seemed to be nothing very much the matter with him. He accepted a drink of milk and then lay back on his fur-coat and surveyed us all with bright eyes. We had just decided that it was a false alarm when he suddenly went limp. In a panic we forced open his clenched jaws and poured a little milk down his throat. Slowly he regained consciousness, lying limp in my cupped hands. He looked at us for a moment and then, summoning up his last remaining strength, poked his tongue out at us and smacked his lips in a last gesture of affection. Then he fell back and died quite quietly.

The house and garden seemed very empty without his minute strutting figure and fiery personality. No longer did the sight of a spider evoke cries of: 'Where's Pavlo?' No longer were we woken up at six in the morning, feeling his cold feet on our faces. He had become one of the family in a way that no other pet had ever done, and we mourned his death. Even the white cat next door seemed moody and depressed, for without Pavlo in it our garden seemed to have lost its savour for her.

BOOK FOUR

The Human Animal

When you travel round the world collecting animals you also, of necessity, collect human beings. I am much more intolerant of a human being's shortcomings than I am of an animal's, but in this respect I have been lucky, for most of the people I have come across in my travels have been charming. In most cases, of course, the fact that you are an animal-collector helps, since people always seem delighted to meet someone with such an unusual occupation, and they go out of their way to assist you.

One of the loveliest and most sophisticated women I know has helped me cram a couple of swans into a taxi-cab boot in the middle of Buenos Aires, and anyone who has ever tried to carry livestock in a Buenos Aires taxi will know what a feat that must have been. A millionaire has let me stack cages of livestock on the front porch of his elegant town house, and even when an armadillo escaped and went through the main flower-bed like a bulldozer, he remained unruffled and calm. The madame of the local brothel once acted as our housekeeper (getting all her girls to do the housework when not otherwise employed), and she once even assaulted the local chief of police on our behalf. A man in Africa – notorious for his dislike of strangers and animals – let us stay for six weeks in his house and fill it with a weird variety of frogs, snakes, squirrels and mongooses. I have had the captain of a ship come down into the hold at eleven at night, take off his coat, roll up his sleeves and set to work helping me clean out cages and chop up food for the animals. I know an artist who, having travelled thousands of miles to paint a series of pictures of various Indian tribes, got involved in my affairs and spent his whole time catching animals and none on painting. By that time, of course, he could not paint anyway, as I had commandeered all his canvas to make snake-boxes. There was the little cockney P.W.D. man who, not having met me previously, offered to drive me a hundred-odd miles, over atrocious African roads, in his brand-new Austin in order that I might follow up the rumour of a baby gorilla. All *he* got out of the trip was a hangover and a broken spring.

At times I have met such interesting and peculiar people I have been tempted to give up animals and take up anthropology. Then I have come across the unpleasant human animal. The District Officer who drawled, 'We chaps are here to help you chaps . . .,' and then proceeded to be as obstructive and unpleasant as possible. The Overseer in Paraguay who, because he disliked me, did not tell me for two weeks that some local Indians had captured a rare and beautiful animal which I wanted, and were waiting for me to collect it. By the time I received the animal it was too weak to stand and died of pneumonia within forty-eight hours. The sailor who was mentally unbalanced and who, in a fit of sadistic humour, overturned a row of our cages one night, including one in which a pair of extremely rare squirrels had just had a baby. The baby died.

Fortunately these types of human are rare, and the pleasant ones I have met have more than compensated for them. But even so, I think I will stick to animals.

MacTootle

When people discover my job for the first time, they always ask me for details of the many adventures they assume I have had in what they will persist in calling the 'jungle'.

I returned to England after my first West African trip and described with enthusiasm the hundreds of square miles of rain-forest I had lived and worked in for eight months. I said that in this forest I had spent many happy days, and during all this time I never had one experience that could, with any justification be called 'hair-raising,' but when I told people this they decided that I was either exceptionally modest or a charlatan.

On my way out to West Africa for the second time, I met on board ship a young Irishman called MacTootle who was going out to a job on a banana plantation in the Cameroons. He confessed to me that he had never before left England and he was quite convinced that Africa was the most dangerous place imaginable. His chief fear seemed to be that the entire snake population of the Continent was going to be assembled on the docks to meet him. In order to relieve his mind, I told him that in all the months I had spent in the forest I had seen precisely five snakes, and these had run away so fast that I had been unable to capture them. He asked me if it was a dangerous job to catch a snake, and I replied, quite truthfully, that the majority of snakes were extremely easy to capture, if you kept your head and knew your snake and its habits. All this soothed MacTootle considerably, and when he landed he swore that, before I returned to England, he would obtain some rare specimens for me; I thanked him and promptly forgot all about it.

Five months later I was ready to leave for England with a collection of about two hundred creatures, ranging from grasshoppers to chimpanzees. Very late on the night the ship was due to sail, a small van drew up with screeching brakes outside my camp and my young Irishman alighted, together with several friends of his. He explained with great glee that he had got me the specimens he had promised. Apparently he had discovered a large hole or pit, somewhere on the plantation he was working on, which had presumably been dug to act as a drainage sump. This pit, he said, was full of snakes, and they were all mine – providing I went and got them.

He was so delighted at the thought of all those specimens he had found for me that I had not the heart to point out that crawling about in a pit full of snakes at twelve o'clock at night was not my idea of a pleasurable occupation, enthusiastic naturalist though I was. Furthermore, he had obviously been boasting about my powers to his friends, and he had brought them all along to see my snake-catching methods. So, with considerable reluctance, I said I would go and catch reptiles; I have rarely regretted a decision more.

I collected a large canvas snake-bag, and a stick with a Y-shaped fork of brass at one end; then I squeezed into the van with my excited audience and we drove off. At half-past twelve we reached my friend's bungalow, and we stopped there for a drink before walking through the plantation to the pit.

'You'll be wanting some rope, will you not?' asked MacTootle.

'Rope?' I said. 'What for?'

'Why, to lower yourself into the hole, of course,' he said cheerfully. I began to feel an unpleasant sensation in the pit of my stomach. I asked for a description of the pit. It was apparently some twenty-five feet long, four feet wide and twelve feet deep. Everyone assured me that I could not get down there without a rope. While my friend went off to look for one which I hoped very much he would not find, I had another quick drink and wondered how I could have been foolish enough to get myself mixed up in this fantastic snake-hunt. Snakes in trees, on the ground or in shallow ditches were fairly easy to manage, but an unspecified number of them at the bottom of a pit so deep that you had to be lowered into it on the end of a rope did not sound at all inviting. I thought that I had an opportunity of backing out gracefully when the question of lighting arose, and it was discovered that none of us had a torch. My friend, who had now returned with the rope, was quite determined that nothing was going to interfere with his plans: he solved the lighting question by tying a big paraffin pressure-lamp on to the end of a length of cord, and informed the company that he personally would lower it into the pit for me. I thanked him in what I hoped was a steady voice.

'That's all right,' he said, 'I'm determined you'll have your fun. This lamp's much better than a torch, and you'll need all the light you can get, for there's any number of the little devils down there.'

We then had to wait a while for the arrival of my friend's brother and sister-in-law: he had asked them to come along, he explained, because they would probably never get another chance to see anyone capturing snakes, and he did not want them to miss it.

Eventually eight of us wended our way through the banana plantation and seven of us were laughing and chattering excitedly at the thought of the treat in store. It suddenly occurred to me that I was wearing the most inadequate clothing for snake-hunting: thin tropical trousers and a pair of plimsoll shoes. Even the most puny reptiles would have no difficulty in penetrating to my skin with one bite. However, before I could explain this we arrived at the edge of the pit, and in the lamplight it looked to me like nothing more nor less than an extremely large grave. My friend's description of it had been accurate enough, but what he had failed to tell me was that the sides of the pit consisted of dry, crumbling earth, honeycombed with cracks and holes that offered plenty of hiding-places for any number of snakes. While I crouched down on the edge of the pit, the lamp was solemnly lowered into the depths so that I might spy out the land and try to identify the snakes. Up to that moment I had cheered myself with the thought that, after all, the snakes might turn out to be a harmless variety, but when the light reached the bottom this hope was shattered, for I saw that the pit was simply crawling with young Gaboon vipers, one of the most deadly snakes in the world.

During the daytime these snakes are very sluggish and it is quite a simple job to capture them, but at night, when they wake up and hunt for their food, they can be unpleasantly quick. These young ones in the pit were each about two feet long and a couple of inches in diameter, and they were all, as far as I could judge, very much awake. They wriggled round and round the pit with great rapidity, and kept lifting their heavy, arrow-shaped heads and contemplating the lamp, flicking their tongues out and in in a most suggestive manner.

I counted eight Gaboon vipers in the pit, but their coloration matched the leaf-mould so beautifully that I could not be sure I was not counting some of them twice. Just at that moment my friend trod heavily on the edge of the pit, and a large lump of earth fell among the reptiles, who all looked up and hissed loudly. Everyone backed away hastily, and I thought it a very suitable opportunity to explain the point about my clothing. My friend, with typical

Irish generosity, offered to lend me his trousers, which were of stout twill, and the strong pair of shoes he was wearing. Now the last of my excuses was gone and I had not the nerve to protest further. We went discreetly behind a bush and exchanged trousers and shoes. My friend was built on more generous lines than I, and the clothes were not exactly a snug fit; however, as he rightly pointed out, the bit of trouser-leg I had to turn up at the bottom would act as additional protection for my ankles.

Drearily I approached the pit. My audience was clustered round, twittering in delicious anticipation. I tied the rope round my waist with what I very soon discovered to be a slip-knot, and crawled to the edge. My descent had not got the airy grace of a pantomime fairy: the sides of the pit were so crumbly that every time I tried to gain a foothold I dislodged large quantities of earth, and as this fell among the snakes it was greeted with peevish hisses. I had to dangle in mid-air, being gently lowered by my companions, while the slip-knot grasped me even tighter round the waist. Eventually I looked down and I saw that my feet were about a yard from the ground. I shouted to my friends to stop lowering me, as I wanted to examine the ground I was to land on and make sure there were no snakes lying there. After a careful inspection I could not see any reptiles directly under me, so I shouted 'Lower away' in what I sincerely hoped was an intrepid tone of voice. As I started on my descent again, two things happened at once: firstly, one of my borrowed shoes fell off and, secondly, the lamp, which none of us had remembered to pump up, died away to a faint glow of light, rather like a plump cigar-end. At that precise moment I touched ground with my bare foot, and I cannot remember ever having been so frightened, before or since.

I stood motionless, sweating with great freedom, while the lamp was hastily hauled up to the surface, pumped up, and lowered down again. I have never been so glad to see a humble pressure-lamp. Now the pit was once more flooded with lamp-light I began to feel a little braver. I retrieved my shoe and put it on, and this made me feel even better. I grasped my stick in a moist hand and approached the nearest snake. I pinned it to the ground with the forked end of the stick, picked it up and put it in the bag. This part of the procedure gave me no qualms, for it was simple enough and not dangerous provided you exercised a certain care. The idea is to pin the reptile across the head with the fork and then get a good firm grip on its neck before picking it up. What worried me was the fact that while my attention was occupied with one snake, all the others were wriggling round frantically, and I had to keep a cautious eye open in case one got behind me and I stepped back on it. They were beautifully marked with an intricate pattern of brown, silver, pink and cream blotches, and when they remained still this coloration made them extremely hard to see; they just melted into the background. As soon as I pinned one to the ground, it would start to hiss like a kettle, and all the others would hiss in sympathy – a most unpleasant sound.

There was one nasty moment when I bent down to pick up one of the reptiles and heard a loud hissing apparently coming from somewhere horribly close to my ear. I straightened up and found myself staring into a pair of angry silver-coloured eyes approximately a foot away. After considerable juggling I managed to get this snake down on to the ground and pin him beneath my stick. On the whole, the reptiles were just as scared of me as I was of them, and they did their best to get out of my way. It was only when I had them cornered that they fought and struck viciously at the stick, but bounced off the brass fork with a reassuring ping. However, one of them must have been more experienced, for he ignored the brass fork and bit instead at the wood. He got a good grip and hung on like a bulldog; he would not let got even when I lifted him clear of the ground. Eventually I had to shake the stick really hard, and the snake sailed through the air, hit the side of the pit and fell to the ground hissing furiously. When I approached him with the stick again, he refused to bite and I had no difficulty in picking him up.

I was down in the pit for about half an hour, and during that time I caught twelve Gaboon vipers; I was not sure, even then, that I had captured all of them, but I felt it would be tempting fate to stay down there any longer. My companions hauled me out, hot, dirty and streaming with sweat, clutching in one hand a bag full of loudly hissing snakes.

'There, now,' said my friend triumphantly, while I was recovering my breath, 'I told you I'd get you some specimens, did I not?'

I just nodded; by that time I was beyond speech. I sat on the ground, smoking a much-needed cigarette and trying to steady my trembling hands. Now that the danger was over I began to realize for the first time how extremely stupid I had been to go into the pit in the first place, and how exceptionally lucky I was to have come out of it alive. I made a mental note that in future, if anyone asked me if animal-collecting was a dangerous occupation, I would reply that it was only as dangerous as your own stupidity allowed it to be. When I had recovered slightly, I looked about and discovered that one of my audience was missing.

'Where's your brother got to?' I asked my friend.

'Oh him,' said MacTootle with fine scorn, 'he couldn't watch any more – he said it made him feel sick. He's waiting over there for us. You'll have to excuse him – he couldn't take it. Sure, and it required some guts to watch you down there with all them wretched reptiles.'

Sebastian

Not long ago I spent some months in Argentina, and it was while there that I first met Sebastian. He was a gaucho, the South American equivalent of the North American cowboy. Like the cowboy, the gaucho is becoming rare nowadays, for most of the farms or estancias in Argentina are increasingly mechanized.

My reasons for being in Argentina were twofold: firstly, I wanted to capture live specimens of the wild animal life to bring back for zoos in this country, and, secondly, I wanted to film these same animals in their natural haunts. A friend of mine owned a large estancia about seventy miles from Buenos Aires in an area noted for its wild life, and when he invited me down there to spend a fortnight I accepted the invitation with alacrity. Unfortunately, when the time arrived my friend had some business to attend to, and all he could do was to take me down to the estancia and introduce me to the place before rushing back to the city.

He met me at the little country station, and as we jogged down the dusty road in the buggy he told me that he had got everything arranged for me.

'I'll put you in charge of Sebastian,' he said, 'so you should be all right.'
'Who's Sebastian?' I asked.

'Oh, just one of the gauchos,' said my friend vaguely. 'What he doesn't know about the animal life of this district isn't worth knowing. He'll be acting host in my absence, so just ask him for anything you want.'

After we had lunched on the veranda of the house, my friend suggested I should meet Sebastian, so we saddled horses and rode out across the acres of golden grass shimmering in the sun, and through the thickets of giant thistles, each plant as high as a man on horseback. In half an hour or so we came to a small wood of eucalyptus trees, and in the middle of it was a long, low, whitewashed house. A large and elderly dog, lying in the sun-drenched dust, lifted his head and gave a half-hearted bark before going back to sleep again. We dismounted and tied up the horses.

'Sebastian built this house himself,' said my friend. 'He's probably round the back having a siesta.'

We went round the house, and there, slung between two slender eucalyptus trees, was an enormous hammock, and in it lay Sebastian.

My first impression was of a dwarf. I discovered later that he measured about five feet two inches, but lying there in that vast expanse of hammock he looked very tiny indeed. His immensely long and powerful arms dangled over the sides, and they were burnt to a rich mahogany brown, with a faint mist of white hair on them. I couldn't see his face, for it was covered by a black hat that rose and fell rhythmically, while from underneath it came the most prolonged and fearsome snores I have ever heard. My friend seized one of Sebastian's dangling hands and tugged at it vigorously, at the same time bending down and shouting in the sleeping man's ear as loudly as he could: 'Sebastian – Sebastian. Wake up, you have visitors.' This noisy greeting had no effect whatever; Sebastian continued to snore under his hat. My friend looked at me and shrugged.

'He's always like this when he's asleep,' he explained. 'Here, catch hold of his other arm and let's get him out of the hammock.'

I took the other arm and we hauled him into a sitting position. The black hat rolled off and disclosed a round, brown chubby face, neatly divided into three by a great curved moustache, stained golden with nicotine, and a pair of snow-white eyebrows that curved up on to his forehead like the horns of a goat. My friend caught hold of his shoulders and shook him, repeating his name loudly, and suddenly a pair of wicked black eyes opened under the white brows and Sebastian glared at us sleepily. As soon as he recognized my friend he uttered a roar of anguish and struggled to his feet: 'Señor!' he bellowed. 'How nice to see you. . . . Ah, pardon me, señor, that I'm sleeping like a pig in its sty when you arrive ... excuse me, please. I wasn't expecting you so early, otherwise I would have been prepared to welcome you properly.'

He wrung my hand as my friend introduced me, and then, turning towards the house, he uttered a full-throated roar: 'Maria – Maria—.' In response to this nerve-shattering cry an attractive young woman of about thirty appeared, whom Sebastian introduced, with obvious pride, as his wife. Then he clasped my shoulder in one of his powerful hands and gazed earnestly into my face.

'Would you prefer coffee or maté, señor?' he asked innocently. Luckily my friend had warned me that Sebastian based his first impressions of people on whether they asked for coffee or maté, the Argentine green herb-tea, for in his opinion coffee was a disgusting drink, a liquid fit only to be consumed by city people and other depraved members of the human race. So I said I would have some maté. Sebastian turned and glared at his wife.

'Well?' he demanded. 'Didn't you hear the señor say he would take maté? Are the guests to stand here dying of thirst while you gape at them like an owl in the sun?'

'The water is boiling,' she replied placidly, 'and they needn't stand, if you ask them to sit down.'

'Don't answer me back, woman,' roared Sebastian, his moustache bristling.

'You must excuse him, señor,' said Maria, smiling at her husband affectionately, 'he always gets excited when we have visitors.'

Sebastian's face turned a deep brick-red.

'Excited?' he shouted indignantly. '*Excited*? Who's excited? I'm as calm as a dead horse ... please be seated, señors ... excited indeed ... you must excuse my wife, señor, she has a talent for exaggeration that would have earned her a wonderful political career if she had been born a man.'

We sat down under the trees, and Sebastian lighted a small and pungent cigar while he continued to grumble good-naturedly about his wife's shortcomings.

'I should never have married again,' he confided. 'The trouble is that my wives never outlive me. Four times I've been married now and as I laid each woman to rest I said to myself, Sebastian, never again. Then, suddenly ... puff! ... I'm married again. My spirit is willing to remain single but my flesh is weak, and the trouble is that I have more flesh than spirit.' He glanced down at his magnificent paunch with a rueful air, and then looked up and gave us a wide and disarming grin that displayed a great expanse of gum in which were planted two withered teeth. 'I suppose I shall always be weak, señor ... but then a man without a wife is like a cow without an udder.'

Maria brought the maté, and the little pot was handed round the circle, while we each in turn took sips from the slender silver maté pipe, and my friend explained to Sebastian exactly why I had come to the estancia. The gaucho was very enthusiastic, and when we told him that he might be required to take part in some of the film shots he stroked his moustache and shot a sly glance at his wife.

'D'you hear that, eh?' he enquired. 'I shall be appearing in the cinema. Better watch that tongue of yours, my girl, for when the women in England see me on the screen they'll be flocking out here to try to get me.'

'I see no reason why they should,' returned his wife. 'I expect they have good-for-nothings there, same as everywhere else.' Sebastian contented himself with giving her a withering look, and then he turned to me.

'Don't worry, señor,' he said, 'I will do everything to help you in your work. I will do everything you want.' He was as good as his word: that evening my friend left for Buenos Aires, and for the next two weeks Sebastian rarely left my side. His energy was prodigious, and his personality so fiery that he soon had complete control of my affairs. I simply told him just what I wanted and he did it for me, and the more extraordinary and difficult my requests the more he seemed to delight in accomplishing them for me. He could get more work out of the peons, or hired men, on the estancia than anyone I met, and, strangely enough, he did not get it by pleading or cajoling them but by insulting and ridiculing them, using a wealth of glittering similes that, instead of angering the men, convulsed them with laughter and made them work all the harder.

'Look at you,' he would roar scathingly, 'just look at you all . . . moving with all the speed of snails in bird-lime . . . it's a wonder to me that your horses don't take fright when you gallop, because even I can hear your eyeballs rattling in your empty skulls . . . you've not enough brain among the lot of you to make a rich soup for a bedbug . . .' And the peons would gurgle with mirth and redouble their efforts. Apart from considering him a humorist, of course, the men knew very well that he would not ask them to do anything he could not do himself. But then there was hardly a thing that he did not know how to do, and among the peons an impossible task was always described as 'something even Sebastian couldn't do.' Mounted on his great black horse, his scarlet-and-blue poncho draped round his shoulders in vivid folds, Sebastian cut an impressive figure. On this horse he would gallop about the estancia, his lassoo whistling as he showed me the various methods of roping a steer. There are about six different ways of doing this, and Sebastian could perform them all with equal facility. The faster his horse travelled, the rougher the ground, the greater accuracy he seemed to obtain with his throws, until you had the impression that the steer had some sort of magnetic attraction for the rope and that it was impossible for him to miss.

If Sebastian was a master with a rope, he was a genius with his whip, a short-handled affair with a long slender thong, a deadly weapon which he was never without. I have seen him, at full gallop, pull this whip from his belt and neatly take the head off a thistle plant as he passed. Flicking cigarettes out of people's mouths was child's play to him. I was told that in the previous year a stranger to the district had cast doubts on Sebastian's abilities with a whip, and Sebastian had replied by stripping the man's shirt from his back, without once touching the skin beneath. Sebastian preferred his whip as a weapon – and he could use it like an elongated arm – yet he was very skilful with both knife and hatchet. With the latter weapon he could split a matchbox in two at about ten paces. No, Sebastian was definitely not the sort of man to get the wrong side of.

A lot of the hunting I did with Sebastian took place at night, when the nocturnal creatures came out of their burrows. Armed with torches, we would leave the estancia shortly after dark, never returning much before midnight or two in the morning, and generally bringing with us two or three specimens of one sort or another. On these hunts we were assisted by Sebastian's favourite dog, a mongrel of great age whose teeth had long since been worn down level with his gums. This animal was the perfect hunting-dog, for even when he caught a specimen it was impossible for him to hurt it with his toothless gums. Once he had chased and brought to bay some specimen, he would stand guard over it, giving one short yap every minute or so to guide us to the spot.

It was during one of these night hunts that I had a display of Sebastian's great strength. The dog had put up an armadillo, and after it had been chased for several hundred yards the creature took refuge down a hole. There were three of us that night: Sebastian, myself, and a peon. In chasing the armadillo the peon and I had far outstripped Sebastian, whose figure did not encourage running. The peon and I reached the hole just in time to see the rear end of the armadillo disappearing down it, so we flung ourselves on to the grass and while I got a grip on its tail the peon grasped its hind legs. The armadillo dug his long front claws into the sides of the hole, and though we tugged and pulled he was as immovable as though he were embedded in cement. Then the beast gave a sudden jerk and the peon lost his grip. The armadillo wriggled farther inside the hole, and I could feel his tail slipping through my fingers. Just at that moment Sebastian arrived on the scene, panting for breath. He pushed me out of the way, seized the armadillo's tail, braced his feet on either side of the hole and pulled. There was a shower of earth, and the armadillo came out of the hole like a cork out of a bottle. With one sharp tug Sebastian had accomplished what two of us had failed to do.

One of the creatures I wanted to film on the estancia was the rhea, the South American ostrich, which, like its African cousin, can run like a racehorse. I wanted to film the rheas being hunted in the old style, by men on horseback armed with boleadoras. These weapons consist of three wooden balls, about the size of cricket balls, each attached to the other by a fairly long string; they are whirled round the head and thrown so that they tangle themselves round the bird's legs and bring it to the ground. Sebastian arranged the whole hunt for me, and we spent my last day filming it. As most of the peons were to appear in these scenes, they all turned up that morning in their best clothes, each obviously trying to outdo the other by the brilliance of his costume. Sebastian surveyed them sourly from the back of his horse:

'Look at them, señor,' he said contemptuously spitting. 'All done up and as shining as partridge eggs, and as excited as dogs on a bowling green, just because they think they're going to get their silly faces on the cinema screen . . . they make me sick.'

But I noticed that he carefully combed his moustache before the filming started. We were at it all day in the boiling sun, and by evening, when the last scenes had been shot, we all felt in need of a rest – all of us, that is, except Sebastian, who seemed as fresh as when he started. As we made our way home, he told me that he had organized a farewell party for me that night, and everyone on the estancia was to be present. There would be plenty of wine and singing and dancing, and his eyes gleamed as he told me about it. I had not the heart to explain that I was dead tired and would much rather go to bed, so I accepted the invitation.

The festivities took place in the great smoke-filled kitchen, with half a dozen flickering oil-lamps to light it. The band consisted of three guitars which were played with great verve. I need hardly say that the life and soul of the party was Sebastian. He drank more wine than everyone else, and yet remained sober; he played solos on the guitar; he sang a great variety of songs ranging from the vulgar to the pathetic; he consumed vast quantities of food. But, above all, he danced; danced the wild gaucho dances with their complicated steps and kicks and leaps, danced until the beams above vibrated with his steps and his spurs struck fire from the stone flags.

My friend, who had driven down from Buenos Aires to pick me up, arrived in the middle of the party and joined us. We sat in the corner, drinking a glass of wine together and watching Sebastian dance, while the peons clapped and roared applause.

'What incredible energy he's got,' I remarked. 'He's been working harder than anyone else today, and now he's danced us all off our feet.'

'That's what a life on the pampa does for you!' replied my friend. 'But, seriously, I think he's quite amazing for his age, don't you?'

'Why?' I asked casually, 'how old is he?'

My friend looked at me in surprise:

'Don't you know?' he asked. 'In about two months' time Sebastian will be ninety-five.'

A Zoo in My Luggage
GERALD DURRELL

A Zoo in My Luggage

For
SOPHIE
In memory of Tio Pepe, Wiener Schnitzel
and dancing kleek to kleek

BOOK ONE

EN ROUTE

Chapter One

The Reluctant Python

MAIL BY HAND

To: The Zoological Officer,
U.A.C. Manager's House,
Mamfe.

Dearest Sir,
  I have once been your customer during your first tour of the Cameroons and get you different animals.
  I send here one animal with my servant, I do not know the name of it. Please could you offer what price you think fit and send to me. The animal has been living in my house almost about three weeks and a half.

   With love, sir.
         I am,
             Yrs. sincerely,
                 Thomas Tambic, *Hunter.*

I had decided that, on the way up country to Bafut, we would make a ten-day stop at a town called Mamfe. This was at the highest navigable point of the Cross River, on the edge of an enormous tract of uninhabited country; and on the two previous occasions when I had been to the Cameroons I had found it a good collecting centre. We set off from Victoria in an impressive convoy of three lorries, Jacquie and myself in the first, our young assistant Bob in the second, and Sophie, my long-suffering secretary, in the third. The trip was hot and dusty, and we arrived at Mamfe in the brief green twilight of the third day, hungry, thirsty and covered from head to foot with a fine film of red dust. We had been told to contact the United Africa Company's manager on arrival, and so our lorries roared up the drive and screeched to a halt outside a very impressive house, ablaze with lights.

The house stood in what was certainly the best position in Mamfe. It was perched on top of a conical hill, one side of which formed part of the gorge through which the Cross River ran. From the edge of the garden, fringed with a hedge of the inevitable hibiscus bushes, you could look straight down four

ion. So, naturally, I went and got the animals first and then set about the task of finding my zoo. This was not so easy as it might seem on the face of it, and looking back on it now I am speechless at my audacity in trying to achieve success in this way.

This, therefore, is the story of my search for a zoo, and it explains why, for some considerable time, I had a zoo in my luggage.

Mail by Hand

From my seat on the bougainvillaea-enshrouded verandah I looked out over the blue and glittering waters of the bay of Victoria, a bay dotted with innumerable forest-encrusted islands like little green, furry hats dropped carelessly on the surface. Two grey parrots flew swiftly across the sky, wolf-whistling to each other and calling 'coo-eee' loudly and seductively in the brilliant blue sky. A flock of tiny canoes, like a school of black fish, moved to and fro among the islands, and dimly the cries and chatter of the fishermen came drifting across the water to me. Above, in the great palms that shaded the house, a colony of weaver-birds chattered incessantly as they busily stripped the palm fronds off to weave their basket-like nests, and behind the house, where the forest began, a tinker-bird was giving its monotonous cry, toink . . . toink . . . toink . . ., like someone beating forever on a tiny anvil. The sweat was running down my spine, staining my shirt black, and the glass of beer by my side was rapidly getting warm. I was back in West Africa.

Dragging my attention away from a large, orange-headed lizard that had climbed on to the verandah rail and was busily nodding its head as if in approval of the sunshine, I turned back to my task of composing a letter.

'The Fon of Bafut,
'Fon's Palace,
'Bafut,
'Bemenda Division, British Cameroons.'

I paused here for inspiration. I lit a cigarette and contemplated the sweat-marks that my fingers had left on the keys of the typewriter. I took a sip of beer and scowled at my letter. It was difficult to compose for a number of reasons.

The Fon of Bafut was a rich, clever and charming potentate who ruled over a large grassland kingdom in the mountain area of the north. Eight years previously I had spent a number of months in his country to collect the strange and rare creatures that inhabited it. The Fon had turned out to be a delightful host, and we had many fantastic parties together, for he was a great believer in enjoying life. I had marvelled at his alcoholic intake, at his immense energy and at his humour, and when I returned to England I had attempted to draw a picture of him in a book I wrote about the expedition. I had tried to show him as a shrewd and kindly man, with a great love of music, dancing, drink and other things that make life pleasant, and with an almost childlike ability for having a good time. I now wanted to revisit him in his remote and beautiful kingdom and renew our friendship; but I was a little bit worried. I had realized – too late – that the portrait I had drawn of him in my book was perhaps open to misconstruction. The Fon might well have thought that the picture was that of a senile alcoholic who spent his time getting drunk amid a bevy of wives. So it was with some trepidation that I sat down to write to him and find out if I would be welcome in his kingdom. That, I reflected, was the worst of writing books. I sighed, stubbed out my cigarette and started.

'My dear friend
'As you may have heard I have returned to the Cameroons in order to catch more animals to take back to my country. As you will remember when I was last here I came up to your country and caught most of my best animals there. Also we had a very good time together.
'Now I have returned with my wife and I would like her to meet you and see your beautiful country. May we come up to Bafut and stay with you while we catch our animals? I would like to stay once more in your Rest House, as I did last time, if you will let me. Perhaps you would let me know?
'Yours sincerely,
'Gerald Durrell.'

I sent this missive off by messenger together with two bottles of whisky which he was given strict instructions not to drink on the way. We then waited hopefully, day after day, while our mountain of luggage smouldered under tarpaulins in the sun, and the orange-headed lizards lay dozing on top of it. Within a week, the messenger returned and drew a letter out of the pocket of his tattered khaki shorts. I ripped open the envelope hastily and spread the letter on the table, where Jacquie and I craned over it.

'Fon's Palace,
'Bafut, Bemenda.
'25th January 1957

'My good friend,
'Yours dated 23rd received with great pleasure. I was more than pleased when I read the letter sent to me by you, in the Cameroons again.
'I will be looking for you at any time you come here. How long you think to remain with me here, no objection. My Rest House is ever ready for you at any time you arrive here.
'Please pass my sincere greetings to your wife and tell her that I shall have a good chat with her when she come here.
'Yours truly,
'Fon of Bafut.'

A Word in Advance

This is the chronicle of a six-month trip that my wife and I made to Bafut, a mountain grassland kingdom in the British Cameroons in West Africa. Our reason for going there was, to say the least, a trifle unusual. We wanted to collect our own zoo.

Since the end of the war I had been financing and organizing expeditions to many parts of the world to collect wild animals for various zoological gardens. Bitter experience over the years had taught me that the worst and most heartbreaking part of any collecting trip came at the end when, after months of lavishing care and attention upon them, you had to part with the animals. If you are acting as mother, father, food-provider and danger eradicator to an animal, half a year is enough to build up a very real friendship with it. The creature trusts you and, what is more important, behaves naturally when you are around. Then, just when this relationship should begin to bear fruit, when you ought to be in a unique position to study the animal's habits and behaviour, you are forced to part company.

There was only one answer to this problem, as far as I was concerned, and that was to have a zoo of my own. I could then bring my animals back knowing what type of cages they were going to inhabit, what sort of food and treatment they were going to receive (a thing which one cannot, unfortunately, be sure about with some other zoos), and secure in the knowledge that I could go on studying them to my heart's content. The zoo, of course, would have to be open to the public so that, from my point of view, it would be a sort of self-supporting laboratory in which I could keep and watch my animals.

There was another and, to my mind, more urgent reason for creating a zoo. I, like many other people, have been seriously concerned by the fact that year by year, all over the world, various species of animals are being slowly but surely exterminated in their wild state, thanks directly or indirectly to the interference of mankind. While many worthy and hard-working societies are doing their best to tackle this problem, I know a great number of animal species which, because they are small and generally of no commercial or touristic value, are not receiving adequate protection. To me the extirpation of an animal species is a criminal offence, in the same way as the destruction of anything we cannot recreate or replace, such as a Rembrandt or the Acropolis. In my opinion zoological gardens all over the world should have as one of their main objects the establishment of breeding colonies for these rare and threatened species. Then, if it is inevitable that the animal should become extinct in the wild state, at least we have not lost it completely. For many years I had wanted to start a zoo with just such an object in view, and now seemed the ideal moment to begin.

Any reasonable person smitten with an ambition of this sort would have secured the zoo first and obtained the animals afterwards. But throughout my life I have rarely if ever achieved what I wanted by tackling it in a logical fash-

hundred feet into the gorge, to where a tangle of low growth and taller trees perched precariously on thirty-foot cliffs of pleated granite, thickly overgrown with wild begonias, moss and ferns. At the foot of these cliffs, round gleaming white sandbanks and strange, ribbed slabs of rock, the river wound its way like a brown, sinuous muscle. On the opposite bank there were small patches of farmland along the edge of the river, and beyond that the forest reared up in a multitude of colours and textures, spreading endlessly back until it was turned into a dim, quivering frothy green sea by distance and heat haze.

I was, however, in no mood to admire views as I uncoiled myself from the red-hot interior of the lorry and jumped to the ground. What I wanted most in the world at that moment was a drink, a bath and a meal, in that order. Almost as urgently I wanted a wooden box to house the first animal we had acquired. This was an extremely rare creature, a baby black-footed mongoose, which I had purchased from a native in a village twenty-five miles back when we had stopped there to buy some fruit. I had been delighted that we had started the collection with such a rarity, but after struggling with her for two hours in the front seat of the lorry, my enthusiasm had begun to wane. She had wanted to investigate every nook and cranny in the cab, and fearing that she might go and get tangled up in the gears and perhaps break a leg I had imprisoned her inside my shirt. For the first half-hour she had stalked round and round my body, sniffing loudly. For the next half-hour she had made several determined attempts to dig a hole in my stomach with her exceedingly sharp claws, and on being persuaded to desist from this occupation, she had seized a large portion of my abdomen in her mouth and sucked it vigorously and hopefully, while irrigating me with an apparently unending stream of warm and pungent urine. This in no way improved my already dusty and sweaty appearance, and as I marched up the steps of the U.A.C. manager's house, with a mongoose tail dangling out of my tightly buttoned, urine-stained shirt, I looked, to say the least, slightly eccentric. Taking a deep breath and trying to seem nonchalant, I walked into the brilliantly-lit living-room, and found three people seated round a card table. They looked at me with a faint air of inquiry. 'Good evening,' I said, feeling rather at a loss. 'My name's Durrell.'

It was not, I reflected, the most telling remark made in Africa since Stanley and Livingstone met. However, a small, dark man rose from the table and came towards me, smiling charmingly, his long black hair flopping down over his forehead. He held out his hand and clasped mine, and then, ignoring my sudden appearance and my unconventional condition, he peered earnestly into my face.

'Good evening,' he said. 'Do you by any chance play Canasta?'

'No,' I said, rather taken aback, 'I'm afraid I don't.'

He sighed, as if his worst fears had been realized. 'A pity... a great pity,' he said; then he cocked his head on one side and peered at me closely.

'*What* did you say your name was?' he asked.

'Durrell... Gerald Durrell.'

'Good heavens,' he exclaimed, realization dawning, 'are you that animal maniac head office warned me about?'

'I expect so.'

'But my dear chap, I expected you two days ago. Where have you been?'

'We would have been here two days ago if our lorry hadn't broken down with such monotonous regularity.'

'These local lorries are bloody unreliable,' he said, as if letting me into a secret. 'Have a drink?'

'I should love one,' I said fervently. 'May I bring the others in? They're all waiting in the lorries.'

'Yes, yes, bring 'em all in. Of course. Drinks all round.'

'Thanks a lot,' I said, and turned towards the door.

My host seized me by the arm and drew me back. 'Tell me, dear boy,' he said in a hoarse whisper, 'I don't want to be personal, but is it the gin I've drunk or does your stomach *always* wriggle like that?'

'No,' I said gravely. 'It's not my stomach. I've got a mongoose in my shirt.'

He gazed at me unblinkingly for a moment.

'Very reasonable explanation,' he said at last.

'Yes,' I said, 'and true.'

He sighed. 'Well, as long as it's not the gin I don't mind *what* you keep in your shirt,' he said seriously. 'Bring the others in and we'll kill a noggin or two before you eat.'

So we invaded John Henderson's house and within a couple of days we had turned him into what must have been the most long-suffering host on the West Coast of Africa. For a man who likes his privacy to invite four strangers to live in his house is a noble deed to start with. But when he has no liking for, and a grave mistrust of, any form of animal life, to invite four animal-collectors to stay is an action so heroic that no words can describe it. Within twenty-four hours of our arrival not only a mongoose, but a squirrel, a bushbaby and two monkeys were quartered on the verandah of John's house.

While John was getting used to the idea of having his legs embraced by a half-grown baboon every time he set foot outside his own front door, I sent messages to all my old contacts among the local hunters, gathered them together and told them the sort of creatures we were after. Then we sat back and awaited results. They were some time in coming. Then, early one afternoon, a local hunter called Agustine appeared, padding down the drive, wearing a scarlet-and-blue sarong and looking, as always, like a neat, eager, Mongolian shopwalker. He was accompanied by one of the largest West Africans I have ever seen, a great, scowling man who must have been at least six feet tall, and whose skin – in contrast to Agustine's golden bronze shade – was a deep soot black. He clumped along beside Agustine on such enormous feet that at first I thought he was suffering from elephantiasis. They stopped at the verandah steps, and while Agustine beamed cheerily, his companion glared at us in a preoccupied manner, as though endeavouring to assess our net weight for culinary purposes.

'Good morning, sah,' said Agustine, giving a twist to his highly-coloured sarong to anchor it more firmly round his slim hips.

'Good morning, sah,' intoned the giant, his voice sounding like the distant rumble of thunder.

'Good morning . . . you bring beef?' I inquired hopefully, though they did not appear to be carrying any animals.

'No, sah,' said Agustine sorrowfully, 'we no get beef. I come for ask Masa if Masa go borrow us some rope.'

'Rope? What do you want rope for?'

'We done find some big boa, sah, for bush. But we no fit catch um if we no get rope, sah.'

Bob, whose speciality was reptiles, sat up with a jerk.

'Boa?' he said excitedly. 'What does he mean . . . boa?'

'They mean a python,' I explained. One of the most confusing things about pidgin English, from the naturalist's point of view, was the number of wrong names used for various animals. Pythons were boas, leopards were tigers and so on. Bob's eyes gleamed with a fanatical light. Ever since we had boarded the ship at Southampton his conversation had been almost entirely confined to pythons, and I knew that he would not be really happy until he had added one of these reptiles to the collection.

'Where is it?' he asked, his voice quivering with ill-concealed eagerness.

' 'E dere dere for bush,' said Agustine, waving a vague arm that embraced approximately five hundred square miles of forest. ' 'E dere dere for some hole inside ground.'

'Na big one?' I asked.

'Wah! Big?' exclaimed Agustine. ' 'E big too much.'

' 'E big like dis,' said the giant, slapping his thigh which was about the size of a side of beef.

'We walka for bush since morning time, sah,' explained Agustine. 'Den we see dis boa. We run quick-quick, but we no catch lucky. Dat snake get power too much. 'E done run for some hole for ground and we no get rope so we no fit catch um.'

'You done leave some man for watch dis hole,' I asked, 'so dis boa no go run for bush?'

'Yes, sah, we done lef' two men for dere.'

I turned to Bob. 'Well, here's your chance: a genuine wild python holed up in a cave. Shall we go and have a shot at it?'

'God, yes! Let's go and get it right away,' exclaimed Bob.

I turned to Agustine. 'We go come look dis snake, Agustine, eh?'

'Yes, sah.'

'You go wait small time and we go come. First we get rope and catch net.'

While Bob hurried out to our pile of equipment to fetch rope and nets, I filled a couple of bottles with water and rounded up Ben, our animal boy, who was squatting outside the back door, flirting with a damsel of voluptuous charms.

'Ben, leave that unfortunate young woman alone and get ready. We're going for bush to catch a boa.'

'Yes, sah,' said Ben, reluctantly leaving his girl friend. 'Which side dis boa, sah?'

'Agustine say it's in a hole for ground. That's why I want you. If this hole is so small that Mr Golding and I no fit pass you will have to go for inside and catch the boa.'

'Me, sah?' said Ben.

'Yes, you. All alone.'

'All right,' he said, grinning philosophically, 'I no de fear, sah.'

'You lie,' I said. 'You know you de fear too much.'

'I no de fear, for true, sah,' said Ben in a dignified manner. 'I never tell Masa how I done kill bush cow?'

'Yes, you told me twice, and I still don't believe you. Now, go to Mr Golding and get the ropes and catch nets. Hurry.'

To reach the area of country in which our quarry was waiting, we had to go down the hill and cross the river by the ferry, a large, banana-shaped canoe which appeared to have been constructed about three centuries ago, and to have been deteriorating slowly ever since. It was paddled by a very old man who looked in immediate danger of dying of a heart attack, and he was accompanied by a small boy whose job it was to bale out. This was something of an unequal struggle, for the boy had a small rusty tin for the job, while the sides of the canoe were as watertight as a colander. Inevitably, by the time one reached the opposite bank one was sitting in about six inches of water. When we arrived with our equipment on the water-worn steps in the granite cliff that formed the landing-stage, we found the ferry was at the opposite shore, so while Ben, Agustine and the enormous African (whom we had christened Gargantua) lifted their voices and roared at the ferryman to return with all speed, Bob and I squatted in the shade and watched the usual crowd of Mamfe people bathing and washing in the brown waters below.

Swarms of small boys leapt shrieking off the cliffs and splashed into the water, and then shot to the surface again, their palms and the soles of their feet gleaming shell pink, their bodies like polished chocolate. The girls, more demure, bathed in their sarongs, only to emerge from the water with the cloth clinging to their bodies so tightly that it left nothing to the imagination. One small toddler, who could not have been more than five or six, made his way carefully down the cliff, his tongue protruding with concentration, carrying on his head an enormous water-jar. On reaching the edge of the water he did not pause to remove the jar from his head, or to take off his sarong. He walked straight into the water and waded slowly and determinedly out into the river until he completely disappeared; only the jar could be seen moving mysteriously along the surface of the water. At length this too vanished. There was a moment's pause, and then the jar reappeared, this time moving shorewards, and eventually, beneath it, the boy's head bobbed up. He gave a tremendous snort to expel the air from his lungs, and then struggled grimly towards the beach, the now brimming jar on his head. When he reached the shore he edged the jar carefully on to a ledge of rock, and then re-entered the water, still wearing his sarong. From some intricate fold in this garment he produced a small fragment of Lifebuoy soap, and proceeded to rub it all over himself and the sarong with complete impartiality. Presently, when he had worked up such a lather all over himself that he looked like an animated pink snowman, he ducked beneath the surface to wash off the soap, waded ashore, settled the jar once more on his head and slowly climbed the cliff and disappeared. It was the perfect example of the African application of time-and-motion study.

By this time the ferry had arrived, and Ben and Agustine were arguing hotly with its aged occupant. Instead of taking us straight across the river, they wanted him to paddle us about half a mile upstream to a large sandbank. This would save us having to walk about a mile along the bank to reach the path that led to the forest. The old man appeared to be singularly obstinate about the proposal.

'What's the matter with him, Ben?' I inquired.

'Eh! Dis na foolish man, sah,' said Ben, turning to me in exasperation, ' 'e no agree for take us for up de river.'

'Why you no agree, my friend?' I asked the old man. 'If you go take us I go pay you more money and I go dash you.'

'Masa,' said the old man firmly, 'dis na my boat, and if I go lose um I no fit catch money again ... I no get chop for my belly ... I no get one-one penny.'

'But how you go lose you boat?' I asked in amazement, for I knew this strip of river and there were no rapids or bad currents along it.

'Ipopo, Masa,' explained the old man.

I stared at the ferryman, wondering what on earth he was talking about. Was Ipopo perhaps some powerful local juju I had not come across before?

'Dis Ipopo,' I asked soothingly, 'which side 'e live?'

'Wah! Masa never see um?' asked the old man in astonishment. ' 'E dere dere for water close to D.O.'s house ... 'e big like so-so motor ... 'e de holla ... 'e de get power too much.'

'What's he talking about?' asked Bob in bewilderment.

And suddenly it dawned on me. 'He's talking about the hippo herd in the river below the D.O.'s house,' I explained, 'but it's such a novel abbreviation of the word that he had me foxed for a moment.'

'Does he think they're dangerous?'

'Apparently, though I can't think why. They were perfectly placid last time I was here.'

'Well, I hope they're still placid,' said Bob.

I turned to the old man again. 'Listen, my friend. If you go take us for up dis water, I go pay you six shilling and I go dash you cigarette, eh? And if sometime dis ipopo go damage dis your boat I go pay for new one, you hear?'

'I hear, sah.'

'You agree?'

'I agree, sah,' said the old man, avarice struggling with caution. We progressed slowly upstream, squatting in half an inch of water in the belly of the canoe.

'I suppose they can't really be dangerous,' said Bob casually, trailing his hand nonchalantly in the water.

'When I was here last I used to go up to within thirty feet of them in a canoe and take photographs,' I said.

'Dis ipopo get strong head now, sah,' said Ben tactlessly. 'Two months pass dey kill three men and break two boats.'

'That's a comforting thought,' said Bob.

Ahead of us the brown waters were broken in many places by rocks. At any other time they would have looked exactly like rocks but now each one looked exactly like the head of a hippo, a cunning, maniacal hippo, lurking in the dark waters, awaiting our approach. Ben, presumably remembering his tale of daring with the bush-cow, attempted to whistle, but it was a feeble effort, and I noticed that he scanned the waters ahead anxiously. After all, a hippo that has developed the habit of attacking canoes gets a taste for it, like a man-eating tiger, and will go out of his way to be unpleasant, apparently regarding it as a sport. I was not feeling in the mood for gambolling in twenty feet of murky water with half a ton of sadistic hippo.

The old man, I noticed, was keeping our craft well into the bank, twisting and turning so that we were, as far as possible, always in shallow water. The cliff here was steep, but well supplied with footholds in case of emergency, for the rocks lay folded in great layers like untidy piles of fossilized magazines, overgrown with greenery. The trees that grew on top of the cliffs spread their branches well out over the water, so that we travelled in a series of fish-like jerks up a tunnel of shade, startling the occasional kingfisher that whizzed across our bows like a vivid blue shooting-star, or a black-and-white wattled plover that flapped away upstream, tittering imbecilically to itself, with its feet grazing the water, and long yellow wattles flapping absurdly on each side of its beak.

Gradually we rounded the bend of the river, and there, about three hundred yards ahead of us on the opposite shore, lay the white bulk of the sandbank, frilled with ripples. The old man gave a grunt of relief at the sight, and started to paddle more swiftly.

'Nearly there,' I said gaily, 'and not a hippo in sight.'

The words were hardly out of my mouth when a rock we were passing some fifteen feet away suddenly rose out of the water and gazed at us with bulbous astonished eyes, snorting out two slender fountains of spray, like a miniature whale.

Fortunately, our gallant crew resisted the impulse to leap out of the canoe *en masse* and swim for the bank. The old man drew in his breath with a sharp hiss, and dug his paddle deep into the water, so that the canoe pulled up short in a swirl and clop of bubbles. Then we sat and stared at the hippo, and the hippo sat and stared at us. Of the two, the hippo seemed the more astonished. The chubby, pinky-grey face floated on the surface of the water like a disembodied head at a séance. The great eyes stared at us with the innocent appraisal of a baby. The ears flicked back and forth, as if waving to us. The hippo sighed deeply and moved a few feet nearer, still looking at us with wide-eyed innocence. Then, suddenly, Agustine let out a shrill whoop that made us all jump and nearly upset the canoe. We shushed him furiously, while the hippo continued its scrutiny of us unabashed.

'No de fear,' said Agustine in a loud voice, 'na woman.'

He seized the paddle from the old man's reluctant grasp, and proceeded to beat on the water with the blade, sending up a shower of spray. The hippo opened its mouth in a gigantic yawn to display a length of tooth that had to be seen to be believed. Then, suddenly, and with apparently no muscular effort, the great head sank beneath the surface. There was a moment's pause, during which we were all convinced that the beast was ploughing through the water somewhere directly beneath us, then the head rose to the surface again, this time, to our relief, about twenty yards up-river. It snorted out two more jets of spray, waggled its ears seductively and sank again, only to reappear in a moment or so still farther up-stream. The old man grunted and retrieved his paddle from Agustine.

'Agustine, why you do dat foolish ting?' I asked in what I hoped was a steady and trenchant tone of voice.

'Sah, dat ipopo no be man . . . na woman dat,' Agustine explained, hurt by my lack of faith in him.

'How you know?' I demanded.

'Masa, I savvay all dis ipopo for dis water,' he explained, 'dis one na woman. Ef na man ipopo 'e go chop us one time. But dis woman one no get strong head like 'e husband.'

'Well, thank God for the weaker sex,' I said to Bob, as the old man, galvanized into activity, sent the canoe shooting diagonally across the river, so that it ground on to the sandbank in a shower of pebbles. We unloaded our gear, told the old man to wait for us and set off towards the python's lair.

The path lay at first through some old native farmland, where the giant trees had been felled and now lay rotting across the ground. Between these trunks a crop of cassava had been grown and harvested, and the ground allowed to lie fallow, so that the low growth of the forest – thorn bushes, convolvulus and other tangles – had swept into the clearing and covered everything with a cloak. There was always plenty of life to be seen in these abandoned farms, and as we pushed through the intricate web of undergrowth there were birds all around us. Beautiful little flycatchers hovered in the air, showing up powder-blue against the greenery; in the dim recesses of convolvulus-covered tree stumps robin-chats hopped perkily in search of grasshoppers, and looked startlingly like English robins; a pied crow flew up from the ground ahead and flapped heavily away, crying a harsh warning; in a thicket of thorn bushes, covered with pink flowers among which zoomed big blue bees, a kurrichane thrush treated us to a waterfall of sweet song. The path wound its way through this moist, hot, waist-high undergrowth for some time, and then quite abruptly the undergrowth ended and the path led us out on to a golden grassfield, rippling with the heat haze.

Attractive though they were to look at, these grassfields were far from comfortable to walk across. The grass was tough and spiky, growing in tussocks carefully placed to trip the unwary traveller. In places, where sheets of grey rocks were exposed to the sun, the surface, sprinkled with a million tiny mica chips, sparkled and flashed in your eyes. The sun beat down upon your neck, and its reflections rebounded off the glittering surface of the rock and hit you in the face with the impact of a blast furnace. We plodded across this sun-drenched expanse, the sweat pouring off us.

'I hope this damned reptile's had the sense to go to ground where there's some shade,' I said to Bob. 'You could fry an egg on these rocks.'

Agustine, who had been padding eagerly ahead, his sarong turning from scarlet to wine-red as it absorbed the sweat from his body, turned and grinned at me, his face freckled with a mass of sweat-drops.

'Masa hot?' he inquired anxiously.

'Yes, hot too much,' I answered, ' 'e far now dis place?'

'No, sah,' he said pointing ahead, ' 'e dere dere. . . . Masa never see dis man I done leave for watch?'

I followed his pointing finger and in the distance I could see an area where the rocks had been pushed up and rumpled, like bedclothes, by some ancient volcanic upheaval, so that they formed a miniature cliff running diagonally across the grass-field. On top of this I could see the figures of two more hunters, squatting patiently in the sun. When they saw us they rose to their feet and waved ferocious-looking spears in greeting.

' 'E dere dere for hole?' yelled Agustine anxiously.

' 'E dere dere,' they called back.

When we reached the base of the small cliff I could quite see why the python had chosen this spot to stand at bay. The rock face had been split into a series of shallow caves, worn smooth by wind and water, each communicating with the other, and the whole series sloping slightly upwards into the cliff, so that anything that lived in them would be in no danger of getting drowned in the rainy season. The mouth of each cave was about eight feet across and three feet high, which gave a snake, but not much else, room for manoeuvring. The hunters had very thoughtfully set fire to all the grass in the vicinity, in an effort to smoke the reptile out. The snake had been unaffected by this, but now we had to work in a thick layer of charcoal and feathery ash up to our ankles.

Bob and I got down on our stomachs and, shoulder to shoulder, wormed our way into the mouth of the cave to try and spot the python and map out a plan of campaign. We soon found that the cave narrowed within three or four feet of the entrance so that there was only room for one person, lying as flat as he could. After the glare of the sunshine outside, the cave seemed twice as dark as it was, and we could not see a thing. The only indication that a snake was there at all was a loud peevish hissing every time we moved. We called loudly for a torch, and when this had been unpacked and handed to us we directed its beam up the narrow passage.

Eight feet ahead of us the passage ended in a circular depression in the rock, and in this the python lay coiled, shining in the torchlight as if freshly polished. It was about fifteen feet long as far as we could judge, and so fat that we pardoned Gargantua for comparing its girth with his enormous thigh. It was also in an extremely bad temper. The longer the torch beam played on it the more prolonged and shrill did its hisses become, until they rose to an eerie shriek. We crawled out into the sunlight again and sat up, both of us almost the same colour as our hunters because of the thick layer of dark ash adhering to our sweaty bodies.

'The thing is to get a noose round its neck, and then we can all pull like hell and drag it out,' said Bob.

'Yes, but the job's going to be to *get* the noose round its neck. I don't fancy being wedged in that passage if it decided to come down it after one. There's no room to manoeuvre, and there's no room for anyone to help you if you do get entangled with it.'

'Yes, that's a point,' Bob admitted.

'There's only one thing to do,' I said. 'Agustine, go quick-quick and cut one fork-stick for me . . . big one . . . you hear?'

'Yes, sah,' said Agustine, and whipping out his broad-bladed machete he trotted off towards the forest's edge some three hundred yards away.

'Remember,' I warned Bob, 'if we *do* succeed in yanking it out into the open, you can't rely on the hunters. Everyone in the Cameroons is convinced that a python is poisonous; not only do they think its bite is deadly, but they also think it can poison you with the spurs under the tail. So if we do get it out it's no good grabbing the head and expecting them to hang on to the tail. You'll have to grab one end while I grab the other, and we'll just have to hope to heaven that they cooperate in the middle.'

'That's a jolly thought,' said Bob, sucking his teeth meditatively.

Presently Agustine returned, carrying a long, straight sapling with a fork at one end. On to this forked end I fastened a slip knot with some fine cord which, the manufacturers had assured me, would stand a strain of three hundredweight. Then I unravelled fifty feet or so of the cord, and handed the rest of the coil to Agustine.

'Now I go for inside, I go try put dis rope for 'e neck, eh? If I go catch 'e neck, I go holla, and then all dis hunter man go pull one time. You hear?'

'I hear, sah.'

'Now if I shout pull,' I said, as I lowered myself delicately into the carpet of ash, 'for Heaven's sake don't let them pull too hard.... I don't want the damn thing pulled on top of me.'

I wriggled slowly up the cave, carrying the sapling and cord with me, the torch in my mouth. The python hissed with undiminished ferocity. Then came the delicate job of trying to push the sapling ahead of me so that I could get the dangling noose over the snake's head. I found this impossible with the torch in my mouth, for at the slightest movement the beam swept everywhere but on to the point required. I put the torch on the ground, propped it up on some rocks with the beam playing on the snake and then, with infinite care, I edged the sapling up the cave towards the reptile. The python had, of course, coiled itself into a tight knot, with the head lying in the centre of the coils, so when I had got the sapling into position I had to force the snake to show its head. The only way of doing this was to prod the creature vigorously with the end of the sapling.

After the first prod the shining coils seemed to swell with rage, and there came echoing down the cave a hiss so shrill and so charged with malignancy that I almost dropped the sapling. Grasping the wood more firmly in my sweaty hand I prodded again, and was treated to another shrill exhalation of breath. Five times I prodded before my efforts were rewarded. The python's head appeared suddenly over the top of the coils, and swept towards the end of the sapling, the mouth wide open and gleaming pinkly in the torchlight. But the movement was so sudden that I had no chance to get the noose over its head. The snake struck three times, and each time I made ineffectual attempts to noose it. My chief difficulty was that I could not get close enough; I was working at the full stretch of my arm, and this, combined with the weight of the sapling, made my movements very clumsy. At last, dripping with sweat, my arms aching, I crawled out into the sunlight.

'It's no good,' I said to Bob. 'It keeps its head buried in its coils and only pops it out to strike... you don't get a real chance to noose it.'

'Let me have a go,' he said eagerly.

He seized the sapling and crawled into the cave. There was a long pause during which we could only see his large feet scrabbling and scraping for a foothold in the cave entrance. Presently he reappeared, cursing fluently.

'It's no good,' he said. 'We'll never get it with this.'

'If they get us a forked stick like a shepherd's crook do you think you could get hold of a coil and pull it out?' I inquired.

'I think so,' said Bob, 'or at any rate I could probably make it uncoil so we can get a chance at the head.'

So Agustine was once more despatched to the forest with minute instructions as to the sort of stick we needed, and he soon returned with a twenty-foot branch at one end of which was a fish-hook-like projection.

'If you could crawl in with me and shine the torch over my shoulder, it would help,' said Bob. 'If I put it on the ground, I knock it over every time I move.'

So we crawled into the cave together and lay there, wedged shoulder to shoulder. While I shone the torch down the tunnel, Bob slowly edged his gigantic crook towards the snake. Slowly, so as not to disturb the snake unnecessarily, he edged the hook over the top coil of the mound, settled it in place, shuffled his body into a more comfortable position and then hauled with all his strength.

The results were immediate and confusing. To our surprise the entire bulk of the snake – after a momentary resistance – slid down the cave towards us. Exhilarated, Bob shuffled backwards (thus wedging us both more tightly in the tunnel) and hauled again. The snake slid still nearer and then started to unravel. Bob hauled again, and the snake uncoiled still farther; its head and neck appeared out of the tangle and struck at us. Wedged like a couple of outsize sardines in an undersized can we had no room to move except backwards, and so we slid backwards on our stomachs as rapidly as we could. At last, to our relief, we reached a slight widening in the passage, and this allowed us more room to manoeuvre. Bob laid hold of the sapling and pulled at it grimly. He reminded me of a lanky and earnest blackbird tugging an outsize worm from its hole. The snake slid into view, hissing madly, its coils shuddering with muscular contraction as it tried to free itself of the hook round its body. Another good heave, I calculated, and Bob would have it at the mouth of the cave. I crawled out rapidly.

'Bring dat rope,' I roared to the hunters, 'quick . . . quick . . . rope.'

They leapt to obey as Bob appeared at the cave mouth, scrambled to his feet and stepped back for the final jerk that would drag the snake out into the open where we could fall on it. But, as he stepped back, he put his foot on a loose rock which twisted under him, and he fell flat on his back. The sapling was jerked from his hands, the snake gave a mighty heave that freed its body from the hook, and, with the smooth fluidity of water soaking into blotting paper it slid into a crack in the cave wall that did not look as though it could accommodate a mouse. As the last four feet of its length were disappearing into the bowels of the earth, Bob and I fell on it and hung on like grim death. We would feel the rippling of the powerful muscles as the snake, buried deep in the rocky cleft, struggled to break our grip on its tail. Slowly, inch by inch, the smooth scales slipped through our sweaty hands, and then, suddenly, the snake was gone. From somewhere deep in the rocks came a triumphant hiss.

Covered with ash and charcoal smears, our arms and legs scraped raw, our clothes black with sweat, Bob and I sat and glared at each other, panting for breath. We were past speech.

'Ah, 'e done run, Masa,' pointed out Agustine, who seemed to have a genius for underlining the obvious.

'Dat snake 'e get power too much,' observed Gargantua moodily.

'No man fit hold dat snake for inside hole,' said Agustine, attempting to comfort us.

' 'E get plenty, plenty power,' intoned Gargantua again, ' 'e get power pass man.'

In silence I handed round the cigarettes and we squatted in the carpet of ash and smoked.

'Well,' I said at last, philosophically, 'we did the best we could. Let's hope for better luck next time.'

Bob, however, refused to be comforted. To have had the python of his dreams so close to capture and then to lose it was almost more than he could bear. He prowled around, muttering savagely to himself, as we packed up the nets and ropes, and then followed us moodily as we set off homewards.

The sun was now low in the sky, and by the time we had crossed the grassfield and entered the abandoned farmland a greenish twilight had settled on the world. Everywhere in the moist undergrowth giant glow-worms gleamed and shuddered like sapphires, and through the warm air fireflies drifted, pulsating briefly like pink pearls against the dark undergrowth. The air was full of the evening scents, wood smoke, damp earth, the sweet smell of blossom already wet with dew. An owl called in an ancient, trembling voice, and another answered it.

The river was like a moving sheet of bronze in the twilight as we scrunched our way across the milk-white sandbank. The old man and the boy were curled up asleep in the bows of the canoe. They awoke, and in silence paddled us down the dark river. On the hill top, high above us, we could see the lamps of the house shining out, and faintly, as a background to the swish and gurgle of our paddles, we could hear the gramophone playing. A drift of small white moths enveloped the canoe as it headed towards the bank. The moon, very fragile and weak, was edging its way up through the filigree of the forest behind us, and once more the owls called, sadly, longingly, in the gloom of the trees.

Chapter Two

The Bald-Headed Birds

MAIL BY HAND

To: Mr G. Durrell,
The Zoological Department,
U.A.C. House,
Mamfe.

Dear Sir,
Here are two animals I am senting you like those animals that you

should me in the pictures. Any tipe of money you want to sent to me try and rapp the money in a small piece of paper and sent it to that boy that brought animals. You know realy that a hunter always be derty so you should try to send me one bar soap.

Good greetings to you.

Yrs.,
Peter N'amabong.

On the opposite bank of the Cross River, eight miles through the deep forest, lay the tiny village of Eshobi. I knew both the place and its inhabitants well, for on a previous trip I had made it one of my bases for a number of months. It had been a good hunting-ground, and the Eshobi people had been good hunters, so, while we were in Mamfe, I was anxious to get in touch with the villagers and see if they could get us some specimens. As the best way of obtaining information or sending messages was via the local market, I sent for Phillip, our cook. He was an engaging character, with a wide, buck-toothed smile, and a habit of walking with a stiff military gait, and standing at attention when addressed; this argued an army training, which, in fact, he had not had. He clumped up on to the verandah and stood before me as rigid as a guardsman.

'Phillip, I want to find an Eshobi man, you hear?' I said.

'Yes, sah.'

'Now,when you go for market you go find me one Eshobi man and you go bring him for here and I go give him book for take Eshobi, eh?'

'Yes, sah.'

'Now, you no go forget, eh? You go find me Eshobi man one time.'

'Yes, sah,' said Phillip, and clumped off to the kitchen. He never wasted time on unnecessary conversation.

Two days passed without an Eshobi man putting in an appearance, and, occupied with other things, I forgot the whole matter. Then, on the fourth day, Phillip appeared, clumping down the drive triumphantly with a rather frightened looking fourteen-year-old boy in tow. The lad had obviously clad himself in his best clothes for his visit to the Metropolis of Mamfe, a fetching outfit that consisted of a tattered pair of khaki shorts, and a grubby white shirt which had obviously been made out of a sack of some sort and had across its back the mysterious but decorative message 'PRODUCE OF GR' in blue lettering. On his head was perched a straw hat which, with age and wear, had attained a pleasant shade of pale silvery green. This reluctant apparition was dragged up on to the front verandah, and his captor stood smugly to attention with the air of one who has, after much practice, accomplished a particularly difficult conjuring trick. Phillip had a curious way of speaking which had taken me some time to understand, for he spoke pidgin very fast and in a sort of muted roar, a cross between a bassoon and a regimental sergeant-major, as though everyone in the world was deaf. When labouring under excitement he became almost incomprehensible.

'Who is this?' I asked, surveying the youth.

Phillip looked rather hurt. 'Dis na man, sah,' he roared, as if explaining something to a particularly dim-witted child. He gazed at his protégé with affection and gave the unfortunate lad a slap on the back that almost knocked him off the verandah.

'I can see it's a man,' I said patiently, 'but what does he want?'

Phillip frowned ferociously at the quivering youth and gave him another blow between the shoulder blades.

'Speak now,' he blared, 'speak now, Masa de wait.'

We waited expectantly. The youth shuffled his feet, twiddled his toes in an excess of embarrassment, gave a shy, watery smile and stared at the ground. We waited patiently. Suddenly he looked up, removed his headgear, ducked his head and said: 'Good morning, sah,' in a faint voice.

Phillip beamed at me as if this greeting were sufficient explanation for the lad's presence. Deciding that my cook had not been designed by nature to play the part of a skilled and tactful interrogator, I took over myself.

'My friend,' I said, 'how dey de call you?'

'Peter, sah,' he replied miserably.

'Dey de call um Peter, sah,' bellowed Phillip, in case I should have been under any misapprehension.

'Well, Peter, why you come for see me?' I inquired.

'Masa, dis man your cook 'e tell me Masa want some man for carry book to Eshobi,' said the youth aggrievedly.

'Ah! You be Eshobi man?' I asked, light dawning.

'Yes, sah.'

'Phillip,' I said, 'you are a congenital idiot.'

'Yes, sah,' agreed Phillip, pleased with this unsolicited testimonial.

'Why you never tell me dis be Eshobi man?'

'Wah!' gasped Phillip, shocked to the depths of his sergeant-major's soul, 'but I done tell Masa dis be man.'

Giving Phillip up as a bad job I turned back to the youth.

'Listen, my friend, you savvay for Eshobi one man dey de call Elias?'

'Yes, sah, I savvay um.'

'All right. Now you go tell Elias dat I done come for Cameroon again for catch beef, eh? You go tell um I want um work hunter man again for me, eh? So you go tell um he go come for Mamfe for talk with me. You go tell um, say, dis Masa 'e live for U.A.C. Masa's house, you hear?'

'I hear, sah.'

'Right, so you go walk quick-quick to Eshobi and tell Elias, eh? I go dash you dis cigarette so you get happy when you walk for bush.'

He received the packet of cigarettes in his cupped hands, ducked his head and beamed at me.

'Tank you, Masa,' he said.

'All right . . . go for Eshobi now. Walka good.'

'Tank you, Masa,' he repeated, and stuffing the packet into the pocket of his unorthodox shirt he trotted off down the drive.

Twenty-four hours later Elias arrived. He had been one of my permanent hunters when I had been in Eshobi, so I was delighted to see his fat, waddling form coming down the drive towards me, his Pithecanthropic features split into a wide grin of glad recognition. Our greetings over, he solemnly handed me a dozen eggs carefully wrapped in banana leaves, and I reciprocated with a carton of cigarettes and a hunting knife I had brought out from

England for that purpose. Then we got down to the serious business of talking about beef. First he told me about all the beef he had hunted and captured in my eight years' absence, and how my various hunter friends had got on. Old N'ago had been killed by a bush-cow; Andraia had been bitten in the foot by a water beef; Samuel's gun had exploded and blown a large portion of his arm away (a good joke, this), while just recently John had killed the biggest bush-pig they had ever seen, and sold the meat for over two pounds. Then, quite suddenly, Elias said something that riveted my attention.

'Masa remember dat bird Masa like too much?' he inquired in his husky voice.

'Which bird, Elias?'

'Dat bird 'e no get bere-bere for 'e head. Last time Masa live for Mamfe I done bring um two picken dis bird.'

'Dat bird who make his house with potta-potta? Dat one who get red for his head?' I asked excitedly.

'Yes, na dis one,' he agreed.

'Well, what about it?' I said.

'When I hear Masa done come back for Cameroons I done go for bush for look dis bird,' Elias explained. 'I remember dat Masa 'e like dis bird *too much*. I look um, look um for bush for two, three days.'

He paused and looked at me, his eyes twinkling.

'Well?'

'I done find um, Masa,' he said, grinning from ear to ear.

'You find um?' I could scarcely believe my luck. 'Which side 'e dere ... which side 'e live ... how many you see ... what kind of place...?'

' 'E dere dere,' Elias went on, interrupting my flow of feverish questions, 'for some place 'e get big big rock. 'E live for up hill, sah. 'E get 'e house for some big rock.'

'How many house you see?'

'I see three, sah. But 'e never finish one house, sah.'

'What's all the excitement about?' inquired Jacquie, who had just come out on to the verandah.

'*Picathartes*,' I said succinctly, and to her credit she knew exactly what I was talking about.

Picathartes was a bird that, until a few years ago, was known only from a few museum skins, and had been observed in the wild state by perhaps two Europeans. Cecil Webb, then the London Zoo's official collector, managed to catch and bring back alive the first specimen of this extraordinary bird. Six months later, when in the Cameroons, I had two adult specimens brought in to me, but these had unfortunately died on the voyage home of aspergillosis, a particularly virulent lung disease. Now Elias had found a nesting colony of them and it seemed we might, with luck, be able to get some fledglings and hand-rear them.

'Dis bird, 'e get picken for inside 'e house?' I asked Elias.

'Sometime 'e get, sah,' he said doubtfully. 'I never look for inside de house. I fear sometime de bird go run.'

'Well,' I said, turning to Jacquie, 'there's only one thing to do, and that's to go to Eshobi and have a look. You and Sophie hang on here and look after the collection; I'll take Bob and spend a couple of days there after *Picathartes*. Even if they haven't got any young I would like to see the thing in its wild state.'

'All right. When will you go?' asked Jacquie.

'Tomorrow, if I can arrange carriers. Give Bob a shout and tell him we're really going into the forest at last. Tell him to sort out his snake-catching equipment.'

Early the next morning, when the air was still comparatively cool, eight Africans appeared outside John Henderson's house, and, after the usual bickering as to who should carry what, they loaded our bundles of equipment on to their woolly heads and we set off for Eshobi. Having crossed the river, our little cavalcade made its way across the grassfield, where our abortive python hunt occurred, and on the opposite side we plunged into the mysterious forest. The Eshobi path lay twisting and turning through the trees in a series of intricate convolutions that would have horrified a Roman road-builder. Sometimes it doubled back on itself to avoid a huge rock, or a fallen tree, and at other times it ran as straight as a rod through all such obstacles, so that our carriers were forced to stop and form a human chain to lift the loads over a tree trunk, or lower them down a small cliff.

I had warned Bob that we would see little, if any, wild life on the way, but this did not prevent him from attacking every rotten tree trunk we passed, in the hopes of unearthing some rare beast from inside it. I am so tired of hearing and reading about the dangerous and evil tropical forest, teeming with wild beasts. In the first place it is about as dangerous as the New Forest in midsummer, and in the second place it does not teem with wild life; every bush is *not* aquiver with some savage creature waiting to pounce. The animals are there, of course, but they very sensibly keep out of your way. I defy anyone to walk through the forest to Eshobi, and, at the end of it, be able to count on the fingers of both hands the 'wild beasts' he has seen. How I wish these descriptions were true. How I wish that every bush did contain some 'savage denizen of the forest' lurking in ambush. A collector's job would be so much easier.

The only wild creatures at all common along the Eshobi path were butterflies and these, obviously not having read the right books, showed a strong disinclination to attack us. Whenever the path dipped into a small valley, a tiny stream would lie at the bottom, and on the damp, shady banks alongside the clear waters the butterflies would be sitting in groups, their wings opening and closing slowly, so that from a distance areas of the stream banks took on an opalescent quality, changing from flame red to white, from sky blue to mauve and purple, as the insects – in a sort of trance – seemed to be applauding the cool shade with their wings. The brown, muscular legs of the carriers would tramp through them unseeingly, and suddenly we would be waist-high in a swirling merry-go-round of colour as the butterflies dipped and wheeled around us and then, when we had passed, settled again on the dark soil which was as rich and moist as a fruit cake, and just as fragrant.

One vast and ancient tree marked the half-way point on the Eshobi road, a tree so tangled in a web of lianas as to be almost invisible. This was a resting place, and the carriers, grunting and exhaling their breath sharply through their front teeth in a sort of exhausted whistle, lowered their loads to the ground and squatted beside them, the sweat glistening on their bodies. I handed round cigarettes and we sat and enjoyed them quietly: in the dim, cathedral-like gloom of the forest there was no breeze, and the smoke rose in straight, swaying blue columns into the air. The only sounds were the incessant, circular-saw songs of the great green cicadas clinging to every tree, and, in the distance, the drunken honking of a flock of hornbills.

As we smoked we watched some of the little brown forest skinks hunting among the roots of the trees around us. These little lizards always looked neat and shining, as though they had been cast in chocolate and had just that second stepped out of the mould, gleaming and immaculate. They moved slowly and deliberately, as if they were afraid of getting their beautiful skins dirty. They peered from side to side with bright eyes as they slid through their world of brown, dead leaves, forests of tiny toadstools and lawns of moss that padded the stones like a carpet. Their prey was the immense population of tiny creatures that inhabited the forest floor, the small black beetles hurrying along like undertakers late for a funeral, the slow, smooth-sliding slugs, weaving a silver filigree of slime over the leaves, and the small, nut-brown crickets who squatted in the shadows waving their immensely long antennae to and fro, like amateur fishermen on the banks of a stream.

Among the dark, damp hollows between the buttress roots of the great tree under which we sat there were small clusters of an insect which had never failed to fascinate me. They looked like a small daddy-longlegs in repose, but with opaque, misty-white wings. They sat there in groups of about ten, trembling their wings gently, and moving their fragile legs up and down, like restive horses. When disturbed they all took to the air and started a combined operation which was quite extraordinary to watch. They rose about eight inches above the ground, formed a circle in an area that could be covered by a saucer and then began to fly round and round very rapidly, some going up and over, as it were, while the others swept round and round like a wheel. The effect from a distance was rather weird, for they resembled a whirling ball of shimmering misty white, changing its shape slightly at intervals, but always maintaining exactly the same position in the air. They flew so fast, and their bodies were so slender, that all you could see was this shimmer of frosty wings. I am afraid that this aerial display intrigued me so much that I used to go out of my way, when walking in the forest, to find groups of these insects and disturb them so that they would dance for me.

Eventually, we reached Eshobi at mid-day, and I found it had changed little from the days when I had been there eight years before. There was still the same straggle of dusty thatched huts in two uneven rows, with a wide area of dusty path lying between them that served as the village high street, a playground for children and dogs and a scratching ground for the scrawny fowls. Elias came waddling down this path to greet us, picking his way carefully through the sprawling mass of babies and livestock, followed by a small boy carrying two large green coconuts on his head.

'Welcome, Masa, you done come?' he called huskily.

'Iseeya, Elias,' I replied.

He grinned at us delightedly, as the carriers, still grunting and whistling, deposited our equipment all over the village street.

'Masa go drink dis coconut?' Elias asked hopefully, waving his machete about.

'Yes, we like um too much,' I said, regarding the huge nuts thirstily.

Elias bustled into activity. From the nearest hut were brought two dilapidated chairs, and Bob and I were seated in a small patch of shade in the centre of the village street, surrounded by a crowd of politely silent but deeply fascinated Eshobites. With quick, accurate strokes of his machete Elias stripped away the thick husk from the coconut. When the tips of the nuts were exposed he gave each of them a swift slice with the end of his machete-blade, and then handed them to us, each neatly trepanned so that we could drink the cool, sweet juice inside. In each nut there was about two and half glassfuls of this thirst-quenching, hygienically-sealed nectar, and we savoured every mouthful.

After the rest, our next job was to get the camp in order. Two hundred yards from the village there was a small stream, and on its banks we chose an area that would not be too difficult to clear. A group of men armed with machetes set to work to cut down all the small bushes and saplings, while another group followed behind with short-handled, broad-bladed hoes, in an effort to level the red earth. At length, after the usual African uproar of insults, accusations of stupidity, sit-down strikes and minor brawls, the area had been worked over so that it resembled a badly ploughed field, and we could get the tents up. While a meal was being prepared we went down to the stream and washed the dirt and sweat from our bodies in the icy waters, watching the pink-and-brown crabs waving their pincers to us from among the rocks, and feeling the tiny, brilliant blue-and-red fish nibbling gently at our feet. We wended our way back to camp, feeling refreshed, and found some sort of organization reigning. When we had eaten, Elias came and squatted in the shade of our lean-to tent, and we discussed hunting plans.

'What time we go look dis bird, Elias?'

'Eh, Masa savvay now 'e be hot too much. For dis time dis bird 'e go look for chop for bush. For evening time when it get cold 'e go for dis 'e house for work, and den we go see um.'

'All right, then you go come back for four o'clock time, you hear? Then we go look dis bird, eh?'

'Yes, sah,' said Elias, rising to his feet.

'And if you no speak true, if we never see dis bird, if you've been funning me I go shoot you, bushman, you hear?'

'Eh!' he exclaimed, chuckling, 'I never fun with Masa, for true, sah.'

'All right, we go see you, eh?'

'Yes, sah,' he said, as he twisted his sarong round his ample hips and padded off towards the village.

At four o'clock the sun had dipped behind the tallest of the forest trees, and the air had the warm, drowsy stillness of evening, Elias returned, wearing, in place of his gaudy sarong, a scrap of dirty cloth twisted round his loins. He waved his machete nonchalantly.

'I done come, Masa,' he proclaimed. 'Masa ready?'

'Yes,' I said, shouldering my field-glasses and collecting-bag. 'Let's go, hunter man.'

Elias led us down the dusty main street of the village, and then branched off abruptly down a narrow alley-way between the huts. This led us into a small patch of farmland, full of feathery cassava bushes and dusty banana plants. Presently, the path dipped across a small stream and then wound its way into the forest. Before we had left the village street Elias had pointed out a hill to me which he said was the home of *Picathartes*, and although it had looked near enough to the village, I knew better than to believe it. The Cameroon forest is like the Looking-glass Garden. Your objective seems to loom over you, but as you walk towards it, it appears to shift position. At times, like Alice, you are forced to walk in the opposite direction in order to get there.

And so it was with this hill. The path, instead of making straight for it, seemed to weave to and fro through the forest in the most haphazard fashion, until I began to feel I must have been looking at the wrong hill when Elias had pointed it out to me. At that moment, however, the path started to climb in a determined manner, and it was obvious that we had reached the base of the hill. Elias left the path and plunged into the undergrowth on one side, hacking his way through the overhanging lianas and thornbushes with his machete, hissing softly through his teeth, his feet spreading out in the soft leaf mould without a sound. In a very short time we were plodding up a slope so steep that, on occasions, Elias' feet were on a level with my eyes.

Most hills and mountains in the Cameroons are of a curious and exhausting construction. Created by ancient volcanic eruption, they had been pushed skywards viciously by the massive underground forces, and this has formed them in a peculiar way. They are curiously geometrical, some perfect isosceles triangles, some acute angles, some cones and some box-shaped. They reared up in such a bewildering variety of shapes that it would have been no surprise to see a cluster of them demonstrating one of the more spiky and incomprehensible of Euclid's theorems.

The hill whose sides we were now assaulting reared up in an almost perfect cone. After you had been climbing for a bit you began to gain the impression that it was much steeper than it had first appeared, and within a quarter of an hour you were convinced that the surface sloped at the rate of one in one. Elias went up it as though it were a level macadam road, ducking and weaving skilfully between the branches and overhanging undergrowth, while Bob and I, sweating and panting, struggled along behind, sometimes on all fours, in an effort to keep pace with him. Then, to our relief, just below the crest of the hill, the ground flattened out into a wide ledge, and through the tangle of trees we could see, ahead of us, a fifty-foot cliff of granite, patched with ferns and begonias, with a tumbled mass of giant, water-smoothed boulders at its base.

'Dis na de place, Masa,' said Elias, stopping and lowering his fat bottom on to a rock.

'Good,' said Bob and I in unison, and sat down to regain our breath.

When we had rested, Elias led us along through the maze of boulders to a place where the cliff face sloped outwards, overhanging the rocks below.

We moved some little way along under this overhang, and then Elias stopped suddenly.

'Dere de house, Masa,' he said, his fine teeth gleaming in a grin of pride. He was pointing up at the rock face, and I saw, ten feet above us, the nest of a *Picathartes*.

At first glance it resembled a huge swallow's nest, made out of reddish-brown mud and tiny rootlets. At the base of the nest longer roots and grass stalks had been woven into the earth so that they hung down in a sort of beard; whether this was just untidy workmanship on the part of the bird, or whether it was done for reasons of camouflage, was difficult to judge. Certainly the trailing beard of roots and grass did disguise the nest, for, at first sight, it resembled nothing more than a tussock of grass and mud that had become attached to the gnarled, water-ribbed surface of the cliff. The whole nest was about the size of a football and this position under the overhang of the cliff nicely protected it from any rain.

Our first task was to discover if the nest contained anything. Luckily a tall, slender sapling was growing opposite, so we shinned up this in turn and peered into the inside of the nest. To our annoyance it was empty, though ready to receive eggs, for it had been lined with fine roots woven into a springy mat. We moved a little way along the cliff and soon came upon two more nests, one complete like the first one, and one half finished. But there was no sign of young or eggs.

'If we go hide, small time dat bird go come, sah,' said Elias.

'Are you sure?' I asked doubtfully.

'Yes, sah, for true, sah.'

'All right, we'll wait small time.'

Elias took us to a place where a cave had been scooped out of the cliff, its mouth almost blocked by an enormous boulder, and we crouched down behind this natural screen. We had a clear view of the cliff-face where the nests hung, while we ourselves were in shadow and almost hidden by the wall of stone in front of us. We settled down to wait.

The forest was getting gloomy now, for the sun was well down. The sky through the tangle of leaves and lianas above our heads was green flecked with gold, like the flanks of an enormous dragon seen between the trees. Now the very special evening noises had started. In the distance we could hear the rhythmic crash of a troupe of mona monkeys on their way to bed, leaping from tree to tree, with a sound like great surf on a rocky shore, punctuated by occasional cries of 'Oink . . . Oink . . .' from some member of the troupe. They passed somewhere below us along the base of the hill, but the undergrowth was too thick for us to see them. Following them came the usual retinue of hornbills, their wings making fantastically loud whooping noises as they flew from tree to tree. Two of them crashed into the branches above us and sat there silhouetted against the green sky, carrying on a long and complicated conversation, ducking and swaying their heads, great beaks gaping, whining and honking hysterically at each other. Their fantastic heads, with the great beaks and sausage-shaped casques lying on top, bobbing and mowing against the sky, looked like some weird devil-masks from a Ceylonese dance.

The perpetual insect orchestra had increased a thousandfold with the approach of darkness, and the valley below us seemed to vibrate with their song. Somewhere a tree-frog started up, a long, trilling note, followed by a pause, as though he were boring a hole through a tree with a miniature pneumatic drill, and had to pause now and then to let it cool. Suddenly I heard a new noise. It was a sound I had never heard before and I glanced inquiringly at Elias. He had stiffened, and was peering into the gloomy net of lianas and leaves around us.

'Na whatee dat?' I whispered.

'Na de bird, sah.'

The first cry had been quite far down the hill, but now came another cry, much closer. It was a curious noise which can only be described, rather inadequately, as similar to the sudden sharp yap of a pekinese, but much more flute-like and plaintive. Again it came, and again, but we still could not see the bird, though we strained our eyes in the gloom.

'D'you think it's *Picathartes*?' whispered Bob.

'I don't know. . . . It's a noise I haven't heard before.'

There was a pause, and then suddenly the cry was repeated, very near now, and we lay motionless behind our rock. Not far in front of our position grew a thirty-foot sapling, bent under the weight of a liana as thick as a bell-rope that hung in loops around it, its main stem hidden in the foliage of some nearby tree. While the rest of the area we could see was gloomy and ill-defined, this sapling, lovingly entwined by its killer liana, was lit by the last rays of the setting sun, so that the whole setting was rather like a meticulous backcloth. And, as though a curtain had gone up on this miniature stage, a real live *Picathartes* suddenly appeared before us.

I say suddenly and I mean it. Animals and birds in a tropical forest generally approach so quietly that they appear before you suddenly, unexpectedly, as if dropped there by magic. The thick liana fell in a huge loop from the top of the sapling, and on this loop the bird materialized, swaying gently on its perch, its head cocked on one side as if listening. Seeing any wild animal in its natural surroundings is a thrill, but to watch something that you know is a great rarity, something that you know has only been seen by a handful of people before you, gives the whole thing an added excitement and spice. So Bob and I lay there staring at the bird with the ardent, avid expressions of a couple of philatelists who have just discovered a penny black in a child's stamp album.

The *Picathartes* was about the size of a jackdaw, but its body had the plump, sleek lines of a blackbird. Its legs were long and powerful, and its eyes large and obviously keen. The breast was a delicate creamy-buff and the back and long tail a beautiful slate grey, pale and powdery-looking. The edge of the wing was black and this acted as a dividing-line that showed up wonderfully the breast and back colours. But it was the bird's head that caught the attention and held it. It was completely bare of feathers: the forehead and top of the head were a vivid sky blue, the back a bright rose-madder pink, while the sides of the head and the cheeks were black. Normally a bald-headed bird looks rather revolting, as if it were suffering from some unpleasant and incurable disease, but *Picathartes* looked splendid with its tricoloured head, as if wearing a crown.

After the bird had perched on the liana for a minute or so it flew down on to the ground, and proceeded to work its way to and fro among the rocks in a series of prodigious leaps, quite extraordinary to watch. They were not ordinary bird-like hops, for *Picathartes* was projected into the air as if those powerful legs were springs. It disappeared from view among the rocks, and we heard it call. It was answered almost at once from the top of the cliff, and looking up we could see another *Picathartes* on a branch above us, peering down at the nests on the cliff face. Suddenly it spiralled downwards and alighted on the edge of one of the nests, paused a moment to look about, and then leaned forward to tidy up a hair-like rootlet that had become disarranged. Then the bird leaped into the air – there was no other way to describe it – and swooped down the hill into the gloomy forest. The other emerged from among the rocks and flew after it, and in a short time we heard them calling to each other plaintively among the trees.

'Ah,' said Elias, rising and stretching himself, ' 'e done go.'

' 'E no go come back?' I asked, pummelling my leg, which had gone to sleep.

'No, sah. 'E done go for inside bush, for some big stick where 'e go sleep. Tomorrow 'e go come back for work dis 'e house.'

'Well, we might as well go back to Eshobi then.'

Our progress down the hill was a much speedier affair than our ascent. It was now so dark under the canopy of trees that we frequently missed our footing and slid for considerable distances on our backsides, clutching desperately at trees and roots as we passed in an effort to slow down. Eventually we emerged in the Eshobi high street bruised, scratched and covered with leaf-mould. I was filled with elation at having seen a live *Picathartes*, but, at the same time, depressed by the thought that we could not hope to get any of the youngsters. It was obviously useless hanging around in Eshobi, so I decided we would set off again for Mamfe the next day, and try to do a little collecting as we passed through the forest. One of the most successful ways of collecting animals in the Cameroons is to smoke out hollow trees, and on our way to Eshobi I had noticed several huge trees with hollow insides, which I thought might well repay investigation.

Early the next morning we packed up our equipment, and sent the carriers off with it. Then, accompanied by Elias and three other Eshobi hunters, Bob and I followed at a more leisurely pace.

The first tree was three miles into the forest, lying fairly close to the edge of the Eshobi road. It was a hundred and fifty feet high, and the greater part of its trunk was as hollow as a drum. There is quite an art to smoking out a hollow tree. It is a prolonged and sometimes complicated process. Before going to all the trouble of smoking a tree the first thing to do, if possible, is to ascertain whether or not there is anything inside worth smoking out. If the tree has a large hole at the base of the trunk, as most of them do, this is a relatively simple matter. You simply stick your head inside and get somebody to beat the trunk with a stick. If there are any animals inside you will hear them moving about uneasily after the reverberations have died away, and even if you can't hear them you can be assured of their presence by the shower of powdery rotten wood that will come cascading down the trunk. Having discovered that there is something inside the tree the next job is to scan the top part of the trunk with fieldglasses and try and spot all exit holes, which then have to be covered with nets. When this has been done, a man is stationed up the tree to retrieve any creature that gets caught up there, the holes at the base of the trunk are stopped. You then light a fire, and this is the really tricky part of the operation, for the inside of these trees is generally dry and tinder-like, and if you are not careful you can set the whole thing ablaze. So first of all you kindle a small bright blaze with dry twigs, moss and leaves, and when this is well alight you carefully cover it with ever-increasing quantities of green leaves, so that the fire no longer blazes but sends up a sullen column of pungent smoke, which is sucked up the hollow barrel of the tree exactly as if it were a chimney. After this anything can happen and generally does, for these hollow trees often contain a weird variety of inhabitants, ranging from spitting cobras to civet cats, from bats to giant snails; half the charm and excitement of smoking out a tree is that you are never quite sure what is going to appear next.

The first tree we smoked was not a wild success. All we got was a handful of leaf-nosed bats with extraordinary gargoyle-like faces, three giant millipedes that looked like Frankfurter sausages with a fringe of legs underneath and a small grey dormouse which bit one of the hunters in the thumb and escaped. So we removed the nets, put out the fire and proceeded on our way. The next hollow tree was considerably taller and of tremendous girth. At its base was an enormous split in the trunk shaped like a church door, and four of us could stand comfortably in the gloomy interior of the trunk. Peering up the hollow barrel of the trunk and beating on the wood with a machete we were rewarded by vague scuffling noises from above, and a shower of powdery rotten wood fell on our upturned faces and into our eyes. Obviously the tree contained something. Our chief problem was to get a hunter to the top of the tree to cover the exit holes, for the trunk swept up about a hundred and twenty feet into the sky as smooth as a walking-stick. Eventually, we joined all three of our rope-ladders together, and tied a strong, light rope to one end. Then, weighting the rope end, we hurled it up into the forest canopy until our arms ached, until at last it fell over a branch and we could haul the ladders up into the sky and secure them. So, when the nets were fixed in position at the top and bottom of the tree, we lit the fire at the base of the trunk and stood back to await results.

Generally one had to wait four or five minutes for the smoke to percolate to every part of the tree before one got any response, but in this particular case the results were almost immediate. The first beasts to appear were those nauseating-looking creatures called whip-scorpions. They cover, with their long angular legs, the area of a soup plate, and they look like a nightmare spider that has been run over by a steamroller and reduced to a paper-like thickness. This enables them to slide in and out of crevices that would allow access to no other beast, in a most unnerving manner. Apart from this they could glide about over the surface of the wood as though it were ice, and at a speed that was quite incredible. It was this speedy and silent movement, combined with such a forest of legs, that made them so repulsive, and made one instinctively shy away from them, even though one knew they were harmless. So, when the first one appeared magically out of a crack and scuttled over my bare arm as I leant against the tree, it produced an extraordinary demoralizing effect, to say the least.

I had only just recovered from this when all the other inhabitants of the tree started to vacate in a body. Five fat grey bats flapped out into the nets, where they hung chittering madly and screwing up their faces in rage. They were quickly joined by two green forest squirrels with pale fawn rings round their eyes, who uttered shrill grunts of rage as they rolled about in the meshes of the nets while we tried to disentangle them without getting bitten. They were followed by six grey dormice, two large greeny rats with orange noses and behinds, and a slender green tree-snake with enormous eyes, who slid calmly through the meshes of the nets with a slightly affronted air, and disappeared into the undergrowth before anyone could do anything sensible about catching him. The noise and confusion was incredible: Africans danced about through the billowing smoke, shouting instructions of which nobody took the slightest notice, getting bitten with shrill yells of agony, stepping on each other's feet, wielding machetes and sticks with gay abandon and complete disregard for safety. The man posted in the top of the tree was having fun on his own, and was shouting and yelling and leaping about in the branches with such vigour that I expected to see him crash to the forest floor at any moment. Our eyes streamed, our lungs were filled with smoke, but the collecting bags filled up with a wiggling, jumping cargo of creatures.

Eventually the last of the tree's inhabitants had appeared, the smoke had died down and we could pause for a cigarette and to examine each other's honourable wounds. As we were doing this the man at the top of the tree lowered down two collecting bags on the end of long strings, before preparing to return to earth himself. I took the bags gingerly, not knowing what the contents were, and inquired of the stalwart at the top of the tree how he had fared.

'What you get for dis bag?' I inquired.

'Beef, Masa,' he replied intelligently.

'I know it's beef, bushman, but what kind of beef you get?'

'Eh! I no savvay how Masa call um. 'E so so rat, but 'e get wing. Dere be one beef for inside 'e get eye big big like man, sah.'

I was suddenly filled with an inner excitement.

' 'E get hand like rat or like monkey?' I shouted.

'Like monkey, sah.'

'What is it?' asked Bob with interest, as I fumbled with the string round the neck of the bags.

'I'm not sure, but I think it's a bushbaby ... if it is it can only be one of two kinds, and both of them are rare.'

I got the string off the neck of the bag after what seemed an interminable struggle, and cautiously opened it. Regarding me from inside it was a small, neat grey face with huge ears folded back like fans against the side of the head, and two enormous golden eyes, that looked at me with the horror-stricken expression of an elderly spinster who had discovered a man in the bathroom cupboard. The creature had large, human-looking hands, with long, slender bony fingers. Each of these, except the forefinger, was tipped with a small, flat nail that looked as though it had been delicately manicured, while the forefinger possessed a curved claw that looked thoroughly out of place on such a human hand.

'What is it?' asked Bob in hushed tones, seeing that I was gazing at the creature with an expression of bliss on my face.

'This,' I said ecstatically, 'is a beast I have tried to get every time I've been to the Cameroons. *Euoticus elegantulus*, or better known as a needle-clawed lemur or bushbaby. They're extremely rare, and if we succeed in getting this one back to England it will be the first ever to be brought back to Europe.'

'Gosh,' said Bob, suitably impressed.

I showed the little beast to Elias.

'You savvay dis beef, Elias?'

'Yes, sah, I savvay um.'

'Dis kind of beef I want *too much*. If you go get me more I go pay you one one pound. You hear.'

'I hear, sah. But Masa savvay dis kind of beef 'e come out for night time. For dis kind of beef you look um with hunter light.'

'Yes, but you tell all people of Eshobi I go pay one one pound for dis beef, you hear?'

'Yes, sah. I go tell um.'

'And now,' I said to Bob, carefully tying up the bag with the precious beef inside, 'let's get back to Mamfe quick and get this into a decent cage where we can see it.'

So we packed up the equipment and set off at a brisk pace through the forest towards Mamfe, pausing frequently to open the bag and make sure that the precious specimen had got enough air, and had not been spirited away by some frightful juju. We reached Mamfe at lunch-time and burst into the house, calling to Jacquie and Sophie to come and see our prize. I opened the bag cautiously and *Euoticus* edged its head out and surveyed us all in turn with its enormous, staring eyes.

'Oh, isn't it *sweet*,' said Jacquie.

'Isn't it a *dear*?' said Sophie.

'Yes,' I said proudly, 'it's a . . .'

'What shall we call it?' asked Jacquie.

'We'll have to think of a good name for it,' said Sophie.

'It's an extremely rare . . .' I began.

'How about Bubbles?' suggested Sophie.

'No, it doesn't look like a Bubbles,' said Jacquie surveying it critically.

'It's an *Euoticus* . . .'

'How about Moony?'

'No one has ever taken it back . . .'

'No, it doesn't look like a Moony either.'

'No European zoo has ever . . .'

'What about Fluffykins?' asked Sophie.

I shuddered.

'If you must give it a name call it Bug-eyes,' I said.

'Oh, yes!' said Jacquie, 'that suits it.'

'Good,' I said, 'I am relieved to know that we have successfully christened it. Now what about a cage for it?'

'Oh, we've got one here,' said Jacquie. 'Don't worry about that.'

We eased the animal into the cage, and it squatted on the floor glaring at us with unabated horror.

'Isn't it sweet?' Jacquie repeated.

'Is 'o a poppet?' gurgled Sophie.

I sighed. It seemed that, in spite of all my careful training, both my wife and my secretary relapsed into the most revolting fubsy attitude when faced with anything fluffy.

'Well,' I said resignedly, 'supposing you feed 'oos poppet? This poppet's going inside to get an itsy-bitsy slug of gin.'

BOOK TWO
BACK TO BAFUT

Chapter Three

The Fon's Beef

MAIL BY HAND

My good friend,

I am glad that you have arrive once more to Bafut. I welcome you. When you are calm from your journeys come and see me.

Your good friend,
Fon of Bafut.

On our return from Eshobi, Jacquie and I loaded up our lorry with the cages of animals we had obtained to date, and set out for Bafut, leaving Bob and Sophie in Mamfe for a little longer to try and obtain some more of the rain-forest animals.

The journey from Mamfe to the highlands was long and tedious, but never failed to fascinate me. To begin with, the road ran through the thick forest of the valley in which Mamfe lay. The lorry roared and bumped its way along the red road between gigantic trees, each festooned with creepers and lianas, through which flew small flocks of hornbills, honking wildly, or pairs of jade-green touracos with magenta wings flashing as they flew. On the dead trees by the side of the road the lizards, orange, blue and black, vied with the pigmy kingfishers over the spiders, locusts and other succulent tit-bits to be found amongst the purple and white convolvulus flowers. At the bottom of each tiny valley ran a small stream, spanned by a creaking wooden bridge, and as the lorry roared across, great clouds of butterflies rose from the damp earth at the sides of the water and swirled briefly round the bonnet. After a couple of hours the road started to climb, at first almost imperceptibly, in a series of great swinging loops through the forest, and here and there by the side of the road you could see the giant tree-ferns like green fountains spouting miraculously out of the low growth. As one climbed higher, the forest gave way to occasional patches of grassland, bleached white by the sun.

Then, gradually, as though we were shedding a thick green coat, the forest started to drop away and the grassland took its place. The gay lizards ran sun-drunk across the road, and flocks of minute finches burst from the undergrowth and drifted across in front of us, their crimson feathering making them look like showers of sparks from some gigantic bonfire. The lorry roared and shuddered, steam blowing up from the radiator, as it made the final violent effort and reached the top of the escarpment. Behind lay the Mamfe forest, in a million shades of green, and before us was the grassland, hundreds of miles of rolling mountains, lying in folds to the farthest dim horizons, gold and green, stroked by cloud shadows, remote and beautiful in the sun. The driver eased the lorry on to the top of the hill and brought it to a shuddering halt that made the red dust swirl up in a waterspout that enveloped us and our belongings. He smiled the wide, happy smile of a man who has accomplished something of importance.

'Why we stop?' I inquired.

'I go piss,' explained the driver frankly, as he disappeared into the long grass at the side of the road.

Jacquie and I uncoiled ourselves from the red-hot interior of the cab and walked round to the back of the lorry to see how our creatures were faring. Phillip, seated stiff and upright on a tarpaulin, turned to us a face bright red with dust. His trilby, which had been a very delicate pearl grey when we started, was also bright red. He sneezed violently into a green handkerchief, and surveyed me reproachfully.

'Dust *too much*, sah,' he roared at me, in case the fact had escaped my observation. As Jacquie and I were almost as dusty in the front of the lorry, I was not inclined to be sympathetic.

'How are the animals?' I asked.

' 'E well, sah. But dis bush-hog, sah, 'e get strong head *too much*.'

'Why, what the matter with it?'

' 'E done tief dis ma pillow,' said Phillip indignantly.

I peered into Ticky, the black-footed mongoose's cage. She had whiled away the tedium of the journey by pushing her paw through the bars and gradually dragging in with her the small pillow which was part of our cook's bedding. She was sitting on the remains, looking very smug and pleased with herself, surrounded by snow-drifts of feathers.

'Never mind,' I said consolingly, 'I'll buy you a new one. But you go watch your other things, eh? Sometime she go tief them as well.'

'Yes, sah, I go watch um,' said Phillip, casting a black look at the feather-smothered Ticky.

So we drove on through the green, gold and white grassland, under a blue sky veined with fine wisps of wind-woven white cloud, like frail twists of sheep's wool blowing across the sky. Everything in this landscape seemed to be the work of the wind. The great outcrops of grey rocks were carved and ribbed by it into fantastic shapes; the long grass was curved over into frozen waves by it; the small trees had been bent, carunculated and distorted by it. And the whole landscape throbbed and sang with the wind, hissing softly in the grass, making the small trees creak and whine, hooting and blaring round the towering cornices of rock.

So we drove on towards Bafut, and towards the end of the day the sky became pale gold. Then, as the sun sank behind the farthest rim of mountains, the world was enveloped in the cool green twilight, and in the dusk the lorry roared round the last bend and drew up at the hub of Bafut, the compound of the Fon. To the left lay the vast courtyard, and behind it the clusters of huts in which lived the Fon's wives and children. Dominating them all was the great hut in which dwelt the spirit of his father, and a great many other lesser spirits, looming like a monstrous, time-blackened beehive against the jade night sky. To the right of the road, perched on top of a tall bank, was the Fon's Rest House, like a two-storey Italian villa, stone-built and with a neatly tiled roof. Shoe-box shaped, both lower and upper storeys were surrounded by wide verandahs, festooned with bougainvillea covered with pink and brick-red flowers.

Tiredly we climbed out of the lorry and supervised the unloading of the animals and their installation on the top-storey verandah. Then the rest of the equipment was off-loaded and stored, and while we made vague attempts to wash some of the red dust off our bodies, Phillip seized the remains of his bedding, his box full of cooking utensils and food and marched off to the kitchen quarters in a stiff, brisk way, like a military patrol going to quell a small but irritating insurrection. By the time we had fed the animals he had reappeared with an astonishingly good meal and having eaten it we fell into bed and slept like the dead.

The next morning, in the cool dawn light, we went to pay our respects to our host, the Fon. We made our way across the great courtyard and plunged into the maze of tiny squares and alleyways formed by the huts of the Fon's wives. Presently, we found ourselves in a small courtyard shaded by an immense guava tree, and there was the Fon's own villa, small, neat, built of stone and tiled with a wide verandah running along one side. And there, at the top of the steps running up to the verandah, stood my friend the Fon of Bafut.

He stood there, tall and slender, wearing a plain white robe embroidered with blue. On his head was a small skull-cap in the same colours. His face was split by the joyous, mischievous grin I knew so well and he was holding out one enormous slender hand in greeting.

'My friend, Iseeya,' I called, hurrying up the stairs to him.

'Welcome, welcome ... you done come ... welcome,' he exclaimed, seizing my hand in his huge palm and draping a long arm round my shoulders and patting me affectionately.

'You well, my friend?' I asked, peering up into his face.

'I well, I well,' he said grinning.

It seemed to me an understatement: he looked positively blooming. He had been well into his seventies when I had last met him, eight years before, and he appeared to have weathered the intervening years better than I had. I introduced Jacquie, and was quietly amused by the contrast. The Fon, six foot three inches, and appearing taller because of his robes, towered beamingly over Jacquie's five-foot-one-inch, and her hand was as lost as a child's in the depths of his great dusky paw.

'Come, we go for inside,' he said, and clutching our hands led us into his villa.

The interior was as I remembered it, a cool, pleasant room with leopard skins on the floor, and wooden sofas, beautifully carved, piled high with cushions. We sat down, and one of the Fon's wives came forward carrying a tray with glasses and drinks on it. The Fon splashed Scotch into three glasses with a liberal hand, and passed them round, beaming at us. I surveyed the four inches of neat spirit in the bottom of my glass and sighed. I could see that the Fon had not, in my absence, joined the Temperance movement, whatever else he had done.

'Chirri-ho!' said the Fon, and downed half the contents of his glass at a gulp. Jacquie and I sipped ours more sedately.

'My friend,' I said, 'I happy too much I see you again.'

'Wah! Happy?' said the Fon. 'I get happy for see you. When dey done tell me you come for Cameroon again I get happy too much.'

I sipped my drink cautiously.

'Some man done tell me that you get angry for me because I done write dat book about dis happy time we done have together before. So I de fear for come back to Bafut,' I said.

The Fon scowled.

'Which kind of man tell you dis ting?' he inquired furiously.

'Some European done tell me.'

'Ah! European,' said the Fon shrugging, as if surprised that I should believe anything told to me by a white person, 'Na lies dis.'

'Good,' I said, greatly relieved. 'If I think you get angry for me my heart no go be happy.'

'No, no, I no get angry for you,' said the Fon, splashing another large measure of Scotch into my glass before I could stop him. 'Dis book you done write ... I like um foine ... you done make my name go for all de world ... every kind of people 'e know my name ... na foine ting dis.'

Once again I realized I had underestimated the Fon's abilities. He had obviously realized that any publicity is better than none. 'Look um,' he went on, 'plenty plenty people come here for Bafut, all different different people, dey all show me dis your book 'e get my name for inside ... na foine ting dis.'

'Yes, na fine thing,' I agreed, rather shaken. I had had no idea that I had unwittingly turned the Fon into a sort of Literary Lion.

'Dat time I done go for Nigeria,' he said, pensively holding the bottle of Scotch up to the light. 'Dat time I done go for Lagos to meet dat Queen woman, all dis European dere 'e get dis your book. Plenty plenty people dey ask me for write dis ma name for inside dis your book.'

I gazed at him open-mouthed; the idea of the Fon in Lagos sitting and autographing copies of my book rendered me speechless.

'Did you like the Queen?' asked Jacquie.

'Wah! Like? I like um too much. Na foine woman dat. Na small small woman, same same for you. But 'e get power, time no dere. Wah! Dat woman get power *plenty.*'

'Did you like Nigeria?' I asked.

'I no like,' said the Fon firmly. ' 'E hot too much. Sun, sun, sun, I shweat, I shweat. But dis Queen woman she get plenty power . . she walka walka she never shweat. Na foine woman dis.'

He chuckled reminiscently, and absent-mindedly poured us all out another drink.

'I done give dis Queen,' he went on, 'dis teeth for elephant. You savvay um?'

'Yes, I savvay um,' I said, remembering the magnificent carved tusk the Cameroons had presented to Her Majesty.

'I done give dis teeth for all dis people of Cameroon,' he explained. 'Dis Queen she sit for some chair an' I go softly softly for give her dis teeth. She take um. Den all dis European dere dey say it no be good ting for show your arse for dis Queen woman, so all de people walka walka backwards. I walka walka backwards. Wah! Na step dere, eh? I de fear I de fall, but I walka walka softly and I never fall . . . but I de fear too much.'

He chuckled over the memory of himself backing down the steps in front of the Queen until his eyes filled with tears.

'Nigeria no be good place,' he said, 'hot too much . . . I shweat.'

At the mention of sweat I saw his eyes fasten on the whisky bottle, so I rose hurriedly to my feet and said that we really ought to be going, as we had a lot of unpacking to do. The Fon walked out into the sunlit courtyard with us, and, holding our hands, peered earnestly down into our faces.

'For evening time you go come back,' he said.. 'We go drink, eh?'

'Yes, for evening time we go come,' I assured him.

He beamed down at Jacquie.

'For evening time I go show you what kind of happy time we get for Bafut,' he said.

'Good,' said Jacquie, smiling bravely.

The Fon waved his hands in elegant dismissal, and then turned and made his way back into his villa, while we trudged over to the Rest House.

'I don't think I could face any breakfast after that Scotch,' said Jacquie.

'But that wasn't drinking,' I protested. 'That was just a sort of mild apéritif to start the day. You wait until tonight.'

'Tonight I shan't drink . . . I'll leave it to you two,' said Jacquie firmly. 'I shall have one drink and that's all.'

After breakfast, while we were attending to the animals, I happened to glance over the verandah rail and noticed on the road below a small group of men approaching the house. When they drew nearer I saw that each of them was carrying either a raffia basket or a calabash with the neck stuffed with green leaves. I could hardly believe that they were bringing animals as soon as this, for generally it takes anything up to a week for the news to get around and for the hunters to start bringing in the stuff. But as I watched them with bated breath they turned off the road and started to climb the long flight of steps up to the verandah, chattering and laughing among themselves. Then, when they reached the top step they fell silent, and carefully laid their offerings on the ground.

'Iseeya, my friends,' I said.
'Morning, Masa,' they chorused, grinning.
'Na whatee all dis ting?'
'Na beef, sah,' they said.
'But how you savvay dat I done come for Bafut for buy beef?' I asked, greatly puzzled.
'Eh, Masa, de Fon 'e done tell us,' said one of the hunters.
'Good lord, if the Fon's been spreading the news before we arrived we'll be inundated in next to no time,' said Jacquie.
'We're pretty well inundated now,' I said, surveying the group of containers at my feet, 'and we haven't even unpacked the cages yet. Oh well, I suppose we'll manage. Let's see what they've got.'
I bent down, picked up a raffia bag and held it aloft.
'Which man bring dis?' I asked.
'Na me, sah.'
'Na whatee dere for inside?'
'Na squill-lill, sah.'
'What,' inquired Jacquie, as I started to unravel the strings on the bag, 'is a squill-lill?'
'I haven't the faintest idea,' I replied.
'Well, hadn't you better ask?' suggested Jacquie practically. 'For all you know it might be a cobra or something.'
'Yes, that's a point,' I agreed, pausing.
I turned to the hunter who was watching me anxiously.
'Na whatee dis beef squill-lill?'
'Na small beef, sah.'
'Na bad beef? 'E go chop man?'
'No, sah, at all. Dis one na squill-lill small, sah . . . na picken.'
Fortified with this knowledge I opened the bag and peered into its depths. At the bottom, squirming and twitching in a nest of grass, lay a tiny squirrel about three and a half inches long. It couldn't have been more than a few days old, for it was still covered in the neat, shining plush-like fur of an infant, and it was still blind. I lifted it out carefully and it lay in my hand making faint squeaking noises like something out of a Christmas cracker, pink mouth open in an O like a choirboy's, minute paws making paddling motions against my fingers. I waited patiently for the flood of anthropomorphism to die down from my wife.
'Well,' I said, 'if you want it, keep it. But I warn you it will be hell to feed. The only reason I can see for trying is because it's a baby black-eared, and they're quite rare.'
'Oh, it'll be all right,' said Jacquie optimistically. 'It's strong and that's half the battle.'
I sighed. I remembered the innumerable baby squirrels I had struggled with in various parts of the world, and how each one had seemed more imbecile and more bent on self-destruction than the last. I turned to the hunter. 'Dis beef, my friend. Na fine beef dis, I like um too much. But 'e be picken, eh? Sometime 'e go die-o, eh?'
'Yes, sah,' agreed the hunter gloomily.
'So I go pay you two two shilling now, and I go give you book. You go

come back for two week time, eh, and if dis picken 'e alive I go pay you five five shilling more, eh? You agree?'

'Yes, sah, I agree,' said the hunter, grinning delightedly.

I paid him the two shillings, and then wrote out a promissory note for the other five shillings, and watched him tuck it carefully into a fold of his sarong.

'You no go lose um,' I said. 'If you go lose um I no go pay you.'

'No, Masa, I no go lose um,' he assured me, grinning.

'You know, it's the most beautiful colour,' said Jacquie, peering at the squirrel in her cupped hands. On that point I agreed with her. The diminutive head was bright orange, with a neat black rim behind each ear, as though its mother had not washed it properly. The body was brindled green on the back and pale yellow on the tummy, while the ridiculous tail was darkish green above and flame orange below.

'What shall I call it?' asked Jacquie.

I glanced at the quivering scrap, still doing choral practice in her palm.

'Call it what the hunter called it: Squill-lill Small,' I suggested. So Squill-lill Small she became, later to be abbreviated to Small for convenience.

While engaged in this problem of nomenclature I had been busy untying another raffia basket, without having taken the precaution of asking the hunter what it contained. So, when I incautiously opened it, a small, pointed, rat-like face appeared, bit me sharply on the finger, uttered a piercing shriek of rage and disappeared into the depths of the basket again.

'What on earth was that?' asked Jacquie, as I sucked my finger and cursed, while all the hunters chorused 'Sorry, sah, sorry, sah,' as though they had been collectively responsible for my stupidity.

'That fiendish little darling is a pigmy mongoose,' I said. 'For their size they're probably the fiercest creatures in Bafut, and they've got the most penetrating scream of any small animal I know, except a marmoset.'

'What are we going to keep it in?'

'We'll have to unpack some cages. I'll leave it in the bag until I've dealt with the rest of the stuff,' I said carefully tying the bag up again.

'It's nice to have two different species of mongoose,' said Jacquie.

'Yes,' I agreed, sucking my finger. 'Delightful.'

The rest of the containers, when examined, yielded nothing more exciting than three common toads, a small green viper and four weaver-birds which I did not want. So, having disposed of them and the hunters, I turned my attention to the task of housing the pigmy mongoose. One of the worst things you can do on a collecting trip is to be unprepared with your caging. I had made this mistake on my first expedition; although we had taken a lot of various equipment, I had failed to include any ready-made cages, thinking there would be plenty of time to build them on the spot. The result was that the first flood of animals caught us unprepared and by the time we had struggled night and day to house them all adequately, the second wave of creatures had arrived and we were back where we started. At one point I had as many as six different creatures tied to my camp-bed on strings. After this experience I have always taken the precaution of bringing some collapsible cages with me on a trip so that, whatever else happens, I am certain I can accommodate at least the first forty or fifty specimens.

I now erected one of our specially built cages, filled it with dry banana leaves and eased the pigmy mongoose into it without getting bitten. It stood in the centre of the cage, regarding me with small, bright eyes, one dainty paw held up, and proceeded to utter shriek upon shriek of fury until our ears throbbed. The noise was so penetrating and painful that, in desperation, I threw a large lump of meat into the cage. The pigmy leaped on it, shook it vigorously to make sure it was dead and then carried it off to a corner where it settled down to eat. Though it still continued to shriek at us, the sounds were now mercifully muffled by the food. I placed the cage next to the one occupied by Ticky, the black-footed mongoose, and sat down to watch.

At a casual glance no one would think that the two animals were even remotely related. The black-footed mongoose, although still only a baby, measured two feet in length and stood about eight inches in height. She had a blunt, rather dog-like face with dark, round and somewhat protuberant eyes. Her body, head and tail were a rich creamy-white, while her slender legs were a rich brown that was almost black. She was sleek, sinuous and svelte and reminded me of a soft-skinned Parisienne *belle-amie* clad in nothing more than two pairs of black silk stockings. In contrast the pigmy mongoose looked anything but Parisienne. It measured, including tail, about ten inches in length. It had a tiny, sharply pointed face with a small, circular pink nose and a pair of small, glittering, sherry-coloured eyes. The fur, which was rather long and thick, was a deep chocolate brown with a faint ginger tinge here and there.

Ticky, who was very much the *grande dame*, peered out of her cage at the newcomer with something akin to horror on her face, watching it fascinated as it shrieked and grumbled over its gory hunk of meat. Ticky was herself a very dainty and fastidious feeder and would never have dreamt of behaving in this uncouth way, yelling and screaming with your mouth full and generally carrying on as though you had never had a square meal in your life. She watched the pigmy for a moment or so and then gave a sniff of scorn, turned round elegantly two or three times and then lay down and went to sleep. The pigmy, undeterred by this comment on its behaviour, continued to champ and shrill over the last bloody remnants of its food. When the last morsel had been gulped down, and the ground around carefully inspected for any bits that might have been overlooked, it sat down and scratched itself vigorously for a while and then curled up and went to sleep as well. When we woke it up about an hour later to record its voice for posterity, it produced such screams of rage and indignation that we were forced to move the microphone to the other end of the verandah. But by the time evening came we had not only successfully recorded the pigmy mongoose but Ticky as well, and had unpacked ninety per cent of our equipment into the bargain. So we bathed, changed and dined feeling well satisfied with ourselves.

After dinner we armed ourselves with a bottle of whisky and an abundant supply of cigarettes and, taking our pressure-lamp, we set off for the Fon's house. The air was warm and drowsy, full of the scents of wood smoke and sun-baked earth. Crickets tinkled and trilled in the grass verges of the road and in the gloomy fruit-trees around the Fon's great courtyard we could hear the fruit bats honking and flapping their wings among the branches. In the courtyard a group of the Fon's children were standing in a circle clapping their hands and chanting in some sort of game, and away through the trees in the distance a small drum throbbed like an irregular heart beat. We made our way through the maze of wives' huts, each lit by the red glow of a cooking fire, each heavy with the smell of roasting yams, frying plantain, stewing meat or the sharp, pungent reek of dried salt fish. We came presently to the Fon's villa and he was waiting on the steps to greet us, looming large in the gloom, his robe swishing as he shook our hands.

'Welcome, welcome,' he said, beaming, 'come, we go for inside.'

'I done bring some whisky for make our heart happy,' I said, flourishing the bottle as we entered the house.

'Wah! Good, good,' said the Fon, chuckling. 'Dis whisky na foine ting for make man happy.'

He was wearing a wonderful scarlet-and-yellow robe that glowed like a tiger skin in the soft lamplight, and one slender wrist carried a thick, beautifully carved ivory bracelet. We sat down and waited in silence while the solemn ritual of the pouring of the first drink was observed. Then, when each of us was clutching half a tumbler full of neat whisky, the Fon turned to us, giving his wide, mischievous grin.

'Chirri-*ho*!' he said, raising his glass, 'tonight we go have happy time.' And so began what we were to refer to later as The Evening of the Hangover.

As the level in the whisky bottle fell the Fon told us once again about his trip to Nigeria, how hot it had been and how much he had 'shweated.' His praise for the Queen knew no bounds, for, as he pointed out, here was he in his own country feeling the heat and yet the Queen could do twice the amount of work and still manage to look cool and charming. I found his lavish and perfectly genuine praise rather extraordinary, for the Fon belonged to a society where women are considered to be nothing more than rather useful beasts of burden.

'You like musica?' inquired the Fon of Jacquie, when the subject of the Nigerian tour was exhausted.

'Yes,' said Jacquie, 'I like it very much.'

The Fon beamed at her.

'You remember dis my musica?' he asked me.

'Yes, I remember. You get musica time no dere, my friend.'

The Fon gave a prolonged crow of amusement.

'You done write about dis my musica inside dis your book, eh?'

'Yes, that's right.'

'And,' said the Fon, coming to the point, 'you done write about dis dancing an' dis happy time we done have, eh?'

'Yes ... all dis dance we done do na fine one.'

'You like we go show dis your wife what kind of dance we get here for Bafut?' he inquired, pointing a long forefinger at me.

'Yes, I like too much.'

'Foine, foine ... come, we go for dancing house,' he said, rising to his feet majestically, and stifling a belch with one slender hand. Two of his wives, who had been sitting quietly in the background, rushed forward and seized the tray of drinks and scuttled ahead of us, as the Fon led us out of his house and across the compound towards his dancing house.

The dancing house was a great, square building, not unlike the average village hall, but with an earth floor and very few and very small windows. At one end of the building stood a line of wickerwork armchairs, which constituted a sort of Royal enclosure, and on the wall above these were framed photographs of various members of the Royal family. As we entered the dancing hall the assembled wives, about forty or fifty of them, uttered the usual greeting, a strange, shrill ululation, caused by yelling loudly and clapping their hands rapidly over their mouths at the same time. The noise was deafening. All the petty councillors there in their brilliant robes clapped their hands as well, and thus added to the general racket. Nearly deafened by this greeting, Jacquie and I were installed in two chairs, one on each side of the Fon, the table of drinks was placed in front of us, and the Fon, leaning back in his chair, surveyed us both with a wide and happy grin.

'Now we go have happy time,' he said, and leaning forward poured out half a tumblerful of Scotch each from the depths of a virgin bottle that had just been broached.

'Chirri-ho,' said the Fon.

'Chin-chin,' I said absent-mindedly.

'Na whatee dat?' inquired the Fon with interest.

'What?' I asked, puzzled.

'Dis ting you say.'

'Oh, you mean chin-chin?'

'Yes, yes, dis one.'

'It's something you say when you drink.'

'Na same same for Chirri-ho?' asked the Fon, intrigued.

'Yes, na same same.'

He sat silent for a moment, his lips moving, obviously comparing the respective merits of the two toasts. Then he raised his glass again.

'Shin-shin,' said the Fon.

'Chirri-ho!' I responded, and the Fon lay back in his chair and went off into a paroxysm of mirth.

By now the band had arrived. It was composed of four youths and two of the Fon's wives and the instruments consisted of three drums, two flutes and a calabash filled with dried maize that gave off a pleasant rustling noise similar to a marimba. They got themselves organized in the corner of the dancing house, and then gave a few experimental rolls on the drums, watching the Fon expectantly. The Fon, having recovered from the joke, barked out an imperious order and two of his wives placed a small table in the centre of the dance floor and put a pressure lamp on it. The drums gave another expectant roll.

'My friend,' said the Fon, 'you remember when you done come for Bafut before you done teach me European dance, eh?'

'Yes,' I said, 'I remember.'

This referred to one of the Fon's parties when, having partaken liberally of the Fon's hospitality, I had proceeded to show him, his councillors and wives how to do the conga. It had been a riotous success, but in the eight years that had passed I had supposed that the Fon would have forgotten about it.

'I go show you,' said the Fon, his eyes gleaming. He barked out another order and about twenty of his wives shuffled out on to the dance floor and formed a circle round the table, each one holding firmly to the waist of the one in front. Then they assumed, a strange, crouching position, rather like runners at the start of a race, and waited.

'What are they going to do?' whispered Jacquie.

I watched them with an unholy glee. 'I do believe,' I said dreamily, 'that he's been making them dance the conga ever since I left, and we're now going to have a demonstration.'

The Fon lifted a large hand and the band launched itself with enthusiasm into a Bafut tune that had the unmistakable conga rhythm. The Fon's wives, still in their strange crouching position, proceeded to circle round the lamp, kicking their black legs out on the sixth beat, their brows furrowed in concentration. The effect was delightful.

'My friend,' I said, touched by the demonstration, 'dis na fine ting you do.'

'Wonderful,' agreed Jacquie enthusiastically, 'they dance very fine.'

'Dis na de dance you done teach me,' explained the Fon.

'Yes, I remember.'

He turned to Jacquie, chuckling. 'Dis man your husband 'e get plenty power ... we dance, we dance, we drink ... Wah! We done have happy time.'

The band came to an uneven halt, and the Fon's wives, smiling shyly at our applause, rose from their crouching position and returned to their former places along the wall. The Fon barked an order and a large calabash of palm wine was brought in and distributed among the dancers, each getting their share poured into their cupped hands. Stimulated by this sight the Fon filled all our glasses again.

'Yes,' he went on, reminiscently, 'dis man your husband get plenty power for dance and drink.'

'I no get power now,' I said, 'I be old man now.'

'No, no, my friend,' said the Fon laughing, 'I be old, you be young.'

'You look more young now den for the other time I done come to Bafut,' I said, and really meant it.

'That's because you've got plenty wives,' said Jacquie.

'Wah! No!' said the Fon, shocked. 'Dis ma wives tire me too much.'

He glared moodily at the array of females standing along the wall, and sipped his drink. 'Dis ma wife dey humbug me too much,' he went on.

'My husband says I humbug him,' said Jacquie.

'Your husband catch lucky. 'E only get one wife, I get plenty,' said the Fon, 'an' dey de humbug me time no dere.'

'But wives are very useful,' said Jacquie.

The Fon regarded her sceptically.

'If you don't have wives you can't have *babies* ... men can't have babies,' said Jacquie practically.

The Fon was so overcome with mirth at this remark I thought he might have a stroke. He lay back in his chair and laughed until he cried. Presently he sat up, wiping his eyes, still shaking with gusts of laughter. 'Dis woman your wife get brain,' he said, still chuckling, and poured Jacquie out an extra large Scotch to celebrate her intelligence. 'You be good wife for me,' he said, patting her on the head affectionately. 'Shin-shin.'

The band now returned, wiping their mouths from some mysterious errand outside the dancing house and, apparently well fortified, launched themselves into one of my favourite Bafut tunes, the Butterfly dance. This was a pleasant, lilting little tune and the Fon's wives again took the floor and did the delightful dance that accompanied it. They danced in a row with minute but complicated hand and feet movements, and then the two that formed the head of the line joined hands, while the one at the farther end of the line whirled up and then fell backwards, to be caught and thrown upright again by the two with linked hands. As the dance progressed and the music got faster and faster the one representing the butterfly whirled more and more rapidly, and the ones with linked hands catapulted her upright again with more and more enthusiasm. Then, when the dance reached its feverish climax, the Fon rose majestically to his feet, amid screams of delight from the audience, and joined the end of the row of dancing wives. He started to whirl down the line, his scarlet and yellow robe turning into a blur of colour, loudly singing the words of the song.

'I dance, I dance, and no one can stop me,' he carolled merrily, 'but I must take care not to fall to the ground like the butterfly.'

He went whirling down the line of wives like a top, his voice booming out above theirs.

'I hope to God they don't drop him,' I said to Jacquie, eyeing the two short, fat wives who, with linked hands, were waiting rather nervously at the head of the line to receive their lord and master.

The Fon performed one last mighty gyration and hurled himself backwards at his wives, who caught him neatly enough but reeled under the shock. As the Fon landed he spread his arms wide so that for a moment his wives were invisible under the flowing sleeves of his robes and he lay there looking very like a gigantic, multicoloured butterfly. He beamed at us, lolling across his wives arms, his skull-cap slightly askew, and then his wives with an effort bounced him back to his feet again. Grinning and panting he made his way back to us and hurled himself into his chair.

'My friend, na fine dance dis,' I said in admiration. 'You get power time no dere.'

'Yes,' agreed Jacquie, who had also been impressed by this display, 'you get plenty power.'

'Na good dance dis, na foine one,' said the Fon, chuckling, and automatically pouring us all out another drink.

'You get another dance here for Bafut I like too much,' I said. 'Dis one where you dance with dat beer-beer for horse.'

'Ah, yes, yes, I savvay um,' said the Fon. 'Dat one where we go dance with dis tail for horshe.'

'That's right. Sometime, my friend, you go show dis dance for my wife?'

'Yes, yes, my friend,' he said. He leant forward and gave an order and a wife scuttled out of the dancing hall. The Fon turned and smiled at Jacquie.

'Small time dey go bring dis tail for horshe an' den we go dance,' he said.

Presently the wife returned carrying a large bundle of white, silky horses' tails, each about two feet long, fitted into handles beautifully woven out of leather thongs. The Fon's tail was a particularly long and luxuriant one, and the thongs that had been used to make the handle were dyed blue, red and gold. The Fon swished it experimentally through the air with languid, graceful movements of his wrist, and the hair rippled and floated like a cloud of smoke before him. Twenty of the Fon's wives, each armed with a switch, took the floor and formed a circle. The Fon walked over and stood in the centre of the circle; he gave a wave of his horse's tail, the band struck up and the dance was on.

Of all the Bafut dances this horsetail dance was undoubtedly the most sensuous and beautiful. The rhythm was peculiar, the small drums keeping up a sharp, staccato beat, while beneath them the big drums rumbled and muttered and the bamboo flutes squeaked and twittered with a tune that seemed to have nothing to do with the drums and yet merged with it perfectly. To this tune the Fon's wives gyrated slowly round in a clockwise direction, their feet performing minute but formalized steps, while they waved the horse's tails gently to and fro across their faces. The Fon, meanwhile, danced round the inside of the circle in an anti-clockwise direction, bobbing, stamping and twisting in a curiously stiff, unjointed sort of way, while his hand with incredibly supple wrist movements kept his horse's tail weaving through the air in a series of lovely and complicated movements. The effect was odd and almost indescribable: one minute the dancers resembled a bed of white seaweed, moved and rippled by sea movement, and the next minute the Fon would stamp and twist, stiff-legged, like some strange bird with white plumes, absorbed in a ritual dance of courtship among his circle of hens. Watching this slow pavane and the graceful movements of the tails had a curious hypnotic effect, so that even when the dance ended with a roll of drums one could still see the white tails weaving and merging before your eyes.

The Fon moved gracefully across the floor towards us, twirling his horse's tail negligently, and sank into his seat. He beamed breathlessly at Jacquie.

'You like dis ma dance?' he asked.

'It was *beautiful*,' she said. 'I liked it very much.'

'Good, good,' said the Fon, well pleased. He leaned forward and inspected the whisky bottle hopefully, but it was obviously empty. Tactfully I refrained from mentioning that I had some more over at the Rest House. The Fon surveyed the bottle gloomily.

'Whisky done finish,' he pointed out.

'Yes,' I said unhelpfully.

'Well,' said the Fon, undaunted, 'we go drink gin.'

My heart sank, for I had hoped that we could now move on to something innocuous like beer to quell the effects of so much neat alcohol. The Fon roared at one of his wives and she ran off and soon reappeared with a bottle of gin and one of bitters. The Fon's idea of gin-drinking was to pour out half a tumblerful and then colour it a deep brown with bitters. The result was guaranteed to slay an elephant at twenty paces. Jacquie, on seeing this cocktail the Fon concocted for me, hastily begged to be excused, saying that she couldn't drink gin on doctor's orders. The Fon, though obviously having the lowest possible opinion of a medical man who could even suggest such a thing, accepted with good grace.

The band started up again and everyone poured on to the floor and started to dance, singly and in couples. As the rhythm of the tune allowed it, Jacquie and I got up and did a swift foxtrot round the floor, the Fon roaring encouragement and his wives hooting with pleasure.

'Foine, foine,' shouted the Fon as we swept past.

'Thank you, my friend,' I shouted back, steering Jacquie carefully through what looked like a flower-bed of councillors in their multicoloured robes.

'I do wish you wouldn't tread on my feet,' said Jacquie plaintively.

'Sorry. My compass bearings are never at their best at this hour of night.'

'So I notice,' said Jacquie acidly.

'Why don't you dance with the Fon?' I inquired.

'I did think of it, but I wasn't sure whether it was the right thing for a mere woman to ask him.'

'I think he'd be tickled pink. Ask him for the next dance,' I suggested.

'What can we dance?' asked Jacquie.

'Teach him something he can add to his Latin American repertoire,' I said. 'How about a rumba?'

'I think a samba would be easier to learn at this hour of night,' said Jacquie. So, when the dance ended we made our way back to where the Fon was sitting, topping up my glass.

'My friend,' I said, 'you remember dis European dance I done teach you when I done come for Bafut before?'

'Yes, yes, na foine one,' he replied, beaming.

'Well, my wife like to dance with you and teach you other European dance. You agree?'

'Wah!' bellowed the Fon in delight, 'foine, foine. Dis your wife go teach me. Foine, foine, I agree.'

Eventually we discovered a tune that the band could play that had a vague samba rhythm and Jacquie and the Fon rose to their feet, watched breathlessly by everyone in the room.

The contrast between the Fon's six-foot-three and Jacquie's five-foot-one made me choke over my drink as they took the floor. Very rapidly Jacquie showed him the simple, basic steps of the samba, and to my surprise the Fon mastered them without trouble. Then he seized Jacquie in his arms and they were off. The delightful thing from my point of view was that as he clasped Jacquie tightly to his bosom she was almost completely hidden by his flowing robes; indeed, at some points in the dance you could not see her at all and it looked as though the Fon, having mysteriously grown another pair of feet, was dancing round by himself. There was something else about the dance that struck me as curious, but I could not pin it down for some time. Then I suddenly realized that Jacquie was leading the Fon. They danced past, both grinning at me, obviously hugely enjoying themselves.

'You dance fine, my friend,' I shouted. 'My wife done teach you fine.'

'Yes, yes,' roared the Fon over the top of Jacquie's head. 'No foine dance dis. Your wife na good wife for me.'

Eventually, after half an hour's dancing, they returned to their chairs, hot and exhausted. The Fon took a large gulp of neat gin to restore himself, and then leaned across to me.

'Dis your wife na foine,' he said in a hoarse whisper, presumably thinking that praise might turn Jacquie's head. 'She dance foine. She done teach me foine. I go give her mimbo . . . special mimbo I go give her.'

I turned to Jacquie who, unaware of her fate, was sitting fanning herself. 'You've certainly made a hit with our host,' I said.

'He's a dear old boy,' said Jacquie, 'and he dances awfully well . . . did you see how he picked up that samba in next to no time?'

'Yes,' I said, 'and he was so delighted with your teaching that he's going to reward you.'

Jacquie looked at me suspiciously. 'How's he going to reward me?' she asked.

'You're now going to receive a calabash of special mimbo . . . palm wine.'

'Oh God, and I can't stand the stuff,' said Jacquie in horror.

'Never mind. Take a glassful, taste it, tell him it's the finest you've ever had, and then ask if he will allow you to share it with his wives.'

Five calabashes were brought, the neck of each plugged with green leaves, and the Fon solemnly tasted them all before making up his mind which was the best vintage. Then a glass was filled and passed to Jacquie. Summoning up all her social graces she took a mouthful, rolled it round her mouth, swallowed and allowed a look of intense satisfaction to appear on her face.

'This is very fine mimbo', she proclaimed in delighted astonishment, with the air of one who has just been presented with a glass of Napoleon brandy. The Fon beamed. Jacquie took another sip, as he watched her closely. An even more delighted expression appeared on her face.

'This is the best mimbo I've ever tasted,' said Jacquie.

'Ha! Good!' said the Fon, with pleasure. 'Dis na foine mimbo. Na fresh one.'

'Will you let your wives drink with me?' asked Jacquie.

'Yes, yes,' said the Fon with a lordly wave of his hand, and so the wives shuffled forward, grinning shyly, and Jacquie hastily poured the remains of the mimbo into their pink palms.

At this point, the level of the gin bottle having fallen alarmingly, I suddenly glanced at my watch and saw, with horror, that in two and a half hours it would be dawn. So, pleading heavy work on the morrow, I broke up the party. The Fon insisted on accompanying us to the foot of the steps that led up to the Rest House, preceded by the band. Here he embraced us fondly.

'Good night, my friend,' he said, shaking my hand.

'Good night,' I replied. 'Thank you. You done give us happy time.'

'Yes,' said Jacquie, 'thank you very much.'

'Wah!' said the Fon, patting her on the head, 'we done dance foine. You be good wife for me, eh?'

We watched him as he wended his way across the great courtyard, tall and graceful in his robes, the boy trotting beside him carrying the lamp that cast a pool of golden light about him. They disappeared into the tangle of huts, and the twittering of the flutes and the bang of the drums became fainter and died away, until all we could hear was the calls of crickets and tree frogs and the faint honking cries of the fruit bats. Somewhere in the distance the first cock crowed, huskily and sleepily, as we crept under our mosquito nets.

Chapter Four

Beef in Boxes

MAIL BY HAND

My good friend,
 Good morning to you all.
 Your note to me received and contents well understood.
 I am a beat relief from that cough but not much.
 I agree for you to hire my landrover as from today on weekly payments. I will also want to bring to your notice that the landrover will be under your charge as from today, but any time I am called for a meeting at Ndop, Bemenda or elsewhere, or any urgent matter, I shall inform you to allow me the motor for the day.
 I want to remind you of the last trip which you hired the landrover and settlement had not yet been made.

Your good friend,
Fon of Bafut.

As soon as Bob and Sophie had joined us in Bafut we set about the task of organizing our already large and ever-growing collection. The great, shady verandah that ran round the upstairs rooms of the Fon's Rest House was divided into three: one section for reptiles, one for birds and one for mammals. Thus each of us had a particular section to look after and whoever finished first lent a hand with somebody else's group. First thing in the morning we would all wander to and fro along the verandah in our pyjamas carefully looking at each animal to make sure it was all right. It is only by this day-to-day routine of careful watching that you can get to know your animals so well that you detect the slightest sign of illness, when to anyone else the animal would appear to be perfectly healthy and normal. Then we cleaned and fed all the delicate animals that could not wait (such as the sunbirds who had to have their nectar as soon as it was light, and the baby creatures that needed their early morning bottles) and then we paused for breakfast. It was during mealtime that we compared notes on our charges. This mealtime conversation would have put any normal mortal off his food, for it was mainly concerned with the bowel movements of our creatures; with wild animals, diarrhoea or constipation is often a good indication as to whether you are feeding it correctly, and it can also be the first (and sometimes the only) symptom of an illness.

On any collecting trip acquiring the animals is, as a rule, the simplest part of the job. As soon as the local people discover that you are willing to buy live wild creatures the stuff comes pouring in; ninety per cent is, of course, the commoner species, but they do bring an occasional rarity. If you want the really rare stuff you generally have to go out and find it yourself, but while you are devoting your time to this you can be sure that all the common local fauna will be brought in to you. So one might almost say that getting the animals is easy: the really hard part is keeping them once you have got them.

The chief difficulty you have to contend with when you have got a newly caught animal is not so much the shock it might be suffering from capture, but the fact that the capture forces it to exist in close proximity to a creature it regards as an enemy of the worst possible sort: yourself. On many occasions an animal may take to captivity beautifully, but can never reconcile itself to the intimate terms on which it has to exist with man. This is the first great barrier to break down and you can only do it by patience and kindness. For month after month an animal may snap and snarl at you every time you approach its cage, until you begin to despair of ever making a favourable impression on it. Then, one day, sometimes without any preliminary warning, it will trot forward and take food from your hand, or allow you to tickle it behind the ears. At such moments you feel that all the waiting in the world was justified.

Feeding, of course, is one of your main problems. Not only must you have a fairly extensive knowledge of what each species eats in the wild state, but you have to work out a suitable substitute if the natural food is unavailable, and then teach your specimen to eat it. You also have to cater for their individual likes and dislikes, which vary enormously. I have known a rodent which, refusing all normal rodent food – such as fruit, bread, vegetables – live for three days on an exclusive diet of spaghetti. I have had a group of five monkeys, of the same age and species, who displayed the most weird idiosyncrasies. Out of the five, two had a passion for hard-boiled eggs, while the other three were frightened of the strange white shapes and would not touch them, actually screaming in fear if you introduced such a fearsome object as a hard-boiled egg into their cage. These five monkeys all adored orange but, whereas four would carefully peel their fruit and throw away the skin, the fifth would peel his orange equally carefully and then throw away the orange and eat the peel. When you have a collection of several hundred creatures all displaying such curious characteristics you are sometimes nearly driven mad in your efforts to satisfy their desires, and so keep them healthy and happy.

But of all the irritating and frustrating tasks that you have to undertake during a collecting trip, the hand-rearing of baby animals is undoubtedly the worst. To begin with, they are generally stupid over taking a bottle and there is nothing quite so unattractive as struggling with a baby animal in a sea of lukewarm milk. Secondly, they have to be kept warm, especially at night, and this means (unless you take them to bed with you, which is often the answer) you have to get up several times during the night to replenish hot-water bottles. After a hard day's work, to drag yourself out of bed at three in the morning to fill hot-water bottles is an occupation that soon loses its charm. Thirdly, all baby animals have extremely delicate stomachs and you must watch them like a hawk to make sure that the milk you are giving them is not too rich or too weak; if too rich, they can develop intestinal troubles which may lead to nephritis, which will probably kill them, and if too weak, it can lead to loss of weight and condition, which leaves the animal open to all sorts of fatal complaints.

Contrary to my gloomy prognostications, the baby black-eared squirrel, Squill-lill Small (Small to her friends) proved an exemplary baby. During the day she lay twitching in a bed of cotton-wool balanced on a hot-water bottle in the bottom of a deep biscuit-tin; at night the tin was placed by our beds under the rays of a Tilley infra-red heater. Almost immediately we were made aware of the fact that Small had a will of her own. For such a tiny animal she could produce an extraordinary volume of noise, her cry being a loud and rapid series of 'chucks' that sounded like a cheap alarm clock going off. Within the first twenty-four hours she had learnt when to expect her feeds and if we were as much as five minutes late she would trill and chuck incessantly until we arrived with the food. Then came the day when Small's eyes opened for the first time and she could take a look at her foster parents and the world in general. This, however, presented a new problem. We happened that day to be a bit late with her food. We had rather dawdled over our own lunch, deep in a discussion about some problem or other, and we had, I regret to say, forgotten all about Small. Suddenly I heard a faint scuffling behind me and, turning round, I saw Small squatting in the doorway of the dining-room looking, to say the least, extremely indignant. As soon as she saw us she went off like an alarm clock and hurrying across the floor hauled herself, panting, up Jacquie's chair and then leapt to her shoulder, where she sat flicking her tail up and down and shouting indignantly into Jacquie's ear. Now this, for a baby squirrel, was quite a feat. To begin with, as I say, her eyes had only just opened. Yet she had succeeded in climbing out of her tin and finding her way out of our bedroom (piled high with camera equipment and film); she had made her way down the full length of the verandah, running the gauntlet of any number of cages filled with potentially dangerous beasts, and eventually located us (presumably by sound) in the dining-room which was at the extreme end of the verandah. She had covered seventy yards over unknown territory, through innumerable dangers, in order to tell us she was hungry. Needless to say, she got her due of praise and, what was more important from her point of view, she got her lunch.

As soon as Small's eyes opened she grew rapidly and soon developed into one of the loveliest squirrels I have ever seen. Her orange head and neat, black-rimmed ears nicely set off her large dark eyes, and her fat body developed a rich moss green tinge against which the two lines of white spots that decorated her sides stood out like cats'-eyes on a dark road. But her tail was her best feature. Long and thick, green above and vivid orange below, it was a beautiful sight. She liked to sit with it curved over her back, the tip actually hanging over her nose, and then she would flick it gently in an undulating movement so that the whole thing looked like a candle flame in a draught.

Even when she was quite grown-up, Small slept in her biscuit-tin by our bed. She awoke early in the morning and, uttering her loud cry, she leaped from the tin on to one of our beds and crawled under the bed-clothes with us. Having spent ten minutes or so investigating our semi-comatose bodies, she jumped to the floor and went to explore the verandah. From these expeditions she would frequently return with some treasure she had found (such as a bit of rotten banana, or a dry leaf, or a bougainvillaea flower) and store it somewhere in our beds, getting most indignant if we hurled the offering out on to the floor. This continued for some months, until the day when I decided that Small would have to occupy a cage like the rest of the animals; I awoke one morning in excruciating agony to find her trying to stuff a peanut into my ear. Having found such a delicacy on the verandah she obviously thought that simply to cache it in my bed was not safe enough, but my ear provided an ideal hiding-place.

Bug-eyes, the needle-clawed lemur we had captured near Eshobi, was another baby, although she was fully weaned when we found her. She had become tame in a short space of time and very rapidly became one of our favourites. For her size she had enormous hands and feet, with long, attenuated fingers, and to see her dancing around her cage on her hind legs, her immense hands held up as though in horror, her eyes almost popping out of her head, as she pursued a moth or butterfly we had introduced, was a delightfully comic spectacle. Once she had caught it she sat there with it clasped tightly in her pink hand and regarded it with a wild, wide-eyed stare, as if amazed that such a creature should suddenly appear in the palm of her hand. Then she stuffed it into her mouth and continued to sit with what appeared to be a fluttering moustache of butterfly wing decorating her face, over which her huge eyes peered in astonishment.

It was Bug-eyes who first showed me an extraordinary habit that bushbabies have, a habit which to my shame I had never noticed before, in spite of the fact that I had kept innumerable bushbabies. I was watching her one morning when she had popped out of her nesting box for a feed of mealworms and a quick wash and brush up. She had, as I said before, large ears which were as delicate as flower petals. They were so fine that they were almost transparent and, presumably to prevent them from becoming torn or damaged in the wild state, she had the power of folding them back against the sides of her head like the furled sails of a yacht. Her ears were terribly important to her as you could tell by watching her. The slightest sound, however faint, would be picked up and her ears would twitch and turn towards it like radar. Now I had always noticed that she spent a lot of time cleaning and rubbing her ears with her hands, but on this particular morning I watched the whole process from start to finish and was considerably startled by what I saw. She began by sitting on a branch, staring dreamily into space while she daintily cleaned her tail, parting the hair carefully and making sure there were no snags or tangles, reminding me of a little girl plaiting her hair. Then she put one of her outsize, puppet-like hands beneath her and deposited in the palm a drop of urine. With an air of concentration, she rubbed her hands together and proceeded to anoint her ears with the urine, rather after the manner of a man rubbing brilliantine into his hair. Then she got another drop of urine and rubbed it carefully over the soles of her feet and the palms of her hands, while I sat and watched her in amazement.

I watched her do this three days in succession before I was satisfied that I was not imagining things, for it seemed to me to be one of the weirdest animal habits I had ever encountered. I can only conclude that the reason for it was this: unless the skin of the ears, so extremely delicate and thin, were kept moistened it must inevitably get dry and perhaps crack, which would have been fatal for an animal that relied so much on hearing. The same would apply to the delicate skin on the soles of her feet and hands, but here the urine would also provide an additional advantage. The soles of feet and hands were slightly cupped, so that as the creature leapt from bough to bough the hands and feet acted almost like the suckers on the toes of a tree-frog. Now, moistened with urine, these 'suckers' became twice as efficient. When, later on in the trip, we obtained a great number of Demidoff's bushbabies (the smallest of the tribe, each being the size of a large mouse) I noticed that they all had the same habit.

This is, to my mind, the best part of a collecting trip, the close daily contact with the animals that allows you to observe, learn and record. Every day, and almost at every moment of the day, something new and interesting was happening somewhere in the collection. The following diary entries show fairly well how each day bristled with new tasks and interesting observations:

February 14: Two patas monkeys brought in; both had severe infestation of jiggers in toes and fingers. Had to lance them, extract jiggers and as precaution against infection injected penicillin. Baby civet did her first adult 'display', making the mane of hair on her back stand up when I approached her cage suddenly. She accompanied this action with several loud sniffs, much deeper and more penetrating than her normal sniffing round food. Large brow-leaf toad brought in with extraordinary eye trouble. What appears to be a large malignant growth, situated behind the eyeball, had blinded the creature and then grown outwards, so that the toad looked as though it was wearing a large balloon over one eye. It did not appear to be suffering so am not attempting to remove the growth. So much for animals being happy and carefree in the wild state.

February 20: At last, after much trial and error, Bob has discovered what the hairy frogs eat: snails. We had previously tried young mice and rats, baby birds, eggs, beetles and their larvae, locusts, all without success. Snails they devour avidly, so we have high hopes of getting the frogs back alive. Have had an outbreak of what appears to be nephritis among the Demidoff's bushbabies. Two discovered this morning drenched in urine as though they had been dipped. Have weakened the milk they get; it may be too strong. Also organized more insect food for them. The five baby Demidoff's are still thriving on their Complan milk, which is curious as this is incredibly rich, and if ordinary dried milk affects the adults one would have thought Complan would have had a similar effect on the babies.

March 16: Two nice cobras brought in, one about six feet long and the other about two feet. Both fed straight away. Best item today was female pigmy mongoose and two babies. The babies are still blind and an extraordinary pale fawn in contrast to the dark brown mother. Have removed babies to hand-rear them as felt sure female would either neglect or kill them if they were put with her.

March 17: Young pigmy mongooses flatly refuse to feed from bottle or from fountain-pen filler. In view of this (since their chances seemed slim) put them into cage with female. To my surprise she has accepted them and is suckling them well. Most unusual. Had two broken leg jobs today: Woodford's owl which had been caught in a gin-trap and a young hawk with a greenstick fracture. I don't think the owl will regain use of leg for all the ligaments appear to be torn, and the bone badly splintered. Hawk's leg should be O.K. as it's a young bird. Both are feeding well. Demidoff's make a faint mewing hiss when disturbed at night, the only sound I have heard them make apart from their bat-like twittering when fighting. Clawed toads have started to call at night: very faint 'peep-peep' noise, rather like someone flicking the edge of a glass gently with finger-nail.

April 2: Young male chimp, about two years old, brought in today. Was in a terrible mess. Had been caught in one of the wire noose-traps they use for antelopes, and had damaged its left hand and arm. The palm of the hand and the wrist were split right open and badly infected with gangrene. The animal was very weak, not being able to sit up, and the colour of the skin was a curious yellowish grey. Attended to wound and injected penicillin. Drove it in to Bemenda for the Dept. of Agriculture's vet to have a look at, as did not like skin colour or curious lethargy in spite of stimulants. He took blood test and diagnosed sleeping-sickness. Have done all we can but the animal appears to be sinking fast. He seems pathetically grateful for anything you do for him.

April 3: Chimp died. They are a 'protected' animal and yet up here, as in other parts of the Cameroons, they are killed and eaten regularly. Big rhinoceros viper fed for first time: small rat. One of the green forest squirrels appears to be developing a bald patch on his back: presume lack of vitamins so am increasing his Abidec. As we now get good supply of weaver-bird's eggs each day all the squirrels are getting them, in addition to their normal diet. The brush-tail porcupines, when disturbed at night, beat rapid tattoo with their hind-feet (like a wild rabbit) then swing their backside round to face danger and rustle bunch of quills on end of tail, producing a sound reminiscent of rattlesnake.

April 5: Have found simple, rapid way of sexing pottos. Nice young male brought in today. Although external genitalia in both sexes is remarkably similar to a superficial glance, have discovered that simplest way is to smell them. The testicles of the male give out a faint, sweet odour, like pear drops, when the animal is handled.

We were not the only ones interested in the animals. Many of the local people had never seen some of the creatures we had acquired, and many called and asked for permission to look round the collection. One day the Headmaster of the local Mission School called and asked if he could bring his entire school of two-hundred-odd boys to see the collection. I was glad to agree to this, for I feel that if you can, by showing live animals, arouse people's interest in their local fauna and its preservation you are doing something worthwhile. So, on the appointed date, the boys came marching down the road in a double column, shepherded by five masters. In the road below the Rest House the boys were divided up into groups of twenty and then brought up in turn by a master. Jacquie, Sophie, Bob and I took up stations at various points in the collection to answer any queries. The boys behaved in a model fashion; there was no pushing or shoving, no skylarking. They wended their way from cage to cage, absorbed and fascinated, uttering amazed cries of 'Wah!' at each new wonder and clicking their fingers in delight. Finally, when the last group had been led round, the Headmaster grouped all the boys at the bottom of the steps and then turned to me, beaming.

'Sir,' he said, 'we are very grateful to you for allowing us to see your zoological collections. May I ask if you would be kind enough to answer some of the boys' questions?'

'Yes, with pleasure,' I said, taking up my stand on the steps above the crowd.

'Boys,' roared the Head, 'Mr Durrell has kindly say that he will answer any questions. Now who has a question?'

The sea of black faces below me screwed themselves up in thought, tongues protruded, toes wiggled in the dust. Then, slowly at first, but with increasing speed as they lost their embarrassment, they shot questions at me, all of which were extremely intelligent and sensible. There was, I noticed, one small boy in the front of the crowd who had, throughout the proceedings, fixed me with a basilisk eye. His brow was furrowed with concentration, and he stood stiffly at attention. At last, when the supply of questions started to peter out, he suddenly summoned up all his courage, and shot his hand up.

'Yes, Uano, what is your question?' asked the Head, smiling down fondly at the boy.

The boy took a deep breath and then fired his question at me rapidly. 'Please, sah, can Mr Durrell tell us why he take so many photographs of the Fon's wives?'

The smile vanished from the Head's face and he threw me a look of chagrin.

'That is not a zoological question, Uano,' he pointed out severely.

'But please, sah, why?' repeated the child stubbornly.

The Head scowled ferociously. 'That is *not* a zoological question,' he thundered. 'Mr Durrell only said he would answer zoological questions. The matter of the Fon's wives is not zoological.'

'Well, loosely speaking it could be called biological, Headmaster, couldn't it?' I asked, coming to the lad's rescue.

'But, sir, they should't ask you questions like that,' said the Head, mopping his face.

'Well, I don't mind answering. The reason is that, in my country, everyone is very interested to know how people in other parts of the world live and what they look like. I can tell them, of course, but it's not the same as if they see a photograph. With a photograph they know exactly what everything is like.'

'There . . .' said the Headmaster, running a finger round the inside of his collar. 'There, Mr Durrell has answered your question. Now, he is a very busy man so there is no more time for further questions. Kindly get into line.'

The boys formed themselves once more into two orderly lines, while the Headmaster shook my hand and earnestly assured me that they were all most grateful. Then he turned once more to the boys.

'Now, to show our appreciation to Mr Durrell I want three hearty cheers.'

Two hundred young lungs boomed out the hearty cheers. Then the boys at the head of the line produced from bags they were carrying several bamboo flutes and two small drums. The Headmaster waved his hand and they started to walk off down the road, led by the school band playing, of all things, 'Men of Harlech.' The Head followed them mopping his face, and the dark looks he kept darting at young Uano's back did not augur well for the boy's prospects when he got back to the classroom.

That evening the Fon came over for a drink and, after we had shown him the new additions to the collection, we sat on the verandah and I told him about Uano's zoological question. The Fon laughed and laughed, particularly at the embarrassment of the Headmaster. 'Why you never tell um,' he inquired, wiping his eyes, 'why you never tell um dat you take dis photo of dis ma wife for show all Europeans for your country dat Bafut women be beautiful?'

'Dis boy na picken,' I said solemnly. 'I think sometime he be too small to understand dis woman palaver.'

'Na true, na true,' said the Fon, chuckling, ' 'e be picken. 'E catch lucky, 'e no get women for humbug him.'

'They tell me, my friend,' I said, trying to steer the conversation away from the pros and cons of married life, 'they tell me tomorrow you go for N'dop. Na so?'

'Na so,' said the Fon, 'I go for two days, for Court. I go come back for morning time tomorrow tomorrow.'

'Well,' I said, raising my glass, 'safe journey, my friend.'

The following morning, clad in splendid yellow and black robes and wearing a curious hat, heavily embroidered, with long, drooping ear flaps, the Fon took his seat in the front of his new Land-Rover. Into the back went the necessities of travel: three bottles of Scotch, his favourite wife and three council members. He waved vigorously to us until the vehicle rounded the corner and was lost from sight.

That evening, having finished the last chores of the day, I went out on to the front verandah for a breath of air. In the great courtyard below I noticed large numbers of the Fon's children assembling. Curiously I watched them. They grouped themselves in a huge circle in the centre of the compound and, after much discussion and argument, they started to sing and clap their hands rhythmically, accompanied by a seven-year-old who stood in the centre of the circle beating a drum. Standing like this they lifted up their young voices and sang some of the most beautiful and haunting of the Bafut songs. This, I could tell, was not just an ordinary gathering of children; they had assembled there for some definite purpose, but what they were celebrating (unless it was their father's departure) I could not think. I stood there watching them for a long time and then John, our houseboy, appeared at my elbow in his unnervingly silent way.

'Dinner ready, sah,' he said.

'Thank you, John. Tell me, why all dis picken sing for the Fon's compound?'

John smiled shyly. 'Because de Fon done go for N'dop, sah.'

'Yes, but why they sing?'

'If the Fon no be here, sah, each night dis picken must for sing inside de Fon's compound. So dey keep dis his compound warm.'

This, I thought, was a delightful idea. I peered down at the circle of children, singing lustily in the gloomy wastes of the great courtyard, to keep their father's compound warm.

'Why they never dance?' I asked.

'Dey never get light, sah.'

'Take them the pressure light from the bedroom. Tell them I send it so that I can help keep the Fon's compound warm.'

'Yes, sah,' said John. He hurried off to fetch the light and presently I saw it cast a golden pool round the circle of children. There was a pause in the singing, while John delivered my message, and then came a series of delighted shrieks and echoing up to me the shrill voices crying, 'Tank you, Masa, tank you.'

As we sat down to dinner the children were singing like larks, and stamping and weaving their way round the lamp, their shadows long and attenuated, thrown halfway across the courtyard by the softly hissing lamp in their midst.

Chapter Five

Film Star Beef

MAIL BY HAND

My good friend,
    Would you like to come and have a drink with us this evening at eight o'clock?'

Your friend,
Gerald Durrell.

My good friend,
    Expect me a 7.30 p.m. Thanks.

Your good friend,
Fon of Bafut.

There are several different ways of making an animal film, and probably one of the best methods is to employ a team of cameramen who spend about two years in some tropical part of the world filming the animals in their natural state. Unfortunately this method is expensive, and unless you have the time and the resources of Hollywood behind you it is out of the question.

For someone like myself, with only a limited amount of time and money to spend in a country, the only way to film animals is under controlled conditions.

The difficulties of trying to film wild animals in a tropical forest are enough to make even the most ardent photographer grow pale. To begin with you hardly ever see a wild animal and, when you do, it is generally only a momentary glimpse as it scuttles off into the undergrowth. To be in the right spot at the right time with your camera set up, your exposure correct and an animal in front of you in a suitable setting, engaged in some interesting and filmable action, would be almost a miracle. So, the only way round this is to catch your animal first and establish it in captivity. Once it has lost some of its fear of human beings you can begin work. Inside a huge netting 'room' you create a scene which is as much like the animal's natural habitat as possible, and yet which is – photographically speaking – suitable. That is to say, it must not have too many holes in which a shy creature can hide, your undergrowth must not be so thick that you get awkward patches of shade, and so on. Then you introduce your animal to the set, and allow it time to settle down, which may be anything from an hour to a couple of days.

It is essential, of course, to have a good knowledge of the animal's habits, and to know how it will react under certain circumstances. For example, a hungry pouched rat, if released in an appropriate setting and finding a lavish selection of forest fruits on the ground, will promptly proceed to stuff as many of them into his immense cheek pouches as they will hold, so that in the end he looks as though he is suffering from a particularly virulent attack of mumps. If you don't want to end up with nothing more exciting than a series of pictures of some creature wandering aimlessly to and fro amid bushes and grass, you must provide the circumstances which will allow it to display some interesting habit or action. However, even when you have reached this stage you still require two other things: patience and luck. An animal – even a tame one – cannot be told what to do like a human actor. Sometimes a creature which has performed a certain action day after day for weeks will, when faced with a camera, develop an acute attack of stage fright, and refuse to perform. When you have spent hours in the hot sun getting everything ready, to be treated to this sort of display of temperament makes you feel positively homicidal.

A prize example of the difficulties of animal photography was, I think, the day we attempted to photograph the water chevrotain. These delightful little antelopes are about the size of a fox-terrier, with a rich chestnut coat handsomely marked with streaks and spots of white. Small and dainty, the water chevrotain is extremely photogenic. There are several interesting points about the chevrotain, one of which is its adaptation to a semi-aquatic life in the wild state. It spends most of its time wading and swimming in streams in the forest and can even swim for considerable distances under water. The second curious thing is that it has a passion for snails and beetles, and such carnivorous habits in an antelope are most unusual. The third notable characteristic is its extraordinary placidity and tameness: I have known a chevrotain, an hour after capture, take food from my hand and allow me to tickle its ears, for all the world as if it had been born in captivity.

Our water chevrotain was no exception; she was ridiculously tame, adored having her head and tummy scratched and would engulf, with every sign of satisfaction, any quantity of snails and beetles you cared to provide. Apart from this she spent her spare time trying to bathe in her water bowl, into which she could just jam – with considerable effort – the extreme rear end of her body.

So, to display her carnivorous and aquatic habits, I designed a set embracing a section of river bank. The undergrowth was carefully placed so that it would show off her perfect adaptive coloration to the best advantage. One morning, when the sky was free from cloud and the sun was in the right place, we carried the chevrotain cage out to the set and prepared to release her.

'The only thing I'm afraid of,' I said to Jacquie, 'is that I'm not going to get sufficient movement out of her. You know how quiet she is ... she'll probably walk into the middle of the set and refuse to move.'

'Well, if we offer her a snail or something from the other side I should think she'll walk across,' said Jacquie.

'As long as she doesn't just stand there, like a cow in a field. I want to get *some* movement out of her,' I said.

I got considerably more movement out of her than I anticipated. The moment the slide of her cage was lifted she stepped out daintily and paused with one slender hoof raised. I started the camera and awaited her next move. Her next move was somewhat unexpected. She shot across my carefully prepared set like a rocket, went right through the netting wall as if it had not been there and disappeared into the undergrowth in the middle distance before any of us could make a move to stop her. Our reactions were slow, because this was the last thing we had expected, but as I saw my precious chevrotain disappearing from view I uttered such a wail of anguish that everyone, including Phillip the cook, dropped whatever they were doing and assembled on the scene like magic.

'Water beef done run,' I yelled. 'I go give ten shillings to the man who go catch um.'

The effect of this lavish offer was immediate. A wedge of Africans descended on to the patch of undergrowth into which the antelope had disappeared, like a swarm of hungry locusts. Within five minutes Phillip, uttering a roar of triumph like a sergeant-major, emerged from the bushes clutching to his bosom the kicking, struggling antelope. When we replaced her in her cage she stood quite quietly, gazing at us with limpid eyes as if astonished at all the fuss. She licked my hand in a friendly fashion, and when tickled behind the ears went off into her usual trance-like state, with half-closed eyes. We spent the rest of the day trying to film the wretched creature. She behaved beautifully in her box, splashing in a bowl of water to show how aquatic she was, eating beetles and snails to show how carnivorous she was, but the moment she was released into the film set she fled towards the horizon as if she had a brace of leopards on her tail. At the end of the day, hot and exhausted, I had exposed fifty feet of film, all of which showed her standing stock still outside her box, preparatory to dashing away. Sadly we carried her cage back to the Rest House, while she lay placidly on her banana-leaf bed and munched beetles. It was the last time we tried to photograph the water chevrotain.

Another creature that caused me untold anguish in the photographic field was a young Woodford's owl called, with singular lack of originality, Woody. Woodfords are very lovely owls, with a rich chocolate plumage splashed and blotched with white, and possessing what must be the most beautiful eyes in the whole of the owl family. They are large, dark and liquid, with heavy lids of a delicate pinky-mauve. These they raise and lower over their eyes in what seems to be slow motion, like an ancient film actress considering whether to make a comeback. This seductive fluttering of eyelids is accompanied by loud clickings of the beak like castanets. When excited the eyelid fluttering becomes very pronounced and the birds sway from side to side on the perch, as if about to start a hula-hula, and then they suddenly spread their wings and stand there clicking their beaks at you, looking like a tombstone angel of the more fiercely religious variety. Woody would perform all these actions perfectly inside his cage and would, moreover, perform them to order when shown a succulent titbit like a small mouse. I felt sure that, if he was provided with a suitable background, I could get his display on film with the minimum of trouble.

So, in the netting room I used for bird photography I set to and created what looked like a forest tree, heavily overgrown with creepers and other parasites, using green leaves and a blue sky as background. Then I carried Woody out and placed him on the branch in the midst of this wealth of foliage. The action I wanted him to perform was a simple and natural one not calculated to tax even the brain of an owl. With a little co-operation on his part the whole thing could have been over in ten minutes. He sat on the branch regarding us with wide-eyed horror, while I took up my position behind the camera. Just as I pressed the button he blinked his eyes once, very rapidly, and then, as if overcome with disgust at our appearance, he very firmly turned his back on us. Trying to remember that patience was the first requisite of an animal photographer, I wiped the sweat from my eyes, walked up to the branch, turned him round and walked back to the camera. By the time I had reached it Woody once more had his back towards us. I thought that maybe the light was too strong, so several members of the staff were sent to cut branches and these were rigged up so that the bird was sheltered from the direct rays of the sun. But still he persisted in keeping his back to us. It was obvious that, if I wanted to photograph him, I would have to rearrange my set so that it faced the opposite way. After considerable labour about a ton of undergrowth was carefully shifted and rearranged so that Woody was now facing the way he obviously preferred.

During this labour, while we sweated with massive branches and coils of creepers, he sat there regarding us in surprise. He generously allowed me to get the camera set up in the right position (a complicated job, for I was now shooting almost directly into the sun) and then he calmly turned his back on it. I could have strangled him. By this time ominous black clouds were rolling up, preparatory to obscuring the sun, and so further attempts at photography were impossible. I packed up the camera and then walked to the branch, murder in my heart, to collect my star. As I approached he turned round, clicked his beak delightedly, executed a rapid hula-hula and then spread his wings and bowed to me, with the mock-shy air of an actor taking his seventeenth curtain call.

Of course not all our stars caused us trouble. In fact, one of the best sequences I managed to get on film was accomplished with the minimum of fuss and in record time. And yet, on the face of it, one would have thought that it was a much more difficult object to achieve than getting an owl to spread his wings. Simply, I wanted to get some shots of an egg-eating snake robbing a nest. Egg-eating snakes measure about two feet in length and are very slender. Coloured a pinkish-brown, mottled with darker markings, they have strange, protuberant eyes of a pale silvery colour with fine vertical pupils like a cat's. The curious point about them is that three inches from the throat (internally, of course) the vertebrae protrude, hanging down like stalactites. The reptile engulfs an egg, whole, and this passes down its body until it lies directly under these vertebrae. Then the snake contracts its muscles and the spikes penetrate the egg and break it; the yolk and white are absorbed and the broken shell, now a flattened pellet, is regurgitated. The whole process is quite extraordinary and had never, as far as I knew, been recorded on film.

We had, at that time, six egg-eating snakes, all of which were, to my delight, identical in size and coloration. The local children did a brisk trade in bringing us weaver-birds' eggs to feed this troupe of reptiles, for they seemed capable of eating any number we cared to put in their cage. In fact, the mere introduction of an egg into the cage changed them from a somnolent pile of snakes to a writhing bundle, each endeavouring to get at the egg first. But, although they behaved so beautifully in the cage, after my experiences with Woody and the water chevrotain, I was inclined to be a bit pessimistic. However, I created a suitable set (a flowering bush in the branches of which was placed a small nest) and collected a dozen small blue eggs as props. Then the snakes were kept without their normal quota of eggs for three days, to make sure they all had good appetites. This, incidentally, did not hurt them at all, for all snakes can endure considerable fasts, which with some of the bigger constrictors run into months or years. However, when my stars had got what I hoped was a good edge to their appetites, we started work.

The snakes' cage was carried out to the film set, five lovely blue eggs were placed in the nest and then one of the reptiles was placed gently in the branches of the bush, just above the nest. I started the camera and waited.

The snake lay flaccidly across the branches seeming a little dazed by the sunlight after the cool dimness of its box. In a moment its tongue started to flicker in and out, and it turned its head from side to side in an interested manner. Then with smooth fluidity it started to trickle through the branches towards the nest. Slowly it drew closer and closer, and when it reached the rim of the nest, it peered over the edge and down at the eggs with its fierce silvery eyes. Its tongue flicked again as if it were smelling the eggs and it nosed them gently like a dog with a pile of biscuits. Then it pulled itself a little farther into the nest, turned its head sideways, opened its mouth wide and started to engulf one of the eggs. All snakes have a jaw so constructed that they can dislocate the hinge, which enables them to swallow a prey that, at first sight, looks too big to pass through their mouths. The egg-eater was no exception and he neatly dislocated his jaws and the skin of his throat stretched until each scale stood out individually and you could see the blue of the egg shining through the fine, taut skin as the egg was forced slowly down his throat. When the egg was about an inch down his body he paused for a moment's meditation and then swung himself out of the nest and into the branches. Here, as he made his way along, he rubbed the great swelling in his body that the egg had created against the branches so that the egg was forced farther and farther down.

Elated with this success we returned the snake to his box so that he could digest his meal in comfort, and I shifted the camera's position and put on my big lenses for close-up work. We put another egg into the nest to replace the one taken, and then got out another egg-eater. This was the beauty of having all the snakes of the same size and coloration: as the first snake would not look at another egg until he had digested the first, he could not be used in the close-up shots. But the new one was identical and as hungry as a hunter, and so without any trouble whatsoever I got all the close-up shots I needed as he glided rapidly down to the nest and took an egg. I did the whole thing all over again with two other snakes and on the finished film these four separate sequences were intercut and no one, seeing the finished product, could tell that they were seeing four different snakes.

All the Bafutians, including the Fon, were fascinated by our filming activities, since not long before they had seen their very first cinema. A mobile ciné van had come out to Bafut and shown them a colour film of the Coronation and they had been terribly thrilled with it. In fact it was still a subject of grave discussion when we were there, nearly a year and a half later. Thinking that the Fon and his council would be interested to learn more about filming, I invited them to come across one morning and attend a filming session and they accepted with delight.

'What are you going to film?' asked Jacquie.

'Well, it doesn't really matter, so long as it's innocuous,' I said.

'Why innocuous?' asked Sophie.

'I don't want to take any risks. . . . If I got the Fon bitten by something I would hardly be *persona grata*, would I?'

'Good God, no, that would never do,' said Bob. 'What sort of thing did you have in mind?'

'Well, I want to get some shots of those pouched rats, so we might as well use them. They can't hurt a fly.'

So the following morning we got everything ready. The film set, representing a bit of forest floor, had been constructed on a Dexion stand, one of our specially made nylon tarpaulins had been erected nearby, under which the Fon and his court could sit, and beneath it were placed a table of drinks and some chairs. Then we sent a message over to the Fon that we were ready for him.

We watched him and his council approaching across the great courtyard and they were a wonderful spectacle. First came the Fon, in handsome blue and white robes, his favourite wife trotting along beside him, shading him from the sun with an enormous orange and red umbrella. Behind him walked the council members in their fluttering robes of green, red, orange, scarlet, white and yellow. Around this phalanx of colour some forty-odd of the Fon's children skipped and scuttled about like little black beetles round a huge, multicoloured caterpillar. Slowly the procession made its way round the Rest House and arrived at our improvised film studio.

'Morning, my friend,' called the Fon, grinning. 'We done come for see dis cinema.'

'Welcome, my friend,' I replied. 'You like first we go have drink together?'

'Wah! Yes, I like,' said the Fon, lowering himself cautiously into one of our camp chairs.

I poured out the drinks, and as we sipped them I explained the mysteries of ciné photography to the Fon, showing him how the camera worked, what the film itself looked like and explaining how each little picture was of a separate movement.

'Dis filum you take, when we go see um?' asked the Fon, when he had mastered the basic principles of photography.

'I have to take um for my country before it get ready,' I said sadly, 'so I no fit show you until I go come back for the Cameroons.'

'Ah, good,' said the Fon, 'so when you go come back for dis ma country we go have happy time and you go show me dis your filum.'

We had another drink to celebrate the thought of my impending return to Bafut.

By this time everything was ready to show the Fon how one set about making a sequence. Sophie, as continuity girl, wearing trousers, shirt, sunglasses and an outsize straw hat, was perched precariously on a small campstool, her pad and pencil at the ready to make notes of each shot I took. Near her Jacquie, a battery of still cameras slung round her, was crouched by the side of the recording machine. Near the set, Bob stood in the role of dramatic coach, armed with a twig, and the box in which our stars were squeaking vociferously. I set up the camera, took up my position behind it and gave the signal for action. The Fon and councillors watched silent and absorbed as Bob gently tipped the two pouched rats out on to the set, and then guided them into the right positions with his twig. I started the camera and at the sound of its high-pitched humming a chorus of appreciative 'Ahs' ran through the audience behind me. It was just at that moment that a small boy carrying a calabash wandered into the compound and, oblivious of the crowd, walked up to Bob and held up his offering. I was fully absorbed in peering through the viewfinder of the camera and so I paid little attention to the ensuing conversation that Bob had with the child.

'Na whatee dis?' asked Bob, taking the calabash, which had its neck plugged with green leaves.

'Beef,' said the child succinctly.

Instead of inquiring more closely into the nature of the beef, Bob pulled out the plug of leaves blocking the neck of the calabash. The result surprised not only him but everyone else as well. Six feet of agile and extremely angry green mamba shot out of the calabash like a jack-in-the-box and fell to the ground.

'Mind your feet!' Bob shouted warningly.

I removed my eye from the viewfinder of the camera to be treated to the somewhat disturbing sight of the green mamba sliding determinedly through the legs of the tripod towards me. I leaped upwards and backwards with an airy grace that only a prima ballerina treading heavily on a tin-tack could have emulated. Immediately pandemonium broke loose. The snake slid past me and made for Sophie at considerable speed. Sophie took one look and decided that discretion was the better part of valour. Seizing her pencil, pad and, for some obscure reason, her camp stool too, she ran like a hare towards the massed ranks of the councillors. Unfortunately this was the way the snake wanted to go as well, so he followed hotly on her trail. The councillors took one look at

Sophie, apparently leading the snake into their midst, and did not hesitate for a moment. As one man, they turned and fled. Only the Fon remained, rooted to his chair, so wedged behind the table of drinks that he could not move. 'Get a stick,' I yelled to Bob and ran after the snake. I knew, of course, that the snake would not deliberately attack anyone. It was merely trying to put the greatest possible distance between itself and us. But when you have fifty panic-stricken Africans, all bare-footed, running madly in all directions, accompanied by a frightened and deadly snake, an accident is possible. The scene now, according to Jacquie, was fantastic. The council members were running across the compound, pursued by Sophie, who was pursued by the snake, who was pursued by me, who in turn, was being pursued by Bob with a stick. The mamba had, to my relief, by-passed the Fon. Since the wave of battle had missed him the Fon sat there and did nothing more constructive than help himself to a quick drink to soothe his shattered nerves.

At last Bob and I managed to corner the mamba against the Rest House steps. Then we held it down with a stick, picked it up and popped it into one of our capacious snake-bags. I returned to the Fon, and found the council members drifting back from various points of the compass to join their monarch. If in any other part of the world you had put to flight a cluster of dignitaries by introducing a snake into their midst, you would have had to suffer endless recriminations, sulks, wounded dignity and other exhausting displays of human nature. But not so with the Africans. The Fon sat in his chair, beaming. The councillors chattered and laughed as they approached, clicking their fingers at the danger that was past, making fun of each other for running so fast, and generally thoroughly enjoying the humorous side of the situation.

'You done hold um, my friend?' asked the Fon, generously pouring me out a large dollop of my own whisky.

'Yes,' I said, taking the drink gratefully, 'we done hold um.'

The Fon leaned across and grinned at me mischievously. 'You see how all dis ma people run?' he asked.

'Yes, they run time no dere,' I agreed.

'They de fear,' explained the Fon.

'Yes. Na bad snake dat.'

'Na true, na true,' agreed the Fon, 'all dis small small man de fear dis snake too much.'

'Yes.'

'I never fear dis snake,' said the Fon. 'All dis ma people dey de run . . . dey de fear too much . . . but I never run.'

'No, my friend, na true . . . you never run.'

'I no de fear dis snake,' said the Fon in case I had missed the point.

'Na true. But dis snake 'e de fear you.'

' 'E de fear me?' asked the Fon, puzzled.

'Yes, dis snake no fit bite you . . . na bad snake, but he no fit kill Fon of Bafut.'

The Fon laughed uproariously at this piece of blatant flattery, and then, remembering the way his councillors had fled, he laughed again, and the councillors joined him. At length, still reeling with merriment at the incident, they left us and we could hear their chatter and hilarious laughter long after they had disappeared. This is the only occasion when I have known a green mamba to pull off a diplomatic *coup d'état*.

Chapter Six

Beef with Hand Like Man

MAIL BY HAND

My good friend,
    Good morning to you all. I received your note, but sorry my sickness is still going on as it was yesterday.
    I was sorry for I failed coming to drink with you, due to the sickness.
    I was grateful for the bottle of whiskey and the medicine which you sent to me. I used the medicine yesterday evening and today morning, but no improvement yet. The thing which is giving me trouble is cough, if you can get some medicine for it, kindly send it me through bearer.
    I think that whiskey will also help, but I do not know yet. Please send me some gin if any.
    I am lying on bed.

Yours good friend,
Fon of Bafut.

Of all the animals one finds on a collecting trip the ones that fascinate me most are, I think, members of the monkey tribe. They are delightfully child-like, with their quick intelligence, their uninhibited habits, their rowdy, eager live-for-the-moment attitude towards life, and their rather pathetic faith in you when they have accepted you as a foster-parent.

In the Cameroons, monkeys are one of the staple items of diet, and, as there are no enforced laws covering the number that are shot or the season at which they are shot, it is natural that a vast quantity of females carrying young are slaughtered. The mother falls from the trees with the baby still clinging tightly to her body, and in most cases the infant is unhurt. Generally the baby is then killed and eaten with the mother; occasionally the hunter will take it back to his village, keep it until it is adult and then eat it. But when there is an animal collector in the vicinity, of course, all these orphans end up with him, for he is generally willing to pay much more than the market price for the living animal. So, at the end of two or three months in a place like the Cameroons you generally find that you are playing foster-parent to a host of monkeys of all shapes and ages.

In Bafut, towards the end of the trip, we had seventeen monkeys (not counting apes and the more primitive members of the tribe, such as pottos and bushbabies) and they caused us endless amusement. Probably the most colourful were the patas, slender monkeys about the size of a terrier, with bright gingery red fur, soot-black faces and white shirt-fronts. In the wild state these monkeys live in the grasslands, rather than the forest, walking about like dogs in large family groups, assiduously searching the grass roots and rotten logs for insects or birds' nests, turning over stones to get worms, scorpions, spiders and other delicacies. Periodically they will stand up on their hind-legs to peer over the grass or, if the grass is too tall, they will leap straight up in the air as though they are on springs. Then, if they see anything that smacks of danger they utter loud cries of 'proup ... proup ... proup' and canter away through the grass, with a swinging stride like little red racehorses.

Our four patas lived in a large cage together, and when they were not carefully grooming each other's fur with expressions of intense concentration on their sad, black faces, they were indulging in weird sorts of Oriental dances. Patas are the only monkeys I know that really do dance. Most monkeys will, during an exuberant game, twirl round and round or jump up and down, but patas have worked out special dance sequences for themselves and, moreover, have quite an extensive repertoire. They would start by bouncing up and down on all fours like a rubber ball, all four feet leaving the ground simultaneously, getting faster and faster and higher and higher, until they were leaping almost two feet into the air. Then they would stop and start a new series of 'steps.' Keeping their back legs and hindquarters quite still they would swing the front of their body from side to side like a pendulum, twisting their heads from left to right as they did so. When they had done this twenty or thirty times they would launch into a new variation, which consisted of standing up stiff and straight on their hind legs, arms stretched above their heads, faces peering up at the roof of their cage, and then staggering found and round in circles until they were so dizzy that they fell backwards. This whole dance would be accompanied by a little song, the lyric of which went like this: 'Waaaaow ... waaaaow ... proup ... proup ... waaaaow ... proup,' which was considerably more attractive and comprehensible than the average popular song sung by the average popular crooner.

The patas, of course, adored live food of any description and they felt their day was incomplete if they did not have a handful of grasshoppers apiece, or some birds' eggs, or a brace of juicy, hairy spiders. But for them the caviare of life was the larva of the palm beetle. Palm beetles are an oval insect about two inches in length, which are very common in the Cameroons. They lay their eggs in rotting tree-trunks, but show a marked preference for the soft, fibrous interior of the palm trees. Here, in a moist, soft bed of food, the egg hatches out and the grub soon grows into a livid white, maggot-like creature about three inches long and as thick as your thumb. These fat, twitching grubs were considered by the patas to be the Food of the Gods, and the shrieks of delight that would greet my appearance with a tinful of them would be almost deafening. The curious thing was that, although they adored eating the larvae, they were really scared of them. After I had emptied the grubs on the floor of the cage, the patas would squat round the pile, still screaming with pleasure, and keep touching the delicacies with trembling, tentative fingers. If the grubs moved, they would hastily withdraw their hands and wipe them hurriedly on their fur. At last one of them would grab a fat larva and, screwing up his face and closing his eyes tightly, he would stuff the end into his mouth and bite hard. The larva, of course, would respond to this unkind decapitation with a frantic dying wriggle and the patas would drop it hastily, wipe his hands again and, still sitting with tightly closed eyes and screwed up face, would munch on the morsel he had bitten off. They reminded me of débutantes being introduced to their first fresh oysters.

Unwittingly one day – under the impression that I was doing them a kindness – I caused pandemonium in the patas cage. An army of local children kept us supplied with live food for the animals and they would arrive just after dawn with calabashes full of snails, birds' eggs, beetle-larvae, grasshoppers, spiders, tiny hairless rats and other strange food that our animals enjoyed. On this particular morning one lad had brought in, as well as his normal offering of snails and palm beetle larvae, the larvae of two Goliath beetles. Goliath beetles are the biggest beetles in the world – an adult measures six inches in length and four inches across the back – so it goes without saying that the larvae were monsters. They were also about six inches long, and as thick as my wrist. They were the same horrid unhealthy white as the palm beetle larvae, but they were much fatter, and their skin was wrinkled and folded and tucked like an eiderdown. They had flat, nut-brown heads the size of a shilling, with great curved jaws that could give you quite a pinch if you handled them incautiously. I was very pleased with these monstrous, bloated maggots, for I felt that, since the patas liked palm beetle larvae so much, their delight would know no bounds when they set eyes on these gigantic tit-bits. So I put the Goliath larvae in the usual tin with the other grubs and went to give them to the patas as a light snack before they had their breakfast.

As soon as they saw the familiar tin on the horizon the patas started to dance up and down excitedly, crying, 'proup . . . proup.' As I was opening the door they sat down in a circle, their little black faces wearing a worried expression, their hands held out beseechingly. I pushed the tin through the door and tipped it up so that the two Goliath larvae fell on to the floor of the cage with a soggy thud, where they lay unmoving. To say that the patas were surprised is an understatement; they uttered faint squeaks of astonishment and shuffled backwards on their bottoms, surveying these barrage-balloons of larvae with a horrified mistrust. They watched them narrowly for a minute or so, but as there was no sign of movement from the larvae, they gradually became braver, and shuffled closer to examine this curious phenomenon more minutely. Then, having studied the grubs from every possible angle, one of the monkeys, greatly daring, put out a hand and prodded a grub with a tentative forefinger. The grub, who had been lying on his back in a sort of trance, woke up at once, gave a convulsive wriggle and rolled over majestically on to his tummy. The effect of this movement on the patas was tremendous. Uttering wild screams of fear they fled in a body to the farthest corner of the cage, where they indulged in a disgracefully cowardly scrimmage, vaguely reminiscent of the Eton wall-game, each one doing his best to get into the extreme corner of the cage, behind all his companions. Then the grub, after pondering for a few seconds, started to drag his bloated body laboriously across the floor towards them. At this the patas showed such symptoms of collective hysteria that I was forced to intervene and remove the grubs. I put them in Ticky the black-footed mongoose's cage, and she, who was not afraid of anything, disposed of them in four snaps and two gulps. But the poor patas were in a twittering state of nerves for the rest of the day and ever after that, when they saw me coming with the beetle larvae tin, they would retreat hurriedly to the back of the cage until they were sure that the tin contained nothing more harmful or horrifying than palm beetle larvae.

One of our favourite characters in the monkey collection was a half-grown female baboon called Georgina. She was a creature of tremendous personality and with a wicked sense of humour. She had been hand-reared by an African who had kept her as a sort of pet-cum-watchdog, and we had purchased her for the magnificent sum of ten shillings. Georgina was, of course, perfectly tame and wore a belt round her waist, to which was attached a long rope; and every day she was taken out and tied to one of the trees in the compound below the Rest House. For the first couple of days we tied her up fairly near the gate leading into the compound, through which came a steady stream of hunters, old ladies selling eggs and hordes of children with insects and snails for sale. We thought that this constant procession of humanity would keep Georgina occupied and amused. It certainly did, but not in the way we intended. She very soon discovered that she could go to the end of her rope and crouch down out of sight behind the hibiscus hedge, just near the gate. Then, when some poor unsuspecting African came into the compound, she would leap out of her ambush, embrace him round the legs while at the same time uttering such a blood-curdling scream as to make even the staunchest nerves falter and break.

Her first successful ambuscade was perpetrated on an old hunter who, clad in his best robe, was bringing a calabash full of rats to us. He had approached the Rest House slowly and with great dignity, as befitted one who was bringing such rare creatures for sale, but his aristocratic poise was rudely shattered as he came through the gate. Feeling his legs seized in Georgina's iron grasp, and hearing her terrifying scream, he dropped his calabash of rats, which promptly broke so that they all escaped, leaped straight up in the air with a roar of fright and fled down the road in a very undignified manner and at a speed quite remarkable for one of his age. It cost me three packets of cigarettes and considerable tact to soothe his ruffled feelings. Georgina, meanwhile, sat there looking as if butter would not melt in her mouth and, as I scolded her, merely raised her eyebrows, displaying her pale pinkish eyelids in an expression of innocent astonishment.

Her next victim was a handsome sixteen-year-old girl who had brought a calabash full of snails. The girl, however, was almost as quick in her reactions as Georgina. She saw the baboon out of the corner of her eye, just as Georgina made her leap. The girl sprang away with a squeak of fear and Georgina, instead of getting a grip on her legs, merely managed to fasten on to the trailing corner of her sarong. The baboon gave a sharp tug and the sarong came away in her hairy paw, leaving the unfortunate damsel as naked as the day she was born. Georgina, screaming with excitement, immediately put the sarong over her head like a shawl and sat chattering happily to herself, while the poor girl, overcome with embarrassment, backed into the hibiscus hedge endeavouring to cover all the vital portions of her anatomy with her hands. Bob, who happened to witness this incident with me, needed no encouragement whatever to volunteer to go down into the compound, retrieve the sarong and return it to the damsel.

So far Georgina had had the best of these skirmishes, but the next morning she overplayed her hand. A dear old lady, weighing about fourteen stone, came waddling and wheezing up to the Rest House gate, balancing carefully on her head a kerosene tin full of groundnut oil, which she was hoping to sell to Phillip the cook. Phillip, having spotted the old lady, rushed out of the kitchen to warn her about Georgina, but he arrived on the scene too late. Georgina leapt from behind the hedge with the stealth of a leopard and threw her arms round the old lady's fat legs, uttering her frightening war-cry as she did so. The poor old lady was far too fat to jump and run as the other victims had, so she remained rooted to the spot, uttering screams that for quality and quantity closely rivalled the sounds Georgina was producing. While they indulged in this cacophonous duet, the kerosene tin wobbled precariously on the old lady's head. Phillip came clumping across the compound on his enormous feet, roaring hoarse instructions to the old lady, none of which she appeared to obey or even hear. When he reached the scene of the battle, Phillip, in his excitement, did a very silly thing. Instead of confining his attention to the tin on the old lady's head, he concentrated on her other end, and seizing Georgina attempted to pull her away. Georgina, however, was not going to be deprived of such a plump and prosperous victim so easily and, screaming indignantly, she clung on like a limpet. Phillip, holding the baboon round the waist, tugged with all his might. The old lady's vast bulk quivered like a mighty tree on the point of falling and the kerosene tin on her head gave up the unequal struggle with the laws of gravity and fell to the ground with a crash. A wave of oil leapt into the air as the tin struck the ground and covered the three protagonists in a golden, glutinous waterfall. Georgina, startled by this new, cowardly and possibly dangerous form of warfare, gave a grunt of fright, let go of the old lady's legs and retreated to the full stretch of her rope, where she sat down and endeavoured to rid her fur of the sticky oil. Phillip stood there looking as though he was slowly melting from the waist down, and the front of the old lady's sarong was equally sodden.

'Wah!' roared Phillip, ferociously, 'you *stupid* woman, why you throw dis oil for ground?'

'Foolish man,' screamed the old lady, equally indignant, 'dis beef come for bite me, how I go do?'

'Dis monkey no go bite you, blurry fool, na tame one,' roared Phillip, 'and now look dis my clothes done spoil . . . na your fault dis.'

'No be my fault, no be my fault,' screeched the old lady, her impressive bulk quivering like a dusky volcano, 'na your own fault, bushman, an' all my dress do spoil, all dis my oil done throw for ground.'

'Blurry foolish woman,' blared Phillip, 'you be bushwoman, you done throw dis oil for ground for no cause . . . all dis my clothes done ruin.'

He stamped his large foot in irritation with the unfortunate result that it landed in the pool of oil and splashed over the front of the old lady's already dripping sarong. Giving a scream like a descending bomb the old lady stood there quivering as if she would burst. Then she found her voice. She only uttered one word, but I knew that this was the time to intervene.

'Ibo!' she hissed malevolently.

Phillip reeled before this insult. The Ibos are a Nigerian tribe whom the Cameroonians regard with horror and loathing, and to call someone in the Cameroons an Ibo is the deadliest insult you can offer. Before Phillip could collect his wits and do something violent to the old lady, I intervened. I soothed the good lady, gave her compensation for her sarong and lost oil, and then somewhat mollified the still simmering Phillip by promising to give him a new pair of shorts, socks and a shirt out of my own wardrobe. Then I untied the glutinous Georgina, and removed her to a place where she could not perform any more expensive attacks on the local population.

But Georgina had not finished yet. Unfortunately I tied her up under the lower verandah, close to a room which we used as a bathroom. In it was a large, circular red plastic bowl which was prepared each evening so that we could wash the sweat and dirt of the day's work from our bodies. The difficulty of bathing in this plastic bowl was that it was a shade too small. To recline in the warm water and enjoy it you were forced to leave your feet and legs outside, as it were, resting on a wooden box. As the bowl was slippery it generally required a considerable effort to rise from this reclining position to reach the soap or the towel or some other necessity. This bath was not the most comfortable in the world, but it was the best we could do in the circumstance.

Sophie adored her bath, and would spend far longer than anyone else over it, lying back luxuriously in the warm water, smoking a cigarette and reading a book by the light of a tiny hurricane lantern. On this particular night her ablutions were not so prolonged. The battle of the bathroom commenced with one of the staff coming and saying, in the conspiratorial manner they always seemed to adopt, 'Barf ready, madam.' Sophie got her book and her tin of cigarettes and wandered down to the bathroom. She found it already occupied by Georgina, who had discovered that the length of her rope and the position in which I had tied her allowed her access to this interesting room. She was sitting by the bath dipping the towel in the water, uttering little throaty cries of satisfaction. Sophie shooed her out, called for a new towel and then, closing the door, she undressed and lowered herself into the warm water.

Unfortunately, as she soon discovered, Sophie had not shut the door properly. Georgina had never seen anyone bathe before and she was not going to let such a unique opportunity pass without taking full advantage of it. She hurled herself against the door and threw it wide open. Sophie now found herself in a predicament: she was so tightly wedged in the bath that she could not get out and shut the door without considerable difficulty, and yet to lie there with the door open was out of the question. With a great effort she leaned out of the bath and reached for her clothes which she had fortunately placed near by. Georgina, seeing this, decided that it represented the beginnings of a promising game and jumping forward she clasped Sophie's clothes to her hairy bosom and ran outside with them. This left only the towel. Struggling out of the bath Sophie draped herself in this inadequate covering and, after making sure that no one was around, went outside to try and retrieve her garments. Georgina, finding that Sophie was entering into the spirit of the game, gave a chattering cry of delight and as Sophie made a dart at her she ran back into the bathroom and hurriedly put Sophie's clothes in the bath. Taking Sophie's cry of horror to be encouragement she then seized the tin of cigarettes and put that in the bath too, presumably to see if it would float. It sank, and forty-odd cigarettes floated dismally to the surface. Then, in order to leave no stone unturned in her efforts to give Sophie pleasure, Georgina tipped all the water out of the bath. Attracted by the uproar I appeared on the scene just in time to see Georgina leap nimbly into the bath and start to jump up and down on the mass of sodden cigarettes and clothes, rather after the manner of a wine-treader. It took some considerable time to remove the excited baboon, get Sophie fresh bath water, cigarettes and clothing, by which time the dinner was cold. So Georgina was responsible for a really exhilarating evening.

But of all our monkey family, it was the apes, I think, that gave us the most pleasure and amusement. The first one we obtained was a baby male who arrived one morning, reclining in the arms of a hunter, with such an expression of sneering aristocracy on his small, wrinkled face that one got the impression he was employing the hunter to carry him about, in the manner of an Eastern potentate. He sat quietly on the Rest House steps watching us with intelligent, scornful brown eyes, while the hunter and I bargained over him, rather as though this sordid wrangling over money was acutely distasteful to a chimpanzee of his upbringing and background. When the bargain had been struck and the filthy lucre had changed hands, this simian aristocrat took my hand condescendingly and walked into our living-room, peering about him with an air of ill-concealed disgust, like a duke visiting the kitchen of a sick retainer, determined to be democratic however unsavoury the task. He sat on the table and accepted our humble offering of a banana with the air of one who is weary of the honours that have been bestowed upon him throughout life. Then and there we decided that he must have a name befitting such a blue-blooded primate, so we christened him Cholmondeley St John, pronounced, of course, Chumley Sinjun. Later, when we got to know him better, he allowed us to become quite familiar with him and call him Chum, or sometimes, in moments of stress, 'you bloody ape,' but this latter term always made us feel as though we were committing *lèse-majesté*.

We built Chumley a cage (to which he took grave exception) and only allowed him out at set times during the day, when we could keep an eye on him. First thing in the morning, for example, he was let out of his cage, and accompanied a member of the staff into our bedroom with the morning tea. He would gallop across the floor and leap into bed with me, give me a wet and hurried kiss as greeting and then, with grunts and staccato cries of 'Ah! Ah!' he would watch the tea tray put in position and examine it carefully to make sure that his cup (a large tin one for durability) was there. Then he would sit back and watch me carefully while I put milk, tea and sugar (five spoons) into his mug, and then take it from me with twitching, excited hands, bury his face in it and with a noise like a very large bath running out, start to drink. He would not even pause for breath, but the mug would be lifted higher and higher, until it was upside down over his face. Then there was a long pause as he waited for the delicious, semi-melted sugar to slide down into his open mouth. Having made quite sure that there was no sugar left at the bottom, he would sigh deeply, belch in a reflective manner and hand the mug back to me in the vague hopes that I would refill it. Having made quite sure that this wish was not going to be fulfilled, he would watch me drink my tea, and then set about the task of entertaining me.

There were several games he had invented for my benefit and all of them were exhausting to take part in at that hour of the morning. To begin with he would prowl down to the end of the bed and squat there, giving me surreptitious glances to make sure I was watching. Then he would insert a cold hand under the bedclothes and grab my toes. I was then supposed to lean forward with a roar of pretended rage, and he would leap off the bed and run to the other side of the room, watching me over his shoulder with a wicked expression of delight in his brown eyes. When I tired of this game I would pretend to be asleep, and he would then walk slowly and cautiously down the bed and peer into my face for a few seconds. Then he would shoot out a long arm, pull a handful of my hair and rush down to the bottom of the bed before I could catch him. If I did succeed in grabbing him, I would put my hands round his neck and tickle his collar bones, while he wriggled and squirmed, opening his mouth wide and drawing back his lips to display a vast acreage of pink gum and white teeth, giggling hysterically like a child.

Our second acquisition was a large five-year-old chimp called Minnie. A Dutch farmer turned up one day and said that he was willing to sell us Minnie, as he was soon due to go on leave and did not want to leave the animal to the tender mercies of his staff. We could have Minnie if we went and fetched her. As the Dutchman's farm was fifty miles away at a place called Santa, we arranged to go there in the Fon's Land-Rover, see the chimp and, if she proved healthy, buy her and bring her back to Bafut. So, taking a large crate with us, we set off very early one morning, thinking we would be back with the chimp in time for a late lunch.

To reach Santa we had to drive out of the valley in which Bafut lay, climb the great Bemenda escarpment (an almost sheer three-hundred-foot cliff) and then drive on into the range of mountains that lay beyond it. The landscape was white with heavy morning mist which, waiting for the sun to drag it into the sky in great toppling columns, lay placidly in the valleys like pools of milk, out of which rose the peaks of hills and escarpments like strange islands in a pallid sea. As we moved higher into the mountains we drove more slowly, for here the slight dawn wind, in frail spasmodic gusts, rolled and pushed these great banks of mist so that they swirled and poured across the road like enormous pale amoebas, and we would suddenly round a corner and find ourselves deep in the belly of a mist bank, visibility cut down to a few yards. At one point, as we edged our way through a bank of mist, there appeared in front of us what seemed, at first sight, to be a pair of elephant tusks. We shuddered to a halt, and out of the mist loomed a herd of the long-horned Fulani cattle which surrounded us in a tight wedge, peering through the Land-Rover windows with serious interest. They were huge, beautiful beasts of a dark chocolate brown, with enormous melting eyes and a massive spread of white horns, sometimes as much as five feet from tip to tip. They pressed closely around us, their warm breath pouring from their nostrils in white clouds, the sweet cattle smell of their bodies heavy in the cold air, while the guide cow's bell tinkled pleasantly with each movement of her head. We sat and surveyed each other for a few minutes and then there was a sharp whistle and a harsh cry as the herdsman appeared out of the mist, a typical Fulani, tall and slender with fine-boned features and a straight nose, somewhat resembling an ancient Egyptian mural.

'Iseeya, my friend,' I called.

'Morning, Masa,' he answered, grinning and slapping the dewy flank of an enormous cow.

'Na your cow dis?'

'Yes, sah, na ma own.'

'Which side you take um?'

'For Bemenda, sah, for market.'

'You fit move um so we go pass?'

'Yes, sah, yes, sah, I go move um,' he grinned and with loud shouts he urged the cows onwards into the mist, dancing from one to the other and beating a light tattoo on their flanks with his bamboo walking-stick. The great beasts moved off into the mist, giving deep, contented bellows, the guide cow's bell tinkling pleasantly.

'Thank you, my friend, walka good,' I called after the tall herdsman.

'Tank you, Masa, tank you,' came his voice out of the mist, against a background of deep, bassoon-like cow calls.

By the time we reached Santa the sun was up and the mountains had changed to golden-green, their flanks still striped here and there with tenacious streaks of mist. We reached the Dutchman's house to find that he had been unexpectedly called away. However, Minnie was there and she was the purpose of our visit. She lived, we discovered, in a large circular enclosure that the Dutchman had built for her, surrounded by a tallish wall and furnished simply but effectively with four dead trees, planted upright in cement, and a small wooden house with a swing door. One gained access to this enclosure by lowering a form of drawbridge in the wall which allowed one to cross the dry moat that surrounded Minnie's abode.

Minnie was a large, well-built chimp about three feet six in height, and she sat in the branches of one of her trees and surveyed us with an amiable if slightly vacuous expression. We regarded each other silently for about ten minutes, while I endeavoured to assess her personality. Although the Dutchman had assured me that she was perfectly tame, I had had enough experience to know that even the tamest chimp, if it takes a dislike to you, can be a nasty creature to have a rough and tumble with, and Minnie, though not very tall, had an impressive bulk.

Presently I lowered the drawbridge and went into the enclosure, armed with a large bunch of bananas with which I hoped to purchase my escape if my estimation of her character was faulty. I sat on the ground, the bananas on my lap, and waited for Minnie to make the first overtures. She sat in the tree watching me with interest, thoughtfully slapping her rotund tummy with her large hands. Then, having decided that I was harmless she climbed down from the tree and loped over to where I sat. She squatted down about a yard away and held out a hand to me. Solemnly I shook it. Then I, in turn, held out a banana which she accepted and ate, with small grunts of satisfaction.

Within half an hour she had eaten all the bananas and we had established some sort of friendship: that is to say, we played pat-a-cake, we chased each other round her compound and in and out of her hut, and we climbed one of the trees together. At this point I thought it was a suitable moment to introduce the crate into the compound. We carried it in, placed it on the grass with its lid and allowed Minnie plenty of time to examine it and decide it to be harmless. The problem now was to get Minnie into the crate without, firstly, frightening her too much and, secondly, getting bitten. As she had never in her life been confined in a box or small cage I could see that the whole operation presented difficulties, especially as her owner was not there to lend his authority to the manoeuvre.

So, for three and a half hours I endeavoured, by example, to show Minnie that the crate was harmless. I sat in it, lay in it, jumped about on top of it, even crawled round with it on my back like a curiously shaped tortoise. Minnie enjoyed my efforts to amuse her immensely, but she still treated the crate with a certain reserve. The trouble was that I realized I should only have one opportunity to trap her, for if I messed it up the first time and she realized what I was trying to do, no amount of coaxing or cajoling would induce her to come anywhere near the crate. Slowly but surely she had to be lured to the crate so that I could tip it over on top of her. So, after another three-quarters of an hour of concentrated and exhausting effort, I had got her to sit in front of the upturned crate and take bananas from inside it. Then came the great moment.

I baited the box with a particularly succulent bunch of bananas and then sat myself behind it, eating a banana myself and looking around the landscape nonchalantly, as though nothing could be farther from my mind than the thought of trapping chimpanzees. Minnie edged forward, darting surreptitious glances at me. Presently she was squatting close by the box, examining the bananas with greedy eyes. She gave me a quick glance and then, as I seemed preoccupied with my fruit, she leant forward and her head and shoulders disappeared inside the crate. I hurled my weight against the back of the box so that it toppled over her, and then jumped up and sat heavily on top so that she could not bounce it off. Bob rushed into the compound and added his weight and then, with infinite caution, we edged the lid underneath the crate, turned the whole thing over and nailed the lid in place, while Minnie sat surveying me malevolently through a knot hole and plaintively crying 'Ooo ... Oooo ... Oooo,' as if shocked to the core by my perfidy. Wiping the sweat from my face and lighting a much-needed cigarette, I glanced at my watch. It had taken four and a quarter hours to catch Minnie; I reflected that it could not have taken much longer if she had been a wild chimpanzee leaping about in the forest. A little tired, we loaded her on to the Land-Rover and set out for Bafut again.

At Bafut, we had already constructed a large cage out of Dexion for Minnie. It was not, of course, anywhere near as big as the one she was used to, but big enough to prevent her feeling too confined to begin with. Later she would have to get used to quite a small crate for the voyage home, but after all her customary freedom I wanted to break her gradually to the idea of being closely confined. When we put her into her new cage she explored it thoroughly with grunts of approval, banging the wire with her hands and swinging on the perches to see how strong they were. Then we gave her a big box of mixed fruit and a large white plastic bowl full of milk, which she greeted with hoots of delight.

The Fon had been very interested to hear that we were getting Minnie, for he had never seen a large, live chimpanzee before. So that evening I sent him a note inviting him to come over for a drink and to view the ape. He arrived just after dark, wearing a green and purple robe, accompanied by six council members and his two favourite wives. After the greetings were over and we had exchanged small chat over the first drink of the evening, I took the pressure lamp and led the Fon and his retinue down the verandah to Minnie's cage which, at first sight, appeared to be empty. Only when I lifted the lamp higher we discovered Minnie was in bed. She had made a nice pile of dry banana leaves at one end of the cage and she had settled down in this, lying on her side, her cheek pillowed on one hand, with an old sack we had given her carefully draped over her body and tucked under her armpits.

'Wah!' said the Fon in astonishment, ' 'e sleep like man.'

'Yes, yes,' chorused the council members, ' 'e sleep like man.'

Minnie, disturbed by the lamplight and the voices, opened one eye to see what the disturbance was about. Seeing the Fon and his party she decided that they might well repay closer investigation, so she threw back her sacking cover carefully and waddled over to the wire.

'Wah!' said the Fon, ' 'e same same for man, dis beef.'

Minnie looked the Fon up and down, plainly thought that he might be inveigled into playing with her, beat a loud tattoo on the wire with her big hands. The Fon and his party retreated hurriedly.

'No de fear,' I said, 'na funning dis.'

The Fon approached cautiously, an expression of astonished delight on his face. Cautiously he leant forward and banged on the wire with the palm of his hand. Minnie, delighted, answered him with a positive fusillade of bangs, that made him jump back and then crow with laughter.

'Look 'e hand, look 'e hand,' he gasped, ' 'e get hand like man.'

'Yes, yes, 'e get hand same same for man,' said the councillors.

The Fon leant down and banged on the wire again and Minnie once more responded.

'She play musica with you,' I said.

'Yes, yes, na chimpanzee musica dis,' said the Fon, and went off into peals of laughter. Greatly excited by her success, Minnie ran round the cage two or three times, did a couple of backward somersaults on her perches and then came and sat in the front of the cage, seized her plastic milk bowl and placed it on her head, where it perched looking incongruously like a steel helmet. The roar of laughter that this manoeuvre provoked from the Fon and his councillors and wives caused half the village dogs to start barking.

' 'E get hat, 'e get hat,' gasped the Fon, doubling up with mirth.

Realizing that it was going to be almost impossible to drag the Fon away from Minnie, I called for the table, chairs and drinks to be brought out and placed on the verandah near the chimp's cage. So for half an hour the Fon sat there alternately sipping his drink and spluttering with laughter, while Minnie showed off like a veteran circus performer. Eventually, feeling somewhat tired by her performance, Minnie came and sat near the wire by the Fon, watching him with great interest as he drank, still wearing her plastic bowl helmet. The Fon beamed down at her. Then he leant forward until his face was only six inches away from Minnie's and lifted his glass.

'Shin-shin!' said the Fon.

To my complete astonishment Minnie responded by protruding her long, mobile lips and giving a prolonged raspberry of the juiciest variety.

The Fon laughed so loud and so long at this witticism that at last we were all thrown into a state of hysterical mirth by merely watching him enjoy the jest. At length, taking a grip on himself, he wiped his eyes, leant forward and blew a raspberry at Minnie. But his was a feeble amateur effort compared to the one with which Minnie responded, which echoed up and down the verandah like a machine gun. So, for the next five minutes – until the Fon had to give up because he was laughing so much and out of breath – he and Minnie kept up a rapid crossfire of raspberries. Minnie was definitely the winner, judged by quality and quantity; also she had better breath control, so that her efforts were much more prolonged and sonorous than the Fon's.

At length the Fon left us, and we watched him walking back across the great compound, occasionally blowing raspberries at his councillors, whereupon they all doubled up with laughter. Minnie, with the air of a society hostess after an exhausting dinner party, yawned loudly and then went over and lay down on her banana-leaf bed, covered herself carefully with the sack, put her cheek on her hand and went to sleep. Presently her snores reverberated along the verandah almost as loudly as her raspberries.

BOOK THREE
COASTWARDS AND ZOOWARDS

Chapter Seven

A Zoo in Our Luggage

MAIL BY HAND

Sir,
   I have the honour most respectfully beg to submit this letter to you stating as follows:

(1) I regret extremely at your leaving me, though not for bad but for good.
(2) At this juncture, I humbly and respectfully beg that you as my kind master should leave a good record of recommendation about me which will enable your successor to know all about me.
(3) Though I have worked with several Masters I have highly appreciated your ways then all.

Therefore should the Master leave some footprints behind on my behalf, I shall price that above all my dukedoms.

> I have the honour to be, Sir,
> Your obedient Servent,
> Phillip Onaga (Cook).

It was time for us to start making preparations to leave Bafut and travel the three-hundred-odd miles down to the coast. But there was a lot to be done before we could set out on the journey. In many ways this is the most harassing and dangerous part of a collecting trip. For one thing to load your animals on to lorries and take them that distance, over roads that resemble a tank-training ground more than anything else, is in itself a major undertaking. But there are many other vital things to arrange as well. Your food supply for the voyage must be waiting for you at the port, and here again you cannot afford to make any mistakes, for you cannot take two hundred and fifty animals on board a ship for three weeks unless you have an adequate supply of food. All your cages have to be carefully inspected and any defects caused by six months' wear-and-tear have to be made good, because you cannot risk having an escape on board ship. So, cages have to be rewired, new fastenings fixed on doors, new bottoms fitted on to cages that show signs of deterioration, and a hundred and one other minor jobs.

So, taking all this into consideration, it is not surprising that you have to start making preparations for departure sometimes a month before you actually leave your base camp for the coast. Everything, it seems, conspires against you. The local population, horrified at the imminent loss of such a wonderful source of revenue, redouble their hunting efforts so as to make the maximum profit before you leave, and this means that you are not only renovating old cages, but constructing new ones as fast as you can to cope with this sudden influx of creatures. The local telegraph operator undergoes what appears to be a mental breakdown, so that the vital telegrams you send and receive are incomprehensible to both you and the recipient. When you are waiting anxiously for news of your food supplies for the voyage it is not soothing to the nerves to receive a telegram which states, 'MESSAGE REPLIED REGRET CANNOTOB VARY GREEN BALAS WELL HALF PIPE DO?' which, after considerable trouble and expense, you get translated as: MESSAGE RECEIVED REGRET CANNOT OBTAIN VERY GREEN BANANAS WILL HALF RIPE DO?

Needless to say, the animals soon become aware that something is in the wind and try to soothe your nerves in their own particular way: those that are sick get sicker, and look at you in such a frail and anaemic way you are quite sure they will never survive the journey down to the coast; all the rarest and most irreplaceable specimens try to escape, and if successful hang around taunting you with their presence and making you waste valuable time trying to catch them again; animals that had refused to live unless supplied with special food, whether avocado pear or sweet potato, suddenly decide that they do not like this particular food any more, so frantic telegrams have to be sent cancelling the vast quantities of the delicacies you had just ordered for the voyage. Altogether this part of a collecting trip is very harassing.

The fact that we were worried and jumpy, of course, made all of us do silly things that only added to the confusion. The case of the clawed toads is an example of what I mean. Anyone might be pardoned for thinking that clawed toads were frogs at first glance. They are smallish creatures with blunt, frog-like heads and a smooth, slippery skin which is most untoadlike. Also they are almost completely aquatic, another untoad-like characteristic. To my mind they are rather dull creatures who spend ninety per cent of their time floating in the water in various abandoned attitudes, occasionally shooting to the surface to take a quick gulp of air. But, for some reason which I could never ascertain, Bob was inordinately proud of these wretched toads. We had two hundred and fifty of them and we kept them in a gigantic plastic bath on the verandah. Whenever Bob was missing, one was almost sure to find him crouched over this great cauldron of wriggling toads, an expression of pride on his face. Then came the day of the great tragedy.

The wet season had just started and the brilliant sunshine of each day was being interrupted by heavy downpours of rain; they only lasted an hour or so, but during that hour the quantity of water that fell was quite prodigious. On this particular morning Bob had been crooning over his clawed toads and when it started to rain he thought that they would be grateful if he put their bowl out in it. So he carefully carried the toads' bowl down the verandah and placed it on the top step, brilliantly positioned so that it not only received the rain itself but all the water that ran off the roof. Then he went away to do something else and forgot all about it. The rain continued to rain as if determined to uphold the Cameroons' reputation for being one of the wettest places on earth, and gradually the bowl filled up. As the water level rose so the toads rose with it until they were peering over the plastic rim. Another ten minutes of rain and, whether they wanted to or not, they were swept out of the bowl by the overflow.

My attention was drawn to this instructive sight by Bob's moan of anguish when he discovered the catastrophe, a long-drawn howl of emotion that brought us all running from wherever we were. On the top step stood the plastic bowl, now completely empty of toads. From it the water gushed down the steps carrying Bob's precious amphibians. The steps were black with toads, slithering, hopping and rolling over and over in the water. In this Niagara of amphibians Bob, with a wild look in his eye, was leaping to and fro like an excited heron, picking up toads as fast as he could. Picking up a clawed toad is quite a feat. It is almost as difficult as trying to pick up a drop of quicksilver; apart from the fact that their bodies are incredibly slippery, the toads are very strong for their size and kick and wriggle with surprising energy. In addition their hind legs are armed with small, sharp claws and when they kick out with these muscular hind legs they are quite capable of inflicting a painful scratch. Bob, alternately moaning and cursing in anguish, was not in the calm collected mood that is necessary for catching clawed toads, and so every time he had scooped up a handful of the creatures and was bounding up the steps to return them to their bath, they would squeeze from between his fingers and fall back on to the steps, to be immediately swept downwards again by the water. In the end it took five of us three quarters of an hour to collect all the toads and put them back in their bowl, and just as we had finished and were soaked to the skin it stopped raining.

'If you must release two hundred and fifty specimens you might at least choose a fine day and an animal that is reasonably easy to pick up,' I said to Bob bitterly.

'I can't think what made me do such a silly thing,' said Bob, peering dismally into the bowl in which the toads, exhausted after their romp, hung suspended in the water, peering up at us in their normal pop-eyed, vacant way. 'I do hope they're not damaged in any way.'

'Oh, never mind about us. We can all get pneumonia galloping about in the rain, just as long as those repulsive little devils are all right. Would you like to take their temperatures?'

'You know,' said Bob frowning, and ignoring my sarcasm, 'I'm sure we've lost quite a lot . . . there doesn't seem to be anything like the number we had before.'

'Well, I am not going to help you count them. I've been scratched enough by clawed toads to last me a lifetime. Why don't you go and change and leave them alone? If you start counting them you'll only have the whole damn lot out again.'

'Yes,' said Bob, sighing, 'I suppose you're right.'

Half an hour later I let Cholmondely St John, the chimp, out of his cage for his morning exercise, and stupidly took my eye off him for ten minutes. As soon as I heard Bob's yell, the cry of a mind driven past breaking point, I took a hasty look round and, not seeing Cholmondely St John, I knew at once that he was the cause of Bob's banshee wail. Hurrying out on to the verandah I found Bob wringing his hands in despair, while on the top step sat Cholmondely, looking so innocent that you could almost see his halo gleaming. Halfway down the steps, upside down, was the plastic bowl, and the steps below it and the compound beyond was freckled with hopping, hurrying toads.

We slithered and slipped in the red mud of the compound for an hour before the last toad was caught and put in the bowl. Then, breathing hard, Bob picked it up and in silence we made our way back to the verandah. As we reached the top step Bob's muddy shoes slipped under him and he fell, and the bowl rolled to the bottom, and for the third time the clawed toads set off joyfully into the wide world.

Cholmondely St John was responsible for another escape, but this was less strenuous and more interesting than the clawed toad incident. In the collection we had about fourteen of the very common local dormouse, a creature that closely resembled the European dormouse, except that it was a pale ash grey, and had a slightly more bushy tail. This colony of dormice lived in a cage together in perfect amity and in the evenings gave us a lot of pleasure with their acrobatic displays. There was one in particular that we could distinguish from all the others for he had a very tiny white star on his flank, like a minute cattle brand. He was a much better athlete than the others and his daring leaps and somersaults had earned our breathless admiration. Because of his circus-like abilities we had christened him Bertram.

One morning, as usual, I had let Cholmondely St John out for his constitutional and he was behaving himself in an exemplary fashion. But a moment came when I thought Jacquie was watching him, and she thought I was. Cholmondely was always on the lookout for such opportunities. When we had discovered our mistake and had gone in search of him we found we were too late. Cholmondely had amused himself by opening the doors of the dormouse sleeping-compartments and then tipping the cage over so that the unfortunate rodents, all in a deep and peaceful sleep, cascaded out on to the floor. As we arrived on the scene they were all rushing frantically for cover while Cholmondely, uttering small 'Oooo's' of delight, was galloping around trying to stamp on them. By the time the ape had been caught and chastised there was not a dormouse in sight, for they had all gone to continue their interrupted slumbers behind our rows of cages. So the entire collection had to be moved, cage by cage, so that we could recapture the dormice. The first one to break cover from behind a monkey cage was Bertram, who fled down the verandah hotly pursued by Bob. As he hurled himself at the flying rodent, I shouted a warning.

'Remember the tail . . . don't catch it by the tail . . .' I yelled. But I was too late. Seeing Bertram wriggling his fat body behind another row of cages Bob grabbed him by his tail, which was the only part of his anatomy easily grabbed. The result was disastrous. All small rodents, and particularly these dormice, have very fine skin on the tail, and if you catch hold of it and the animal pulls away the skin breaks and peels off the bone like the finger of a glove. This is such a common thing among small rodents that I am inclined to think it may be a defence mechanism, like the dropping of the tail in lizards when caught by an enemy. Bob knew this as well as I did, but in the excitement of the chase he forgot it, and so Bertram continued on his way behind the cage and Bob was left holding a fluffy tail dangling limply between finger and thumb. Eventually we unearthed Bertram and examined him. He sat plumply in the palm of my hand, panting slightly; his tail was now pink and skinless, revoltingly reminiscent of an ox-tail before it enters a stew. As usual when this happens, the animal appeared to be completely unaffected by what is the equivalent in human terms, of having all the skin suddenly ripped off one leg, leaving nothing but the bare bone and muscle. I knew from experience that eventually, deprived of skin, the tail would wither and dry, and then break off like a twig, leaving the animal none the worse off. In the case of Bertram, of course, the loss would be a little more serious as he used his tail quite extensively as a balancing organ during his acrobatics, but he was so agile I did not think he would miss it much. But, from our point of view, Bertram was now useless, for he was a damaged specimen. The only solution was to amputate his tail and let him go. This I did, and then, very sorrowfully, we put him among the thick twining stems of the bougainvillaea that grew along the verandah rail. We hoped that he would set up house in the place and perhaps entertain future travellers with his acrobatic feats when he had grown used to having no tail.

He sat on a bougainvillaea stem, clutching it tightly with his little pink paws, and looking about him through a quivering windscreen of whiskers. Then, very rapidly, and apparently with his sense of balance completely unimpaired, he jumped down on to the verandah rail, from there to the floor, and then scurried across to the line of cages against the far wall. Thinking that perhaps he was a bit bewildered I picked him up and returned him to the bougainvillaea. But as soon as I released him he did exactly the same thing again. Five times I put him in the bougainvillaea and five times he jumped to the verandah floor and made a bee-line for the cages. After that, I tired of his stupidity and carried him right down to the other end of the verandah, put him once more in the creeper and left him, thinking that this would finish the matter.

On top of the dormouse cage we kept a bundle of cotton waste which we used to change their beds when they became too unhygienic, and that evening, when I went to feed them, I decided that they could do with a clean bed. So, removing the extraordinary treasure trove that dormice like to keep in their bedrooms, I pulled out all the dirty cotton waste and prepared to replace it with clean. As I seized the bundle of waste on top of the cage, preparatory to ripping off a handful, I was suddenly and unexpectedly bitten in the thumb. It gave me a considerable shock, for not only was I not expecting it, but I also thought for a moment that it might be a snake. However, my mind was quickly set at rest for as soon as I touched the bundle of cotton waste an indignant face poked out of its depths and Bertram chittered and squeaked at me in extremely indignant terms. Considerably annoyed, I hauled him out of his cosy bed, carried him along the verandah and pushed him back into the bougainvillaea. He clung indignantly to a stem, teetering to and fro and chittering furiously. But within two hours he was back in the bundle of cotton waste.

Giving up the unequal struggle we left him there, but Bertram had not finished yet. Having beaten us into submission over the matter of accommodation, he started to work on our sympathies in another direction. In the evening, when the other dormice came out of their bedroom and discovered their food plate with squeaks of surprise and delight, Bertram would come out of his bed and crawl down the wire front of the cage. There he would hang, peering wistfully through the wire, while the other dormice nibbled their food and carried away choice bits of banana and avocado pear to hide in their beds, a curious habit that dormice have, presumably to guard against night starvation. He looked so pathetic, hanging on the wire, watching the others stagger about with the succulent titbits, that eventually we gave in, and a small plate of food was placed on top of the cage for him. At last his cunning served its purpose: it seemed silly, since we had to feed him, to let him live outside, so we caught him and put him back in the cage with the others, where he settled down again as if he had never left. It merely seemed to us that he looked a trifle more smug than before. But what other course could one adopt with an animal that refused to be released?

Gradually we got everything under control. All the cages that needed it were repaired, and each cage had a sacking curtain hung in front, which could be lowered when travelling. The poisonous snake-boxes had a double layer of fine gauze tacked over them, to prevent accidents, and their lids were screwed down. Our weird variety of equipment – ranging from mincers to generators, hypodermics to weighing machines – was packed away in crates and nailed up securely, and netting film tents were folded together with our giant tarpaulins. Now we had only to await the fleet of lorries that was to take us down to the coast. The night before they were due to arrive the Fon came over for a farewell drink.

'Wah!' he exclaimed sadly, sipping his drink, 'I sorry too much you leave Bafut, my friend.'

'We get sorry too,' I replied honestly. 'We done have happy time here for Bafut. And we get plenty fine beef.'

'Why you no go stay here?' inquired the Fon. 'I go give you land for build one foine house, and den you go make dis your zoo here for Bafut. Den all dis European go come from Nigeria for see dis your beef.'

'Thank you, my friend. Maybe some other time I go come back for Bafut and build one house here. Na good idea dis.'

'Foine, foine,' said the Fon, holding out his glass.

Down in the road below the Rest House a group of the Fon's children were singing a plaintive Bafut song I had never heard before. Hastily I got out the recording machine, but just as I had it fixed up, the children stopped singing. The Fon watched my preparations with interest.

'You fit get Nigeria for dat machine?' he inquired.

'No, dis one for make record only, dis one no be radio.'

'Ah!' said the Fon intelligently.

'If dis your children go come for up here and sing dat song I go show you how dis machine work,' I said.

'Yes, yes, foine,' said the Fon, and roared at one of his wives who was standing outside on the dark verandah. She scuttled down the stairs and presently reappeared herding a small flock of shy, giggling children before her. I got them assembled round the microphone and then, with my fingers on the switch, looked at the Fon.

'If they sing now I go make record,' I said.

The Fon rose majestically to his feet and towered over the group of children.

'Sing,' he commanded, waving his glass of whisky at them.

Overwhelmed with shyness the children made several false starts, but gradually their confidence increased and they started to carol lustily. The Fon beat time with his whisky glass, swaying to and fro to the tune, occasionally bellowing out a few words of the song with the children. Presently, when the song came to an end, he beamed down at his progeny.

'Foine, foine, drink,' he said, and as each child stood before him with cupped hands held up to their mouths he proceeded to pour a tot of almost neat whisky into their pink palms. While the Fon was doing this I wound back the tape and set the machine for playback. Then I handed the earphones to the Fon, showed him how to adjust them, and switched on.

The expressions that chased one another across the Fon's face were a treat to watch. First there was an expression of blank disbelief. He removed the headphones and looked at them suspiciously. Then he replaced them and listened with astonishment. Gradually as the song progressed a wide urchin grin of pure delight spread across his face.

'Wah! Wah! Wah!' he whispered in wonder, 'na wonderful, dis.' It was with the utmost reluctance that he relinquished the earphones so that his wives and councillors could listen as well. The room was full of exclamations of delight and the clicking of astonished fingers. The Fon insisted on singing three more songs, accompanied by his children, and then listening to the playback of each one, his delight undiminished by the repetition.

'Dis machine na wonderful,' he said at last, sipping his drink and eyeing the recorder. 'You fit buy dis kind of machine for Cameroons?'

'No, they no get um here. Sometime for Nigeria you go find um . . . maybe for Lagos, I replied.

'Wah! Na wonderful,' he repeated dreamily.

'When I go for my country I go make dis your song for proper record, and then I go send for you so you fit put um for dis your gramophone,' I said.

'Foine, foine, my friend,' he said.

An hour later he left us, after embracing me fondly, and assuring us that he would see us in the morning before the lorries left. We were just preparing to go to bed, for we had a strenuous day ahead of us, when I heard the soft shuffle of feet on the verandah outside, and then the clapping of hands. I went to the door and there on the verandah stood Foka, one of the Fon's elder sons, who bore a remarkable resemblance to his father.

'Hallo, Foka, welcome. Come in,' I said.

He came into the room carrying a bundle under his arm, and smiled at me shyly.

'De Fon send dis for you, sah,' he said, and handed the bundle to me. Somewhat mystified, I unravelled it. Inside was a carved bamboo walking stick, a small heavily embroidered skull cap, and a set of robes in yellow and black, with a beautifully embroidered collar.

'Dis na Fon's clothes,' explained Foka. ' 'E send um for you. De Fon 'e tell me say dat now you be second Fon for Bafut.'

'Wah!' I exclaimed, genuinely touched. 'Na fine ting dis your father done do for me.'

Foka grinned delightedly at my obvious pleasure.

'Which side you father now. 'E done go for bed?' I asked.

'No, sah, 'e dere dere for dancing house.'

I slipped the robes over my head, adjusted my sleeves, placed the ornate little skull cap on my head, grasped the walking stick in one hand and a bottle of whisky in the other, and turned to Foka.

'I look good?' I inquired.

'Fine, sah, na fine,' he said, beaming.

'Good. Then take me to your father.'

He led me across the great, empty compound and through the maze of huts towards the dancing house, where we could hear the thud of drums and the pipe of flutes. I entered the door and paused for a moment. The band in sheer astonishment stopped dead. There was a rustle of amazement from the assembled company, and I could see the Fon seated at the far end of the room, his glass arrested halfway to his mouth. I knew what I had to do, for on many occasions I had watched the councillors approaching the Fon to pay homage or ask a favour. In dead silence I made my way down the length of the dance hall, my robes swishing round my ankles. I stopped in front of the Fon's chair, half crouched before him and clapped my hands three times in greeting. There was a moment's silence and then pandemonium broke loose.

The wives and the council members screamed and hooted with delight, the Fon, his face split in a grin of pleasure, leapt from his chair and, seizing my elbows, pulled me to my feet and embraced me.

'My friend, my friend, welcome, welcome,' he roared, shaking with gusts of laughter.

'You see,' I said, spreading my arms so that the long sleeves of the robe hung down like flags, 'You, see, I be Bafut man now.'

'Na true, na true, my friend. Dis clothes na my own one. I give for you so you be Bafut man,' he crowed.

We sat down and the Fon grinned at me.

'You like dis ma clothes?' he asked.

'Yes, na fine one. Dis na fine ting you do for me, my friend,' I said.

'Good, good, now you be Fon same same for me,' he laughed.

Then his eyes fastened pensively on the bottle of whisky I had brought.

'Good,' he repeated, 'now we go drink and have happy time.' It was not until three thirty that morning that I crawled tiredly out of my robes and crept under my mosquito net.

'Did you have a good time?' inquired Jacquie sleepily from her bed.

'Yes,' I yawned. 'But it's a jolly exhausting process being Deputy Fon of Bafut.'

The next morning the lorries arrived an hour and a half before the time they had been asked to put in an appearance. This extraordinary circumstance – surely unparalleled in Cameroon history – allowed us plenty of time to load up. Loading up a collection of animals is quite an art. First of all you have to put all your equipment into the lorry. Then the animal cages are placed towards the tailboard of the vehicle, where they will get the maximum amount of air. But cages cannot be pushed in haphazardly. They have to be wedged in such a way that there are air spaces between each cage, and you have to make sure that the cages are not facing each other, or during the journey a monkey will go and push its hand through the wire of a cage opposite and get itself bitten by a civet; or an owl (merely by being an owl and peering), if placed opposite a cage of small birds, will work them into such a state of hysteria that they will probably all be dead at the end of your journey. On top of all this you must pack your cages in such a way that all the stuff that is liable to need attention *en route* is right at the back and easily accessible. By nine o'clock, the last lorry had been loaded and driven into the shade under the trees, and we could wipe the sweat from our faces and have a brief rest on the verandah. Here the Fon joined us presently.

'My friend,' he said, watching me pour out the last enormous whisky we were to enjoy together, 'I sorry too much you go. We done have happy time for Bafut, eh?'

'Very happy time, my friend.'

'Shin-shin,' said the Fon.

'Chirri-ho,' I replied.

He walked down the long flight of steps with us, and at the bottom shook hands. Then he put his hands on my shoulders and peered into my face.

'I hope you an' all dis your animal walka good, my friend,' he said, 'and arrive quick-quick for your country.'

Jacquie and I clambered up into the hot, airless interior of the lorry's cab and the engine roared to life. The Fon raised his large hand in salute, the lorry jolted forward and, trailing a cloud of red dust, we shuddered off along the road, over the golden-green hills towards the distant coast.

The trip down to the coast occupied three days, and was as unpleasant and nerve-racking as any trip with a collection of animals always is. Every few hours the lorries had to stop so that the small bird cages could be unloaded, laid along the side of the road, and their occupants allowed to feed. Without this halt the small birds would all die very quickly, for they seemed to lack the sense to feed while the lorry was in motion. Then the delicate amphibians had to be taken out in their cloth bags and dipped in a local stream every hour or so, for as we got down into the forested lowlands the heat became intense, and unless this was done they soon dried up and died. Most of the road surfaces were pitted with potholes and ruts, and as the lorries dipped and swayed and shuddered over them we sat uncomfortably in the front seats, wondering miserably what precious creature had been maimed or perhaps killed by the last bump. At one point we were overtaken by a heavy rainfall, and the road immediately turned into a sea of glutinous red mud, that sprayed up from under the lorry wheels like bloodstained porridge; then one of the lorries – an enormous four-wheel-drive Bedford – got into a skid from which the driver could not extricate himself, and ended on her side in the ditch. After an hour's digging round her wheels and laying branches so that her tyres could get a grip, we managed to get her out; and fortunately none of the animals were any the worse for their experience.

But we were filled with a sense of relief as the vehicles roared down through the banana groves to the port. Here the animals and equipment were unloaded and then stacked on the little flat-topped railway waggons used for ferrying bananas to the side of the ship. These chugged and rattled their way through half a mile of mangrove swamp and then drew up on the wooden jetty where the ship was tied up. Once more the collection was unloaded and stacked in the slings, ready to be hoisted aboard. On the ship I made my way down to the forward hatch, where the animals were to be stacked, to supervise the unloading. As the first load of animals was touching down on the deck a sailor appeared, wiping his hands on a bundle of cotton waste. He peered over the rail at the line of railway trucks, piled high with cages and, then he looked at me and grinned.

'All this lot yours, sir?' he inquired.

'Yes,' I said, 'and all that lot down on the quay.'

He went forward and peered into one of the crates.

'Blimey!' he said, 'These all animals?'

'Yes, the whole lot.'

'Blimey,' he said again, in a bemused tone of voice, 'You're the first chap I've ever met with a zoo in his luggage.'

'Yes,' I said happily, watching the next load of cages swing on board, 'and it's my own zoo, too.'

Chapter Eight
Zoo in Suburbia

POSTCARD

Yes, bring the animals here. Don't know what the neighbours will say, but never mind. Mother very anxious to see chimps so hope you are bringing them as well. See you all soon. Much love from us all.

Margo.

Most people who lived in this suburban road in Bournemouth could look out on their back gardens with pride, for each one resembled its neighbour's. There were minor differences, of course: some preferred pansies to sweet peas, or hyacinths to lupins, but basically they were all the same. But anyone looking out at my sister's back garden would have been forced to admit that it was, to say the least, unconventional. In one corner stood a huge marquee, from inside which came a curious chorus of squeaks, whistles, grunts and growls. Alongside it stretched a line of Dexion cages from which glowered eagles, vultures, owls and hawks. Next to them was a large cage containing Minnie, the Chimp. On the remains of what had once been a lawn, fourteen monkeys rolled and played on long leashes, while in the garage frogs croaked, touracos called throatily, and squirrels gnawed loudly on hazel-nut shells. At all hours of the day the fascinated, horrified neighbours stood trembling behind their lace curtains and watched as my sister, my mother Sophie, Jacquie and I trotted to and fro through the shambles of the garden, carrying little pots of bread and milk, plates of chopped fruit or, what was worse, great hunks of gory meat or dead rats. We had, the neighbours felt, taken an unfair advantage of them. If it had been a matter of a crowing cockerel, or a barking dog, or our cat having kittens in their best flower-bed, they would have been able to cope with the situation. But the action of suddenly planting what amounted to a sizeable zoo in their midst was so unprecedented and unnerving that it took their breath away, and it was some time before they managed to rally their forces and start to complain.

In the meantime I had started on my search for a zoo in which to put my animals. The simplest thing to do, it occurred to me, was to go to the local council, inform them that I had the contents of a fine little zoo and wanted them to let me rent or purchase a suitable site for it. Since I already had the animals, it seemed to me in my innocence that they would be delighted to help. It would cost them nothing, and they would be getting what was, after all, another amenity for the town. But the Powers-that-Be had other ideas. Bournemouth is nothing if not conservative. There had never been a zoo in the town, so they did not see why there should be one now. This is what is known by local councils as progress. Firstly, they said that the animals would be dangerous; then they said they would smell; and then, searching their minds wildly for ideas, they said they had not got any land anyway.

I began to get a trifle irritable. I am never at my best when dealing with the pompous illogicalities of the official mind. But I was beginning to grow worried in the face of such complete lack of co-operation. The animals were sitting in the back garden, eating their heads off and costing me a small fortune weekly in meat and fruit. The neighbours, now thoroughly indignant that we were not conforming to pattern, kept bombarding the local health authorities with complaints, so that on an average twice a week the poor inspector was forced to come up to the house, whether he wanted to or not. The fact that he could find absolutely nothing to substantiate the wild claims of the neighbours made no difference: if he received a complaint he had to come and investigate. We always gave the poor man a cup of tea, and he grew quite fond of some of the animals, even bringing his little daughter to see them. But I was chiefly worried by the fact that winter was nearly upon us, and the animals could not be expected to survive its rigours in an unheated marquee. Then Jacquie had a brilliant idea.

'Why not let's offer them to one of the big stores in town as a Christmas show?' she suggested.

So I rang every big store in town. All of them were charming but unhelpful; they simply had not the space for such a show, however desirable. Then I telephoned the last on my list, the huge emporium owned by J. J. Allen. They, to my delight, expressed great interest and asked me to go and discuss it with them. And 'Durrell's Menagerie' came into being.

A large section of one of their basements was set aside, roomy cages were built with tastefully painted murals on the walls depicting a riot of tropical foliage, and the animals were moved out of the cold and damp which had already started, into the luxury of brilliant electric light and a constant temperature. The charge for admission just covered the food bills, and so the animals were warm, comfortable and well fed without being a drain on my resources. With this worry off my mind I could turn my attention once more to the problem of getting my zoo.

It would be wearisome to go into all the details of frustration during this period, or to make a catalogue of the number of mayors, town councillors, parks superintendents and sanitary officers I met and argued with. Suffice it to say that I felt my brain creaking at times with the effort of trying to persuade supposedly intelligent people that a zoo in any town should be considered an attraction rather than anything else. To judge by the way they reacted one would have thought I wanted to set off an atomic bomb on one of the piers.

In the meantime the animals, unaware that their fate hung in the balance, did their best to make life exciting for us. There was, for example, the day that Georgina the baboon decided that she wanted to see a little more of Bournemouth than the inside of J. J. Allen's basement. Fortunately it was a Sunday morning, so there was no one in the store: otherwise I dread to think what would have happened.

I was sipping a cup of tea, just before going down to the store and cleaning and feeding the animals, when the telephone rang. Without a care in the world I answered it.

'Is that Mr Durrell,' inquired a deep, lugubrious voice.

'Yes, speaking.'

'This is the Police 'ere, sir. One of them monkeys of yours 'as got out, and I thought I'd better let you know.'

'Good God, which one is it?' I asked.

'I don't know, sir, really. It's a big brown one. Only it looks rather fierce, sir, so I thought I'd let you know.'

'Yes, thanks very much. Where is it?'

'Well, it's in one of the windows at the moment. But I don't see as 'ow it'll stay there very long. Is it liable to bite, sir?'

'Well, it may do. Don't go near it. I'll be right down,' I said, slamming down the receiver.

I grabbed a taxi and we roared down to the centre of the town, ignoring all speed limits. After all, I reflected, we were on police business of a sort.

As I paid off the taxi the first thing that greeted my eyes was the chaos in one of the big display windows of Allens. The window had been carefully set out to exhibit some articles of bedroom furniture. There was a large bed, made up, a tall bedside light and several eiderdowns tastefully spread over the floor. At least, that was how it had been when the window dresser had finished it. Now it looked as if a tornado had hit it. The light had been overturned and had burned a large hole in one of the eiderdowns; the bedclothes had been stripped off the bed and the pillow and sheets were covered with a tasteful pattern of paw marks. On the bed itself sat Georgina, bouncing up and down happily, and making ferocious faces at a crowd of scandalized church-goers who had gathered on the pavement outside the window. I went into the store and found two enormous constables lying in ambush behind a barricade of turkish towelling.

'Ah!' said one with relief, 'there you are, sir. We didn't like to try and catch it, see, because it didn't know us, and we thought it might make it worse, like.'

'I don't think anything could make that animal worse,' I said bitterly. 'Actually she's harmless, but she makes a hell of a row and looks fierce ... it's all bluff, really.'

'Really?' said one of the constables, polite but unconvinced.

'I'll try and get her in the window there if I can, but if she breaks away I want you two to head her off. Don't, for the love of Allah, let her get into the china department.'

'She came through the china department already,' said one of the constables with gloomy satisfaction.

'Did she break anything?' I asked faintly.

'No, sir, luckily; she just galloped straight through. Me and Bill was chasing 'er, of course, so she didn't stop.'

'Well, don't let's let her get back in there. We may not be so lucky next time.'

By this time Jacquie and my sister Margo had arrived in another taxi, so our ranks had now swelled to five. We should, I thought, be able to cope with Georgina between us. I stationed the two constables, my sister and wife at suitable points guarding the entrance to the china department, and then went round and entered the window in which Georgina was still bouncing up and down on the ruined bed, making obscene faces at the crowd.

'Georgina,' I said in a quiet but soothing voice, 'come along then, come to Dad.'

Georgina glanced over her shoulder in surprise. She studied my face as I moved towards her, and decided that my expression belied my honeyed accents. She gathered herself and leapt through the air, over the still smouldering eiderdown, and grabbed at the top of the great rampart of turkish towelling that formed the background of the window display. This, not having been constructed to take the weight of a large baboon hurtling through the air, immediately collapsed, and Georgina fell to the ground under a cascade of many-hued towelling. She struggled madly to free herself, and just succeeded in doing so as I flung myself forward to catch her. She gave a hysterical squawk and fled out of the window into the interior of the shop. I unravelled myself from the towelling and followed her. A piercing shriek from my sister told me of Georgina's whereabouts; my sister always tends to go off like a locomotive in moments of crisis. Georgina had slipped past her and was now perched on a counter, surveying us with glittering eyes, thoroughly enjoying the game. We approached her in a grim-faced body. At the end of the counter, suspended from the ceiling, hung a Christmas decoration made out of holly, tinsel and cardboard stars. It was shaped somewhat like a chandelier, and looked, as far as Georgina was concerned, ideal for swinging. She poised herself on the end of the counter and as we ran forward she leaped up and grabbed at the decoration in a manner vaguely reminiscent of the elder Fairbanks. The decoration promptly gave way, and Georgina fell to the ground, leapt to her feet and galloped off wearing a piece of tinsel over one ear.

For the next half-hour we thundered to and fro through the deserted store, always with Georgina one jump ahead of us, as it were. She knocked down a huge pile of account books in the stationery department, paused to see if a pile of lace doilies was edible, and made a large and decorative puddle at the foot of the main staircase. Then, just as the constables were beginning to breathe rather stertorously and I was beginning to despair of ever catching the wretched animal, Georgina made a miscalculation. Loping easily ahead of us she came upon what looked like the perfect hiding-place constructed of rolls of linoleum arranged on end. She fled between the rolls and was lost, for the rolls had been arranged in the form of a hollow square, a three-sided trap from which there was no escape. Quickly we closed in and blocked the entrance to the linoleum trap. I advanced towards her, grim-faced, and she sat there and screamed wildly, begging for mercy. As I made a lunge to grab her she ducked under my hand, and as I swung round to prevent her escape I bumped into one of the massive rolls of linoleum. Before I could stop it this toppled forward like a gigantic truncheon and hit one of the constables accurately on the top of his helmet. As the poor man staggered backwards, Georgina took one look at my face and decided that she was in need of police protection. She rushed to the still swaying constable and wrapped her arms tightly round his legs, looking over her shoulder at me and screaming. I jumped forward and grabbed her by her hairy legs and the scruff of her neck, and dragged her away from the constable's legs.

'Cor!' said the constable, in a voice of deep emotion, 'I thought I'd 'ad me chips that time.'

'Oh, she wouldn't have bitten you,' I explained, raising my voice above Georgina's harsh screams. 'She wanted you to protect her from me.'

'Cor!' said the constable again. 'Well, I'm glad *that's* over.'

We put Georgina back in her cage, thanked the constables, cleared up the mess, cleaned and fed the animals and then went home to a well-earned rest. But for the rest of that day, every time the telephone rang I nearly jumped out of my skin.

Another animal that did his best to keep us on our toes was, of course, Cholmondely St John, the chimp. To begin with, after establishing himself in the house and getting my mother and sister well under control, he proceeded to catch a nasty chill that rapidly developed into bronchitis. Having recovered from this he was still very wheezy, and I therefore decreed that he should, for the first winter at any rate, wear clothes to keep him warm. As he lived in the house with us he already was wearing plastic pants and paper nappies, so he was used to the idea of clothes.

As soon as I had made this decision my mother, a delighted gleam in her eye, set to work, her knitting-needles clicking ferociously, and in record time had provided the ape with a variety of woolly pants and jerseys, in brilliant colours and the most complicated Fair-Isle patterns. So Cholmondely St John would loll on the window-sill of the drawing-room, nonchalantly eating an apple, clad in a different suit for each day of the week, completely ignoring the fascinated groups of local children that hung over our front gate and watched him absorbedly.

The attitude of people towards Cholmondely I found very interesting. Children, for example, did not expect him to be anything more than an animal with a curious resemblance to a human being, and with the ability to make them laugh. The adults who saw him, I'm afraid, were much less bright. On numerous occasions I was asked by apparently intelligent people whether he could talk. I always used to reply that chimps have, of course, a limited language of their own. But this is not what my questioners meant; they meant could he talk like a human being, could he discuss the political situation or the cold war, or some equally fascinating topic.

But the most extraordinary question I was ever asked about Cholmondely was asked by a middle-aged woman on the local golf-links. I used to take Cholmondely up there on fine days and let him scramble about in some pine trees, while I sat on the ground beneath, reading or writing. On this particular day Cholmondely had played for half an hour or so in the branches above me and then, growing bored, he had come down to sit on my lap and see if he could inveigle me into tickling him. Just at that moment this strange woman strode out of the gorse bushes and, on seeing Cholmondely and me, stopped short and looked at us. She displayed none of the surprise that most people evince at finding a chimpanzee in a Fair-Isle pullover occupying the golf-links. She came closer and watched Cholmondely closely as he sat on my lap. Then she turned to me and fixed me with a gimlet eye.

'Do they have souls?' she inquired.

'I don't know, madam,' I replied. 'I can't speak with any certainty for myself on that subject, so you can hardly expect me to vouch for a chimpanzee.'

'Um,' she said, and walked off. Cholmondely had that sort of effect on people.

Having Cholmondely living in the house with us was, of course, a fascinating experience. His personality and intelligence made him one of the most interesting animals I have ever kept. One of the things about him that impressed me most was his memory, which I considered quite phenomenal.

I possessed at that time a Lambretta and side-car, and I decided that, providing Cholmondely sat well in the side-car and didn't try to jump out, I would be able to take him for excursions into the countryside. The first time I introduced him to it, I took him for a round trip of the golf-links, just to see how he would behave. He sat there with the utmost decorum, watching the passing scenery with a regal air. Apart from a tendency to lean out of the side-car and try to grab any cyclist we overtook, his behaviour was exemplary. Then I drove the Lambretta down to the local garage to have her filled up with petrol. Cholmondely was as fascinated with the garage as the garage man was with Cholmondely. The ape leaned out of the side-car and carefully watched the unscrewing of the petrol tank; and the introduction of the hose and splash and gurgle of the petrol made him 'Ooo' softly to himself in astonishment.

A Lambretta can travel an incredible distance on a very small amount of petrol and, as I did not use it a great deal, about two weeks had passed before she needed filling up again. We had just come back from a local water-mill where we had been visiting Cholmondely's friend, the miller. This kind man, a great admirer of Cholmondely's, always had a brew of tea ready for us, and we would sit in a row above the weir, watching the moorhens paddling by, sipping our tea and meditating. On the way home from this tea party I noticed that the Lambretta was getting low on fuel, so we drove down to the garage.

As I was passing the time of day with the garage man, I noticed that he was gazing over my shoulder, a somewhat stupefied expression on his face. I turned round quickly to see what mischief the ape was up to. I found that Cholmondely had climbed out of the side-car on to the saddle, and was busy trying to unscrew the cap of the petrol tank. Now this was surely quite a feat of memory. Firstly, he had only seen the filling-up process once, and that had been two weeks previously. Secondly, he had remembered, out of all the various gadgets on the Lambretta, which was the correct one to open in these circumstances. I was almost as impressed as the garage man.

But the time Cholmondely impressed me most, not only with his memory but with his powers of observation, was on the occasions when I had to take him up to London, once to appear on TV and later for a lecture. My sister drove me up to London, while Cholmondely sat on my lap and watched the passing scenery with interest. About half-way to our destination I suggested that we stopped for a drink. You had to be rather careful about pubs when you had Cholmondely with you, for it was not every landlord that appreciated a chimpanzee in his private bar. Eventually we found a pub that had a homely look about it, and stopped there. To our relief, and Cholmondely's delight, we found that the woman who ran the pub was a great animal lover, and she and Cholmondely took an immediate fancy to each other. He was allowed to play catch-as-catch-can among the tables in the bar, he was stuffed with orange juice and potato crisps, he was even allowed to get up on the bar itself and do a war dance, thumping his feet and shouting 'Hoo ... Hoo ... Hoo.' In fact he and the landlady got on so well that he was very reluctant to leave the place at all. If he had been an R.A.C. inspector he would have given that pub twelve stars.

Three months later I had to take Cholmondely up for the lecture; by that time I had forgotten all about the pub in which he had had such a good time, for we had, since then, been in many other licensed establishments which had given him a warm welcome. As we drove along Cholmondely, who was sitting on my lap as usual, started to bounce up and down excitedly. I thought at first he had seen a herd of cows or a horse, animals in which he had the deepest interest, but there was not a farm animal to be seen. Cholmondely went on bouncing, faster and faster, and presently started 'Oo ... ooing' to himself. I still could not see what was exciting him. Then his 'Ooing' rose to a screaming crescendo, and he leaped about on my lap in an ecstacy of excitement, and we rounded a corner and there, a hundred yards ahead, was his favourite pub. Now this meant that he had recognized the countryside we were passing through, and had connected it with his memory of the good time he had had in the pub, a mental process which I had not come across in any other animal. Both my sister and I were so shaken by this that we were very glad to stop for a drink, and let Cholmondely renew his acquaintance with his friend the landlady, who was delighted to see him again.

In the meantime I was still continuing my struggle to find my zoo, but my chance of success seemed to recede farther and farther each day. The collection had to be moved from J. J. Allen's, of course, but here Paignton Zoo came to my rescue. With extreme kindness they allowed me to board my collection with them, on deposit, until such time as I could find a place of my own. But this, as I say, began to seem more and more unlikely. It was the old story. In the initial stages of a project, when you need people's help most, it is never forthcoming. The only solution, if at all possible, is to go ahead and accomplish it by yourself. Then, when you have made a success of it, all the people who would not help you launch it gather round, slap you on the back and offer their assistance.

'There must be an intelligent local council *somewhere*,' said Jacquie one evening, as we pored over a map of the British Isles.

'I doubt it,' I said gloomily, 'and anyway I doubt whether I have the mental strength to cope with another round of mayors and town clerks. No, we'll just have to get a place and do it ourselves.'

'But you'll have to get their sanction,' Jacquie pointed out, 'and then there's Town and Country Planning and all that.'

I shuddered, 'What we should really do is to go to some remote island in the West Indies, or somewhere,' I said, 'where they're sensible enough not to clutter their lives with all this incredible red tape.'

Jacquie moved Cholmondely St John from the portion of the map on which he was squatting.

'What about the Channel Isles?' she asked suddenly.

'What about them?'

'Well, they're a very popular holiday resort, and they've got a wonderful climate.'

'Yes, it would be an excellent place, but we don't know anyone there,' I objected, 'and you need someone on the spot to give you advice in this sort of thing.'

'Yes,' said Jacquie, reluctantly, 'I suppose you're right.'

So, reluctantly (for the idea of starting my zoo on an island had a very strong appeal for me) we forgot about the Channel Islands. It was not until a few weeks later that I happened to be in London and was discussing my zoo project with Rupert Hart-Davis that a gleam of daylight started to appear. I confessed to Rupert that my chances of having my own zoo now seemed so slight that I was on the verge of giving up the idea altogether. I said that we had thought of the Channel Islands, but that we had no contact there to help us. Rupert sat up, and with an air of a conjurer performing a minor miracle, said he had a perfectly good contact in the Channel Islands (if only he was asked) and a man moreover who had spent his whole life in the islands and would be only too willing to help us in any way. His name was Major Fraser, and that evening I telephoned him. He did not seem to find it at all unusual that a complete stranger should ring him up and ask his advice about starting a zoo, which made me warm to him from the start. He suggested that Jacquie and I should fly across to Jersey and he would show us round the island, and give us any information he could. And this accordingly we arranged to do.

So we flew to Jersey. As the plane came in to land the island seemed like a toy continent, a patchwork of tiny fields, set in a vivid blue sea. A pleasantly carunculated rocky coastline was broken here and there with smooth stretches of beach, along which the sea creamed in ribbons. As we stepped out on to the tarmac the air seemed warmer, and the sun a little more brilliant. I felt my spirits rising.

In the car park Hugh Fraser awaited us. He was a tall, slim man, wearing a narrow-brimmed trilby tilted so far forward that the brim almost rested on his aquiline nose. His blue eyes twinkled humorously as he shepherded us into his car and drove us away from the airport. We drove through St Helier, the capital of the island, which reminded me of a sizeable English market town; it was something of a surprise to find, at a cross-roads, a policeman in a white coat and white helmet, directing the traffic. It suddenly gave the place a faintly tropical atmosphere. We drove through the town and then out along narrow roads with steep banks, where the trees leaned over and entwined branches, turning it into a green tunnel. The landscape, with its red earth and rich green grass, reminded me very much of Devon, but the landscape was a miniature one, with tiny fields, narrow valleys stuffed with trees, and small farmhouses built of the beautiful Jersey granite, which contains a million autumn tints in its surface where the sun touches it. Then we turned off the road, drove down a long drive and suddenly, before us, was Hugh's home, Les Augres Manor.

The Manor was built like an E without the centre bar; the main building was in the upright of the E, while the two cross pieces were wings of the house, ending in two massive stone arches which allowed access to the courtyard. These beautiful arches were built in about 1660 and, like the rest of the building, were of the lovely local granite. Hugh showed us round his home with obvious pride, the old granite cider-press and cow-sheds, the huge walled garden, the small lake with its tattered fringe of bulrushes, the sunken water-meadows with the tiny streams trickling through them. At last we walked slowly back under the beautiful archways and into the courtyard, flooded with sunshine.

'You know, Hugh, you've got a wonderful place here,' I said.

'Yes, it is lovely . . . I think one of the loveliest Manors on the island,' said Hugh.

I turned to Jacquie. 'Wouldn't it make a wonderful place for our zoo?' I remarked.

'Yes, it would,' agreed Jacquie.

Hugh eyed me for a moment. 'Are you serious?' he inquired.

'Well, I *was* joking, but it would make a wonderful site for a zoo. Why?' I asked.

'Well,' said Hugh, thoughtfully, 'I'm finding the upkeep too much for my resources, and I want to move to the mainland. Would you be interested in renting the place?'

'Would I?' I said. 'Just give me the chance.'

'Come inside, dear boy, and we'll discuss it,' said Hugh, leading the way across the courtyard.

So, after a frustrating year of struggling with councils and other local authorities, I had gone to Jersey, and within an hour of landing at the airport I had found my zoo.

The Last Word

My zoo in Jersey has now been open to the public for nearly a year. We are probably the newest zoo in Europe and, I like to think, one of the nicest. We are small, of course (at the moment we have only about six hundred and fifty mammals, birds and reptiles), but we will continue to expand. Already we have on show a number of creatures which no other zoo possesses and we hope in the future when funds permit to concentrate on those species which are threatened with extinction.

Many of the animals on show are ones I collected myself. This is, as I said before, the best part of having one's own zoo; one can bring the animals back for it, watch their progress, watch them breed, go out and visit them at any hour of the day or night. This is the selfish pleasure of one's own zoo. But also I hope that, in a small way, I am interesting people in animal life and in its conservation. If I accomplish this I will consider that I have achieved something worthwhile. And if I can, later on, help even slightly towards preventing an animal from becoming extinct, I will be more than content.

Acknowledgements

Britain

All the members of the expedition are very grateful to the following manufacturers who supported them in a most generous way:

S. Allcock & Co. Ltd.	Fishing lines
Ashton Brothers & Co. Ltd.	Bedding
Black & Decker Ltd.	Drill
Bovril Ltd.	Food
Brand & Co. Ltd.	Food
British Bata Shoe Co.	Baseball boots
British Berkefeld Filters Ltd.	Filters
British Nylon Spinners Ltd.	Clothing
Cerebos Ltd.	Food
Coleman Quick Lite Co. Ltd.	Lighting and heating
Joseph Cookson Ltd.	Rope
Cussons Sons & Co.	Toilet goods
W. M. Delf (L'pool) Ltd.	Disinfectant
Electrical Equipment Co.	Generator
Ever-Ready Co. (GB) Ltd.	Batteries
Joseph Farrow & Co. Ltd.	Food
Granta Works	Folding canoe
Horlicks Ltd.	Food
Hugon & Co. Ltd.	Food
Jeyes-Ibco Sales Ltd.	Disinfectant
Percy Jones (Twinlock) Ltd.	Files
G. B. Kalee Ltd.	Ciné equipment
Kimberly-Clark Ltd.	Tissues
Latex Upholstery Ltd.	Foam rubber
Linen Thread Company Ltd.	Special line
Lustraphone Ltd.	Microphone
Marmite Ltd.	Food
William Marples & Sons Ltd.	Tools
Minnesota Mining & Manufacturing Co. Ltd.	Tapes
Don S. Momand Ltd.	Alka-Seltzer
The Nestlé Company Ltd.	Food
Olympia Ltd.	Typewriter
Oxo Ltd.	Food
Pifco Ltd.	Lighting
Polarisers (UK) Ltd.	Sunglasses
Prestige Group Ltd.	Cooking equipment
Rael-Brook Ltd.	Clothing
Reckitt & Colman Ltd.	Medical supplies
Revlon	Toilet goods
Ross Ensign Ltd.	Binoculars

Geo. Salter & Co. Ltd.	Scales
Adhesive Tapes Ltd.	Sellotape
Scott & Turner	Vitamin food
Selfset Ltd.	Traps
The Sheffield Twist Drill & Steel Co. Ltd.	Drills
Smiths Clocks and Watches Ltd.	Watches
Spear & Jackson Ltd.	Spades
Spong & Co. Ltd.	Mincers
Smith & Nephew Ltd.	Medical supplies
Stanley Works (G.B.) Ltd.	Tools
Tate & Lyle Ltd.	Food
Templeton Patents Ltd.	Dried foods
Joseph Tetley & Co. Ltd.	Tea
Tilley Lamp Co. Ltd.	Lamps and heaters
United Yeast Co. Ltd.	Yeast
Venesta Ltd.	Plymax board
Venner Accumulators Ltd.	Batteries for recorder
Vitamins Ltd.	Bemax
Windolite Ltd.	Windolite
Yeo Bros. Paull Ltd.	Tent
S. Young & Sons (Misterton) Ltd.	Animal equipment

Manufacturers whose products were of tremendous value and without which the expedition would have been seriously hampered were:

Allen & Hanburys	Entavet
Barnards Ltd.	Wire netting
B.D.H.	Medical supplies
British Nylon Spinners Ltd., Pontypool	Tarpaulins, etc.
Dexion Ltd.	Dexion
Glaxo Labs Ltd.	Animal food
Greengate & Irwell Rubber Co. Ltd.	Nylon tarpaulins
Joseph Gundry & Co. Ltd.	Special nets
Halex Ltd.	Plastic goods
Kenneth G. Hayes Ltd.	Finch nest baskets
Hounsfield Ltd.	Camp beds
Imperial Chemical (Pharmaceuticals) Ltd.	Medical supplies
The Oppenheimer Casing Co. (UK) Ltd.	Polythene bags
Parke-Davis & Co. Ltd.	Medical supplies
William Smith (Poplar) Ltd.	Tarpaulins, tent, etc.
Thomas's Ltd.	Cages and special equipment
J. H. Thompson (Cutlery) Ltd.	Cutlery
Transatlantic Plastics Ltd.	Polythene bags
Varley Dry Accumulators Ltd.	for ciné camera
Wire-Bands Ltd.	Banding machine.

London: Mr Miles, of Grindlay's Bank Shipping Department, without whose efforts no members of the expedition would ever have arrived in the Cameroons.

Cameroons

Victoria: Mr Eric Saward, Acting Manager, U.A.C., and his wife, Sheila, who generously welcomed us to the Cameroons.

Mr MacCarney, Manager U.A.C., who went out of his way to help us.

Mr Walker, of Elders and Fyffes Ltd., who saw that all food supplies for the animals were safely put upon the ship.

Mr Dudding, Assistant Commissioner, for all his help in arranging all our permits to catch animals.

Mr Austin, of the Agricultural Co-operative, who most kindly sent a large truck all the way up from the coast to Bafut to ensure that both we and our animals caught the ship on time.

Kumba: Dr William Crewe, who so lavishly entertained both us and our animal cargo on our way down to the coast.

Mr Gordon, Manager U.A.C., who supplied us with a 4-wheel drive Bedford truck to take our animals down to the coast.

Mamfe: Mr John Henderson, Manager U.A.C., for whom our gratitude knows no bounds.

Mr John Topham, who invited both us and our animals to invade his house at the dead of night and did everything he could to assist us. He also provided a truck to take the animals down to the coast.

Mr John Thrupp, District Officer of the Mamfe Division, who bore our complaints and protests with fortitude.

Mr Martin Davis, Forestry Officer, who helped us in every way and brought us Tavy, our second black-footed mongoose.

Bamenda: Dr Paul Gebauer, of the Cameroons Baptist Mission, who, as on previous expeditions, suffered much at our hands yet always welcomed us.

Mr Brandt, Manager, U.A.C., and his wife Rona, who did everything they could to make our stay in Bamenda enjoyable.

Mr Shadock, A.D.O., who helped us in many ways to smooth our departure.

Mr Macfarlane, Veterinary Officer of the Cameroons, who gave us invaluable assistance with our animal charges.

Mr Stan Marriot, of the Agricultural Department, who recharged our camera batteries and repaired our Land-Rover on countless occasions. Mr Dennison, Manager U.A.C., who helped us in any way he could.

Tiko: Mr Bowerman, of C.D.C., who made all arrangements for us to stay in the Rest House prior to our sailing.

Our thanks also to the Captain, officers and men of the M.V. *Nicoya*, and in particular to Mr Terrance Huxtable, the Chief Steward, who bore with us and our animals with great fortitude and understanding.

Last of all we would like to thank our good friend, the Fon of Bafut, for giving us 'a happy time.'

The Whispering Land

GERALD DURRELL

The Whispering Land

This is for
BEBITA
who, by leaving Argentina, has deprived me of
my best reason for returning

In calling up images of the past, I find the plains of Patagonia frequently pass across my eyes; yet these plains are pronounced by all to be wretched and useless. They can be described only by negative characters; without habitation, without water, without trees, without mountains, they support merely a few dwarf plants. Why, then, and the case is not peculiar to myself, have these arid wastes taken so firm a hold on my memory?

CHARLES DARWIN: THE VOYAGE OF H.M.S.
BEAGLE

A Word in Advance

Some time ago I wrote a book (called *A Zoo in my Luggage*) in which I explained that after travelling to different parts of the world for a number of years, collecting live animals for various zoos, I became bored.

I was not bored, I hasten to add, with the expeditions, still less with the animals I found. I was bored with having to part with these animals when I returned to England. The only answer to this was to start my own zoo, and how I set out to West Africa to gather the nucleus for this project, brought them home, and eventually founded my zoo on the island of Jersey, in the Channel Islands, I told about in *A Zoo in my Luggage*.

This, then, is really a sort of continuation of that book, for in this I describe how my wife and I, accompanied by my indefatigable secretary, Sophie, went to spend eight months in Argentina, in order to bring back a nice South American collection for the Jersey Zoo, and how, in spite of many setbacks, this was what we did. If any praise for the collection is due it must go to Sophie, for, although she does not figure largely in these pages, she bore perhaps the greatest burden of the trip. Uncomplainingly she stayed in Buenos Aires and looked after the incessant flow of animals which I kept reappearing with from various places, and looked after them, moreover, in a way that would have done credit to a veteran collector. For this, and for many other reasons, I am deeply in her debt.

BOOK ONE

The Customs of the Country

Buenos Aires, decked out for spring, was looking her best. The tall and elegant buildings seemed to gleam like icebergs in the sun, and the broad avenues were lined with jacaranda trees covered with a mist of mauvy blue flowers, or *palo borracho*, with their strange bottle-shaped trunks and their spindly branches starred with yellow and white flowers. The spring-like atmosphere seemed to have infected the pedestrians, who fled across the road through the traffic with even less caution than usual, while the drivers of the trams, buses and cars vied with each other in the time-honoured Buenos Aires game of seeing how close they could get to each other at the maximum speed without actually crashing.

Not having a suicidal streak in me, I had refused to drive in the city, and so we swept on our death-defying way in the Land-Rover with Josefina at the wheel. Short, with curly auburn hair and big brown eyes, Josefina had a smile like a searchlight that could paralyse even the most unsusceptible male at twenty paces. By my side sat Mercedes, tall, slim, blonde and blue-eyed; she habitually wore an expression as though butter would not melt in her mouth, and this successfully concealed an iron will and grim, bulldog-like tenacity of purpose. These two girls were part of my private army of feminine pulchritude that I used in dealing with officialdom in the Argentine. At that precise moment we were heading towards the massive building that looked like a cross between the Parthenon and the Reichstag in whose massive interior lurked the most formidable enemy of sanity and liberty in Argentina: the Aduana, or Customs. On my arrival, some three weeks earlier, they had let all my highly dutiable articles of equipment, such as cameras, film, the Land-Rover and so on, into the country without a murmur; but, for some reason known only to the Almighty and the scintillating brains in the Aduana, they had confiscated all my nets, traps, cage-fronts and other worthless but necessary items of collecting equipment. So, for the past three weeks Mercedes, Josefina and I had spent every day in the bowels of the massive Customs House, being passed from office to office with a sort of clockwork-like regularity which was so monotonous and so frustrating that you really began to wonder if your brain would last out the course. Mercedes regarded me anxiously as Josefina wove in and out of fleeing pedestrians in a way that made my stomach turn over.

'How are you feeling today, Gerry?' she asked.

'Wonderful, simply wonderful,' I said bitterly; 'there's nothing I like better than to get up on a lovely morning like this and to feel that I have the whole sunlit day lying ahead in which to get on more intimate terms with the Customs.'

'Now, please don't talk like that,' she said; 'you promised me you wouldn't lose your temper again; it doesn't do any good.'

'It may not do any good, but it relieves my feelings. I swear to you that if we are kept waiting half an hour outside an office to be told by its inmate at the end of it that it's not *his* department, and to go along to Room Seven Hundred and Four, I shall not be responsible for my actions.'

'But today we are going to see Señor Garcia,' said Mercedes, with the air of one promising a sweet to a child.

I snorted. 'To the best of my knowledge we have seen at least fourteen Señor Garcias in that building in the past three weeks. The Garcia tribe treat the Customs as though it's an old family firm. I should imagine that all the baby Garcias are born with a tiny rubber-stamp in their hands,' I said, warming to my work. 'As christening presents they receive faded portraits of San Martin, so that when they grow up they can hang them in their offices.'

'Oh dear, I think you'd better sit in the car,' said Mercedes.

'What, and deprive me of the pleasure of continuing my genealogical investigation of the Garcia family?'

'Well, promise that you won't say anything,' she said, turning her kingfisher-blue eyes on me pleadingly. 'Please, Gerry, not a word.'

'But I never do say anything,' I protested, 'if I really voiced my thoughts the whole building would go up in flames.'

'What about the other day when you said that under the dictatorship you got your things in and out of the country without trouble, whereas now we were a democracy you were being treated like a smuggler?'

'Well, it's perfectly true. Surely one is allowed to voice one's thoughts, even in a democracy? For the last three weeks we have done nothing but struggle with these moronic individuals in the Customs, none of whom appears to be able to say anything except advise you to go and see Señor Garcia down the hall. I've wasted three weeks of valuable time when I could have been filming and collecting animals.'

'De hand . . . de hand . . .' Josefina said suddenly and loudly. I stuck my arm out of the window, and the speeding line of traffic behind us screeched to a shuddering halt as Josefina swung the Land-Rover into the side turning. The shouts of rage mingled with cries of '*janimál!*' faded behind us.

'Josefina, I do wish you would give us all a little more warning when you're going to turn,' I said. Josefina turned her glittering smile on to me.

'Why?' she inquired simply.

'Well, it helps you know. It gives us a chance to prepare to meet our Maker.'

'I 'ave never crash you yet, no?' she asked.

'No, but I feel it's only a matter of time.'

We swept majestically across an intersection at forty miles an hour, and a taxi coming from the opposite direction had to apply all its brakes to avoid hitting us amidships.

'Blurry Bas-tard,' said Josefina tranquilly.

'Josefina! You must not use phrases like that,' I remonstrated.

'Why not?' asked Josefina innocently. 'You do.'

'That is not the point,' I said severely.

'But it is nice to say, no?' she said with satisfaction. 'And I 'ave learn more; I know Blurry Bastard and . . .'

'All right, all right,' I said hastily. 'I believe you. But for Heaven's sake don't use them in front of your mother, otherwise she'll stop you driving for me.'

There were, I reflected, certain drawbacks to having beautiful young women to help you in your work. True, they could charm the birds out of the trees, but I found that they also had tenacious memories when it came to the shorter, crisper Anglo-Saxon expletives which I was occasionally driven to using in moments of stress.

'De hand . . . de hand,' said Josefina again, and we swept across the road, leaving a tangle of infuriated traffic behind us, and drew up outside the massive and gloomy façade of the Aduana.

Three hours later we emerged, our brains numb, our feet aching, and threw ourselves into the Land-Rover.

'Where we go to now?' inquired Josefina listlessly.

'A bar,' I said, 'any bar where I can have a brandy and a couple of aspirins.'

'O.K.,' said Josefina, letting in the clutch.

'I think tomorrow we will have success,' said Mercedes, in an effort to revive our flagging spirits.

'Listen,' I said with some asperity, 'Señor Garcia, God bless his blue chin and eau-de-cologne-encrusted brow, was about as much use as a beetle in a bottle. And you know it.'

'No, no, Gerry. He has promised tomorrow to take me to see one of the high-up men in the Aduana.'

'What's *his* name . . . Garcia?'

'No, a Señor Dante.'

'How singularly appropriate. Only a man with a name like Dante would be able to survive in that Inferno of Garcias.'

'And you nearly spoilt everything,' said Mercedes reproachfully, 'asking him if that was a picture of his father. You knew it was San Martin.'

'Yes, I know, but I felt if I didn't say something silly my brain would snap like a pair of ancient elastic-sided boots.'

Josefina drew up outside a bar, and we assembled at a table on the edge of the pavement and sipped our drinks in depressed silence. Presently I managed to shake my mind free of the numbing effect that the Aduana always had on it, and turn my attention to other problems.

'Lend me fifty cents, will you?' I asked Mercedes. 'I want to phone up Marie.'

'Why?' inquired Mercedes.

'If you must know she's promised to find me a place to keep the tapir. The hotel won't let me keep it on the roof.'

'What is a tapir?' asked Josefina interestedly.

'It's a sort of animal, about as big as a pony, with a long nose. It looks like a small elephant gone wrong.'

'I am not surprised that the hotel won't let you keep it on the roof,' said Mercedes.

'But this one's only a baby . . . about the size of a pig.'
'Well, here's your fifty cents.'
I found the phone, mastered the intricacies of the Argentine telephone system and dialled Marie's number.
'Marie? Gerry here. What luck about the tapir?'
'Well, my friends are away so you can't take him there. But Mama says why not bring him here and keep him in the garden.'
'Are you sure that's all right?'
'Well, it was Mama's idea.'
'Yes, but are you sure she knows what a tapir is?'
'Yes, I told her it was a little animal with fur.'
'Not exactly a zoological description. What's she going to say when I turn up with something that's nearly bald and the size of a pig?'
'Once it's here, it's here,' said Marie logically.
I sighed.
'All right. I'll bring it round this evening, O.K.?'
'O.K., and don't forget some food for it.'
I went back to where Josefina and Mercedes were waiting with an air of well-bred curiosity.
'Well, what did she say?' inquired Mercedes at length.
'We put Operation Tapir into force at four o'clock this afternoon.'
'Where do we take it?'
'To Marie's house. Her mother's offered to keep it in the garden.'
'Good God, no!' said Mercedes with considerable dramatic effect.
'Well, why not?' I asked.
'But you cannot take it there, Gerry. The garden is only a small one. Besides, Mrs Rodrigues is very fond of her flowers.'
'What's that got to do with the tapir? He'll be on a leash. Anyway, he's got to go somewhere, and that's the only offer of accommodation I've had so far.'
'All right, take him there,' said Mercedes with the ill-concealed air of satisfaction of one who knows she is right, 'but don't say I didn't warn you.'
'All right, all right. Let's go and have some lunch now, because I've got to pick up Jacquie at two o'clock to go and see the shipping people about our return passages. After that we can go and pick up Claudius.'
'Who's Claudius?' asked Mercedes, puzzled.
'The tapir. I've christened him that because with that Roman snout of his he looks like one of the ancient Emperors.'
'Claudius!' said Josefina, giggling. 'Dat is blurry funny.'
So, at four o'clock that afternoon we collected the somewhat reluctant tapir and drove round to Marie's house, purchasing en route a long dog-leash and a collar big enough for a Great Dane. The garden was, as Mercedes had said, very small. It measured some fifty feet by fifty, a sort of hollow square surrounded on three sides by the black walls of the neighbouring houses, and on the fourth side was a tiny verandah and French windows, leading into the Rodrigues establishment. It was, by virtue of the height of the building surrounding it, a damp and rather gloomy little garden, but Mrs Rodrigues had done wonders to improve it by planting those flowers and shrubs which flourish best in such ill-lit situations. We

had to carry Claudius, kicking violently, through the house, out of the French windows, where we attached his leash to the bottom of the steps. He wiffled his Roman snout appreciatively at the scents of damp earth and flowers that were wafted to him, and heaved a deep sigh of content. I placed a bowl of water by his side, a huge stack of chopped vegetables and fruit, and left him. Marie promised that she would phone me at the hotel the first thing the following morning and let me know how Claudius had settled down. This she dutifully did.

'Gerry? Good morning.'

'Good morning. How's Claudius?'

'Well, I think you had better come round,' she said with an air of someone trying to break bad news tactfully.

'Why, what's the matter? He's not ill, is he?' I asked, alarmed.

'Oh, no. Not ill,' said Marie sepulchrally. 'But last night he broke his leash, and by the time we discovered him, he had eaten half Mama's begonias. I've got him locked in the coal cellar, and Mama's upstairs having a headache. I think you had better come round and bring a new leash.'

Cursing animals in general and tapirs in particular, I leapt into a taxi and fled round to Marie's, pausing on the way to buy fourteen pots of the finest begonias I could procure. I found Claudius, covered with coal-dust, meditatively chewing a leaf. I reprimanded him, put on his new and stronger leash (strong enough, one would have thought, to hold a dinosaur) wrote a note of apology to Mrs Rodrigues, and left, Marie having promised to get in touch immediately should anything further transpire. The next morning she rang me again.

'Gerry? Good morning.'

'Good morning. Everything all right?'

'No,' said Marie gloomily, 'he's done it again. Mama has no begonias left now, and rest of the garden looks as if a bulldozer's been at work. I think he will have to have a chain, you know.'

'Dear God,' I groaned, 'what with the Aduana and this bloody tapir, it's enough to drive one to drink. All right, I'll come round and bring a chain.'

Once more I arrived at the Rodrigues establishment, carrying a chain that could have been used to anchor the *Queen Mary*, and bearing another herbaceous border in pots. Claudius was enchanted with the chain. He found it tasted very nice if sucked loudly, and better still, it made a loud and tuneful rattling if he jerked his head up and down, a noise that suggested there was a small iron-foundry at work in the Rodrigues garden. I left hurriedly before Mrs Rodrigues came down to ascertain the cause of the noise. Marie phoned me the following morning.

'Gerry? Good morning.'

'Good morning,' I said, with a strong premonition that it was going to turn out to be anything but a good morning.

'I'm afraid Mama says you will have to move Claudius,' said Marie.

'What's he done *now*?' I asked in exasperation.

'Well,' said Marie, with the faintest tremor of mirth in her voice, 'Mama gave a dinner party last night. Just as we had all sat down there was a terrible noise in the garden. Claudius had managed to get his chain loose from the railings, I don't know how. Anyway, before we could do anything sensible he burst in through the French windows, dragging his chain behind him.'

'Good God!' I said startled.

'Yes,' said Marie, starting to giggle helplessly, 'it was so funny. All the guests leaping about, quite terrified, while Claudius ran round and round the table, clanking his chain like a spectre. Then he got frightened at all the noise and did a ... you know ... a *decoration* on the floor.'

'Dear Heaven,' I groaned, for I knew what Claudius could do in the way of 'decoration' when he put his mind to it.

'So Mama's dinner was ruined, and she says she is very sorry, but could you move him. She feels that he is not happy in the garden, and that anyway, he's not a very *simpatico* animal.'

'Your mother is, I presume, upstairs having a headache?'

'I think it's a bit more than a headache,' said Marie judiciously.

'O.K.' I sighed, 'leave it to me. I'll think of something.'

This, however, appeared to be the last of a series of bedevilments we had suffered, for suddenly everything seemed to go right. The Customs released my equipment, and, more important still, I suddenly found not only a home for Claudius, but the rest of the animals as well: a small house on the outskirts of Buenos Aires had been lent to us to keep our collection in as a temporary measure.

So, with our problems solved, at least for the moment, we got out the maps and planned our route to the south, to the Patagonian coastline where the fur seals and elephant seals gambolled in the icy waters.

At first sight everything seemed to be quite straightforward. Marie had managed to obtain leave from her job, and was to come with us to act as interpreter. Our route was planned with the minute detail that only people who have never been to an area indulge in. The equipment was checked and double-checked, and carefully packed. After all the weeks of frustration and boredom in Buenos Aires we began to feel that at last we were on our way. Then, at our last council of war (in the little café on the corner), Marie produced an argument that she had obviously been brooding upon for some considerable time.

'I think it would be a good idea if we take someone who knows the roads. Gerry,' she said, engulfing what appeared to be a large loaf of bread stuffed with an exceptionally giant ox's tongue, a concoction that passed for a sandwich in Argentina.

'Whatever for?' I asked. 'We've got maps, haven't we?'

'Yes, but you have never driven on those Patagonian roads, and they are quite different from anywhere else in the world, you know.'

'How different?' I inquired.

'Worse,' said Marie, who did not believe in wasting words.

'I'm inclined to agree,' said Jacquie. 'We've heard the most awful reports of those roads from everyone.'

'Darling, you know as well as I do that you *always* hear those sort of reports about roads, or mosquitoes, or savage tribes, wherever you go in the world, and they are generally a lot of nonsense.'

'Anyway, I think Marie's suggestion is a good one. If we could get someone who knows the roads to drive us down, then you know what to expect on the way back.'

'But there *is* no one,' I said irritably, 'Rafael is in college, Carlos is up in the North, Brian is studying . . .'

'There is Dicky,' said Marie.

I stared at her.

'Who is Dicky?' I asked at length.

'A friend of mine,' she said carelessly, 'he is a very good driver, he knows Patagonia, and he is a very nice person. He is quite used to going on hunting trips, so he does not mind suffering.'

'By "suffering" do you mean roughing it, or are you insinuating that our company might be offensive to his delicate nature?'

'Oh, stop being facetious,' said Jacquie. 'Would this chap come with us, Marie?'

'Oh, yes,' she said. 'He said he would like it very much.'

'Good,' said Jacquie, 'when can he come and see us?'

'Well, I told him to meet us here in about ten minutes' time,' said Marie. 'I thought Gerry would want to see him in case he did not like him.'

I gazed at them all speechlessly.

'I think that's a very good idea, don't you?' asked Jacquie.

'Are you asking my opinion?' I inquired. 'I thought you had settled it all between you.'

'I am sure you will like Dicky . . .' began Marie, and at that moment Dicky arrived.

At first glance I decided that I did not like Dicky at all. He did not look to me the sort of person who had ever suffered, or, indeed, was capable of suffering. He was exquisitely dressed, too exquisitely dressed. He had a round, plump face, with boot-button eyes, a rather frail-looking moustache like a brown moth decorated his upper lip, and his dark hair was plastered down to his head with such care that it looked as if it had been painted on to his scalp.

'This is Dicky de Sola,' said Marie, in some trepidation.

Dicky smiled at me, a smile that transformed his whole face.

'Marie have told you?' he said, dusting his chair fastidiously with his handkerchief before sitting down at the table, 'I am delight to come with you if you are happy. I am delight to go to Patagonia, whom I love.'

I began to warm to him.

'If I am no useful, I will not come, but I can advise if you will allow, for I know the roads. You have a map? Ah, good, now let me explanation to you.'

Together we pored over the map, and within half an hour Dicky had won me over completely. Not only did he have an intimate knowledge of the country we were to pass through, but his own brand of English, his charm and infectious humour had decided me.

'Well,' I said, as we folded the maps away, 'if you can really spare the time, we'd like you to come very much.'

'Overwhelmingly,' said Dicky, holding out his hand.

And on this rather cryptic utterance the bargain was sealed.

Chapter One

The Whispering Land

The plains of Patagonia are boundless, for they are scarcely passable, and hence unknown; they bear the stamp of having lasted, as they are now, for ages, and there appears no limit to their duration through future time.

CHARLES DARWIN: THE VOYAGE OF H.M.S. BEAGLE.

We set off for the south in the pearly grey dawn light of what promised to be a perfect day. The streets were empty and echoing, and the dew-drenched parks and squares had their edges frothed with great piles of fallen blooms from the *palo borracho* and jacaranda trees, heaps of glittering flowers in blue, yellow and pink.

On the outskirts of the city we rounded a corner and came upon the first sign of life we had seen since we had started, a covey of dustmen indulging in their early morning ballet. This was such an extraordinary sight that we drove slowly behind them for some way in order to watch. The great dustcart rumbled down the centre of the road at a steady five miles an hour, and standing in the back, up to his knees in rubbish, stood the emptier. Four other men loped alongside the cart like wolves, darting off suddenly into dark doorways to reappear with dustbins full of trash balanced on their shoulders. They would run up alongside the cart and throw the dustbin effortlessly into the air, and the man on the cart would catch it and empty it and throw it back, all in one fluid movement. The timing of this was superb, for as the empty dustbin was hurtling downwards a full one would be sailing up. They would pass in mid air, and the full bin would be caught and emptied. Sometimes there would be four dustbins in the air at once. The whole action was performed in silence and with incredible speed.

Soon we left the edge of the city, just stirring to wakefulness, and sped out into the open countryside, golden in the rising sun. The early morning air was chilly, and Dicky had dressed for the occasion. He was wearing a long tweed overcoat and white gloves, and his dark, bland eyes and neat, butterfly-shaped moustache peered out from under a ridiculous deer-stalker hat which he wore, he explained to me, in order to 'keep the ears heated.' Sophie and Marie crouched in strange prenatal postures in the back of the Land-Rover, on top of our mountainous pile of equipment, most of which, they insisted, had been packed in boxes with knife-like edges. Jacquie and I sat next to Dicky in the front seat, a map spread out across our laps, our heads nodding, as we endeavoured to work out our route. Some of the places we had to pass through were delightful: Chascomus, Dolores, Necochea, Tres Arroyos, and similar delicious names that slid enticingly off the tongue. At one point we passed through two villages, within a few miles of each other, one called 'The Dead Christian' and the other 'The Rich Indian.' Marie's explanation of this strange nomenclature was that the Indian was rich because he killed the Christian, and had stolen all his money, but attractive though this story was, I felt it could not be the right one.

For two days we sped through the typical landscape of the Pampa, flat golden grassland in which the cattle grazed knee-deep; occasional clumps of eucalyptus trees, with their bleached and peeling trunks like leprous limbs; small, neat *estancias*, gleaming white in the shade of huge, carunculated *ombù* trees, that stood massively and grimly on their enormous squat trunks. In places the neat fences that lined the road were almost obliterated under a thick cloak of convolvulus, hung with electric-blue flowers the size of saucers, and every third or fourth fence-post would have balanced upon it the strange, football-like nest of an oven-bird. It was a lush, prosperous and well-fed-looking landscape that only just escaped being monotonous. Eventually, in the evening of the third day, we lost our way, and so we pulled in to the side of the road and argued over the map. Our destination was a town called Carmen de Patagones, on the north bank of the Rio Negro. I particularly wanted to spend the night here, because it was a town that Darwin had stayed in for some time during the voyage of the *Beagle*, and I was interested to see how it had changed in the last hundred years. So, in spite of near-mutiny on the part of the rest of the expedition, who wanted to stop at the first suitable place we came to, we drove on. As it turned out it was all we could have done anyway, for we did not pass a single habitation until we saw gleaming ahead of us a tiny cluster of feeble lights. Within ten minutes we were driving cautiously through the cobbled streets of Carmen de Patagones, lit by pale, trembling street-lights. It was two o'clock in the morning, and every house was blank-faced and tightly shuttered. Our chances of finding anyone who could direct us to a hostelry were remote, and we certainly needed direction, for each house looked exactly like the ones on each side of it, and there was no indication as to whether it was a hotel or a private habitation. We stopped in the main square of the town and were arguing tiredly and irritably over this problem when suddenly, under one of the street lights, appeared an angel of mercy, in the shape of a tall, slim policeman clad in an immaculate uniform, his belt and boots gleaming. He saluted smartly, bowed to the female members of the party, and with old-world courtesy directed us up some side-roads to where he said we should find an hotel. We came to a great gloomy house, heavily shuttered, with a massive front door that would have done justice to a cathedral. We beat a sharp tattoo on its weather-beaten surface and waited results patiently. Ten minutes later there was still no response from the inhabitants, and so Dicky, in desperation, launched an assault on the door that would, if it had succeeded, have awakened the dead. But as he lashed out at the door it swung mysteriously open under his assault, and displayed a long, dimly-lit passageway, with doors along each side, and a marble staircase leading to the upper floors. Dead tired and extremely hungry we were in no mood to consider other people's property, so we marched into the echoing hall like an invading army. We stood there and shouted '¡*Holà¡*' until the hotel rang with our shouts, but there was no response.

'I think, Gerry, that sometime they are all deceased,' said Dicky gravely.

'Well, if they are I suggest we spread out and find ourselves some beds,' I said.

So we climbed the marble staircase and found ourselves three bedrooms, with beds made up, by the simple expedient of opening every door in sight. Eventually, having found a place to sleep, Dicky and I went downstairs to see if the hotel boasted of any sanitary arrangements. The first door we threw open in our search led us into a dim bedroom in which was an enormous double-bed hung with an old-fashioned canopy. Before we could back out of the room a huge figure surged out from under the bedclothes like a surfacing whale, and waddled towards us. It turned out to be a colossal woman, clad in a flowing flannel nightie, who must have weighed somewhere in the neighbourhood of fifteen stone. She came out, blinking, into the hallway, pulling on a flowing kimono of bright green covered with huge pink roses, so the effect was rather as if one of the more exotic floral displays of the Chelsea Flower Show had suddenly taken on a life of its own. Over her ample bosoms spread two long streamers of grey hair which she flicked deftly over her shoulder as she did up her kimono, smiling at us with sleepy goodwill.

'*Buenas noches*,' she said politely.

'*Buenas noches, señora*,' we replied, not to be outdone in good manners at that hour of the morning.

'¿*Hablo con la patrona?*' inquired Dicky.

'*Si, si, señor*,' she said, smiling broadly, '¿*que queres?*'

Dicky apologized for our late arrival, but *la patrona* waved away our apologies. Was it possible, Dicky asked, for us to have some sandwiches and coffee? Why not? inquired *la patrona*. Further, said Dicky, we were in urgent need of a lavatory, and could she be so kind as to direct us to it. With great good humour she led us to a small tiled room, showed us how to pull the plug, and stood there chatting amiably while Dicky and I relieved the pangs of nature. Then she puffed and undulated her way down to the kitchen and cut us a huge pile of sandwiches and made a steaming mug of coffee. Having assured herself that there was nothing further she could do for our comfort, she waddled off to bed.

The next morning, having breakfasted, we did a rapid tour of the town. As far as I could see, apart from the introduction of electricity, it had changed very little since Darwin's day, and so we left and sped down a hill and across the wide iron bridge that spanned the rusty red waters of the Rio Negro. We rattled across the bridge from the Province of Buenos Aires to the Province of Chubut, and by that simple action of crossing a river we entered a different world.

Gone were the lush green plains of the Pampa, and in their place was an arid waste stretching away as far as the eye could see on each side of the dusty road, a uniform pelt of grey-green scrub composed of plants about three feet high, each armed with a formidable array of thorns and spikes. Nothing appeared to live in this dry scrub, for when we stopped there was no bird or insect song, only the whispering of the wind through the thorn scrub in this monochromatic Martian landscape, and the only moving thing apart from ourselves was the giant plume of dust we trailed behind the vehicle. This was terribly tiring country to drive in. The road, deeply rutted and potholed, unrolled straight ahead to the horizon, and after a few hours this monotony of scene numbed one's brain, and one would suddenly drop off to sleep, to be awoken by the vicious scrunch of the wheels as the Land-Rover swerved off into the brittle scrub.

The evening before we were due to reach Deseado this happened on a stretch of road which, unfortunately, had recently been rained upon, so that the surface had turned into something resembling high-grade glue. Dicky, who had been driving for a long time, suddenly nodded off behind the wheel, and before anyone could do anything sensible, both Land-Rover and trailer had skidded violently into the churned-up mud at the side of the road, and settled there snugly, wheels spinning like mad. Reluctantly we got out into the bitter chill of the evening wind, and in the dim sunset light set to work to unhitch the trailer and then push it and the Land-Rover separately out of the mud. Then, our feet and hands frozen, the five of us crouched in the shelter of the Land-Rover and watched the sunset, passing from hand to hand a bottle of Scotch which I had been keeping for just such an emergency.

On every side of us the scrubland stretched away, dark and flat, so that you got the impression of being in the centre of a gigantic plate. The sky had become suffused with green as the sun sank, and then, unexpectedly, turned to a very pale powder-blue. A tattered mass of clouds on the western horizon suddenly turned black, edged delicately with flame-red, and resembled a great armada of Spanish galleons waging a fierce sea-battle across the sky, drifting towards each other, turned into black silhouette by the fierce glare from their cannons. As the sun sank lower and lower the black of the clouds became shot and mottled with grey, and the sky behind them became striped with green, blue and pale red. Suddenly our fleet of galleons disappeared, and in its place was a perfect archipelago of islands strung out across the sky in what appeared to be a placid, sunset-coloured sea. The illusion was perfect: you could pick out the tiny, white rimmed coves in the rocky, indented shoreline, the occasional long, white beach; the dangerous shoal of rocks formed by a wisp of cloud at the entrance to a safe anchorage; the curiously-shaped mountains inland covered with a tattered pelt of evening-dark forest. We sat there, the whisky warming our bodies, watching enraptured the geography of this archipelago unfold. We each of us chose an island which appealed to us, on which we would like to spend a holiday, and stipulated what the hotel on each of our islands would have to provide in the way of civilized amenities.

'A very, *very* big bath, and very deep,' said Marie.

'No, a nice hot shower and a comfortable chair,' said Sophie.

'Just a bed,' said Jacquie, 'a large feather bed.'

'A bar that serves real ice with its drinks,' I said dreamily.

Dicky was silent for a moment. Then he glanced down at his feet, thickly encrusted with rapidly drying mud.

'I must have a man to clean my feets,' he said firmly.

'Well, I doubt whether we'll get any of that at Deseado,' I said gloomily, 'but we'd better press on.'

When we drove into Deseado at ten o'clock the next morning, it became immediately obvious that we could not expect any such luxuries as feather beds, ice in the drinks, or even a man to clean our feets. It was the most extraordinarily dead-looking town I had ever been in. It resembled the set for a rather bad Hollywood cowboy film, and gave the impression that its inhabitants (two thousand, according to the guide-book) had suddenly packed up and left it alone to face the biting winds and scorching sun. The empty, rutted streets between the blank-faced houses were occasionally stirred by the wind, which produced half-hearted dust-devils, that swirled up for a moment and then collapsed tiredly to the ground. As we drove slowly into what we imagined to be the centre of the town we saw only a dog, trotting briskly about his affairs, and a child, crouched in the middle of a road, absorbed in some mysterious game of childhood. Then, swinging the Land-Rover round a corner, we were startled to see a man on horseback, clopping slowly along the road with the subdued air of one who is the sole survivor of a catastrophe. He pulled up and greeted us politely, but without interest, when we stopped, and directed us to the only two hotels in the place. As these turned out to be opposite each other and both equally unprepossessing from the outside, we chose one by tossing a coin and made our way inside.

In the bar we found the proprietor, who, with the air of one who had just suffered a terrible bereavement, reluctantly admitted that he had accommodation, and led us through dim passages to three small, grubby rooms. Dicky, his deer-stalker on the back of his head, stood in the centre of his room, pulling off his white gloves, surveying the sagging bed and its grey linen with a cat-like fastidiousness.

'You know what, Gerry?' he said with conviction. 'This is the stinkiest hotel I ever dream.'

'I hope you never dream of a stinkier one,' I assured him.

Presently we all repaired to the bar to have a drink and await the arrival of one Captain Giri, whom I had an introduction to, a man who knew all about the penguin colonies of Puerto Deseado. We sat round a small table, sipping our drinks and watching the other inhabitants of the bar with interest. For the most part they seemed to consist of very old men, with long, sweeping moustaches, whose brown faces were seamed and stitched by the wind. They sat in small groups, crouched over their tiny tumblers of cognac or wine with a dead air, as though they were hibernating there in this dingy bar, staring hopelessly into the bottoms of their glasses, wondering when the wind would die down, and knowing it would not. Dicky, delicately smoking a cigarette, surveyed the smoke-blackened walls, the rows of dusty bottles, and the floor with its twenty-year-old layer of dirt well trodden into its surface.

'What a bar, eh?' he said to me.

'Not very convivial, is it?'

'It is so old . . . it has an air of old,' he said staring about him. 'You know, Gerry, I bet it is so old that even the flies have beards.'

Then the door opened suddenly, a blast of cold air rushed into the bar, the old men looked up in a flat-eyed, reptilian manner, and through the door strode Captain Giri. He was a tall, well-built man with blond hair, a handsome, rather aesthetic face and the most vivid and candid blue eyes I had ever seen. Having introduced himself he sat down at our table and looked round at us with such friendliness and good humour in his child-like eyes that the dead atmosphere of the bar dropped away, and we suddenly found ourselves becoming alive and enthusiastic. We had a drink, and then Captain Giri produced a large roll of charts and spread them on the table, while we pored over them.

'Penguins,' said the Captain meditatively, running his forefinger over the chart. 'Now, down here is the best colony ... by far the best and biggest, but I think that that is too far for you, is it not?'

'Well, it is a bit,' I admitted. 'We didn't want to go that far south if we could avoid it. It's a question of time, really. I had hoped that there would be a reasonable colony within fairly easy reach of Deseado.'

'There is, there is,' said the Captain, shuffling the charts like a conjuror and producing another one from the pile. 'Now, here, you see, at this spot ... it's about four hours' drive from Deseado ... all along this bay here.'

'That's wonderful,' I said enthusiastically, 'just the right distance.'

'There is only one thing that worries me,' said the Captain, turning troubled blue eyes on to me. 'Are there enough birds there for what you want ... for your photography?'

'Well,' I said doubtfully, 'I want a fair number. How many are there in this colony?'

'At a rough estimate I should say a million,' said Captain Giri. 'Will that be enough?'

I gaped at him. The man was not joking. He was seriously concerned that a million penguins might prove to be too meagre a quantity for my purpose.

'I think I can make out with a million penguins,' I said. 'I should be able to find one or two photogenic ones among that lot. Tell me, are they all together, or scattered about?'

'Well, there are about half or three-quarters concentrated *here*,' he said, stabbing at the chart. 'And the rest are distributed all along the bay *here*.'

'Well, that seems perfect to me. Now what about somewhere to camp?'

'Ah!' said Captain Giri. 'That is the difficulty. Now, just here is the *estancia* of a friend of mine, Señor Huichi. He is not on the *estancia* at the moment. But if we went to see him he might let you stay there. It is, you see, about two kilometres from the main colony, so it would be a good place for you to stay.'

'That would be wonderful,' I said enthusiastically. 'When could we see Señor Huichi?'

The Captain consulted his watch and made a calculation.

'We can go and see him now, if you would like,' he said.

'Right!' I said, finishing my drink. 'Let's go.'

Huichi's house was on the outskirts of Deseado, and Huichi himself, when Captain Giri introduced us, was a man I took an instant liking to. Short, squat, with a weather-browned face, he had very dark hair, heavy black eyebrows and moustache, and dark brown eyes that were kind and humorous, with crow's feet at the corners. In his movements and his speech he had an air of quiet, unruffled confidence about him that was very reassuring. He stood silently while Giri explained our mission, occasionally glancing at me, as if summing me up. Then he asked a couple of questions, and, finally, to my infinite relief, he held out his hand to me and smiled broadly.

'Señor Huichi has agreed that you shall use his *estancia*,' said Giri, 'and he is going to accompany you himself, so as to show you the best places for penguins.'

'That is very kind of Señor Huichi ... we are most grateful,' I said. 'Could we leave tomorrow afternoon, after I have seen my friend off on the plane?'

'*¿Si, si, como no?*' said Huichi when this had been translated to him. So we arranged to meet him on the morrow, after an early lunch, when we had seen Dicky off on the plane that was to take him to Buenos Aires.

So, that evening we sat in the depressing bar of our hotel, sipping our drinks and contemplating the forlorn fact that the next day Dicky would be leaving us. He had been a charming and amusing companion, who had put up with discomfort without complaint, and had enlivened our flagging spirits throughout the trip with jokes, fantastically phrased remarks, and lilting Argentine songs. We were going to miss him, and he was equally depressed at the thought of leaving us just when the trip was starting to get interesting. In a daring fit of *joie de vivre* the hotel proprietor had switched on a small radio, strategically placed on a shelf between two bottles of brandy. This now blared out a prolonged and mournful tango of the more cacophonous sort. We listened to it in silence until the last despairing howls had died away.

'What is the translation of that jolly little piece?' I asked Marie.

'It is a man who has discovered that his wife has T.B.,' she explained. 'He has lost his job and his children are starving. His wife is dying. He is very sad, and he asks the meaning of life.'

The radio launched itself into another wailing air that sounded almost identical with the first. When it had ended I raised my eyebrows inquiringly at Marie.

'That is a man who has just discovered that his wife is unfaithful,' she translated moodily. 'He has stabbed her. Now he is to be hung, and his children will be without mother or father. He is very sad and he asks the meaning of life.'

A third refrain rent the air. I looked at Marie. She listened attentively for a moment, then shrugged.

'The same,' she said tersely.

We got up in a body and went to bed.

Early the next morning Marie and I drove Dicky out to the airstrip, while Sophie and Jacquie went round the three shops in Deseado to buy necessary supplies for our trip out to Huichi's *estancia*. The airstrip consisted of a more or less level strip of ground on the outskirts of the town, dominated by a moth-eaten-looking hangar, whose loose boards flapped and creaked in the wind. The only living things were three ponies, grazing forlornly. Twenty minutes after the plane had been due in there was still no sign of her, and we began to think that Dicky would have to stay with us after all. Then along the dusty road from the town came bustling a small van. It stopped by the hangar, and from inside appeared two very official-looking men in long khaki coats. They examined the wind-sock with a fine air of concentration, stared up into the sky, and consulted each other with frowning faces. Then they looked at their watches and paced up and down.

'They must be mechanics,' said Dicky.

'They certainly look very official,' I admitted.

'Hey! Listen!' said Dicky, as a faint drone made itself heard. 'She is arrive.'

The plane came into view as a minute speck on the horizon that rapidly grew bigger and bigger. The two men in khaki coats now came into their own. With shrill cries they ran out on to the airstrip and proceeded to drive away the three ponies, who, up till then had been grazing placidly in the centre of what now turned out to be the runway. There was one exciting moment just as the plane touched down, when we thought that one of the ponies was going to break back, but one of the khaki-clad men, launched himself forward and grabbed it by the mane at the last minute. The plane bumped and shuddered to a halt, and the two men left their equine charges and produced, from the depths of the hangar, a flimsy ladder on wheels which they set against the side of the plane. Apparently Dicky was the only passenger to be picked up in Deseado.

Dicky wrung my hand.

'Gerry,' he said, 'you will do for me one favour, yes?'

'Of course, Dicky,' I said, 'anything at all.'

'See that there is no bloody bastard horses in the way when we go up, eh?' he said earnestly, and then strode off to the plane, the flaps of his deerstalker flopping to and fro in the wind.

The plane roared off, the ponies shambled back on to the runway, and we turned the blunt snout of the Land-Rover back towards the town.

We picked up Huichi at a little after twelve, and he took over the wheel of the Land-Rover. I was heartily glad of this, for we had only travelled a couple of miles from Deseado when we branched off the road on to something so vague that it could hardly be dignified with the term of track. Occasionally this would disappear altogether, and, if left to myself, I would have been utterly lost, but Huichi would aim the Land-Rover at what appeared to be an impenetrable thicket of thorn bushes, and we would tear through it, the thorns screaming along the sides of the vehicle like so many banshees, and there, on the further side, the faint wisp of track would start again. At other points the track turned into what appeared to be the three-feet-deep bed of an extinct river, exactly the same width as the Land-Rover, so we were driving cautiously along with two wheels on one bank – as it were – and two wheels on the other. Any slight miscalculation here and the vehicle could have fallen into the trough and become hopelessly stuck.

Gradually, as we got nearer and nearer to the sea, the landscape underwent a change. Instead of being flat it became gently undulating, and here and there the wind had rasped away the topsoil and exposed large areas of yellow and rust-red gravel, like sores on the furry pelt of the land. These small desert-like areas seemed to be favoured by that curious animal, the Patagonian hare, for it was always on these brilliant expanses of gravel that we found them, sometimes in pairs, sometimes in small groups of three or four. They were strange creatures, that looked as though they had been put together rather carelessly. They had blunt, rather hare-like faces, small, neat, rabbit-shaped ears, neat forequarters with slender forelegs. But the hindquarters were large and muscular in comparison, with powerful hindlegs. The most attractive part of their anatomy was their eyes, which were large, dark and lustrous, with a thick fringe of eyelashes. They would lie on the gravel, sunning themselves, gazing aristocratically down their blunt noses, looking like miniature Trafalgar Square lions. They would let us approach fairly close, and then suddenly their long lashes would droop over their eyes seductively, and with amazing speed they would bounce into a sitting position. They would turn their heads and gaze at us for one brief moment, and then they would launch themselves at the heat-shimmered horizon in a series of gigantic bounding leaps, as if they were on springs, the black and white pattern on their behinds showing up like a retreating target.

Presently, towards evening, the sun sank lower and in its slanting rays the landscape took on new colours. The low growth of thorn scrub became purple, magenta and brown, and the areas of gravel were splashed with scarlet, rust, white and yellow. As we scrunched our way across one such multi-coloured area of gravel we noticed a black blob in the exact centre of the expanse, and driving closer to it we discovered it was a huge tortoise, heaving himself over the hot terrain with the grim determination of a glacier. We stopped and picked him up, and the reptile, horrified by such an unexpected meeting, urinated copiously. Where he could have found, in that desiccated land, sufficient moisture to produce this lavish defensive display was a mystery. However, we christened him Ethelbert, put him in the back of the Land-Rover and drove on.

Presently, in the setting sun, the landscape heaved itself up into a series of gentle undulations, and we switchbacked over the last of these and out on to what at first looked like the level bed of an ancient lake. It lay encircled by a ring of low hills, and was, in fact, a sort of miniature dust-bowl created by the wind, which had carried the sand from the shore behind the hills and deposited it here in a thick, choking layer that had killed off the vegetation. As we roared across this flat area, spreading a fan of white dust behind us, we saw, in the lee of the further hills, a cluster of green trees, the first we had seen since leaving Deseado. As we drew nearer we could see that this little oasis of trees was surrounded by a neat white fence, and in the centre, sheltered by the trees, stood a neat wooden house, gaily painted in bright blue and white.

Huichi's two peons came to meet us, two wild-looking characters dressed in *bombachas* and tattered shirts, with long black hair and dark, flashing eyes. They helped us unload our gear and carry it into the house, and then, while we unpacked and washed, they went with Huichi to kill a sheep and prepare an *asado* in our honour. At the bottom of the slope on which the house was built, Huichi had prepared a special *asado* ground. An *asado* needs a fierce fire, and with the biting and continuous wind that blew in Patagonia you had to be careful unless you wanted to see your entire fire suddenly lifted into the air and blown away to set fire to the tinder-dry scrub for miles around. In order to guard against this Huichi had planted, at the bottom of the hill, a great square of cypress trees. These had been allowed to grow up to a height of some twelve feet, and had then had their tops lopped off, with the result that they had grown very bushy. They had been planted so close together in the first place that now their branches entwined, and formed an almost impenetrable hedge. Then Huichi had carved a narrow passage-way into the centre of this box of cypress, and had there chopped out a room, some twenty feet by twelve. This was the *asado* room, for, protected by the thick walls of cypress, you could light a fire without danger.

By the time we had washed and changed, and the sheep had been killed and stripped, it was dark; we made our way down to the *asado* room, where one of the peons had already kindled an immense fire. Near it a great stake had been stuck upright in the ground, on this a whole sheep, split open like an oyster, had been spitted. We lay on the ground around the fire and drank red wine while waiting for our meal to cook.

I have been to many *asados* in the Argentine, but that first one at Huichi's *estancia* will always remain in my mind as the most perfect. The wonderful smell of burning brushwood, mingling with the smell of roasting meat, the pink and orange tongues of flame lighting up the green cypress walls of the shelter, and the sound of the wind battering ferociously against these walls and then dying to a soft sigh as it became entangled and sapped of its strength in the mesh of branches, and above us the night sky, trembling with stars, lit by a fragile chip of moon. To gulp a mouthful of soft, warm red wine, and then to lean forward and slice a fragrant chip of meat from the brown, bubbling carcase in front of you, dunk it in the fierce sauce of vinegar, garlic and red pepper, and then stuff it, nut-sweet and juicy, into your mouth, seemed one of the most satisfying actions of my life.

Presently, when our attacks on the carcase became more desultory, Huichi took a gulp of wine, wiped his mouth with the back of his hand, and beamed at me across the red, pulsating embers of the fire, lying like a great sunset on the ground.

'¿Mañana,' he said, smiling, 'we go to the *pinguinos*?'

'Si, si,' I responded sleepily, leaning forward in sheer greed to detach another strip of crackling skin from the cooling remains of the sheep, '*mañana* the *pinguinos*.'

Chapter Two

A Sea of Headwaiters

It was a brave bird; and till reaching the sea, it regularly fought and drove me backwards.

CHARLES DARWIN: THE VOYAGE OF H.M.S. BEAGLE.

Early the next morning, while it was still dark, I was awoken by Huichi moving around the kitchen, whistling softly to himself, clattering the coffee-pot and cups, trying to break in on our slumbers gently. My immediate reaction was to snuggle down deeper under the pile of soft, warm, biscuit-coloured guanaco skins that covered the enormous double-bed in which Jacquie and I were ensconced. Then, after a moment's meditation, I decided that if Huichi was up I ought to be up as well; in any case, I knew I should have to get up in order to rout the others out. So, taking a deep breath, I threw back the bed-clothes and leapt nimbly out of bed. I have rarely regretted an action more: it was rather like coming freshly from a boiler-room and plunging into a mountain stream. With chattering teeth I put on all the clothes I could find, and hobbled out into the kitchen. Huichi smiled and nodded at me, and then, in the most understanding manner, poured two fingers of brandy into a large cup, filled it up with steaming coffee and handed it to me. Presently, glowing with heat, I took off one of my three pullovers, and took a malicious delight in making the rest of the party get out of bed.

We set off eventually, full of brandy and coffee, in the pale daffodil-yellow dawn light and headed towards the place where the penguins were to be found. Knots of blank-faced sheep scuttled across the nose of the Land-Rover as we drove along, their fleeces wobbling as they ran, and at one point we passed a long, shallow dew-pond, caught in a cleft between the gentle undulation of hills, and six flamingoes were feeding at its edge, pink as cyclamen buds. We drove a quarter of an hour or so, and then Huichi swung the Land-Rover off the main track and headed across country, up a gentle slope of land. As we came to the top of the rise, he turned and grinned at me.

'*Ahora*,' he said, '*ahora los pinguinos.*'

Then we reached the top of the slope and there was the penguin colony.

Ahead of us the low, brown scrub petered out, and in its place was a great desert of sun-cracked sand. This was separated from the sea beyond by a crescent-shaped ridge of white sand-dunes, very steep and some two hundred feet high. It was in this desert area, protected from the sea wind by the encircling arm of the dunes, that the penguins had created their city. As far as the eye could see on every side the ground was pock-marked with nesting burrows, some a mere half-hearted scrape in the sand, some several feet deep. These craters made the place look like a small section of the moon's surface seen through a powerful telescope. In among these craters waddled the biggest collection of penguins I had ever seen, like a sea of pigmy headwaiters, solemnly shuffling to and fro as if suffering from fallen arches due to a lifetime of carrying overloaded trays. Their numbers were prodigious, stretching to the furthermost horizon where they twinkled black and white in the heat haze. It was a breath-taking sight. Slowly we drove through the scrub until we reached the edge of this gigantic honeycomb of nest burrows and then we stopped and got out of the Land-Rover.

We stood and watched the penguins, and they stood and watched us with immense respect and interest. As long as we stayed near the vehicle they showed no fear. The greater proportion of birds were, of course, adult; but each nesting burrow contained one or two youngsters, still wearing their baby coats of down, who regarded us with big, melting dark eyes, looking rather like plump and shy debutantes clad in outsize silver-fox furs. The adults, sleek and neat in their black and white suits, had red wattles round the base of their beaks, and bright, predatory street-pedlar eyes. As you approached them they would back towards their burrows, twisting their heads from side to side in a warning display, until sometimes they would be looking at you completely upside down. If you approached too close they would walk backwards into their burrows and gradually disappear, still twisting their heads vigorously. The babies, on the other hand, would let you get within about four feet of them, and then their nerve would break and they would turn and dive into the burrow, so that their great fluffy behinds and frantically flapping feet was all that could be seen of them.

At first the noise and movement of the vast colony was confusing. As a background to the continuous whispering of the wind was the constant peeting of the youngsters, and the loud prolonged, donkey-like bray of the adults, standing up stiff and straight, flippers spread wide, beaks pointing at the blue sky as they brayed joyfully and exultingly. To begin with you did not know where to look first, and the constant movement of the adults and young seemed to be desultory and without purpose. Then after a few hours of getting used to being amongst such a huge assemblage of birds, a certain pattern seemed to emerge. The first thing that became obvious was that most of the movement in the colony was due to adult birds. A great number stood by the nest burrows, obviously doing sentry duty with the young, while among them vast numbers of other birds passed to and fro, some making their way towards the sea, others coming from it. The distant sand-dunes were freckled with the tiny plodding figures of penguins, either climbing the steep slopes or sliding down them. This constant trek to and fro to the sea occupied a large portion of the penguins' day, and it was such a tremendous feat that it deserves to be described in detail. By carefully watching the colony, day by day, during the three weeks we lived among it, we discovered that this is what happened:

Early in the morning one of the parent birds (either male or female) would set out towards the sea, leaving its mate in charge of the nestlings. In order to get to the sea the bird had to cover about a mile and a half of the most gruelling and difficult terrain imaginable. First they had to pick their way through the vast patchwork of nesting burrows that made up the colony, and when they reached the edge of this – the suburbs, as it were – they were faced by the desert area, where the sand was caked and split by the sun into something resembling a gigantic jig-saw puzzle. The sand in this area would, quite early in the day, get so hot that it was painful to touch, and yet the penguins would plod dutifully across it, pausing frequently for a rest, as though in a trance. This used to take them about half an hour. But, when they reached the other side of the desert they were faced with another obstacle, the sand-dunes. These towered over the diminutive figures of the birds like a snow-white chain of Himalayan mountains, two hundred feet high, their steep sides composed of fine, loose shifting sand. We found it difficult enough to negotiate these dunes, so it must have been far worse for such an ill-equipped bird as a penguin.

When they reached the base of the dunes they generally paused for about ten minutes to have a rest. Some just sat there, brooding, while others fell forwards on to their tummies and lay there panting. Then, when they had rested, they would climb sturdily to their feet and start the ascent. Gathering themselves, they would rush at the slope, obviously hoping to get the worst of the climb over as quickly as possible. But this rapid climb would peter out about a quarter of the way up; their progress would slow down, and they would pause to rest more often. As the gradient grew steeper and steeper they would eventually be forced to flop down on their bellies, and tackle the slope that way, using their flippers to assist them in the climb. Then, with one final, furious burst of speed, they would triumphantly reach the top, where they would stand up straight, flap their flippers in delight, and then flop down on to their tummies for a ten-minute rest. They had reached the half-way mark and, lying there on the knife-edge top of the dune, they would see the sea, half a mile away, gleaming coolly and enticingly. But they had still to descend the other side of the dune, across a quarter of a mile of scrub-land and then several hundred yards of shingle beach before they reached the sea.

Going down the dune, of course, presented no problem to them, and they accomplished this in two ways, both equally amusing to watch. Either they would walk down, starting very sedately and getting quicker and quicker the steeper the slope became, until they were galloping along in the most undignified way, or else they would slide down on their tummies, using their wings and feet to propel their bodies over the surface of the sand exactly as if they were swimming. With either method they reached the bottom of the dune in a small avalanche of fine sand, and they would get to their feet, shake themselves, and set off grimly through the scrub towards the beach. But it was the last few hundred yards of beach that seemed to make them suffer most. There was the sea, blue, glittering, lisping seductively on the shore, and to get to it they had to drag their tired bodies over the stony beach, where the pebbles scrunched and wobbled under their feet, throwing them off balance. But at last it was over, and they ran the last few feet to the edge of the waves in a curious crouching position, then suddenly straightened up and plunged into the cool water. For ten minutes or so they twirled and ducked in a shimmer of sun ripples, washing the dust and sand from their heads and wings, fluttering their hot, sore feet in the water in ecstasy, whirling and bobbing, disappearing beneath the water, and popping up again like corks. Then, thoroughly refreshed, they would set about the stern task of fishing, undaunted by the fact that they would have to face that difficult journey once again before the food they caught could be delivered to their hungry young.

Once they had plodded their way – full of fish – back over the hot terrain to the colony, they would have to start on the hectic job of feeding their ravenous young. This feat resembled a cross between a boxing- and an all-in wrestling-match, and was fascinating and amusing to watch. There was one family that lived in a burrow close to the spot where we parked the Land-Rover each day, and both the parent birds and their young got so used to our presence that they allowed us to sit and film them at a distance of about twenty feet, so we could see every detail of the feeding process very clearly. Once the parent bird reached the edge of the colony it had run the gauntlet of several thousand youngsters before it reached its own nest-burrow and babies. All these youngsters were convinced that, by launching themselves at the adult bird in a sort of tackle, they could get it to regurgitate the food it was carrying. So the adult had to avoid the attacks of these fat, furry youngsters by dodging to and fro like a skilful centre-forward on a football field. Generally the parent would end up at its nest-burrow, still hotly pursued by two or three strange chicks, who were grimly determined to make it produce food. When it reached home the adult would suddenly lose patience with its pursuers, and, rounding on them, would proceed to beat them up in no uncertain fashion, pecking at them so viciously that large quantities of the babies' fluff would be pecked away, and float like thistledown across the colony.

Having routed the strange babies, it would then turn its attention to its own chicks, who were by now attacking it in the same way as the others had done, uttering shrill wheezing cries of hunger and impatience. It would squat down at the entrance to the burrow and stare at its feet pensively, making motions like someone trying to stifle an acute attack of hiccups. On seeing this the youngsters would work themselves into a frenzy of delighted anticipation, uttering their wild, wheezing cries, flapping their wings frantically, pressing themselves close to the parent bird's body, and stretching up their beaks and clattering them against the adult's. This would go on for perhaps thirty seconds, when the parent would suddenly – with an expression of relief – regurgitate vigorously, plunging its beak so deeply into the gaping mouths of the youngsters that you felt sure it would never be able to pull its head out again. The babies, satisfied and apparently not stabbed from stem to stern by the delivery of the first course, would squat down on their plump behinds and meditate for a while, and their parent would seize the opportunity to have a quick wash and brush up, carefully preening its breast-feathers, picking minute pieces of dirt off its feet, and running its beak along its wings with a clipper-like motion. Then it would yawn, bending forward like someone attempting to touch his toes, wings stretched out straight behind, beak gaping wide. Then it would sink into the trance-like state that its babies had attained some minutes earlier. All would be quiet for five minutes or so, and then suddenly the parent would start its strange hiccupping motions again, and pandemonium would break out immediately. The babies would rouse themselves from their digestive reverie and hurl themselves at the adult, each trying its best to get its beak into position first. Once more each of them in turn would be apparently stabbed to the heart by the parent's beak, and then once more they would sink back into somnolence.

The parents and young who occupied this nest-burrow where we filmed the feeding process were known, for convenient reference, as the Joneses. Quite close to the Joneses' establishment was another burrow that contained a single, small and very undernourished-looking chick whom we called Henrietta Vacanttum. Henrietta was the product of an unhappy home-life. Her parents were, I suspected, either dim-witted or just plain idle, for they took twice as long as any other penguins to produce food for Henrietta, and then only in such minute quantities that she was always hungry. An indication of her parents' habits was the slovenly nest-burrow, a mere half-hearted scrape, scarcely deep enough to protect Henrietta from any inclement weather, totally unlike the deep, carefully dug villa-residence of the Jones family. So it was not surprising that Henrietta had a big-eyed, half-starved,

The Whispering Land

ill-cared-for look about her that made us feel very sorry for her. She was always on the look-out for food, and as the Jones parents had to pass her front door on their way to their own neat burrow, she always made valiant attempts to get them to regurgitate before they reached home.

These efforts were generally in vain, and all Henrietta got for her pains was a severe pecking that made her fluff come out in great clouds. She would retreat, disgruntled, and with anguished eye watch the two disgustingly fat Jones babies wolfing down their food. But one day, by accident, Henrietta discovered a way to pinch the Jones family's food without any unpleasant repercussions. She would wait until the parent Jones had started the hiccupping movements as a preliminary to regurgitation, and the baby Joneses were frantically gyrating round, flapping their wings and wheezing, and then, at the crucial moment, she would join the group, carefully approaching the parent bird from behind. Then, wheezing loudly, and opening her beak wide, she would thrust her head either over the adult's shoulder, as it were, or under its wing, but still carefully maintaining her position behind the parent so that she should not be recognized. The parent Jones, being harried by its gaping-mouthed brood, its mind fully occupied with the task of regurgitating a pint of shrimps, did not seem to notice the introduction of a third head into the general mêlée that was going on around it. And when the final moment came it would plunge its head into the first gaping beak that was presented, with the slightly desperate air of an aeroplane passenger seizing his little brown paper bag at the onset of the fiftieth air-pocket. Only when the last spasm had died away, and the parent Jones could concentrate on external matters, would it realize that it had been feeding a strange offspring, and then Henrietta had to be pretty nifty on her great, flat feet to escape the wrath. But even if she did not move quickly enough, and received a beating up for her iniquity, the smug look on her face seemed to argue that it was worth it.

In the days when Darwin had visited this area there had still been the remnants of the Patagonian Indian tribes left, fighting a losing battle against extermination by the settlers and soldiers. These Indians were described as being uncouth and uncivilized and generally lacking in any quality that would qualify them for a little Christian charity. So they vanished, like so many animal species when they come into contact with the beneficial influences of civilization, and no one, apparently, mourned their going. In various museums up and down Argentina you can see a few remains of their crafts (spears, arrows, and so on) and inevitably a large and rather gloomy picture purporting to depict the more unpleasant side of the Indians' character, their lechery. In every one of these pictures there was shown a group of long-haired wild-looking Indians on prancing wild steeds, and the leader of the troupe inevitably had clasped across his saddle a white woman in a diaphanous garment, whose mammary development would give any modern film star pause for thought. In every museum the picture was almost the same, varying only in the number of Indians shown, and the chest expansion of their victim. Fascinating though these pictures were, the thing that puzzled me was that there was never a companion piece to show a group of civilized white men galloping off with a voluptuous Indian girl, and yet this had happened as frequently (if not more frequently) than the rape of white women. It was a curious and interesting sidelight on history. But nevertheless these spirited but badly-painted portraits of abduction had one interesting feature. They were obviously out to give the worst possible impression of the Indians, and yet all they succeeded in doing was in impressing you with a wild and rather beautiful people, and filling you with a pang of sorrow that they were no longer in existence. So, when we got down into Patagonia I searched eagerly for relics of these Indians, and questioned everyone for stories about them. The stories, unfortunately, were much of a muchness and told me little, but when it came to relics, it turned out, I could not have gone to a better place than the penguin metropolis.

One evening, when we had returned to the *estancia* after a hard day's filming and were drinking *maté* round the fire, I asked Señor Huichi – via Marie – if there had been many Indian tribes living in those parts. I phrased my questions delicately, for I had been told that Huichi had Indian blood in him, and I was not sure whether this was a thing he was proud of or not. He smiled his slow and gentle smile, and said that on and around his *estancias* had been one of the largest concentrations of Indians in Patagonia, in fact, he went on, the place where the penguins lived still yielded evidence of their existence. What sort of evidence, I asked eagerly. Huichi smiled again, and, getting to his feet he disappeared into his darkened bedroom. I heard him pull a box out from under his bed, and he returned carrying it in his hands and placed it on the table. He removed the lid and tipped the contents out on to the white tablecloth, and I gasped.

I had seen, as I say, various relics in the museums, but nothing to compare with this; for Huichi tumbled out on to the table a rainbow-coloured heap of stone objects that were breathtaking in their colouring and beauty. There were arrow-heads ranging from delicate, fragile-looking ones the size of your little fingernail, to ones the size of an egg. There were spoons made by slicing in half and carefully filing down big sea-shells; there were long, curved stone scoops for removing the edible molluscs from their shells; there were spear-heads with razor-sharp edges; there were the balls for the *boleadoras*, round as billiard-balls, with a shallow trough running round their equators, as it were, which took the thong from which they hung; these were so incredibly perfect that one could hardly believe that such precision could be achieved without a machine. Then there were the purely decorative articles: the shells neatly pierced for ear-rings, the necklace made of beautifully matched green, milky stone rather like jade, the seal-bone that had been chipped and carved into a knife that was obviously more ornamental than useful. The pattern on it was simple arrangements of lines, but carved with great precision.

I sat poring over these objects delightedly. Some of the arrowheads were so small it seemed impossible that anyone could create them by crude chipping, but hold them up to the light and you could see where the delicate wafers of stone had been chipped away. What was more incredible still was that each of these arrowheads, however small, had a minutely serrated edge to give it a bite and sharpness. As I was examining the articles I was suddenly struck by their colouring. On the beaches near the penguins almost all the stones were brown or black; to find attractively coloured ones you had to search. And yet every arrowhead, however small, every spearhead, in fact every piece of stone that had been used had obviously been picked for its beauty. I arranged all the spear- and arrowheads in rows on the tablecloth, and they lay there gleaming like the delicate leaves from some fabulous tree. There were red ones with a darker vein of red, like dried blood; there were green ones covered with a fine tracery of white; there were blue-white ones, like mother-of-pearl; and yellow and white ones covered with a freckling of blurred patterns in blue or black where the earth's juices had stained the stone. Each piece was a work of art, beautifully shaped, carefully and minutely chipped, edged and polished, constructed out of the most beautiful piece of stone the maker could find. You could see they had been made with love. And these, I reminded myself, were made by the barbarous, uncouth, savage and utterly uncivilized Indians for whose passing no one appeared to be sorry.

Huichi seemed delighted that I should display such obvious interest and admiration for his relics, and he went back into the bedroom and unearthed another box. This one contained an extraordinary weapon carved from stone: it was like a small dumb-bell. The central shaft which connected the two great, misshapen balls of stone fitted easily into the palm of your hand, so that then you had a great ball of stone above and below your fist. As the whole thing weighed about three pounds it was a fearsome weapon, capable of splitting a man's skull like a puffball. The next item in the box – which Huichi reverently unwrapped from a sheet of tissue paper – looked as though, in fact, it had been treated with this stone club. It was an Indian skull, white as ivory, with a great splinter-edged gaping hole across the top of the cranium.

Huichi explained that over the years, whenever his work had taken him to the corner of the *estancia* where the penguins lived, he had searched for Indian relics. He said that the Indians had apparently used that area very extensively, for what particular purpose no one was quite sure. His theory was that they had used the great flat area where the penguins now nested as a sort of arena, where the young men of the tribe practised shooting with bow and arrow, spear-throwing, and the art of entangling their quarry's legs with the *boleadoras*. On the other side of the great sand-dunes, he said, were to be found huge piles of empty sea-shells. I had noticed these great, white heaps of shells, some covering an area of a quarter of an acre and about three feet thick, but I had been so engrossed in my filming of the penguins that I had only given them a passing thought. Huichi's theory was that this had been a sort of holiday resort, as it were, the Margate of the Indians. They had come down there to feed on the succulent and plentiful shellfish, to find stones on the shingle beach from which to make their weapons, and a nice flat area on which to practise with these weapons. What other reason would there be for finding these great piles of empty shells, and, scattered over the sand-dune and shingle patches, such a host of arrow- and spearheads, broken necklaces, and the occasional crushed skull? I must say Huichi's idea seemed to me to be a sensible one, though I suppose a professional archaeologist would have found some method of disproving it. I was horrified at the thought of the number of delicate and lovely arrowheads that must have been splintered and crushed beneath the Land-Rover wheels as we had gaily driven to and fro over the penguin town. I resolved that the next day, when we had finished filming, we would search for arrowheads.

As it happened, the next day we had only about two hours' decent sunshine suitable for filming, and so the rest of the time we spent crawling over the sand-dunes in curious prenatal postures, searching for arrowheads and other Indian left-overs. I very soon discovered that it was not nearly as easy as it seemed. Huichi, after years of practice, could spot things with uncanny accuracy from a great distance.

'*Esto, una,*' he would say, smiling, pointing with the toe of his shoe at a huge pile of shingle. I would glare at the area indicated, but could see nothing but unworked bits of rock.

'*Esto,*' he would say again, and bending down pick up a beautiful leaf-shaped arrowhead that had been within five inches of my hand. Once it had been pointed out, of course, it became so obvious that you wondered how you had missed it. Gradually, during the course of the day, we improved, and our pile of finds started mounting, but Huichi still took a mischievous delight in wandering erect behind me as I crawled laboriously across the dunes, and, as soon as I thought I had sifted an area thoroughly, he would stoop down and find three arrowheads which I had somehow missed. This happened with such monotonous regularity that I began to wonder, under the influence of an aching back and eyes full of sand, whether he was not palming the arrowheads, like a conjuror, and pretending to find them just to pull my leg. But then my unkind doubts were dispelled, for he suddenly leant forward and pointed at an area of shingle I was working over.

'*Esto,*' he said, and, leaning down, pointed out to me a minute area of yellow stone protruding from under a pile of shingle. I gazed at it unbelievingly. Then I took it gently between my fingers and eased from under the shingle a superb yellow arrowhead with a meticulously serrated edge. There had been approximately a quarter of an inch of the side of the arrowhead showing, and yet Huichi had spotted it.

However, it was not long before I got my own back on him. I was making my way over a sand-dune towards the next patch of shingle, when my toe scuffed up something that gleamed white. I bent down and picked it up, and to my astonishment found I was holding a beautiful harpoon-head about six inches long, magnificently carved out of fur seal bone. I called to Huichi, and when he saw what I had found his eyes widened. He took it from me gently and wiped the sand off it, and then turned it over and over in his hands, smiling with delight. He explained that a harpoon-head like this was one of the rarest things you could find. He had only ever found one, and that had been so crushed that it had not been worth saving. Ever since he had been looking, without success, for a perfect one to add to his collection.

Presently it was getting towards evening, and we were all scattered about the sand-dunes hunched and absorbed in our task. I rounded a spur of sand and found myself in a tiny valley between the high dunes, a valley decorated with two or three wizened and carunculated trees. I paused to light a cigarette and ease my aching back. The sky was turning pink and green as it got towards sunset time, and apart from the faint whisper of the sea and the wind it was silent and peaceful. I walked slowly up the little valley, and suddenly I noticed a slight movement ahead of me. A small, very hairy armadillo was scuttling along the top of the dunes like a clockwork toy, intent on his evening search for food. I watched him until he disappeared over the dunes and then walked on. Under one of the bushes I was surprised to see a pair of penguins, for they did not usually choose this fine sand to dig their nest burrows in. But this pair had chosen this valley for some reason of their own, and had scraped and scrabbled a rough hole in which squatted a single fur-coated chick. The parents castanetted their beaks at me and twisted their heads upside down, very indignant that I should disturb their solitude. I watched them for a moment, and then I noticed something half hidden in the pile of sand which they had dug out to form their nest. It was something smooth and white. I went forward and, despite the near hysterics of the penguins, I scraped away the sand. There lying in front of me was a perfect Indian skull, which the birds must have unearthed.

I sat down with the skull on my knee and smoked another cigarette while I contemplated it. I wondered what sort of a man this vanished Indian had been. I could imagine him, squatting on the shore, carefully and cleverly chipping minute flakes off a piece of stone to make one of the lovely arrowheads that now squeaked and chuckled in my pocket. I could imagine him, with his fine brown face and dark eyes, his hair hanging to his shoulders, his rich brown guanaco skin cloak pulled tight about him as he sat very straight on a wild, unshod horse. I gazed into the empty eye-sockets of the skull and wished fervently that I could have met the man who had produced anything as beautiful as those arrowheads. I wondered if I ought to take the skull back to England with me and give it a place of honour in my study, surrounded by his artistic products. But then I looked around, and decided against it. The sky was now a vivid dying blue, with pink and green thumb-smudges of cloud. The wind made the sand trickle down in tiny rivulets that hissed gently. The strange, witch-like bushes creaked pleasantly and musically. I felt that the Indian would not mind sharing his last resting place with the creatures of what had once been his country, the penguins and the armadillos. So I dug a hole in the sand and placing the skull in it I gently covered it over. When I stood up in the rapidly gathering gloom the whole area seemed steeped in sadness, and the presence of the vanished Indians seemed very close. I could almost believe that, if I looked over my shoulder quickly, I would see one on horseback, silhouetted against the coloured sky. I shrugged this feeling off as fanciful, and walked back towards the Land-Rover.

As we rattled and bumped our way back in the dusk towards the *estancia*, Huichi, talking to Marie, said very quietly:

'You know, *señorita*, that place always seems to be sad. I feel the Indians there very much. They are all around you, their ghosts, and one feels sorry for them because they do not seem to be happy ghosts.'

This had been my feeling exactly.

Before we left the next day I gave Huichi the harpoon-head I had found. It broke my heart to part with it, but he had done so much for us that it seemed very small return for his kindness. He was delighted, and I know that it is now reverently wrapped in tissue-paper in the box beneath his bed, not too far from where it ought to be, buried on the great shining dunes, feeling only the shifting sand as the penguins thump solidly overhead.

Chapter Three

The Golden Swarm

They appeared to be of a loving disposition, and lay huddled together, fast asleep, like so many pigs.

CHARLES DARWIN: THE VOYAGE OF H.M.S. BEAGLE.

The penguin colony near Huichi's *estancia* had been our southernmost goal. Now, leaving Deseado behind us we drove northward across the flat purple scrub-land towards Peninsula Valdes, where, I had been assured, I would find large colonies of fur seal, and the only remaining colony of elephant seals in Argentina.

Peninsula Valdes lies on the coast of the province of Chubut. It is a mass of land rather like an axe-head, some eighty miles long by thirty broad. The peninsula is almost an island, being connected to the mainland by such a narrow neck of land that, as you drive along it, you can see the sea on both sides of the road. Entering the peninsula was like coming into a new land. For days we had driven through the monotonous and monochrome Patagonian landscape, flat as a billiard-table and apparently devoid of life. Now we reached the fine neck of land on the other side of which was the peninsula, and suddenly the landscape changed. Instead of the small, spiky bushes stretching purply to the horizon, we drove into a buttercup-yellow landscape, for the bushes were larger, greener and each decked with a mass of tiny blooms. The countryside was no longer flat but gently undulating, stretching away to the horizon like a yellow sea, shimmering in the sun.

Not only had the landscape changed in colouring and mood but it had suddenly become alive. We were driving down the red earth road, liberally sprinkled with backbreaking potholes, when suddenly I caught a flash of movement in the undergrowth at the side of the road. Tearing my eyes away from the potholes I glanced to the right, and immediately trod on the brakes so fiercely that there were frenzied protests from all the female members of the party. But I simply pointed, and they became silent.

To one side of the road, standing knee-deep in the yellow bushes, stood a herd of six guanacos, watching us with an air of intelligent interest. Now guanacos are wild relatives of the llama, and I had been expecting to see something that was the same rather stocky shape as the llama, with a dirty brown coat. At least, I remembered that the one I had seen in a Zoo many years before looked like that. But either my memory had played me false or else it had been a singularly depressed specimen I had seen. It had certainly left me totally unprepared for the magnificent sight these wild guanacos made.

What I took to be the male of the herd was standing a little in front of the others and about thirty feet away from us. He had long, slender racehorse legs, a streamlined body and a long graceful neck reminiscent of a giraffe's. His face was much longer and more slender than a llama's, but wearing the same supercilious expression. His eyes were dark and enormous. His small neat ears twitched to and fro as he put up his chin and examined us as if through a pair of imaginary lorgnettes. Behind him, in a tight and timid bunch, stood his three wives and two babies, each about the size of a terrier, and they had such a look of wide-eyed innocence that it evoked strange anthropomorphic gurgles and gasps from the feminine members of the expedition. Instead of the dingy brown I had expected these animals almost glowed. The neck and legs were a bright yellowish colour, the colour of sunshine on sand, while their bodies were covered with a thick fleece of the richest biscuit brown. Thinking that we might not get such a chance again I determined to get out of the Land-Rover and film them. Grabbing the camera I opened the door very slowly and gently. The male guanaco put both ears forward and examined my manoeuvre with manifest suspicion. Slowly I closed the door of the Land-Rover and then started to lift the camera. But this was enough. They did not mind my getting out of the vehicle, but when I started to lift a black object – looking suspiciously like a gun – to my shoulder this was more than they could stand. The male uttered a snort, wheeled about, and galloped off, herding his females and babies in front of him. The babies were inclined to think this was rather a lark, and started gambolling in circles, until their father called them to order with a few well-directed kicks. When they got some little distance away they slowed down from their first wild gallop into a sedate, stiff-legged canter. They looked, with their russet and yellow coats, like some strange gingerbread animals, mounted on rockers, tipping and tilting their way through the golden scrub.

As we drove on across the peninsula we saw many more groups of guanacos, generally in bunches of three or four, but once we saw a group of them standing on a hill, outlined against a blue sky, and I counted eight individuals in the herd. I noticed that the herds were commoner towards the centre of the peninsula, and became considerably less common as you drove towards the coast. But wherever you saw them they were cautious and nervous beasts, ready to canter off at the faintest hint of anything unusual, for they are persecuted by the local sheep-farmers, and have learnt from bitter experience that discretion is the better part of valour.

By the late afternoon we were nearing Punta del Norte on the east coast of the peninsula, and the road had faded away into a pair of faint wheel-tracks that wended their way through the scrub in a looping and vague manner that made me doubt whether they actually led anywhere. But, just when I was beginning to think that we had taken the wrong track, I saw up ahead a small white *estancia*, its shutters tightly fastened, and to the left of it a large Dutch barn or *galpón*. Knowing that a *galpón* was generally the centre of any activity on an *estancia*, I drove up to it and stopped. Three large, fat dogs immediately appeared, barked at us vigorously, and then, obviously thinking that their duty was done, set about the fascinating task of irrigating the Land-Rover wheels. Three peons came out from inside the barn, brown, lean, rather wild-looking men with wide, eager smiles. They were obviously delighted to see us, for strangers there were a rarity. They insisted that we go into the barn, brought chairs for us to sit on, and within half an hour they had killed a sheep and an *asado* was being prepared, while we sat and drank wine and told them why we had come.

They were fascinated by the thought that I should have come all the way from England just to catch and film *bichos*, and doubtless thought I was more than a little mad, though they were far too well-mannered to say so. On the subject of elephant seals and fur seals they were very informative and helpful. The elephant seals, they explained, had now had their babies and reared them. This meant that they were no longer to be found in one spot on the beach near the fur seals, which acted, as it were, as their maternity ward. Now they drifted up and down the coast as the mood took them, and were difficult to find, though there were two or three places which they were particularly fond of where they might be located. These favourite haunts were called charmingly enough, the *elefanterías*. The peons marked on the map the areas in which the *elefanterías* were to be found, and then they showed me where the biggest concentration of fur seals lived. These, they said, would be easy, for they still had young, and were therefore packed on the beach and easily accessible. Moreover, the peons went on, there was a good camping area just near the fur seal colony, a flat grassy space, sheltered from the wind on all sides by a gentle rise in the ground. Cheered by this news we drank more wine, ate large quantities of roast sheep, and then clambered into the Land-Rover again and set off to look for the camp site.

We found it without too much difficulty, and it was as good as the peons had promised, a small, level plain covered with coarse grass and occasional clumps of small, twisted dead bushes. On three sides it was protected by a curving rim of low hills, covered in yellow bushes, and on the third side a high wall of shingle lay between it and the sea. This offered us some cover, but even so there was a strong and persistent wind blowing from the sea, and now that it was evening it became very cold. It was decided that the three female members of the party would sleep inside the Land-Rover, while I slept under it. Then we dug a hole, collected dry brushwood and built a fire to make tea. One had to be very careful about the fire, for we were surrounded by acres and acres of tinder-dry undergrowth, and the strong wind would, if you were not careful, lift your whole fire up into the air and dump it down among the bushes. I dreaded to think what the ensuing conflagration would be like.

The sun set in a nest of pink, scarlet and black clouds, and there was a brief green twilight. Then it darkened, and a huge yellow moon appeared and gazed down at us as we crouched around the fire, huddled in all the clothes we could put on, for the wind was now bitter. Presently the Land-Rover party crept inside the vehicle, with much grunting and argument as to whose feet should go where, and I collected my three blankets, put earth on the fire, and then fashioned myself a bed under the back axle of the Land-Rover. In spite of the fact that I was wearing three pullovers, two pairs of trousers, a duffel-coat and a woolly hat, and had three blankets wrapped round me, I was still cold, and as I shivered my way into a half-sleep I made a mental note that on the morrow I would reorganize our sleeping arrangements.

I awoke in that dimly-lit silence just before dawn, when even the sound of the sea seems to have hushed. The wind had switched direction in the night, and the wheels of the Land-Rover now offered no protection at all. The hills around were black against the blue-green of the dawn sky, and there was no sound except the hiss of the wind and the faint snore of the surf. I lay there, shuddering in my cocoon of clothes and blankets, and debated whether or not I should get up and light the fire and make some tea. Cold though I was under my clothes, it was still a few degrees warmer than wandering about collecting brushwood, and so I decided to stay where I was. I was just trying to insinuate my hand into my duffel-coat pocket for my cigarettes, without letting a howling wind into my cocoon of semi-warmth, when I realized that we had a visitor.

Suddenly a guanaco stood before me, as if conjured out of nothing. He stood some twenty feet away, quite still, surveyed me with a look of surprise and displeasure, his neat ears twitching back and forth. He turned his head, sniffing the breeze, and I could see his profile against the sky. He wore the supercilious expression of his race, the faint aristocratic sneer, as if he knew that I had slept in my clothes for the past three nights. He lifted one forefoot daintily, and peered down at me closely. Whether, at that moment, the breeze carried my scent to him I don't know, but he suddenly stiffened and, after a pause for meditation, he belched.

It was not an accidental gurk, the minute breach of good manners that we are all liable to at times. This was a premeditated, rich and prolonged belch, with all the fervour of the Orient in it. He paused for a moment, glaring at me, to make sure that his comment on my worth had made me feel properly humble, and then he turned and disappeared as suddenly as he had come, and I could hear the faint whisper of his legs brushing through the little bushes. I waited for a time to see if he would come back, but he had obviously gone about his business, so I lit my cigarette and lay shivering and smoking until the sun came up.

Once we had breakfasted and everyone was more or less conscious, we unhitched the trailer, removed all our equipment from inside the Land-Rover and piled it on the ground under tarpaulins, checked the camera equipment, made sandwiches and coffee, and then set off to look for the fur seals. The peons had told us that if we drove half a mile or so down the track and then branched off, across country, towards the sea, we should easily find the colony. What they had not told us, of course, was that driving across country was a nerve- and spine-shattering experience, for the ground was corrugated and pitted in the most extraordinary way, and most of these death-traps were concealed by the bushes, so you would crash into them before you knew they were there, while the bushes screeched along the sides of the Land-Rover in what sounded like an ecstasy of shrill, maniacal laughter. At last I decided that, unless we wanted a broken spring or puncture, we had better continue the hunt on foot, so, finding a more or less level piece of country I parked the Land-Rover and we got out. At once I became aware of a strange sound, like the frenzied roar of a football crowd heard distantly. We walked through waist-high golden scrub until we came out on the edge of a small cliff, and there on the shingle beach below us, at the edge of the creaming waves, lay the fur seal colony.

As we reached this vantage point the noise of the animals smote us, roar, bleat, gurgle and cough, a constant undulation of sound, like the boiling of an enormous cauldron of porridge. The colony, consisting of about seven hundred animals, lay strung out along the beach in a line some ten or twelve deep, and so tightly packed together that, as they shifted and moved in the sun, they gleamed gold, like a restless swarm of bees. Forgetting all about filming I just squatted on the edge of the cliff, staring down at this wonderful collection of animals, completely entranced.

At first we found – as we had done with the penguin colony – that there was so much going on, so much confusion and noise, that you were bewildered, and your eyes were moving constantly up and down this immense moving plate of animals in an effort to catch and translate every movement, until you began to feel dizzy. But, after the first hour, when the shock of seeing such a magnificent mass of animals at close range had worn off somewhat, you found you could concentrate.

It was the adult bulls that first caught and held your attention, for they were so massive. They were quite the most proud and extraordinary-looking animals I have ever seen. They sat with their faces pointed skywards, their shaggy necks bent back so that the fat was scalloped into folds, their snub-noses and fat beery faces peering up into the sky with all the pompous arrogance of the Tenniel illustration of Humpty Dumpty. They had physiques like boxers, the tremendous muscular shoulders tapering down to slender hindquarters, and ending, incongruously, in a pair of limbs that were quite ridiculous. The feet had long slender fingers, carefully webbed, so the impression was that the seal was wearing, for some reason best known to himself, a pair of very elegant frogmen's flippers. Sometimes you would see one old bull stretched out asleep in the sand, blubbering and snoring to himself, while at the end of his body he would be waving his large flippers to and fro, pointing the slender fingers with all the grace and delicacy of a Balinese dancer. When they walked these huge frog-like feet stuck out on either side, and, as the motion of the animal's body was very like a rumba, the effect was extremely funny. Their colouring ranged from chocolate to a rich biscuit brown, fading to russet on the shaggy fur round their shoulders and necks. This made a nice contrast to the wives who were very much smaller and decked out in silver or golden coats. Whereas their husbands were enormous blundering tanks of animals, the wives were slim, sinuous and sexy, with their neat pointed faces and big melting eyes. They were the personification of femininity, graceful to a degree, beautiful, coquettish and at the same time loving. They were heavenly creatures, and I decided that should I ever have the chance of being an animal in this world I would choose to be a fur seal so that I might enjoy having such a wonderful wife.

Although they had some six miles of beach to use, the colony chose to lie in a tight conglomeration, covering an area about a quarter of a mile in length. It seemed to me that if they had spaced themselves out a bit more they would have halved the troubles of the colony, for, packed tightly like this, each bull was in a constant state of nerves over his little group of wives, and throughout the colony there were fights breaking out all the time. A lot of the blame for these, I am afraid, was due to the females who – as soon as they thought their husband was not watching – would undulate gracefully across the sand towards the next group, and sit there watching the bull with languishing eyes. It would take a very staunch Presbyterian fur seal to resist the appeal of those pleading melting eyes. But before any infidelity could take place the husband would suddenly make a rapid count and discover that he was a wife short. As soon as he spotted her, he would surge after her, his enormous bulk scattering the shingle like spray, and from his mouth, with its great white fangs, would issue a prolonged, lion-like belching roar. Reaching her he would catch her by the scruff of the neck and shake her savagely from side to side. Then, with a jerk of his head, he would send her spinning across the sand towards his harem.

By this time the other bull would have worked himself into a state of nerves. He would feel that the husband was too close to *his* wives for safety, and so he would lunge forward with open mouth, uttering fearsome gurgling cries, and the two would join in battle. Most of these fights were merely mock combats, and after a good deal of mouth-opening, roaring and lunging, honour would be satisfied. But occasionally both bulls would lose their tempers, and then it was incredible and frightening to watch how two such ponderous and dropsical-looking creatures could turn into such swift, deft and deadly fighters. The shingle would be churned up as the two colossal creatures snapped and barged at each other's fat necks, and the blood spurted out over the fascinated audience of wives and babies. One of the favourite gambits during these fights was to undulate across the shingle towards your opponent, waving your head from side to side, like a boxer feinting. Then, when you got near enough you would lunge forward and, with a sideways and downwards bite, try and slash open the thick hide of your antagonist's neck. Most of the old bulls on the beach had fresh wounds or white scars decorating their necks, and one I saw looked as though someone had slashed him with a sabre, for the wound was some eighteen inches long and appeared to be about six inches deep.

When a bull waddled back to his wives after such a battle they would gather round him in admiration and love, elongating their sinuous necks so that they could reach up and nuzzle and kiss his face, rubbing their gold and silver bodies against his barrel chest, while he stared up into the sky arrogantly, occasionally condescending to bend his head and bite one of his wives gently on the neck.

A lot of the nervous tension that the bulls with wives suffered from, and a lot of the actual fighting, was due to the bachelor bulls. These were gay young bulls, much slimmer and less muscular than the old ones, who had been unable to acquire a wife or wives for themselves at the beginning of the breeding season when the courtship battles take place. These young bulls spent most of their time just sleeping in the sun, or swimming about in the shallow water at the sea's edge. But, every now and then, they would be smitten with an impish desire to irritate their elders and betters. They would swagger slowly along the colony, their great frog's feet stuck out, gazing about them with a benign air of innocence, as though there was not an evil thought in their heads. Then, as they passed a family group in the centre of which squatted an old bull star-gazing, the young bachelor would suddenly swerve and break into an undulating run, getting faster and faster as he approached the group. The females would scatter wildly as he burst through their circle, he would hurl himself at the old bull, give him a quick bite on the neck, and then undulate rapidly away before the old bull really knew what was happening. Then, with a roar of rage the old bull would give chase, but by then the gay bachelor had reached the sea and plunged in, so the old bull, grumbling to himself, would return to round up his scattered wives, and settle himself in their midst for another period of astronomical research.

The ones that seemed to lead the most carefree and pleasant lives were the young, but fully adult bulls, who had only succeeded in getting themselves one wife. They generally lay a little apart from the main colony, their wife and cub alongside them, and spent a lot of time sleeping. They could afford to do this, as it was obviously easier to control one of these high-spirited female seals than to try and cope with the vagaries of six or seven. It was with one of these young newlywed couples that I was lucky enough to see the consummation of their marriage, as it were, and I have never seen such a delicate and beautiful piece of love-play between two animals.

The young bull had dug himself the fur seal equivalent of a honeymoon cottage in the shingle near the base of the cliff from which I was filming. This cottage consisted of a large, deep hole scraped out with his fore-flippers, so that the top layer of sun-heated shingle was scraped off, and the cool damp shingle beneath was exposed. He lay in this hole with his wife in a very typical attitude, his great head resting on her back as she lay asleep, at right-angles to him. They had lain like this, almost unmoving, for the whole morning. Now, at midday with the fierce sun directly overhead, they began to get restless. The bull started to wave his hind flipper to and fro in the air, shift his bulk about uneasily, and scoop great flippersful of damp shingle and shovel them on to his back, in an effort to keep cool. His wife, disturbed by his movements, woke up, looked about her, yawned widely, and then lay down again with a deep, contented sigh, gazing around placidly with her great, dark eyes. After a few minutes' contemplation she shifted her body round so that she was lying parallel to the bull, thus depriving him of his head-rest. He gave a low grunt of annoyance at this, and heaving up his bulk he flopped down on top of her back, so that she was half-hidden by his body. Then he closed his eyes and prepared for sleep. But his wife, with her spouse's great bulk half covering her, had other ideas. She wriggled sideways so that the bull's barrel-shaped body slipped off her back and settled into the shingle with a scrunch. Then she leant forward and started to bite at his mouth and chin, very delicately, and in a slow and languorous manner. The bull kept his eyes tightly shut, and put up with these caresses, only occasionally snorting as if he were very embarrassed. But at last the female's love-play seduced him, and he opened his eyes and started to bite at the back of her glossy neck. With these signs of affection from her lord the female became as excited as a puppy, rolling and wriggling under his great head as he bit her, nibbling at his pigeon-chest and uttering subdued 'woofing' noises through her nose, so that her long whiskers stood out like fans of spun glass round her neat muzzle. As she writhed on the shingle he bent his head and delicately sniffed at her hindquarters, like some bloated old gourmet savouring the bouquet of a rare brandy. Then he hauled himself slowly and ponderously on top of her and entered her. Now she was straining up her face to his so that their whiskers entwined, biting his muzzle, his nose and his throat, and he in his turned engulfed her neck or her throat in savagely restrained bites. Their hindquarters undulated together, not quickly, urgently and crudely as in most animals, but slowly and carefully, the movement as smooth and precise as honey pouring from a jar. Presently, closely entwined, they reached their shuddering climax and then relaxed. The bull hauled himself off his wife and flopped down beside her, where they lay gently nibbling one another's mouths and faces with a tenderness that was remarkable. The whole act had been beautiful to watch, and was a lesson in restrained love-making which a lot of human beings would do well to emulate.

I have not as yet mentioned the fur seal pups which were such an important and amusing part of the colony. There were hundreds of them, and they moved continuously through the mass of sleeping, love-making, bickering adults, looking like animated black ink-blots. They would lie sleeping on the shingle in the most extraordinary abandoned attitudes, as though they were really balloon animals that had suddenly been half deflated. Then, suddenly, one would wake up and discover that its mother was not there, and it would hoist itself on to its flippers and move sturdily down the beach, employing the strange rumba-like movement of the adult seal. Planting its flippers in the shingle with great determination, it would pause every few yards to open wide its pink mouth and bleat forlornly, like a lamb. Then, after it had wandered some distance in search of its parents, its bravado and strength would desert it, and it would give one more despairing bleat and then flop down on its tummy and sink almost immediately into a deep and refreshing sleep.

There appeared to be a rather vague crèche system in operation for some of the pups, for in places there would be groups of them, perhaps ten or twenty together, looking like heaps of curiously shaped coal. There would be a young bull or a couple of females sleeping nearby who were apparently in charge of these crèches, for if one of the babies wandered outside the invisible area that formed the crèche, one of the adults would rouse itself, undulate after it, catch it up in its vast mouth, give it a good shaking and throw it back into the nursery again. In spite of careful watching I was never able to decide satisfactorily whether these groups of babies were the progeny from one family of seals, or whether they were a mixture from several families. If they came from several families then these groups of babies would be, in effect, a sort of nursery-school or kindergarten where the babies were dumped while the parents went down to the sea to swim or feed. I wanted to film the daily behaviour of the pups, but in order to do this one had to pick out one particular baby, and as they were all identical in size and colour this was difficult. Then, just when I had begun to despair, I saw a pup that was recognizable. He had obviously been born later than the others, for he was only half their size, but what he lacked in inches he more than made up for in determination and personality.

When I first noticed Oswald (as we christened him) he was busily engaged in stalking a long ribbon of glittering green seaweed that lay on the shingle, and which he was obviously under the impression was some sort of monstrous sea-serpent which was threatening the colony. He shambled towards it, bleary-eyed, and stopped a yard or so away to sniff. A slight wind twitched the end of the seaweed, and at this obviously threatening display Oswald turned and lolloped off as fast as his flippers would carry him. He stopped a safe distance away and peered over his shoulder, but the wind had died now and the seaweed lay still. Carefully he approached it again, stopping some six feet away to sniff, his fat little body taut and trembling, ready to run should he see the slightest movement. But the seaweed lay quiet in the sun, shining like a ribbon of jade. He approached it slowly and carefully, giving the impression that he was almost tiptoeing on his great fat flippers, and holding his breath in case of accidents. Still the seaweed made no movement. Cheered by this display of cowardice, Oswald decided that it was his duty to save the colony from this obviously dangerous enemy, which was liable to take them unawares. He shuffled his bottom to and fro ridiculously, so that his hind flippers got a good grip in the shingle, and then launched himself at the seaweed. In his enthusiasm he rather overshot the mark, and ended up on his nose in a fountain of shingle, but with a large section of the seaweed firmly grasped in his mouth. He sat up, the seaweed dangling from either side of his mouth like a green moustache, looking very pleased that his first bite had apparently disabled the enemy completely. He shook his head from side to side, making the weed flap to and fro, and then, shambling to his flippers, he galloped off along the beach trailing the weed on each side of him, occasionally shaking his head vigorously, as if to make sure his victim was really dead. For a quarter of an hour he played with the weed, until there was nothing left but a few tattered remnants. Then he flung himself down on the shingle, exhausted, the remains of the weed wound round his tummy like a cummerbund, and sank into a deep sleep.

Presently, when he woke up, he remembered that originally he had been looking for his mother, before his attention was distracted by the weed. So he shambled to his feet and made off down the beach, bleating soulfully. Suddenly in the middle of his grief he noticed a seagull squatting on the shingle near him. Forgetting about his mother he decided that the seagull should be taught a lesson, so he humped himself up indignantly and rumbaed towards it ferociously. The gull watched his approach from the corner of one cold, inimical eye. Oswald undulated across the shingle, panting a little, a look of grim determination on his face, while the gull watched him sardonically. Each time Oswald charged it side-stepped neatly, pattering a few paces on its webbed feet, with the air of a professional matador eluding a very inexperienced bull. Four times this happened, and then the gull grew bored. At the next charge he opened his wings, gave a couple of lazy flaps, and glided off down the beach to a more restful spot.

Oswald, the object of his wrath having vanished, suddenly remembered his mother and started out to search for her, bleating loudly. He made his way towards the most crowded part of the colony, a jumbled mass of cows and bulls all enjoying a siesta. Oswald ploughed his way through them, treading with complete impartiality on cows and bulls alike, scrambling over their backs, treading on their tails, and planting his flippers in their eyes. He left behind him a wake of infuriated adults who had been woken from a refreshing sleep by a large flipper covered with shingle being planted in the most vulnerable portion of their anatomy. At one point he discovered a cow lying on her back, exposing her teats to the rays of the sun, and he decided that it would be a suitable opportunity to stop for a snack. He had just taken a firm hold of one of the teats, and was preparing to imbibe life-giving nourishment, when the cow woke up and looked down at him. For a second she gazed at him fondly, for she was still half asleep, but then she suddenly realized that he was not her son, but some dastardly interloper helping himself to a free drink. With a grunt of wrath she bent down, pushed her nose under his fat tummy, and, with a quick flip of her head, sent Oswald somersaulting through the air to land on the head of a sleeping bull. The bull was not amused, and Oswald had to be pretty nifty on his flippers to escape punishment. He plodded on over the mountain ranges of sleeping seals with grim determination. Then, at last, he slipped while negotiating a particularly rotund female, and fell on top of a young bull who was sleeping next door to her. The bull sat up, snorted indignantly, and then bent down and seized Oswald in his great mouth before the pup could get away. Oswald dangled there by the scruff of his neck, without movement, while the bull decided what was the best thing to be done with him. At last he decided that a little swimming lesson would do Oswald no harm, and so he flopped his way down to the sea, Oswald dangling from his mouth as limp as a glove.

I had often watched the bulls giving the pups swimming lessons, and it was a frightening sight. I felt quite sorry for Oswald. The bull paused at the end of the surf and started to shake Oswald to and fro, until one felt certain that the pup's neck was broken, and then hurled him some twenty feet out into the waves. After a prolonged submersion Oswald surfaced, flapping his flippers desperately, spluttering, and coughing, and struck out towards the shore. But the bull lumbered into the water and caught him by the neck again, long before he was in his depth, and then proceeded to hold him under the water for five or ten seconds at a time, eventually releasing his hold so that Oswald popped up like a cork, gasping for breath. After this had happened three or four times Oswald was so frightened and exhausted that he tried to attack the bull's great bulk with open mouth, uttering spluttering yarring cries. This, of course, had about as much effect as a pekinese attacking an elephant. The bull simply picked Oswald up, shook him well and flung him out to sea again, and repeated the whole process. Eventually, when it was obvious that Oswald was so exhausted that he could hardly swim, the bull took him into the shallows and let him rest for a little while, but standing guard over him so that he could not escape. When he was rested Oswald was picked up and thrown out to sea again, and the whole lesson was repeated. This went on for half an hour and would have gone on longer, but another bull came and picked a quarrel with Oswald's instructor, and while they were fighting it out in the shallows Oswald made his escape, scrambling back to shore as fast as he could, wet, bedraggled and thoroughly chastened.

These swimming lessons, as I say, were to be seen very frequently, and were agony to watch, for not only was the terror of the pups so piteous, but I was always convinced that the bulls might go too far and actually drown one of them. But the babies appeared to have the elasticity of mind and body that allowed them to survive these savage swimming lessons, and none of them seemed any the worse.

The adults spent ninety per cent of the day sleeping, and only occasionally the young bulls and cows would venture into the water, but it was not until evening that the colony as a whole went swimming. As the sun sank lower and lower a restlessness would prevail throughout the colony, and presently the females would hump themselves down to the water's edge, and the water ballet would begin. First two or three cows would enter the shallows and start swimming up and down, slowly and methodically. For some time the bull would watch them in a lordly manner, and then he would lift his huge bulk and shoulder his way into the surf with the air of a heavyweight boxer entering the ring. There he would pause and survey the sinuous shapes of his wives before him, while the foam made an Elizabethan ruff of white round his fat neck. His wives, desperately trying to get him to join in their game, would tumble and curve in the water ahead, their coats now gleaming and black with sea-water. Then, suddenly, the bull would submerge, his portly form disappearing beneath the water with a speed and grace that was startling. His blunt, snub-nosed head would appear between the bodies of his wives, and the entire picture would change. Whereas before the female's movements had been slow, gentle curvings of the body on the surface and beneath the water, now the tempo of their play quickened, and they would close in round the bull, making him the focal point of their game. Their movements as smooth as a flow of oil, they would curve over and under him, so that he was like a stocky maypole with the slim, swift ribbon of female seals drifting and fluttering around him. He would sit there with his massive head and neck out of the water, peering with supreme smugness into the sky, while his wives formed a whirlpool around him, weaving and gliding faster and faster, demanding his attention. Suddenly he would yield and, bending his head, he would open his mouth and bite playfully at a passing body. This was the signal for the ballet proper to begin.

The females' arrow-swift bodies and the bulk of the male would entwine like a gleaming back plait, curving and twisting through the water, assuming the most graceful and complicated shapes like a pennant whipped by the wind. As they rolled and curved through the water, leaving a foam-smudged track behind them, you could see them biting at each other with a sort of languorous lovingness, the gentle bites of affection, possession and submission. The tide would be coming in so gently that there was hardly any movement of the sea, but the seals would create in miniature their own seascape: sometimes they would slide free of the water, leaving no ripple on the surface, and at other times they would burst from the depths in a white rose of foam, their shining bodies curving up into the air like black boomerangs, before turning and plunging into the water again with a clean cut that scarcely disturbed the even surface.

Occasionally one of the young, unattached bulls would attempt to join one of these family groups in their play, and immediately the old bull would forget his game. He would submerge and suddenly reappear at the young bull's side in a crumple of foam, uttering a sort of gargling roar that had started beneath the surface. If the young bull was quick he would hurl himself sideways in the water, and the old bull's leap would be abortive and he would land on the water surface with a crack like a cannon going off, and the noise would roll and echo down the coast. Then it would be a question of who recovered first, the young bull from his awkward sideways leap, or the old bull from his belly-splitting charge. If the old bull recovered first he would seize the younger one by the neck and they would roll and thrash in the water, roaring and biting in a tidal wave of foam, while the females glided round them watching lovingly the progress of the battle. Eventually the young bull would break free from the savage grip of his adversary and plunge beneath the waves with the old bull in hot pursuit. But in swimming under water the young bull would have the slight advantage that he was not so bulky and therefore slightly faster, and he would generally escape. The old bull would swim pompously back to his wives and squat in the water, staring grandly up into the sky while they swam round him, reaching their pointed faces out of the water to kiss him, gazing at him with their huge melting eyes in an ecstasy of admiration and love.

By this time the sun would have sunk into a sunset of pink, green and gold, and we would make our way back to camp to crouch shivering over the fire, while in the distance, carried by the night wind, steady and bitterly cold, we could hear the noises of the seals, belching and roaring and splashing in the black and icy waters along the empty coast.

Chapter Four

The Bulbous Beasts

They did not remain long under water, but rising, followed us with outstretched necks, expressing great wonder and curiosity.

CHARLES DARWIN: THE VOYAGE OF H.M.S. BEAGLE.

After we had spent some ten days filming the fur seals I decided that, reluctant though I was to leave these beautiful and fascinating animals, we really ought to move on and try and locate the elephant seals before they left the peninsula in their southward migration. So, for the next four days, we drove to and fro about the peninsula searching for the *elefantería*, and seeing a variety of wild-life, but no elephant seals.

I was amazed and delighted at the numbers of creatures we saw on the Valdes peninsula. When I thought that, a few miles away across the isthmus, lay hundreds of miles of scrub-land which we had driven through without seeing a single living creature, and yet on the peninsula life abounded, it seemed incredible. It was almost as if the peninsula and its narrow isthmus was a *cul-de-sac* into which all the wild-life of Chubut had drained and from which it could not escape. I wish that it were possible for the Argentine

Government to make the whole peninsula into a sanctuary, for which it seems to have been designed by nature. To begin with you have a wonderful cross-section of the Patagonian fauna, all concentrated in a limited area, and most of it very easy to see. Secondly the whole area could be easily and effectively controlled by virtue of the narrow isthmus connecting it to the mainland; a check point on this could keep an adequate control on the people who entered and left the area, and keep an eye out for the sort of 'sportsmen' (of which there are some in every country throughout the world) who would think it fun to chase guanaco in fast cars, or pepper the bull fur seals with buckshot. I do not think that the fact of the peninsula being divided up into several large sheep *estancias* is of great importance. True, the guanaco and the fox are shot, the first because it is supposed to eat grazing that would be better employed feeding sheep, and the latter because it is big enough to take lambs and chickens. Yet, in spite of having the *estancias* against them, both these animals, when we were there, seemed very common. Provided the sheep-farmers behaved sensibly, I think a balance between the domestic and the wild animal could be maintained. If the peninsula could be declared a wild-life sanctuary now, then, when Southern Argentina is opened up still further (which seems inevitable), and when decent roads make the peninsula less inaccessible, it could well turn out to be a tourist attraction of considerable value.

In our search for the *elefantería* we covered a lot of the peninsula, and the commonest bird we saw was undoubtedly the martineta, a species of tinamu. It is a plump, partridge-shaped little bird, about the size of a bantam. Its plumage is a rich array of autumn browns, speckled and streaked with golds, yellows and creams in an intricate and lovely pattern. Its cheeks are a pale cream colour, with two black stripes showing up well on this background, one running from the corner of the eye to the neck and the other running from the edge of the beak to the neck. On its head there is an elongated crest of dark feathers, which curves like a half-moon over its head. It has large, dark eyes, and a general air of innocent hysteria.

Martinetas were to be seen everywhere along the rough roads in little groups of five or ten. Ridiculously tame, they would stand in the middle of the road, watching the Land-Rover's approach with wide eyes, bobbing their heads so that their silly crests twitched and fluttered, not bothering to move until you slowed down within a few feet of them and blew the horn. Then, stretching out their necks and holding their heads low, as if searching the ground for something they had lost, they would scuttle off into the scrub. They were most reluctant to fly, and in order to make them do so you had to pursue them for considerable distances through the undergrowth. Then, when they felt you were coming too near, they would launch themselves into the sky with an air of desperation. It was a curious, laboured flight, like that of a bird which has never learnt to use its wings properly. They would give four or five frantic flaps of their wings, and then glide until their fat bodies had almost dragged them to earth again, when they would give another series of wild flaps and then glide on a bit further. As they flew the rush of wind through their feathers produced a curious wailing note, that rose and fell flute-like, as they flapped and glided away. Their partiality for sitting in the middle of the road was due to the fact, I think, that it was only on these bare earth surfaces that they could construct the best dust-baths. In many places they had scooped out quite deep depressions in the red earth, and you could see three or four of them standing patiently waiting their turn, while one member of the flock rolled and kicked absurdly in the bath, fluttering its wings to throw the dust over its body.

These lovely, slightly imbecile birds are, of course, ground-nesting, and I think that they themselves, their eggs and their young, form an important item of diet among the carnivorous mammals of the peninsula, particularly the pampas fox, which was a common predator in the area. They are slim, grey, dainty little animals, with incredibly slender and fragile-looking legs. They appeared to hunt as much by day as by night, and were usually to be seen in pairs. They would suddenly dash across the road in front of us as we drove along, their bushy tails streaming out behind them like puffs of grey smoke, and on reaching the other side of the road they would skid to a halt and, squatting on their haunches, examine us craftily.

At one of the places in which we camped a pair of these little foxes paid us a visit, the only animal apart from the guanaco to do so. It was about five in the morning, and from my bed under the rear axle of the Land-Rover I was watching the sky turn green with dawn, while, as usual, trying to pluck up the courage to quit the warmth of my blankets and light the fire for breakfast. Suddenly, from the yellow scrub around us, the two foxes appeared as unexpectedly and as silently as ghosts. They approached the camp cautiously, with the conspiratorial air of a couple of schoolboys raiding an orchard, with many pauses to sniff the dawn wind. It was fortunate, at that precise juncture, that no one was snoring. I can put it on record that there is nothing quite so effective for scaring off wild animals as three women in the back of a Land-Rover, all snoring in different keys.

Having circled the camp without mishap, they grew bolder. They approached the ashes of the fire, sniffed at them deeply, and then frightened each other by sneezing violently. Recovering from this shock they continued their investigation and found an empty sardine tin, which, after a certain amount of low bickering, they proceeded to lick clean. Their next discovery was a large roll of bright pink toilet paper, one of the few luxury articles in our equipment. Having proved that it was not edible, they then discovered that if it was patted briskly with a paw it unravelled itself in the most satisfactory manner. So, for the next ten minutes, they danced and whirled on their slender legs, hurling the toilet roll to and fro, occasionally taking streamers of it in their mouths and leaping daintily into the air, returning to earth with the paper wrapped intricately round their necks and legs. This game was conducted so silently and so gracefully that it was a delight to watch, and their agile bodies were well set off against the green sky, the yellow-flowered bushes and the pink paper. The whole camp site was taking on a gay carnival air, when somebody in the Land-Rover yawned. The foxes froze instantly, one of them with a piece of toilet paper dangling from his mouth. The yawn was repeated, and the foxes vanished as silently as they had come, leaving – as a souvenir of their visit – some hundred and twenty feet of pink paper fluttering in the breeze.

Another creature that we saw very frequently was the Darwin's rhea, the South American counterpart of the African ostrich. These birds were smaller than the rheas from Northern Argentina, more delicate in build and a more pearly grey in colour. They were generally in small flocks of five or six, and on many occasions we saw them moving through the scrub in conjunction with a flock of guanaco. I think one of the loveliest sights we saw on the peninsula was a herd of six guanaco with three graceful cinnamon-coloured babies, trotting slowly through the golden scrub in company with four Darwin's rheas, who were ushering along a swarm of twelve young, each dressed in its striped baby plumage, so that they looked like a line of tiny fat wasps running close to their parents' great feet. While the baby rheas were very sedate and orderly, like a school crocodile, the baby guanacos were more exuberant and unruly, dancing about in amongst the adults, in exciting, daring and complicated gambols. One of them carried out such an intricate gambol that he bumped into one of the adults and received a sharp kick in the stomach as punishment, after which he became very subdued and trotted quietly along behind his mother.

If undisturbed the rheas would pace along in a very regal manner. But, occasionally, we would come upon them when they were on the road and immediate panic would ensue. Instead of swerving off into the scrub, they would set off in a disorderly cluster down the road, running with the slightly effeminate grace of professional footballers. As we drove the Land-Rover closer and closer they would increase their speed, lowering their long necks groundwards, their feet coming up so high with each step that they almost touched what passes for a chin in a rhea. One I paced in this manner ran six feet in front of the Land-Rover bonnet for a distance of half a mile, averaging between twenty-five and thirty miles an hour. Eventually, when you had followed them like this for some considerable time, it would suddenly occur to them that they might be safer in the scrub. So they would put on a sudden burst of speed, open their pale wings in a graceful gesture, swerve off the road with a ballet-like grace and go bouncing away into the distance.

These rheas, like the common rhea of the north, have communal nests, that is to say several females lay their eggs in one nest. This is a mere scrape in the ground, lined with some dry grass or a few twigs, and you can find as many as fifty eggs in the one nest. As in the common rheas the male Darwin's rhea does the hard work of incubating the eggs and rearing the young when they hatch. The highly-polished eggs are a fine green colour when just laid, but the side that is towards the sun soon fades, first to a dull mottled green, then yellowish, then to pale blue and finally to white. The rheas are so prolific that their eggs, and, to a large extent, their young, form an important item of diet for the predators of the peninsula.

Another creature which was very common, and which we frequently met on the roads, was the *pinche* or hairy armadillo. We saw them just as much by day as by night, but the time they were most frequently seen was towards evening in the rays of the setting sun, trotting to and fro over the road surfaces, sniffing vigorously, looking like strange clockwork toys, for their little legs moved so fast they were a mere blur beneath the shell. They are fairly thickly cloaked with a long, coarse white hair, but I should not have thought that this would have provided them with any protection from the cold in the winter. I presume they must hibernate in the winter months, for there could be nothing for them to eat as the ground is frozen to a depth of several feet. All the ones we caught were covered with a tremendously thick layer of fat, and their pale pink, heavily wrinkled bellies were always bulging with food. Their main diet must consist of beetles, their larvae, and the young and eggs of ground-nesting birds like the martineta, though sometimes they may come across a windfall in the shape of a dead sheep or guanaco. Frequently they could be seen right down on the sea-shore, trotting briskly along the tide line, looking like small, rotund colonels on a Bournemouth seafront, imbibing the health-giving ozone, though they would occasionally spoil the illusion by stopping to have a light snack off a dead crab, a thing I have never seen a colonel do.

Watching all this wild-life was, of course, fascinating, but it was still not bringing us any nearer to our objective, which was the elephant seals. We had, by now, covered quite a large area of the coast, without any success, and I began to think we were too late, and that the elephant seals were already drifting southwards towards Tierra del Fuego and the Falkland Islands. But just when I had given up hope we discovered an *elefantería* which no one had told us about, and then we only found it by luck. We had been walking along a fairly high cliff, pausing every quarter of a mile or so to examine the beach below us for signs of life. Presently, we rounded a small headland and came to a bay where the beach at the base of the cliff was covered in a tumbled mass of rocks. Some of these rocks were so large that, from our vantage point, we could not tell what might be lying behind them, so, after searching along the cliff for a short way, we found a rough path which led us down to the shore, and made our way down to investigate.

The beach was of bright mottled shingle, each pebble sea-polished so that it shone in the evening sun. The boulders, some as large as a cottage, lay tumbled haphazardly along the beach, grey and fawn in colour. Some of them were so large and fretted into such weird shapes by the wind and the sea, that it was a major operation scrambling over them, weighted down as we were with the cameras and equipment. We struggled through and over them for some distance, and then decided that what we needed was food. So, choosing a rock that had been moulded to make a natural seat, we sat down and unpacked our food and wine. I was convinced by then that there was not an elephant seal for miles, and I was thoroughly depressed and irritated with myself for having spent so much time on the fur seals.

'Well, we might find some tomorrow,' said Jacquie soothingly, handing me a sandwich that appeared to have three-quarters of the Patagonian topsoil adhering to it.

'No,' I said, viewing this sustenance with a jaundiced eye, and refusing to be comforted, 'they've gone south now. They've had their babies and left. If I hadn't spent so much time on those damned fur seals we might have found them.'

'Well, it's your own fault,' said Jacquie logically. 'I kept telling you that you had enough film of the fur seal, but you kept insisting we spent just one more day.'

'I know,' I said gloomily, 'but they were such wonderful creatures, I couldn't tear myself away.'

Marie, with the air of one who is making the best of a disaster, seized a bottle of wine, and as the cork popped out of the bottle a large, slightly elongated and egg-shaped boulder some ten feet away gave a deep and lugubrious sigh, and opened a pair of huge, gentle, liquid-looking eyes of the deepest black, and gazed at us placidly.

Once it had thus revealed itself as an elephant seal, one wondered why one had ever thought it was anything else; and a close and excited scrutiny of the surrounding beach showed us that we were, in fact, sitting next to twelve of the gigantic beasts, which had all remained calmly sleeping while we had walked up to them, seated ourselves, and unpacked our food like trippers at Margate. They so closely resembled the rocks amongst which they lay that I began to wonder how many other groups we had walked past in our search for them. After watching the fur seals, I had expected the elephant seal colony to be a much more boisterous and vivacious lot, whereas here they were, lying about the beach in attitudes of relaxed abandon, displaying about as much boisterousness as could be expected from a convention of dropsy sufferers having a chess tournament in a Turkish bath. We walked among the huge, snoring carcases, and by investigation we discovered that of the twelve animals there three were males, six were females, and three were well-grown young. The babies measured about six feet in length, and the females about twelve to fourteen feet. The real bulk was reserved for the males. Two of these were young bulls, each about eighteen feet in length, while the last was a fully adult bull, and measured twenty-one feet in length.

This bull was a magnificent beast, with a huge barrel-like body, and a great carunculated nose, like that of a confirmed gin-drinker. He lay on the shining shingle like a colossal blob of putty, occasionally sighing deeply so that his nose wobbled like a jelly, or every so often waking up sufficiently to ladle some damp shingle on to his back with one of his flippers. His placidity towards our intrusion was extraordinary, for we approached within three or four feet to measure and take photographs, and all he did was to open his eyes, survey us dreamily, and sink back into sleep again.

For me this was a tremendously exciting experience. Other people may have a burning ambition to see the Leaning Tower of Pisa, or visit Venice, or see the Acropolis before they die. But my ambition had been to see a live elephant seal in his natural environment, and here I was, lying on the shingle eating sandwiches within five feet of one, who lay there looking not unlike a baby barrage balloon which has, unaccountably, been filled with dough. With a sandwich in one hand and a stop-watch in the other I checked on his breathing, which is one of the many remarkable things about an elephant seal. They breathe fairly regularly some thirty times during five minutes, and then they stop breathing for a time, which varies from five to eight minutes. Presumably this is of great use to them when they are at sea, for they can rise to the surface, breathe, and then sink below the water and hold their breath for this considerable period without having to resurface and refill their lungs. I was so carried away, lying there with this gigantic and fantastic animal within touching distance, that I proceeded to give the others a lecture on the elephant seal.

'It's quite extraordinary the soundness of their sleep. Do you know there was one naturalist who actually went and lay on top of an elephant seal without waking it?'

Jacquie surveyed the colossal animal in front of me.

'Rather him than me,' she said.

'Apparently the females don't become sexually mature until they are two years old. They have this delayed implantation thing as well ... you know, where they're mated and retain the sperm for varying lengths of time in their bodies before allowing it to develop. Now those babies over there are this year's brood. That means they won't be ready to breed ...'

'*This* year's brood?' Jacquie interrupted in astonishment. 'I thought they were about a year old.'

'No, I should say they are four or five months old.'

'How big are they when they're born, then?'

'Oh, about half that size, I should think.'

'Good God!' said Jacquie with feeling. 'Fancy giving birth to a thing *that* size.'

'There you are,' I said. 'It just goes to show that there's always someone worse off than you are.'

The elephant seal, as if in agreement, gave a deep, heart-rending sigh.

'Do you know that the intestine of an adult bull can measure six hundred and sixty-two feet?' I inquired.

'No, I didn't,' said Jacquie, 'and I think we'd all enjoy our sandwiches more if you refrained from divulging any more secrets of their internal anatomy.'

'Well, I thought it would interest you.'

'It does,' said Jacquie, 'but not when I'm eating. It's the sort of information I prefer to acquire between meals.'

There were several things that struck one immediately about the elephant seals, once one had got over incredulity at their mere size. The first thing was, of course, their ridiculous hindquarters. The fur seal (which is really a sea lion) has the hind limbs well developed as legs, so that when they move they hoist themselves up on to all four legs and walk as a dog or a cat would. But in the elephant seal, which is a true seal, the hind limbs are minute and pretty useless, with stupid flippers that make it look as though the animal has had a couple of empty gloves attached to its rear end. When the creature moves all the propulsion comes from the front flippers, and the humping of the massive back, a slow, ungainly method of movement that was painful to watch.

There was quite a colour variation among the herd. The old bull was a rich, deep slate-grey, tastefully speckled here and there with green, where some marine alga was apparently growing on his tough hide. The young bulls and the cows were a much paler grey. The babies were not bald and leathery like their parents, but each was wearing a fine fur coat of moon-white hair, close and tight as plush. The adults had so many folds and wrinkles all over them that they looked rather as if they were in need of a square meal to fill out the creases, as it were, whereas the babies were so rotund and glossy they looked as though they all had just been blown up with bicycle pumps, and would, if they were not careful, take to the air.

From the point of view of filming the elephant seal colony was, to say the least, difficult. All they wanted to do was sleep. The only real movement they made was to open and close their huge nostrils as they breathed, and occasionally one would shovel some shingle on to its back; but as there was no preliminary warning to this action it took me some time to get it on film. Sometimes one of them would hump itself forward, eyes tightly shut, burrowing its great nose through the shingle like a bulldozer. Even when I had got all these actions on film it still did not seem to me that the elephant seals were showing themselves to advantage; they lacked action, which, after all, is one of the things necessary for a moving picture. One of the extraordinary things about these seals is the flexibility of the backbone. In spite of their bulk and vast quantities of blubber, they can bend themselves backwards, like a hoop, until the head touches the uplifted tail. How to get them to demonstrate this for me to film, when they were all lying about displaying the animation of a group of opium smokers, was somewhat of a puzzle. At last, however, we were successful with the old bull, by the simple expedient of throwing handfuls of fine gravel on to his tail. The first handful made him stir slightly and sigh deeply, without opening his eyes. The second handful made him open his eyes and stare at us in mild surprise. With the third handful he raised his head, drew back his snout so that it wrinkled like a concertina, opened his mouth and uttered a hissing roar, and then fell back on to the shingle as if exhausted by this effort and went back to sleep again.

Eventually, however, our bombardment got on his nerves. It did not, of course, hurt him, but a constant rain of shingle on your rear-end when you are trying to get to sleep can be extremely irritating. He suddenly became very wide awake and reared up so that he was like the letter J with his head high in the air, his mouth opened wide uttering the loud hissing roar, an oddly reptilian sound for such a monstrous mammal to make. Four times he reared up like this, and then, seeing that the display was having no detrimental effect on our morale, he did what all seals do in moments of crisis: he burst into tears. Great, black tears oozed out of his eyes and trickled forlornly down his cheeks. He lowered himself full length on to the shingle, and proceeded to move backwards towards the sea, like a gargantuan caterpillar, humping his body up with tremendous effort, the fat along his back rippling into waves as he moved. At last, with a final plaintive roar and another flood of tears, he backed into the water, and an incoming wave broke in a garland of white foam around his shoulders. The rest of the herd became alarmed at their lord and master's disappearance, and they all raised their heads and started to look at us uneasily. Then one of the babies panicked, and hunched its way down to the sea, tears streaming down its white face. This was the final straw, and within a minute the whole herd was rushing seawards, looking like a flock of huge maggots in pursuit of a cheese.

Sadly we packed up our equipment and started up the cliff, sadly because we had just completed our last task, and this meant that we must leave the peninsula with its wonderful animal life, and head back to Buenos Aires and the next stage of the expedition. As we made our way along the twilit cliff path we saw the old bull elephant seal for the last time. His head appeared out of a wave, his dark eyes surveyed us puzzledly. He snorted, a reverberating noise that echoed along the cliffs and made his nose vibrate. Then, still watching us sadly, he sank slowly beneath the icy waters and disappeared.

BOOK TWO

The Customs of the Country

The plane taxied out across the darkened airfield to where the runway lay, between two strips of diamond-bright lights. Here it paused, revved up its engine until every bone in the plane's metal body seemed to screech out in protest, and then suddenly rushed forward. The strip-lights fled past, and then suddenly we were airborne, the plane tipping from side to side like a slightly drunken swallow as it climbed higher and higher. Then, below me, Buenos Aires lay spread in the warm night like a chessboard of multicoloured stars. I unfastened my safety belt, lit a cigarette and lay back in my seat, feeling very mellow and full of farewell brandy. At last I was on my way to a place I had long wanted to visit, a place with a magical name: Jujuy.

When we had returned from the south the effects of the car crash we had had soon after arrival in Argentina (in which Jacquie was the only one hurt) had begun to make themselves felt; the terrible jolting we had undergone on the Patagonian roads, and the rough conditions under which we had been forced to live, had resulted in her getting blinding headaches. It was obvious that she could not continue the trip, so we had decided to send her back to England. She had departed the week before, and this left Sophie and me to finish the trip. So, while Sophie remained in our little villa with its garden already stuffed with animals which she had to minister unto, I made tracks for Jujuy, to try and add to the collection.

As the plane droned on through the night I dozed in my seat and tried to remember all I knew about Jujuy, which was precious little. It is a north-western province of Argentina, bordered on the one side by Bolivia, and on the other by Chile. It is a curious place in many ways, but chiefly because it is like a tropical tongue, as it were, inserted into Argentina. On the one side you have the mountains of Bolivia, on the other the curious, desiccated province of Salta, and between the two the lush tropical area of Jujuy, which compares favourably with anything to be found in Paraguay or southern Brazil. Here I knew that you could find the colourful, exciting tropical fauna, just starting to encroach on the Pampa and grassland fauna, and it was these creatures I was after. Thinking about all these magnificent animals I fell into a deep sleep, and was just dreaming that I was catching a particularly malevolent jaguar with a lassoo, when I was awoken by the steward shaking my arm. Apparently we had arrived at some godforsaken place, and all passengers had to dismount while the plane refuelled. Plane travel has never been my favourite form of transportation (except for very small planes, where you get a real sense of flying), so to be roused from a brandy-soothed sleep at two in the morning and be forced to stand around in a tiny bar that did not offer anything more exciting than luke-warm coffee did not improve my temper. As soon as they would allow I got on the plane again, settled down in my seat and tried to sleep.

Almost immediately I was roused by what appeared to be a ten-ton weight descending on my arm. I extricated it with difficulty, before any bones were broken, and glared at the person responsible. This was not very effective, as the interior of the plane was lit by what appeared to be a series of fireflies suffering from pernicious anaemia. All I could see was that the next seat to me (until then mercifully empty) was now being inundated – there is no other word – by a female of colossal proportions. The various portions of her anatomy which she could not cram into her own seat she had generously allowed to overflow into mine.

'*Buenas noches*,' she said pleasantly, exuding sweat and scent in equal quantities.

'*Buenas noches*,' I mumbled, and hastily closed my eyes and huddled into what was left of my seat, in order to put an end to the conversation. Fortunately, my companion, after this exchange of pleasantries, settled herself down for sleep, with much grunting and shifting and deep shuddering sighs that were vaguely reminiscent of the elephant seals. Presently she twitched and mumbled her way into sleep, and then started a prolonged and interesting snore that sounded like someone rhythmically rolling small potatoes down a corrugated iron roof. Lulled, rather than disturbed by this sound, I managed to drop off myself.

When I awoke it was light, and I surreptitiously examined my still sleeping companion. She was, as I say, a fine figure of a woman – all twenty stone of her. She had clad her generous body in a silk dress in yellow and green, and she was wearing scarlet shoes, both now reclining some distance from her feet. Her hair was bright glossy black and carefully arranged in tiny curls all over her head, and to crown this she was wearing a straw hat to which half the fruit and vegetable produce of Argentina appeared to have been attached. This breath-taking horticultural achievement had slipped during the night, and now reclined over one of her eyes at a saucy angle. Her face was round and dimpled, and separated from her ample bosom by a lava-flow of chins. Her hands, I noticed, were folded demurely in her lap, and though they were reddened and work-roughened they were tiny and beautifully formed, like the hands of so many fat people. As I was watching her she suddenly gave a great, shuddering sigh and opened large, pansy-dark eyes and gazed about her with the vacant expression of an awakening baby. Then she focused on me and her dumpling face spread into a dimpled smile.

'*Buenos dias, señor*,' she said, inclining her head.

'*Buenos dias, señora*,' I replied, also inclining my head gravely.

From somewhere under the seat she hoicked out a handbag the size of a small cabin-trunk and proceeded to repair the damage that the night's sleep had done to her face. This was little enough, as far as I could see, for her complexion was as perfect as a magnolia petal. Satisfied at last that she was not going to let her sex down, she put away her bag, resettled her bulk, and turned her bright, kindly eyes on me. Wedged as I was there was no escape.

'Where are you travelling to, *señor*?' she asked.

'Jujuy, *señora*,' I replied.

'Ah, Jujuy?' she said, opening wide her dark eyes and raising her eyebrows, as though Jujuy was the most interesting and desirable place in the world.

'You are German?' she asked.

'No, English.'

'Ah, English?' with again the delighted surprise, as though to be English was something really special.

I felt it was time I took a more active part in the conversation. 'I do not speak Spanish at all,' I explained, 'only a very little.'

'But you speak *beautifully*,' she said, patting my knee, and then qualified it by adding, 'and I will speak slowly so that you may understand.'

I sighed and gave myself up to my fate; short of jumping out of the window on my left there was nothing else I could do. Having decided that my knowledge of Spanish was limited she came to the conclusion that I would get a better grasp of her conversation if she shouted, so now the whole plane was party to our exchange of confidences. Her name, it appeared, was Rosa Lillipampila and she was on her way to visit her married son in Salta. She had not seen him for three years, and this was to be a terrific reunion. This was also her first flight in a plane, and she was taking a child-like delight in it. She kept breaking off her conversation with shrill cries (which made the more nervous of the other passengers jump) in order to lean over me, enveloping me in scent and bosom, to peer at some landmark passing below. Several times I offered to change seats with her, but she would not hear of it. When the steward came round with morning coffee she fumbled for her bag to pay, and when it was explained that it was free she was so delighted that you would have thought the rather grubby paper cup full of gritty liquid was a magnum of champagne which the benevolent air company had bestowed upon her. Presently the red lights went on to tell us that we were landing yet again at some obscure township to refuel, and I helped her struggle to get the safety belt round her enormous girth. This was a strenuous task, and her shrieks of merriment at our efforts echoed up and down the plane.

'You see,' she panted, between gusts of laughter, 'when one has had six children and one likes to eat, one loses control over the size of one's body.'

At last, just as the plane touched down, we got the belt hitched round her.

We clambered out on to the tarmac, stiff and crumpled, and I found that my girl-friend moved with the grace and lightness of a cloud. She had obviously decided that I was to be her conquest of the trip, and so, with a courteous, old world gesture I offered her my arm, and she accepted it with a beaming, coquettish smile. Linked together like a courting couple we made our way towards the inevitable small café and toilets that decorated the airport. Here she patted my arm, told me she would not be long, and drifted to the door marked 'Señoras,' through which she passed with difficulty.

While she was communing with nature I took the opportunity to examine a large bush which grew alongside the little café. It was about the size of the average hydrangea, and yet on its branches and among its leaves (after only a cursory inspection) I found fifteen different species of insect and five species of spider. It was obvious we were nearing the tropical area. Then I spotted a very old friend of mine, a praying mantis, perched on a leaf, swaying from side to side and glaring about with its pale, evil eyes. I detached it from its perch and was letting it stalk its way up my arm, when my girl-friend returned. On seeing the creature she let out a cry that could, with a following wind, have been heard in Buenos Aires, but, to my surprise, it was not a cry of horror, but a cry of delighted recognition.

'Ah, the Devil's Horse!' she cried excitedly. 'When I was a child we often used to play with them.'

This interested me, for, as a child in Greece, I used to play with them as well, and the local people had also called them the Devil's Horse. So, for ten minutes or so, we played with the insect, making it run up and down each other's arms, and laughing immoderately, so that all the other passengers obviously doubted our sanity. At last we returned the mantis to his bush and went to have a coffee, but just at that moment an official arrived, and with much apologetic hand-spreading informed us that we would be delayed two hours. Groans of rage rose from the assembled passengers. There was, however, the official went on, a company bus which would run us into town, and there, at a hotel, the air company had arranged for us to have anything we wanted at their expense. My girl-friend was delighted. Such generosity! Such kindness! I helped her into the bus, and we rattled over the dusty road into the town and drew up outside a curiously Victorian-looking hotel.

Inside, the hotel was so ornate that my lady friend was quite overcome. There were huge, brown, imitation marble pillars, pots and pots of decayed-looking palms, flocks of waiters who looked like ambassadors on holiday, and a sort of mosaic of tiny tables stretching away, apparently, to the farthest horizon. She held very tight to my arm as I steered her to a table and we sat down. All this splendour seemed to bereave her of speech, so in my halting Spanish I ordered lavishly from one of the ambassadors (who did not appear to have shaved since his last official function) and settled back to enjoy it. Soon, under the influence of five large cups of coffee with cream, a plate of hot *medialunas* and butter, followed by six cream cakes and half a pound of grapes, my companion lost her awe of the place, and even ordered one of the ambassadors to fetch her another plate to put her grape-pips on.

Presently, replete with free food, we made our way outside to the coach. The driver was sitting on a mudguard, moodily picking his teeth with a matchstick. We inquired if we were now ready to return to the airport. He gazed at us with obvious distaste.

'*Media hora*,' he said, and returned to the cavity in his back molar, in which he obviously hoped to find a rich deposit of something, maybe uranium.

So my girl-friend and I went for a walk round the town to kill time. She was delighted to have this chance to act as guide to a real foreigner, and there was nothing she did not show and explain to me. This was a shoe-shop ... see, there were shoes in the window, so one knew, without a shadow of a doubt, that it was a shoe-shop. This was a garden, in which they grew flowers. That was a donkey, over there, that animal tethered to a tree. Ah, and here we had a chemist's shop, where you purchased medicines when you were not well. Oblivious to the people trying to force their way past on the pavement, she insisted on standing in front of the chemist's window and giving such a realistic display of suffering that I expected someone to call for an ambulance, if the town toasted of such an amenity. Altogether our tour was a great success, and I was quite sorry when we had to return to the bus and be driven back to the airport.

Once more in the plane we had the Herculean task of lashing her into her seat, and then unlashing her once we were airborne on the last leg of our journey. Hitherto the country we had been flying over had been typical Pampa, with here and there an occasional outcrop of small hills, but by and large the view from the plane had been flat and featureless. But now the hills became more and more frequent, and higher and higher, covered with scrub and gigantic cacti like huge green surrealist candelabra. And then the air-pockets started.

The first was quite a big one, and one felt one's stomach had been left at least a hundred feet up as the plane dropped. My companion, who had been in the middle of an intricate and – to me – almost incomprehensible story about some remote cousin, opened her mouth wide and uttered a cry of such a piercing quality that the whole of the aircraft was thrown into confusion. Then, to my relief, she burst into peals of happy laughter.

'What was that?' she asked me.

I did my best, in my limited Spanish, to explain the mysteries of air-pockets, and managed to get the basic fact across to her. She lost all interest in the story about her cousin, and waited expectantly for the next air-pocket to make its appearance so that she could enjoy it to the full, for, as she explained, she had not been prepared for the first one. She was soon rewarded with a real beauty, and greeted it with a scream of delight and a flood of delighted laughter. She was like a child on a switchback in a fair, and she treated the whole thing as a special treat which the air company had provided for her enjoyment, like the meal we had just eaten. The rest of the passengers, I noticed, were not treating the air-pockets in the same light-hearted way, and they were all glowering at my fat friend with faces that were growing progressively greener. By now we were flying over higher and higher ground, and the plane dropped and rose like a lift out of control. The man across the gangway had reached a shade of green I would not have thought the human countenance could have achieved. My friend noticed this too, and was all commiseration. She leant across the gangway.

'Are you ill, *señor*?' she inquired. He nodded mutely.

'Ah, you poor thing,' she said and burrowing into her bag produced a huge bag of very sticky and pungent sweets which she thrust at him.

'These are very good for sickness,' she proclaimed. 'Take one.'

The poor man took one look at the terrible congealed mass in the paper bag and shook his head vigorously. My friend shrugged, gave him a glance of pity, and popped three of the sweets into her mouth. As she sucked vigorously and loudly she suddenly noticed something that had escaped her sharp eyes before, the brown paper bag in a little bracket attached to the back of the seat in front of us. She pulled it out and peered inside, obviously wondering if some other magnificent largesse from the kindly air company was concealed inside it. Then she turned a puzzled eye on me.

'What is this for?' she asked in a penetrating voice.

I explained the necessity of the paper bag. She held it aloft and examined it minutely.

'Well,' she said at last, 'if I wanted to get sick I should want something *much* larger than *that*.'

The man across the gangway cast a look at her ample form and the size of the brown paper bag, and the vision conjured up by her words was obviously too much for him, for he dived precipitously for his own bag and buried his face in it.

When the plane eventually touched down my girl-friend and I were the only ones who dismounted without looking as though we had just been through a hurricane. In the foyer of the airport her son was waiting, a pleasant-faced man who was identical in shape to his mother. Uttering shrill cries they undulated towards each other and embraced with a fat-quivering crash. When they surfaced, I was introduced and commended for the care I had taken of my protégée *en route*. Then, because the driver who was to meet me was nowhere to be seen, the entire Lillipampila family (son, wife, three children and grandmother) hunted round the airport like foxhounds until they found him. They saw me to the car, embraced me, told me to be sure to look them up when I was in Salta, and stood, a solid façade of fat, beaming and waving as I drove off on my way to Calilegua, the place where I was to stay. Kindness in Argentina is apt to be overwhelming, and after having been embraced by the entire Lillipampila family I felt every bone in my body aching. I gave the driver a cigarette, lit one myself and leant back and closed my eyes. I felt I deserved a few moments' relaxation.

Chapter Five

Jujuy

The elegance of the grasses, the novelty of the parasitical plants, the beauty of the flowers, the glossy green of the foliage, but above all the general luxuriance of the vegetation, filled me with admiration.

CHARLES DARWIN: THE VOYAGE OF H.M.S. BEAGLE.

Calilegua was primarily a sugar-producing estate, though it also grew a certain amount of the more tropical varieties of fruit for the Buenos Aires market. It was a flat plain that lay cupped in a half-moon of mountains that were covered with thick, tropical forest. It was curious how suddenly you came upon this lushness of vegetation. We left the airport and for the first hour or so drove throught a desiccated landscape of semi-eroded hills, sun-baked, scrub-covered, dotted here and there with the great swollen trunks of the *palo borracho* trees, their bark as thickly covered with spines as a hedgehog's back, and here and there you saw one of the giant cacti rearing up, perhaps twenty feet high, decorated with strange curving branches. These again were spine-covered and unfriendly. Then we sped round a couple of corners, down a hill and into the valley of Calilegua, and the vegetation changed, so suddenly that it was almost painful to the eye. Here were the vivid greens of the tropics, so many shades and some of such viridescence that they make the green of the English landscape look grey in comparison. Then, as if to assure me that I was back in the tropics, a small flock of parakeets swooped across the road, wheezing and chittering. Shortly afterwards we passed a group of Indians, dressed in tattered shirts and trousers and gigantic straw hats. They were short and squat, with Mongolian features and the curious sloe-coloured eyes over which there seems to be a bloom like a plum that covers thought and expression. They glanced at the car incuriously as we passed. After being among Europeans so long, and in the flat scenery of the Pampa and Patagonia, the Indians, the parakeets and the vividness of the country through which we drove went to my head like wine.

Presently the driver slowed down and swung off the main road on to a rough track that was thickly lined on both sides by thick clumps of gigantic bamboos, some of the canes being as thick as a man's thigh and pale honey-coloured, tiger-striped with green. These huge canes bent gracefully over the road and intertwined their fluttering green leaves overhead so thickly that the road was gloomy, and it was like driving down the nave of a cathedral. The sunlight flickered and flashed between the giant stems as we drove down the rutted track, and above the noise of the car engine I could hear the strange groans and squeaks that bamboos make when swayed by the wind. Presently we came to a villa half-hidden in a riot of flowers and creepers, and here the car stopped. Joan Lett, who, with her husband Charles, had invited me to Calilegua, came out to greet me, took me inside and gave me the most welcome cup of tea. Presently, when Charles returned from his work, we sat on the balcony in the fading indigo evening night and discussed my plan of campaign.

It has always been my experience in most parts of the world that if you go to an area which is fairly well populated you can obtain most of your common local fauna without much difficulty, for the local people keep the creatures either as pets, or rear them until they are old enough to form the basis for a meal. So your first job should be to go round every ranch and village in the vicinity and buy what you can. Then you can review your collection and try and fill in the gaps (which are generally the rare creatures) yourself. I propounded this philosophy to Charles, as the ice tinkled musically in our gin-and-tonics, but to my dismay he was not inclined to agree with me. He said that he did not think the Indians in Calilegua kept anything in the livestock line, except the usual run of cats, dogs and chickens. However, he promised that the next day he would get one of his more intelligent helpers to make inquiries in the village, and let me know the result. I went to bed fortified by gin but in a gloomy frame of mind, wondering if after all I had come to the wrong place. Even the faint whisper of crickets outside in the garden and the huge trembling stars that told me I was back in the tropics did little to cheer me.

The next morning, however, things looked brighter. After breakfast I was out in the garden watching a flock of gold, blue and silver butterflies feeding on the scarlet blooms of a bush when Luna arrived. I had heard him singing, in a pleasant tenor voice, as he came down the avenue of bamboo, and as he reached the gate he paused in his song, clapped his hands in the customary manner of anyone in South America when arriving at your house, opened the gate and joined me by the bush and the butterflies. He was a tiny man, about five feet in height, and as slender as a fourteen-year-old boy. He had a handsome, faintly skull-like face, with huge dark eyes, and black hair that was cropped close to his head. He held out a hand that looked as fragile as the butterflies we were surrounded by.

'Señor Durrell?' he inquired.

'Yes,' I replied, shaking his hand gently, for fear it should break off at the wrist.

'I am Luna,' he said, as if this should be sufficient explanation.

'Señor Lett sent you?' I asked.

'*Si, si,*' he answered, giving me a smile of great charm and sweetness.

We both stood and watched the butterflies drifting round the red blooms, while I racked my brains for the right Spanish phrases.

'*¡Que lindo,*' said Luna, pointing at the butterflies, '*que bicho más lindos!*'

'*Si,*' I said. There was another pause, and we smiled at each other amiably.

'You speak English?' I inquired hopefully.

'No, very small,' said Luna, spreading his hands and smiling gently, as if deploring this terrible gap in his education.

It was obvious that his knowledge of my language was about as extensive as mine was of his. This later proved to be true. Both of us could understand a quite complicated conversation in each other's language, but both were incapable of doing more in speech than string a few ungrammatical nouns and verbs together.

'You ... I ... go Helmuth,' suggested Luna suddenly, waving a delicate hand.

I agreed, wondering what a Helmuth was; it was a new word to me, and, as far as I was concerned, could have been anything from a new type of jet-engine to a particularly low night-club. However, I was willing to try anything once, especially if it turned out to be a night-club. We walked down the musically squeaking, creaking, groaning and rustling avenue of bamboo, and then came to a large area of lawn, dotted with gigantic palm-trees, their trunks covered with parasitic plants and orchids. We walked through these towards a long, low red brick building, while the humming-birds flipped and whirred around us, gleaming and changing with the delicate sheen one sees on a soap bubble. Luna led me through gauze-covered doors into a large cool dining-room, and there, sitting in solitary state at the end of a huge table, devouring breakfast, was a man of about thirty with barley-sugar coloured hair, vivid blue eyes, and a leathery, red, humorous face. He looked up as we entered and gave us a wide, impish grin.

'Helmuth,' said Luna, pointing to this individual, as if he had performed a particularly difficult conjuring trick. Helmuth rose from the table and extended a large, freckled hand.

'Hullo,' he said, crushing my hand in his, 'I'm Helmuth. Sit down and have some breakfast, eh?'

I explained that I had already had some breakfast, and so Helmuth returned to his victuals, talking to me between mouthfuls, while Luna, seated the other side of the table, drooped languidly in a chair and hummed softly to himself.

'Charles tells me you want animals, eh?' said Helmuth. 'Well, we don't know much about animals here. There *are* animals, of course, up in the hills, but I don't know what you'll get in the villages. Not much, I should think. However, when I've finished eating we go see, eh?'

When Helmuth had assured himself, somewhat reluctantly, that there was nothing edible left on the table, he hustled Luna and myself out to his station-wagon, piled us in and drove down to the village, over the dusty, rutted roads that would, at the first touch of rain, turn into glutinous mud.

The village was a fairly typical one, consisting of small shacks with walls built out of the jagged off-cuts from the saw mill, and whitewashed. Each stood in its own little patch of ground, surrounded by a bamboo fence, and these gardens were sometimes filled with a strange variety of old tins, kettles and broken barrels each brimming over with flowers. Wide ditches full of muddy water separated these 'gardens' from the road, and were spanned at each front gate by a small, rickety bridge of roughly-nailed branches. It was at one of these little shanties that Helmuth stopped. He peered hopefully into the riot of pomegranate trees, covered with red flowers, that filled the tiny garden.

'Here, the other day, I think I see a parrot,' he explained.

We left the station-wagon and crossed the rickety little bridge that led to the bamboo gate. Here we clapped our hands and waited patiently. Presently, from inside the little shack, erupted a brood of chocolate-coloured children, all dressed in clean but tattered clothing, who lined up like a defending army and regarded us out of black eyes, each, without exception, sucking its thumb vigorously. They were followed by their mother, a short, rather handsome Indian woman with a shy smile.

'Enter, señores, enter,' she called, beckoning us into the garden.

We went in, and, while Luna crouched down and conducted a muttered conversation with the row of fascinated children, Helmuth, exuding goodwill and personality, beamed at the woman.

'This señor,' he said, gripping my shoulder tightly, as if fearful that I might run away, 'this señor wants *bichos*, live *bichos*, eh? Now, the other day when I passed your house, I saw that you possessed a parrot, a very common and rather ugly parrot of a kind that I have no doubt the señor will despise. Nevertheless, I am bound to show it to him, worthless though it is.'

The woman bristled.

'It is a beautiful parrot,' she said shrilly and indignantly, 'a very beautiful parrot, and one, moreover, of a kind that is extremely rare. It comes from high up in the mountains.'

'Nonsense,' said Helmuth firmly, 'I have seen many like it in the market in Jujuy, and they were so common they were practically having to give them away. This one is undoubtedly one of those.'

'The señor is mistaken,' said the woman, 'this is a most unusual bird of great beauty and tameness.'

'I do not think it is beautiful,' said Helmuth, and added loftily, 'and as for its tameness, it is a matter of indifference to the señor whether it be tame or as wild as a puma.'

I felt it was about time I entered the fray.

'Er . . . Helmuth,' I said tentatively.

'Yes?' he said, turning to me and regarding me with his blue eyes flashing with the light of battle.

'I don't want to interfere, but wouldn't it be a good idea if I saw the bird first, before we start bargaining? I mean, it might be something very common, or something quite rare.'

'Yes,' said Helmuth, struck by the novelty of this idea, 'yes, let us see the bird.'

He turned and glared at the woman.

'Where is this wretched bird of yours?' he inquired.

The woman pointed silently over my left shoulder, and turning round I found that the parrot had been perching among the green leaves of the pomegranate tree some three feet away, an interested spectator of our bargaining. As soon as I saw it I knew that I must have it, for it was a rarity, a red-fronted Tucuman Amazon, a bird which was, to say the least of it, unusual in European collections. He was small for an Amazon parrot, and his plumage was a rich grass-green with more than a tinge of yellow in it here and there; he had bare white rings round his dark eyes, and the whole of his forehead was a rich scarlet. Where the feathering ended on each foot he appeared to be wearing orange garters. I gazed at him longingly. Then, trying to wipe the acquisitive look off my face I turned to Helmuth and shrugged with elaborate unconcern, which I am sure did not deceive the parrot's owner for a moment.

'It's a rarity,' I said, trying to infuse dislike and loathing for the parrot into my voice, 'I must have it.'

'You see?' said Helmuth, returning to the attack, 'the señor says it is a very common bird, and he already has six of them down in Buenos Aires.'

The woman regarded us both with deep suspicion. I tried to look like a man who possessed six Tucuman Amazons, and who really did not care to acquire any more. The woman wavered, and then played her trump card.

'But this one *talks*,' she said triumphantly.

'The señor does not care if they talk or not,' Helmuth countered quickly. We had by now all moved towards the bird, and were gathered in a circle round the branch on which it sat, while it gazed down at us expressionlessly.

'Blanco . . . Blanco,' cooed the woman, '¿como te vas, Blanco?'

'We will give you thirty pesos for it,' said Helmuth.

'Two hundred,' said the woman, 'for a parrot that talks, two hundred is cheap.'

'Nonsense,' said Helmuth, 'anyway, how do we know it talks? It hasn't said anything.'

'Blanco, Blanco,' cooed the woman in a frenzy, 'speak to Mama . . . speak Blanco.'

Blanco eyed us all in a considering way.

'Fifty pesos, and that's a lot of money for a bird that won't talk,' said Helmuth.

'*Madre de Dios*, but he talks all day,' said the woman, almost in tears, 'wonderful things he says . . . he is the best parrot I have ever heard.'

'Fifty pesos, take it or leave it,' said Helmuth flatly.

'Blanco, Blanco, speak,' wailed the woman, 'say something for the señores ... please.'

The parrot shuffled his green feathering with a silken sound, put his head on one side and spoke.

'*Hijo de puta*,' he said, clearly and slowly.

The woman stood as though transfixed, her mouth open, unable to believe in the perfidy of her pet. Helmuth uttered a great sigh as of someone who knows the battle is won. Slowly, and with a look of utter malignancy, he turned to the unfortunate woman.

'So!' he hissed, like the villain in a melodrama. 'So! This is your idea of a talking parrot, eh?'

'But, señor ...,' began the woman faintly.

'Enough!' said Helmuth, cutting her short. 'We have heard enough. A stranger enters your gates, in order to help you by paying you money (which you need) for a worthless bird. And what do you do? You try and cheat him by telling him your bird talks, and thus get him to pay more.'

'But it *does* talk,' protested the woman faintly.

'Yes, *but what does it say*?' hissed Helmuth. He paused, drew himself up to his full height, took a deep breath and roared:

'It tells this good-natured, kindly señor that he is the son of a whore.'

The woman looked down at the ground and twiddled her bare toes in the dust. She was beaten and she knew it.

'Now that the señor knows what disgusting things you have taught this bird I should not think he will want it,' continued Helmuth. 'I should think that now he will not even want to offer you fifty pesos for a bird that has insulted not only him, but his mother.'

The woman gave me a quick glance, and returned to the contemplation of her toes. Helmuth turned to me.

'We have got her,' he said in a pleading tone of voice, 'all you have to do is to try and look insulted.'

'But I am insulted,' I said, trying to look offended and suppress the desire to giggle. 'Never, in fact, in a long career of being insulted, have I been so insulted.'

'You're doing fine,' said Helmuth, holding out both hands as if begging me to relent. 'Now give in a bit.'

I tried to look stern but forgiving, like one of the less humorous saints one sees in ikons.

'All right,' I said reluctantly, 'but only this once. Fifty, you said?'

'Yes,' said Helmuth, and as I pulled out my wallet he turned again to the woman. 'The señor, because he is the very soul of kindness, has forgiven you the insult. He will pay you the fifty pesos that you demanded, in your greed.'

The woman beamed. I paid over the grubby notes, and then approached the parrot. He gazed at me musingly. I held out my finger, and he gravely climbed on to it, and then made his way up my arm to my shoulder. Here he paused, gave me a knowing look, and said quite clearly and loudly:

'*¿Como te vas, como te vas, que tal?*' and then giggled wickedly.

'Come on,' said Helmuth, revitalized by his session of bargaining. 'Let's go and see what else we can find.'

We bowed to the woman, who bowed to us. Then, as we closed the bamboo gate behind us and were getting into the car, Blanco turned on my shoulder and fired his parting shot.

'*Estupido,*' he called to his late owner, '*muy estupido.*'

'That parrot,' said Helmuth, hastily starting the car, 'is a devil.'

I was inclined to agree with him.

Our tour of the village was not entirely unproductive. By careful questioning and cross-questioning nearly everyone we met we managed to run to earth five yellow-fronted Amazon parrots, an armadillo and two grey-necked guans. These latter are one of the game-birds, known locally as *charatas*, which is an onomatopoeic name resembling their cry. They look, at first glance, rather like a slim and somewhat drab hen pheasant of some species. Their basic colouring is a curious brown (the pale colour a stale bar of chocolate goes) fading to grey on the neck. But, see them in the sun and you discover that what you thought was a matt brown is really slightly iridescent with a golden sheen. Under the chin they have two drooping red wattles, and the feathers on their heads, when they get excited, stand up in a kind of crest that looks like a lengthy crew-cut. They were both young birds, having been taken from the nest when a few days old and hand-reared, so they were ridiculously tame. The Amazon parrots were also tame, but none of them had the knowingness or the vocabulary of Blanco. All they could do was to mutter '*Lorito*' at intervals, and whistle shrilly. Nevertheless, I felt for one morning's work we were not doing too badly, and so I carried my purchases back in triumph to the house, where Joan Lett had kindly allowed me to use their empty garage as a sort of storehouse for my creatures.

As I had no cages ready for the reception of my brood, I had to let them all loose in the garage and hope for the best. To my surprise this arrangement worked very well. The parrots all found themselves convenient perches, just out of pecking range of each other, and, though it had obviously been agreed that Blanco was the boss, there was no unmannerly squabbling. The guans also found themselves perches, but these they only used to sleep on, preferring to spend their days stalking about the floor of the garage, occasionally throwing back their heads and letting forth their ear-splitting cry. The armadillo, immediately on being released, fled behind a large box, and spent all day there meditating, only tip-toeing out at night to eat his food, casting many surreptitious and fearful glances at the sleeping birds.

By the following day the news had spread through the village that there had arrived a mad *gringo* who was willing to pay good money for live animals, and the first trickle of specimens started. The first arrival was an Indian carrying, on the end of a length of string, a coral snake striped in yellow, black and scarlet, like a particularly revolting Old School tie. Unfortunately, in his enthusiasm, the Indian had tied the string too tightly about the reptile's neck, and so it was very dead.

I had better luck with the next offering. An Indian arrived clasping a large straw hat tenderly to his bosom. After a polite exchange of greetings I asked to see what he had so carefully secured in his hat. He held it out, beaming hopefully at me, and then looking into the depths of the hat I saw reclining at the bottom, with a dewy-eyed expression on its face, the most delightful kitten. It was a baby Geoffroy's cat, a small species of wild cat which is getting increasingly rare in South America. Its basic colouring was a pale fawny yellow, and it was dappled all over with neat, dark brown spots. It regarded me with large bluey-green eyes from the interior of the hat, as if pleading to be picked up. I should have known better. In my experience it is always the most innocent-looking creatures that can cause you the worst damage. However, misled by its seraphic expression, I reached out my hand and tried to grasp it by the scruff of the neck. The next moment I had a bad bite through the ball of my thumb and twelve deep red grooves across the back of my hand. As I withdrew my hand, cursing, the kitten resumed its innocent pose, apparently waiting to see what other little game I had in store for it. While I sucked my hand like a half-starved vampire, I bargained with the Indian and eventually purchased my antagonist. Then I tipped it, hissing and snarling like a miniature jaguar, out of the hat and into a box full of straw. There I left it for an hour or so to settle down. I felt that its capture and subsequent transportation in a straw hat might be mainly responsible for its fear and consequent bad temper, for the creature was only about two weeks old, as far as I could judge.

When I thought it had settled down and would be willing to accept my overtures of friendship, I removed the lid of the box and peered in hopefully. I missed losing my left eye by approximately three millimetres. I wiped the blood from my cheek thoughtfully; obviously my latest specimen was not going to be easy. Wrapping my hand in a piece of sacking I placed a saucer of raw egg and minced meat in one corner of the box, and a bowl of milk in the other, and then left the kitten to its own devices. The next morning neither of the two offerings of food had been touched. With a premonition that this was going to hurt me more than the kitten, I filled one of my feeding-bottles with warm milk, wrapped my hand in sacking and approached the box.

Now I have had, at one time and another, a fair amount of experience in trying to get frightened, irritated or just plain stupid animals to feed from a bottle, and I thought that I knew most of the tricks. The Geoffroy's kitten proceeded to show me that, as far as it was concerned, I was a mere tyro at the game. It was so lithe, quick and strong for its size that after half an hour of struggling felt as though I had been trying to pick up a drop of quicksilver with a couple of crowbars. I was covered in milk and blood and thoroughly exhausted, whereas the kitten regarded me with blazing eyes and seemed quite ready to continue the fight for the next three days if necessary. The thing that really irritated me was that the kitten had – as I knew to my cost – very well-developed teeth, and there seemed no reason why it should not eat and drink of its own accord, but, in this stubborn mood, I knew that it was capable of quite literally starving itself to death. A bottle seemed the only way of getting any nourishment down it. I put it back in its box, washed my wounds, and was just applying plaster to the deeper of them when Luna arrived, singing cheerfully.

'Good morning, Gerry,' he said, and then stopped short and examined my bloodstained condition. His eyes widened, for I was still bleeding profusely from a number of minor scratches.

'What's this?' he asked.

"A cat ... *gato*,' I said irritably.

'Puma ... jaguar?' he asked hopefully.

'No,' I said reluctantly, '*chico gato montes.*'

'*Chico gato montes,*' he repeated incredulously, 'do this?'

'Yes. The bloody little fool won't eat. I tried it on the bottle, but it's just like a damned tiger. What it really needs is an example . . . ' my voice died away as an idea struck me. 'Come on, Luna, we'll go and see Edna.'

'Why Edna?' inquired Luna breathlessly as he followed me down the road to Helmuth's flat.

'She can help,' I said.

'But, Gerry, Helmuth won't like it if Edna is bitten by a *gato montes,*' Luna pointed out in Spanish.

'She won't get bitten,' I explained. 'I just want her to give me a kitten.'

Luna gazed at me with dark, puzzled eyes, but the conundrum was too much for him, and so he merely shrugged and followed me round to Helmuth's front door. I clapped my hands and went into Helmuth's and Edna's comfortable sitting room, where Edna was ensconced over a huge pile of socks, darning placidly and listening to the gramophone.

'Hullo,' she said, giving us her wide, attractive smile, 'the gin is over there, help yourself.'

Edna had a beautiful and placid nature: nothing seemed to worry her unduly. I am sure that if you walked into her sitting-room with fourteen Martians in tow she would merely smile and point out the location of the gin.

'Thank you, dear,' I said, 'but I didn't come for gin, strange though it may sound.'

'It does sound strange,' agreed Edna, grinning at me mischievously. 'Well, if you don't want gin, what do you want?'

'A kitten.'

'A kitten?'

'Yes . . . you know, a small cat.'

'Today Gerry is *loco,*' said Luna with conviction, pouring out two liberal measures of gin and handing one to me.

'I have just bought a baby *gato montes,*' I explained to Edna. 'It's extremely wild. It won't eat by itself, and this is what it did to me when I tried to feed it on the bottle.' I displayed my wounds. Edna's eyes widened.

'But how big is this animal?' she asked.

'About the size of a two-week-old domestic cat.'

Edna looked stern. She folded up the sock she was darning.

'Have you put disinfectant on those cuts?' she inquired, obviously preparing herself for a medical orgy.

'Never mind the cuts . . . I washed them . . . But what I want from you is a kitten, an ordinary kitten. Didn't you say the other day that you were infested with kittens over here?'

'Yes,' said Edna, 'we have plenty of kittens.'

'Good. Well, can I have one?'

Edna considered

'If I give you a kitten will you let me disinfect your cuts?' she asked cunningly. I sighed.

'All right, blackmailer,' I said.

So Edna disappeared into the kitchen quarters, from whence came a lot of shrill exclamations and much giggling. Then Edna returned with a bowl of hot water and proceeded to minister unto my cuts and bites, while a procession of semi-hysterical Indian maids filed into the room, carrying in their arms groups of kittens of all shapes and colours, from ones still blind to ones that were half grown and looked almost as wild as my Geoffroy's cat. Eventually I chose a fat, placid female tabby which was approximately the same size and age as my wild cat, and carried it back in triumph to the garage. Here I spent an hour constructing a rough cage, while the tabby kitten purred vigorously and rubbed itself round my legs, occasionally tripping me up. When the cage was ready I put the tabby kitten in first, and left it for an hour or so to settle down.

Most wild animals have a very strong sense of territory. In the wild state, they have their own particular bit of forest or grassland which they consider their own preserve, and will defend it against any other member of their own species (or other animals sometimes) that tries to enter it. When you put wild animals into cages the cages become, as far as they are concerned, their territory. So, if you introduce another animal into the same cage, the first inmate will in all probability defend it vigorously, and you may easily have a fight to the death on your hands. So you generally have to employ low cunning. Suppose, for example, you have a large vigorous creature who is obviously quite capable of looking after itself, and it has been in a cage for a period of a few weeks. Then you get a second animal of the same species, and you want to confine them together, for the sake of convenience. Introduce the new specimen into the old one's cage, and the old one may well kill it. So the best thing to do is to build an entirely new cage, and into this you introduce the weaker of the two animals. When it has settled down, you then put the stronger one in with it. The stronger one will, of course, still remain the dominant animal, and may even bully the weaker one, but as far as he is concerned he has been introduced into someone else's territory, and this takes the edge off his potential viciousness. It's a sort of Lifemanship that any collector has to practise at one time or another.

In this case I was sure that the baby Geoffroy's was quite capable of killing the domestic kitten, if I introduced the kitten to *it*, instead of the other way round. So, once the tabby had settled down, I seized the Geoffroy's and pushed it, snarling and raving, into the cage, and stood back to see what would happen. The tabby was delighted. It came forward to the angry Geoffroy's and started to rub itself against its neck, purring loudly. The Geoffroy's, taken aback by its greeting as I had hoped, merely spat rather rudely, and retreated into a corner. The tabby, having made the first overtures of friendship, sat down, purring loudly, and proceeded to wash itself with a self-satisfied air. I covered the front of the cage with a piece of sacking and left them to settle down, for I was sure now that the Geoffroy's would do the tabby no real harm.

That evening, when I lifted the sacking, I found them lying side by side, and the Geoffroy's, instead of spitting at me as it had done up until now, contented itself with merely lifting its lip in a warning manner. I carefully inserted a large bowl of milk into the cage, and a plate containing the finely-chopped meat and raw egg, which I wanted the Geoffroy's to eat. This was the crucial test, for I was hoping that the tabby would fall upon this delicious fare and, by example, encourage the Geoffroy's to eat. Sure enough, the tabby, purring like an ancient outboard engine, flung itself at the bowl of milk, took a long drink and then settled down to the meat and egg. I had retreated to a place where I could see without being seen, and I watched the Geoffroy's carefully. To begin with it took no interest at all, lying there with half-closed eyes. But eventually the noise the tabby was making over the egg and meat – it was a rather messy feeder – attracted its attention. It rose cautiously and approached the plate, while I held my breath. Delicately it sniffed round the edge of the plate, while the tabby lifted a face that was dripping with raw egg and gave a mew of encouragement, slightly muffled by the portion of meat it had in its mouth. The Geoffroy's stood pondering for a moment, and then, to my delight, sank down by the plate and started to eat. In spite of the fact that it must have been extremely hungry it ate daintily, lapping a little raw egg, and then picking up a morsel of meat which it chewed thoroughly before swallowing. I watched them until, between them, they had cleaned both plates, then I replenished them with more milk, egg and meat, and went to bed well satisfied. The next morning both plates were spotless, and the Geoffroy's and the tabby were locked in each other's arms, fast asleep, their stomachs bulging like two little hairy balloons. They did not wake up until midday, and then they both looked distinctly debauched. But when they saw me approaching with the plates of food they both displayed considerable interest, and I knew that my battle with the Geoffroy's was won.

Chapter Six

A City of Bichos

The excitement from the novelty of objects, and the chance of success, stimulate him to increased activity.

CHARLES DARWIN: THE VOYAGE OF H.M.S. BEAGLE.

Ever since my arrival in Calilegua, Luna had been pestering me to accompany him to a town called Oran, which lay some fifty miles away, and where, he assured me, I would get plenty of *bichos*. I was a bit chary about this idea, for I knew how easy it is to rush frantically from one place to another on a collecting trip, and, though each place in itself might be a good centre, you achieve very little by virtue of your grasshopper-like activities. I decided to discuss it with Charles, and so, that evening, as we sat gently imbibing gin and watching a moon with a blue halo silvering the palm fronds, I put my problem to him.

'Why is Luna so keen on Oran?' I asked.

'Well,' said Charles drily, 'it's his home town, for one thing, but this might prove an advantage, for it means that he knows everyone. I think you could do worse than go and investigate, Gerry. It's got a much bigger population than Calilegua, and in view of what you've found here, I should think you'd get twice as much stuff there.'

'Can Luna get the time off?' I asked.

Charles smiled his gentle smile.

'I don't think that we would notice his absence for three days,' he said, 'and that should give you time to denude Oran of whatever fauna is lurking there.'

'Could we leave on Monday?' I inquired hopefully.

'Yes,' said Charles, 'that would be all right.'

'Wonderful,' I said, finishing my drink, 'and now I must go across and see Edna.'

'Why Edna?'

'Well, someone's got to feed my animals while I'm away, and I'm hoping Edna has a kind heart.'

I found Helmuth, Edna and Luna arguing over the relative merits of two folk-songs which they kept playing over and over again on the gramophone. Edna pointed silently to the drinks and I helped myself, and then went and sat on the floor at her feet.

'Edna,' I said, during a lull in the argument, 'I love you.'

She raised one eyebrow sardonically and regarded me.

'If Helmuth wasn't bigger than me I would suggest that we elope,' I went on, 'since the first day I saw you I have been mad about you, your eyes, your hair, the way you pour gin . . .'

'What do you want?' she inquired.

I sighed.

'You have no soul,' I complained. 'I was just getting into my stride. Well, if you must know, Charles says that Luna and I can go to Oran for three days. Will you look after my animals for me?'

'But, of course,' she said, surprised that there should have been any doubt in my mind.

'But, of course,' echoed Helmuth. 'Gerry, you are very stupid. I tell you we will help all we can. You have only to ask. We will try and do anything for you.'

He splashed more gin into my glass.

'Except,' he added reluctantly, 'let you elope with my wife.'

So, early on Monday morning, Luna and I set out in a small station-wagon driven by a gay, semi-inebriated individual, sporting a moustache so large it looked like a Nature Reserve. We took with us only the bare essentials of travel: Luna's guitar, three bottles of wine, my wallet well stuffed with pesos, recording machine and cameras. We also had a clean shirt each, which our driver had placed reverently and tenderly in a pool of oil. All the previous night it had rained with a loudness and thoroughness that only the tropics can achieve; this now had thinned out to a fine grey drizzle, but the earth road had turned into something resembling the consistency of a badly-made blancmange. Luna, undeterred by the weather, the surface of the road and the doubtful driving capabilities of our driver, the fate of our clean shirts and the fact that the roof of the station-wagon leaked daintily but persistently, sang happily to himself as we slithered and swooped along the road to Oran.

We had been travelling some three-quarters of an hour when our driver, concentrating more on harmonizing with Luna in a mournful song than on the car, rounded a corner on two wheels, and as we slithered miraculously on to the straight again I saw something ahead that made my heart sink. Before us lay a torrent of red, froth-flecked water some four hundred yards across. At the edge of this, like a line of depressed elephants, stood three lorries, while in mid-stream, twisted to one side by the force of the water, another lorry was being laboriously dragged across to the opposite bank by a thing like a gigantic tractor, fitted with a winch and steel cable. Our driver joined the line of waiting lorries, switched off his engine and beamed at us.

'*Mucho agua*,' he pointed out to me, in case my eyesight should be defective and I had missed noticing the miniature Bay of Biscay we had to cross. I knew that the previous day this broad torrent had probably been a mere trickle of water, shallow and glinting over its bed of pebbles, but one night's rain had swollen it suddenly and out of all proportion. I knew, from experience, how a tiny stream can grow into a fierce full-sized river in next to no time, for once in West Africa I had had my camp almost washed away by a stream that started by being a mere three feet wide and four inches deep, and had, in the course of an hour or so, turned into something resembling the upper reaches of the Amazon. No one who had not seen this sudden transformation can believe it, but it can be one of the most irritating (and sometimes dangerous) aspects of travel in the tropics.

At last, after an hour of waiting, the last of the lorries had been hauled over and it was our turn. The hawser was attached to our bumper and gingerly we were drawn into the flood. Slowly the water rose higher and higher, and became stronger, until it was rustling and lapping along one side of the station-wagon like a miniature tidal wave. The water spurted in through the cracks of the door and trickled across the floor under our feet. Gradually the water rose until it covered our shoes. We were now approximately half-way across, and the force of the water was kindly but firmly pushing us downstream so that, although to begin with we had been opposite the tractor and the winch, we were now some fifty yards downstream from them. The hawser was taut, and I felt as though we were some gigantic and misshapen fish that the two laconic-looking Indians on the tractor were playing. The water had now reached the level of the seats; here it paused for a moment and then overflowed generously under our behinds. At this crucial moment, sitting in half an inch of icy water, we heard the winch stop.

'Arrrr!' roared our driver, sticking his head out of the window, his moustache quivering impressively, '*¿que pasa?*'

One of the Indians leapt off the tractor, and loped slowly off down the road; the other pushed his big straw hat on to the back of his head and slowly approached the bank of the river.

'*Nafta no hay*,' he explained, scratching his stomach with every evidence of satisfaction.

'Fine bloody time for them to run out of petrol,' I said irritably to Luna.

'Yes,' said Luna despondently, 'but the other Indian has gone for some. He will not be long.'

Half an hour passed. Then an hour. By now our nether regions were so frozen that we were all shifting uneasily in our seats to try and get some feeling back, making noises like a troupe of hippopotami enjoying a wallow in a particularly succulent swamp. At last, to our relief, the Indian appeared loping down the road carrying a can of petrol. He and the other Indian then had a long argument as to the best method of putting the life-giving fluid into the tractor, while our driver roared insults at them from between chattering teeth. But at last they had finished this highly complicated operation, the tractor sprang into life, the hawser tightened and we were drawn slowly but inexorably towards the bank, while the water-level in the wagon fell.

When we eventually reached dry land we all got out, removed our trousers and wrung them out, while our driver soundly berated the Indians for their attempted homicide, while they both grinned amiably at us. Then the driver, in his shirt-tails, opened the bonnet of the car and peered into the engine, his moustache twitching, muttering to himself. He had carefully wrapped in cotton waste certain vital parts of the internal organs of our vehicle before we entered the flood, and these he now unwrapped, and then proceeded to dry other parts of the engine. Eventually, he climbed in, pressed the starter, and with a wide grin of pride, heard the engine roar into life. We piled in and jolted off down the road, the Indians waving their straw hats in gay farewell.

We had travelled some five miles and were just beginning to dry out when we met our next water hazard. The road here ran along the lower slopes of the mountains, and the terrain was intersected at intervals by deep, narrow gorges through which the water from the mountains drained. Where the road crossed one of these narrow but powerful rivers one would have thought that the simplest engineering method would have been to throw a small bridge across from bank to bank. Apparently the vast numbers of these rivers made this too costly, and so another method was employed. A slightly concave apron of cement was laid across the river bed, which at least gave your wheels some purchase. In the dry season, of course, this looked merely like a continuation of the road, but when the waters from the mountains stormed down they roared over the apron, sometimes four feet deep, and then dropped into a graceful ten foot waterfall the other side to join the river lower down. A few days covered with water and the cement developed a surface like glass, owing to the algae that adhered to it, and so it was considerably more hazardous than the original river-bed would have been.

Here there was no winch to help us, and the driver nosed the station-wagon carefully into the red water, scowling fearfully behind his bristling moustache. We had got half-way across the invisible cement apron, when the engine stalled. We sat and looked at each other mutely, until suddenly the force of the water piling up against the side of the vehicle shifted it an inch or so in the direction of the waterfall on our right, and then we were all suddenly galvanized into activity. We none of us wanted to be sitting in the station-wagon if the torrent suddenly got a good grip on her and swept her over the edge and downstream among the tangle of rocks we could see. We left the vehicle as one man.

'Push . . . we must all push,' said Luna, raising his voice above the noise of the falls. He was clinging to the side of the station-wagon with both hands, for the force of the water was considerable. He was so slight in build that I expected at any moment to see him plucked away by the current and swept over the waterfall like a feather.

'Go round the other side of the car,' I shouted, 'the water won't sweep you away there.'

Luna realized the force of this argument, and made his way round the wagon in a starfish-like manner, until it stood between him and the waterfall. Then we laid our shoulders to the wagon and started to push. It was quite one of the most unrewarding tasks I have ever undertaken, for not only were we trying to push the wagon up the opposite slope of the cement apron, but we were also pushing against the current which all the time was trying to twist the wagon round at an angle. After about ten minutes of struggling we had managed to shift our vehicle approximately three feet nearer the opposite bank, and the current had moved it three feet nearer the edge of the waterfall. I began to get really worried, for at this rate I could see the wagon plunging gracefully over the waterfall in a matter of another half-hour, for the three of us alone had not the strength to push her up the slope *and* against the current. We had a rope in the back of the wagon and, if it was long enough, the only thing I could suggest was that we tethered the wagon to a tree on the opposite bank, and just sat there until the waters subsided. I was just about to try and put this plan into Spanish, when round the corner of the road on the opposite bank appeared a Fairy Godmother, heavily disguised as a wheezing, snorting lorry, which, in spite of its age and rust, looked powerful and phlegmatic. We greeted it with shouts of joy. The driver of the lorry took in our predicament in a glance, and slowing down, drove the vast bulk of his vehicle slowly into the red torrent until he was within a few feet of us. Hastily we got out our rope and shackled the two vehicles together; then the lorry went into reverse and gently drew our vehicle out of the flood and on to dry land. We thanked the lorry driver, gave him a cigarette, and watched enviously as he drove his mighty steed through the torrent as if it had not been there. Then we turned our attention to the laborious and messy process of drying out our engine.

Eventually we reached Oran at two o'clock in the afternoon, having had to navigate three more water hazards, none of which, fortunately, was as bad as the first two. Nevertheless, we arrived at Luna's house all looking as though we had spent our entire day in the river, which was not so far from the truth. Luna's charming family greeted us with delight, whipped our clothes away to be dried, cooked us an enormous meal, and sat us down to eat it in an indoor courtyard, overflowing with flowers, where the frail sunlight was just starting to make its heat felt. While we ate and drank good, warming red wine, Luna sent an apparently endless stream of his smaller relatives on mysterious missions to different parts of the town, and they kept reappearing to whisper reports to him, whereupon he would nod his head portentously and smile, or else scowl ferociously, according to the news that was being vouchsafed to him. Everyone had an air of suppressed excitement, and stiffened expectantly if Luna so much as coughed or looked in their direction. I began to feel as though I was having lunch with the Duke of Wellington on the eve of Waterloo. At last he leant forward, poured us both out a last glass of wine, and then grinned at me, his big black eyes sparkling with suppressed excitement.

'Gerry,' he said in Spanish, 'I have found you some *bichos*.'

'Already?' I asked. 'But how?'

He waved a hand at his small army of relatives, standing in a grinning line.

'I have sent my family to make inquiries, and they have discovered a number of people who have *bichos*. Now it only remains for us to go and buy them if they are the *bichos* you want.'

'Wonderful,' I said enthusiastically, finishing my wine at a gulp, 'let's go, shall we?'

So, in ten minutes' time, Luna and I set off to quarter Oran like huntsmen, preceded by our pack of Luna's young and excited relatives. The town was not really so large, but rather straggling, built on the typical Argentine chessboard pattern. Everywhere we went, as Charles had predicted, Luna was greeted with cries of joy, and we had to refuse many invitations of the more bibulous variety. But Luna, with a reluctant gleam in his eye, sternly turned his back on such frivolity, and we continued on our way. Eventually, one of the younger members of our retinue ran on ahead and beat a loud tattoo on a most impressive-looking door of a large house. By the time we had reached it the door had been opened by an ancient woman dressed in black, which made her look like a somewhat dilapidated cockroach. Luna paused in front of her and gave her a grave good evening, to which she bowed slightly.

'I know that you have in your house a parrot,' said Luna with the air of a policeman daring a criminal to deny the existence of a corpse which he knows to be concealed beneath the sofa.

'That is so,' said the woman, mildly surprised.

'This English señor is collecting for his *jardin zoologico* in England,' Luna went on, 'and it is possible that he may wish to purchase this bird of yours.'

The woman surveyed me from dark, dry eyes, without curiosity.

'You are welcome to him,' she said at last, 'for he is a dirty bird and he does not talk. My son brought him to me, but if I can sell him I will be only too glad. Come in, señores, and see him.'

She shuffled ahead of us and led us into the inevitable courtyard of potted plants, forming the well of the house. When I saw the bird it was all I could do to stifle a yelp of delight, for the creature was a yellow-naped macaw, a rare member of the parrot family. It was sitting on the remains of a wooden perch which it had obviously, over the past week, demolished slowly and systematically until scarcely anything remained. It glanced up at us as we gathered round it, a fine sliver of wood in its beak, uttered a short gurking noise, and returned to its work of demolition. Luna gave me a quick glance from his brilliant eyes, and I nodded my head vigorously. He took a deep breath, surveyed the macaw with loathing, and then turned to the woman.

'One of the commoner ones, I see,' he said carelessly, 'but even so the señor is interested in buying it. You realize, of course, that for such a common, destructive bird, and one, moreover, that does not talk, we cannot afford to be generous. The señor would not dream of considering paying anything more than, say, twenty-five pesos for such a creature.'

Then he folded his arms and looked at the woman, waiting for her outburst of indignation at the mere mention of such a low price.

'All right,' said the woman, 'you can have him.'

While Luna regarded her open-mouthed she picked up the macaw, plonked him unceremoniously on my shoulder, and held out her wrinkled palm for the notes which I was hastily counting out from my wallet before she changed her mind. We were back in the street again, with the macaw making surprised and pleased gurking noises in my ear, before Luna recovered the power of speech. Then he shook his head despondently.

'What's the matter, Luna?' I asked. 'It's a wonderful bird, and to get it so cheap is incredible.'

'For your sake,' said Luna gloomily, 'I am glad. But it makes me fear for the future of Argentina when I meet someone who will not bargain, but accepts the first price offered. Where would we all be if everyone did that?'

'Life would probably be a lot cheaper,' I pointed out, but he refused to be comforted, and continued to grumble over the woman's behaviour for the rest of our tour of the town, though a brisk half-hour exchange with a man who drove a hard bargain over another parrot shortly restored his faith in humanity.

We continued on our way through the town until it grew dark, by which time all of us were carrying what amounted to a small zoo. There were five parrots (including, to my delight, another yellow-naped macaw), two pigmy Brazilian rabbits, with ginger paws and white spectacles of fur round their eyes, and an orange-rumped agouti, a large rodent with dark eyes, slender legs and the disposition of a racehorse suffering from an acute nervous breakdown. We carried this assortment of wild life back to Luna's house and let them all loose in the patio, while Luna organized his band of relatives once more and sent them scurrying in all directions to fetch empty boxes, wire-netting, saws, hammers, nails and other accoutrements of the carpenter's trade. Then, for the next two hours we were fully occupied building suitable habitations for my acquisitions. At length, when the last of the creatures had been placed in its cage, Luna and I sat at the table nearby and ate and drank heartily, while from the pile of wooden boxes came the faint scufflings and squawks which are such music to the animal collector's ears. Presently, a large tumbler of good wine by my side, I sat down in front of the cages to examine my charges by lamplight, while Luna called for his guitar and sang the soft, mournful folk-songs of Argentina, occasionally, where the music required it, using the deep wooden belly of his guitar as a drum.

The parrots we had acquired were all blue-fronted Amazons, all rather scruffy because of bad feeding, but all reasonably tame and able to mutter the inevitable '*Lorito*' which is the Argentine equivalent of 'Polly.' As they were all much the same size and age we had caged them together, and now in the lamplight they sat in a row, like a highly coloured jury, regarding me with the ancient, reptilian and falsely-wise expressions that parrots are such masters at adopting. I was pleased with them in spite of their tattered appearance, for I knew that a few weeks of good feeding would make a world of difference, and that, at their next moult, their feathers would glow with lemon-yellow, blue and a multitude of greens that would make a collection of emeralds look dowdy in comparison. Gently I lowered a piece of sacking over the front of their cage and heard them all fluff and rearrange their feathers (a sound like someone riffling through a pack of cards) preparatory to sleep. Next I turned my attention to the yellow-naped macaws, and gloated over them for some time. We had, experimentally, caged them together, and the way they had immediately taken to each other and started to bill and coo inclined me to think that they were a true pair. They sat on the perch now and regarded me solemnly, occasionally turning their heads on one side as if to see whether I looked any more attractive that way. Basically their colouring was a deep, rush green, only relieved on the neck where they had a broad half-moon-shaped patch of feathers which were bright canary-yellow. For macaws – which are as a rule the largest of the parrots – they were diminutive, being slightly smaller and more slender than the common Amazon parrots. They gurked gently to me and to each other, their pale eyelids drooping sleepily over their bright eyes, so I covered them up with sacking and left them.

Next to the macaws the Brazilian rabbits were the creatures I was most delighted to have obtained, for they were animals I had long wanted to meet. The two we had got were only babies, and I lifted them out of their cage and they sat, one in each hand, comfortably filling my palms with the soft, fat warmth of their bodies, their noses wiffling with all the strange scents of food and flowers with which the patio was filled. At first glance you would have taken them for the young of the common European rabbit, but closer inspection soon showed the differences. To begin with their ears were very short for their size, and very neat and slender. The basic colouring on the back was a dark rich brown, flecked and patterned with rusty-coloured patches and blobs. Their feet and part of the leg was a bright, rich ginger, and, as I said before, they had a fine circle of white hair round each eye. Their nose and lips, I now noticed, were faintly outlined in white as well. When they were fully adult, I knew, they would still be among the dwarfs of their breed, being only half the size of the European wild rabbit. As far as I knew, no zoo in the world possessed these interesting little creatures, and I was delighted to have got them, though I had faint qualms about being successful in taking them back to Europe, for the rabbit and hare family do not, on the whole, take kindly to captivity, and are reputedly difficult. However, these were very young, and I had hopes that they would settle down satisfactorily.

When I lifted the sacking off the front of the agouti's cage she leapt straight up into the air, and landed with a crash in her straw bed, quivering in every limb, with the expression of an elderly virgin who, after years of looking under the bed, has at last found a man there. However, with the aid of a piece of apple I managed to soothe her into a fairly reasonable state, and she actually allowed me to stroke her. Agoutis are, of course, rodents, members of that enormous and interesting family that includes creatures like the harvest mouse, which would hardly fill the bowl of a teaspoon, to capybaras that are the size of a large dog and in between these two extremes a great variety of squirrels, dormice, rats, porcupines and other unlikely beasts. Agoutis are not, let us admit at once, the most prepossessing of their family. To be perfectly frank, they look like a cross between one of the smaller forerunners of the horse, and a rather lugubrious rabbit. Their basic colouring is a rich, shining mahogany, fading to reddish-ginger on their rumps. Their legs are chocolate brown, very long and slender and racehorse-like, ending in a bunch of frail, artistic toes which give them the ancient-horse look. Their hind legs are powerful in order to support a backside that is out of all proportion to the forequarters, so that the creature looks, if I might put it like this, as though it had a hump-behind. The head is rabbit-like, but again slightly elongated so that there is still a faint suggestion of horse about it. They have large, fine eyes, neat rounded ears and a mass of black whiskers which are in a constant state of agitation about everything. Combine all this with the beast's temperament, its constantly neurotic state, its wild leaps into the air at the slightest sound followed by a period of acute ague, and you begin to wonder how the species survives at all. I should imagine that a jaguar would only have to growl once and every agouti within a hundred yards radius would die of heart-failure immediately. Musing on this I lowered the sacking over the front of my agouti's cage, and she immediately leapt once more into into the air and came down shaking in every limb. However, within a few minutes she had recovered from this terrible experience sufficiently to make an attack on the apple I had left in the cage for her. Luna had now, by the application of song and wine, worked himself into a pleasant state where he sat at the table, humming softly like a drowsy bee. We had a final glass of wine as a nightcap, and then yawning prodigiously, stumbled off to bed.

I was awoken at what seemed to me to be a most uncivilized hour of the morning by a burst of song from Luna's bed, in the opposite corner of the room. Song and music ran through Luna's being as naturally as the blood flowed through his veins. When he was not talking he was singing or humming, and he is the only man I have ever met who can stay up until three in the morning and rise at five, bursting into song before he is even out of bed. But he sang so pleasantly and with such obvious pleasure that you forgave him, even at that hour of the morning, and, after knowing him some time, you took no more notice of it than you would have done of a dawn chorus of birds.

'The moon is like a little white drum in the sky,' he sang from under a pile of bedclothes, 'leading me to my love with the dark hair and the magic eyes, behind the mountains of Tucuman.'

'If you sing to all your female acquaintances at this hour of the morning,' I said drowsily, 'I should think you lead a pretty lonely life in bed. These things get around, you know.'

He chuckled and stretched luxuriously.

'Today is going to be a fine day, Gerry,' he said. I wondered how he knew, for the shutters on the two windows were tightly closed. The night air, in which the Argentine will sit as late as he pleases without any harm to his being, becomes, as soon as he retires to bed, a deadly gas waiting to strangle him. So all shutters must be tightly closed to guard against such a dangerous experience. However, when we had dressed and gone out into the patio to breakfast, I found he was right, for it was flooded with sunshine.

We were finishing our last cup of coffee when our troupe of spies appeared to report. Apparently they had been out and about at the crack of dawn, and they made their reports to Luna as he sat there, sipping his coffee, and occasionally giving a lordly nod. Then one of the younger of the spies was dispatched with money to purchase provisions for my specimens, and, on his return, the spies stood wide-eyed and watched me while I chopped up food and vegetables, filled bowls with milk or water, and generally ministered to my animals. When the last one had been fed, we filed out into the sunlit street and started once more on our search of the town. This time Luna used our retinue slightly differently. While we made our way to a house which we knew contained some wild pet, our young helpers fanned out and explored every alley and street in the immediate vicinity, clapping their hands outside people's doors, and questioning complete strangers as to what pets they kept. Everyone was most good-humoured about this intrusion of their privacy, and, even if they had no creatures themselves, would sometimes direct us to another house in which lurked some member of the local fauna. By this means, during the morning, we ran to earth three more pigmy rabbits, another parrot, two seriemas, a strange, leggy type of bird, and two coatimundis, the odd little raccoon-like predator of South America. We took them back to Luna's house, caged them, ate a hearty lunch and then, exhilarated by our morning's success, set out to explore the outer limits of Oran with the aid of an ancient car, lent to us by one of Luna's friends.

Luna had learnt, by some M.I.5 methods of his own, that in one of the more far-flung portions of the town was a man who possessed a wild cat of some sort, but no one was quite sure who it was or the exact location of his house. Eventually, however, we narrowed our search down to one rambling street, and by the simple process of knocking or clapping outside every house we eventually found the man we were looking for. He was a large, dark, sweating and unclean-looking man of about forty, with an unhealthy paunch and beady black eyes that were alternately cringing or cunning. Yes, he admitted, he had got a wild cat, an ocelot; and then, with all the fiery eloquence of a pre-election politician, he proceeded to tell us about the animal's beauty, grace, tameness, value, coloration, size, appetite, until I began to feel that he was trying to sell me an entire zoo instead of one animal. Breaking in on his asthmatic eulogy on the feline tribe in general and his specimen in particular, we asked to see it. He led us round into one of the filthiest backyards I had been in to date, for in Oran and in Calilegua, however poor and tiny the house, the backyard was always neat and full of flowers. This looked like a council rubbish dump, with old broken barrels, rusty tin cans, piles of old wire-netting, bicycle wheels and other flotsam and jetsam. Our host lumbered over to a rough wooden cage in one corner which would have been small for the average rabbit. He opened the door, caught hold of a chain inside and hauled out on to the ground one of the most pathetic sights I have seen. It was a half-grown ocelot, and how it managed to fit in such a small cage was a mystery. But it was its condition that was so appalling. Its coat was so matted with its own filth that you could only just discern the natural pattern of the skin. It had a large, running sore on one flank, and it was so thin that you could, under its matted coat, see its ribs and backbone clearly. Indeed, it was so weak that it wavered from side to side, like a drunk, when it was dropped on to the ground, and eventually gave up the attempt to stay upright, and sank dejectedly down on to its dirty belly.

'You see how tame it is?' inquired the man, giving us a display of tattered yellow teeth in an ingratiating grin. 'She is very tame with everybody. Never has she been known to bite.' He was patting the cat as he spoke, with one great sweaty palm. I could see that it was not tameness that stopped the animal from turning on him, but sheer inertia due to lack of food. She had almost reached the point of no return, where she felt so weak that she just did not care.

'Luna,' I said, making a valiant attempt to keep my temper, 'I will pay fifty pesos for this cat. No more. Even that is too much, for she will probably die. I won't bargain, so you can tell this bloated illegitimate son of an inadequate whore that he can take it or leave it.'

Luna translated my message tactfully leaving out my character rendering. The man clasped his hands in horror. Surely we were joking? He giggled feebly. For such a magnificent animal three hundred pesos would be a beggarly sum to pay. Surely the señor could see what a wonderful creature . . . and so on. But the señor had seen enough. I spat loudly and accurately into the remains of a barrel, lovingly entwined with a bicycle-wheel, gave the man the dirtiest look I could achieve, turned on my heel and walked back to the road. I got into our ancient car and slammed the door with such violence that, for a moment, I thought the whole thing was going to fall to pieces in the road. I could hear Luna and the man arguing, and presently, when I detected a weakening note in the repulsive man's voice, I leant out of the window and roared at Luna to come on and not waste time. Within thirty seconds he appeared.

'Give me the money, Gerry,' he said. I gave him the fifty pesos, and presently he appeared with the box and put it in the back seat. We drove off in silence. Presently, when I had finished mentally working out what I would like to have done to the cat's late owner, which would not only have been painful but have made his marital state, if any, difficult in the extreme, I sighed and lit a cigarette.

'We must get home quickly, Luna. That animal's got to have a decent cage and some food or she's going to die,' I said. 'Also I shall want some sawdust.'

'Si, si,' said Luna, his dark eyes worried. 'I have never seen anyone keep an animal like that. She is half dead.'

'I think I can save her,' I said. 'At least, I think we've got a fifty-fifty chance.'

We drove in silence along the rutted road for some way before Luna spoke.

'Gerry, you do not mind stopping once more, only for a minute?' he inquired anxiously. 'It is on our way. I hear of someone else that has a cat they might sell.'

'Yes, all right, if it's on the way. But I hope to God it's in better condition than the one we've got.'

Presently Luna ran the car off the road on to a sizeable stretch of greensward. On one corner of this stood a dilapidated-looking marquee, and near it a small, battered-looking merry-go-round and a couple of small booths made of striped canvas now so faded as to be almost white. Three fat, glossy horses, one a bright piebald, grazed near by, and around the marquee and the booths trotted a number of well-fed looking dogs, who had the air of professionals.

'What is this? It looks like a circus,' I said to Luna.

'It is a circus,' said Luna, grinning, 'only a very small one.'

I was amazed that any circus, even a small one, could make a living in a place as remote and small as Oran, but this one appeared to be doing all right for, although the props were somewhat decrepit, the animals looked in good condition. As we left the car a large ginger-haired man appeared, ducking out from under a flap of the marquee. He was a muscular individual with shrewd green eyes and powerful, well-kept hands, who looked as though he would be capable of doing a trapeze act or a lion act with equal skill. We shook hands, and Luna explained our business.

'Ah, you want my puma,' he grinned. 'But I warn you I want a lot of money for her ... she's a beauty. But she eats too much, and I can't afford to keep her. Come and see her, she's over here. A real devil, I can tell you. We can't do a thing with her.'

He led us to a large cage in one corner of which crouched a beautiful young puma, about the size of a large dog. She was fat and glossy, and still had her baby paws which, as in all young cats, look about three times too big for the body. Her coat was a rich amber colour, and her piercing, moody eyes a lovely leaf green. As we approached the cage she lifted one lip and showed her well-developed baby teeth in a scornful snarl. She was simply heavenly, and a joy to look at after the half-starved creature we had just bought, but I knew, fingering my wallet, that I should have to pay a lot for her.

The bargaining lasted for half an hour and was conducted over a glass of very good wine which the circus proprietor insisted we drank with him. At length I agreed to a price which, though high, seemed to me to be fair. Then I asked the man if he would keep her until the following day for me, if I paid for her evening meal, for I knew that she would be in good hands, and I had no cage ready for her reception. This our amiable ginger friend agreed to and the bargain was sealed with another glass of wine, and then Luna and I drove back home to try and resurrect the unfortunate ocelot.

When I had built a cage for her, and one of Luna's lesser relatives had appeared with a large sackful of sweet-smelling sawdust, I got the poor creature out of her evil-smelling box and dressed the wound on her thigh. She just lay on the ground apathetically, though the washing of the wound must have hurt considerably. Then I gave her a large shot of penicillin, which again she took no notice of. The third operation was to try and dry her coat out a bit, for she was drenched with her own urine, and already the skin of her belly and paws were fiery red, burnt by the acid. All I could do was literally to cover her in sawdust, rubbing it well into the fur to absorb the moisture, and then gently dusting it out again. Then I unpicked the more vicious tangles in her fur, and by the time I had finished she had begun to look faintly like an ocelot. But she still lay on the floor, uncaring. I cut the filthy collar away from her neck, and put her in her new cage on a bed of sawdust and straw. Then I placed in front of her a bowl containing one raw egg and a small quantity of finely-minced fresh steak. At first she displayed no interest in this, and my heart sank, for I thought she might well have reached the stage of starvation where no amount of tempting offerings would induce her to eat. In sheer desperation I seized her head and ducked her face into the raw egg, so that she would be forced to lick it off her whiskers. Even this indignity she suffered without complaint, but she sat back and licked the dripping egg off her lips, slowly, carefully, like someone sampling a new, foreign and probably dangerous dish. Then she eyed the dish with a disbelieving look in her eye. I honestly think that the animal, through ill-treatment and starvation, had got into a trance-like state, where she disbelieved the evidence of her own senses. Then, while I held my breath, she leant forward and lapped experimentally at the raw egg. Within thirty seconds the plate was clean, and Luna and I were dancing a complicated tango of delight round the patio, to the joy of his younger relatives.

'Give her some more, Gerry,' panted Luna, grinning from ear to ear.

'No, I daren't,' I said. 'When a creature's that bad you can kill it from overfeeding. She can have a bowl of milk later on, and then tomorrow she can have four small meals during the day. But I think she'll be all right now.'

'That man was a devil,' said Luna shaking his head.

I drew a deep breath and, in Spanish, gave him my views on the cat's late owner.

'I never knew you knew so many bad things in Spanish, Gerry,' said Luna admiringly. 'There was one word you used I have never heard before.'

'I've had some good teachers,' I explained.

'Well, I hope you say nothing like that tonight,' said Luna, his eyes gleaming.

'Why? What's happening tonight?'

'Because we are leaving tomorrow for Calilegua, my friends have made an *asado* in your honour, Gerry. They will play and sing only very old Argentine folk-songs, so that you may record them on your machine. You like this idea?' he asked anxiously.

'There is nothing I like better than an *asado*,' I said, 'and an *asado* with folk-songs is my idea of Heaven.'

So, at about ten o'clock that evening, a friend of Luna's picked us up in his car and drove us out to the estate, some distance outside Oran, where the *asado* had been organized. The *asado* ground was a grove near the *estancia*, an area of bare earth that told of many past dances, surrounded by whispering eucalyptus trees and massive oleander bushes. The long wooden benches and trestle tables were lit with the soft yellow glow of half a dozen oil-lamps, and outside this buttercup circle of light the moonlight was silver brilliant. There were about fifty people there, many of whom I had never met, and few of them over the age of twenty. They greeted us uproariously, almost dragged us to the trestle-tables which were groaning under the weight of food, and placed great hunks of steak, crisp and sizzling from the open fires, in front of us. The wine-bottles passed with monotonous regularity, and within half-an-hour Luna and I were thoroughly in the party spirit, full of good food, warmed with red wine. Then these gay, pleasant young people gathered round while I got the recorder ready, watching with absorbed attention the mysteries of threading tape and getting levels. When, at last, I told them I was ready, guitars, drums and flutes appeared as if by magic, and the entire crowd burst into song. They sang and sang, and each time they came to the end of a song, someone would think of a new one, and they would start again. Sometimes a shy, grinning youth would be pushed to the front of the circle as the only person there capable of rendering a certain number, and after much encouragement and shouts of acclamation he would sing. Then it would be a girl's turn to sing the solo refrain in a sweet-sour voice, while the lamps glinted on her dark hair, and the guitars shuddered and trembled under the swiftly-moving brown fingers of their owners. They danced in a row on a flagstoned path, their spurs ringing sparks from the stone, so that I could record the heel-taps which are such an intricate part of the rhythm of some of their songs; they danced the delightful handkerchief dance with its pleasant lilting tune, and they danced tangos that made you wonder if the stiff, sexless dance called by that name in Europe was a member of the same family. Then, shouting with laughter because my tapes had run out and I was in despair, they rushed me to the table, plied me with more food and wine, and sitting round me sang more sweetly than ever. These, I say again, were mostly teenagers, revelling in the old and beautiful songs of their country, and the old and beautiful dances, their faces flushed with delight at my delight, honouring a stranger they had never seen before and would probably never see again.

By now they had reached the peak. Slowly they started to relax, the songs getting softer and softer, more and more plaintive, until we all reached the moment when we knew the party was over, and that to continue it longer would be a mistake. They had sung themselves from the heavens back to earth, like a flock of descending larks. Flushed, bright-eyed, happy, our young hosts insisted that we travelled back to Oran with them in the big open back of the lorry in which they had come. We piled in, our tightly-packed bodies creating a warmth for which we were grateful, for the night air was now chilly. Then as the lorry roared off down the road to Oran, bottles of red wine were passed carefully from hand to hand, and the guitarists started strumming. Everybody, revived by the cool night air, took up the refrain, and we roared along through the velvet night like a heavenly choir. I looked up and saw the giant bamboos that curved over the road, now illuminated by the lorry's headlights. They looked like the talons of some immense green dragon, curved over the road, ready to pounce if we stopped singing for an instant. Then a bottle of wine was thrust into my hand, and as I tipped my head back to drink I saw that the dragon had passed, and the moon stared down at me, white as a mushroom-top against the dark sky.

Chapter Seven

Vampires and Wine

The vampire bat is often the cause of much trouble, by biting the horses on their withers.

CHARLES DARWIN: THE VOYAGE OF H.M.S. BEAGLE.

On my return from Oran the garage almost overflowed with animals. One could scarcely make oneself heard above the shrill, incomprehensible conversations of the parrots (interspersed occasionally with a shrill scream, as if some local female was being raped), the harsh rattling cries of the guans, the incredibly loud trumpeting song of the seriemas, the chittering of the coatimundis, and an occasional dull rumble, as of distant thunder, from the puma, whom I had christened Luna in the human Luna's honour. As a background to this there was a steady scrunching noise that came from the agouti cage, for it was always engaged in trying to do alterations to its living quarters with its chisel-like teeth.

As soon as I had got back I had begun constructing cages for all our various creatures, leaving the caging of Luna until last, for she had travelled in a large packing-case that gave her more than enough room to move about in. However, when all the other animals were housed, I set about building a cage worthy of the puma, which, I hoped, would show off her beauty and grace. I had just finished it when Luna's godfather arrived, singing lustily as usual, and offered to help me in the tricky job of getting Luna to pass from her present quarters into the new cage. We carefully closed the garage doors so that, if anything untoward happened, the cat would not go rampaging off across the countryside and be lost. It also had the advantage, as the human Luna pointed out, that we would be locked in with her, a prospect he viewed with alarm and despondency. I soothed his fears by telling him that the puma would be far more frightened than we were, and at that moment she uttered a rumbling growl of such malignance and fearlessness that Luna paled visibly. My attempt to persuade him that this growl was really an indication of how afraid the animal was of us was greeted with a look of complete disbelief.

The plan of campaign was that the crate in which the puma now reposed would be dragged opposite the door of the new cage, a few slats removed from the side, and the cat would then walk from the crate into the cage without fuss. Unfortunately owing to the somewhat eccentric construction of the cage I had built, we could not wedge the crate close up to the door: there was a gap of some eight inches between crate and cage. Undeterred, I placed planks so that they formed a sort of short tunnel between the two boxes, and then proceeded to remove the end of the crate so that the puma could get out. During this process a golden paw, that appeared to be the size of a ham, suddenly appeared in the gap and a nice, deep slash appeared across the back of my hand.

'Ah!' said Luna gloomily, 'you see, Gerry?'

'It's only because she's scared of the hammering,' I said with feigned cheerfulness, sucking my hand. 'Now, I think I've removed enough boards for her to get through. All we have to do is wait.'

We waited. After ten minutes I peered through a knot hole and saw the wretched puma lying quietly in her crate, drowsing peacefully, and showing not the slightest interest in passing down our rickety tunnel and into her new and more spacious quarters. There was obviously only one thing to do, and that was to frighten her into passing from crate to cage. I lifted the hammer and brought it down on the back of the crate with a crash. Perhaps I should have warned Luna. Two things happened at once. The puma, startled out of her half-sleep, leapt up and rushed to the gap in the crate, and the force of my blow with the hammer knocked down the piece of board which was forming Luna's side of the tunnel. In consequence he looked down just in time to see an extremely irritable-looking puma sniffing meditatively at his legs. He uttered a tenor screech which I have rarely heard equalled, and leapt vertically into the air. It was the screech that saved the situation. It so unnerved the puma that she fled into the new cage as fast as she could, and I dropped the sliding door, locking her safely inside. Luna leant against the garage door wiping his face with a handkerchief.

'There you are,' I said cheerfully, 'I told you it would be easy.'

Luna gave me a withering look.

'You have collected animals in South America and Africa?' he inquired at length. 'That is correct?'

'Yes.'

'You have been doing this work for fourteen years?'

'Yes.'

'You are now thirty-three?'

'Yes.'

Luna shook his head, like a person faced with one of the great enigmas of life.

'How you have lived so long only the good God knows,' he said.

'I lead a charmed life,' I said. 'Anyway, why did you come to see me this morning, apart from wanting to wrestle with your namesake?'

'Outside,' said Luna, still mopping his face, 'is an Indian with a *bicho*. I found him with it in the village.'

'What kind of *bicho*?' I asked as we left the garage and went out into the garden.

'I think it is a pig,' said Luna, 'but it's in a box and I can't see it very clearly.'

The Indian was squatting on the lawn, and in front of him was a box from which issued a series of falsetto squeaks and muffled grunts. Only a member of the pig family could produce such extraordinary sounds. The Indian grinned, removed his big straw hat, ducked his head, and then, removing the lid of the box, drew forth the most adorable little creature. It was a very young collared peccary, the common species of wild pig that inhabits the tropical portions of South America.

'This is Juanita,' said the Indian, smiling as he placed the diminutive creature on the lawn, where it uttered a shrill squeak of delight and started to snuffle about hopefully.

Now, I have always had a soft spot for the pig family, and baby pigs I cannot resist, so within five minutes Juanita was mine at a price that was double what she was worth, speaking financially, but only a hundredth part of what she was worth in charm and personality. She was about eighteen inches long and about twelve inches high, clad in long, rather coarse greyish fur, and a neat white band that ran from the angle of her jaw up round her neck, so that she looked as though she was wearing an Eton collar. She had a slim body, with a delicately tapered snout ending in a delicious retroussé nose (somewhat like a plunger), and slender, fragile legs tipped with neatly polished hooves the circumference of a sixpence. She had a dainty, lady-like walk, moving her legs very rapidly, her hooves making a gentle pattering like rain.

She was ridiculously tame, and had the most endearing habit of greeting you – even after only five minutes' absence – as if you had been away for years, and that, for her, these years had been grey and empty. She would utter strangled squeaks of delight, and rush towards you, to rub her nose and behind against your legs in an orgy of delighted reunion, giving seductive grunts and sighs. Her idea of Heaven was to be picked up and held on her back in your arms, as you would nurse a baby, and then have her tummy scratched. She would lie there, her eyes closed, gnashing her baby teeth together, like miniature castanets, in an ecstasy of delight. I still had all the very tame and less destructive creatures running loose in the garage, and as Juanita behaved in such a lady-like fashion I allowed her the run of the place as well, only shutting her in a cage at night. At feeding time it was a weird sight to see Juanita, her nose buried in a large dish of food, surrounded by an assortment of creatures – seriemas, parrots, pigmy rabbits, guans – all trying to feed out of the same dish. She always behaved impeccably, allowing the others plenty of room to feed, and never showing any animosity, even when a wily seriema pinched titbits from under her pink nose. The only time I ever saw her lose her temper was when one of the more weak-minded of the parrots, who had worked himself into a highly excitable state at the sight of the food plate, flew down squawking joyously, and landed on Juanita's snout. She shook him off with a grunt of indignation and chased him, squawking and fluttering, into a corner, where she stood over him for a moment, champing her teeth in warning, before returning to her interrupted meal.

When I had got all my new specimens nicely settled, I paid a visit to Edna to thank her for the care and attention she had lavished on my animals in my absence. I found her and Helmuth busy with a huge pile of tiny scarlet peppers, with which they were concocting a sauce of Helmuth's invention, an ambrosial substance which, when added to soup, removed the roof of your mouth with the first swallow, but added a flavour that was out of this world. An old boot, I am sure, boiled and then covered with Helmuth's sauce, would have been greeted with shouts of joy by any gourmet.

'Ah, Gerry,' said Helmuth, rushing to the drink cupboard, 'I have got good news for you.'

'You mean you've bought a new bottle of gin?' I inquired hopefully.

'Well, that of course,' he said, grinning. 'We knew you were coming back. But apart from that do you know that next week-end is a holiday?'

'Yes, what about it?'

'It means,' said Helmuth, sloshing gin into glasses with gay abandon, 'that I can take you up the mountains of Calilegua for three days. You like that, eh?'

I turned to Edna.

'Edna,' I began, 'I love you . . . '

'All right,' she said resignedly, 'but you must make sure the puma can't get out, that is all I insist upon.'

So, the following Saturday morning, I was awoken, just as dawn was lightening the sky, by Luna, leaning through my window and singing a somewhat bawdy love-song. I crawled out of bed, humped my equipment on to my back, and we made our way through the cool, aquarium light of dawn to Helmuth's flat. Outside it was a group of rather battered-looking horses, each clad in the extraordinary saddle that they use in the north of Argentina. The saddle itself had a deep, curved seat with a very high pommel in front, so that it was almost like an armchair to sit in. Attached to the front of the saddle were two huge pieces of leather, shaped somewhat like angel's wings, which acted as wonderful protection for your legs and knees when you rode through thorn scrub. In the dim dawn light the horses, clad in these weird saddles, looked like some group of mythical beasts, Pegasus for example, grazing forlornly on the dewy grass. Nearby lounged a group of four guides and hunters who were to accompany us, delightfully wild and unshaven-looking, wearing dirty *bombachas*, great wrinkled boots and huge, tattered straw hats. They were watching Helmuth, his corn-red hair gleaming with dew, as he rushed from horse to horse, stuffing various items into the sacks which were slung across the saddles. These sacks, Helmuth informed me, contained our rations for the three days we should be away. Peering into two of the sacks I discovered that our victuals consisted mainly of garlic and bottles of red wine, although one sack was stuffed with huge slabs of unhealthy-looking meat, the blood from which was dripping through the sacking, and whose curious shape gave one the rather unpleasant impression that we were transporting a dismembered body. When everything was to Helmuth's satisfaction, Edna came out, shivering in her dressing gown, to see us off, and we mounted our bony steeds and set off at a brisk trot towards the mountain range which was our goal, dim, misty and flecked here and there with gold and green in the morning light.

At first we rode along the rough tracks that ran through the sugar-cane fields, where the canes whispered and clacked in the slight breeze. Our hunters and guides had cantered on ahead, and Luna and I and Helmuth rode in a row, keeping our horses at a gentle walk. Helmuth was telling me the story of his life, how, at the age of seventeen (as an Austrian) he had been press-ganged into the German Army, and had fought through the entire war, first in North Africa, then Italy and finally in Germany, without losing anything except the top joint of one finger, which was removed by a land-mine that blew up under him and should have killed him. Luna merely slouched in his great saddle, like a fallen puppet, singing softly to himself. When Helmuth and I had settled world affairs generally, and come to the earth-shaking conclusion that war was futile, we fell silent and listened to Luna's soft voice, the chorus of canes, and the steady clop of our horses' hooves, like gentle untroubled heart-beats in the fine dust.

Presently the path left the cane fields and started to climb up the lower slopes of the mountains, passing into real forest. The massive trees stood, decorated with trailing epiphytes and orchids, each one bound to its fellow by tangled and twisted lianas, like a chain of slaves. The path had now taken on the appearance of an old watercourse (and in the rainy season I think this is what it must have been) strewn with uneven boulders of various sizes, many of them loose. The horses, though used to the country and surefooted, frequently stumbled and nearly pitched you over their heads, so you had to concentrate on holding them up unless you suddenly wanted to find yourself with a split skull. The path had now narrowed, and twisted and turned through the thick under-growth so tortuously that, although the three of us were riding almost nose to tail, we frequently lost sight of each other, and if it had not been for Luna's voice raised in song behind me, and the occasional oaths from Helmuth when his horse stumbled, I could have been riding alone. We had been riding this way for an hour or so, occasionally shouting comments or questions to each other, when I heard a roar of rage from Helmuth, who was a fair distance ahead. Rounding the corner I saw what was causing his rage.

The path at this point had widened, and along one side of it ran a rock-lined ravine, some six feet deep. Into this one of our pack horses had managed to fall, by some extraordinary means known only to itself, for the path at this point was more than wide enough to avoid such a catastrophe. The horse was standing, looking rather smug I thought, in the bottom of the ravine, while our wild-looking hunters had dismounted and were trying to make it climb up on to the path again. The whole of one side of the horse was covered with a scarlet substance that dripped macabrely, and the animal was standing in what appeared to be an ever-widening pool of blood. My first though was to wonder, incredulously, how the creature had managed to hurt itself so badly with such a simple fall, and then I realized that the pack that the horse was carrying contained, among other things, part of our wine supply. The gooey mess and Helmuth's rage were explained. We eventually got the horse back on to the path, and Helmuth peered into the wine-stained sack, uttering moans of anguish.

'Bloody horse,' he said, 'why couldn't it fall on the *other* side, where the meat is?'

'Anything left,' I asked.

'No,' said Helmuth, giving me an anguished look, 'every bottle broken. Do you know what that means, eh?'

'No,' I said truthfully.

'It means we have only twenty-five bottles of wine to last us,' said Helmuth. Subdued by this tragedy we proceeded on our way slowly. Even Luna seemed affected by our loss, and sang only the more mournful songs in his extensive repertoire.

We rode on and on and on, the path getting steeper and steeper. At noon we dismounted by a small, tumbling stream, our shirts black with sweat, bathed ourselves and had a light meal of raw garlic, bread and wine. This, to the fastidious, may sound revolting, but when you are hungry there is no finer combination of tastes. We rested for an hour, to let our sweat-striped horses dry off, and then mounted again and rode on throughout the afternoon. At last, when the evening shadows were lengthening and we could see glimmers of a golden sunset through tiny gaps in the trees above, the path suddenly flattened out, and we rode into a flat, fairly clear area of forest. Here we found that our hunters had already dismounted and unsaddled the horses, while one of them had gathered dry brushwood and lighted a fire. We dismounted stiffly, unsaddled our horses and then, using our saddles and the woolly sheepskin saddle-cloth, called a *recado*, as back-rests we relaxed round the fire for ten minutes, while the hunters dragged out some of the unsavoury-looking meat from the sacks and set it to roast on wooden spits.

Presently, feeling a bit less stiff, and as there was still enough light left, I decided to have a walk round the forest in the immediate area of our camp. Very soon the gruff voices of the hunters were lost among the leaves as I ducked and twisted my way through the tangled, sunset-lit undergrowth. Overhead an occasional humming-bird flipped and purred in front of a flower for a last-night drink, and small groups of toucans flapped from tree to tree, yapping like puppies, or contemplating me with heads on one side, wheezing like rusty hinges. But it was not the birds that interested me so much as the extraordinary variety of fungi that I saw around me. I have never, in any part of the world, seen such a variety of mushrooms and toadstools littering the forest floor, the fallen tree-trunks, and the trees themselves. They were in all colours, from wine-red to black, from yellow to grey, and in a fantastic variety of shapes. I walked slowly for about fifteen minutes in the forest, and in that time I must have covered an area of about an acre. Yet in that short time, and in such a limited space, I filled my hat with twenty-five different species of fungi. Some were scarlet, shaped like goblets of Venetian glass on delicate stems; others were filigreed with holes, so that they were like little carved ivory tables in yellow and white; others were like great, smooth blobs of tar or lava, black and hard, spreading over the rotting logs, and others appeared to have been carved out of polished chocolate, branched and twisted like clumps of miniature stag's antlers. Others stood in rows, like red or yellow or brown buttons on the shirt-fronts of the fallen trees, and others, like old yellow sponges, hung from the branches, dripping evil yellow liquid. It was a Macbeth witches' landscape, and at any moment you expected to see some crouched and wrinkled old hag with a basket gathering this rich haul of what looked like potentially poisonous fungi.

Soon, it became too dark to see properly between the trees, and I made my way back to camp, spread out my fungi in rows, and examined them by the firelight. The unsavoury-looking meat had by now turned into the most delicious steaks, brown and bubbling, and we each with our own knife kept leaning forward cutting any delicate slivers away from the steaks, dunking them in Helmuth's sauce (a bottle of which he had thoughtfully brought with him) and popping the fragrant result into our mouths. Except for an occasional belch the silence was complete. The wine was passed silently, and occasionally someone would lean forward and softly rearrange the logs on the fire, so that the flames flapped upwards more brightly, and the remains of the steaks sizzled briefly, like a nest of sleepy wasps. At last, surfeited with food, we lay back against the comfortable hummocks of our saddles, and Luna, after taking a deep pull at the wine bottle, picked up his guitar and started to strum softly. Presently, very gently, he started to sing, his voice scarcely travelling beyond the circle of fire-light, and the hunters joined him in a deep, rich chorus. I put on my poncho (that invaluable garment like a blanket with a hole in the middle) wrapped myself tightly in it – with one hand free to accept the wine bottle as it drifted round the circle – rolled my sheepskin *recado* into a warm, comfortable pillow and lay back, listening to the haunting songs, and watching a white moon edge its way very slowly through the black fretwork of branches above our heads. Then, suddenly, without any preliminary drowsiness, I was deeply asleep.

I awoke, still staring up into the sky, which was now a pale blue, suffused with gold. Turning on my side I saw the hunters already up, the fire lit, and more strips of meat hung to cook. Helmuth was crouching by the fire drinking a huge mug of steaming coffee, and he grinned at me as I yawned.

'Look at Luna,' he said, gesturing with his cup, 'snoring like a pig.'

Luna lay near me, completely invisible under his poncho. I extricated my leg from my own poncho and kicked vigorously at what I thought was probably Luna's rear end. It was, and a yelp greeted my cruelty. This was followed by a giggle and a burst of song as Luna's head appeared through the hole in his poncho, making him look ridiculously like a singing tortoise emerging from its shell. Presently, warmed by coffee and steaks, we saddled up and rode off into the forest, damp and fragrant with dew, and alive with ringing bird-calls.

As we rode my mind was occupied with the subject of vampire bats. I realized that, in the short time at our disposal up the mountains, we had little chance of catching any really spectacular beasts, but I knew that our destination was infested with these bats. At one time an attempt had been made to start a coffee plantation up where we were going, but no horses could be kept because of the vampires, and so the project had been abandoned. Now, I was extremely keen to meet a vampire on its home ground, so to speak, and, if possible, to catch some and take them back to Europe with me, feeding them on chicken's blood, or, if necessary, my own or that of any volunteers I could raise. As far as I knew they had never been taken back to any European zoo, though some had been kept successfully in the United States. I only hoped that, after being so long neglected, all the vampires at the coffee farm had not moved on to more lucrative pastures.

Our destination, when we reached it an hour or so later, proved to be a dilapidated one-roomed hut, with a small covered verandah running along one side. I gave it approximately another six months before it quietly disintegrated and became part of the forest: we had obviously only just arrived in time. All the hunters, Helmuth and Luna, treated this hut as though it was some luxury hotel, and eagerly dragged their saddles inside and argued amicably over who should sleep in which corner of the worm-eaten floor. I chose to sleep out on the verandah, not only because I felt it would be a trifle more hygienic, but from there I could keep an eye on the tree to which the horses were tethered, for it was on them that I expected the bats to make their first attack.

After a meal we set off on foot into the forest, but, although we saw numerous tracks of tapir and jaguar and lesser beasts, the creatures themselves remained invisible. I did manage, however, by turning over every rotten log we came across, to capture two nice little toads, a tree-frog and a baby coral snake, the latter much to everyone's horror. These I stowed away carefully in the linen bags brought for the purpose when we returned to our hut for the evening meal. When we had finished we sat round the glowing remains of the fire, and Luna, as usual, sang to us. Then the rest of them retired into the hut, carefully closing the window and the door so that not a breath of deadly night air should creep in and kill them (though they had slept out in it quite happily the night before), and I made up my bed on the verandah, propped up so that I could get a good view of the horses, silvered with moonlight, tethered some twenty feet away. I settled myself comfortably, lit a cigarette, and then sat there straining my eyes into the moonlight for the very first sign of a bat anywhere near our horses. I sat like this for two hours before, against my will, dropping off to sleep.

I awoke at dawn, and, furious with myself for having slept, I struggled out of my poncho and went to inspect the horses. I discovered, to my intense irritation, that two of them had been attacked by vampires while I lay snoring twenty feet away. They had both been bitten in exactly the same place, on the neck about a hand's length from the withers. The bites themselves consisted of two even slits, each about half an inch long and quite shallow. But the effect of these small bites was quite gruesome, for the blood (as in all vampire bites) had not clotted after the bat had finished licking up its grisly meal and flown off, for the vampire's saliva contains an anticoagulant. So, when the bloated bat had left its perch on the horses' necks, the wounds had continued to bleed, and now the horses' necks were striped with great bands of clotted blood, out of all proportion to the size of the bites. Again I noticed that the bites, as well as being in identical positions on each horse, were also on the same side of the body, the right side of the animal if you were sitting on it, and there was no sign of a bite or an attempted bite on the left side of either horse. Both animals seemed quite unaffected by the whole thing, and seemed mildly surprised at the interest I was taking in them.

After breakfast, determined that the vampire bats must be lurking somewhere nearby, I organized the rest of the party in a search. We spread out and hunted through the forest in a circle round the hut, going about a quarter of a mile deep into the forest, looking for hollow trees or small caves where the vampires might be lurking. We continued in this fruitless task until lunch-time, and when we reassembled at the hut the only living specimens we could really be said to have acquired were some three hundred and forty black ticks of varying ages and sizes, who, out of all of us, seemed to have preferred the smell of Luna and Helmuth, and so had converged on them. They had to go down to the stream nearby and strip; then, having washed the more tenacious ticks off their bodies, they set about the task of removing the others from the folds and crannies of their clothing, both of them perched naked on the rocks, picking at their clothes like a couple of baboons.

'Curious things, ticks,' I said conversationally, when I went down to the stream to tell them that food was ready, 'parasites of great perception. It's a well-known natural history fact that they always attack the more unpleasant people of the party . . . usually the drunks, or the ones of very low mentality or morals.'

Luna and Helmuth glared at me.

'Would you,' inquired Helmuth interestedly, 'like Luna and me to throw you over that waterfall?'

'You must admit it's a bit peculiar. None of our hunters got ticks, and they are all fairly good parasite-bait, I would have thought. *I* didn't get ticks. You two were the only ones. You know the old English proverb about parasites?'

'What old English proverb?' asked Helmuth suspiciously.

'Birds of a feather flock together,' I said, and hurried back to camp before they could get their shoes on and follow me.

The sun was so blindingly hot in the clearing when we had finished eating that everyone stretched out on the minute verandah and had a siesta. While the others were all snoring like a covey of pigs, I found I could not sleep. My head was still full of vampires. I was annoyed that we had not found their hideout, which I felt sure must be somewhere fairly near. Of course, as I realized, there may have been only one or two bats, in which case looking for their hideout in the local forest was three times as difficult as the usual imbecile occupation of looking for needles in haystacks. It was not until the others had woken, with grunts and yawns, that an idea suddenly occurred to me. I jumped to my feet and went inside the hut. Looking up I saw, to my delight, that the single room had a wooden *ceiling*, which meant that there must be some sort of loft between the apex of the roof and the ceiling. I hurried outside and there, sure enough, was a square opening which obviously led into the space between roof and ceiling. I was now convinced that I should find the loft simply stuffed with vampire bats, and so I waited impatiently while the hunters fashioned a rough ladder out of saplings and hoisted it up to the hole. Then I sped up it, armed with a bag to put my captures in and a cloth to catch them with without being bitten. I was followed by Helmuth who was going to guard the opening with an old shirt of mine. Eagerly, holding a torch in my mouth, I wriggled into the loft. The first discovery I made was that the wooden ceiling on which I was perched was insecure in the extreme, and so I had to spread myself out like a starfish to distribute my weight, unless I wanted the whole thing to crash into the room below, with me on it. So, progressing on my stomach in the manner of a stalking Red Indian, I set out to explore the loft.

The first sign of life was a long, slender tree-snake, which shot past me towards the hole that Helmuth was guarding. When I informed him of this and asked him to try and catch it he greeted this request in the most unfriendly manner, interspersed with a number of rich Austrian oaths. Luckily for him, the snake found a crack in the ceiling and disappeared through that, and we did not see it again. I crawled on doggedly, disturbing three small scorpions, who immediately rushed into the nearest holes, and eight large revolting spiders of the more hirsute variety, who merely shifted slightly when the torch beam hit them, and crouched there meditatively. But there was not the faintest sign of a bat, not even so much as a bat dropping to encourage me. I was just beginning to feel very bitter about bats in general and vampire bats in particular, when my torch-beam picked out something sitting sedately on a cross-beam, glaring at me ferociously, and I immediately forgot all about vampires.

Squatting there in the puddle of torchlight was a pigmy owl, a bird little bigger than a sparrow, with round yellow eyes that glared at me with all the silent indignation of a vicar who, in the middle of the service, has discovered that the organist is drunk. Now, I have a passion for owls of all sorts, but these pigmy owls are probably my favourites. I think it is their diminutive size combined with their utter fearlessness that attracts me; at any rate I determined to add the one perching above me to my collection, or die in the attempt. Keeping the torch beam firmly fixed on his eyes, so that he could not see what I was doing, I gently brought up my other hand and then, with a quick movement, I threw the cloth I carried over him, and grabbed. He uttered a squeak of indignation, and fluttered wildly, sinking his small but sharp talons into my fingers through the cloth. Placing the torch on the floor I wrapped him up tightly in the cloth and then put the whole bundle inside my shirt and buttoned it up for further safety. Then, having made quite sure once more, that there was not a bat in the loft, I started to make my way back to the entrance. This was, to say the least, difficult, for the owl was reposing against my chest, so I had to travel on my back. This gave me a wonderful view of the spiders overhead, all of which now seemed to be the size of soup-plates and each ready to drop on me if I made a false move. Fascinating as I find spiders, I prefer to keep the larger and more hairy varieties at a distance. At last I reached the opening and levered myself out into the sunshine.

To my surprise the hunters were excited and delighted with my capture of the pigmy owl. I was puzzled by this, until they explained that it was a common belief in Argentina that if you possessed one of these little birds you would be lucky in love. This answered a question that had been puzzling me for some time. When I had been in Buenos Aires I had found one of these owls in a cage in the local bird market. The owner had asked a price that was so fantastic that I had treated it with ridicule, until I realized that he meant it. He refused to bargain, and was quite unmoved when I left without buying the bird. Three days later I had returned, thinking that by now the man would be more amenable to bargaining, only to find that he had sold the owl at the price he had asked for. This had seemed to me incredible, and I could not for the life of me think of a satisfactory explanation. But now I realized I had been outbid by some lovesick swain; I could only hope that the owl brought him luck.

That night was to be our last spent in the mountains, and I was grimly determined that I was going to catch a vampire bat if one showed so much as a wing-tip that night. I had even decided that I would use myself as bait. Not only would it bring the bats within catching range, but I was interested to see if the bite was really as painless as it was reputed to be. So, when the others had retired to their airless boudoir, I made up my bed as near to the horses as I felt I could get, without frightening off the bats, wrapped myself up in my poncho but left one of my feet sticking out, for vampires, I had read, were particularly fond of human extremities, especially the big toe. Anyway, it was the only extremity I was prepared to sacrifice for the sake of Science.

I lay there in the moonlight, glaring at the horses, while my foot got colder and colder. I wondered if vampires liked frozen human big toe. Faintly from the dark forest around came the night sounds, a million crickets doing endless carpentry work in the undergrowth, hammering and sawing, forging miniature horseshoes, practising the trombone, tuning harps, and learning how to use tiny pneumatic drills. From the tree-tops frogs cleared their throats huskily, like a male chorus getting ready for a concert. Everything was brilliantly lit by moonlight, including my big toe, but there was not a bat to be seen.

Eventually, my left foot began to feel like something that had gone with Scott to the Pole, and had been left there, so I drew it into the warmth of the poncho and extended my right foot as a sacrifice. The horses, with drooping heads, stood quite still in the moonlight, very occasionally shifting their weight from one pair of legs to another. Presently, in order to get some feeling back into my feet, I went and hobbled round the horses, inspecting them with the aid of a torch. None of them had been attacked. I went back and continued my self-imposed torture. I did a variety of things to keep myself awake: I smoked endless cigarettes under cover of the poncho, I made mental lists of all the South American animals I could think of, working through the alphabet, and, when these failed and I started to feel sleepy, I thought about my overdraft. This last is the most successful sleep eradicator I know. By the time dawn had started to drain the blackness out of the sky, I was wide awake and feeling as though I was solely responsible for the National Debt. As soon as it became light enough to see without a torch I hobbled over to inspect the horses, more as a matter of form than anything. I could hardly believe my eyes, for two of them were painted with gory ribbons of blood down their necks. Now, I had been watching those horses – in brilliant moonlight – throughout the night, and I would have staked my life that not a bat of any description had come within a hundred yards of them. Yet two of them had been feasted upon, as it were, before my very eyes. To say that I was chagrined is putting it mildly. I had feet that felt as if they would fall off at a touch, a splitting headache, and felt generally rather like a dormouse that had been pulled out of its nest in mid-October.

Luna and Helmuth, of course, when I woke them up, were very amused, and thought this was sufficient revenge for my rude remarks the previous day about parasites. It was not until I had finished my breakfast in a moody and semi-somnambulistic state, and was starting on my third mug of coffee, that I remembered something that startled me considerably. In my enthusiasm to catch a vampire bat, and to be bitten by one to see what it felt like, I had completely forgotten the rather unpleasant fact that they can be rabies carriers, so being bitten by one might have had some interesting repercussions, to say the least. I remembered that the rabies vaccine (which, with the usual ghoulish medical relish, they inject into your stomach) is extremely painful, and you have to have a vast quantity of the stuff pumped into you before you are out of danger. Whether this is necessary, or simply because the doctors get a rake-off from the vaccine manufacturers, I don't know, but I do know – from people that have had it – that it is not an experience to be welcomed. The chances of getting rabies from a bat in that particular area would be extremely slight, I should have thought, but even so, had I been bitten, I would have had to undergo the injections as a precautionary measure; anyone who has ever read a description of the last stages of a person suffering from rabies would be only too happy to rush to the nearest hospital.

So, without bats or bites, and with my precious pigmy owl slung round my neck in a tiny bamboo cage, we set off down the mountains back to Calilegua. By the time we reached the cane fields it was green twilight, and we were all tired and aching. Even Luna, riding ahead, was singing more and more softly. At length we saw the glow of lights from Helmuth's flat, and when we dismounted, stiff, sweaty and dirty, and made our way inside, there was Edna, fresh and lovely, and by her side a table on which stood three very large ice-cold gin-and-tonics.

Chapter Eight

A Wagon-Load of Bichos

In conclusion, it appears to me that nothing can be more improving to a young naturalist than a journey in distant countries.

CHARLES DARWIN: THE VOYAGE OF H.M.S. BEAGLE.

I have, during the course of my perambulations about the world, met a number of curious and interesting human beings. If I were to make a list of these characters the top places would be occupied by two people I met during my last ten days at Calilegua.

Helmuth came in one morning and informed me that he had to travel to an *estancia* some distance away from Calilegua, for some purpose or other, and that near his destination was another *estancia* run by a man who (he had been informed) kept animals as pets. So while he conducted his business he would drop me off at the other *estancia* to see what bargains I could discover. As we drove along Helmuth told me something about the man I was to meet.

'I have never seen him, but all the local people say that he comes from a very good European family. They say he used to entertain kings and princes when his father was chief minister of one of the Balkan states. I don't know how much is true ... you know what it's like in this sort of place, Gerry, eh? They say anything about your past life, and if they can't think of anything about your past life, they simply say that you are not married to your wife, or that you are a drunk or a homosexual, or something of the sort.'

'Yes, I know what it's like,' I said, 'I once lived in a cosy English village where you couldn't pass the time of day with any female between the ages of seven and seventy without being accused of rape.'

'Still,' said Helmuth philosophically, 'if he has *bichos* for you, who cares what he is.'

After driving for a couple of hours we turned off the road and made our way along bumpy tracks through sugar-cane fields. Presently we came to a pleasant, small, one-storied house, surrounded by a well-tended garden. The lawn was scattered with the evidence of children: a rocking-horse, a battered teddy bear, a rough cement paddling-pool with a small yacht listing heavily to starboard floating in it.

'Here we are,' said Helmuth. 'Out you get. I'll pick you up in a couple of hours' time. O.K.?'

'O.K.,' I agreed, as I got out. 'What's this chap's name, anyway?'

'Caporal,' said Helmuth, and drove off, leaving me standing in a cloud of dust.

Here I might say that the person in question was not called Caporal, but I have not used his real name for a variety of reasons, the chief one being that he did not give me permission to write about him. Anyway, when I had sneezed some of the dust out of my nose, I clapped dutifully outside the gate, and then opened it and walked towards the house. As I was nearing the broad verandah, a man appeared from round the side of the house. He was tall, well-built, and dressed in the usual costume of long, wrinkled boots, plus-four-like *bombachas*, a dirty shirt, and a battered felt hat with a wide brim.

'*Buenos dias*,' he said as he approached me.

'*Buenos dias*. I wish to see Señor Caporal. Is he in the house?' I asked.

He came up to me and swept off his hat.

'I am Caporal,' he said. He took my extended hand, clicked his heels together and bowed very slightly. The gesture was not theatrical, but automatic. He had a fine brown face, with dark eyes that were full of kindness. He sported a carefully trimmed black moustache under his eagle-beak nose, but his cheeks and chin were covered with a black stubble.

'Do you,' I inquired hopefully, 'speak English?'

'But, of course,' he answered at once, in an impeccable accent that must have been the result of some public school. 'I don't speak it very well, you understand, but I manage to converse fairly well. But please don't stand out here. Come inside and have some coffee, and you can tell me what I may do for you.'

He ushered me through the door which led straight into a small dining-room-cum-sitting-room. The floor was highly polished and gay with locally-woven mats, and the few simple pieces of furniture were similarly polished and glowing. He poked his head through another door and called '*Maria, café para dos, por favor*,' and then turned back to me, smiling.

'This is a great pleasure,' he said sincerely, 'I very seldom get a chance to practise my English. But first, will you excuse me for a brief moment?

The coffee will be ready soon . . . here are cigarettes . . . please make yourself at home.'

He bowed again slightly, and left the room. I took a cigarette absently and then suddenly, with surprise, noticed that the box that contained them was silver, and with a beautiful and intricate design worked on the lid. Looking about the room I noticed other silver objects, a lovely slender-stemmed vase full of scarlet hibiscus flowers; on the sideboard a pair of beautifully-worked candlesticks and, between them, a massive fruit bowl that must have weighed a couple of pounds when empty. I began to wonder if perhaps the stories about Caporal were true, for these silver articles were not made in Argentina, and together they were worth a lot of money. He came back in an amazingly short space of time, and I saw that he had washed, shaved and changed into clean *bombachas*, boots and shirt.

'Now I am more fitted to entertain you,' he said smiling, as the Indian maid padded into the room with a tray of coffee, 'what may I do for you?'

I explained about having my own zoo in the Channel Isles, and how I had come to Argentine to collect specimens for it, and he was deeply interested. It turned out that, until quite recently, he had had some wild animals as pets, which he had kept to amuse his children, but as the animals grew bigger and less trustworthy he had sent them all down to the zoo in Buenos Aires. This had been some three days before my arrival in Jujuy, so my feelings can be imagined.

'I had two ostrich,' he said, smiling at my glum expression, 'a fox, an ocelot and a wild pig. I am so sorry I sent them. If I had only known that you were coming . . .'

'Never mind,' I said. 'But if you do get anything during the next ten days, would you send it to Calilegua for me, or send me a message and I'll pick it up?'

'But, of course,' he said, 'with the greatest pleasure.'

He poured me out some more coffee, and we talked about other things. He had the most impeccable manners and the air of a man who had not only been used to money but to a position of authority as well. I began to wonder more and more about him, but he was far too well mannered to talk about himself, and instead tried to steer the conversation into channels which he thought would be of interest to me. Then an idea came to me. During a slight lull in the talk, I turned to him and said:

'Do please excuse me, but ever since you brought me in I have been admiring your candlesticks. They are quite beautiful. I've never seen anything quite like them before.'

His face lit up delightedly.

'Ah, yes, they are beautiful, aren't they,' he said staring at them. 'They are a little bit of the old régime that I managed to keep . . . those and the other bits of silver you see in here.'

I kept silent, but let myself look faintly puzzled.

'You see,' he went on, 'I am Hungarian. My father was chief minister there before the war. But, after the war, when the Communists came, my father was dead, and I had a wife and three children . . . I did not want them to grow up under such a régime. We escaped, and we only managed to bring a few of my family things with us, most of which we had to sell when we reached Buenos Aires in order to eat. I had some difficulty in getting a job: I had only been trained to be a gentleman.'

He smiled at me shyly, as if ashamed at having bored me with his private reminiscences.

'Still,' he said, offering me a cigarette, 'it is nice to have a few things to remind me of the happy parts of one's life. You would, I think, have liked Hungary in those days. There were plenty of animals there then; what shooting parties we used to have. You like shooting, or do you like the animals too much?'

'No, I don't object to shooting,' I said honestly, 'providing that the animals are not exterminated indiscriminately.'

His eyes glowed eagerly.

'Perhaps,' he said tentatively, 'you would like to see some photographs ... ?' His voice died away on a faintly interrogative note.

I said I would love to see some photographs, and he went quickly into another room and soon reappeared with a large, beautifully-carved oak chest, which he put on the floor.

He pulled up the lid and tipped out on to the mat a huge heap of photographs, which he shuffled through swiftly. Photograph after photograph he pulled out of the pile, thrusting them excitedly into my hands, wanting to try and communicate some of the happiness they brought back to him. To him they represented hunts he would never forget, and the people that figured in the photographs meant little or nothing to him.

'This is the biggest wild boar we ever shot ... it was during a drive for the King of Sweden ... see what a magnificent creature, it was almost a shame to shoot him ... look at those tusks.'

There the monstrous boar lay on the ground, his lip lifted scornfully over his great tusks, while the King of Sweden stood stiffly, gun in hand, behind him.

'Now, look at this. The best duck drive we had, for the Prince of Siam, five hundred odd brace of ducks ... it was a wonderful day, the sky was black with ducks ... like locusts ... your feet were frozen and your gun barrels were red-hot but you couldn't stop shooting. ... '

So we looked at photographs for an hour or so, photographs of a parade of animals, royalty and nobility. Then, at last, I pulled out from the pile a large flashlight photograph that showed a massive, panelled dining-room. The chandeliers were like half-grown Christmas-trees, turned upside down, hanging over a long table laden with silver and glass. At the table were seated men and women, beautifully dressed, while at the head of the table sat an elderly man, and on his right a bejewelled and turbaned Indian potentate, and on the other side of the table I recognized my host, immaculate in evening dress. It looked like a scene out of *The Prisoner of Zenda*.

'Oh,' he said carelessly, 'that was a banquet we gave for the Maharajah. Now here, look, see these roedeer, what magnificent heads? Only in Hungary did you get heads like that.'

Presently I heard Helmuth honking his horn in the road outside, and, reluctantly I rose to go. My host shovelled the photographs back into the chest and closed the lid.

'I am so sorry,' he said contritely, 'I have been boring you with my photographs. If my wife had been here, she would have entertained you more amusingly.'

I protested that I had enjoyed them very much, and, as we went out on to the verandah, there was one question I felt I must ask, whether it was good manners or not.

'Tell me, Señor Caporal,' I said, 'don't you ever miss all that? After having that wonderful life, with money and hunting and influential friends? Don't you find Argentina, to say the least, a little dull?'

He looked at me and laughed.

'Señor Durrell,' he said, 'that which I have been showing you is past, like a dream. It was wonderful while it lasted. But now I have a new life. I am saving a bit of money, so that I may send my children to school in Buenos Aires, and I will have enough left over, I hope, to buy a very small *estancia* for myself and my wife when my children are grown up. What more do I want?'

I pondered on this for a moment, while he watched me, smiling.

'Then you like your job here,' I asked, 'managing this *estancia*?'

'But, of course,' he said. 'It is much better than the first job I had when I first came to Argentina.'

'What was that?' I inquired curiously.

'Castrating bulls in Cordoba,' he said chuckling.

I walked down to join Helmuth in the car, feeling very thoughtful. It seemed that I had been privileged to spend the last two hours with a very unusual human being: a truly happy man, and one without bitterness.

By now my collection of creatures had grown to such an extent that it was a whole-time job looking after it. No longer could I go off for three or four days at a time and leave poor Edna to cherish my creatures. Also I was busy building cages for those tame animals which, up until now, had either been at complete liberty, or spent their time tethered, but on leashes. I had originally intended to fly my collection back to Buenos Aires, but the air freight estimate, when it arrived, looked as if it had been worked out by the Astronomer Royal in light-years.

There was nothing for it, I would have to go by train, a two-day and three-night journey that I did not relish, but there was no alternative. Charles arranged the whole thing for me with a speed and efficiency that was typical of him. This in spite of the fact that he had his own work to do, as well as being extremely worried over his wife Joan, who was ill in hospital. So I hammered and sawed in the garden, getting cages ready for my train-journey, and keeping a stern eye on those animals which were still loose and therefore liable to get up to mischief.

The biggest of the still un-caged animals were the coatimundis, Martha and Mathias, who, on collars and chains, were tethered under the trees. I am fond of coatimundis, though they are not everyone's idea of the most charming of animals. But I find something very appealing about their long, rubbery, tip-tilted noses, their pigeon-toed, bear-like walk, and the way they hold their long, ringed tails straight up in the air when they move, like furry exclamation marks. In the wild state they are gregarious, travelling through the forest in quite large parties, uprooting logs and stones, snuffling in every nook and cranny with their vacuum-cleaner-like noses for their prey, which may range from beetles to birds and from fruit to mushrooms. Like most small, gregarious mammals they have quite an extensive vocabulary, and the conversations of a troupe of coatimundis would, I am sure, repay investigation. Mathias would converse with me by the hour in a series of bird-like squeaks and trills; if, when investigating a rotten log or a stone, he thought he was nearing a succulent beetle or slug, the sounds would turn to snuffling grunts, pitched in different keys, and interspersed with a strange champing noise made by chattering his teeth together at great speed. When in a rage he would chitter violently, his whole body shaking as if with ague, and give prolonged, piercing whistling cries that would almost burst your ear drums.

Both the coatimundis had fairly long leashes which were attached to a convenient tree. When they had uprooted and investigated every log and stone within the circle of the leash, they were moved to a fresh tree. Every time this happened, Mathias would spend ten minutes or so marking out his circle of territory with the scent gland at the base of his tail. He would solemnly shuffle his way round in a circle, a look of immense concentration on his face, squatting down at intervals to rub his hindquarters on a convenient rock or stick. Having thus, as it were, hoisted the coatimundi equivalent of the flag, he would relax and settle down to the task of beetle-hunting with a clear conscience. If any of the local dogs were so misguided as to approach his territory they never did it a second time. He would walk slowly towards them, champing his teeth alarmingly, his tail erect, stiff as a poker, and puffed up to twice its normal size. Having got within range he would suddenly dart forward in a curious, rolling run, uttering his piercing, ear-splitting screams. This ghastly noise had the effect of undermining the morale of any but the bravest dog, and, when they had hurriedly retreated, Mathias, quietly chattering and trilling to himself, would wend his way round in a circle, re-marking his entire territory. During all this, Martha would be sitting at the extreme limit of her chain, watching Mathias with adoring eyes, and uttering tiny squeaks of encouragement.

All the other creatures I had acquired were doing splendidly. Juanita, the peccary, grew fatter and more charming each day, and lorded it over the parrots. My precious yellow-naped macaws had given me heart-failure by appearing to go into a decline; I eventually discovered that they were not ill but, for some obscure reason, wanted to sleep inside a box at night, a fact that I discovered quite by accident. As soon as they were supplied with a sleeping box their appetites revived and they started to do well. Among the cats the little Geoffroy's was now quite reconciled to captivity, and played such strenuous games of hide-and-seek with his tabby kitten companion, as well as a game they had invented which appeared to be called 'Strangle Your Neighbour,' that I began to wonder if I would get them to Buenos Aires alive, let alone Jersey. Luna the puma had tamed down a lot, and even condescended to allow me to scratch her behind the ears, while she rumbled contentedly deep in her throat. The poor half-starved ocelot was now fat and glossy. Having lost the apathy of starvation, she was now very full of herself, and regarded the interior of her cage as sacred, so the process of cleaning her out or feeding her was fraught with danger. Thus are one's kindnesses sometimes repaid.

Among the new creatures which I had added to my collection were two of the most enchanting members of the monkey tribe, a pair of douroucoulis which had been caught in the forest by an Indian hunter. He had been a very good hunter, but unfortunately I had paid him rather too lavishly for the monkeys, and, overcome by the size of the payment, he had retired to the village and stayed drunk ever since, so these were the last specimens I got from him. There is quite an art in paying the right amount for an animal, and by paying too much you can easily lose a good hunter, for between your camp and the forest always lies a series of gin-shops, and hunters are notoriously weak-willed.

Douroucoulis are the only nocturnal monkeys in the world, and from that point of view alone would be remarkable. But when you add to that the fact that they look like a cross between an owl and a clown, that they are the gentlest of monkeys, and that they spend a lot of time clasped in each others arms exchanging the most human kisses, then douroucoulis become, so far as I am concerned, irresistible. They have the huge eyes, typical of a nocturnal creature, surrounded by a white facial mask edged with black. The shape of the mouth gives you the impression that they are just about to break into a rather sad, slightly pitying smile. Their backs and tails are a pleasant shade of greenish-grey, and they possess great fluffy shirt-fronts that vary from pale yellow to deep orange, according to age. In the wilds these monkeys, like the coatimundis, are gregarious, travelling through the trees with silent leaps in troupes of ten to fifteen animals. The only time they make any sound is when feeding, and then they converse among themselves with loud, purring grunts which swell their throats up, or a series of bird-like tweets, cat-like mewing, pig-like snufflings and snake-like hissings. The first time I heard them feeding among the dark trees in the forest I identified them as each of these animals in turn, and then became so muddled I was convinced I had found something new to science. I used to dig large red beetles out of the rotting palm-trees for the douroucoulis, insects of which they were inordinately fond. They would watch my approach with the titbits, their eyes wide, their hands held out beseechingly, trembling slightly, uttering faint squeaks of excitement. They would clasp the wriggling beetles in their hands with the awkward grace of a young child accepting a stick of rock, and chew and scrunch their way through them, pausing now and again to utter squeaks of joy. When the last piece had been chewed and swallowed, they would carefully examine their hands, both back and front, to make sure there was none left, and then examine each other for the same reason. Having convinced themselves that no fragment remained, they would clasp each other and kiss passionately for five minutes or so, in what appeared to be an orgy of mutual congratulation.

It was just after I had acquired these delightful monkeys that I had my second encounter with a curious human being, and my introduction to him was due to Luna. He appeared one morning and said that business was to take him to a place a few miles away from Calilegua. In this village he had to visit he had heard rumours of a man who was interested in animals and even kept them as pets.

'All I can find out is that his name is Coco, and that everyone there says he is *loco*, Gerry,' said Luna. 'But you might like to come and see.'

'All right,' I said, nothing loath to leaving my sweat-provoking carpentry for a while, 'but can you wait until I've cleaned and fed the animals?'

'O.K.,' said Luna, and lay patiently on the lawn scratching Juanita's stomach until I had finished my chores.

The village, when we reached it, proved to be a large, straggling one, with a curious dead air about it. Even the houses, constructed as usual with the off-cuts from tree-trunks, had an ill-kempt, dirty look. Everything looked scruffy and depressed. But everyone appeared to know Coco, for when we inquired in the local bar where he lived a forest of hands directed us, and everyone smiled and said, 'Ah, yes, Coco,' as if they were referring to the village idiot. Following directions we found his house easily enough. It would have been very noticeable anyway, for in comparison to the rest of the village, it gleamed like a gem. It had been carefully whitewashed, so that it shone; its front garden was neatly tended and, incredibly, a real gravel path, neatly raked, led up to the house. I decided that if this was the house of the village idiot, then I very much wanted to meet him. In response to our clapping a slight, dark woman appeared, who looked as though she might be Italian. She admitted to being Coco's wife, but said that he was not at home: he worked during the day at the local saw-mill, which we could hear humming in the distance like all the bees in the universe having a conference. Luna explained my mission, and the wife's face lighted up.

'Oh,' she said, 'I will send one of the children to fetch him. He would never forgive me if he missed meeting you. Please come round to the back and wait . . . he will come in a few moments.'

The garden at the back of the house was as well tended as the front, and, to my surprise, contained two well-constructed and spacious aviaries. I peered into them hopefully, but they were both empty. We did not have to wait long for Coco's appearance. He appeared from the path leading to the saw-mill at a brisk trot, and arrived, breathing deeply, in front of us and doffed his straw hat. He was a short, well-built man with coal-black, curly hair and (unusual in Argentina) a thick black beard and moustache, carefully trimmed. His eyes were dark, and shone with eagerness as he held out a well-shaped brown hand to Luna and myself.

'Welcome, welcome,' he said, 'you must excuse, please, my English . . . she is not good for I have no chance to practise.'

The fact that he could speak English at all amazed me.

'You have no idea what this means to me,' he said eagerly, wringing my hand, 'to speak with someone who has an interest in Nature . . . if my wife had not called me I would never have forgiven her . . . I could not believe it when my son told me . . . an Englishman to see me, and about animals, too.'

He smiled at me, his face still slightly awe-stricken at this miracle that had happened. One would have thought that I had come to offer him the Presidency of Argentina. I was so overwhelmed at being greeted like a newly-descended angel that I was almost at a loss for words.

'Well,' said Luna, having obviously decided that he had done his job by bringing one lunatic in contact with another, 'I will go and do my work and see you later.'

He drifted off, humming to himself, while Coco seized my arm gently, as though it were a butterfly's wing that he might damage, and urged me up the steps and into the living-room of his house. Here his wife had produced wonderful lemonade from fresh lemons, heavily sweetened, and we sat at the table and drank this while Coco talked. He spoke quietly, stumbling occasionally in his English and saying a sentence in Spanish when he realized I knew enough of the language to follow. It was an extraordinary experience, like listening to a man who had been dumb for years suddenly recover the power of speech. He had been living for so long in a world of his own, for neither his wife, children nor anyone in the fly-blown village could understand his interests. To him I was the incredible answer to a prayer, a man who had suddenly appeared from nowhere, a man who could understand what he meant when he said that a bird was beautiful, or an animal was interesting, someone, in fact, who could speak this language that had been so long locked up inside him, which no one around him comprehended. All the time he spoke he watched me with an embarrassing expression, a mixture of awe and fear – awe that I should be there at all, and fear that I might suddenly disappear like a mirage.

'It is the birds that I am particularly studying,' he said, 'I know the birds of Argentina are catalogued, but who knows anything about them? Who knows their courtship displays, their type of nests, how many eggs they lay, how many broods they have, if they migrate? Nothing is known of this, and this is the problem. In this field I am trying to help, as well as I can.'

'This is the problem all over the world,' I said, 'we know what creatures exist – or most of them – but we know nothing of their private lives.'

'Would you like to see the place where I work? I call it my study,' he explained deprecatingly, 'it is very small, but all I can afford . . .'

'I would love to see it,' I said.

Eagerly he led me outside to where a sort of miniature wing had been built on to the side of the house. The door that led into this was heavily padlocked. As he pulled a key from his pocket to open this he smiled at me.

'I let no one in here,' he explained simply, 'they do not understand.'

Up until then I had been greatly impressed with Coco, and with his obvious enthusiasm for animal life. But now, being led into his study, I was more than impressed. I was speechless.

His study was about eight feet long and six feet wide. In one corner was a cabinet which housed, as he showed me, his collection of bird and small mammal skins, and various birds' eggs. Then there was a long, low bench on which he did his skinning, and nearby a rough bookcase containing some fourteen volumes on natural history, some in Spanish, some in English. Under the one small window stood an easel, and on it the half-finished water colour of a bird, whose corpse lay nearby on a box.

'Did you do *that*?' I asked incredulously.

'Yes,' he said shyly, 'you see, I could not afford a camera, and this was the only way to record their plumage.'

I gazed at the half-finished picture. It was beautifully done, with a fineness of line and colouring that was amazing. I say amazing because the drawing and painting of birds is one of the most difficult of subjects in the whole natural history field. Here was work that was almost up to the standards of some of the best modern bird painters I had seen. You could see that it was the work of an untrained person, but it was done with meticulous accuracy and love, and the bird glowed on the page. I had the dead specimen in my hand to compare the painting with, and I could see that this painting was far better than a lot I had seen published in bird books.

He pulled out a great folder and showed me his other work. He had some forty paintings of birds, generally in pairs if there was any sexual difference in the plumage, and they were all as good as the first one I had seen.

'But these are terribly good,' I said, 'you must do something with them.'

'Do you think so?' he inquired doubtfully, peering at the paintings.

'I have sent some to the man in charge of the Museum at Cordoba, and he liked them. He said we should have a small book printed when I have enough of them, but this I think is doubtful, for you know how costly a production would be.'

'Well, I know the people in charge of the Museum at Buenos Aires,' I said. 'I will speak to them about you. I don't guarantee anything, but they might be able to help.'

'That would be wonderful,' he said, his eyes shining.

'Tell me,' I said, 'do you like your work here in the sawmill?'

'Like it?' he repeated incredulously, *'like it?* Señor, it is soul-destroying. But it provides me with enough to live on, and, by careful saving I have enough left over to buy paints. Also I am saving to buy a small ciné-camera, for however skilful you are as a painter there are certain things that birds do which can only be captured on film. But these ciné-cameras are very expensive, and I am afraid it will be a long time before I can afford it.'

He talked on for an hour or so, quickly, enthusiastically, telling me what he had accomplished and what he hoped to do. I had to keep reminding myself that this was a man – a peasant, if you prefer the term – who worked in a saw-mill and lived in a house which, though spotless, no so-called 'worker' in England would be seen dead in. To have discovered Coco in the outskirts of Buenos Aires would not have been, perhaps, so incredible, but to find him here in this remote, unlikely spot, was like suddenly coming across a unicorn in the middle of Piccadilly. And, although he explained to me the difficulties of saving enough money to buy paints, and enough to buy his dream ciné-camera, there was never once the slightest suggestion that financial aid might be forthcoming from me. He was simply, with the naïveté of a child, discussing his problems with someone he felt would understand and appreciate what he was doing. To him I must have represented a millionaire, yet I knew that if I offered him money I would cease to be his friend, and become as the other inhabitants of the village, a person who did not understand. The most I could do was to promise to speak to the Museum in Buenos Aires (for good bird-painters are not two a penny) and to give him my card, and tell him that if there was anything that he wanted from England which he could not obtain in Argentina, to let me know and I would send it to him. When, eventually, Luna reappeared and we simply had to leave, Coco said goodbye wistfully, rather like a child who had been allowed to play with a new toy, and then had it taken away. As we drove off he was standing in the centre of the dusty, rutted street, watching the car and turning my card over and over in his hands, as if it were some sort of talisman.

Unfortunately, on my way down to Buenos Aires I lost Coco's address, and I did not discover the loss until I got back to England. But he had mine, and I felt sure that he would write and ask me to send him a bird book or perhaps some paints, for such things are hard to get in Argentina. But there was no word from him. Then, when Christmas came, I sent him a card, and in it I reiterated my offer to send him anything he needed. I sent the card care of Charles, at Calilegua, who kindly drove out and delivered it to Coco. Then Coco wrote to me, a charming letter, in which he apologized for his bad English, but he thought that, nevertheless, it was improving slightly. He gave me news of his birds and his painting. But there was not a single request in the letter. So, at the risk of offending him, I packed up a parcel of books that I thought would be of the greatest use to him, and shipped them off. And now, when I get disgruntled with my lot, when I get irritated because I can't afford some new animal, or a new book, or a new gadget for my camera, I remember Coco in his tiny study, working hard and enthusiastically with inadequate tools and money, and it has a salutary effect on me. On the way back to Calilegua Luna asked me what I had thought of Coco, since everyone in the village thought he was *loco*. I said he was, in my opinion, one of the sanest men I had ever met, and certainly one of the most remarkable. I hope that some day I have the privilege of meeting him again.

On the way back to Calilegua we stopped briefly at another village where Luna had heard a rumour that some *bicho* was being kept. To my delight it turned out to be a fully adult male peccary, ridiculously tame, and the perfect mate for Juanita. He was called, by his owner, Juan, and so we purchased him, and put him, grunting excitedly, into the back of the car and drove back to Calilegua in triumph. Juan, however, was so large, clumsy and eagerly tame that I felt he might, in all innocence, damage Juanita, who was only a quarter his size, and very fragile, so I was forced to cage them separately until Juanita had grown sufficiently. However, they touched noses through the bars, and seemed to be delighted with each other, so I had hope of eventually arranging a successful marriage.

At last the day came when I had to leave Calilegua. I did not want to leave a bit, for everyone had been too kind to me. Joan and Charles, Helmuth and Edna, and the human nightingale Luna, had accepted me, this complete stranger, into their lives, allowed me to disrupt their routine, showered me with kindness and done everything possible to help in my work. But, although I had been a stranger on arrival in Calilegua, such was the kindness shown to me that within a matter of hours I felt I had been there for years. To say that I was sorry to leave these friends was putting it mildly.

My journey was, in the first stages, slightly complicated. I had to take the collection on the small railway that ran from Calilegua to the nearest big town. Here everything had to be transhipped on to the Buenos Aires train. Charles, realizing that I was worried about the transhipment side of the business, insisted that Luna travelled with me as far as the main town, and that he, Helmuth and Edna (for Joan was still ill) would drive into the town and meet us there, to sort out any difficulties. I protested at the amount of trouble this would put them to, but they shouted my protests down, and Edna said that if she was not allowed to see me off she would give me no more gin that evening. This frightful threat squashed my protests effectively.

So, on the morning of departure, a tractor dragging a giant flat cart arrived outside Charles's house, and the crates of animals were piled up on it and then driven slowly to the station. Here we stacked them on the platform, and awaited the arrival of the train. I felt distinctly less happy when I examined the railway lines. They were worn right down, obviously never having been replaced for years. In places the weight of the train had pushed both the sleeper and the track so far into the ground that, from certain angles, they seemed to disappear altogether. There was such a riot of weeds and grass growing all over the track anyway, that it was difficult enough to see where the railway began and the undergrowth ended. I estimated that if the train travelled at anything more than five miles an hour on such a track we were going to have the train crash of the century.

'This is nothing,' said Charles proudly, when I protested at the state of the lines, 'this is good compared to some parts of the track.'

'And I thought the plane I came in was dangerous enough,' I said, 'but this is pure suicide. You can't even call them railway *lines*, they're both so bent they look like a couple of drunken snakes.'

'Well, we haven't had an accident yet,' said Charles. And with this cheerful news I had to be content. When the train eventually came into view it was so startling that it drove all thoughts about the state of the track out of my head. The carriages were wooden, and looked like the ones you see in old Western films. But it was the engine that was so remarkable. It was obviously an old one, again straight out of a Wild West film, with a gigantic cowcatcher in front. But someone, obviously dissatisfied with its archaic appearance, had attempted to liven it up a bit, and had streamlined it with sheets of metal, painted in broad orange, yellow and scarlet stripes. It was, to say the least, the gayest engine I had ever seen; it looked as though it had just come straight from a carnival as it swept down towards us at a majestic twenty miles an hour, the overgrown track covering the rails so successfully that the thing looked as though it was coming straight across country. It roared into the station with a scream of brakes, and then proudly let out a huge cloud of pungent black smoke that enveloped us all. Hastily we pushed the animal crates into the guard's van, Luna and I went and got ourselves a wooden seat in the compartment next door, and then, with a great jerk and a shudder, the train was off.

For most of the way the road ran parallel with the railway, only separated by a tangle of grass and shrubs and a low barbed-wire fence. So Charles, Helmuth and Edna, drove along parallel with our carriage, shouting insults and abuse at us, shaking their fists and accusing Luna and myself of a rich variety of crimes. The other passengers were at first puzzled, and then, when they realized the joke, they joined in heartily, even suggesting a few choice insults we could shout back. When Helmuth accused Luna of having a voice as sweet as that of a donkey suffering from laryngitis, the orange that Luna hurled out of the train window missed Helmuth's head by only a fraction of an inch. It was childish, but it was fun, and the whole train joined in. At each of the numerous little stations we had to stop at, the idiots in the car would drive on ahead, and be there on the platform to present me with a huge bouquet of wilting flowers, after which I would make a long and impassioned speech in modern Greek out of the train window, to the complete mystification of the passengers who had only just joined the train, and obviously thought that I was some sort of visiting politician. So we enjoyed ourselves hugely until we reached the town where I was to change trains. Here we piled the collection carefully on the platform, posted a porter in charge to keep people from annoying the animals, and went to have a meal, for there were several hours to wait before the Buenos Aires train got in.

When we reassembled dusk had fallen, and the Buenos Aires train puffed and rumbled its way into the station in an impressive cloud of sparks and steam. But it was just an ordinary engine, and bore not the remotest resemblance to the vivid, lurching dragon that had transported us so nobly from Calilegua. Helmuth, Luna and I carefully stacked the animals into the van that I had hired, and which proved to be far smaller than I anticipated. Charles, meanwhile, had run my sleeping berth to earth, and put my things inside. I was to share it with three other people, but none of them was present, and so I could only hope that they would be interesting. Then, with nothing to do but wait for departure, I squatted on the steps leading down from the carriage, while the others gathered in a group around me. Edna fumbled in her bag, and then held up something that glinted in the dim lights of the station. A bottle of gin.

'A parting present,' she said, grinning at me wickedly, 'I could not bear to think of you travelling all that way without any food.'

'Helmuth,' I said, as Luna went off in search of tonic water and glasses. 'You have a wife in a million.'

'Maybe,' said Helmuth gloomily, 'but she only does this for you, Gerry. She never gives me gin when I go away. She just tells me that I drink too much.'

So, standing on the station, we toasted each other. I had just finished my drink when the guard's whistle squealed, and the train started to move. Still clutching their drinks the others ran alongside to shake my hand, and I nearly fell out of the train kissing Edna goodbye. The train gathered speed, and I saw them in a group under the dim station lights, holding up their glasses in a last toast, before they were lost to view, and I went gloomily to my compartment, carrying the remains of the gin.

The train journey was not quite as bad as I had anticipated, although, naturally, travelling on an Argentine train with forty-odd cages of assorted livestock, is no picnic. My chief fear was that during the night (or day) at some station or other, they would shunt my carriage-load of animals into a siding and forget to reattach it. This awful experience had once happened to an animal-collector friend of mine in South America, and by the time he had discovered his loss and raced back to the station in a hired car, nearly all his specimens were dead. So I was determined that, whenever we stopped, night or day, I was going to be out on the platform to make sure my precious cargo was safe. This extraordinary behaviour of leaping out of my bunk in the middle of the night puzzled my sleeping companions considerably. They were three young and charming footballers, returning from Chile where they had been playing. As soon as I explained my actions to them, however, they were full of concern at the amount of sleep I was losing, and insisted on taking turns with me during the night, which they did dutifully during the rest of the trip. To them the whole process must have appeared ludicrous in the extreme, but they treated the matter with great seriousness, and helped me considerably.

Another problem was that I could only get to my animals when the train was in a station, for their van was not connected by the corridor to the rest of the train. Here the sleeping car attendant came into his own. He would warn me ten minutes before we got to a station, and tell me how long we were going to stay there. This gave me time to wend my way down the train until I reached the animal van, and, when the train pulled up, to jump out and minister to their wants.

The three carriages I had to go through to reach the animal van were the third-class parts of the train, and on the wooden benches therein was a solid mass of humanity surrounded by babies, bottles of wine, mothers-in-law, goats, chickens, pigs, baskets of fruit, and other necessities of travel. When this gay, exuberant, garlic-breathing crowd learned the reason for my curious and constant peregrinations to the van at the back, they united in their efforts to help. As soon as the train stopped they would help me out on to the platform, find the nearest water-tap for me, send their children scuttling in all directions to buy me bananas or bread or whatever commodity was needed for the animals, and then, when I had finished my chores, they would hoist me lovingly on board the slowly-moving train, and make earnest inquiries as to the puma's health, or how the birds were standing up to the heat, and was it true that I had a parrot that said '*hijo de puta*'? Then they would offer me sweetmeats, sandwiches, glasses of wine or pots of meat, show me their babies, their goats or chickens or pigs, sing songs for me, and generally treat me as one of the family. They were so charming and kind, so friendly, that when we eventually pulled slowly into the huge, echoing station at Buenos Aires, I was almost sorry the trip was over. The animals were piled into the lorry, my hand was wrung by a hundred people, and we roared off to take the creatures, all of whom had survived the journey remarkably well, to join the rest of the collection in the huge shed in the Museum grounds.

That evening, to my horror, I discovered that a good friend of mine was giving a cocktail party to celebrate my return to Buenos Aires. I hate cocktail parties, but could think of no way of refusing this one without causing offence. So, tired though we were, Sophie and I dolled up and we went. The majority of people there I had never met, and did not particularly want to, but there was the sprinkling of old friends to make it worthwhile. I was standing quietly discussing things of mutual interest with a friend of mine when I was approached by a type that I detest. It is the typical Englishman that seems, like some awful weed, to flourish best in foreign climes. This particular one I had met before, and had not liked. Now he loomed over me, wearing, as if to irritate me still further, his old school tie. He had a face empty of expression, like a badly-made death-mask, and the supercilious, drawing voice that is supposed to prove to the world that even if you have no brains you were well brought up.

'I hear,' he said condescendingly, 'that you've just got back from Jujuy.'

'Yes,' I said shortly.

'By train?' he inquired, with a faint look of distaste.

'Yes,' I said.

'What sort of trip down did you have?' he asked.

'Very nice . . . very pleasant,' I said.
'I suppose there was a very ordinary crowd of chaps on the train,' he said commiseratingly. I looked at him, his dough-like face, his empty eyes, and I remembered my train companions; the burly young footballers who had helped me with the night watches; the old man who had recited *Martin Eierro* to me until, in self-defence, I had been forced to eat some garlic too, between the thirteenth and fourteenth stanzas; the dear old fat lady whom I had bumped into and who had fallen backwards into her basket of eggs, and who refused to let me pay for the damage because, as she explained, she had not laughed so much for years. I looked at this vapid representative of my kind, and I could not resist it.

'Yes,' I said sorrowfully. 'They were a very ordinary crowd of chaps. Do you know that only a few of them wore ties, *and not one of them could speak English?*'

Then I left him to get myself another drink. I felt I deserved it.

The Customs of the Country

When you have a large collection of animals to transport from one end of the world to the other you cannot, as a lot of people seem to think, just hoist them aboard the nearest ship and set off with a gay wave of your hand. There is slightly more to it than this. Your first problem is to find a shipping company who will agree to carry animals. Most shipping people, when you mention the words 'animal cargo' to them grow pale, and get vivid mental pictures of the Captain being eviscerated on the bridge by a jaguar, the First Officer being slowly crushed in the coils of some enormous snake, while the passengers are pursued from one end of the ship to the other by a host of repulsive and deadly beasts of various species. Shipping people, on the whole, seem to be under the impression you want to travel on one of their ships for the sole purpose of releasing all the creatures which you have spent six hard months collecting.

Once, however, you have surmounted this psychological hurdle, there are still many problems. There are consultations with the Chief Steward as to how much refrigerator space you can have for your meat, fish and eggs, without starving the passengers in consequence; the Chief Officer and the Bosun have to be consulted on where and how your cages are to be stacked, and how they are to be secured for rough weather, and how many ships' tarpaulins you can borrow. Then you pay a formal call on the Captain and, generally over a gin, you tell him (almost with tears in your eyes) you will be so little trouble aboard that he won't even notice you are there – a statement which neither he nor you believe. But, most important of all, you generally have to have your collection ready for embarkation a good ten days or so before the ship is scheduled to leave, for a number of things may happen in some ports that will put the sailing date forward, or, more irritatingly, backward, and you have to be on the spot to receive your orders. If there is something like a series of dock strikes to delay a ship, you may be sitting round kicking your heels for a month or more, while your animals' appetites appear to increase in direct proportion to your dwindling finances. The end of a trip is, then, the most harrowing, frustrating, tiring and frightening part. When people ask me about the 'dangers' of my trips I am always tempted to say that the 'dangers' of the forest pale into insignificance as compared with the dangers of being stranded in a remote part of the world with a collection of a hundred and fifty animals to feed, and your money running out.

However, we had now, it seemed, surmounted all these obstacles. A ship had been procured, consultations with the people on board had been satisfactory, food for the animals had been ordered, and everything appeared to be running smoothly. It was at this precise juncture that Juanita, the baby peccary, decided to liven up life for us by catching pneumonia.

The animals, as I have said, were now in a huge shed in the Museum grounds, which had no heating. While this did not appear to worry any of the other animals unduly (although it was the beginning of the Argentine winter and getting progressively colder) Juanita decided to be different. Without so much as a preliminary cough to warn us, Juanita succumbed. In the morning she was full of beans, and devoured her food avidly; in the evening, when we went to cover the animals for the night, she looked decidedly queer. She was, for one thing, *leaning* against the side of her box as if for support, her eyes half-closed, her breathing rapid and rattling in her throat. Hastily I opened the door of the cage and called her. She made a tremendous effort, stood upright shakily, tottered out of the cage and collapsed into my arms. It was in the best cinematic tradition, but rather frightening. As I held her I could hear her breath wheezing and bubbling in her tiny chest, and her body lay in my arms limp and cold.

In order to husband our rapidly decreasing money supplies two friends in Buenos Aires had rallied round and allowed Sophie and me to stay in their respective flats, in order to save on hotel bills. So, while Sophie was ensconced in the flat of Blondie Maitland-Harriot, I was occupying a camp-bed in the flat of one David Jones. At the moment when I discovered Juanita's condition David was with me. As I wrapped her up in my coat I did some rapid thinking. The animal had to have warmth, and plenty of it. But I knew we could not provide it in that great tin barn, even if we lit a bonfire like the Great Fire of London. Blondie already had a sick parrot of mine meditatively chewing the wallpaper off the bathroom in her flat, and I felt it was really carrying friendship too far to ask if I could introduce a peccary as well into her beautifully appointed flat. David had now returned at the double from the Land-Rover whence he had gone to get a blanket to wrap the pig in. In one hand he was clasping a half-bottle of brandy.

'This any good?' he inquired, as I swaddled Juanita in the blanket.

'Yes, wonderful. Look, heat a drop of milk on the spirit stove and mix a teaspoonful of brandy with it, will you?'

While David did this, Juanita, almost invisible in her cocoon of blanket and coat, coughed alarmingly. Eventually, the brandy and milk were ready, and I managed to get two spoonfuls down her throat, though it was a hard job, for she was almost unconscious.

'Anything else we can do,' said David hopefully, for, like me, he had grown tremendously fond of the little pig.

'Yes, she's got to have a whacking great shot of penicillin and as much warmth and fresh air as she can get.'

I looked at him hopefully.

'Let's take her back to the flat,' said David, as I had hoped he would. We wasted no more time. The Land-Rover sped through the rain-glistening streets at a dangerous pace, and how we arrived at the flat intact was a miracle. While I hurried upstairs with Juanita, David rushed round to Blondie's flat, for there Sophie had our medicine chest with the penicillin and the hypodermic syringes.

I laid the by now completely unconscious Juanita on David's sofa, and, although the flat was warm with the central heating, I turned on the electric fire as well, and then opened all the windows that would not create draughts. David was back in an incredibly short space of time, and rapidly we boiled the hypodermic and then I gave Juanita the biggest dose of penicillin I dared. It was, almost, kill or cure, for I had never used penicillin on a peccary before, and for all I knew they might be allergic to it. Then, for an hour, we sat and watched her. At the end of that time I persuaded myself that her breathing was a little easier, but she was still unconscious and I knew she was a very long way from recovery.

'Look,' said David, when I had listened to Juanita's chest for the fourteen-hundredth time, 'are we doing any good, just sitting here looking at her?'

'No,' I said reluctantly, 'I don't think we'll really see any change for about three or four hours, if then. She's right out at the moment, but I think the brandy has a certain amount to do with that.'

'Well,' said David practically, 'let's go and get something to eat at Olly's. I don't know about you, but I'm hungry. We needn't be more than three-quarters of an hour.'

'O.K.,' I said reluctantly, 'I suppose you're right.'

So, having made sure that Juanita was comfortable and that the electric fire could not set fire to her blankets, we drove down to Olly's Music Bar in 25 de Mayo, which is a street that runs along what used to be the old waterfront of Buenos Aires. It is a street lined with tiny clubs, some of which have the most delightful names like 'My Desire,' 'The Blue Moon Hall of Beauties,' and, perhaps slightly more mysteriously, 'Joe's Terrific Display.'

It was not the sort of street a respectable man would be seen in, but I had long ceased to worry about respectability. With my various friends we had visited most of these tiny, dark, smoky bars, and drunk drinks of minute size and colossal price, and watched the female 'hostesses' at their age-old work. But, of all the bars, the one we liked best was Olly's Music Bar, and we always made this our port of call. There were many reasons for liking Olly's. Firstly, was the walnut-wrinkled Olly himself and his lovely wife. Secondly, Olly not only gave you fair measure in your glass, but frequently stood you a drink himself. Thirdly, his bar was well-lit, so that you could actually see your companions; in the other bars you would have had to be a bat or an owl to observe clearly. Fourthly, his hostesses were not allowed to irritate you by constantly suggesting you bought them drinks, and fifthly, there was a brother and sister with a guitar who sang and played delightfully. Lastly, and perhaps most importantly, I have seen the hostesses at Olly's, when their night's work was done, kiss Olly and his wife goodnight as tenderly as if they had been the girls' parents.

So David and I made our way down the stairs into Olly's, and were greeted with delight by Olly and his wife. The reason for our depression being explained the whole bar was full of commiseration; Olly stood us both a large vodka, and the hostesses gathered round us to tell us how they were sure Juanita would get well, and generally tried to cheer us up. But, as we stood there eating hot sausages and sandwiches and consuming vodka, not even the gay *carnavalitos* the brother and sister played and sang specially for us could cure my depression. I felt sure that Juanita was going to die, and I had grown absurdly fond of the little creature. Eventually, when we had eaten and drunk, we said goodbye and climbed the steps that led to the road.

'Come tomorrow and tell us how the animal is,' called Olly.

'*Si, si,*' said the hostesses, like a Greek chorus, 'come tomorrow and tell us how the *pobrecita* is.'

By the time we had got back to David's flat I was convinced that we should find Juanita dead. When we went into the living-room I gazed at the pile of blankets on the sofa, and had to force myself to go and look. I lifted one corner of the blanket gently and a twinkling dark eye gazed up at me lovingly, while a pink plunger-shaped nose wiffled, and a faint, very faint, grunt of pleasure came from the invalid.

'Good God, she's better,' said David incredulously.

'A bit,' I said cautiously. 'She's not out of danger yet, but I think there's a bit of hope.'

As if to second this Juanita gave another grunt.

In order to make sure that Juanita did not kick off her blanket during the night and make her condition worse I took her to bed with me on the sofa. She lay very quietly across my chest and slept deeply. Though her breathing was still wheezy it had lost that awful rasping sound which you could hear with each breath she took to begin with. I was awoken the following morning by a cold, rubbery nose being pushed into my eye, and hearing Juanita's wheezy grunts of greeting. I unwrapped her and saw she was a different animal. Her eyes were bright, her temperature was normal, her breathing was still wheezy, but much more even, and, best of all, she even stood up for a brief, wobbly moment. From then she never looked back. She got better by leaps and bounds, but the better she felt the worse patient she made. As soon as she could walk without falling over every two steps, she insisted on spending the day trotting about the room, and was most indignant because I made her wear a small blanket, safety-pinned under her chin, like a cloak. She ate like a horse, and we showered delicacies on her. But it was during the nights that I found her particularly trying. She thought this business of sleeping with me a terrific idea, and, flattering though this was, I did not agree. We seemed to have different ideas about the purposes for which one went to bed. I went in order to sleep, while Juanita thought it was the best time of the day for a glorious romp. A baby peccary's tusks and hooves are extremely sharp, and their noses are hard, rubbery and moist, and to have all these three weapons applied to one's anatomy when one is trying to drift off into a peaceful sleep is trying, to put it mildly. Sometimes she would do a sort of porcine tango with her sharp hooves along my stomach and chest, and at other times she would simply chase her tail round and round, until I began to feel like the unfortunate victim in *The Pit and the Pendulum*. She would occasionally break off her little dance in order to come and stick her wet nose into my eye, to see how I was enjoying it. At other times she would become obsessed with the idea that I had, concealed about my person somewhere, a rare delicacy. It may have been truffles for all I know, but whatever it was she could make a thorough search with nose, tusks and hooves, grunting shrilly and peevishly when she couldn't find anything. Round about three a.m. she would sink into a deep, untroubled sleep. Then, at five-thirty, she would take a quick gallop up and down my body to make sure I woke up in good shape. This lasted for four soul-searing nights, until I felt she was sufficiently recovered, and then I banished her to a box at night, to her intense and vocal indignation.

I had only just pulled Juanita round in time, for no sooner was she better than we got a message to say that the ship was ready to leave. I would have hated to have undertaken a voyage with Juanita as sick as she had been, for I am sure she would have died.

So, on the appointed day, our two lorry-loads of equipment and animal-cages rolled down to the dock, followed by the Land-Rover, and then began the prolonged and exhausting business of hoisting the animals on board, and arranging the cages in their places on the hatch. This is always a nerve-racking time, for as the great nets, piled high with cages, soar into the air, you are always convinced that a rope is going to break and deposit your precious animals either into the sea or else in a mangled heap on the dockside. But, by evening, the last cage was safely aboard, and the last piece of equipment stowed away in the hold, and we could relax.

All our friends were there to see us off, and, if in one or two people's eyes was a semi-repressed expression of relief, who was to blame them, for I had made martyrs of them all in one way or another. However, we were all exhausted but relaxed, ploughing our way through a series of bottles I had had the foresight to order in my cabin. Everything was on board, everything was safe, and now all we had to do was to have a farewell drink, for in an hour the ship was sailing. Just as I was replenishing everyone's glass for the fifth toast, a little man in Customs uniform appeared in the cabin doorway, rustling a sheaf of papers. I gazed at him fondly, without any premonition of danger.

'Señor Durrell?' he asked politely.

'Señor Garcia?' I inquired.

'*Si*,' he said, flushing with pleasure that I should know his name, 'I am Señor Garcia of the Aduana.'

It was Marie who scented danger.

'Is anything wrong?' she asked.

'*Si, si, señorita*, the señor's papers are all in order, but they have not been signed by a *despachante*.'

'What on earth's a *despachante?*' I asked.

'It is a sort of man,' said Marie worriedly, and turned back to the little Customs man. 'But is this essential, señor?'

'*Si, señorita,*' he said gravely, 'without the *despachante*'s signature we cannot let the animals be taken. They will have to be unloaded.'

I felt as though someone had removed my entire stomach in one piece, for we had about three-quarters of an hour.

'But is there no *despachante* here who will sign it?' asked Marie.

'Señorita, it is late, they have all gone home,' said Señor Garcia.

This is, of course, the sort of situation which takes about twenty years off your life. I could imagine the shipping company's reaction if we now went to them and told them that, instead of gaily casting off for England in an hour's time, they would be delayed five hours or so while they unloaded all my animals from the hatch, and, what was worse, all my equipment and the Land-Rover which were deep in the bowels of the ship. But by now my friends, unfortunate creatures, were used to crises like this, and they immediately burst into activity. Mercedes, Josefina, Rafael and David went to argue with the Chief of Customs on duty, while Willie Anderson, another friend of ours, went off with Marie to the private home of a *despachante* he knew. This was on the outskirts of Buenos Aires, so they would have to drive like the devil to get back in time. The happy farewell party burst like a bomb and our friends all fled in different directions. Sophie and I could only wait and hope, while I mentally rehearsed how I would phrase the news to the Captain, without being seriously maimed, if we had to unload everything.

Presently the party who had been arguing with the Chief of Customs returned despondently.

'No use,' said David, 'he's adamant. No signature, no departure.'

'He is very much what you call a stupid buggler,' said Josefina, and then, struck by a thought, 'Gerry, tell me what does this word buggler mean? I look her up in dictionary and all I find is a man who plays a buggle. That is not insulting, no?'

But I was in no condition to help Josefina out with her English translations. We had twenty minutes to go. At that moment we heard a car screech to a halt on the dock outside. We piled out on to the deck, and there, coming up the gangway, smiling triumphantly, were Marie and Willie, waving the necessary document, all beautifully signed by what must be the finest, noblest *despachante* in the business. So, with ten minutes to go we all had a drink. I even gave Señor Garcia one.

Then the steward poked his head in to say that we could be casting off in a moment, and we trooped on to the deck. We said our goodbyes, and our tribe of friends made their way down on to the quay. Ropes were cast off, and slowly the gap between the ship and the dock widened, so that we could see the shuddering reflection of the quay lights in the dark waters. Presently the ship gained speed, and soon our friends were lost to sight, and all we could see was the great heap of multicoloured lights that was Buenos Aires.

As we turned away from the rail and made our way to our cabins, I remembered Darwin's words, written a century before. When speaking of the travelling naturalist he said: '*he will discover how many truly kind-*

hearted people there are with whom he had never before had, or ever again will have, any further communication, who yet are ready to offer him the most disinterested assistance.'

Stop Press

For those that are interested here is an up-to-date account of the creatures we brought back. Claudius the tapir, whom I could once lift up in my arms – at the risk of a rupture – is now the size of a pony, and eagerly awaiting a bride when we can afford one.

Mathias and Martha, the coatimundis, have settled down to domestic bliss and have produced two sets of children. Martha, at the time of writing, is again in an interesting condition.

Juan and Juanita, the peccaries, also had two sets of babies, and are expecting a third.

Luna, the puma, the ocelot and the Geoffroy's cat are all flourishing, getting fatter with each passing day.

Blanco, the Tucuman Amazon, still says '*Hijo de puta*,' but very softly now.

All the other birds, beasts and reptiles are equally well, and many showing signs of wanting to breed.

Which leaves me with only one thing to say and thus, I hope, stop people writing to ask me: my zoo is a private one, but it is open to the public every day of the year except Christmas Day.

So come and see us.

Acknowledgements

As always after an expedition there are those people to whom one's gratitude is so immense that there is no way of adequately thanking them. All I can do is reiterate once more how much I appreciated their help and encouragement.

Buenos Aires

The entire de Sota family; the entire Rodrigues family; our dear friend Bebita Ferreyra; Lassie Greenslet; David Jones; Josefina Pueyrredon; Dicky de Sola; Brian Dean; Bill Partridge; and Willie Anderson.

All these people assisted us in countless ways, giving advice and helping us clear our equipment through the Customs; entertaining us lavishly and acting as drivers, translators, guides, carpenters and cooks, on our behalf.

People whose patience we tried, and whose houses and places of work we infested with our animals are: Blondie Maitland-Harriot; Mrs Dorothy Krotow; Dr Mario Teruggi. To them all we – and our animals – are most grateful.

To Dr Carlos Godoy, my special thanks, as he was so efficient and helpful over our collecting permits and in furnishing us with letters of introduction to many throughout the Argentine.

Dr Cabrera, was extremely helpful in giving us information regarding the Argentine fauna.

Mr Salmon of Bovril, Ltd was most kind and helpful. Mr Blackburn of Chadwick Weir arranged for the transportation of the entire collection and equipment from the Argentine, a massive undertaking.

Puerto Deseado

To Señor Huichi for his help we simply cannot express our gratitude enough. Captain Giri was instrumental in introducing us to Señor Huichi and for helping us find the penguin colonies. For both of these things we were most grateful. Mr Bateman, the British Vice-Consul, and his wife assisted us in every way possible, as did Mr and Mrs Roberts the local Postmaster and his wife. All these people did their utmost to make our stay in Deseado a pleasant one.

Puerto Madryn

The manager of the Hotel Playa, not only provided us with accommodation but lent us money, sent telegrams for us and helped us in every other way he could.

Jujuy

Charles and Joan Lett; Edna and Helmuth Vorbach; Luna, a very good friend, and everyone at Calilegua accepted me into their midst and did everything to help me build up my collection of animals, make my film and arrange everything for my comfort and salvation. Without them all I would have been lost.

Mendoza

Dr Menoprio, who was so kind to us in many ways.

Britain

Mr Peter Newborne of C.A.P., who was his usual helpful self and did all he could to assist us in the complicated matters of customs facilities, etc. Dr Don Alberto Candiotti the former Argentine Ambassador in London, who gave the whole expedition his official blessing and encouraged us in every way. Mr Lawton Johnson of Bovril, arranged for us to visit the various Bovril estates in the Argentine, which, unfortunately, we were unable to do; Mr Flack and Mr Aggett of Blue Star Line, arranged passages for us all. The South American Saint Line, kindly agreed to transport my entire collection and all my equipment from Buenos Aires to England, and in this connection I would like to thank the Captain and crew of the M.V. *St John* for enabling the return voyage to go smoothly, which was due entirely to their help and kindness.

The following British manufacturers supplied us with various equipment, without which the expedition would have been a complete failure. The Rover Company supplied us with our Land-Rover, in which we were able to travel all over the Argentine, and Mr Baldwin and Mr Bradley of the Company's Sales and Publicity Dept were extremely kind and helpful in enabling us to have this vehicle.

The Directors of William Smith (Poplar) Ltd, The British Nylon Spinners Ltd, and Greengate & Irwell Rubber Co. Ltd, continue to earn our deep gratitude for the wonderful tarpaulins and animal shelters that they gave us on a previous trip. These articles, which are in constant use have proved absolutely invaluable.

Finally, may we thank all those both here and in the Argentine who have helped us in many small ways, but without whose help the expedition could not have been successful.

Menagerie Manor
GERALD DURRELL

Menagerie Manor

For
HOPE AND JIMMY
In memory of overdrafts, tranquillizers
and revolving creditors

Explanation

Dear Sir,
We should like to draw your attention to the fact that your account with us is now overdrawn ...

Most children at the tender age of six or so are generally full of the most impractical schemes for becoming policemen, firemen or engine drivers when they grow up, but when I was that age I could not be bothered with such mundane ambitions; I knew exactly what I was going to do: I was going to have my own zoo. At the time this did not seem to me (and still does not seem) a very unreasonable or outrageous ambition. My friends and relatives – who had long thought that I was mental owing to the fact that I evinced no interest in anything that did not have fur, feathers, scales or chiton – accepted this as just another manifestation of my weak state of mind. They felt that, if they ignored my oft-repeated remarks about owning my own zoo, I would eventually grow out of it. As the years passed, however, to the consternation of my friends and relatives, my resolve to have my own zoo grew greater and greater, and eventually, after going on a number of expeditions to bring back animals for other zoos, I felt the time was ripe to acquire my own.

From my last trip to West Africa I had brought back a considerable collection of animals which were ensconced in my sister's suburban garden in Bournemouth. They were there, I assured her, only temporarily because I was completely convinced that any intelligent council, having a ready-made zoo planted on its doorstep, would do everything in its power to help one by providing a place to keep it. After eighteen months of struggle, I was not so sure of the go-ahead attitude of local councils, and my sister was utterly convinced that her back garden would go on forever looking like a scene out of one of the more flamboyant Tarzan pictures. At last, bogged down by the constipated mentality of local government and frightened off by the apparently endless rules and regulations under which every free man in Great Britain has to suffer, I decided to investigate the possibility of starting my zoo in the Channel Islands. I was given an introduction to one Major Fraser who, I was assured, was a broad-minded, kindly soul, and would show me round the Island of Jersey and point out suitable sites.

My wife, Jacquie, and I flew to Jersey where we were met by Hugh Fraser who drove us to his family home, probably one of the most beautiful manor houses on the Island: here was a huge walled garden dreaming in the thin sunlight; a great granite wall, thickly planted with waterfalls of rock plants; fifteenth-century arches, tidy lawns and flowerbeds brimming over with colour. All the walls, buildings and outhouses were of beautiful Jersey granite which contains all the subtle colourings of a heap of autumn leaves and they glowed in the sunshine and seduced me into making what was probably the silliest remark of the century. Turning to Jacquie, I said:

'What a marvellous place for a zoo.'

If Hugh Fraser, as my host, had promptly fainted on the spot, I could scarcely have blamed him: in those lovely surroundings the thought of implanting the average person's idea of a zoo (masses of grey cement and steel bars) was almost high treason. To my astonishment Hugh Fraser did not faint but merely cocked an enquiring eyebrow at me and asked whether I really meant what I said. Slightly embarrassed, I replied that I had meant it, but added hastily that I realized it was impossible. Hugh said he did not think it was as impossible as all that. He went on to explain that the house and grounds were too big for him to keep up as a private individual, and so he wanted to move into a smaller place in England. Would I care to consider renting the property for the purpose of establishing my zoo? I could not conceive a more attractive setting for my purpose, and, by the time lunch was over, the bargain had been sealed and I was the new 'Lord' of the Manor of Les Augres in the Parish of Trinity.

The alarm and despondency displayed by all who knew me when I announced this, can be imagined. The only one who seemed relieved by the news was my sister, who pointed out that, although she thought the whole thing was a hare-brained scheme, at least it would rid her back garden of some two hundred assorted denizens of the jungle, which were at that time putting a great strain on her relationship with the neighbours.

To complicate things even more, I did not want a simple straightforward zoo, with the ordinary run of animals: the idea behind my zoo was to aid in the preservation of animal life. All over the world various species are being exterminated or cut down to remnants of their former numbers by the spread of civilization. Many of the larger species are of commercial or touristic value, and, as such, are receiving the most attention. Yet, scattered about all over the world, are a host of fascinating small mammals, birds and reptiles, and scant attention is being paid to their preservation, as they are neither edible nor wearable, and of little interest to the tourist who demands lions and rhinos. A great number of these are island fauna, and as such their habitat is small. The slightest interference with this, and they will vanish forever: the casual introduction of rats, say, or pigs could destroy one of these island species within a year. One has only to remember the sad fate of the dodo to realize this.

The obvious answer to this whole problem is to see that the creature is adequately protected in the wild state so that it does not become extinct, but this is often easier said than done. However, while pressing for this protection, there is another precaution that can be taken, and that is to build up under controlled conditions breeding stocks of these creatures in parks or zoos, so that, should the worst happen and the species become extinct in the wild state, you have, at least, not lost it forever. Moreover, you have a breeding stock from which you can glean the surplus animals and reintroduce them into their original homes at some future date. This, it has always seemed to me, should be the main function of any zoo, but it is only recently that the majority of zoos have woken up to this fact and tried to do anything about it. I wanted this to be the main function of my zoo. However, like all altruistic ideas, it was going to cost money. It was, therefore, obvious the zoo would have to be run on purely commercial lines to begin with, until it was self-supporting. Then one could start on the real work of the zoo: building up breeding stocks of rare creatures.

So this is the story of our trials and tribulations in taking the first step towards a goal which I think is of great importance.

Chapter One
Menagerie Manor

Dear Mr Durrell,
I am eighteen years old strong in wind and limb having read your books can I have a job in your zoo . . .

It is one thing to visit a zoo as an ordinary member of the public but quite another to own a zoo and live in the middle of it: this at times can be a mixed blessing. It certainly enables you to rush out at any hour of the day or night to observe your charges, but it also means that you are on duty twenty-four hours a day, and you find that a cosy little dinner party disintegrates because some animal has broken its leg, or because the heaters in the Reptile House have failed, or for any one of a dozen reasons. Winter, of course, is your slack period, and sometimes days on end pass without a single visitor in the grounds and you begin to feel that the zoo is really your own private one. The pleasantness of this sensation is more than slightly marred by the alarm with which you view the mounting of your bills and compare them to the lack of gate-money. But in the season the days are so full and the visitors so numerous that you hardly seem to notice the passing of time, and you forget your overdraft.

The average zoo day begins just before dawn; the sky will be almost imperceptibly tinged with yellow when you are awakened by the bird-song. At first, still half asleep, you wonder whether you are in Jersey or back in the tropics, for you can hear a robin chanting up the sun, and, accompanying it, the rich, fruity, slightly hoarse cries of the touracous. Then a blackbird flutes joyfully, and as the last of his song dies the white-headed jay thrush bursts into an excited, liquid babble. As the sky lightens, this confused and cosmopolitan orchestra gathers momentum, a thrush vies with the loud, imperious shouts of the seriamas, and the witches' cackle from the covey of magpies contrasts with the honking of geese and the delicate, plaintive notes of the diamond doves. Even if you survive this musical onslaught and can drift into a doze again, you are suddenly and rudely awakened by something that resembles the strange, deep vibrating noise that a telegraph pole makes in a high wind. This acts upon you with the same disruptive effect of an alarm clock, for it is the warning that Trumpy has appeared, and if you have been foolish enough to leave your window wide open you have to take immediate defensive action. Trumpy is a grey-winged trumpeter, known to his more intimate ornithologist friends as *Psophia crepitans*. His function in the Zoo is three-fold – combined guide, settler-in and village idiot. He looks, to be frank, like a badly made chicken, clad in sombre plumage as depressing as Victorian mourning: dark feathers over most of his body and what appears to be a shot-silk cravat at his throat. The whole ensemble is enlivened by a pair of ash-grey wings. He has dark, liquid eyes and a high, domed forehead which argues a brainpower which he does not possess.

Trumpy – for some reason best known to himself – is firmly convinced that his first duty of each day should be to fly into one's bedroom and acquaint one with what has been going on in the Zoo during the night. His motives are not entirely altruistic, for he also hopes to have his head scratched. If you are too deeply asleep – or too lazy – to leap out of bed at his greeting cry, he hops from the window-sill on to the dressing table, decorates it extravagantly, wags his tail vigorously in approval of his action, and then hops on to the bed and proceeds to walk up and down, thrumming like a distraught cello until he is assured that he has your full attention. Before he can produce any more interesting designs on the furniture or carpet, you are forced to crawl out of bed, stalk and catch him (a task fraught with difficulty, since he is so agile and you are so somnambulistic), and push him out on to the window-ledge and close the window so that he cannot force his way in again. Trumpy now having awakened you, you wonder sleepily whether it is worth going back to bed, or whether you should get up. Then from beneath the window will come a series of five or six shrill cries for help, apparently delivered by a very inferior soprano in the process of having her throat cut. Looking out into the courtyard, on the velvet-green lawns by the lavender hedge, you can see an earnest group of peahens searching the dewy grass, while around them their husband pirouettes, his shining and burnished tail raised like a fantastic, quivering fountain in the sunlight. Presently he will lower his tail, and throwing back his head will deafen the morning with his nerve-shattering cries. At eight o'clock the staff arrive, and you hear them shouting greetings to each other, amid the clank of buckets and the swish of brushes, which all but drowns the bird-song. You slip on your clothes and go out into the cool, fresh morning to see if all is right with the Zoo.

In the long, two-storied granite house – once a large cider press and now converted for monkeys and other mammals – everything is bustle and activity. The gorillas have just been let out of their cage, while it is being cleaned, and they gallop about the floor with the exuberance of children just out of school, endeavouring to pull down the notices, wrench the electric heaters from their sockets or break the fluorescent lights. Stefan, brush in hand, stands guard over the apes, watching with a stern eye, to prevent them from doing more damage than is absolutely necessary. Inside the gorillas' cage Mike, rotund and perpetually smiling, and Jeremy, with his Duke of Wellington nose and his barley-sugar-coloured hair, would be busy, sweeping up the mess that the gorillas' tenancy of the previous day entailed and scattering fresh, white sawdust in snowdrifts over the floor. Everything, they assure you, is all right: nothing has developed any malignant symptoms during the night. All the animals, excited and eager at the start of a new day, bustle about their cages and shout 'Good morning' to you. Etam, the black Celebes ape, looking like a satanic imp, clings to the wire, baring his teeth at you in greeting and making shrill, chuckling noises. The woolly-coated orange-eyed mongoose lemurs bound from branch to branch, wagging their long thick tails like dogs, and calling to each other in a series of loud and astonishingly pig-like grunts. Farther down, sitting on his hind-legs, his prehensile tail wrapped round a branch, and surveying his quarters with the air of someone who has just received the freedom of the city, is Binty, the binturong, who suggests a badly-made hearthrug, to one end of which has been attached a curiously oriental-like head with long ear-tufts and circular, protuberant and somewhat vacant eyes. The next door cage appears to be empty, but run your fingers along the wire and a troupe of diminutive marmosets comes tumbling out of their box of straw, twittering and trilling like a group of canaries. The largest of these is Whiskers, the emperor tamarin, whose sweeping snow-white Colonel Blimp moustache quivers majestically as he gives you greeting by opening wide his mouth and vibrating his tongue rapidly up and down.

Upstairs, the parrots and parakeets salute you with a cacophony of sound: harsh screams, squeakings resembling unoiled hinges, and cries that vary from 'I'm a very fine bird,' from Suku, the grey parrot, to the more personal 'Hijo de puta,' squawked by Blanco, the Tucuman Amazon. Farther along, the genets, beautifully blotched in dark chocolate on their golden pelts, move as quicksilver through the branches of their cage. They are so long and lithe and sensuous that they seem more like snakes than mammals. Next door, Queenie, the tree ocelot, her paws demurely folded, gazes at you with great amber eyes, gently twitching the end of her tail. A host of quick-footed, bright-eyed, inquisitive-faced mongooses patter busily about their cages, working up an appetite. The hairy armadillo lies supine on its back, paws and nose twitching, and its pink and wrinkled stomach heaving as it dreams sweet dreams of vast plates of food. You reflect, as you look at it, that it is about time it went on a diet again, otherwise it will have difficulty in walking, and you make a bet with yourself as to how many visitors that day would come to tell you that the armadillo was on its back and apparently dying: the record to date had been fifteen visitors in one day.

Outside, the clank of a bucket, the burst of whistling, herald the approach of Shep, curly-haired and with a most disarming grin. As his real name is John Mallet it was inevitable that he should be called Shepton Mallet which, in turn, has degenerated into Shep. You walk up the broad main drive with him, past the long twelve-foot-high granite wall ablaze with flowering rock plants, and down to the sunken water-meadow where the swans and ducks swim eagerly to welcome him as he empties out the bucket of food at the edge of the water. Having ascertained from Shep that none of his bird charges have during the night sickened or died or laid eggs, you continue on your tour.

The Bird House is aburst with song and movement. Birds of every shape and colour squabble, eat, flutter and sing, so the whole thing would resemble a market or a fairground alight with bright colours. Here a toucan cocks a knowing eye at you and clatters his huge beak with a sound like a football rattle; here a black-faced lovebird, looking as though he had just come from a minstrel show, waddles across to his water-dish and proceeds to bathe himself with such vigour that all the other occupants of the cage receive the benefit of his bathwater; a pair of tiny, fragile diamond doves are dancing what appears to be a minuet together, turning round and round, bowing and changing places, calling in their soft, ringing voices some sort of endearments to each other.

You pass slowly down the house to the big cage at the end where the touracous now live. The male, Peety, I had hand-reared while in West Africa. He peers at you from one of the higher perches and then, if you call to him, he will fly down in a graceful swoop, land on the perch nearest to you and start to peck eagerly at your fingers. Then he will throw back his head, his throat swelling, and give his loud, husky cry: 'Caroo ... Caroo ... Caroo ... coo ... coo ... coo.' Touracous are really one of the most beautiful of birds. Peety's tail and wings are a deep metallic blue, while his breast, head and neck are a rich green, the feathering so fine and shining that it looks like spun glass. When he flies, you can see the undersides of his wings, which flash a glorious magenta red. This red is caused by a substance in the feathers, called turacin, and it is possible to wash it out of the feathers. Place a touracou's wing feather in a glass of plain water, and presently you will find the water tinged with pink, as though a few crystals of permanganate of potash had been dissolved in it. Having dutifully listened to Peety and his wife sing a duet together, you now make your way out of the Bird House.

Dodging the exuberant welcome of the chimpanzees who prove their interest in your well-being by hurling bits of fruit – and other less desirable substances – with unerring accuracy through the wire of their cage, you walk to the Reptile House. Here in a pleasant temperature of eighty degrees the reptiles doze. Snakes regard you calmly with lidless eyes, frogs gulp as though just about to succumb to a bout of sobs, and lizards lie draped over rocks and tree-trunks, exquisitely languid and sure of themselves. In the cage which contains the Fernand skinks I had caught in the Cameroons, you can dig your hands into the damp, warm soil at the bottom of it and haul them out of their subterranean burrow, writhing and biting indignantly. They have recently shed their skins, and so they look as though they have been newly varnished. You admire their red, yellow and white markings on the glossy black background, and then let them slide through your fingers and watch as they burrow like bulldozers into the earth. John Hartley appears, tall and lanky, bearing two trays of chopped fruit and vegetables for the giant tortoises. The previous night had been a good feeding one, he tells you. The boa-constrictors had had two guinea pigs each, while the big reticulated python had engulfed a very large rabbit, and lies there bloated and lethargic to prove it. The horned toads, looking more like bizarre pottery figures than ever, had stuffed themselves on baby chickens, and, according to their size, the smaller snakes were busily digesting white rats or mice.

Round the back of the house are some more of the monkey collection that have just been let out into their outdoor cages: Frisky, the mandrill, massive and multi-coloured as a technicolored sunset, picks over a huge pile of fruit and vegetables, grunting and gurgling to himself; farther along, Tarquin, the cherry-crowned mangabey, with his grey fur, his mahogany-coloured skull-cap and his white eyelids, goes carefully through the fur of his wife, while she lies on the floor of the cage as though dead. Periodically he finds a delectable fragment of salt in her fur and pops it into his mouth. One is reminded of the small boy who had witnessed this operation with fascinated eyes and had then shouted: 'Hi, Mum, come and see this monkey eating the other one.'

Up in their paddock the tapirs, Claudius and Claudette, portly, Roman-nosed and benign, play with Willie, the black and white cat, who guards the aviaries nearby from the rats. Willie lies on his back and pats gently at the whiffling, rubbery noses of the tapirs as they sniff and nuzzle him. Eventually tiring of the game, he would rise and start to move off, whereupon one of the tapirs would reach forward and tenderly engulf Willie's tail in its mouth and pull him back, so that he would continue this game of which they never seemed to tire. In the walled garden the lions, butter-fat and angry-eyed, lie in the sun, while near them the cheetahs would be languidly asprawl amid the buttercups, merging with the flowers so perfectly that they became almost invisible.

At ten o'clock the gates open and the first coach-loads of people arrive. As they come flooding into the grounds, everyone has to be on the alert, not, as you may think, to ensure that the animals do not hurt the people, but to ensure that the people do not hurt the animals. If an animal is asleep, they want to throw stones at it or prod it with sticks to make it move. We have found visitors endeavouring to give the chimpanzees lighted cigarettes and razor-blades; monkeys have been given lipsticks which, of course, they thought were some exotic fruit and devoured accordingly, only to develop acute colic. One pleasant individual (whom we did not catch, unfortunately) pushed a long cellophane packet full of aspirins into the chinchilla cage. For some obscure reason one chinchilla decided that this was the food it had been waiting for all its life and had eaten most of it before we came on the scene: it died the next day. The uncivilized behaviour of some human beings in a zoo has to be seen to be believed.

Now, there might be any one of fifty jobs to do. Perhaps you go to the workshop where Les, with his craggy face and bright eyes, is busy on some repair work or other. Les is one of those people who are God's gift to a zoo, for no job defeats him and his ingenuity is incredible. He is like a one-man building firm, for he can do anything from welding to dovetailing, from cementing to electrical maintenance. You discuss with him the new line of cages you are planning, their size and shape, and whether they should have swing doors, or whether sliding doors would be more convenient.

Having thrashed out this problem, you remember that one of the giant tortoises had to have an injection. On your way to deliver this, you pass an excited crowd of North country people round the mandrill cage, watching Frisky as he stalks up and down, grunting to himself, presenting now his vivid, savagely beautiful face, and now his multi-coloured rear to their eyes.

'Ee,' says one woman in wonderment, 'you can't tell front from back.'

Lunchtime comes and so far the day has progressed smoothly. As you sit down to eat, you wonder if there will be a crisis during the afternoon: will the ladies' lavatories overflow, or, worse still, will it start to rain and thus put off all the people who are intending to visit the Zoo? Lunch over, you see that the sky is, to your relief, still a sparkling blue. You decide to go down and look at the penguin pond, for which you have certain ideas of improvement.

You scuttle surreptitiously out of the house, but not surreptitiously enough, for both your wife and your secretary catch you in rapid succession and remind you that two reviews and an article are a week overdue and that your agent is baying like a bloodhound for the manuscript you promised him eighteen months previously. Assuring them, quite untruthfully, that you will be back very shortly, you make your way down to the penguins.

On the way you meet Stefan grinning to himself, and on asking him what the joke is, he tells you that he was in one of the lions' dens, cleaning it out, when, glancing over his shoulder, he was surprised to see a visitor standing there, using the place as a lavatory.

'What are you doing?' enquired Stefan.

'Well, this is the gents', isn't it?' replied the man peevishly.

'No, it isn't. It's the lions' den,' replied Stefan.

Never had an exit been so rapidly performed from a public convenience, he told me.

Having worked out a complicated but very beautiful plan for the penguin pool, you then have to work out an equally complicated and beautiful plan for getting the scheme passed by Catha, the administrative secretary, who holds the Zoo's purse-strings in a grip so firm it requires as much ingenuity to prise money out of it as it would do to extract a coin from a Scotsman's sporran. You march to the office, hoping to find her in a sunny, reckless mood, instead of which she is glowering over an enormous pile of ledgers. Before you can start extolling the virtues of your penguin pond idea, she fixes you with a gimlet green eye and in a voice like a honey-covered razor-blade informs you that your last brilliant idea came to approximately twice what you had estimated. You express bewilderment at this and gaze suspiciously at the ledger, implying, without saying so, that her addition must be wrong. She obligingly does the sum in front of you, so that there will be no argument. Feeling that this precise moment is not perhaps the best one to broach the subject of the penguin pond, you back hastily out of the office and go back into the Zoo.

You are spending a pleasant ten minutes making love to the woolly monkeys through the wire of their cage, when suddenly your secretary materializes at your elbow in the most unnerving fashion, and before you can think up a suitable excuse she has reminded you once more about the reviews, the article and the book, and has dragged you disconsolately back to your office.

As you sit there racking your brains to try to think of something tactful to say about a particularly revolting book that has been sent to you for review, a constant procession of people appear to distract your attention. Catha comes in with the minutes of the last meeting, closely followed by Les who wants to know what mesh of wire to put on the new cage. He is followed by John who wants to know if the mealworms have arrived, as he is running short, and then Jeremy appears to tell you that the dingos have just had eleven pups. I defy any writer to write a good review when his mind is occupied with the insoluble problem of what to do with eleven dingo pups.

Eventually, you manage to finish the review and slip once more into the Zoo. It is getting towards evening now and the crowds are thinning out, drifting away up the main drive to the car park, to wait for their buses or coaches. The slanting rays of the sun floodlight the cage in which the crowned pigeons live: giant powder-blue birds with scarlet eyes and a quivering crest of feathers as fine as maidenhair fern. In the warmth of the setting sun they are displaying to each other, raising their maroon-coloured wings over their backs, like tombstone angels, bowing and pirouetting to one another and then uttering their strange, booming cries. The chimpanzees are starting to scream peevishly, because it is nearing the time for their evening milk, but they pause in their hysterical duet to utter greeting to you as you pass.

Up in the Small Mammal House the night creatures are starting to come to life, creatures that all day long have been nothing but gently snoring bundles of fur: bushbabies with their enormous, perpetually horrified eyes, creep out of their straw beds and start to bound about their cages, silently as thistledown, occasionally stopping by a plate to stuff a handful of writhing mealworms into their mouths; pottos, looking like miniature teddy-bears, prowl about the branches of their cage, wearing guilty, furtive expressions, as though they were a convention of cat burglars; the hairy armadillo, you are relieved to see, has roused itself out of its stupor and is now the right way up, puttering to and fro like a clockwork toy.

Downstairs, with growls of satisfaction, the gorillas are receiving their milk. Nandy likes to drink hers lying on her stomach, sipping it daintily from a stainless steel dish. N'Pongo has no use for this feminine nonsense and takes his straight from the bottle, holding it carefully in his great black hands. He likes to drink his milk sitting up on the perch, staring at the end of the bottle with intense concentration. Jeremy has to stand guard, for when N'Pongo has drained the last dregs he will just simply open his hands and let the bottle drop, to shatter on the cement floor. All round, the monkeys are gloating over their evening ration of bread and milk, uttering muffled cries of delight as they stuff their mouths and the milk runs down their chins.

Walking up towards the main gate you hear the loud ringing cries of the sarus cranes: tall, elegant grey birds with heads and necks the colour of faded red velvet. They are performing their graceful courting dance in the last rays of the sun, against a background of blue and mauve hydrangea. One will pick up a twig or a tuft of grass, and then, with wings held high, will twirl and leap with it, tossing it into the air and prancing on its long slender legs, while the other one watches it and bows as if in approval. The owls are now showing signs of animation. Woody, the Woodford's owl, clicks his beak reprovingly at you, as you peer into his cage, and over his immense eyes he lowers blue lids with sweeping eyelashes that would be the envy of any film star. The white-faced Scops owls that have spent all day pretending to be grey, decaying tree stumps, now open large, golden eyes and peer at you indignantly.

Shadows are creeping over the flower beds and the rockery. The peacock, as exhausted as an actor at the end of a long run, passes slowly towards the walled garden, dragging his burnished tail behind him and leading his vacant-eyed harem towards their roosting place. Sitting on top of the granite cross that surmounts the great arch leading into the courtyard, is our resident robin. He has a nest in a crevice of the wall, half hidden under a waterfall of blue-flowered rock plants. So, as his wife warms her four eggs, he sits on top of the cross and sings his heart out, gazing raptly at the western sky where the setting sun has woven a sunset of gold and green and blue.

As the light fades, the robin eventually ceases to sing and flies off to roost in the mimosa tree. All the day noises have now ceased and there is a short period of quietness before the night cries take over. It is started inevitably by the owls – beak-clicking and a noise like tearing calico from the whitefaced Scops owls, a long, tremulous and surprised hoot from the Woodford's owl, and a harsh, jeering scream from the Canadian horned owls. Once the owls have started, they are generally followed by the Andean fox who sits forlornly in the centre of his cage, throws back his head and yaps shrilly at the stars. This sets off the dingos in the next cage and they utter a series of gently melodious howls that are so weird and so mournful they make you want to burst into tears. Not to be outdone, the lions take up the song – deep, rasping, full-throated roars that tail off into a satisfied gurgle that sounds unpleasantly as though they have just found a hole in the wire.

In the Reptile House snakes that had been so lethargic all day now slide round their cages, bright-eyed, eager, their tongues flicking as they explore every nook and cranny for food. The geckos, with enormous, golden eyes, hang upside down on the roof of their cage, or else with infinite caution stalk a dishful of writhing mealworms. The tiny, yellow and black corroboree frogs (striped like bulls' eyes and the size of a cigarette butt) periodically burst into song: thin, reedy piping that has a metallic quality about it, as if someone were tapping a stone with a tiny hammer. Then they relapse into silence and gaze mournfully at the ever-circling crowd of fruit flies that live in their cage and form part of their diet.

Outside, the lions, the dingos and the fox are quiet; the owls keep up their questioning cries. There is a sudden chorus of hysterical screams from the chimpanzees' bedroom and you know that they are quarrelling about who should have the straw.

In the Mammal House the gorillas are now asleep, lying side by side on their shelf, pillowing their heads on their arms. They screw up their eyes in your torch beam and utter faint indignant growls that you should disturb them. Next door, the orang-utans, locked passionately in each other's arms, snore so loudly that it seems as though the very floor vibrates. In all the cages there is deep relaxed breathing from sleeping monkeys, and the only sound apart from this is the steady patter of claws as the nine-banded armadillo, who always seems to suffer from insomnia, trots about his cage, making and remaking his bed, carefully gathering all the straw into one corner, smoothing it down, lying on it to test its comfort, and then deciding that the corner is not a suitable one for a bedroom, removing all the bedding to the opposite end of the cage and starting all over again.

Upstairs, the flying squirrels gaze at you with enormous, liquid eyes, squatting fatly on their haunches, whilst stuffing food into their mouths with their delicate little hands. Most of the parrots are asleep, but Suku, the African grey, is incurably inquisitive, and, as you pass, never fails to pull his head out from under his wing and watch to see what you are doing. As you make your departure, he shuffles his feathers – a whispering silken noise

– and then in a deep, rather bronchial voice says: 'Good night, Suku,' to himself in tones of great affection.

As you lie in bed, watching through the window the moon disentangling itself from the tree silhouettes, you hear the dingos starting again their plaintive, flute-like chorus, and then the lions cough into action. Soon it will be dawn and the chorus of bird-song will take over and make the cold air of the morning ring with song.

Chapter Two

A Porcupine in the Parish

Dear Mr Durrell,
I would like to join one of your expeditions. Here are my qualifications and faults:
36 years old, single, good health, a sport, understand children and animals, except snakes; devoted, reliable, excellent; young in character. My hobbies are playing the flute, photography and writing stories. My nerves are not too steady; am disagreeable if anybody insults my country or my religion (Catholic). In the event of my accompanying you, it would be everything paid – on the other hand, if you are a snob and you don't mean what you write, I regret to say I do not wish to know you. Hoping to hear from you soon. . . .

I soon found, to my relief, that Jersey appeared to have taken us to its heart. The kindness that has been shown to us during the five years of our existence is tremendous, both from officials and from the Islanders themselves. After all, when living on an island eight miles by twelve you may be pardoned for having certain qualms when someone wants to start a zoo and import a lot of apparently dangerous animals. You have vivid mental pictures of an escaped tiger stalking your pedigree herd of Jersey cows, of flocks of huge and savage deer browsing happily through your fields of daffodils, and gigantic eagles and vultures swooping down on your defenceless chickens. I have no doubt that a lot of people thought this, especially our nearest neighbours to the Manor, but nevertheless they welcomed us without displaying any symptoms of unease.

In a zoo of five or six hundred animals the variety and quantity of food they consume is staggering. It is the one thing that must not be stinted if they are to be kept healthy and happy; and, above all, the food must not only be plentiful, but good. Cleanliness and good food go a very long way to cutting down disease. A creature that is well fed and kept in clean surroundings has, in my opinion, an eighty per cent better chance of escaping disease, or, if it contracts a disease, of recovering. Unfortunately, a great many people (including, I am afraid, some zoos) still suffer from the extraordinary delusion that anything edible but not fit for human consumption is ideal for animals. When you consider that, in the wild state, most animals – unless they are natural carrion feeders – always eat the freshest of food, such as fresh fruit and freshly killed meat, it is scarcely to be wondered at when they sicken and die if fed on a diet that is 'not fit for human consumption.' Of course, in all zoos a lot of such food *is* fed, but in most cases there is nothing at all wrong with it. For example, a greengrocer opens a crate of bananas and finds that many of the fruit have black specks or blotches on the skin. There is nothing wrong with the fruit, but his customers demand yellow bananas, and will not buy discoloured ones. If a zoo did not buy it, the fruit would be wasted. Sometimes the greengrocer has fruit or vegetables which have reached that point of ripeness where another twenty-four hours in the shop and the whole lot will have to be thrown away. In that case they are sold to a zoo that can use them up rapidly.

Some time ago a greengrocer telephoned us, enquiring if we would like some peaches. He explained that his deep-freeze had gone wrong and that it contained some South African peaches which had gone black just round the seed. There was absolutely nothing wrong with them, he reassured us, but they were unsaleable. We said we would be delighted to have them, thinking that a couple of crates of peaches would be a treat for some of the animals. A few hours later, a huge lorry rolled into the grounds, stacked high with boxes. There must have been anything up to thirty or forty, and the financial loss this represented to the greengrocer must have been staggering. They were some of the largest and most succulent peaches I have ever seen; we tipped cratefuls of them into the cages, and the animals had a field day. Within half an hour all the monkeys were dripping peach juice and could hardly move; several members of the staff, too, were surreptitiously wiping peach-juice off their chins. There was, as I say, nothing wrong with the peaches: they were just unsaleable. But it might happen that someone else, in the most kindly way, would bring us a whole lorry load of completely rotten and mildewed peaches, and be hurt and puzzled when we refused them on the grounds that they were unfit for animal consumption. One of the biggest killers in a zoo is that rather nebulous thing called enteritis, an infection of the stomach. This, in itself, can cause an animal's death, but even if it is only a mild attack it can weaken the creature, and thus open the door to pneumonia or some other deadly complaint. Bad fruit can cause enteritis quicker than most things; thus care must be taken over the quality of the fruit fed to the animals.

As soon as the people of Jersey knew what our requirements were in the matter of food, they rallied round in the most extraordinarily generous way. Take the question of calves, for instance. In Jersey most of the bull-calves are slaughtered at birth and, until we arrived, they were simply buried, for they were too small to be marketable. We discovered this quite by accident, when a farmer telephoned us and asked, rather doubtfully, if a dead calf was any use to us. We said we would be delighted to have it, and when he brought it round he asked us if we would like any more. It was then that we found out there was this wonderful source of fresh meat: meat which – from the animal point of view – could not have been more natural, for not only was it freshly killed (sometimes still warm), but they could also have the hearts, livers and other internal organs which were so good for them. Gradually, the news spread among the farmers, and before long – at certain times of the year – we were receiving as many as sixteen calves a day, and farmers were travelling from one end of the Island to the other, delivering them to us. Other farmers, not to be outdone, offered us tomatoes and apples, and would bring whole lorry-loads round, or let us go to collect as many as we could take away. One man telephoned to say he had a 'few' sunflowers, the heads of which were now ripe, would we like them? As usual we said yes, and he turned up in a small open truck piled high with gigantic sunflower heads, so that the whole thing looked like a sun chariot. The heads were not fully ripe, which meant that the kernel of each seed was soft and milky; we simply cut up the heads as if they were plum cakes and put big slices in with such creatures as the squirrels, mongooses and birds. They all went crazy about the soft seeds and simply gorged themselves.

But these are all the more normal types of food. In a zoo you can use a great many very unusual items of diet, and in acquiring these we were again helped by the local people. There was one elderly lady who used to cycle up to the Zoo once or twice a week on an antediluvian bicycle and spend the afternoon talking to the animals. Whenever she saw me she would back me into a corner and for half an hour or so tell me what tricks her favourite animals had been up to that day. She was, I discovered, a lavatory attendant in St Helier. One day I happened to meet her when I had been out collecting some acorns for the squirrels. She watched entranced while the squirrels sat up on their hind legs, twirling the acorns round and round in their paws as they chewed them. She then told me that she knew of a great many churchyards in which grew fine oak trees, and vowed that she would, herself, bring some acorns for the squirrels at the end of the week. Sure enough, on the Sunday she appeared, pedalling strenuously up to the Zoo on her ancient bicycle, the front basket of which was filled to the brim with plump acorns, and there was another large carrier-bagful strapped – somewhat insecurely – to the back of her vehicle. Thereafter, she used to bring us a regular supply of acorns every week, until the squirrels became quite blasé about them and even started to store them in their beds.

Another food item for which we are always grateful is what could be loosely called 'live food,' that is to say earwigs, woodlice, grasshoppers, moths and snails. Here a great many people come to our rescue, and they turn up at the Zoo with jam-jars full of woodlice and other creatures, and biscuit-tins full of snails, of which they are, of course, only too glad to see the last. The earwigs, woodlice and so on are fed to the smaller reptiles, the amphibians and some of the birds. The snails we feed to the larger lizards, who scrunch them up with avidity, eating shell and all as a rule.

In order to pad out the animals that I had brought back from West Africa and South America, we had, of course, to acquire from different sources several other creatures. The most amusing of these was, undoubtedly, the bird I mentioned before, Trumpy, the trumpeter. Not only had he appointed himself the Zoo's clown but also the Zoo's settler-in. As soon as we got a new creature, Trumpy managed to hear of it, and would come bouncing along, cackling to himself, to settle it in. He would then spend twenty-four hours standing by the cage (or preferably in it, if he could), until he thought that the new arrival was firmly established, whereupon he would bounce back to his special beat in the Mammal House. Sometimes Trumpy's settling efforts were on the risky side, but he seemed to be too dimwitted to realize the danger. When Juan and Juanita, the white-collared peccaries, were first released into their paddock there was Trumpy to settle them in. The pigs did not seem to mind in the slightest, and so Trumpy did his twenty-four-hour stint and departed. But later on, when Juan and Juanita had just had their first litter, and had brought them out into the paddock for the first time, Trumpy flew gaily over the fence to settle in the babies. Now, Juan and Juanita had not minded this for themselves, but they thought that Trumpy's efforts on behalf of their piglets held some hidden menace. They converged on Trumpy (who was standing on one leg and eyeing the piglets benignly), their fur bristling, their tusks clattering like castanets. Trumpy woke out of his trance with a start, and only a skilful bit of dodging and a wild leap saved him. It was the last time he attempted to go into the peccary paddock. When we dammed up the little stream in the sunken water-meadow and constructed a small lake for the black-necked and coscoroba swans I had brought back from South America, Trumpy was there to supervise the work, and when the swans were eventually released he insisted, in spite of all our entreaties, on standing up to his ankles in water for twenty-four hours to settle them in. It did not appear to have any effect on the swans, but Trumpy enjoyed it.

Another new acquisition was the fine young male mandrill, Frisky. With his blue and red behind, and his blue and red nose, Frisky was a fine sight. If you went near his cage he would peer at you with his bright, amber-coloured eyes, lift his eyebrows up and down, as if in astonishment, and then, uttering throaty little grunts, he would turn round and present his backside to you, peering over his shoulder to see what effect his sunset-rear was achieving. Frisky was, of course, exceedingly inquisitive, like all members of his family, and one bright spring day this was his undoing. We were having the tops of the monkey cages repainted in a pleasant shade of mushroom, and Frisky had been watching this operation with the keenest interest. He was obviously under the impression that the paint pot contained some delicious substance, probably like milk, which would repay investigation. He had not had a chance to find out, however, for the painter, in the most selfish and boorish manner, had kept the paint pot close beside him. But patience is always rewarded, and after a few hours Frisky had his chance. The painter left the pot unguarded while he went to fetch something, and Frisky seized the opportunity. He pushed his arm though the wire, grabbed the edge of the paint pot and pulled. The next moment he was spluttering and choking under a waterfall of mushroom-coloured paint, and almost instantly, he discovered, he had turned into a mushroom-coloured mandrill. There was really not much that we could do, for you cannot take a half-grown mandrill out of its cage and wash it as though it were a poodle. However, when the paint had dried as hard as armour on his fur, he looked so miserable that we decided to put him into the next door cage, which contained a female baboon and two female drills, in the hope that they would clean him. When Frisky was let in with them, they viewed him with alarm, and it was some time before they plucked up enough courage to approach him. When they did, however, and found out what was the matter with him, they gathered round enthusiastically and set about the task of giving Frisky a wash and brush up. The trouble was that the paint had dried so hard on to the fur that the three females had to use a great deal of force, and so, although at the end of two days they had removed all the paint, they had also removed a vast amount of Frisky's fur with it. Now, instead of a mushroom-coloured mandrill, we had a partially bald and slightly shame-faced looking mandrill.

Another newcomer was our lion, who went under the time-honoured name of Leo. He was one of the famous Dublin Zoo lions, and was probably about the fiftieth generation born in captivity. On his arrival he was only about the size of a small dog, and so he was housed in a cage in the Mammal House, but he grew at such a pace that it was soon imperative that we find him more spacious quarters. We had just finished construction on a large cage for the chimpanzees, and decided we would put Leo in that until we could get around to building him a cage of his own. So Leo was transferred, and settled down very happily. I was glad to see, when his mane started to develop, that he was going to be a blond lion, for in my experience the lions with blond manes, as opposed to dark manes, have always nice, if slightly imbecile, characters. This theory has been amply born out by Leo's behaviour. He had in his cage a large log as a plaything, and a big, black rubber bucket in which he received his water ration. This bucket fascinated him, and after he had drunk his fill he would upset the remains of the water and then pat the bucket with his great paws, making it roll round the cage so that he could stalk it and pounce on it. One day I was in the grounds when a lady stopped me to enquire whether we had acquired Leo from a circus. Slightly puzzled, I said, 'No,' and asked her why she should think so. 'Because,' she replied, 'he was doing such clever tricks.' I discovered that he had, by some extraordinary means, managed to wedge the rubber bucket on his head, and was walking round and round the cage proudly, wearing it like a hat.

In his second year Leo decided, after mature reflection, that it was a lion's duty to roar. He was not awfully sure how to go about it, so he would retire to quiet corners of his cage and practise very softly to himself, for he was rather shy of this new accomplishment and would stop immediately and pretend it was nothing to do with him if you came in view. When he was satisfied that the timbre was right and his breath control perfect, he treated us to his first concert. It was a wonderful moonlight night when he started, and we were all delighted that Leo was, at last, a proper lion. A lion roaring sounds just like someone sawing wood on a gigantic, echoing barrel. The first coughs or rasps are quick and fairly close together, and you can imagine the saw biting into the wood; then the coughs slow down and become more drawn out, and suddenly stop, and you instinctively wait to hear the thud of the sawn-off piece hitting the ground. The trouble was that Leo was so proud of his accomplishment that he could not wait until nightfall to give us the benefit of his vocal cords. He started roaring earlier and earlier each evening, and would keep it up solidly all night, with five-minute intervals for medition in between each roar. Sometimes, when he was in particularly good voice, you could imagine that he was sitting on the end of your bed, serenading you. We all began to be somewhat jaded. We found that if we opened the bedroom window and shouted, 'Leo, *shut up*,' this had the effect of silencing him for half an hour; but at the end of that time he would decide that you had not really meant it and would start all over again. It was a very trying time for all concerned. Now, however, Leo has learnt to roar with a certain amount of discretion, but even so there are nights – especially at full moon – when the only thing to do is to put the pillow over your head and curse the day you ever decided you wanted a zoo.

We also obtained in our first year two South African penguins, called Dilly and Dally. I hasten to add that they were not christened by us, but arrived with these revolting names stencilled on their crate. We had prepared a pool for them in the shade of some trees bordering the main drive, and here they seemed quite content. Trumpy, of course, spent twenty-four hours in their pen with them, and seemed faintly disgruntled that the pool was too deep for him to join Dilly and Dally in it. After settling them in, he took a great fancy to the penguins and paid them a visit every morning, when he would stand outside the wire, making his curious booming cry, while Dilly and Dally would point their beaks skywards and bray to the heavens, like a couple of demented donkeys.

I am not quite sure when the rift in this happy friendship appeared, or for what reason, but one morning we saw Trumpy fly over into the penguin enclosure and proceed to beat up Dilly and Dally in the most ferocious manner. He flew at them, wings out, feathers bristling, pecking and scratching, until the two penguins (who were twice his size) were forced to take refuge in the pool. Trumpy stood on the edge of the pond and cackled triumphantly at them. We chased Trumpy out of the enclosure and scolded him, whereupon he shuffled his feathers carelessly and stalked off nonchalantly. After that we had to watch him, for he took advantage of every opportunity to fly over the wire and attack poor Dilly and Dally who, at the sight of him, would flop hysterically into the water. One morning he did this once too often. He must have flown over very early, before anyone was about, intent on giving Dilly and Dally a bashing, but the penguins had grown tired of these constant assaults, and rounded on him. One of them, with a lucky peck, must have caught him off balance and knocked him into the pool, from which – with his waterlogged feathers – he could not climb out. This was the penguins' triumph, and as Trumpy floundered helplessly, they circled round, pecking at him viciously with their razor-sharp beaks. When he was found, he was still floating in the pond, bleeding profusely from a number of pecks, and with just enough strength to keep his head above water. We rushed him into the house, dried him and anointed his wounds, but he was a very sick and exhausted bird, and black depression settled on the Zoo, for we all thought he would die. The next day there was no change, and I felt it was touch and go. As I was sipping my early morning tea on the third day, I suddenly heard, to my amazement, a familiar thrumming cry. I slipped out of bed and looked out of the window. There, by the lavender hedge in the courtyard, was Trumpy, a slightly battered and tattered trumpeter who limped a little, but still with the same regal air of being the owner of the property. I saluted him out of the window, and he cocked a bright eye at me. Then he shuffled his torn feathering to adjust it to his liking, gave his loud, cackling laugh and stalked off towards his beat in the Mammal House.

Another new arrival that caused us a certain amount of trouble, one way and another, was Delilah. She was a large female African crested porcupine, and she arrived up at the airport in a crate that looked suitable for a couple of rhinoceros. Why she had been crated like this became obvious when we peered into the crate, for even in that short air journey she had succeeded in nearly demolishing one side with her great yellow teeth. When she saw us looking into the crate, she uttered a series of such fearsome roars and gurks that one would have been pardoned for thinking it contained a pride of starving lions. She stamped her feet petulantly on the floor of the crate, and rattled and clattered her long black and white quills like a crackle of musketry. It was quite obvious that Delilah was going to be a personality to be reckoned with.

On our return to the Zoo we had to chivy her out of her rapidly disintegrating crate and into a temporary cage, while her permanent home was under construction. During this process she endeared herself to at least one member of the staff by backing sharply into his legs. The experience of having several hundred extremely sharp porcupine quills stabbed into your shins is not exactly an exhilarating one. By the time Delilah was installed in her temporary home there were several more casualties, and the ground was littered with quills, for Delilah, like all porcupines, shed her quills with gay abandon at the slightest provocation.

The old fable of a porcupine being able to shoot its quills out like arrows is quite untrue. What acutally happens is this. The quills, some of them fourteen inches long, are planted very loosely in the skin of the back. When the animal is harried by an enemy, what it does is to back rapidly into the adversary (for all the quills point backwards), jab the quills into him as deeply as possible, and then rush forward again. This action not only drives the quills into the enemy, but pulls them loose from the porcupine's skin, so the enemy is left looking like a weird sort of pin cushion. This action is performed so rapidly that, in the heat of battle, as it were, you are quite apt to get the impression that the porcupine *has* shot its adversary full of quills. This delightful action Delilah used to indulge in with great frequency, and, therefore, at feeding and cleaning times you had to be prepared to drop everything and leap high and wide at a moment's notice.

Porcupines are, of course, rodents, and the giant crested species – since it spreads from Africa into parts of Europe – has the distinction of being the largest European rodent, bigger even than the beaver. It is also the largest of the porcupines, for, although there are many different species scattered about the world, none of them come anywhere near the size of the crested one. In North and South America the porcupines are, to a large extent, arboreal, and the South American kind even have prehensile tails to assist them in climbing. The other porcupines found in Africa and Asia are rather small, terrestrial species, that generally have fairly long tails ending in a bunch of soft spines like the head of a brush, and this they rattle vigorously in moments of stress. Without doubt, as well as being the biggest, the great crested porcupine is the most impressive and handsome member of the family.

It was not long before we had Delilah's new home ready, and then came the great day on which we had to transport her to it from one end of the Zoo to the other. We had learnt from bitter experience that trying to chivy Delilah into a crate was worse than useless. She simply put up all her spines, gurked at us fiercely, and backed into everything in sight, parting with great handfuls of quills with a generosity I have rarely seen equalled. The mere sight of a crate would send her off into an orgy of foot-stamping and quill-rattling. We had learnt that there was only one way to cope with her: to let her out of the cage and then two people, armed with brooms, to chivy her along gently. Delilah would stride out like one of the more muscular and prickly female Soviet athletes, and as long as you kept her on a fairly even course by light taps from the brushes you could keep her going for any distance.

This was the method we decided to employ to transfer her to her new quarters, and to begin with all went well. She started off at a great lick down the main drive, Jeremy and I panting behind with our brushes. We successfully made her round the corner into the courtyard, but once there a suspicion entered her head that she might be doing exactly what we wanted her to do. Feeling that the honour of the rodents was at stake, Delilah proceeded to run round and round the courtyard as though it was a circus-ring, with Jeremy and me in hot pursuit. Then, whenever she had got us going at a good pace, she would suddenly stop and go into reverse, so that we would have to leap out of the way and use our brushes as protection. After a few minutes of this, there appeared to be more quills sticking in the woodwork of the brushes than there were in Delilah. Eventually, however, she tired of this game, and allowed us to guide her down to her new cage without any further ado.

She lived very happily in her new quarters for about three months before the wanderlust seized her. It was a crisp winter's evening when Delilah decided there might be something in the outside world that her cage lacked, and so setting to work with her great curved yellow teeth she ripped a large hole in the thick interlink wire, squeezed her portly form through it and trotted off into the night. It so happened that on that particular evening I had gone out to dinner, so the full honours of the Battle of the Porcupine go to John.

At about midnight my mother was awakened by a car which had driven into the courtyard beneath her bedroom window and was tooting its horn vigorously. Mother, leaning out of the window, saw that it was one of our nearest neighbours from the farm over the hill. He informed Mother that there was a large and, to judge by the noises it was making, ferocious creature stamping about in his yard, and would we like to do something about it. Mother, who always has a tendency to fear the worst, was convinced that it was Leo who had escaped, and she fled to the cottage to wake John. He decided from the description that it must be Delilah, and pausing only for a broom, he leapt into the Zoo van and drove up to the farm. There, sure enough, was Delilah, stamping about in the moonlight, gurking to herself and rattling her quills. John explained to the farmer that the only way to get Delilah back to the Zoo was to brush her, as it were, along the half mile or so of road. The farmer, though obviously thinking the whole procedure rather eccentric, said that if John would undertake that part of it, he would undertake to drive the Zoo van back again.

So John set off, clad in his pyjamas, brushing a snorting, rattling Delilah down the narrow moonlit road. John said he had never felt such a fool in his life, for they met several cars full of late-night revellers, and all these screeched to a halt and watched in open-mouthed astonishment the sight of a man in pyjamas brushing along a plainly reluctant porcupine. Several of them, I am quite sure, must have hurried home to sign the pledge, for after all, the last thing you expect to find wandering about a respectable parish is an infuriated porcupine pursued by a highly embarrassed man in night attire. But at last John brought her safely back to the Zoo and then, to her great indignation, locked her up in the coal cellar. For, as he explained, it had a cement floor and two-foot thick granite walls, and if she could break out of that she deserved her freedom and, as far as he was concerned, she could have it.

Not long afterwards, Delilah caused trouble in quite another context. As the Zoo needs every form of publicity it can obtain, television was clearly one of the best mediums, and so I tried to popularize it by this means whenever possible. A television producer once said to me that if he could produce a programme without a television personality or professional actor he would be a happy man. I could see his point, but he did not know that there could be something infinitely more harrowing than putting on a programme with a televison personality or a professional actor. He had never undertaken one with live wild animals, the difficulties of this making the strutting and fretting of television personalities and actors fade into insignificance. When making a programme with animals, they either behave so badly that you are left a jittering mass of nerves in the end, or else they behave so well that they steal the show. Whichever way it is, you cannot win, and anyone (in my considered opinion) who undertakes to do such a job, should be kindly and firmly conducted by his friends to the nearest mental home. If you let him do the programme, he will end there anyway, so you are merely anticipating.

One of the first programmes I did was devoted to the primates, or monkey family, of which the Zoo boasted a rather fine collection. For the first time, live, on television, I could show the great British public a splendid array of creatures ranging from the tiny, large-eyed bushbabies, through the lorises, the Old and New World monkeys, to the gorilla and chimpanzee, with myself thrown in as an example of *Homo sapiens*. I had no qualms about this: the monkeys and apes were all extremely tame, the bushbabies would be confined in glass-fronted cases, and the lorises would be on upright branches where, I knew, they would simply curl up and sleep until awakened by me during the programme. At least, that is how it should have worked, but unfortunately I had not taken into consideration the effects of the journey, for the Island of Jersey is an hour's flying time from the City of Bristol where the programme was to be recorded. By the time the animals had been crated, flown to Bristol and unloaded in the dressing-room which had been put at their disposal, they were all in a highly neurotic state of mind. So was I.

When the time for the first rehearsal approached, all the monkeys had to be removed from their travelling crates, have belts and leashes attached to them, and be tethered (one to each compartment) on a construction that resembled a miniature cow stall. The monkeys, hitherto always tame, placid and well-behaved, took one look at the cow stall and had what appeared to be a collective nervous breakdown. They screamed, they bit, they struggled; one broke his leash and disappeared behind some piled scenery, from which he was extracted – yelling loudly and covered with cobwebs – after about half an hour's concentrated effort. Already rehearsal was fifteen minutes overdue. At last we had them all in position and more or less quiet. I apologized to the producer and said that we would be ready in next to no time, for all we had to do was to put the lorises on their respective tree trunks, and this – with such lethargic animals – would be the work of a moment. We opened the cage doors, expecting to have to chivy the sleepy lorises out on to their trees, but instead they stalked out like a couple of racehorses, their eyes blazing with indignation, uttering loud cat-like cries of disgust and warning. Before anyone could do anything sensible, they had rushed down their tree trunks and were roaring across the studio floor, their mouths open, their eyes wide. Technicians departed hurriedly in all directions, except a few of the bolder ones who, with rolled-up newspapers as weapons, endeavoured to prevent the determined lorises from getting among the scenery, as the monkey had done. After further considerable delay we managed to return the lorises to their travelling crates, and the Props Department was hurriedly summoned to attach to the bottom of each tree a cardboard cone that would prevent the creatures from getting a grip and so climbing down on to the floor. Rehearsals were now an hour overdue. At last we were under way, and by this time I was in such a state of nerves that the rehearsal was a shambles: I forgot my lines; I called most of the animals by the wrong names; the slightest sound made me jump out of my skin, for fear something had escaped, and to cap it all Lulu, the chimp, urinated copiously, loudly and with considerable interest in her own achievement, all over my lap. We all retired to lunch with black circles under our eyes, raging headaches and a grim sense of foreboding. The Producer, with a ghastly smile, said she was sure it would be all right, and I, trying to eat what appeared to be fried sawdust, agreed. We went back to the studio to do the recording.

For some technical reason that defeats me, it is too expensive or too complicated to cut a tele-recording. So it is exactly like doing a live programme: if you make a mistake, it is permanent. This, of course, does not help to bolster your confidence in yourself; when you are co-starring with a number of irritated and uninhibited creatures like monkeys you start going grey round the temples before you even begin. The red light went on, and with shaking hands I took a deep breath, smiled a tremulous smile at the camera, as if I loved it like a brother, and commenced. To my surprise, the monkeys behaved perfectly. My confidence started to return. The bushbabies were wonderful, and I felt a faint ray of hope. We reached the lorises and they were magnificent. My voice lost its tremolo and, I hoped, took on a firm, manly, authoritative note. I was getting into my stride. Just as I was launching myself with enthusiasm into the protective postures of a potto – believe it or not – the Studio Manager came over and told me that there had been a breakdown in the tele-recording and we should have to start all over again.

Of course, after an experience like this, one is mental to even try to do any more television. But I had agreed to do five more. The five I did, I must admit, were not quite as trying as the monkey programme, but some of the highlights still live vividly in my memory, and occasionally I awake screaming in the night and have to be comforted by Jacquie. There was, for example, the programme I did on birds. The idea was to assemble as many different species as possible, and show how their beaks were adapted for their varying ways of life. Two of the birds were to be 'star' turns, because they did things to order. There was, for instance, Dingle the chough. This member of the crow family is extremely rare in Great Britain now, and we are very lucky to have him. They are clad in funereal black feathering, but with scarlet feet and a long, curved scarlet beak. Dingle, who had been hand-reared, was absurdly tame. The second 'star' was a cockatoo named – with incredible originality by its previous owner – 'Cocky.' Now, this creature would, when requested, put up its amazing crest and shout loudly, a most impressive sight. All the other birds taking part in the programme did nothing at all: they were all, very sensibly, content to just sit there and be themselves. So my only problems were Dingle and Cocky, and I had great faith in both of them.

The programme was to open with me standing there, Dingle perched on my wrist, while I talked about him. During rehearsals this worked perfectly, for if you scratch Dingle's head he goes off into a trance-like state, and remains quite still. However, when it came to the actual recording, Dingle decided that he had been scratched enough, and just as the red light went on he launched himself off my wrist and flew up into the rafters of the studio. It took us half an hour with the aid of ladders and bribes in the shape of mealworms, meat and cheese (of which he is inordinately fond) to retrieve him, whereupon he behaved perfectly and sat so still on my wrist that he appeared to be stuffed. All went smoothly until we came to Cocky. Here I made the mistake of telling my audience what to expect, which is the one thing not to do with animals. So, while five million viewers gaped expectantly waiting to see Cocky put up his crest and scream, I made desperate attempts to persuade him to do it. This went on for five soul-searing minutes, while Cocky just sat on his perch as immobile as a museum specimen. In despair I eventually moved on to the next bird, and as I did so Cocky erected his crest and screamed mockingly.

There was the occasion, also, of the programme devoted to reptiles. Here I felt I was on safer ground, for, on the whole, they are fairly lethargic creatures and easily handleable. The programme, however, was a chore for me, as I was just in the middle of a bout of influenza, and my presence in the studio was entirely due to the efforts of my doctor who had pumped me full of the most revolting substances to keep me on my feet for the required time. If you are nervous anyway – which I always am – and your head is buzzing under the influence of various antibiotics, you tend to give a performance closely resembling an early silent film. During the first rehearsals all the technicians realized that I was feeling both lousy and strung up, and so when it came to a break they each took it in turn to back me into a corner and try to restore my morale, with little or no effect. We came to the second rehearsal and I was worse than before. Obviously something had to be done, and somebody was inspired enough to think of the answer. During my discourse on members of the tortoise family I mentioned how the skeleton of the beast was, as it were, welded into the shell. In order to show this more clearly I had a very fine tortoise shell and skeleton to demonstrate. The bottom half of the shell was hinged, like a door, and upon opening it all the mysteries and secrets of the tortoise's anatomy were revealed. Having done my little introduction on the tortoise family, I then opened the underside of the shell and, to my surprise, instead of just finding the skeleton therein, I found a piece of cardboard on which the words 'NO VACANCIES' had been carefully printed. It was a few minutes before order was restored in the studio, but I felt much better, and the rest of the rehearsal went off without a hitch.

Delilah cropped up in a programme which I did on adaptation. I thought she would be a very good example of the way an animal protects itself, and certainly she showed this off to advantage. When we came to put her into the crate, she charged wildly in all directions, backing into us and the woodwork, and leaving spines embedded in the sides of the crate and in the end of the brushes. She gurked and roared and rattled her quills throughout the trip to Bristol, and the studio hands, who unloaded her on arrival there, were for some considerable time under the impression that I had brought a fully grown leopard with me. Then we had to transfer Delilah from her travelling box and into the special studio cage that had been built for her. This took half an hour and by the time we had achieved it Delilah had stuck so many quills into so much of the studio scenery that I began to wonder whether she would be completely bald for her debut on television. During the actual transmission she behaved, to my amazement, perfectly, doing all the things that I wanted: she gurked fearsomely, she stamped her feet and rattled her quills like castanets, as though she were a born television star. By the end of the show I was feeling quite friendly towards her and beginning to think that I might well have misjudged her. Then came the moment of inducing her out of the studio cage back into her travelling crate. It took eight of us three-quarters of an hour. One stagehand received a sharp stab in the calf of his leg; two pieces of scenery were irretrievably damaged, and the entire set was pierced so full of porcupine quills it looked as though we had been fighting off a Red Indian attack. I was thankful to get a by then quill-less Delilah back to the Zoo and into her own cage again.

I suppose that the terrible things that occur tend to live in one's memory more vividly than the pleasant happenings, and so I look back on the television shows I have done with animals rather in the way that one remembers a nasty series of accidents. There is, however, one incident on which I look back with extreme pleasure, and that was the occasion when the B.B.C. wanted our young gorilla N'Pongo to take part in a programme. They even went to the unprecedented lengths of chartering a small plane to fly us over to Bristol. They also sent a camera man to cover the trip with his camera – a timid individual who confessed to me that he did not like flying, as it made him sick. We took off in brilliant sunshine, and almost immediately dived into black cloud filled to capacity with air pockets.

N'Pongo, sitting back in his seat, like a seasoned traveller, thoroughly enjoyed everything. He accepted six lumps of barley sugar to counteract the popping in his ears, peered with interest and excitement out of the window, and when the air pockets began, he fetched out the sick-bag and put it on his head. The poor photographer had become progressively greener, while attempting to film N'Pongo's antics, but when he put the bag on his head this reminder acted in a devastating way, and he dived for his own receptacle and treated it in the way for which it was designed.

Chapter Three

The Cold-blooded Cohort

Dear Mr Durrell,
At a garden fête the other day a lizard was found in the ice-cream container ...

I know that it is a confession of acute and depraved eccentricity, but nevertheless I must admit that I am very fond of reptiles. They are not, I grant you, over-burdened with intelligence. You do not get the same reaction from them that you would from a mammal, or even a bird, but still I like them. They are bizarre, colourful, and in many cases graceful, so what more could you want?

Now, the majority of people will confess to you (as though it is something quite unique) that they have an 'instinctive' loathing for snakes, and with much eye-rolling and grimacing they will give you many different reasons for their fear, ranging from the sublime ('it's instinctive') to the ridiculous ('they're all sort of slimy'). I have been, at one time or another, bored by so many snake complex admissions that as soon as the subject of reptiles crops up in conversation with anyone, I want to run away and hide. Ask the average person their views on snakes and they will, within the space of ten minutes, talk more nonsense than a brace of politicians.

To begin with, it is not 'natural' for human beings to fear snakes. You might just as well say that they were naturally afraid of being run over by a bus. Most people, however, are convinced they are born with a built-in anti-snake feeling. This can be quite simply disproved by handing a harmless snake to a child who is too young to have its head filled with a lot of nonsense about these creatures; the child will hold the reptile and play with it quite happily and without a trace of fear. I remember once putting this point to a woman who had been gurgling on about her snake phobia for what seemed like years.

She was most indignant.

'I've never been taught to fear snakes, I've always been like it,' she said, haughtily, and then added in triumph, 'and my mother was like it, too.'

Faced with such logic, what could one reply?

People's fears of snakes seem to be based on a series of misconceptions. The most common one is the conviction that all these creatures are poisonous. In actual fact, the non-poisonous ones outnumber the poisonous ones by about ten to one. Another very popular idea is that these reptiles are slimy to touch, whereas snakes are dry and cold, and feel no different from a pair of snakeskin shoes or a crocodile-skin handbag. Yet people will insist that they cannot touch a snake because of its sliminess, and think nothing of handling a wet cake of soap.

Our Reptile House is fairly small, but we have a pretty good cross-section of reptiles and amphibia on show. I derive a lot of innocent amusement out of going in there when it is crowded and listening to the general public airing its ignorance with an assurance that is breathtaking. For instance, the snake's tongue: this is purely a scent organ with which the creature smells – hence the way it is flicked rapidly in and out of the mouth; it is also used as a feeler, in the same way that a cat uses its whiskers. The snake experts, however, who visit the Reptile House, know better.

'Cor, Em,' they'll shout excitedly, 'come and look at this snake's sting ... coo, wouldn't like to be stung by *that*.'

And Em will hurry over and peer horrified at the innocent grass snake, and then give a delicious shudder. All reptiles can, of course, spend long periods completely immobile, when even their breathing is difficult to detect, unless you look closely. The classic remark was delivered by a man who, having peered into several cages in which the reptiles lay un-moving, turned to his wife with an air of one who has been swindled, and hissed:

'They're *stuffed*, Milly.'

A snake moving along the ground or through the branches of a tree is one of the most graceful sights in the world, and when you consider that the creature is walking with its ribs the whole thing becomes even more remarkable. If you watch a moving snake carefully, you can sometimes see the ribs moving beneath the skin as the snake draws itself along. The creature's unblinking stare (another thing to which people object) is not due to the fact that the snake is trying to hypnotise you, but simply that it has no eyelids. The eye is covered with a fine, transparent scale, like a watch-glass. This is very clearly noticed when a snake sheds its skin, which they all do periodically. The skin comes loose around the lips, and then, by rubbing itself against rocks or branches, the snake gradually peels off its old skin. If you examine this shed skin, you can see that the eye scales have been shed as well.

All snakes are adapted for feeding in the same way, but their methods of obtaining their food varies. The non-poisonous ones and the constrictors (like the pythons) grab their prey with their mouths, and then try to throw two or three coils of their body round the victims as rapidly as possible, thus holding and crushing at the same time. The poisonous one, on the other hand, bites its victim and then waits for the poison to take effect, which is generally very soon. Once the prey has undergone its last convulsions, then it can be eaten. The poison fangs, of course, are in the upper jaw, and usually near the front of the mouth. When not in use, they fold back against the gum, like the blade of a pen-knife; as the snake opens its mouth to strike, they drop down into position. The fangs are hollow, similar to a hypodermic needle, or else they have a deep groove running down the back. The poison sac, to which they are connected, lies above the gum. As the snake bites, the poison is forced out and trickles down the groove or hollow in the fang and so into the wound. However, whatever the method of attack, once the prey is dead, the swallowing process is the same in all snakes. The lower jaw is jointed to the upper one in such a way that it can be dislocated at will, and, of course, the skin of the mouth, throat and body is extremely elastic, and so this allows the snake to swallow a creature considerably larger than its own head. Once the food is in the stomach, the slow process of digestion starts. Any portions of the animal that are impossible to assimilate, such as hair, are regurgitated in the form of pellets at a later date. On an occasion a large python was killed, and in its stomach were found four round balls of hair, the size of tennis balls and very hard. On being cut open, each one was found to contain the hoof of a wild pig. These sharp hooves could have damaged the lining of the python's stomach, and so each one had been carefully covered with a thick smooth layer of hair.

In the majority of zoos nowadays they feed dead creatures to the snakes. This is not because it is better for the snakes, or that they prefer it, but simply due to misplaced kindness on the part of the general public, who imagine that a white rat or a rabbit suffers terribly when put into a cage with a snake. That this is nonsense I have proved to my complete satisfaction, for I have seen, in a Continental zoo, a rabbit perched on the back of a python (obviously not hungry), cleaning its whiskers with tremendous sang-froid. The Director of the zoo told me that if white rats were fed to the snakes, it was imperative they should be removed if they were not eaten straight away, otherwise they proceeded to gnaw holes in the snake's body.

While snakes are passive and rather expressionless beasts, lizards can display considerable intelligence and character. One such reptile we had was a mastigure, which I christened Dandy, owing to his great partiality for dandelion flowers. One must, I think, face the fact that mastigures are not the most attractive of lizards, and Dandy was a particularly unattractive member of his species. Nevertheless, his eager personality made him a likeable creature. He had a blunt, rounded head; a fat, flattened body; and a heavy tail covered with short, sharp spikes. His neck was rather long and thin, and this made him look as though he had been put together out of bits of two totally unrelated species. His colour could only be described as a rich, dirty brown. Dandy, as I say, had a liking for dandelion flowers, which amounted to an obsession. He had only to see you approaching the Reptile House with something yellow in your hands, and he would immediately rush to the front of his cage and scrabble wildly against the glass. If it was a dandelion flower you were carrying, you had only to slide back the glass front of his cage and he would gallop out on to your arm, panting with emotion; and then, closing his eyes, he would stretch out his long neck and, like a child waiting to have a sweet popped into its mouth, would open his jaws. If you pushed the flower into his mouth, he would munch away in ecstasy, the petals dangling outside his mouth and making him look as though he had a bright yellow military moustache. He was the only lizard I have known that would genuinely play with you. If he was lying on the sand, and you let your hand creep slowly towards him, as though you were stalking him, he would watch you, his eyes bright, his head on one side. As soon as you were close enough, he would suddenly whip his tail round, give you a gentle bang on the hand with it, and then scuttle away to a new position, and you were then expected to repeat the whole performance. That this was real play I have no doubt, for the blows he dealt you with his tail were very gentle, whereas I have seen him bash other lizards with it and not only send them flying, but draw blood.

Not long after we had Dandy, we had trouble with teguexins. These are large, handsome and very intelligent lizards from South America. They can grow to about three and a half feet in length, and their skin is very beautifully patterned in yellow and black. They are very quick-witted, belligerent creatures, and the female we had was quite the most vicious in the Reptile House. Tegus, as they are called for short, have three methods of attack, all of which they employ – together or separately – very cheerfully and without any provocation at all. They will either bite, scratch with their well developed claws, or lash you with their tails. Our female preferred to start hostilities with her tail. As you opened her cage she would regard you with obvious dislike and mistrust, inflate her throat and start to hiss, and at the same time curve her body into a half-moon shape like a bow. Once your hand came near enough, she would suddenly straighten out, and her tail would lash round like a stockwhip. If she found that this method of defence did not deter you, she would run forward and try to grab you with her mouth. If she succeeded, she would hang on with the tenacity of a bulldog, at the same time bringing up reinforcements in the shape of her sharp, curved hind claws, which could tear chunks off you. I did not think this tegu's character was an exception. After a fair amount of experience with tegus in their natural state, I had come to the conclusion that they were by far the most evilly-disposed of the lizards, and were, moreover, so fast and intelligent that they were a force to be reckoned with when in captivity. We were always suffering at the hands, or rather the tail, of our female tegu, and so it was with somewhat mixed feelings that we discovered her lying dead in her cage one morning. I was puzzled by her sudden death, for she had appeared to be in the very pink of fighting condition, having bitten me vigorously only a couple of days previously. So I decided to do a rough post-mortem and try to find a clue as to the cause. To my astonishment, on opening the stomach, I found a huge mass of whitish substance, not unlike soft fish roe, which I took to be a gigantic growth of some sort. Wanting to find out more about this mysterious growth, I shipped the body off for a more detailed and expert post-mortem, and awaited the results with interest. When they came through, they were terse and to the point: the mass of white substance had not been a growth, but a large quantity of pure fat. The lizard had died of heart trouble brought on by this fatty condition, and it was suggested that we fed less abundantly in future. On reflection, it was plain, for in the wild state tegus are very active creatures. Therefore, if you confine them in a limited area and give them a rich and continuous food supply, they are bound to become over-fat. I vowed that the next tegus we obtained would be treated very differently.

Our chance came not long afterwards, when a dealer offered us a pair.

On arrival they turned out to be wonderful specimens, well marked and with glossy skins: the male with a great, heavy head and fleshy jowls; the female with a longer, more slender head. Contrary to our expectations, they did not prove to be typical tegus at all. Instead of being fierce and unhandleable, they were as tame as kittens, and liked nothing so much as to lie in your arms, being gently rocked, and drowse off to sleep. If you went and stood by their cage, they would make the most frantic and flattering efforts to climb through the glass and into your arms. Apart from these bursts of social activity, they showed little desire to do anything very much, except to lie around in abandoned attitudes, gazing benignly at any human beings who happened to be around in the Reptile House. As a result of all this feverish activity, of course, they grew fatter and fatter, and, viewing their increasing girth with alarm, we decided that something would have to be done, or we would have another couple of heart failures on our hands. The answer was exercise; so, every morning, John would let them both out to wander round the Reptile House, while he did his work. To begin with – for the first two or three days – this worked like a charm, and the tegus, breathing heavily, pottered about the Reptile House for a couple of hours each morning. Then, however, they discovered that by climbing over a low barrier they could get into the tortoise pen, over which hung an infra-red light. So, each morning when they were let out, they would rush shortwindedly over to the tortoise pen, climb in and settle themselves under the infra-red light and go to sleep. The only answer to this was to cut down on their food, and consequently they were dieted as rigorously as a couple of dowager duchesses at a health resort. Needless to say, they took a very poor view of this, and would gaze plaintively through the glass as they watched the other inmates of the Reptile House enjoying such delicacies as raw egg, mincemeat, dead rats and chopped fruit. We hardened our hearts, though, and continued with the diet, and within a very short time they had regained their sylph-like figures, and were much more active as a result. Now we let them eat what they like, but at the least sign of corpulence back they will go to the diet until their size is respectable again.

The one Reptile House inhabitant that never seemed to become overweight, no matter how much he ate, was our dragon, known as George. He was a Guiana dragon, a rather rare and interesting kind of lizard from the northern parts of South America. They measure about two feet six inches in length, and have large, heavy heads with big, dark, intelligent eyes. The body and tail are very crocodile-like in appearance, the tail being heavily armoured and flattened on top, whereas the back is covered with heavy scales which are bean-shaped and protrude above the surface of the skin. The colouring is a warm rusty brown, fading to yellowish on the face. They are slow, thoughtful and attractive lizards, and George had a very mild and likeable character.

Probably one of the most remarkable things about Guiana dragons is their feeding habits. Before George arrived we had read up all we could on the species, but none of the text-books was very helpful. However, they seemed to be perfectly normal lizard-type creatures, so we thought that their diet would be similar to that of any large carnivorous lizard. So George duly arrived, was petted, admired and placed reverently in a large cage which had been prepared for him, with a special pond of his own. This amenity he appeared to appreciate fully, for the moment he was released into his quarters he made straight for the pond and plunged in. He spent half an hour or so squatting in the water, occasionally ducking his head beneath the surface for a few minutes at a time and peering thoughtfully about the bottom of the pond. That evening we gave him a dead rat, which he regarded with considerable loathing. Then we tried him on a young chicken, with the same result. Fish he retreated from as if it were some deadly poison, and we were in despair, for we could think of nothing else that he might like. Just when we were convinced that George was going to starve himself to death, John had an idea. He went off and fetched a handful of fat garden snails and tossed them into George's pond. George, who had been sitting on a tree trunk at the back of the cage and looking very regal, eyed this floating, frothing largesse with his head on one side. Then he came down to the pool, slid into the water and nosed interestedly at a snail, while we watched hopefully. Delicately he picked up the snail in his mouth and, throwing back his head, allowed it to slide to the back of his mouth. Now that his mouth was open I could see that he had the most astonishing teeth I had ever seen in a lizard: teeth that were, of course, perfectly adapted for eating snails. Those in the front of the mouth were fairly small, pointed and inclined slightly backwards into the mouth. These were the grasping teeth, as it were. Once they had hold of the snail, the lizard threw back his head so that the mollusc slid and rested on the teeth at the back of the mouth. These were huge, shoe-box-shaped molars with caruncular surfaces which looked more like miniature elephant's teeth than anything else. With the aid of his tongue, George manoeuvred the snail until it rested between these ponderous molars, and then closed his jaws slowly. The snail cracked and splintered, and when he was quite sure that the shell was broken he shifted the whole into the centre of his mouth and, by careful manipulation of his tongue, extracted all the bits of broken shell and spat them out. Then the smooth, shell-less body of the snail was swallowed with every evidence of satisfaction. The complete process took about a minute and a half, after which George sat there for a bit, licking his lips with his black tongue, and musing to himself. After a time he leant forward and daintily picked up another snail, which he despatched in the same manner. Within half an hour he had eaten twelve of these molluscs, and we were jubilant, for, having now discovered George's preference, we knew there would be no more difficulty in keeping him.

It is always a relief when a reptile starts to feed itself, for if it refuses food for a certain length of time it has to be force-fed, and that is a tricky and unpleasant job. Many of the constricting snakes refuse food on their arrival, and have to be force-fed until they have settled down, but it is not an operation one relishes, since, with their fragile jaws and teeth, it is very easy to break something and thus set up an infection in the mouth. I think the worst force-feeding job we ever had was with a pair of young gharials. These are Asiatic members of the crocodile family, and in the wild state feed on fish. Instead of the strong, rather blunt jaws of the alligators and crocodiles, the gharial's jaws are long and very slender, resembling a beak more than anything. Both the jaws and the teeth are very fragile, the teeth especially so, for they appear to fall out if you look at them. In consequence, when our two young gharials arrived and steadfastly refused all food, including live fish in their pond, our hearts sank, as we realized we would have to force-feed them. The process was tedious, protracted and difficult, and had to be done once a week for a year before the gharials would feed on their own. First, you take a firm grip on the back of the creature's neck and his tail. Then you lift him out of the tank and place him on a convenient flat surface. Whoever is helping you, then slides a flat, smooth piece of wood between the jaws at the back of the mouth, immediately behind the last teeth. When the jaws are prised a little apart, you slightly release your grip on the reptile's neck and slide your hand forward, push your thumb and forefinger between the jaws and hold them apart. This is generally much easier than it sounds. The other person then arms himself with a long, slender stick and a plateful of raw meat chunks or raw fish. Impaling a piece of meat or fish on the end of the stick, he inserts it into the reptile's mouth and pushes it towards the back of the throat. This is the tricky part, for in all members of the crocodile family the throat is closed by a flap of skin: this arrangement allows the creature to open its mouth beneath the surface without swallowing vast quantities of water. The food has to be pushed past this flap of skin and well down into the throat. Then you massage the throat until you feel the food slide down into the stomach. As I say, it is a tedious task, as much for the gharial as for you.

By and large, the creatures that seem to cause the least trouble in the Reptile House are the amphibians. They usually feed well, and they do not seem to suffer from the awful variety of cankers, sores and parasites that snakes and lizards contract, though I must admit they can come up with one or two choice complaints of their own on occasions, just to enliven things for you. The pipa toads were a good example of this. These extraordinary creatures come from British Guiana, and look, quite frankly, like nothing on earth. Their bodies are almost rectangular, with a leg at each corner, so to speak, and a pointed bit between the front legs that indicates where the head is supposed to be. The whole affair is very flattened and a dark blackish brown colour, so the creature looks as though it had met with a nasty accident some considerable time ago and has been gently decomposing ever since. The most extraordinary thing about these weird beasts is their breeding habits, for the pipa toads carry their young in pockets. During the breeding season the skin on the female's back becomes thickened, soft and spongy, and then she is ready for mating. The male clasps her, and as soon as she is ready to lay she protrudes a long ovipositor which curves up on to her back, underneath the male's stomach. As the eggs appear, he fertilizes them and presses them into the spongy skin of the back. They sink in until only a small proportion of the egg is above the surface of the skin. This exposed portion of egg hardens. So, inside their individual pockets, the tadpoles undergo their entire metamorphosis until they change into tiny replicas of their parents. When they are ready to hatch, the hardened top of the shell comes loose, and the tiny toads push it back and climb out, looking rather like someone getting out of a bubble-car.

I had once been fortunate enough to witness the hatching of some baby pipa toads, and I was anxious to see if we could breed them in the Zoo. So

I ordered a pair from a dealer, and on their arrival duly installed them in the Reptile House. We kept them in a large aquarium full of water, for, unlike other toads, pipas are entirely aquatic. They settled down very well, and were soon devouring monstrous great earthworms by the score. All we had to do now, I thought, was to wait for them to breed. One morning John came to me and said that one of the pipas had apparently bruised itself on the stomach, though he could not see how this had happened. I examined the toad and discovered that what appeared to be a bruise was something which looked like a gigantic blood blister. It was difficult to know what to do. If the toads had not been aquatic and had had dry skin, I would have anoited the area with penicillin. Within twenty-four hours both pipas were dead, their bodies covered with red blisters which were full of blood and mucous. I sent them away for post-mortem, and the report came back that they were suffering from an obscure disease called red-leg. I had a strong feeling that this had something to do with the water in which they had been kept: it was ordinary tap water but rather acid. So I purchased another pair of pipas, and this time we kept them in pond water only. This has, so far, proved successful, and, at the time of writing, both toads are flourishing. With a bit of luck, I might get around to breeding pipa toads yet, unless they can think up something new to frustrate me.

Another amphibian with almost as fascinating breeding habits as the pipas is the little pouched frog. We had five of these delightful tubby little frogs, handsomely marked in green and black, which were brought to us from Ecuador. They did very well, eating prodigiously, but they showed no signs of wanting to breed. So we moved them into a bigger tank where they had more land and water space, and this did the trick. Out of the breeding season, the female's pouch, which is on her lower back, is scarcely noticeable. If you look closely, you can see a faint line down the skin, with a slightly puckered edge, as if at one time the skin had been torn and healed up rather badly. However, when the breeding season comes round, the slit becomes much more obvious. The frogs begin to sing to each other, and presently you will see the females going off into quiet corners and indulging in a very curious action. They manage, by great contortion, to get one hind leg at a time up over their backs, insert the toes into their pouches and proceed to stretch the skin. When the pouch is stretched to their satisfaction, they are ready to breed. The method by which they put the eggs into the pouch is still a mystery to me, for, unfortunately, I missed the actual egg-laying. The next thing we knew was that the female had a bulging pouchful of spawn which protruded from her back and made her look as though she had been disembowelled. The female carries the eggs around until she knows, by some means or other, that the tadpoles are ready to hatch, whereupon she goes and sits in the water. The tadpoles wriggle free of the gelatine-like spawn and swim off on their own, the mother taking no further interest in them. We found that the tadpoles did very well on strips of raw meat and white worms, the tiny worms that fish fanciers breed as food. When they grew their legs and came out on land, we fed them on fruit flies and tiny earthworms, until they were old enough to graduate to house-flies and bluebottles.

Amphibians are much easier to breed than reptiles, for you do not have to worry about the moisture. Reptiles lay eggs with a parchment-like shell which is either soft or hard. If the temperature of the cage is not right, and if the moisture content of the air is too great or not enough, the contents of the egg will either dry up or else go mildewed. Although we have had some successes with hatching reptile eggs, the chances against are always ninety to one. One success we did achieve, of which we were rather proud, was in hatching some Greek tortoise eggs. The Greek tortoise is probably one of the commonest pets, and they invariably lay eggs with monotonous regularity, but these very seldom hatch. Thinking that this batch of eggs was going to be no more successful than all the others had been, John did not worry overmuch about them. He buried them in the sand at the bottom of one of the cages which had what he thought was a suitable temperature. Week after week passed, and eventually he forgot all about them. He was, therefore, considerably astonished one morning to find a baby tortoise perambulating about the cage. He called me and we dug up the rest of the eggs. Out of the six, four were in the process of hatching. In one egg the baby was almost out, but in the other three the babies had only just started to breach the shell. We placed them in a small aquarium on a saucer of sand, in order to watch the hatching more conveniently. The eggs were almost the size of ping-pong balls, and much the same shape; the parchment-like shell was tough, and it was clearly an exhausting job for the babies to break out of their prisons. The one who had made the biggest hole in his shell could be seen quite plainly inside, as he twisted round and round, now using his front feet and now his back ones to enlarge the hole. On his nose he had the little horny 'beak' which baby tortoises are supposed to use to make the first breach in the shell; this later drops off. But I did not see this one use his 'beak' at all – all the hard work was done with the front and hind legs, with frequent pauses for him to regain his strength. It took him three-quarters of an hour to break out, and then the egg split in half and he trundled off across the sand wearing one half on top of his carapace, like a hat. When they emerged from the egg, their shells were spongy, misshapen and extremely soft, and they were each the diameter of a two-shilling piece. However, after an hour or so a change had taken place; it was as though someone had inflated them with a bicycle pump. The shell had filled out, and, instead of being flattened, it was now handsomely domed and looked much harder, although it was, in actual fact, still as soft as damp cardboard. They were now so much larger than the egg that, unless I had watched them hatching myself, I would have said they could not possibly have emerged so recently from such a small prison. I noticed that their nails, when they hatched, were very long and sharp, presumably to help them break through the egg shell. Within a very short time, though, they had worn down to a normal length.

I had spent several hours watching this hatching process, and it was worth every minute of it. I had the greatest admiration for these rotund and earnest little tortoises, for breaking out of the egg was no easy matter. What amused me most, I think, was the way – after he had been using the hind feet to enlarge the hole – the tiny reptile would swivel round inside the shell, and the next moment a minute, wrinkled and rather sad little face would be poked through the hole in the shell, as if the tortoise wanted to reassure himself that the outside world was still there and still as attractive as it had been when he last looked. We were very lucky to have been able to hatch these tortoises, but what was even luckier was the fact that Ralph Thompson, the illustrator, happened to be staying with me at the time, and was thus able to draw the whole of the hatching process from start to finish, which he assured me he thoroughly enjoyed, in spite of the fact that, owing to the high temperature in the Reptile House, his glasses kept misting over.

Chapter Four

Claudius Among the Cloches

Dear Mr Durrell,
Do you ever stuff your animals? If you ever wanted to stuff your animals I could stuff them for you, as I have a great experience in stuffing animals . . .

On acquiring new animals, one of the many problems that face you is the process of settling them in, for until they have learnt to look upon their new cage as home, and have also learnt to trust you, they are unsettled. There are many different ways of making animals feel at home, and these vary according to the species. Sometimes special titbits have to be given, so that the animal forgets its fear of you in its eagerness for the food. With highly nervous creatures you may have to provide them with a box in which they can hide, or cover the front of the cage with sacking until they have decided that you mean them no harm. There are times when the most extraordinary methods have to be used to give an animal confidence and the trouble we had with Topsy was a case in point.

I was in an animal dealer's shop in the North of England one cold winter's day, looking around to see if he had anything interesting I could buy for the Zoo. As I walked round the shop I suddenly noticed a very dank, dark cage in one corner, and peering at me from behind the bars was one of the most pathetic little faces I had ever seen. It was coal-black with large, lustrous eyes that seemed to be perpetually full of tears. The fur surrounding this face was reddish-brown, short and thick like the pile on an expensive carpet. I looked closer and saw that the face belonged to a baby woolly monkey, one of the most charming of the South American primates. This one could not have been more than a few weeks old, and was far too young to have been separated from its mother. It crouched miserably on the floor of the cage, shivering and coughing, its nose streaming, its fur matted and tangled with filth. From the condition and smell of the cage I could see that it had enteritis as well as a cold which looked as though it was bordering on pneumonia. It was not an animal that anyone in their right senses would contemplate buying. But then it peered up at me with its great, dark eyes filled with despair, and I was lost. I asked the dealer how much he wanted for the baby. He said that he would not dream of selling it to me, as I was a good customer and the baby was sure to die. I replied that I realized the animal was a bad risk, but that if he would let me have it I would pay him if it lived, but not if it died. Rather reluctantly he agreed to this, and we bundled the plaintively squealing baby into a box full of straw, and I hurried back to Jersey with it. I knew that unless it was treated rapidly, it would die, and already it might well be too late.

On my return to Jersey, we put the baby, which someone christened Topsy, into a warm cage and examined her. First, I realised she would have to have antibiotic and vitimin injections to combat the enteritis and the cold. Secondly, her thick fur, matted with her own extreta, would have to be cleaned, for if it was left in that state she could develop skin rash and eventually lose all her fur. Our chief problem, though, was how to get Topsy to allow us to do these things. Most baby monkeys will, within a matter of hours, take to a human foster-parent, and they are generally no trouble at all. As Topsy's experience of human beings had obviously been of the worst possible kind, she threw herself in fits of screaming hysterics (as only a woolly monkey can) if we so much as opened the door of her cage. To manhandle her was, therefore, going to do more harm than good, and yet she had to have treatment or die. Then we had a brainwave: if Topsy would not accept us as foster parents, would she accept something else? How about a teddy-bear? We were all a bit doubtful about this, but we had to try something, and so we obtained one. The bear had a pleasant, if slightly vacuous expression, and was just about the size that Topsy's mother would be, so we put it in the cage and awaited results. At first, Topsy would not go near it, but at last her curiosity got the better of her and she touched it. As soon as she discovered that it was cuddly and furry, she took to it, and within half an hour was clinging to it with a fierce, possessive passion that was quite touching.

Now, a complete change came over Topsy. As long as she was clinging to her teddy-bear with arms, legs and tail, she lost her fear of human beings. We just simply lifted the bear out of the cage with Topsy stuck to it, like a limpet, and she would allow us to do what we liked. We were thus able to inject her and clean up her matted fur, and within a few days she was well on the road to recovery, and looked a different monkey. But then came another problem: as the days passed, the teddy-bear became more and more unhygienic, until finally we decided he would have to be removed from Topsy's cage to be washed and disinfected. So, to Topsy's extreme annoyance, we removed the bear. Immediately she threw a screaming fit. Of all the monkey family, the woolly monkeys have the most powerful and excruciating scream you have ever heard, a scream that goes through you and makes your blood run cold, like the screech of a knife on a plate, magnified a million times. We blocked our ears, and consoled ourselves with the thought that she would stop in about ten minutes when she realized that she was not going to have her bear back, but Topsy did not stop. She screamed solidly all morning, and by lunch-time our nerves were in shreds. There was only one thing to do: we took the van and rushed down into the town and, after visiting several toy shops, managed to buy a teddy-bear closely resembling

Topsy's original one. Then we hurried back to the Zoo and stuffed it hastily into Topsy's cage. She stopped in mid-scream, gave a loud squeak of joy and flung herself on to the new teddy-bear, wrapped her arms, legs and tail tightly round it, and immediately fell into a deep and exhausted sleep. After that, the teddy-bears took it in turn: while one was being washed, the other took over the duties of foster mother, and this arrangement Topsy found eminently satisfactory.

At last Topsy had grown so big that she was bigger than her teddy-bears, and we decided that we would have to wean her off them, as it were, for eventually she would have to go into a big cage with other woolly monkeys, and she could not take her bears with her. It was time, we felt, that she grew used to the idea of having a companion in the cage with her, and so we chose a large ginger guinea-pig of placid disposition and no brain. He was introduced into Topsy's cage, and at first she ignored him, except when he went too near to her precious bear, whereupon she could clout him. It was not long, however, before Topsy discovered that the guinea-pig had one great advantage over the bear as a sleeping companion, and that was it had built-in central heating. The guinea-pig – whom we now called Harold for convenient reference – took, I think, a rather dim view of all this. To begin with, if he possessed a thought in his head at all, that thought was food. Harold's life-work was to test the edibility of everything into which he came in contact, and he did not like having his life's work mucked about by a domineering woolly monkey. Topsy, on the other hand, had very strict ideas about the correct time to get up, go to bed, play, and so on, and she did not see why she should have to change these to fit in with Harold's feeding habits. It seemed to Harold that no sooner had he found a respectable piece of carrot, or something, than Topsy would decide it was bedtime, and he was seized by the hind-leg and hauled off to their box of straw, in the most undignified manner. Here, to add insult to injury, Topsy would climb on to his back, wrap her arms, legs and tail tightly round him to prevent his escape, and sink into a deep sleep looking like an outsize jockey on a small and very rotund ginger horse.

Another thing that Harold found rather disquieting was Topsy's firm conviction that, if given the opportunity, he would be able to leap about in the branches with the same agility that she herself displayed. She was sure that, if only she could get him *up* into the branches, he would turn out to be a splendid climber, but the job was to lift Harold off the ground. She could only spare one hand to hold him with, and he was fat, heavy and unco-operative. She would, after considerable effort, tuck him under one arm, and then start to climb, but before she was more than a few inches up the wire Harold would slip out from under her arm and plop back to the floor of the cage. Poor Harold, I think he suffered a great deal at Topsy's hands, but he served our purpose, for very soon Topsy had forgotten all about her teddy-bears, and was able to take her place in the big cage with the rest of the woolly monkeys. Harold was returned to the guinea-pig pen where he spends all day up to his knees in vegetables, champing his way through them with grim determination.

Another creature that gave us a certain amount of trouble during his settling-in period was Fred, a patas monkey from West Africa. He was a fully adult male, one of the largest patas I have ever seen, and he had been the personal pet of some people in England. How they managed to keep him up to that size without being severely bitten was a mystery, for Fred's canines were a good two inches long and as sharp as razors. Apparently, right up to the time that Fred came to us, he used to go into the house each evening and watch television.

But the really awful thing about Fred was his clothing. Patas monkeys are covered with thick, bright ginger-coloured fur, and Fred arrived wearing a knitted jumper in a startling shade of pillar-box red. This combination of colours made even the most un-sartorial members of the staff blench. The trouble was that Fred missed his television and his rides in the car, and decided that we were in some way responsible for depriving him of these, and so he loathed us all from the very start with complete impartiality. If anyone went near his cage he would leap at the wire and shake it vigorously, baring all his teeth in a ferocious grimace. Until, if ever, he showed any signs of trusting and liking us, we could do nothing about removing his terrible jacket. Fred just sat among the branches in his cage, wearing his scarlet jacket and showing no signs of forgiving us. The trouble was that, as the days passed, the jumper grew more and more grubby and dishevelled until he looked as though he had just emerged from some poverty-stricken slum. We tried every method to rid him of this insanitary garment, but without success. Fred seemed rather proud of it, and would become very annoyed if we tried to take it off him. We began to wonder how long it would take the wool to disintegrate naturally and fall off, but whoever had knitted the jumper had chosen really tough wool, and it was obvious that it would be several years before it fell to pieces. Then fate played into our hands. We had a heat-wave, and the temperature in the Mammal House where Fred lived soared up. At first, he enjoyed it, but soon it became too much even for him, and we noticed that he was pulling meditatively at his jumper. The next morning we found the offending garment hanging neatly over a branch in Fred's cage, and managed to hook it out with the aid of a long stick. From that day onwards, Fred grew increasingly placid; he will never be really trustworthy, but at least he is now less inclined to treat human beings as his enemies.

Still another creature that gave us a certain amount of trouble in the early stages was Millicent, the Malabar squirrel. Malabars are the largest members of the squirrel family, and hail from India. They measure about two feet in length, with sturdy bodies and long, very bushy tails. Their undersides are saffron yellow, their upper parts a rich mahogany red, and they have very large ear-tufts that are like a couple of black sporrans perched on their heads. They are, like all squirrels, very alert, quick moving and inquisitive, but, unlike most squirrels, they do not have that nervous desire to gnaw everything with which they come into contact. The exception to this was, of course, Millicent. Her view was that nature had provided her with a pair of very prominent, bright orange teeth for the sole purpose of demolishing any cage in which she was confined. This was not from any desire to escape, because having gnawed a large hole in one side of the cage she would then move over to the other side and start all over again. She cost us a small fortune in repairs until we had a cage specially lined with sheet metal, and thus put a stop to her activities. However, feeling that she would miss her occupational therapy, we gave her large logs of wood, and she proceeded to gnaw her way through these, like a buzz saw.

At first, Millicent was anything but tame, and would not hesitate to bury her teeth in your finger, should you be foolish enough to give her the chance. No amount of bribery on our part, with the aid of such things as mushrooms and acorns, would make her any the less savage, and we came to the conclusion that she was just one of those animals which never became tame. But then a peculiar thing happened: Millicent was found one day lying in the bottom of her cage in a state of collapse. She had no obvious symptoms, and it was a little difficult to tell exactly what was wrong with her. When I find an animal suffering from some mysterious complaint like this, I do two things: I give it an antibiotic and keep it very warm. So Millicent had an injection and was moved down to the Reptile House, for this is the only place where the heat is kept on throughout the summer months.

Within a few days Millicent was recovering satisfactorily, but was still languid. The extraordinary fact was the change in her character. From being acutely anti-human, she had suddenly become so pro-*Homo sapiens* that it was almost embarrassing. You had only to open her cage door and she would rush out into your arms, nibbling your fingers gently and peering earnestly into your face, her long whiskers quivering with emotion. She liked nothing better than to lie along your arm, as though it were the branch of a tree, and in this position doze for hours if you let her. Since she was now such a reformed character, she was allowed out of her cage first thing each morning, to potter round the Reptile House. Millicent very soon discovered that the tortoise pen provided her with everything a self-respecting Malabar could want: there was an infra-red lamp that cast a pleasant, concentrated heat; there were the backs of the giant tortoises which made ideal perches; and there was an abundance of fruit and vegetables. So the giant tortoises would move ponderously round their pen, while Millicent perched on their shells. Occasionally, when one of them found a succulent piece of fruit and was just stretching out his neck to engulf it, she would hop down from his back, pick up the fruit, and jump back on to the shell again before the tortoise really knew what was happening. When the time came that Millicent was well enough to return to the Small Mammal House, I think the giant tortoises were glad to see the back of her, for not only had she been an additional weight on their shells, but the constant disappearance of titbits from under their very noses was having a distressing effect on their nerves.

It is amazing how wild-caught animals (as opposed to hand-reared ones) differ in settling down in captivity. Some take a considerable time to adjust themselves, while others, from the moment of arrival, carry on as if they had been born in the Zoo. A dealer sent us a pair of brown woolly monkeys which he had just received direct from Brazil. We found that the male was a magnificent specimen, fully adult, and must have been about twelve or fourteen years old. We were not very pleased with this, for an adult monkey of that age would, we felt, take a long time to adjust itself to captivity, and might even pine and die. We released him into his cage with his mate, and went and fetched them some fruit and milk. As soon as he saw these, he became very excited, and when the door of the cage was opened, to our complete astonishment, he came straight down and ate and drank while we were still holding the dishes, as if he had been with us for years instead of a matter of minutes. Right from the start he was perfectly tame, and ate well and seemed to thoroughly enjoy his new life.

There are many creatures which, on being settled in, make the most determined attempts to escape from their cages, not because they want their freedom but simply because they miss their old territory: the travelling crate to which they have grown used and which they look upon as their home. I have known an animal that was removed from its tiny, travelling crate and placed in a spacious, well-appointed cage spend three days endeavouring to break out, and when it was finally successful it made a bee-line to its old travelling box and was found sitting inside it. The only answer to this problem was to place the travelling crate inside the new cage. This we did, and the animal used it thereafter as its bedroom and settled down quite happily.

There are again some creatures, of course, which, when they manage to escape, present you with considerable problems. For instance, there was the night I shall never forget, when Claudius, the South American tapir, contrived to find a way out of his paddock. The person who had been in to give him his night feed had padlocked the gate carefully but without sliding the bolt into position. Claudius, having a nocturnal perambulation round his territory, found to his delight that the gate which he had hitherto presumed to be invulnerable now responded to his gentle nosings. He decided that this was a very suitable night to have a short incursion into the neighbouring countryside. It was a suitable night from Claudius' point of view, because the skies were as black as pitch and the rain was streaming down in torrents that I have rarely seen equalled outside the tropics.

It was about quarter past eleven, and we were all on the point of going to bed, when a rather harassed and extremely wet motorist appeared and beat upon the front door. Above the roar of the rain, he said that he had just seen a big animal in the headlights of his car, which he felt sure must be one of ours. I asked him what it looked like, and he said it looked to him like a misshapen Shetland pony with an elephant's trunk. My heart sank, for I knew just how far and how fast Claudius could gallop if given half a chance. I was in my shirt sleeves and only wearing slippers, but there was no time to change into more suitable attire against the weather, for the motorist had spotted Claudius in a field adjoining our property and I wanted to catch up with him before he ventured too far afield. I rushed round to the cottage and harried all those members of the staff who lived in. In various stages of night attire they all tumbled out into the rain and we headed for the field into which the motorist assured us our tapir had disappeared. This was quite a large field and belonged to our nearest neighbour, Leonard du Feu. Leonard had proved himself to be the most long suffering and sympathetic of neighbours, and so I was determined that Claudius was not going to do any damage to his property if we could possibly avoid it. Having made this mental resolve, I then remembered to my horror that the field in which Claudius was reputedly lurking had just recently been carefully planted out by Leonard with anemones. I could imagine what Claudius' four hundredweight could do to those carefully planted rows of delicate plants, particularly as, owing to his short-sightedness, his sense of direction was never too good at the best of times.

We reached the field, soaked to the skin, and surrounded it. There, sure enough, stood Claudius obviously having the best evening out he had had in years. The wet as far as he was concerned was ideal: there was nothing quite like a heavy down-pour of rain to make life worth while. He was standing there, looking like a debauched Roman emperor under a shower, meditatively masticating a large bunch of anemones. When he saw us, he uttered his greeting – a ridiculous, high-pitched squeak similar to the noise of a wet finger being rubbed over a balloon. It was quite plain that he was delighted to see us and hoped that we would join him in his nocturnal ramble, but none of us was feeling in any mood to do this. We were drenched to the skin and freezing cold, and our one ambition was to get Claudius back into his paddock with as little trouble as possible. Uttering a despairing and rather futile cry of 'don't tread on the plants,' I marshalled my band of tapir-catchers and we converged on Claudius in a grim-faced body. Claudius took one look at us and decided from our manner and bearing that we did not see eye to eye with him on the subject of gambolling about in other people's fields at half-past eleven on a wet night, and so he felt that, albeit reluctantly, he would have to leave us. Pausing only to snatch another mouthful of anemones, he set off across the field at a sharp gallop, leaving a trail of destruction behind him that could only have been emulated by a runaway bulldozer. In our slippered feet, clotted with mud, we stumbled after him. Our speed was reduced not only by the mud but by the fact that we were trying to run between the rows of flowers instead of on them. I remember making a mental note as I ran that I would ask Leonard in future to plant his rows of flowers wider apart, as this would facilitate the recapture of any animal that escaped. The damage Claudius had done to the flowers was bad enough, but worse was to follow. He suddenly swerved, and instead of running into the next field, as we had hoped (for it was a grazing meadow), he ran straight into Leonard du Feu's back-garden. We pulled up short and stood panting, the rain trickling off us in torrents.

'For God's sake,' I said to everyone in general, 'get that bloody animal out of that garden before he wrecks it.' The words were hardly out of my mouth when from inside the garden came a series of tinkling crashes which told us too clearly that Claudius, trotting along in his normal myopic fashion, had ploughed his way through all Leonard's cloches. Before we could do anything sensible, Claudius having decided that Leonard's garden was not to his liking, crashed his way through a hedge, leaving a gaping hole in what hitherto had been a nice piece of topiary, and set off into the night at a brisk trot. The direction he was taking presented yet another danger, for he was heading straight for our small lake. Tapirs in the wild state are very fond of water and they are excellent swimmers and can submerge themselves for a considerable length of time. The thought of having to search for a tapir in a quarter of an acre of dark water on a pitch black, rainy night made the thought of hunting for a needle in a haystack pale into insignificance. This thought struck the other members of my band at the same moment, and we ran as we had never run before and just succeeded at the very last minute in heading off Claudius. Coming up close to his rotund behind, I launched myself in a flying tackle and, more by luck than judgement, managed to grab him by one hind leg. In thirty seconds I was wishing that I had not. Claudius kicked out and caught me a glancing blow on the side of the head, which made me see stars, and then revved up to a gallop, dragging me ignominiously through the mud, but by now I was so wet, so cold, so muddy and so angry that I clung on with the determination of a limpet in a storm. My tenacity was rewarded, for my dragging weight slowed Claudius down sufficiently to allow the others to catch up, and they hurled themselves on various portions of his anatomy. The chief difficulty with a tapir is that there is practically nothing on which to hold: the ears are small and provide a precarious grip, the tail is minute, there is no mane, so really the only part you can grip with any degree of success are its legs, and Claudius' legs were fat and slippery with rain. However, we all clung on grimly, while he bucked and kicked and snorted indignantly. As one person loosened their hold, another one would grab on until eventually Claudius decided he was using the wrong method of discouragement. He stopped pirouetting about, thought to himself for a moment and then just simply lay down and looked at us.

We stood round him in a sodden, exhausted circle and looked at each other. There were five of us and four hundred-weight of reluctant tapir. It was beyond our powers to carry him, and yet it was quite obvious that Claudius had no intention of helping us in any way. He lay there with a mulish expression on his face. If we wanted to get him back to the Zoo it implied, we would jolly well have to carry him. We had no more reinforcements to call on, and so it appeared that we had reached an impasse. However, as Claudius was prepared to be stubborn, I was prepared to be equally so. I sent one of my dripping team back to the Zoo for a rope. I should, of course, have brought this very necessary adjunct of capture with me, but in my innocence I had assumed that Claudius could be chivied back to his paddock with no more trouble than a domestic goat. When the rope arrived, we attached it firmly round Claudius' neck, making sure that it was not a slip-knot. I thought one drenched member of the staff was heard to mutter that a slip-knot would be ideal. Then two of us took hold of the rope, two more took hold of his ears, and the fifth took hold of his hind legs, and by the application of considerable exertion we raised him to his feet and wheel-barrowed him all of ten feet, before he collapsed again. We had a short pause to regain our breath and started off again. Once more we carted him for about ten feet, in the process of which I lost a slipper and had my hand heavily trodden on by one of the larger and weightier members of my team. We rested again, sitting dejectedly and panting in the rain, longing for a cigarette and unanimously deciding that tapirs were animals that should never in any circumstances have been invented.

The field in which these operations took place was large and muddy. At that hour of night, under the stinging rain, it resembled an ancient tanks training ground which had been abandoned because the tanks could no longer get through it. The mud in it appeared to have a glue-like quality not found elsewhere in the Island of Jersey. It took us an hour and a half to get Claudius out of that field, and at the end of it we felt rather like those people must have felt who erected Stonehenge – that none of us was ruptured was a miracle. A final colossal effort and we hauled Claudius out of the field and over the boundary into the Zoo. Here we were going to pause for further recuperation, but Claudius decided that since we had brought him back into the Zoo grounds and would, it appeared, inevitably return him to his paddock, it would be silly to delay. He suddenly rose to his feet and took off like a rocket, all of us desperately clinging to various parts of his body. It seemed ludicrous that for an hour and a half we should have been making the valiant attempt to get him to move at all and now we were clinging to his fat body in an effort to slow him down for fear that in his normal blundering way he would run full tilt into one of the granite archways and hurt or perhaps even kill himself. We clung to him like sucker-fish to a speeding shark, and, to our intense relief, managed to steer our irritating vehicle back into its paddock, without any further mishap, and so we returned to our respective bedrooms, bruised, cold and covered with mud. I had a hot bath to recuperate, but as I lay in it drowsily, I reflected that the worst was yet to come: the following morning I had to telephone Leonard du Feu and try to apologize for half an acre of trampled anemones and twelve broken cloches.

Jacquie, as always, was unsympathetic. As I lay supine in the comforting warmth of the bath, she placed a large whisky within easy reach and summed up the night's endeavour:

'It's your own fault,' she said, 'you would get this blasted Zoo.'

Chapter Five

The Nightingale Touch

Dear Mr Durrell,
You are the most evil man I know. All God's creatures should have their freedom, and for you to lock them up is against His Will. Are you a man or a devil? You would be locked up in prison for the rest of your life if I had my way ...

Whether you run a pig farm, a poultry farm, a mink farm or a zoo, it is inevitable that occasionally your animals will damage themselves, become diseased, and eventually that they will die. In the case of death, however, the pig, mink or poultry farmer is in a very different position from the person who owns a zoo. Someone who visits a pig farm and enquires where the white pig with the black ears has gone, is told that it has been sent to market. The enquirer accepts this explanation without demur, as a sort of porcine kismet. This same person will go to a zoo, become attracted to some creature, visit it off and on for some time, and then, one day, will come and find it missing. On being told that it has died, they are immediately filled with the gravest suspicion. Was it being looked after properly? Was it having enough to eat? Was the vet called in? And so on. They continue in this vein, rather like a Scotland Yard official questioning a murder suspect. The more attractive the animal, of course, the more searching do their enquiries become. They seem to be under the impression that, while pigs, poultry or mink die or are killed as a matter of course, wild creatures should be endowed with a sort of perpetual life, and only some gross inefficiency on your part has removed them to a happier hunting ground. This makes life very difficult, for every zoo, no matter how well-fed and cared-for are its animals, has its dismal list of casualties.

In dealing with the diseases of wild animals you are venturing into a realm about which few people know anything, even qualified veterinary surgeons, so a lot of the time one is working, if not in the dark, in the twilight. Sometimes the creature contracts the disease in the zoo, and at other times it arrives with the disease already well established, and it may well be a particularly unpleasant tropical complaint. The case of Louie, our gibbon, was a typical one.

Louie was a large, black gibbon with white hands, and she had been sent to us by a friend in Singapore. She had been the star attraction in a small R.A.F. zoo where – to judge by her dislike of humans, and men in particular – she had received some pretty rough handling. We put her in a spacious cage in the Mammal House, and hoped that, by kind treatment, we would eventually gain her confidence. For a month all went well. Louie ate prodigiously, actually allowing us to stroke her hand through the wire, and would wake us every morning with her joyous cries, a series of ringing 'whoops' rising to a rapid crescendo and then tailing off into what sounded like a maniacal giggle. One morning, Jeremy came to me and said that Louie was not well. We went down to have a look at her, and found her hunched up in the corner of her cage, looking thoroughly miserable, her long arms wrapped protectively round her body. She gazed at me with the most woebegone expression, while I racked my brains to try to discover what was wrong with her. There seemed to be no signs of a cold, and her motions were normal, though I noticed her urine was very strong and had an unpleasant pungent smell. This indicated some internal disorder, and I decided to give her an antibiotic. We always use Tetramycin, for this is made up in a thick, sweet, bright red mixture, which we have found by experience that very few animals can resist. Some monkeys would, if allowed, drink it by the gallon. At first, Louie was clearly so poorly that she would not even come to try the medicine. At last, after considerable effort, we managed to attract her to the wire, and I tipped a teaspoonful of the mixture over one of her hands. Hands, of course, are of tremendous importance to such an agile, arboreal creature as a gibbon, and Louie was always very particular about keeping her hands clean. So to have a sticky pink substance poured over her fur was more than she could endure, and she set to work and licked it off, pausing after each lick to savour the taste. After she had cleaned up her hand to her satisfaction, I pushed another teaspoonful of Tetramycin through the wire, and to my delight she drank it greedily. I continued this treatment for three days, but it appeared to be having no effect whatsoever, for Louie would not eat and grew progressively weaker. On the fourth day I caught a glimpse of the inside of her mouth, and saw that it was bright yellow. It seemed obvious that she had jaundice, and I was most surprised, for I did not know that apes or monkeys could contract this disease. On the fifth day Louie died quite quietly, and I sent her pathetic corpse away to have a post-mortem done, to make sure my diagnosis was correct. The result of the post-mortem was most interesting. Louie had indeed died of jaundice, but this had been caused by the fact that her liver was terribly diseased by an infestation of filaria, a very unpleasant tropical sickness that can cause, among other things, blindness and elephantiasis. We realized, therefore, that, whatever we had tried to do, Louie had been doomed from the moment she arrived. It was typical that Louie, on arrival, had displayed no symptoms of disease, and had, indeed, appeared to be in quite good condition.

This is one of the great drawbacks of trying to doctor wild animals. A great many creatures cuddle their illnesses to themselves, as it were, and show no signs of anything being wrong until it is too late – or almost too late – to do anything effective. I have seen a small bird eat heavily just after dawn, sing lustily throughout the morning, and at three o'clock in the afternoon be dead, without having given the slightest sign that anything was amiss. Some animals, even when suffering from the most frightful internal complaints, look perfectly healthy, eat well, and display high spirits that delude you into believing they are flourishing. Then, one morning, it looks off-colour for the first time, and, before you can do anything sensible, it is dead. And, of course, even when a creature is showing obvious symptoms of illness, you have to make up your mind as to the cause. A glance at any veterinary dictionary will show a choice of several hundred diseases, all of which have to be treated in a different manner. It is all extremely frustrating.

Generally, you have to experiment to find a cure. Sometimes these experiments pay off in a spectacular way. Take the case of the creeping paralysis, a terrible complaint that attacks principally the New World monkeys. At one time there was no remedy for this, and the disease was a scourge that could wipe out your entire monkey collection. The first symptoms are very slight: the animal appears to have a certain stiffness in its hips. Within a few days, however, the creature shows a marked disinclination to climb about, and sits in one spot. At this stage both hind limbs have become paralysed, but still retain a certain feeling. Gradually the paralysis spreads until the whole of the body is affected. At one time, when the disease reached this stage, the only thing to do was to destroy the animal.

We had had several cases of this paralysis, and lost some beautiful and valuable monkeys as a result. I had tried everything I could think of to effect a cure. We massaged them, we changed the diet, we gave them vitamin injections, but all to no purpose. It worried me that I could not find a cure for this unpleasant disease, since watching a monkey slowly becoming more paralysed each day is not a pretty sight.

I happened to mention this to a veterinary surgeon friend, and said that I was convinced the cause of the disease was dietary, but that I had tried everything I could think of without result. After giving the matter some thought, my friend suggested that the monkeys might be suffering from a phosphorus deficiency in their diet, or rather that, although the phosphorus was present, their bodies were unable, for some reason, to assimilate it.

Injections of D_3 were the answer to this, if it was the trouble. So the next monkey that displayed the first signs of the paralysis was hauled unceremoniously out of its cage (protesting loudly at the indignity) and given an injection of D_3. Then I watched it carefully for a week, and, to my delight, it showed distinct evidence of improvement. At the end of the week it was given another injection, and within a fortnight it was completely cured. I then turned my attention to a beautiful red West African patas monkey, who had had the paralysis for some considerable time. This poor creature had become completely immobile, so that we had to lift up her head when she fed. I decided that, if D_3 worked with her, it would prove beyond all doubt that this was the cure. I doubled the normal dose and injected the patas; three days later I gave her another massive dose. Within a week she could lift her head to eat, and within a month was completely cured. This was a really spectacular cure, and convinced me that D_3 was the answer to the paralysis. When a monkey now starts to shuffle, we no longer have that sinking feeling, knowing that it is the first step towards death; we simply inject them, and within a short time they are fit and well again.

Another injection that we use a lot with conspicuous success is vitamin B_{12}. This acts as a general pick-me-up and, more valuable still, as a stimulant to the appetite. If any animal looks a bit off-colour, or starts to lack interest in its food, a shot of B_{12} soon pulls it round. I had only used this product on mammals and birds, but never on reptiles. Reptiles are so differently constructed from birds and mammals that one has to be a bit circumspect in the remedies you employ for them, as what may suit a squirrel or a monkey might well kill a snake or a tortoise. However, there was in the Reptile House a young boa constrictor which we had obtained from a dealer some six months previously. From the day it arrived it had shown remarkable tameness, but what worried me was that it steadfastly declined to eat. So, once a week, we had to haul the boa out of its cage, force open its mouth and push dead rats or mice down its throat, a process which he did not care for, but which he accepted with his usual meekness. Force-feeding a snake like this is always a risky business, for, however carefully you do it, there is always a chance that you might damage the delicate membranes in the mouth, and thus set up an infection which would quickly turn to mouth canker, a disease to which snakes are very prone, and which is very difficult to cure. So, with a certain amount of trepidation, I decided to give the boa a shot of B_{12} and see what happened. I injected halfway down his body, in the thick, muscular layer that covers the backbone. He did not appear to even notice it, lying quite quietly coiled round my hand. I put him back into his cage and left him. Later on that day he did not seem to be any worse for his experience, and I suggested to John that he put some food in the cage that night. John placed two rats inside, and in the morning reported to me delightedly that not only had the boa eaten the rats, but had actually struck at his hand when he had opened the cage. From that moment on the boa never looked back. As it had obviously only done good to the snake, I experimented with B_{12} on other reptiles. Lizards and tortoises I found benefited greatly from periodical shots, especially in the colder weather, and on several occasions the reptiles concerned would certainly have died but for the injections.

Wild animals, of course, make the worst possible patients in the world. Any nurse who thinks her lot is a hard one, handling human beings, should try her hand at a bit of wild animal nursing. They are rarely grateful for your ministrations, but you do not expect that. What you do hope for (and never, or hardly ever, receive) is a little co-operation in the matter of taking medicines, keeping on bandages, and so forth. After the first few hundred bitter experiences you reconcile yourself to the fact that every administration of a medicine is a sort of all-in wrestling match, in which you are more likely to apply more of the healing balm to your own external anatomy than to the interior of your patient. You soon give up all hope of keeping a wound covered, for nothing short of encasing your patient entirely in plaster of Paris is going to prevent it from removing the dressings within thirty seconds of their application. Monkeys are, of course, some of the worst patients. To begin with, they have, as it were, four hands with which to fight you off, or remove bandages. They are very intelligent and highly-strung, on the whole, and look upon any medical treatment as a form of refined torture, even when you know it is completely painless. Being highly-strung means that they are apt to behave rather like hypochondriacs, and quite a simple and curable disease may kill them because they just work themselves into a state of acute melancholy and fade away. You have to develop a gay, hearty bedside manner (rather reminiscent of a Harley Street specialist) when dealing with a mournful monkey which thinks he is no longer for this world.

Among the apes, with their far superior intelligence, you are on less shaky ground, and can even expect some sort of co-operation occasionally. During the first two years of the Zoo's existence we had both the chimps, Chumley and Lulu, down with sickness. Both cases were different, and both were interesting.

One morning I was informed that Lulu's ear was sticking out at a peculiar angle, but that, apart from this, she looked all right. Now Lulu's ears stuck out at the best of times, so I felt it must be something out of the ordinary for it to be so noticeable. I went and had a look at her and found her squatting on the floor of the cage, munching an apple with every sign of appetite, while she gazed at the world, her sad, wrinkled face screwed up in intense concentration. She was carefully chewing the flesh of the apple, sucking at it noisily, and then, when it was quite devoid of juice, spitting it into her hand daintily, placing it on her knee and gazing at it with the air of an ancient scientist who has, when he is too old to appreciate it, discovered the elixir of life. I called to her and she came over to the wire, uttering little breathless grunts of greeting. Sure enough, her ear looked most peculiar, sticking out at right angles to her head. I tried to coax her to turn round so that I could see the back of the ear, but she was too intent in putting her fingers through the wire and trying to pull the buttons off my coat. There was nothing for it but to get her out, and this was a complicated procedure, for Chumley became most jealous if Lulu went out of the cage without him. However, I did not feel like having Chumley as my partner during a medical examination. So, after much bribery, I managed to lure him into her bedroom and lock him in, much to his vocal indignation. Then I went into the outer cage, where Lulu immediately came and sat on my lap and put her arms round me. She was an immensely affectionate ape, and had the most endearing character. I gave her a lump of sugar to keep her happy, and examined the ear. To my horror, I found that, behind the ear on the mastoid bone, there was an immense swelling, the size of half an orange, and the skin was discoloured a deep purplish black. The reason this had not been noticed in the early stages was that Lulu had thick hair on her head, and particularly behind her ears, so that – until the swelling became so large that it pushed the ear out of position – nothing was noticeable. Also Lulu had displayed no signs of distress, which was amazing when one considered the size of the lump. She allowed me to explore the exact extent of the swelling gently, without doing anything more than carefully and politely removing my fingers if their pressure became too painful. I decided, after investigation, that I would have to lance it, as it was obviously full of matter, so I picked Lulu up in my arms and carried her into the house, where I put her down on the sofa and gave her a banana to keep her occupied until I had everything ready.

Up till now, the chimps had only been allowed in the house on very special occasions, and Lulu was, therefore, charmed with the idea that she was getting an extra treat without Chumley's knowledge. She sat on the sofa, her mouth full of banana, giving a regal handshake and a muffled hoot of greeting to whoever came into the room, rather as though she owned the place and you were attending one of her 'At Homes.' Presently, when everything was ready, I sat down beside her on the sofa and gently cut away the long hairs behind the ear that was affected. When it was fully exposed, the swelling looked even worse than before, a rich plum colour, and the skin had a leathery appearance. I carefully swabbed the whole area with disinfected warm water, searching to see if I could find a head or an opening to the swelling, for I was now convinced that it was a boil or ulcer that had become infected, but I could find no opening at all. Meanwhile, Lulu, having carefully and thoroughly scrutinized all the medical paraphernalia, had devoted her time to consuming another banana. I took a hypodermic needle and gently pricked the discoloured skin all over the swelling without causing her to deviate from the paths of gluttony, so it was obvious that the whole of the discoloured area was dead skin.

I was faced with something of a problem. Although I was fairly sure that I could make an incision across the dead skin, and thus let out the pus, without Lulu suffering any pain, I was not absolutely certain about it. She was, as I have remarked, of a lovable and charming disposition, but she was also a large, well-built ape, with a fine set of teeth, and I had no desire to enter into a trial of strength with her. The thing to do was to keep her mind occupied elsewhere while I tackled the job, for, like most chimps, Lulu was incapable of thinking of more than one thing at a time. I enlisted the aid of my mother and Jacquie, to whom I handed a large tin of chocolate biscuits, with instructions that they were to feed them to Lulu at intervals throughout the ensuing operation. I had no fears for their safety, as I knew that if Lulu was provoked into biting anyone it would be me. Uttering up a brief prayer, I sterilized a scalpel, prepared cotton wool swabs, disinfected my hands and went to work. I drew the scapel blade across the swelling, but, to my dismay, I found that the skin was as tough as shoeleather, and the blade merely skidded off. I tried a second time, using greater pressure, but with the same result. Mother and Jacquie kept up a nervous barrage of chocolate biscuits, each of which was greeted with delighted and slightly sticky grunts from Lulu.

'Can't you hurry up?' enquired Jacquie, 'these biscuits won't last forever.'

'I'm doing the best I can,' I said irascibly, 'and a nurse doesn't tell a doctor to hurry up in the middle of an operation.'

'I think I've got some chocolates in my room, dear,' said my mother helpfully, 'shall I fetch them?'

'Yes, I should, just in case.'

While Mother went off to fetch the chocolates, I decided that the only way to break into the swelling was to jab the point of the scalpel in and then drag it downwards, and this I did. It was successful: a stream of thick putrid matter gushed out from the incision, covering both me and the sofa. The smell from it was ghastly, and Jacquie and Mother retreated across the room hastily. Lulu sat there, quite unperturbed, eating chocolate biscuits. Endeavouring not to breathe more often than was necessary, I put pressure on the swelling, and eventually, when it was empty, I must have relieved it of about half a cupful of putrefying blood and pus. With a pair of scissors I carefully clipped away the dead skin and disinfected the raw area that was left. It was useless trying to put a dressing on, for I knew that Lulu would remove it as soon as she was put back in her cage. When I had cleaned it up to my satisfaction, I picked Lulu up in my arms and carried her back to her cage. Here she greeted Chumley with true wifely devotion, but Chumley was deeply suspicious. He examined her ear carefully, but decided that it was of no interest. Then, during one of Lulu's hoots of pleasure, leant forward and smelt her breath. Obviously, she had been eating chocolate, so Lulu, instead of receiving a husbandly embrace, received a swift clout over the back of the head. In the end, I had to go and fetch the rest of the chocolate biscuits to placate Chumley. Lulu's ear healed up perfectly, and within six months you had to look very closely to see the scar.

About a year later Chumley decided that it was his turn to fall ill, and of course he did it – as he did all things – in the grand manner. Chumley, I was told, had tooth ache. This rather surprised me, as, not long before, he had lost his baby teeth and acquired his adult ones, and I thought it was a bit too soon for any of them to have decayed. Still, there he was, squatting forlornly in the cage, clasping his jaw and ear with his hand and looking thoroughly miserable. He was obviously in pain, but I was not sure whether it was his ear or his jaw that was the cause of it. The pain must have been considerable, for he would not let me take his hand away to examine the side of his face, and when I persisted in trying he became so upset that it was clear I was doing more harm than good, so I had to give up. I stood for a long time by the cage, trying to deduce from his actions what was the matter with him. He kept lying down, with the bad side of his head cuddled by his hand, and whimpering gently to himself; once, when he had climbed up the wire to relieve himself, he lowered himself to the ground again rather awkwardly, and as his feet thumped on to the floor of the cage he screamed, as though the jar had caused him considerable pain. He refused all food and, what was worse, he refused all liquids as well, so I could not give him any antibiotics. We had to remove Lulu, as, instead of showing wifely concern, she bounded round the cage, occasionally bumping into Chumley, or leaping on to him and making him cry out with pain.

I became so worried about his condition by the afternoon that I called into consultation Mr Blampier, a local veterinary surgeon, and our local doctor. The latter, I think, was somewhat surprised that he should be asked to take a chimpanzee on to his panel, but agreed nevertheless. It was plain that Chumley's jaw and ear would have to be examined carefully, and I knew that, in his present state, he would not allow that, so it was agreed that we would have to anaesthetize him. This is what had to be done, but how to do it was another matter. Eventually, it was decided that I should try to give Chumley an injection of a tranquillizer which would, we hoped, have him in an agreeable frame of mind by the evening to accept an anaesthetic. The problem was whether or not Chumley was going to let me give him the injection. He was lying huddled up in his bed of straw, his back towards me, and I could see he was in great pain, for he never even looked round to see who had opened the door of his cage. I talked to him, in my best bedside manner, for a quarter of an hour or so, and at the end of that time he was allowing me to stroke his back and legs. This was a great advance, for up till now he had not let me come within stroking distance. Then, plucking up my courage, and still talking feverishly, I picked up the hypodermic and swiftly slipped the needle into the flesh of his thigh. To my relief, he gave no sign of having noticed it. As gently and as slowly as I could, I pressed the plunger and injected the tranquilliser. He must have felt this, for he gave a tiny, rather plaintive hoot, but he was too apathetic to worry about it. Still talking cheerful nonsense, I closed the door of his bedroom and left the drug to take effect.

That evening Dr Taylor and Mr Blampier arrived, and I reported that the tranquilliser had taken effect: Chumley was in a semi-doped condition, but, even so, he still would not let me examine his ear. So we repaired to his boudoir, outside of which I had rigged up some strong lights and a trestle table on which to lay our patient. Doctor Taylor poured ether on to a mask, and I opened Chumley's bedroom door, leant in and placed the mask gently over his face. He made one or two half-hearted attempts to push it away with his hand, but the ether, combined with the tranquillizer was too much for him, and he slipped into unconsciousness quite rapidly. As soon as he was completely under, we hauled him out of the cage and laid him on the trestle table, still keeping the mask over his face. Then the experts went to work. First, his ear was examined, and found to be perfectly healthy; just for good measure, we examined his other ear as well, and that, too, was all right. We then opened his mouth and carefully checked his teeth: they were an array of perfect, glistening white dentures without a speck of decay on any of them. We examined his cheeks, his jaw and the whole of his head, and could not find a single thing wrong. We looked at his neck and shoulders, with the same result. As far as we could ascertain, there was nothing the matter with Chumley whatsoever, and yet *something* had been causing him considerable pain. Dr Taylor and Mr Blampier departed, much mystified, and I carried Chumley into the house, wrapped in a blanket, and put him on a campbed in front of the drawing-room fire. Then Jacquie brought more blankets, which we piled on top of him, and we sat down to wait for the anaesthetic to wear off.

Lying there, his eyes closed, breathing out ether fumes stertorously, he looked like a slightly satanic cherub who, tired out after a day's mischief-making, was taking a well-earned rest. The amount of ether he was expelling from his lungs made the whole room reek, so that we were forced to open a window. It was about half an hour before he began to sigh deeply and twitch, as a preliminary to regaining consciousness, and I went over and sat by the bedside with a cup of water ready, since I knew from experience the dreadful thirst that assails one when you come out from under an anaesthetic. In a few minutes he opened his eyes, and as soon as he saw me he gave a feeble hoot of greeting and held out his hand, in spite of the fact that he was still half asleep. I held up his head and put the cup to his lips and he sucked at the water greedily before the ether overcame him again and he sunk back into sleep. I decided that an ordinary cup was too unwieldy to give him drinks, as a considerable quantity of liquid was spilt. I managed, by ringing up my friends, to procure an invalid's cup, one of those articles that resemble a deformed teapot, and the next time Chumley woke up this proved a great success, as he could suck water out of the spout without having to sit up.

Although he recognized us, he was still in a very drugged and stupid state, and so I decided that I would spend the night sleeping on the sofa near him, in case he awakened and wanted anything. Having given him another drink, I made up my bed on the sofa, turned out the light and dozed off. About two o'clock in the morning I was awakened by a crash in the far corner of the room. I hastily put on the light to find that Chumley was awake and wandering round the room, like a drunken man, barging into all the furniture. As soon as the light came on and he saw me, he uttered a scream of joy, staggered across the room and insisted on embracing and kissing me before gulping down a vast drink of water. I then helped him back on to his bed and covered him with his blankets, and he slept peacefully until daylight.

He spent the day lying quietly on his bed, staring up at the ceiling. He ate a few grapes and drank great quantities of glucose and water, which was encouraging. The most encouraging thing, however, was that he no longer held the side of his face and did not appear to be suffering any pain. In some extraordinary way we seemed to have cured him without doing anything. When Dr Taylor telephoned later that day to find out how Chumley was faring I explained this to him, and he was as puzzled as I. Then, later on, he rang up to say that he had thought of a possible explanation: Chumley might have been suffering from a slipped disc. This could have caused intense pain in the nerves of jaw and ear, without there being anything externally to show what caused it. When we had Chumley limp and relaxed under the anaesthetic we pulled his head around quite a lot during our examination, and probably pushed the disc back into place, without realizing it. Mr Blampier agreed with this diagnosis. We had no proof, of course, but certainly Chumley was completely cured, and there was no recurrence of the pain. He had naturally lost a lot of weight during his illness, and so for two or three weeks he was kept in a specially heated cage and fed up on every delicacy. Within a very short time he had put on weight and was his old self, so that whenever anyone went near his cage they were showered with handfuls of sawdust. This, I presume, was Chumley's way of thanking one.

Sometimes animals injure themselves in the most ridiculous way imaginable. Hawks and pheasants, for example, are the most hysterical of birds. If anything unusual happens they get into a terrible state, fly straight up, like rockets, and crash into the roof of their cage, either breaking their necks or neatly scalping themselves. But there are other birds equally stupid. Take the case of Samuel.

Samuel is a South American seriama. They are not unlike the African secretary bird. About the size of a half-grown turkey, they have long, strong legs, and a ridiculous little tuft of feathers perched on top of their beaks. In the wild state seriamas do not fly a great deal, spending most of their time striding about the grasslands in search of snakes, mice, frogs and other delicacies. I had purchased Samuel from an Indian in Northern Argentina, and as he had been hand-reared he was, of course, perfectly (and sometimes embarrasingly) tame. When I finally shipped him back to Jersey with the rest of the animals, we took him out of his small travelling crate and released him in a nice, spacious aviary. Samuel was delighted, and to show us his gratitude the first thing he did was to fly up on to the perch, fall off it and break his left leg. There are times when animals do such idiotic things that you are left bereft of words.

Fortunately, for Samuel, it was a nice clean break, half-way down what would be the shin in a human being. We made a good job of splinting it, covered the splint with plaster of Paris bandage, and, when it was dry, put him in a small cage so that he could not move around too much. The following day his foot was slightly swollen, so I gave him a penicillin injection – which he took great exception to – and his foot returned to normal size as a result. When we eventually took off the splint, we found the bones had knitted perfectly, and today, as he strides importantly around his aviary, you have to look very closely to see which leg it was that he broke. Knowing Samuel for the imbecile he is, it would not surprise me in the least if he did not repeat the performance at some time in the future . . . probably on a day when I am up to my eyes in other work.

During the course of your Florence Nightingale work you become quite used to being bitten, scratched, kicked and bruised by your patients, and on many occasions, having performed first-aid on them, you have to perform it on yourself. Nor is it always the bigger creatures that are the most dangerous to deal with. A squirrel or a pouched rat can inflict almost as much damage as a flock of Bengal tigers when they put their minds to it. While anointing a fluffy, gooey-eyed bushbaby once for a slight skin infection on the tail, I was bitten so severely in the thumb that it went septic, and I had to have it bandaged for ten days. The bushbaby was cured in forty-eight hours.

Human doctors are covered by the Hippocratic Oath. The wild animal doctor employs a variety of oaths, all rich and colourful, but which would, I feel, be frowned upon by the British Medical Council.

Chapter Six

Love and Marriage

Dear Mr Durrell,
I am seven years old and I have just had a baby tortoise ...

You can tell if an animal is happy in captivity in a number of different ways. Principally, you can tell by its condition and appetite, for a creature which has glossy fur or feathering, and eats well to boot, is obviously not pining. The final test that proves beyond a shadow of doubt that the animal has accepted its cage as 'home' is when it breeds.

At one time, if an animal did not live very long in captivity, or did not breed, the zoos seemed to be under the impression that there was something wrong with it, and not something wrong with their methods of keeping it. So-and-so was *'impossible'* to keep in captivity, they would say, and, even if it did manage to survive for a while, it was *'impossible'* to breed. These sweeping statements were delivered in a wounded tone of voice, as if the wretched creature had entered into some awful conspiracy against you, refusing to live or mate. At one time there was a huge list of animals that, it was said, were impossible to keep or breed in confinement, and this list included such things as the great apes, elephants, rhinoceros, hippopotamus, and so on. Gradually, over the years, one or two more agile brains entered the zoo world, and to everyone's surprise and chagrin it was discovered that the deaths and lack of babies were not due to stubbornness on the part of the creature, but due to lack of knowledge and experiment on the part of the people who kept them. I am convinced there are precious few species of animals which you cannot successfully maintain *and* breed, once you have found the knack. And by knack I mean once you have discovered the right type of caging, the best-liked food, and, above all, a suitable mate. On the face of it, this seems simple enough, but it may take several years of experiment before you acquire them all.

Marriages in zoos are, of course, arranged, as they used to be by the eighteenth-century Mammas. But the eighteenth-century Mamma had one advantage over the zoo: having married off her daughters, there was an end to it. In a zoo you are never quite sure, since any number of things may happen. Before you can even lead your creatures to the altar, so to speak, it is quite possible that either the male or the female may take an instant dislike to the mate selected, and so, if you are not careful, the bride or groom may turn into a corpse long before the honeymoon has started. A zoo matchmaker has a great number of matters to consider, and a great number of risks to take, before he can sit back with a sigh of relief and feel the marriage is an accomplished fact. Let us take the marriage of Charles, as a fairly typical one.

Charles is – rather unzoologically – what is known as a Rock ape from Gibraltar. He is, of course, not an ape at all, but a Macaque, one of a large group of monkeys found in the Far East. Their presence in North Africa is puzzling, but obviously they have been imported to the Rock of Gibraltar, and have thus gained the doubtful distinction of being the only European monkey. We were offered Charles when the troop on the Rock underwent its periodical thinning, and we were very pleased to have him. He was brought over from Gibraltar in style on one of Her Majesty's ships, and we duly took possession of him. He stood two feet six inches high, when squatting on his haunches, and was clad in an immensely long, thick, gingery brown coat. His walk was very dog-like, but with a distinct swagger to it, as befits a member of the famous Rock garrison. He had bright, intelligent brown eyes, and a curious pale pinkish face, thickly covered with freckles. He was undoubtedly ugly, but with an ugliness that was peculiarly appealing. Curiously enough, although he was a powerful monkey, he was excessively timid, and an attempt to keep him with a mixed group of other primates failed, for they bullied him unmercifully. So Charles was moved to a cage of his own, and a carefully worded letter was despatched to the Governor of Gibraltar, explaining in heart-rending terms, Charles' solitary confinement, and hinting that he would be more than delighted if a female Rock ape should be forthcoming. In due course we received a signal to say that Charles' condition of celibacy had been reviewed and it had been decided that, as a special concession, a female Rock ape, named Sue, was going to be sent to us. Thus another of Her Majesty's ships was pressed into service, and Sue duly arrived.

By this time, of course, Charles had settled down well in his new cage, and had come to look upon it as his own territory, and so we had no idea how he would treat the introduction of a new Rock ape – even a female one – into his bachelor apartments. We carried Sue in her travelling crate and put it on the ground outside Charles' cage, so that they could see each other. Sue became very excited when she saw him, and chattered away loudly, whereas Charles, after the first astonished glance, sat down and stared at her with an expression of such loathing and contempt on his freckled face that our hearts sank. However, we had to take the plunge, and Sue was let into the cage. She sprang out of her crate with great alacrity, and set off to explore the cage. Charles, who had been sitting up in the branches dissociating himself from the whole procedure up till then, decided the time had come to assert himself. He leapt down to the ground and sprang on Sue before she realized what was happening and could take evasive action. Within a second she had received a sharp nip on the shoulder, had her hair pulled and her ears boxed, and was sent tumbling into a corner of the cage. Charles was back on his branch, looking around with a self-satisfied air, uttering little grunts to himself. We hastily went and fetched two big bowls of fruit and put them into the cage, whereupon Charles came down and started to pick them over with the air of a gourmet, while Sue sat, watching him hungrily. Eventually, the sight of the grape juice trickling down Charles' chin was too much for her, and she crept forward timidly, leant towards the bowl and took a grape, which she hastily crammed into her mouth, in case Charles went for her. He completely ignored her, however, after one quick glance from under his eyebrows, and, gaining courage, she again leant forward and grabbed a whole handful of grapes. Within a few minutes they were both feeding happily out of the same dish, and we sighed with relief. An hour later, when I passed by, there was Charles, lying on his back, eyes closed, a blissful expression on his face, while Sue, with a look of deep concentration, was searching his fur thoroughly. It seemed that his original attack on Sue was merely to tell her that it was *his* cage, and that, if she wanted to live there, she had to respect his authority.

Sometimes one acquires mates for animals in very curious ways. One of the most peculiar was the way in which we found a husband for Flower. Now, Flower was a very handsome North American skunk, and when she first came to us she was slim and sylph-like and very tame. Unfortunately, Flower decided that there were only two things in life worth doing: eating and sleeping. The result of this exhausting life, which she led, was that she became so grossly overweight that she was – quite literally – circular. We tried dieting her, but with no effect. We became somewhat alarmed, for overweight can kill an animal as easily as starvation. It was plain that what Flower needed was exercise, and equally plain that she had no intention of going out of her way to obtain it. We decided that what she needed was a mate, but, at that particular time, skunks were in short supply and none were obtainable, so Flower continued to eat and sleep undisturbed. Then, one day, Jacquie and I happened to be in London on business, and, being a bit early for our appointment, we walked to our destination. On rounding a corner, we saw approaching us a little man dressed in a green uniform with brass buttons, carrying in his arms – above all things – a baby chimpanzee. At first, with the incongruous combination of the uniform and the ape, we were rather taken aback, but as he came up to us I recovered my wits and stopped him.

'What on earth are you doing with a chimpanzee?' I asked him, though why he should not have a perfect right to walk through the streets with a chimpanzee I was not quite sure.

'I works for Viscount Churchill,' he explained, 'and he keeps a lot of queer pets. We've got a skunk, too, but we'll 'ave to get rid of that, 'cos the chimp don't like it.'

'A skunk?' I said eagerly. 'Are you sure it's a skunk?'

'Yes,' replied the little man, 'positive.'

'Well, you've met just the right person,' I said. 'Will you give my card to Viscount Churchill and tell him that I would be delighted to have his skunk, if he wants to part with it?'

'Sure,' replied the little man, 'I should think he'd be pleased to let you 'ave it.'

We returned to Jersey full of hope that we might have found a companion, if not a mate, for Flower. Within a few days I received a courteous letter from Viscount Churchill, saying that he would be very pleased to let his skunk come to us, and that, as soon as he had had a travelling cage constructed, he would send him. The next thing I received was a telegram.

Its contents were simple and to the point, but I cannot help feeling that it must have puzzled the postal authorities. It read as follows:

'GERALD DURRELL ZOOLOGICAL PARK LES AUGRES JERSEY CI: GLADSTONE LEAVING FLIGHT BE 112 AT 19 HOURS TODAY THURSDAY CAGE YOUR PROPERTY.   CHURCHILL.'

Gladstone, on being unpacked, proved to be a lovely young male, and it was with great excitement that we put him in with Flower and stood back to see what would happen. Flower was, as usual, lying in her bed of straw, looking like a black and white, fur-covered football. Gladstone peered at this apparition somewhat short-sightedly and then ambled over to have a closer look. At that moment Flower had one of her brief moments of consciousness. During the day she used to wake up periodically for about thirty seconds at a time, just long enough to have a quick glance around the cage to see if anyone had put a plate of food in while she slept. Gladstone, suddenly perceiving that the football had a head, stopped in astonishment and put up all his fur defensively. I am quite sure that for a moment he was not certain what Flower *was*, and I can hardly say I blame him, for when she was just awakened from a deep sleep like that she rarely looked her best. Gladstone stood staring at her, his tail erect like an exclamation mark; Flower peered at him blearily and, because he was standing so still and because she had a one track mind, Flower obviously thought he was some new and exotic dish which had been put in for her edification. She hauled herself out of her bed and waddled across towards Gladstone.

Flower walking looked, if anything, more extraordinary than Flower reclining. You could not see her feet, and so you had the impression of a large ball of black and white fur propelling itself in your direction in some mysterious fashion. Gladstone took one look, and then his nerve broke and he ran and hid in the corner. Flower, having discovered that he was only a skunk, and therefore not something edible, retreated once more to her bed to catch up on her interrupted nap. Gladstone steered clear of her for the rest of the day, but towards evening he did pluck up sufficient courage to go and sniff her sleeping form and find out *what* she was, a discovery that seemed to interest him as little as it had done Flower. Gradually, over a period of days, they grew very fond of one another, and then came the great night when I passed their cage in bright moonlight and was struck dumb with astonishment, for there was Gladstone chasing Flower round and round the cage, and Flower (panting and gasping for breath) was actually enjoying it. When he at length caught her, they rolled over and over in mock battle, and, when they had finished, Flower was so out of breath she had to retire to bed for a short rest. But this was only the beginning, for after a few months of Gladstone's company Flower regained her girlish figure, and before long she could out-run and out-wrestle Gladstone himself.

So zoo marriages can be successful or unsuccessful, but if they are successful they should generally result in some progeny, and this again presents you with further problems. The most important thing to do, if you can, is to spot that a happy event is likely to take place as far in advance as possible, so that the mother-to-be can be given extra food, vitamins and so forth. The second most important thing is to make up your mind about the father-to-be: does he stay with the mother, or not? Fathers, in fact, are sometimes more of a problem than the mothers. If you do not remove them from the cage, they might worry the female, so that she may give birth prematurely; on the other hand, if you do remove them, the female may pine and again give birth prematurely. If the father is left in the cage, he might well become jealous of the babies and eat them; on the other hand, he might give the female great assistance in looking after the young: cleaning them and keeping them amused. So, when you know that a female is pregnant, one of your major problems is what to do with Dad, and at times, if you do not act swiftly, a tragedy may occur.

We had a pair of slender loris of which we were inordinately proud. These creatures look rather like drug-addicts that have seen better days. Clad in light grey fur they have enormously long and thin limbs and body; strange, almost human, hands; and large lustrous brown eyes, each surrounded by a circle of dark fur, so that the animal appears as though it is either recovering from some ghastly debauchery, or a very unsuccessful boxing tournament. They have a reputation for being extremely difficult and delicate to keep in captivity, which, by and large, seems to be true. This is why we were so proud of our pair, as we had kept them for four years, and this was a record. By careful experiment and observation, we had worked out a diet which seemed to suit them perfectly. It was a diet that would not have satisfied any other creature *but* a slender loris, consisting as it did of banana, mealworms and milk, but nevertheless on this monotonous fare they lived and thrived.

As I say, we were very proud that our pair did so well, so you can imagine our excitement when we realized that the female was pregnant: this was indeed going to be an event, the first time slender loris had been bred in captivity, to the best of my knowledge. But now we were faced with the father problem, as always; and, as always, we teetered. Should we remove him or not? At last, after much deliberation, we decided not to do so, for they were a very devoted couple. The great day came, and a fine healthy youngster was born. We put up screens round the cage, so that the parents would not be disturbed by visitors to the Zoo, gave them extra titbits, and watched anxiously to make sure the father behaved himself. All went well for three days, during which time the parents kept close together as usual, and the baby clung to its mother's fur with the tenacity and determination of a drowning man clasping a straw. Then, on the fourth morning, all our hopes were shattered. The baby was lying dead at the bottom of the cage, and the mother had been blinded in one eye by a savage bite on the side of her face. To this day we do not know what happened, but I can only presume that the male wanted to mate with the female, and she, with the baby clinging to her, was not willing, and so the father turned on her. It was a bitter blow, but it taught us one thing: should we ever succeed in breeding slender loris again, the father will be removed from the cage as soon as the baby is born.

In the case of some animals, of course, removing the father would be the worst thing you could do. Take the marmosets, for instance. Here the male takes the babies over the moment they are born, cleans them, has them both clinging to his body and only hands them over to the mother at feeding time. I had wanted to observe this strange process for a long time, and thus, when one of our cotton-eared marmosets became pregnant, I was very pleased. My only fear was that she would give birth to the baby when I happened to be away, but luckily this did not happen. Instead, very early one morning, Jeremy burst into my bedroom with the news that he thought the marmoset was about to give birth, so, hastily flinging on some clothes, I rushed down to the Mammal House. There I found the parents to be both unperturbed, clinging to the wire of their cage and chittering hopefully at any human who passed. It was quite obvious from the female's condition that she would give birth fairly soon, but she seemed infinitely less worried by the imminence of this event than I. Getting myself a chair, I sat down to watch. I stared at the female marmoset, and she stared at me, while in the corner of the cage her husband – with typical male callousness – sat stuffing himself on grapes and mealworms, and took not the slightest notice of his wife.

Three hours later there was absolutely no change, except that the male marmoset had finished all the grapes and mealworms. By then my secretary had arrived and, as I had a lot of letters to answer, I made her bring a chair and sit down beside me in front of the marmoset cage while I dictated. I think that visitors to the Zoo that day must have thought slightly eccentric the sight of a man dictating letters, while keeping his eyes fixed hypnotically on a cageful of marmosets. Then, about midday, someone arrived whom I had to see. I was away from the cage for approximately ten minutes, and on my return the father marmoset was busy washing two tiny scraps of fur that were clinging to him vigorously. I could quite cheerfully have strangled the female marmoset: after all my patient waiting, she went and gave birth during the short period I happened to be away.

Still, I could watch the father looking after the babies, and I had to be content with that. He looked after the twins with great care and devotion, generally carrying them slung one on each hip, like a couple of panniers on a donkey. His fur was so thick and the babies so small that most of the time they were completely hidden; then, suddenly, from the depths of his fur, a tiny face, the size of a large hazel nut, would appear, and two bright eyes would regard you gravely. At feeding time the father would go and hang on the wire close alongside the mother, and the babies would pass from one to the other. Then, their thirst quenched, they would scramble back on to father again. The father was extremely proud of his babies, and was always working himself up into a state of panic over their welfare. As the twins grew older, they became more venturesome, and would leave the safety of their father's fur to make excursions along the nearby branches, while their parents eyed them with pride, as well as a little anxiously. If you approached too near the cage when the twins were on one of their voyages of exploration, the father would get wildly agitated, convinced that you had evil designs on his precious offspring. His fur would stand on end, like an angry cat's, and he would chitter loud and shrill instructions to the twins, which were generally ignored as they grew older. This would reduce him to an even worse state of mind, and screaming with rage and fear, he would dive through the branches, grab the twins and sling them into place, one on each hip; then, muttering dark things to himself – presumably about the disobedience of the modern generation – he would potter off to have a light snack to restore his nerves, casting dark glances at you over his shoulder. Watching the marmoset family was an enchanting experience, more like watching a troupe of strange little fur-covered leprechauns than monkeys.

Naturally, the biggest thrill is when you succeed in breeding some creature which you know from the start is going to be extremely difficult. During my visit to West Africa I had managed to acquire some Fernand's skinks, probably one of the most beautiful of the lizard family, for their big, heavy bodies are covered with a mosaic work of highly polished scales in lemon yellow, black, white and vivid cherry-red. By the time the Zoo in Jersey was established I had only two of these magnificent creatures left, but they were fine, healthy specimens, and they settled down well in the Reptile House. Sexing most reptiles is well-nigh impossible, so I did not know if these skinks were a true pair or not, but I did know that, even if by some remote chance they were a true pair, the chances of breeding them were one in a million. The reason for this lay in the fact that reptiles, by and large, lay the most difficult eggs to hatch in captivity. Tortoises, for example, lay hard-shelled eggs which they bury in earth or sand. But if you do not get the temperature and humidity just right in the cage, the eggs will either become mildewed or else the yolk will dry up. A lot of lizards, on the other hand, lay eggs which have a soft, parchment-like shell, which makes matters a bit more difficult, for they are even more sensitive to moisture and temperature.

Knowing all this, I viewed with mixed feelings the clutch of a dozen eggs which the female Fernand's skink laid one morning in the earth at the bottom of her cage. They were white, oval eggs, each about the size of a sugared almond, and the female (as happens among some of the skinks) stood guard over them and would attack your hand quite fearlessly should you put it near the eggs. With most lizards the female walks off, having laid her batch, and forgets all about it; in the case of some of the skinks, however, the female guards the nest and, lying on top of the soil in which the eggs are buried, urinates over the nest at intervals to maintain the right moisture content, in order to keep the delicate shells from shrivelling up in the heat. Our female skink appeared to know what she was doing, and so all we could do was to sit back and await developments, without any great hope that the eggs would hatch. As week after week passed, our hopes sank lower and lower, until, eventually, I dug down to the nest, expecting to find every egg shrivelled up. To my surprise, however, I found that only four eggs had done so; the rest were still plump and soft, though discoloured, of course. I removed the four shrivelled ones and carefully opened one with a scalpel. I found a dead but well-developed embryo. This was encouraging, for it proved at least that the eggs were fertile. So we sat back to wait again.

Then, one morning, I was down in the Reptile House about some matter, and as I passed the skink's cage, I happened to glance inside. As usual, the cage looked empty, as the parent skinks spent a lot of their time buried in the soil at the bottom of the cage. I was just about to turn away when a movement among the dry leaves and moss attracted my attention. I peered more closely to see what had caused it, and suddenly, from around the edge of a large leaf, I saw a minute pink and black head peering at me. I could hardly believe my eyes, and stood stock still and stared as this tiny replica of the parents slowly crept out from behind the leaf. It was about an inch and a half long, with all the rich colouring of the adult, but so slender, fragile and glossy that it resembled one of those ornamental brooches that women wear on the lapels of their coats. I decided that if one had hatched, there might be others, and I wanted to remove them as quickly as possible for, although the female had been an exemplary mother till now, it was quite possible that either she or the male might eat the youngsters.

We prepared a small aquarium and very carefully caught the baby skink and put him into it. Then we set to work and stripped the skinks' cage. This was a prolonged job, for each leaf, each piece of wood, each tuft of grass had to be checked and double checked, to make sure there was no baby skink curled up in it. When the last leaf had been examined, we had four baby Fernand's skinks running round in the aquarium. When you consider the chances of any of the eggs hatching at all, to have four out of twelve was, I thought, no mean feat. The only thing that marred our delight at this event was that the baby skinks had decided to hatch at the beginning of the winter, and as they could only feed off minute things the job of finding them enough food was going to be difficult. Tiny mealworms were, of course, our standby, but all our friends with gardens rallied round, and would come up to the Zoo once or twice a week, bearing biscuit-tins full of woodlice, earwigs, tiny snails and other dainty morsels that gave the babies the so necessary variety in diet. Thus the tiny reptiles thrived and grew. At the time of writing, they are about six inches long, and as handsome as their parents. I hope it will not be long before they start laying eggs, so that we can try to rear a second generation in captivity.

There are, of course, some animals which could only with the greatest difficulty be prevented from breeding in captivity, and among these are the coatimundis. These little South American animals are about the size of a small dog, with long, ringed tails which they generally carry pointing straight up in the air. They have short, rather bowed legs, which give them a bear-like, rolling gate; and long, rubbery, tip-tilted noses which are forever whiffling to and fro, investigating every nook and cranny in search of food. They come in two colours: a brindled greenish-brown, and a rich chestnut. Martha and Mathias, the pair I had brought back from Argentina, were of the brindled kind.

As soon as these two had settled down in their new cage in the Zoo they started to breed with great enthusiasm. We noticed some very interesting facts about this which are worth recording. Normally, Mathias was the dominant one. It was he who went round the cage periodically 'marking' with his scent gland so that everyone would know it was his territory. He led Martha rather a dog's life, pinching all the best bits of food until we were forced to feed them separately. This Victorian male attitude was only apparent when Martha was not pregnant. As soon as she had conceived, the tables were turned. She was now the dominant one, and made poor Mathias's life hell, attacking him without provocation, driving him away from the food, and generally behaving in a very shrewish fashion. It was only by watching to see which was the dominant one at the moment, that we could tell, in the early stages, whether Martha was expecting a litter or not.

Martha's first litter consisted of four babies, and she was very proud of them, and proved to be a very good mother indeed. We were not sure what Mathias's reactions to the youngsters was going to be, so we had constructed a special shut-off for him, from which he could see and smell the babies without being able to sink his teeth into them, should he be so inclined. It turned out later that Mathias was just as full of pride in them as Martha, but in the early stages we were not taking any risks. Then the great day came when Martha considered the babies were old enough to be shown to the world, and so she led them out of her den and into the outside cage for a few hours a day. Baby coatimundis are, in many ways, the most enchanting of young animals. They appear to be all head and nose, high-domed, intellectual-looking foreheads, and noses that are, if anything, twice as rubbery and inquisitive as the adults. Then they are natural clowns, forever tumbling about, or sitting on their bottoms in the most human fashion, their hands on their knees. All this, combined with their ridiculous rolling, flat-footed walk, made them quite irresistible. They would play follow-my-leader up the branches in their cage, and when the leader had reached the highest point he would suddenly go into reverse, barging into the one behind, who, in his turn, was forced to back into the one behind him, and so on, until they were all descending the branch backwards, trilling and twittering to each other musically. Then they would climb up into the branches and do daring trapeze acts, hanging by their hind paws, or one fore paw, swinging to and fro, trying their best to knock each other off. Although they often fell from quite considerable heights on to the cement floor, they seemed as resilient as india-rubber and never hurt themselves.

When they grew a little older and discovered they could squeeze through the wire mesh of the cage, they would escape and play about just inside the barrier rail. Martha would keep an anxious eye on them during these excursions, and should any real or imaginary danger threaten they would come scampering back at her alarm cry, and, panting excitedly, squeeze their fat bodies through the wire mesh and into the safety of the cage. As they grew bolder, they took to playing farther and farther afield. If there were only a few visitors about, they would go and have wrestling matches on the main drive that sloped down past their cage. In many ways this was a nuisance, for at least twenty times a day some kindly and well-intentioned visitor would come panting up to us with the news that some of our animals were out, and we would have to explain the whole coatimundi set-up.

It was while the babies were playing on the back drive one day that they received a fright which had a salutary effect on them. They had gradually been going farther and farther away from the safety of their cage, and their mother had been growing increasingly anxious. The babies had just learnt how to somersault, and were in no mood to listen to their mother's warnings. It was when they had reached a point quite far from their cage that Jeremy drove down the back drive in the Zoo van. Martha uttered her warning cry, and the babies, stopping their game, suddenly saw they were about to be attacked by an enormous roaring monster that was between them and the safety of their home. Panic-sticken they turned and ran. They galloped flat-footedly down past the baboon cage, past the chimps' cage, past the bear cage, without finding anywhere to hide from the monster that pursued them.

Suddenly, they saw a haven of safety, and the four of them dived for it. The fact that the ladies' lavatory happened to be empty at that moment was entirely fortuitous. Jeremy, cursing all coatimundis, crammed on his brakes and got out. He glanced round surreptitiously to make sure there were no female visitors around, and then dived into the ladies' in pursuit of the babies. Inside, they were nowhere to be seen, and he was just beginning to wonder where on earth they had got to when muffled squeaks from inside one of the cubicles attracted him. He discovered that all four babies had squeezed under the door of one of these compartments. What annoyed Jeremy most of all, though, was that he had to put a penny in the door *to get them out*.

Still, whatever tribulations they might give you, the babies in the Zoo provide tremendous pleasure and satisfaction. The sight of the peccaries playing wild games of catch-as-catch-can with their tiny piglets; the baby coatimundis rolling and bouncing like a circus troupe; the baby skinks in their miniature world, carefully stalking an earwig almost as big as themselves; the baby marmosets dancing through the branches, like little gnomes, hotly pursued by their harassed father: all these things are awfully exciting. After all, there is no point in having a Zoo unless you breed the animals in it, for by breeding them you know that they have come to trust you, and that they are content.

Chapter Seven

A Gorilla in the Guestroom

Dear Mr Durrell,
Could you please have our Rhesus monkey? He is growing so big and jumping on us from trees and doing damage and causing so much trouble. Already my mother has been in bed with the doctor three times . . .

It was towards the end of the second year that I decided, the Zoo now being well established, it must cease just being a mere showplace of animals, and start to contribute something towards the conservation of wildlife. I felt that it would be essential to gradually weed out all the commoner animals in the collection and to replace them with rare and threatened species. That is, species which were threatened with extinction in the wild state. The list of these was a long and melancholy one; in fact – without reptiles – it filled three fat volumes. I was wondering which of this massive list of endangered species we could start with, when the decison was taken out of my hands. An animal dealer telephoned and asked me if I wanted a baby gorilla.

Gorillas have never been exceptionally numerous as a species and with the state that Africa was in (politically speaking) at that moment it seemed to me that they might well become extinct within the next twenty years, for newly emergent governments are generally far too busy proving themselves to the world for the first few years to worry much about the fate of the wildlife of their country, and history has proved, time and time again, how rapidly a species can be exterminated, even a numerous one. So the gorilla had been high on my list of priorities. I was not convinced, however, that the animal in question really was a gorilla. In my experience, the average animal dealer can, with difficulty, distinguish between a bird, a reptile and a mammal, but this is about the extent of his zoological knowledge. I felt that it was more than likely that the baby gorilla would turn out to be a baby chimpanzee. However, I could not afford to turn the offer down, in case it really *was* a baby gorilla.

'How much are you asking for it?' I enquired, and took a firm grip of the telephone.

'Twelve hundred pounds,' said the dealer.

A brief vision of my Bank Manager's face floated before my eyes, and I repressed it sternly.

'All right,' I said, in what I hoped was a confident voice, 'I'll meet it at London Airport and, if it's in good condition, I'll have it.'

I put down the telephone to find Jacquie regarding me with a basilisk eye.

'What are you going to have?' she enquired.

'A baby gorilla,' I said nonchalantly.

'Oh, how lovely,' said Mother enthusiastically, 'they're such dear little things.'

Jacquie was more practical.

'How much?' she asked.

'As a matter of fact it's very reasonable,' I said, 'you know how rare gorillas are, and you know that our policy now is to concentrate on the rare things. I feel this is a wonderful opportunity ...'

'How much?' Jacquie interrupted brutally.

'Twelve hundred pounds,' I replied and waited for the storm.

'Twelve hundred pounds? *Twelve hundred pounds?* You must be *mad*. You've got an overdraft the size of the National Debt and you go and say you'll pay twelve hundred pounds for a gorilla? You must be out of your mind. Where d'you think we're going to find twelve hundred pounds, for Heaven's sake. And what d'you think the Bank Manager's going to say when he hears? You must be stark staring *mad*.'

'I shall get the money from other sources,' I said austerely. 'Don't you realize that this island is infested with rich people who do nothing all day long but revolve from one cocktail party to another, like a set of Japanese waltzing mice. It's about time they made a contribution towards animal conservation. I shall ask them to contribute the money.'

'That's an even stupider idea than saying you'll have the gorilla in the first place,' said Jacquie.

Ignoring my wife's pessimistic and anti-social outlook, I picked up the telephone and asked for a number.

'Hallo? Hope? Gerry here.'

'Hallo,' said Hope resignedly. 'What can I do for you?'

'Hope, I want you to give me a list of all the richest people on the Island.'

'All the richest people?' said Hope in bewilderment, 'now *what* are you up to?'

'Well, I've just been offered a baby gorilla at a very reasonable price ... twelve hundred pounds ... only I don't happen to have twelve hundred pounds at the moment....'

The rest of my sentence was drowned by Hope's rich laughter.

'So you hope to get the wealthy of the Island to buy it for you?' she said, chortling. 'Gerry, really, you're *dotty*.'

'I don't see what's wrong with the idea,' I protested, 'they should be glad to contribute towards buying such a rare creature. After all, if breeding colonies of things like gorillas aren't established in captivity soon, there won't be any left at all. Surely these people *realize* this?'

'I'm afraid they don't,' said Hope. 'I realize it and you realize it, but I'm afraid the average person either doesn't or couldn't care less.'

'I suppose you're right,' I said gloomily, 'anyway, I think it's worth a try, don't you?'

'It's worth a try, but I wouldn't pin too much faith to their generosity, if I were you,' said Hope. 'Anyway, give me half an hour and I'll ring you back.'

Half an hour later Hope dictated a list of about fifty people over the telephone, while I wrote them down feverishly. Then I looked up the telephone numbers, took a deep breath and started.

'Good morning, Mrs Macgurgle? Gerald Durrell from the Zoo here, I'm so sorry to worry you, but we've just been offered a baby gorilla ... at a very reasonable price ... twelve hundred pounds ... well, yes, but it's not expensive for a gorilla ... well, I was wondering if you'd care to purchase a small portion of it ... say a leg or something? You would? That's immensely kind of you ... thank you very much indeed ... Goodbye.'

By lunch-time I had collected two hundred pounds. Only another thousand to go and the gorilla was mine. It was at this point that I discovered the next person on the list was Major Domo. I had never met him and I had no idea how he would react to the suggestion that he might buy a bit of gorilla. To my immense relief, the suggestion seemed to amuse him, for he chuckled.

'How much is it?' he asked.

'Twelve hundred pounds,' I said.

'And how much have you collected already?'

'Two hundred pounds.'

'Well,' said Major Domo, 'you'd better come along this afternoon and I'll find you the balance.'

To say I was speechless means nothing. When I had gone to the telephone I thought there might be a chance of getting twenty-five pounds, possibly even fifty. A hundred would have been beyond the dreams of avarice. And here was Major Domo virtually handing me a baby gorilla on a plate, so to speak. I stammered my thanks, slammed down the telephone and rushed round the Zoo, telling everyone of the fact that we were going to have a baby gorilla.

The great day came and I flew over to London airport to collect the ape. My one fear now was that when I arrived there it would turn out to be a chimpanzee after all. The dealer met me and escorted me to a room in the R.S.P.C.A. Animal Shelter. He threw open the door, and the first thing I saw was a couple of baby chimpanzees sitting on a table meditatively chewing bananas. My heart sank and I had visions of having to go back to Jersey empty-handed. But the dealer walked over to a crate in the corner, opened the door and N'Pongo walked into my life.

He stood about eighteen inches high and was quite the most handsome and healthy-looking baby gorilla I had ever seen. He strolled stockily across the room towards me and then held up his arms to be lifted up. I was amazed at how heavy he was for his size, and I soon realized that this was all solid bone and muscle; there was not a spare ounce of fat on him. His light chocolate-coloured fur was thick and soft, and the skin on his hands, feet and face was soft and glossy as patent leather. His eyes were small and deep set, twinkling like chips of coal. He lay back in my arms and studied me carefully with an unwinking stare, and then lifted a fat and gentle forefinger and investigated my beard. I tickled his ribs and he wriggled about in my arms, giggling hoarsely, his eyes shining with amusement. I sat him down on a convenient table and handed him a banana which he accepted with little bearlike growlings of pleasure, and ate very daintily compared to the chimpanzees who were stuffing their mouths as full as they could. I wrote out the cheque and then we bundled N'Pongo – growling protests – back into the crate, and went off to catch the plane for Jersey.

When we landed at the airport I took N'Pongo out of his crate and we drove to the Zoo with him sitting on my lap, taking a great interest in the cows we passed, and occasionally turning round so that he could peer up into my face. When we arrived I carried him up to our flat, for his cage was not quite ready and I had decided that he would have to spend a couple of days in our guestroom. His grave, courteous manner and his rather sad expression immediately won over both Jacquie and my mother, and before long he was lolling back on the sofa while they plied him with delicacies, and the staff came upstairs one by one to pay homage to him as though he was some black potentate. Having previously suffered by keeping Chumley the chimpanzee in the house, I knew from bitter experience that there was nothing like an ape for turning a civilized room into something closely resembling a bomb site in an incredibly short space of time, so I watched N'Pongo like a hawk. When he became bored with lying on the sofa, he decided to make a circuit of the room to examine anything of interest. So he walked slowly round like a small black professor in a museum, pausing now to look at a picture, now to stroke an ornament, but doing it so gently that there was never any danger that he would break anything. After the attitude I was used to with Chumley, I was captivated by N'Pongo's beautiful behaviour. You would have thought that he had been brought up in a house, to watch him. Apart from a slight lapse when he wet the floor (and he could not be expected to know that this was not done in the best circles), his behaviour was exemplary, so much so that, by the time we put him to bed, my mother was doing her best to try to persuade me to keep him in the house permanently. I had, however, learnt my lesson with Chumley, and I turned a deaf ear to her pleas.

N'Pongo, of course, did not leave the guestroom in the condition that he found it, but this was only to be expected. Although his manners were exemplary, he was only a baby and could not be expected to automatically assume civilized behaviour, because he was living in the house. So the guestroom, when he left it, bore numerous traces of his presence: on one wall, for instance, was something that resembled a map of Japan drawn by one of the more inebriated ancient mariners. This was nicely executed in scarlet and was due to the fact that I had thought N'Pongo might like some tinned raspberries. He had liked them, and his enthusiasm at this new addition to his diet had resulted in the map of Japan. There was also straw. Next to paraffin, I know of no other commodity that manages to worm its way – in a positively parasitic fashion – into every nook and cranny before you are aware of it. For months after N'Pongo's sojourn in our guestroom we were apologizing to guests for the floor which, in spite of hoovering, looked like a sixteenth-century ale-house. There was also the fact that the handle on the door drooped at rather a depressed angle since N'Pongo, after receiving his meal, had attempted to follow me out of the room. Knowing that the handle by some magical means opened and closed the door, but not knowing exactly how to manipulate it he had merely pulled it downwards with all his strength. As I tried, unsuccessfully, to bend the handle back into position again, I reflected that N'Pongo was only about two years old and that his strength would increase in proportion to his size.

One of the things which particularly interested me about him was his different approach to a problem or a situation. If, for example, a baby chimpanzee is used to being brought out of its cage, on being reincarcerated it will carry on like one of the more loquacious heroines in a Greek tragedy, tearing its hair, rolling with rage on the floor, screaming at the top of its voice and drumming its heels on every available bit of woodwork. N'Pongo was quite otherwise. Although deploring it, he would accept the necessity of being locked up again in his cage. He would try his best to divert you from this course of action, but when he realized that it had become inevitable he would submit with good grace. His only protest would be a couple of sharp and faintly peevish screams, as he saw you disappear, whereas the average chimpanzee of his age and with his background would have gone on having hysterics for a considerable length of time. Owing to his attractive appearance and disposition, his good manners and his very well-developed sense of humour, N'Pongo was in a very short space of time the darling of the Zoo. Every fine afternoon he was brought out on to the lawn in front of the yew hedge and there he would show off to his admirers: either lolling in the grass, with a bored expression on his face, or else, with a wicked gleam in his eye, working out how he could pose for his photograph to be taken by some earnest visitor and then rush forward at the crucial moment, grasp the unfortunate person's leg and push it from under him – a task that gave him immense amusement and generally resulted in the visitor sustaining a slipped disc and having an excellent picture of a completely empty section of lawn.

Within twelve months N'Pongo had almost doubled his size, and I felt it was now time to try, by fair means or foul, to obtain a mate for him. Unless they lack finances, I have no use for zoos that acquire animals purely for exhibition and make no effort to provide them with a mate; this applies particularly to apes. The problem does not arise while they are young, for they accept the human beings around them as their adopted, if slightly eccentric, family. Then comes the time when they are so powerful that you do not, if you have any intelligence, treat them in the same intimate way. When a gorilla or chimpanzee or an orang-utan at the age of three or four pulls your legs from under you, or jumps from a considerable height on to the back of your neck, it tests your stamina to the full and is done because you are the only companion with whom he has to play. If he is left on his own, and he is a nice-natured ape, he will try to play the same games with you when he is eleven and twelve; this means a broken leg or a broken neck. So if this friendly, exuberant animal is kept on his own and deprived of both the company of his own kind and that of human beings, you can hardly be surprised if he turns into a morose and melancholy creature. Not wanting to see N'Pongo degenerate into one of those magnificent but sad and lonely anthropoids that I have seen in many zoos (including some that had ample resources at their disposal for providing a mate), I thought the time had come to try to procure a wife for N'Pongo, even though I knew that our funds would probably not stretch that far. I telephoned the dealer from whom we had N'Pongo and asked him about the possibilities of obtaining a female gorilla. He told me he had just been offered one, a year or so younger than N'Pongo, but now, owing to the political state in Africa, the price had increased and he was asking £1,500. There followed two days of soul searching. I knew we could not afford that amount of money in a lump sum, but we might be able to do it if it were spread over a period. Once again I telephoned the dealer and asked him whether he would consider letting us have the animal on hire purchase terms. To his credit and to my relief he agreed and said that his representative would bring her over to Jersey in a week's time. The whole Zoo waited for that day with bated breath. I, prompted by a slightly acrimonious conversation with my bank manager, spent the week by having a collecting box made, over which hung the notice: 'We have bought Nandy on the instalment plan, please help us to keep up the instalments.'

So Nandy arrived, crouched in a crate that I would have considered small for a squirrel. She, like N'Pongo, appeared to be in perfect condition: her fur was glossy, she was fat, and her skin had a sheen like satin, but at first sight of her it was her eyes that impressed me most. N'Pongo's eyes, as I have said, were small and deepset, calculating and full of humour. Nandy's eyes were large and lustrous, and when she looked sideways, she showed the whites of them; but they were frightened eyes that did not look at you squarely. They were the eyes of an animal that had had little experience of human beings, but even that limited experience had given her no reason to trust or respect them. When we released her from her cage, I could see the reason: right across the top of her skull was a scar which must have measured six or seven inches in length. Obviously, when she was being caught, some over-enthusiastic and intrepid human being had given her a blow with a machete which had split her scalp like a razor slash. It must have been a glancing blow, or else her skull would have been split in two. With such an introduction to the human race, you could hardly blame Nandy for being a little anti-social. This great slash was by now completely healed and there was only the long white scar to be seen through the hair of her head, which reminded me of the curious imitative and quite unnecessary partings that so many Africans carve in their hair with the aid of a razor.

We kept Nandy in a separate cage for twenty-four hours, so that she could settle down. The cage was next to N'Pongo's, to enable her to see her future husband, but she evinced as little interest in him as she evinced in us. If you tried to talk to her and looked directly at her face, her eyes would slide from side to side, only meeting yours for a sufficient length of time to judge what your next action might be. Eventually deciding that the wire between us rendered us comparatively harmless, and rather than look at us, she turned her back. She had such a woebegone, frightened face that one longed to be able to pick her up and comfort her, but she had been too deeply hurt, and this was the last thing she would have appreciated. It would take us, I reckoned roughly, at least six months to gain her confidence, even with the example of the pro-human N'Pongo.

The morning when we let her into the cage with N'Pongo was a red-letter day, but fraught with anxiety. He had by now become so well established and was such a fearfully extroverted character that he obviously considered he was the only gorilla in the world and that all human beings were his friends. We did not know how he would react to Nandy's sullenness and anti-human attitude. Although for twenty-four hours he could see her in the cage alongside him, he had shown absolutely no interest in her presence. Thus when the great moment of introduction came, we stood by with buckets of water, brushes, nets and long sticks, just in case the engagement party did not come off with the same romantic swing that one expects from reading women's magazines. When all was ready, we opened the shutters and Nandy, looking thoroughly distrustful, sidled her way from the small cage into N'Pongo's comparatively palatial quarters. There she put her back to the wall and squatted, her eyes darting to and fro with a curiously suspicious, yet belligerent, expression on her face. Now she was actually in the cage with N'Pongo, who was sitting up on a branch, watching her with the same expression of uninterested mistrust that he reserved for some new item of diet, we could see that she was very much smaller than he – in fact only about half his size. They sat steadily contemplating each other for some minutes, while we on the other side of the wire did hasty checks to make sure that all our buckets of water, nets, sticks and so on were easily accessible.

This was the critical moment: the two gorillas and ourselves were frozen into immobility. To any spectator, who did not know the circumstances, we would have appeared like one of the more bizarre of Madame Tussauds' exhibits. Then N'Pongo stretched out a black hand with fingers the size of chipolata sausages, clasped the wire and rolled himself carefully to the ground. There he paused and examined a handful of sawdust, as though it were the first time he had ever come across such a commodity. Then, in a casual, swaggering manner, he sauntered in a semi-circle which took him close to Nandy, and then, without looking at her, but with the utmost speed, he reached out a long, powerful arm, gripped a handful of her hair and pulled it, and then hurried along the perimeter of the cage as though nothing had happened. Nandy by nature has always been – and I fear will always be – a little slow in the uptake, and so N'Pongo was some six feet away before she realized what had happened. By then the baring of her teeth and her grunt of indignation were quite useless. The first round, therefore, went to N'Pongo, but before he could get exalted views of male superiority I felt that we should bring up our second line of defence. We removed the buckets and nets and produced two large dishes full of a succulent selection of fruits. One was presented to N'Pongo and one to Nandy. There was one slight moment of tension when N'Pongo, having examined his own plate, decided that possibly Nandy's contained additional delicacies, which his lacked, and went off to investigate. Nandy, however, was still smarting under the indignity of having had her hair pulled and she greeted N'Pongo's investigation of her plate with such a display of belligerence that N'Pongo, being essentially a good humoured and cowardly creature, retreated to his own pile of food. For the next half an hour they both fed contentedly at opposite ends of the cage. That night N'Pongo, as usual, slept on his wooden shelf, while Nandy, looking like a thwarted suffragette, curled up on the floor. All through the following day they had little jousts with each other to see who would occupy what position. They were working out their own protocol: should Nandy be allowed to swing on the rope when N'Pongo was sitting on the cross beam? Should N'Pongo be allowed to pinch Nandy's carrots even though they were smaller than his own? It had the childishness of a General Election but was three times as interesting. However, by that evening, Nandy had achieved what amounted to Votes for Female Gorillas, and both she and N'Pongo shared the wooden shelf. Judging by the way N'Pongo snuggled up to her, he was not at all averse to this invasion of his bedroom.

It was obvious from the first that the marriage of the gorillas was going to be a success. Although they were so different in character, they quite plainly adored one another. N'Pongo was the great giggling clown of the pair, while Nandy was much quieter, more introspective and watchful. N'Pongo's bullying and teasing of her was all done without any malice and out of a pure sense of fun, and this Nandy seemed to realize. Occasionally, however, his good humoured teasing would drive her to distraction: it must have been rather like being married to a professional practical joker. When she reached the limit of her endurance, she would lose her temper, and with flashing eyes and open mouth would chase him round the cage while he ran before her, giggling hysterically. If she caught him, she would belabour him with her fists while N'Pongo lay on the ground curled up in a ball. Nandy might just as well have tried to hurt a lump of cement – in spite of her strength – for he would just lie there, laughing to himself, his eyes shining with good humour. As soon as she tired of trying to make some impression on his muscular body, Nandy would stalk off to the other end of the cage, and N'Pongo would sit up, brush the sawdust from himself, beat a rapid tattoo of triumph on his breast or stomach and then sit there with his arms folded, his eyes glittering, working out what other trick he could play to annoy his wife.

To have acquired such a pair of rare and valuable animals was, I considered, something of an achievement, but now, I discovered, we were to live in a constant state of anxiety over their health and well-being: every time one of them got sawdust up its nose and sneezed, we viewed this with alarm and despondency – was it a prelude to pneumonia or something worse? The functioning of their bowels became a daily topic of conversation. I had had installed a magnificent communication apparatus in the Zoo, for, small though it was, it could take a considerable length of time to locate the person required at the moment you wanted them. So at various salient points throughout the grounds, small black boxes were screwed to the walls, through which the staff could speak with the main office and vice versa. One of these boxes was also installed in our flat, so that I could be apprised of what was going on and be warned should any crisis arise. The occasion when I had doubts as to the wisdom of this system was the day when we were entertaining some people that we did not know very well. In the middle of one of those erudite and futile conversations one has to indulge in, the black box on the bookcase gave a warning crackle, and, before I could leap up to switch it off, a sepulchral and disembodied voice said:

'Mr Durrell, the gorillas have got diarrhoea again.'

I know of no equal to this remark for putting a blight on a party. However, N'Pongo and Nandy grew apace, and to our intense relief developed none of the diseases that we feared they might contract.

Then came N'Pongo's first real illness. I had just arranged to spend three weeks in the South of France, which was to be a sort of working holiday, for we were to be accompanied by a B.B.C. producer whom I hoped to convince of the necessity for making a film about life in the Camargue. Hotels had been booked, numbers of people, ranging from bull-fighters to ornithologists, had been alerted for our coming, and everything seemed to be running smoothly. Then four days before we were due to depart, N'Pongo started to look off colour. Gone was his giggling exuberance; he lay on the floor or on the shelf, his arms wrapped round himself, staring into space, and only just taking enough food and milk to keep himself alive. The only symptom was acute diarrhoea. Tests were hurriedly made and the advice of both the vet and medical profession acted upon, but what he was suffering from remained a mystery. As with all apes, he lost weight with horrifying rapidity. On the second day he stopped eating altogether and even refused to drink his milk, so this meant we could administer no antibiotic. Almost as you watched, his face seemed to shrink and shrivel and his powerful body grow gaunt. What had once been a proudly rotund paunch now became a ghastly declivity where his ribs forked. Now his diarrhoea was quite heavily tinged with blood and at this symptom I think most of us gave up hope. We felt that if he would only eat something, it might at least give him some stamina to withstand whatever disease he was suffering from, as well as rouse him out of the terrible melancholia into which he was slipping, as most of the anthropoids do when they are ill.

Jacquie and I went down to the market in St Helier and there we walked among the multi-coloured stalls that surrounded the charming, Victorian fountain with its plaster cherubim, its palms and its maidenhair fern and its household cavalry – the plump scarlet goldfish. It was difficult to know what to choose for N'Pongo that would tempt his appetite, for he had such an excellent variety of food in his normal diet. So we bought out-of-season delicacies that cost us a small fortune. Then, when we were loaded down with exotic fruits and vegetables, I suddenly noticed on a stall that we were passing an immense green and white water melon. Water melon is not to everyone's taste, but I personally prefer it to ordinary melon. It occurred to me that the bright pink-coloured, scrunchy, watery interior with its glossy black seeds might be something that would appeal to N'Pongo, for, as far as I knew, he had never sampled it before. We added the gigantic melon to our loads and drove back to the Zoo.

By now, through lack of food and drink, N'Pongo was in a very bad way. Jeremy had managed to persuade him to drink a little skimmed milk by the subterfuge of rubbing a Disprin on his gums. The Disprin, of course, dissolved rapidly and the taste not being to his liking, N'Pongo was only too happy to take a couple of gulps of the milk to wash out his mouth. One by one we presented him with the things we had obtained in the market, and one by one he viewed them with an apathetic glance and refused the hothouse grapes, the avocado pears and other delicacies. Then we cut him a slice of water melon, and for the first time he displayed signs of interest. He prodded the slice with his finger and then leant forward and smelt it carefully. The next minute he had the slice in his hands, and to our great delight had started to eat. But we did not become too jubilant, for we knew that the water melon contained practically no nutriment, but at least it had aroused his interest in food again. The next thing was to try to administer an antibiotic, as by now the consensus of expert opinion was that he was suffering from a form of colitis. Since he still refused to take any quantity of liquid in which we could mix medicines, there was only one way to get the antibiotic into him, and that was by injection.

We enticed N'Pongo out of his cage and kept Nandy shut up; he would be sufficiently difficult to deal with, in spite of his emaciated condition, without having any assistance from his, by now, extremely powerful wife. He squatted on the floor of the Mammal House, staring about him with dull, sunken eyes. Jeremy squatted one side of him, with a supply of water melon to try to maintain his interest, while I on the other side hastily prepared the syringe for the injection. N'Pongo watched my preparations with a mild interest and once put out his hand gently to try to touch the syringe. When I was ready, Jeremy endeavoured to distract his attention with pieces of water melon, and as soon as his head was turned away from me I pushed the needle into his thigh and pressed the plunger home. N'Pongo gave no sign of having even noticed this. He followed us obediently back into his cage and, with a small piece of water melon, retired to his shelf where he curled up on his side, his arms folded, and stared at the wall. The following morning he showed very slight signs of improvement, and using the same subterfuge we managed to give him another injection. For the rest of the day there seemed no change in him, and although he ate some of the melon and drank a little skimmed milk he did not show any radical signs of progress.

I was now in a quandary: in twenty-four hours' time I was due to leave for France. There I had organized and stirred up a bees' nest of helpers and advisers. The B.B.C. were also under the impression that the trip was a foregone conclusion. If I put it off at this juncture, I would have put a tremendous amount of people to a lot of trouble for nothing, and yet I felt

I could not leave N'Pongo unless I was satisfied that he was either on the mend or else beyond salvation.

Then, the day before I was due to leave, he suddenly turned the corner. He started drinking his Complan – a highly concentrated form of dried milk – and eating a variety of fruits. By the evening of that day he showed considerable signs of improvement and had eaten quite a bit of food. The next morning I went down very early to look at him, for I was due to catch my plane to Dinard at eight-thirty. He was sitting up on the shelf, and although he still looked emaciated and unwell his eyes had a sparkle in them that had been lacking for the past few days. He ate quite well and drank his Complan, and I felt that he was at last on the road to recovery. I drove down to the airport and caught the plane to Dinard, and we motored down to the South of France. It cost a small fortune in trunk-calls to Jersey to keep myself apprised of N'Pongo's progress, but, every time I telephoned, the reports got better and better, and when Jeremy informed me that N'Pongo had drunk one pint of Complan and eaten three slices of water melon, two bananas, one apricot, three apples and the white of eight eggs, I knew there was no further cause for alarm.

By the time I returned from France, N'Pongo had put on all the weight he had lost, and when I went into the Mammal House there he was to greet me, his old self: massive, black and rotund, his eyes glittering mischievously as he tried to inveigle me close enough to the wire so that he could pull the buttons off my coat. I reflected, as I watched him rolling on his back and clapping his hands vigorously in an effort to attract my attention, that, though it was delightful to have creatures like this – and of vital importance that they should be kept and bred in captivity – it was a two-edged sword, for the anxiety you suffered when they became ill made you wonder why you started the whole thing in the first place.

Chapter Eight

Animals in Trust

Dear Mr Durrell,
You will probably be astonished to receive a letter from a complete stranger . . .

The Zoo has now been in existence for five years. During that time we have worked steadily towards our aim of building up our collection of those animals which are threatened with extinction in the wild state. Examples of these are our chimpanzees, a pair of South American tapirs, but, perhaps, the pair of gorillas are one of the most important of our acquisitions and one of which we are extremely proud. Apart from these, we have over the past year obtained a number of valuable creatures. It is not always possible to buy or collect these animals, so recently in exchange for an ostrich we had our binturong, a strange, small, bear-like animal with a long prehensile tail, which comes from the Far East; and a spectacled bear, whom we have christened Pedro.

Spectacled bears are the only members of the family to be found in South America, inhabiting a fairly restricted range high in the Andes. They are a blackish brown colour with fawn or cinnamon spectacled markings round the eyes and short waistcoats of a similar colour. They grow to be as large as the ordinary black bear, but Pedro, when he arrived, was still quite a baby and only about the size of a large retriever. We soon found that he was ridiculously tame and liked nothing better than to have his paws held through the bars while he munched chocolate in vast quantities. He is an incredible pansy in many ways, and several of the attitudes he adopts – one foot on a log while he leans languidly against the bars of his cage, with his front paws dangling limply – remind one irresistibly of the more vapid and elegant young men one can see at cocktail parties. He very soon discovered that if he did certain tricks the flow of chocolates and sweets increased a hundredfold, and so he taught himself to do a little dance. This consisted of standing on his hind legs and bending over backwards as far as he could, without actually falling, and then revolving slowly – a sort of backward waltz. This never failed to enchant his audience. To give him something with which to amuse himself, we hung a large empty barrel from the ceiling of his cage, having knocked both ends out of it: this formed a sort of circular swing and gave Pedro a lot of pleasure. He would gallop round the barrel and then dive head first into it, so that it swung to and fro vigorously. Occasionally, he would dive a bit too strenuously and come shooting out of the other end of the barrel and land on the ground. At other times, when he was feeling in a more soulful mood, he would climb into his barrel and just lie there, sucking his paws and humming to himself, an astonishingly loud vibrant hum as though the barrel contained quite a large dynamo.

Pedro was, at first, in temporary quarters, but, as we hoped to get him a mate eventually, we had to build him a new cage. During the period while his old quarters were being demolished and his new one being erected, he was confined in a large crate to which, at first, he took grave exception. However, when we moved it next to one of the animal kitchens and the fruit store, he decided that life was not so bad after all. The staff were constantly in view and nobody passed his crate without pushing a titbit to him through the bars. Then, two days before he was due to be moved into his new home, it happened. Jacquie and I were up in the flat, having a quiet cup of tea with a friend, when the inter-communication crackled and Catha's voice, as imperturbable as though she were announcing the arrival of the postman, said:

'Mr Durrell, I thought you would like to know Pedro is out.'

Now, although Pedro had been small when he arrived, he had grown with surprising rapidity and was now quite a large animal. Also, although he still appeared ridiculously tame, bears, I am afraid, are some of the few creatures in this world which you cannot trust in any circumstance. So, to say that I was alarmed by this news would be putting it mildly. I fled downstairs and out of the back door. Here, where the animal kitchen and fruit store form an annexe with a flat roof, I saw Pedro. He was galloping up and down on the roof, obviously having the time of his life. The unfortunate thing was that one of the main windows of the flat overlooked this roof, and if he went through that he could cause a considerable amount of havoc in our living quarters. Pedro was plainly unfamiliar with the substance called glass, and, as I watched, he bounded up to the window, reared up on his hindlegs and hurled himself hopefully forward. It was lucky that it was an old-fashioned sash window with small panes of glass, and this withstood his onslaught. If it had been one big sheet of glass, he would have gone straight through it and probably cut himself badly. But with a slightly astonished expression on his face he rebounded from it: what appeared to be a perfectly good means of getting into the flat was barred by some invisible substance. I rushed round to where the crate was, in an endeavour to lift up the sliding door which, as always happens in moments of this sort of crisis, stuck fast. Pedro came and peered at me over the edge of the roof and obviously thought that he should come down to my assistance, but the long drop made him hesitate. I was still struggling with the door of the cage when Shep appeared with a ladder.

'We'll never get him down without this,' he said, 'he's frightened to jump.'

He placed the ladder against the wall, while I continued my struggles with the door of the crate. Then Stefan came on the scene and was coming to my aid, when Pedro suddenly discovered the ladder. With a little 'whoop' of joy, he slid down it like a circus acrobat and landed in an untidy heap at Stefan's feet.

Now, Stefan was completely unarmed and so was I, but fortunately Stefan kept his head and did the right thing: he stood absolutely still. Pedro righted himself and, seeing Stefan standing next to him, gave a little grunt, reared up on his hind legs and placed his paws on Stefan's shoulders, who went several shades whiter but still did not move. I looked round desperately for some sort of weapon with which I could hit Pedro, should this be a preliminary to an attack on Stefan. Pedro, however, was not interested in attacking anyone. He gave Stefan a prolonged and very moist kiss with his pink tongue and then dropped to all fours again and started galloping round and round the crate, like an excited dog. I was still trying ineffectually to raise the slide when Pedro made a miscalculation. In executing a particularly complicated and beautiful gamble, he rushed into the animal kitchen. It was the work of a second for Shep to slam the door, and we had our escapee safely incarcerated. Then we freed the reluctant slide and pushed the crate up to the kitchen, opened its door, and Pedro re-entered his quarters without any demur at all. Stefan vanished and had a strong cup of tea to revive himself. Two days later we released Pedro into his spacious new quarters, and it was a delight to watch him rushing about, investigating every corner of the new place, hanging from the bars, pirouetting in an excess of delight at finding himself in such a large area.

When owning a zoo, the question of Christmas, birthday and anniversary presents is miraculously solved: you simply give animals to each other. To any harassed husband who has spent long sleepless nights wondering what gift to present to his wife on any of these occasions, I can strongly recommend the acquisition of a zoo, for then all problems are answered. So, having been reminded by my mother, my secretary and three members of the staff that my twelfth wedding anniversary was looming dark and forbidding on the horizon, I sat down with a pile of dealers' lists, to see what possible specimens I could procure that would have a two-fold value of both gladdening Jacquie's heart and enhancing the Zoo. The whole subterfuge had this additional advantage: I could spend far more money than I would have done otherwise, without the risk of being nagged for my gross extravagance. So, after several mouth-watering hours with the lists, I eventually settled on two pairs of crowned pigeons, birds which I knew Jacquie had always longed to possess. They are the biggest of the pigeon family and certainly one of the most handsome, with their powder-blue plumage, and scarlet eyes and their great feathery crests. Nobody knows how they are faring in the wild state, but they seem to be shot pretty indiscriminately both for food and for their feathering, and it is quite possible, before many years have passed, that crowned pigeons will be on the danger list. I saw that at that precise moment the cheapest crowned pigeons on the market were being offered by a Dutch dealer. Fortunately, I have a great liking for Holland and its inhabitants, so I thought it would be as well if I went over personally to select the birds, for, as I argued to myself, it would enable me to choose the very finest specimens (and for a wedding anniversary, surely nothing but the best would do?), and at the same time give me a chance to visit some of the Dutch zoos which are, in my opinion, among the finest in the world. Having thus salved my conscience, I went across to Holland.

It was just unfortunate that the very morning I called at the dealers to choose the crowned pigeons, a consignment of orang-utans had arrived. This put me in an extremely awkward position. First, I have always wanted to have an orang-utan. Secondly, I knew that we could not possibly afford them. Thirdly, owing in part to this trade in these delicate and lovely apes, their numbers have been so decimated in the wild state that it is possible within the next ten years they may well become extinct. As an ardent conservationist what was I to do? I could not report the dealer to anyone, for the simple reason that now they had managed to reach Holland there was no law against him having them in his possession. I was in a quandary. I could either not even look at the apes and leave them to his tender mercies, or else I could, as it were obliquely, encourage a trade of which I strongly disapproved, by rescuing them.

By this time I was so worked up over the conservation aspect of this problem that the financial side of it had disappeared completely from my mind. Knowing full well what would happen, I went and peered into the crate containing the baby orang-utans and was immediately lost. They were both bald and oriental-eyed; the male, who was the slightly larger of the two, looked like a particularly malevolent Mongolian brigand, while the female had a sweet and rather pathetic little face. As usual, they had great pot-bellies, owing to the ridiculous diet of rice on which the hunters and dealers insist on feeding them and which does them no good whatsoever, except to distend their stomachs and give them internal disorders.

They crouched in the straw, locked in each others arms; to each the other was the one recognizable and understandable thing in a horrifying and frightening world. They both looked healthy, apart from their distended tummies, but they were so young I knew the chances of their survival were risky. The sight of them, however, clutching each other and staring at me with such obvious terror, decided me, and (knowing that I should never hear the end of it) I sat down and wrote out a cheque.

That evening I telephoned the Zoo to tell Jacquie that all was well and that I had not only managed to buy the crowned pigeons she wanted, but also two pairs of very nice pheasants. On hearing this, both Catha and Jacquie said that I should not be allowed to go shopping in animal dealers by myself and I had no sense of economy and why was I buying pheasants when I knew the Zoo could not afford them, to which I replied that they were rare pheasants and that was sufficient excuse. I then carelessly mentioned that I had also bought something else.

What, they enquired suspiciously, had I bought?

'A pair of orang-utans,' I said airly.

'Orang-utans?' said Jacquie. 'You must be mad. How much did they cost? Where are we going to keep them? You must be out of your mind.'

Catha, on being told the news, agreed with her. I explained that the orang-utans were so tiny that they would practically fit in your pocket and that I could not possibly leave them to just die in a dealer's shop in Holland.

'You'll love them when you see them,' I said hopefully, to which Jacquie's answer was a derisive snort.

'Well,' she said philosophically, 'if you have bought them, you have bought them, and I suggest you come back as quickly as possible before you spend any more money.'

'I am returning tomorrow,' I replied.

So the following day I sent the crowned pigeons and the pheasants off by air and travelled myself by sea with my two waifs. They were very suspicious and timid, although the female was more inclined to be trusting than the male, but after a few hours of coaxing they did take titbits from my hand. I decided after much deliberation to call the male Oscar and the female Bali, since it had some vague connotation with the area of the world from which they originated. Little was I to know that this would give rise to Jeremy perpetrating a revolting pun 'that when Oscar was wild, this made Bali high.'

I had decided to travel by sea with them because, first of all, I never travel by air if I can possibly avoid it. I am absolutely convinced that every aeroplane pilot who flies me has just been released from Broadmoor, suffering from acute angina pectoris. Also I felt the trip would be more leisurely and would give me a chance to establish some sort of contact with my charges. As regards the latter, I was perfectly correct: Bali had begun to respond quite well and Oscar had bitten me twice by the time I arrived.

As I anticipated, as soon as I returned to the Zoo with my two bald-headed, pot-bellied, red-haired waifs, everyone immediately fell in love with them. They were crooned over and placed in a special cage which had been prepared for them in advance, and hardly a moment of the day passed without someone or other going to peer at them and give them some delicacy. It was a month before they showed signs of recovering their self-confidence and began to realize that we were not the ogres they thought. Then their personalities blossomed forth and they very soon became two of the most popular inmates of the Zoo. I think it was their bald heads, their strange slant eyes, and their Buddha-like figures that made them so hilariously funny to watch as they indulged in the most astonishing all-in-wrestling matches that I have ever seen. Owing to the fact that their hind legs can, it seems, swivel round and round on the ball and socket joint of the hip in a completely unanatomical manner, these wrestling matches had to be seen to be believed. Gasping and giving hoarse chuckles, they would roll over and over in the straw, banging their great pot-bellies together, and so inextricably entwine their arms and legs that you began to wonder how on earth they would ever disentangle themselves. Occasionally, if Oscar became too rough, Bali would protest: a very reedy, high-pitched squeak which was barely audible and quite ridiculous from an animal of that size.

They grew at an astonishing rate and very soon had to be moved into a new cage. Here Jeremy had designed and had had constructed for them a special piece of furniture for their edification. It was like a long iron ladder slung from the ceiling. This gave them masses of handholds and they enjoyed it thoroughly; they took so much exercise on this that their tummies soon reduced to a more normal size.

In character they were totally different. Oscar was a real toughy; he was a terrible coward, but never lost an opportunity for creating a bit of mischief if he could. He is definitely the more intelligent of the pair and has shown his inventive genius on more than one occasion. In their cage is a recessed window; the window ledge we had boarded over to form a platform on which they could sit, and, leading up to it, an iron-runged ladder. Oscar decided (for some reason best known to himself) that it would be a good idea to remove all the boards from the windowsill. He tried standing on them and tugging, but his weight defeated his object. After considerable thought, he worked out the following method of dislodging the planks, which is one of the most intelligent things I have seen done by an ape. He found out that the top rung of the iron ladder lay some two inches below the overlap of the shelf. If he could slide something into this gap and press it downwards it would act as a lever, using the top rung of the ladder as fulcrum; and what better tool for his purpose than his stainless-steel dish? By the time we had found out that we had a tool-using ape in our midst, Oscar had pried up six of the boards and was enjoying himself hugely.

It is unfortunate that, like many apes, Oscar and Bali have developed some rather revolting characteristics, one of which is the drinking of each other's urine. It sounds frightful, but they are such enchanting animals and do it in such a way that you can only feel amused to see Oscar sitting up on his iron ladder urinating copiously, while Bali sits below with open mouth to receive the nectar, and then savours it with all the air of a connoisseur. She puts her head on one side, rolling the liquid round her mouth as if trying to make up her mind from which vineyard it came and in what year it was bottled. They also, unfortunately, enjoy eating their own excreta. As far as I know, these habits in apes apply only to specimens in captivity. In the wild state apes are on the move all the time and to a greater or lesser extent are arboreal, so that their urine and faeces drop to the forest floor below, and therefore they are not tempted to test their edibility. Once they start this habit in captivity, it is virtually impossible to break them of it. It does not appear to do them any harm, except, of course, that if they do happen to be infected with any internal parasites (of which you are endeavouring to cure them), they are constantly reinfecting themselves and each other by this means.

Other new arrivals of great importance from the point of view of conservation were a pair of tuataras from New Zealand. These astonishing reptiles had at one time had a wide range but were exterminated on the mainland, and are now found only in a few scattered groups of small islands off the coast of New Zealand. They are rigidly protected by the New Zealand Government and, only occasionally, the odd specimen is exported for some zoo. On a brief visit I paid to that country, I explained to the authorities the work I was trying to do in Jersey and they – somewhat unwisely – asked me if there was any member of the New Zealand fauna which I would particularly like to have. Resisting the impulse to say 'everything' and thus appear greedy, I said that I was very interested in tuatara. The Minister concerned said that he was sure they could see their way to letting me have one, to which I replied that I was not interested in having one, although this seemed like looking a gift horse in the mouth. I explained that my idea was to build up breeding colonies, and it was difficult, to say the least, to form a breeding colony with one animal. Could I, perhaps, have a pair? After due deliberation, the authorities decided that they would let me have a true pair of tuatara. This was indeed a triumph, for, as far as I know, we are the only Zoo in the world to have been allowed to have a true pair of these rare reptiles.

The climate of New Zealand is not unlike that of Jersey. Previously, when I had seen tuataras at various zoos, they had always been incarcerated in Reptile Houses in cages, the temperature of which fluctuated between 75° and 80°F. At the time this had not occurred to me as being a bad thing, but when I went to New Zealand and saw the tuataras in their wild state, I suddenly realized that the mistake the majority of European zoos had been making was to keep the tuatara as though it were a tropical reptile: this accounted for the fact that very few of these creatures kept in Europe had lived for any great length or time. Having obtained permission to have a pair of tuatara, I was quite determined that their cage must be the best possible, and that I would keep them at temperatures as near to the ones to which they were accustomed as we could manage. So when I was alerted from the Wildlife Department of New Zealand that the tuataras would be sent to me very shortly, we started work on their housing. This, in fact, resembles a rather superior greenhouse: it is twenty-one feet in length and eleven feet wide, with a glass roof. This roof is divided into windows, so that we can keep a constant current of air flowing through the cage and thus make sure that the temperature does not rise too much. A large quantity of earth and rock-work was then arranged and planted out, so as to resemble as closely as possible the natural habitat of the reptiles. We sank one or two pipes into the earth to act as burrows, should the tuataras not feel disposed to make their own, and then we waited for their arrival excitedly.

At last the great day came and we went down to the airport to collect them. They were carefully packed in a wooden box, the air holes of which did not allow me to see if they had survived the journey, and I remained in a state of acute frustration all the way back from the airport to the Zoo. There I could lay my hand on a screwdriver and remove the lid of the box, to see how our new arrivals had fared on their travels. As we removed the last screw and I prepared myself to lift the lid off, I uttered up a brief prayer. I lifted off the lid, and there, gazing at me benignly from the depths of the container, were a pair of the most perfect tuatara I had ever beheld. In shape they resemble a lizard, though anatomically they are so different that they occupy a family all of their own. They have, in fact, come down from prehistoric times virtually unchanged, and so if anything in the world can be dignified with the term prehistoric monster, the tuatara can.

They have enormous, lustrous dark eyes and a rather pleasant expression. Along the back is a fringe of triangular spines, white and soft, rather like the frill on a Christmas cake. This is more accentuated in the male than in the female. A similar row of spines decorates the tail, but these are hard and sharp, like the spikes on the tail of a crocodile. Their bodies are a sort of pale beige, mottled with sage green and pale yellow. They are, altogether, very handsome creatures with an extremely aristocratic mien.

Before releasing the tuataras into their new home, I wanted to be sure that the journey had not upset them too much, and that they would feed, so we left them in their travelling box over-night and put twelve dead baby rats in with them. The next day, to my delight, the box contained no trace of baby rats but a couple of rather portly and smug tuataras. It was obvious that a plane journey of thousands of miles to creatures of such ancient lineage was a mere nothing, and so we released them into their new quarters. Here, I am glad to say, they have settled down very well and have now grown so tame that they will feed from your hand. I hope that in the not too distant future we may make zoological history by breeding them, for, as far as I know, no zoo outside Australia and New Zealand has succeeded in hatching baby tuataras.

Now that the Zoo was solvent and had acquired so many pairs of threatened species, I felt the time had come to take the next big step forward. It was essential, if we were to do the work of saving threatened species which was my aim, that we had to have outside financial assistance and that the whole operation had to be put on an intelligent scientific footing. The answer, therefore, was for the Zoo to cease being a limited company and to become a proper scientific Trust.

On the face of it, this seems a fairly simple manoeuvre, but in practice it is infinitely more difficult. First you have to gather together a council of altruistic and intelligent people who believe in the aims of the Trust, and then launch a public appeal for funds. I shall not go into all the wearisome details of this period, which can be of no interest to anyone but myself. Suffice it to say that I managed to assemble a council of hard working and sympathetic people on the Island, who did not consider my aims so fantastic as to qualify me for a lunatic asylum, and with their help the Jersey Wildlife Preservation Trust came into being. We launched a public appeal for funds, and once more the people of Jersey came to my rescue, as they had done in the past with calves, or tomatoes, or snails, or earwigs. This time they came forward with their cheque books, and before long the Trust had acquired sufficient money to take over the Zoo.

This means that after twenty-two years of endeavour I shall have achieved one of the things that I most desired in the world, and that is to help some of the animals that have given me so much pleasure and so much interest during my lifetime. I realize that the part we can play here is only a very small one, but if by our efforts we can prevent only a tiny proportion of threatened species from becoming extinct, and, by our efforts, interest more people in the urgent and necessary work of conservation, then our work will not have been in vain.

Final Demand

Dear Sir,
Once again may we point out that your account is still overdrawn . . .

I don't know whether you, who are reading this, have read any of my other books, but if you have, or if you have only read this one with pleasure, it is the animals that have made it enjoyable for you. Whether your work is in the countryside, or whether it is in a broker's office, or in a factory, animals – although you may not realize it – like the forests and fields in this world, are of importance to you, if only for the reason that they provide people like myself with material to write about, which entertains you. A world without birds, without forests, without animals of every shape and size, would be one that I, personally, would not care to live in. The rate of man's progress and, in consequence, his rape of an incredibly beautiful planet accelerates month by month, and year by year. It is up to everyone to try to prevent the awful desecration of the world we live in, which is now taking place, and everybody can help in this in however a humble capacity. I am doing what I can in the only way that I know, and I would like your support. As a rule, I frown on touting, but in a case as urgent and as necessary as this, I throw my scruples overboard. If you feel that you want to help in this work, please write to the address below:

> Jersey Wildlife Preservation Trust
> c/o Jersey Zoological Park
> Les Augres Manor
> Trinity
> Jersey
> Channel Islands.

In the meantime, while there are still animals and green places left in the world, I shall do my best to visit them and write about them.

TITLES IN THIS SERIES

Eric Ambler
The Mask of Dimitrios
Passage of Arms
The Schirmer Inheritance
Journey into Fear
The Light of Day
Judgement on Deltchev

John le Carré
The Spy Who Came in from the Cold
Call for the Dead
A Murder of Quality
The Looking-Glass War
A Small Town in Germany

Raymond Chandler*
Farewell My Lovely
The Lady in the Lake
Playback
The Long Goodbye
The High Window
The Big Sleep

Joseph Conrad
Lord Jim
The Nigger of the 'Narcissus'
Typhoon
Nostromo
The Secret Agent

Catherine Cookson
The Round Tower
The Fifteen Streets
Feathers in the Fire
A Grand Man
The Blind Miller

Catherine Cookson
The Mallen Streak
The Girl
The Gambling Man
The Cinder Path
The Invisible Cord

Monica Dickens
One Pair of Hands
The Happy Prisoner
Mariana
Kate and Emma
One Pair of Feet

Gerald Durrell
My Family and Other Animals
The Bafut Beagles
The Drunken Forest
Encounters with Animals
The Whispering Land
Menagerie Manor
A Zoo in My Luggage

F. Scott Fitzgerald*
The Great Gatsby
Tender is the Night
This Side of Paradise
The Beautiful and Damned
The Last Tycoon

Ian Fleming
Dr. No
Thunderball
Goldfinger
On Her Majesty's Secret Service
Moonraker
From Russia, With Love

C. S. Forester
The Ship
Mr Midshipman Hornblower
The Captain from Connecticut
The General
The Earthly Paradise
The African Queen

E. M. Forster
Where Angels Fear to Tread
The Longest Journey
A Room with a View
Howards End
A Passage to India

Fourteen Great Plays*

John Galsworthy
The Forsyte Saga:
The Man of Property
In Chancery
To Let
A Modern Comedy:
The White Monkey
The Silver Spoon
Swan Song

Erle Stanley Gardner
Perry Mason in the Case of
  the Gilded Lily
The Daring Decoy
The Fiery Fingers
The Lucky Loser
The Calendar Girl
The Deadly Toy
The Mischievous Doll
The Amorous Aunt

Richard Gordon
Doctor in the House
Doctor at Sea
Doctor at Large
Doctor in Love
Doctor in Clover
The Facemaker
The Medical Witness

Graham Greene
The Heart of the Matter
Stamboul Train
A Burnt-out Case
The Third Man
Loser Takes All
The Quiet American
The Power and the Glory

Graham Greene
Brighton Rock
The End of the Affair
It's a Battlefield
England Made Me
The Ministry of Fear
Our Man in Havana

Ernest Hemingway*
For Whom the Bell Tolls
The Snows of Kilimanjaro
Fiesta
The Short Happy Life of Francis
    Macomber
Across the River and into the Trees
The Old Man and the Sea

Georgette Heyer
These Old Shades
Sprig Muslin
Sylvester
The Corinthian
The Convenient Marriage

Henry James
The Europeans
Daisy Miller
Washington Square
The Aspern Papers
The Turn of the Screw
The Portrait of a Lady

Franz Kafka*
The Trial
America
In the Penal Settlement
Metamorphosis
The Castle
The Great Wall of China
Investigations of a Dog
Letter to his Father
The Diaries 1910-1923

Rudyard Kipling
The Jungle Book
The Second Jungle Book
Just So Stories
Puck of Pook's Hill
Stalky and Co.
Kim

Norah Lofts
Jassy
Bless This House
Scent of Cloves
How Far to Bethlehem?

D. H. Lawrence
Sons and Lovers
St. Mawr
The Fox
The White Peacock
Love among the Haystacks
The Virgin and the Gipsy
Lady Chatterley's Lover

D. H. Lawrence
Women in Love
The Ladybird
The Man Who Died
The Captain's Doll
The Rainbow

Robert Ludlum*
The Scarlatti Inheritance
The Osterman Weekend
The Matlock Paper
The Gemini Contenders

Thomas Mann*
Death in Venice
Tristan
Tonio Kröger
Doctor Faustus
Mario and the Magician
A Man and His Dog
The Black Swan
Confessions of Felix Krull,
    Confidence Man

W. Somerset Maugham
Cakes and Ale
The Painted Veil
Liza of Lambeth
The Razor's Edge
Theatre
The Moon and Sixpence

W. Somerset Maugham
Sixty-five Short Stories

Ed McBain*
Cop Hater
Give the Boys a Great Big Hand
Doll
Eighty Million Eyes
Hail, Hail, the Gang's All Here!
Sadie When She Died
Let's Hear it for the Deaf Man

James A. Michener*
The Source
The Bridges at Toko-Ri
Caravans
Sayonara

George Orwell
Animal Farm
Burmese Days
A Clergyman's Daughter
Coming up for Air
Keep the Aspidistra Flying
Nineteen Eighty-Four

George Orwell
Down and Out in Paris & London
Homage to Catalonia
Selections from Essays and Journalism: 1931-1949
The Road to Wigan Pier

Jean Plaidy
St. Thomas's Eve
Royal Road to Fotheringay
The Goldsmith's Wife
Perdita's Prince

Nevil Shute
A Town Like Alice
Pied Piper
The Far Country
The Chequer Board
No Highway

Georges Simenon
Ten Maigret Stories

Wilbur Smith
When the Lion Feeds
The Diamond Hunters
Eagle in the Sky
Gold Mine
Shout at the Devil

Wilbur Smith
Hungry as the Sea
The Sound of Thunder
The Eye of the Tiger

John Steinbeck*
The Grapes of Wrath
The Moon is Down
Cannery Row
East of Eden
Of Mice and Men

Mary Stewart
The Crystal Cave
The Hollow Hills
Wildfire at Midnight
Airs Above the Ground

Evelyn Waugh
Decline and Fall
Black Mischief
A Handful of Dust
Scoop
Put Out More Flags
Brideshead Revisited

H. G. Wells
The Time Machine
The Island of Dr. Moreau
The Invisible Man
The First Men in the Moon
The Food of the Gods
In the Days of the Comet
The War of the Worlds

Morris West
The Devil's Advocate
The Second Victory
Daughter of Silence
The Salamander
The Shoes of the Fisherman

Dennis Wheatley
The Devil Rides Out
The Haunting of Toby Jugg
Gateway to Hell
To the Devil—A Daughter

John Wyndham
The Day of the Triffids
The Kraken Wakes
The Chrysalids
The Seeds of Time
Trouble With Lichen
The Midwich Cuckoos

*Not currently available in Canada for copyright reasons

OFFICERS MESS LIBRARY
R.A.F. LYNEHAM

Peter Monteath was born in B and in Germany. He has taug of Queensland, Griffith University, University, The University of Western Australia and The University of Adelaide. He has also been Adjunct Professor at The University of Missouri–St. Louis and the Technical University of Berlin, where he was an Alexander von Humboldt Fellow. Currently at Flinders University, he teaches modern European history and is Director of Research in the Faculty of Social and Behavioural Sciences.

P.O.W.
Australian prisoners of war in Hitler's Reich

PETER MONTEATH

MACMILLAN
Pan Macmillan Australia

First published 2011 in Macmillan by Pan Macmillan Australia Pty Limited
1 Market Street, Sydney

Reprinted 2011

Copyright © Peter Monteath 2011
The moral right of the author has been asserted.

All rights reserved. No part of this book may be reproduced or transmitted by any person or entity (including Google, Amazon or similar organisations), in any form or by any means, electronic or mechanical, including photocopying, recording, scanning or by any information storage and retrieval system, without prior permission in writing from the publisher.

National Library of Australia
Cataloguing-in-Publication data:

Monteath, Peter.

P.O.W. : Australian prisoners of war in Hitler's Reich / Peter Monteath.

9781742610085 (pbk.)

World War, 1939–1945 – Prisoners and prisons, German – Personal narratives.
World War, 1939–1945 – Personal narratives, Australian.

940.5472

The author and the publisher gratefully acknowledge permission granted to reproduce material from the Australians at War Film Archive (AAWFA).

Typeset in Sabon 11.5/15pt by Midland Typesetters, Australia
Maps by Laurie Whiddon, Map Illustrations
Printed in Australia by McPherson's Printing Group

Papers used by Pan Macmillan Australia Pty Ltd are natural, recyclable products made from wood grown in sustainable forests. The manufacturing processes conform to the environmental regulations of the country of origin.

The author and the publisher have made every effort to contact copyright holders for material used in this book. Any person or organisation that may have been overlooked should contact the publisher.

*In memory of Keith Hooper
and those like him*

Contents

List of maps ix
Introduction: The Plight of the POW 1

Part 1: Capture

1 To War 13
2 From the Skies 22
3 From the Seas 38
4 Desert War 46
5 Greece 59
6 Crete 75
7 Syria 93
8 Into the Reich 98

Part 2: Captivity

9   Hitler's Behemoth 123
10 The World of the Camps 140
11 Göring's Empire 161
12 Comrades Unarmed 177
13 Kriegie Life 196
14 Working for the Führer 221
15 Crime and Punishment 243

Part 3: Into the Abyss

16	Total War	269
17	The Great Escape	276
18	Sojourn in Buchenwald	290
19	Himmler Steps In	299
20	The Small Fortress	309
21	Holidaying for Hitler	318

Part 4: Freedom

22	Escape	345
23	Exchanges and Repatriation	369
24	On the Move	377
25	Liberation	393

Aftermath	417
Glossary	431
Placenames	435
Notes	437
Bibliography	481
Acknowledgements	503
Index	505

List of Maps

North Africa circa 1942 — x
Greece — xi
Crete — xii
The Middle East circa 1942 — xiii
Major camps for Australian and other British POWs, 1942 — xiv–xv

North Africa
circa 1942
SCALE
0
600
Kilometres
TURKEY
GREECE
Crete
Cyprus
Mediterranean
Sea
SYRIA
(French Mandate)
Palestine
BRITISH
MANDATE
Trans-
Jordan
Bardia
Sidi
Barrani
Mersa
Matruh
Alexandria
El Daba
Port Said
Derna
Benghazi
Tobruk
Cyrenaica
El Alamein
Suez Canal
Suez
CAIRO
LIBYA
Giarabub
Qattara
Depression
Nile
River
EGYPT
Red
Sea

N
S
W
E
BULGARIA
YUGOSLAVIA
ALBANIA
Florina
Vevi
Salonika
Servia
Mount Olympus
Tempe Gorge
Larissa
GREECE
Volos
Aegean
Sea
Brallos Pass
Lamia
Brallos
Gravia
Evvoia
Levadia
Thebes
Gulf of Corinth
Megara
ATHENS
Corinth
Piraeus
Nafplion
Tolos
Ionian
Sea
Kalamata
Monemvasia
Greece
SCALE
0
100
Kilometres

Sea of Crete
N
W
E
S
Galatas
Canea
Maleme
Suda Bay
Skines
Georgioupolis
Retimo
Heraklion
Sphakia
CRETE
Mediterranean Sea
Crete
SCALE
0
100
Kilometres

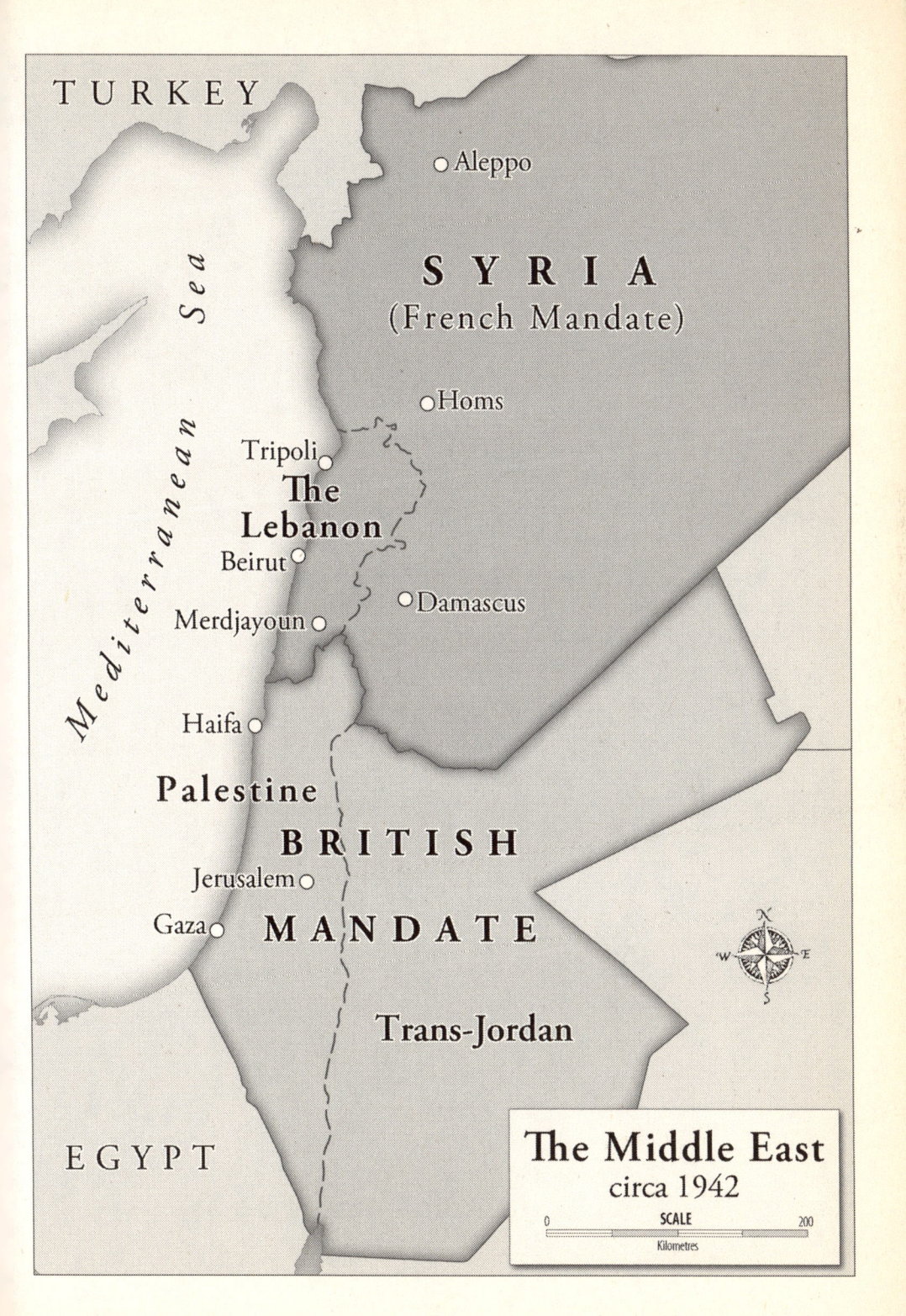

The Middle East
circa 1942

- TURKEY
- Aleppo
- **SYRIA** (French Mandate)
- Homs
- Tripoli
- **The Lebanon**
- Beirut
- Merdjayoun
- Damascus
- Mediterranean Sea
- Haifa
- **Palestine**
- **BRITISH MANDATE**
- Jerusalem
- Gaza
- Trans-Jordan
- EGYPT

Scale: 0 – 200 Kilometres

Map of Germany showing POW camp locations during WWII:

- North Sea
- DENMARK (Occupied)
- Sassnitz
- Stalag Luft I Barth
- Oflag X C Lübeck
- Rostock
- Swinemunde
- Stalag X B Sandbostel
- Hamburg
- Marlag-Milag Nord
- Stettin
- Stalag Luft IV Gross Tychow
- Bremen
- Stalag XI B/357 Fallingbostel
- Hanover
- Stalag III A Luckenwalde
- ★ BERLIN
- Genshagen
- Stalag Luft III Sagan
- NETHERLANDS (Occupied)
- Oflag VI B Warburg
- Oflag IX A/H Spangenberg
- Stalag IV B Mühlberg
- Leipzig
- Stalag VIII A Görlitz
- Düsseldorf
- Oflag IX Ziegenhain
- Buchenwald
- Oflag IV C Colditz
- Dresden
- Cologne
- Oflag IX A/Z Rotenburg
- BELGIUM (Occupied)
- Wetzlar
- Theresienstadt
- Dulag Luft Oberursel
- Frankfurt
- GERMANY
- Prague
- Stalag XIII C Hammelburg
- BOHEMIA (Protectorate)
- Saarbrücken
- Stalag XIII D Nuremberg
- Stalag 383 Hohenfels
- Stuttgart
- Steinburg
- Oflag VII B Eichstätt
- Stalag VII A Moosburg
- Danube
- FRANCE (Occupied)
- Oflag V B Biberach
- Munich
- Oflag VII C Laufen
- Berne
- SWITZERLAND (Neutral)
- Stalag XVIII A Wolfsberg
- Geneva
- Stalag XVIII D Marburg
- Vichy France (Axis)
- ITALY (Axis)

xiv

Baltic Sea
Stalag Luft VI Heydekrug
Reichskommissariat
Ostland
(Occupied)
Königsberg
Danzig
Oflag XXI B
Schubin
Vistula
Stalag XX A
Thorn
Warsaw
River
Reichskommissariat
Ukraine
(Occupied)
General
Government
of Poland
(Occupied)
Stalag Luft VII
Bankau
Breslau
River
Stalag VIII B/344
Lamsdorf
Auschwitz
Krakow
Lemberg
(Lvov)
Stalag VIII B Teschen
MORAVIA
(Protectorate)
SLOVAKIA
Bratislava
Vienna
River
Budapest
HUNGARY
(Axis)
CROATIA
Major camps for Australian and other British POWs, 1942
Oflag (for officers)
Stalag (for other ranks)
Stalag Luft (for airmen)
0
SCALE
400
Kilometres

INTRODUCTION
The Plight of the POW

Prisoner of War! That is the least unfortunate kind of prisoner to be, but is nevertheless a melancholy state. You are in the power of your enemy. You owe your life to his humanity, and your daily bread to his compassion. You must obey his orders, go where he tells you, stay where you are bid, await his pleasure, possess your soul in patience. Meanwhile the war is going on, great events are in progress, fine opportunities for action and adventure are slipping away. Also the days are very long. Hours crawl like paralytic centipedes. Nothing amuses you. Reading is difficult; writing impossible. Life is one long boredom from dawn till slumber.

Winston Churchill[1]

A stint in a POW camp in Pretoria during the Boer War taught the young war correspondent Winston Churchill the misery of military captivity. Indeed, the lot of the prisoner of war had always been a wretched one, as he well knew. Plucked from the field of battle, the POW could expect at the very best a stint of unrelieved boredom, accompanied by the ignominy of prolonged absence from his assigned duty on the field of battle. Moreover, posterity merely underlines that ignominy – history books typically consign POWs to their footnotes. At the other end of his range of hopes or expectations, an abrupt and violent death might await the POW in the very near future, or perhaps a life of drudging slavery, far removed from the familial warmth and comforts of his homeland.

In the ancient world those bleaker outcomes were commonly confronted. The Old Testament's book of Samuel speaks eloquently of the uncompromising measures meted out to the vanquished: 'Now go and smite Amalak, and utterly destroy all that they have, and spare them not; but slay both man and woman, infant and suckling, ox and sheep, camel and ass.'[2] Deuteronomy, too, by no means counselled compassion, insisting instead that the Israelites prosecute the most ruthless – yet divinely sanctioned – treatment of the gamut of foes: 'thou shalt utterly destroy . . . the Hittites, and the Amorites, the Canaanites, and the Perizzites, the Hivites, and the Jebusites; as the Lord thy God hath commanded thee: That they teach you not to do after their abominations, which they have done unto their gods; so should ye sin against the Lord your God.'[3] Wittingly or otherwise, armies in Biblical times appeared to have followed these injunctions with some relish.

Yet clemency too was not unknown in the ancient world. At the end of hostilities Egyptian soldiers would check the battlefield for bodies, both living and dead. The dead were counted, the dying executed, but the living, including those who had surrendered, were taken captive and presented to the pharaoh, to whom they automatically belonged, and who held the power of life and death over them. In most cases, it was the power of life which held sway, so that the prisoners were returned as slaves to their captors as a reward, given their freedom after swearing loyalty to the pharaoh, or returned to Egypt as labourers or hostages. Some might even enter service in the Egyptian army. For an unfortunate minority, typically high officials or royalty, ceremonial execution awaited, after which their bodies were paraded through conquered territories and through Egypt as a salutary lesson to all who viewed them.

To the stark alternatives of death, enslavement and enlistment in the foe's army, Roman history added a new option. In the Battle of Cannae, Carthaginian forces managed to take some 10,000 Roman soldiers prisoner; Hannibal then offered to ransom them. The Roman senate, however, refused the offer, and the prisoners were sold into slavery. According to the historian Livy, one of the senators, T. Manlius Torquatus, went so far as to brand the captives cowards, since they had chosen surrender over fighting to the death and were therefore to be regarded as of no value for the state.[4] They were words that Hitler and Stalin were to echo many centuries later. In the end, pity re-emerged, and when Hannibal was finally defeated at Zama, Scipio Africanus brought home all the Roman POWs he could still find.

All of those options from the ancient world – execution, enslavement, exchange (whether for money or other prisoners) and enlistment in the enemy's forces – were bequeathed to the centuries that followed. Extractions of ransom, for example, were a feature of the Hundred Years War (1337–1453), even if relatively few combatants became POWs. In almost all cases those concerned were aristocrats or royalty, precisely because their capture could be exploited for considerable financial or political gain. Indeed, prisoners generally were worth taking only if they might bring a handsome reward. The rule of thumb was that a ransom would be set at such a level as not to ruin a captive. A king's ransom was typically a huge sum, and with such a value attached to him, a captured king could expect to be well treated. It is recorded that the King of France, Jean II, needed twelve wagons when he was returned to France from captivity in 1360. When the French did not meet the instalments on the king's ransom that were still owed, the king returned voluntarily to English captivity at various sites, including the Savoy and Berkhamsted Castle, where he was treated in a manner befitting a king. At the other end of the social scale, where prisoners might be considered as good as worthless, exposure to the most brutal treatment was a real possibility. The currency of chivalry had its limits.

If the modern world brought progress, then it was in codification. Over centuries wars would commonly be preceded by the making of arrangements relating to prisoners and sundry other conditions of hostility. But by the seventeenth century the notion that the common elements of such arrangements might become a body of law applicable to all wars gained traction. An early attempt in this direction was a book by Hugo Grotius in the year 1625. In *De Jure Belli ac Pacis* Grotius sought to establish the limits on what might be done to captured soldiers, thus breaking with the notion that their treatment might be entirely at the whim of the captor. Yet the limits he sought to impose were generous, to say the least, at least from the captors' perspective. It was entirely at their discretion as to whether the POWs might be ransomed; killing them remained an option too.[5] A generation later the Treaty of Westphalia set the bar markedly higher, insisting as it did that all prisoners be released without ransom when hostilities concluded. A century beyond that, and in a similar vein, the French philosopher the Baron de Montesquieu withdrew murder as a legitimate option. Conquest completed, the killing of an enemy could be justified only in self-defence. Indeed, if Montesquieu had had his way, enslavement too would have been forbidden.[6]

In a similarly enlightened vein, Jean-Jacques Rousseau favoured a rational justification and codification of human rights. He vehemently rejected any notion that the victor in war acquired any right to kill the vanquished. War, after all, was a relationship between states, not between individuals. While a soldier might be viewed as an instrument of his state in war, once war was completed and the soldier was defeated, his status should automatically default to that of the citizen, in full possession of the rights conferred by citizenship. The state, he argued, was entitled to deprive captured soldiers of the capacity once more to become instruments of their state, that is, they could be disarmed and prevented from returning to the field of battle. Having ceased to act as soldiers, however, 'they become simply men again, and there is no longer any right over their lives'.[7]

In modern times, in Europe and indeed across the globe, no organisation has been more influential in regulating the conduct of war than the Red Cross. As early as 1864 it played a role in the codification of the treatment of the wounded. In that year the representatives of twelve powers became signatories to the

Convention of Geneva 'For the Amelioration of the Condition of Sick and Wounded Armies in the Field'. The unwieldy title betrays the document's focus on medical treatment, but the implications for POWs were clear enough. Article 6 of the convention stipulated that, in the event of their capture, sick and wounded soldiers should be returned immediately to their own forces or as soon as their health had improved after battle. Their health fully restored, they would be returned home on a pledge to take no further part in hostilities. As was reiterated more firmly in the 1906 Geneva Convention – which now dedicated seven articles to POWs – the signatories had taken upon themselves the responsibility of looking after the sick and wounded regardless of their nationality. This could only be interpreted to include the wounded on both sides.

The urge to codify did not wane with the arrival of a new century. The Hague Conventions of 1899 and 1907 represented progress in international POW law because they dealt with POWs not as a category of the sick and wounded but as a group in their own right, a group whose proper treatment, whether injured or not, needed to be clarified further. The main focus of both conventions, though, was the customs of waging war on land – indeed, both were labelled conventions 'With Respect to the Laws and Customs of War on Land'. The first convention of 1899 devoted 17 articles to POWs. Their effect was to establish that captured combatant and non-combatant members of armed forces enjoyed the status of POWs, their confinement was to be no more restrictive than necessary, and they were entitled to keep all their possessions, with the exception of their weapons and military papers. The principle was accepted that POWs could be used for labour, but only if it was not excessive and not related to military activities. In terms of food, clothing and shelter, the detaining power was obliged to treat POWs on a par with its own troops. Attempted escape, however, could not be subject to disciplinary punishment. As for the POW himself, he was obliged to provide his captor with his name and rank but no further information.[8]

The 1907 convention introduced a number of alterations with ramifications for the world wars that followed, and indeed even beyond. Officers, it determined, had to be paid by their captors and could not be required to work. For those states which were unquestionably bound by the Hague Conventions, the Great War posed a significant test of their efficacy, not least because the capture of POWs on both sides was on a hitherto unimaginable scale. Moreover, the very nature of this first 'total war' of the twentieth century revealed the Hague Conventions' inadequacies, allowing unforeseen maltreatment and exploitation of POWs. In an early instance of the strategy of deploying human shields, for example, in May 1917 German authorities moved British POWs to the middle of German towns such as Freiburg, trusting that this would persuade the British to cease bombardment of such locations. The British duly responded by adopting the very same tactic.[9] Questionable behaviour on both sides drew attention to the need both to fill some of the Hague Conventions' unintended loopholes and to ensure that codes of this kind were universally adopted.

Some of those loopholes, at least, were filled by a document commonly known as 'The Geneva Convention' of 1929, though its proper title is 'The Convention Relating to Prisoners of War'. Together with a revamped version of the earlier Geneva convention dealing with the sick and wounded, the Geneva Convention of 1929 set the standard for the treatment of prisoners of war in the first half of the twentieth century. Among its signatories on that auspicious day in Geneva, 27 July 1929, were Australia and Germany. This, in theory at least, was the document that would guarantee that the misery of POWs over the course of human history would not be repeated. For those, at least, who met the agreed definition of 'combatant', the pendulum of human progress had swung decisively in their favour.

Yet by the time Germany ratified the treaty five years later, on 29 March 1934, the pendulum was swinging back. By that time Adolf Hitler was Chancellor. Of course, Hitler could choose to apply to the letter the Geneva Convention in dealing with the millions who were to fall into his hands during the war he provoked. As a keen student of history, he could also look back on the history of warfare and be aware that multiple possibilities stood at his disposal. As Australians – among many others – were to discover, he was to use all of them.

Australians were as familiar with the evils of war as any other modern soldiers; they had witnessed their share of death, mutilation and captivity too. In the last year of the nineteenth century, when war broke out in South Africa, Australian troops were sent to join the British campaign against the Boers. A small number of Australians – estimates suggest not more than a dozen – were captured and held for a period of not more than a few weeks.[10] This by itself was not remarkable; it was on the other side of the coin that controversy was generated. That controversy related to the Australian treatment of captured Boers.

The figure at the centre of attention was Harry 'Breaker' Morant. Though British by birth, Morant had honed his skills as a horseman in Australia before enlisting in the 2nd Contingent of the South Australian Mounted Rifles in 1899. It was during a second tour of South African service that he joined one of the units – the Bush Veldt Carbineers – consisting of colonial troops charged with countering Boer insurgency. The irregularity of the unit's activities famously brought about the undoing of both Morant and fellow carbineer Peter J. Handcock at the cynical hands of British military justice. The case was complex; its nub, however, was the maltreatment and murder of captured soldiers and a civilian. The condemned men's plea that they had acted according to an age-old practice, and indeed the specific order, of taking no prisoners, did not spare them the firing squad.[11]

Many Australians became POWs in the Great War, the first of them during the Gallipoli campaign, when not only soldiers but the crew of the submarine *AE2* fell into Turkish hands. Then, as well as in campaigns in Mesopotamia and Sinai–Palestine, over two hundred Australians became captives of Ottoman Turkey. They did not have it easy, enduring severe privation, inadequate medical and other supplies, as well as gruelling work. In an experience which anticipated uncannily the experience of POWs of the Japanese a generation later, some Australians were employed in the building of a railway in the Taurus Mountains. The harshness of the work and the inadequacy of their food supplies condemned about a quarter of them to death.[12]

Numerically more telling, and of greater consequence for Australians in the next world war as well, was the taking of prisoners on both sides on the Western Front. Though they have largely been written out of the history of that war, 3850 Australians were captured by German forces in France and Belgium, especially during the ambitious German spring offensive of 1918.[13] Generally their lot compared favourably with that of their compatriots in Turkish hands. True, supplies were often scarce due to the blockade of German ports, but enough food parcels were supplied by the Red Cross to save them from starvation; indeed, in this regard they were better provided for than many German civilians.

Like those in Turkish hands, Australian other ranks were obliged to work for the enemy, a fate which could only sharpen the indignity of captivity. By an already established principle – observed in Turkey and in Germany – officers were exempted and sat out the war in relative comfort. But the other ranks commonly found themselves working long and arduous hours in mines or even in armaments production. Their experiences, too, anticipated those of their countrymen in World War II, who shared with millions of others the task of keeping the German war economy running. The experience of those Australians in German POW camps and work detachments, and of the Germans who became acquainted with their Australian enemies through capture, did much to frame military relations and even attitudes between the two nations. Those relations and attitudes, formed in captivity as well as on the field of battle, were to re-emerge when the world was plunged into war again just two decades later.

In its scale alone the Second World War was like no other. Some 100 million human beings took up arms. By some estimates more than a third of them – around 35 million – spent a shorter or longer period in captivity. And of these, something in the order of five million died while in captivity.[14] Their stories, however, are not well known.

In the broader scheme of things, Australians were a drop in the proverbial ocean, yet in so many ways their experiences mirror those of others in that war. The worst of it was the wretched lot of those who fell into the hands of the Japanese, whose government had not ratified the Geneva Convention, and who treated their prisoners with a barbarism which stunned the men and women who experienced it at first hand. In time it also shocked the Australian public when details of what the Japanese had done became known. Not all of those in Japanese captivity lived to tell the tale. Of 21,652 prisoners, 7780 – something like 35 per cent – never saw Australia again.[15] But when the surviving 65 per cent did finally return from August 1945, their emaciated, broken bodies spoke more eloquently of their experiences than their words alone could. Then, and in many cases even years later, the physical impact of captivity was plain for all to see.

As for the 8400 or so who returned from German captivity, it is true they had had it easier. They did not lament the same horrific death tally among their number as the prisoners of the Japanese did; their bodies were not marked by the ravages of war as visibly as the bodies of the men captured, used and abused by the Japanese were. Many of the 'Europeans' arrived home while war in the Pacific still raged – still willing, though barely able, to take up arms again. With victory not yet secured, theirs was a modest homecoming. Over weeks and months they melted quietly back into the ordinary civilian lives from which they had come – or so it seemed. Yet they had remarkable stories to tell of life and death in Hitler's Reich – stories of the pain, the fear, the boredom, the privation, the adventure and the frustration of life as a POW. What they missed was an audience to listen to them and, in time, they lost as well the inclination to tell their stories.

PART I

Capture

1

To War

In the early hours of 1 September 1939, German forces commenced an invasion of Poland. Having reached an agreement with Stalin just over a week earlier, Hitler could be confident that the Soviet Union would not spring to its western neighbour's defence. Indeed, Stalin knew all too well from the secret protocols of his pact with Hitler that within days of the expected German triumph eastern Poland would be his. Britain's government found itself skewered on the horns of a dilemma. Should it meet its treaty obligations to the people of Poland, pledging military support to a state on the far side of Europe, already being overrun by vastly superior forces, or should it accept Hitler's express intention of redrawing the map of eastern Europe and expanding his Greater German Reich?

It was not a decision to make in haste. Not until 3 September did Britain declare war on Germany. In return, as at the commencement of the Great War a generation earlier, there was no formal German declaration of war on Britain. For Hitler, the war with Britain was not the war he had sought, but in the absence of an alternative, he would bludgeon both Britain and its empire into submission.

CAPTURE

For the Australian Prime Minister, Robert Gordon Menzies, the decision to commit Australia to the war was regrettable but not difficult. He made it within an hour of Neville Chamberlain's declaration of war, without consulting his parliament, and indeed without seeking the counsel of his Cabinet colleagues. Instead, via radio broadcast he performed his 'melancholy duty' to inform the country that 'in consequence of a persistence by Germany in her invasion of Poland, Great Britain had declared war upon her and that, as a result, Australia is also at war.'[1]

Since the Great War it had become a tenet of the British Commonwealth that the Dominions should undertake their own defence. With the winding back of defence budgets after 1918, a trend confirmed by the restraints imposed by the Depression, this goal was never realised; the Dominions still instinctively sought the haven afforded by Britannia and her Royal Navy. Conversely, it remained an article of faith that in the event of Britain facing a security crisis of its own, the Dominions would display unstinting loyalty. Thus it was a matter of course that Australia would follow the British lead headlong into war with Hitler's Reich.

Australia's Labor opposition did not demur in its unreserved endorsement of Britain's decision, though it did emphatically remind the conservative Australian government of its longstanding opposition to conscription for overseas service, and it gave voice to a widely held anxiety. With tensions emerging in Asia as Japan's imperial ambitions unfolded, and with British military power focused on continental Europe, many pondered whether an Australian commitment to a war in Europe, in global circumstances quite different from 25 years earlier, would leave the country dangerously exposed to Japanese aggression. Yet Menzies' pledge to Britain's war on Germany was fully met. Unwanted though the war was, and unprepared though all branches of its armed services were, Australia braced for a conflict which, in terms of its envisaged enemy and theatre of operations, appeared at first an uncanny copy of the Great War. And in that catastrophe, seared on the national psyche, 332,000 had left the continent for overseas service, of whom nearly one-fifth were never to return.

The first steps were taken to spring to Britain's aid soon after the declaration of war. Apart from a puny permanent army of just 3572 personnel, there was a peacetime military force, the Australian Citizens Military Force – the CMF, or simply the Militia – consisting of some 80,000 part-time volunteers.[2] Neither Australian law nor a potent tradition allowed the overseas deployment of the Militia. If the declaration of war against Germany were to be met with the sending of some kind of expeditionary force, then it would be necessary in 1939, as it had been in 1914, to raise an Australian Imperial Force composed entirely of volunteers. That was precisely what happened. Proudly conscious of the tradition of voluntary overseas service set in 1914 – and the stubborn rejection of conscription – the force raised from 1939 for war against the Third Reich was labelled the Second AIF. In effect a 'two armies' policy applied, with the Militia to serve at home and the Second AIF to be sent to serve once more overseas, though for some time its destination remained unknown.

In the middle of September it was announced that the entire Militia would be called up in two drafts, each of 40,000 men, who would receive four weeks of solid training. As compulsory training had been abandoned in 1929, the need for it was dire. At about the same time, the government set in motion the raising of a first division of volunteers for overseas service. This was to be done outside the existing framework of the Militia, but with the expectation that most of the men would have some kind of Militia background. Yet not all were at liberty to sign up. To protect the needs of an Australian economy just beginning to gear up for war, occupation restrictions were applied. Nor could professional soldiers enlist unless, like some of those from barred professions, they made false statements about their occupation. Others took liberties with information they provided about previous service or military experience so as to make the cut. Still others made extravagant claims about their age, either to boost themselves to the legal minimum age or to conceal the signs of advancing years. Some of those who succeeded in this last deception came to regret it – they were to discover that the physical demands of this new war bordered on the unbearable.

But for all the horrors of the Great War, they were prepared to do it again.

In the end, fewer than half the men who signed up for overseas service in the new division of the 2nd AIF – the 6th Division – were drawn from the Militia. Militia officers tended to discourage their men from moving across from one army to the other, fearing that their units would be unduly weakened. Besides, rates of pay in the Militia were higher than in the AIF. But where Militia officers took up commands in the AIF, their men often moved with them.

The destination of the 6th Division was a subject of much speculation. Had the Japanese threat in Asia crystallised further, it might well have been Singapore. But in late 1939 there seemed little likelihood that Japan would challenge the British Empire in Asia, with the result that in November Cabinet resolved that the soldiers of the 6th Division would follow in the wake of their forebears in the original AIF and sail to the Middle East. The British presence in Egypt and Palestine would provide facilities for training and the anticipated deployment to France, bracing itself for a German onslaught while the 'phoney war' prevailed. On 10 January 1940 the first contingents of the 6th Division left Australia's shores, setting course for the Middle East and arriving there the following month.

In naval matters there was little scope for debate about overseas service. The longstanding principle that the Royal Australian Navy should be regarded as an integral part of the Royal Navy continued to apply. Within a week of the commencement of war in Europe, the Admiralty asked for, and received, the release of a number of vessels for operations far from Australian waters. Just two months later, on 7 November, Cabinet agreed that all RAN vessels would be placed under the Admiralty's strategic control. Yet the Australian government retained the prerogative to recall Australian vessels for duties closer to home where required, as indeed was deemed necessary well before Japanese entry into the war. The German menace to Australian shipping extended into the Indian and Pacific oceans, most notoriously in the annals of Australian naval history in the form of the raider *Kormoran*. Moreover, the

Australian government expanded the capabilities of the RAN by boosting both manpower and the number of vessels at its disposal. Reservists were called up, the RAN's establishment increased, and vessels were requisitioned to serve as minesweepers and armed merchant cruisers. Whether serving close to home or as far away as the Mediterranean, whether among the crew of Australian or British vessels, the outbreak of war made naval service dangerous. Australian merchant seamen, too, working on vessels in oceans around the globe, daily risked potentially lethal encounters with the German navy, the Kriegsmarine.

The third of the branches of Australia's armed forces was by no means the last, certainly not in terms of popularity. More acutely than the other services, the Royal Australian Air Force confronted the bigger issue of how Australia would balance its obligations to Britain and its global Empire with its need to protect itself. When war was declared, one RAAF squadron was already stationed in Britain, where it was placed under the command of the Royal Air Force's Coastal Command. Later that month the Australian government offered a kind of aerial version of an 'expeditionary force' in the form of four bomber and two fighter squadrons, to be placed fully at the RAF's disposal. The very offer signalled the parlous state of the Empire's air defences, because, if accepted, it would have left the RAAF with few options to play any kind of role in defending Australia. A new approach was desperately sought, and its makings were to be found in an idea which had been around for a few years.

The idea, championed most stridently by the Australian High Commissioner in London, Stanley Bruce, was to create a kind of Empire air force by pooling the Empire's air training resources. More specifically, the proposal put forward by Bruce suggested that basic training would be carried out in the individual dominions, then more advanced training would be offered in Canada before graduates joined squadrons in Britain. With the endorsement and adoption of the so-called Empire Air Training Scheme (EATS), Menzies' offer to send further RAAF squadrons to Britain was withdrawn, because the scheme was calculated to meet Britain's needs by other means. Indeed, if anything, EATS did more to tip the balance in favour of the RAF's immediate European concerns than the interests of the RAAF, which to a large extent became a kind of training organisation. Then when Australian servicemen entered service in Britain after training in Australia and Canada, they commonly joined 'Empire' crews of various nationalities, most of them in British squadrons.

While it is true that ultimately eighteen RAAF squadrons were formed, most Australian airmen joined other crews. And most of them found themselves in Bomber Command, which of all the British Commonwealth forces came to make the rueful boast of the highest operational loss rate. In any case, whether with RAAF squadrons under RAF command, or whether integrated directly into RAF crews, whether serving in bombers or fighters, Australian airmen in Europe more than any other servicemen found themselves removed from the charge of their government back home.

This had absolutely no impact on the enlistment of Australians, who displayed all the enthusiasm and commitment for the cause which had marked the outbreak of the Great War. Six months after the commencement of hostilities in Europe, no fewer than 68,000 young Australian men had volunteered to join the air force. As for the army, by that time a decision had been reached to raise a 7th Division of the 2nd AIF to join the 6th in the Middle East. By the end of March some 22,000 men were in AIF uniform, with more to follow after the announcement of the raising of an 8th Division in June 1940, and a 9th in September. Around 7000 had volunteered for naval service.[3]

As most of the 6th Division steamed towards the Middle East, it must have been difficult to avoid a collective sense of déjà vu. In the Great War Australian soldiers commonly went to the Middle East to receive training before being introduced to the horrors of twentieth century combat, whether in Turkey or on the Western Front. The members of the 6th Division were entitled to expect something similar. When the Division's three brigades underwent training and equipping after arrival in Egypt, officers and men assumed it was a staging point for the defence of France. But this time Europe was not to be their destination, because events on the Continent had taken an astonishing turn for the worse.

Having failed to take Paris after more than four years of desperate battle in the Great War, in May 1940 German forces swept down through Holland and Belgium to enter France, rendering the Maginot Line an irrelevance. Employing the tactics of *Blitzkrieg* – lightning war – characterised by the precise coordination of startlingly mobile air and ground forces, the Wehrmacht – the German armed forces – not so much marched but drove south to take the French capital by 14 June. If the capitulation of Polish forces the previous September was not enough, the precipitous collapse of Holland, Belgium and France proved that a new era of warfare had begun. Armies could move at hitherto unimagined speed, giving them the power to entrap and capture huge swathes of enemy forces even before they had a genuine chance to establish a credible line of defence. In a chilling portent of things that were to come in North Africa, Greece and Crete, the Germans took into captivity, often with barely a whimper, the armies of western Europe which had dared to stand in their way. As for the British Expeditionary Force, it was famously stranded at Dunkirk but allowed to evacuate, the humbled beneficiaries of an act of misguided munificence. In these desperate circumstances there could be no repeat of the Australians' Western Front heroics of a generation earlier. The Germans would have to be confronted elsewhere.

Not only in the military but also in the international political realm, things had deteriorated in such a way as to alter drastically the role Australian forces would play. With France on its knees, Italy entered the war on Germany's side on 10 June 1940, immediately bringing to bear a strategic interest in the region where Australian forces were already present. As far as Mussolini was concerned, the Mediterranean was *mare nostrum*, 'our sea'. His vision was of a recreated Roman Empire embracing all sides of the sea, including an expanded African empire. There could be no place for outposts of British imperialism, the centrepiece of which in that region was Egypt. Together with the successes of Hitler, the ambitions of Mussolini meant that, despite all expectations, the first theatre of war for the men of the 6th Division was to be North Africa. Indeed, with British forces already spread thinly, Australian troops were to provide the foundation on which the engagement with Italy in North Africa was to be built.

THE MEN WHO signed up for service in the 2nd AIF came from all parts of Australia, from cities but also from the bush, where a larger proportion of the population lived back then. Most came from families touched in some tragic way by the Great War. Fathers, brothers and uncles had been lost back then, others returned bearing the visible and invisible scars of war: limbs had been blasted off, lungs ravaged by chemical warfare and faces mangled by gunshot wounds, while others were 'shell-shocked' and retreated into a private hell.

The so-called '39ers', the men who enlisted in the first months of war, had been touched too by the Depression. Farms and family businesses had gone bust, their parents had spent years looking for work, an unhappy burden they passed on to their children at an all-too-early age, and with scarcely better chances of success. People resigned themselves to meagre diets of whatever they could lay their hands on, or whatever charity would spare. They had little choice but to live by their wits, moving as necessary to wherever a job might present itself, and acquiring with speed whatever skills might help to feed them.

It was the scarcity of work which had driven many to join the Militia. It offered comradeship and a paltry income in straitened times. For many it also offered certain challenges they had not confronted in their civilian lives. Military life imposed an authority and discipline that many found difficult to accept. It was a challenge which remained with those who transferred over to the AIF, and confronted those men who joined the AIF directly from their civilian lives. The training they received at places like Puckapunyal or Northam or Ingleburn or Woodside was a trial not just for their bodies but for their minds as well.

For those who were to find themselves prisoners of the Reich, the hardships of the cruel decade of the 1930s had a silver lining. Their capacity to fashion solutions from the most meagre resources, to adapt to new and testing circumstances, was an ideal preparation for captivity. Many of the Australians had a toughness, a resilience and a canniness that had been tempered in the rotten years of the 1930s, and which held them in good stead in the even grimmer years of the war. And it was just as well, because in their training they received no instruction at all to prepare them for the prospect of captivity. Some might have had relatives or acquaintances who had spent some part of the Great War in a German or even Turkish POW camp, but these were experiences that had been neatly erased from the collective memory of that war.

All of the men who joined the AIF were volunteers. Just what drove them to enlist is not always clear. The war correspondent Chester Wilmot got to know a number of them in North Africa. Wilmot claimed that if asked his motivation an Australian might have been inclined to answer, 'Oh, I wanted a bit of fun,' or 'Well, all my cobbers were joining up and so I went along too.' But Wilmot also speculated that the reasons might have run much deeper. The need for fun or a change does not itself explain a determination to risk one's life in battle. If pressed, the soldier might articulate a belief in freedom, a fair go, and a life without violence. 'It was because they felt that the battle was being fought for things like these, which mattered directly to them, that the Mallee farmer and the Kalgoorlie miner, the Bendigo bank-clerk and the Sydney solicitor made the soldiers of Tobruk just as they had made those of Gallipoli.'[4]

Even if fathers and uncles had made similar journeys just a generation earlier, these men had little idea what awaited them as they left Australia's shores. They were, as one of them, Ray Corbett, reflected decades later, 'like schoolboys on a picnic'.[5] There were any number of matters that might have played on their minds, death surely among them. But as was the case for their predecessors crammed on troopships heading for Gallipoli or the Western Front, captivity was not one of them.

2

From the Skies

It was a fascination with the technology and grace of modern flight that drew young Australians to service in the air force. Responses to the call for aircrew bordered on the overwhelming, even as the government was still planning Australia's most telling contribution to the war. Six months after the declaration of hostilities, nearly 70,000 had applied to become aircrew or ground staff. The Empire Air Training Scheme could not cope with such numbers.[1] The necessarily gradual climb in enlistments towards the target of 10,000 per year barely curbed enthusiasm, yet first reports of the nature of the war over Europe might have given cause for reflection. In the end, the air force proved the most perilous of the services.

With EATS behind them, the Australian airmen underwent the final stage of preparation in Britain, where adjustments had to be made to the different flying conditions there as well as to aircraft. For those deployed to the squadrons in Bomber Command in particular, the heavy four-engined machines such as the widely used Halifaxes and Lancasters, laden with bombs, were a vastly different proposition from the training craft the men had known earlier.

The first Australian airmen entered the European fray well before their infantry countrymen. Even before the RAAF squadrons were formed in Britain, Australians were integrated into aircrew in RAF squadrons, in which four in ten men were from 'the Dominions'.[2] In time RAAF squadrons too played their roles in the battles waged against both Germany and Italy. Whether in the RAF or the RAAF, the airmen's tasks were manifold and the range of their operations vast. Most numerously they fought in Bomber Command, flying operations over Germany with the aim of destroying enemy industry and morale. But they also served in Coastal Command, entrusted with the task of sinking enemy shipping and submarines, as well as laying mines to achieve similar goals. Australians served in Fighter Command, too, joining airmen of many nationalities in seeking famously to repel the doomed German efforts through the summer and autumn of 1940 to bludgeon Britain into submission and then, with the tide turning, taking the fight to the enemy.

The areas of operations extended far beyond the skies over Britain, Germany and the seas between. In Europe alone, Australians served – and were shot down – in skies as far apart as those over France, Belgium, Holland, Italy and Poland. They supported campaigns against German and Italian forces in North Africa – at the time of the Battle of El Alamein there were five Australian squadrons in the Middle East.[3] Australian airmen even established a presence as far east as Iraq to protect crucial strategic and resource interests there. In September 1942, 454 Squadron RAAF with its Blenheims and its 500 ground crew were sent to a location just outside Mosul.[4] By the end of hostilities there were some 16,000 RAAF personnel in locations as varied as the UK, Western Europe, Gibraltar, Iceland, the Azores and at points around the Mediterranean and Middle East.[5]

Understandably, the ones who were most likely to fall into German hands were those serving in Bomber Command, flying raids over Germany and German-occupied Europe. It was in a lumbering heavy bomber over enemy territory or the icy waters of the North Sea that the yawning chasm between adolescent fantasies of heroic flight and the realities of a vicious industrialised aerial war became most apparent. No matter which position the airman occupied, the combination of prolonged discomfort and privation on the one hand and moments of acute, witless terror on the other was a harsh and inescapable reality.

The role of gunner might appear the most unenviable. Typically on the four-engined bombers there were two gunners, one in the upper middle of the aircraft, the other its tail; both scanned the skies for lightning-fast fighter attacks launched from behind or above. Lancasters were also equipped with guns in the nose to be operated by the bomb aimer. The rear gunner was not only in the loneliest position in the aircraft, perched at the very back and exposed to temperatures so cold as to demand the donning of electric suits, he was also the most directly vulnerable. Tales of the shattered remains of gunners being washed out of the rear turrets with a hose at the end of missions were apocryphal, yet they expressed an understandable and widespread anxiety.

Gunners in fact did not suffer the highest death rates among bomber crews – wireless operators perished at almost double the rate. In truth when a heavy bomber was targeted by flak batteries or fighter aircraft seeking desperately to bring it down, whether before or after dropping its lethal payload, all the crew – a full contingent in a Lancaster, for example, consisted of the two gunners, the wireless operator, the pilot, the flight engineer, the bomb aimer and navigator – were in mortal danger. In the worst case, a direct strike on a heavy bomber could cause the immediate death of all on board. Even in the more favourable circumstances of the aircraft being stricken without being blown out of the air, odds were not good. The otherwise much-praised Lancasters in particular were tough to escape from. The number of men surviving from a seven-man crew averaged just 1.3. As the wireless operator, the upper gunner and the navigator were all in the middle of the plane, the chances of them squeezing through the fuselage of a viciously pitching, plummeting machine, past equipment and the main wing spar, burdened with their vests and parachute harnesses, were small.[6]

Aircrew were all too aware just how the odds were stacked. The great hope was to survive enough operations to be transferred to other duties. Initially the target was 200 hours of flying which, the Air Ministry calculated, would give aircrew a fifty-fifty chance of survival. Then in 1943 it became policy that an airman's 'tour' would consist of 30 operations, after which he would be eligible for a six-month stint at a training school. Where aircrew survived a first tour, their next tour would consist of just twenty sorties. By 1943 only one in six crews could expect to survive their first tour, just one in forty a second.[7] In this regard, the airmen were far worse off than their comrades on the ground or at sea. Indeed, the life expectancy of an airman was less even than that of an infantry officer on the Western Front in the hellish year of 1916.[8]

The statistics for Australians paint a chillingly clear picture of the perils of this kind of warfare. Fatal casualties in the RAAF over the duration of the war in Europe were 5397, of whom the lion's share – 3486 – had served in Bomber Command, compared with 191 in Fighter Command, 408 in Coastal Command and 1312 in training and other units. Middle Eastern operations, too, claimed a high price in RAAF fatalities, reaching 1135.[9]

Anticipations of captivity were less pressing, yet not entirely absent. Though statistically less likely than death, it soon became clear that the chances of airmen forcibly aborting their mission on or over enemy territory were sufficiently high to occupy the minds of their superiors and of the men themselves. In the cold military logic of the war in Europe, airmen were invaluable assets. Should they be brought down, efforts had to be made to give them the best possible chance to make their way back to Britain. Airmen thus came to carry escape kits, consisting of some high energy food, a map printed on silk in the form of a handkerchief, and a small compass. Providing they had a good sense of where they had parachuted or crash-landed, and providing their bodies were still sufficiently intact, they were expected to make their way to neutral or friendly territory.

The activities of Australian airmen extended across the greatest part of the war's duration, and in this regard their experiences of the conflict differed from those of the infantry. If they did not manage to escape, these men captured in the first year of hostilities spent close to five long years behind bars. At the other extreme, the last of the Australians to become POWs were also airmen, shot down over the Reich as it drew its final breaths.

The first of the Australian airmen POWs forfeited their freedom during the Battle of France. On 12 May 1940, as British forces were throwing their weight behind the French defence, Flight Lieutenant Guy E. Grey-Smith, an RAF bomber pilot hailing from Wagin in Western Australia, fell into enemy hands, eventually finding himself in Stalag Luft III. Shortly thereafter another young Australian, Flight Lieutenant Hedley Nevile Fowler, suffered a similar fate.

Bill Fowler, as he was called, was born in London in 1916, the son of a paymaster-commander of the Royal Navy and of the grand-daughter of Sir Henry Ayers, a Premier of South Australia. The family moved to South Australia in 1920, but Bill was sent to England to attend school at Rugby before returning to Australia. He enlisted in the RAAF in 1936 but then was among the many seconded for service in the RAF the following year, though he was permitted to continue wearing his dark-blue RAAF uniform.[10] In mid-November 1939 he was sent to France, and six months later, soon after the German invasion, he saw action, bringing down two Me 109s and a Dornier 17 in the very first days, before he himself fell victim to a Dornier while escorting a bombing mission over the Meuse River. He managed to eject from his Hurricane by tipping it on its side and letting himself fall out. His parachute set him down gently in the Ardennes forest below, where his first encounter was not with invading German forces but with French engineers, left behind in a withdrawal to destroy bridges over the Meuse. As sundry stray infantrymen and civilians joined them in a retreat west, they were intercepted by a German tank detachment. Fowler was taken into captivity by a gun-wielding German officer emerging from one of the tanks. Whatever ignominy might have been attached to his capture was relieved a couple of years later when he joined the impressive list – as we shall see later – of those who escaped.[11]

Even during the Battle of Britain in the summer and autumn of 1940, the RAF had ventured not only to thwart German bombing raids and the planned invasion – Operation *Seelöwe* (*Sea-Lion*) – but also to send some bombing missions of its own to stalk German targets. By 1941, with *Seelöwe* removed from Hitler's agenda and his focus in Europe's east and south-east, the RAF ramped up its capabilities in European airspace, aided by a steady flow of Australian and other EATS graduates.

From 1942, Bomber Command became a more formidable fighting force; its capacity to strike German interests began to reach far beyond maritime targets and leaflet raids. Under the determined command of Air Chief Marshal Arthur Harris – who came to be known in the vernacular as 'Bomber Harris' – Bomber Command grew as its teeth were sharpened with the provision of superior aircraft, weaponry and equipment. In particular Lancasters, operational since the previous July, were arriving in large numbers to strike fear into German air defences as far away as the north-eastern port towns of Rostock and Warnemünde. Then Harris focused his sights on some of the large centres of population such as Cologne and Hamburg, raids on which came to comprise over 1000 bombers.

Geoff Cornish was one of the Australian pilots serving in the RAF as it sought to take the war to Germany in the face of fierce opposition. In an operation targeting Düsseldorf just before Easter 1941, Cornish was blown out of his Hampden, which had collided freakishly with a Messerschmitt fighter. In a dazed and disoriented state Cornish, the sole survivor, managed to pull his rip-cord – a testament to the RAF's thorough training regime. He fell slowly towards a Dutch forest and then landed with an almighty thud in a farmyard. A young Dutch lad appeared, perhaps a year shy of Cornish's own age of nineteen, and helped the Australian to his house, that of the local schoolmaster. Another of the thirteen children, a daughter, proceeded to inform him in perfect English that the dramatic events that had been played out in the skies above were observed from below both by the locals and by Germans. Before she had finished speaking a German arrived, pointed a revolver at the airman's head and announced that for him the war was over.[12]

CAPTURE

The so-called Battle of the Ruhr – targeting that river valley's enormous coal, steel and armaments production – reached a climax in the middle months of 1943. In sardonic recognition of the perils of any flight over the Ruhr Valley, the airmen came to dub it 'Happy Valley'. One of its early casualties was the Sydneysider Charles 'Chuck' Lark. He was the observer on a flight returning from 'Happy Valley' in mid-1942 when his aircraft came under attack from a night fighter near the Dutch coast. One bullet pierced both Lark's astrodome and his right shoulder, another thudded into his right hip, while still a third penetrated his right temple, making its exit via the socket of his right eye. It took most of the eye with it, though it still dangled on the end of a stringy mess. The pain came later – only after Lark landed in a Dutch lake, where with his intact eye he spotted its partner floating near its owner's nose, still attached. In Lark's case the ensuing capture was not only unavoidable, it was fortunate. As for so many airmen horrifically injured in their aircraft or thudding into the ground, capture at least brought with it an urgently needed stint in hospital. It was to be some time before Lark would find himself in a POW camp.[13]

Luckier than Lark – much luckier – on his flight to 'Happy Valley' in the following year was Queenslander Joe Herman, flying his 33rd operation in a Halifax. He was approaching Bochum when German searchlights fixed on him – in airmen's parlance 'coned' him. Evasive manoeuvres could not shake them before flak thudded into the plane and sent it into a wild spin, shaking it apart as it fell out of the sky. Herman had been unable to pull on a parachute before the inevitable disintegration. He free-fell perhaps three terrifying kilometres, contemplating the ground he could not see but which he knew was hurtling towards him. In the most incredible of tales of cheating death, Herman managed to embrace a fellow crewmember, John 'Irish' Vivash, in the very moment when Vivash opened his chute. The double-weight meant that they hit the ground hard but otherwise well enough at least to attempt evasion. They were both captured, but no airman could have felt more fortunate to enter captivity alive than Joe Herman.[14]

FROM THE SKIES

By the end of August 1943 the people of Hamburg, too, were experiencing the RAF's full wrath, as did other targets in central Germany. One of them was Kassel, pounded by a raid on the night of 22 October. A gunner in the mid-upper turret of one of the Lancasters on that raid was Ron Zwar, another graduate of the Empire Air Training Scheme. After training in Wellingtons and Lancasters he joined RAF 61 Squadron in August 1943. His fateful encounter with a German fighter occurred on his ominous thirteenth operation. Struck on its starboard wing, his plane caught fire, and the order was given to bale out. With a calmness which surprised him he clambered down into the body of the craft, donned his parachute, and prepared to exit just as it exploded, pushing him out in the process. Stunned by the explosion, when he came to he found himself dangling on his parachute, having unwittingly tugged it open. But the release buckle had been damaged; only one of the straps was still attached to it, and that one strap was around his leg, leaving him dangling upside down, the strap working its way under the force of gravity towards his knee. Should it have slipped to his lower leg, he would have plummeted to certain death. To add to his concerns, a German fighter shot at him, an inviting target silhouetted against a moonlit sky.

Neither gravity nor the fighter prevailed and, though badly hurt, he landed just in time to hear the fading drone of the bombers heading for home. Released from the single strap, he crawled to a copse of pine trees and excavated a rough shelter among the needles for the night. The next morning he awoke at daylight and noticed in the distance a farmhouse where he might seek medical help. He waved down a truck and in the most basic English explained to the two civilian occupants that he was an English airman in need of a hospital. They proved friendly, and delivered him to a medical facility in the nearest village, where a doctor obligingly explained he would need to operate. Two crush fractures continued to cause pain, but the operation was a success. The following day, although still laid up, he was judged fit for a first interview, to be conducted by a military officer in the company of a translator. She was a girl of some ten years of age, and presumably had distinguished herself in her school English lessons. Compared with the kind of interrogations soon to be faced, it was innocuous, and the nurses remained attentive to his needs as he recuperated. In time, however, the ineluctable escort arrived to take him, along with a Canadian airman, to Frankfurt and to the Luftwaffe's interrogation centre just outside it.

Frankfurt itself was the target of a raid in which RAAF 466 Squadron participated on the night of 20 December 1943. For one of its Halifax bombers it was the period just after the dropping of its payload that was fateful. An attack by a German fighter, the most dangerous enemy of the heavy bomber, set the aircraft ablaze. Not all the crew were able to bale out, leaving the pilot, the 20-year-old Pat Edwards, to perish as it crashed. But the wireless operator, Bruce Loane, made his way to the escape hatch in time and managed to squeeze himself out and open his chute. The force of striking the ground knocked him out. When he came to, he buried his chute and turned to his escape kit. But in poor light and with injured eyes, neither the map nor tiny compass it contained were of much help. As he searched for road signs to establish his bearings he was approached by uniformed Germans who escorted him to the local jail. Brief spells in other jails followed, but his inevitable destination was the interrogation centre.[15]

Gordon Stooke's path to captivity in contrast was a circuitous one. By the time he was just 20 years of age he was serving in one of the RAAF squadrons in Bomber Command, 460 Squadron. Piloting a Lancaster on a sortie targeting the German town of Wuppertal on 24 June 1943, his plane was hit by flak fire on its return journey. With two engines crippled and one in its death throes, the crew had no option but to abandon their plane. As its captain, Stooke baled out last, late enough to witness the Lancaster's fiery demise and to be hopelessly separated from his six crewmates. Though he could not have known it in the middle of the night, he had landed near the town of Alken in northern Belgium, in the heart of German-occupied territory, yet his capture was still weeks away.

Eager to gain some distance between himself and his aircraft before dawn, he quickly ditched his silk parachute, his 'Mae West' (inflatable life-vest) and his helmet in a hedgerow. He set off to the south with vague hopes of following an evasion route through France into Spain. Hampered by severe ankle soreness incurred on a painful landing, he struggled to reach a woodshed on a farm before daybreak. When the farm's owner, an elderly Flemish-speaking woman, came across him the next day, she arranged for him to be guided by sympathetic countrymen to a railway station. Playing the role of a deaf mute, he was able to evade the strong German military and security presence, travelling by train, tram and foot to a sympathetic contact, arranged by his initial guides, in a village called Bonne Espérance.

A prolonged stay in any place in occupied Europe represented at least as much danger to his hosts as it did to him. He was passed from one resistance cell to another, including a stint in a Belgian monastery, before a nest of traitors brought about his betrayal in Paris. As a sundry group of Allied airmen and hunted resisters made their way to the station to continue their journey south, they were set upon by German security forces who, plainly, had been tipped off. The evil deed, it seems, was the work of Florentine Léonarda Maria Louisa Giralt – she preferred the alias Annie – the Spanish-born mistress of the Belgian traitor Prosper de Zitter.[16] It was more than a month since Stooke had parachuted onto Belgian soil. Interrogated initially at a Gestapo facility in Paris, Stooke and the other airmen were then delivered, on 27 July, to the notorious Gestapo-controlled prison at Fresnes, just south of Paris. There Stooke was confined to a single cell for a period of a couple of weeks, creating for him an unwelcome opportunity to reflect on his parlous circumstances. Just four months after his twentieth birthday, he was in enemy territory, quite on his own, and with little idea of how the Gestapo might deal with a man who, as they pointed out, was captured not in his RAAF uniform but in civilian clothes, and who might therefore be taken to be a spy or saboteur. Reflecting on this desperately lonely time in his memoirs many decades later, Stooke recalled that he sat himself on the single wooden chair in his cell, placed his elbows on the table, covered his eyes with his hands to obliterate his surroundings and sought to conjure images of Australia, of family and his friends.[17]

CAPTURE

For RAAF and RAF airmen, Berlin was the most intimidating target of all. The Reich's capital was armed to the teeth against bombers. Ron Zwar recalls that it was the kind of target that would make your knees knock. From over 100 kilometres out from their targets the airmen would be confronted with a mass of anti-aircraft bursts before them, knowing they would need to negotiate a perilous path through them to drop their load. Nonetheless, during the so-called Battle of Berlin, which lasted from November 1943 to March 1944, some 9000 raids were launched on the Reich capital, with the loss of nearly 600 aircraft.[18]

Berlin was Bert Stobart's target when his Lancaster in 460 Squadron set out across the English Channel, but a German night fighter ensured that the bomber barely reached the continent. Stobart had the dubious fortune of occupying the position of rear gunner. In a Lancaster the space assigned the hapless rear gunner was so small that there was no room even for a parachute. In the event of an emergency the gunner had to hope that there was time to exit his turret, don his parachute inside the fuselage and still bale out. The night fighter struck at the Lancaster soon after it crossed the Dutch coast, setting a starboard engine on fire and sending it into a rapid descent. Stobart extracted himself from his turret and went to the aid of the mid-upper gunner, whom he helped out of the plane before himself baling out. Only later did he learn that the pilot attempted a crash landing, at the cost of his own life and of the others who had remained on board. Of the descent in the parachute he remembers little but for the wild swinging from side to side and the landing, hard enough to concuss him. Nausea overcame him, blurring his memory of capture by Dutch policemen and the handover to German authorities.[19]

At the end of January 1944, Peter Giles came much closer to the Reich's capital before coming to grief. A native of the township of Clare, north of Adelaide, Giles served as a bomb-aimer in a mainly Australian crew of a Lancaster in 463 Squadron. For his Lancaster, too, a night fighter played the role of nemesis, this time just short of the operation target, bristling with anti-aircraft defences. Suddenly the tail gunner spied a night fighter and shouted to the pilot to weave, but almost immediately a burst of fire penetrated the plane, cutting communications. Giles, who had been lying flat out in the nose of the aircraft, got up to help the engineer struggling with wires. Having taken barely a step towards him, Giles was thrown to the floor and along it. He grabbed at the escape ring on the escape hatch but missed it, and was hurled into the perspex cone of the plane from where he was given an unexpected glimpse of the fires of Berlin. Before falling unconscious, his last thought was, 'This is it.' The cone, in fact, had been the best place to be at that moment, for as the plane exploded he was blown out like a cork from a bottle.[20]

When he came to with cords slapping him in the face, he was falling through the air. Instinctively he reached for his parachute pull but could not find it. A voice inside him calmly reminded him that he had put his parachute on back to front. This time he found it, pulled it, and promptly fell back into unconsciousness. He had come around just long enough to open his chute. The next thing he knew he was in a snow-covered clearing in a forest, being pulled along by his chute. Despite his injuries he had the presence of mind to step to the side to collapse the parachute. As it happened, he was very close to an anti-aircraft gun, but as its crew were still firmly focused on the sky above, Giles managed to make good his exit. Eventually he came to a river and, having stripped and bundled his clothes, he swam across to the other side, only to have his bundle unfurl and with it his clothes, drenched in the freezing water, and his identification medals – crucial proof of his identity – lost forever.

At that point other elements of his training came to the fore. Badly bruised and sporting a head wound, he walked and walked until reaching a point of utter exhaustion. After a couple of days heading vaguely in the direction of France, he was rudely awakened in the morning as a big German farmer kneed him in the side and gestured to him to jump onto his cart. By this point Giles was so weak after making his way through the swamp that he had to be helped onto it. After riding some distance, the farmer offered his captive an apple – it was plain to see that Giles was famished, and the offer was gratefully accepted. The farmer took him to his home, where he was the object of the wide-eyed stares of the entire family. In due course officers from the nearby aerodrome arrived to collect him, not missing the opportunity to vent their anger at him as a representative of the 'murderers' who had been wreaking havoc among the German population.

At the aerodrome he was brought before the commandant who, with the help of an interpreter, asked the standard questions about name, number and rank, which he answered, but declined to state his squadron number. Eventually he was taken to Tempelhof airport in Berlin, where he joined a motley and sorry lot of Allied airmen shot down in the previous days. From there they, too, were packed off to Frankfurt for interrogation.

Though flak batteries remained a constant threat, by 1945 the Allies ruled the German skies and could drop their huge and deadly loads with relative impunity. January was a bad month for night flying, but by February the heavy bomber squadrons were making up for lost opportunities with a vengeance. Included in their targets was the Saxon city of Dresden, which was pulverised and burnt in raids conducted on 13 and 14 February. Among the bombers were 56 RAAF Lancasters, one of them piloted by Alex Jenkins of 460 Squadron. For him and his crew it was a night not easily forgotten. Although 20,000 feet in the air, the huge fire plume over the city gave a good sense of what was happening below. As they pulled out of the target zone the intercom system on the plane and the radio transmitter system keeping them in touch with other bombers were uncharacteristically busy with remarks of the scale of the destruction: 'You could sense that the crews were furious about this raid.' Back at the airfield the debriefing officer asked him his impressions of the raid, to which he replied, 'My impressions are unfit to print, and as for the raid itself I don't think we'll ever hear the end of this.'[21]

Dresden had brought the crew's morale to a low ebb, yet the very next evening a new operation – Jenkins' dreaded seventh – was flown, this time against the industrial target of Dortmund in the Ruhr Valley. The raid itself ran according to plan, but not the return flight. Electronic aids warned him of the rapid approach of a night fighter; his evasive action, wrestling the Lancaster into a series of stomach-churning manoeuvres, came too late to avoid a fatal hit to the inside of the starboard wing. That was the location of the fuel tanks, while in the bomb-bay there was still a 'hanger', a bomb that had not been released. There was barely a pause between the disintegration of the wing, and then of the entire stricken aircraft, giving the crew no time to don parachutes. Jenkins, still in his armour-plated seat atop his chute, was thrown out of the flaming wreck, unconscious. The time between his involuntary ejection and the ground below while in free-fall would be about two and a half minutes. With moments to spare, Jenkins came to, saw the snow-covered ground beneath him, kicked off the remnants of his seat and, despite a great gash across his forehead, still had the composure to open his chute. His clearest recollection as the plane's debris hurtled ahead of him to the ground was of not wanting to be impaled backside-first on a church spire he saw below. Badly burned though the chute was, it did its job well enough to land him in the snow with a great thud, but still in one piece and alive.

At that late point of the war the Western Front was being pushed across Belgium towards Germany proper. Jenkins had contrived to land at a place called Linkhaut in the thick of the hostilities, but just on the German side. Yet there was fortune in this misfortune, because he was captured by Luftwaffe personnel and taken to a field hospital for treatment. Even better, within days the Allied forces claimed the location, with its field hospital, its medical staff and its patients. In a few days he was back with his squadron, having served one of the briefest stints as a POW, never experiencing any of the camps. Indeed, he was never properly registered as a POW. Leaving the trauma of the previous days behind him, and refusing to be sent back to Australia as an 'LMF' (Lacking Moral Fibre), he continued to fly operations over Europe until the end of the war.

Jenkins was incredibly lucky, yet he knew of an even more fortunate Allied airman, a rear gunner, who did become a POW. On an operation over Germany the entire rear section of his aircraft was severed from the rest by gunfire. Serendipitously this rear end of the plane – tail section, vertical rudder and the rear gunner's compartment, complete with guns and the rear gunner himself – displayed remarkable aerodynamic qualities. Rather than falling from the sky like a brick, it semi-glided onto a snow-covered mountainside. Strapped inside, the gunner braced for the thud of landing, was shaken free and rolled from his makeshift cocoon and down the mountain and onto a road. The Germans collected him there and duly transported him to a new home behind barbed wire. The disappointment of capture must surely have been outweighed by the elation of such far-fetched survival.

The last raid flown by the RAAF's 460 Squadron, and indeed by Jenkins himself, had a primarily symbolic target, namely Hitler's 'Eagle's Nest' in Berchtesgaden, mooted as the Reich's National Redoubt, but in reality a military triviality. For the Australians the token value of the operation stemmed in good part from the date, 25 April. Anzac Day four years earlier had brought with it the inglorious rout of ANZAC forces in Greece; in 1945 the airmen of 460 Squadron could feel that a natural moral and military order had been restored. Within weeks the war was over and Jenkins was using his flying talents to ferry former POWs from Bari in Italy to Britain.

While the great majority of Australian airmen who became POWs served in Bomber Command, there were fighter pilots, too, who were shot down over enemy territory and managed to survive. One of them was the Sydneysider John Ulm, son of the famed aviator Charles Ulm. As a Spitfire pilot in the RAF's 145 Squadron, John Ulm was deployed to Africa and then Italy. His brief there was to attack German ground targets.[22]

In early March 1945 he was involved in an attack on a German train north-west of Venice. He dive-bombed it and then pulled away to swing around and strafe the locomotive, but during the dive, flying at some 500 kilometres an hour at just ten metres or so of height, he felt a great thump on the Spitfire's side. His instincts told him to duck the flak and seek cover below the tree line before then climbing to height at full power in anticipation of the engine cutting out. When it did he was out over the Adriatic, from where he could either ditch in the sea – and possibly drown – or, as he decided, glide down to farmland and take his chances with the locals. He spiralled steeply to his chosen field, using the tops of trees as a brake, and landed heavily, taking a blow to the head but still preserving the presence of mind to radio a fellow pilot, anxious that word of his fate should be passed on to his mother. Then he followed standard ditching procedure, taking a red cartridge from his vest and firing it into the plane so that it would burn and the Germans could make no use of it.

Soon a group of about a dozen farmers clumped across the field, took hold of him and escorted him away before offering him a seat and a glass of water. Just as the hope dawned that he might have had the good fortune to be among well-disposed Italians, two German uniforms emerged over a brush fence; their wearers soon made their intentions clear. As was always the case with airmen, whether bombers or fighters, the Germans took great care to ensure that Ulm was carefully watched over the following days, until his transfer north into the Reich, in the company of an American and two South Africans who had suffered similar fates, could be arranged. It was interrogation that awaited them.

3

From the Seas

The German raider *Kormoran* occupies a sinister place in Australian history, for it was *Kormoran* which brought the demise of the cruiser *Sydney*. Captain Theodor Detmers engaged in an act of deception by flying a Dutch flag as *Sydney* approached her some 200 kilometres south-west of Carnarvon in the Indian Ocean. *Sydney*'s Captain J. Burnett allowed the German too close; by the time he realised his mistake the sinking of both vessels was in train. *Kormoran*, at least, had time to release boats and rafts, so that 315 German officers and ratings became POWs in Australia. The 645 crew of *Sydney* were less fortunate; all of them found watery graves. Sent unceremoniously to the bottom on 19 November 1941, *Sydney* was not found until 2008.

It was not the first time *Kormoran* and other German armed merchant cruisers had caused heartache in the Antipodes. These were speedy merchant vessels converted for military use as auxiliary cruisers soon after the outbreak of war. When she was launched a year before the war, *Kormoran* was *Steiermark*, but after her refitting to disguise her she became HSK *Kormoran* – HSK standing for *Handelsstörkreuzer* or 'commerce disruption cruiser'. The acronym neatly expressed its function of disrupting allied shipping, though it revealed nothing of the deceptions employed to that end. The disguises adopted could include the flying of other flags, the erection of additional masts, or even the installation of a second funnel to allay suspicions. Though armed as well, it was the capacity for deception which brought success, initially in the South Atlantic but then in the Pacific and Indian Oceans as well. *Sydney* was the last and largest of ten vessels sunk by Detmers and his men.

Apart from *Sydney*, there was one other Australian victim, and that was SS *Mareeba*. We know something of the fate of *Mareeba* through an account based on the experiences of a man who was himself destined to become a POW, namely W.A. 'Syd' Jones. He was British-born but had adopted Australia as his homeland after the Great War, eventually opting for a career at sea. He became a cook aboard *Mareeba*, a ship of the Australian United Steam Navigation Company. According to Jones' account, while sailing from Singapore to Colombo on 25 June 1941, *Mareeba* was approached by a vessel flying a Japanese flag and bearing a Japanese name, *Kinka Maru*. The true identity – it was *Kormoran* – was not revealed until she swiftly de-camouflaged and turned her broadside on the unarmed *Mareeba* and opened fire. According to *Kormoran*'s artillery report, in just 30 seconds she fired seven 15-centimetre shells in three salvos, three of them striking their target.[1] With some haste a boarding and scuttling party reached *Mareeba*. Jones managed to get aboard a lifeboat before *Mareeba* went down; he soon found himself among altogether 48 prisoners gathered on the deck of their nemesis. There he joined a bedraggled collection of humanity, including Yugoslavs and Indians, awaiting transfer to the Reich.

In the following months boredom and privation were punctuated with moments of suspense. *Kormoran* was in no hurry to offload her human cargo, as she continued to seek enemy shipping. The next victim was a Greek vessel, *Stamatios G. Embirikos*, which had the misfortune to cross paths with *Kormoran* on 26 September. The number of prisoners joining Syd Jones swelled further, the overcrowding below decks relieved only when a meeting with a supply vessel in early November enabled a transfer. Twelve days

CAPTURE

later, on 17 November, Jones and his fellow prisoners were handed over to yet another vessel for the long voyage to Europe.[2]

Kormoran was the largest of a fleet of ten such raiders operated by the Kriegsmarine – the German navy – in World War II. In most cases they needed to be refuelled and provisioned by German supply vessels or through visiting Japanese island bases, but they could also replenish themselves from their victims before sinking them. In both the Indian and the Pacific oceans they wreaked havoc.

In June 1940 one of them, *Orion*, laid mines off the New Zealand coast and then cruised along Pacific routes, entering the Coral Sea and then the Tasman. Near Noumea she sank the French steamer *Notou* on 16 August; her next victim, just four days later, was the freighter *Turakina*, plying the route from Sydney to Wellington. One of those aboard *Turakina* was Port Melbourne-born merchant seaman Edward Sweeney, who rushed onto the deck when he heard the first enemy salvo. As darkness approached, the rough wintry seas caused both hunter and prey to roll and pitch wildly; the German gunners took a while to find their range. *Turakina* could at best respond with the single 4.7-inch gun mounted on her afterdeck as the crew braced themselves for a direct hit. When it came, it took the foremast, which crashed into the deck and then bounced overboard, taking the lookout with it. A second direct hit destroyed the wireless room, killing the two radio officers who had been sending out news of *Turakina*'s plight. Further strikes caused more casualties and also set *Turakina* alight; her captain had no choice but to order the abandonment of the ship; even as lifeboats were launched, salvos continued from both sides.

It was from a lifeboat tossed like a cork that Sweeney observed *Turakina*'s demise, slipping stern-first into the sea. He was the first of the survivors to be hauled aboard *Orion*. He climbed the Jacob's ladder hurled from above with great apprehension, as *Turakina* had offered stubborn resistance and had refused German orders not to radio her position. His fears were allayed when greeted on deck with the words, 'Are you OK?' and a mug of hot tea, the finest he had ever tasted. In this way he and twenty others, plucked from lifeboats or the sea, became prisoners of the Germans.[3]

Sweeney's memoirs have *Orion* heading west to the Indian Ocean, laying mines off Albany in Western Australia on the way, but within weeks she was back in the Pacific, rendezvousing in early October with the supply ship *Regensburg* off the Marshall Islands before teaming up with another raider, *Komet*, newly arrived in the Pacific.[4]

The combined brief of *Orion* and *Komet*, supported by the supply ship *Kulmerland*, was to intercept shipping off New Zealand's east coast, which they managed with some success camouflaged as Japanese vessels. One of their hapless victims was RMS *Rangitane*. On the morning of 27 November 1940 *Rangitane* was about 600 kilometres out of Auckland, bound for England with 312 passengers and crew, most of them from either Britain or New Zealand. Among her passengers were a number of New Zealand recruits for both the Royal Navy and the Royal Air Force.[5] The German vessels' actions were tightly coordinated and ruthless. *Orion* fired on *Rangitane* and damaged her. Boarding parties from both raiders found bounty that 'made their eyes bulge and their mouths water'.[6] *Rangitane* was packed with meat and dairy products. Alas, there was little time for shopping, as *Rangitane* was taking water. Her crew and passengers were removed by motor launch before their erstwhile home was dealt its death blows with torpedoes and gunfire.

Among those killed was 44-year-old South Australian Doris Beeston.[7] Surviving passengers and crew – including Australians – either joined Sweeney and his fellow POWs aboard *Orion* or were transferred to *Komet* which, like *Orion*, had purpose-built barrack-style rooms below deck to accommodate prisoners. *Kulmerland*, too, took some of the prisoners. With large numbers hauled on board, they became dirty, overcrowded and, when adjacent to the engine-room, incessantly tormented by heat and noise.[8]

Rangitane was not the last of the victims. Maureen White was a passenger on board *Triona* bound for Ocean Island – like Nauru, a phosphate mining island – when she saw *Orion*, *Komet* and the supply vessel *Kulmerland* approach, all flying Japanese flags. Their true identity was revealed when they fired on the defenceless *Triona*, landing one clear hit which killed a number of the Filipino crew. *Triona* was abandoned, her passengers and crew seeking refuge in lifeboats, which in due course were intercepted by boats sent out from the raiders. Some of the captives were allowed to re-embark *Triona* and gather some belongings. Among them were White and her mother, who threw what they could into a suitcase. As they awaited their renewed departure, her mother said, 'Well now, you know this is very serious. We are in a very difficult situation. I think we should all say a prayer.' The prayer said, her mother added, 'Now, I think we all better have a drink!' Fortunately a bottle of brandy was on hand to mark the end of their freedom.[9]

White was transferred to *Orion*, where the crew were assembled on the deck, agape at the arrival in their midst of a very young woman – she was just 17 at the time. She does not recall feeling frightened at that moment, but she does remember her knees knocking uncontrollably. She had been separated from her mother and other passengers, and soon found herself in the bowels of *Orion*, reunited with the captain of *Triona*, but not at all sure what the future held for her. The space was very hot and sparsely equipped, formerly the provisional home of some of the passengers of *Rangitane*. She was at least fed, though the food was 'very greasy and very German'.[10]

Shortly before Christmas, and after less than three trying weeks on *Orion*, the captain brought Maureen White and her fellow captives good news: 'Ladies, it's nearly Christmas and I have a lovely Christmas present for you. We are going to land you at an island which is in the Bismarck Archipelago.' The island he had in mind was Emirau, or New Island, a tiny German possession before the First World War, and hardly equipped to deal with a sizeable influx of hungry men and women. Through releasing them, the Germans relieved themselves of a logistical conundrum, transferring it in effect to the small population of the island and the nearly 500 reluctant visitors themselves. Huddled around a lagoon, the freed prisoners did what they could to arrange food and shelter until evacuation by ship could be arranged. Soon they were back in Australia, where Maureen White, her mother and many others were feted, until news of Australian victories over Italian forces in North Africa forced them from the front pages and, soon enough, into oblivion altogether.

The several hundred merchant seamen imprisoned on *Orion* were not as fortunate as Miss White. The young South Australian Vic Marks was among those merchant seamen captured on 8 December 1940 when *Komet* seized his vessel *Triadic* off Nauru. A long and circuitous voyage to Europe awaited him.[11] The hopes of Edward Sweeney, who had already spent four months below decks on *Orion*, were similarly dashed, as he was among those destined now to commence the arduous voyage to Germany and several years of captivity. They were later transferred to *Ermland*, which made her way to Bordeaux, aggravating her charges' discomfort by picking up a further load of unfortunates from the pocket battleship *Admiral Scheer* in the South Atlantic.[12] *Komet*, in the meantime, reappeared off Nauru, this time to blast shells into the phosphate plant and put it out of action.

By this time the Indian Ocean was proving no less perilous for merchant shipping. After a tour of duty in the Pacific, during which she laid mines off the Australian coast and sent three merchantmen to the bottom, the German raider *Pinguin* returned to the Indian Ocean, sank a further three cargo vessels and joined *Atlantis* to wreak further damage. Among the victims of *Atlantis* was the Norwegian tanker M/T *Teddy*, whose crew included four Australians. It was in the Bay of Bengal on the night of 8 November 1940 that *Atlantis* intercepted *Teddy*, boarding her almost before the crew knew what had occurred. The Australians, including Merchant Seaman Charles Lacey, were taken aboard *Atlantis*. Later they were transferred to a captured tanker where they were placed, alongside some 600 other prisoners, in the dark and dank holds for the long voyage to Europe. Not until February of 1941 did they reach Bordeaux, their temporary home, until they were transferred into the Reich itself.[13]

Among the merchant sailors there were some fortunate exceptions who were spared the full length and danger of the voyage to Europe. One of them was an engineer by the name of A. Denholm.[14]

He was serving aboard the vessel *Commissaire Ramel*, a French passenger ship commandeered by the Royal Navy after the fall of France and heading from Australia to the UK in September 1940. Out of Fremantle she encountered a German raider and was sunk when the captain defied German wishes and attempted to use the radio. Denholm and 62 other seamen launched their lifeboats, were duly picked up by the German vessel and escorted below deck to join some 120 other British seamen, survivors of several other vessels recently sent to the bottom.

Denholm's new home, he soon established, was the prison room of *Atlantis*.[15] Some weeks later he was transferred from *Atlantis* to the captured Yugoslav vessel *Durmitor*, in effect now functioning as a floating prison, inadequate to the task of feeding and accommodating its miserable human cargo of nearly 300.[16] The holds, Denholm wrote, were infested with rats: 'We often wondered what they lived on because, as can well be imagined, there were none of our scraps left.'[17] After a month Italian Somaliland came into view. The prisoners were disgorged at an Italian outpost called Warsheik, where there was a garrison manned by some 100 indigenous troops. From there the next stop was a prison at Mogadsicio, a relic of the Abyssinian war, and a formal handing over to Italian authority. After three months of a diet of macaroni and rice, a new home was found in a prison at Muka, eighty kilometres to the south.

It was then that Denholm's luck changed for the better, because by this time – early 1941 – British forces were making advances into Somaliland from Kenya. Indeed, the British advance was so rapid that the prisoners were not moved; rescue came on 25 February in the form of the King's African Rifles. From a Somaliland now firmly under the British thumb, Denholm was evacuated to Mombasa in Kenya, and from there eventually returned to Australia.[18]

Altogether over 4000 merchant seamen from British and Allied merchant ships – covering a range of 29 nationalities – fell into German hands. One source finds 82 Australians among them.[19] Next to these merchant seamen, whom the Germans regarded as a special category, there were also seamen from naval rather than merchant vessels who were to spend a good part of the war in the Reich. These men did not, however, come from RAN vessels, even if RAN vessels – sometimes because of their advanced age referred to disparagingly as the 'scrap-iron flotilla' – did serve in the Mediterranean, on numerous occasions running the gauntlet of German or Italian forces as they supplied Allied forces in Africa or evacuated them from mainland Greece or Crete. Indeed, the crew of just one RAN vessel was delivered into enemy hands in World War II, and they were from HMAS *Perth*, sunk by Japanese forces in March 1942.

So apart from the merchant seamen, the only Australian sailors who became captives of the Germans were serving aboard Royal Navy vessels, on which they comprised a very small percentage of the crew. Official figures showed that there were just 25 of them, all of whom were to survive captivity.[20] One of them was Norman 'Nobby' Hayes, who was aboard *Voltaire*, an armed merchant cruiser, when on 4 April 1941 she was sunk in the Atlantic by the German raider *Thor*. Badly injured, Hayes spent a number of hours in the sea before rescue and, eventually, transfer to dry land. The circumstances of his capture were not unlike those of many merchant mariners; indeed, many aspects of his treatment were the same as theirs. Like merchant mariners, men serving in the Royal Navy were transported to Germany and sent to the facility for naval prisoners at Westertimke in Lower Saxony. But at Westertimke, as we shall see, the Germans began to draw their distinctions between merchant and naval POWs.

4

Desert War

As an episode in the history of POWs in the Second World War, the first campaign fought by the 6th Division was remarkable above all for the capture of Italians, not of Germans. On 13 September 1940 Italian forces had commenced their Libyan campaign with the goal of pushing eastwards across Egypt towards Alexandria and Cairo, fantasies of an Italian empire stretching down the East African coast playing on their minds. An initial advance was halted at Sidi Barrani in north-western Egypt, giving the Italian commander, Marshal Rudolfo Graziani, pause to think about how he might reach the humbler goal of Alexandria. For Graziani's enemies it proved a pregnant pause, as they gathered whatever forces were at their disposal to mount a counterattack. Among those forces was the Australian 6th Division, now well acclimatised, trained and equipped, along with the British 7th Armoured Division and, in the opening phase, the 4th Indian Division. Under the command of General Sir Archibald Wavell, they were ready to launch a counteroffensive on 9 December, taking the Italians by surprise and expelling the best part of three divisions westwards to the Libyan border. There they would attempt to make a stand.

The successful Australian participation in action around Sidi Barrani in December and then in the weeks that followed won universal praise. It was at the coastal town of Bardia on 3 January 1941 – just a few days short of the first anniversary of its departure from Australia – that the Australian 6th Division first saw action. Indeed, it was the first significant land action of the war involving an Australian formation anywhere, and it was 'a colossal Australian achievement'.[1] Within just a couple of days, the Italian garrison was overrun in the first of a series of rapid victories. After Bardia the Australians pushed on to Tobruk, Derna, Benghazi and Giarabub, Italian resistance crumbling before them. Large though the Italian 10th Army was, it was shoddily equipped, poorly trained and woefully led. It fell back to Tripolitania to await German assistance and a dramatic change of fortune.

Some 130,000 Italians had fallen into Allied hands, along with large quantities of equipment and supplies. At Bardia alone more than 40,000 Italians became POWs. Captured as they were by Commonwealth forces, most spent the rest of the war in British hands, some as far away as in Australia, where they might have served out the war working in the tomato gardens of Murchison or the wheatbelt farms of Western Australia.

For Hitler, the Italian humiliations in North Africa and elsewhere were intolerable. Apart from the disastrous loss of prestige for the Axis, there were important strategic considerations in the Mediterranean, even as Hitler was sharpening his focus on targets much further north and east. Were all of Libya to fall into Allied hands, the Mediterranean would be open for British shipping; even the Italian mainland might be exposed. The humiliation felt on the Italian home front could conceivably lead to the toppling of Il Duce and a precipitate Italian exit from the war. Action was urgently required, and it was soon forthcoming. In North Africa it meant the dispatch of the 10th Air Corps from Norway to lend clout to Italian attacks on British shipping. Operating from Sicily, the Luftwaffe could attack Allied targets in the Mediterranean and North Africa, making an impact from Malta through to the Suez.

Troops followed. When his men had first tasted a reversal of fortunes in Egypt, Mussolini had proudly spurned a German offer of an armoured division; after the calamities on Libyan soil in January, the repeated offer of assistance was too good to refuse. On 12 February 1941 a large German force arrived in Tripoli, having been requested by Italy but sent under terms set by Germany. The inspired appointment to the position of 'commander of the German army troops in Libya' was Lieutenant General Erwin Rommel. On 12 February he arrived in Tripoli, mentally armed with a plan to deploy his swift and potent motorised units to drive the British from their Mediterranean coastal nests. The face of the war in North Africa was about to change, and along with it the lives of the men of the 2nd AIF.

Events on the other side of the Mediterranean stoked Rommel's ambitions in Africa. During March 58,000 British and Commonwealth troops – Australians included – were transferred to Greece in anticipation of an invasion by German forces there. In fact, Rommel himself believed that those very forces should have been deployed to North Africa, rendering the Balkan campaign superfluous.[2] Be that as it may, he was the primary beneficiary of the weakened Allied opponent in the Western Desert. As the Allies committed to Churchill's folly of defending Greece, Rommel threw caution to the wind and pressed home the advantage eastwards across the coastal plains of Cyrenaica.

His Axis counteroffensive commenced at the end of March, a good month earlier than expected, deploying his 5th Light Division in combination with Italian units. At this point a miserly 21 Australian soldiers had fallen into enemy hands, but Rommel was to change all that in what seemed the blink of an eye.[3] His move displayed a boldness not easily countered. Initial success encouraged ever greater audacity, driving Rommel to acts of daring well in excess of the expectations of the Allies and of his own superiors back in the Reich. Buoyed by easy and early success, on 3 April he decided to conquer all of Cyrenaica.[4] The chief of staff of the German High Command, General Halder, went so far as to comment that Rommel had gone 'stark mad'.[5]

Over the following two weeks British controlled forces were being chased out of Cyrenaica in a spectacular Axis advance. The rapid Allied retreat towards Egypt entered Australian military folklore as the 'Benghazi Handicap', and it was during that race back towards Tobruk that significant numbers of Australians – members of the 24th Anti-Tank Company – fell into Rommel's hands. And if those who eluded Rommel at this point could not soon break his momentum, then the swastika would soon be fluttering over Cairo.

The formidable task of stopping Rommel in his tracks fell in good part to Australian forces. On the one hand, the Australian presence in the Middle East had been bolstered by the arrival of the 7th and 9th Divisions. On the other hand, the Australian presence in the Western Desert had been weakened by the deployment of the Australian 6th Division to Greece. The men deployed in Africa soon learned that in the Afrika Korps they confronted a much more wily and determined opponent than the Italians had proven to be. Rommel coordinated his infantry and armour superbly; the speed with which his men adapted to the tricky desert conditions, and with which they launched their offensives, was astonishing.

It was during the confusion of the eastward retreat that one of the most unusual acts of capture of Australian forces during the Second World War occurred. It stemmed from a convincingly executed act of German deceit. Near the town of Derna the retreating forces became separated on 6 April. Some headed for the provisional haven of Tobruk, while others, including twelve vehicles of the 2/8th Field Ambulance under the command of Major Raymond Thomas Binns, mistakenly turned down a road towards the Derna airfield. Aware that his party had become separated from the main convoy, Binns consulted a man dressed in an Australian uniform, complete with slouch hat, who directed him along the Derna road. Alas, a trap had been set, and the Australians proceeded unwittingly to a dry basin in the Wadi El Fetei, where a German unit bearing small arms and machine-guns lay in wait.[6]

Binns was among many Australians and others duped in this way, including his own quartermaster, Captain G. Gilbert, and

39 men. One of them was Edwin Broomhead, a chaplain. He, too, thought that his vehicle was delivering him to Tobruk, only to find himself confronted with the blunt reality of his captivity. 'We were formed up in two ranks, hands above heads, and in this humiliating attitude were led off, heavily guarded, from the side of the road.' While the chaplain comforted his men with the assurance that they were in God's hands now and would be alright, gruffer German voices herded them to a collecting point. The instruction was neither to move from that spot nor to light a cigarette or they would be shot. 'That grim phrase,' Broomhead later wrote, 'which we heard many times in the days ahead, strikes into the heart of the newly-captured prisoner not so much a sensation of fear as of deep abject humiliation.'[7]

These field ambulance men were more than useful booty and were soon set to work, setting up a dressing station to treat the wounded under the direction of Major Binns. As Broomhead later recalled, wounded Britons and Germans of 'mangled bone and flesh' were treated 'under the skilled untrembling hands of this shy little man'.[8] In time the men were sent to Derna hospital in trucks across desert roads. For patients it was a hellish journey: 'Every jolt, every tremble, shot maddening claws of pain into them. Smashed feet, ripped bowels, torn thighs, pink smears of flesh, and we could do nothing.'[9] In Derna for several months the medical staff treated the wounded of various nationalities, including Australian airmen and soldiers. And in time they began to see less of their captors, the Germans, and more of their new masters, the Italians. Ultimately they were transferred to Tripoli and then Italy. Their services – and those of a dozen ambulance wagons that fell with them into enemy hands – would have been more than useful at the destination they never reached: Tobruk.[10]

This transfer of POWs from German to Italian hands, typically sooner rather than later, was standard procedure in North Africa. If it was German military skill which led to the capture of most of the POWs there, the Italians could at least offer the logistical wherewithal to take them out of harm's way, and, eventually, transfer them to Italy. The Germans readily conceded the principle that

Africa was the Italians' theatre of war, but largely because in most cases caring for masses of prisoners was at best a hindrance. The Binns contingent was a small one, but soon much larger numbers were to follow.

The Benghazi Handicap having been negotiated successfully by the more fortunate, plans for stopping the Afrika Korps in their tracks in Libya focused on the port town of Tobruk, where the 9th Division, the 18th Brigade of the 7th Division, and some other Commonwealth units dug in grimly. For as long as the Australians were there, Rommel could not take it. Amid the spectacular reconquest of Cyrenaica in under a week, the failure to take Tobruk stuck in Rommel's craw. The Australians for their part knew that if they could not hold Tobruk, Rommel would open up lines of supply by sea which would be invaluable in a march on Egypt and the strategically precious Suez Canal.

On 10 April 1941 the German attack, and with it the legendary siege of Tobruk, began. In a series of bloody battles on that day and through the rest of April 1941, German and Italian forces pummelled Tobruk and its defenders. When ground attacks failed, air attacks proceeded by day and night. Yet every unit Rommel threw at Tobruk in mid-April got every bit as good as it gave. The Australians held firm, earning from Rommel the sobriquet 'Rats of Tobruk'. Though intended pejoratively, for the Australians it became a badge of pride. Over some eight nerve-jangling months the Axis siege was resisted, but at great cost of human life, and at the cost, too, of large numbers of Australians falling into enemy hands. The siege of Tobruk alone cost 467 Australians their freedom.[11]

One of them was Bill Cousins of the 2/24th Infantry Battalion. He had completed the Benghazi Handicap, reaching Tobruk after a scampering retreat and occupying a position near the coast. But several weeks into the siege the Germans launched the 'May Show', an intensified effort to take the port. It did not succeed, but it did snare Cousins and a handful of fellow Rats. Heavy fire forced them from their underground refuge. Although badly wounded himself, Cousins emerged into the light at one end of a stretcher, carrying an even more seriously wounded mate, only to be greeted with what was to become a standard refrain: 'For you the war is over.' The voice was amicable enough, but also fractured in a characteristically German way. Cousins and others were whisked away to a German field hospital and then to a German-run hospital in Benghazi where, in his opinion, the captured men were treated every bit as well as wounded Germans. Only after his recovery was he transferred into Italian hands.[12]

The Afrika Korps could not take Tobruk, but neither could British forces break the siege. The territory around the Egyptian–Libyan border was still Rommel's, even as Hitler cast his gaze elsewhere, massing his divisions on the Soviet border in preparation for launching Operation *Barbarossa*. In Hitler's broader scheme of things, North Africa was little more than a sideshow. A stalemate was preserved as the German war machine recorded the most spectacular of its victories on battlefields almost a world away. Failure to take Tobruk, and with it failure to shorten crucial supply lines, meant that a full-scale assault on Egypt was out of the question. For a time, both sides had to await the outcome of dramas being staged in other theatres of war.

In May 1942 Rommel chose to go on the offensive once more in North Africa, as he still eyed the prize of Egypt and the Suez Canal. By now his target was the Allied forces assembled in the Qattara Depression, where they were well entrenched. For weeks on end Rommel threw everything he had at his enemy, culminating on 30 August 1942 in a final desperate effort to pierce British defences and race towards Cairo. But the gamble of attempting to crash through did not pay off; failure at that Battle of Alama el Halfa forced him into a series of defensive manoeuvres from which his forces would never fully recover. Initiative had been wrested by the British, who could begin plotting a campaign of counteroffensives.

In the inexorable turn of the screws over the following months, one battle stood out for Australians. Its name was provided by a humble railway siding, El Alamein. Just hours before the Battle of El Alamein commenced, Lieutenant General Leslie Morshead predicted in his diary that it would be 'by far the greatest battle ever fought in the Middle East'.[13] In the firing line – literally – were the men of the Australian 9th Division, who after British tanks failed to break enemy lines were required to advance on enemy lines, pulling the full force of German army and infantry towards themselves. As they did so, British armoured forces to the south would penetrate vulnerable German lines and then sweep north to capture enemy forces and relieve the Australians. Bold in its conception, in execution it was to cost large numbers of lives, because it provoked vicious resistance from the Afrika Korps and their Italian allies.

In some secrecy – the men were ordered not to wear their distinctive slouch hats, and the tan boots too were to be disguised – the 7th Division was moved from its garrison duties in Syria back through Palestine and Egypt towards El Alamein to confront Rommel's redoubled efforts. Heading south towards Egypt, the men were at first unsure of their final destination, and some understandably hoped it would be Australia, by now at war with Japan. But as they proceeded across the Suez Canal and through Cairo, it became an open secret, both to them and the Arab population, that there was urgent business to attend to further west.

South Australian Ray Jones of the 2nd/48th Battalion was among those who, having managed to hold Tobruk the previous year, were thrown back into the Western Desert in July 1942 to stop Rommel. He was the driver of a Bren gun carrier, and on 22 July 1942 he and the two men with him manoeuvred the gun, loaded with ammunition, to a position from where it would support an infantry assault on German lines. But the gun carrier ran over a landmine which blew the track off it and rendered it useless. When the ammunition was hit by German fire, the entire carrier was blown to bits. Trapped unarmed in the midst of an assault gone awry, Jones' sergeant had to guess in which direction to take his driver and gunner to safety. He guessed wrongly. The position to which they eventually headed during a lull in hostilities was in German hands; the Germans saw them coming and welcomed them with words which made it clear that they knew exactly with whom they were dealing: 'Come on, Aussie, for you the war is over.' They were words Jones never forgot.[14]

On this occasion just three disoriented Australians fell into German – and soon Italian – hands. Many more were to follow within a matter of days. Western Australian Patrick Toovey was among those forces transferred from Syria to the El Alamein line. The Australians' distinctive brown boots were a giveaway to all those who saw them marching westwards through Egypt to throw their weight behind the British Eighth Army. Toovey's 2/28th Infantry Battalion soon saw action at the northern section of the line, where it was exposed to the measured might of German machine guns and Stuka dive-bombers. Near the end of July the Battalion was given the ambitious task of taking the crucial strategic position of Sanyet el Miteiriya – better known to Australians as 'Ruin Ridge' because of the remains of a building on its crest. The attack, the last of a series designed to crack open the Axis front, was to be carried out in the middle of the night from 26 to 27 July.

Initially, at least, the 2/28th achieved remarkable success, pushing forward stubbornly in the face of counter-fire despite the loss of 65 men. The ridge was occupied, the Australians themselves took prisoners and held their position for several hours to await the arrival of support in the form of British tanks. But as day dawned, so too did the realisation that a hard-fought triumph could not be consolidated. Without successes elsewhere and without the arrival of the expected back-up, a German counterattack was a certainty. Tanks appeared, and not the hoped-for British but rather German tanks, followed closely by well-armed infantry determined to retake the ridge. Against tanks and armoured vehicles the Australians, armed only with rifles and Bren guns, had little chance. The Australians' commanding officer, Major Lew McCarter, raised his hands in surrender. For Patrick Toovey and 489 others, the German advance had been so rapid and overwhelming that even the contemplation of escape was fleeting and futile.[15]

One of those 489 others was Phil Loffman, also from the Western Australian 2/28th Battalion. He had survived a six-month stint defending Tobruk, and then several actionless months in a remote, northern Syrian outpost guarding against a feared Turkish entry into the fray on the Axis side. He recalls clearly the night assault on Ruin Ridge and its long-term consequences for him. It had begun with a barrage of artillery fire which lit the night horizon like a bushfire, Loffman awaiting the signal to advance in a saucer-shaped depression short of the target. The cold light of morning brought with it the German counteroffensive and, for Loffman, a voice emanating from a German half-track, intoning in an English voice infused with what seemed a Scottish accent, 'Get out, you English swine, before I blast you out.' Thereupon the half-track fired a couple of shots to prove that this was no idle threat. Loffman hurriedly buried beneath his feet a Luger gun he had recently looted from captured German soldiers, before being herded into a big group of freshly captured Allied soldiers. As it happened, he also had in his possession – although he was not supposed to – a German-made Carl Zeiss camera, of which he was duly relieved. The capturing officer properly issued a receipt for it, consoling his captive that if he did not take it then someone else further down the line would, and as he was the one who had captured him, he deserved it. 'Well of course you do', Loffman agreed, bowing to the inevitable: 'Take the bloody thing.' His watch, wisely, he hurriedly hid in his pants.[16]

The Germans were eager to usher their captives from the front line, fearing a British counterattack at any moment. The swiftness of his removal from danger did nothing to quell Patrick Toovey's tumultuous sense of guilt, shame and misery at being captured, an event for which his training had in no way prepared him.[17] Jim Paterson, also of the 2/28th, felt the same. Those early hours of captivity 'were the loneliest hours of our lives. Little was said. What could be said? Our thoughts turned within, seeking strength and determination to face the future with courage and fortitude.'[18]

Behind the lines the Germans methodically followed a standard procedure whereby the wounded and officers were separated out, the former for transfer to hospital, the latter for a flight from a nearby airfield across the Mediterranean to Italy. As for the exhausted but still able-bodied other ranks, their immediate fate was to be marched in a column through the desert, with empty stomachs and parched throats, and exposed to the occasional 'friendly fire' of British artillery some kilometres distant. Their destination was a crude wire enclosure at a place called El Daba, run by Italians, and it was here that the formal handover from German to Italian authority occurred. As Lawrence Calder remembers, the German commanding officer was apologetic in pointing out to him as a sergeant that there was no choice in the matter – the Italians bore sole responsibility for POWs.[19] Though captured by Germans, the 'processing' of these men at El Daba and their fate for the next year or so was now a matter for the Italians.

The transfer to new masters rankled with the Australians, whose first-hand experiences had bred a contempt for the military qualities of Mussolini's forces. As Jim Paterson puts it, 'To be delivered into the care of the "Ities" had added salt to our deep psychological wounds. The humiliation of having to send our first communication home indicating we were prisoners of the Italians was the last straw.'[20] Relieved to be freed of these POWs and to return their attention to the combat zone, the Germans too might have wondered what awaited the Australians. Ted Faulkes remembers that when the Germans handed him and his fellow captives over to Italian control, the Germans bade the Australians 'good luck'.[21] They would need it.

The Italians typically shunted POWs westwards towards Benghazi. In mid-1942 the journey west must have stirred some wistful thoughts of more propitious times more than a year earlier. Finally at Benghazi they were deposited at a camp inaptly known as 'The Palms'; in reality it offered no lush tropical foliage but rather was 'a stinking dustbowl . . . It was filthy and smelly, with overflowing open latrines'.[22]

After about a month of being tortured by hunger and thirst and set upon by lice 'as big as white ants' the men were moved to a much larger camp in Benghazi, populated by POWs from many parts of the British Empire.[23] There they awaited transfer to Italy from the nearby port, hoping against hope that the perilous voyage to Brindisi through submarine-infested waters would not send them to an ironically watery grave, having barely survived the war in the desert.

For Patrick Toovey the route to Italy proved more painful and circuitous than for most. A back injury, together with a bout of dysentery, qualified him for a brief respite in an Italian hospital in Benghazi, and then transfer to another camp, divested of all his possessions but the clothes he wore. Alas, the new camp was little improvement on the dreaded 'Palms'; indeed, the authorities there appeared to have acquired a heightened disdain for Australians and New Zealanders. He and another Australian swapped their identities with two South Africans, and as a consequence were not shipped to Italy with other Australians but instead evacuated further west to Tripoli. For all the travails of the long journey, the camp there was even worse than he had experienced in Benghazi. Above all the goading omnipresence of lice stuck in his memory for decades to come.

The survivors of the Ruin Ridge calamity were not the last to fall into Rommel's hands and be passed to the Italians. Albeit in much smaller numbers, over the following weeks and months others followed. Among them was Ernest Brough, already a veteran of desert warfare. In May 1941 in Tobruk he had unwittingly joined the man destined to become Australia's most famous POW, Edward 'Weary' Dunlop. Brough's job back then had been to make tours of duty to the front line, normally for about three weeks at a time. But with the rest of his division he too was sent to Palestine and then Syria, before returning to Africa just as Rommel threatened El Alamein. It was this second tour of duty in the Western Desert, with the turning of the tide in Africa within sight, that cost him his freedom.

On the last day of October 1942, and in the vicinity of a place called Barrel Hill, he and his unit were approached by a formation of German tanks. In the absence of artillery support, and with no anti-tank guns of their own, Brough and fifteen companions had no choice but to raise their hands in the time-honoured tradition of surrender. That moment unleashed in them feelings of sadness and humiliation. Their captors ushered them away from the front lines across sand dunes to a nearby beach. Removed from immediate danger, Brough was questioned by a German officer, who appeared surprised to have captured a sergeant of just 22 years of age. A search ensued which left him with nothing but the clothes on his back, though there was no unduly rough treatment or – to his surprise – interrogation. Brough was among those bundled into a truck and transported via Bardia, Tobruk and Benghazi to Tripoli.[24]

It would have been cold comfort to Brough that early in the following month, to be precise on 4 November 1942, a decisive tank battle produced a clear victory for British forces. From that point, Rommel had no option but to stage a series of retreats all the way to Tripoli. His war was by no means over, but his dreams of African conquest were, and the pendulum that had been the war in the desert refused to swing again. By that time 4863 Australians had been killed or wounded in North Africa, while 1941 had drawn the straw of captivity. Captured in their vast majority by German forces, they were in Italian hands, and soon were to experience the dubious pleasures of life in wartime Italy.[25]

5

Greece

It was not just into the North African segment of his envisioned *mare nostrum* that Mussolini's vainglorious misadventures drew the Wehrmacht. In Greece, too, it was becoming increasingly apparent that a mixture of Italian bungling and spirited Greek resistance would, in the absence of a Teutonic *deus ex machina*, end in tears.

As early as in 1939 Mussolini had established a beachhead across the Aegean by occupying Albania. That, at least, was achieved without embarrassment. Since then his Axis partner had recorded a series of stunning victories in eastern, northern and western Europe, triumphs which Mussolini had observed with a combination of awed reverence and deep envy. The war was proceeding so well for the Germans that even in the second half of 1940 Hitler's alliance with Italy seemed little more than an irrelevance. In any case, for Hitler the Mediterranean was not the main game. With western and northern Europe subdued, albeit in the absence of victory over Britain, Italy's allotted function extended to no more than keeping the Mediterranean region and the Balkans quiet. This was the firm message delivered in August 1940.[1]

Yet the Italians were not persuaded that German strategic

interests in what they regarded as their own broader sphere of influence were entirely innocent. A tangible cause for suspicion was the sending of German advisers into Romania, without any consultation with their ally. What Mussolini did not realise was that this was part of the general preparations for the invasion of the Soviet Union, still many months away. In ignorance of this, and aware that the territorial spoils of their alliance had hitherto been claimed almost entirely by Hitler, Mussolini could not dismiss the gnawing suspicion that Hitler might even harbour designs on the Balkans.

When he learned of the Wehrmacht's move into Romania, Mussolini was angry. On 12 October 1940 he explained ominously to his foreign minister Count Ciano, 'Hitler always faces me with a fait accompli. This time I am going to pay him back in his own coin. He will find out from the papers that I have occupied Greece. In this way the equilibrium will be re-established.'[2] And this, Mussolini boldly assumed, his military could manage on its own.

When Mussolini duly decided that it was time for Italy to invade Greece and seek the 'equilibrium' he cherished, he delayed passing any official word to his ally until the last moment. If this discourtesy displeased the Germans, the course of the invasion could only provoke ill temper and frustration. Anticipating the possibility of invasion, the Greeks had positioned their defences wisely; initial advances were halted with remarkable ease. A Greek counter-offensive mounted by mid-November forced the Italians back; by early 1941 a stalemate founded on mutual exhaustion prevailed. In a predicament entirely of their own making, Italian forces found themselves confronting an enemy every bit as determined as that which had stopped them in North Africa, where a collapse was imminent. In desperation Mussolini resorted to what one historian has labelled a public relations stunt – he sent all Cabinet members under the age of 45 to the Albanian front.[3] If this had provoked the deposing of Il Duce it might have made a difference, but Italians had to endure many more travails before that came to pass.

Hitler faced a genuine dilemma in Greece as in North Africa. Had both Italian campaigns gone well, they would have helped the German cause; as both had developed dismally, Hitler's plans for Europe were in grave jeopardy. Though he did not reckon the Mediterranean to be part of Germany's natural *Lebensraum* (living space), and he could not welcome the diversion of valuable military resources away from his eastern European goals, he could not afford to let Mussolini fail. Italian capitulation would have exposed the southern and Balkan underbelly of his vast imperial project. Moreover, the centrepiece of that project – the conquest of the Soviet Union – could fall into place only if south-eastern Europe were firmly bound into the German sphere of influence.

At first German aid to Italy assumed a modest form – in December 1940 transport aircraft were sent to help the Italian air force shift troops and supplies across the Adriatic. That alone could not force victory. If an intervention with ground forces were to occur, then the combination of winter weather and mountainous terrain along the Greek–Bulgarian border dictated a delay until the spring of the following year. In any case, preparations on the scale required for a quick and successful operation would take time, involving transports across Hungary, Romania and Bulgaria. The last was the obvious entry point into Greece, since Albania was reachable only via Italy and across the Adriatic.

As it happened, a further strategic development not directly connected to Italy confirmed the wisdom of sending forces south; indeed, it prompted Hitler into immediate action. On 27 March 1941 the Yugoslav government, sympathetic to the German cause, was overthrown in a coup; a pro-British regime was installed. Moreover, there was mounting evidence of expanding British influence, not to mention a growing British military presence, in Greece itself. It was an issue on which the Greeks were deeply divided. Not all shared the king's Anglophilia, and as the Italians were being held in check on the Albanian front, there was little sense in provoking a German intervention. But events further north forced Hitler's hand. He resolved to invade and occupy both Yugoslavia and Greece, and sooner rather than later. Not only would such a step haul Mussolini from his self-made Greek mire, it would protect the Reich's southern flank as it prepared for its assault on the Soviet Union.[4]

If developments in Greece had distracted Hitler, they presented Winston Churchill with a conundrum. British sympathy for the cause of Greek liberty could be traced back at least as far as the poet, adventurer and freedom-fighter Lord Byron, who lost his life siding with the Greeks against their Turkish oppressors. True, he had succumbed to marsh fever rather than the cut of a sword, just as in 1915 his spiritual descendant Rupert Brooke died of malaria en route to confront the more modern incarnation of the same foe, but the myth possessed a potent resonance in World War II. With such a tradition in mind, how could Britain permit Greece to be crushed between a revived Italian incursion from Albania and the German juggernaut descending from the north? More prosaically, how might Britain meet the guarantee to Greece it had delivered when Italy had first occupied Albania?

If a combination of emotion, tradition and strategic self-interest spoke for a British intervention in Greece, a more compelling suite of counter-arguments counselled against it. The power and scale of the impending German invasion were predictable, not least on the basis of recent and bitter British experience. The hurried commitment of anything like adequate forces to the Greek mainland was a looming logistical nightmare. Moreover, those forces, both men and equipment, could only be gathered together for a Greek campaign if they were removed from elsewhere. Wherever they were currently deployed, they were desperately needed, not least in North Africa, where Australian and Allied forces had fought brilliantly, but from February were staring down a more formidable enemy in the person of Rommel. Finally, the prospect of defeating German forces and turning the tide of war in Europe was at best minuscule.

Australians might also argue that a further British tradition entered political and military thinking in favour of intervention in Greece, and that was the tradition of the foolhardy and vainglorious commitment of Empire forces to entirely avoidable military catastrophes. As First Lord of the Admiralty, Winston Churchill had been the advocate and author of the century's greatest example, the preposterous Gallipoli campaign. While German forces gathered to strike Greece, it was Churchill once more, now as British Prime Minister, who sought to extract himself from his dilemma by committing Empire troops to a doomed enterprise. He extended the hand of military aid to Greece, a hand the Greeks had long been reluctant to shake. If they had coped heroically with the Italian version of an invasion on the Albanian front, they did not want to provoke the Germans, with whom they had no particular truck.

Churchill had General Archibald Wavell, his commander in chief in the Middle East, prepare to send to Greece the largest possible force he could spare. Given the delicate state of the war in North Africa, this was no easy task, but in Cairo Wavell began to prepare a combined force, including the Australian 6th Division. Nonetheless, Wavell elected to wait a few days before conveying his intentions to General Thomas Blamey, who commanded Australian forces in the Middle East. Neither was Blamey consulted on which Australian troops would be selected for deployment to Greece, even if the terms of Blamey's charter from the Australian government insisted that Blamey's consent was required for the separate deployment of AIF forces. And despite the central place of the Australians in the contingent to be sent to Greece, Blamey was overlooked for its command. That role was to be given to a British general, Sir Henry Maitland 'Jumbo' Wilson.[5]

Blamey had good cause for reservations, and Prime Minister Menzies, too, was justifiably becoming anxious about developments in the Balkans. He had visited Australian forces in the Middle East in early February, and he had held discussions with Wavell there. Thereafter he had been in London as German forces marched into Bulgaria. That a further German move into Greece was now becoming a likelihood did not escape him. Moreover, by the second week of March Blamey was not only harbouring reservations about Wavell's plans but was prepared to express them to the Menzies government – as indeed was his chartered duty. But by the time he could bring himself to give voice to his reticence, it was all too late.[6] The die of intervention was cast on 11 February; not until the end of the month was Australia formally told of the role envisaged for Australian troops in the Greek expedition.[7] Menzies acquiesced, later making an exculpatory gesture to Churchill's strength of personality, so tangible 'you felt it like a physical blow'.[8] Others would take the view that the Australian Prime Minister had been trapped in a snare carefully laid by his British counterpart.[9] In any case, whatever the misgivings, there was to be no last-minute reversal. The belated, pessimistic advice from Blamey could have offered no comfort, but by early March preparations for sending a contingent to Greece were well underway. By this time the Greek government, too, had finally bowed to British pressure.[10]

Operation *Lustre* was the ill-fitting name for the Allied expedition to Greece. In truth there was little that was lustrous about its conception, its preparation or its execution. The Australians, who were to make up about two-fifths of *Lustre* Force, began to arrive in the port of Piraeus in March; soon a convoy including most of the Australian 6th Division and the New Zealand Division was dispatched from Alexandria, arriving in Greece to be rushed to its allotted defensive positions.

The German invasion of Yugoslavia and Greece was Operation *Marita*. On 6 April 1941 German multi-pronged assaults on Yugoslav and Greek territory were staged simultaneously by German, Italian and Hungarian forces. They were spectacularly successful. Belgrade was bombed mercilessly from the start; Yugoslavia capitulated on 17 April and awaited its dismemberment. In Greece, as in so many other parts of Europe earlier, the Luftwaffe signalled the horrors that were to come. On the very first night of the invasion Piraeus was bombed, the harbour wrecked and shipping destroyed.

For the planned ground invasion the Germans assembled three army corps: XVIII Mountain Corps (consisting of two mountain divisions, one infantry division, and one infantry regiment), XXX Corps (two infantry divisions) as well as divisions of XXXX (motorised) army corps. These included the 9th Armoured Division but also an SS division, namely the SS *Leibstandarte* Adolf Hitler. Bristling with modern equipment, and with every expectation of unstinting close air support from the Luftwaffe, these three corps were considered sufficient to get the job done in Greece.[11]

GREECE

The strategy to be adopted against the ground invasion was to establish lines of defence in the very north of Greece to halt the German advance. The first barriers erected by the Greeks were along the so-called Metaxas Line in the very north-east. British allies were immediately sceptical as to the prospect of holding a position so adjacent to the assembled German forces in Bulgaria, but the seamless collaboration of Greek and Allied forces was never a feature of the campaign. The launching of *Marita* did trigger the tenacious defence of the Metaxas Line, prompting the commander of the German 5th Mountain Division to the sardonic observation, 'It looks like the Greeks are ready to sacrifice themselves for England down to the last man.'[12] But to defend the line was a hopeless brief, not just because of the weight and power of forces pushing south from Bulgaria but because the simultaneous conquest of Yugoslavia opened new launching pads further to the west. There the German Second Armoured Division smashed through a south-eastern pocket of Yugoslavia to expose the rear of the Greek defences, opening up a path towards the strategically vital Aegean coast and the ancient port city of Salonika. The Greek forces trapped in this manoeuvre had no escape; they offered the Germans their capitulation on 8 April. When German forces entered Salonika the following day some 60,000 Greek soldiers became their prisoners, at least for a short time.

With Salonika and the north-east lost, a combined Greek and British defence was hurriedly assembled at the so-called Aliakmon Line, named for a river in northern Greece. It was in the village of Servia on that river that the Australians had established their 6th Division headquarters, and it was along a line formed by the Aliakmon that the Australians, including those scurrying back from the abandoned northern positions, braced themselves for the next stage of the invasion, as German troops poured south through the breached Metaxas Line and, further to the west, through southern Yugoslavia.

The number and power of the German ground forces were matched with a superiority in the air. Australians and their allies in Greece were repeatedly exposed to the frightening qualities of the

German *Blitzkrieg* strategy as Stuka dive-bombers targeted a piece of a defensive line, opened up a gap and allowed mobile ground forces to flood through it. Encounters with the whining, dive-bombing Stukas were a chilling and often fatal experience. Reg Worthington witnessed a mate, Jack Kidston, desperately seeking shelter against an embankment formed by a bridge, but the bomb got him anyway – 'we couldn't find enough of him to bury him'.[13] The Germans, in stark contrast, encountered next to no opposition in the skies. For the Australians fighting in Greece, the acronym 'RAF' came to mean 'Rare As Fairies'.

The formal constitution of an ANZAC force during the defence of Greece lifted morale and hardened resolve, invoking as it did the spirit of Gallipoli. But morale and resolve were ultimately no match for a vastly better equipped and better organised enemy. ANZAC units doggedly countered the advances of German ground forces and the attentions of the Luftwaffe around Servia, but in time the Aliakmon Line, like the Metaxas Line before it, was becoming porous. There was a very real risk that units would be trapped by well rehearsed German encirclement manoeuvres. Recognising the possibilities, the German commanders threw the soldiers of the Waffen SS *Leibstandarte* Adolf Hitler against the growing number of pressure points along the Aliakmon Line. They forced a further retreat, albeit without effecting the desired encirclement and wholesale capture of Greek and ANZAC forces, who set up new lines of defence yet further south around Thermopylae.

For the ANZACs whose school curriculum might have included at least a smattering of ancient Greek history, Thermopylae was a familiar term. Many might well have wished themselves back in school when the battles in and around Thermopylae and the Brallos Pass commenced, because history was about to repeat itself. The invaders from the north, superior in numbers and weaponry, encountered bitter resistance, but they were ultimately an ineluctable force. This time, too, there was a hint of Greek betrayal, since by this point the Greek government could see little sense in merely delaying the inevitable at a high price, to be paid in Greek lives. The Italian reactivation of the Albanian front played a role in

Greek deliberations too. As Greek resistance crumbled, it was no longer a question of whether the Greek government would capitulate but when. On 14 April the British government ordered the High Command in Cairo to prepare a possible evacuation of the expeditionary corps from Greece. If that order was not compelling enough, within two days Greek General Papagos himself was suggesting that Jumbo Wilson consider evacuation in order to spare Greece further destruction.[14] By 20 April, Hitler's birthday, Greek forces had capitulated.[15]

In these circumstances British tactical thinking took a purely practical turn. The ever-shifting lines of defence were to serve the purpose of buying time to implement Operation *Demon*, that is, the evacuation of British forces from the Greek mainland. Pessimistic though Wavell was about the chances of evacuating in large numbers to Crete and Egypt – let alone saving much of the matériel deployed on the mainland – retreat at least offered some prospect of confronting the Germans again and under more favourable terms. For many Australians the evacuations – scheduled to take place from 24 April – came all too late, as they were caught by the rapid advance of German forces which encircled them. They were to assemble at designated evacuation points north of and around Athens; once those points fell into enemy hands, they would have to cross the Corinth Canal and enter the Peloponnesian peninsula, hoping that the Royal Navy might still whisk them to safety from beaches there.

In a further echo of Gallipoli, after a botched campaign the withdrawal at least was executed with exemplary courage and tactical aplomb. To win precious time, ANZAC troops offered dogged resistance on the battlefield and destroyed bridges and tunnels as they withdrew south under intense pressure. Simultaneously they had to free up men to allow large numbers to stage a retreat to the designated evacuation points. As if to remind them how easily the balance between defence and flight might be upset, on the very day of the first scheduled evacuation, German forces attacked the crucial Thermopylae Line, stretching from the coast to the mountains. For every hour it was held, the defenders knew, the more of their comrades would survive to fight another day.

CAPTURE

The next day – 25 April – was Anzac Day, the most miserable since the very first in 1915. On that day in 1941 the German 5th Armoured Division finally pierced the Thermopylae Line and headed for Thebes. This was no day of celebration for the Australians and the New Zealanders fighting beside them. For all the courage they were showing on the field of battle, humiliation stared them squarely in the face as they battled to salvage what they might from a campaign they should never have fought. And salvage they did – on that day, as on those that followed, evacuations were performed with an unremitting sense of urgency. The grimness of the situation stemmed from the sure knowledge that the fate of those left behind was reduced to a simple formula – death or capture. As for the Germans, though pleased with their breakthrough of the Thermopylae Line, their commanders were disappointed that their POW booty was so meagre.[16]

Those Australians captured in the north would be delivered as soon as it could be arranged to Salonika, the largest city of northern Greece, where a transit camp for POWs was established. Depending on where they were captured, these men might pass through rough staging camps in Lamia or Larissa; their provisional lodging might be in a field, a cottage or a schoolhouse.

In the confusion of retreat George Morley was one who found himself in a mixed group of Australians and New Zealanders desperately trying to halt the German advance north of Athens. He and those with him were vigorously defending the beach side of a hill. From there they could see the German forces across a level field and could take pot shots at them if there were signs of movement. The Germans responded by sending a captured British officer to the embattled unit to warn them that if they did not surrender then a nearby village would be destroyed by a bombing raid. That tactic producing no immediate result, a further ruse was ventured the same evening, when a voice called up to Morley and his colleagues advising them to descend from their position. What had appeared to be the voice of a British officer had on this occasion in fact been that of a German paratroop officer. He and some fifty fellow paratroops, a number of whom spoke perfect English, greeted the astonished Morley at the bottom of the hill. The Germans made no effort to hinder the men in disposing of their weapons in a well; their sole objective was to herd the soldiers into captivity. At first that took the form of a warehouse, followed by the grounds of a hospital and, a train ride later, a provisional camp in Larissa. But for POWs in Greece, ultimately all roads and railway lines led to Salonika, and Morley was no exception.[17]

As fate would have it, the Victorian signalman Frank Cox was one of the men who suffered the indignity of finding himself in captivity – 'in the bag' – on the afternoon of Anzac Day itself. Over the preceding days, as he beat a path south, he had been exposed to the technological sophistication of the German advanced forces. For Cox the contrast to the easy victories over Italian forces in the Western Desert in the not so distant past was striking. The Germans used mortars to stunning effect – he could draw little comfort from a more experienced soldier's advice: 'Don't worry, son – you'll never hear the one that hits you.' For the first time, too, he witnessed the frightening spectacle of tracer bullets.[18]

When the members of his unit realised that the Germans had already passed south behind them, they hid in the hills and plotted an escape by sea to neutral Turkey. The plan was short-lived, as at five o'clock on 25 April 1941, the modern-day ANZAC Cox found himself staring down the barrel of a German gun. To this day he does not know why its owner did not pull the trigger. He and some two dozen members of the 16th Brigade had been surrounded. Bearded, unkempt and fatigued, they were loaded into a truck and taken to Volos and from there the very next day to Salonika.

For Alf Stone, too, Greece was a series of hurried retreats, from the slopes of Mt Olympus south past Larissa and then to Megara, a nominated evacuation point about halfway between Athens and the Corinth Canal. He and his corporal missed their chance at Megara so headed south, hoping to cross the Corinth Canal and make their way to an evacuation point called Kalamata on the south of the Peloponnesian peninsula. It was not easy. The railway bridge over the canal had been destroyed, and the journey on foot was so painfully slow as to allow German paratroops to land to their south and block their path. Their capture was just a matter of time, though it came in an act of subterfuge – climbing into a passing Australian ambulance, Stone and his companions found that it was being driven by Germans. They had commandeered it near Athens. The first moments of more than four years captivity had begun almost before he knew it. Three days later he was in the POW camp the Germans had set up at Corinth.[19]

The Tasmanian Barney Roberts was another among the unlucky who did not make it to an evacuation point in time. Stranded at Megara when evacuations ceased, and driven almost mad by thirst, he and 180 others saw no choice but to surrender themselves at a German airfield north-west of Athens. Their captors soon found use for them in levelling the runways, until they transferred them to further work duties at the already well-populated Corinth camp.[20]

The retreating troops who did manage to make it safely across the Corinth Canal continued the risky act of holding up the German advance while as many men as possible were loaded onto vessels. The evacuations had to be performed at night, otherwise the destroyers and other vessels would have been subjected to the unwanted attention of the Luftwaffe. They needed to be well clear of the Greek coastline before daybreak, and even then the journey to Alexandria or Suda Bay was fraught with danger. Capacities aboard the vessels were limited too; they already had full complements of sailors on board. And as the Wehrmacht pushed south, the number of beaches from which the evacuations could be performed sank with alarming rapidity. The very last of these operations took place from the southern port town of Kalamata. The bravery of the navy allowed many to make good their escape, as the control of the town for a time was disputed. But finally it was at Kalamata that the Germans recorded their greatest success in rounding up the hapless many who were stranded there. An advance German unit made a preliminary strike, was dislodged, but then finally asserted its control. Thousands of agitated soldiers, Australians and others, still awaiting nightfall and the vain hope of evacuation were taken captive.[21]

GREECE

Tasmanian John Crooks was among the desperately unlucky who witnessed the fall of Kalamata and the capture of the expectant masses assembled there. The first opportunity presented to him and his men had been from the port of Nafplion on Anzac Day. But there was to be no evacuation from Nafplion, so Crooks, an officer, gathered his men together and shepherded them into a convoy heading further south to Kalamata, where night evacuations were occurring. By the time Crooks and his men reached Kalamata it was too late to undertake the night embarkation of a motley force of some 8000 troops – ANZACs, Greeks, Yugoslavs, Cypriots, Indians and Palestinians. The Royal Navy vessels would need time the following morning to sail clear of the mainland to escape harassment by the Luftwaffe. That night – 28 April – saw the evacuation from Kalamata of just 330 men in small boats sent from a destroyer, and Crooks was not one of them.[22]

The local commander of the British forces had little choice but to negotiate a ceasefire to take effect at dawn on 29 April. Word of the surrender spread rapidly through the olive groves, where the men anxiously waited. Later in the morning a solitary German strolled into Crooks' unit, his rifle casually slung over his shoulder, and gathered the men together to escort them through the town of Kalamata itself and then into an open field, forming the most primitive of POW compounds. Officers were separated from the other ranks, and two machine guns were set up to guard against the possibility that members of either group might harbour thoughts that their war was not over after all. Crooks' first night as a POW was spent under the stars. The next morning the men were marched to a station, entrained and delivered to Corinth, where disused army barracks would provide a roof over their heads for some weeks. Their neighbours were hundreds of Italian POWs, captured by the Greeks in Mussolini's bungled campaign, and not yet released by their Axis partners as they set about setting in place a harsh regime of occupation.[23]

Doug Nix, too, having beaten a disheartening retreat from northern Greece, finally found his options evaporate at Kalamata. Having missed the last of the evacuations, just one final and desperate hope presented itself in the form of a commandeered fishing vessel. The men had vague notions of evading the Germans' reach by sailing south and away from the mainland, but their boat was bombed. They dived overboard and swam to safety, finding refuge in a cave just south of Kalamata. Soon Nix and his mate Crofton 'Teddy' Barnes went in search of food, only to be surprised by a paratrooper announcing unceremoniously the end of their freedom. In case there was any doubt, a *Feldwebel* soon arrived to confirm the news in flawless English: 'For you the war is over.'

The men were escorted back to Kalamata, where they joined those already in the cage near the beach there. It was little more than a barbed wire enclosure, patrolled by a handful of Germans. The only shelter Nix found was that of the olive trees. For the first days the only food was olives. With a strong aversion to the only source of nourishment available, Nix spent the first days of captivity like a vegetarian in an abattoir. Not until the third day were Greek hard biscuits provided; softened with olive oil they became edible and gave urgently needed sustenance. Over two weeks the diet did not change, while the incidence of lice, bugs and dysentery took a sharp turn for the worse.[24]

Others were caught and held elsewhere. An unusual case was that of the South Australian Ralph Churches, who came tantalisingly close to escaping the German grasp. After beating a southerly retreat he found himself stranded in the village of Tolos near the head of the Gulf of Nafplion at the end of April. By now the enemy was closing in; the chances of evacuation had evaporated. Rather than await his fate with hundreds of mainly British troops, he set out along the beach until, with three other Australians, he found a dinghy which they requisitioned and sailed south, converting an oar to a mast and a blanket to a sail. The plan was to make the southernmost point of the mainland – Cape Maleas – and from there to island-hop via Kythira and Antikythira to Crete, dodging German vessels and aircraft but otherwise assuming the identities of Greek fishermen. Alas, on land and at sea German forces pressed south more rapidly than these faux Greek sailors could. The Australians made it to a beach outside the village of Monemvais, not far from their first major target, Cape Maleas, but while sleeping the deep sleep of the weary they were rudely awakened by a group of armed Germans demanding surrender. Nearby were two powerboats that had been captured by a seaborne troop. Their captors displayed no ill-will towards their erstwhile quarry, indeed offered them cigarettes to calm their nerves, motioned to the Australians to gather their few things together and escorted them to their captain, who in halting English pronounced their capture.[25]

By the time the main German forces reached and occupied the southern tip of the Peloponnese on 30 April, any chance of mass evacuations was well and truly lost. And yet on a smaller and more clandestine scale they continued. Those like Charles Granquist of 2/4 Battalion, who managed to get clear of the mainland without the help of the Royal Navy, were hunted as they headed for the Greek islands. Granquist was one of those who had tried to block the German advance at the Brallos Pass, had missed out on evacuation at Megara beach and joined the stream of men fanning across the Peloponnese, only to miss his second chance at evacuation. At that point fortune flashed a brief smile, allowing him to seize a small Greek boat with some fellow stragglers, and that weary boatload made it to the island of Milos. It soon proved a poor choice, because the Kriegsmarine took the island and all those who had sought refuge there. Granquist could only lament, 'The sense of guilt and shame was still strong; that I had failed as a soldier, failed my mates and failed myself.'[26]

With the capture of all the major Greek islands – except Crete – by 3 May, the Greek campaign was over. As early as the end of April some of the German forces were withdrawn – Hitler had other plans for them, plans that would be realised before long. Italian forces, for whom neither Greek soldiers nor civilians bore any respect, arrived to aid an occupation notable above all for its viciousness.

For the Australians, too, the scale of the tragedy inflicted on them gradually became clear. Of the 17,125 troops sent there, 814 lost their lives. But more than double that number – 2065 – became POWs, most of them doomed to sit out the rest of the conflict in the Reich. An unknown number, but probably some hundreds, managed to evade capture, melting into the landscape, surviving on a combination of their own wits and the courageously offered assistance of Greek families. Those who fell in with partisans were able to continue their war by other means. Some, it is recorded, even spent the rest of their lives in the country they came to love.[27]

As for the rest, they were whisked away on perilous voyages across the Mediterranean to regroup, inviting the attention of the Luftwaffe and the Italian navy as they went. For many the destination was Alexandria; others were jumping unwittingly from the frying pan of mainland Greece into the fire about to start on the island of Crete.

6

Crete

If the Greek campaign was an unmitigated disaster, Crete offered the ANZACs some chance of redemption. To hold the island would have been to win a substantial consolation prize after the mainland's loss, since both the size and the location of Crete guaranteed its masters some strategic advantages in the Mediterranean theatre of war. The island dominates the eastern Mediterranean; it is a crucial stage on any transit by air or by sea from north to south and from east to west. If it remained in Allied hands, Romanian oilfields would be within reach of Allied bombers. From Cretan ports the British could conduct naval thrusts into the Aegean. Moreover, hegemony in Crete had a symbolic dimension. Greek legend has it that Europa, the princess who was to give a continent its name, had been seduced by Zeus, appearing in the form of a snow-white bull. From the eastern shores of the Mediterranean he had spirited her across the seas to Crete, the cradle of European civilisation.

In 1941 the definition of European civilisation was up for grabs. Hitler's version of it was already on the march; victory in Crete as much as anywhere else on the continent would hail the triumph of the fascists. Hitler's ruminations on Crete were emboldened by a sense of the Reich's invincibility, a sense which even some of its enemies were grudgingly prepared to countenance by the spring of 1941. In that atmosphere a daring plan put to him by General Kurt Student was likely to win Hitler's favour. Student was already well known to his Führer as the driving force behind the formation of parachute regiments and an architect of the military deployment of gliders. Abetted by an enthusiastic Hermann Göring, Student made the case for an airborne assault on Crete. The idea was not entirely untested: gliders bearing parachutists had delivered the telling element of surprise in a successful raid on the Belgian fort of Eben Emael in May 1940. Yet it was as well known to Student as it was to any other strategist of aerial warfare that the spectacle was matched by the danger – an operation targeting Rotterdam had nearly cost Student his life when a sniper's bullet pierced his skull.[1]

Nonetheless, on 21 April 1941, his mood perhaps leavened by his 52nd birthday the previous day, Hitler announced to a gathering of the Luftwaffe's representatives his decision to conquer Crete.[2] The ambitious Student was commissioned to devise an invasion by paratroops and airborne infantry. A Hitler directive issued on 25 April gives a clear sense of German strategic objectives: 'The occupation of the island of Crete (Operation *Merkur*) is to be prepared in order to have a base for conducting the air war against England in the Eastern Mediterranean.'[3] If delivery of a crushing blow to the British Empire was foremost in his mind, the coming war against the Soviet Union, already well advanced in its planning, was not forgotten. To this end the directive added, 'The transport movements must not lead to any delay in the strategic concentration for *Barbarossa*.'[4]

Those transport movements entailed amassing air power on the Greek mainland and manoeuvring naval supply capabilities to within striking distance of Crete. The key forces to be deployed were Student's XI Air Corps, which would provide the paratroops and other landing forces, and Richthofen's VIII Air Corps, which would provide the necessary air support in the form of bombers, fighters and reconnaissance aircraft. A total of 1280 aircraft were to participate.[5] From mainland airfields it was envisaged that a series of coordinated attacks would be launched on targets across the coast of northern Crete, the most vital being the airfields. Once they were taken, transport aircraft would be able to land troops and secure the entire island. Crete's defences, German intelligence predicted on the eve of battle, would be weak; Cretan troops had been deployed on the mainland against the Italians, while the remaining British garrison was estimated at just 5000 men. Evacuations from the mainland, it was wrongly assumed, had proceeded directly to Egypt. So poor was the intelligence that Retimo – where a good part of the Australian forces was gathered – was thought to be undefended.[6]

In military intelligence, and in military intelligence alone, the Allies were better served than the Germans, because those who planned the island's defence had in their possession so-called 'Ultra' intelligence. This took the form of decrypts, achieved with the aid of 'Enigma' machines, of coded German military communication. Ultra decrypts relating to Crete gave the island's defenders a pretty good sense not only that the Germans were intending an invasion, but also how they planned to pull it off. It was one of the tragedies of the Cretan campaign that the precious intelligence was squandered by those who possessed it.

Even before the disasters unfolded on the mainland, a garrison was established on Crete consisting of just the British 14th Brigade, some anti-aircraft and other units, and several thousand ill-equipped Greek troops. A huge boost came then with the scurrying evacuation of forces from the mainland. Of these evacuees, some 30,000 were landed on the island from 23 April. On Anzac Day alone, while Germans were wreaking havoc further north, 5000 evacuees arrived at Crete's main port of Suda Bay to find at least temporary respite.

They and those who followed were placed under the command of the New Zealand General Bernhard Freyberg, a highly decorated veteran of both the First World War and the debacle that had just played out on the mainland. In the days that followed his own arrival in Crete on 29 April, Freyberg was commanded to reorganise the defences of the island in preparation for an expected German invasion, whether launched by air or by sea. Just a day earlier, Churchill had issued Archibald Wavell in Cairo with a message which was both chilling and characteristically pugnacious: 'It seems clear', the Prime Minister warned, 'that a heavy airborne attack by German troops and bombers will soon be made on Crete . . . It ought to be a fine opportunity for killing the parachute troops. The island must be stubbornly defended.'[7]

Churchill, Wavell and Freyberg were among the elite charged with the responsibility of protecting their precious Ultra secrets while also using them to their best advantage. They achieved the former while failing dismally in the latter. As Churchill at least appears to have grasped, the Germans were throwing the bulk of their eggs in the basket of an airborne invasion. The best chance of defending the island would have been provided by concentrating all available men and matériel on rendering the airfields impregnable. To be sure, forces were allocated to the island's airfields, but precious resources were held ready for the expected accompanying seaborne assault. Men were disposed along beaches that did not figure in Student's plans.

In all some 6500 Australians, along with British, New Zealand and Greek forces numbering about 34,000, dug in across the island's northern coast and narrow coastal plain. There were four locations which needed special attention: the island capital Canea and its airfield at Maleme in the north-west, the harbour formed by Suda Bay just to the east of Canea, Retimo and its airfield a further 30 kilometres east, and finally Heraklion, a gateway to the eastern end of the island with its own airfield.

One of the main concentrations of Australians was near Retimo on the central north coast, where Lieutenant Colonel Ian Campbell and his men, drawn mainly from the 2/1st and 2/11th battalions, were to defend the airfield. On the island's north-west, men of the 2/7th and 2/17th battalions were deployed with New Zealand forces in the crucial area around Maleme, where they, too, had among their tasks the defence of an airfield. Between those two concentrations, at Georgioupolis, Brigadier George

CRETE

Vasey, who commanded Australian forces on the island, set up his headquarters. Wherever they were disposed along the island's north coast, the Australians' determination to dig in was from the very beginning hampered by the absence of adequate equipment; their predicament was well illustrated by their resourceful – yet pitiful – use of steel helmets to scoop out trenches.[8] Much of their weaponry had been abandoned on the mainland; artillery, especially, was in short supply, and the RAF was as rare in the skies overhead as it had been in Greece. With all those disadvantages in mind, together with the freshly painful experience of the campaign just ended, the men of 'Creforce' braced themselves for combined assaults from sea and air.

The date for the assault was finally set for 20 May, by which time the Germans had dedicated a full week to bombing land and naval targets. Envisaged was an early morning assault in the Maleme and Canea area in the island's north-west. Later on the same day the airfields further east at both Retimo and Heraklion would be attacked with paratroops, who would in due course be supported by reinforcements and supplies delivered by air and using captured airfields. The paratroops would be delivered to their target zones by Junkers transport aircraft and by gliders, themselves protected by a combination of dive-bombers – the already notorious Stukas – as well as fighter and reconnaissance aircraft. Support would arrive by sea, too, though as time would soon tell, this dimension of the invasion would be successfully thwarted by the Royal Navy.

At dawn of the scheduled day the attack began with the arrival of Richthofen's fighters and bombers; their job was to scatter and demoralise the defences in preparation for the landing of the glider and parachute troops.[9] When that first wave appeared at the western end of the island early on the appointed day, they filled the sky. Ray Corbett, perched above Suda Bay, saw them gather over the northern horizon 'like a load of gnats'. Soon they were so close he could see the smiles on the pilots' faces.[10] When a second wave of aircraft arrived to drop its human load, it was apparent that 20 May was not to be just another day of softening up Creforce; it was a full-scale aerial assault.

CAPTURE

The paratroops were in for a nasty surprise. Though the men in the field knew nothing better, General Freyberg at his Canea HQ had received the Ultra intelligence that told him the significance of that day. When the bombers arrived as he took breakfast, he allegedly merely grunted, examined his watch and remarked at the Germans' punctuality.[11] For all the flaws in the preparation of 'Fortress Crete', at least the intelligence was reliable. Though more might have been done to protect the airfields, they all boasted some defences, all of which were in readiness.

As the paratroops floated down to their target areas, many were picked off mercilessly before landing. Their vulnerability as they dangled towards the ground, the sound of arms fire cracking in their ears, must have been a ghastly shock. Defenders were given word to aim for the invaders' boots to adjust for their rapid descent; in countless cases the parachutes delivered nothing more than a corpse, which on landing was covered by a silken shroud. The occupants of the gliders that followed also received a ferocious greeting. About forty of them landed in the river bed of the Tavronitis just west of the Maleme airfield, only to be confronted with infantrymen emerging from slit trenches and firing on the Germans as they emerged from their unlikely craft.[12]

The first stages of the invasion had not gone well for the Germans; back in Athens Student was shocked to learn of the scale and intensity of the island's defence. For a time the German footholds were at best tenuous, and casualties were higher than any had imagined. On that first day alone 1856 paratroopers fell victim to the resistance offered by Creforce and the local Cretan population, determined as ever to repel invaders.

At no point was the repulsion of the German forces more determined than at Retimo, where Ian Campbell organised the defence of the town itself – left largely in the capable hands of the local gendarmerie – and the nearby airfield. Australians of the 2/1st and the 2/11th battalions, though poorly equipped and down on manpower, staged spirited, even aggressive opposition. On the morning of the invasion a glance at the skies gave them some sense of what awaited them. Campbell and his men saw German aircraft passing overhead, towing gliders towards Suda Bay to the west. But at four in the afternoon it was their turn. As a large force of fighters and fighter bombers attacked the area, the Australians remained in their well-camouflaged positions. Then came the troop planes, which spewed out some 1600 paratroops, easy prey for the defenders as they dangled from their parachutes, and even on landing readily dealt with by the defenders. Twelve German planes were brought down, and apart from some 900 dead, in Campbell's reckoning 529 Germans were captured around the airfield they thought was theirs for the taking.[13]

Terry Fairbairn remembers camping among the trees around the Retimo airfield when the first wave of German planes arrived, heading to Suda Bay to the west. A more vivid memory is that of the wave targeting Retimo itself, dropping paratroops from the lowest possible height. In reality no height was safe; around the airfield the Germans thought undefended, the Australians lay in wait and attacked them at the first opportunity. Fairbairn's sergeant said to him, 'I'll never go duck shooting again' – to him as an experienced duck shooter in civilian life, that was how it seemed. Tragically, on a second count he was right too – the sergeant was killed the next day.[14]

Had they placed greater trust in Ultra and ignored the slim chance of revealing their secret, Creforce would have saved all the airfields. Like Retimo, Heraklion further east was also successfully defended. The advantage the Germans had, however, was that they required just one weak point, one airfield, to fall into their hands. Then they could fly in reinforcements and supplies. That weak point was Maleme, where the airfield was overrun by German forces, albeit at the cost of many lives.

Even then the defence of Crete might yet have been salvaged, if only the Germans could have been dislodged from Maleme within hours. The necessity of a counterattack was recognised, but the actions which might have achieved it did not eventuate. Freyberg needed to redeploy troops in a hurry; instead he sought to keep his forces dug in near the coast in expectation of mass landings by sea while merely isolating the landed paratroops.[15] A Maori battalion did make a brave attempt to wrestle Maleme and its crucial Hill 107 from the Germans, staging a blood-curdling bayonet charge. But to the eternal regret of nearby members of the Australian 2/7th and 2/8th battalions, the Maori initiative was not supported. Instead a tactical withdrawal allowed the consolidation of the German foothold. It was just a matter of time before they pushed their advantage eastwards across the northern coastal plains of the island and its major population centres, airfields and harbours.

Over three crucial days, from 21 to 23 May, the Germans landed some 7500 men at Maleme – not a single one touched ground at Retimo in the same period. The breakthrough in the west made all the difference, opening a path to Canea and the nearby port at Suda Bay. Though not part of the original assault, German naval forces granted control of the port facilities at Suda Bay would in time be able to furnish by sea all the reinforcements and supplies the occupiers needed.

Their paratroops having paid a high price for the Maleme airstrip, the Germans bolstered numbers on the island by flying in a mountain regiment to complement the surviving paratroops. Piece by piece an imposing force was accumulated to perform a task blindingly apparent to both sides. Over a period of days it would roll back Creforce from west to east. Tentative footholds would be expanded into strongholds from which any resistance from any source, military or civilian, would be crushed.

With confirmation of the failure around Maleme and Canea, by 26 May Freyberg knew the game was up. He reported to Cairo that dwindling supplies and persistent German air attacks had rendered Creforce's situation hopeless. Within a day permission was granted for another evacuation, following painfully quickly on the heels of the abandonment of the Greek mainland. A first evacuation was staged from Suda Bay; commandos landed with vain hopes of stopping the German advance were replaced in the hold of their vessel by the sick and wounded. From Heraklion evacuations were carried out by Royal Navy ships around the eastern end of the island and on to Egypt, albeit at some cost. The crippled vessel *Imperial* had to be sunk, and 260 men lost their lives when

Orion was dive-bombed and her bridge raked with machine-gun fire. Among those who left Heraklion but never reached Alexandria were 48 Australians of the 2/4th Battalion and the 2/3 Light Anti-Aircraft Regiment.[16]

Further west, though, at Retimo Ian Campbell and his men were not even presented with the option of evacuation. Having led his men superbly in defending the airfield, Campbell ultimately saw no alternative but to perform a formal act of surrender to the Germans who were approaching from the west to encircle them, blocking any chance of the Australians escaping east to Heraklion. A communications failure meant that Campbell and his men had not received the message to hurry south across the island to an evacuation point there. In an act steeped in both tradition and sheer bravery, Campbell heralded the surrender of his men by striding across the airfield towards the German forces, waving a towel on a stick, and no doubt hoping against hope that among soldiers on both sides any urge to pull a trigger would be resisted. It was a moment he recalled soberly years later:

> I was not shot at as I walked towards the Germans on the north side of the airstrip, but they continued firing with four light mountain guns at my troops on the ridge behind me, until I ran over and shouted to them to stop. All firing then ceased. A polite German major, who spoke good English, asked me a few questions until General Student, who was the celebrated commander of their renowned parachute division, arrived and I was asked a few more questions. I well remember he was amazed and appalled at the large number of his men we had killed.[17]

Just as the Australians became POWs, the Germans they had captured earlier were given their freedom. The atmosphere, one Australian later observed, resembled that 'at the end of a hard-fought football match, with the Germans laughing and joking and taking souvenirs'.[18] One German account has it that Campbell and his men were 'not in any way dispirited. They are friendly and calm and simply declare: "We do not want any more", just as if they had given up a sporting test match.'[19] All up some 450 men of 'Retimo

Force', including Campbell himself, entered captivity, spending their first dismal night as POWs confined in the local school before being sent west to a future behind barbed wire.[20]

Not all the Australians at Retimo followed Campbell. The Western Australian Ray Sandover led a group of men away from Retimo in the nick of time, recognising instinctively that to have any chance of evacuation they would need to make their way with all haste to the southern coast of the island. The great hope of many who were veterans of the mainland campaign was that lightning would strike twice; the Royal Navy would intervene once more to pluck them from the jaws of the Germans and deliver them to safety across the seas, this time to Egypt.

What Sandover and his men did instinctively, other members of Creforce deployed further to the west did on instruction. The plan was for the men to make their way south to a place called Sphakia, a little fishing village on the central southern coast. But to reach Sphakia was by itself no easy task. Though not wide, Crete was mountainous, and the trek along half-made roads and goat tracks led through the island's central snow-capped spine before descending to an escarpment and then, as a final torture, a precipitous descent to the village and its little harbour. It was an arduous journey in the most favourable of circumstances, but on this occasion it had to be completed by dispirited men already on half-rations, and with well-armed adversaries hot on their tails.

Battered, bruised and half-starving, most reached the coast, and over the last four nights of the month May 1941 the Royal Navy once more rescued men who would live to fight another day. But from 1 June that option was cut off, and unlike at Heraklion, thousands were stranded at Sphakia.[21] They huddled in the nearby groves, gullies and caves to await what now seemed an inexorable fate. While plucky rearguard actions, well rehearsed on the Greek mainland, had delayed the enemy's march south, there was no prospect of halting the German advance altogether. The mood among the men was predictably bleak. One of the New Zealanders, James Kinder, noted in his diary:

One Aussie blew his brains out but that didn't help much and the rest of us prepared for the arrival of the enemy. Most of us were wondering whether the Jerries would feed us, as we were all getting weak with dysentery which was rife. The latter was the worse of the two and many men were now mere skeletons. We set to work and piled our arms and equipment and then destroyed any papers which might be of use to the enemy.[22]

The arrival of the German forces was experienced by the men in a multitude of ways. Keith Hooper's capture was distinctive because he was blissfully unaware of it. As a member of the 2/17th composite Battalion, he was part of the rearguard action staged near Sphakia, holding back the Germans as the last evacuations took place. In a swoop by German Messerschmitts he was sprayed with stones flung around by gunfire, fell some metres and was knocked unconscious. Only when he came to some time later, already bandaged, did he learn that he was now a POW; the pain of this realisation and that of his wounds struck him simultaneously. One of his captors, a Württemberger, handed him a British biscuit with bully beef on it. It was a small act of chivalry not uncommon among front-line troops but, as Hooper and others were to discover, a much rarer commodity behind barbed wire.[23]

Ray Corbett recalls an eerie silence preceding his capture at Sphakia. Having declined an opportunity for evacuation the previous evening, he was wakened on the morning of his capture by intense mortar bombing and then, at about 9 o'clock, silence punctuated only by anxious whispering, 'the silence of the tomb'. A New Zealander told all those within earshot that the island had been surrendered. Having had just enough time to wrap his possessions in a ground sheet and bury them, Corbett was presented with the image of a unit of young Austrian alpine troops, tommy-guns slung over their shoulders. Their leader, knowing exactly with whom he was dealing, announced, 'Hey, you Aussies, come here.' Rounded up, they were given just one hunk of bread to prepare them for the long trek back over the island. Camped on a plateau at the end of that woeful day,

Corbett swapped his wristwatch for more bread. Waking the next morning with a full day's march still ahead of him, he had to scratch himself to confirm the events of the previous day. The mental adjustment to captivity was difficult enough, but it was made all the harder by the guards' assurances that they had ten years of labour for the Reich ahead of them.[24]

Laurie West and others of the 2/6th Infantry Battalion were ill-equipped and exhausted after beating a retreat south past the imposing White Mountains towards Sphakia. On the morning after their arrival an officer delivered the news that Allied forces were to capitulate. Hardware had to be destroyed – the men removed bolts from their rifles and smashed their sights – as they nervously awaited the inevitable. In due course the mountain troops arrived to take the surrender and ordered the men down onto the beach. For West it was an anticlimactic event. He and the men of the platoon he commanded quietly contemplated the harsh reality of captivity as they joined the gathered throngs on the beach. Though there was no doubt who was in control, the scene for a time was shambolic and subdued. The tortuous march back north through the White Mountains stood before them.[25]

Charlie Parrott, too, was captured at Sphakia. The German who approached him knew exactly with whom he was dealing, addressing him as 'Aussie'. For Parrott the emotions triggered by his capture remained for decades as difficult to express as they were to forget: 'Nobody can explain the feeling of being taken a prisoner. It's such a dreadful feeling that you're useless. You can't do anything. All your ego's gone. There's nothing left.'[26] Charles Jager, also among the 5000 or so rounded up ignominiously around Sphakia, choked with bitterness as in the presence of his new masters he had to hurl his Remington onto a growing mound of discarded weapons, followed by his six-shooter. As he commenced his penitential trek north he was mortified 'by the contrast between our bedraggled selves and the superbly equipped and seasoned 18-year-olds who've taken us.'[27] That dejection accompanied him all the way back across the island, picking his way through the detritus of rushed retreat. 'Every yard,' he recalled, 'is shameful, littered with abandoned gear; rifles, bayonets, ammo, waterbottles, banjos, an officer's blue dress uniform spilling from a suitcase. But as I hop barefoot, picking a tortuous way over stones as sharp as razors, handicapped by stubbed toes, diarrhea and an empty belly, nothing's so painful as the humiliation of surrender.'[28]

The sense of humiliation knew no boundaries of status or rank. Among the men who fell into German captivity on 1 June in the vicinity of the beach at Sphakia was one of the most distinguished and decorated of Australia's POWs. He was Lieutenant Colonel Leslie Le Souef, who commanded the 2/7th Field Ambulance and was the senior Australian medical officer in Crete. His medical skills had already brought relief and solace to countless members of the 6th Division during the campaigns in North Africa and on the Greek mainland. He had been evacuated from Greece to bolster forces on Crete, but as the island was overrun by Germans, he and his men joined the dispirited retreat south across the island's imposing mountainous spine. He, his orderlies and his patients awaited the arrival of the Royal Navy to snatch them to Egypt. Alas, at that point, exhausted, famished and thirsty like everyone, hope of rescue deserted them. With further evacuations impossible, and with rearguard actions against pursuing and then enveloping German patrols ultimately doomed, the order to surrender had come from Major General E.C. Weston, who commanded the forces still left on the island.[29]

Le Souef's was a capture made not in the heat of battle but painfully contemplated in advance. As he awaited the inevitable, he pursued his duties in the makeshift hospital in the tiny village of Komitades. It was his solemn duty to inform the troops gathered there of the capitulation, a missive greeted with a mixture of resignation, consternation and incredulity. Indeed, some of those Le Souef addressed opted to seek any kind of vessel to chance a hazardous voyage to Egypt; others took the more perilous path of evading capture to seek out the goodwill of the Cretans, even to join them in their resistance to German occupation. Le Souef's first responsibilities were to the wounded, even if that meant accompanying them into captivity. The surrender negotiated, the Germans indeed wanted the wounded transported back across the island to its northern coast. Crippled with exhaustion, with too few stretchers and too little food, Le Souef and his men drew deep breaths as their German captors prodded them on on their way to the Maleme airfield. From there the seriously wounded were to be flown to medical facilities in Athens. As for Le Souef, he was taken to the docks in Suda Bay, where, as a variation on a sickening theme, a German officer pronounced in halting schoolboy French, 'La guerre est fini pour vous.'[30]

Others were captured elsewhere on the island. Arthur Leggett was among those men of the 2/11th Battalion who, following Ray Sandover's lead, had taken flight from Retimo and reached the south coast. First he had zigzagged hurriedly back west to battalion headquarters and from there joined the gathering exodus south across the island.[31] Leggett and his companions followed a crude track through the mountains until an armed Cretan shepherded them to a holding point where, with hundreds of others, Leggett waited in vain for evacuation. One afternoon a German officer, accompanied by an interpreter, strolled casually into the camp, requested to speak to the senior officer and convincingly conveyed the hopelessness of the situation. Thereupon he made the offer that the ragged remainder of the Allied forces might spend the next two hours contemplating giving themselves up and becoming prisoners. Two hours later the Germans returned in numbers to learn that their offer had been accepted. At the moment of capture the thought that occupied Leggett's mind was, 'How am I going to tell my Mum?'[32] It was a sentiment shared by his fellow Western Australian Hal Finkelstein, because as far as he knew 'no-one ever dreamed of being a prisoner of war. They'd thought of being killed and wounded and crippled but I only ever met one man who thought he might be a prisoner of war.'[33]

Just as on the mainland, there were those who successfully evaded the Germans or, having been captured, broke out of the provisional camps and fled into the hills. Altogether there might have been some 600 Australians among perhaps 1000 Allied soldiers whose horror at the prospect of captivity drove them to take on the privations and perils of life on the run rather than give themselves over to the enemy.[34] Records show that 139 Australians who had been 'on the run' in Crete made it back to their units in the Middle East.[35]

Ray Sandover was one whose bold bid to preserve his freedom paid off. The initial chance of evacuation missed, Sandover headed for the hills. His patience was rewarded, and he was among 125 who boarded the Royal Navy submarine HMS *Torbay* heading for Alexandria on 20 August.[36] Another evader was Reg Saunders, who later in the war was to become the first indigenous commanding officer in the Australian armed forces. But in June 1941 he was among the hapless members of the 2/7th Battalion stranded around Sphakia when the evacuations were halted. His life on the run extended almost an entire year until he secured a place on a clandestine naval evacuation in May 1942. He was able to rejoin the 2/7th, but for him and his battalion there was now a new enemy – Japan – and a new theatre of war much closer to home.

Others were less fortunate, and their time on the run was called to a halt through some conspiracy of misfortune or privation. Michael Clarke, a lieutenant in the 2/3rd Field Regiment with a good knowledge of German, experienced the most civilised of captures after a time on the run. He and some of his men had taken refuge in a taverna in a small village when half a dozen Germans walked in to dine. The Australians were taken by surprise. The German commanding officer approached their table and fell into an affable conversation with Clarke, who shared his experiences of visiting Austria. As the officer himself was Tyrolean, Clarke's story piqued some interest, but the Australian identity of his interlocutor left the Austrian with little choice. For a moment he struggled for words but then gathered his thoughts enough to declare, 'I have to inform you, Herr Oberleutnant, that you and your men are the prisoners of the German army.' Rather than interrupt their meal, however, the Austrian insisted they complete it, noting it might be their last decent one for some time. Having returned to his own table – and posted a man to guard Clarke and his men – the Austrian capped his generous performance by sending over a bottle of ouzo. It would be their last decent drink for a while, too.[37]

As for the luckier ones who retained their freedom, there were those who understood the act of evasion as not merely a preservation of liberty but a means to prosecute the war by other means. These men made the brutal German occupation of most of the island – and the Italian occupation of its eastern end – as uncomfortable as they possibly could. In this they were aided by Cretans, who paid a high price in Cretan lives for their open resentment of the occupiers and their spirited resistance. In this they and the evaders were aided by the clandestine operations of the SOE, the British Special Operations Executive, and MI9. The latter was formed with the express intention of helping escapers and evaders in enemy-occupied territory.

As late as the second half of 1943 there were still at least four ANZACs on Crete, including the Australians Tom Spriggs and Norm Scott. The latter's case was an extraordinary one, as he managed to inhabit a Cretan cave for all of 34 months until an act of betrayal eventually did deliver him to the Germans, who duly transferred him to Germany via an Athenian hospital. Eventually he was diagnosed as suffering from beriberi – a condition caused by severe vitamin deficiency.[38]

For all the bravery of the escapers and evaders and the nuisance they presented the occupiers, the ledger of Australia's Cretan campaign, like that on the mainland before it, was deeply in deficit. Put more bluntly, Crete was an almost unequivocal disaster. Recriminations were inevitable, though the men labouring across the island under German guard had other things on their minds. Their perspective from below – and many felt they could not sink much lower than entering captivity as a result of a military cock-up – had been foreshadowed in graffiti spied on a British troopship: 'Never before in the history of human endeavour have so many been buggered about by so few'.[39]

As the dust settled, the Australian casualties were counted – 781. Each had been desperately unlucky to find himself on the losing side of a campaign plagued with avoidable error. The POWs, too, had good reason to curse as they were being led behind wire, most of them for years to come. Their official tally was put at 3102 – many times the number of dead.[40]

If some cold comfort could be drawn from the defeat, then it was that the Australians and their allies could savour at least some *Schadenfreude* of their own. The Germans had won, but at great cost. Operation *Merkur* had led to the death or wounding of nearly a third of the German forces. In addition, 150 of Student's precious aircraft had been completely destroyed and a further 165 badly damaged.[41]

The German mood was further soured by chilling revelations of the mutilations of the bodies of the German dead. Later investigations laid much of the blame with civilians, who on this ancient island fought invaders by ancient means. But Creforce, too, was not above suspicion. A German report noted:

> During an attack which a German Mountain Battalion mounted on the Pirgos Heights in the direction of Suda Bay, the battalion had to retreat provisionally in the face of superior enemy forces and leave wounded behind. The enemy was comprised of Australians and New Zealanders. After the end of the battle it was established that the wounded officers, NCOs and other ranks of the battalion who had been left behind had in the meantime been killed. Four officers and at least 10 NCOs and other ranks had had their skulls crushed by rifle butts. Numerous other members of the battalion had puncture wounds. As the battle had been solely an exchange of fire and not led to hand-to-hand combat, there is no doubt that all these injuries were inflicted on the wounded afterwards.[42]

Whatever the truth may have been, the accusations alone will have done little to endear the Creforce POWs to their new masters. They could expect few favours before their transfer to the mainland.

With the burying of the dead on both sides, the Cretan campaign was over. The surviving Australians who had escaped captivity would not stay in Egypt long. Another theatre of war already awaited them. As for Hitler, he could now launch Operation *Barbarossa* as planned, just three weeks after the swastikas began fluttering in Canea. Never again, however, would Hitler attempt a major airborne invasion of enemy territory.

7

Syria

If the campaigns the Australians fought in North Africa, Greece and Crete have found their place in Australian military folklore, the 2nd AIF's role in Syria has slipped silently into oblivion. But for a small number of Australian soldiers – including a handful of POWs – it was an integral part of their war experience, hardening them for the horrors that were still to come.

The enemy in this instance was neither German nor Italian but rather the Vichy French. In the wake of the German victory over France in June 1940, Hitler occupied northern France and set up a harsh regime of military rule there. But in the south of France, with the town of Vichy as its nominated capital, a puppet regime was established under the leadership of Marshal Philippe Pétain. Like many French, Pétain and his supporters found little to object to in Hitler's Nazism or Mussolini's fascism; they willingly collaborated with their German vanquishers. Some of those of a different persuasion were to join the ranks of the Resistance, remaining in France to undermine German and Vichy rule. Still others fled France to throw in their lot with the so-called Free French. Their leader was Charles de Gaulle, quintessentially Gallic in both name and countenance; his forces fought alongside the Allies to liberate France from the detested Germans and their equally reviled collaborators.

Like Britain, France had entered the Second World War in possession of an empire, in size and population far greater than France itself. With the fall of France, the Empire's fate was up for grabs. Of interest to Allied forces in the Middle East was the future of Syria, which bordered British-administered Palestine and which, were it to fall under Axis control, would threaten British oil supplies. It was Vichy forces which took control of Syria under Commissioner Henri Dentz, presenting Britain with the very real danger that the French would welcome the arrival of the Germans with open arms. Indeed, from very early in the piece Dentz issued the Germans with the rights to use Syrian airfields, rendering British interests further east in Iraq vulnerable. It was a German foothold in the Middle East which might easily be extended.

This was a possibility which needed to be nipped in the bud – control of Syria had to be shifted from the Vichy French to the Free French. A preventive campaign was fought from 7 June to 11 July 1941 – in the wake of the Cretan campaign just concluded across the Mediterranean to the west. Before Germany had any opportunity to accept a Vichy invitation, a mixture of Australian 7th Division and 6th Division units, in combination with British, Indian and Free French troops, launched an attack from Palestine north into Lebanon and Syria.

The enemy was no pushover. One Australian had predicted with exuberant over-confidence, 'We will only have to walk in, wave and walk on,' but military realities soon set him and others straight.[1] Fortunately by this time German preparations for *Barbarossa* were at fever-pitch. The only practical help Hitler offered was to allow Vichy forces to shift supplies and troops across the Mediterranean from North Africa, as well as by train from France across German-controlled Europe to Salonika, by now under German occupation. Nonetheless, General Dentz had 28,000 French and African troops at his disposal, along with some 10,000 Lebanese and Syrians.[2] They knew the terrain well, and they readily grasped the defensive possibilities it offered.

SYRIA

From 7 June Allied forces poured north from their bases in Palestine along three main routes. Of those ground forces, more than half – some 18,000 of 34,000 troops – were Australians.[3] An RAAF squadron and Australian naval vessels were also committed to the campaign. Of the ground forces involved in the invasion, all three prongs dared a lightning drive north. At multiple points, however, the enemy held firm and offered spirited resistance, leading to loss of life and capture.

One of the areas which offered particular advantages to defenders was around Merdjayoun, set in mountainous inland terrain. For a time Australian forces were concentrated in the Merdjayoun area, participating in a series of attacks and counterattacks which ultimately bore fruit, albeit with loss of lives and captures recorded on both sides. Only with great persistence and the diversion of crucial support could that sector be held, as the success of the entire campaign hung tenuously on a thread. Before Merdjayoun could be taken, two men of the 2/3rd Australian Machine Gun Battalion, Tom Keays and Frank Crouch, became prisoners of the Vichy French. They spent the remainder of the Syrian campaign as POWs at Homs. Only when the campaign was concluded and an armistice signed could their platoon commander, Nobby Clarke, make the trek to Homs to retrieve them.[4]

Wally Summons, too, was taken prisoner, but he had a different tale to tell. A lieutenant in the 2/2nd Pioneer Battalion, Summons was involved in efforts to re-take the fort at Merdjayoun. As he lay in a dusty depression contemplating how to seize it, the sound of feet behind him, followed immediately by the sight of men walking up the road with their hands in the air, informed him that the French defenders had artfully approached from the rear. Summons and the other Australians with him were marched through the fort's main gate, though not in triumph. For their part the French defenders were hardly trumpeting their success either. Some continued playing cards, while the commander apologised to the Australians for capturing them and arranged to fetch the wounded after nightfall.[5] Twenty Australians were captured that day.[6] Under armed escort the healthy captives were taken to the nearby village, allowed to drink from the village well, given a little chocolate and deposited at the brigade HQ. As an officer, Summons was separated from his men and joined another Australian officer who had strayed inadvertently behind French lines. Both were trucked to Beirut.

Meanwhile on other fronts things ran more smoothly. Australian forces were diverted to the more amenable terrain of the coastal road, reinforcing units heading towards the Syrian capital Damascus.[7] On 21 June, the day before *Barbarossa* was unleashed on an unsuspecting Stalin, Damascus fell. Australians were in the thick of the action, claiming the crucial high ground and occupying forts. Before midday of that day the combined Australian and Free French column which had advanced rapidly from the south secured a surrender.

The next major objective was Beirut, from where General Dentz directed a stubborn but doomed rearguard action. When paths to the city were opened up from both the south and the east, and with only exhausted and demoralised troops at his disposal, Dentz knew his war was over. On 10 July, Beirut succumbed to the superior Allied forces. Just four days later – on Bastille Day – an armistice was signed and, for better or worse, Syria was placed in the hands of de Gaulle and his Free French.

By this time Wally Summons had long departed Beirut. He was flown to Athens, visibly under German occupation – indeed, he and his fellow officers were inspected by Germans. From there they were flown on to Salonika, just as clearly under a heavy German thumb, yet their hosts were French and looked after them well. Summons was aware of the contrasting treatment of his fellow Australians who at that time were being unloaded on Salonika's wharves after their voyages from Crete. With Vichy French forces superfluous to Axis needs in Greece, they headed for home – with their prisoners. So it was that Summons and 52 fellow officers, including three other Australians, found themselves on a train with a French escort and a German liaison officer heading north through German-controlled territory, eventually entering the Reich itself. But for Summons it was a mercifully fleeting visit; his train crossed the Rhine and entered occupied France through Mulhouse, eventually arriving on 4 August at their destination, Toulon, located in Vichy territory. Their new home was yet another fort, Fort St Catherine, where they were held under the watchful eyes of the French regiment Chasseurs Alpins.[8]

Summons had indeed experienced rare good fortune. He had travelled through the Reich from east to west in relative comfort at the height of the war. Yet that good luck was balanced by some misfortune as well. He had been whisked from Syria on the eve of an armistice agreement that, if signed earlier, would have rendered his travels through Greece and Germany superfluous. As early as 9 August his luck turned again, in lock-step with the march of international politics. Agreements had been reached for the return by both sides of the officers each held. Summons and his co-captives were bundled onto a French vessel and cruised across the Mediterranean – travelling within sight of the mountains of Crete to Beirut and a joyful reunion with their units.[9]

Summons' war was not over, however. He was among those sent back east. As an intelligence officer in *Blackforce* he was deployed to Java, where he was captured once more. Summons spent the best part of the rest of the war acquainting himself with the unrelieved misery of Japanese captivity.[10]

8

Into the Reich

Such was the success of the Wehrmacht in the first two years of the war that by the summer of 1941 Hitler's Reich stretched its ascendancy from Norway in the north down to the Mediterranean, indeed to the deserts of North Africa, to the south. It controlled Europe from the coasts of France, Belgium and Holland in the west to the heartland of Russia in the east.

Hitler exercised his hegemonic fantasies in a number of ways. The so-called Greater German Reich itself was expanded to the east and south. Yet German authority over the largest part of the continent was established not through direct incorporation into the Reich but in different ways, ranging from strategic alliance, as in the already established cases of Hungary, Finland, Bulgaria and Romania, through nominally independent but subordinate regimes such as those in Croatia and Slovakia. Denmark preserved the fig-leaf of sovereignty well, as both the king and parliament remained in place, while Germany pulled the strings through an administration of just a few hundred. Vichy France and Norway were favourably disposed towards the Reich, while puppet regimes obedient to Hitler were set up in Greece, Serbia and the Protectorate of Bohemia–Moravia. In reality the authorities there did not behave much differently from the Netherlands, where a Reich commissioner was installed to rule via the secretaries-general of the civil service; the Belgian variation meanwhile had the civil service answerable to German military authorities. In all cases it was ultimately the Germans who ruled with a trademark iron will, though nowhere was their exertion of authority more apparent than in the east, where beyond the incorporated territory of Poland a vicious general government and Reich commissariats held sway, while in the vicinity of the ever-changing eastern front the Wehrmacht combined with its own and with Heinrich Himmler's security forces to impose a draconian but fragile peace.

The logic in all of this was to commit as few German forces as possible to the maintenance of stability in incorporated, occupied and allied territories, as indeed the vast scale of the enterprise demanded. In this Hitler could draw on the example of the British Empire, maintained in parts with a veritable handful of men co-ordinating existing administrative and political frameworks. For him Ukraine was to be a kind of new Indian Empire, while the eastern front would become a German north-west frontier, 'where generations of officers would win their spurs and preserve the martial virtues of the Aryan race'.[1] In Europe's south, which Hitler by and large was prepared to concede to Mussolini's sphere of influence, the logistical burden of occupation was shared with the Axis partner. In Greece, including Crete, the German military withdrew after the completion of operations – they had bigger fish to fry elsewhere – leaving the bare bones of a German presence in zones of occupation. An Italian regime of occupation, too, was set up, much to the disgust of large parts of the Greek population, whose contempt for their Italian masters had both long and short roots.

Australian POWs, as we have seen, were captured both inside and outside the Reich, in rare instances even on the other side of the world. Yet in accordance with the terms of the Geneva Convention, it was the German practice to transfer POWs into the Reich and into accommodation designed to contain them until the end of hostilities. Next to the capture itself, which might have been effected in the heat of battle, the period of temporary detention in makeshift holdings or in transit camps, followed by transport into the Reich, was for many POWs the most perilous and unpleasant they were to experience.

The longest of POW travels into the Reich were made by those captured in the Indian and Pacific Oceans. The collecting point for most of those who made their way from the oceans of the world was Frontstalag 221 at St Médard en Jalles in France. Later some others, including Syd Jones from *Mareeba*, were taken to *U-boot* bases at Lorient or St Nazaire. After months in the bowels of *Kormoran*, Jones and his fellow captives had been transferred to a supply vessel, which was sunk by an unidentified submarine. A *U-boot* plucked survivors – including nineteen Australians – from the Atlantic and deposited them at Lorient.[2] But 27 unluckier Australians lost their lives when the supply ship *Spreewald* was dispatched to a watery grave.[3]

To set foot on solid French ground was a massive relief after prolonged periods at sea, tossed around in squalid conditions under deck and exposed to the perils of submarine warfare. Yet privation remained a daily test even on dry land. The combination of miserable food, rough wooden barracks and crude sanitary conditions brought no consolation to the hundreds of men and women delivered unceremoniously to France. Even the modest gratification to be gained from writing to loved ones was long postponed.[4]

In early April 1941 all of those gathered at St Médard were packed into a train and sent north into Germany. Civilians and officers travelled in third-class carriages, while an uncomfortable five-day journey in cattle-trucks awaited others. At the end of this trial a further indignity confronted them in the form of an 11-kilometre march from the train station to Stalag X B at Sandbostel outside Bremen. At the gates of the camp they passed two more purgatorial hours in the rain before being permitted the dubious pleasure of entering the long rows of drab wooden barracks. In no way did the camp offer any improvement on the tribulations of Frontstalag 221. Soon, at least, they were to be allocated to new camps. The civilians, men and women, would be sent to *Ilags*, internment camps, any servicemen to POW camps, and the merchant seamen to Sandbostel's naval compound. In time, however, a new facility became available to them in the form of a purpose-built camp at Westertimke near Bremen. This was Marlag-Milag Nord, which became the home of captured naval seamen – in the Marlag (Marine-Lager) – and captured merchant seamen in the Milag (Marine-Internierten-Lager).[5]

For almost all the Australians captured in Greece or Crete, there was a common denominator in their POW experience – almost all passed through a transit camp at Salonika in northern Greece. The few exceptions who avoided Salonika were captured very early in the Greek campaign, on the night of 10–11 April, in the far north of Greece near Vevi. They were concentrated at Florina, and some were interrogated. The Germans wondered why it was that they were fighting in Greece. A group of four Australians could name no higher purpose: 'It was just war and as good soldiers they had to fight against us. The question whether they knew anything about English war aims in Greece they answered in the negative. They had simply been brought here and received the order to fight against us.'[6] Before long these men and others were packed into cattle-trucks and sent to a camp at Marburg in the annexed Slovenian part of Yugoslavia.[7]

But for everyone else captured in Greece and Crete, Salonika was part of their Greek sojourn, whether for days, weeks or even months. Almost without exception it was an experience those sent there would much rather forget. The judgment is universal – Salonika was a hellhole.

A series of empires had left their mark on Salonika – or Thessaloniki – over a period stretching back two millennia. Macedonians, Romans (of both western and eastern varieties), Bulgarians, Venetians and Ottomans had at various points shown more than a passing interest in the city located at one of the most congested crossroads of civilisation. Among its inhabitants were a large number of Jews – indeed, for more than two centuries Salonika was the city with the world's largest Jewish population.

In April 1941 Hitler's version of a German empire took an interest in Salonika also, capturing it early in the Greek campaign and keeping it under occupation until the end of October 1944. Though just over three years in duration, the German occupation proved fateful for Salonika's Jews, some 11,000 of whom were deported to the Reich and to extermination. But before Nazi racial mania caught up with the Jews, the Wehrmacht designated Salonika as a gathering point for POWs captured on the Greek mainland and on Crete. They installed their transit camp – Dulag (*Durchgangslager*) 183 – in former Turkish and Greek army barracks.

For the Australians the tribulations of Salonika began with the journey there. If captured north of the Corinth Canal, that typically meant transport in cramped train carriages from their provisional holding pens – whether jail, warehouse, schoolhouse, hospital grounds or whatever was available – to Salonika. But large numbers of men had retreated to evacuation points on the lower end of the Greek mainland, south of the Corinth Canal. Those men, as we have seen, were held for various periods in provisional camps nearer their place of capture before being transported north.

From their crude cage at Kalamata, John Crooks and his fellow POWs were transferred to a camp at Corinth. The Corinth camp had been set up in late April to accommodate some 12,000 POWs captured on the Peloponnese.[8] As the Red Cross inspectors noted when they visited that camp in the middle of May 1941, Corinth might have been fine for its original purpose as army barracks, but it was quite inadequate for the mass of humanity, 'British' and Yugoslav, gathered behind barbed wire there, many exposed to the full force of the sun by day and sleeping under the stars at night.[9] Among the thousands of 'British' POWs enduring their first days behind wire were, according to German sources, 889 Australians.[10]

For Crooks his seven weeks in the Corinth camp were on the one hand a chance to recover from the exhaustion of battle and retreat. This was possible in part through the intervention of local Greeks, who for a time at least were able to supplement the prisoners' scanty rations through establishing a kind of spontaneous market at the wire boundary. It was here that he acquired his first taste of lentils. And although the atmosphere of the camp as he experienced it was not unpleasant, one feature provoked serious problems. Included in the camp population were Italian soldiers, captured by Greek forces during their attempted invasion of Greece and not yet released by their Axis partners. The continued presence of the Italians exacerbated the overcrowding, and sanitation in particular was in a parlous state. The Italian latrines, he remembered, 'were such that the concrete floor was awash with urine and faeces, indeed, as high as the uppers of army boots'.[11]

Captured as he was at the very southern tip of the Greek mainland, for Ralph Churches the road to the so-called 'Corinth Cage' was a circuitous one. From the site of their capture, Churches and his fellow POWs were trucked to a school building in a village in Sparta, where on the upper floor they joined a group of some fifteen others whom a similar fate had befallen. Conditions were, well, Spartan, as there was neither bedding nor sanitation, with the exception of three buckets emptied morning and evening. Soon they were moved on once more, this time packed like sardines in the back of a lorry heading north via Tripoli in the central Peloponnese towards the Corinth Canal. At Corinth they were unceremoniously unloaded and escorted through the barbed wire gates of the Corinth camp to join the languishing masses.[12]

Here Churches was prepared for a longer stay – he was registered, issued with a blanket and a palliasse, and directed to a stack of mildewed straw to fill it. At Corinth there were some wooden huts, but the sanitation facilities were pitifully inadequate for the numbers; many preferred to remain unwashed rather than battle for access to the single block with its handful of cold water taps and basins. To avoid the use of the latrine altogether was, however, no option. It stretched at a spade's width across the compound, a distance of some 70 metres, from the entrance to the rear. Undernourished on arrival, Churches' hunger pangs only grew with the tightly rationed diet of thin potato soup. Between the two daily servings of soup there was nothing to do but vegetate in the lice-infested filth.[13]

There was one thing worse than vegetating in the Corinth Cage, and that was leaving it for Salonika. In the early hours of 5 June the clearing out of the camp began. The first group of some hundreds of POWs marched 12 kilometres to the train line at Kalamaki on the northern side of the Corinth Canal, carrying their belongings with them. Having reached the line, they boarded a train which took them as far as Gravia near Levadhia. From there they had to march once more, this time through the Brallos Pass, which Australian forces had fought vainly to defend some weeks earlier. For all the hardship he endured during the war, Reg Worthington still recalls the day he marched across the Brallos Pass as the worst in his life. To the weight of his gear was added the burden of an exhausted member of his unit, Ernie Shelswell. With the help of two others he carried and cajoled his mate across the pass. 'That was a terrible dark day.'[14]

On the other side of the pass near Lamia they entrained once more; packed into cattle-trucks they were delivered to Salonika, where they marched through crowded streets to Dulag 183. Similar movements of POWs from Corinth continued over the following days; by 11 June the Corinth camp had been emptied out.[15]

It was no easier for the men captured in Crete. They might have entered captivity later than those on the mainland, but their experiences were just as harsh, and Salonika no more welcoming when they got there. Starting with the foot-slog across the island, they had much to endure before they, too, undertook their journeys to faraway Salonika. The severely wounded were flown to a military hospital at Kokkinia near Athens on the mainland, where the unevacuated members of the 2/5th Australian General Hospital, working with other British staff under German supervision, could care for them.[16] Officers, too, could reckon with a relatively brief stay on the island. But the unwounded or lightly wounded had to endure privation in crude temporary holdings on Crete before being loaded onto vessels for transfer to Salonika from early July.[17]

On the northern side of the island the Germans established a collecting point in a sandy coastal area five kilometres west of Canea. Many of the prisoners knew it as the Galatas Camp; for the Germans it was Dulag Kreta. As the abject, bedraggled columns making their way from Sphakia reached the camp, the inadequacy of its facilities soon became apparent. Most of the newly arrived simply lay down wherever they could, taking whatever measures available to protect themselves from the harsh Cretan sun during the day. Thirsts could be quenched only after standing in a queue at an old well; sickness and hunger added to the sepulchral gloom settling over the camp.[18]

At first Galatas was little more than a large holding pen surrounded by a six-foot wire fence; men could scramble out at night to forage for food and return before dawn.[19] But in time security became more elaborate, patrolled as the camp was by trigger-itchy youths, as nervous of their captives as their captives were of them. That these young men took their duties seriously was confirmed traumatically with the brazen murder of the Australian Ken 'Bluey' Atock, shot on the night of 13 July while attempting escape. The Germans left his body hanging from the wire until sunset the following day to dispel any others' thoughts of escape.[20]

Overcrowding soon forced the Germans to disperse their prisoners across a number of areas – the New Zealanders to a coastal holding below Galatas, the British, Greeks and Cypriots nearby, and most of the Australians to a site near Skines, located 16 kilometres south of Galatas.[21] The accommodation at Skines had little to recommend it; above all the evidence of the compound's previous inhabitants – Italian POWs brought to Crete all the way from the Albanian front – was horrifying. Charles Robinson noted, 'Unfortunately during the battle it had been bombed in error and the ground was pockmarked with craters. The first batch of Australians found bits of Italian bodies littering the area, attracting swarms of flies. Although these remnants were immediately collected and buried, the flies stayed on to spread dysentery, and when we arrived there over 3000 [. . .] were affected, some seriously.'[22]

Food was in woefully short supply, though at one memorable point it was supplemented temporarily by a donkey, which within moments of being ridden through the gates into the enclosure was butchered and prepared for a meal, much to the astonishment of its rider.[23] The standard of shelter was no better. There were no barracks or huts at Skines, just, as Roy East remembers, 'dirt, no water, no latrines and next to no food. We dug slit trenches for latrines, and the place was full of body lice.'[24] Charlie Parrott recalls the latrines at Skines all too well. A large hole in the ground had logs placed over it in a crisscross fashion, leaving a number of holes about 30 centimetres along each side. Struck with dysentery, many of the men lay beside the holes, 'too frightened to move away because they were so weak'.[25]

For almost all the POWs the journey to Salonika, already being cleared of the men captured on the mainland, was by boat departing from Suda Bay. These were typically aging cargo vessels, not built for passenger comfort. Indeed, sanitary requirements were lacking altogether. The poor sods confined to the holds were provided with nothing more than a bucket to meet their needs. If allowed on deck, they had to make do with a flimsy structure erected at the side of the ship, but for those weakened by dysentery or some other debilitating condition, to climb onto it was more than their physical states could manage.[26]

Crammed in the hold of one ancient freighter, Arthur Leggett recalls that all below deck had barely enough room to sit. The heat soon drained their bodies of fluid. By the time they arrived in Salonika some of the men, clad only in shirt and shorts and with just sacking wound around their feet as footwear, 'were so debilitated and physically weak they could hardly stand, and we were all covered with the dirt and filth of the freighter's hold'.[27]

Arrival at Salonika's port brought no immediate relief. Ahead of them still was the escort through the streets of the city to the camp that was to be their provisional home. Guiding them were guards, no longer the front-line troops of Crete but a new yet older complement eager to impose discipline. Commonly, the Australians soon learned, they lacked the sort of respect for the enemy that might have been created in the crucible of battle. The torture in Salonika thus began with a lengthy harbourside parade in full sun, followed by the march, or stagger, through the streets. For all the sympathy directed to them from the local population watching on, the suffering was unrelieved: 'Dirty, starved, some half naked, we were belted, bashed, ridiculed and humiliated before the population lining the streets.'[28]

Lindsay Lawrence had the good fortune to avoid the hold for his passage from Suda Bay to Salonika. His great luck was to be given a place on the deck of the rusty old steamer *Arcadia*, and with it exposure to fresh air. After one night at sea the hatches were opened to release the stench emanating from the writhing humanity below deck, where a mixture of seasickness and dysentery had wreaked havoc. Those on deck had been able to put their bums overboard to relieve themselves, an option unavailable to those down below, who moreover had to cope with stinking bilge water as it rose and fell with the vessel's pitch. It took five days to reach the wharves at Salonika, where they were disembarked and paraded to their new home past the locals, themselves adjusting painfully to the realities of Nazi occupation.[29]

Whether they arrived from somewhere further south on the mainland or from Crete, it was in the Salonika camp that the degradation reached its apogee. Laurie West, himself a survivor of Skines, recalls that by the time of arrival in Salonika the men were already seriously undernourished and filthy, proving a striking contrast to their German guards cajoling them to their new accommodation. The originally Turkish army barracks were long brick buildings with concrete floors. Here the men's Australian uniforms and boots were removed, and they were issued with new clothing; West himself received an improbably archaic ensemble of baggy pants, long underwear, a cavalryman's overcoat and wooden clogs for footwear. Completely inappropriate for the middle of summer, West nonetheless had to don them for the parades conducted for hours on end in the burning Greek sun. In the evening, in contrast, there was a strictly enforced confinement to barracks.[30]

There was nothing to recommend Salonika. According to the official New Zealand history of the war, daily rations comprised 'three-quarters of a hard Italian army biscuit, about four ounces of bread, sometimes mouldy, a pint of watery lentil soup with an occasional flavouring of horseflesh, and two hot drinks of German "mint" tea.'[31] It was plainly not enough to stave off hunger and disease, especially among men who had just endured the physical exhaustion of battle, capture and forced transfer. As the camp population reached its height from the summer of 1941, with captives from Crete being crammed in with those remaining from the mainland, the incidence of malnutrition rose alarmingly. Some invaluable dietary supplements were provided courtesy of the Greek Red Cross, but not enough to stave off the hundreds of cases of famine oedema and beriberi reported by Captain Cochrane of the Royal Australian Medical Corps.[32]

Charlie Parrott recalls men of many nationalities dying in Salonika, including his good friend the Victorian Jimmy Greer, who perished on 2 September. The precipitate decline in Greer's health seemed to be accompanied by a matching trajectory in his mental outlook, triggered by the act of capture: 'Jimmy had great difficulty accepting the fact that he was a prisoner of war. He'd sit on his right ankle for hours on end staring at nothing. The doctors said he died of starvation.'[33]

One of those who only narrowly escaped death was Frank Atkins, who had already spent weeks in an Athens hospital before being transferred by an Italian vessel to Salonika, still with a raging temperature and bleeding badly from the nose. In the Salonika camp he was placed among men with a range of ailments, including an Australian mate Phillip Gillon, who was suffering from beriberi. His face and jowls were so swollen that Atkins did not at first recognise him. His bed, consisting of wire springs with no mattress, was debugged by burning the hollow springs with gum leaves and putting small tins of water under each leg.[34]

Many to this day recall the exquisite torture of flies, fleas and, worst of all, the lice which swarmed all over the men. For Alex McClelland the worst feature of Salonika was the bedbugs, which would appear at night as a creeping mass, covering the normally white sheets to turn them black. If they were squashed the odour released would mix with the general stench of urine and excreta given off by the men who were gravely ill with typhoid, malaria or dysentery. The only relief McClelland could conjure was to leave the lights on at night to keep the bugs at bay.[35] Skines had been hellish in multiple ways, but at least, as Ray Corbett recalls, sleeping in sand there he was not plagued by lice. At Salonika, however, they were a constant irritation, because even if the men managed to remove them they were reinfected 'night after night after bloody night'. So abundant were they, Philip Brown remembers, 'you could scrape them off by the handful'.[36]

At least at one point the Germans took steps to combat them. Albert Gibb, who had already survived the trials of Corinth, recollected that in Salonika he and others were marched down to the sea, stripped naked in a seemingly endless line of humanity and disinfected with backpack spray units: 'They immediately sprayed you all over, including your privates and your test-timonials. Heaven knows what was in that delousing spray concoction, but from the hellish burning of the crotch, I guess it was Spirit of Salts. I thought I was going to be a permanent boy soprano.'[37]

The latrines, too, were no improvement on Skines. In Hal Finkelstein's memory, there was a trough with a tap at one end and a gravity-fed slope; the men had to squat on two concrete foot pieces raised above the floor and shit through holes about 25 centimetres in diameter into the gutter below. The tap would then be turned on to wash the shit away. 'There were rats living in those gutters that were the biggest rats I'd even seen in my life and they were as brazen as you liked and when you squatted you had to make sure there wasn't a rat underneath. They appeared out of holes in the floor and they were whoppers.'[38]

If the time spent in Salonika varied, what awaited all who survived it was entrainment and transfer into the Reich. They commonly remember the French lettering on the sides of the 'cattle-trucks' which took them there – *40 Hommes ou 8 Chevaux* – 40 men or 8 horses. These wagons had indeed delivered horses to the Wehrmacht in Greece; the POWs were sometimes grateful for the hay left behind, but not the shit.

Used now for human transport, the recommendation of 40 men was treated with scant respect. Severe overcrowding meant the men could neither sit nor lie comfortably, at least not for any length of time. The overcrowding added to another aspect of their discomfort – the heat. Most were transported at the tail-end of the European summer. After the doors slammed shut the only ventilation was provided by a narrow slit at one end of the truck. Not only was the food provided inadequate for the several days ahead, more pressing in the sauna-like conditions was the shortage of water. For days on end the men were tortured with a thirst they had no way of slaking.

Toilet facilities were nonexistent. As they drank at most sparingly, they seldom had need to urinate, and generally could do so through cracks in the floor. But diarrhoea and dysentery caused other problems. As Arthur Leggett remembered, 'Shirts were torn into pieces and space made available on the crowded floor while an embarrassed, apologetic, miserably-sick man dealt with his problem. When this was over the four corners of the rag were brought together and the bundle lifted to be poked through a space in the barbed wire covering the opening. Socks and donated rags were eventually used after the final scraps of the individual's shirt had disappeared through the opening.'[39]

Lindsay Lawrence was one of 50 men prodded into a car still covered with the straw and droppings left by its previous load. Each man was issued with a tin of meat to last five days; fortunately in his wagon there was a tin opener. The tins were useful also for toilet functions, especially as dysentery was rife: 'To piddle in a tin of this size was no effort, but to pass a motion, while the train was in motion without spillage was a rare feat. When you had completed your toiletries you then had to empty the contents out of the window, which measured twelve inches by eighteen inches and was crisscrossed with barbed wire.'[40] Even the best-laid plans came unstuck, especially in the face of widespread dysentery. In the middle of the journey the train stopped at an unnamed station, giving some small opportunity to recover some of their humanity. Some of the men were so weak with dysentery that their mates held them while washing and wiping their bums with their shirt tails.[41]

By the end of September Dulag 183 was practically cleared – only a skeleton medical staff and some of their serious cases remained.

Yet these were not the last of the deportations from Salonika. In early 1943 Adolf Eichmann sent a trusted deputy to Salonika to prepare the 'final solution'. On Sunday 15 March of that year a train was loaded in Salonika with some 2800 Jews, around 80 per wagon. Five days later the train arrived at Auschwitz, the final destination for almost all of them. In most cases their murders occurred within hours of their arrival at Auschwitz II–Birkenau. Horrific though the journeys of the Australians had been, not one would have swapped places with the Jews of Salonika who followed.[42]

Australian POWs were sent to many parts of the Reich. The shortest journey was that made by those whose cattle-trucks opened in Marburg on the Drau. Before this town had been known by its Slovenian name, Maribor on the river Drava, but it had been incorporated as part of a sliver of formerly Yugoslav territory into the 'Greater German Reich'. Relatively short though his journey was, Ralph Churches nonetheless recalls four quite hellish days of travel. True, on isolated stretches of track, removed from the sight and possible supplications of the local population, they were fed and watered twice a day and snatched precious fresh air. But the wagon's only window could not release the foul and fetid air; the sensation inside the wagon, he remembers, was like drowning in a sea of sewage.[43]

Others went not much further, commonly to Wolfsberg, which, like Marburg, was in Military District XVIII. That was in southern Austria, since March 1938 part of the 'Greater German Reich'. A few days later a similarly large group of about 1000 Australians were delivered to Moosburg, just outside Munich. Here, too, the reception appears to have been good, with not only the German authorities tending to their new charges' needs, but the existing population of French POWs proving solicitous and sympathetic to their new neighbours.[44] It was the beginning of a relationship between Australians and Moosburg which lasted to the very last days of the war.

As for the officers, the first load of them out of Salonika was taken to a camp in Military District V in Baden Württemberg. From the train station they were marched to Oflag V B

CAPTURE

Biberach. After weeks of hardship they had some cause to be pleasantly surprised. Officers, by and large, were treated well, and in Biberach they found before them a camp with an existing British officer population, who had already organised the basic necessities of a plain but not entirely uncomfortable existence. Other officers, however, were subjected to the discomfort of a journey to the very north of the Reich, to Oflag X C near the Baltic port of Lübeck.

A large load of prisoners – some 1000 Australians – was taken to Hammelburg, 80 kilometres east of Frankfurt am Main, in mid-August 1941. By the time they arrived there they were in poor condition, as even their new host acknowledged at the train station. The camp commandant 'stormed up and down the platform saying he was to take delivery of a thousand colonial prisoners, not a thousand sick men'. To fortify the men for the walk to the camp containers of gruel were brought as a makeshift meal.[45]

In September and October painfully long journeys awaited those assigned to the massive camp at Lamsdorf in Silesia. Ray Corbett was one of them; in his recollection the journey was ten or twelve days from Greece. On arriving at the camp they were greeted by British POWs, clean-shaven and well-dressed, and speaking a babble of British dialects. Captured at Dunkirk or Calais, they were already well acquainted with the rhythms and logic of German POW camp life. Their greatcoats were the envy of the dishevelled interlopers, still dressed in the scraps of the uniforms they had worn through a Greek summer. The British marshalled their ANZAC protégés into huts with wooden bunks and straw palliasses, but the greatest joy of all was the arrival in carts of Red Cross food parcels, from the UK or Canada, which were distributed one to a man – for whom it would need to last two weeks. Thereafter the men were shorn, showered and deloused, processed like cattle through a dip, emerging as quite different creatures from those who had been bundled stiff-limbed and weak from cattle-trucks just hours earlier. As Corbett put it, 'The scars and degradation of battle and capture slipped away like a discarded cloak.'[46]

Among the last to bid farewell to Salonika were the medical personnel. Leslie Le Souef should have been aboard a transport of some 500 officers and men, provisioned with four days' rations for a journey which might last as many as ten, and loaded into the by now customary cattle-trucks. The officers enjoyed the relative luxury of being packed into a small third-class carriage. But the indisposed Le Souef gained a reprieve. The extra time in Dulag 183 was happily enhanced by the arrival of a new commandant, a man of a character vastly different from his predecessor. The new commandant was so kind as to drive Le Souef and another officer around the ancient town, including a visit to the British cemetery. But three weeks later his reprieve ended when he and some 200 patients gathered at the Salonika station to board a German hospital train for a journey through the remnants of Yugoslavia and Austria. It then snaked its way into Germany proper, depositing the sick and wounded at a variety of medical facilities, until he and some 100 wounded reached their final destination – Dieburg, just outside Frankfurt am Main – where the army hospital attached to Stalag IX B awaited his services.[47]

Mussolini's misadventures in North Africa and Greece in late 1940 had come at some cost. Lives had been lost, soldiers and matériel had fallen into enemy hands en masse, and Italy's reputation as a military power had taken a severe pounding. The situation was salvaged only through swift and telling German intervention. In the case of Greece the Germans not only rescued their partner from the fiasco of its Albanian campaign, they also defeated in short time an assembled Allied military force and, moreover, took on the responsibility of transferring captured personnel back into the Reich. In North Africa, however, even where Australians and others were captured by German forces, they were almost invariably handed as soon as possible to Italian authorities. For these men, if it were to occur at all, then their transfer into the Reich was a long and circuitous process.

From their camps in Benghazi or Tripoli the Australians and other British POWs were marched to the harbour, packed into the dank holds of cargo vessels and sent across the Mediterranean to Naples or Bari, and from there they were distributed to camps at Sulmona, Padulla, Turturano, Chiavari, Servigliano, Gravina, Capua or, most commonly, Gruppignano near Udine.[48] The last was the location of Campo PG (Prigioneri di Guerra) 57. These journeys within Italy were the easy bit; the greatest dangers were to be encountered on the voyages from Africa to Italy. Quite apart from the discomforts comparable with those endured between Suda Bay and Salonika, the journeys to Italy through waters teeming with submarines were downright dangerous, especially for the masses huddled below decks.

One tragedy above all illustrates the perils of these voyages. *Nino Bixio* was a freighter charged in August 1941 with transferring POWs from Benghazi in Libya to Italy. On the second day out of Benghazi she was torpedoed by an Allied submarine with huge loss of life – whether through the initial blast or the drowning of those trapped in the hold – including 37 of 201 Australian POWs.[49] It was the greatest single loss of Australian POW life during the war. The lucky ones escaped the hold and were pulled onto the deck, staying with the stricken vessel until it was towed by an escorting destroyer to the Greek coast at Navarino. Only after an unscheduled stay in Greece, and still in a state of shock, did the passengers finally reach the port of Bari in Italy.

Jim Reeves suffered a similar fate four months later. Crammed with some 2000 other POWs in the hold of *Sebastiano Venier*, he was headed from Benghazi to Italy when the British submarine *Porpoise* crippled the Italian vessel with a torpedo. As in the case of *Nino Bixio*, there was great loss of life below decks, yet the stricken ship limped to the Greek coastline to disgorge its surviving human cargo. Reeves' second sojourn in Greece was no happier than the first, and in due course he, too, found himself in PG 57, but at least alive. Records show that 500 less fortunate passengers aboard *Sebastiano Venier* would all too happily have joined him there.[50]

Ernest Brough was one of those who disembarked unwashed and famished at Reggio Calabria on the toe of Italy's boot. With other

POWs he entrained there, eleven men squeezed into a compartment devoid of toilet facilities. For those like Brough still suffering dysentery, that meant perching themselves with exposed buttocks on a windowsill, supported from within by fellow passengers. The train headed north past Mount Vesuvius and Naples on its way to Gruppignano in Italy's very north-east.[51]

The officers were held in their own compound, but neither they nor the other ranks had it easy in the camp. Men who had been captured in Egypt or Libya often arrived at Gruppignano in a severely malnourished state, in many cases presenting with signs of beriberi or other diseases caused by food deficiency.[52] Malaria, too, reared its ugly head there, and it was only the supply of quinine from the British Red Cross that kept it in check. Deaths from diseases occurred at the rate of about one per month.[53] Survival prospects were not aided by the parlous state of hygiene. Water restrictions inhibited thorough washing, latrines were of the open pit variety, and the Italian authorities did little to adjust the camp's facilities to the growing numbers of men housed there.

First among the culprits in the maltreatment of POWs was Vittorio Calcaterra, the camp commandant. Calcaterra allegedly had painted on the wall above his desk a motto pilfered from a Mussolini speech: 'The English are cursed, but how much more cursed is any Italian who treats them well.' Among the litany of the commandant's misdeeds was the jailing of prisoners for trivial offences; the first half of a thirty-day sentence would be spent in irons and on Italian half-rations, with no access to books, cigarettes or writing materials.[54] His underlings were inclined to follow his example. Lawrence Calder recalls guards patrolling the Australian and New Zealand section around the clock: 'And they were all fascists. They had no hesitation walking up to you and giving you a good clip across the ears with a rifle butt if they didn't like the look of you.'[55]

Bill Cousins witnessed just how cruel Calcaterra's men could be. At a cricket match a very popular Western Australian by the name of 'Socks' Symons – probably Edward William Symons – aided by a stealthily acquired bottle of wine, began barracking with an enthusiasm which irked one of the guards. When the guard attempted to escort the ebullient Symons away, the Australian resisted. Cousins and another man tried to calm Symons but, in a flash, events took a dramatically tragic turn: 'The guard, at close range, shot Socks in the chest. Socks fell backwards, blood spurted from his chest wound and he died in seconds. We were all shocked by this murderous act, but unfortunately there was nothing we could do about it.'[56]

From their camps the other ranks were sent out to work detachments in many parts of Italy to perform a variety of tasks. Like Germany, Italy was desperately short of labour, and POWs were used to fill gaps. The more fortunate POWs were sent to agricultural detachments, which at least helped to guarantee sufficient food, even if the work could be back-breaking. Many Australians found themselves at Campo 106, a complex of camps in the vicinity of the Piedmontese town of Vercelli, where they engaged in rice-farming, at least until word got around that fascist Italy was on the brink of collapse.

Officially Italy's miserable war was brought to an end in 1943. A perfect storm of military calamities had made Mussolini's political survival untenable. Italy's ever-tenuous hold in Africa was lost when Italian forces fighting on the eastern front in Tunisia were trounced, and Allied raids brought the war to Italy's citizens with a vengeance. With the Allied landing in Sicily in May the knives were drawn among both fascists and the military men close to the king. A vote taken on the Fascist Grand Council forced Mussolini's ousting and then arrest on 25 July, triggering the collapse of the entire fascist house of cards. A new government under Marshal Pietro Badoglio was hurriedly installed to negotiate an armistice, finally signed on 3 September.

Fearing that Allied prisoners in Italian POW camps might be caught perilously between battle fronts after the Allies landed in the south and the Germans sent reinforcements from the north to hold Italy, British POWs were told to stay put to await the arrival of Allied forces.[57] It was MI9, an organisation formed in good part to aid POWs, which sent the messages into the Italian camps. Indeed, officers were instructed to take necessary disciplinary action to ensure that individual prisoners did not make any effort to rejoin their units.[58] Most of those who received this message duly stayed put. One source has it that the POWs were directed, 'Keep cool, keep calm, and you will be collected.'[59]

As the Italian camps were mainly in central and northern Italy, this advice played into German hands. Those who stayed put in their camps – as altogether about 52,000 out of 80,000 did – were easily gathered together as German forces descended from the north, collected the men and deported them to the overflowing camps of the Reich, to places like Moosburg, Görlitz, Spittal or Lamsdorf.[60] With haste and determination, the Germans asserted control over central and northern Italy as well as over Albania, the Italian islands in the Aegean, and Italian occupation zones in France, Yugoslavia and Greece. And now that he could do as he pleased, Hitler seized control of the South Tyrol and most of north-eastern Italy, declaring these areas 'Operational Zones'.[61]

The flood of German troops south was soon countered by movements in the opposite direction. It was quite a patchwork of humanity which headed into the Reich, most of it against its will. Apart from the POWs there were Italian servicemen, now recruited against their will into the swelling ranks of the Reich's labour force. In reality they themselves were effectively POWs, captives of their erstwhile ally, but German authorities were careful not to label them as such. In official parlance they were now 'Italian military internees' (*Italienische Militärinternierte*), and thousands upon thousands soon found themselves in German POW camps and on work detachments, where even the slightest hint of sympathetic treatment from their hosts was a rarity. Among those sent north were also, in time, Italian Jews. Under Mussolini's rule Italy had bowed to German pressure to adopt anti-Semitic legislation in 1938. But the Italian commitment to the extermination program adopted in the second half of 1941 was desultory. That changed when the Germans themselves stepped in to control the operation with the type of dedication to the cause of ridding Europe of its Jews they were already exhibiting elsewhere.

CAPTURE

Yet the Germans did not dispatch a full set of Allied POWs into the Reich. Many either did not receive the message to stay put or simply ignored it when the chance to grasp their freedom presented itself. As most of the work camps with Australians were in the north-west of Italy, the obvious destination was neutral Switzerland. One calculation has it that 545 Australians made it safely to Swiss soil after an arduous alpine trek.[62] Others made it to Yugoslavia, where after Italy's defeat there was the hope of meeting up with partisans.

Still others remained in Italy, avoiding the grasp of Germans and their Italian collaborators, awaiting the day when they would be liberated by American and British forces pressing inexorably north. The lucky ones could count on the hospitality of Italians, who in large numbers made their homes available to these British and Australian POWs on the run, at some risk to their lives. When, many years later, the historian Roger Absalom asked these courageously hospitable Italians what had motivated them to house and feed the Australians, a not uncommon reply was, 'Maybe, somewhere, my boy, if he's captured, might need help.'[63] Half a world away, there were thousands of Italian POWs who, like the Australians in Italy, had come to depend on the hospitality and goodwill of their erstwhile foes.

Among the fortunate was Ray Jones, who spent some eighteen months living among hospitable Italians – and doing his best to avoid fascists of both the Italian and German varieties – before gratefully coming across an American unit.[64] But not all were so lucky, and not all of the evaders lived long enough to witness liberation. James McCracken was one of the ill-fated. By February 1944 he had joined partisans fighting German occupation forces in the vicinity of Milan. In April he was caught at Varallo, north-east of Milan, and as he was wearing civilian clothes he was treated as a partisan. Before being executed – stood against a wall and shot in the back – he was permitted to write home to his family in Bendigo: 'Just a line to tell you that I will not see you again as I am going to be shot.' He was one of perhaps 39 Australians who lost their lives in this way.[65]

INTO THE REICH

*

FOR CAPTURED AUSTRALIAN airmen, paths into the Reich were many and varied. Not all bombing raids conducted from the UK targeted Germany itself. During the build-up to Operation *Seelöwe* – the planned but never executed invasion of Britain – coastal and port facilities in France and Belgium were targeted. Moreover, bombing raids with German targets were faced with enemy fire before or not uncommonly after the raid had been carried out. Crews were often forced to bale out over Holland, Belgium or France, in which case both their training and their instincts drove them to evade capture and seek a way back to Britain with the aid of sympathetic locals. As numerous Australians found, this was no easy task, as Allied airmen were the highly prized quarry of German security forces and their local collaborators.

Gordon Stooke of 460 Squadron, shot down over Belgium after a night raid on 'Happy Valley', eventually was caught and taken to Fresnes prison near Paris. He was far from the only airman to pass through Fresnes on the way into the Reich. Along with two Australians from his Lancaster crew, Clarrie Craven and Norm Conklin, he was taken under Luftwaffe guard by train via Paris and Saarbrücken to Frankfurt, where at the main station their welcome was hostile. A guard foolishly announced his prisoners to be *'englische Terrorflieger'*, English terror flyers, eliciting a spontaneous and bitter wave of spitting, jostling and abuse. The prisoners were hustled to a suburban railway station where another journey would bring Stooke and his fellow airmen to the place which almost all Allied air force POWs came to know, namely the Luftwaffe's transit camp Dulag Luft, at that time located in Oberursel just outside Frankfurt. Stooke's interrogations were not yet over, he was ravenously hungry, but he was also safer than he had been since his Lancaster had taken off from England several weeks earlier.[66]

The RAAF's Wilf Hodgson, shot down near Nantes in March 1943, spent time in a Gestapo facility in Poitiers before transfer to Fresnes. In his single cell there he noticed a neat description divulging something of the cell's history: 'Stone walls do not a prison make nor iron bars a cage.' It was signed by a British army captain, a padre captured at Dunkirk. Below it in an untidier script was a pithy appendix, the work of a sergeant RAF air gunner: 'No but they bloody well help.'[67]

One of the longest and most circuitous of the Australian airmen's paths to captivity was undertaken by Henry Bastian. His 33 Squadron Hurricane was brought down on the wrong side of the lines at El Alamein in August 1942. He tried to reach Allied positions by walking at night, only to have his plans foiled by the foulest of luck. A group of Germans stumbled upon him while they were hunting antelope. As he was an airman, they had no interest in handing Bastian over to the Italians. Instead they packed him into a JU 52, the Luftwaffe's reliable workhorse, which flew him via Maleme to Athens. From there he unwittingly replicated the train journey of thousands of Australians about a year earlier, travelling north through Belgrade into the Reich, passing through the capital and then reaching his provisional yet ineluctable destination, Dulag Luft.[68]

Whether they made their journeys into the Reich from Africa, Norway, Italy, Holland or France, for the airmen all roads led to Dulag Luft, but it was not to be their permanent home. When their interrogators had extracted from them whatever they could, the airmen were packed off east, typically to one of the camps which Hermann Göring included in his growing empire.

PART 2

Captivity

9

Hitler's Behemoth

The Third Reich is unimaginable without Hitler. There is barely an aspect of its history which does not in some way, great or small, bear the stamp of his authority. Whether he intervened personally or simply set the tone for others to follow, Hitler imposed his trademark Führer-principle from the time of his ascent to power through to the Reich's collapse. In military matters above all else, Hitler was the Reich's permanent puppet-master, pulling the strings of all the major figures of a theatre which he himself had largely built. Though the Australians could not know it, it was in good part an unholy mix of Hitler's will and whim which dictated how they would spend their captivity in the Reich.

Institutionally his power was unchallenged. The vicious murders committed in Hitler's name on the Night of the Long Knives convinced the leaders of the then Reichswehr – Germany's armed forces – that Hitler had their best interests at heart. He would not allow the Storm Troopers, a party organisation, to challenge the place of the armed forces. With the death of President Paul von Hindenburg a few weeks later in August 1934, Hitler collapsed the offices of Chancellor and President into one. His place as Führer of his beloved Nazi Party was expanded to encompass the state as well. Thereafter all army officers were obliged to swear an oath of loyalty to him personally.

In 1938 Hitler used a potentially damaging scandal to expand his control of what was now the Wehrmacht. At the centre of the scandal was his war minister and commander-in-chief of the Wehrmacht, Field Marshal Werner von Blomberg. Blomberg had a reputation for competence in things military, earning him respect not only from leading figures in the armed forces but from Hitler himself. That professional reputation counted for little when it was revealed that the woman he had married, 35 years his junior, was a former prostitute and model for pornographic photographs.[1] Hitler had been among the wedding guests. The affront to the Reich and its officer corps could not be tolerated. Presented with the evidence, Hitler was incredulous. How could the man in whom he had invested so much trust place his love for a woman above the interests of the Nazi state?[2] Momentarily shaken by the unexpected turn of events, Hitler soon recovered to plot a characteristically bold path through the crisis – Blomberg retired 'on health grounds' and the former Austrian lance-corporal declared himself commander-in-chief of the Wehrmacht.[3]

When most of the Australians were delivered into the Reich in the summer and autumn of 1941, Hitler's power and popularity were at their apogee. For, whatever reservations the career military men might have had in 1934 or 1938, by 1941 Hitler's successes as a military leader fell nowhere short of the spectacular. In military matters, including the comparatively arcane realm of POW affairs, Hitler brooked no rival. What was it, then, that drove Hitler's thinking on POWs? There are two elements which stand out above all others. The first is history. It was his favourite subject at school and a passion he maintained throughout his life. The history of warfare, especially as it concerned Germany, was a particular preoccupation, complementing as it did his own experiences on the battlefields of the Western Front in the Great War.

The second is what might be labelled the reciprocity principle. Here, too, Hitler's thinking drew heavily on his memory of the

Great War. He had seen the horrors of that conflict, in which he had fought bravely and suffered some of the physical consequences of modern industrialised warfare. He took from that war the view that when nations pitched themselves against each other in mortal combat, the only moral standard to apply was that each would treat the other in the same manner, thus any step deeper into barbarism would be countered by a similar step taken by the other side.

Into the mix of factors which coloured Hitler's policies and practices must be added two more. One was ideology. As a Nazi and therefore an unstinting racist, Hitler had firm views on the qualities of the millions who entered into German captivity and how they deserved to be treated. The place of this racial mania can be monitored in any assessment of how the Reich treated its POWs. Quite alien to Hitler's world view, in contrast, is the concept of universally valid human rights which might be upheld through a codified law. Hitler was no fan of universalism in any of its forms. And yet in matters of the treatment of POWs, he was at the very least aware that Germany had been one of the signatories to the Geneva Convention in 1929. More than that, he knew all too well that Germany had ratified the Convention in 1934 – when he was Chancellor.

As FÜHRER AND commander-in-chief of the Wehrmacht, it was Hitler who decided which of the Reich's enemies would be sent into captivity and remain there. History resonates powerfully through the choices he made. All those nationalities which fought against Germany in the Great War were counted among those whose soldiers were held captive in the next World War: British (including Australian), French, American, Serb and even Italian. But those who had remained neutral in the First World War or who had fought alongside Germany – the Norwegians, Dutch and Danish – were soon set free in the Second World War.

A couple of specific cases are strikingly insightful. One is Belgium. In the First World War the Germans had imprisoned the French-speaking Walloons, but the Dutch-speaking Flemings remained at large.[4] History repeated itself in 1940. As for Yugoslavia, itself a creation of the postwar era, it meant little to Hitler in 1941. As in the Great War, the Serbs were taken into captivity and stayed there. Croatians and others from regions once part of the Austro-Hungarian Empire were typically granted their freedom – except if they were Jewish.[5]

There is one instance which does not quite fit this theory – at least not at first blush – namely that of Greece. In the First World War, Greece did eventually enter the conflict against Germany, but reluctantly and under great pressure. For that reason the Germans were disinclined to see the Greeks as enemies back then – or in World War II. So it came about that in 1941 Greek soldiers, many of whom had served alongside Australians in Greece and Crete, were soon set free after capture. The exceptions were Cretan-born soldiers who had fought the Germans. On Hitler's wishes they remained in captivity for the duration, collectively punished for mutilating the German dead.[6]

Italy, too, defies easy explanation, because after eventually joining the Entente in the Great War, Italy formed part of the Axis in the Second. Germans and Italians thus fought side by side, at least until the Italian surrender in September 1943. At that point the memory of Italy's treachery in the First World War seems to have assumed a very central place in Hitler's thinking. Hundreds of thousands of Italian soldiers were taken captive by their erstwhile allies. With a kind of terminological sleight of hand, most of the Italians were labelled 'military internees' and in German camps suffered for their own putative failings and for those of a previous generation as well.

Customary though it is to point to Nazi racism in explaining the appalling German treatment of Soviet POWs, the memory of the Great War should not be brushed aside. It can help to explain not only why they remained in captivity – having been among Germany's enemies in the Great War – but also how they were treated in captivity. Large numbers of German soldiers had fallen into the hands of the Tsar's armies in the First War, and very large numbers perished there miserably. Of course, there were many Germans who fell into British, and indeed even into Australian, hands in the First World War, but by and large they were treated well and lived to tell the tale. Behind Russian lines, mortality rates in the east were higher than in the west – and in popular memory they were higher still. The persistence of that memory helped condemn millions of Red Army soldiers to mass death and suffering from the summer of 1941.[7]

If history had been the only determinant of Hitler's policy on POWs, the Australians might have experienced mixed blessings. They had counted among Germany's enemies in the First World War, thus there was no hope of an early release in the Second. But in the days before the Geneva Convention of 1929, both sides had generally treated each other's prisoners with a good deal of respect. That, at least, might augur well the second time around.

As for Hitler's tacit acceptance of a reciprocity principle in POW matters, it manifested in multiple ways, some of which affected Australians. Even if they generally categorised the Australians as 'British', the German authorities knew that the Australian government had under its control considerable numbers of German POWs. That in itself was a bone of some contention, as the Reich argued that as captives of the British, its men should have been accommodated safely in British camps and not subjected to the perils of a long voyage. But the British government remained firm, and some 1500 Germans were duly delivered to Australia, mostly to northern Victoria, where there was an officers' camp at Dhurringile and a camp for other ranks at nearby Murchison. Some of the Germans found themselves on work camps in the forests of the far south-west of the continent, where they cut and hauled timber until the end of the war and their return home – whether they wanted to or not.

Reciprocity meant that these German POWs in Australia were unwitting aids to the proper treatment of Australians in Hitler's Reich. As we shall see, however, they were by no means rock-solid guarantors. Nonetheless, for the duration of the war the German authorities took a keen interest in how their POWs were being treated in Australia, just as the Australian government wanted to know how its men were faring in Europe.

Reciprocity could, of course, cut two ways. Applied positively, it meant that the belligerent parties held each other to an agreed level of behaviour. Herein lay the value of the Geneva Convention, which in effect set the gold standard for the treatment of POWs. It was a convenient benchmark by which each could determine whether the other was taking seriously its obligations as a detaining power. Moreover, its application could entail the useful invocation of a neutral third party to check on whether the standard was being met. Applied in this way, the reciprocity principle could only work to the good of POWs. But it worked the other way, too, triggering a downward spiral of a kind with which Australian POWs, among others, became all too familiar. The great exemplar of this in the Second World War was the so-called Shackling Crisis.

The crisis originated in a botched Canadian raid on the French port of Dieppe in August 1942, during which Allied commandos shackled German prisoners. This action had an echo in a similar commando raid on the island of Sark in October, after which the bodies of Wehrmacht personnel with their hands bound behind their backs were uncovered. The evidence pointed to them being shot while attempting to flee from captivity.[8] The Germans argued that the shackling of prisoners – typically in the form of the tying or chaining together of their wrists – was a breach of international law. Moreover, they pointed to evidence suggesting that the British had instructed commandos engaged in close combat to preserve their prisoners' lives only for as long as it was convenient. In other words, not only the shackling but maltreatment and even execution had become a standing operational order from above, and a flagrant breach of law.[9] The Reich thus demanded that the British government renounce and discontinue the practice. Churchill did no such thing, declaring that British forces had a right to tie up enemy soldiers.

What began as a series of accusations and counter-accusations escalated to a number of practical steps which added to the already considerable woes of both British and German POWs. When Churchill refused to renounce the practice of tying up prisoners, Hitler ordered that the British soldiers taken in the Dieppe raid be put in manacles. Churchill shackled an equivalent number of German POWs. Like Hitler, Churchill was not a man to back down, even if his hard line was not universally condoned throughout the Commonwealth, the Australian government voicing its concern that the escalation might spread as far as Australian POWs in Japanese captivity.[10] Hitler's next move was to triple the number of British POWs required to don the manacles, at which point Australian POWs, too, became involved.[11] They were among the British POWs in seven camps across the Reich who became the pawns in a game of diplomatic tit-for-tat.[12] By October more than 5500 British and German POWs were in chains.[13]

Among them were some Australians at the officers' camp at Eichstätt in Bavaria. When a Red Cross inspector visited the camp in November 1942, he noted that handcuffs of the common police type had arrived from Berlin and were being applied to some 320 officers and orderlies, from 8 in the morning to midday and then from 1 in the afternoon to 9 at night. The shackled men, the inspector observed, 'make it a point of honour not to show how deeply they resent this treatment'.[14] One of those men was the Australian Terry Fairbairn, who in time learned to adjust. He and others were always able to work one hand free, but at night they would keep one cuff on in case guards entered unexpectedly. The worst of it was during toilet visits, when a man at the door would have to unlock one handcuff. Eating was similarly difficult – generally it was done by lifting a bowl directly to the lips with a cuffed wrist.

In the *Stalag* for other ranks at Lamsdorf in Silesia – one of those affected by the crisis – a neat solution presented itself. With some wriggling, the key on bully beef tins, it was discovered, could spring the lock on the cuffs.[15] And at the major British camp for NCOs, too, at Bavarian Hohenfels, as Keith Hooper remembers, the guards became so lax that in the end the prisoners would hang the cuffs behind the door and collect them in the evening.[16]

The stalemate held for many months, despite the interventions of the International Red Cross and the Vatican. In the end a solution came only when military circumstances changed so as to persuade the German authorities of the advantages of abandoning the practice. With Rommel finally driven out of Africa, thousands of German POWs remained behind there in British hands, many of them sick or wounded. They had no prospect of repatriation while the shackling standoff continued. The practice was dropped by both sides in November 1943, a significant moment allowed to pass without public comment.[17]

If the shackling was abandoned, the reciprocity principle was not. Indeed, the Germans abided by it to the bitter end. In early 1945 there were reports that German POWs were being maltreated at a British POW camp in Egypt. Once again the men at Eichstätt were among those who bore the brunt of the reprisals. A Swiss inspector noted in his report at the end of January that special measures such as the withdrawal of palliasses, the closure of leisure facilities and the removal of tables and chairs had been introduced as a reprisal for the alleged ill-treatment of Germans at camp 306 in Egypt. Similar measures were imposed at Stalag 357.[18] The war might well have been lost by now, but the tit-for-tat of POW affairs knew no end.

What role, then, did ideology play in the way Hitler treated POWs? For all the evidence of the role played by history, reciprocity and the Geneva Convention, it is also clear that Hitler felt bound by none of them. There were times when he stepped beyond parameters set by tradition, law or convention, and as the war turned sour for the Germans, they became more common. Looming defeat provoked lurches towards more radical policies and practices; in these circumstances Nazi ideology raised its ugly head ever higher.

The first major example of Hitler thumbing his nose at law and tradition was the *Kommissarbefehl*, the Commissar Order. In a meeting with his generals at the end of March 1941, with the launching of *Barbarossa* still three months away, Hitler outlined his most sinister intentions in dealing with the 'judeo-bolshevist' foe.[19] Commissars in the Red Army, that is, those charged with the indoctrination of the Soviet troops, were to be murdered after capture. In accordance with Hitler's wishes expressed on this occasion, the Wehrmacht's High Command, together with the legal department within the Army High Command, formulated a decree which determined that any commissars active in operational areas deemed guilty of acting against the interests of German forces were to be separated from other POWs and 'finished off'. An identical fate would await those commissars operating behind the combat zones. They were to be handed over to the Einsatzgruppen and Einsatzkommandos, the 'special action' groups and commandos under SS command which followed the Wehrmacht into Soviet territory.[20]

Guidelines for the treatment of these commissars were distributed to army commanders before *Barbarossa* was launched.[21] They were then passed on orally to officers and soldiers in the field, where they were received with mixed levels of enthusiasm. Where they were eagerly embraced, the consequences for the hapless commissars were horrendous, as they were murdered en masse from the time the Soviet border was breached. In the minds of Hitler and those who followed him, these disseminators of 'bolshevism' were indistinguishable from Jewry. The policy of killing commissars translated into the practice of killing male Jews. Within weeks this slaughter unleashed on the commissars had taken a genocidal turn. Commonly with the witting collusion of the Wehrmacht, by early August the SS death squads began targeting Jewish women and children too.[22] If prisoners were taken, it was only to dispatch them to their deaths.

This initiative of Hitler's had little impact on his war with the West, but another did. The raids on Dieppe and Sark which gave rise to the Shackling Crisis triggered another of Hitler's pet hates in military matters, and that was the role of commandos. For Hitler, the commando units of the kind that the Western allies deployed to carry out furtive raids on German military and other targets were an affront. His secretly issued 'Commando Order' insisted that:

> all enemies on so-called commando missions in Europe or Africa challenged by German troops, even if they are to all appearances soldiers in uniform or demolition troops, whether armed or unarmed, in battle or in flight, are to be slaughtered to the last man. It does not make any difference whether they are landed from ships and aeroplanes for their actions, or whether they are dropped by parachute. Even if these individuals, when found, should

apparently be prepared to give themselves up, no pardon is to be granted them on principle.[23]

The order had tragic consequences for a number of British soldiers. After a raid on Glomfjord in Norway, seven British and Canadian commandos were captured and executed in cold blood; just a month later another commando raid in Norway led to double the number of executions of British commandos.[24] Commandos who were apprehended in occupied territories by security forces such as the police were to be delivered alive into the hands of the Wehrmacht and then to the Reich's Security Service, the SD.[25] It was a topic about which the judges who presided over the Nuremberg trials were to learn a great deal. They were not impressed with this flagrant breach of the Geneva Convention. Like the Commissar Order, the Commando Order showed that, when Hitler wished it, ideology had its place.

As Commander-in-Chief of the Wehrmacht, Hitler not only bore ultimate responsibility for the treatment of POWs captured by German forces, he clearly showed more than a passing interest in them. If he set the tone, the day-to-day business of looking after POWs was the preserve of his Wehrmacht. Having undergone breakneck expansion with the introduction of conscription in 1935 – at which time the old title Reichswehr was abandoned – the Wehrmacht emerged as an institutional colossus. In peacetime its fixation was on the almost frenzied preparation for war, and in those preparations POWs barely rated a mention. When war was finally triggered on 1 September 1939, arrangements for the care of a flood of POWs had to be put in place, and quickly.

The institutional structures of POW affairs in Germany were complex and changed over time. With those first fateful incursions into Polish territory in the early morning of 1 September 1939, no-one could have guessed that over the coming years the Reich would take over ten million POWs.[26] To administer such a mass of humanity – to transport, accommodate, feed and clothe them – was a logistical challenge on an unprecedented scale.

Hitler's aide, secretary, chief-of-staff and immediate subordinate in military matters was General (later Field Marshal) Wilhelm Keitel, who headed the Wehrmacht's High Command, the Oberkommando der Wehrmacht (OKW). The responsibility for POWs captured outside the Reich, and for as long as they remained outside the Reich, rested with Army High Command, Oberkommando des Heeres (OKH). In operational areas a department within the OKH with the cumbersome title of the Department for POW Administration of the Army's General Quartermaster – Abteilung Kriegsverwaltung des Generalquartiermeisters des Heeres or OKH/Gen.Qu./Abt. K.V. – had to deal with the POWs. Placing this responsibility on the shoulders of the General Quartermaster gives more than a hint that this was regarded as above all a logistical issue. After all, the POWs had to be transported away from the front lines, accommodated and fed. About half of them – something in the order of five million, including all Australian and other Western allied POWs – would be transported into the Reich itself, where responsibility was passed from the OKH to the OKW.[27]

In its first years, as we have seen, the war was fought mainly on non-German soil – most of the Australian POWs were captured in North Africa, Greece and Crete. The front-line *Stalags* (*Front-Stalags* or, more properly, *Front-Stamm-Mannschaftslager*, front base camps for other ranks) established there were usually rough, makeshift affairs – fields with barbed wire thrown up around them, or collections of buildings such as old army barracks which would have to do until transport back into the Reich could be arranged. As the Australians discovered to their dismay, these provisional camps were often woefully inadequate in multiple ways. In some cases, like Salonika and Galatas, they took on the more formal status of a transit camp (*Durchgangslager* or *Dulag*). With the exception of just one, Dulag Luft, these transit camps were all outside the territory of the Reich and were closed down when the men were moved on.

It was in the *Dulags* that the formal transfer of responsibility from OKH to OKW occurred. Under Wilhelm Keitel the OKW was divided into a number of departments. The key one for POW matters was the Allgemeines Wehrmachtsamt (AWA, General Military Forces Office), headed by a dyed-in-the-wool

Nazi, General Hermann Reinecke.[28] POW matters were just one element in Reinecke's expansive brief, handled by his Department of Wehrmacht Casualties and POW Affairs (Abteilung Wehrmachtverluste und Kriegsgefangenwesen). This department itself was divided into five sections or groups, of which two were of particular importance for Australian POWs. Group I dealt with foreign POWs in Germany, while Group V fulfilled some of the Reich's obligations under the Geneva Convention. It comprised the Wehrmacht Information Bureau for War Casualties and Prisoners of War (Wehrmachtauskunftstelle für Kriegsverluste und Kriegsgefangene, or sometimes simply WASt).[29] Australia, too, and other signatories of the Geneva Convention established such an office – in Australia's case the Prisoners of War Information Bureau, in Melbourne – so that belligerent states could keep account of their losses through death or capture.

Such was the growth of POW numbers during the early part of the war that from the beginning of 1942 POW Affairs became an independent department within the AWA. The office was now that of the Head of POW Affairs in the OKW (Chef Kriegsgefangenenwesen im OKW, or simply Chef Kgf).[30] Its incumbent was from that point Brigadier Hans von Graevenitz, Reinecke's desired appointee.[31] Its headquarters were in the Berlin district of Schöneberg. In effect, it was from here that the growing empire of POW Affairs was ruled. At its height it had a staff of about 4000, charged with keeping tabs on German POWs in foreign hands and foreign POWs in the Reich. Moreover, the regulations and orders stemming from this office applied in the OKH area as well, even if its own administrative functions were performed within the Reich, and that meant above all the running of the POW camps. Graevenitz held his post until April 1944, when he was replaced by Colonel Adolf Westhoff. As we shall see later, the most dramatic change in the incumbency occurred just six months later, when the office was filled not by another Wehrmacht officer but an SS General, Gottlob Berger.

Alongside the Head of POW Affairs, and in recognition of the spiralling volume of POW work, a position at first clumsily titled

General for Special Deployment in POW Affairs (General z.b.V. für das Kriegsgefangenenwesen) was created.[32] Brigadier von der Schulenburg was the first occupant of the post. In time he came to be known more succinctly as the Inspector of POW Affairs (Inspekteur Kriegsgefangenenwesen). Von der Schulenburg's main tasks consisted of ensuring that the German POW system followed the terms of the Geneva Convention, dealing with aid organisations such as the International Red Cross, negotiating with the Protecting Powers and inspecting relevant institutions – above all POW camps. He had to work closely with the Head of POW Affairs, as their duties were closely meshed. Ultimately, in April 1943 von der Schulenburg was dismissed and his duties simply absorbed by von Graevenitz, a move which brought some administrative neatness but also signalled the gradual downgrading of the commitment to the letter of the Geneva Convention.[33]

Just as the role of inspector was being downgraded, a different office, albeit with a similar name – General Inspector of POW Affairs (Generalinspekteur für das Kriegsgefangenenwesen) was created in the middle of 1943. Placed in the job was Major General Otto Roettig. His role was first and foremost to look after security in the camps – a response to a rash of successful breakouts which were embarrassing the OKW and giving Heinrich Himmler cause to interfere in POW matters. But Roettig was answerable to the OKW, not to Himmler's SS, and he set about running a taut ship to keep Himmler and his acolytes at bay – at least for the time being.[34]

Hitler's reign was guided by the Führer Principle. In theory the Third Reich was like a pyramid: all power flowed down from Hitler at the top. But in practice the Reich was notorious for its administrative untidiness. The division – and competition – between the institutions of party and state was part of that. Yet it was more complicated as well, as centres of power and interest formed in the Reich and sought to press their own claims before those of their rivals. In these circumstances a favoured underling like Heinrich Himmler could build an empire of his own, pitched in almost daily struggle against his rivals and prevailing through a wink or nod from the Führer. Göring, too, could establish and grow his own fiefdom, jealously claiming then abusing the platforms of power that Hitler allocated him.

The Third Reich was, then, as the German social scientist Franz Neumann noted perceptively as early as 1944, a kind of behemoth, a monster. Its structure was characterised by the distribution and redistribution of power among multiple agencies and individuals. The guiding philosophy in the exercise of authority was a Nazi variant on the theme of Social Darwinism. Sometimes bitter rivals sought to gain ascendancy by winning the favour of the Führer by 'working towards' him. And they understood that the pleasure of the Reich's ultimate arbiter was most likely to be achieved through the proffering of drastic solutions to the Reich's problems. It was a system whose internal dynamics led to a kind of 'cumulative radicalisation', that is, a process in which one bold step led to ever more radical measures. If the inevitable descent into barbarism was initiated from above, it was achieved through the tireless efforts of those below, desperate both to please their leader and to reap the rewards conferred on the favoured ones.

POW matters were no exception. The role of the Wehrmacht was institutionally predetermined. Yet the fate of Australian and other POWs in the Reich cannot be comprehended solely in terms of Hitler, his Wehrmacht, and the agencies for which it was responsible. Others, too, craved their piece of the action.

One of those other institutions with a perfectly legitimate role to play in POW matters was the German Foreign Office, the Auswärtiges Amt. Its involvement was essential, because the Foreign Office regulated both Nazi Germany's and the prisoners' contacts with the rest of the world. Even the act of passing on basic information relating to capture ran via the German Foreign Office and, in the case of Australia, the Department of External Affairs in Canberra. Dealings with the Protecting Power – that is, the neutral state nominated to look after the interests of a belligerent state's POWs – were handled via the conduit of the respective foreign offices. In addition, the German Foreign Office took on a role in matters of propaganda in relation to foreigners and foreign countries. As far as foreign minister Joachim von Ribbentrop and his office were concerned, that entailed access to and work with POWs, via whom particular images of the Third Reich might be presented to the outside world.[35]

The Third Reich's security apparatus also had a legitimate involvement in POW Affairs from the very beginning. Yet as much as any other area, the security services illustrated the deleterious consequences of the Reich's administrative chaos. The military had its own intelligence arm, the Abwehr. Military intelligence sought to extract whatever information it could from captured men, especially officers. But the military also had an interest in ensuring that the POW camps it ran were not security risks; their prisoners therefore had to be monitored, any thoughts of escape or uprising nipped in the bud. Thus each camp was assigned one or more Abwehr officers, integrated into the commandant's staff.[36]

Yet the Reich's security and intelligence network spread far beyond the military. Germany's police services had an obvious interest in ensuring that POW facilities did not pose a threat to the German population. Escaped prisoners had to be captured with all haste, as did airmen who landed on the territory of the Reich. Relatively small though it was, one particular branch of the German police, the Secret State Police or Gestapo (*Geheime Staatspolizei*), thought it well within its remit to involve itself in POW matters. Whether inside POW camps or outside them, as far as the Gestapo was concerned, POWs were a security concern, and the security of the Reich was the very raison d'être of the Gestapo. That was the unambiguous view championed by Heinrich Himmler, who counted among his minions not only the various state police services but also those whose origins lay not in the state but in the Nazi Party, above all the SS. The most important of the security agencies were bundled together in the Reich Security Main Office (Reichssicherheitshauptamt, RSHA). The RSHA's relations with military intelligence were not always cordial, yet it too insisted it had a role in POW matters, whether the Abwehr liked it or not.

Since most POWs, as we shall see, were required to work, the Ministry of Labour (Reichsarbeitsministerium) also became involved in POW matters, along with the huge network of employment offices throughout the Reich which were controlled by the ministry. In addition, such was the rising importance of labour that Hitler created a special position in March 1942, that of Plenipotentiary for Labour (Generalbevollmächtigter für den Arbeitseinsatz). That person, too, had an interest in the massive reservoir of potential labourers in German POW camps. The first plenipotentiary was Hitler's trusted Gauleiter of Thuringia, Fritz Sauckel, who relished the massive and growing responsibilities which came with the job.[37] Part of his brief, as Hitler formulated it, was to 'direct POW forced labour'.[38] In following his Führer's wishes, Sauckel took control of the network of employment offices, and got millions of POWs into workplaces to perform labour for the benefit of the Reich. It was no easy task, as the Reich's appetite for work was insatiable. Moreover, the role of POWs in labour prompted the Reich Food Ministry (Reichernährungsministerium) to take more than a passing interest in them. Alongside the millions of forced labourers hauled into the Reich, POWs, too, were put into service around the Reich to keep its citizens – and its army – fed.

And then there was Joseph Goebbels and his Ministry of Popular Enlightenment and Propaganda (Reichsministerium für Volksaufklärung und Propaganda). Just why such a ministry would stick its fingers in the POW pie is not immediately apparent, and indeed it was never clear to many outside the ministry. Certainly the understanding of the Foreign Office was that in matters of propaganda there was a simple division of labour: the Foreign Office looked after propaganda directed to the outside world, while the Goebbels outfit was responsible for propaganda within the Reich. But Goebbels was reluctant to have parameters set on his ministry's activities, and he intruded in POW affairs wherever he could. His radio network, for example, allowed Australian POWs to send greetings to their loved ones via a special service called 'Anzac Tattoo', though it is not known how many might have made use of it. A similar service recited the names of men who fell into German captivity.[39]

For the most part, however, Goebbels' interest was of a more nefarious nature. Across the pages of his beloved Nazi Party organ, the *Völkischer Beobachter*, were splashed his diatribes against Allied airmen involved in bombing raids on German cities – the so-called 'Terror Fliers'. Under the titles 'Now is Enough' and 'A Comment on Enemy Air Terror', Goebbels demanded that any Allied airmen guilty of targeting civilians be killed like mad dogs. A series of letters to the paper showed that he was not alone in his views.[40]

Last, but by no means least, the Nazi Party, the Nationalsozialistische Deutsche Arbeiterpartei or NSDAP, signalled that it, too, envisaged a role for itself in POW matters, and not just through its Führer and an array of ministers. Martin Bormann, Hitler's secretary who headed the Nazi Party Chancellery, was given to intemperate interventions in any number of affairs. His trademark boorishness was targeted not only at enemy airmen but also – as he made abundantly clear in an address to local party leaders, the Gauleiter, in March 1944 – to those errant members of the *Volk* who were displaying insufficient contempt for their foe. He chided them for 'not maintaining a distance in keeping with the severity of the war'. He then went on to warn that cases of 'malevolent intentions' or 'misconstrued sympathy' would lead to 'assignment to a concentration camp and disclosure in the newspapers'.[41]

Though they might well have felt abandoned in their camps throughout the Reich, the Australian POWs, along with all the others, were in reality exercising the minds of many. While for a good part of the war it was the moderate elements in the armed forces and the Foreign Office who held sway in the Reich, that, as we shall see, was all to change in 1944, when Himmler and the radicals won the day.

10

The World of the Camps

The world of the military is one of distinctions and divisions of seemingly endless kinds. Whether in the Australian armed forces or the German, officers inhabited a different world than did the other ranks. And then the non-commissioned officers, the NCOs, occupied a grey zone distinguished by a view in two directions, upwards to the privilege of higher rank, and down to the subservient uniformity of the many. Of course, in battle, those distinctions could be provisionally erased, as all ultimately faced their trials under fire with their common humanity. But with capture the hierarchies were rapidly restored, the proper military order of things held sway, albeit within the larger context of a new set of masters. However they were captured, the Australians sooner or later were sorted into their military identities as officers, NCOs, other ranks or, perhaps, orderlies. It was a process which had a profound effect on how they spent the next phase of their lives.

The question of which branch of the armed forces they belonged to had its consequences too. In Germany more than in Australia a clear division was observed. While the OKW retained control over the running of the system, Hermann Göring's Luftwaffe and the Kriegsmarine were permitted to run their own POW camps. Such was the scale and distinctiveness of Göring's POW empire it deserves a chapter of its own (see following chapter).

Then there were geographical divisions in the world of the POW camps. There were, as we have seen, provisional camps and *Dulags* established outside the Reich, but as for the Reich itself, it was divided into military districts, each of which had its POW camps. It was by no means uncommon for POWs to spend time in camps in more than one district. Nonetheless, it is also true that the experiences that the Australians and others had as POWs were shaped very powerfully by the blind fortune that determined which part or parts of the Reich would provide their new home.

Typically POWs were held at first in the vicinity of the front line, close to the point of capture, at very crude and provisional collecting points. The army, which was responsible for them there, labelled such facilities *Armee-Kriegsgefangenensammelstellen* (AGSST) or, in a smaller number of cases, *Kgf.-Auffanglager*, that is, POW collection points or POW reception camps.[1] But the Geneva Convention insisted that POWs be moved quickly to safer accommodation well behind the lines, typically to a *Front-Stalag* or to a *Dulag*, where they would await transfer to the Reich proper.

The Reich was divided into 17 military districts (*Wehrkreise*) identified, strangely, with Roman numerals I to XXI. The discrepancy arises because there were no military districts XIV, XV, XVI or XIX. The districts extended south into annexed Austria (Districts XVII and XVIII) and east into East Prussia and annexed western Poland. From 18 February 1941 each military district also appointed its own *Kommandeur der Kriegsgefangenen* – Commander of POWs – located in the district headquarters and responsible for all the POWs in the district.[2]

Even on the limited scale of a single military district this job was no picnic. The commander in each district had to provide adequate and secure accommodation not only in the camps but also, as we shall see, on the work detachments which dotted the countryside of just about every district. He was in a sense a victim of the Germans' own stunning early military successes, as with each campaign more

POWs flooded into the Reich. According to the German military authorities themselves, by August 1944 the 17 districts were home to 2,882,695 POWs.[3] On top of that, the men who staffed the camps, the commandant, his officers and guards, were all his responsibility too.

Each military district typically had a range of camps which might include varying numbers of the following types. There were camps for officers (*Offizierslager*, or *Oflags*), and there were camps for other ranks (*Stamm-Mannschaftslager*, or *Stalags*, perhaps best – if clumsily – translated as base camps for other ranks). The total number of camps varied over time, but there were always more *Stalags* than *Oflags*. One count puts the overall number of *Oflags* at 99, compared with 220 *Stalags*.[4]

The designation of the camps typically ran like this: first came the Roman numeral designating the district where the camp was located, followed by a letter of the alphabet, beginning with the letter 'A' for the first such camp in the district, and so on. There was, then, no such camp as Stalag XIII, for example, as featured in the television series *Hogan's Heroes*, but there was a Stalag XIII A and a Stalag XIII B and so on – Military District XIII was in the Franconian region of northern Bavaria.

There were exceptions to this pattern. *Front-Stalags* and *Dulags* were commonly given Arabic numbers. The camp at Salonika, for example, was Dulag 183. Such camps were outside the Reich's military districts. But within the Reich, too, there were occasionally camps formed which were allocated Arabic numerals. This delivered the minor administrative benefit that they might be shifted from district to district with ease, though commonly they stayed put. One such camp housed a lot of Australians. Initially it was Stalag VIII B in Lamsdorf in Silesia, but in October 1943 the designation 'VIII B' was passed to the camp at Teschen in the same district, while Lamsdorf became Stalag 344. Another variation was the addition of the letter 'Z' to indicate a satellite camp or *Zweiglager* of a main camp. Then there were other kinds of camps with other functions. *Heilag* was the abbreviation for *Heimkehrerlager*, a type of camp at which POWs would be assembled in preparation for repatriation. Then there were *Ilags*, that is, *Internierungslager*, for civilian internees, but run by the OKW.

Like the system of concentration camps, the German POW camp system could not have operated without a good level of self-rule within the camps. While the German officers and guards imposed a regime in which their own authority was never in question, the day-to-day running of the camps was left as far as possible in the hands of the POWs themselves. Of course order had to be preserved, and security was paramount. But within certain parameters the POWs could organise and fend for themselves. That meant having a point of contact between captors and captives to negotiate and regulate room for manoeuvre. For the Australians and the other British POWs in *Oflags*, this was the Senior British Officer, the SBO. If the SBO wanted to achieve minimal German intervention in the daily lives of the POWs, he had to convince the German authorities that the British compound was observing the rules and regulations imposed from above and that they could be trusted to manage their own affairs. In the *Stalags* it was the so-called Man of Confidence, the *Vertrauensmann*, usually an NCO elected by the other ranks from the NCOs in their midst. Like the SBOs in the *Oflags*, the Men of Confidence were the senior authority figures within the POW population, and they were the key interface between the German authorities and the prison population. If the Man of Confidence could convince his masters that all was running smoothly within his compound, then a minimum of interference from outside could be won. Moreover, they were a window to the outside world, since they could air their own grievances or those of their men to the representatives from the International Committee of the Red Cross (ICRC) or the Protecting Power – in the absence of the Germans.[5]

In another respect the POW camps were quite different from concentration camps. With a couple of extraordinary exceptions, the concentration camps were not subjected to any regime of external control. They had no place in the Geneva Convention. But the Convention did insist on a couple of control mechanisms that ensured that POW camps were subjected to some level of international scrutiny. One was via the requirement that the camps be open to visits by delegates of the ICRC. Those delegates, in effect playing the role of inspectors, would attempt to tour the camps of a military district every three or four months and would prepare detailed reports on conditions in the camps. The Young Men's Christian Association (YMCA) was permitted to do the same in Germany, Australia and a number of other belligerent states. When their inspections or consultations revealed deficiencies, these could be discussed with the commandant to be addressed at his level. But they were also included in the reports which made their way via the OKW and the German Foreign Office to British authorities. Where Australians were concerned, these reports would even make their way to Australia.

The role of the Protecting Power, also codified in the Geneva Convention, similarly guaranteed some level of transparency. Each belligerent state nominated a neutral power, among whose obligations was to protect the interests of the POWs from the state it represented. For Australia it was the United States which played that role, at least until December 1941, when the United States itself entered the war. From that time, it was Switzerland. American and then Swiss representatives claimed – and were granted – the right to enter POW camps, observe conditions there, and consult with both the German authorities and the POWs' representatives. Like the ICRC and YMCA reports, the Protecting Power reports give us some useful insight into just what was going on behind the barbed wire.

STALAGS WERE USUALLY designed to hold around 10,000 POWs. Typically they would consist of multiple compounds, each designated for a nationality. Because Australian POWs were regarded as British, they almost always found themselves in British compounds. A *Stalag*'s administration would have a staff of around 130. The implement of guards consisted of two security battalions (*Landesschutzbataillonen*) comprising about 1000 men. Usually these men were middle-aged or older; the younger men were usually unfit for front-line duties for whatever reason – often due to war wounds. They were drawn from the local military district, but ultimately operated under the administrative authority of the *Ersatzheer*, the Replacement Army. Also on staff in the camps were a doctor, who would work together with captured doctors or medical orderlies in looking after the prisoners' health, and the already mentioned Abwehr officer. His brief included preventing escape, censoring mail, gathering information and guarding against sabotage.[6]

Over the course of the war, Australians found themselves in numerous *Stalags* across the Reich, sometimes in quite small numbers. But together with the other British POWs they tended to find themselves in particular military districts. Not surprisingly, many of the men sent by train from Greece were unloaded in the military districts in Austria – and that meant districts XVII and XVIII – and also in southern Germany, especially Military District VII in Bavaria.

That so many of the Australians spent so much of their time in Austria can be regarded in hindsight as good fortune. The POW death rates were lower in Austria than in other parts of the Reich.[7] Moreover, there is some reason to believe that by and large the commandants there were not as 'Nazified' as those in the 'old' Reich. When Austria was annexed to the Reich by Hitler in March 1938, political reservations meant that many Austrian officers were not taken into the Wehrmacht. Only later, when their numbers were sorely needed, were they taken on, and then often only in roles not accorded high priority – such as POW administration.[8]

One of the Austrian camps with a sizeable Australian population for a time was at Marburg, which nowadays goes by its Slovenian name Maribor. When the Australians arrived there in 1941, the territory where Maribor lay had been incorporated into the Greater German Reich and the town Germanised as Marburg. It was there that the Germans built Stalag XVIII D. When the Australians arrived, there were already large numbers of French POWs in the camp and, indeed, even with multiple arrivals from Salonika the French remained in the majority.[9]

When the Australians first arrived after their torturous journey in box cars from Salonika, the authorities were still not quite ready for them, as the early Red Cross reports from Marburg show.[10] At the time of their first visit, 21 July, there were 4320 prisoners in the British compound, 414 of them Australians, 183 New Zealanders, 417 Palestinians, and the rest English. They were doing it tough: there was still no Man of Confidence, no postal service had been established for the men to send the customary 'capture cards' to their families back home, a great number of the prisoners were accommodated in tents, and their uniforms were in poor condition.[11] Moreover, they were disastrously short of the long trousers, the coats and the blankets to help them survive the cooler climate and the looming end of summer. While the inspectors acknowledged that the Germans were working hard to create acceptable conditions, they reported numerous urgent requests, above all for shoes, blankets, uniforms and tobacco.[12]

When a new inspection took place in October, things were no better. The ICRC was by no means given to intemperate language in its reporting, but in this instance the camp was described as 'very primitive', its general impression 'miserable'. Most damningly, the sanitary conditions were labelled 'deplorable'.[13] The POWs themselves were even more keenly aware of the deficiencies. One of the prisoners, for example, recalls that the German guards 'used to throw crusts of bread from upstairs windows to the starving crowds of POWs in the yard below, and watch while they fought over the crumbs'.[14]

It was by far the worst of the camps in Military District XVIII, and the Germans knew it. One of the Red Cross inspectors went so far as to say that it must have been 'about the worst camp in Germany'.[15] By June 1942 all the British POWs had been sent out to work detachments, and in August of the same year the camp was made into an annex of Stalag XVIII B Wagna and rebadged as Stalag XVIII B/Z. By November it had been abandoned altogether, and the work detachments based there were passed on to the administrative responsibility of the major *Stalag* in that district at Wolfsberg.[16]

Stalag XVIII A Wolfsberg was in the mountainous Carinthian region of Austria. Initially it had been an *Oflag* and then had taken on a mainly French population, before making the adjustments for the influx of British POWs. One of the new arrivals in the middle of 1941 was the Australian Harry Giesen, struck by the town's sublime alpine setting. For him it was like a scene from a Grimm's fairytale. 'Cobbled streets, quaint gabled houses painted in the most unlikely colours, and the romantic old castle with its battlements and towers completed the illusion.'[17]

The idyllic setting deceived. At Wolfsberg, like Marburg, painful adaptations were being made to accommodate the new arrivals. The first large convoy arrived at the camp on 1 July 1941. They had been sent north to make space at Salonika for men captured on Crete. Of just over 5000 British POWs reported to be there by October 1941, some 800 were Australians. They had to make do with makeshift accommodation – those in the *Stalag* lived in three converted stables – and even as winter approached had just one blanket each.[18] The men were shabbily and inadequately clothed, they had no benches or tables, the latrines were primitive, three men had died of dysentery, and some 80 were currently being treated for malaria. There were no books or games, and nowhere to play any sport. And, as at Marburg, the main request was for shoes and uniforms – the British were not prepared to accept the French uniforms with which the Germans could have provided them immediately.[19]

It took time for things to improve, as accommodation remained at a premium. Lack of space was the main complaint of a report lodged by the Protecting Power in March 1942, by which time the camp was clearly straining to contain large numbers of Soviet soldiers. 'Three tiers of each bunk,' the inspectors complained, 'are fully occupied and men sleeping on the lowest tier close to the stone floor are lodged in unhealthy conditions.' Poor heating, a shortage of straw in the mattresses, unhygienic latrines and insufficient washing facilities did nothing to lighten the inspectors' mood.[20]

On the one hand, space could be won by sending the men out to the hundreds of work detachments based at Wolfsberg, but then new POWs arrived, including the Soviets. With the collapse of Italy in 1943, still more British POWs were hauled to Wolfsberg after their sojourns in Italian POW camps. Records show that the British POW population reached its zenith in February 1944, when there were 11,017 on the books.[21] While the Germans did not distinguish the various British nationalities, happily the Red Cross did, and the ICRC reports show 1417 Australians in Wolfsberg in late October 1944.[22]

ICRC reports from the latter part of the war create the impression that Wolfsberg became a good camp. To some degree the improvement can be attributed to its commandant, Captain Steiner, judged by one of the Australian POWs, Ray Norman, to have been 'a very fair and good man'.[23] Steiner in fact was himself a former POW. Even more impressively, he had an escaper's pedigree. The story was that he had been captured by Russian forces in the First World War but managed to escape and make his way across Russia to Harbin in China. Proud as he was of this achievement, it was a story he was happy to share with his captives, as Harry Giesen became aware: 'If through our *Vertrauensmann* [Man of Confidence] we were to complain about our rations or any other problem, he'd immediately come back with "You don't know what bad conditions are! When I was a prisoner in Russia. . ."' Though the telling of the story might have provoked much rolling of eyes, Steiner did earn the respect of many. On one occasion, as Giesen again recalls, Steiner was required to pass judgment on a Maori soldier who, like Giesen, had been captured on Crete. Provoked by a Wolfsberg guard, the Maori had grabbed the man's rifle and rammed its bayonet so far into a tree that the guard could not remove it. Steiner extracted a confession from the Maori that this was indeed true but then turned to the guard to mock him: 'So! You, a German soldier under my command, allowed yourself to be disarmed by a one-eyed nigger!' The charges against the Maori were dropped.[24]

Some of the accolades for improvements in the British compound should also be heaped on the British Man of Confidence, who was the Australian Warrant Officer Ernest Ferdinand Stevenson, elected to that post in December 1942 and serving in it until the end of hostilities.[25] A Swiss inspector was sufficiently impressed with what he observed on a December 1944 visit to Wolfsberg that he noted, 'The Australians appear to be particularly successful in "handling affairs" and the Delegate wishes to mention in this connexion the Chief Man of Confidence, Warrant Officer Ernest Ferdinand Stevenson.'[26] Indeed, Stevenson's efforts were recognised after the war, when he was awarded an MBE for his 'Energetic attitude improving POW conditions'.[27]

Other Australians made it further north into the 'old' Reich, that is, the Reich as it was before the annexation of Austria. A common destination was Military District VII in the southern German region of Bavaria. Stalag VII A at Moosburg, some 50 kilometres north of Munich, became home for many of the other ranks. The camp had been founded in 1939 and then expanded with the aid of POW labour in 1940 before taking in part of the wave of British POWs from the Mediterranean theatre.[28] Records show that by the end of 1941 there were some 2000 British POWs there, including nearly 1000 Australians.[29]

As in many of the camps with British POWs, Moosburg's commandant had a good grasp of his British captives' language, as Lindsay Lawrence noted. When the senior Australian NCO was presented to the commandant on arrival, the latter learned that the man's name was Roy Fury and responded, 'Fury by name and not by nature, I hope.'[30]

The commandant might have been generally well-disposed towards his prisoners, but by early 1942 some alarm bells were ringing as far away as the Prime Minister's Department in Canberra on the basis of Red Cross reports. In response the High Commissioner's Office in London was urged to 'enter the strongest possible protest'. The reports received suggested that in the main camp at Moosburg and in one of the work detachments food restrictions were being applied, there was a lack of dental attention and work pay was low. This, the Prime Minister's Office claimed – tacitly invoking the reciprocity principle – contrasted 'most unfavorably with the humane treatment of German P.W. in Australia'.[31] The delegate from the Red Cross voiced his reservations too. The men were dressed in a 'medley of odd uniforms'; with winter around the corner – this report stemmed from a November 1941 visit – men captured in Crete were still clothed in shorts and had neither tunics nor boots; moreover, discipline was 'very severe'. Dogs were commonly let loose to force the men back into their barracks, at times not without taking a bite out of their quarry, as a number of cases in the camp infirmary showed.[32]

By the following year the High Commissioner reported that the dogs had been withdrawn and conditions in the main camp improved, though Work Detachment 2780 with 212 Australians was still overcrowded, its sanitary and hygiene arrangements unsatisfactory and work conditions 'gruelling'.[33] But by the end of the year here, too, things had taken a turn for the better, and under a new camp leader the Protecting Power now judged it to be 'a good camp'. Indeed, by the same time, the Protecting Power was reporting that the men from another work detachment based at Moosburg, 2780A, which included some 2500 British POWs, were particularly fortunate: 'Their favourite occupation was cleaning garbage in the streets of the city for then they were allowed more freedom (indeed POW state that with a 2 oz. tin of tea they received preferential treatment at the brothels of Munich).'[34]

Sooner or later, large numbers of Australians were sent northeast into Military District VIII, in Silesia, where there was strong demand for POW labour. The main *Stalags* in the district were VIII A Görlitz and VIII B Lamsdorf, later Stalag 344. Lamsdorf was to become the biggest 'British' camp in the Reich, with nearly 20,000 POWs, well ahead of the second largest, Wolfsberg, with just over 10,000.[35] It also had a very large Soviet compound. Trying though conditions were in Lamsdorf's *'Britenlager'*, they were nothing compared with the notorious *'Russenlager'*, from which in time thousands of prisoners were dispatched to nearby Auschwitz, where few lived beyond a month.[36]

Indeed Lamsdorf, which today goes by its Polish name Łambinowice, was an ugly place with an ugly history well before World War II. Its military use can be traced back to Prussian times, when it was established as an artillery range. As early as the

Franco–Prussian war it was used for holding French POWs; decades later, in the First World War, it served the same purpose, taking prisoners of many nations. Records show that 83 Englishmen died there. The re-established camp took its first prisoner of the Second World War, a hapless Pole, on 3 September 1939. Many thousands more were to follow. By the time evacuations began in 1945, there were some 51,000 souls, overwhelmingly British and Soviet, behind its barbed wire.[37]

As for the Australians, Red Cross records through 1942 and 1943 show that the number of Australians in VIII B hovered just under the 900 mark but then jumped as high as 1593 at the end of October 1943.[38] And the Red Cross inspectors noted in September 1942 that these Australians had some reason to be unhappy – they had received neither letters nor individual parcels from home for many months.[39] After the re-designation as Stalag 344, there was still much to bemoan. Happily, the entertainment offerings in this large camp were impressive, especially in theatre and sport. For some precious hours, at least, the men's minds could be drawn away from their grumbling stomachs and crowded huts.[40]

Close to a thousand Australians, both NCOs and other ranks, were sent to Military District XIII in mid-August 1941. There they found that Stalag XIII C Hammelburg was a vast improvement on Salonika. When an American official toured the camp in early September, he was able to gain a frank assessment from the Australian Man of Confidence, William Brown of Perth, who reassured him that the treatment there was 'splendid' after Greece, even if the men still needed decent clothing and blankets.[41]

Oflags were smaller affairs than the *Stalags*, designed to cater for about 1000 officers, offering the kinds of comfort to which their caste was accustomed. That could include up to seven orderlies, depending on the rank and nationality of the officers in question.[42] This separation of officers from the rank and file was entirely in accordance with the Geneva Convention and with the practices adopted in other belligerent countries, including Australia. The *Oflags* observed the same numbering system as the *Stalags*. The only difference was that there were *Oflags* which were attached administratively to a *Stalag*; their label was thus identical to that of the *Stalag* with the addition of either *Zweiglager Oflag* or *Teillager Oflag* (annex *Oflag*).

Typically the officers were separated from the other ranks soon after capture and from then had virtually no contact with their men until their liberation. The exceptions were the non-medical orderlies who remained with the officers, functioning essentially as personal servants or batmen. They commonly considered life in an *Oflag* catering to the wishes of an officer preferable to life in a *Stalag* or, almost inevitably for the other ranks, labouring on a work detachment. Of course, if they happened to find themselves at the beck and call of an overbearing tyrant, they might well have had second thoughts.

Though generally better treated than the other ranks, the officers could not expect kid gloves. After weeks in the lice-ridden discomfort of Salonika many were not spared a taxing journey to the very furthest northern part of Germany, to Lübeck. Ian Campbell, who had offered his surrender at Retimo on Crete, was one of those who finally got to his destination – Oflag X C – on 29 July 1941. At that time the Battle of Britain was still raging, and it was not at all clear to the OKW whether it would need to offer long-term accommodation to British officers. When it was clear that Britain would neither be invaded nor brought to the negotiating table, the OKW set about concentrating British officers in dedicated British *Oflags*. So in October Campbell and others in Lübeck were packed off south to Oflag VI B Warburg near Kassel in Westphalia, which became a major *Oflag* for British officers. By early 1942 even Warburg was considered too small, and Campbell was among those sent from there to Oflag IXA Spangenberg to ease the strain.[43]

Other early destinations for officers were in the very south of Germany. One was Oflag VII C Laufen in Bavaria, and the other, in the south-western corner of the Reich, was Oflag V B Biberach. It consisted of a series of one-storey brick huts, with inside latrines and running water, and was located on a plateau blessed with pleasant views.[44] Initially used to house French POWs, it accepted the first British POWs in June 1941, and by the middle of the following month counted 56 Australians among its numbers. Most of the men had been sent there directly from Salonika, although 13 of the Australians had spent time at Oflag X C.[45] Despite some early signs of overcrowding noted by an inspector just a few weeks after its establishment, Oflag V B was not a bad camp. Moreover, it provided an almost irresistible enticement – aspiring escapers contemplated the manageable distance of just 60 kilometres to neutral Switzerland.[46]

That temptation was removed in due course. By late 1941 large numbers of British, including Australian, officers from Biberach and elsewhere were concentrated at the Warburg camp, formerly the home of civilian workers. Wherever they came from, the officers arriving at Warburg were in for an unpleasant surprise, as the camp was overcrowded, rat-infested and flea-ridden. The Red Cross agreed. This, its delegates chided, was 'the worst camp we have seen in Germany'.[47] The 1000 officers, they recommended, should be sent elsewhere.

The Germans had other plans, expanding and improving the camp over the following months. Yet it never afforded the kind of comfort that might have persuaded the men to resign themselves to serving out the war there, and it was from Warburg, as we shall see, that one of the famed British escape bids was launched. Thereafter Warburg was closed, its prisoners dispersed among the *Oflags* at Spangenberg, Rotenburg in central Germany and at Schubin in distant Poland. The biggest contingent, comprising mainly younger and more junior officers, made their home at Eichstätt in Bavaria. This was an altogether more satisfactory arrangement than dreary Warburg. Consisting of old cavalry barracks, Eichstätt was blessed with spectacular mountainous surroundings and boasted among its facilities two makeshift tennis courts.[48] By the last year of the war it was Eichstätt which had the largest population of Australian officers, with over a hundred. By then the second-largest population – with 38 just a third of those in Eichstätt – was at Oflag V A Weinsberg.[49]

CAPTIVITY

*

THAT NCOs WERE to be treated differently from both officers and other ranks was enshrined in the Geneva Convention. The biggest difference concerned work. Officers could not be obliged to work, whereas the other ranks had little choice and typically were shunted off to work detachments after allocation to their *Stalag*. NCOs, however, could not be obliged to work, though they could be requested to perform supervisory duties. To relieve the boredom of POW life they could, however, consent to work, and it was an option which some embraced for the sake of their sanity.

German authorities were at first reluctant to acknowledge that they could not force the NCOs to work, with the result that they were commonly sent out to work detachments along with the other ranks whether they wanted to be or not. In time those who did not want it became aware of their rights; there was nothing ambiguous about the Geneva Convention. The grudging German response was to allocate the non-working NCOs to particular camps where, indeed, they did not have to work. One was Stalag XX A at Thorn in Poland, situated in an old fortress with a dry moat. But the best known, and indeed possibly the best, of the NCOs' camps was in Bavaria in the south. It was Stalag 383 Hohenfels, and it became home to about 500 Australians, some of whom were relocated there from Thorn. Hohenfels had been set up originally for officers, so the NCOs were pleased to find accommodation and facilities befitting their superiors. One of them gushed that Hohenfels

> . . . must be the best camp in Germany. We have extensive playing fields, theatres, even dance rooms, educational classes on every subject under the sun, our own internal newspaper and many little conveniences . . . The Germans leave us pretty much to ourselves and but for searches which are caused through the activities of the 'Moles' we would only see the enemy on morning check parade. We've even got a swimming pool 22 yards long with its [water] Polo Club. We are free to do anything we like inside the barbed wire and there is plenty of room to do it in.[50]

THOUGH ANSWERABLE ULTIMATELY to the OKW, the Kriegsmarine looked after its own POWs. For the Australians, as we have seen, that meant not only men serving with the Royal Navy who fell into German hands, but also merchant sailors. And as we have seen also, the first of those when taken into the Reich were housed at Stalag X B at Sandbostel outside Bremen. But by 1942 the Kriegsmarine had established its own dedicated facility at Westertimke, on the featureless sandy plains between the Weser and the Elbe. This was known as Marlag-Milag Nord. Clumsy though it was, the title indicated that it was both a *Marlag*, that is a *Marine-Lager* for naval seamen, and a *Milag*, that is a *Marine-Internierten-Lager* for merchant seamen.[51] The Marlag and the Milag were physically quite separate from each other, albeit within the same complex, and there was only limited contact between them.

There were never large numbers of Australians there, but they were to be found in both the Marlag and Milag. A report from November 1941 put the number of Australian merchant seamen at 26, while the number of naval personnel at that time was 19.[52]

The Marlag had all the trappings of any other POW camp, including high barbed-wire perimeter fences and sentry boxes from which guards kept an eagle eye on the two compounds. The larger compound – sometimes known as Marlag 'O' – accommodated petty officers and leading seamen, while the other – Marlag 'M' – contained a smaller and more elite group of officers and orderlies.[53] There were never more than about 1300 prisoners all up in the Marlag. The number jumped after Italy's capitulation, but it remained at manageable levels. In any case, sending the ratings off to work camps acted as a pressure valve. Order and discipline were maintained effectively. One of the British captains held there observed that the Marlag 'was run as a ship'. The rooms were regularly cleaned and everything scrubbed down.[54] The passion for cleanliness extended to the men. Each week a batch of officers and ratings were taken about a kilometre from the camp to a bathhouse for a warm shower.[55]

Security was tight and enthusiastically enforced by one of the German officers, Lieutenant Güssefeld, who had an excellent command of English thanks to a stint as a journalist in the United States. Nonetheless his command of the language fell short of perfection, as he demonstrated on one notable occasion after a thorough but fruitless search of the barracks. He mocked a group of grinning officers, 'So! You think I know fucking nothing. Well, let me tell you, I know fuck all!'[56]

The Milag was larger and came to house some 3000 Merchant Navy personnel of all ranks, from captains of merchant vessels through to stokers and even some passengers. Those gathered in the Milag formed a polyglot community, including citizens of states in all corners of the globe who just happened to find themselves on the wrong vessel at the wrong time.

CIVILIANS WERE NOT prisoners of war in any technical sense, of course, and yet they, too, could find themselves detained if considered a security risk. That applied to Australians living in Germany just as it did to Germans living in Australia. On both sides there were stories to be told of injustice and ill-treatment, and of lives ruptured by the onset and travails of war.

There were Australian civilians in Germany when war broke out. At that time there was no such thing as an Australian citizen in a technical sense: Australians were regarded as British subjects and treated as such. Some had good reason to get out sooner rather than later. Famously the Queensland-born aviator–spy Sidney Cotton was one of them. After clandestinely photographing some of the Reich's military installations, Cotton made good his departure with the last civilian aircraft to leave Berlin before the outbreak of hostilities.[57]

Others could make their exit in hurried yet less dramatic circumstances. In the first week of the war some 1610 British subjects departed the Reich. Records show that five Australians were among those granted exit permits by the Reich government.[58] In the first two months of the war only a few hundred British subjects were interned, overwhelmingly men of military age. Whether married or single, they found themselves in an internment camp at Wülzburg. This was Internierungslager, or Ilag, XIII A.[59]

In those early weeks of the war it was not at all clear how the internees would be treated. Unlike for POWs, in 1939 there was no accepted international convention dedicated to civilians, though a draft of an international agreement comparable to the Geneva Convention on the Treatment of POWs had been approved by the Fifteenth International Conference of Red Cross Societies in Tokyo in 1934. Alas, a conference scheduled for 1940 to formalise those terms never took place. Instead, the International Red Cross Committee invited the belligerents either to accept the draft convention or to use the terms of the Geneva Convention on the Treatment of POWs as the basis for the treatment of civilians as well. The government of the Reich opted for the latter.[60]

If the internment of British women was rare, it was also very revealing, in part because it involved Australians, and in part also because it showed that here, too, the principle of reciprocity was at least as important as any legal convention. When the German authorities gained wind that seven women with German citizenship had been locked up unceremoniously in Sydney's Long Bay jail, they looked for an identical number of Australian women in Germany to treat in the same way. They soon found them. Among the first to be arrested were a couple of holiday-makers, Alma Graf and Angelina Gomm, who were seized by plain-clothes policemen and detained in a police station at Berlin's Alexanderplatz. It was made clear to them that their fate rested very heavily on whether the Australian government gave the word for the release of the German internees in Sydney. The arrest was not without some potential embarrassment for the German authorities, as the Australians carried with them a letter of recommendation from a Nazi official in Melbourne, a certain Mr Wildermuth, which was extracted from the women and destroyed. A more public form of embarrassment might have arisen from the arrest of Mrs Anne Carter, who was visiting her daughter in Hamburg when she was arrested. Her son-in-law soon engaged a local law firm in the hope of a quick release, but to no avail.[61]

It might all have been quite different in Germany if things had developed differently in the Antipodes. According to the

German Foreign Office, in 1942 there were 29 German women and nine children being interned in Australia. There were 47 Australian women in the Reich, of whom only four were interned. The possibility that each side might simply repatriate the other's women internees was raised, of course, but the German women in Australia would not consider an unconditional repatriation – they would only go if their interned husbands or sons accompanied them.[62] So it was that they served out most of the war in the internment camp at Tatura, where a compound was dedicated to Germans sympathetic to Hitler's Reich, while the Australians stayed put in the Reich.

In one variation of this diplomatic to and fro, the German cause might have been better served if the woman in question was paraded before the public rather than locked away. That was the case of an Adelaide woman by the name of Hester Burden, who was eager to present her fascist bona fides to her hosts. She wrote that even before leaving Australia she had spent more than six years as a member of the 'Fascist Union of Australia'; moreover, she had joined similar organisations in Britain and Greece since making her way to Europe. But now she wanted to marry a German and devote herself fully to the Greater German Reich, for which she was prepared to do propaganda work if required. If not, such was her desire to avoid deportation that she declared her preparedness to spend the rest of the war in police custody in Graz. In short, she was prepared to do anything 'to do her duty as a German woman'. Far from seeking permission to leave the Reich, she was begging the authorities to allow her to stay.[63]

Less politically passionate was the Western Australian soprano Lorna Sidney-Smith, who had just commenced a season at the Berlin Opera, to which she had been appointed by none other than Hermann Göring. When war broke out, she tried to make her way over the border into Hungary but was turned back. Numerous efforts to secure her release were in vain – she was to take her place among the Australian internees. By March 1940 word came through that the Australians had released the German women in Sydney, but even then Miss Sidney-Smith remained in internment in Vienna. The authorities were not entirely persuaded by the Australian assurances, apparently because the released women in Australia had declined repatriation. By the time Miss Sidney-Smith was told she could leave the country, in July 1940, her circumstances had changed – she too now wanted to marry a German. Internment had not quite had the consequences the Germans had intended.[64]

The *Ilag* for men at Wülzburg had little to recommend it. Consisting of a dilapidated castle, it was overcrowded, but things improved for the internees when many were transferred to a new camp at Tost near Gleiwitz in Silesia in late 1940.[65] Here by September 1941 there were 24 Australians.[66] The most famous of their fellow internees, as an American inspector noted on a visit to Tost in November 1940, was P.G. Wodehouse.[67] Any qualms they might have had about being housed in a former lunatic asylum were doused by the recognition that the facilities were fundamentally sound. They were sound, at least, until Tost, too, became hopelessly overcrowded. In response yet another *Ilag* was opened up in April 1942, this time in Kreuzberg in Silesia. Kreuzberg held some 300 British subjects including, interestingly, all British civilian Jews. They served out most of the war there until January 1945, when they were shifted away from the approaching Red Army to Ilag XVIII at Spittal in Austria.[68]

The other major camp for British subjects was Ilag VII H Laufen, a castle dating back to medieval times which became home to some 450 British subjects, most of them from the Channel Islands, now under German occupation. At Liebenau in Germany's deep south, there was a smaller camp for women and children from October 1940. The internees had been living in Germany or Poland. The inspector sent by the Protecting Power a year later noted five Australian women still at the camp, the Canadian and South African women having already been released into the community.[69] It was something of a model camp, even when its numbers more than doubled to 320 when some 200 British women were transferred from Holland a year later.[70]

There was an *Ilag* for British subjects at Biberach, too, founded in September 1942 when the *Oflag* was shut down, but apparently without Australians. It had a big contingent of Channel Islanders, causing it to become overcrowded. At least the arrival of Red Cross parcels meant that the unfortunates condemned to this camp were adequately fed.[71] With their stomachs full, the boredom of life devoid of work and diversion sat heavily on them; most found no relief for close to the full duration of the war.

When German forces entered neighbouring countries such as France and Denmark, small numbers of Australian civilians were deposited in internment camps there too. At Store Grundet near Velje in Denmark, for example, the Protecting Power's inspector in October 1941 noted among the forty British subjects five Canadian, three South African and three Australian nationals.[72] In France there were camps with significant numbers of British internees at St Denis and Vittel.[73]

Last but by no means least in the world of the camps were the doctors and medical orderlies. They inhabited a kind of twilight world, neither POWs in any strict sense, but not civilians either. If the Geneva Convention were followed to the letter, they should technically have been released after capture. But an agreement struck between Britain and Germany entitled both to hold an appropriate number of medical personnel to care for their countrymen.

In one crucial sense their circumstances differed from those of their fighting brothers. Medical staff were not necessarily accommodated among men of the same nationality – indeed, Australians might find themselves performing medical duties alongside doctors of a variety of nationalities. As for the Western Australian Leslie Le Souef, captured on Crete and exposed for longer than he could have wished to the tribulations of Salonika, he served in a number of medical facilities in the Reich, working tirelessly to save lives and to lend succour to men of many nations. For a time he was in a dedicated medical facility in Elsterhorst in Military District IV, where he became Senior British Medical Officer. But he also served in a number of *Oflags* and *Stalags*, where he proved to be a firm and fearless advocate of the rights of his patients.

11

Göring's Empire

The larger-than-life Nazi Air Minister and jack-of-all-trades Hermann Göring insisted that airmen who became POWs were his responsibility. In this sense the Luftwaffe was treated like the Kriegsmarine, but while the navy built its modest establishment for POWs at Westertimke, Göring built a veritable empire. His Luftwaffe controlled a network of camps which it jealously guarded as its own territory – at least for as long as it could.

The centrepiece of Göring's POW empire was a facility established near Frankfurt in the modest Hessian town of Oberursel. It is commonly referred to as Dulag Luft, as it was a *Durchgangslager*, a transit camp, for airmen on the sometimes tortuous route from capture to one of the *Stalags* run by the Luftwaffe. But in fact what is commonly referred to simply as Dulag Luft was not just one but two facilities. It was a transit camp offering POWs short-term accommodation before allocation to a *Stalag*, but it was also an Intelligence Assessment Centre, the so-called Auswertestelle West. The function of the Intelligence Assessment Centre was to assemble and assess intelligence gained both from enemy airmen who fell into German hands – primarily through interrogation – and also from the crashed or force-landed aircraft, which were meticulously scoured for their equipment and any documents they might contain.

The forensic examination of the aircraft and their singed contents gave up much valuable information, yet it is for the interrogation of the airmen that Oberursel is best known. It was a widely shared experience. Over the course of the war at least 25,000 Allied airmen, including an unknown number of Australians – were subjected to questioning there.[1]

It was only after the outbreak of war that the site acquired by Nazi Party interests in Oberursel was made over to military uses. At first the intention was to house and interrogate captured army officers there, but in time the Luftwaffe's unexpected need to deal with British airmen gained the ascendancy.[2] That need reached the point of urgency over the summer of 1940, the summer of the Battle of Britain, during which the RAF became increasingly determined to answer the German bombing of British targets with regular sorties over Germany. Nonetheless in those early months of the war the German treatment of British airmen – especially the officers – was archaically chivalrous, as inspection reports reveal. Apart from comfortable accommodation, one of the early liberties granted some was the freedom to leave the camp on parole. After one visit the American inspector complained that he had been unable to speak to the British Man of Confidence, who apparently had absented himself from the camp for a spot of skiing. Another inspector noted that when prisoners returned from such excursions 'the Commandant usually meets them with a bottle of cognac!'[3]

With the appointment of a new commandant, Erich Killinger, and a turn in the Reich's military fortunes at the end of 1941, the tone at Oberursel began to change. Killinger had been shaped in the 'hard but fair' mould. Like many commandants of POW camps, he was a veteran of the Great War, indeed he had been a prisoner of war of the Russians, before escaping and fleeing east via Siberia to China, Japan and the US before returning to Germany.[4] A former pilot himself, he knew something of the mentality of his captives. He also supervised a rapid expansion of Dulag Luft's capacity to cope with growing numbers of airmen passing through. That meant the construction of more cells but also the employment of more interrogators. Under his rule Oberursel came to consist of some fourteen buildings, the largest in a U shape and containing some 150 solitary cells. This was colloquially known as 'The Cooler' and was the provisional home of thousands of Western Allied airmen whose ill-fated flights had commenced in the UK, Africa or Italy. Soviet airmen were sent to another facility.[5]

With the transit section – the *Dulag* – bursting at its seams, it was separated from the intelligence gathering section in September 1943. The latter stayed at Oberursel, but the *Dulag* was shifted to the city of Frankfurt and installed near the Palm Garden, a short distance from the main railway station.[6] In international law this was a dubious step, because it placed the POWs in an area subject to bombing. The British government registered its objection through the Protecting Power – by now Switzerland – but to no avail.[7]

If Göring thought these 'human shields' would protect Frankfurt from Allied raids, he was sadly mistaken. Frankfurt was pounded in an air raid, and Dulag Luft became collateral damage. As it happens, one of the POWs who witnessed the raid from inside the camp was the Australian Ron Zwar. One of the blasts knocked him off his feet as he watched it through a hut window. When he got back up he sought refuge in the open and displayed a remarkable presence of mind in recognising the opportunity which the raid offered. Apart from heavy explosives, the RAF was dropping small incendiaries, some of which he saw after they had fallen inside the camp. He grabbed a shovel to lift one of them and place it next to one of the pine camp perimeter posts in the hope of burning it down and bringing its barbed wire down with it; he lobbed a second incendiary towards a guard. His actions did not bring about his escape, but on the following morning he and his fellow POWs could at least observe from inside their camp the damage done by the bombs which had hit their industrial targets the previous night.[8]

Then on the night of 22 to 23 March 1944 a massive raid on Frankfurt totally destroyed the *Dulag*. It was something of a minor miracle that only two POWs lost their lives.[9] In quick time a new facility was constructed in Wetzlar, some 50 kilometres north of Frankfurt.[10] There it remained until the end of the war, though the POWs themselves, as ever, only remained in Dulag Luft as long as it took to be packed off to one of the permanent *Stalag Luft* facilities further to the east, usually within a month.[11]

While the *Dulag* shifted twice, interrogation always took place at Oberursel. One part of Oberursel, the Captured Materials Evaluation Section (Beute- und Nachrichtenauswertung), was responsible for the forensic examination of any material or documents that had been gathered from crashed or force-landed Allied aircraft. The information was recorded in a complex but efficient index card system and then made available to the interrogators working in the nearby interrogation facility. Many are the accounts by captured POWs revealing their astonishment at the facts presented to them by their interrogators, and in truth the assessment facility was a richer source of intelligence than the interrogation centre ever was.[12]

In the postwar popular imagination the 'Master Interrogator' at Oberursel was a certain Hanns Joachim Scharff. In 1978 a hagiographic biography of Scharff was published, feeding a cultural appetite during the Cold War for German characters of honourable repute.[13] In reality Scharff was just one of many interrogators at Oberursel. By November 1944 there was a staff of about 160, of whom about 55 were officers performing interrogations.[14] These men were generally well educated, often had specialist technical knowledge, especially concerning aircraft types, and had excellent English language skills. Those skills may well have been gained during prolonged stays in English-speaking countries in the interwar period.[15] Scharff himself, for example, had lived for eleven years in South Africa.[16]

For captured airmen the interrogation was just the most intimidating phase of a gruelling process. Efforts to extract intelligence began from the moment of capture. Prisoners were taken to Oberursel as soon as feasible, typically by train to Frankfurt and then tram. Written documents were to be removed from the prisoner at the location of capture, placed in bags and also forwarded to Oberursel with the guards. Badly wounded airmen were delivered to the Luftwaffe's hospital at Hohemark, where they remained in single rooms until fit to be interrogated.[17]

At Oberursel the men undressed and any further possessions – such as their escape kits – were removed and registered; a receipt was issued to the prisoner for all clothing and personal possessions, but watches were treated as military equipment and confiscated, while currency was sent to a central currency office in Berlin. The men were photographed, both in portrait and in profile, and together with their fingerprints the photographs were attached to an identity card (*Personalkarte*), along with other information about the prisoner. After treatment with a delousing agent, the men were then placed in single cells.

The Australian Calton Younger recalls how stark and uninviting these isolation rooms were, engendering a sense of utter blankness: 'There were none of the traditional bugs to tame, not even nails in the door to count.'[18] Exceptionally, for a time in the summer of 1944 men were placed in shared rooms in the 'snake pit', so named, as one of its American denizens gloomily recalled, 'because of its nightmarish aspects. It was extremely dirty and smelly; the guards were vicious and treated everyone as a snake. Life within these walls was a veritable hell.'[19]

The next step was a preliminary interview, carried out by the reception officer and interpreters. The officer would hand the prisoner's identity card and a survey form to a colleague, who would accompany the prisoner to a cell and seek to persuade him to fill in the form, which was allegedly from the Red Cross. Indeed, until the autumn of 1943 these forms were adorned with the letterhead and logo of the Red Cross.[20] The purpose, so the prisoner was informed, was merely to let the Protecting Power and, above all, the relatives know his whereabouts. By the terms of the Geneva Convention the prisoner was obliged to give just his name, rank and service number, but these forms extended to a series of questions about both military and civilian experiences.[21] Many fell for this trick, at least until 1944, from which time airmen were better informed about the kind of ruses they might encounter in captivity.[22]

CAPTIVITY

The faux Red Cross forms filled a second function as well. Depending on the prisoner's response to filling one in, the reception officer would assemble a crude psychological profile, assessing whether the captive was likely to be a helpful interviewee. That early profile might well determine how much effort would be invested in contact with the prisoner. When large numbers of airmen were flowing through Oberursel, it was useful to know early on who were most likely to spill some beans. If the preliminary interview suggested that the prisoner was the talkative type, then that prisoner was likely to have a longer stay at the interrogation centre than his taciturn comrades.[23]

After the preliminary interview, the prisoners were guided to cells where they would await interrogation proper. In their size, in their appearance, and in the meagre sustenance offered their inhabitants, these spaces were clearly designed to dispel any desire for a lengthy stay. Fed minimal rations and placed in putrid and grimy lodgings, the prisoner could only wish to put the interrogation centre behind him as quickly as possible. That, too, the Germans hoped, was an invitation to loquacity.[24]

The next stage was interrogation itself. One officer was ideally suited to conducting interrogations with Australians, and indeed may have been responsible for a good number of them. That was Lieutenant Otto-Walter Recknagel, who had been born in Denver, Colorado, in 1893 and who had spent a good part of his youth in New Zealand, South Africa and Britain. In Oberursel he acted as a reception officer but also carried out interrogations.[25] Geoff Taylor was interrogated by an officer who could identify Taylor's Australian accent. The German knew the accent, he said, because 'I was out there myself before the war. A lovely climate, isn't it?' The German was clearly something of a linguistic prodigy, since he had the language of a British airman down pat. 'Everything was spot-on, gen, clued-up, bang-on, wizard or ropey. Listening to him I could have been yarning with the flight-commander of an RAF squadron discussing mutual acquaintances at my last station.'[26]

In good part the sorts of strategies that Recknagel and others used at Oberursel to extract intelligence derived from a sophisticated combination of deception, keen psychological insight and cunning. Yet a first approach was often a very simple one, and involved introducing the prisoner to a calm and pleasant atmosphere. A German guide to interrogation gives some insight into how such an approach would work in practice: 'The contrast between the bareness of his single cell and the agreeable cleanliness and friendliness of the interrogation room is helpful. It is well lit, often decorated with flowers, familiar maps are hanging on the wall, as well as pictures of familiar aircraft types, and long-denied cigarettes lie enticingly within easy reach.'[27]

This welcoming atmosphere was complemented by a congenial host, who typically eschewed military formalities. According to one British report, if through force of habit the prisoner saluted the interrogating officer before him, 'This salute was seldom returned, and was usually acknowledged by a friendly smile and *Won't you sit down?*'[28] Thereafter the officer's apparently easy command of English would further set the prisoner at ease, subtly persuading him that the cordial and debonair gentleman seated opposite him could hardly be the barbaric Teuton he had expected. Such geniality could ideally not only elicit the answers to direct questions but even induce the prisoner to offer information not requested.[29]

Many POWs recall the disarming effect of their interrogators confronting them with a surprisingly sophisticated range of knowledge about them and their mission. So efficiently did the German index card system function that the prisoner might be confronted with complete dossiers about his civilian and military career, his unit, the sorties flown and the names of his comrades. Just how this apparent minor intelligence miracle was achieved was revealed at a postwar military tribunal, where a certain Lieutenant Bauer-Schlichtegroll described the process thus:

> The interrogator took the [reception] sheet, which had a number in accordance [. . .] with the crash, and went to the casualty recording department where all these crash numbers and the crews belonging to them were put down on a list or a card index, and he would find out whether [. . .] other prisoners belonged to this [. . .] and asked whether the department had got

any other information [. . .]. Then he went to the department of evaluation of documents, gave the crash number and asked [. . .] for documents which might be of use. He might find a wallet, a target map. [. . .] Then the interrogator went to the intelligence room where the information from the various interrogators and evaluators of documents was coordinated. Pinned on the wall were various sheets giving the crews that had been participating in various attacks, and there were also maps showing the various methods of attack which had been used on recent targets. Files containing the interrogation and evaluation reports lay on the table. Next he might go to the squadron history department and get the files containing information about the squadron he suspected the prisoner belonged to. These [. . .] histories contained [. . .] details such as the names of the commanders, incidents [. . .], photographs [. . .], a list of members shot down and those still active in the Service, and so on.[30]

Temporarily stunned by the interrogator's revelations and apparent omniscience, the captive might have been misled into divulging what might to him have seemed much less impressive fragments of information. Ron Zwar was one of the Australians taken aback in this way. By the time he was presented for interrogation, the Germans already knew what squadron he was from, where exactly he had lived in Australia and even his mother's name. Nonetheless, they wanted still more, and to that end adopted a couple of widely used ploys.

One was the gambit with the Red Cross form, though this was one Zwar readily countered, as he could inform his interrogator that his registration as a POW had already been carried out during his detention in hospital. The other was to ease the captive into a state of relaxation, creating the circumstances in which the casual transfer of titbits of information might occur, a step heralded in this instance by the offering of cigarettes.

If such strategies failed – as they did miserably in Zwar's case – then means might be employed to unsettle the prisoner, undermining expectations and appearing to redefine the relationship of captor and captive. A more aggressive demeanour, for example, which might involve shouting at the prisoner to break him down and intimidate him into cooperation, might swiftly follow a failed friendly approach. Yet in doing so it was recognised that the interrogating officer must never be seen to lose his self-control, which would hand the psychological advantage back to the captive. Even signs of tiredness or a tremulous voice might undermine all hope of a breakthrough.[31] The best interrogators, as the staff in Oberursel well knew, were not violent Nazis but rather 'native Germans of comparatively liberal background who had spent part of their lives in England or America'.[32]

Over time the intimidation strategy became more widely used as the Germans noted that the Allied airmen – with the benefit of better training – had grown immune to affability. The interrogators had to work harder and longer and resort to new techniques.[33] Some of them were designed to force compliance through breeding fear. One well-known source of fear was the Gestapo, and the German interrogators did resort to threatening recalcitrant prisoners with delivery to the Gestapo, whose notoriety had spread far beyond the borders of the Reich and who, from early 1944, had a permanent presence at Oberursel.[34]

Usually this was bluff, but there were occasions when the bluff was called and the prisoner was passed on to the SD, the Security Service, which, like the Gestapo, was part of Heinrich Himmler's massive police and security empire.[35] In rare instances – and it is unclear whether at any point Australians were involved – Dulag Luft prisoners were delivered to the Gestapo. In the latter stages of the war, and especially after Himmler took on overall responsibility for POW matters, the chances of the involvement of security forces were greater, even if Göring's Luftwaffe did not welcome the incursion. Indeed, it seems that the Luftwaffe's interrogation officers treated the interlopers with disdain, secretly deriding their poor language skills and disinclined to share with them any information they had already gleaned. Indeed, after the war Allied investigators concluded that the Luftwaffe's commandant at Oberursel 'put all possible obstacles in the way of prisoners going to the notorious Shelter (the popular name for the Gestapo building at Auswertestelle

West), and this non-cooperation extended to passing on prisoners in whom the Gestapo would be interested before [they] had a chance to know of their arrival.'[36]

If a prisoner did nonetheless find himself in the hands of the Gestapo, two options presented themselves. One was that he would be murdered; the other was that, having divulged information under duress, he was returned to the interrogation centre, where a Luftwaffe officer would offer an apology and maintain that such treatment would never have occurred in the custody of the Luftwaffe.[37] Yet Luftwaffe officers themselves had little compunction in threatening their prisoners that a failure to answer questions would be interpreted as evidence of espionage or sabotage, the punishment for which was commonly execution.[38]

One strategy to which some of the Luftwaffe officers themselves stooped was to overheat the cells in which the airmen were held in order to 'soften' them for interrogation. After the war investigations were held into allegations to this effect made by a number of RAF airmen.[39] As a result, some of the interrogators soon found the boot placed on the other foot – they were hauled before a military tribunal and forced to explain their behaviour in the so-called 'heating affair'.[40] The court heard of a number of cases of the use of overheating to entice a timely response to the interrogator's questions during the year 1943. One witness, a British pilot by the name of Victor Bain, recalled:

> I asked him [ie the interrogator] to turn the heat off. He asked if I had filled in the form. I said that I had filled in all that was necessary but that that had nothing to do with it. [. . .] He repeated, 'The heating system has gone wrong. If you fill in my form I will see that you are transferred to another cell.' Having seen the switch turned off earlier in the day I knew this to be a lie [. . .]. I am afraid I lost my temper and I shouted at him, 'If you don't get out of here I'll punch your bloody head.' He withdrew quickly and locked the door.[41]

The Australian Jack Liley was not a witness at the trial, but he was subjected to the heating ploy. His Wellington had been shot out of the sky over North Africa in April 1943. After Liley's capture he was delivered across the Mediterranean and Italy, and finally to Oberursel. After stubbornly resisting the deception with the bogus Red Cross form, he noticed his single cell becoming very hot, prompting him to remove his clothes down to his underpants. In another room he heard a fellow prisoner beating on the door and begging to be let out because it was so hot. Only later did Liley gather that both of them had been subjected to a form of torture.[42] The Germans attempted one more fruitless interrogation of Liley, but then tacitly admitted defeat in packing him off to Stalag Luft I at Barth.

Henry Bastian, a Hurricane pilot shot down near El Alamein, recalls the opposite problem – his accommodation was too cold. His cell had a steam radiator, but it rarely worked. So severe was the cold that he rang the bell to request a blanket, only to be surprised by the identity of the guard responding to his plea:

> The door flew open, and a big sod with an Aussie accent swept into the room asking rather crossly, what the bloody hell was I making such a fuss about. I said, 'You sound like an Australian.' He said, 'I am, but don't think you will get any favours from me, because you bastards kicked us all out of Australia at the end of the last war.' He had been born here, and the whole family were interned when he was in his early teens. They must have liked the place because he was still very much against us Aussies.[43]

Another Australian airman at Oberursel was John Mathews. His case is a revealing one, because it gives an indication of the gamut of tactics the interrogators employed. Via a jail in Hamburg – by now a city reduced to an 'unutterable mess', Mathews was delivered by train to Oberursel. His accommodation there was a single, spartan cell housing just a bed, and quite devoid of natural light. He recalls spending about ten days there, facing interrogations with an officer who spoke impeccable English. The worst of it was awaiting the initial interrogation; after that conditions were improved, and he felt well prepared to cope with whatever techniques the interrogators might apply. He was determined to remain 'objectively polite' and to offer no more than what the Geneva Convention required, that is, name, rank and service number.

To his astonishment his interrogator, rather than objecting to his captive's reticence, began to provide him with details of the raids over Germany in which he had participated and the names of people in his squadron. Having done his utmost to impress Mathews with the extent of his knowledge, he then guided him into a room containing some of the RAF equipment, requesting advice on how it worked. But Mathews resisted the attempts over a number of days, sometimes being summoned in the morning, sometimes in the afternoon.

Although his interrogator was no doubt disappointed, there were at this stage no recriminations. Rather, the German adopted a different tack when one night a beautiful blonde woman appeared in his cell with a tray of enticing food and a bottle of wine. Mathews was neither surprised at this ploy – it was one of an array of techniques he had been warned of in training – nor tempted to succumb to it; he was especially wary of the wine, which he suspected might have been laced with chemicals. His guest's womanly wiles, too, elicited no information. After a couple of hours she left.

The next day was quite different. The attempt at seduction was replaced by the interrogator's rudeness and then brazen threats. Pointing to the absence of brevets on his prisoner's insignia, the officer accused Mathews of being a spy, the punishment for which was execution. He produced a pistol and pointed it at Mathews' head for some thirty minutes while directing a barrage of accusations at him along with a torrent of abuse in German. The moment the interrogator placed the gun down on the desk Mathews knew that he had won. Unlike the previous day's episode, the gun threat was unexpected and traumatic, but when it was concluded it gave him an extra strength which was to hold him in good stead.

The Jekyll and Hyde charade resumed the next morning, when the interrogator offered a profuse apology, reverting once more to his perfect English as he engaged his captive in wide-ranging small talk. His last gambit was to offer Mathews release if he would only explain how the captured equipment worked, but this time too he drew a blank. He conceded that the Australian had been a tough nut to crack, and then wondered why Mathews was fighting a war in Europe when, after all, Australia was under attack from the Japanese. And then came the greatest surprise of all – he claimed that he himself had been educated at the University of Adelaide. Mathews was so shattered at this news that he says he might finally have divulged information, but that very afternoon he was released from Oberursel. Unfortunately, he never learned his interrogator's name.[44]

FROM THE DULAG LUFT – whether at the time it was in Oberursel, Frankfurt or Wetzlar – the airmen were sent off to the permanent camps for airmen, called *Stalags Luft* to distinguish them from the *Stalags* for soldiers, and each designated with a roman numeral, from I eventually through to VII.

At the beginning of hostilities the Germans could have had little idea of just how many such facilities they would need; it was a system which demanded constant growth and revision in the light of military developments. These Luftwaffe camps were under the supervision of the Supreme Command of the Luftwaffe (OKL), though ultimately, like the OKL itself, they were answerable to the OKW. They contained men of all ranks and, like the camps run directly by the OKW, the POWs were held in separate compounds along national lines. For the Australians, whether they were serving in the RAF or the RAAF, that meant finding themselves in barracks with 'British' POWs who could, for example, be English, Canadian, Polish, Czech or South African. It was the uniform that counted.

The first such camp was installed near the Pomeranian fishing village of Barth. At first it was simply called Stalag Luft, but with the construction of a second such camp in the middle of 1941 it became Stalag Luft I. Its four compounds were well equipped, and there were few complaints from its guests, but it soon needed to be supplemented by other camps. In Henry Bastian's view, Barth was probably the best camp in the country: 'six per room, plenty of showers and flushing toilets, the first that worked since Egypt. The C/O was a von Müller, a very decent type, with impeccable manners, and he had been a lino salesman in England.'[45] The Red Cross inspectors who turned up to pass judgment on Barth in the summer of 1942 could not fault it. It was, they agreed, 'an excellent camp'.[46]

In April 1942 most of Stalag Luft I's prisoners were transferred to Stalag Luft III at Sagan (now Żagań) in Silesia, making Sagan into essentially an officers' camp. As more airmen were captured, still more facilities were constructed, right down to Stalag Luft VII at Bankau, also in Poland. The locations of these camps – in the far east of Germany, or even further east in occupied territory – were a clear sign of the importance the Germans attached to keeping the most feared of their enemies, the airmen, as far as possible from home and a renewed chance of wreaking havoc on the Reich.

Stalag Luft III was the biggest of the camps run by the Luftwaffe. Its notoriety stems neither from its size nor its conditions, which in fact were generally good, but rather from the 'Great Escape' which was launched from there in March 1944, and from the escape's appalling consequences. Located in a pine forest, Stalag Luft III initially had just two compounds accommodating both officers and NCOs, but over time it was to expand substantially.[47] In April 1943 a new north compound was added, largely to deal with the growing numbers of American POWs, and a few months later a south compound followed. The last of the compounds came on line by the middle of 1944, creating a total of six, half of which were dedicated to British personnel, including Australians. The other three compounds held Americans.[48]

Yet even the sprawling Sagan complex did not meet the Reich's growing needs for accommodation for captured airmen. Stalag Luft IV was opened up at Gross Tychow in Pomerania between Danzig and Stettin; its four compounds were designed to accommodate air force NCOs.[49] Stalag Luft VI, which took on large numbers of Australian airmen when NCOs were sent there from Barth and Sagan, was at Heydekrug, a town halfway between Tilsit and Memel in East Prussia. When Stalag Luft VII opened at Bankau, it took new prisoners from Dulag Luft, but it also caught an overflow of RAF NCOs who had spent time at Stalag VII A in Moosburg.[50]

They were not the only airmen to spend time in an OKW camp. Indeed, because of overcrowding issues there were many airmen who spent almost all their captivity in OKW camps. One of those camps with a dedicated RAF compound was Stalag IV C Mühlberg in Saxony. An Australian who arrived there in October 1943 was Geoff Taylor, and his first impressions did not give him great cause for optimism. It was 'an ugly and alien place in this land of farms and crops, and featureless except for the stilted guard-towers along the wire. Maybe the wind was blowing towards us from the direction of the camp but we could certainly smell the place a mile before we reached it. It was not a pleasant smell.'[51]

Coming as he had straight from Dulag Luft, Taylor assumed that some kind of mistake had been made. The barrack to which he was allocated was a menagerie-like mess:

> The brick-floored, barn-like barrack was almost entirely occupied by rickety wooden bunks; bunks that rose in layers almost to the ceiling; bunks on which men crawled, crouched, squatted, stood and sprawled, craning their heads to see if they could recognize friends amongst us newcomers; bunks crowded together in tiers of three and blocks of twelve like grotesque, gloomy burlesques of those structures you see toddlers climbing in playgrounds.[52]

Soon he became aware of the adjoining compound full of army POWs. Separated by nothing more than barbed wire, it was nonetheless a different world. The army men had been prisoners longer, enduring years behind barbed wire as a kind of community of suffering, strengthened by the similarities in its members' experience of capture and captivity. It was, Taylor noted with a tinge of envy, 'a brotherhood born of fighting comradeship in the Libyan desert and Greek campaigns where most of them were captured. They have a democratic, community spirit stronger than ours, which, so far, is mainly apparent only with bomber crews or their close-knit survivors.' The airmen, in contrast, came to Mühlberg at different times and in widely varying circumstances; they cultivated a sense of identity based not on the discipline of the collective but the stubborn insistence on the worth of the individual: 'We are cheerfully disrespectful of the army's parade-ground manners and take a pride in "messing the Jerries around". Ours is a tradition of no tradition.'[53]

The other OKW camp which had a sizeable airmen's compound was the *Stalag* at Lamsdorf. It contained what amounted to an Australian barrack holding 84 Australian airmen.[54] Its origins, according to one of the Australian airmen held there, Raphael Sherman, lay in the Shackling Crisis which commenced in September 1942. Australian airmen were among the 'British' POWs shackled at Lamsdorf, but then they were exempted – the camp authorities told Sherman that as Australian authorities had not followed the British lead in shackling German POWs in Australia, the Australians would be released from their shackles in Lamsdorf.[55] It is a story confirmed in the diary of another prisoner, Raymond Ryan, who wrote in 1943, 'The Germans are unchaining the Australians and have issued us with passes stating we are "nicht zu fesseln" [not to be shackled].'[56]

For their part, the Australians refused to be unchained. Ryan wrote that 'by unanimous vote all the Australians have decided to hand all the non-chained passes back to the Germans and tell them we do not wish for preferential treatment.' They insisted on taking their share of the discomfort and hardship. Eventually the Germans broke the impasse by placing the Australians together in one barrack where no shackles were applied. It was clear to the Australians, Raphael Sherman contended later, that the Germans were trying to drive a wedge between the Dominion and the United Kingdom personnel, but the POWs would have none of it.[57]

12

Comrades Unarmed

The conflict unleashed by Hitler in September 1939 became a genuinely global conflagration, a reality reflected in the composition of the POW population collected in the Reich. The Australians were a tiny segment of a massive multiracial and multicultural world. Moreover, for most official purposes they were not even 'Australians', rather, they were British, and it was with this diverse population of 'Britons' that Australian POWs spent most of their time behind barbed wire.

On 1 January 1945 there were 168,640 'British' POWs in German captivity.[1] Though by this point their situation was deteriorating rapidly, relative to other POW groups they were still in an unusually privileged position. Apart from being in a state of war in which the enemy, too, agreed to respect the conditions of the Geneva Convention, Britain was the only power at war with the Reich from the beginning of hostilities which was neither conquered nor occupied. And even if their numbers were initially small – that changed dramatically later – the British had under their control German civilians and POWs who could function as an effective bargaining chip.

CAPTIVITY

Anglo–German relations on POW matters began on a positive note. Early in the piece Britain and the Reich mutually agreed, for example, to a rapid exchange of information about the identities of each other's captured POWs. In cases of the serious or fatal wounding of POWs, both sides agreed that enquiries would be held and the Protecting Power would be informed.[2] The Reich's dealings with POWs from various parts of the Commonwealth, it was determined, would be conducted for the sake of convenience via London, so that the Foreign Office became the crucial conduit for any negotiations with Australian authorities. But with time those good relations soured and, with the Shackling Crisis, descended into rancour and recrimination. By the last months of the war, as we shall see, outright hostility prevailed, and Hitler counted the British – especially airmen – among the most despised of his enemies.

One of the complicating factors in the relationship between Germany and Britain was that the British POWs were such a diffuse lot. There were those who came from the British Isles, who were English, Welsh, Scottish or Irish. Large numbers of these, something in the region of 40,000, were members of the British Expeditionary Forces taken into captivity during Germany's western offensive in May and June 1940. Most had some five miserable years of captivity ahead of them.[3]

Then there were those who hailed from the so-called Dominions, in principle regarded as autonomous and equal members of the British Empire. At the time of the Second World War the title of 'Dominion' was carried by Great Britain itself and five other countries – Australia, New Zealand, the Irish Free State, Canada and the South African Union. All but Ireland chose to join Britain in declaring war on Germany, though the Canadians needed a week to think about it. In addition there were the many colonies and the mandated territories which made up the remainder of the Empire on which the proverbial sun never set, and which had no choice but to follow their British masters into conflict as so many had a generation earlier, whether they liked it or not.[4]

The largest single contingent came from India – something in the order of 2.5 million men.[5] Altogether the Empire managed to put about 6 million men into the field. Whatever the colour of their skin or the corner of the globe from which they hailed, of the 170,000 or so who were to spend time in German captivity, all were regarded as British. That is not to say, however, that colour and race played no role, as the fate of the Indians neatly illustrates. Although regarded as 'British', in practice they were commonly placed by the Germans in separate compounds. Black Africans too, though from Commonwealth countries, were treated in the same way.

To add an extra level of complexity, there were in addition many men serving in British forces who were neither from Britain nor its Commonwealth. This is true for all branches of the armed services, where Poles, Czechs, Belgians, Dutch, Spaniards and Frenchmen were to be found. The Australian airman Calton Younger even shared a hut with a Uruguayan who had joined the RAF.[6] As far as the Germans were concerned, it was the uniform rather than the country of origin that counted.

For all the variety among the 'British' POWs, it is possible to perceive a quasi-official German view of them, which in a strange way was not so far removed from the view that many of the 'British' had of themselves. While Germans who had adopted a racialised schema for judging their fellow humans grudgingly conceded to the British a status not so far below their own, British POWs were similarly inclined to view themselves among the most gifted of the races. Yet they were not disposed to allocate themselves a rung on the racial ladder anywhere below the Germans, an attitude which seems to have manifested itself in their attitudes and behaviour in POW camps. This at least was the gist of a letter written by the OKW's Department of Prisoner of War Affairs to the German Foreign Office in the middle of 1941. In observing the levels of order and cleanliness in the camps, it was noted that the British camps were distinguished by their low standards when compared with French, Belgian or Polish camps. The British camps indeed were marked by their 'disorder and uncleanliness', a feature particularly evident among younger officers, who practised a tacit opposition to camp authorities, 'apparently on the basis that English pride does not tolerate in any fashion the lifting of a finger in the service of order in the barracks, because the Englishman is very well accustomed throughout the entire world to being served.'[7]

This was a view confirmed by reports that Germany's security agencies collected around the country where civilians came in contact with British POWs. One report from central Germany in August 1943 claimed that British POWs manifested 'an attitude of self-confidence often bordering on arrogance'. Another from Danzig spoke of the impressive physical bearing of the British, their fine state of health and perfect clothing. On the locals they made an even more favourable impression than did the German replacement units being trained there. The British, it was noted, did not hesitate to mock the Reich, its institutions and its leading figures.[8]

Of course, that did not mean that the Australians themselves did not preserve a sense of national identity even when thrown together with other British POWs. There are many instances where a critical mass of Australians permitted the cultivation of a distinctively Australian identity. Laurie West was one of the Australian NCOs in the camp at Hohenfels, where he counted among his friends a couple of Basque commandos captured in Crete. But he saw his fellow Australians as a distinct group who stuck together and preferred not to be labelled 'English'. He recalls that the men of the 2/11th (City of Perth) Infantry Battalion from Western Australia, a battalion captured almost in its entirety after its dogged defence of Retimo, preserved a strong sense of their origins in their two barracks. In particular the Australians distinguished themselves through a combination of mateship and dedicated self-reliance. As for the blokes in his own battalion, the 2/6th Infantry Battalion, they were bushies, physically tough if not imposing, and well equipped to deal with the hardships and vicissitudes of POW life. In contrast the English, many of them taken prisoner earlier than the Australians and commonly as very young men, were less worldly than the Australians and less adaptable to the tribulations of confinement.[9]

The spirit of ANZAC too, invoked in the defence of Greece, omoted close bonds between the Australians and the New

Zealanders who had fought side by side with them before capture. It was a spirit which was preserved in the camps. At Stalag IV B, for example, where there were airmen and soldiers from both sides of the Tasman, Anzac Day was commemorated. Britons, South Africans and Canadians, too, would join the Australians and New Zealanders. After a religious service at the 'Empire Theatre', a parade would take place on the camp's major thoroughfare; Major Whyte of the Royal Army Medical Corps and other officers took the salute.[10]

It was with other British POWs that the Australians were accommodated in the camps, but that does not mean that they were entirely deprived of contact with other POWs. While men of non-Commonwealth nationalities were housed in other compounds, there was fleeting contact through the wire, and in some cases there was more sustained contact in the kitchens or medical facilities. If those who had donned British uniforms to fight the war were themselves a motley bunch, the other nationalities thrown behind barbed wire expanded still further the cultural horizons of the Australians.

As German forces swooped through the Ardennes forest and into France in May 1940, French soldiers were captured en masse. Many had five years of captivity ahead of them. When the armistice was signed, some 150,000 were transported into the Reich to join those already there, pressed into work for the enemy. Most struck a Faustian deal. They resigned themselves to the new arrangements, toiling honestly while accepting France's defeat and subservience. In time there was some modest reward for their gentle compliance – in early 1941 a portion of the French POWs were sent back to France to perform work duties there. Of those who remained in the Reich, some 250,000 were later granted 'favoured status', which meant they were released from captivity and worked alongside German civilians. After a probationary period they were fully released into civilian life. These favours were, however, not made available to professional soldiers or Jews.[11]

When Doug Nix arrived at the *Stalag* at Wolfsberg there was already a well-established French compound there. Even at that early time – the summer of 1941 – his impression was that the French soldiers already had 'a fairly free run of the place', treated more like guest workers than POWs.[12] An Englishman, Christopher Burney, later had the opportunity to observe close at hand French inmates in the Buchenwald concentration camp. True, these men were political prisoners rather than POWs, yet Burney's characterisation of them rings true for the Frenchmen throughout the Reich's camps, men who had entered captivity early, without salvaging much pride during their rapid defeat. In Burney's estimation the French prisoners 'were cowed by the enemy's show of force and had little faith in themselves to make the necessary moral come-back to join us. Perhaps, too, they resented us. They were painfully aware of the depths to which they had fallen, publicly as well as really, and thought that to do anything but patronise us would be beneath their dignity. It was a pity. We had no wish to appear condescending, we only wanted to see a flicker of their real spirit.'[13]

On a similar level to the French in the hierarchy were POWs from Belgium, Holland and Norway. Like the French, they were from countries under German occupation and, also like the French, they could benefit from the visits staged by delegations of the ICRC and the Protecting Powers. Among the Belgians the Walloons and the Flemish POWs were treated differently. The latter were generally allowed to remain in Belgium and, like Dutch and Norwegian POWs, were released from captivity, but the Walloons were transported to the Reich to work as forced labourers.[14]

A rung below the French, Belgians, Dutch and Norwegians were the POWs from south-eastern Europe, most numerously Serbs. An indicator of their place in the system was their work pay – they received only a third of what British POWs received. The Serbs were particularly disadvantaged by the German decision not to allow them the allocation of a Protecting Power. As they were not citizens of a recognised state, so the argument ran, the protection of international law could not extend to them.[15]

The same argument was applied to the Poles, who until Operation *Barbarossa* suffered the unenviable distinction of occupying the lowest rung on the POW ladder. As Poland had been excised from the map of Europe, the Geneva Convention had no place in the treatment of Polish POWs. Indeed, the Poles were treated with barefaced contempt, commonly finding themselves, for example, working in armaments industries, an egregious breach of the Geneva Convention.[16]

Then there were the Italians. When German forces swooped south across the Alps after the signing of an Italian armistice in September 1943, it was not only the Australian and other POWs in Italian camps who were caught in the German net. Next to them were their erstwhile enemies, Italian soldiers, more than 550,000 of whom were seized and transported north. Far from handling their former comrades in arms with kid gloves, German exasperation at Italian military inadequacies and ultimate treachery sparked bitter recriminations. Some 6000 Italians were killed during capture, another 13,000 died during transport to the Reich, and 20,000 perished between their arrival in the Reich and the end of the war in 1945.[17] If the Italians thought in September 1943 that their inglorious war was finally over, they were sadly mistaken. For many the worst of their travails were only just beginning.

Below them in the POW hierarchy were solely the Soviets, millions of them, treated from beginning to end as the lowest of the low. During World War II some 5.5 million Soviet soldiers fell into German hands; of them 3.3 million were murdered or perished.[18] The numbers are staggering and by themselves convey something of the abyss which distinguished their treatment from that of the Australians.

The Germans could seek to justify their ill-treatment of Soviets by pointing to Stalin's failure to ratify the Geneva Convention on the Treatment of Prisoners of War. This was true, although the Soviets had ratified the Geneva Convention on the Treatment of the Wounded. Had that commitment been honoured in the deed then the suffering of many of those captives would have been eased. In reality, wounded and sick Red Army soldiers were either pitilessly left to their fate or actively delivered to it through execution. Moreover, if Geneva were not adhered to, then in international law the default position should have been the Hague Convention of 1907, the terms of which at least guaranteed some level of decency in dealing with POWs. Indeed, on 17 July 1941, less than a month into *Barbarossa*, the Soviet Union offered to follow the terms of the Hague Convention if the Germans did also. In the following month the Soviet government announced that it had established a POW Information Bureau in Moscow in compliance with the Hague Convention.[19]

Hitler was not interested. His response to the Soviet offer was brusque and unambiguous – in light of multiple breaches of international law by the Soviet government since the commencement of hostilities, Germany rejected the Hague Convention in its dealings with the Soviet Union. As for the Geneva Convention on the Treatment of Wounded – which the Soviets *had* signed and ratified – Hitler saw no place for it. His formal rejection of Stalin's offer was disseminated among his own men and outside Germany as well.[20] For his part Stalin soon made it known that no mercy would be shown to the fascist invaders. Neither, for that matter, could Soviet soldiers who fell into German hands – let alone threw in their lot with the other side – expect clemency from the Man of Steel. Soviet soldiers in Stalin's view did not become POWs – they fought to the death to defend their country. As it happened, Stalin's own son Jacob became a POW as early as 16 July 1941. To escape the disgrace of captivity he had himself shot by a German guard on 14 April 1943.[21]

Yet in a war of rapid movement, whatever the determination among commanders and soldiers alike to avoid capture, the large-scale seizure of enemy forces, indeed of entire armies, was a military inevitability. Millions were captured on both sides, and every soldier knew all too well to expect no quarter. Of the more than three million Germans captured by Soviet forces, a third never saw their homeland again; many of the luckier ones did not finally make their way home until a decade after the war.[22]

Most Soviet POWs never made it into the Reich in the first place. Red Army POWs who survived the initial slaughter unleashed by the Commissar Order could not expect much better. Countless thousands were starved to death or died of disease in barbaric provisional camps in the Wehrmacht's operational areas, typically devoid of shelter. The survivors were marched westwards until, as one observer noted, they looked 'more like the skeletons of animals than humans'.[23] Within just six months of the beginning of *Barbarossa* some two million of the Soviet POWs were dead.[24]

If *Barbarossa* had gone as planned, then Hitler's clear preference was to keep the Reich untainted by the presence of Soviet POWs. That they did begin to enter the Reich had much to do with the changing fortunes of the Wehrmacht. By the autumn of 1941 the time of Blitzkrieg was over, and it was adapting to the kind of long and draining affair Hitler had been so keen to avoid. It was turning into a war which would engage the home-front on a scale he feared. Those initial hopes dashed, in late October 1941 Hitler permitted the use of Soviet POW labour in the Reich; by the end of the year contingencies had forced him to abandon his reservations about Soviet labour altogether.[25]

In their camps and on work detachments, Australian POWs witnessed the horrific treatment of the Soviet POWs. In Wolfsberg, for example, Albert Gibb became aware of their presence after his arrival from Salonika. For all the hardship he himself had just suffered, he acknowledged that the Soviets had it far worse. Fortunately he was able to communicate with one of them, who gave them some insight into their travel through Germany, 'without being allowed out of cattle trucks for sanitary purposes, starved, beaten, and of the 1200 on that hell train, a quarter had died on the journey. On the trucks there were signs with wording "These are the Bolsheviks" and "This is what Bolshevism will do to Germany!"'[26]

Frank Cox arrived at Wolfsberg at a similar time and has memories of the Soviets that will not disappear. He too became aware that they had been paraded around Germany for some weeks 'as animals'. 'The sight of these poor people sickens me today, some died as they were unloaded from the trucks, others were stripped of their rags and pushed under showers and collapsed and died where they lay.'[27] Doug Nix describes them as looking like they had been dragged along the road by a truck for 100 miles. Yet the Germans attempted to nip any act of sympathy in the bud, warning him and others, 'You feed them, you're dead.' Nonetheless when an opportunity arose bread was hurled over the fence into the Soviet compound. There the Soviets were left to their fate by their captors, who would lock the gates at night, only to bring out the bodies in carts the next morning.[28]

Similar scenes were played out further south in the *Stalag* at Marburg. Arthur Buxton had arrived there from Greece when a train load of Soviets, clearly distressed from long periods spent in cattle-trucks, reached the camp. 'Many were dead and dying, all very weak from typhus and some had resorted to cannibalism – up to 10 a day died and over 2000 were buried in the first few months – the dead were put in horse carts and pulled by our men.'[29]

Lawrence Calder not only saw Soviet POWs in their compound, he was given the gruesome task of recovering their bodies for burial outside the camp. In some cases he noted that the corpses had been lifeless for a number of days. The Russians would appear in groups of three to receive their meagre daily ration; one of them would take delivery of a pint of potato soup. But one of the group was already dead, his body dragged along to entitle his two undertakers to an increased ration. But after some days the body would have to be dispensed with, and for a time Calder collected onto a cart the Soviets whose usefulness, living or dead, had expired. The cart was pulled by oxen – all the horses were on the eastern front – to a provisional cemetery outside the camp, where the unidentified bodies would be dispatched unceremoniously into a mass grave.[30]

Melbourne-born rear gunner Bert Stobart was one of the airmen taken to the OKW's Stalag IV B Mühlberg, which also had a Soviet compound. From his airmen's compound he could see little of them, yet they made a strong impression on him. He remembers seeing Russians missing arms or legs, hobbling around in a pitiful quest for something to eat. On one occasion the Germans sent in a German shepherd to impose some order in the Soviet compound, but before long the dog's carcass was hanging outside a hut; it had been killed, gutted and turned into a meal.[31]

In the Nazi racial hierarchy, the Soviet 'Slavs' occupied a low rung, but not the lowest. That they were treated so much worse than others categorised as Slavs – such as Poles and Serbs – had as much to do with politics as race. The Soviets bore the awful brunt of the Nazis' virulent anti-Bolshevism. The dubious distinction of occupying the lowest rung on the Nazis' racial ladder was borne by the Jews, who had good reason to be concerned for their fate if seized in battle. The Commissar Order had guaranteed that Jews in the Red Army would be slaughtered soon after capture. Jews in other armies, however, were generally spared the awful fate of the Soviets. Indeed, as a general rule, and with the egregious exception of Soviet Jews, one of the safest places for a Jew to be in the Reich was a POW camp.

There were Jews in the armed forces of the British Commonwealth, the United States, the Soviet Union, Poland, the Free French and Yugoslavia, and of them perhaps 200,000 became POWs. The first to fall into German hands were Poles. Most of them were released from captivity in the war's first winter – the Wehrmacht did not wish to be encumbered with people it no longer regarded as security risks and whom it would have to feed and house indefinitely. But by February 1940 the decision was made no longer to release them but to engage the ones still in captivity as civilian workers, keeping, however, those deemed security risks, and that meant, above all, the officers. Later, after the launch of the Holocaust from the summer of 1941, the SS attempted to seize Polish officers from the Wehrmacht, but the Wehrmacht would not hand them over, arguing that the Poles were allied with the British, and therefore any maltreatment of these Jewish officers would invite equivalent mistreatments of Germans in British hands.[32]

Many of the Jews in the French army were from Alsace, part of the Second Reich as it existed from 1871 to 1918. Captured as soldiers in World War II, they could, if they chose, have themselves released by declaring themselves to be German. That, however, would prove to be an unwise choice; to be a German Jew in time led inexorably to tragedy. Though they could not know its benefits at the time, it was better to remain a POW, especially as the Germans rejected the idea of separate camps for Jewish POWs. Moreover, the Vichy government sought to curry favour with the

CAPTIVITY

French population by assuming responsibility for POWs detained on French soil. The wives and children of French POWs, too, remained the responsibility of the Vichy government, provided the men remained POWs, and regardless of whether they and their family members were Jewish.[33]

As we have seen, many Yugoslav POWs were soon released from captivity, but Serbs and Jews were not among them. There were some 650 Yugoslav Jewish officers who were led by a military rabbi by the name of Hermann Helfgott, who took good care of his charges in Oflag VI C in Osnabrück-Eversheide. Like the French, they were much better off being inside POW camps. But unlike the French, their families were not protected by their POW status, and while the officers whiled away the war in Germany, their parents, wives and children were murdered. Foolishly, twelve Serbian Jews applied for transport back to Serbia in 1942. On arrival they were murdered by the Gestapo.[34]

And then there were Jews in the British forces, too, the largest single group Palestinians. Palestine was a British mandate territory, and the British raised companies of both Arabs and Jews on their territory. In the Mediterranean campaigns they served with the Australians, and something like 1500 of them entered captivity alongside the Australians in Greece and Crete.[35] Waiting in vain for evacuation at places like Kalamata, they must have been desperately anxious about the prospect of falling into German hands. If the Holocaust proper was yet to be unleashed, they were perfectly acquainted with Nazi anti-Semitism. Some of the Jews in the Palestinian brigades were indeed Germans who had left their homeland for good reason. Their officers, it seems, 'thought that the Jewish soldiers would be safer being captured together with the British, and feared that individuals caught while attempting to escape would fare worse'.[36]

At Kalamata the Jews' anxieties were shared by some 400 Arabs. As the Jews prepared for surrender, cleaning themselves up and destroying their weapons, they were approached by representatives of the Arabs, requesting that they surrender together, as the Arabs were without a commander. One of the Jewish commanders accepted the proposal, then divided his men into groups of thirty to march together towards the Germans and into captivity. 'At first, the Jews proceeded in despair and fear, and I who led the column assumed all these fears and my heart turned to water. I saluted the German commander . . . reported precisely on our numbers and informed him that henceforward the responsibility for these people was in his hands.'[37] In fact, at this point the Germans showed little interest in interrogating the troops; only later, at Corinth, did interrogations begin and the extent of a Jewish Palestinian presence become apparent.

The Palestinians, like a good proportion of the Australians, were taken to camps in the annexed southern part of the Reich, in particular Marburg and Wolfsberg. Here the Palestinian Jews were segregated from other POWs and then divided among themselves; Jews of German or Austrian origin were not allowed to join the work detachments outside the camps. There were rumours that further measures might be taken to distinguish Jews from other POWs – for example by the wearing of a yellow star being imposed on civilians at that time – but they came to nothing. The OKW's Office for POW Affairs, the Kriegsgefangenenwesen, issued an order in early 1942 which stated, 'The marking of Jews in the Reich with a star is a German Government step to facilitate the identification of Jews in the streets, shops, etc. Jewish Prisoners of War are exempted from wearing any Jewish star; they are, however, to be segregated as far as possible from the other prisoners.'[38]

From Wolfsberg the Jews were sent on to the large British camp at Lamsdorf.[39] At Stalag XVIII D Marburg, too, they were accommodated separately for a time after their arrival from Salonika, as a Red Cross inspector noted in July 1941. The Jews were kept in the *Vorlager*, a compound at the entrance to the main camp. Separated though they were, the inspector noted that they were otherwise treated in the same way as everyone else.[40]

Later, too, there were cases where the Palestinian Jews were kept separately from other British POWs. In Silesia there was at least one labour detachment which consisted entirely of 'British' Jews, as a

Red Cross report noted in January 1945. It was Work Detachment (Arbeitskommando) E 595 at Schomberg, based at Stalag XVIII B Teschen, and all 414 of the men – almost certainly Palestinian Jews – were involved in coalmining. Their German masters deigned to give them every third Sunday off.[41] Little did they know that they were the luckiest Jews in Silesia.

Life in the mines was brutal for Jews and non-Jews alike. Discipline was imposed ruthlessly, and with violence if deemed necessary. There were reports of the beating of Jewish POWs by German guards in coalmines in Polish Jawozno. These reports were investigated by the Red Cross and by the representatives of the Swiss Protecting Power, but the investigators concluded that the treatment of Jews was identical to that of non-Jews, which in effect meant that it was equally harsh. During the same period, according to one account, seven Australian and seven other British POWs were shot and killed in the mines in that area, while several British were shot for attempting escape.[42] The killing of the Australians suggests an evenly applied ruthlessness; it was not just Jewish POWs who suffered. In the work detachments as in the POW camps, there were acts of anti-Semitism, but they usually sprang from the personal initiative of guards, not from orders from above.[43]

Early cases of the segregation of Palestinian POWs were noted in the Prisoners of War Department in the British War Office, albeit without triggering panic. After all, the segregation of POWs along racial lines could be interpreted as entirely consistent with Article 9 Paragraph 3 of the Geneva Convention. It was a part of the Convention with which the British had no quarrel – they would certainly not expect, for example, that Englishmen would be accommodated with Indians in captivity. Nonetheless, the War Office was interested in knowing whether Jews in British units other than the Palestinian battalions were also being segregated. There is no clear evidence of this occurring, and certainly not in any systematic kind of way. Indeed, it would have been very difficult for the Germans to identify individual Jews among British POWs. As the War Office noted, many had in any case taken the precaution of having other religions inscribed on their identity disks,[44] but to play it safe it requested the Protecting Power to monitor any German step towards the segregation of Jews.[45] When the query was put to the Swiss Legation in Berlin – without sharing the concerns with the German government for fear of giving it ideas – the reply confirmed that 'Generally speaking it cannot be said that Jews are receiving different treatment than other p/w.'[46] The Swiss did note, however, that 'in exceptional circumstances German officers and NCOs abused their authority toward certain Jewish prisoners of war'.[47]

It is unclear just how many members of the Australian armed forces were Jewish. By one reckoning there were just twenty.[48] When Australians enlisted they were asked their religion, and this of course offers some guide. Yet identity is a complex issue, and as far as the Third Reich was concerned, Jewishness was not a question of religion but of race. Whether one followed the faith was neither here nor there.

One of the Australian Jews to serve in the Second World War was Paul Alfred Cullen, by any measure a great Australian. Over a long and varied life he has distinguished himself in business, as a farmer, in charity work, in advocacy for refugees, and as one of the finest soldiers and military minds this country has produced. In war he is known above all for his contribution to the victories over Japanese forces on the Kokoda Track and in other battles in the New Guinea campaign.[49]

Cullen entered that campaign as a battle-hardened veteran. He had fought in North Africa at the end of 1940 and through the first months of 1941. Then with the 6th Division he was sent to Greece to withstand the expected German invasion. Forced into retreat when the Germans breached the Yugoslav border and, one by one, the lines of defence to its south, Cullen and his men escaped the Greek mainland by the skin of their teeth. Cullen's tunic was pierced in the Battle of Tempe Gorge by German machine-gun bullets, but its wearer survived. With a timely display of bravado under pressure, Cullen made good his escape from the Greek mainland in a cockleshell. The island-hopping which ensued in this and other vessels provided him and those in his charge with another chance to insert sticks in the wheels of the German juggernaut – on Crete. With that

CAPTIVITY

battle lost, Cullen, along with thousands of others, found himself near the fishing village of Sphakia, desperately hoping for a place on an evacuation vessel sailing for Alexandria. On the last of the four nights of evacuations, Cullen was the final man to find a place on the very last landing craft. No man came closer to capture by the Germans than Paul Cullen.[50]

At that time of his life Paul Cullen's name was Paul Cohen. He was Jewish, the grandson of the prominent Sydney businessman George Judah Cohen and the son of Sir Samuel Cohen, knighted in 1937 for his services to education.[51] Before the war Paul Cohen distinguished himself as a tireless advocate for refugees seeking a haven in Australia – Jewish refugees fleeing persecution in Nazi Germany. After the campaigns in Greece and Crete – and his narrow escapes in both – Paul Cohen chose to become Paul Cullen in case of capture by German forces. His brother George and some of their cousins in the UK who had entered the armed services made the same decision. The reason, as Cullen's biographer explains, was that the possibility of becoming a POW in Europe 'meant that they would be at great risk of ill-treatment by the Germans if they retained what was clearly a Jewish name'.[52]

Other Australian Jews were unable to evade the Germans. Among these men the record of Wolfe Greenstein is a particularly intriguing one. Greenstein was a Russian Jew born in Odessa in 1899. The humble printer from Sydney, all of five feet two in height, enlisted in the AIF in June 1918, eager to serve his adoptive homeland. He arrived in Europe too late to see active service, but then he did not miss the chance to see action when the Second World War broke out, enlisting in Paddington in June 1940 and joining the 2/1st Battalion.[53]

Greenstein was captured on Crete and taken to Salonika. Keith Hooper later recalled his fellow soldier coming to the attention of the Germans at the waterfront there. The men were lined up, standing to attention, as a German officer came along. The officer said, 'Any Jews, step forward.' Apart from Wolfe Greenstein, there was one other Jew among the Australians, Mark Phillips, who had also enlisted in the 2/1st in Paddington a couple of weeks before

Greenstein. In contrast to Greenstein, Hooper remembered, Phillips was well over six feet tall and had a classical Jewish countenance. The men stepped forward, but on seeing the relatively modest figure of Greenstein, the officer said he could step back. Later, records show, he was repatriated from Germany, and Phillips too eventually returned to Australia safe and sound.[54]

The Western Australian Hal Finkelstein, captured on Crete, similarly remembers that on arrival in Salonika Jews were asked to step forward. The demand, he recalls, came from a British Armoured Corps sergeant major, who had married a German and thrown in his lot with the enemy. Finkelstein, himself a Jew, swayed forward but was persuaded by friends in the nick of time to stay put. Later he took further steps to ensure that his Jewish identity would play no role in his treatment. He got rid of his identity disks – they had his religion entered on them – and he burnt his pay book so as to expunge his religious affiliation: 'I put a hot coal on the cover and burnt through several pages and it just went through and cut out my religion – about 3 pages. I kept it because I didn't want to lose my book; that was an important thing to me.'[55]

While in the camp, he came to know an older Jewish man from Perth who, like Wolfe Greenstein, had served in the 1st AIF. This time around, a greater sense of caution, or perhaps a visceral hunch that the enemy was now of a different moral order, had persuaded him also to take an unusual step. When he left this time, he arranged with his wife that if taken prisoner he would change his name, but she would know it was he. This, though, was the exception.[56]

If racial mania alone had driven the German treatment of POWs, then indigenous Australians too might have had cause for anxiety. Unlike the New Zealanders, who had separate Maori battalions, the Australians had relatively few Aborigines who were integrated into units, and even fewer who became POWs. One of them, Reg Saunders, had a very narrow escape, smuggled from Crete aboard a British submarine and able to continue his war against a new enemy, the Japanese.[57]

CAPTIVITY

The Western Australian Harry Davis was one who did not get away. Lawrence (Jack) Calder remembers him in the Benghazi camp under Italian control. The two of them had been captured on the same day. Davis sought Calder's assistance in Benghazi because he had been told by the Italian authorities that he would be put in with the black South Africans, a fate he was eager to avoid. Fortunately they were able to persuade the guards not to take that step, and for future reference his Australian mates devised a small pass for Davis to carry with him, indicating that he was Australian and so was to remain with Australian forces. Davis remained among Australians until he was in Italy, where he eventually joined those with the opportunity and the gumption to make their way to Switzerland after the Italian surrender.[58]

Jim Brennan had a similar story to tell. He too hailed from Western Australia, where he worked as a stockman before enlisting in the 2/28th Battalion in the Perth suburb of Claremont. He saw service in North Africa until his capture at El Alamein. From there he was passed into Italian hands and shipped to Italy. With the Italian capitulation he too had the nous and the courage to leave his camp, but rather than find refuge in Switzerland, he joined partisans, conducting guerrilla operations against German forces.[59] He must have been recaptured, however, because by June 1944 he was in a train heading north to Stalag VII A Moosburg in Bavaria.[60]

It is unclear just how many Aborigines might have ended up in the Reich. A photograph in the Australian War Memorial's archive displays the uniformed, pipe-smoking image of Tommy 'Negus' Green – almost certainly Thomas Harold Green of the 2/1st Battalion, hailing from Baryulgil in country New South Wales – as a POW at Stalag XIII C Hammelburg. Green had reportedly been named 'Negus' by the German guards at the camp. Though his surname and origins are unknown, there is a recollection of one other Aborigine in the Reich. Alex McClelland recalls coming across him in a punishment camp at Gersdorf in Czechoslovakia.[61] He went by the name of Dave and was one of the men from the 2/11th Battalion who had fought at Retimo in Crete before his capture. There were some tough men in Gersdorf, including a 'razor gang' led by an Englishman bearing the nickname Duke. At one point Duke and his gang threatened Dave, waving a razor under his throat. When this became known to the other Australians, one of them turned the tables on Duke, grabbing him by the scruff of the neck and informing him sternly, 'If one of your mob looks sideways at Dave again we will cut every one of your bloody throats.' With that the talk of razors came to an end.[62]

Whatever it was that had landed Dave in Gersdorf, it is certain that it was something he did, not who he was. At most the Germans might have viewed the Aborigines as a curiosity, but they treated them according to the uniform they wore. In that sense, at least, Aborigines were no worse off than in their homeland.

13

Kriegie Life

For the Australians, that moment of entering the gates of an *Oflag* or *Stalag* was an ambivalent one. On the one hand it signalled the end of a period of danger, of privation, even of trauma. It delivered a sense of security that, after the travails of the recent past, could only be welcomed. On the other hand, that moment also represented a formal passing into the grim and dreary world of captivity, any prospect of further glory on the field of battle – or above it – abandoned. Ahead lay the painful adjustments to the strains and arcane logic of an environment quite unlike anything they had known before. As Churchill had learned in the Boer War, it was 'a melancholy state', odious for the unremitting requirement to obey the orders of the enemy, and humiliating for the nagging reminders of the deprivation of freedom.[1] Loathe it or not, the men were now *Kriegsgefangene*, prisoners of war, or in their own parlance simply 'kriegies'.

Kriegie life officially commenced with the completion of formalities on arrival at camp. A card was prepared for each POW – a double-sided so-called *Personalkarte* with a photo portrait, a description of physical attributes, civilian occupation and a home address. Next to the photo was placed a print from the index finger of the right hand. There was also a second card on which any money or valuables removed from the POW's possession were recorded.[2] The POW had an individual POW number, and this was entered both on the registration cards and on a small metal tag perforated in the centre. The cards and the tag would accompany the POW wherever he was transferred. Were the POW to die, the tag would be snapped along the perforation, one side to be sent home with the prisoner's personal belongings, the other to be buried with the body[3] and his cards sent to the Armed Forces Information Office in Berlin.[4]

Doug Nix recalls well his own registration at Stalag XVIII A Wolfsberg. He was asked his name, his unit, his place of capture and his religion. Then he was given his tag, perforated down the middle. On it was recorded the key information, in his case: 'Stalag XVIII A Wolfsberg Kriegsgefangener Nr. 197'. Most wore the tag around their necks, but in a minor triumph of individual expression in a strictly regulated world, Nix tied it around his wrist. Like other POWs, he nonetheless recognised that it was important not to lose it. Even in the case of escape – indeed, perhaps especially in the case of escape – it could be vital on recapture to prove one's identity as a kriegie and thereby stake an ironic claim for the protection of the Wehrmacht.[5]

The Wehrmacht's protection was not without its value. In exercising its duty of care towards the Australians, the Wehrmacht was diligent while falling some distance short of being generous. Overall, and with significant exceptions, the *Stalags* and *Oflags* were safe environments. They at least provided the POWs with basic necessities to maintain their existence: food, clothing and shelter.

For the shelter they were dependent on the Germans and the Germans alone. If they did have to scurry in some cases to build or find accommodation, and even if for longer or shorter periods the Australians had to make do with overcrowded or provisional lodgings, for most of the war they could count on at least a roof over their heads and a degree of warmth, albeit at times coming as much from their fellow captives as from the ovens and fuel their hosts provided. In the last months of the war, as we shall see, an acute accommodation crisis was to re-emerge, as POWs were marched for weeks on end across war-ravaged Europe, finding refuge where they could until finally the luckier would be allocated a chilled, lice-infested space in a camp bursting at its seams.

Clothing, too, was a German responsibility, as the Geneva Convention made clear, but in practice it was not borne by the Germans alone. The uniforms the Australians wore at the time of their capture could not serve them through their captivity. Those captured in the heat of North Africa, Greece or Crete could not hope to survive a German winter in the threadbare clothes on their backs. Civilian clothing would not do – for security reasons. It would raise suspicions that the wearer was planning an escape.[6] Even on work detachments, any work apparel had to be worn in conjunction with a uniform. The Australian airman Calton Younger was deprived of his distinctive RAAF blue battledress on the grounds that it would be too easily mistaken for civilian clothing.[7]

In pressing circumstances a number of creative solutions to the uniform shortage were found. One was to dye discarded German uniforms, another to recycle the motley collection of uniforms the Germans had assembled from diverse vanquished forces.[8] The provisional garb provided by the Germans sometimes bestowed on the POWs the appearance of walking, bedraggled advertisements for the defunct League of Nations. The trousers, for example, might be French but the shirt Belgian, while many had to endure the discomfort of Dutch-style clogs, a genuine handicap for those sent on work detachments. When he arrived at Moosburg, Lindsay Lawrence was sporting pants 'that were meant to be worn with leggings from Poland and a grey jacket with yellow facings from Yugo-Slavia and my own army boots with holes worn through their soles. The only under-clothing issued to us was a singlet made from wood which was full of splinters and itchy.'[9]

Some of the clothing needs were met by deliveries received all the way from loved ones in Australia. In theory this was entirely possible, but it was far from satisfactory. After a long and perilous voyage, the package had to be forwarded to its addressee, whose location might well have changed since the parcel was sent. This remained a particular frustration for many Australian POWs. Sympathy for their plight stares from the pages of a Red Cross report on a visit to the *Stalag* at Marburg – by this time an annex of Spittal – on the very southern fringes of the Reich. The poor Australians, the delegate noted in September 1942, were desperately short of underwear and socks. As it happened, on the day before the Red Cross inspection – and thus about a year after the Australians arrived there from Salonika – the first larger consignment of private parcels from Australia was delivered, having been posted many months earlier. 'This arrival gave a great encouragement to the Australian prisoners some of whom already believed that they were quite forgotten.'[10] Ron Zwar received just one clothing parcel during his captivity, only to find out after the war that four had been sent.[11]

Only the engagement of the Red Cross brought about a more satisfactory solution, because in time the Red Cross could deliver uniforms into the Reich from various belligerent states. For the Australians this usually meant the provision of English battledress to supplement whatever they were wearing at the time of capture, but that at least was a vast improvement on the motley wardrobe they had been enduring.

Of the most basic POW needs, food was a bone of contention from the very start. For anyone with ready access to food, the exquisite daily torture of hunger is difficult to comprehend. To the sheer discomfort of an empty belly is added the dimension of time – hunger pangs could stab the afflicted for days, months, years on end. One of its sufferers, Gordon Stooke, put it nicely: 'As I tried to sleep through the onset of dysentery, I fantasized uproarious orgies where the main attraction was not a shapely wench bursting out of a monstrous cake but the cake itself.'[12] The hungriest times were typically shortly after capture and then again in the final, chaotic weeks of the war. But whether in its acute or its duller forms, hunger was the POW's permanent, despised companion.

Some sought a provisional reprieve in tobacco, generally in good supply in British compounds. When Earle Nelson arrived at Stalag Luft III his more experienced comrades told him he could take the edge off his hunger by smoking. Nelson duly followed the advice, including the instruction to be sure to inhale the smoke. A spell of violent coughing and spluttering ensued, but it did help appease the hunger. The cost, alas, was an addiction to nicotine.[13]

Presented with the evidence of the men's suffering, the Germans stuck doggedly to their hard line. They set POW rations at the equivalent of what German soldiers who were living at home received, and they would not budge. It was a policy which provoked a good deal of rancour among the POWs and those who advocated for them.[14] German troops not accommodated in barracks had ample opportunities to supplement the rations provided them simply by purchasing more food. The POWs, however, argued compellingly that their rations should have been set at the same level as German troops stationed in barracks, because in both cases the men were fully dependent on what was provided for them by those in whose care they stood. Powerful though the argument was, and well grounded in the Geneva Convention to boot, it consistently fell on deaf ears. True, the POWs could spend the meagre wages they received for their labour at the camp canteens, but they were woefully stocked.

What rations the Germans did provide, typically prepared in the camp kitchen, were both inadequate and bland. Of course there were regional and seasonal variations, but a basic POW diet might consist of ersatz tea or coffee for breakfast, a midday bowl of soup with some vegetables such as potato or swede and perhaps a few lumps of horseflesh floating in it, followed in the afternoon by a slice of some kind of bread or biscuits.[15] On one occasion Hal Finkelstein was confronted with a cut of meat whose sole virtue was the exercise it offered his jaws – a cow's udder: 'You could have as easily eaten a motor tyre.'[16]

An unknown number of POWs were saved from starvation through the unstinting efforts of the Red Cross and the package service it provided.[17] From Geneva the International Committee of the Red Cross, the ICRC, coordinated delivery into the Reich of standard parcels, directed not to individual prisoners but to camps and work detachments, where they were received with undying gratitude. As a supplement to the meagre rations the camp authorities provided, for as long as they were accessible the Red Cross parcels ensured that the POWs had at least an adequate diet. If there was a drawback, it was that commonly the camp administrations took the parcels as an excuse to cut further the rations they made available.[18] This too appeared a clear breach of the Geneva Convention, yet it remained German policy.

Australia was not among the countries from which these parcels were sourced. The Australian Red Cross came to an agreement with the British Red Cross that it would fund parcels sourced and packed in the United Kingdom. In any case, the Australian POWs in their British compounds received parcels from many parts of the Commonwealth, and even on occasion from Argentina. The most desired of the parcels, it seems, were those from the Canadian Red Cross. Typically they contained: '1 lb tin butter, 16 oz. bully beef, 16 oz. powdered milk, 8 oz. pork roll, 1 large tin sardines, 8 oz. milk chocolate, 8 oz. sugar; 1 cake toilet soap; 1 oz. fine salt; 1 packet dry biscuits, 8 oz. salmon, 12 oz. pkt. raisins, ½ lb sultanas, 16 oz. tin marmalade, 4 oz. pkt. cheese and 4 oz. pkt. tea.'[19] Mundane elements of civilian life they all were, yet for kriegies such a parcel was a veritable cornucopia.

The need to make the most of scarce food, whatever combination of Red Cross and German rations it might have been, was the source of much POW ingenuity and invention. In Stalag VIII B Lamsdorf the guards forbade the use of open flames to heat food, but they approved an oven designed and built by the Australian Charlie Parrott. He collected biscuit tins from Red Cross parcels, and when he had 86 of them in his possession he opened them and flattened out the tin, forming doubled edges with the aid of an improvised hammer. He then joined them to build the wall and base of an oven, packing them with mud and providing an insert to separate the food from the oven walls. He added a top, a fire box with flue and finally a door. It was invaluable, for the oven could effectively heat cans from Red Cross packages with steak and kidney or meat and vegetables, and it could even make tea and coffee. The ultimate test was the preparation of a Yorkshire pudding, a test it passed with flying colours.[20] The Germans, it seems, did not quite know what to make of it: 'About half an hour before dinner, we had a visit from a German officer and two of the guards. I don't know what this was about. No one said anything. The officer stood in the doorway and looked at the table. A couple of minutes later, he shook his head and the three walked off. As for the blokes, they thought Christmas was terrific under the circumstances.'[21]

As for drinks, the kind most highly valued in breaking the unremitting boredom of kriegie life was alcoholic. True, in some cases the camp canteens offered watery beer to at best numb the monotony but barely alleviate it. For a more serious exit from their everyday woes the POWs were left to their own devices. Happily there was no shortage of will or creativity in this regard. The comforts of alcohol were particularly seductive in the depths of the German winter. Ray Corbett recalls being invited by a fellow Australian, Ted Kelly, to a hut at the Blechhammer work camp where triple-distilled potato juice was put to humorous use, delighting the huddled onlookers. A tall Welsh Guardsman imbibed a quantity of the brew and then, as Corbett recorded it, 'dragged himself out of his bunk and bent over the table, having dropped his slacks. His mate, the urger – "Come on mate, we got fags! Let 'er rip!" Maybe it was the pressure of the table. The mate flicked his lighter and a reasonably long tongue of flame emanated from the hairy fundamental orifice.'[22]

Mentally and physically, the challenges of kriegie life extended far beyond having a roof over their heads, clothes on their backs and food in their stomachs. For all the variety among the camps, each provided a most unusual social environment, the apparent stability of which masked the inner turmoils in those who had no choice but to endure it – or literally go crazy.

Survival in the camps was possible only through some form of tenacious, forgiving and enduring solidarity. A decade or so after the war, the Australian airman Calton Younger wrote perceptively of the kind of communities which were formed within barbed wire.

There were those who, enduring the shock of captivity, pared back their social existence to the most basic unit – the individual. They retreated into 'a kind of inward solitude', a condition which on the one hand was enviable, because such men did not rely on the support of others. At the same time, as Younger recognised, it was dangerous, because it could lead to a 'miasma of self-pity', and in extreme cases the melancholic, far from freeing his fellow POWs of a responsibility, became a burden, 'sometimes a menace'.[23]

Indeed, there were those who did not find a way to live in the camps. Frank Cox witnessed the shooting of a fellow Australian in Spittal. The man was suffering from what POWs referred to as 'barbed wire happies', that is, the rules and restrictions of camp life had driven his mental state to the edge and, on this horrifying occasion, over it. On this day he walked steadily towards the barbed wire perimeter, initially attracting no attention. But as he continued the guards started shouting at him, as too did fellow prisoners. Undeterred and unheeding, he proceeded to the fence, and after he came in contact with the wire the guards shot him dead. In effect he had committed suicide.[24]

Camps were not the ideal environments in which to deal with the sorts of trauma which had surrounded and preceded capture. Thomas Fielder, an airman held in Stalag IV B Mühlberg, found little opportunity to work through his recent experiences with his fellow POWs. All 200 men in his hut had had different experiences. Some were sole survivors of operations, having lost not just fellow crew but close friends. Many, he knew, needed the release of telling their story to people who would understand. Yet the hut was ill-equipped to meet that need. When the men spoke openly, they were inclined to tell unlikely stories of derring-do, with the result that all within earshot would 'in unison and a tone of derision chant the well known airforce routine: "And there I was, upside down at 20,000 feet and nothing on the clock . . ." with the result that not only did the "skite" shut up but it silenced every other person who needed the release as a natural therapy'.[25] Rather than working through their problems, the men's mental anguish manifested as nightmares or antisocial behaviour. Fielder's abiding memory of life in hut 34 B was utter boredom: 'The days were too long and the nights also were too long.'[26]

Troubled minds who were so inclined could turn to chaplains for support – if they were available. Technically they were not counted among the POWs, but like the medical orderlies in many cases they remained among the men to offer them succour through testing times. They could be as rare as the proverbial hen's teeth. When in September 1942 a YMCA inspector visited the largest of the British camps, the *Stalag* at Lamsdorf, he noted only two chaplains serving the needs of thousands, and neither of them was from the Church of England. There was a Catholic and a Baptist, the latter Frank Hiddlestone from Melbourne, who told the inspector something of his work. In the previous week he had held 24 services in the camp, the hospital and at work detachments. The previous Sunday the church, which had space for 600, was overfilled with 800. Moreover there were many private discussions with the men. Hiddlestone expressed his thanks to the YMCA for providing him with a typewriter to ease some of the burden of his work.[27]

Others found ways to preserve their sanity by seeking temporary relief from the company of their fellow POWs. Among the men at Stalag Luft I Barth and then Stalag Luft IV Heydekrug, Jack Liley observed that some who descended into a depressive funk would retreat to their bunks for hours or days, emerging only to present themselves for rollcalls. The depression they suffered could be triggered by any number of events, great and small, but commonly some kind of news from home.[28]

In Stalag Luft III at Sagan the RAAF Wireless Air Gunner Ron Mackenzie went a step further. He found temporary refuge from the strains of close and crowded confinement by occasionally committing an offence to earn a few days' isolation in a single cell in the so-called bunker. The simplest provocation was to smoke on parade. The Germans regarded such an activity as unsoldierly and routinely punished it with a week of solitary confinement. The prisoner had to make do with a diet of bread and water, but for provisional relief it was as good as a holiday. The idea caught on, and in time it was almost a case of the men having to book their turn to commit the one offence which guaranteed just a week or less to rediscover their individual identities.[29]

More commonly a kind of mateship or camaraderie grew. It was a phenomenon acutely observed by Calton Younger in Stalag Luft III. He reflected insightfully on the distinctive dynamics of the all-male community which had formed behind the barbed wire. The men there, he wrote, 'drew upon qualities which were innate but never before needed to the same degree, and the tiny skeletons of ephemeral kindnesses created a structure of unyielding tolerance'.[30] In Sagan he noted the initial formation of 'combines', that is, groups of ten POWs who would pool their rations and share their chores. But in time these broke down under the stress of tensions and dissent into small groups of just two, three or four. These tiny groups became the most fundamental building blocks of camp life, functioning in effect as substitutes for the kind of family most had known in civilian life. Of course, there were still those 'lone wolves' who chose the task of uncompromising individualism, but even they were known as 'one-man combines'.[31]

While the Australian tradition of mateship might have contributed to the formation of these basic units of camp life, the combines were not the achievements of the Australians alone. Indeed at one point Younger counted 23 nationalities in his block.[32] There is no shortage of cases of Australians forming close bonds with men from other parts of the Commonwealth as well as with fellow Australians. In Younger's case, his tight-knit group of three consisted of Dick, the son of a Southampton doctor, and Toby, 'a chunky little Canadian'.[33] Their lives were inextricably interwoven for some three years in three separate camps. On the one hand they were thrown together through the exigencies of war, yet captivity also allowed them the choice of their ersatz family. Such was the intensity of the relationship that it might even be compared with marriage, marked by an intensity of the kind made possible, as Younger knew, 'only where men are thrown together in such a way that they cannot avoid each other, cannot choose when they will meet, when separate. Even the husband-wife relationship is not so taut, is less absorbing, less demanding.'[34] As in a marriage, the closest of mates in the camp 'shared with you your hours of melancholy, nursed you in illness, and accepted, without complaint, the spite you felt in your heart for the other fellows, but which, to preserve the peace, you vented upon him'.[35]

The company of other POWs could also provide the most pleasurable, indeed even the most uproariously comic, of times. It was as if the pervasive abjection of the world around them could serve to heighten those rare moments of joy. It was precisely the company of men, for all its vagaries, that brought about those treasured moments of transcendence. Laughter, as Younger noted, 'came not cheaply, not easily, but it did come and was for ever sought'.[36]

Some desires were never easily met in the all-male world of the camps, and sex was one of them. Poor diet, the everyday anxieties of POW life and a punishing work regime stifled the sex drive of many, and yet the absence of women was not just a sexual but also a social deprivation. What was lacking in these men's lives for a period of close to four years in some cases was, in the words of a medical report from the time, 'the whole sphere of association between the sexes and all that it entails'. This, the author warned, 'was not only a fundamental but the fundamental factor in the formation of the prisoner of war attitude. Deeply within the prisoner, but seldom expressed, there lies the fear of becoming a forgotten man.' Evidence of this acute fear could be observed in the meticulous care with which the POWs pored over every word in letters from home.[37]

In matters of sex, a basic need conflicted with deep-seated Nazi miscegenation anxieties. While some concentration camps had their own brothels, POW camps were strictly all-male affairs, and sexual relations between German women and prisoners of war were strictly forbidden. Even before the bulk of the Australians entered captivity, the 'Decree for the Protection of the Defensive Strength of the German People' (*Verordnung zum Schutze der Wehrkraft des deutschen Volkes*) was issued in August 1940, expressly forbidding German women from taking any actions which might compromise the 'well-being of the Volk'. Among the misdemeanours which would cause offence were not just sexual but even social intercourse with non-Germans, and that might include dances, walks or visits to public establishments. These sorts of interactions were regarded as 'sex crimes' (*Geschlechtsverkehr-Verbrechen*) with potentially serious consequences for all concerned. Hitler himself demanded that POWs who had sexual or simply 'friendly' relations with German women were to be shot, while the women were to have their heads shorn and be sent to a concentration camp.[38] The more moderate OKW for its part directed that any POWs found to have had sexual relations with German women were to be sentenced to ten years' jail or even execution.[39]

In any case officers and NCOs had little opportunity to pursue any kind of relations with German women. But the other ranks did have possibilities, especially through their allocation to work detachments. At the workplace they commonly came into contact with women, who themselves were forming a crucial part of the Reich's workforce while the menfolk served in the armed forces. Moreover on rural work detachments it was not at all unusual for the POWs to be quartered in the immediate vicinity of German families, in which younger males were a rarity.

Interestingly the records for Military District XVIII in southern Austria, where there were good numbers of Australians, suggest that cases of British POWs pursuing relations with German women were relatively rare, though this was not because fear stifled passions between the local women and the many young males in their midst. On the contrary, clearly many liaisons were formed between Frenchmen and Austrian women – an estimated 90 per cent of the illicit relations were of this nature. Wondering why not more British POWs took such steps, the Security Service in Graz concluded, 'Sexual relations between British POWs and German women and girls occur relatively seldom. The main reason for this would have to be that the English display a strongly developed sense of national consciousness which prevents them from pursuing sexual relations with members of an enemy people.'[40] If asked, the French transgressors might well have proffered quite different explanations for their behaviour.

The temptations for Australians were present. Don Luckett recalls one such occasion on a work detachment in southern

Austria: 'We were at work on this particular morning, on a stage overlooking the road that led into the village, when a young girl of about twenty was seen walking along the road, she was quite attractive and smartly dressed, carrying a string bag that held a round loaf, something like 25 pairs of eyes followed the progress in silence, then a very Aussie voice was heard to remark – "Bloody hell! Look at that loaf!"'[41] One Australian who did succumb to the temptation, risking a long spell in jail or even execution, was Harry Burton from Sydney, who, on a rural work detachment in southern Austria, pursued a relationship with a young woman by the name of Maria Annerer from Neudorf bei Ilz. Maria became pregnant, but fortunately gave birth to her child on 19 May 1945, after the war's end. At the time she did not imagine that she and Burton would marry, even though 'he was very nice, very, very nice. Back then love was just crazy [*keck*].' But Burton decided that he did want to stay on in Styria; he and Maria married in early 1946 and bore five children. In 1973 he died without ever having returned to Australia.[42]

Relations with non-German women, though not condoned by the German authorities, were seen in a different light. At least the spectre of miscegenation did not raise its ugly head, though the authorities could hardly have welcomed the prospect of a valuable worker falling pregnant and giving birth to another unwanted extra mouth to feed. Ray Corbett knew of men at his Blechhammer work detachment in Silesia who pursued relations with French women workers. It had to be done surreptitiously, or with the turning of a guard's blind eye with the help of cigarettes, but it raised morale on all sides.

Some men no doubt met their sexual needs with their kind. There was homosexuality in POW camps as there was in any part of the population. It was a topic which, as Calton Younger noted in the 1950s, appeared to elicit a good deal of attention, albeit in the form of circuitous probing rather than direct questions. He himself knew of no case in the barracks he shared, nor indeed did he even hear the rumour of homosexual relations occurring. In POW barracks 'you could not even turn the page of a book without someone seeing you do it, and at any moment of the night, in every room, half a dozen cigarettes burned restlessly'.[43] Ron Mackenzie was aware of homosexuality in Stalag Luft III but agrees that opportunities were limited. Where there was an awareness of men with homosexual inclinations, they were treated 'with courtesy and a sort of baffled sympathy'.[44]

A comical and probably self-ironic manifestation of sexual frustration was occasionally provoked by theatrical productions in the camps. The roles of women were necessarily played by men. Basil Brudenell-Woods, who after capture near Benghazi eventually found himself at Lamsdorf, recalls that the performances in that camp's productions were at times so convincing 'that quite a few of the boys got really randy and followed them back to their quarters after the show'. Brudenell-Woods was quick to point out that nothing 'untoward' happened, though he did note that the senior Allied officer saw fit to call a parade at which the padre 'gave us a lecture on women-hungry men amongst men'.[45]

For officers and NCOs especially, confined to the camps and not required to work, the need to keep mind and body active was a burning existential necessity. Theatre was one of those activities which enabled men to divert their energies in other directions, to take their minds from their misery and even to save their sanity. Despite the multiple constrictions of a POW camp in the midst of a war, the entertainment offered in the form of theatre and revues achieved an astounding variety and quality. In some cases the productions were of such a standard that the Germans would be sure to occupy the best seats in the house. In the NCOs' camp at Hohenfels the shows were, in Laurie West's opinion, every bit as good as anything London had to offer. Moreover the camp had a superb multinational orchestra whose members could readily knock up a tune to support a waltz or a foxtrot; when the Canadians arrived after Dieppe, jiving and jitterbugging were added to the dance-card.[46]

When a representative of the YMCA visited Stalag VIII B Lamsdorf at the beginning of September 1943, he was privileged to witness one of the theatrical performances put on by the men.

A uniformed usher met him at the door to escort him to his place of honour next to the Man of Confidence. 'The curtain,' he recorded in his report, 'rose over the funniest play I had ever seen. The men in this camp are excellent musicians and artists. No words can adequately describe how much these entertainments mean to the prisoners.'[47]

Even the Blechhammer work detachment – albeit a very large one – managed to put together a series of shows, despite the men's heavy work commitments. One of the most active of participants was Ray Corbett, who performed to appreciative audiences, British and German, within the camp. Such was the quality of the production of the *Mikado* that it was taken to the 'holiday camp' at Genshagen, where the crème-de-la-crème of POW theatrical and musical endeavour was presented to enthusiastic applause.[48]

Many POWs had their eyes on postwar civilian lives as they sought to occupy their minds, taking advantage of educational opportunities that some camps offered in abundance. Hohenfels was a veritable hive of educational activity. The 'Hohenfellows' embraced and encouraged educational opportunities to such an extent that a visiting Red Cross delegation could barely hide its enthusiasm. From originally quite primitive facilities – just two classes in one room with no materials and no textbooks – by September 1942 the POWs on their own initiative and by their own labour had constructed an institution of higher learning. The creative use of wood salvaged from Red Cross packages had served to divide a large building into no fewer than seven separate classrooms where a vast array of topics was taught. An inspector gushed:

> The 23 original subjects are still on the programme, but now there are no less than 84 subjects taught! This may appear to be the height of folly, ridiculously over-ambitious. But one has only to consider the many diverse occupations of the men congregated inside these strands of wire: men from all parts of the Empire; men from all walks of life; men from every trade or profession known in Britain or the Dominions. Consider those, and remember that, as far as is humanly possible, every individual must be catered for – and the number of classes becomes explicable. Notice

also the variegated examinations that have been applied for and one will realize that the need is very real.[49]

Of the 4686 men in Hohenfels on 1 October 1943, the inspector noted, over half – 2373 to be exact – were 'in school'. A copy of the timetable shows subjects ranging from algebra and stockbroking through to Maori, Welsh and 'Sheep Aust.', which ran concurrently with 'Sheep NZ'. The most popular subject was agriculture, with all of 200 students, followed by first aid (183) and matriculation-level maths (165).[50]

The airmen were well provided for too. In the *Stalags Luft* more than 170 Australians took correspondence courses provided through the British War Office, the RAAF Educational Services in Australia, London University and other institutions. The camps at Barth and Sagan built up impressive libraries with the aid of books sent from Oxford's New Bodleian Library via the Red Cross.[51] Sagan developed close links with Oxford University, whose Examinations Department would send papers out to the camps and arrange for their assessment on return. The Australian Ron Mackenzie was one of many beneficiaries, not only learning new things but giving lectures in his own area of expertise, accountancy.[52] The YMCA, too, played its part in providing the camps with reading materials, though like other suppliers it had to tread carefully with the German authorities. The OKW insisted on certain limits being set: 'Scientific literature and theoretical texts are admissible without limitation as far as they are not the works of Jews or emigrants, do not contain maps and are in accordance with German demands. These writings of course may not contain practical instructions on the production and use of radios, weapons, incendiaries, poisons, secret inks etc . . .'[53]

Then there were some less formal pastimes. In Hohenfels, Laurie West was able to complete two years of the University of London's commerce degree, but he also kept his mind active by learning Spanish from a Basque POW, whose colourful career had led him to a British commando unit on Crete and then to Hohenfels. Others read as much for entertainment as edification, as some of the camps built up well-stocked libraries. A 'British Prisoners of War Books and Games Fund' was set up in Britain to send reading material of all kinds to camps in Germany. Here, too, the sensitivities of the detaining power had to be respected. Edgar Rice Burroughs' *Tarzan the Untamed* and *Return of Tarzan* as well as E.L. Long's *Young Flynn* were banned on the grounds that they defamed Germans.[54] Perhaps, too, they might have encouraged the kind of adventurous spirit and yearning for freedom best left untapped in a POW.

On the other hand, not all the reading material made available would necessarily have appeared on the prisoners' wish lists. Ron Mackenzie remembers that in Sagan the first books to arrive were Bibles, printed on India-type paper. Everything was read, but for these Bibles, soft to the touch, a double use was found. The scene of the second use was the camp latrine – a crude affair of a long pole suspended over a similarly proportioned cesspit, with a support pole running parallel. The facility could accommodate up to forty or fifty at a time: 'All reading the Bible.'[55]

The Germans made a modest and self-serving contribution to keeping their captives' minds active, producing an illustrated newspaper called *The Camp* for English-speaking POWs throughout the Reich.[56] With its egregious distortions, it was not favoured reading among the POWs, who preferred to publish their own newspapers, albeit with limited means. As long as the content did not offend, the German authorities had no objection to such publications, but shortages of paper normally meant that the final product was a one-off, displayed on a prominent wall in the camp for all to enjoy.

The talents of the POWs and the grudgingly suspended parsimony of the Germans did, though, on occasion lead to more substantial outcomes, such as the magazines *The Quill* and *Touchstone* produced at Oflag VII B or *The Observer* at Stalag IV B.[57] Keith Hooper had already worked as a journalist before enlisting. The camp newspaper at Hohenfels gave him an invaluable opportunity to practise and hone his skills; similarly, those with artistic skills could both give them free rein and entertain their fellow prisoners. While these rough newspapers were permitted by the camp authorities, radios, on the other hand, were strictly illegal, and the Germans went to considerable lengths to locate them. They were constructed from parts filched from or bartered with civilians, or hidden undetected inside parcels. It was a measure of POW ingenuity that the Germans were so seldom successful at finding them. Hiding places might include a gramophone, a hollowed-out copy of *Mein Kampf*, an accordion, and even a football.[58] 'Stooges' would keep watch while the radio was being used to ensure that the guards did not intervene.

Most of the writing done in camps was correspondence with loved ones. In principle the men in *Stalags* were permitted to send four postcards and two letters per month, though many remember a more miserly reality. Ron Zwar, for example, recalls being permitted to send at most one letter and three postcards a month.[59] Officers were allowed an extra letter, but the most privileged were medical orderlies, permitted a grand total of eight cards and six letters.[60] Post could even be sent by airmail, providing the prisoner covered the cost – a letter by air to Australia would cost 0.45 Reichsmarks, payable in the form of the otherwise almost worthless camp money, *Lagergeld*.[61] There were limitations of other kinds, too. Templates existed for both cards and letters which had to be filled in with pencils, and correspondence had to be in the writer's mother tongue or in German. Most restrictive, though, was the censorship to which all mail was subjected by the censors working under the direction of the intelligence (Abwehr) officer stationed in every camp.

To receive letters from home could, of course, help to haul a POW from the gloom engendered by capture and confinement. Much joy was to be gleaned from knowing that all was well at home, and that their return was eagerly awaited by loved ones. But correspondence could work both ways. Ron Mackenzie recalls a line in a letter received by a fellow prisoner in Sagan. It said, 'If you'd been a man, you'd have got killed when they shot you down.'[62] Most dreaded, though, were letters from girlfriends or fiancées announcing that, despite their very best of intentions, they were not prepared to wait after all and, indeed, had met someone else. These were 'Dear John' letters, and they could pitch their recipients into deep depression, utterly helpless in the face of the news from afar, and with little prospect of confining a lost relationship to the past by 'moving on'.

From the end of 1943 British and German authorities agreed to an exchange of films, though this too troubled the censors. The Ministry of Popular Enlightenment and Propaganda complained bitterly in October 1944 that the movie *The Three Stooges Back from the Front* disparaged the figures of both Hitler and Göring, while lines such as 'We are Nazis, we need no brain' mocked National Socialism. The film was duly banned.[63]

Card games were a much more readily accessible way to urge the hours and days to pass. In Mühlberg Gordon Stooke took to contract bridge, the most popular game played in the camp. Together with his Australian partner John (Doc) Haines from Gosford, he played in-barrack, inter-barrack, inter-services and ultimately international bridge, finding talented French, Danish and Dutch opposition. The stakes were cigarettes.[64]

Whether playing for cigarettes, potatoes or perhaps *Lagergeld* as the medium of exchange, and whether using coins, dice or cards, Australians found gambling a useful antidote to the tedium of barrack life. Doug Nix remembers a gambling mat fashioned in the *Stalag* at Wolfsberg from a Red Cross parcel. It was the sole piece of equipment required for the dice game Crown and Anchor. Signed by hundreds of participants in the games, it is nowadays to be found in the collection of ephemera at the Australian War Memorial.[65]

Some pastimes were distinguished by nothing other than their inanity. John Mathews remains grateful for the Red Cross parcels that contained items of woollen clothing. Though clothing was always welcome, what was more valuable for him about these items was their capacity to provide him and his fellow POWs with hours of distraction, even entertainment. In particular he had a scarf which he pulled apart and then reknitted perhaps twenty times. Others, too, would sit around knitting in groups, no doubt a strange sight for guards and non-knitters. But as a way to take their minds off the acute privations of the war's final days, it was a blessing.[66]

Then, of course, there were those pastimes which demanded a good deal more physical exertion than a book or a game of cards. For the Australians, sports became the most popular of POW pastimes remarkably quickly. A team of Red Cross inspectors arrived at the Wolfsberg camp not long after large numbers of Australians and other Allied POWs had been delivered from Crete and Greece, most still dressed in the khaki shorts appropriate to the Mediterranean summer. In the Red Cross delegation was a photographer whose work documented the participation of the POWs, soon after enduring the travails of capture and a hellish rail journey, in a sports day held in the camp. This event is likely to have been the brainchild of the camp commandant, who might have thought it a useful distraction for men still coming to terms with a dramatic reversal of fortune. He might even have conceived of the event as a means to impress his Swiss visitors. In any case, the enthusiasm written across the faces of both participants and spectators is easy to read.

The camps for airmen were no different. When a YMCA delegate turned up at Stalag Luft III Sagan in September 1942 he enthused:

> Without doubt the greatest interest among the prisoners is in sport. It was on a hot, sunny day that my visit took place. Everywhere one saw young, powerful men, all beautifully tanned by the sun, most wearing shorts, engaged in various sporting activities. On the large sport field football, basketball, volleyball and athletics competitions were being staged. A boxing ring, assembled with great effort, was available also. In both compounds there were ponds where one could bathe on these hot days.[67]

What might have appeared a remarkably liberal policy on the part of the captors had precious little to do with altruism. In the *Stalags* the men were viewed as an invaluable reservoir of labourers. To work well their morale had to be high and their bodies had to be in good shape. The Chief of POW Affairs made it clear that the purpose of the various forms of entertainment the POWs were permitted to organise for themselves was not to amuse them but rather 'to make the POW willing and able to work and to promote in him the psychological preparedness to commit himself fully to his work performance'.[68] Moreover, just as was the case with less physical forms of diversion, the Germans recognised that it was ultimately in their own interests, too, to keep their captives occupied, soaking up energies which might otherwise be put to more troublesome use.

Camp authorities naturally had to be wary that requests for sporting activity were not veiled efforts to create escape opportunities. Such had been their humiliating experience at Stalag Luft III in October 1943, when one of the bolder and more enterprising escape bids was made. As men exercised on a wooden vaulting horse in an open space inside the camp, one or two men hidden inside the horse dug a tunnel, carefully sealing its entrance at the end of each session. Eventually the hole enabled three of them to make their way to freedom, an escape immortalised in the 1950 movie *The Wooden Horse*.[69] Thereafter the Germans displayed a heightened attentiveness to such ruses and the opportunities that sporting activities might provide.

As by its nature the game of cricket did not invite conjecture that it might conceal a bid for escape, or indeed that it might entail any form of physical or mental exertion, one wonders what the Germans might have made of it. Why, they must have pondered, would one team be represented by just two players at a time, the other nine simply sitting and watching? Their curiosity piqued, in many camps they tolerated the playing of cricket, albeit without going to any lengths to offer ideal facilities and equipment. That, as was typically the case in matters of sport, was left largely to the prisoners themselves and the YMCA.

At the *Milag* at Westertimke on the flat plains of northern Germany the merchant seamen POWs counted cricket among a variety of sports they played to stave off boredom. Whether spectators shared the benefits is not clear, but cricket was played on the cinder-sandy surface of the camp's *Platz*, its central square. One of the players was an Englishman who, many years later, was to become known to Australians as the endearingly eccentric cricket umpire Arthur 'Dicky' Bird. In his memoirs, Bird describes the spectacle of the cricket matches arranged by the Milag Sports Organisation, which in 1942 put no fewer than seventeen teams into the field on a barrack basis. Balls were produced ingeniously by winding Red Cross parcel string around a pebble; seamen would then apply their expertise with rope to cover the outside with a series of 'fancy work' hitches. Bats were carved from wood, but pads were unavailable to batsmen and wicketkeepers alike. By the second season things improved when the owners of the ship on which Bird had been captured supplied a set of equipment; the Germans contributed by laying a strip of concrete, duly covered with matting, to form a pitch in a sandy stretch called 'Siberia'.[70]

Bird recalls that 'Test' matches provoked a high level of excitement in the camp, conceding that despite the relatively few men from which to pick a team the Australians acquitted themselves remarkably well. 'Ashes' matches were played in 1942 and in 1943 and in both cases were won by the Australian Eleven, allowing them to take possession of a replica, carved Ashes trophy. Alas for the England team, the 1944 series was not completed, and despite winning the first four matches they were unable to claim the trophy, which the South Australian Vic Marks stubbornly kept in his possession, proudly displaying it on the cover of his own POW memoirs.[71]

Cricket was played at a number of other camps too. Stalag 383 Hohenfels, Stalag Luft VI Heydekrug, Oflag IX A/H Spangenberg and Stalag VIII B Lamsdorf all staged matches.[72] At the last venue one of the outstanding Australian players was Alan Snedden, a right-arm bowler who, in a match against New Zealand, achieved the figures of 5/13 and 9/18.[73] One assessment avers that he bowled 'at a lively pace with a Jeff Thomson-like slinging action and was able to get considerable cut from the off on the matting wicket'.[74] A less graceful but nonetheless effective player was the RAAF airman G.S. 'Pat' Ferrero, who captained Australia in a mock 'Ashes' series played at Lamsdorf, earning a reputation as a shrewd and popular captain, impervious to the pressure from crowds of

CAPTIVITY

up to 2500.[75] Stalag Luft III Sagan seems to have been similarly blessed with Australian cricketing talent. Among the prisoners there was Flight Lieutenant Keith Carmody, an Australian batsman who in 1943, before his capture, had captained an Australian XI against England. The following year he was in Sagan with Flying Officer Peter Pearson, a more than handy left-hand bowler whose wicket-taking was decisive in another Australian 'Test' victory over England played behind barbed wire.[76]

Football was already the World Game and was widely played not only in *Stalags* and *Oflags* but even in some of the bigger labour detachments like E3 Blechhammer. E3 had its own soccer pitch, made by POW labour, which had also fashioned the string from Red Cross parcels into goal nets. With some talented British players in the camp, Ray Corbett resigned himself to playing in goal, but he made a good fist of it. Competitions were played between rooms and blocks.[77]

Rugby, too, was widely played in camps with British POWs, though not altogether without reservations on the part of the Germans. At Oflag XVII A Edelbach in Austria the commandant went so far as to ban the game because of the damage it caused to the playing field.[78] More commonly, and especially in the latter part of the war, when men's constitutions weakened under poor diets, the full-contact version of the game had to be abandoned for health reasons.

At Hohenfels, with its sizeable Australian population, the Reich received its first and modest exposure to the joys of Australian football, albeit with modified rules that forbade the hip and shoulder and tackling a man to the ground. About half the 500 Australians in the camp were from the Australian football-playing states, and by the end of 1942 had adapted a rugby ball and a football pitch to their purposes. By the following year the Australians were running their own competition among four teams: Kangaroos, Emus, Kookaburras and Wallabies, with two other teams, the Snakes and Goannas, as reserves. With makeshift jerseys and footwear, it was a crude affair played on the camp's parade ground.[79] One particular highlight was the staging of a kind of state-of-origin match between

Western Australians and Victorians in late May 1943. The Western Sandgropers ran out winners thanks to some inaccurate kicking by the eastern Vics. For the record, the score was 10.8 (68) to 8.19 (67).[80] But in that same year a doctor put a stop to Australian football altogether because of the many broken bones and other injuries incurred on the hard ground.[81]

As the makeshift carnival recorded on camera by the Red Cross at Wolfsberg had shown, athletics was the purest and most readily adaptable of the sporting contests. If Ray Corbett had struggled to adapt to the unfamiliar space between football goalposts in Blechhammer, his natural athleticism lent him a great advantage in various athletic disciplines. His superior height and strength gave him an unassailable advantage over his mainly English opponents. The camera which he, almost incredibly, kept in his possession in captivity records one of his many triumphs on the athletics field, capturing him in the moment of clearing the high-jump bar.

At other camps, too, Australians excelled in athletics. The YMCA went so far as to sponsor an athletics carnival in the Silesian camp of Görlitz in June 1944 as a way of celebrating the YMCA's centenary, apparently with great success. The ANZACs were declared the winners; one of their star performers was an Australian who set a new camp record of 11 seconds flat for the 100 metres dash.[82]

Other sporting achievements are remarkable for having taken place at all. Photographic evidence exists of a surf carnival march-past at Stalag 344, complete with a bamboo flagpole, home-made reel and costumes consisting of singlets and shorts.[83] For one bizarre moment, at least, a small corner of the Reich was most distinctively Australian. One of the more basic requirements for surf-lifesaving – namely water – was present in the camp in the form of a reservoir, there primarily to help douse any fire that might break out. But as Charles Willoughby and others recalled, even if the water was not changed for years on end, the reservoir served as a venue for a range of aquatic sports. Willoughby himself was a member of the camp's Australian Water Polo Team; its group portrait, along with images of various swimming teams, is held in the Australian War Memorial. His other chosen sporting pastime in the camp was boxing – he was a member of the 'Four Post Club' for both boxers and wrestlers. Both sports were well suited to working off some of the frustrations and tensions of kriegie life. Alas, Willoughby does not record who his opposition was, with the exception of one boxing tournament in which he managed to floor his Palestinian Jewish opponent with a left hook, much to the dismay of the many who had placed their money on the Palestinian.[84]

Weirdly, too, there was a golf course of sorts at Stalag Luft III Sagan. The sandy soil there presented problems for tunnellers, but it was well suited to the construction of a crude, links-style nine-hole golf course. Prepared with POW labour – even the most Anglophile of the Germans had little appreciation of the game, let alone an interest in facilitating it – the holes varied in length from 50 to 120 metres. The challenges came then not from daunting fairways but rather from the requirement that the player provide his own ball and book in advance the one club available.[85]

Whatever the sport of preference or necessity was, its benefits were apparent to all. Sport brought with it the prospect of transcendence, an escape from the cruel monotony and troubles of kriegie life to the comforting certainties of their most elemental, physical selves. And for a short time, at least, sport was a chance to forget – or perhaps to remember – who the real enemy was.

14

Working for the Führer

In the popular understanding of life as a POW in Germany, whether gleaned from books, movies or from *Hogan's Heroes*, the men allowed the days to pass idly by, at most exercising their minds and limbs preparing some devious plot to fool Jerry and effect a daring escape. For the great majority of POWs, life in captivity was nothing like that at all. Most spent the bulk of their days labouring hard for the Reich, typically against their will and at untold cost to their health, both then and later.

When large numbers of Australians fell into German hands in the middle of 1941, the German authorities had no inkling of how important POW labour was to become to them. It was only when the campaign in the East became mired on Russia's plains that the German demand for labour grew exponentially and attitudes to POWs changed. They were to become an indispensable part of the German war economy. After murdering and starving nearly three million Soviets for months, from February of 1942 the Nazi regime shifted the 1.1 million survivors and newcomers into its burgeoning labour force. There they joined the existing POW labour force, along with 2.1 million civilian workers already conscripted into labour ranks before *Barbarossa* was unleashed. By 1944, with total war in full swing, there were eight million foreign workers and POWs in the Reich and a further two million working under German command outside it.[1]

The Australians were just a drop in the ocean. For the most part they laboured under tolerable work conditions, yet one cannot assume that all Australians experienced identical conditions, or that the provisions of Geneva were applied consistently. Treatment could depend very heavily on the temperament or even the whim of the employer.

Officers enjoyed the privilege enshrined in the Geneva Convention of not being required to work. NCOs occupied a kind of twilight world, since they could legitimately be required to perform supervisory duties, but not to offer their own labour. Should they choose to, however, they could work and in doing so hope to keep their minds and bodies fit, avoiding the danger of slipping into the tedium of life behind the wire. Some of these men might have had one eye on the prospect of escape, easier to contemplate from the rough accommodation of a work detachment than behind the watch towers and barbed wire of a camp. But others took the view that any kind of work was a contribution to the German war effort, and far from aiding one's health, a bad detachment with long hours, hard labour and poor conditions could be injurious. They refused, as was their right as NCOs, and from late 1942 many of the Australians found themselves in Stalag 383 Hohenfels in Bavaria. They were joined by some other ranks who granted themselves 'Stalag promotions', claiming to have lost their pay book and enjoying inactivity as NCOs until truth caught up with them.[2] Frank Cox had the good fortune of meeting in his camp at Spittal a more than competent forger who 'organised' some promotion documents which fooled the camp authorities. From that time on, Cox was no longer a humble signalman but a corporal and, in theory at least, no longer working for the Führer.[3]

Airmen were classified as either officers or NCOs, so they could not be set to work. That meant that there were no work detachments based at Göring's *Stalag Luft* camps. But there were airmen's compounds at Silesian Lamsdorf and Saxon Mühlberg, and there were airmen who were known to swap identities with captured soldiers with the specific aim of joining a work detachment based outside the camp. The idea, of course, was not to work but to use the opportunity a work detachment might provide for escape. With those exceptions, however, the airmen did not join the ranks of the Reich's forced labourers.

Jack Parsons of the Australian Army Medical Corps was indisputably exempted from work according to the Geneva Convention, and on two counts. He was an NCO – his rank was that of lance-sergeant – and as a member of the Australian Army Medical Corps he was protected personnel. Captured in Crete along with Leslie Le Souef, the Germans pressed him to work after his arrival in the Reich, but Parsons knew the terms of the Geneva Convention and refused. The guard called together a firing squad and placed Parsons up against a wall, but he still refused to work. Even as the firing squad raised their rifles, Parsons remained obstinate: 'If you shoot I can't: if you don't, I won't.' Indeed they did not shoot, and Parsons did not work.[4]

If the NCOs felt at best ambivalent about the prospect of working, it was an ambivalence which came to be shared by their captors. POWs could indeed be a handy labour force in times of chronic labour shortages, but they also needed to be adequately fed, clothed and housed outside their *Stalags*.[5] Above all, they needed to be watched with an eagle eye, not just to prevent escape but to counter their natural inclination to shirk. The British NCOs in particular proved to be at best a troublesome and recalcitrant bunch, not least because of the well-founded suspicion that they engaged in acts of sabotage. When push came to shove, the Germans were happy for NCOs who had second thoughts about making their labour available to be returned to their camps. An OKW order from June 1942 stated: 'British NCOs who have agreed in writing to work but who are now no longer prepared to work are to be sent back to their camps. The NCOs are not to be regarded as shirkers. The deployment of British NCOs has had so many disadvantages that they far outweigh the benefits.'[6] Only from 1944, when the need for POW labour was desperate, was this policy reversed.[7]

As for members of the other ranks, whose obligation to work was not disputed, the OKW could exercise its claim on them from the very beginning of their captivity. And from the time that the Germans recognised how crucial POW labour was going to be for the war effort, they made it clear that the direction to work had the status of a military order; the guards were instructed to apply force of arms if necessary.[8] The detaining power was, however, obliged to pay the men, although this was hardly an impediment to exploiting them. Pay rates were less than handsome. Theoretically they received about 60 per cent of what a civilian worker performing identical work would earn, but in practical terms the payment was as good as meaningless anyway. It came from the employer, who paid it not to the POW but to the *Stalag*, who credited it to the men or paid it as *Lagergeld* – camp money – which was recognised in one place and one place only, namely the camp canteen, typically devoid of any products worthy of purchase.[9]

One historian of POWs in Japanese captivity claims that Australians made the best workers. In order of working ability, Gavan Daws calculates, it was a case of 'Australians 1, English 2, Americans 3, Dutch 4'. This quasi-official ranking was complemented by an unofficial saying: 'One Aussie, fifteen Englishmen, four hundred Dutchmen.'[10] But in Germany the Australian POWs seem to have developed a knack and a reputation for avoiding work. The Germans themselves came to notice this. In December 1942 the Chief of the Security Police received information under the heading 'Report on Inadequate Work Performance of POWs'. It claimed that from all over the Reich reports were being received of shirking by POWs in both rural and factory employment. The complaints, it was stated, 'concern not only French and Belgian POWs but to an equal extent English, Australian POWs and those of other nations'. Indeed, attempts to improve work performance by loosening security arrangements – following a secret decree issued by the OKW on 20 March 1942 – had only led to a slackening of attitude and performance by Western POWs.[11]

German photograph of Australian troops captured in the Greek campaign, Corinth, April 1941. bpk | Bayerische Staatsbibliothek | Archiv Heinrich Hoffmann

The moment of capture. British forces defending Crete surrender to German paratroops, May 1941. Bundesarchiv, Bild 1011-166-0509-16, Photographer: Franz Peter Weixler

German forces inspect weaponry and equipment left behind by British forces captured at Sphakia on the south coast of Crete, June 1941. Bundesarchiv, Bild 1011-166-0516-09, Photographer: Strassl

One of the victors in the Battle for Crete, a German sergeant major (*Oberfeldwebel*) of the mountain infantry, decorated with the Iron Cross First Class and Second Class. Bundesarchiv, Bild 1011-166-0516-08, Photographer: Strassl

Colonel General (later Field Marshal) Erwin Rommel, flanked on his left by General Fritz Bayerlein, walks past recently captured British POWs at Tobruk, circa June 1942. Bundesarchiv, Bild 1011-785-0299-24A, Photographer: Moosmüller

The main entrance to the Italian prisoner of war camp PG 57 at Gruppignano in northern Italy, circa 1941. By October 1942 there were more than 1200 Australians and 1000 New Zealanders held in this camp. AWM P02793.001

Left: POWs being evacuated from Italy to Germany in a cattle truck, September 1943.
Leighton McLeod Hill, DA-11319, War History Collection, Alexander Turnbull Library

Right: A shackled POW at Stalag VIII B Lamsdorf holds a Red Cross parcel, 1943. © CICR

Below: View of 'ANZAC Avenue' in Stalag 383, a camp for NCOs at Hohenfels in Bavaria. The avenue is bordered by the living quarters of Australian and New Zealand POWs. A watch tower is visible in the right background.
AWM 072850

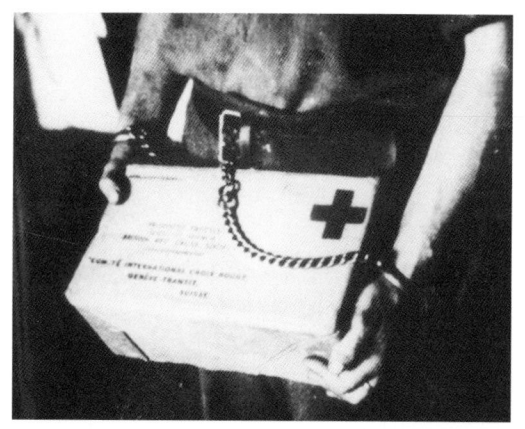

Reclining POW airmen sun themselves outside their barracks at Stalag Luft I Barth, the first and the best of the airmen's camps. The photograph was taken during a Red Cross inspection in July 1941. © CICR

Heinrich Himmler looks through a barbed wire fence to inspect Soviet POWs, circa 1941. © CORBIS

A group of Jewish POWs from Palestine, captured during the Greek campaign, being held separately at Stalag XVIII D Marburg. The image is the work of a photographer accompanying Red Cross delegates visiting the camp on 21 July 1941. © CICR

Tommy 'Negus' Green, POW at Stalag XIII C Hammelburg, smoking a pipe. Green, an Aboriginal serviceman, had been named 'Negus' by the German guards at the camp. AWM P04379.003

Group portrait of Australian and New Zealand POWs on stage following a concert called 'Anzacs on Parade' in Stalag 383. Identified are: Sergeant David William Barry, 2/4th Battalion (standing, third from right), and Spence Hill, New Zealand Infantry (standing, centre wearing a grey short sleeved shirt).
AWM P0376.005

Prisoners of war attend a class given by a fellow POW in Stalag VIII B Lamsdorf, the largest of the 'British' camps, in 1942. © CICR

A composite Australian and New Zealand rugby union team at E3 Blechhammer. Holding the ball in the front row is Ray Corbett. Ray Corbett collection.

Ray Corbett clears the high jump bar at E3 Blechhammer. Ray Corbett collection.

Group portrait of POWs at Stalag 383 Hohenfels who made up the Australian water polo team. They are posed in front of the fire-fighting reservoir, which was used for swimming; the water was not changed for three years. AWM P02071.032

A Red Cross delegate, Dr Descoeudres, visits the worksite of a detachment based at Stalag XVIII A Wolfsberg. © CICR

'British' POWs on a detachment from Stalag VIII B Lamsdorf working inside a Silesian coal mine. © Photothèque CICR (DR)

Group portrait in Stalag 383 Hohenfels. Identified are: Tim West (front row, left); Les Fox (middle row, second from left); Colin McClure (middle row, third from left); Diamond Jim (middle row, fourth from left); New Zealander Spence Hill standing, left); Frank Bourne (standing, second from left), Joe Rogini (standing, third from left). AWM P00110.037

German officers at Stalag XVIII A Wolfsberg examine supplies of Red Cross parcels.
© CICR

Portrait of Flight Sergeant James Gwilliam and Flight Sergeant Eric L. Johnston, both of No. 78 (Halifax) Squadron. Shot down on 22 June 1944 en route to a bombing mission in northern France, they were later transported to Buchenwald Concentration Camp, Germany, then transferred to Stalag Luft III Sagan.
AWM P02961.002

SS General Gottlob Berger, who as Chef Kriegsgefangenenwesen took over the running of POW Affairs in the Reich from October 1944.
Bundesarchiv, Bild 183-S73321

Group portrait of Australian POWs at the 'Holiday Camp' at Genshagen outside Berlin in October 1944. This photograph was made into a postcard for POWs to send home to their families. AWM P00877.001

A group of POWs from the Genshagen 'Holiday Camp' enjoying a tour of Berlin. The provision of new uniforms and decent food, along with the freedom to tour the Reich capital supervised by just a single guard with a side-arm, was designed to entice them to join the British Free Corps. Ray Corbett collection.

A disguised John Peck and his Italian collaborator, Oreste Ferrari, in Luino, December 1943, a month before their arrest by the Gestapo. Ferrari was responsible for arranging guides to take escaped POWs to the Swiss border. He spent the rest of the war in concentration camps in Fossoli and Mauthausen.
AWM PR03098.005

Repatriated Australians in conversation with the Vice-President of the Swedish Red Cross, 1943. Photothèque CICR (DR)/CHRISTIANSSON, Thure

Exchange of POWs between Germany and the Allies. The German Ambassador to Spain, Dr Hans Dieckhoff, watches Australian POWs disembark from a German ship in Barcelona. Pictures Collection, State Library of Victoria

The moment of liberation, 13 April 1945. A jeep from the US 3rd Armoured Division enters a farm at Wimmelburg, where Allied POWs from Oflag IX A/Z Rotenburg had been billeted by their German guards. The guards had abandoned them on the previous evening. Leighton McLeod Hill, 1/4-069779-F, War History Collection, Alexander Turnbull Library

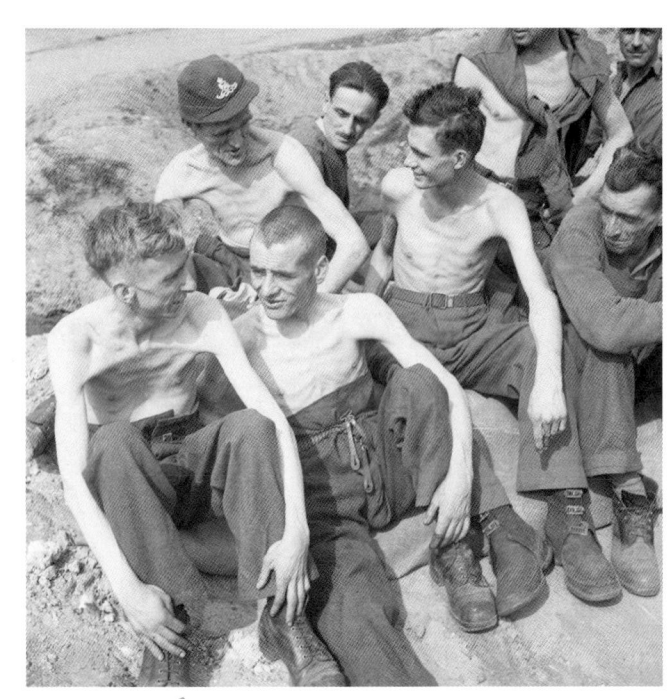

Emaciated former POWs at Stalag XI B Fallingbostel, 17 April 1945, soon after liberation by British forces.
Imperial War Museum BU 3865

Australian Private Lawrence Phillip Saywell, 17th Brigade Company (wearing glasses), Private Sydney O.C. Kerkham of New Zealand (far left) and two Russians, in 1942. In January 1943 they escaped from a work detachment in Bohemia during a route march. Private Saywell was murdered – shot in the head by a German SS Patrol on 8 May 1945 (VE Day), the last Australian killed in Europe. AWM P02551.006

Drawing from 1945 by the Australian war artist Alan Moore. It depicts recovered Australian prisoners of war in (possibly) a German staff car passing by a column of German soldiers. Two of the Australians are giving a mock Nazi salute. AWM ART25518

RAAF ex-POWs outside Somers House, Brighton, where Australian Red Cross workers supplied them with refreshments in the place known as 'Kriegies Corner', 8 August 1945. AWM UK3136

Arrival in Sydney on 23 May 1945 of the first group of Australian POWs liberated by the Western allies in Europe. Shown are Private R.V. Morrison and his wife and other members of his family. AWM 108023

The attitude of the Western POWs was the subject of a further security report filed in August 1943. The British POWs, an observer from central Germany claimed, 'all show an outwardly self-confident demeanour bordering on arrogance'.[12] Another report, this time from Danzig, complained of the disrespectful conduct of the POWs. 'The general conduct of the British POWs toward the Reich is absolutely hostile. They mock the Reich, its institutions and its leading personalities at every available opportunity.'[13] And if that was not troubling enough, it was added that the negative attitudes of British POWs were spreading to other foreign workers, leading to a general decline in performance.[14]

There was no reason for the attitudes of the POWs to improve as the war continued. Even in the relative isolation of POW camps or work detachments, the POWs knew broadly about the course of the war; after D-Day in 1944, they were well aware that in both the East and the West Allied forces had gained the upper hand. As their captors' desperation grew, so too did the determination of the POWs not to contribute in any way to the German economy.

Just how soon the men could be pressed into service is apparent from tales set in the Mediterranean. In Greece the rapid German deployment of POW labour was driven by the logistical needs of the provisional camps and of other German facilities. That meant tasks like loading and unloading of supply depots, repairing damaged infrastructure, or helping out in camp and hospital kitchens. Given the shortage of food in the provisional early camps, work in kitchens was often considered a desirable alternative to vegetating among the hungry masses. But all other work was more perilous and unpleasant. Men in the Corinth camp, for example, were subjected to German regulations which said quite explicitly, 'The English prisoners must be put immediately in work detachments. They must rebuild all that they have destroyed.'[15] Other ranks, under the supervision of sergeants, were formed into detachments and sent out from the camp under tight guard; among their jobs was the repair of roads and bridges or even the removal of bombs and dud shells scattered across the area.[16]

Reg Worthington was one of those men captured at Kalamata

and dumped in the Corinth camp who was set to work. He considered himself lucky to be assigned to a work party, because it meant extra rations – in the misery of Corinth an extra half-biscuit was highly desirable. In Salonika he behaved no differently, because there too work offered the prospect of extra rations and the chance to maintain a level of fitness in preparation for the unknown. So when the Germans guards approached to request working parties, he made it his business to join. Others, though, insisted that they 'were not going to work for the Huns'.[17]

Captured on Crete near Sphakia like so many others, Arthur Marshall spent time in a Suda jail before working for the Germans, reburying their dead and harvesting grain.[18] Roy Heron and Charlie Parrott too were among the Australians given the grisly task of burying the dead at the Suda Bay war cemetery.[19] In the aftermath of the vicious battles around the bay, Parrott remembers, the stench of decaying bodies hung over the island's north coast. Some of them had been just crudely half buried, so Parrott's job was to retrieve the German bodies, already dead about a fortnight, and place them in coffins for cemetery burial. His brother attempted the procrustean task of inserting a long body into a coffin plainly too short. He called a German guard over to seek advice, whereupon the guard took a pick and bashed the shins until the legs could be doubled up and he could report, 'He'll fit now.' Such was the jumble of rotting body parts that some coffins received just one leg, others three.[20]

Australians rendered a further service to the German war dead. Though Charles Jager himself did not do so – he managed to escape from the Galatas camp and make his way to Africa – he was aware that it was POW labour which built a monument to fallen German soldiers, the so-called Eagle of the Paratroopers, on the slopes overlooking Galatas. It was puzzling, he pondered many years later when visiting the island, 'that after the war the Cretans didn't take to it with sledgehammers but, no, they respect it as a memorial to the enemy's dead'.[21]

From the Skines camp, men like Roy East were taken down to the wharf at Suda Bay or the airfield at Maleme to unload ammunition from ships and airplanes. Apart from breaching the Geneva

Convention, which expressly forbade the war-related employment of POWs, the work was punishing for men who had been on half-rations even before capture and had not fared any better since. East fell down on many occasions, only to be beaten across the back or neck with rifle butts.[22]

Lew Lind was one of those who managed to escape from Crete by submarine, but before he did so the Germans found multiple uses for him. For a time he cleared the airfield at Maleme – another clear breach of Geneva – and when it was serviceable he had to load and unload German transport aircraft. Then he was assigned to building a jetty before, as he puts it, 'swallowing his pride' and becoming a batman to a German officer before once more performing loading duties. Shirkers were unwelcome; he remembers them being beaten across the shoulders with a piece of timber.[23]

In Africa, too, Australian POWs could find themselves working for the enemy. One of the strangest cases, and one which does not sit comfortably in the memory of Australians who spent time there, was at Gargaresc near Derna. It was unusual because this was initially an Italian camp where the German practice of handing their captives over to their Italian partners had been observed. But on this occasion the Germans in effect took their POWs back, deciding that they needed their labour, and so the unpleasant Italian Campo 59 became the genuinely nasty German Feldpost 12545.[24] The apparently innocuous military postcode masked something much more sinister, because at Feldpost 12545 the Germans set about exploiting POW labour for purposes in egregious breach of the Geneva Convention, requiring them to unload German military supplies in brutal conditions, and working long hours from sunrise to sunset. Moreover, a good percentage of the men drafted into this back-breaking labour were medical orderlies, a further violation of Geneva. One of them was the Australian John Milbank of the 2/8th Field Ambulance, who spent four and a half arduous months at Feldpost 12545 handling military supplies.[25]

The hapless Australian chaplain Ted Broomhead had a similar tale to tell about Feldpost 12545. After capture he was shunted off to Derna under Italian supervision, and from there he was taken to a camp in Tripoli. But then the Germans chose to take him and the medical personnel captured with him back into their control. In his case for over seven months, and sometimes for seven days a week, Broomhead slaved for the Germans alongside about 120 Australians and some 180 other British men, inhabiting a kind of enclave of German forced labour in territory where otherwise Italians ruled the roost.[26] The work days were long and their routines so repetitive that they melted into each other: 'Coffee, bread and a cubic inch of jam for breakfast; barely time to wash; the bawling and hectoring of parade; and the roaring lorries in the dark. By 4 o'clock in the morning the slave gangs had arrived at their destinations and started work, while the hot midsummer day commenced. They arrived home at eleven o'clock that night, lined up for a ladle of stew and ate their meal beside their bunks, in the darkness of the barracks. The next morning the call came at 4.'[27]

A similar fate befell the 'Rat of Tobruk' Bill Cousins of the 2/24th Infantry Battalion. Snatched from his Benghazi camp, he was required to work for the Germans unloading ammunition from barges bringing ammunition from ships anchored in the harbour. Then the POWs had to transfer it from the barges onto trucks. It was heavy work, potentially lethal in the event of an air raid. Moreover, there was no joy in the knowledge that the ammunition would then make its way to the front to be used against his countrymen, but there was one consolation. When the guards were looking the other way, the men would allow quantities of ammunition to slip overboard into the water.[28]

For the other ranks transferred to Italy, the POW camps and work detachments there became their new workplaces. The story of Ray Jones stands for that of many. After capture in North Africa and transfer to Italy, he was taken north to Campo PG 57 at Udine. From there, he and many other Australians were taken to Campo 106 in the Po Valley near Vercelli in north-west Italy. It was a rice-growing area, and Jones found himself with some 50 other Australians working on a rice farm. Planting the rice was women's work; they worked in great lines, singing as they went. The POWs worked at a distance from them, preparing the ground and performing long hours of manual labour to ensure that the channels they dug in the earth diverted the right amount of water into the fields. Jones was lucky. As a former driver of a Bren gun carrier, he scored the task of driving a tractor, a rare Italian example of mechanisation in agriculture. He was the envy of his mates, who worked on their feet all day long using more traditional tools. What they all came to share after many months in the fields was a hatred of rice.[29]

Inside the Reich there was a queue of German authorities waiting to secure the POWs' services. Outside the Reich, of course, the army exercised a complete monopoly, but inside it had some rivals in the labour market: Hermann Göring had ministerial responsibilities in the area as well as his own war enterprises, Albert Speer ran munitions factories, Fritz Sauckel built a foreign labour empire, Himmler's SS had a massive economic arm, while countless small and large businesses throughout the Reich desperately sought to counter chronic labour shortfalls. Each of them, including the OKW itself, jealously guarded its labour pool. The Wehrmacht's district commanders commonly struck convenient arrangements with their local employment offices and were reluctant to transfer their POWs to other districts.[30]

Broadly, two possibilities awaited the Australian other ranks on entering the Reich. They might be employed in agricultural labour – in the *Landwirtschaft* – or they might have one of a very large range of jobs in the German *Gewerbewirtschaft*, in industry. The former option was likely to entail participation in a relatively small work detachment – an *Arbeitskommando* – under conditions which varied hugely depending on the location, the season, and above all on the employer. It was almost invariably some form of farm work, and that brought with it the not inconsiderable advantage of access to food, an almost constant thought on the POW's mind. With its often makeshift security arrangements, the agricultural work detachment also offered the potential benefit of relative ease of escape.

Transported north from Salonika, most Australian POWs were delivered to camps in Austria or Bavaria, parts of the Reich which were known not for their industry but for their farmland and rolling pasture. After arrival at camps such as Marburg or Wolfsberg it was often just a short time before the men were allocated to farms in the surrounding areas, from where the young men had been conscripted into the Reich's armed forces, and those left behind were coping as well as they could. Unwilling and often inexperienced POWs were generally considered a poor substitute for the dead or absent loved ones, yet from the farmers' viewpoint they were better than no substitute at all.

Farmers needing extra assistance would turn to the local employment office, the Arbeitsamt, which would seek to meet their needs from the pool of forced labourers and POWs who had entered the Reich. If the pool included workers from the nearest *Stalag*, then either the men would be allocated directly to farms or, in a variation on the tradition of the cattle market, the farmers themselves would choose from an assembly of available men. The POWs had little say in where they were employed, what kind of work they were to perform and how long they were to stay there. Some might stay for years on the same farm, whereas others worked in different kinds of labour at a variety of locations over the course of their captivity, even sent from one part of the Reich to another.

Starvation was an unlikely outcome of farm work, yet it was no picnic either. To the uninitiated especially, farm labour could be tough, the employer could be ill-disposed to his hireling, and even the landscape, picturesque though it often was, could provide challenges of its own. One Australian sent to a farm near Markt Pongau in southern Austria joked that the fields were so steep that 'farmers used to look up the chimney to see if the cows were coming home'.[31]

Reg Worthington was one of the Australians allocated to a work detachment on an Austrian farm, together with nine Englishmen. Worthington brought with him farm experience from Australia, but on the small-scale German farms things were different. Where in Australia he had milked 80 cows, the German farm had just four, two of which were used for ploughing in the absence of horses. Happily, he got on well with the farmer, Adolf, with whom he worked twelve hours a day through winter, fourteen in summer.

The farmer's wife was less welcoming: 'She was tougher. She was more pro-German than Adolf was.' One of the sons would visit on leave from the Eastern front and managed to converse with Worthington, becoming ever more fluent in German, without animosity. 'He was a German doing his bit. I was an Australian doing my bit. So we didn't hate each other, we understood each other.'[32] Here as on many other farms it was customary for the POWs to eat with the farmer's family, but accommodation was elsewhere in a crowded room.

For Jack Wooding, too, farm work was a mixed blessing. Sent out from the *Stalag* at Franconian Hammelburg, he shuffled around in completely unsatisfactory footwear – wooden clogs, the curse of countless POWs, concentration camp inmates and impecunious workers alike. His clothing was threadbare, and it took more than twelve months before the first mail arrived from Australia. But the food was the redeeming feature: 'We were now getting meals three times a day. In the morning, a big slice of farm-made rye bread with ersatz coffee (roast oats) and perhaps a piece of cheese, midday bread again with a piece of German sausage again home-made and in the evening there was something like a stew, often with small dumplings, plenty of potatoes, which were steamed never boiled in water.'[33]

Laurie West was also deposited initially at Hammelburg, but then drew the short straw. Although a sergeant and therefore as an NCO not required to work according to the provisions of the Geneva Convention, he was placed in a work camp at Fladungen in the Rhön Mountains of northern Bavaria. There he and his men performed heavy manual labour under civilian supervision, extracting rocks from a creek bed for use in road building. But then his fortune turned for the better, as he and a number of other Australians happily accepted the offer of transfers to farming detachments. He found himself living in the town of Hallstadt, also in northern Bavaria. There he and some 14 other POWs were accommodated in an ancient brick mill, constructed, as the date inscribed in its wall proclaimed, in the year 1594. The Australians lived upstairs, sleeping in double-tiered bunks, their guards nearby and their hosts downstairs. Of course, the farming methods were those practised for hundreds of years, and quite different from Australia, but although working hours were long it was a more agreeable way to pass the time than building roads.

Some further dignity was restored with the arrival of British battledress and boots to replace the tawdry collection of vestments they had received in Salonika. Moreover, the living arrangements were such that the POWs would break bread and exchange stories with their hosts in what rudiments of German they had acquired. After some eight months, this all came to an end when word was received that NCOs indeed could not be required to work, and for all the advantages that farm life offered, West exercised his prerogative not to make any kind of contribution to the enemy's labour needs and, acting out of soldierly duty, returned 'to the wire', to Hohenfels, his home for the next two-and-a-half years.[34]

In many instances the goodwill of the farmer and guards was in short supply. Peter Barrett was accommodated in an old ski chalet in Bavaria, where he and others were expected to sleep on bagged-up straw on the ground. When they asked for proper bedding, they were lined up, and some were butted in the face with rifles. Barrett had some of his teeth knocked out.[35] Stanley Leonard had a similar experience on a Bavarian farm in Oberstreu. He was so disenchanted with the treatment meted out to him by the farmer that he applied on numerous occasions for a transfer, but his requests were turned down. When he made a further attempt, as he recalled in a statutory declaration after the war, his farmer, enthusiastically assisted by a guard and the local *Bürgermeister* 'locked me in a room and commenced to bash me around, whilst lying on floor Burgomeister [sic] and Wutischer [the farmer] kicked me in the ribs, and on previous occasion Wutischer struck me with horse-whip, he had a vile temper, and all day he called me English swine and British dog'.[36]

Another Australian POW, John McTigue, had a similarly disposed farmer, as he recalled in the 1950s:

> We moved to Grauthorn in January 1942 and were each billeted on farms.
> I have to remark here that a certain prominent politician said in Federal

Parliament that he understood that 'prisoners on Austrian farms had quite a good time'. Mine was at Eganfald – the name of the farmer, 'Furstl'. The prisoner on this farm before I went there, died in the unheated stone hut in which I lived. I was five weeks on this farm and collapsed from exposure, malnutrition, and the skin complaint that goes with these things. I literally crawled to the doctor in the village some kilometres away, who ordered me immediately back to Stalag. [. . .] V.C. Makepeace, 2/4th Battalion, who was unlucky enough to succeed me at Furstl's farm, died within three weeks, supposedly of Meningitis, nobody ever knew; as Makepeace had no medical attention, nobody to lay him out, but his comrades who discovered his twisted up body in the unheated stone hut, and no clergyman to officiate at his graveside when his cobbers buried him.[37]

Even in Austria most work detachments were in some branch of industry, the Gewerbewirtschaft.[38] Doug Nix was a case in point. Though based at the *Stalag* in Wolfsberg and a veteran of a number of working detachments, he never worked on a farm. Mostly he was allocated to factory jobs, but for him the toughest of the work was railway work. After bombing raids, his gang would fill in craters and lay down new sleepers. At times trucks had to be loaded and unloaded, perilous work when trains, too, were becoming the targets of accurate Allied bombing. He was almost killed working on a train at the small Austrian town of St Lambrecht when Allied fighters raided the railyard.[39]

Patrick Toovey was another. From his *Stalag* at Markt Pongau in Austria he was required to perform a range of duties, from heavy labour building air-raid shelters in Graz – so heavy as to lead to a stint in hospital – to various lighter jobs in numerous places. In the end he could claim that he knew Austria better than he knew his home state of Western Australia. One of the more unusual jobs was at a hospital, which was being expanded to take larger numbers of German soldier casualties being sent back into the Reich from the Eastern Front. He aided in the expansion of the facility, adding prefabricated wards at the rate of as many as six a day. But the flow of patients never eased, as he became aware while transferring casualties from trains to the hospital. The most common wounds were from frostbite rather than gunshots, but whatever the cause of hospitalisation it was evident that the steady stream of the wounded from the East was a reality to which the German authorities preferred not to expose its civilian population. For that reason, POW labour was worth tapping.[40]

Red Cross inspectors agreed that the industrial working parties from Wolfsberg were no holiday. A report from October 1944 recorded sympathetically, 'Work is hard, tiring and dirty in the industrial working parties. Only a few town detachments provide work which corresponds to the prisoners' civilian occupations; all the other working parties continue from 10 to 12 hours daily, very often on piecework.'[41] Neither did the German authorities shy away from repeating the breaches of the Geneva Convention perpetrated outside the Reich. In Military District XVIII alone there were six armaments factories which employed British POW labour.[42]

Inside the 'Old Reich', Bavarian camps offered a comparable palette of work options. Numbers of Australians were transported from Salonika straight to Stalag VII A at Moosburg, just north of Munich. One of those was Lyle Cullinger of the 2/7th Infantry Battalion, who after arrival in Moosburg was soon allocated to work outside the camp. He was sent to a detachment providing labour for a contractor building air-raid shelters: 'Many tools went into the concrete mix. If Munich was bombed, we were sent out to clear the rubble at the site destroyed. We shared this task with Concentration Camp inmates from Dachau. Slave labour.'[43]

There was a work detachment also in Munich's West End. By the time John Williamson was sent there it was the winter of 1941–42, and in the freezing cold he was put to work digging sewers and mending streets, 'from dark until dark'. Then he and sixteen others were sent to the district of Waldfriedhof, marching into the city every day to labour in asphalt manufacturing works before going out to repair streets and shovel snow from footpaths. It was a cold winter, and the only footwear they had was clogs and pieces of cloth for socks.[44]

Lindsay Lawrence recalls the routine of being sent by train from Moosburg to the West End railyards, where the selection of workers for various duties had all the charm of a slave market. The men were marched into a paddock where prospective employers ogled them; one even felt the muscles of their legs and arms. It reminded the Australians of a sheep sale, so of course they started to bleat, persuading the guards that the men must be allocated their jobs in groups and on the basis of their appearance alone. Lawrence duly found himself in a group of about 140 working for the construction company Liebherr.[45]

One work detachment based at Moosburg earned a certain notoriety. This was work detachment 2780, and its specialty was road clearing. When Red Cross inspectors visited the detachment in 1942, they noted that most of the men there – 212 of the 362 – were Australians, and they were doing it tough. The camp was overcrowded, the latrines were insufficient in number and approachable only via deep mud or snow, three of them had seats which were 'repulsively filthy', and the work was long and arduous. The men often had to spend a good part of the day just getting to their workplace, rising as early as 4 am to travel up to 22 kilometres on foot, arriving back at camp as late as 7.30 pm. With little chance to catch up on rest – they regularly worked Sundays – it was little wonder that the inspector noted an atmosphere of discontent bordering on mutiny.[46]

For the Australians sent to *Stalags* in the Silesian Military District VIII – and from there to work detachments in occupied Poland or even in Czechoslovakia – the balance was tipped even more heavily towards industrial work. By March 1942 the vast camp Stalag VIII B Lamsdorf alone was the base for some 260 work detachments of vastly varying sizes, from just a handful of men up to thousands.[47] A list of detachments based at another Silesian camp, Stalag VIII A Görlitz, gives some indication of the gamut of labour options, ranging from work in paper factories, quarries, brickworks, iron foundries, sugar factories, flax mills, gas works, clay pits, railways and coal mines through to forestry and town administration. Two of the detachments, 11501 and 11502 at Rothenburg, are listed as 'aircraft factories'.[48]

Some of the Australians found themselves doing work they would not have dreamed of. Sent straight from Salonika to

Lamsdorf, Ray Corbett soon found himself processing sugar beet. If he had to work, this seemed at first not such a terrible option: a sugar factory would surely offer shelter, warmth and food through the depths of a Silesian winter. All the greater was the dashing of their expectations, since in reality labour at the sugar factory stretched over twelve miserable hours a day, from before dawn to twilight or beyond, six days a week. A horse-drawn cart would deliver the beet to the icy slush of the factory compound, where Corbett and his fellow POWs, many wearing just clogs or foot-cloths to protect their feet, would receive it and guide it through the stages of its processing under the watchful eyes of the guards.[49]

George Blanch, also one of those sent straight from Salonika to Silesia, was allocated to a cement factory. His first job there was to load a barge:

> We had to unload 250 tons of cement out of a rail truck into a barge, eight men, four down in the barge and four unloading the cement out of the rail truck, the cement was red hot having just come from the cement factory. We were given some tape to put on our fingers but it only lasted about one hour and then we had to handle the bags of cement without any tape so our fingers were bleeding all the time and the bags of cement had blood all over them but we still had to keep going and unload the 250 tons or we didn't get anything to eat that night. We had German guards standing over us all the time to make sure we didn't break any of the bags. After I had been there for about six months I developed 35 boils on my stomach so the Doctor sent me back to Stalag VIII B [Lamsdorf] where I was put in a Hospital for a little over a week.[50]

John Williamson shared this fate, perhaps even on the same detachment. He had earlier been in a quarry, which he had left when he broke his false teeth and was unable to eat the hard biscuit ration. But it was a case of leaving the frypan for the fire, because he too had to handle cement at his new workplace, at a further cost to his health. 'Handling the hot bags of cement was torture, it burnt our hands, and we had no respite, the only thing to do was to throw a bag in such a manner that it fell and spilled the contents [. . .] Then of course we had to sweep every bit of spilt cement and the air was thick with cement dust which got into one's lungs and caused coughing.'[51]

From Lamsdorf many of the Australians found themselves allocated to detachments serving the huge industrial sites the Germans were establishing in that part of the world. What all of them had in common was their brief – to serve the growing needs of the German military–industrial complex. To achieve that end, they developed an ever more insatiable appetite for whatever kind of labour they could get their hands on.

The most notorious of all was at Auschwitz, a complex in three parts. While more notorious for its concentration camp in the town of Auschwitz itself, and the nearby extermination facilities at Birkenau, the epicentre of the Holocaust, the Auschwitz complex also included an industrial plant, variously called Auschwitz III or Monowitz or even Buna. Monowitz had massive resources allocated to it in the vain hope of producing synthetic rubber, vital for the war effort. Among the labourers there were POWs, including British POWs, drawn from labour detachments based at Silesian *Stalags*. Though they lived in different worlds and were imprisoned for quite different reasons, in the workplace concentration camp inmates and POWs at times laboured alongside each other. The most famous of the Jewish survivors of Monowitz, the Italian chemist Primo Levi, later wrote of his contact with British soldiers. Indeed, Levi's acquaintance Henri came to benefit greatly from the presence of the POWs, having learned that 'in exchange for a single cigarette you can make enough in the Lager not to starve for a day'.[52]

Whether there were Australians among the British POWs working at Monowitz is unclear, but there does exist at least one specific reference to Australian POWs in an Auschwitz-based work detachment. They are named and identified on a list of members of a POW work detachment transferred in January 1944 from Ottmachau in Upper Silesia to an Auschwitz detachment at Trzebinia, where there was an oil refinery. All 45 members of the detachment were from Commonwealth countries; three of them are listed as Australians.[53]

Then there was a huge complex employing POW labour at Blechhammer in Upper Silesia. At its height Blechhammer had some 20,000 POW and slave labourers, including Jews. The latter were accommodated separately, yet at the workplace the POWs would come in contact with them and could see just how abominably they were treated. Blechhammer was a series of factories spread over a site of some twelve square kilometres. The common speciality was the production of synthetic products ranging from oil to petrol and coke.[54] In that sense, Blechhammer was not unlike Buna or Monowitz, yet it had its redeeming features too. The commandant of the British camp there was a certain Rittmeister Prinz zu Hohenlöhe, a soldier of aristocratic pedigree who treated his charges with decency and even a degree of latitude, leading ultimately to his dismissal. Even the guards there under his command appear to have been of a more liberal bent than others. As so often, the degree of liberality could depend on the offer of cigarettes. A deal struck in this way at Blechhammer saw the guards turn a blind eye while the POWs exited through the wire at night, swam across the Adolf Hitler Canal and paid a visit to a civilian brothel, where a different kind of favour could be purchased with a bar of Red Cross chocolate.[55]

Ray Corbett remembers Blechhammer well. His E3 detachment was home to some 800 men, among them just a handful of Australians. It was one of the larger work camps, with eight low-set timber huts of six rooms. One block was set apart for administration and a sick bay, while another contained a recreation area, including not just a stage but an orchestra pit. In addition there were bathhouses with hot water, a cook-house, a tailor's shop and a coal shed. The strong British character of the camp was reflected in the ironic names bestowed on the cinder roads separating the buildings: Mayfair, Red Cross Street, The Old Kent Road and so on.[56]

Corbett enjoyed liberties he might only have dreamt of elsewhere. He found work for the Telefunken company, work that gave him the opportunity to travel from location to location, to take up contact with civilians, to pilfer and barter and do deals. Such were the liberties of his Telefunken job that he fashioned his own identity card as a Telefunken worker, complete with a small photograph of himself, and in time gained not only possession of a camera but access to developing agents and a darkroom. The camera had to be jealously guarded, strapped to the inside of his leg to avoid detection in searches, but saved as it and its products were to the end of the war, it preserves a remarkable record of POW life at Blechhammer and elsewhere.[57]

Just across the border in Czechoslovakia – or technically, at that time, the annexed Sudetenland – was another giant complex. It was the Sudetenländische Treibstoffwerke (Sudetenland Fuel Works), part of the industrial branch of the empire Hermann Göring had established for himself to benefit from the Third Reich's insatiable thirst for armaments and fuel. Built largely with slave labour, the complex was located in the Sudetenland town of Brüx (now Most); its main task was to convert coal to liquid fuel.

By the time the Western Australian Phil Loffman arrived there in January 1944, the demands on all labourers attached to the works were enormous. From his work detachment located in Obergeorgental he and his fellow POWs walked an hour to the factory to commence work by 6 am. After a twelve-hour shift they walked back to their camp, seven days a week. Loffman did a variety of tasks there: he fumigated huts, disposed of chemical waste, worked in the tar cellar and constructed new shelters. From May 1944 sites such as Brüx were receiving the full attention of the RAF and the USAAF; while the work regime itself threatened the men's well-being, the most acute danger was posed by bombing raids – POWs were not given passes to the new air-raid shelter bunkers, only to slit trenches. And if they survived the raids, Allied leaflets warned of another peril lurking in the ruins – time-fuse bombs which would explode after raids.[58]

Of all the men sent to labour in Silesia, the shortest of straws was drawn by those sent down the infamous Silesian coalmines, as many men from Lamsdorf were. By 1944 there were altogether 4000 POWs, including an unknown number of Australians, working at fifteen mining detachments from Stalag VIII B.[59] The harshness of the conditions in the mines has been recorded by some of those who survived the experience. Arthur Leggett was just one who, after a stint in Bavaria, was sent east to Upper Silesia to work in a Polish coalmine near Lamsdorf. Conditions underground in the mine, as he recalls,

> though not brutal, were extremely harsh. We worked three weeks day shift followed by three weeks night shift shovelling at the coalface until bribery and black market dealing with Red Cross cigarettes and chocolate manoeuvred me into less demanding underground activities. Nevertheless, rheumatism and sinusitis were developed due to the damp conditions; especially in the winter when months of heavy snow and not seeing sunlight for weeks on end added to the misery of our existence.[60]

Other Australians made the same woeful journey, from Salonika to Moosburg to the coalmines of Lamsdorf. Norm Tuckwell did his time in a coalmine near Krakow, though also served for periods in a sawmill, oil refinery, steel works in Beuthen and, finally, a quarry. Collectively those workplaces impacted permanently on his health. A badly crushed finger was his souvenir of the quarry, while a bashing with a rifle butt incurred in the coalmine led to three back operations after the war.[61] Roy East, also a veteran of Moosburg, was sent down a coalmine, where he worked closely with a Polish civilian; together they had to put out 15 skips of coal each day or night on their 11-hour shifts. Water dripped constantly, the ground was wet underfoot, and of the two days break they were to receive every two weeks, one had to be 'donated' to the Führer.[62]

Then there was Charlie Parrott, sent east to Lamsdorf in February 1943, and from there, although he had no experience whatsoever in mining, down the mines. His first was the Paris mine at Dabrova in the Sisnowiet/Kattowitz/Beuthen area. Each day he and the other POWs would leave their huts at 4 am, walk to the mine and be put into lifts in which they descended into a huge black cavern. There were three levels of mining, of which he was allocated to the lowest, some 350 metres below ground. Fortunately he had sufficient guile to note that POWs with glasses were not required to work at the coalface. He duly donned his glasses and worked replacing posts and timbers where slides had occurred. He hated the work, which he had to do up to 20 days in succession, but he had no choice.[63]

It was dangerous, too. One day he worked in a shaft where there had been a collapse. His job was to break up the huge lumps of coal with a sledgehammer to unblock the shaft. As he worked, a second collapse occurred, striking him on the hand and leg. He did not realise it immediately, but he had suffered a knee injury which later almost cost him his life. Only the skill and commitment of a South African doctor, who eventually performed an operation on the leg without anaesthetic to remove a severe infection, saved him. The after-effects were grave – a prolonged loss of consciousness followed by the peeling away of his skin. He remembers discovering the loss of his skin as he went to do some washing: 'All the palms of my hand hung down about a foot below my hand. On both hands that was. I asked them to get the doctor to come out and he just cut the skin off. Over a period of six months I lost every bit of skin off my body. The soles of my feet were the last to come off. That's thick. I wouldn't believe the sole of my feet was so thick.'[64]

Conditions in major work detachment at mines, quarries and factories were monitored by the inspectors from the ICRC and the Swiss Protecting Power, who took a particular interest in what was happening down the mines. And they were happy to share their findings. One ICRC report on detachments from Lamsdorf, sent to the British Foreign Office in August 1943, hardly minced its words:

> The norms are long and there is always Sunday work. In some cases 1 Sunday out of 2, 2 out of 3, 3 out of 4. As regards working conditions at E. 543 (Dombzowa) men sometimes work in water without rubber boots and at E.538 (Sosnowice) there is a high percentage of rheumatism

and 'athlete's foot'. At E. 535 (Milovitz) men work also in water without proper miners' protective helmets.[65]

The Swiss Protecting Power was equally forthright in its views, citing to the German authorities egregious examples of the exploitation of POW labour. One report on a mine in Saxony observed the men were getting up at 3 in the morning, leaving the camp at 4 and not returning until 7.30 in the evening, while POWs at Detachment E 744 in Silesia were working shifts of 11.5 hours with one day's rest in 20.[66]

Such reports caused much consternation at the Foreign Office and on the Imperial Prisoners of War Committee, whose Australian representative was High Commissioner Stanley Bruce. But beyond registering displeasure, there was little to be done. Forcefully worded appeals to the authority of the Geneva Convention to the effect that the work was overly harsh were sent to the Germans via Switzerland. But the Germans simply countered that coalmining was not in contravention of the Convention and that the work norms for POWs were no different from those imposed on civilians.[67]

The issue came to a head in the case of a tank factory at Austrian Gneixendorf, which used both POWs and concentration camp inmates drawn from Mauthausen and Gusen. It did not allow its workers even a single day of rest.[68] Complaints registered through the Protecting Power that the lack of that rest day was a breach of Geneva were stubbornly blocked by the German Foreign Office. The overriding principle, the Germans maintained, was that POW working conditions should match those of civilian workers. And if civilian workers were being deprived of a day of rest, then the POWs would just have to wear that as well.[69]

15

Crime and Punishment

POW camps and their work detachments were not penal institutions; theoretically their denizens were not treated in the same way as the inmates of jails or concentration camps. Yet POWs inhabited a strictly regulated world, its parameters set by international law but also by German military law and regulations – and indeed sometimes even by German civilian law. There was a broad gamut of infractions ranging from the trivial to the severe, and there was an equivalently broad range of sanctions, from the disapproving glance to the firing squad. Australians were subjected to all of them.

Amidst the many official sanctions to which a POW might be subjected there was a place, too, for whim. The daily lives of POWs were determined to a very great extent by the soldiers who guarded them, or by the civilians who supervised their work. The relationship could be, and not uncommonly was, one of mutual respect, where both parties tacitly acknowledged that beneath the division into the roles of captive and captor there was a common humanity. It could also be one of mutual contempt, grounded perhaps in ideology or in destructive feelings of resentment and revenge. In those circumstances, the life of the POW was bound to be one of unrelieved misery.

CAPTIVITY

Immediately after capture in North Africa, Greece or Crete, the first men to guard the Australians were German or Austrian front-line troops. Australians captured in this way often refer to the basic decency of the men effecting their capture; it was a respect forged in the crucible of battle. As Reg Worthington, captured at Kalamata, put it, 'The fighting soldier is alright. He understood that we were fighting soldiers too.'[1]

But for those front-line troops the guarding of POWs was a temporary distraction. They had other work to do. Those who had completed their tasks so efficiently in the campaigns in Greece and Crete were soon needed elsewhere. They handed their duties on to rear echelon soldiers, generally older men who did not share the same regard for their charges. In Greece Worthington observed that the Germans 'brought in these older and not so fit troops and they weren't real good fellows'.[2] The driving raison d'être of the new shift was to discipline, to punish and ultimately to break the morale of their prisoners. The attitude they adopted was condensed in a list of 'Ten Commandments' the OKW provided them. Guards were warned not to engage in misplaced camaraderie; there was to be no offering of cigarettes or private conversations. The last of the commandments neatly summarised the favoured position: 'Hold back and preserve the dignity of the German soldier. The enemy remains the enemy.'[3]

In the Reich itself the camps were characterised by strictly hierarchical structures of authority. The Germans were keen that their captives be fully integrated into those structures, only to encounter some opposition from Australian POWs, distrustful of authority and dismissive of officers' cant at the best of times. Charlie Parrott recalls that the one thing the commandant at Stalag VII A Moosburg did not like about the Australians was that they would not salute him. To teach them a lesson, the commandant posted officers at 20-metre gaps around the parade ground and marched the prisoners around to salute each officer as they passed. 'We were buggers', Parrott remembers. 'We weren't there to make him happy.'[4] Lindsay Lawrence was in the same camp, and he too recalls the lengths Australians would go to to avoid gestures of subservience: 'With the approach of a German officer you would immediately kneel down and do up your bootlaces, if you had a pair of boots. Other means of non-compliance were to turn away from the approaching officer and point to some object in the far distance or to turn around and proceed in the same direction as he was heading.'[5]

Security duties in the camps and also in the work detachments were performed by teams of guards, the so-called Wachmannschaften or simple Wam, who were drawn from Landesschutzbataillonen, the security battalions in the relevant military district. The regular guards were typically older men, very often veterans of the Great War, or, if they were younger, they were generally there because they had been wounded in battle – they might have lost a limb in the mountains of Greece or digits in the snow of Stalingrad and now, for the sake of filling the growing ranks of guards, in exchange for their sacrifice at the front had been granted the tedium and drudgery of patrolling barbed wire. For many of these younger men it was a formula for a brooding resentment. Given the opportunity, some at least were inclined to vent it on their charges.

These regular guards, young and old, were all members of the Wehrmacht, but as POW numbers climbed, the OKW found it impossible to meet the recommended ratio of one guard to ten POWs and so drew ever more heavily on teams of auxiliary guards – Hilfswachmänner – from the civilian population. In principle these auxiliary forces were only ever to be used in a supportive role. In time, however, they became indispensable, with results that were at best mixed.[6] If filling the stocks of regular guards entailed some scraping of the Wehrmacht barrel, the filling of the auxiliary ranks demanded a plumbing of new depths. In some cases it no doubt turned up some bottom feeders, eager to exercise every piece of power they could extract. But at the other extreme it also turned up gentler and more humane souls who carried the rod of authority lightly and used it sparingly, if at all. As among the POWs themselves, the full range of humanity was on display in the ranks of the guards.

The guards carried arms, but in theory at least strict conditions were placed on when and how they might use them. Should a prisoner attempt escape, the guard was obliged to call 'Halt' three times before firing, and then at first only a warning shot. In cases of sabotage and crime, too, or if they considered their own lives at risk, the guards could discharge their weapons, though strictly speaking not as a means of punishment. In practice, of course, there were some guards who interpreted these regulations generously, shooting at and even killing prisoners where little more than suspicion of foul intent was present.[7] If a cooler head prevailed, a guard might also apply his powers of arrest, which could be invoked if a POW exhibited insubordination, whether in deed or simply in word, directed against either the German state or the armed forces. From the prisoners' viewpoint it was difficult to predict which course of action was more likely, as much still depended on the mood of the guard at the crucial moment, and generally caution was the better part of valour.

For all their superficial properness and dedication to duty, the guards were by no means beyond susceptibility to corruption. Indeed, their superiors knew perfectly well that these men were being subjected to temptation on an almost daily basis. They expressly warned their men, 'Whoever accepts gifts, even if it is only a cigarette, is acting in neglect of his duty and criminally.'[8] Commonly such injunctions fell on deaf ears; indeed, the guards' willingness to take bribes from POWs only increased as the war dragged on. Guards and their families suffered from dire shortages of luxury items and then of bare necessities. The POWs, in contrast, provided they preserved their access to the manna that was the Red Cross parcels, were comparatively well off and could use their position to advantage. A report put together on the basis of information gleaned from RAF POWs noted in the last year of hostilities:

> The great majority of Germans seem to be quite willing to sell information of both military and escape importance to Ps/W for a few cigarettes or some chocolate, coffee, etc. This traitorous streak is not confined only to other ranks but is found just as frequently among the officers. It is

amazing what risks German personnel will take in order to obtain a few extra luxuries. The stupidity of the lower ranking Germans has to be seen to be believed.

By early 1945 German morale had decayed so severely that 'it was difficult to find an incorruptible German'.[9]

Ray Corbett came to witness with his own eyes this decaying morale at his Blechhammer work camp. In the last phase of the war in particular, when both the quality and quantity of the cigarettes received by the British POWs were vastly superior to anything the Germans might have had, tobacco could even be employed for punishment as well as reward:

> If a nasty guard wanted to play rough, nothing gave us greater pleasure than to pull out a new pack of Players cigarettes during a rest break and devilishly stand to windward, letting the smoke drift in his direction . . . then eye-ball him, as the butt was ground into the dirt. It was a terrible thing to do. He might carry the rifle, but we had the artillery. We became the arrogant ones and adopted a superior role, knowing that the pop-gun on his shoulder was useless against such mental torture.[10]

So widespread did the guards' vulnerability to bribes become that the security services became aware of it. In one of the reports from the Reich prepared for them, it was noted that the POWs were making their guards more amenable by offering them treats from their parcels. This had had an impact on the guards who, it was noted, treated their captives more leniently, allowing them, for example, to be exempted from working on Sundays.[11] An extreme case of the guards' susceptibility to temptation was noted by the airman Calton Younger at Heydekrug. So covetous was one of the German NCOs of the treasures the POWs possessed that he purveyed pornographic photographs he had taken of his wife.[12]

There was another reason why guards' attitudes and behaviour towards prisoners changed in the last months of the war, and that was the increasingly obvious reversal in the Reich's military fortunes. This could cut two ways. Among some, typically the younger guards whose formative years had been spent under Nazi rule, the threat to the very survival of the Reich provoked almost fanatical devotion and commitment. The corollary was an intensified hatred of the Reich's declared enemies and a willingness to punish them at any opportunity. But for the older guards, socialised well before Hitler came to power, and having witnessed the misery and defeat of the First World War, a resigned pragmatism came to the fore. By 1944 they were sick of the war and wanted it to end, even in the ignominy of defeat. Nothing was to be gained from displays of cruelty against the representatives of the forces who would soon rule the German roost.[13]

The range of misdemeanours punishable within the camp was wide, as was the range of punishments meted out. Most infractions entailed some kind of expression of insubordination, whether practised individually or collectively, but they extended too to attempted escape, or, even more severe, the threatening of a guard. Perhaps one of the more unusual was the sexual abuse of a goat. The offender was given a stint of 12 days in an isolation cell.[14] The so-called 'cooler' was the most common form of punishment, with sentences ranging up to 30 days, the most severe sanction for attempted escape allowed by the Geneva Convention. That upper limit aside, just how long offenders might be obliged to cool down and reconsider their behaviour was left to the discretion of the commandants, who were generally disposed to deal more severely with repeat offenders.

In rare instances punishment might be meted out by the prisoners themselves. From their perspective one of the gravest of infractions committed in a POW camp was theft, above all the theft of food from a fellow POW. And yet it did happen, as the severe pangs of hunger frequently wrestled with the pangs of conscience and won. In the *Stalag* at Mühlberg, Geoff Taylor became familiar with the unofficial code of justice prevailing among the POWs. He witnessed the treatment of a British soldier who had been caught stealing food in a barrack occupied by paratroopers and commandos. 'Beaten up by the man he stole from, he is carried to the deep, ice-encrusted sewage pit inside the entrance to the barrack. Into this stinking, freezing cesspool he is thrown wearing the only clothes he has.' The man emerged fouled and reduced to tears, and yet Taylor condones the brutality of the treatment in the context of a camp. 'Toleration of thieving could plunge our prison community into a way of life where we would become animals in anarchy.'[15]

The world outside the *Stalags* – in the labour detachments – brought with it the temptation of other forms of behaviour to trouble the Germans. One of them was shirking. Even if they were not employed in war-related work, many Australians felt that to perform any kind of labour was an aid to the enemy and therefore to be avoided if at all possible. The Germans for their part were keen to stamp out shirking, regardless of the identity of the offender.

The task of coaxing greater efforts from POW labourers fell to the guards and auxiliary guards. Though the civilian supervisors had an interest in boosting productivity, technically, at least, Geneva did not permit them to step in and drive the POWs to greater efforts. Indeed, the Germans' own regulations made it clear that this was among the duties of the guards. Faced with the need for improved output, a May 1943 supplement to the German document 'The Foreign Worker in Germany' impressed on its readers the role of the guards and the extent to which they should go if they suspected a POW of shirking: 'Every Prisoner of War liable for work and able-bodied is expected to exert himself to the full. Should he fail to do so the guards or auxiliary guards who fail to take such action will themselves be held responsible and severely punished. They are entitled to enforce their orders by force of arms.'[16]

Demands for full commitment to work became even shriller as Germany's defeat loomed. At Stalag XVIII A Wolfsberg and its hundreds of labour detachments the authorities went so far as to invoke Paragraph 139 of the German Military Penal Code, as the Red Cross noted in a report filed in December 1944. A *Stalag* order cautioned, 'POWs, who without reason report sick, thereby shirking work, will have to make up the lost work. Furthermore a detailed report will be submitted to the Court Martial on the ground of false statements made, §139 MStGB [Military Penal

Code]. This may lead to anything up to 5 years imprisonment, in aggravating circumstances up to 15 years hard labour.'[17]

Even with this kind of threat hovering over them, the Australians were never fully persuaded and sought ways to withdraw or minimise their labour. The subterfuges employed to this end were legion. 'Stomach ulcers', for instance, showed up as nasty black spots on X-rays caused by prisoners swallowing the silver paper from cigarette packets. That enabled the initial crafty concocters of that ruse to be confined and fed special Red Cross rations. In time the German supervising doctors were alerted to the ploy when further X-rays showed the spots had moved on![18]

Others resorted to more painful measures. Charlie Parrott witnessed men placing their hands on a table and having a mate smash their fingers with a stick to get time off. Others would scratch an open wound in their arm, rub in salt and bandage the wound to make it go septic. One fellow scratched his arm and then heightened his chances of infection by having another squeeze the pus from a boil onto the wound before bandaging it. It worked – the man became 'really, really sick'.[19] Lawrence Calder was among Australians on a work detachment in Graz digging tunnels for air-raid shelters. He invented a finger-breaking machine. For five cigarettes he would break the little finger of the left or right hand, without leaving a suspicious mark. A broken digit would suffice for the German doctor to pardon the POW from work duties.[20] Doug Nix saw POWs strap their arms to their bunks so as to roll out and break them. Others tied wet towels around their knee and then beat them until they swelled far beyond their normal size, while still others would bang their teeth out, all in the service of ensuring that they were sent anywhere but the workplace.[21]

Widely practised though it was, shirking was also a high-risk game. It was the sort of strategy which might trigger violent responses from supervisors and guards. One source has it that in 1943 seven Australians and seven British POWs were shot and killed in the mines around Jawozno in Silesia.[22] Refusal to work might well have been the cause.

CRIME AND PUNISHMENT

POW labourers could also find more active ways of undermining the Reich's war effort. While options were limited for those working on farms – by themselves they could hardly sabotage a crop – there were various possibilities for those in industrial employment. They could, for example, surreptitiously pour sand or gravel into grease-boxes, drive pick axes through cabling being laid, mix concrete foundations with an excess of sand or drop nuts and bolts into machinery. As Ron Mackenzie puts it, they applied their own variation to a Churchillian dictum, 'Give us the job and we will finish the tools.'[23] Charlie Parrott, sent to work building a canal in Bavaria, recalls the POWs holding a competition among themselves to see who could bury the most shovels.[24]

Sabotage, as many saw it, was a way to prosecute the war by other means; a timely and successful act could indeed inflict embarrassment or harm. Edwin Broomhead at Feldpost 12545 near Tripoli used the opportunity of working in a fuel dump to add sugar to canisters of petrol meant for German tanks.[25] Doug Nix took similar risks at an Austrian papermill in Frantschach near Stalag XVIII A Wolfsberg. With some fellow POWs he decided to make a home-made bomb using a cigarette tin as its casing. The tin itself was acquired easily enough; more difficult was one of the crucial elements, carbide. Its most common source was bullets, but it was no easy task for a POW to acquire bullets. The men turned to one of the guards, who with the help of a generous incentive to conquer his qualms eventually made the required bullet available. With a lengthy fuse the makeshift bomb was carefully deposited in a place designed to cause maximum damage at the end of a shift. It worked, setting off a fire and forcing the removal of the POW detachment back to their base camp at Wolfsberg, temporarily, at least, removed from the Reich's labour force.[26]

A similar act of sabotage occurred in the same district. At a sawmill, Alf Stone and his fellow workers suddenly found themselves confronted with a fire in the mill. Like their German supervisors, they assumed it was the work of partisans crossing from neighbouring Slovenia. Stone and his mates did their best to hinder the fire-fighting efforts, digging spikes and rakes into the hose to lessen the pressure. Only at a reunion 35 years later did he learn that it was his own mates who had started the fire.[27]

The other temptation to misconduct experienced on the work detachments was to abscond. Escape played on the minds of many in the *Stalags* and *Oflags* too, but the detachments generally presented greater possibilities. To escape was, technically, no crime, since the Geneva Convention explicitly recognised the right of POWs to attempt escape. If recaptured they could be subjected to disciplinary measures, but not to prosecution before any form of court. Indeed, Geneva dictated that the severest form of punishment for attempted escape was a stint in a cell which could not exceed a month.[28]

There was, however, another kind of punishment which Geneva did not dictate – indeed, did not allow. It was a punishment generally reserved for repeat escapers or those who otherwise distinguished themselves by a steadfast inclination to disturb the order of the camps in other ways. It was the *Straflager* or punishment camp, sometimes known also as a *Bewährungslager*. Officially no such thing existed, and the German Foreign Office went to some effort to fudge the reality of the camps, noting simply that recalcitrant POWs were to be placed in *Sonderkompanien* (special companies) within their *Stalags*. In theory this meant little more than denial of leisure activities with the maintenance of full access to food and mail.[29] But for those condemned to such companies the reality was harsher than the bureaucrats in Berlin would ever know.

An unknown number of Australians were among them, and they knew very well what the camps were for and why they were there. Some recall being categorised on the basis of their escape-prone or unruly behaviour as a *Disziplinär*, a POW earmarked for disciplinary treatment. For some it became a badge of pride, but it did have consequences. Just what they might comprise was confirmed through the neutral services of the ICRC, which in April 1944 received a revealing report from one of its inspectors in Military District XVIII. He was touring the labour detachments based at Stalag XVIII A Wolfsberg when he called in at Bewährungslager

1025/GW Steinach and came across 34 British POWs, all of them recaptured escapees. Nearly half of them, he reported, were unfit for the particularly heavy work demanded on that detachment. Moreover, he noted that the German authorities were continuing to ignore a warning issued the previous year, pressing for proper medical examinations of the 'disciplinaries' before any allocation to heavy labour. The Germans' shortcomings led to what the Red Cross delegate called an 'unpleasant controversy' with the German doctor, prompting the tactful intervention of the commandant. A short time later, 16 men were on the way back to the *Stalag* for a careful examination, while the delegate reminded his hosts that they were breaching Article 32 (2) of the Convention, which states 'Condition of work shall not be rendered more arduous by disciplinary measures.'[30]

Charles Granquist became a *Disziplinär* because he was an incorrigible escaper. His five failed attempts landed him in a number of punishment camps performing hard labour. The first was at Leoben in Styria, where he performed back-breaking railway repair work. Yet the stint of hard labour did nothing to relieve his urge to flee. Unlike the many who resigned themselves to a war of boredom behind barbed wire, Granquist found that engaging in 'criminal' activities helped wash away a lot of the guilt he had felt at becoming a POW. So it was that he spent time in a quarry at Hermigor in Slovenia as well, and later still at a punishment camp at St Georgen.[31]

Reg Worthington was another. He found himself in trouble because, in the position of Man of Confidence on a work detachment, he had allowed his fellow prisoners to attempt an escape. With a pilfered hacksaw and the willing aid of Worthington, two Englishmen in his work detachment cut their way to freedom, at least for a short time. As Man of Confidence and witting accomplice, Worthington was sent to a *Straflager* at Markt Pongau, where he sat out the war, expecting a court martial which mercifully never came.[32]

Doug Nix, suspected (quite rightly) of involvement in the act of sabotage at the Frantschach papermill, was sent with

20 other Wolfsberg POWs to a nearby *Straflager* at Waldenstein. The miscreants were placed on the top floor of a three-storey stone building constructed as a fortress, indeed, even surrounded by a moat. Escape, the men were advised on arrival, was out of the question. That advice was all the more reason to take up the challenge, spurred on by the knowledge that failure to escape would condemn them to days spent breaking stones in the courtyard. They observed a chute running straight down the building connecting lavatories. On just their second night of incarceration there they tied together their hessian bed-sacks, emptied of straw, and descended the chute, breaking their way through the grate at the bottom. Having exited their impregnable fortress, they rubbed salt into their captors' wound by marching back to the *Stalag* at Wolfsberg and announcing their return to an incredulous sentry and commandant.[33]

In distant Silesia, Leslie 'Aussie' Osborn made the mistake of attempting to hit a civilian worker with a shovel in an altercation. He was sent back to the main camp – Lamsdorf – where he sat out a period of solitary confinement. Instead of then being returned to a work detachment, he was told he was to be sent to a punishment camp. It entailed railway work, lifting heavy railway lines; the quarry had been a pleasure by comparison.[34]

In Bavaria, Lyle Cullinger was sent to a quarry near Deggendorf. Part of his punishment seems to have been to share for a night the Russian barracks. 'I did not know whether they wanted to eat me or root me. So much for German humour.'[35] Cullinger managed to escape from the quarry but on recapture was sent to work in a Silesian coalmine near a town called Kutz.[36] The move was part of a much larger trend to attempt to raise coal production. In July 1943 Hitler had envisaged the use of some 200,000 Soviet POWs in the coal-mining industry, but by the end of that year the Germans were prepared to cast their net more widely. In December new measures were put forward to cover the shortage of labour, and one of them was the use of POWs other than the hapless Soviets. For good reason the men perceived this at the very least as a hardship posting, if not as crude punishment for recalcitrant behaviour. The plan envisaged that the inmates would be released from such camps only when they were no longer capable of doing the work.[37]

The most notorious of camps designed to deal with recalcitrants was Oflag IV C Colditz in Saxony. While film and television have endowed it with the status of the archetypal POW camp, in reality Colditz was a world of its own; the experiences of those who had the misfortune to enter Colditz bore only a passing resemblance to those of the mass of POWs held elsewhere.

Colditz is a small Saxon town some 40 kilometres south-east of Leipzig. The camp was installed in the town's castle, originally the hunting lodge of Augustus the Strong, who was both King of Poland and Elector of Saxony.[38] As an *Oflag* in World War II it became at various stages the home to officers from Britain and the Commonwealth, but also to French, Belgian, Dutch and Polish officers whom the Germans deemed worthy of special attention.

One of the distinctive features of Colditz was that it contained prisoners from all branches of the armed services: army, navy and air force. What most of the captives had in common was that they were considered to pose a particular threat to the Reich; they were considered '*deutschfeindlich*' – hostile to Germany. That attitude might have exhibited itself in a number of ways, among them a proclivity to escape. The great advantage of Colditz Castle as a repository for these troublesome types, so the German authorities thought, was that it was considered 'escape proof'.[39] Not only did the imposing solid stone structure appear to relegate any thought of escape to the realm of fantasy, the camp was staffed with guards so numerous as to outnumber the prisoners. Its very reputation, of course, only encouraged its denizens to disabuse their hosts of their faith in its impregnability. In the final escape tally, 300 were caught in various attempts, 130 managed to get clear of the castle, and 32 made successful 'home runs', that is, they reached their own forces, including fourteen French, nine British (among them, as we shall see, the Australian Bill Fowler), six Dutch and one Pole.[40]

As early as 1941 the then American Protecting Power inspectors noted that Colditz was characterised by its strained relations between the prisoners and their captors. In October of that year, on the last of the American visits, the inspector recorded 'considerable tension and bad feeling on both sides'. In his view the bulk of the blame had to be placed at the feet of the commandant: 'Though he can be very charming on occasions, he seems to lack the prisoner "point of view" and regards his charges as a group of "bad prisoners" who have not behaved in other camps and have been sent to him for special watching, and who must therefore be kept under strict discipline.'[41]

From 1942 the Germans began to collect in Colditz a number of high-profile prisoners whom they labelled *Prominente*. In most cases their prominence derived from their relationships with even more well-known individuals. One, for example, was Winston Churchill's nephew Giles Romilly, who had earlier escaped the Germans' grasp dressed as a woman.[42] Another was the Earl of Hopetoun, the son of the Marquess of Linlithgow, Viceroy of India since 1936, and a third was Captain the Earl Haig, only son of Field-Marshal Douglas Haig.[43] More were added to this gallery of the impeccably connected as the war developed, forming a group which, ultimately, would possess great value for their captors as potential hostages.

Their arrival did nothing to improve the atmosphere of the camp, as they resented their imprisonment as keenly as all the others. The prevailing mood in Colditz was well captured by a Red Cross inspector who paid a visit in early 1943 and wrote, 'The impression this camp gives is not pleasant. One feels that there is a very strained atmosphere resulting from the frantic wish on one side to escape, and on the other the stern decision to prevent this.' The atmosphere had little to do with the accommodation, since the castle was well situated and was less crowded than many officer camps. Rather, it had much to do with the obdurate personalities of those who were most likely to end up there. They were, in the words of one inspector, 'an excellent elite of remarkably strong characters, stubborn, proud and uncompromising'.[44] The clash of two hardened objects could only mean friction.

There were no Australians among the *Prominente*, but there were a number elsewhere in the castle at various times. As one would expect in an *Oflag*, the majority of Australians were officers – 13 in number, though not all at the same time. Then there was a doctor, Captain Roger Playoust. Finally there were seven non-medical orderlies, charged with tending to the officers' needs.[45]

The Australians were as keen as anyone to leave this *Oflag* behind them. The first to attempt to do so was Malcolm McColm, born aboard his father's ship in a Welsh port before being baptised in Australia in 1914.[46] He had arrived at Colditz as a result of an achievement of outstanding heroism followed by an act of witless stupidity. Baling out of his RAF Blenheim over Holland, he was captured, interrogated at Dulag Luft and delivered to Stalag Luft I. He escaped via a tunnel and managed to make his way to the northern port city of Lübeck, where he hid under the steering gear cover of a Swedish vessel. In a state of exhaustion he fell asleep; when at sea his snoring alerted a deckhand, who handed him over to the captain. Although Sweden was neutral, Swedish vessels were placed under German pilotage when making their way through mined waters. McColm was handed to a German pilot, transferred to a German vessel and taken back to Stalag Luft I. In time the Germans decided that for a man of McColm's skills and inclinations, Colditz was a safer home. He entered the castle on 8 October 1941.[47]

Another itchy-footed Australian in Colditz was the fighter pilot Vincent 'Bush' Parker, a man whose escape talents had brought him to Colditz, where he was able to put them on surreptitious display to his admiring fellow captives. Parker had a particular penchant for performing sleights of hand. Some were of the innocuous variety – pulling cigarettes from behind friends' ears, counting cards and the like – but others were of practical use to would-be escapists. His talent for picking locks, a veritable passport to the rabbit-warren that was Colditz Castle, acquired legendary status. His fellow Australian Don Donaldson witnessed Parker's first attempt to gain access to the castle attic, armed only with a tube of toothpaste. With his ear pressed against the door, Parker would strain to work the lock dials: 'When a tumbler lifted he injected the toothpaste to hold it in the open position. Finally he manoeuvred all of the tumblers the right way, and the door swung open. Within a week Bush could master a lock in thirty seconds without using the toothpaste.'[48]

CAPTIVITY

The only Australian to escape Colditz and record a 'home run' was the airman Bill Fowler, one of the first Australians to enter captivity in Europe, in his case as early as 15 May 1940. He had arrived at Colditz by a circuitous route. After the customary stint at Dulag Luft in Oberursel he was sent to Oflag II A at Prenzlau, a camp mainly for Polish officers. A month later he was in Stalag Luft I at Barth on the Baltic coast of Pomerania.[49] It was here that his penchant for escape surfaced. He exploited his position in the camp's parcel office to assemble a bogus German uniform, which he used to make his first brazen bid for freedom, swapping the uniform for a set of civilian clothes when he was clear of the camp. His destination was to be Sweden, which he hoped to reach by ship from Sassnitz, but he was nabbed short of his goal. As punishment he was sent to Colditz. There he joined a group which devised an ingenious escape scheme. It entailed digging a tunnel into a storeroom from the office of the German RSM, Stabsfeldwebel Gephard. From the storeroom the escape would be staged with the aid of assembled German uniforms, in which they would walk brazenly past the sentries to freedom.

Gaining regular access to Gephard's office was no pushover, but the manufacture of a key and the careful posting of 'stooges' to keep a lookout for guards solved that problem. By 8 September 1942 all was in readiness for the team of six and their two accomplices. After the evening rollcall, they hid in the sick-bay until that section of Colditz was locked down. Then they made their way to Gephard's office and locked themselves inside it. The two accomplices finished the last piece of the tunnel so that the chosen six could enter the storeroom and make final preparations. These entailed donning two German uniforms and outfits worn by the Polish orderlies who worked in the clothing store.

The guard commencing duty at seven the next morning – 9 September 1942 – would not have been aware if anyone was already in the clothing store, so saw nothing untoward in the emergence of the disguised men who had picked the clothing store lock. In full view of the new sentry, they relocked the door behind them. Two more guards were passed, each duly saluting the POW dressed as an officer. A moment of drama followed when, at the last gate, the skeleton key fashioned by one of the three Dutchmen in the group failed to do its job. Just as they contemplated abandoning their performance and jumping the gate, a sentry arrived with a key which fitted the lock, apologising for not having done so earlier.[50]

Outside both castle and barbed wire, the six men made for a nearby wood where they destroyed their uniforms and donned the civilian clothes they had acquired with some difficulty inside the camp and taken with them. All had forged papers, Fowler's identifying him as a Belgian worker on two weeks' leave with permission to travel by train. A convincing touch was added in the form of a small attaché case.

The men paired off into three groups, each containing a Briton and a Dutchman. The Dutch were considered highly desirable escape companions, because they could speak German and knew the country well. The three pairs headed in quite different directions. Coupled with Lieutenant Commander Damiaen van Doorninck, Fowler headed for Switzerland via Stuttgart. Having reached a station some 30 kilometres from Colditz, they caught a train to Plauen. Train services were severely disrupted, so that it was not until very late at night that they finally reached Stuttgart, too late to make a final strike at the frontier. After a night in a hotel, they resumed their quest the next morning. The last part of their journey was by foot, considered a less risky choice than train, though at one point they were stopped and checked – without consequence – by a patrol. Having left Colditz on 9 September, it was not until the early hours of 13 September that they spied a Swiss customs hut and knew that they had reached freedom.[51]

In international law POWs were free once they had left the territory of the detaining power, but Fowler had more work to do to complete his home run. From Switzerland he made his way with the aid of a secret network of helpers across France and into Spain, where his movements included an unpleasant stint incarcerated in Figueras. The timely intervention of the British consulate set the escape back on track, so that Fowler and other RAF personnel were released and escorted south to Gibraltar and from there to

Britain. Tragically, Bill Fowler was killed in March 1943 while testing a Typhoon dive-bomber.[52]

Just one other Australian managed to make an escape from Colditz – at least temporarily – and that was Johnny Rawson, formerly of the *Oflag* at Warburg. He, too, made his escape via the main gate, successfully executing an act of deceit. He swapped identities with a New Zealand dentist, Captain A.H. Aitken, having learned that Aitken was to be transferred to the NCOs' compound at Stalag IV B Mühlberg. With the permission of Escape Officer Tom Stallard and the willing complicity of Aitken himself, the swap was effected, and Rawson was marched out of Colditz and delivered to Mühlberg. There he befriended a number of Australian airmen, confiding to them his true identity and revealing his plan to get onto a work detachment outside the camp as the next step to escape.[53]

Indeed this plan had developed a degree of urgency, as Rawson was expected to perform the work of the dentist he purported to be. When he saw no option but to reveal his identity to the senior British officer, the latter showed little sympathy, accusing Rawson of impersonating protected personnel; he was impervious to Rawson's argument that it was every officer's duty to escape by whatever means available. Rawson was duly handed over to the Germans and returned to Colditz.[54]

Rawson's fate was the same as almost all recaptured escapers. They were typically sent back to their *Oflag* or *Stalag* and given a stint in the cooler, the length of which would not exceed a month but was otherwise at the commandant's discretion. Repeat offenders could expect a longer term, which might be followed by allocation to a punishment camp. And those who had absconded from their work detachment could expect, after a period of punishment, to find themselves working for the Führer once more, but not at the same location. Escapers were pests, and by the middle of the war they were considered serious pests, but generally they were not considered criminals. In the drama of war, German authorities generally accepted that the role of the POWs was to escape, just as it was theirs to thwart them.

There were other offences which were viewed much more gravely and fell outside the remit of the commandant and his staff. Article 45 of the Geneva Convention laid down that POWs would be subject to the laws, regulations and orders of the armed forces of the detaining power.[55] In short, this meant that offences which required more than disciplinary measures meted out by the camp commandant were to be dealt with by German military courts. As a result Australian POWs could find themselves being dealt with by the very same courts that passed judgment on German soldiers accused of serious breaches of German military law. If found guilty, they could end up in the same military prisons or, worse, facing a death sentence to be carried out by German military authorities.

Cases of Australian and other British POWs being sent before German military courts were relatively rare, though not as rare as the British government would have liked. In July 1943 it was arguing the case via the Swiss Protecting Power that the Germans were finding all too frequent recourse to judicial proceedings and, as a consequence, British POWs were receiving heavier sentences than if the matters in question had been handled internally in the relevant camps. It also demanded that an agreement be put in place so that those POWs who did find themselves in prison would benefit from the sorts of conditions they took for granted in POW camps – access to packages and correspondence as well as exercise. The British contended that similar cases of German POW misbehaviour in British camps were being dealt with by normal disciplinary measures imposed within the camp.[56]

It was an argument the Germans rejected. Discipline among POWs in Germany, they contended, had to be accorded a much higher value than in, say, distant Canada or Australia, far removed from hostilities. In any case, the OKW insisted that the British accusations of the callous treatment of their POWs were unfounded: 'In their behaviour toward their guards and camp officers, the British POWs are becoming ever more challenging and are offering even more passive resistance. In order to maintain discipline among the POWs the firmest action is required.

A German soldier who makes use of a weapon against an unruly Briton is acting in accordance with his orders and not illegally.'[57]

Oddly enough, the sentences handed down on POWs by German military courts generally became milder as the war progressed. The most common charges over the course of the war were of two kinds. The first related to breaches of discipline and failure to obey orders. The second, interestingly, concerned accusations of relations pursued by POWs with German women. Such relations were strictly forbidden, and indeed the charge was typically brought under paragraph 92 of the Military Penal Code dealing with disobedience to a service order. The charge sometimes included the statement that by his actions the accused had 'endangered the security of the German Reich'.[58]

James Edward Steward of Manly in Sydney was among more than 300 sailors of the Royal Navy captured by German forces in the Atlantic and transferred to the German MS *Portland* in February 1941. *Portland* was actually a merchant vessel, but was placed under military command to carry out the task of delivering the prisoners to land, where they would be interned. But 30 of the men, including Steward, and led by the Englishman Arthur Fry, attempted a rebellion onboard the ship. It failed, and although some damage was done to the vessel – the rebels had laid a fire – the German crew was able to retain control and eventually to bring the prisoners to land, where the 30 accused of involvement in the rebellion were brought before a military court in Hamburg. Steward got off relatively lightly, receiving a prison sentence of six months,[59] but Fry was sentenced to death. The British government conveyed its displeasure to the Germans through the Protecting Power, by that time Switzerland. The British view was that cases like Fry's should not even come before military courts, since to attempt to escape was part of the accepted military code of honour, as recognised in Articles 50, 51 and 52 of the Geneva Convention.[60] And according to Geneva, the maximum sanction for attempted escape was 30 days' detention. Nonetheless, the sentence stuck.

The centre of the German military justice system was in Torgau. Though better known as the place where American and Soviet troops met in 1945, this Saxon town on the Elbe had much more sinister connotations for German soldiers and POWs alike. There were two military prisons there, one the so-called Bridgehead Prison, the other Fort Zinna, which dated back to Napoleonic times. German soldiers were sent to Torgau for a wide range of crimes, ranging from insubordination to – ever more commonly – desertion. At Torgau they could expect no kid gloves if jailed; many arrived there with the sure knowledge they would never leave. An unknown number were executed there. As for POWs, theoretically as soldiers they were subjected to the same punishment as German soldiers of equivalent rank. If sentenced in a court-martial they might well, like German soldiers, end up in Torgau, where in Fort Zinna there was a dedicated penal facility for British POWs. It was devoid of all the modest comforts of a *Stalag* – above all there was no ready access to Red Cross parcels to content the stomach or cheer the soul. Torgau was a desolate place.

One of the Australians who had the misfortune to do time in Fort Zinna was Ian Ramsay. At his *Stalag* in Wolfsberg he overstepped a crucial line – after a failed escape bid he struck out at a German NCO, a reckless act which landed him a stint in the town jail rather than in the camp cooler. More troubling was that his transgression now warranted an appearance before a military court. The trial went badly, so he was sent to Torgau to serve the bulk of a nine-month sentence.[61]

For all its harshness the rhythm of life in his POW compound followed the same pattern as that inside a *Stalag* or work detachment. For most that meant daily work, and as befitted a military prison, it was tough. The British POWs were marched for an hour to a bank of the Elbe, where they were handed sledgehammers and commanded to break boulders before loading them into a barge. For Ramsay the rigours of Fort Zinna were relieved only by a spell in a POW hospital to cure a bout of dysentery, after which he was deposited back at Torgau. Then at the end of 1942 all the British POWs in the fort were transferred to a different penal institution, a jail in Graudenz (today in Polish Grudziadz) in Military District XX. At first this appeared to be a positive development. After all,

Australia had rushed into war on the coat-tails of Britain's spirited commitment to Poland; surely, Ramsay reasoned, the Polish jail staff would be sympathetic to British and Commonwealth prisoners. He was soon disabused of that hope: 'The Poles in German uniform were greedy, self-interested and anxious to obey German commands in order to satisfy their masters and improve their lot.'[62] Graudenz proved every bit as miserable as Torgau.

Bill Trainor of Warracknabeal was another of the unfortunates dispatched to Torgau, where he had an even tougher time than Ramsay. The Germans found Trainor a handful. He was brought before a military court on a charge of violent assault against a guard. The incident had allegedly occurred in October 1941, when Trainor was in Stalag XVIII A Wolfsberg. Like so many Australians in that camp, he had served in North Africa and then Greece before being captured near Corinth. The charge was of striking the guard in charge of his work detachment, though Trainor's version of events was that he had been provoked and the guard had hit him first. In any case, Trainor found himself before a court in the regional centre of Klagenfurt, where he was found guilty and sentenced to a year in prison.[63]

Ian Ramsay remembered seeing Trainor in Fort Zinna, where he was doing it tough. The two men became acquainted until, as Ramsay records, Trainor was eventually segregated from his fellow POWs 'for his increasing conflicts with the Huns'.[64] One of the punishments meted out to Trainor – because, according to Ramsay, he refused to interpret German orders despite his good knowledge of German – was acutely painful. A New Zealander witnessed it and recalled after the war that Trainor was 'hung up by his wrists through an iron door. He was hung in such a position so as his feet were off the ground, and all the weight of his body was taken on his wrists. He lost the use of his arms for four days and was not allowed to see a doctor. The time he was hung up was 1 hour 20 minutes.'[65]

Worse was to follow. After his release in September 1943, Trainor was sent to Stalag XX A Thorn and from there to a work detachment in the Polish district of Briesen. There, with a number of other British POWs, he worked for a farmer, with whom he soon developed a relationship of intense loathing. For the guard, too, Trainor felt only contempt, a feeling which seems to have been shared in equal measure. The guard, it appears, a man by the name of Vater, had been punished because of an earlier escape by Trainor and had never forgiven his charge.

On 8 July 1944 latent antagonism spiralled into open and lethal violence. Postwar evidence suggests that the farmer's foreman complained about the woeful work performance of the POWs, prompting the farmer to hold Trainor responsible and attempt to ride him down with his horse. Trainor sought to protect himself with a pitchfork, sending the farmer off to report the incident to the guard. Trainor, too, indicated that he would lodge a complaint against the farmer, but as he made his way along the road he was met by both the farmer and the guard. A heated exchange of words ensued, culminating in Vater drawing his pistol and shooting Trainor at point blank range through the heart.[66] Today his body lies in the Malbork Commonwealth War Cemetery outside Gdansk.

PART 3

Into the Abyss

16

Total War

Nineteen forty-three was not a good year for the Reich. It began poorly with defeat at Stalingrad – and with it the humiliating capture of General Friedrich Paulus' Sixth Army – and it just got worse. By September Axis partner Italy was out of the war, the tide had turned against German U-boats in the Atlantic, and such was the superiority of British and American air power in the skies over the Reich that massive raids were becoming sickeningly regular. In their hearts many Germans knew that the war was already lost. Yet Hitler's own will to victory in the face of setback after setback remained undiminished. He would battle to the death, and he expected the same of his countrymen. If that meant fighting an ever more desperate campaign, abandoning whatever veneer of civilisation the conduct of modern warfare might hitherto have preserved, then so be it. It did not augur well for POWs.

The signs of desperation were there for all to see or hear. In February 1943 Propaganda Minister Joseph Goebbels delivered an ominous address to a hand-picked audience, crammed into Berlin's Sportpalast. After outlining the level of sacrifice needed to achieve victory, he asked the Nazi zealots assembled before him whether they were prepared to give their utmost to secure victory. Two more chilling questions followed: 'Do you want total war?' and, when the wild applause and affirmation had died down, 'Do you want it, if necessary, more total and more radical than we can imagine it today?'[1] The answer to this question, in the Sportpalast at least, was no less fervent. Around the Reich, as Germans pushed their ears to their radios, there must have been many more tremulous souls who were beginning to grasp the scale of the calamity to which Goebbels and his ilk were condemning them.

'Total War' would cast a long and sinister shadow across the field of battle as well. If a barbarisation of warfare was already well underway in the East, it soon became clear that in its vicious campaigns to defend the Reich in the West, too, the regime would dispense with any semblance of civility. Foremost among those to feel the Germans' ire were airmen, held responsible for the all too regular bombing of German towns and cities and branded *Terrorflieger*, literally 'terror flyers', by regime and nerve-racked civilians alike. In the year 1943 alone some 100,000 Germans fell victim to Allied bombing raids, which were deliberately designed to terrify the populations of large cities and industrial areas, even to hobble the German economy by killing large numbers of workers.[2] Fighter aircraft wreaked havoc among civilians, pursuing the goal of proving the Luftwaffe's weakness and the imminence of defeat.

The Nazi leadership sought to make the most of the groundswell of anger and despair generated by the Allied raids. It was eager that the palpable anger should be directed at the enemy, and not at the Nazi regime for failing in its promises to spare the population the horrors of Allied bombs. As early as May 1943 the local Nazi Party leader (the so-called *Gauleiter*) in Mecklenburg, a man by the name of Hildenbrandt, had informed Hitler's Chancellery that the population enjoyed watching when every English airman emerging alive from his aircraft was shot on the spot.[3] It was a barbaric action which Reichsführer SS Heinrich Himmler saw fit to endorse. On 10 August 1943 he issued advice which would send a shudder down the spine of any airman flying over Europe. It is not the task of the police, Himmler proclaimed, 'to intervene in confrontations between Germans and English and American terror flyers who have parachuted to the ground'.[4] The lynching of shot-down airmen, in other words, had become permissible behaviour. From this point on guards escorting airmen had the double duty of ensuring they did not escape and protecting their charges from angry civilians.[5]

A tone was thereby set which Propaganda Minister Goebbels was only too keen to follow. He embraced the use of the word *Terrorflieger* and then added '*Luftgangster*' (air gangsters) to the Nazi lexicon to demonise the Allies. His media campaign reached a ghoulish climax of sorts in November 1943, when a crewmember of an American bomber, Lieutenant Kenneth Williams, was captured and his image strewn across the pages of Nazi newspapers in the following days. On the back of the hapless airman's leather flying jacket the words 'Murder Inc.' were visible – it was the practice of American crews to give their aircraft names, and not always wisely chosen ones, which would then be added to each crewman's jacket.[6]

Hitler, typically, had a word to say on this matter too. His anger at the strategies of Allied bombers and fighters alike moved him to contemplate putting men like Williams on trial for war crimes and having them killed.[7] In the end he went so far as to identify the circumstances under which captured Allied airmen were to be shot. The execution was to be carried out immediately if the airmen had fired on German airmen in parachutes or in force-landed aircraft, if they had fired on trains operating as public transport, or if in low swoops they had fired their guns on civilians.[8]

If such trials do not seem to have come about, there is no doubt that lynchings did take place from 1943 through to the end of hostilities. The exact number can never be known, as despite the open condoning of these actions the perpetrators might still have feared some ultimate retribution; many bodies would have been recorded as dead on discovery. Estimates range from a cautious 30 through to 350.[9] In these circumstances, of course, it is impossible to know whether any – or how many – Australians were among them.

One Australian, at least, appears to have witnessed such an atrocity vicariously. The wireless operator John Mathews, a member of the mixed crew of a Flying Fortress in 214 Squadron, flew operations over Germany in the last month of the war. For him it was the 45th mission, targeting Harburg in the vicinity of Hamburg, that was fateful. It was neither flak nor a German night fighter which paralysed his aircraft, rather, it was the novice crew of a Lancaster which unwittingly crippled the Flying Fortress with 'friendly fire'.

Despite a head wound, with a good turn of speed Mathews managed on landing to evade angry locals armed with pitchforks, but was then – perhaps fortunately – seized by a local official who took him into custody. The official resisted all efforts to have him released to anyone but the Luftwaffe; producing a photograph, he explained to Mathews that he himself had a son who was a POW in English captivity. At least one of Mathews' crewmates, the rear gunner, was not so lucky. Mathews was in earshot of him after they both landed in their parachutes close to each other, and he heard enough for him to conclude that the gunner had been caught and pitchforked to death. Three others, he conjectured, might have shared that fate. In any case, they were reported as having baled out, but their bodies were never recovered.[10]

In other regards, too, the German prosecution of the war plumbed new depths as the prospect of defeat loomed. Aside from his rage at the 'terror flyers' who menaced the Reich from the air, Hitler adopted a keen loathing for Allied commando units, who in attacks staged from the sea and on land were proving remarkably effective in penetrating German defences.

Through the middle of 1942, Allied commando forces had launched a series of raids on German targets in western Europe, culminating in a raid on Dieppe. This action, and a similar raid on Sark, had not only triggered the Shackling Crisis, they had also stirred a deep animosity in Hitler towards this brand of warfare and its practitioners. His Commando Order, issued, as we have seen, in October 1942, was in effect a death sentence for those who in Hitler's view had forfeited the protection of the Geneva Convention.

That death sentence was not to be carried out by the Wehrmacht but by Heinrich Himmler's security forces. Quite apart from its dire consequences for captured commandos, the Commando Order was a portent of a development which would affect all POWs – the ever expanding role of Himmler and his henchmen in POW matters.

Himmler in truth had long been building an empire for himself. The former chicken farmer had been Chief of German Police since 1936; he was handed control of the Reichssicherheitshauptamt (RSHA, Reich Security Main Office) in 1939. There was almost no limit to his control over the Reich's security operations. All of the security forces were ultimately under Himmler's command, from the local constable through the Gestapo to the Security Service and the various branches of the SS, which by now possessed a mammoth and still growing military arm, the Waffen SS. When in 1943 he added the mantle of Minister of the Interior to his vast portfolio, Himmler cemented his place in the Reich's inner sanctum. Only Hitler was more powerful. 'Reichsheini', as Himmler was contemptuously known by his legion of enemies, had a finger in just about every pie.

His claim to a larger say on POW issues was based above all on security concerns. Not without some justification, he claimed that this was a problem for him to deal with, and indeed it was a growing problem. POW escapes in particular were becoming a huge headache for military and civilian authorities in the Reich alike. German records show that by August 1942, almost 80,000 POWs had made successful escape attempts, about half of them on the territory of the Reich. Dealing with this massive and growing number, Himmler insisted, was a major security issue, and security was his brief.[11] That meant not just a role for his forces in rounding up the escapees but in stopping them from escaping in the first place. Even more ominously, if Himmler had his way, it would also mean that he and his men would assume responsibility for punishing the escapers they recaptured.

In these circumstances one of the Reich's trademark demarcation disputes was unavoidable. The Wehrmacht would resist any incursion into the domain of POW matters, and it would certainly be cranky about any effort by security forces to establish a toehold in its *Oflags* and *Stalags*. But Himmler was not the sort of person to seek to resolve the emerging dispute through diplomatic niceties. His hand was strengthened not only by his close relationship with Hitler but by the fact that escapes from the Wehrmacht's camps showed no sign of abating.

Bit by ineluctable bit Himmler got his way. At first most of the POWs would not have noticed any difference, but a new POW order was being constructed in the Reich. *Stalag* commandants were instructed to establish contact with the nearest branch of the Nazi Party and with local police authorities. Within the Reich's Office of Criminal Police a central bureau was set up under the codename 'C2K' to coordinate searches for escaped POWs. It was this central bureau which would plan searches and engage wherever necessary police and Nazi Party personnel, including even Hitler Youth, in tracking down escapees.[12] By the end of 1943 the camp commandants had lost their right to exclude police forces from their camps, and officers of the Criminal Police were now dubbed 'Representatives of the RSHA for the Prevention of POW Escapes'.[13]

Just what Himmler's men might do with recaptured POWs outside the camps became strikingly clear with the confidential issuing of the so-called *Kugel-Erlass*, the Bullet Decree. On 3 March 1944 the Reich Security Main Office directed all offices under its control that all escaped and then recaptured POW officers and non-working NCOs were not to be sent back to their camps but rather were to be handed over under maximum security to the Mauthausen Concentration Camp in Austria. To disguise its intent the codename *Stufe III* (Stage III) was applied, and news of the recapturing of the prisoners was suppressed.[14] But it was the name Bullet Decree which betrayed the final act in this furtive drama – most of those recaptured were murdered with bullets fired in the backs of their necks. Others were gassed, starved or tortured to death. One gruesome way or another, it is estimated that some 5040 POWs lost their lives in Mauthausen this way. The vast majority – in the region of 4300 – were the wretched Soviets.[15]

British and American POWs were exempted from the Bullet Decree. Himmler specifically directed, 'In case escaped British and

American officers or non-working NCOs are recaptured, then at first for security reasons these are to be kept outside POW camps and not in view of POWs. If Wehrmacht facilities are not available, then they are to be kept in police custody. The decision on whether they should be handed over to the Head of the Security Police and the SD is to be requested immediately by the Military District Commanders on a case by case basis from the Chief of POW Affairs.'[16]

That, at least, was the theory, a sign that even as the war descended into barbarism the Western POWs were still viewed differently from the rest. But the reality could be something else again, as British POWs in Stalag Luft III were to find to their horror in March 1944, the very month in which the Bullet Decree was issued.

17

The Great Escape

In the 1963 movie *The Great Escape*, James Coburn botches the accent of the Australian he plays, while the scriptwriters botch the plot. Based on the escape of 76 airmen from the north compound of the airmen's camp Stalag Luft III at Sagan in what is now Poland in March 1944, the movie strains at the limits of credibility. The Coburn character makes good his escape via France and Spain, one of just three who recorded a 'home run'. That three made it back safely to the UK is true, but there was no Australian among them.

Stalag Luft III was the largest of the camps in Göring's POW empire. By the time it was built to cope with the growing numbers of airmen being captured, the Germans knew a thing or two about preventing escapes, and they were especially leery of tunnels. On the one hand the soil at Sagan, sandy and dry, lent itself to digging, but its very lightness presented the seemingly insuperable problem to any would-be tunneller of stabilising it. As extra insurance the Germans made sure that the camp huts were far removed from the outer fences, so that any tunnel would need to burrow well over 100 metres to clear the camp. And if all that were not enough, microphones were installed to detect any underground activity occurring within about 10 metres of the surface.

THE GREAT ESCAPE

Despite all those obstacles, when Sagan's North Compound was completed and populated in March 1943, its first inhabitants included a number who immediately turned their thoughts to escape. They formed an escape committee bearing the name 'Organisation X'. For these airmen the precautions taken by their captors were understood as challenges rather than hindrances. They set about dealing with them, one by one.

The ingenuity of Organisation X and of the some 500 men who worked on not just one but three tunnels – Tom, Dick and Harry – over a year has long found its place in folklore and popular culture. The entrances were ingeniously disguised; systems of lighting and of feeding air into the tunnels were developed, along with a track and pulley system for the men to haul themselves across the large distances required. Timber from inside the huts, scrounged above all from their bunks, could serve for shoring up the tunnels, while a very long and very deep tunnel would avoid detection both before and during the moment of escape.

Most ingenious, perhaps, was the method devised for the distribution of the sandy soil extracted from the tunnels. This was the work of 'penguins', men who suspended inside their trouser legs cloth cylinders filled with the soil. With the aid of pieces of string inside their pockets, they could pull the pin at the bottom of the cylinders. This they would do as unobtrusively as possible – often with the help of diversions such as boxing matches – as they stood or walked in open sections of the camp, shuffling their feet to make the soil blend in with its surroundings. At the height of the tunnel construction phase, up to 150 'penguins' were spreading dirt around their German cage.[1]

The airmen's inventiveness did not stop with the surreptitious digging of tunnels. Equally crucial were the preparations for the moment the escapees left the tunnel behind them. Detailed knowledge not just of the local area around Sagan but far beyond as well was a necessity. Escape routes in numerous directions for over 200 men had to be carefully plotted, train timetables established, uniforms and forged papers produced. And all this had to be done under the very noses of the Germans and their 'ferrets', the men whose job it was to go down any holes being dug.

There is no better example of the skill, persistence and ingenuity which enabled the escape than the contribution of the Sydney-born Albert Hake. He was the maker of compasses, a necessary item in any escape kit. His countryman and fellow-POW Paul Brickhill was unstinting in his praise of Hake's work. The bases of Hake's compasses, Brickhill recalled after the war, were made of melted down gramophone records, pressed into a mould. Camp artists would then paint compass points on pieces of paper fitted into the base, while a gramophone needle was inserted to support the compass needle, fashioned from a magnetised razor blade or sewing needle. The process of magnetising was performed with a magnet Hake had 'liberated' from a guard; it had to be passed over the blade or needle for hours, always in the same direction.[2] To the needle a pivot point was attached, soldered either from melted down silver paper from cigarette packets or the tops of bully-beef tins. Then to seal the compass, glass was taken from window shards, of which there was no shortage in the camp. Hake cut the glass to shape under water to avoid cracking or chipping. It was fitted when the rims of the compass were heated to make them malleable, so that the sides would fit the glass so perfectly as to make the compass waterproof. Perhaps the neatest thing, though, in Brickhill's estimate of Hake's handiwork, was the inscription carved in the base. Each compass bore the words 'Made in Stalag Luft III'.[3]

Preparations both in the tunnels and outside them were plagued by difficulties. In late autumn 1943 most of the Americans were moved to a new compound, the South Compound, depriving the efforts in the North Compound of crucial manpower.[4] Worse followed when Tom was detected during a routine hut search. It was duly dynamited. Dick and Harry remained undetected, but a period of caution and low activity had to be observed through winter. When heightened activity was resumed, efforts were focused on Harry, its entrance under a stove in hut 104, though in a stroke of genius a use for Dick was found as a repository for the mass of soil gouged from Harry.[5]

Eventually the moonless night of 24 March 1944 was nominated as the time at which 220 airmen would make their way to freedom.

Conditions were less than perfect. It was bitterly cold, and the snow on the ground would preserve the escapees' tracks. But fearing the Germans were growing increasingly suspicious, no-one was prepared to wait another month for the next moonless night.

It was the combination of cold and snow which delayed entry to the tunnel entrance at the appointed hour, jamming the boards and causing exasperating delays. Others followed due to cave-ins and trolley derailments. The greatest threat to success, however, was revealed when the tunnel exit was unblocked. It fell short of the woods outside the camp; escapers would have to make their way across a patch of open ground within sight of a nearby guard tower. A tug on a string from an observer in the wood would advise each man of the appropriate moment to stage his dash, but it was fraught with risk. Sure enough, eventually it was the shortfall of several metres that foiled the hopes to give over 200 their freedom. It was a single warning shot ringing out through the early morning that signalled a guard's discovery of the tunnel exit. He had been alerted to the movement across the open ground, and the escape was put to a sudden end. By that time 76 had gone.[6]

Escapes always triggered manhunts following standard procedures, but the scale of this escape resulted in a pursuit on an unheard of magnitude. Camp Commandant Colonel Friedrich-Wilhelm von Lindeiner-Wildau threw all his resources into the chase, but the steps he set in motion necessarily engaged the security forces, who were not under his command. Everyone from local police forces up to – eventually – Himmler and indeed Hitler were informed and searchers mobilised.

For Himmler in particular this news was merely confirmation that the Luftwaffe was grossly incompetent in the exercise of its security obligations. As for Hitler, the thought of some of those 'terror flyers' returning home to strike at the Reich all over again was unbearable. While Lindeiner-Wildau was deeply humiliated by the breach of security in his camp – which would not only cost him his job but trigger a court-martial – Hitler, Himmler and others contemplated how to punish the miscreants and ensure that such an escape would never recur.[7] It was Hitler himself who, in conference with Keitel, Göring, Himmler and others at Berchtesgaden, decreed that captured escapees were to be shot. While Göring argued against an all-out massacre – it might be greeted by similar measures against German airmen in Allied captivity and would be impossible to cover up – Himmler suggested a figure of 50. As so often, Himmler got his way.[8]

The chain of command correspondingly did not run through the military men Keitel or Göring, but through Himmler and his man Ernst Kaltenbrunner, the then head of the Reich Security Main Office in Berlin. Kaltenbrunner in turn passed on the order to his Gestapo chief Heinrich Müller and his Criminal Police (Kripo) Chief Arthur Nebe. Apart from unleashing the manhunt that standard procedures demanded, Müller and Nebe plotted the formation of execution squads in egregious breach of any principle or letter of international law.[9]

The 76 escapees, in the meantime, made hell for leather in various directions, some heading south in the hope of reaching France and Spain, others heading north to find their way to neutral Sweden. The plan had it that some 40 would make their way by train, but not all managed that part of their assignment. Most, then, made their way on foot through the snow and slush of a prolonged winter, aiming to put as much distance between themselves and Sagan before the light of a new day set a cast of thousands in pursuit.

There were a number of Australians on the list of would-be escapees. Number 150 on the list was Flight Lieutenant Peter Kingsford-Smith. In his debriefing after the war, he described how all was put in readiness for the nominated night: papers, clothing and rations were gathered together. Then the chosen many collected in the vicinity of the tunnel entrance. From about 9.30 all seemed to proceed smoothly as far as Kingsford-Smith could judge, when an air-raid forced a frustrating halt. Then the news of the guards' detection of the tunnel at about 5 am leaked back, prompting furious efforts to destroy maps, documents and compasses. Soon heavily armed guards surrounded the hut before calling the men out and telling them to strip. If they were not quick enough, shirts and vests were torn off them. The men were then called out singly for identification.[10] The time they spent stripped was miserable – it was bitterly cold and an icy wind chilled them to the bones until their clothes were returned. Each person was searched for an average of fifteen minutes. Eventually, when the number of escapees had been established, they were returned to the barracks, and all were told they would be punished. In fact, of the men left behind only the Australian Group Captain D.E.L. Wilson was punished, sentenced in the usual manner to two weeks in the camp 'cooler'.[11]

There were six Australians among the 76 who got clear of the camp. One was Squadron Leader James Catanach, 22 years of age and a member of 455 Squadron; his Hampden had crash-landed in Norway in September 1942. Another was John E.A. 'Willy' Williams, 24 years of age when he attempted his escape from Sagan. A member of 450 Squadron, he had gone missing during operations in the Middle East at the end of October 1942.[12] In Sagan he had proved his value as the head of the tunnel carpentry department.[13] Then there was the 29-year-old Flight Lieutenant Reginald V. 'Rusty' Kierath of 450 Squadron, a captive for a year and a day when he broke out from Sagan. Thomas B. Leigh, one of the Australians serving in the RAF – in 76 Squadron – had been shot down in his Halifax in August 1941. For a long time it was not recognised that Leigh was Australian. Another was the compass-maker Warrant Officer Albert Hake, 27 years of age, whose 72 Squadron Spitfire had been shot down two years earlier. Last and luckiest was Paul Gordon Royle, who was a flight lieutenant in the RAAF's 53 Squadron. Western Australian by birth, 30-year-old Royle was also the oldest of the Australians in the escape group. He had also been in captivity longer than the others, shot down in his Blenheim on 18 May 1940 near Fontaine aux Pires.[14]

Royle, number 54 out of the tunnel, was the lucky one because he survived. He was paired off with the British airman Edgar 'Hunk' Humphreys, and together they struck out to the south after clearing the camp, reaching and crossing the main road that connected Berlin with Breslau. Like other escapees their progress was slowed by snow and slush, which forced them to take the risk of using roads. This was in all likelihood the cause of their misfortune, because on the second night of their freedom they were approached and surrounded by three men who, judging by their green uniforms, were probably members of the Landwehr, the home-guard. With insufficient knowledge of German and three armed men before them, there was no hope of bluffing their way through or taking flight. They were once again 'in the bag' and promptly deposited in the local jail. There they were joined by three other escapees, and then all were taken by van to the jail in Sagan, little more than a stone's throw from the camp they had fled. Nineteen abject airmen, their escapes nipped in the bud, were collected there.[15]

What Royle and the other eighteen might reasonably have expected at this point was that all of them would be returned to the camp, where they might have to endure a stint of anything up to four weeks in the 'cooler'. But in this case their captors were not reading from the pages of the Geneva Convention. From the Sagan jail the group was transported through the night to Görlitz, where they were deposited in tiny cells in the town jail, four in each one. Altogether 35 escapees were collected in the Görlitz jail, cold, hungry, bitterly disappointed, and with little sense of what awaited them.[16] After languishing there for a day, they were escorted, one by one, across town to the grey stone Gestapo district headquarters, where they were questioned about their exploits. Royle savoured the provisional freedom of the escorted walk across town, only to have any sense of relief soured by the oppressive atmosphere inside those headquarters and the surly demeanour of the men inside. He answered questions curtly, fending off any implication that he might have harboured any intentions of sabotage. He was duly escorted back to the jail, but this time was placed among new cell-mates, also escapees from Stalag Luft III.[17]

Then the story became even more curious. Royle and his new cell-mates noted that the letter 'S' was chalked on their door, though its meaning was unclear. As they sat in the cell they observed a party of eight prisoners being escorted under heavy guard from the jail, destination unknown. A second group of half a dozen or more soon followed, and yet another later in the morning. As for those in the 'S' cell, they stayed put for another day, until they too were removed from the jail and returned to their camp. Yet the others moved before them were not there. Had the 'S' stood for 'Sagan'? As expected, having re-entered Stalag Luft III they were sent to the 'cooler', so full that they had company in what normally were isolation cells. But the mystery of what had happened to those removed from Görlitz before them remained unanswered.[18]

It was a new commandant who informed the senior British officer in the camp, Group Captain Herbert Massey, that 41 of the escapees had been shot dead, either in resisting apprehension or in attempting renewed escape. Massey's incredulity only grew when he heard the commandant's answer to the question how many of the airmen had been wounded. The answer was 'none'. That every man halted by gunfire would die of his wounds defied all odds. Massey asked for a list of the dead; he also wrote to the Protecting Power and to Göring, requesting a personal interview. When the news was passed on to his fellow POWs, it was greeted with stunned silence.[19]

Days later a list of the dead arrived. By now it included 47 names, among them that of Paul Royle's travelling partner, 'Hunk' Humphreys. Also on the list was the name of a man seen in Görlitz to be suffering from frostbite so dreadful as to deprive him of his mobility – it was the Australian compass-maker Albert Hake.[20] How could a man in such a condition have been attempting escape? Finally the urns with the ashes of the dead men arrived in the camp, each urn marked with the place of the man's death. With the cremation of their bodies any chance of an investigation into the cause of death was lost.[21]

Only in time did the course of events become clearer in Stalag Luft III and the wider world. Williams and Kierath, it appears, were in a group of twelve pretending to be foreign workers. Their leader was a Pole, Jerzy Mondschein, a fluent German speaker. From Sagan they had headed for the railway station at Tschiebsdorf, a couple of hours by foot from the camp. There they bought tickets for Boberohrsdorf, some 80 kilometres to the south, and in the vicinity of Hirschberg. From there the plan was they would walk some 60 kilometres to the Czech border, and at that point divide up to take their separate chances.[22] But in reality those 60 kilometres in thick snow proved an ordeal. Now in a group of four, Williams and Kierath were apprehended by a military patrol and escorted to the nearest town, Reichenberg – today Liberec. Both, it seems, were executed in cold blood with their two travelling companions on 29 March. Williams' murderer was a Gestapo officer by the name of Lux; Kierath's never firmly established. The urns with the ashes of both men were sent to Sagan; they bore the name 'Brüx' – today the Czech city of Most – in all likelihood the place of their cremation and perhaps their execution as well.[23]

Catanach was headed north, making it as far as Flensburg, an impressive achievement in itself. But it was in Flensburg, close to the Danish border, that his trek, and his life, came to an end. It seems that he, too, was murdered on 29 March, five days after the escape. His killer was the Gestapo officer Johannes Post, who held the SS rank of Sturmbannführer, and whose distinguishing feature was the moral vacuousness of the dyed-in-the-wool Nazi he so proudly was. Post made a point of not sparing his victims the awful truth of their imminent execution. For him, as he explained after the war, it was a point of pride to announce to the condemned well in advance what he was about to do.[24]

Testimony given at his postwar trial suggests Post indulged this penchant as he conducted Catanach to his murder. The recaptured airman was seated near Post in a car travelling through Kiel towards the nominated point of execution. After pointing out numerous landmarks – some of them familiar to the airman from a different perspective – Post informed the Australian, 'We must get on. I have to shoot you.' The incredulous Catanach queried the threat which had been delivered so casually, but Post merely repeated it. Thinking that Post's attempt at black humour had to be treated with humour of his own, Catanach reportedly responded, 'Another time. I have an appointment in the cooler at Stalag Luft III. I've done nothing wrong except go under the wire. You can't shoot me.' Eventually the car reached a field and stopped. In Post's testimony, by this time Catanach was in no doubt as to his fate. Before carrying out the deed, Post repeated that he had orders to shoot the airman. If he was resigned to his fate, Catanach's incredulity was undiminished. He merely asked 'Why?'[25] Catanach's body was cremated at Kiel; his ashes, too, were sent back to Sagan.[26]

The RAF man Thomas Leigh was among a group captured not far from Sagan and taken to Görlitz jail. That was where Albert Hake, too, was deposited after his capture, suffering from severe frostbite, just south of Sagan. Neither Leigh nor Hake was among the select few chosen for return to the camp, at least not alive. The unlucky majority, including those two Australians, were moved in black cars on 30 and 31 March, never to be seen again. Those who saw Hake being moved from the Görlitz prison speculated that he might have been taken to hospital to treat his frostbite. In fact, both the Australians were being escorted to their death.[27]

The perpetrators in this instance were the Gestapo officers Scharpwinkel and Lux. From a Moscow prison after the war, Scharpwinkel gave some insight into the process. The first of the shootings of the men hauled from the Görlitz prison involved six of them, among them the Australians Thomas Leigh, Albert Hake and the Maori John (or Porokoru Patapu) Pohe. The Gestapo murder squad took the men from the prison to the Gestapo headquarters, where, according to Scharpwinkel's testimony, they were told they had been sentenced to death by order of the Supreme Military Commander – Hitler. Then the condemned were driven away and, according to Scharpwinkel, when the *Autobahn* was reached the executions were performed: 'The prisoners were placed in position. It was revealed to them that the sentence was about to be carried out. The prisoners showed considerable calm, which surprised me very much. The six prisoners stood next to one another in the wood. Lux gave the order to fire and the detachment fired. Lux shot with them. By the second salvo the prisoners were dead.' So shameless was the killing it took place on 31 March in broad daylight.[28]

Of the 76 who escaped, only three recorded the fabled 'home run': the Norwegians Peter Bergsland and Jens Muller, who made their way to Sweden, and the Dutchman Bram van der Stok, who reached England via France, Spain and Gibraltar. What all three had in common was a good dose of luck and a command of German.

As for the other 73, Paul Royle was among 20 who were returned to Stalag Luft III. Six men were recaptured and sent to the Sachsenhausen concentration camp just outside Berlin. Four of those six managed to escape from Sachsenhausen and ultimately returned safely to their homelands. One of them, curiously, was Major Johnnie Dodge, who was related to Winston Churchill. Dodge was recaptured after making good his escape from Sachsenhausen but then was released into Switzerland before the end of the war. Two Czech RAF airmen upon recapture were sent to Colditz to sit out the rest of the war there. The other 50 had all been murdered in cold blood.[29]

Himmler would have preferred to keep the whole atrocious business secret, but in time the awful truth would come out, aided as it was by an unlikely conduit. The key figure in all this was a senior Wehrmacht officer, Colonel Adolf Westhoff, who at that time was still deputy to the Chief of POW Affairs, Major General Fritz von Graevenitz, but destined very soon to take over from him. Westhoff was a career soldier with a most distinguished record, including the Iron Cross First Class and Second Class as well as a stint in a British POW camp at the end of the Great War. In the Second World War he had already served with distinction on the Eastern Front, earning the reputation of an exemplary officer.[30]

We know something of Westhoff's views on the matter of the Sagan escape because he was obliged to answer some awkward questions after the war. He was a very useful witness, because he was present at the meeting hosted by Hitler at Berchtesgaden on 26 March. The agenda was simple – come up with a plan in response to the breakout from Stalag Luft III. In Westhoff's recollection, Hitler wanted all those airmen recaptured by the police and other security forces to be shot; Keitel expressed his concurrence at the need to set an example for others and went so far as to suggest sending the ashes of the dead to the camp. Moreover, Keitel levelled some of the blame at Westhoff, though for no good reason. Sagan was one of Göring's camps; Westhoff had nothing to do with security arrangements there.[31]

In his testimony, Westhoff stated that he had condemned the suggestion to murder the airmen and moreover reminded all present that it was forbidden to cremate the bodies of POWs. Graevenitz, too, at that point still Chief of POW Affairs in the OKW, had his qualms and told Westhoff after the meeting, 'You could see that nothing was to be done. What can be done when the Gestapo has its hand in it? We can only make sure that our people do not get involved after the Gestapo has carried out the shootings.'[32] Westhoff was not so pessimistic and saw the possibility of taking some action. His motivation – or so at least he claimed after the war – was to make Hitler understand that the orders he was giving had to be reversed.[33]

If Westhoff could not win the day at that fateful meeting, he was able to strengthen his position through his elevation to Chief of POW Affairs on 1 April.[34] In that role he could at least do two things to foil efforts to hide the truth. Firstly, he was able to use his promotion to proceed with the repatriation of Group Captain Massey. Massey had been told that 41 men had been shot in the act of escape or resisting recapture and had reacted with due scepticism, and through the connivance of Westhoff – above all in circumventing Keitel, who would surely have vetoed the request – the repatriation went ahead.[35] He was sent to the *Heilag* (*Heimkehrerlager*, repatriates' camp) at Annaburg to await his journey home.[36] In fact, in Annaburg Massey learned the truth was worse than he had thought. He was informed there that the number of dead was 47, not 41 as originally reported. Indeed, it seems that on the day the 41 deaths were reported, six others were being led to their execution.[37] Massey would have no compunction in sharing this information with all who would listen when he returned to Britain.

The second part of Westhoff's plan was to ensure that a scheduled inspection by the Protecting Power went ahead. Thus on 17 April, shortly after Massey was taken to Annaburg, Stalag Luft III received a visit from Gabriel Naville, who was head of the British Interests Division at the Swiss legation in Berlin. At Stalag Luft III he, like Massey and other British officers in the camp, was fed the lie about men being shot dead while resisting capture or attempting to escape after capture. By now there was just one variation – in the new version of the Germans' story 47 had been killed, while 14 were still at large.[38] Naville was not fooled. It was his prerogative to interview senior POW officers in the absence of their captors, and they told a different story. It was inconceivable, they pointed out, that the murdered men would have resisted arrest. Moreover, from the recaptured men had come reports that they had seen 30 of their fellow escapees in handcuffs and under heavy police escort as they were taken by truck from a prison in Görlitz.[39] Naville shared the officers' suspicions, and he passed them on to British authorities via Clifford Norton, the British minister in Geneva.[40]

In mid-May Norton reported to London, where an indignant War Cabinet instructed the Swiss government to take up the issue with the highest German authorities, demanding a full report on the loss of life. From the government the news of the suspected atrocity spilled into the pages of the British press, prompting Foreign Secretary Anthony Eden to make a statement to the House of Commons. By then the cat was well and truly out of the bag, and the investigations took on a momentum of their own.[41]

In June, Naville made another visit to Stalag Luft III, learning that the true figure of the number of dead was now set at 50, with 11 men still missing. More accurate though this information was, it was not delivered in an atmosphere of amiable transparency. On the contrary, a chill had settled over the camp, and Naville was told that the camp was now in the hands of the Gestapo, not the military authorities. Two of the returned officers, Naville established, had been told they would be shot, while another was threatened with decapitation if he did not answer questions.[42]

With knowledge of the killings now having crossed the Channel, formal processes of enquiry could be set in motion. As Switzerland was the relevant Protecting Power, it was the Swiss who posed awkward questions about the escape and its consequences. These enquiries were made via the German Foreign Office in Berlin, which had received information on the escape from both the OKW

– which had limited knowledge – and from the RSHA, which had little interest in making known the full extent of its actions. The report handed to the Swiss Legation satisfied no-one, following as it did the already established line that the dead escapees had been shot while resisting recapture.[43]

If the German authorities bit their tongues, the POWs were more forthcoming. Naville learned a great deal from the fortunate officers who had been returned to the camp. One had been subjected to an interrogation in which his interlocutor had gone some way to letting the cat out of the bag – he told the airman that he was in the hands of the Gestapo, might never return to camp, and that any escapee caught in civilian clothes could not claim the protection of the Geneva Convention. Other returned escapees gave similar accounts of interrogation and intimidation. One gave an account which provided further insight into the fate of Albert Hake, who had been sighted at Görlitz. Naville was told, 'if any man at Görlitz had been shown an open door and told they could walk out all would have refused. Everybody was very hungry, exhausted and the weather outside was hopeless.' Poor Hake's last hours on earth, like those of the other dead men, are likely to have been wretched in the extreme.[44]

By now a much clearer picture had emerged. The accusing finger could be pointed with much greater certainty at the Gestapo and its allied security services. The buck stopped with Himmler. Moreover, Naville could now report more accurately that 50 escaped officers of altogether 11 nationalities had been murdered.[45] On 23 June Eden briefed the House of Commons on the newest findings, presenting the official German excuse that the actions were a response to unprecedented numbers of escapes and commando activities, yet conveying his government's outrage at the events of 24–25 March. Calling on the sworn evidence of men including the repatriated Massey, he recounted the events of that fateful night and their deadly aftermath. It was abundantly clear, he concluded, that all 50 had been murdered in overt breach of the Geneva Convention. The culprits, he promised, would be brought to 'exemplary justice' when the war was over.[46]

18

Sojourn in Buchenwald

Adolf Westhoff was not the only member of the Wehrmacht who despaired at the course of the war and the Reich's inexorable slide into amorality under Hitler's leadership. On 20 July 1944 Claus Graf Schenck von Stauffenberg famously attempted to assassinate the Führer. He very soon paid for his failure with his own life, and in the wake of the attempt co-conspirators were tracked down, rounded up and subjected to Nazi justice by the most brutal means. Hitler reportedly took sadistic pleasure in watching film footage of his alleged enemies dangling from piano wire. His blood lust did not stop at Stauffenberg's circle, rather it reached opponents of even quite different political persuasions.

If the revelations of the murderous upshot of the Great Escape had brought embarrassment to the Reich, the Nazi leaders did not show it. With their enemies both within and outside the Reich gaining strength, international prestige was the least of their concerns. The first lesson Himmler in particular drew from the escape was that the Luftwaffe was negligent in its security obligations. As far as he was concerned, the Sagan fiasco proved that his role needed to grow, not shrink. The security dilemmas facing the Reich demanded not the kid-gloves offered by the Wehrmacht but the trademark ruthlessness on which he and his men prided themselves.

A second episode in 1944 demonstrated that Himmler's star in POW matters was indeed on the rise. Once again, the victims were airmen, and once again there were Australians among them. Unlike the men of Stalag Luft III, these POWs were delivered into the hands of the German security services after capture until, sooner or later, they were delivered to the most emblematic of the Reich's institutions, a concentration camp.

In the Nazis' camp universe, concentration camps and the POW camps were in principle separate planets. One was ruled by Himmler's SS, the other by the Wehrmacht. Yet at certain points they did collide. Allocated to their work detachments, Australian and other POWs on occasion came into direct contact with the inmates of concentration camps, an invaluable source of slave labour to the Nazi regime. In rarer instances the POWs encountered the concentration camps themselves. Charlie Parrott, for example, in getting to his place of work in Bavaria would pass the entrance to the Dachau concentration camp. 'We could see the prisoners at work inside the camp.'[1]

The concentration camp at Buchenwald in Thuringia was one of the centrepieces of the German concentration camp system. It was the largest of the camps in central Germany, just as Dachau near Munich was the dominant camp in the south and Sachsenhausen near Berlin in the north. Buchenwald was just outside the town of Weimar, intimately associated with German classicism and its leading representatives Johann Wolfgang von Goethe and Friedrich Schiller. But as Goethe's Faust put it, there were two souls in the German breast, and from 1937 Weimar's second soul found ominous expression in the concentration camp built on the Ettersberg, a hillside outside the town. In a telling emblem of a descent into barbarism, the watchtowers and the barbed wire strung between them enclosed the Goethe Oak, a tree much visited and praised by Goethe himself well over a century earlier.

While the men who bore the stigma of the 'red triangle' – a badge worn by the 'political' prisoners such as Communists and Social Democrats – bore the brunt of Buchenwald's prewar evil, during the war both the range and the number of victims expanded.

There were homosexuals and Jehovah's Witnesses, common criminals and Christian anti-fascists. Above all as the war progressed there were Jews with their distinctive yellow star badges. Germans and non-Germans among them, they came to Buchenwald from near and far to assume their by now accustomed place in the Reich as the lowest of the low. Of the more than sixty thousand victims of Buchenwald tallied in the aftermath of war, it was the Jews who easily outnumbered all the other groups.

To this already diverse assortment of the wretched were added, extraordinarily, in August 1944, 168 airmen. All of them were transferred there from the Gestapo prison at Fresnes on the outskirts of Paris. Nearly half of them were from the United States, the rest from Canada, Australia, New Zealand and the United Kingdom.

The Buchenwald Archive holds the records of the arrivals dated 20 August 1944, among them a group categorised as 'police prisoners' (*Polizeihäftlinge*). The nine Australian names on the list, together with their allocated Buchenwald inmate numbers, are Mervyn Fairclough (78427), James Gwilliam (78423), Eric Johnston (78421), Kevin Light (78381), Thomas Malcolm (78379), Keith Mills (78426), Robert Mills (78405), Raymond Perry (78356) and Les Whellum (78442). Fairclough and Perry were Western Australians, Gwilliam and Light New South Welshmen, Johnston and Malcolm Victorians, Robert Mills (the baby of the group at just 20 when he walked through Buchenwald's gates) and Leslie Whellum were South Australians, while Keith Mills – no relation to Robert – hailed from Mackay in Queensland. The remaining 159 men came from many places, but the senior officer among them, who took on a huge burden in representing their interests to the camp authorities, was a New Zealander, Philip Lamason.

The adventurous tales of these men – explaining how they had been rounded up by the Gestapo and delivered to Buchenwald via Fresnes – have been told before. Generous though the support of French anti-Nazis had been, it was also very perilous, and the Gestapo had been successful in infiltrating escape and evasion networks. Many of the Buchenwald men, and countless others before and after them, had walked unwittingly into carefully laid traps.

SOJOURN IN BUCHENWALD

RAAF Flight Sergeant Ray Perry's story was typical. On 7 May 1944 he was shot down over France. He was serving as the bomb-aimer in an all-Australian crew flying a Halifax in the RAAF's 466 Squadron; their target that night was railway yards west of Paris. It was that crew's thirteenth operation together, and indeed on this occasion the number proved itself entirely worthy of the apprehension it engendered. After it dropped its load, it was struck and crippled by a German night fighter. The crew had no choice but to bale out.[2]

All the crewmembers had the good fortune to exit in time and parachute to the ground, albeit in different locations. Perry had the particular fortune of announcing his presence at a house where his plight was understood intuitively and empathetically. Its occupants gave him new clothes, a French identity card, and awkwardly conveyed instructions to follow a guide to a safe house. The following day Perry was moved to another village, Rouvre, where an elderly couple accommodated him. He had plainly slipped into the care of the Resistance.[3]

Two weeks later he was moved to another village, where he was taught French and given access to a radio through which, in time, he could follow the fortunes of the Normandy invasion. Eventually he and two RAF officers were shifted into the lion's den, to Paris, with the advice that in due course they would be shifted south, ultimately to Gibraltar, and flown to England.[4]

The appointed day of the next move held a nasty surprise. Perry and five other airmen were picked up by car, driven past some of the sights of Paris, and then driven off the street into a courtyard. The driver announced that they had reached Gestapo headquarters, and they were now prisoners of the Germans. Incredulous at the dramatic change of fortune, the airmen were ushered into a room one at a time to record name, rank and number, and then placed in a cell. In time they were led outside once more to join a ragged assembly of captives. They sported a variety of clothing, yet the 20 or so of them were all airmen like Perry, victims of an act of betrayal.[5]

From the Fresnes prison they were loaded onto cattle trucks on 15 August and commenced a journey, their destination unknown.

They passed through Frankfurt am Main, a city Perry had seen from above eight months earlier. For these men there was not to be the customary airman's visit to the Luftwaffe's interrogation centre at Oberursel and then Dulag Luft; instead, the train headed further east. Perry remembers that in the last stage of the journey the train passed through a forest, until a sign hailed their arrival at Buchenwald.[6]

From the platform they saw on one side the buildings of the munitions factory and striped-pyjama workforce. But their new home was along the road known as the 'Caracho Weg', leading to the main entrance of the camp with its trademark clock and its wrought-iron gates proclaiming to all who passed through them the sinister platitude, *'Jedem das Seine'* – To Each His Own. After entering the gates the airmen and other captives were led down the hill to the delousing facility, where they surrendered what possessions they had, including their clothes; they were thoroughly shaved and showered and given striped clothes from the store. From there they were led to their accommodation in the most miserable part of the camp, the *Zeltlager*. For the time being, at least, Perry and his comrades would be living in tents. The date was 20 August; it was Perry's 21st birthday.[7]

Captured earlier or later, the other 167 Allied airmen had similar stories to tell, from the point of baling out to betrayal, a stint in Fresnes, and a cattle-car ride to the Ettersberg. A common denominator in many stories was the nefarious role of traitors. In Belgium the worst of them was a certain Prosper de Zitter, a Belgian who had returned from Canada just before the war and who had offered his services to German military intelligence – the Abwehr – soon after hostilities commenced. 'The Captain', as he was sometimes known, adopted the habit of directing RAF men straight into the hands of the enemy they were so desperately trying to evade.[8] Then in France there was another Belgian, Jacques Desoubrie, who posed as a Resistance figure guiding airmen to safety, but who in reality had struck his own Faustian bargain with the Gestapo. He did more than anyone else to destroy the 'Comet' escape line by which Allied airmen sought passage south to the Pyrenees and Spain. Not only airmen but French and Belgian Resistance workers, too, were betrayed by 'Captain Jacques' and suffered the consequences.[9]

The men arrived at a time when Buchenwald was already overfilled and taking more than it could accommodate with any modicum of humane treatment. On the day of their entry alone, there were 1650 new arrivals at a camp bursting at the seams with 88,000 inmates.[10] The tent camp where the airmen were accommodated – along with countless other inmates – had been built in the recent past to cope with an influx of 2000 Frenchmen. There were five tents, allegedly with a capacity of 200 each, and as a postwar report established, at first with 'no beds, blankets, seating, any sort of water to drink or wash with, no underwear, latrines, drainage system, medications, dishes or spoons'. Only the feverish efforts of prisoners had rendered the space habitable, yet still far from agreeable.[11] Deaths from an unholy combination of disease and undernourishment were a daily occurrence. One of the Australian airmen, Bob Mills, was for a time coerced into operating the cart which bore the bodies of the dead from the 'Small Camp' containing the *Zeltlager* to the crematorium.

After their initial time in the *Zeltlager*, room was found for the airmen in Block 45, near the corner of the camp which had the storage building and the delousing facility. Camp records show that this occurred on 28 August, eight days after their arrival, and after medical inspections had been carried out.[12] The two-storey stone building was a vast improvement on the tent accommodation. The rhythm of camp life they now adopted was similar to that of the more established inmates. After a morning rollcall they received rye bread with margarine as breakfast. At 11 am they drank a cup of ersatz coffee, and at 4 in the afternoon they took their main meal, soup, which every second day would contain a small portion of sausage.[13] The key difference between these men and most inmates was that the airmen did not have to work. They simply languished, having no sense of when they would leave or indeed if they would leave at all.

These men were not the first POWs to arrive at Buchenwald. That dubious honour had been accorded Soviet POWs from late 1941. For most of them their stay in Buchenwald was mercilessly brief. The camp authorities had installed a special killing facility in converted horse stables. Duped into thinking they were being given a medical examination, the Soviet officers were executed through a single pistol shot administered to the back of the neck. Over 7000 of them lost their lives in this way.[14]

There were also some members of the British Special Operations Executive (SOE) in Buchenwald; indeed, they were still there when the airmen arrived in August. Hitler's by now well-established abhorrence of commandos meant they were denied the status of POWs. There were 43 such men, English and French, almost all brought to Buchenwald from France in the same month as the airmen. In the first half of September, 16 of them were executed by hanging in the cellar of the camp crematorium.[15] On 5 October a further 20 were executed. Of this group only a handful experienced liberation, among them the Englishman Christopher Burney. Burney had been captured at Caen in August 1942 after being parachuted into France. He arrived in Buchenwald only after enduring interrogations and 18 months of solitary confinement, then spent all of fifteen months in the horror that was Buchenwald and lived to write his story.[16]

Shortly before the airmen arrived, Buchenwald had received a very special and brutally brief visit. As they vegetated in a train limping east towards Weimar, the long incarcerated head of the banned German Communist Party, Ernst Thälmann, was delivered to Buchenwald. Himmler's men had hauled him from his prison cell in the Bautzen jail and delivered him to the concentration camp for execution. From his cell in Bautzen, Thälmann had played no role in the plot concocted by Stauffenberg and the 'Men of the 20th of July' to assassinate Hitler, but a month after his narrow escape, Hitler was still lashing out mercilessly at the swelling ranks of his enemies. After a meeting with Hitler on 14 August, Himmler recorded in his diary, 'Thälmann ist zu exekutieren' – Thälmann is to be executed. On 18 August at Buchenwald, Thälmann was led by his SS guard to the crematorium where, in its small courtyard, he was shot dead. Covering their tracks immediately, the killers burned the fully clothed body.[17]

The SS later tried to claim that Thälmann had been killed during an Allied bombing raid on Buchenwald's adjoining armaments works on 24 August. That was a barefaced lie, though there was indeed a raid on that date. Altogether 129 aircraft of the US 8th Air Force unleashed half an hour of fury through the middle of the day.[18] If the airmen had not yet arrived when Thälmann was killed, they did feel the full force of more than a thousand bombs dropped around them, as the Americans preferred, during daylight. All 168 of the airmen emerged unscathed, but others were not so lucky. The socialist politician Rudolf Breitscheid was one of the privileged prisoners in a special barrack, housing also his wife and Princess Mafalda, daughter of the former King Emanuel of Italy. The two women survived the bombs, but Breitscheid was dead.[19]

Other arrivals were more welcome. A large contingent of some 1700 Danish policemen arrived in the camp when the airmen were there. Placed in huts near the airmen, the Danes were so generous as to share their Red Cross parcels with their unlikely fellow inmates.[20] Despite their good state of health on entry, and despite the rare privilege of access to the parcels, the Danes did not cope well with Buchenwald. Within four months, 60 of them were dead.[21]

The airmen were more fortunate, or at least most of them were. Buchenwald records show that on 19 October 156 'terror-flyers' from Block 58 were transferred from the camp.[22] The same records do not name the destination; in reality it was Stalag Luft III at Sagan. By machinations which remain unclear, the Luftwaffe learned that there were airmen being held in a concentration camp, and was ultimately able to assert its right to get its hands on them. A representative of the Luftwaffe duly appeared in Buchenwald to organise the men's departure. On the appointed day the men were handed the civilian clothing they were wearing when captured, along with whatever effects had been confiscated from them on arrival. As they were being escorted through the camp's main gate, they must have thought themselves cheating hell. One of the Americans in that group, Jim Fore, recalls the moment of departure: 'As we left Buchenwald, people hung onto the inner wire and watched us with their staring eyes inside gaunt faces and bodies. Their eyes were pleading, "why, why, why?"[23]

That fortunate group included all the Australian airmen with the one exception of Thomas Malcolm. He was among 14 sick men who remained behind. At the crucial time he was suffering a severe bout of erysipelas, a highly contagious condition affecting the skin and kidneys and liable, in extreme cases like Malcolm's, to lead to delirium.[24] Thankfully Malcolm was among the small group who departed the camp more than a month later than the others – on 28 November. But two of the airmen, the Englishman Philip Hemmens and the American L.C. Beck, never left Buchenwald, and never experienced liberation.[25]

19

Himmler Steps In

As the airmen languished in Buchenwald, ominous changes were taking place in Berlin. If Heinrich Himmler had long shown more than a passing interest in POW affairs, and commonly intervened as he saw fit, from the beginning of October he took over completely.

Himmler's star had long been on the rise, and Claus von Stauffenberg's fateful misjudgment only played into Himmler's hands. The plans hatched by Stauffenberg and his co-conspirators entailed a crucial role for the Ersatzheer, the German Replacement Army or Home Army, which in the envisaged state of emergency after the assassination would foil any attempt by Himmler and his men to seize control of the Reich. Though assiduously wooed by the plotters, the Commander in Chief of the Replacement Army, Friedrich Fromm, remained at best ambivalent about his proposed role in a post-Hitler world and downright fretful about the consequences of a bungled plot. In the end his ambivalence counted for naught. When Hitler emerged scathed but alive from the ruins of the Wolf's Lair, Fromm sought to cover the tracks pointing to him by ordering the hasty and brutal murder of the plotters who knew too much. In the end, though, it was just a matter of time before the general himself faced the firing squad.

Command of the Replacement Army was passed immediately to Himmler, whose loyalty Hitler did not doubt. It was a move with consequences for POWs, because it granted Himmler even greater licence to interfere in POW matters. Moreover the Wehrmacht, whose competence in POW matters was already in question, plummeted in Hitler's esteem. It was now Himmler who loomed irresistibly over POWs.

Himmler's ascent was noted in London. With the tragedy of Stalag Luft III still in mind, the War Office thought fit to let the Prisoners of War Department in the Foreign Office know of Himmler's expanded role. The fear was that an alleged proclivity on behalf of the German armed forces to wash its hands of any maltreatment of POWs, passing the blame to the Gestapo, might gain momentum. The War Office made it clear that any such protestations of innocence on behalf of the Wehrmacht would be unacceptable. Nonetheless, the possible implications of Himmler's swelling portfolio had to be faced: 'We feel that the unification of the Army in Germany and the Gestapo under one command may perhaps result in the methods of the latter being adopted as the standard for the treatment of all Allied Prisoners of War.'[1]

In the camps themselves the men knew nothing of these ructions, though they did detect a change of mood among their captors. It was especially evident among the younger Germans, those who had been socialised and indoctrinated in the Third Reich and would serve it to the end. Unfazed by D-Day and the assassination attempt on their Führer, their resolve to serve the Reich and punish its enemies merely hardened. The signs of the new mood were unmistakable. In the middle of 1944 a poster began to appear in the camps. 'TO ALL PRISONERS OF WAR', it proclaimed, 'THE ESCAPE FROM PRISON CAMPS IS NO LONGER A SPORT'. While Germany had observed its international legal obligations, the poster insisted, its British enemy had stooped to illegal warfare in non-combat zones 'in the form of gangster commandos, terror bandits and sabotage troops'. But the Reich was determined to ensure its security and to this end had created 'death zones', areas in which all unauthorised trespassers would be shot on sight. As if that were not clear enough, the poster reiterated,

> Escaping prisoners of war, entering such death zones, will certainly lose their lives. They are therefore in constant danger of being mistaken for enemy agents of sabotage groups. <u>Urgent warning is given against making future escapes!</u> In plain English: Stay in the camp where you will be safe! Breaking out of it is now a damned dangerous act. <u>The chances of preserving your life are almost nil!</u>[2]

The posters alone had little effect. Escapes continued, some of the escapers motivated by the steady approach of the Allies from both West and East. German anxieties only grew, conjuring frightening visions in which POW camps were transformed into enemy strongholds from which the Reich would be overwhelmed from within. Hitler became convinced that only the uncompromising ruthlessness of Himmler and his men could keep the massive population of POWs under control. On 25 September he issued a directive that from the first day of the next month control over POW affairs was to be passed formally to Himmler. The directive explicitly transferred to the Reichsführer SS 'the safekeeping of all POWs and internees as well as all POW camps and facilities with their guard personnel'.[3]

In international law this was at best a dubious move, and the Germans knew it. According to Geneva, POWs were the responsibility of the armed forces, not the police or security forces. To surmount this obstacle Himmler had all his Higher SS and Police Leaders (HSSPF) relabelled as Generale der Polizei und Gruppenführer der Waffen-SS – Generals of the Police and Group Leaders of the Waffen SS.[4] Even at the point of recapture of escaped POWs, this veneer of legality was preserved and polished. An escaped POW seized by the Gestapo would be formally released from captivity as a POW, his name stricken from the list of POWs held by the Wehrmacht's POW Information Bureau, and the POW thereby placed beyond the reach of his own government, the Protecting Power and the Red Cross. It was a perilous predicament.[5]

The sheen of legal propriety masked fundamental structural changes in the way the Reich dealt with its POWs. The office of the Chief of POW Affairs in the General Wehrmacht Office, the AWA, was now declared to be an independent entity within the Wehrmacht. An SS General was then appointed to the role of Chief of POW Affairs. Because he headed an independent office, he was not answerable to any Wehrmacht superiors but rather to the Head of the Replacement Army. And as we know, by this time that was Heinrich Himmler. Things worked differently, too, at the level of the Military Districts. Each district's Commander of POWs – responsible for the running of the POW camps – had hitherto been subordinate to the district's Deputy General Commander – responsible for the units of guards in the camps. Under the new arrangements, both the camps and their guards were transferred to the district's Higher SS and Police Leader, who was Himmler's man and not part of a Wehrmacht command structure. And at the most basic level, inside the POW camps security men were installed and placed on the same level as the camp commandants, who thereby abandoned some of their powers to Himmler's representatives.[6]

To appease international opinion, assurances were given that the Geneva Convention was being respected, and that meant that POW matters were still assigned to the military. In a couple of crucial ways this was true. In the operational areas adjacent to the fronts, the OKH remained in charge, as had always been the case.[7] The other area left for the sake of appearances in the hands of the military was the conduct of relations with the outside world. That meant that it was the Wehrmacht and its offices that dealt with the Protecting Powers and the inspection agencies, stubbornly maintaining the fiction that the Geneva Convention was being universally respected. But in all internal matters of substance, the strings were being pulled from the top by Himmler, and priorities shifted to his obsession – security.

Colonel Adolf Westhoff, no friend of the SS, felt the changes more keenly than most. Relieved of the role of Chief of POW Affairs, now handed to the SS, Westhoff was given as a consolation prize the revived office of Inspekteur Kriegsgefangenenwesen

HIMMLER STEPS IN

– Inspector of Prisoner of War Affairs. His job description was implicit in Hitler's directive of 25 September 1944.[8] On matters of the observation of international law – in relation to foreign POWs in the Reich and German POWs abroad – Westhoff was Germany's face to the rest of the world. But in the bigger scheme of things, as Westhoff well knew, this was small beer. The issues that really counted by now, namely security and the exploitation of labour, had shifted to the SS. Like many other members of the Wehrmacht, Westhoff had to adjust to the indignity of carrying out the wishes of men whose moral code, if they had one at all, bore only a passing resemblance to his own.

These structural changes did nothing at all to curb Hitler's own abiding interest in POWs. If anything, it only grew. Even as he tracked the misfortunes of his men in the field and dreamed of mounting crushing counteroffensives, he watched with a growing sense of anger and vindictiveness those enemies whose fate he thought he could control – the POWs.

As defeat loomed, the desperation of the measures he contemplated against them deepened. A notable nadir was the fire-bombing of Dresden on 13 and 14 February 1945. In its aftermath Hitler was livid with fury at what he saw as the wanton malevolence of the Allies. Goebbels proposed to him that POWs should be shot in numbers equivalent to those killed in Dresden as a deterrent against future raids.[9] But on this occasion Hitler's ire was directed at the airmen specifically. As an act of vengeance he demanded the shooting of all Western Allied Air Force officers – and that would include the Australian airmen.[10] He also pondered the idea of a 'human shield'. In this scheme, 5000 of the Allied officers would be placed daily on the central square of Berlin, the Wilhelmplatz, to deter bombings of the capital.[11] In the following month, March 1945, the memory of Dresden still fresh in his mind, Hitler issued yet another in a long line of murderous orders concerning POWs: henceforth all downed enemy airmen would be shot on capture.[12] By April, with what was left of the Reich being crushed in the pincers of the Allied forces and defeat imminent, Hitler considered shifting

100,000 POWs as hostages to an Alpine redoubt in the deep, mountainous south.[13]

If the worst did not eventuate, then it was not for lack of will on Hitler's part. Others around him contemplated what amounted to the wholesale abandonment of Geneva with trepidation. They anticipated the application of the reciprocity principle, and with it the consequences for the growing number of German POWs in enemy hands. Others, having accepted the inevitability of defeat, were no doubt clinging to some hope of saving their own skins in the great postwar reckoning they could not avoid. If the counter-arguments put to Hitler did not convince him, they at least caused delays, until the Führer's wrath locked onto a new target. Though they knew nothing of it at the time, the airmen in particular had had a very narrow escape.

Some credit for the avoidance of POW bloodbaths must be given to Adolf Westhoff. In the toothless role of Inspector of POW Affairs, he did what he could to uphold the Geneva Convention, which he knew backwards. Fully aware of what had happened after the Sagan escape, he knew better than anyone how Himmler's quiet coup had impacted on POWs.[14] Even after the war his irritation at Himmler's longstanding habit of meddling in Wehrmacht business was still palpable:

> From the beginning Himmler attempted time and time again to get his hands on the POWs, and because he did not, he constantly made difficulties for the OKW. Despite ongoing resistance from the OKW he finally managed in October 1944 to push his claims through at the highest level. Party Chancellory, Reich Security Main Office, Propaganda Ministry, Plenipotentiary for Labour, the Speer Ministry, the German Labour Front, they were all stronger and got all their wishes granted by Hitler against the OKW.[15]

The other man to whom Australians and other POWs should be grateful is an implausible object of admiration. That was SS General Gottlob Berger, who was given Westhoff's former job of Chief of POW Affairs. Theoretically Berger's office was still located within the OKW, and indeed its personnel were still drawn from the ranks of the Wehrmacht, but Berger was answerable to the Commander of the Replacement Army, and that was Himmler. His brief was challenging, to say the least. From 1 October 1944, his first day in office, he would be responsible for guaranteeing the security of the camps and, if further escapes were to occur, the conduct of searches and the recapture, interrogation and punishment of escapees. Through all this he still needed to ensure that the POW population was being exploited to its maximum potential to provide the Reich with the labour force it needed to sustain the conduct of Total War.[16]

Berger had got the job thanks to his record as a ruthlessly efficient administrator. Born in 1896, he had seen some service on the Western Front in the First World War and had been wounded. Where the stereotype of the evil Nazi has a scar etched across the face, Berger's multiple wounds were more discreetly placed. Among them was a massive scar – 34 centimetres – across his stomach. After that war he pursued a career as a school-teacher, and by his own account he became politically active for the Nazi Party even before the putsch attempt of November 1923. In 1930 he became a storm trooper, a member of Ernst Röhm's SA, but left it as early as May 1933, long before the Night of the Long Knives. His career was to be made in the SS, which he joined in November 1935. By 1938 he was Head of the Recruitment Office in the SS Main Office in Berlin, but it was the war which was to give him numerous opportunities to demonstrate his commitment to the Nazi cause, above all in the wake of *Barbarossa*.

In July 1942 he became the SS's Head of Liaison with the Reich Ministry for the Occupied Territories. Outstanding service in Slovakia – distinguished above all by his ruthless suppression of Slovak resistance – brought him the Iron Cross First Class and promotion in 1943 to the rank of SS-*Obergruppenführer* and General in the Waffen-SS.[17] Needing a multi-skilled and loyal workaholic to run POW Affairs, Himmler appeared to have made an excellent choice.[18] Hitler, too, seems to have approved, relishing the prospect, as he confided to Berger personally, that with the SS in control the security issue would be settled and any repeat of the Sagan fiasco avoided.[19]

At first Berger gave every impression that he was delivering to his masters everything they could desire. His was a harsher regime in which settling German security anxieties were the first priority. There was a more thorough searching of Red Cross parcels, a more insistent warning to POWs of the risks of escape, and a greater likelihood that escape attempts would be dealt with uncompromisingly, especially if the escapees fell into the hands of the security services. And yet in truth Berger was no yes-man. While he was not the type to defy his Führer openly, his tenure in POW Affairs is distinguished by a series of acts of subtle resistance or non-compliance. In October 1944 Hitler got wind of what appeared to be relatively lavish supplies of food available to POWs in the form of Red Cross parcels, available in such quantities as to be stockpiled at some of the camps. Struck by the apparently privileged position of this enemy within, and troubled moreover by the knowledge that the possession of tinned foods and cigarettes aided escape attempts, Hitler ordered excess supplies to be distributed among the German population. It was Gottlob Berger who skilfully ensured that the order was not carried out.[20] Similarly, Hitler wanted to put an end to Red Cross inspection visits, but Berger had other ideas, and quietly he won his way.[21]

There were other acts which appeared to border on the downright philanthropic. One was his organisation of a medical conference dealing with POW health issues, held in Berlin in March 1945. Just as Hitler was contemplating the murder of POWs, Berger was arranging discussions of their health. On 22 April, at his last meeting with the Führer, Berger was ordered to transfer all British and American officer POWs to the Tyrol. According to his own postwar recollections, Berger's response to Hitler was, 'Order impossible to carry out.'[22]

His final and most extraordinary act of munificent defiance followed shortly thereafter. Himmler ordered the evacuation of the *Prominente*, the very special prisoners, from Colditz. If they were to be of any use at all in armistice negotiations, they had to be kept in German hands, well clear of the fronts approaching from East and West. In the early hours of 13 April their final odyssey began. Churchill's nephew Giles Romilly contrived to escape along the way, but the others were whisked south into Austria and to a *Stalag* with which a number of Australians were familiar – Markt Pongau. It was at that stage of their journey that they were introduced to the man who would determine their fate – it was none other than Gottlob Berger.[23]

It soon became apparent to the *Prominente* that Berger was eager to ingratiate himself with them, insisting on drawing a distinction between his Waffen SS and the other, in his now apostate view, more sinister branches of the SS. He regaled the *Prominente* not only with comforting words but liberal quantities of whisky and cigarettes. His audience appropriately engaged, Berger came to the nub. Hitler had ordered that the *Prominente* be shot, but Berger had chosen in this instance to ignore the Führer's wishes. By this time Hitler was already dead, yet Berger reported that RSHA chief Ernst Kaltenbrunner remained determined to carry out the order. Berger, however, was prepared to go so far as to escort the *Prominente* to the safety of American lines. 'Gentleman', he reportedly declared, 'these are probably the last orders I shall give as a high official of the Third Reich.'[24]

In fact Berger had negotiated this flamboyant display of defiance with the Swiss. On the evening of 3 May, he met with the Protecting Power's representative, Dr Feldscher, at Kirchdorf in the Tyrol. Feldscher impressed upon Berger the hopelessness of the German situation and the desirability of currying favour with the inevitable victors by saving the lives of the *Prominente*, best achieved by handing them over as soon as possible to the Protecting Power. Berger was persuaded. With his connivance, an American car with diplomatic plates and Swiss registration collected the *Prominente* from Markt Pongau and, with the help of two commandeered lorries, drove the *Prominente* towards liberty.[25]

Before their destination was reached, they had one more encounter with Berger, who greeted all of them individually before delivering a pathos-laden valedictory speech as the *Prominente* dined. It was a last vain appeal that his guests might finally recognise that Germans and the British were blood brothers who should unite in common cause against the 'red' enemy. If the *Prominente* were moved, they were not swayed. In a parting gesture, Berger ceremoniously passed an ivory-inlaid pistol boasting the enamelled monogram of the SS – allegedly a gift to Berger from the Führer himself – to Lord Elphinstone, and then he wished them a safe return to Allied hands. The following day that wish, at least, became reality, and the *Prominente* were delivered to American forces.[26]

Had the rabid Nazi Gottlob Berger at some point undergone some kind of road to Damascus experience after taking on the role of Chief of POW Affairs? Had he recognised the errors of his brutal ways and committed himself to saving lives rather than expending them? On balance the answer is probably no. By the time Berger accepted the job of Chief of POW Affairs, he knew that the Reich he had faithfully served was heading for defeat. A family man, he was probably looking to save his skin. The Western Australian POW doctor Leslie Le Souef was one, at least, who was not convinced by Berger's ostensible change of heart. Though not among the privileged number invited to Berger's medical conference in Berlin, Le Souef's interpretation was sensibly sceptical. He learned of the proceedings in Berlin from one of the British medical delegates, D.H. Thompson. The latter reported the presence there of representatives of the Red Cross, the Swiss Protecting Power and of various German medical agencies. The conference goal – presumably dictated by Berger without Hitler's knowledge – was to alleviate the suffering of British POWs. On its final day, 21 March, with Soviet guns trained on Berlin, an address was held on 'Malaria in Europe', followed by a concert of chamber music. For Leslie Le Souef there was no doubt that this was a shameless exercise in unalloyed cynicism.[27]

20

The Small Fortress

The Australian and other POWs in their camps and work detachments scattered across the Reich knew nothing of the Machiavellian machinations of German high politics. The name Berger would not have meant a thing to them. They might well have been aware of the increased incursion of security personnel into what had hitherto been the jealously guarded realm of the German armed forces. They will have noticed, too, sharpened security measures in their camps and ever more dire warnings of the consequences of escape. Those were by no means empty threats. Unruly and uncooperative behaviour among POWs was treated harshly, and escape was a genuinely hazardous activity, especially if escapers fell into the hands of the security forces rather than the military. They could by no means rely on being graciously shepherded back to their camps and given a rap over the knuckles in the form of a stint in an isolation cell.

The Australians who found themselves in Buchenwald were not the only ones to see the inside of a German concentration camp. Many decades after the war, and in the face of the conventional wisdom insisting that POWs were not held in concentration camps, a Concentration Camp Committee set up by the Hawke government decided that 27 Australian POWs spent time in such institutions – 17 from the AIF and 10 airmen. An ex-gratia payment of $10,000 was made to each of them. Apart from the cases of the airmen in Buchenwald, recognition was given to men who claimed to have been in Auschwitz, Dachau, Flossenbürg, Lublin (the site of the Majdanek camp), Mauthausen, Stutthof and Theresienstadt.[1]

The last of these cases is an intriguing one. Theresienstadt, a fortress town located north of Prague, is known today by its Czech name, Terezín. The large fortress, which dated from the late eighteenth century, had been designed to thwart invasion from the north. In the wars of the twentieth century other tasks were found for the fortress – rather than keeping enemies out, it served as a prison to keep them in. In Nazi times it achieved notoriety as the site of a ghetto to which some 150,000 Jews, primarily from Czechoslovakia, Austria and Germany, were sent. It was actively promoted by the Nazis as a kind of privileged ghetto, catering to the needs of the elderly. In reality it was a site of misery and ultimately of mass death. For many it was also a sinister halfway house on the way to the extermination camps further north in Auschwitz and Treblinka.

Just across the river from the 'Large Fortress' there was a smaller but no less malevolent site, known as the 'Small Fortress' or, in German, the *Kleine Festung*. Its landlord during the war was the Gestapo, which soon converted it into a cabinet of horrors. Its main functions were to incarcerate and to punish the occupation regime's political opponents, most of them Czechs. But with trademark zeal the Gestapo delivered to the Small Fortress inmates accused of a variety of crimes, including that of simply being born Jewish. From 1940 to 1945 some 32,000 men, women and children passed through its gate, the numbers growing with every desperate year. By the final year of the war the prison, ludicrously overcrowded, was home to some 5500.[2] For many, their stay in the Small Fortress was brief. They were sent on to other prisons, to concentration camps or to death camps. Others, however, stayed longer, and some 2500 of them stayed there forever.[3]

THE SMALL FORTRESS

If overcrowding, disease and vermin did not make life in the Small Fortress insufferable enough, the behaviour of its commandant and guards commonly stepped into the realm of unrestrained depravity, as postwar trials and testimonies revealed. Commandant Heinrich Jöckel was a staunch Nazi who did not shy away from personally delivering fierce beatings to the newly arrived. His complement of guards appears to have comprised almost without exception the most morally vacuous and pathologically violent dregs the Gestapo could lay its hands on. One of them, Albin Storch, 'threw people from the fortress walls, beat them to death, drowned them in the filth of the moat, the manure pit or barrels of excrement'.[4]

After the war, yet at glacial pace, a most surprising aspect of the history of the Small Fortress was revealed. Among the inmates of this Gestapo prison had been a number of English-speaking POWs, though the exact tally was never established. They were prisoners of war, or at least should have been treated as such. Their clothing could deceive, as some wore just the tattered shreds of battledress or the ragged remains of civilian clothes. Among them were Americans as well as representatives of various parts of the Commonwealth – Britons, Canadians, New Zealanders (including a number of Maoris) and at least six Australians. They were Walter Wise and Wal Riley from Tasmania – though Riley was born in Scotland – and Herb Cullen, his mate Frederick Lawrence, Alexander McClelland and Wal Steilberg from New South Wales. There might have been others, too, but the passing of decades has blurred details.[5]

What these men seem to have had in common was that they were incorrigible escapists. The most devoted of all was Wal Steilberg, a strapping lad who hailed originally from Port Macquarie. As his name suggests, he was of German heritage, yet that did not endear him to his captors when a German patrol boat nabbed him off the coast of Greece in 1941. For their part the Germans did not endear themselves to him either, sowing the seeds of a mutual antipathy which lasted the length of the war. One German officer provoked him with the question, 'Steilberg, why are you fighting against the fatherland?', to which Steilberg responded abruptly, 'I'm a bloody

Australian!' Another German officer intervened, 'Australian, are you? Why aren't you black?'⁶ As the Germans delighted in their ignorance, Steilberg made a solemn commitment to a mate: 'These bastards aren't going to keep me. I'm not going to work for them and I'm going to make it as hard as I possibly can for them to keep me in captivity.'⁷ They were prophetic words; Steilberg's elusiveness became such a thorn in the German side that his eight escapes ultimately earned him a British Empire Medal. Before then, however, he earned himself a long and wretched stint in the Small Fortress.

Steilberg's first escape was staged in April 1943. With one other man, he broke from his work detachment in Austria and made it across the Yugoslav border. They made their way down the river Mur on a barge, finally crashing into a bridge on the Hungarian border. Here they were arrested and thrown into jail at Siklos. At least they had fled the Reich, but they were behind bars. There they joined a number of others whose escape efforts had gone similarly awry, among them the Englishman Douglas Collins. In his memoirs of captivity Collins later wrote of Steilberg as 'a huge Australian who had once been a lifeguard on the Sydney beaches', and as a man who had 'a giant's good nature and spoke with the easy drawl of a man who is hard to ruffle'. Accordingly he bore the nickname 'Tiny'.⁸

A month passed before Steilberg escaped Siklos. Once more in the company of a friend, the two men lowered themselves from a window with sheets tied together. Free of the prison, they walked eastwards for four days to reach the Danube, only to be recaptured and returned to Siklos. However, Siklos was no more escape-proof than earlier, and by August 1943 Steilberg was out once more, this time with a couple of Scots, aiming to join up with partisans in the vicinity of Derventa.⁹ On this occasion his recapture landed him back in a *Stalag* – VIII B Lamsdorf – which was similarly deficient in dealing with the Australian's Houdini-esque talents. Escapes from there, and then from work detachments, ensued. For the Germans, the last of them was the straw that broke the camel's back. Recaptured in September 1944, he was taken via the Gestapo's Pankrác prison in Prague to the Small Fortress.¹⁰ His arrival augured badly. One of the guards, Stefan Rojko, walked along the line of the new arrivals, reading names from a list. In reciting Steilberg's name he added a sneering comment to the effect that Steilberg was Jewish. When Steilberg pointed out that he was an Australian soldier and POW, Rojko punched him in the face; two other guards joined in the beating.[11]

After an imposed change of clothing – Steilberg and his fellow POWs reluctantly had to abandon the remnants of their battle-dress – Rojko delivered further troubling news. Everywhere else they might have been POWs, but here they were inmates of a prison. As they had been caught escaping, they would be treated as civilians.[12] There followed a grisly induction into the horrors of the Small Fortress, where, as Steilberg soon learned, beatings and even murders were a regular occurrence, many of them observed with diminishing incredulity as they took place in the yard outside the POWs' cells. Entirely unanticipated by Steilberg's previous experience of *Stalags* and work detachments, it was a nightmare existence stretching over months: 'It wasn't just the hunger. There was absolutely no communication with anyone. We were just cut off from everything. Death and stink was all around us, we could hear the killing going on. I think the worst thing was we never knew which day it'd be when our turn would come. We'd just disappeared and we didn't know if they had any ideas for us.'[13]

By 1945 the number of POWs in the Small Fortress was increasing, though precise figures will probably never be known.[14] POW camp populations in the East were being marched westwards to avoid the Red Army. One of the key evacuation routes from Silesia towards Bavaria passed through Czech territory. In all likelihood the new POW arrivals in the Small Fortress in the late winter of 1945 were men who had slipped out of the weary lines of men trudging towards unknown destinations further West. It was an extraordinarily dangerous thing to do. Rounded up by the security forces, some of these men were hauled to Terezín and bundled into the cell with Steilberg and others.

It is not recorded exactly when Walter Wise entered the gates of the Small Fortress. He too was an escape artist. Captured during the disastrous Cretan campaign, he was also a veteran of four escapes.

In the Small Fortress, he was charged with a gruesome task – he had to load a cart with corpses. By March 1945 the Theresienstadt crematorium was no longer functional, so pits were dug near the vegetable garden to dispose of the bodies. Wise would pull the cart to and from the grave sites, where others dealt with the corpses: 'They had Jews pulling the bodies off the cart and dumping them into lime pits. Some of them were still alive. At first the guards told me I was not supposed to see this and they ordered me to stand with my back to the pits. But after a while they stopped worrying about what I saw.'[15]

Herb Cullen had been captured after the spirited defence of Retimo. But he had broken out of the camp at Salonika and spent close to a year in Greece on the run, aided by the bold generosity of the Greeks. After recapture he was packed off to Lamsdorf and then work detachments before giving his hosts the slip once more, in early 1945. As it was for many, his stint in the Small Fortress was prefaced with a brief stay in the Gestapo's Pankrác prison in Prague before being trucked north to Terezín. If Pankrác had been nightmarish, the Small Fortress was infernal, as he recognised immediately on arrival. Unwittingly he rehearsed Dante's injunction to abandon all hope:

> We arrived at Terezín at night. I can't remember what happened when we got there. I can't even remember getting out of the truck. It's a funny thing, that. I think once I saw what sort of place this was I just didn't seem to put things in my brain any more. I knew this place was different, you could see it in the faces of the people who were already there, they were like skeletons. I think I thought to myself, this is the end of the line, you've done it this time.[16]

Walter Riley was a veteran of five escape attempts, two of them in Italy. With a New Zealand Maori, his latest effort had been from a work camp near the Czech border. Their recapture and arrival at the Small Fortress were accompanied by an orgy of beatings and humiliations. Riley recalled receiving some sage advice from a Czech inmate: 'Keep your head down. There is nothing you can do.' He followed the advice as best he could, stuck close to his Maori mate Tami Tamaki and an Englishman – he did not encounter other Australians – and he survived.[17]

Alex McClelland, too, did not encounter other Australians while he was in the Small Fortress. He had been captured at Retimo and spent time in various camps, until by early 1945 he was in a work detachment called Bismarckhütte. When that detachment was evacuated in the winter of 1945, the men headed south through Czech territory. McClelland grasped the opportunity to flee, only to find himself a short time later in Pankrác, and again shortly thereafter in one of the mass cells in the Small Fortress, Cell 44. In Prague he had been told, 'You men have caused us so much trouble, we are putting you in a place where you will cause us no further trouble.'[18] He soon recognised that his cellmates were Soviet soldiers dressed in dirty rags – all that was left of their uniforms. It was an unwelcome sight, not least because he knew well that with the Soviets came lice, and with the lice came typhus.[19] Indeed, the hygiene conditions were catastrophic, because the Soviets 'didn't use the toilets, so they made a heap on the floor and urinated up against the wall. As most of them, like us, had some form of stomach trouble, an awful mess seeped its way down from the rear of the cell to where we were down near the door. It made life almost unbearable.'[20]

To make matters worse, McClelland's health was already compromised. His left leg was infected; one day he woke to find it swollen like a sausage. Fellow prisoners lanced it with a shard scrounged in the cell, releasing the pressure and easing the pain. Beyond that there was no medical attention to be had. The diet, too, was not designed to boost recovery, being nothing more than water and a small square of bread per day.[21]

McClelland was disadvantaged in other ways, too. On 4 April the British POWs were called from their cells, shepherded out through the gates of hell and sent as a ghostly column of perhaps 180 men to join other POWs being force-marched west into the Reich.[22] But no-one thought to check cell 44, with the result that McClelland stayed on. With that his chances of surviving his ordeal dropped dramatically, as the camp authorities contemplated a bloody finale for their charges.[23] There was indeed a frenzy of blood-letting in the final days, and typhus too wrought havoc among the inmates, costing some 1000 lives before the Red Army arrived to liberate Terezín on 9 May.[24]

After the war there were suspicions that other British POWs had lost their lives in the Small Fortress, but they could never be verified beyond doubt.[25] Unusually for the POWs in Terezín, there was a point at which they were called upon to work. Most of the time they simply vegetated in their cells, subsisting on their meagre diet and picking lice from their bodies. But in mid-March a number of them were escorted outside the fortress to participate in the digging – in good part with their bare hands – of an anti-tank ditch. The guards assigned to the project were drawn from a nearby SS Air Signals school, and in some accounts they behaved with the utmost cruelty, making no allowance for the weakened condition of the prisoners. They imposed order with whips and truncheons, and in at least one man's memory, their rifles came into use too.

Wal Steilberg was one who was exposed not only to the rigours of labour on what was illegal, war-related work, but also to the brutality imposed by a regime of unleavened sadism:

> On this tank trap, most of the people there could barely walk, let alone work, and the kapos [inmates assigned authority roles] and the SS, well you know, he just flogged them with anything they could get their hands on – rifle butts, sticks, shovels, and those truncheons. Oh, they used all sorts of ways of killing them. I saw this one old chap, he'd fallen on his knees and couldn't get up. I saw a kapo pick up a spade and split his head open straight down the middle with the edge of it. This chap's head just sort of fell apart on to his shoulders. Oh, it was horrible, you couldn't imagine anything like it. I saw another chap fall down and this SS guard started shooting him and went up his legs, just shot him in the ankle and then the knees and finally killed him.[26]

Despite his poisoned leg, one day Alex McClelland had been dragged out to work on the anti-tank ditch and thereafter received daily beatings from one of the guards in his cell. Finally – in McClelland's recollection it was 5 May – there was a change of routine, and the morning knock on the door was followed by the shouted command, 'All Englishmen out!' The British and the Americans of cell 44 stumbled out into the compound, leaving the Soviets and Czechs behind. 'We trudged along. As for myself, with fibrosis of the lung, I was only glad to be out in the clean open air after that ghastly stench of unwashed bodies, urine and excrement, after being packed into that cell almost like sardines in a can.'[27] Finally, he, too, was leaving the Small Fortress, and leaving it alive. But like the other Australians who had departed earlier, in his mind McClelland would go on revisiting the Small Fortress for the rest of his life.

21

Holidaying for Hitler

A strange thing happened to Ray Corbett in June 1943. At his work camp at Blechhammer in Silesia he was instructed by a guard to report to the Commandant's office the next morning. Fearful that bad news awaited him, he sought the advice of the Regimental Sergeant Major, who agreed to accompany Corbett to his meeting with the Commandant at the appointed hour. The RSM, too, had no inkling of Corbett's fate.

The news was that Corbett, together with one other British POW, a corporal, was to be transferred away from the work detachment. The order stemmed not from the Commandant but from much higher up, from the High Command of the Armed Forces, the OKW. Soon Corbett and the British POW were being escorted through the forest outside the camp to the nearest railway station. Corbett's mind was 'on a razor's edge' – perhaps removed from the camp the guards would take the opportunity to do away with their charges? Yet it seems that the guards also had no idea of their destination beyond the nearest railway station. Corbett speculated that he was being repatriated. He knew that repatriations were occurring, but these were generally reserved for the sick and wounded. It did not make sense – he was fully fit. As far as he was concerned, this was an unwelcome development. Work detachment E3 at Blechhammer had provided a convivial atmosphere which allowed freedoms – including the possession and use of a camera – which could only have been dreamt of elsewhere.

He might well have been dreaming. The guards delivered their charges to the station, Ehrenforst. There they joined a number of other prisoners under guard, scattered among civilians, who boarded first-class carriages with leather seats in a train headed for Berlin. From there they were bussed to Genshagen, some 20 kilometres south-west of the city. Their destination was one of the most extraordinary camps in Hitler's Reich. It was a *Ferienlager*, a holiday camp.

At Genshagen they were allocated to new accommodation. There were impressive entertainment facilities, new slit trenches, and the food was good. Over the following days more men arrived, usually in twos and threes. In larger groups the men were then taken on sightseeing tours of Berlin, accompanied by just a single guard bearing nothing more than a side-arm. They saw numerous sights – the Brandenburg Gate, the Berlin Cathedral, the Olympic Stadium, and much more. Further hours of leisure were spent pleasantly in the company of a dance band conducted by Jimmy Howe, brought in from Lamsdorf to play the hits of the day, including, as Corbett fondly remembers, *Lili Marleen*.

In these early days of the Genshagen camp there was a variety of POWs – non-commissioned officers and other ranks – who had been brought there from many parts of the Reich. Apart from the short-term visitors were those destined to become the permanent staff, including, as Corbett remembers, an Englishman by the name of John 'Busty' Brown. He was a controversial figure, as many of the POWs resented both his apparently cosy relationship with his German superiors and the relative opulence of his living quarters. Corbett remembers him as a 'fat overblown-looking sergeant', distrusted by his fellow POWs.[1]

Then Corbett was invited to a discussion with a German who, as a result of his accent and language skills acquired on a lengthy stay in the United States, was known as 'American Joe'. He identified himself as a representative of the German Foreign Office. At this point the real purpose of the holiday camp became abundantly clear. 'American Joe' lectured Corbett on the battle against Communism, in which surely the British and the Germans should join forces. Germany was a great country; it had much in common with Britain and its Empire. If the need to battle the common Soviet enemy were recognised, then the opportunity was available to POWs to play their role in vanquishing the Communist threat. In this spirit 'American Joe' continued for a while before inviting Corbett to join that battle for humanity's future by signing up for the British Free Corps. If he did so, he would be asked to fight against only the Soviets, he would receive a new uniform, good food and accommodation plus the freedom to travel. Corbett allowed 'American Joe' to say his piece, but his answer to the question at the end of it was blunt and unambiguous: 'See this uniform? I'm an Australian. Up yours!'[2]

His stay at Genshagen did not last much longer. He was returned to Blechhammer, this time not in the comfort of leather seats but rather in the form of transport to which POWs were accustomed: cattle-trucks. Along the way his train stood in Berlin for two days and nights during heavy bombing raids. The exposure to bombing, he assumed, was deliberate. In the end it was with great relief that he arrived back in Blechhammer.[3]

There were other Australians who spent time in this most unusual of camps. Although he arrived some time later, Alex McClelland – later to land in the Small Fortress – tells a story similar to Corbett's. He too was taken by train to Genshagen, in his case from his camp at Lamsdorf, in September 1943. He remembers being asked to sign a pledge that he would not attempt to escape but refused to do so, fearing that at some point his complicity with the Germans might be held against him. Happily his refusal did not compromise his hosts' hospitality; soon McClelland and his fellow vacationers were taken on a sightseeing trip to Berlin, where they viewed the Olympic Stadium, blighted by some bomb damage. Elsewhere in the Reich capital, too, the scars of air raids were everywhere to be seen. In Potsdam, in contrast, not a single crater was visible; he marvelled at the untainted grandeur of Sans Souci Palace.

A second trip into Berlin was for medical purposes: he was to have his troublesome lungs examined. During a change of train, McClelland and three other POWs were separated from their guard and the two other POWs, leaving them to make their way unguarded to the Friedrichstrasse station in the middle of the city. The absence of supervision piqued the curiosity of a nearby officer, who in flawless English enquired, 'Excuse me, gentlemen, where is your guard?' When they accounted for their separation from the guard the officer conveyed his gratitude and relayed the explanation to his fellow officers, who thought it was a huge joke. Fortunately the guard and the two other POWs soon arrived, so that the group could make its way to the famous Charité Hospital, where McClelland's lungs could receive the most expert attention.

In due course McClelland, too, was asked if he would place his services in the hands of the Germans' anti-Communist cause. He gave the same answer as Ray Corbett before him, and so he too was soon back at his work detachment.[4]

And then there is the tale of the Tasmanian Barney Roberts, who came to learn of Genshagen in January 1944, when the unlikely offer was relayed to him by a guard. At that time Roberts was part of a work detachment located in the Austrian village of Eichberg, where he and his comrades inhabited a castle. The offer was of a stint in the designated 'holiday camp' in Genshagen. Despite his reservations, and with the aid of some friendly prompting from the guard ('You go for a bloody holiday or I shoot you'), Roberts began his journey on 20 January, travelling via his *Stalag* at Wolfsberg and Berlin, so extensively damaged by bombs that it chilled him. Coming from the relative peace of rural Austria, this was new and frightening. It took some time to get used to it.[5]

In his estimation there were at this time about 200 prisoners at Genshagen, along with 32 staff. His expectation was that he, like the others, would enjoy a month's holiday and then be transferred back to his 'home' camp. On 30 January he enjoyed the first of many camp concerts – only for it to be interrupted by an air raid on nearby Berlin. A soccer match played on that same day had seen England defeat Scotland. A host of lectures, albeit of questionable entertainment and intellectual value, soon followed: the first by a German professor holding forth on postwar economics, the next by a fellow Tasmanian, Captain Rex Dakers of the 2/7th, who spoke on 'Love and War'.[6]

A man of considerable talent himself, Roberts had the chance to express his own creative side while in the camp. He recited one of his own poems before an appreciative audience and then wrote a play ('Krieg fertig'), which by the middle of February was ready for performance.

His active participation in the camp's rich entertainment program soon drew the attention of the camp leader, the same John Brown Ray Corbett had come to know. The relative opulence in which Brown lived – he had an entire room to himself – stirred Roberts' curiosity as it had Corbett's. On the wall was a framed photograph of a young opera singer. In his recollections it was of the Nazi Elisabeth Schwarzkopf,[7] and it was, as Brown explained to his Australian guest, a personal gift from 'a wonderful lady'.[8] The other possibility is that it was a photograph of the British opera singer Margery Booth, who had married a wealthy German, settled in the Reich and was working at the Berlin Opera when the war began. She did indeed befriend John Brown, going so far as to pay a visit to the Genshagen camp, where she performed for the POWs.[9]

Brown then proceeded to hold forth to Barney Roberts on the subject of his political philosophy: 'There are some of us', he opined, 'who see more clearly than others the tragedy of two great Teutonic peoples fighting each other. Our real enemy comes from the East.'[10] He prodded Roberts for his views on the war, but in the end the discussion turned to a less weighty topic, namely the coming fancy-dress ball and the trip to Berlin to collect the necessary costumes.[11]

Just how Roberts spent some of his time in Genshagen – and at large outside it – is revealed in his diary entry for 22 February 1944:

> Last few days very busy. Now in volley-ball finals – boxing training with Tip, English heavyweight, very fast. Air raid 3 a.m. Sunday – Two picture

shows – Concert. We lost debate (judges biased). Went to Berlin to get fancy dress as planned on the 18th. Ball most successful, gorgeous flamboyant outfits. Germans arranged for photographers. Took lots of pictures. Then (on 18th) and again today dressed in civvies. Saw over Potsdam – old and new palaces with ghosts of the past, Kaisers and kings (William II, with the withered arm, the last of them). Bach, Bismarck, Voltaire.

Long and pleasant walks through parks and gardens, long and pleasant enough to imagine for a short time there was no war, no ugliness; turf under my feet, ducks on a lake even, peace, trees, very old trees. [. . .] We crossed more lawns and gardens, up the 131 steps and the glass terraces to Sans Souci; inspecting the pomp and splendour, visualizing the spilt blood, the plunder, the cost of satisfying an idle whim. How many million shells came from where, for the Shell Room?[12]

The excursion to Potsdam meant that Roberts missed a lecture by a Professor Pfeffer on 'English and German home life'.[13] It is a pity that the Tasmanian's and Professor Pfeffer's paths did not cross. The professor in question is almost certainly Karl Heinz Pfeffer, Nazi Germany's foremost expert on the British Empire, who knew a thing or two about Australia. After study at Stanford, the Sorbonne and the London School of Economics, Pfeffer toured Australia with the aid of the Rockefeller Foundation and worked on his postdoctoral dissertation, a study of Australian society.[14] By the time he got back to Germany he was married to an Englishwoman and Hitler was chancellor. From 1937 Pfeffer himself was a Nazi, gained a Chair, and in 1943 was Dean of the Faculty of International Studies (*Auslandswissenschaftliche Fakultät*) at the University of Berlin.[15] He may well have welcomed the opportunity to take a small break from his duties in Berlin to spend some time with the Britons and Australians he imagined he knew so well.

Incredibly, in April 1944 Roberts was still in Genshagen, and still having the sort of time that beggared even his own belief. On the 13th he enjoyed a spectacularly lucky day that went something like this: 'Went to Berlin on the 11th and again today. Lucky thirteen! Unter den Linden, Brandenburger Tor with the six great columns, and a Wagner opera at the Berlin Opera House, *Lohengrin*. The wonder was not in the story – I understood little of it – but in the music, the scenery, the stage setting, and the complete unreality of *being there*.'[16] Alas, by the end of the month he was no longer there; he was back working in southern Austria. Even four months of regal treatment had not persuaded him to sign on to the bargain he had been offered.

And then there is the case of the South Australian Jim Reeves, in all likelihood among the last of any nationality to witness the bizarre world of Genshagen. Reeves was a latecomer to Germany, having spent the first months of captivity in Italy, followed by over four months in hiding. But when he was snaffled the Germans wasted little time in sending him to work. For several months he performed back-breaking labour, digging trenches in Dresden. As a reward for unpleasant work over a lengthy period he was invited, as he remembers it, to a 'rest camp'. Sure enough it was Genshagen, and by now it was already October 1944. With Allied forces well established in France, the Germans were no more likely to persuade Reeves to join the enemy than any of his predecessors, and sure enough they did not.

Reeves, though, was happy enough to have a good time, albeit a short one of just three weeks. He was taken by train to the camp, located in the midst of a pine forest. Armed with some idea of what awaited him, he was not disappointed: 'The food was plentiful, our beds extremely comfortable, and we were treated well. There were British, American and German films to watch, and other entertainment, including a play put on by the prisoners, in which they dressed in costumes provided by our hosts.' Reeves, too, was regaled with a sightseeing trip to Berlin, more than ever before bearing the scars of Allied bombs, and including a visit to the Olympic Stadium. That, at least, had been spared devastation, allowing Reeves to sit in the deserted stands, 'imagining the roar of the crowds, the presence of Hitler, and the parade of athletes'.[17]

The camp authorities will have had no truck with the tone of the letter he sent back to his mother in Adelaide on 22 October 1944:

Dear Mum,

I hope this finds you well and happy. The last letter I had from you was dated 4 August, and I was glad to hear you were feeling better. I am writing from a 'holiday camp'. This camp was formed about a year ago and has monthly sessions. One or two men of the same nationality are selected from each working camp. There are over a hundred of us Aussies [!] here and it is great to renew acquaintances. There is a library, large recreation room, football field, hot showers etc., trips to Berlin etc. We have been here over a week now and have seen several English, American and German films. We also heard a very well-known German pianist in a recital [. . .][18]

Two weeks later he had left Genshagen, but before being assigned a new work camp, he recalls, he was sent to a transit camp, visited some time later by two German soldiers. One of them he recognised as an Australian he had known at Genshagen. 'He was immaculately dressed in German uniform and appeared to be quite happy.'[19]

What, then, was this holiday camp all about? As their prospects for victory dimmed during 1943, the Germans doubled their efforts to win others to their cause. In some quarters they recorded resounding successes. Their vicious regimes of occupation in Europe's north, south, east and west could only be sustained with the collaboration of the many, not just the few. And on the field of battle, men of many nations allowed themselves to be drafted into the German military. POWs, including British and Commonwealth POWs, were among those to be wooed. The militant Indian nationalist leader Subhas Chandra Bose arrived in Berlin as early as 1941 to recruit Indian POWs for a cause which wedded Nazi and 'Free India' interests. Whatever charismatic appeal and rhetorical skills he attributed to himself, for the most part Bose's words fell on deaf ears. Relatively few persuaded themselves to join the Free India Legion.[20]

An even smaller Arab Legion was formed with the assistance of the Grand Mufti of Jerusalem, hoping similarly to play on the national liberationist sentiments of his Arab countrymen, and holding out the prospect that draftees would serve in the Middle

East. The few who signed up wore 'Free Arabia' patches on their arms, but they were a military irrelevance, characterised by low morale and poor discipline.[21]

Irishmen, too, were a target of German recruitment efforts. Ireland remained neutral in World War II, leading Germans to harbour hopes that they might coax some Irishmen to throw in their lot against a longstanding enemy. Indeed, a precedent for Irish pro-German attitudes had been set in the Great War by Roger Casement, a former member of the British consular corps who had been knighted in 1911. During the war Casement went to Germany to attempt to organise into a military unit a number of Irish soldiers captured while serving with British forces. The unit's goal would be to invade Ireland, but with just 52 men won for his misadventure, Casement's dream came to naught.[22]

Efforts made in World War II bore similarly rotten fruit. True, the treacherous propagandist William Joyce, better known as Lord Haw Haw, was an Irishman of sorts, born in the United States of Irish parents. But among most Irishmen, POWs and others, any contempt for Britain did not convert to support for the Nazi cause. That did not stop the Germans trying. A special camp for the Irish was established in Brandenburg's Havelland.[23] Others were assembled at the POW camp at Luckenwalde south of Berlin which, as not only these Irishmen but Indians and British POWs found, was no holiday camp – it was an altogether unpleasant environment. The POWs were delivered there by the army from operational areas before they got a true taste of life in the Reich. With these POWs the German strategy seems to have been to persuade them that joining the British Free Corps offered vast advantages over languishing in a *Stalag*.[24] But none of the target groups was particularly susceptible to this kind of argument, and the small number who did sign up for the enemy in all likelihood did so out of fear rather than conviction. As far as the Irish were concerned, Casement's original farce repeated itself as failure. One account has it that the Irishmen left over from these doomed conversion attempts ended up in a concentration camp, in all likelihood Buchenwald. It was feared they knew too much.[25]

Some Australians were first-hand witnesses to this doomed enterprise. The Irish-born platoon commander Terry Fairbairn was one of them. After capture in Crete and a period of convalescence in an Athens hospital, Fairbairn was transferred to the transit camp at Salonika. Having informed his captors that he had been born in Ireland, he was interviewed by an officer claiming to be from the German Foreign Office. 'He was nicely spoken; no accent; no anger; no malice; no politics – just a friendly German Officer – if there ever was such a thing.'[26] Three weeks later Fairbairn was among five officers separated from the other POWs and transported, together with 92 other ranks from British units, to a camp at Wustermark outside Berlin.

Fairbairn's own suspicion was that the Germans 'were trying to establish a World War I Roger Casement type of Irish Brigade'. His group was addressed by a putative Irish priest; thereafter Fairbairn was interviewed once more by the German officer from the Foreign Office, who by this stage had acquired an astounding knowledge of his interlocutor. Fairbairn was dumbfounded when the German told him that two of his brothers had joined the army and served with the 2/2nd Machine Gun Battalion in the Middle East, while another had left the police to join the AIF. He knew the full names of Fairbairn's parents and sister as well as the precise place of his birth in Ireland. 'The Huns', Fairbairn pondered, 'knew more about me than I knew myself.'[27] Disarming though this was, it did not persuade Fairbairn to throw in his lot with the Germans. A period of solitary confinement was followed by transfer to the *Oflag* at Warburg.[28]

Laurie West, who ended up at the NCOs' camp at Hohenfels, was also exposed to these sorts of recruitment attempts. In that camp the Germans made it known that they were trying to form an Irish Brigade and asked for volunteers in the camp. Their efforts were not without success, at least superficially. As West recalls, after the recruitment drive about twenty volunteers marched out of the camp – and there was not a single genuine Irishman among them. They all came back in due course, perhaps having reasoned that a short break from camp routine pending the discovery of their true identities was better than no break at all.[29]

As the experiences of these men suggest, there were two guiding forces behind German efforts. One was the OKW – the Wehrmacht's High Command – which was responsible for all POWs who entered the Reich. The OKW had its own propaganda section which, among its broad range of activities, included the attempt to influence the hearts and minds of POWs. Although the OKW did not normally distinguish among the various groups of British POWs, in January 1942 it ordered the collection of separate lists of the names of all Australians and New Zealanders in POW camps 'for propagandistic purposes'.[30]

The other was the German Foreign Office, which, like the OKW, had an unavoidable interest in POW matters, responsible as it was for conducting the Reich's relations with the rest of the world. Like the OKW, the Foreign Office was concerned with propaganda – indeed, it assumed that the propaganda directed to the world outside the Reich was the proper business of the Foreign Office. A 1943 order from Hitler explicitly tasked the Foreign Office with mounting a systematic propaganda campaign among British POWs.[31] Given the nature of the work – it could hardly be performed without direct access to the POWs in their camps – the Foreign Office began to work collaboratively with the OKW.

A document produced within the Foreign Office in April 1944 gives a useful summary of the propaganda work that was being done through this partnership of the OKW and the Foreign Office. Its author was a man by the name of Schmidt, the head of the Prisoner of War Organisation in the Foreign Office.[32] Apart from its central staff, this organisation, according to Schmidt's report, had a series of country-based committees: for England, the United States, France and Italy. There was no such service for the Soviet Union – any propaganda work with Soviet POWs lay in the domain of the Ministry for the Occupied Territories. On each of the four committees were representatives of both the OKW and Joseph Goebbels' Propaganda Ministry. In addition, via the head of the Foreign Ministry's Legal Department, the country committees liaised with the Interior Ministry, the Reich Main Security Office, the Ministry of Justice and other Reich authorities. Moreover, these country committees had their representatives in various POW camps around the Reich. Their goal was to advise the camp commandants on how to influence the POWs psychologically, especially in terms of raising their work morale, but also to use propaganda directly on the POWs to convince them of the merits of the Nazis' anti-Bolshevik, anti-Semitic cause.[33]

For Australian POWs the committee that mattered was the England Committee, headed by Dr Fritz Hesse. The Baghdad-born Nazi Dr Hesse had worked in London for the German news agency DNB, but soon after the outbreak of war was recruited into the German Foreign Office to make the most of his close knowledge of England.[34] One of the England Committee members appears to have been Arnold Hillen Ziegfeld, also a Nazi party member, who had been born in Japan but educated in Germany. Before joining the Foreign Office in July 1943, Ziegfeld had worked in Goebbels' Ministry for Popular Enlightenment and Propaganda.[35] According to one British report, he was the author of two books on England and a former German press representative in London.[36] As early as 1939 Dr Hesse had been directed by Hitler himself to influence English and French prisoners. In 1942 the very same Dr Hesse had received an order from Hitler to intensify his propaganda efforts with English POWs in particular. The arsenal of propaganda weapons Dr Hesse and his colleagues on the England Committee could draw upon was well stocked. One took the form of the weekly publication of an English-language newspaper called *The Camp*, which by 1944 had reached a circulation of 25,000. Then there were propaganda pamphlets with such edifying titles as 'Are the Soviets human beings?', 'Jews in the American Administration' and its equally provocative sequel 'Jews in the English Administration'. There were also numerous books, with the notable exception, however, of an English translation of *Mein Kampf*, the entire print-run having been destroyed in a bombing raid on Leipzig.[37]

Finally, there were the holiday camps, one for British officers and one for NCOs and other ranks. The initiative came from within the German Foreign Office, though its precise origins are not entirely clear. A memorandum prepared by a repatriated British officer for the War Office suggests the seminal figure might have been the Anglophile Adam von Trott zu Solz, who worked in the German Foreign Office, and who had stated in July 1943 that as early as 1941 he had suggested showing British POWs the 'better side of Germany' and implied 'that the so-called "holiday camps" had grown out of his suggestion'.[38] Foreign Minister Joachim von Ribbentrop had made representation to Hitler, who had approved the idea, which was then carried out on the order of the OKW's General Field Marshal Keitel.[39] Their purpose, according to the Foreign Office itself, was to step up the propaganda work with POWs. That the Genshagen establishment offered a standard of comfort far superior to that of the normal *Stalags* or work detachments is apparent enough from the accounts given by Australians like Corbett, McClelland and Roberts. In fact, the holiday camp for NCOs and other ranks had initially been established as Stalag III D in the Berlin district of Steglitz.[40] When moved to Genshagen it became Special Detachment 517; its capacity was limited to just 270.[41] It was a wise move, as Genshagen was relatively safe from the bombing raids over the Reich's capital which were becoming all too frequent.

The officers' camp, originally known as Special Detachment 999 and located in a villa in the Berlin suburb of Zehlendorf, was re-established on 4 May 1944 at a very safe distance far to the south at Steinburg near Regensburg. Officially it was attached to the NCOs' camp Stalag 383 Hohenfels. It is not known whether any Australian officers ever spent any time at this camp, but it is clear that conditions there were even more comfortable than at Genshagen. As was the case in all *Oflags*, fewer men were held at Steinburg, but even they must have been surprised at the level of freedom they were accorded. A report by Swiss delegates from June 1944 provided the following general impression: 'Any officer having the chance to stay for four weeks at this camp benefits enormously both physically and mentally. The Delegate spoke to most of the officers and they all agreed in emphasizing the great change it makes to any POW to stay a few weeks here, after a protracted captivity in an ordinary Oflag.'[42] The building in which the men were accommodated was described as 'a medium sized country mansion' just 12 kilometres from the town of Straubing, boasting a stove in every room. 'When arriving in camp every officer received 100 Reichsmarks, spend at his discretion. Can shop in the nearby village, sunbathing and swimming possible, regular walks. Prisoners attend a cinema performance at Straubing once a week.'[43]

Accounts by a number of British officers confirm the Swiss delegate's favourable impressions. Lieutenant Stewart Walker of the 9th Durham Light Infantry reported, 'On arrival we found a comfortable white building situated on its own grounds. There were four sentries to patrol the area, which was on parole all day, everything, in fact, was on parole except by night. Fifty officers were gathered here, including many colonels and ten naval officers.'[44] A British captain by the name of Wilson sent there from Marlag Nord formed a similar opinion. He attended a performance by a quartet from the Bavarian Symphony Opera Company and was allowed to take long walks on parole through the surrounding countryside. Another officer from Westertimke confirmed the sense of pleasure derived from the change of scenery and circumstances. The castle at Steinburg seemed 'quite beautiful to us after the barbed wire enclosure in the bleak countryside we had grown accustomed to'.[45] In a similar spirit the New Zealander Brigadier George Clifton, who was there in September 1944, observed that 'those who went into the bag so early in Norway and France benefitted very much from their month or six weeks' complete change of air, scenery and conditions.'[46]

In the thinking of those who created them, these two holiday camps would have two purposes, one quite general and one more specific. In terms of their propaganda work with British POWs, it was reasoned, they would do much to curry favour in the English-speaking world, creating the impression that Germany was treating its POWs well. After all, Germany was not the real enemy of the British Empire.[47]

Beyond that general propaganda purpose, there was a more specific and sinister goal, and that was the raising of a legion of British soldiers fighting for the German cause.[48] In its origins this concept of a British legion can be traced back to the English traitor John Amery, the son of a former British cabinet minister and a man with firm links to the diverse misfits who populated the European Far Right. Amery's idea fell on fertile ground. By the end of 1942 Hitler had made it known to his Foreign Office that he supported the idea of an 'English Legion'.[49] Amery himself had favoured the name 'British Legion of St George', only to discover that the naming rights and then the recruiting drive were taken out of his hands. Before long the running was being made by the Foreign Office and the German military, who located what was now officially the British Free Corps (BFC) in an old monastery in Hildesheim. Even with its friends in high places, however, the BFC's growth was at best stunted, reaching just fifty or so recruits from Britain and the Commonwealth; only a handful of members ever found themselves risking their lives for the cause.[50]

In their goal of winning British POWs for the Nazi cause, the Foreign Office and the OKW did not have the field entirely to themselves. As we have already seen, in the 'polycratic'[51] power structures of the Third Reich, shared ideological interests could also manifest themselves as institutional rivalries, and POW propaganda was turning out to be a case in point. While many individuals and institutions wanted access to POWs and plotted to win them for the Nazi cause, they could not always agree on whose job this really was.

These internecine Nazi rivalries were reaching a climax during the existence of the holiday camps. They had an unashamedly propagandistic purpose. In the Third Reich the man who claimed propaganda as his territory was Joseph Goebbels, the Minister for Popular Enlightenment and Propaganda, whose appearance was spectacularly un-Aryan. In December 1943 Goebbels raised the topic of propaganda among British POWs with Hitler, offering the services of his ministry. It was a topic in which Hitler had a particular interest. Many years earlier in *Mein Kampf* he had regretted the superiority of the British over the German propaganda efforts in the First World War. Indeed, Hitler seems to have been receptive to the idea that a sophisticated level of propaganda work among British POWs, including exposing them to the virtues of German culture, was required. Encouraged by Hitler's response, by February 1944 Goebbels was arguing for a greater role for himself and his spin doctors, inevitably at the expense of both the Foreign Office and the OKW.[52]

As far as both of the latter were concerned, Goebbels' efforts were an unwelcome intrusion and had to be nipped in the bud.[53] The head of the Foreign Office's Prisoner of War Organisation Schmidt did exactly that. By detailing his organisation's work over many years he was in effect urinating all over the territory of POW propaganda to remind Goebbels and others who its true owner was, just in case Goebbels had not picked up the scent. Schmidt argued forcefully against Goebbels' attempted incursions by pointing out that Goebbels' ministry was already involved in the various country committees, albeit without showing much interest. And as for the idea that Hitler wanted to involve his Propaganda Ministry in these POW matters, Schmidt insisted that was true only insofar as Hitler expected work morale among POWs to be improved. Anything else was the work of the Foreign Office.[54]

If the Foreign Office and its collaborators in the OKW were able to keep Goebbels at bay, they faced a tougher proposition in their other great rival in this field, Heinrich Himmler, especially from the time Himmler and his men took over the running of POW affairs.

When it came to wooing British POWs to the Nazi cause, Himmler had played his first hand as early as 1942. One of the hats he wore at that time was that of Reichskommissar für die Festigung des deutschen Volkstums (Reich Commissar for the Consolidation of German Ethnicity). It entitled him to more than a passing interest in the racial makeup of the ever-growing POW population. His representatives toured POW camps holding Commonwealth POWs to identify those of German descent. Among Australian POWs they drew a blank, as was reported to Heinrich Himmler in June 1942.[55] It was assumed – wrongly, in fact – that the Australian army had not drafted Germans or German descendants into its ranks. Moreover, the pessimistic assessment formed by the SS itself was that any attempts to win such people over were likely to be met by passive resistance, if not outright rejection.[56] Himmler nonetheless asked to be kept informed on developments in this matter.[57] Moreover, he supported the idea that if descendants of Germans were eventually found among British, Australian and American POWs then they should be considered for placement in a special camp (*Sonderlager*).[58] This, he insisted, was part of his brief, and plans were made for such a camp for American POWs in the Austrian region of Styria. The idea, as Himmler himself put it, was that the SS would take control of these POWs, who would have German parents or grandparents, 'and in a clever way influence this lost German people [*dieses verlorene Deutschtum*] in order to win it back gradually.'[59]

By 1944 Himmler was still occupied with POWs, but for different reasons. When once he had contemplated winning Aryans of the diaspora back into the fold, his great obsessions by now were security and labour. Hare-brained schemes to pamper POWs in low security camps – especially if they were dreamed up by the career bureaucrats in the OKW and the Foreign Office – were now likely to get short shrift from him and his acolytes.

It so happened that in October 1944 an SS officer by the name of Jürgen Stroop got wind of the holiday camp for officers at Steinburg. His indignation on learning that the enemy's POWs were living in veritable luxury moved him to write to his boss. At that point, it seems, Himmler and his SS knew nothing about what the Foreign Office and the OKW were up to in Genshagen and Steinburg. Stroop complained:

> On checking the POW camps in my district I have established that on a rotating basis English officers are transferred by the responsible Officer Camps (Oflags) to the POW-Holiday Camp at Steinburg near Regensburg for periods of 3 to 4 weeks. In this Holiday Camp the officers enjoy enormous privileges, they meet with German women, come into contact with the civilian population without any hindrance and can gather whatever information they desire. [. . .] A similar Holiday Camp apparently exists in Genshagen near Berlin. On the basis of the points raised above, I request that the closure of these holiday camps be instituted.[60]

Stroop was a nasty piece of work. A member of the SS since 1932, he is most notorious for overseeing the merciless destruction of the Warsaw Ghetto, but he had also fought with the 3rd Death's Head SS Division on the Eastern Front and carried out security tasks in the Soviet Union, Poland and Greece before assuming the command of an SS administrative district in the Rhineland in late 1943.[61] Himmler took Stroop's concerns seriously, sending a directive to his freshly appointed Chief of POW Affairs Gottlob Berger to investigate Stroop's claims and in the interim to stop any further transfers to the camps. He closed with the cutting remark, 'If this information is true, then one does not have to wonder why the enemy has such an outstanding spy network in Germany.'[62]

Before the month was out Berger, still learning the ropes as Chief of POW Affairs, had a good idea of what was going on in both camps. A report prepared for him stated that the *Oflag* at Steinburg had been open since May, it took officers who had been imprisoned for a long time, and it sought to influence them through propaganda over a period of four to six weeks. The choice of just who was sent there was made by the commandant and the Wehrmacht's propaganda officer in the camp, but the senior British officer could make suggestions also. As for Genshagen, it was attached to Stalag III D in Berlin, was designed for some 270 NCOs and other ranks deemed deserving of a four-week break as reward for their labours. They, too, were to be introduced to 'the German way of seeing things' through exposure to German culture, including excursions to nearby Potsdam and Berlin. John Brown was given specific mention in this report to Berger, as were the liberties he enjoyed. Indeed, it was suggested that the camp authorities resented the extent of Brown's independence, but he argued he was answerable only to Arnold Hillen Ziegfeld in the Foreign Office.[63]

Early in the following month Berger's report duly arrived on Himmler's desk, confirming the essential truth of Stroop's suspicions – these holiday camps did exist, and they had been established on the orders of the OKW in collaboration with the Foreign Office. The latter, Berger was aware, saw a role for itself in propaganda directed to the outside world and thought of POWs as useful conduits. Berger told Himmler that he did not share Stroop's security concerns; the camps' denizens were not the sort of inveterate escape artists who languished in punishment camps. Nonetheless he announced that further transfers to the holiday camps had stopped until decisions were made in principle about the future of the camps.

Berger then offered his opinion of what that future might be. He conceded that their division of labour was messy. The commandant of the nearest *Stalag* provided the guards and intelligence officers to attend to security issues in the camps, while the Foreign Office and its personnel inside the camp attended to the very casual inner workings of the establishments and their propaganda functions. In Berger's view this arrangement was unsustainable. His advice was to hand the camps over entirely to the Foreign Office, to close them completely, or to run them without any Foreign Office involvement. He was very sceptical about the chances of influencing British officers who, he believed, were set in their ways. As for the other ranks, they were more likely to be receptive to new ideas, but Berger feared that offering them the carrot of a complete break from work would achieve at best the illusion of success.[64] He was probably right.

The Foreign Office for its part sought to impress on Himmler that this was its territory, and that its propaganda work in the camps was successful.[65] It cited a written agreement which had been reached with Colonel Westhoff – back in September when he was still Chief of POW Affairs – which guaranteed the Foreign Office sole control of the camps. An order to this effect had been presented to General Field Marshal Keitel for signing. Alas, Keitel's signature was never gained, because in the meantime Himmler as Commander of the Replacement Army had taken over POW Affairs.[66] And that, indeed, was the crucial point which sealed the fate of the camps. Himmler's reply to Berger was that under no circumstances could they continue to be run under the aegis of the Foreign Office.[67]

When Adolf Westhoff was obliged to issue word of the impending closures he fudged the real reasons behind the decision. On 18 December he told Swiss authorities that the decision 'was caused by the attitude of the British Government who would not authorise the prisoners of war interned in these camps, to give their parole not to escape'.[68] By the beginning of 1945 Genshagen, at least, was no more. On 16 January one of the YMCA's POW camp inspectors, Henry Soderberg, reported to the British Military Attaché in Stockholm that the holiday camp 'was closed two weeks ago, as it was failing to fulfil the propaganda purposes for which it was erected. [. . .] The Germans have abandoned propaganding British officers.'[69] For the Australians and many others, the holidays were over.

Despite all the indignation and posturing emanating from the OKW and the Foreign Office, in truth any sober assessment would probably have labelled the camps a dismal failure. No officer at Steinburg was ever persuaded to switch sides.[70] The testimonies of men like Corbett, McClelland, Roberts and Reeves suggest that Australians, and probably other British POWs as well, adopted a purely pragmatic attitude to the unexpected offer of a holiday. If it was there for the taking, then they might as well make the most of it. Even if it was just for a few weeks, it gave them an invaluable break from their work routine and a chance to recharge their batteries in relative comfort. If the Germans were sufficiently naive to believe that they might be persuaded to switch sides, then that was their problem. And after D-Day in 1944, why would they throw in their lot with what was clearly a lost cause?

There was one other factor that tipped the balance away from the men in the Foreign Office and the OKW. John Brown, the senior British NCO at Genshagen and acquaintance of both Ray Corbett and Barney Roberts, was a double agent.[71] Contrary to carefully cultivated appearances presented to German and Briton alike, Brown had worked hard to win – and then to betray – the Germans' confidence. To do this he had needed to foster the distrust and even the contempt of his countrymen, as he played the role of the enthusiast for the British Free Corps and the Nazi cause. Captured at Dunkirk in May 1940, Quartermaster Sergeant Brown was taken to the Blechhammer Camp in Silesia. It was of some interest to his captors that Brown had once been a member of the British Union of Fascists. What he did not reveal, however, was that before leaving England he had participated in a course for spies operating in enemy hands.[72]

His apparently promising political credentials led Brown to be transferred to the Berlin-Steglitz prototype of Genshagen for an initial assessment. It was here that he made a couple of interesting acquaintances. One was Major Heimpel, who claimed to be in charge of counter-espionage in POW camps. The other was his room-mate in Berlin, Lieutenant Ralph Holroyd, an Australian who had been captured in Greece after being shot in the ankle. The reason why Heimpel and others were interested in Holroyd soon became clear. Holroyd was born in Hamburg; his mother was German. As it happened, she was in Germany when the war broke out, but as a German national she was not interned. Holroyd fell into the category of those who, so the Germans hoped, might be turned with a ploy involving both a carrot and a stick. At Lamsdorf he was told that it might be possible to see his mother regularly, 'if I did what they wanted'. Like Brown, he was given the dubious pleasure of an audience with William Joyce, Lord Haw-Haw.[73] But like Brown, Holroyd was no rat, as Brown well knew. The stint in Colditz on Holroyd's service record suggests he was more trouble than he was worth.[74]

Having gathered a sense of the Germans' intentions, Brown returned to Blechhammer to take up contact with Captain Julius Green, the camp dentist, who provided Brown with the codes and the means to pass intelligence to London via the MI9 Escape and Evasion Network. When confirmed in the role of senior NCO at Genshagen, his undercover work could begin in earnest. Though not trusted by many of the men under his supervision, Brown was in fact using coded letters to feed vital information such as bombing coordinates back to London. Assisting him in this task was opera singer Margery Booth, who in one – perhaps apocryphal – account of her heroics sang before Hitler himself with ciphers hidden inside her costume.[75] Far from helping the Germans put together their projected British Free Corps, Brown and his network were skilfully subverting recruitment to it.[76]

In time his German masters indeed grew suspicious and confronted Brown. While Brown affirmed his dedication to the Nazi cause, distrust remained, and ultimately Heinrich Himmler ordered his arrest. Booth, too, was arrested. Both managed to escape their captors' grasp, but in Allied hands they found themselves confronted with similar accusations of treachery. When information surfaced of Brown's undercover work he was not only released but awarded the Distinguished Conduct Medal and called upon as a prosecution witness at 20 treason trials.[77] His account of his exploits ends with the words, 'I was only able to do what I did because of my Christian belief which sustained me in durance vile through not only the danger, but the hopeless dreariness of prisoner-of-war life'.[78]

One cannot conclude, however, that the Germans' efforts in seduction stirred no-one. It is not easy to establish just how many Australians might have been tempted to join the BFC, and it is even harder to work out what might have motivated them. The line between feigning an interest for selfish short-term benefit on the one hand and visceral commitment to Nazism is not easily drawn. The passing of time makes neither the collection of evidence nor the assignation of motives easier.

One source has an Australian doing his bit to recruit men into the BFC from at least one POW camp. A British private at a work detachment from Stalag XX A Thorn (today in Polish Toruń) recalls the visit of a German officer accompanied by a man wearing a BFC uniform. The man's identity is unknown, but the private suggests it was an Australian captured on Crete who proceeded to deliver his recruitment spiel. When his intent became obvious to the POWs they reacted furiously, 'and several made threatening moves toward the Australian, calling him some unprintable names and telling him in no uncertain terms exactly what they would do with him when they got hold of him'. Only the intervention of the guards with fixed bayonets, followed by the hasty retreat of the ostensible Australian with his German escort, brought the incident to a conclusion.[79] The identity of the man cannot be known, indeed there can be no certainty that he was Australian. And yet there is no doubt that there were a few Australians who at the very least toyed with the idea of succumbing to the temptations placed before them.

We know the names of four Australians who definitely did so; further evidence points to one individual taking part in broadcasts on German radio. The three soldiers who signed up were the Yorkshire-born Robert Chipchase, the Western Australian Albert James Stokes and the Victorian Lionel Herbert Battinson Wood, all members of the 9th Division's 2/32 Battalion, and all of them captured in North Africa for transfer initially to Italian POW camps and then, in September 1943, to Stalag XVIII A Wolfsberg, where they learned of the BFC. One of these men, Wood, was among those who spent time in early 1944 at Genshagen. His postwar testimony suggests he had gone to the holiday camp in the hope of finding an opportunity to escape. Receptive as he must have been to the entreaties of Genshagen's masters, he was transferred after five weeks to the BFC's base in Hildesheim to enlist. In time, as his testimony insists, he realised the impossibility of escape and asked to be removed from the camp.[80]

Chipchase was also a 'vacationer' at Genshagen in early 1944, and he too was subsequently transferred to Hildesheim. But in his testimony he claims to have recognised his mistake and not signed recruitment papers. For his sins he was sent to a punishment camp at Drönnewitz, where he served out the war.[81] Albert Stokes arrived at Hildesheim from a camp in District XVII in March 1944. He, too, was to claim after the war that his dalliance with the BFC was part of a ploy to escape. As it happened, he remained with the BFC until the end of the war.[82]

MI5 knew of these Australians, even if it did not know their names. A report of 27 March 1945 lists among 39 BFC recruits 'Aussie 1', 'Aussie 2' and 'Aussie 3'. Of the first two it suggests that they might have allowed themselves to be recruited 'to dodge trouble', while the third was allegedly anti-German and intending to escape.[83]

To the names of the three soldiers can be added that of a merchant seaman, Ronald David Barker of Goulburn, who also used the surname Voysey after the Sydney woman who adopted him.[84] Barker/Voysey fell into German hands in 1941 as a cabin-boy aboard *British Advocate*, captured in the Indian Ocean by the German pocket battleship *Admiral Scheer*.[85] He was taken to the merchant seamen's compound at Marlag-Milag Nord, from where he was recruited to Hildesheim. One explanation of his apostasy has it that at Marlag-Milag Nord he befriended a German woman in the censorship office, and when the relationship was revealed he was confronted with the stark choice of joining the BFC or being sent to a concentration camp.[86]

Whatever mixture of naivety, idiocy or ideological passion might have driven these men into the arms of the enemy, neither the war nor the time thereafter went for them as they and their hosts had envisaged. While they were in Hildesheim the BFC recruits 'generally seem to have made a nuisance of themselves, getting drunk, returning to barracks beyond curfew and so on'.[87] Towards the end of 1944 they were sent to Dresden, in good time to witness the vicious raid of February 1945; indeed, some took part in the clean-up that followed. From there the small and motley bunch was deployed to the far north, joining the 11th SS Nordland Division in the expectation that they would finally see some real action. But the commanding SS General Felix Steiner had little interest in sending the BFC into combat, and by this point the men themselves appear to have lost whatever taste for it they might once have had. The merchant seaman Barker/Voysey in particular 'had been collecting and smoking aspirins as a means of getting himself sick and removed from the unit, a task in which he obviously succeeded'.[88]

The end of the war could bring them no joy. Private Wood was lucky; he received no punishment at all for his stint in Hildesheim. Chipchase, too, does not appear to have been called to account. But for Barker/Voysey and Stokes it was a different story. Their names were on a 'British renegades warning list', which meant the Allied forces took a keen interest in them when hostilities ended. Stokes was found guilty by a military tribunal of aiding the enemy and received a year in prison, part of which he served in

Fremantle Prison. Barker/Voysey was arraigned in London on charges of 'assisting the enemy' under the Emergency Powers (Defence) Regulations Act 1939. He received two years' imprisonment with hard labour.[89]

PART 4

Freedom

22

Escape

Morale at P/W camp is NOT maintained solely by Concerts and Gramophone Records. Real Morale comes from a maintenance of a determination to escape. Watch and plan – don't be content to abandon yourself to the situation. That way lies depression – the destruction of initiative and a feeling of dull hopelessness – the effects may well be permanent. Maintenance of the Offensive Spirit – a constant determination to escape – therein lies the way to high Morale. Keep fit – YOU WILL REQUIRE TO BE FIT TO ESCAPE SUCCESSFULLY – it will help you to be on the alert.[1]

This was one official British view of escape, delivered in the form of lectures to those who faced that prospect. Even if not successful, the very effort of planning an escape was considered valuable in itself. It guarded against the morale-sapping effects of prolonged detention.

The Germans, too, formed views on why it was that their captives might seek to make themselves scarce. So curious were they to peer inside the minds of escapees that they conducted a survey among them. In Military District XVIII – where there were good numbers of Australians – they asked recaptured POWs what had motivated them to take flight. The answers they got ranged from a feeling of depression, through longing for home, boredom at the workplace, unjust treatment by guards or civilian overseers, to soldierly duty to escape. Next to the last reason were added the words, 'especially among the British'.[2]

Australians could name some other reasons, too. One of them, Charles Granquist, who by his own reckoning had failed five escape attempts, candidly acknowledged later that escape could help POWs assuage the guilt they felt at having ended their war prematurely through surrender. To engage repeatedly in the 'criminal' activity of escape, as Granquist did, 'washed away a lot of the guilt that I felt about becoming a POW'.[3] Another, Jim Paterson, who was destined to become a successful escaper, claimed that the motivation could be something as apparently trivial as the desire to remove a particularly loathed guard: any perception of a dereliction of duty in allowing the escape would typically lead to his reassignment, in all likelihood to tougher duties. In a small camp the prisoners would decide among themselves who would escape, perhaps by tossing a coin. The winner would duly take flight but set course for district headquarters and hand himself in: 'Any hardship suffered by the escapee was considered worthwhile if the desired result was achieved.'[4]

Another motive for absconding was what Paterson called the 'search for solace', which meant exiting the all-male community of the work detachment to seek out the company of a female forced labourer or, much more perilously, a German woman. And then, finally, there was the 'just for kicks' rationale, whereby the escaper would flee his detachment for the sake of breaking the mind-numbing monotony of the camp/work routine, at least for a short and precious time.[5]

Having said that, escape was not for everyone. A majority became resigned to the inevitability of prolonged detention, choosing to direct their energies to the simple yet herculean task of developing the skills to see themselves through to liberation, whenever that might be. They reached the prudent judgment that little was to be gained be making a break into the unknown world beyond the barbed wire, where countless dangers lurked. Even as the Reich lurched towards defeat, a cold reckoning would insist that it was safer to stay put than risk the mounting ire of the enemy or the misjudgment of a friend. Some even resented the efforts of their itchy-footed comrades. Successful or not, the consequences of their actions were likely to take the form of heightened security, soured relations with the guards and an even more oppressive regime for those left behind. One man's act of heroism could be another's vainglory, and there were many who had resolved to sit out the war without causing unnecessary danger to themselves and their mates.

For all those reasons and perhaps some others as well, over the course of the Second World War 6039 British POWs successfully escaped from German or Italian captivity to make their way to the UK.[6] In kriegie parlance this was known as a 'home run', though for many of the estimated 266 Australians who achieved this great feat it was something of a misnomer – Britain was not their home, they had never been there in their lives.[7]

Just how impressive the escape statistics are can be highlighted through a simple comparison with German POWs. They managed just one home run, performed of course in the reverse direction by a certain Franz Xaver Baron von Werra. A flamboyant airman – he kept his pet lion Simba as a mascot at the aerodrome – von Werra was shot down in England in September 1940 and sent as a POW to Canada. From there he escaped to the US – still neutral at the time – and then made his way back to the Reich via Mexico, Brazil, Spain and Italy.[8] The Australian figures look all the more impressive if evaders, too, are recognised, that is, those who were in German occupied territory but managed to avoid capture and make their way to safety. By that reckoning the tally climbs to 747.[9] On the other hand, if we narrow our gaze to omit the evaders and those who gave the Italians the slip, then we arrive at the more modest tally of 89.[10]

Escape from Germany, then, was not easy, and the risks were huge, as not only the men of Stalag Luft III came to realise. At the very least, flight from a camp or work detachment brought anxiety, privation and exhaustion; at worst it brought death. From the autumn of 1942 German guards were directed to call 'Halt' three times to a fleeing POW but then to shoot if the man did not respond. (For the shooting of a Soviet POW no warning call was required.)[11] Records show that nine Australians were killed in attempting to escape enemy hands.[12]

The risks had to be balanced against the benefits. Successful escape might give the opportunity to return to the fray, to confront the enemy once more on the field of battle. In the more likely event of recapture, the escaper could at least derive some satisfaction that his efforts had cost the Reich the expenditure of manpower to track him down, recapture him and haul him back to camp. With the onset of Total War, it was manpower the Reich could hardly spare. The cost to the POW himself, in contrast, could, according to the Geneva Convention, amount to no more than a month in an isolation cell. Successful or not, escape attempts were in effect the waging of war by other means. Even short-term escapes, undertaken with every expectation of failure, were valuable because, as Ron Zwar puts it, they had 'nuisance value'.[13]

Some things worked in the escapers' favour in Europe in ways they did not in Asia. If they were lucky, the Australians in Europe could rely on some local help. The lives of those who evaded capture or escaped in places like Greece, Crete, Yugoslavia, France, Belgium or Holland were in the hands of courageous and sympathetic locals. In this regard the Australians in Europe were better off than those in Japanese captivity; they found it much easier to melt into the local population and disappear from the enemy's view. And if they were particularly fortunate they might be able to draw on some help from MI9, founded by the Director of British Military Intelligence in late 1939 expressly to facilitate escapes. In time, MI9 agents penetrated many parts of occupied Europe, establishing crucial havens for escapees and lines of escape to guide them to freedom.

Airmen had some advantages denied those in the army. Though there would hardly have been a man in the AIF who did not contemplate his own mortality on the eve of battle, barely anyone wasted a thought on the prospect of captivity. But increasingly Australian airmen were able to benefit from training given in the UK in the art of evasion and escape. They were told in no uncertain terms, as MI9 records show, that if they were brought down then capture was a last resort. And then if they were captured, their first priority must be 'to escape at the EARLIEST OPPORTUNITY'.[14] They were equipped with cleverly devised and concealed escape aids which might, in the event of a safe landing behind enemy lines, make the difference between captivity and freedom.[15] The miniature armoury of the potential escaper or evader consisted of such items as a silk map, compass, identity card and money and food such as chocolate or Benzedrine tablets for energy.[16]

In one vital regard, however, the men of the AIF had it easier, or at least the other ranks did. Where airmen and army officers spent their wars in *Stalags Luft* and *Oflags*, surrounded by barbed wire fences and watchtowers, the other ranks were sent to the typically less secure arrangements of the work detachments. The burden of labouring for the Reich was at least compensated by the greater ease of escape. Crucially, at their workplaces the men had opportunities to make contacts with civilians, contacts which could make all the difference in the planning and execution of a breakout. Moreover, their daily journeys to their worksites gave them the sort of knowledge of the lie of the land that the airmen and officers could only dream of.

The best time to escape was soon after capture. Detention arrangements in operational areas were provisional and porous; the bold and the fit could take advantage of them, if only they did not tarry. Charles Jager was one of them. He found himself in the camp at Skines in Crete. With two mates he climbed the camp wire and disappeared, melting rapidly into the local Cretan population. Most were sympathetic to the Commonwealth troops, but Jager drew the short straw and was dobbed in by a treacherous Cretan near Canea and found himself back in a camp, this time at Galatas. He sat out a period of solitary confinement as punishment. Neither that experience nor the tighter security at Galatas dissuaded him from a renewed attempt. Temporary though it was, Galatas had turned into 'an efficiently-run POW camp, without any obvious weakness, patrolled by trigger-itchy youths'.[17]

Permission to escape was solicited from Leslie Le Souef, the only commissioned officer left in the camp. By Jager's account the doctor gave it hesitantly – he was concerned that a botched escape attempt would have unfortunate consequences for the local population, since already the Germans had earned a reputation for harsh dealing with unsympathetic locals. Grudging though Le Souef's approval was, it was given, and the attempt was well executed. Jager with two mates scaled the wires of Galatas and, as planned, found a boat and made their way to Mersa Matruh on the North African coast. Jager rejoined his battalion and then transferred to the Navy, performing service in the Pacific.[18]

Arthur Burton was an indirect witness to one successful escape from a holding camp near Athens. The Germans ordered a snap parade for counting as two men had got over the wall and made good their escape. One of them was Max Derbyshire, Tasmanian by birth, whom Burton knew from school in Wagga. He was assisted by a Greek family who had once had a shop in Wagga and, with their help, managed to get back to Palestine.[19]

Salonika, too, could leak POWs. For a time the favoured method of escape was via the sewerage system. Entry via a manhole inside the camp could lead via the stinking sewers to an exit hidden from the prying eyes of the guards. One who took this route and gained at least provisional freedom was Percy Cusack, who made good his escape along with six other British and seven Cypriot POWs via the Salonika sewer. By his reckoning he had crawled along the sewer floor on his belly for about 500 yards before exiting the system and finding refuge in a Greek home. But multiple accounts record how this escape route was stemmed. At some point a Cypriot passed out at a bend in the sewer, blocking the path of all those behind, who had no choice but to retreat to the humiliation of, in effect, capture *inside* the camp. Cusack recorded in his diary, 'Last night I heard some shots fired and was informed this morning by Mine Host that 4 men had been shot while attempting to escape.'[20]

ESCAPE

Some of the best opportunities to give the Germans the slip in Greece were during transport, whether to or from Salonika. The railway lines had been badly damaged during the campaign; train travel was slow and punctuated by stretches on foot, when tired and inattentive guards might soon be outwitted by a fleet-footed POW. Keith Hooper was one who contemplated escape on his train journey north to Salonika after release from an Athens hospital. At one point on a watercourse the bridge had been destroyed, so the men had to leave the train on one side of the watercourse and make their way to the other, where their journey would continue in another train. The brief walk offered a slender opportunity to escape, or so Hooper thought. He ducked under the train, made his way to a stone wall and jumped over it, only to see some twenty metres ahead of him a German guard relieving himself. 'He looked at me, I looked at him, we smiled at each other and just walked back to the train.'[21]

Frank Atkins witnessed a more fruitful manoeuvre on his journey north from Salonika. One night near the Macedonian/Bulgarian border some Australians opened the door to their wagon using a saw fashioned from a table knife; a number of men escaped. The train was halted as searchlights were set up to scour the darkness so the guards could hunt their quarry. An unknown number eluded them, their fates unknown, their best prospects to take up contact with Yugoslav partisans.[22] Lindsay Lawrence witnessed something similar. From the bushes beside a railway station where his train to Germany had halted, loaves of bread of unknown origin were hurled at men milling on the platform. They were, of course, gratefully received, especially those in which blades had been secreted. One such loaf made its way into a wagon adjacent to that carrying Lawrence, enabling its occupants to cut a hole in the floor and some ten of them to escape as the train made a slow ascent.[23]

Norm Tuckwell was another of the escapers from a train headed from Salonika to Germany. With an Englishman, a Scotsman and a Welshman, he jumped from the moving train on its second night and spent nearly a week on the loose before being reported to authorities by Bulgarian civilians. After being marched to Belgrade, the men were subjected to an interrogation, during which Tuckwell was bashed over the head and face, losing his two front teeth.[24] But Teddy Barnes was luckier, as Doug Nix recalls. In the same train as Nix heading north towards Belgrade, Barnes extracted a hook from the wall of the horse-car and attacked the half-rotten floor boards until a hole appeared to reveal the axles and sleepers beneath. At an appropriate moment he made his escape, risking the possibility that the base of his prison carriage might snuff out his life at the very moment of self-liberation. Only some years after the war did Nix learn that his old mate had joined partisans to make his way to Turkey and then on to Egypt and Australia.[25]

For the sheer adventure of train-jumping, however, it is hard to trump the story of Francis Barrett. He was packed in a wagon delivering him to Austria, but just as the train reached a station he managed to jump onto the brake car of a train travelling in the opposite direction. More than a day later he found himself in a suburb of Belgrade, where locals offered him food and shelter before secreting him under a tarpaulin on a goods train heading south – to Greece! As the citation for Barrett's award of a Distinguished Conduct Medal stresses, it required great persistence and determination on Barrett's part and the courageous assistance of numerous Greeks to deliver him finally to neutral Turkey, where a British consul collected him and the stray fellow escapees he had collected along the way.[26]

From other parts of Europe, too, the train journey into the Reich was the Germans' Achilles heel. The merchant seaman Edward Sweeney, captured by the raider *Orion* in the Tasman Sea, was to be transferred from St Médard en Jalles in France to Germany. The train journey offered him and his Scottish mate Frank Quinn an opportunity they could not resist. They jumped train, and with the aid of numerous sympathetic French men and women eventually found their way back south through France to Spain, Gibraltar and freedom.[27] At a later date and on a much larger scale, a group of 102 men, including 13 Australians, abandoned a train heading from Italy to Germany after the

Italian defeat. Among them were a father and son from Queensland, the Sharps, who from the point at which they jumped from the train at Le Viss near Trento spent seven days hiking through the Alps to Switzerland and freedom.[28]

Stalags and *Oflags* were difficult nuts to crack, but not impossible. There were four ways out – under the wire, through the wire, over the wire, or out the gate – the last requiring some kind of cunningly devised and executed subterfuge. One daring example of the exit through an open gate was the brainchild of the Australian Johnny Rawson, whom we have already met in Colditz, and indeed it had a distinctively Australian quality. Rawson was an officer in the 2/6th Battalion, captured on Crete and taken via Lübeck to the *Oflag* at Warburg. Rawson observed that the Germans cleared piles of used tins from Red Cross parcels with a tractor-drawn cart. His plan was a simple one, namely, to conceal himself in the cart as it was driven from the camp. The trick was to deal with the inspection of the cart by guards, who would prod the load with large iron spikes, potentially skewering any stowaway. Rawson's solution was to don the kind of garb made famous by Ned Kelly – indeed, he recalled once seeing Kelly's suit of armour. The suit fashioned for Rawson and his co-escaper Andy Benns – also an Australian – consisted of materials from two disused stoves, beaten into plates for their backs, legs and heads, which were then to be strapped onto them before they were to be helped into a cart. If struck during the search, the armour would not pierce but deflect the spike harmlessly and without raising suspicion. The date of the cart's departure would be known in advance since the Germans would pass the information to the British corporal in charge of the working party.[29]

Rawson's bold plan was approved by the Warburg escape committee. In time it was further refined, the would-be escapers equipped, and a number of rehearsals staged. Eventually the attempt was set for 15 June 1942, when a load of tins was scheduled to be taken from the cart to the train station, and from there to an industrial site for recycling. Rawson and Benns had to spend several hours in position in the cart before the tractor arrived. It was duly checked by the guards, thrusting the spikes into the load, but not drawing blood or provoking screams. The cart proceeded through the gate as planned to the railway station.[30]

Not until that point did the well-hatched plan begin to go awry. The tractor duly stopped at the railway station for unloading. As he contemplated his next move, curiosity got the better of Benns, who raised his head from the bottom of the cart to establish his whereabouts, only to find himself staring into the incredulous face of a guard. Benns was ordered out of the cart, but incredibly Rawson's presence was not revealed. After an astutely timed delay, Rawson's emergence was in the presence not of guards but of British orderlies, who removed his suit of armour and smuggled him into a rail truck, once again concealing him among tins. Rawson had only to wait until nightfall and the train's departure.[31]

His downfall was cramp. Rawson was unable to fight if off without moving, and eventually a severe attack led him to swing a leg forward, disturbing tins and setting off a noise which alerted nearby guards. Rawson, like Benns before him, was apprehended and returned to camp. Yet he did not suffer the fate of Ned Kelly – indeed, he was not at all chastened by the experience. For him and for other compulsive escapers it was something of a badge of honour that, as we know, he was eventually sent to Colditz, where his talents would be put to an even sterner test than Warburg could offer.[32]

It was the *Oflag* at Warburg which also produced a fabled over-the-wire escape attempt, and with some success. On this occasion, too, Australian officers played leading roles. The plan entailed four teams of 10 men making rapid and tightly coordinated assaults on the perimeter fences in the vicinity of huts. They would carry ladders constructed in such a way that they could be propped against the wire, and then an extension platform attached to them could be thrown across to the outer perimeter. In this way the extended ladders would straddle both the inner and outer perimeter fences. The men would climb up the ladders, cross the extension, suspend themselves from a trapeze bar and then drop to freedom before running from the camp as fast as they could. By whatever means available they would get to Holland, and from there to Britain.[33] That, at least, was the plan.

A key figure in the preparation was Jack Champ, an officer of the 2/6th Infantry Battalion, who had been captured on the island of Milos while trying to make his way from Greece to Crete. He had been in Biberach before his transfer to Warburg. Allocated to his team was Rex Baxter, who had also become a POW in Greece, in his case while recuperating in an Athens hospital as the city was overrun. The leader of one of the other teams was the Queenslander Doug Crawford, captured in Greece, and in the *Oflag* at Warburg after stints in Lübeck and Biberach.[34]

On the appointed evening the plan worked smoothly for the team of Champ and Baxter, who made their way over the fence and to safety before they heard the first shots being fired behind them. Elation instantly turned to despair, however, as they encountered a group of armed Germans demanding their surrender. Altogether six were recaptured and ushered back into camp, where an interrogation was followed by a return to their quarters.[35]

In the full light of the following day they pieced together the fate of the others. All twenty men of the first two teams had got over the fence, six from Doug Crawford's team had made it, and two from the fourth team. Of those 28, six had been recaptured almost immediately. Others, like Doug Crawford, were able to savour their freedom for longer, though not permanently. Crawford made it over the fence and headed south towards Frankfurt for several days, until he ran into an occupied dug-out and was apprehended. Like a number of others, he soon found himself in a new home, the *Oflag* in Eichstätt in northern Bavaria.[36]

Three among the 28 did, however, achieve a 'home run', as a coded letter received by one of the unsuccessful escapers revealed some six months later. It read, 'Darling David, I have just returned from a most interesting journey. Your two cousins send their kind regards. I trust you are well. Your affectionate aunt, Henrietta.' Indeed, three Englishmen had managed to reach Holland, contact Dutch sympathisers and smuggle themselves along an escape line via Belgium and France and ultimately back to England.[37]

As for the Australians Champ, Crawford and Baxter, their involvement in what became known as the Warburg Wire Job was a black mark against their names, and in all three cases the accumulation of black marks was to lead them to stretches in Colditz. It was a move which did little to dim their creativity as escape artists; it merely set them a stiffer challenge.

THERE IS A statistic which says much about how tough the airmen had it in executing escapes from their camps. As we have seen, one of them, Bill Fowler, achieved the rare feat of escape from Colditz and successful return to England. Just three other Australian airmen recorded 'home runs', and all of them did so from work detachments, not from camps. The trick was to swap identities with a soldier and thereby 'qualify' for work. Keith Chisholm made his break from a detachment at Gleiwitz and managed to get to Paris, where he was liberated. Allan McSweyn left his detachment to reach England via Spain and Gibraltar, while William Reed abandoned his fellow-workers to reach Stettin, where he boarded a ship for Sweden. As was often the case in successful escapes, he was wise enough to take with him a German-speaking fellow POW, an Austrian-born Jew from Palestine by the name of Henry Toch.[38]

The third man, Allan McSweyn, earned his home run the hard way. He had attempted to steal an ME 110 fighter from a German airfield three days after he was shot down over Bremen in the middle of 1943. For a time a member of the ground crew had even assisted in McSweyn's efforts to start the engine, only to realise that the would-be pilot was an unkempt ring-in. Via Spangenberg McSweyn arrived at the Warburg *Oflag*, only to be thwarted in the 'Warburg Wire Job'. A later attempt involved swapping identities before entering Stalag Luft III so as to take on the identity of an orderly. With this new persona he played the recalcitrant, eventually earning himself a transfer to Lamsdorf. From there he qualified for posting to a work detachment, from which he duly absconded, only to be nabbed after reaching a Swedish ship in Danzig and sent back to Lamsdorf. A later effort with a New Zealander,

N.G. Williamson, saw him cross into France by train. The target was neutral Spain, but the arduous trek was too much for Williamson, who perished, as did a Basque guide. McSweyn reached Spain and headed for Gibraltar, from where he made England after some six months of unstinting devotion to the task of gaining his freedom.[39]

The Germans were in a bind. They desperately needed every source of labour they could lay their hands on, but they found it ever more difficult to guarantee the security of the work detachments. At first they sought to provide one guard for every 10 POWs, but by 1942 most rural work detachments, even much larger ones, had just one guard, perhaps supported by an auxiliary drawn from the civilian population, usually a retiree.[40] It was a formula for escape. As long as the POWs were fit and eager, then giving their geriatric guards the slip during a moment of inattention was child's play. It occurred on countless occasions. The larger challenge for the escapees was to sustain their freedom, to find food, shelter and a path to freedom while guarding permanently against the chance of recapture.

The easiest of the escapes from work detachments were those from the rice fields of Vercelli in north-western Italy after the Italian surrender. At Ray Jones' detachment, the guards even encouraged flight, confiding to their charges that all of them – prisoners and guards – were best served leaving the dubious comforts and security of the humble camp to chance their futures elsewhere.[41]

By and large those prisoners like Jones and his group of five Australians who left their camps could count on the goodwill and in countless cases even the active assistance of Italians, who had grown weary of fascism and soon resented the occupation of their country by their erstwhile Axis partners. Yet mixed into the population were unreconstructed fascists and lackeys of the occupation regime, keen to curry favour with their new masters. To be on the loose in Italy was perilous; a single act of betrayal could mean recapture and even sudden death.

For many of the prisoners the aim was to put themselves out of harm's way as soon as possible by making their way to neutral Switzerland. This was more easily said than done. Although the camps and work detachments were largely in the north of Italy, the passage to Switzerland was across dangerous and, in the last part, rugged alpine terrain. Without reliable guides, uncompromised physical condition and a good dose of luck, reaching the border was an unlikely prospect. Ray Jones was one of those who, having reached the Alpine foothills and contemplated what lay before him, reconsidered his options. He had the good fortune of falling in with sympathetic local partisans, who fed him and his four companions well and protected them from danger while fighting tenaciously against the Germans and their collaborators. He and his group took the calculated risk of remaining with them in the vicinity of Cogolo rather than risk capture or serious injury in a bid to cross the Alps. And so he remained in the company of partisans from soon after exiting his camp with the collusive nod of his Italian guards through to his cautious approach to – and then acceptance by – an American armoured unit more than a year and a half later. After so many months on the run, it was 'a bloody relief', and the celebrations that followed with their liberators were long and hard.[42]

The Western Australians Syd Shove, Newt Moore and Fred Price made it further – indeed, they were among the 420 Australians who made it to Switzerland. They too had left Vercelli behind them, one of their guards going so far as to guide them through the town to the river Sesia. In parting company he gave them instructions to follow the river north to the Swiss border. With food and shelter provided by farmers, the group was matched with a guide to take them closer to Switzerland and to higher altitudes. They caught up with another group of POWs and, under a new guide, climbed via Macugnaga to the border, which they reached at Monte Moro. The last 500 metres were tortuous. At the border they were welcomed by Swiss border guards and representatives of the Red Cross. Their new home in Switzerland was Saas-Grund.[43]

Fred Vardy made it further after he, too, decided to risk leaving his Vercelli work camp on 10 September 1943. Together with two other Australians, the Victorian Jack Fullarton and the Queenslander Bert Lockie, he crossed the River Po and reached the village of Santa Maria, surviving for several weeks on a diet of grapes. Their first plan was to head for the coast at Genoa, commandeer a boat and head for Corsica, but the coast was crawling with Germans, so they turned inland again, finding refuge with villagers and living on their generosity. In the new year the next plan was to head south, hoping to cross lines and meet up with Allied troops. Yet breaking the lines was no easy task, and only after some months did they have the good fortune of falling into the hands of Poles fighting with British forces. Their war was over – they were back in Perth by October 1944.[44]

For others their freedom in Italy was short-lived. South Australian Jim Reeves, too, absented himself from Vercelli, but by the time he ventured towards the Swiss Alps, even the foothills were crawling with Germans, their eyes peeled for POWs on the run. With several other POWs, and with the sympathy of a Po Valley farmer, he remained at large for over four months. But then his luck ran out, courtesy of a rare Italian who saw fit to exchange the whereabouts of the POWs for a reward offered by his new masters. Months behind the schedule set by many others, Reeves, too, was soon heading north towards the Reich by train. In Milan he glanced from his truck to another just like it, noting with some unease the expressionless face of a much older, bearded man. In all likelihood it was the face of an Italian Jew, also destined for a long train ride north into the Reich, but with no prospect of returning to his homeland.[45]

Other escapees from the Vercelli labour camps fell into the wrong hands with tragic results. John 'Ticker' Nicholls, Ernie Wolfe, William Harvey, Harold Blain, Clive Liddel and an unknown Englishman were murdered, it seems, by Black Shirts in Piccone on 8 May 1944. A fellow POW learned from locals near Villaboit that the group had been captured by the Fascists, forced to dig their own graves and then shot.[46] Nicholls had expressed his objections, with the result that his tongue was removed before he was shot. Jim Brennan, an Aboriginal soldier from Western Australia taken at Ruin Ridge on 27 July 1942, witnessed an atrocity when he, too, left Vercelli in the direction of Switzerland. With a group of

POWs he headed north, finding shelter along with some escaped New Zealanders in an old cattle hut at Biella, where they were well fed by locals. On Anzac Day 1944 he was awakened by the sound of machine-gun fire and saw that the hut was surrounded by Fascists. He and the other men were taken from the hut and lined up against a wall, where he noticed that two New Zealanders and an Australian were already lying nearby, having been shot in the chest. With vigorous protestations that he and those with him were English, he himself narrowly avoided being shot.[47]

Escape from work detachments in the Reich presented a different array of obstacles. The men could under no circumstances rely on the goodwill of locals. If they escaped during the colder months of the year, then merely feeding and clothing themselves was a major challenge. The Germans had adopted the tactic of puncturing any tins of Red Cross food on distribution; it could not be hoarded in preparation for escape. And while the men might have accumulated local knowledge, had perhaps even made contact with sympathetic locals, the world beyond was a mystery, to be negotiated with instinct or a trust in some kind of divine guidance.

For men based in the east, as so many of them were, the geographical quandary had no easy solution. To make their way hundreds of kilometres north to a Baltic port and the slim possibility of stowing away to freedom was to invite failure, but any path directly west led into the jaws of the Reich. East was the Front and the disarming prospect at best of an encounter with Soviet forces. South of Silesia was Czechoslovakia – or the Reich's Protectorate of Bohemia and Moravia – ruled since Reinhard Heydrich's time by a merciless occupation regime, as the men who landed in Terezín's Small Fortress found. Hungary, at first an axis partner of the Reich and then, in 1944, overrun by its partner, was no more alluring. On the other hand, proximity to Switzerland or, late in the war, to Yugoslavia as the occupation fell apart under partisan pressure from within, was a great advantage. That meant that detachments in the Bavarian Military District (VII) or in one of the Austrian districts (XVII and XVIII) were much more auspicious starting points.

ESCAPE

Based at Stalag VIIA Moosburg, David Lang, captured in Crete in June 1941, was sent to a work detachment in Munich. Would-be escapers in that part of Germany typically thought of neutral Switzerland as a destination. In March 1942, well over a year before Switzerland became the preferred destination for men fleeing Italian POW camps, Lang plotted his own route from Munich to Switzerland. With maps stolen from the sides of stationary trains, and with civilian clothes nicked from an excavator, he secreted himself under the front part of a train headed across the border to St Margarethen. Security checks did not extend to the underside of the train. Some fourteen hours later, and blackened by soot, Lang emerged from his hiding place, only to be apprehended by Swiss police and placed in prison. His travels were by no means over. A visit from the British Legation ensured his release and then guided travel through France and Spain to Gibraltar and, finally, England.[48]

Lawrence Calder was in District XVIII, where he managed to have himself assigned to a work party in Graz responsible for cleaning up the railway yards after bombing raids. One night during a particularly heavy raid Calder, his Welsh mate Taffy, and a number of others took advantage of the confusion caused by the raid to escape into the nearby hills. Resting during the day and travelling by night, they made their way south across the Drau – or the Drava – in the direction of Bulgaria. Eventually they came across Red Army forces, only to find them suspicious. Rather than alleviate any doubts, the metal POW tags they carried were taken as evidence that the strangers were Germans. Fortunately a woman doctor in the Red Army unit piped up at a crucial moment, 'Are you fellows in trouble?' She had been trained in London, and although she could not place Calder's accent, she at once identified Taffy's accent as that of a Welshman. Less impressively, she even guessed his nickname. The doctor arranged a pass to allow them to travel in a truck ferrying wounded to Romania. With the war by this time nearly over, the path to freedom soon took a new direction – north to American forces gathering on the banks of the Elbe.[49]

Other Australians, too, crossed the Drau heading south, most of them into Slovenia in northern Yugoslavia. For the men in the

Stalag at Wolfsberg in District XVIII, the Drau came to seem little more than a stone's throw. And as the German occupation forces in Yugoslavia retreated north, the proximity of the Drau took on ever greater psychological significance. South of it, they knew, were Slovenian partisans, locked in a war to turf out the German invaders, just as the Italians had already been sent on their way. Extraordinarily, there was even contact from within the Wolfsberg camp to Slovenian partisans. British POWs built a tunnel from their compound to a position directly under the guard house at the camp entrance, and from there were able to establish radio contact with a radio station in partisan territory, run by Special Service agents parachuted into the area.[50]

The escape tales of two Australians, Ralph Churches and Jim Paterson, highlight the possibilities but also the peculiar gamut of dangers confronting those who contemplated a break across the Drau.

Captured in Greece despite determined efforts at evasion, Churches had been sent to the *Stalag* at Marburg and from there to various work detachments. Having acquired a good knowledge of German and the respect of his fellow POWs, in March 1943 Churches was elected Man of Confidence for his detachment, a motley mixture of Australians and other British POWs.[51] At that time the detachment was building roads north of Marburg; later in the year they were given railway work close to Marburg itself. By that time the temptation to head south in search of partisans was becoming irresistible.

Having determined to make a break in August 1944, Churches worked to establish contacts with Slovenian partisans. To prepare the escape he abandoned his position as Man of Confidence, keen to spend as much time as possible covertly making plans with his close English mate Les Laws. On the eve of the break, the small circle of the initiated extended to the other men in the barracks. At the appointed time on the day Churches had set, seven men were able to abscond from the railway worksite and, under the guidance of Churches, make their way to the arranged rendezvous with partisans.[52]

ESCAPE

At that point the enterprise took an ambitious turn. On Churches' pressing, and despite the clearly voiced misgivings of his fellow escapers, it was agreed with the partisans to risk a return to the detachment and secure, by force of arms if necessary, the release of the remainder of the 80 or so men working there. And so it was that within a day of the original escape, 79 unsuspecting POWs were added to the original seven who had placed their fate in the hands of Slovenians. Among the escapees were twelve Australians, including Churches himself, the unofficial leader of the group and negotiator with the Slovenians. Both partisans and escapees recognised that the first priority was to put some distance between themselves and Marburg, since the Germans would hardly tolerate such a massive loss of POWs without undertaking some measure to track them down immediately.[53]

On the second night after the escape they came across another group of partisans, about 100 strong. From that unit a group of ten was tasked with guiding the POWs further away from German positions and south towards the Sava River, receiving shelter and sustenance from sympathetic farmers along the way. As they approached the Slovenian capital of Ljubljana, at the time renamed Laibach, German forces snapped at their heels. A further source of constant concern was the indigenous forces of the Bela Garde, the White Guards, Slovenian quislings who were the sworn enemies of the partisans gathered under the broad banner of Tito's anti-fascist movement.[54]

The capital itself would be too dangerous and so was to be avoided. The group finally came to the Sava, which would need to be crossed in secrecy. In the dark of a September night, the river was safely negotiated by a small fleet of boats. They were now within reach of the border with Croatia and in the hands of new escorts, who kept watchful eyes out for Croatian fascists, the Ustasha. The march continued south, largely through heavily wooded territory for the sake of camouflage, its destination the village of Semic near the Croatian border. In Semic there was an Allied Mission under the command of an American, Captain Jim Goodwin, who coordinated efforts to clear airstrips for Allied aircraft supplying the partisan campaigns. To the great relief of Churches and his fellow marchers, they reached their goal on 13 September, and there they learned that these airstrips could also be used to ferry people out of Yugoslavia. So it was that, five days later, Churches was among the first to be ferried by an American Dakota out of Yugoslavia, across the Adriatic to Bari, and freedom.[55] Churches had led an extraordinarily successful mass breakout from German captivity, a feat acknowledged with a British Empire Medal and, later, an upgraded citation which read, 'for gallant and distinguished conduct in the field'. It was a rare distinction indeed for a former POW.[56]

Jim Paterson's escape was later, by which time he confronted a new assortment of hurdles. From his work detachment he had been able to contact partisans, with the help of whom a group of six POWs fled their work camp in December 1944, immediately finding refuge on a farm run by partisans, where they were well fed and cared for. Apart from the one Australian, Paterson, there were four Britons and a New Zealander. On New Year's Eve their journey continued, as with two guides they crossed the Drau heading south to join a small band of partisans just in time to celebrate with them the dawning of a hopeful new year. From there they were guided to an entire battalion of partisans allied with Tito, where Paterson found a welcome place alongside 36 other escaped POWs on the run. Their brief was not to fight but to carry equipment and the wounded among their mobile hosts; they were almost permanently on the move to avoid both Germans and the dreaded Serb Cetniks – not pro-German, but no friends of Tito's partisans. As with Ralph Churches' group earlier, the plan was to guide the POWs to the airstrip at Semic for evacuation to Italy.[57]

With the benefit of hindsight Paterson would eventually learn that he had unwittingly become a member of the 2nd Battalion Kolzjanski Brigade of Tito's Liberation Army. At the time the precise composition of the battalion was obscure. The fact that all wore caps with red stars and addressed each other as 'Tovarich' gave an indication of the ideological glue that held the group together. As much as ideology, though, it was the persona of Tito who drew together different national groups in a common cause, so successfully as to win the support of none other than the British Prime Minister.

Nonetheless, the resistance movement in Yugoslavia comprised at best a fragile unity. As an outsider, Jim Paterson had to be wary of the dangers to his very life of the internecine struggles that had ripped Yugoslavia apart after the German invasion. For all the theatre of bonhomie, he was well aware that his new comrades were a mixed bunch with differing visions of a postwar order. Apart from Communists and nationalists there were others, he noted, 'who, to avoid certain arrest and possible liquidation, had fled to the mountains for safety and, since September 1943, there were Italians amongst them who had decided to ignore their country's capitulation and throw in their lot with the Yugoslav Communists. There were even conscripts plucked from under the very nose of the Germans, and a sprinkling of foreign workers who had escaped the clutches of their masters, plus, for good measure, a couple of German deserters.'[58] Alien, too, for Paterson after years in POW camps was that it was not an all-male community – there were women among the partisans, mostly medical personnel.

The greatest danger for Paterson lay with the deteriorating military circumstances. He had not fluked the good timing of Ralph Churches, because by early 1945 the presence of German forces in northern Yugoslavia had intensified as they sought desperately to secure the borders of the Reich. So grave were the dangers that Paterson parted company from the battalion, seeing out the best part of the rest of the war living in a hayloft, then a small cave, entirely dependent on the goodwill, the moral integrity and the tangible generosity of locals. There were no comforts as he sat out the rest of winter and the tentative beginnings of spring, but in time the war ended. Eventually he was able to make his way via Semic to Ljubljana and Trieste, which he did not reach until the end of May, the war well and truly over.[59]

People like Jim Paterson, Ralph Churches, Allan McSweyn, Walter Steilberg and Ralph Granquist were among a very special band of the brave and restive who constantly sought opportunities to give their captors the slip. There were many who needed the fingers of more than one hand to tally the number of times they had given their captors grief. For feats of evasion and escape, altogether 83 Australians received decorations or were mentioned in dispatches.[60]

For sustained pluck and almost unremitting derring-do in matters of escape, however, it is hard to go past the story of John Peck. Sydney-born and Victorian-raised Peck was among those captured near Sphakia on Crete. He had managed to escape within a few days of capture, finding helpful Cretans in the vicinity of Georgioupolis, but then the Germans caught up with him again and threw him into solitary confinement for a month. Placed then in the POW camp at Galatas, he escaped again ten days later and made his way back to Georgioupolis and from there to the eastern end of the island, which was under Italian supervision. And so it came about that Peck was captured by an Italian patrol, who transferred him and those with him to a POW facility on the island of Rhodes, also under Italian control. Yet the Italians were no more successful in keeping Peck behind barbed wire than the Germans had been; with his companions – three Czechs and the Australian Noel Dunne – he escaped once more, this time stealing a boat and heading for neutral Turkey.[61]

That attempt too was thwarted, this time by a combination of a storm at sea and an Italian destroyer. For Peck there was a considerable measure of luck in his misfortune, because he alone survived the storm which sank the tiny vessel. For a time he was passed into German hands on mainland Greece but was then handballed once more to Italian authorities, who decided that it was best to send him to Italy. Thus by May 1942, almost a year after his initial capture on Crete, Peck found himself at PG 57 Gruppignano outside Udine, where large numbers of Australians captured in North Africa would keep him company, at least until he seized the opportunity to continue the cycle of escape and capture.[62]

When that opportunity came, he was well prepared. He took time as a POW to learn Italian, so that when he escaped from his lightly guarded work detachment at Vercelli he could call on local assistance as he made for the Swiss border. Indeed, on the first attempt at an escape from Vercelli he calculates that he made it over the Swiss border, only to turn back into Italy to request food from an Italian shepherd. Instead of bringing food the shepherd brought a patrol, with the result that soon Peck found himself in solitary confinement in Vercelli. But with the announcement of the Armistice in September he was freed once more, and the opportunity to reach the border all over again unexpectedly presented itself.[63]

He took it, and covering familiar territory made it halfway there before being halted, this time by the pangs of his own conscience. He recognised that he could place his experience of the language, the people and the routes to Switzerland in the service of fellow POWs, so he retraced his steps to establish, with Italian participation, an organisation devoted to helping former POWs leave the country. And so a network was born which offered a haven to countless Allied servicemen. Peck was its founder and one of its guides, escorting men across the border to safety, as well as its chief planner of staging points, secret routes and safe houses.

The dangers inherent in Peck's selfless labours stemmed not just from the occupying German forces but also from the fascists and their sympathisers who were waging a kind of civil war against the partisans of northern Italy. With the armistice many fascists might have gone underground, but they had not disappeared altogether. Peck and his collaborators constantly risked betrayal and, with it, summary execution. He counted among his enemies both German occupying powers and Blackshirts. As his work against both those groups expanded to include sabotage, even with the benefit of disguises his identity became more widely known.[64] Indeed, it was while wearing a captured German officer's uniform during a sabotage operation that he once more fell into enemy hands, and by this stage of the war and in these circumstances – consorting with partisans – the consequences were likely to extend far beyond a spell of solitary confinement. German security officials surprised him in the middle of the night, arrested him and interrogated him. Dispassionate in tone though it is, Peck's own account of his arrest gives some insight into the perils to which he had exposed himself in trying to help others:

I was captured in the house of my second-in-command Oreste Ferrari, and was dressed in the uniform of a German officer. I attempted to shoot my way out but failed, and when taken was put against the wall of the house for execution. While searching the house the SS found certain documents which they wanted me to explain before I was shot, but I refused. They tore the German uniform from my body and belted me with their fists, boots and rifles, but after an hour of this and I wouldn't talk they gave up and took me down to German H.Q. at Luino. There I was tortured, with others of my band, for three days and nights, but finally they sent me to Varese. From there I went to Como for Court-martial on 16.2.1944.[65]

A farcical trial was staged at Como, where Peck was sentenced to death. He awaited execution in the San Vittore prison in Milan.[66]

In the meantime, with the aid of a Resistance contact inside the prison, he was put on a bomb disposal squad, a position which, for all its obvious dangers, offered at least some hope of escape while on outside duty. During an RAF bombing raid he shook his guards, escaping Milan and, on this occasion, escaping Italy for good as he crossed over into Switzerland on 22 May 1944.[67] The cycle of capture and escape was broken, and yet despite his brush with death in Milan he continued to venture into northern Italy from his Swiss haven, playing the role of liaison officer with Communist partisans.[68]

23

Exchanges and Repatriation

There were safer paths to freedom than escape, but they were open only to the few. Those few consisted of two groups. The first were those who enjoyed the privilege of 'protected status', and that usually meant medical personnel such as doctors, nurses and medical orderlies but could also include soldiers who had received dedicated training as auxiliary nurses or stretcher bearers. It extended too to padres or chaplains. The second group consisted of those unfortunates whose state of health – whether through the wounds of battle or illness or injury incurred in captivity – entitled them to an early journey home. The Geneva Convention allowed for the repatriation of prisoners from both these categories, typically in the form of exchanges. Over the course of the war in Europe – but overwhelmingly as Hitler's downfall approached – 1329 Australians took this path home.[1]

Geneva was quite explicit about how repatriation along medical lines would occur. The crucial point was to determine which men came into consideration on the grounds that illness or injury rendered any further military role in the conflict impossible. Entrusted to make this decision was a Mixed Medical Commission consisting of three doctors, one to be appointed by the detaining power – in this case the Reich – but the majority appointed by the International Committee of the Red Cross in consultation with the Protecting Power (for Australia that meant Switzerland from December 1941). The commission would be chaired by one of the latter; a simple majority would set the outcome of every deliberation.

The prisoner – according to the Convention at least – could put himself forward for examination, but he could also be recommended by his camp's medical officer or a senior prisoner, even by his own government. Of course he might need to wait until the commission visited the camp in question, and then the decision was not always straightforward. Loss of a limb or paralysis were automatic cases, but where other wounds were concerned the judgment had to be made whether they would render the POW an invalid for at least a year. At first blush the legless British pilot Douglas Bader might have appeared a strong case for repatriation, but as his loss of limbs predated the war, he was not a contender. Some conditions like blindness, deafness, epilepsy or chronic skin diseases were readily diagnosed, but with others like gastrointestinal or psychological disorders there was room for scepticism and disagreement among the three wise men entrusted with the decision-making. That many worthy Australian and other candidates were not repatriated but had to endure painful injuries and illnesses for the duration of the war is a sorry reflection on the repatriation system.

As for 'Protected Personnel', in theory their services should have been redundant in captivity, since the detaining power was obliged to provide medical and pastoral care. In principle, then, these men – unlike in the Far East, there were no female Australian nurses captured in the European theatre of war – should have been repatriated without delay. But provisions in the Convention allowed for agreements to be struck between belligerent powers to detain protected personnel where their services were needed by their countrymen. Moreover, an abiding sense of duty and commitment to their countrymen in their hours of acute need persuaded many men in these categories to remain in detention. For the succour they provided in trying times, countless POWs were eternally grateful.

As for those who eventually sought repatriation, commonly alongside the ill and injured, they too were destined to become the playthings of *Realpolitik* as it was practised by the Reich.[2]

Repatriations were typically conducted in the form of the exchange of eligible personnel from both sides. But to make exchanges a reality was no easy task, as experience soon showed. Commonly the goodwill that existed on both sides foundered on the rocks of complexity, exigency and political point-scoring. Even with the Red Cross offering its services as an honest broker, there was much that could, and did, go wrong.

The first efforts to arrange exchanges took place early in the war. British and German authorities, drawing on the services of the United States as the Protecting Power, agreed to the creation of the Mixed Medical Commissions required for the exchange of the sick and wounded, and indeed in both the UK and in Germany such commissions had commenced tours of camps by the end of 1940.[3] In the following year it appeared that a first exchange would take place. After months of sparring over who might be included on the lists of the respective belligerents, the nominated persons on both the British and German side were transported to the respective harbours to commence their voyages to freedom: Newhaven and Dieppe. The exchange was scheduled for early October 1941.

Hitler was the fly in the ointment, even if the OKW could see the advantages of freeing up beds and medical personnel for the war in the East.[4] But Hitler discovered that the agreement reached entailed the exchange of over 1000 British for just 100 or so Germans. The reasons for the imbalance were obvious enough – in the first two years of the conflict many more British than German soldiers entered captivity. Three weeks before the exchange was to take place, the Germans let it be known through the Protecting Power that the imbalance was unacceptable. In this they did not have Geneva on their side – Article 68 of the Convention insisted that exchange was to be 'without regard to rank and numbers'. To correct the imbalance they began to negotiate for the exclusion of greater numbers of German civilian internees – among whom, unlike the British, they would include merchant seamen. With no prospect of equal numbers in sight, the operation was abandoned amid shrill accusations of deceit and treachery. The British POWs were sent with heavy hearts back into the Reich.[5]

Later that year, in November 1941, the Germans made a second attempt at an exchange, this time involving not just POWs but also civilian internees and protected personnel. A Mixed Medical Commission visited camps and examined over 1700 Commonwealth and British POWs, of whom 1153 were recommended for repatriation.[6] The new categories were understood to present the possibility of achieving parity this time around, as there were significant numbers of German civilians who came into consideration. On this occasion a stumbling block formed on the other side of the Atlantic. As the German proposal was being discussed, the US entered the war and the Canadian government wanted to wait and see if it should participate in an agreement involving both its neighbour and the Reich. The Canadian misgivings were significant, because large numbers of German POWs were located there, much to Hitler's chagrin. On this occasion, too, the goodwill which no doubt existed among the officials on both sides came to nothing. The Germans not surprisingly took the Canadian recalcitrance as evidence of an Allied strategy of excluding the great bulk of German POWs from any deal.[7] The British POWs slated for exchange had been gathered in Rouen, only to experience the bitterest disappointment shortly before Christmas.

The Italian authorities, on the other hand, proved much more amenable. Australian and other Commonwealth forces had captured large numbers of Italians in North Africa; in East Africa, too, Italians had been captured in droves. In these circumstances Rome was receptive to a British proposal put in September 1941 to exchange the sick and wounded. An agreement was reached in January 1942, with the result that a first exchange was carried out at the neutral Turkish port of Smyrna on 8 April. The imbalance clearly favoured the Italians, of whom over 900 were released from captivity. The ships bringing the British to Alexandria by contrast contained 59 sick and wounded along with 69 protected personnel. There were just 11 Australians among them.[8] With that modest success further exchanges were planned. The second and third did not involve Australians, but the fourth, also carried out at Smyrna in June 1943, brought 80 Australians, a mixture of protected personnel and wounded, their freedom.[9]

One of the fortunate beneficiaries was the Australian George Worledge, who had been captured when the motor launch he captained was sunk by an Italian destroyer during a daring raid on Tobruk in September 1942. He found himself in camps in Bari and then Sulmona, but after six months of Italian captivity he was told, much to his surprise, that he had been selected to be exchanged for an Italian naval officer. The two appointed vessels swapped their human cargo off the Turkish coast. Worledge could not have known it at the time, but the exchange probably saved him from a spell in German captivity. Instead he was able to return to Australia via Alexandria and continue his war there.[10]

By 1943 exchange negotiations with German authorities were more fruitful. The Shackling Crisis had died a quiet death; more importantly, the state of the war had changed, and there were now many more Germans in British captivity. Defeat in Africa in May had been a turning point. The Germans initiated an exchange plan sent via Berne and entailing large numbers drawn from all categories of personnel. Exchanges were to take place via ports in Sweden, Spain and French North Africa. The first stage took place in Gothenburg on 20 October 1943. By train and ferry the Germans conveyed British repatriates, while the British prisoners reached the Swedish port in three vessels. On the very same day German sick and wounded in Tunisia were collected by their countrymen from Oran.

The final stage of the scheme took place a week later in Barcelona, where some 1000 Germans held in the Middle East were exchanged with a similar number of British and Commonwealth POWs; from there the Australians, New Zealanders, South Africans and Indians could be taken home. To reach Barcelona the Australians and others were sent by train to Marseilles and from there sailed to Spain aboard *Aquileia* and *Djenné*.[11]

Of these men 180 were Australians, one of them the medical orderly Hal Finkelstein. Although entitled to repatriation as an orderly, he was given a medical examination. Even then the wheels turned slowly. Eventually he was taken from his labour detachment to his *Stalag* and from there by train through France to Marseilles. From Marseilles a vessel sailed to Barcelona and docked. Then came the wait until all was in readiness for the handover, a British vessel with German POWs visible nearby. And then it happened: 'One lot went through the wharf shed and the other lot went round the end of the wharf shed. I can't remember which was which. We went round and onto the British ship. We were on protected voyages and were lit up. They took our names and numbers because up until then they didn't know who was coming.'[12] From Barcelona they sailed to Alexandria and were placed in a camp. He was home in his native Western Australia by 19 January 1944, but, with war still raging in Europe and the Pacific, to no fanfare. His own thoughts on leaving Germany had been deeply ambivalent. He had cared for many men for a long time, but his identity as a Jew, signalled by his name, was an ongoing source of anxiety.

Frank Atkins was entitled to feel less ambivalent. He had been among those whose patience had been sorely tested by the delays in organising the first of the German exchanges. From Stalag VIII B he was loaded into a hospital train which, stopping and picking up further POWs along the way, proceeded to Marseilles, where the men were loaded onto a small Italian hospital ship. Among those welcoming the men in Barcelona was the British Ambassador to Spain, Sir Samuel Hoare, and his daughter. Though the sympathies of the Franco government were with Hitler, the Spaniards handled the men correctly. It was a great relief to board a hospital ship flying a British flag. By this time many of the men had imbibed a good quantity of beer, fanning their high spirits. The 'snooty' English captain conveyed his disapproval of their unruly behaviour, but by the time the Australians in the exchange reached Egypt they no longer had reason to fear German or English censure. There they boarded *Oranje*, a Dutch vessel loaned to the Australian and New Zealand governments as a hospital ship.[13]

Charles Robinson had made his way to Barcelona from his camp at Hammelburg. He remembers that during a moment of boisterous hilarity after the exchange was effected an Australian woman came on board ship. Her escorting sergeant struggled to impose an atmosphere of appropriate decorum for the visit: 'Shut up, you bastards! Can't you see there's a bloody lady present!'[14] Female company had been a rarity for a very long time; the excitement was hard to contain. Soon it would be contact with Germans which would be consigned to the past, as the vessel carrying German soldiers prepared to leave the wharf, accompanied by enthusiastic cries of 'Heil Hitler'.

> As their troopship turned its stern came near to our vessel and the Germans started singing 'Und wir fahren gegen England'. We countered with shouts of 'Have a look at Frankfurt as you go past' and 'Deutschland kaputt'. We sailed the following morning and the wharves were bare of spectators. Our only farewell was from a chap in a small rowing boat painting the rudder of an anchored merchantman. He gave a furtive 'V' sign as we steamed close by and headed for the open sea.[15]

A further exchange took place in Barcelona on 18 May 1944. Four trainloads of POWs left Germany for Marseilles, and from there the hospital ship *Gradisca* delivered the men to Barcelona. On this occasion the Swedish ship *Gripsholm*, which earlier had delivered eligible German repatriates from Canada, carried 1043 British POWs – including 61 Australians – to Algiers before taking the remainder to Belfast and back to Canada.[16] Three Australians were lucky to make the exchange. The German report on the exchange noted that three drunken Australians were found in a cabin on the lowest deck of *Gradisca* an hour after the rest of the passengers had disembarked.[17]

After D-Day, Barcelona could no longer be used for exchanges – the Germans had no access through France. But Gothenburg was still an option, and it was used once more on 10 September 1944. This time the eligible Allied POWs travelled by ferry to Trelleborg from the German port of Sassnitz on the Baltic coast; 107 Australians were among those sent on via transit camps in Gothenburg to Liverpool and Eastbourne.[18] One of them was Frank Cox, whose camp at Spittal had been visited by a Mixed Medical Commission in early 1944. Assessed as deserving of repatriation, he was taken north into Germany proper, avoiding Berlin itself, and to the north coast for transport to Gothenburg. From there he sailed via England to India and back to Australia, finally arriving aboard *General Anderson* in November 1944.[19]

The last of the German exchanges involving Australians took place on 6 February 1945.[20] Once more Gothenburg hosted the proceedings, this time involving 75 Australians.[21] The trial of the long sea voyage back to Australia was still ahead of them. As far as trials go, though, it was a picnic compared to what the men left behind still faced.

24

On the Move

From the summer of 1944, the Allies were pushing in on the Reich. The D-Day landings finally opened a Western front. In the south, fraught German efforts to hold the Allied advance through Italy were giving ground, piece by precious piece. More alarmingly, in the East the Red Army was turning Hitler's dreams of a Nazi Empire into a nightmare from which there was to be no waking.

For those dealing with POWs, the steady march of the Red Army presented a headache, because large numbers of POWs were held in the eastern reaches of the Reich. Farther to the east, at the Reich's very limits, there was a camp which held Allied airmen, including Australians, and they were to be among the first who would be subjected to the turmoil and pain of being force-marched away from the Soviets. That place was one of Göring's collection of camps for airmen, Stalag Luft VI, located at Heydekrug near the Baltic port of Memel. As the Red Army approached in July 1944, word was given for the camp to be abandoned. All the POWs would have to be moved west. If there was one group of men the Germans did not want returning to combat, it was the airmen.

Some of them had it relatively good – they were put on a train and taken to Stalag XX A in Thorn – but others, including the South Australian airman Peter Giles, shot down in his Lancaster near Berlin early in the year, had unwittingly drawn the short straw.[1]

With just 24 hours' notice he and his fellow POWs at Heydekrug were told to pack their belongings and prepare to leave. Nearby Königsberg had been captured by the Red Army; the evacuation of Stalag Luft VI was now a matter of great urgency. He took everything he could and headed to the port at Memel. There the men were loaded onto a Russian collier which the Germans had commandeered and renamed *Insterburg*. Offloaded onto the deck of the vessel, one by one they had to descend a rope ladder into the pitch-black depths of the hold, where they were cramped together under a pall of coal dust. For three and a half days they travelled across the Baltic, not knowing their destination but permanently fearful of mines and submarines. The only food available was the scant supplies they carried with them.

Henry Bastian, captured in Africa, was another Australian who had been sent all the way east to Heydekrug until he, too, found himself being packed into the dark and dank hold of *Insterburg* in Memel. Like the other survivors, he recalls all too clearly the nightmarish voyage for three days and nights through perilous waters. There were no toilet facilities in the coal dust–covered hold; the only relief came from brief and infrequent visits to the deck. Water was passed down into the hold in a bucket on a rope, losing the best part of its load as it tangled with the ladder. It was barely enough for the men to wet their lips, and the Germans offered no food at all.[2] Even after arriving at their destination, Swinemunde, the men had to spend another night in the hold. When they finally emerged the next day, they were covered in coal dust, sick and tired. Two of the men, as Bastian remembers, were so affected by the prolonged confinement that they entered a mad frenzy and attempted a break, only to be gunned down by the guards.[3]

For the others a further journey, this time in a cattle wagon, was in store. The men were manacled together in pairs, but just as they prepared to entrain the Americans launched an air-raid on the port, where German warships were at anchor. A massive smokescreen was thrown up, as the prisoners were ordered to take shelter under the train. With that ordeal behind them, the men emerged, still shackled, and the loading of the cars with their battered and weary human cargo continued.

As the train pushed westwards, the men were not permitted even to stretch their legs on sidings. Finally they detrained at Kiefheide – nowadays Podborsko – where a daunting welcoming committee awaited them. It consisted of members of the Kriegsmarine – and senior Hitler Youth members, all with fixed bayonets. Presiding over the whole operation, in Peter Giles' recollection, was an SS officer, directing both men and a number of dogs straining at their leashes.

The POWs crossed the road, taunted by locals, and then entered a forest. Then they were given the order to run. It was at that point that chaos broke out. Carrying what possessions they could while still chained together, their undernourished bodies stiff from several days of cramped transport in the ship's hold and the cattle wagons, the prisoners were in no condition to run the several kilometres to their destination. Those who slowed down were bayoneted or beaten with rifle butts. The dogs were set mercilessly onto any perceived stragglers. As if that were not intimidating enough, on both sides of the furrow through the woods were machine guns. The word was passed around to stay together at all costs.

Another South Australian airman, Thomas Roberts, was in the same group. He found that carrying his pack was almost impossible while handcuffed to another man, so the two of them attempted to discard bundles of their possessions as they were driven mercilessly forward. Those unfortunates who stumbled over their packs were soon set upon by dogs or by guards wielding bayonets or rifle butts. By the end of the run, Roberts had seen dozens of bayonet wounds and dog bites, along with a number of rifle butts smashed on the skulls and bodies of POWs. Their packs discarded, the men had nothing but the clothes they stood in as they entered the raw haven of the new camp.[4]

And then there was the Victorian pilot Jack Liley, who

experienced the descent of what began as an orderly march into a rabble, inflamed by loud shouting, vicious dogs and jabbing bayonets. The one brief moment of levity was provided by a Canadian in front of him in the column. The 'Canuck' was clubbed by a member of the Kriegsmarine and responded – at a timely moment crossing a bridge – by executing the ice-hockey version of a hip-and-shoulder on the German, knocking him into the water. The Canadian, Liley recalls, 'ran off as if nothing had happened, confident in the knowledge that his captor would never recognise him'.[5]

'The run up the road', as this horrific event came to be known, ended at a makeshift campsite which was to be the new home for the POWs. There had been no urgency to reach it – the planned accommodation was not yet available to the men who arrived, beaten, bayoneted and exhausted. The run had served only to satisfy the sadism of the guards and their commanding officers. On arrival there was no prospect of relief from pain, hunger and thirst. The men lay on the ground, tending their wounds and begging for water which seemed to take an eternity to arrive. To fill their grumbling bellies there was still nothing.

Not all the Germans approved of what had happened. Some of the older German guards, as Peter Giles observed, shook their heads in censure, while Henry Bastian's elderly guard had shown the decency to remove the manacles before the run commenced. But during the run itself it was the young men of the Kriegsmarine who clubbed and stabbed.[6] Relatively unscathed for a good part of the run, Bastian's luck ran out when he stopped to help a fellow POW to his feet. A vicious guard took advantage of Bastian in that brief, vulnerable moment: 'The bastard bayoneted me up the rectum and with witnesses I must have broken the standing broad jump record. By the time I reached the camp, both my boots were full of blood.'[7] The run was over but, like others, Bastian was to wear the scars – physical and mental – for the rest of his life.[8]

The unfinished camp that was to be their new home was Stalag Luft IV Gross Tychow, located between the villages of Kiefheide and Gross Tychow (Tychowo). As was immediately obvious to the new arrivals, the camp authorities were still scurrying to throw together barracks that would offer at least provisional shelter. In the meantime, the tortures of the run were followed by the discomfort and indignity of makeshift arrangements. The first night in the new camp was spent in pain, in cold, indeed in the open air. In time accommodation in the form of so-called 'dog boxes' was set up, but the permanent barracks were still a work in progress. For the older hands among these airmen POWs, the comforts of Stalag Luft I at Barth must have seemed a very distant memory.

The 'run up the road' was a sinister precedent of what was to come for most other POWs in the early months of the following year. If the summer of 1944 delivered pressure on German forces from three sides, the winter of early 1945 brought one crushing blow after the other. In January the Red Army went for the German jugular. On the 12th of that month it staged a massive offensive stretching from the Baltic in the north to the Carpathians in the south. Something like six million Soviet troops were thrown against two million German soldiers and about 190,000 others in a series of battles that would determine the outcome of the war.[9]

The German policy of generally holding POWs at locations farthest from their homelands meant that it was these military developments in the East that had the greatest impact on British and Australian POWs, and not just the airmen. As the Soviets approached, at times with a startling rapidity as German front lines crumbled, the POWs had to be evacuated west into the heart of the Reich. British and American POWs were not to be permitted to fall into enemy hands. An order to that effect had come from Hitler himself, delivered on 12 February 1945, and passed down the lines of command ultimately to the camps, charged with the Sisyphean task of guarding and provisioning thousands upon thousands of men on the move. 'Political reasons' were given for the order that these POWs were not to be lost to the Reich by falling into enemy hands.[10]

There were three main areas to which they were to be taken – in the region of Lübeck in the far north, in Saxony-Anhalt south and south-west of Berlin in central Germany, and to Bavaria in the south.[11] With rail stock devoted primarily to military use, the evacuations of almost all the camps had to be on foot, commonly over distances of hundreds of kilometres. Typically the men were formed into columns of perhaps 250 or 300 men who, despite years of captivity and poor diets, were expected to march between 20 and 40 kilometres a day. All of this was to take place through the depths of a German winter, when food and accommodation were in desperately short supply and competition for them fierce. The only reward for a day's march was at best a provisional billet in a barn, a factory, a church or even in the open. Arrival at a final destination – usually a *Stalag* in the central north, centre or south of the Reich – brought little respite, because these camps were chaotic, overcrowded towers of Babel. The German penchant for orderliness and the strict separation of the POWs into their national groups buckled under the weight of exigency.

As if the men of Stalag Luft VI had not already suffered enough through their evacuation to Gross Tychow, the arrival of a new year brought with it a fresh move, this time still further to the west. Peter Giles was in the group which, with a heavy heart, departed Gross Tychow on 6 February. He had no inkling of how long he would be marching or what his destination might be. Over cobbled roads they trudged, foraging for food as they went, their Red Cross parcels having soon run out. Many predictably became ill and fell out of the bedraggled line. Dysentery decimated their ranks, the men's bowels producing only a greeny-coloured liquid. They were given charcoal, but that served only to turn the liquid black. Lice covered their bodies like a living hairnet, burrowing into every crease and crevice and tormenting their hosts incessantly. On warmer days they might spend time picking lice out of their clothes and hair, but to little avail.

The goal, as they eventually discovered, was Fallingbostel, about 60 kilometres north of Hanover in Lower Saxony, where there were two *Stalags*, XI B and 357. They finally arrived in late March 1945 after weeks on the road, yet then they were instructed to leave within a day. Fallingbostel was hopelessly overcrowded with POWs flooding in from the east; Giles and the others from Gross Tychow could not even gain some food by begging. Incredibly, then, they headed back eastwards across the Elbe, until the approach of Red Army forces persuaded the guards to change direction yet again. These men were condemned to plod across the north German plains until, finally, they would encounter Allied troops and gain their freedom. But that would take weeks.

The more fortunate evacuees from Heydekrug who had been taken by train to Thorn had it better, but not much. Ron Mackenzie was one of them. The sojourn in Thorn was brief, until they too were shifted to Fallingbostel. Mackenzie was at least spared the later march there, but his journey in a goods wagon was itself a torture. The heat of late summer and the shortage of water drove the men crazy with thirst. At some cost in cigarettes they negotiated with the guards at least to keep the doors open for periods to deliver vital air to the fetid wagons. At Fallingbostel the discomforts of train travel were soon replaced by the acute privations of a severe winter in a camp already overpopulated with French, Soviet and other British POWs. There was virtually no food except what the POWs themselves might scrounge, frequent air-raids heightened fears of instant death by 'friendly fire', and those who ventured to take a bath had first to chip the ice from the top of the brick well. Desperately short of all three elements required for survival – namely food, warmth and sleep – Mackenzie witnessed men beginning to die 'from practically anything'.[12] There were perils outside the camps, too. The men in the columns wandering the German countryside in search of a temporary or permanent billet risked attack from the skies. From great heights, Allied pilots could scarcely distinguish between POWs and columns of German soldiers.

The Australian airman Allen Campbell, a veteran of Heydekrug and Thorn, was among those evacuated once more from Fallingbostel in the general direction of Lübeck in the far north. To get there they had to cross the Lüneburg Heath, at that time a war zone; Allied aircraft patrolled night and day, often flying overhead. 'We stayed on the road hoping they would recognize us. When we camped, bundles of hay were put out to spell POW. We were not molested, but on one occasion a fighter flew over us and attacked movement on another road with rockets. Sad to say it was a column of POWs.'[13]

There was, indeed, a recorded case of a column of POWs from Fallingbostel strafed by a formation of British Typhoon fighters. In moments they created a scene of carnage, as their cannon and anti-personnel bombs scythed through the luckless POWs. The pilots did not recognise their error; a second attack was launched at those who invested their last energies in a dash across open fields. There were perhaps 60 to 70 dead.[14]

Stalag Luft III at Sagan, the biggest of the airmen's camps and still with some 10,000 men spread through its six compounds as the final year of the war began, was evacuated from 27 January 1945, and in something of a hurry. Thousands of Red Cross parcels, as well as clothes, blankets and literally millions of cigarettes were left behind in the stores.[15] By coincidence the order to evacuate arrived on the very day the Red Army entered Auschwitz to find the grotesque remains of the horrors perpetrated there. There were numerous destinations for Stalag Luft III's British and American airmen, reached by a combination of foot and train. A lot of the Americans went to Nuremberg. For the others, including the Australians, the major destinations were Luckenwalde just south of Berlin, but also the naval camp at Westertimke, or the *Stalags* at Fallingbostel, Hammelburg or Moosburg.[16] Sometimes these, too, proved purely provisional havens.[17]

Wilf Hodgson was one of the airmen in Stalag Luft VII in Silesian Bankau (today Bąków) who on 19 January, with about 1500 others, was given Red Cross supplies and packed off westwards to cross the Oder and make his way to Stalag III A Luckenwalde, an army camp south of Berlin. When the men arrived there on 8 February, a nightmarish scenario confronted them. All of the compounds here, too, were by this time hopelessly congested. Hodgson and his fellow airmen found themselves crammed 300 men to a hut. The concrete floor was covered with straw, but within a short time the straw had become filthy and lice-infested. It was disposed of and not replaced, leaving the men to sleep on a bare concrete floor, tortured by hunger. There were no Red Cross parcels to be had; at best an extortionate barter carried out with more fortunate French prisoners – Luckenwalde too was by now a bulging multinational affair – permitted meagre supplements to what was at best a starvation diet.[18]

Another Australian airman, James Beecroft from Melbourne, was in the same group. As the men set wearily forth at three in the morning on that bitterly cold mid-winter's day, the parting threat to fortify their step was that for every man who fell out, five would be shot. With that prospect ever present in their minds, the airmen covered the 236 kilometres in 17 days, only to find their achievement crowned with arrival in the desolation that was Luckenwalde.

There were airmen, too, in the *Stalag* in Silesian Lamsdorf. Both they and the much larger numbers of soldiers – some of whom had already been transferred from Stalag VIII B Teschen – had to be evacuated from the second half of January. On 22 January a large group containing airmen and soldiers was marched from Lamsdorf towards Görlitz, some 250 kilometres away.[19] Sleeping rough in barns or factories and trudging through snow in subzero temperatures, they took two weeks to reach their destination on 3 February. Görlitz could offer only cold comfort. As one of the survivors of that trek, Reg Centillon, recorded, 'The barracks we are taken to are filthy having just been vacated by Russian prisoners that morning. 450 men in a barrack designed for 100. One block of beds for 54 men being 3 layers 12' x 10'. One block of beds collapsed first night but fortunately no one hurt. No Red Cross and rations very poor. We have to live, eat and sleep at bed space.'[20]

In any case the stay in the *Stalag* at Görlitz offered these men only a fleeting respite. It was located in Silesia in the eastern reaches of a shrinking Reich, so that it, too, soon had to be evacuated. Thus the interlopers from Lamsdorf were forced onto an even longer trek west, one group heading to the *Stalag* at Ziegenhain in District IX, some 800 kilometres from their original starting point. If an army marches on its stomach, these men over a period of more than a month marched on thin soup, some scraps of bread and occasional brews of ersatz coffee or tea. Of those who reached Ziegenhain, most could barely walk. Men dropped out to uncertain fates along the way; others arrived with ailments ranging from frostbite to dysentery and hunger oedema.[21] Just short of Ziegenhain, Reg Centillon took a protein shot from an unlikely source. As the men sheltered in a barn during an air raid, an American chased a rabbit inside, but did not know how to kill it without attracting the guards' attention. The Australians offered to help if the spoils would be shared. One of them was a country lad 'and managed the job without a murmur from the rabbit. It was quickly skinned and seven of us ate it raw while it was still warm.'[22]

The evacuations from Görlitz led in other directions, too. Doug Butterworth's group headed towards Duderstadt: 'Many suffered from dysentery and the state of hygiene can well be imagined. On leaving this hell hole we got mixed up with fleeing civilians and beat-up units of the German army. It was pitiful and chaotic, especially when fresh German units were being sent to the front on the same road in the opposite direction!'[23] Duderstadt offered respite, but of the most primitive kind. This time the billet was a brickworks. Four large kegs of soup protected by a man with a machine gun awaited thousands of hungry men. 'After spending three to four hours getting near the kegs, the air raid sirens would blow and supper was called off. Another attempt was made on the "All Clear". More often than not the kegs would be empty on your arrival.'[24]

Unlike the airmen, most of the soldiers were on their work detachments when the orders came to head west. In early 1945, these men were scattered across the Reich, but with a heavy concentration in Silesia as the Red Army drew nearer. Not just the starting points, but the routes heading west, too, were numerous. Many had to contend with the mountain ranges of the Sudetenland. The luckier ones might arrive at Königrätz, from where a train journey might deliver them to Stalag XIII D Nuremberg. Others kept heading towards the south-west into Bavaria.[25]

Ray Corbett's labour detachment E3 Blechhammer was evacuated on 21 January. With a Soviet spearhead rapidly approaching, they hurriedly prepared packs and some sledges and set off across the Oder heading south-west towards Bavaria. These were the darkest times of his captivity, constituting what he now calls a 'black memory':

> For three weeks, the temperature was anything from 0 degrees to 20 degrees below zero C. Sledges made the going easier for some wounded. Then came the thaw. Tracks became quagmires. Boots, such as they were, began to leak and feet were soaked day and night. Food became a scarcity after 2 weeks. The German rations each evening were for the most part unfit for a self respecting pig to eat (but after all, we were not much better, according to some German minds). I don't wish to recall here some of the tragic sights I've seen caused by hunger. But those of us who have witnessed it, know how it can change completely a man's appearance . . . self respect is lost, cleanliness becomes a forgotten virtue. Men will fight and argue over a rotten potato . . .[26]

Mercifully after some weeks Red Cross food parcels reached the men, just as starvation loomed large. After entering Bavaria, Corbett's column – by now comprising not just POWs but Jews, gypsies, political prisoners and others – found some relief in a tiny village near Bayreuth. He counted losses at about 200, attributing them to 'beri-beri, anaemia, nervous diseases, frostbite, even the lack of the will to live, to face further privations. All these took their toll as every morning many were left in villages or hamlets.'[27] A week later the column was on the move again, finally reaching Moosburg on 13 April.

On a work detachment in a Silesian coalmine, Arthur Leggett received word of the impending march in the form of the camp leader's announcement, 'No work today. We are leaving in 24 hours.' Possessions gathered over years of captivity had to be abandoned if they were to keep ahead of the advancing Red Army. On cue a day later they were lined up, counted and herded through the main gate, destination unknown. For four weeks they trudged through snow and blizzards, flanked by cantankerous guards, seeking shelter in the barns of villages they reached at the end of a day's tramping. It was usually at this time that they would take their one 'good' meal of the day, drawing on precious Red Cross parcels to consume perhaps half a tin of meat between two men. In the freezing conditions the remaining half was easily stored for the next evening in the open tin. The evenings were also the time to try to dry socks and boots in straw, yet only ever imperfectly. 'Next morning the socks would crackle as they were pulled on and the boots were stiff with a thin coating of ice inside them.'[28] Leggett's new destination, a small village in northern Bavaria, offered little solace after the travails of the coalmines and the long march. He and others were almost immediately dispatched to further work details, helping to clear the damage caused by bombing raids on Regensburg.[29]

Evacuation exposed Leggett and those in his predicament to some ghoulish sights along the way. POWs were not the only ones trudging along the Reich's wintry roads and lanes. As it battled its way west, the Red Army pushed a wave of Germans and non-Germans, prisoners and guards, labourers and bosses, young and old, before it. In the vicinity of Fallingbostel, for example, Ron Mackenzie's column came across a column of Polish women, almost certainly forced labourers, being marched under guard: 'Rickety, dirty, deformed, half-clad, many without shoes or stockings, others with heavy boots on spindly legs, disheveled and with faces so completely hopeless as to wring any heart not completely dead to human decency, faces almost animal in their fear but without the life that illumines the face of the animal; the guards hustling them along with rifle butt and barrel, shouting, bullying and pushing.'[30]

Heading south-west from Silesia, Arthur Leggett noted a column of political prisoners in striped clothing – perhaps concentration camp inmates – ahead of him. Even more poorly nourished than the POWs, not all could be cajoled to their daily destinations. At times he would pass a political prisoner on the roadside, 'a bullet hole drilled neatly through his forehead. His thin coat, wrapped around his gaunt, bone-protruding body, was occasionally wind-ruffled before it, too, became frozen and buried beneath the blanket of whiteness stretching to the horizon. Ah well; what's another body? They're all over the place.'[31]

George Anderson fell in with a large and motley marching group that was very nearly claimed by the Red Army. Moved out from his work detachment at the Dombrova coalmine near Krakow on 20 January in temperatures well below freezing point, his original column of 600 reached 1400; in the vicinity of Auschwitz it picked up further numbers, as inmates from the camps there fell in. Here, too, a chilling warning was issued – anyone falling out of the column would be shot. That the threat was no idle one was confirmed by the presence along the roadside of the bodies of dead Soviets and political prisoners.[32] Not until the end of March did Anderson's group reach Regensburg; the fit still had another 90 kilometres ahead of them on the way to Moosburg.

Not all made it to their destination in the Reich, at least not alive. Bill Williams was one of those who had been sent north to Silesia from Italy in September 1943. After a series of heavy-duty work detachments – among them a quarry and then a coalmine – his health was probably compromised before the forced march towards Bavaria even began. In his last postcard to his mother, dated 3 December 1944, he reported, as he invariably did, that he was 'still kicking'. Then the communication stopped. Only after the war could Bill Williams' mother learn from her son's good mate and fellow POW Bill Bosse just what had happened to her Bill on that dreadful long march. Six weeks into it, Bill Bosse explained in a letter, Bill took sick. For nearly three weeks he was carried on a horse-drawn cart, spending the nights in barns with his mates. But then his health took a sharper turn for the worse, and he was delivered to a hospital. The next day, 23 March, the news was that Bill had died overnight of an ulcerated stomach. Bill Bosse had done all that he possibly could, in the end to no avail. As they slept in the barn with the cattle, he recalled, 'I would go and see if I could do anything for him, all he wanted was some milk, so I would get someone to watch to see the Germans didn't come, while I milked a cow for him.'[33]

Officers and NCOs had it better, as they were more likely to stay in one place. But they, too, were feeling the pinch in the last months of the war. By this time the *Oflag* at Eichstätt in Bavaria had about 100 Australians. In the appalling winter of 1945 one of them lamented, 'This place is like an ice chest . . . there are long pieces of ice hanging from the ceiling . . . I have one blanket 3' by 4'6" . . . we get one bucket of coal a week to cook on and for heat.'[34] The Red Cross inspectors agreed. A February 1945 report damned the conditions and also noted the clear signs that long periods of incarceration were having deleterious effects on the minds of the men:

> The effects of long captivity are telling on a number of officers and other ranks, most of whom are under thirty years of age, and over half of whom have been nearly five years in captivity. The camp is more overcrowded than ever; lighting is worse than before, the shortage of fuel is making this winter particularly uncomfortable; and the non-arrival of Red Cross supplies and private parcels means that food is short.[35]

Eventually these men, too, were marched out of camp, in their case to the *Stalag* at Moosburg, no better equipped to deal with a swelling population.

At the NCOs' camp at Hohenfels, the men could at least stay put as the war raged around them, but they too were not exempt from the Reich's creeping logistical catastrophe. From December 1944 to February 1945, no Red Cross parcels got through; the 500 Australians could see the flesh wasting away from their bodies. For a time they even recorded their atrophy, noting an average weight loss for those months of over 5 kilos per man, prompting them to stop the measurements for fear of their effect on morale. The Red Cross inspector who arrived in March 1945 was struck by the deterioration in conditions since his last visit. Even if the camp authorities were doing their best, supply networks had collapsed and the POWs' health, he warned, was in peril.[36]

The most fortunate in all this were the men in the two military districts in Austria. In District XVIII there were large numbers of

Australians, whether in the *Stalag* at Wolfsberg or its work detachments. They stayed put, at least for the time being. After all, they were in effect already in the heart of the Reich, albeit in its deepest south, and there was nothing to be gained from marching them through the Alps to the muddled and overflowing *Stalags* further north. In any case, the military threat from the south was less urgent than that coming from the east or even the west. In time, though, it would come.

In April the men on their work detachments in the eastern border regions under threat were recalled to *Stalags* or collecting centres to commence their marches to the west. In late April Wolfsberg's sick were packed into carriages and sent to Stalag XVIII C Markt Pongau, while their healthy colleagues set out on foot.[37] It was an exercise in futility, because by now it was just a matter of time before Allied forces – whether Soviets from the north-east, Americans from the north-west, or British from the south – would liberate them.

Among the Germans all but the most fanatical Nazis recognised that the end was near and nothing was to be gained from continuing to send men onto the roads, at great risk to their lives, and at the very least at the cost of creating yet another logistical nightmare for the Reich when it was least able to cope with it. For some time, the Allied powers kept a close watch on what was happening with their POWs and urged the German authorities to desist from marching the men from camp to camp.

As they became aware of the hardships the men were suffering, Britain and the United States put to the Reich government the suggestion that their POWs should simply stay put in their camps, with the Allied assurance that on liberation they would not be deployed to fight the war. On 20 April – Hitler's 56th and last birthday – German authorities formally offered to leave prisoners in their camps as German forces retreated.[38]

The offer was formally accepted by all the Allied governments, including the USSR, on 23 April, and thereby came into effect as the 'POW Standstill Agreement'.[39] On Anzac Day the Australian Prime Minister's Department in Canberra received a cablegram from London bearing the good tidings: the German government had agreed to leave POWs located near the front in situ, providing that they would not be redeployed in the war against Germany.[40] It was a sensible agreement, driven on the German side by necessity. As the Reich collapsed into itself, the options for moving men evaporated. Confirmation that the agreement was working finally arrived on 1 May, when the British and Americans received assurances from the Protecting Power that prisoner movements had ceased, the bulk of the POWs collected in large *Stalags* open to visits from the ICRC and the Protecting Power.[41]

For the thousands already on the road as the agreement came into effect, it was next to meaningless, doing little to staunch the chaotic flow of desperate humanity from one atrophied limb of the Reich to the next. As for those still in the camps, they and their representatives could not be absolutely confident that the Reich would respect the terms of the agreement. Not only had the Reich sullied its representation as an upholder of international law, in reality the life-and-death decisions about the fate of POWs had devolved to those on the ground who had the men in their immediate care. Fully aware of this, the Allied leaders saw fit to issue a dire warning to all Germans who might contemplate acting to the detriment of prisoners, declaring: 'Any person guilty of maltreating or allowing any Allied prisoner of war to be maltreated whether in the battle zone, on the lines of communication, in a camp, hospital, prison or elsewhere, will be ruthlessly pursued and brought to punishment.'[42]

25

Liberation

It was already bad enough that the POWs faced the travails of an ineffably harsh winter, the perils of being marched across the Reich as it collapsed around them, and the anxieties about what Hitler and his acolytes might have in store as the endgame neared. But then high politics intervened to add an extra degree of difficulty to their task of saving themselves.

By the last months of 1944, it was becoming clear that large numbers of British and American POWs were going to fall into Soviet hands. Allied leaders had to start giving some thought to what this might mean. When British Foreign Secretary Anthony Eden attended the Moscow Conference in October 1944, he extracted from Stalin a personal assurance that all care would be given to Commonwealth POWs from the moment of liberation.[1] Sure enough, over the weeks and months that followed, the Red Army did liberate the soldiers of their Western Allies, whether by entering camps or occupying territory in which men who had given the Germans the slip were seeking refuge. How these men would be treated was going to depend to a very large extent on how much goodwill the Soviets would muster. Equally, the treatment of the Soviet soldiers and citizens liberated by advancing Western Allies would depend on the level of benevolence the British and Americans would bring to the bargaining table.

By the winter of 1944–45 there were some worrying signs that goodwill was in short supply. The great concern was that the Western POWs who fell into Soviet hands would be used as pawns in the game of chess that would determine the postwar order. If these men were to be treated well and handed over in a timely and orderly way, then the demands of the Soviets would need to be listened to. In this game, the Western Allies, too, were not without their players, because large numbers of Soviet citizens – POWs and civilians – were falling into Western Allied hands. Unlike their Western brethren, not all of them wanted to head home after the war – indeed, they had very compelling reasons to stay in the West if they possibly could. That was especially true of the more than 22,000 Soviets who were taken prisoner while wearing German uniforms.[2]

The POW issue was just one of many to be hammered out at a conference the Allied powers scheduled for early February. Stalin, never keen to venture from the Soviet Union, would host it at Yalta in the Crimea. In the weeks leading to the conference, the Allies scrambled to reach agreements ripe for signing when the leaders turned up, pens in hand, ready to pose for the world's press.

In POW matters, as in so many other areas, the Australian government had left the negotiations in the hands of the British, but in the lead-up to Yalta there were signs that the Australians' confidence that Churchill would have the POWs' very best interests at heart was limited. As British officials scrambled to find common ground with the Soviets, they were also having to heed the supplications of a querulous Australian government.

When on 20 January the Soviets presented a draft reciprocal agreement for the treatment of POWs and civilians, the UK government liked what it read. The draft envisaged that prior to being handed back to their respective forces, the POWs could be engaged in labour by their provisional masters. Former Soviet POWs were already working in the UK, and, it was pointed out, SHAEF (the Supreme Headquarters of the Allied Expeditionary Forces) took the pragmatic view that if they were not working the Soviet POWs would be difficult to control.[3] Viscount Cranborne, the UK Secretary of State for Dominion Affairs, expressed his optimism: as the terms of the proposal would ensure tolerable work conditions, he therefore recommended its acceptance. He asked all the Dominion governments concerned to let their thoughts be known.[4]

The Australian government responded that it was not an issue on which it would fall obsequiously into line. If the offending paragraph of the Soviet proposal were agreed to, then it would mean that large numbers of Australian POWs, after years of working for Hitler, would soon be working for Stalin.[5] The line to Whitehall from Canberra was firm and forthright:

> These men are all volunteers, many of them airmen. It would be impossible to justify it to public opinion in Australia if, on their release from a rigorous and in many cases prolonged captivity, they were subjected to compulsion to labour service for whatever purpose. [. . .] We regret therefore that the Australian Government cannot be a party to any arrangement with the Soviet Government which includes a provision such as that in paragraph 4 of your telegram. The only attitude which we feel it possible to take is that we expect and assume that on release Australian prisoners-of-war will automatically resume their military status and that the Soviet authorities will be ready to cooperate in arranging their immediate repatriation.[6]

Cranborne's reply has the character of a double-take, unaccustomed as he no doubt was to taking 'no' for an answer from Dominion governments. He tried to press his case again, arguing the urgency of putting into place some kind of binding and mutually agreeable arrangement with the Soviets. But he also suggested a compromise in the form of a modification to the disputed paragraph 4, according to which work by ex-POWs and civilians would be voluntary, not compulsory. Next to the suggestion of a compromise was a thinly veiled threat: 'Should be glad to learn from you most immediately whether you would wish your prisoners of war and civilians to be excluded from the agreement on this modified basis.'[7] In other words, if the Australians did not agree, the British would push ahead with the agreement and simply exclude the Australians.

Neither the sweetener nor the threat was enough for the Australian government to change its mind, and it let Cranborne know immediately that the performance of even voluntary work would be quite unacceptable, notwithstanding the practical need for an agreement with the Soviets.[8] Extra ammunition was added to a follow-up telegram two days later:

> Labour on a voluntary basis would probably lead to invidious distinctions and might well produce special anomalies. Reports recently received indicate the very serious effect from the point of view of both mental and physical fitness of prisoners who have long been in German hands. We do not feel that any of them should be submitted either to the strain of labour after their liberation or to the necessity of making individual decisions which would differentiate them from their comrades.[9]

As for the threat of exclusion, the mere suggestion of it, Canberra complained, 'seems to us hardly a proper one because as you have charge of the negotiations we have no alternative but to rely on you for securing proper treatment of all Australian service personnel who may come into the hands of the Soviet Command'. The appeal closed with a none too subtle reminder that the immediate return of Australian personnel was a matter of urgency – in the Pacific Australia's needs were 'great and urgent'.[10]

Despite the Australian objections, Churchill pushed on with negotiations on the basis that voluntary work would be permitted. Cranborne told Curtin of this on 9 February, citing Churchill's reasoning that it would be best to have an agreement covering men from all parts of the Commonwealth, pointing out that the Canadians, New Zealanders and South Africans had conveyed their support. Should Australia not fall into line, Churchill indicated that in a final agreement the Australian position would be treated as reserved.[11]

Convinced that the well-being of Australian POWs – and indeed those of other Commonwealth states as well – was not exactly the UK government's first priority, Australian Minister for External Affairs Herbert Evatt contacted his man in Moscow, Minister to the Soviet Union J.J. Maloney,[12] asking him to handle the POW matter 'with Soviet authorities on highest necessary level'. He should even go so far as to arrange to visit camps where Australians were accommodated, reporting back as soon as possible on what facilities were required and at what cost.[13]

At Yalta the British and Soviets did finally manage to nail down an agreement on the treatment of their respective POWs. It was signed on 11 February, when the Australian POWs were either trekking west to avoid the Red Army or, bit by bit, were falling into Soviet hands. In essence both sides undertook a duty of care to the other's POWs, and that meant the provision of food, clothing, shelter and adequate medical care in designated collection points until a transfer could be arranged. In the meantime repatriation officers would be given direct access to their countrymen. On the thorny issue of work, a compromise of sorts was reached which forbade any form of forced work outside the collecting points.[14] Even so, the particular concerns of the Australian government were given expression. British Foreign Minister Anthony Eden drew attention in a special note that his signature for the Government of Australia did not apply to point '6' of the agreement, which dealt with the issue of POWs and civilian labour.[15]

In the end, Australian disappointments were not so much with the terms of the agreement signed at Yalta but with the Soviet breaches of it. Australia established a legation in Moscow to facilitate the transfer of POWs, and in doing so to work hand-in-glove with the British Military Mission operating there. Repatriation officers, one for the AIF and one for the RAAF, were sent into occupied Polish territory as the terms of the Yalta Agreement had anticipated, yet they found the Soviets less than forthcoming with assistance. While it was clear to the Australians and other British authorities that there were at the very least hundreds of Australian stragglers making their way eastwards towards the port of Odessa in the Crimea, typically under their own steam or with the aid of sympathetic Polish civilians rather than with any help from the Red Army, the Soviets claimed that the POWs had already been cared for and guided to Odessa.[16]

The Australian representatives on the ground were not slow to seek improvements. In the immediate aftermath of Yalta, Maloney, a tenacious former Boot Trade Union secretary, had requested an audience with the Soviet Foreign Minister Molotov, but to no avail. He did at least manage to present a note to Dekanazov, the Assistant People's Commissar for Foreign Affairs of the Soviet Union. Dekanazov promised to place the matter before his government, but he also reassured Maloney that it was not the Soviet intention to keep Allied POWs on Soviet territory any longer than necessary.[17] When things did not improve as promised, Maloney wrote once more to Molotov recording his disappointment. He did not get much joy when he finally received a reply.[18] Progress had indeed been slow, and there were still many Australians impatiently awaiting repatriation in Odessa or still making their way there.

Maloney was like a dog with a bone, and he found natural allies in the British, who also suspected that the Soviets were not being entirely honest. The British expectation of the agreement struck at Yalta was that they would have access to their ex-POWs at 'points of concentration' in Soviet-controlled territory. British repatriation teams visited Lublin, Lemberg (about to be renamed Lvov) and Volkovysk but, in their view, were not being allowed to do their jobs properly – and, in the last case, were instructed by the Soviets to leave while there were still British former-POWs in the camp. And at Odessa the British team was not permitted to live in the camp to minister to the needs of the former POWs – indeed, they were required to enter the camp under Soviet escort. Reports suggested that other former POWs were still to arrive in the Black Sea port, but some of these 'stragglers' were being subjected to Soviet maltreatment or were even being used to dismantle industrial facilities for transfer to the east.[19] The whereabouts of an unknown number of British troops who, simple logic insisted, must be somewhere in Eastern Europe remained unknown. As for the

Australians who must have been among them, at the beginning of March the Soviets were still taking the fanciful line that none had been liberated by the Red Army![20]

Three weeks later the Department of External Affairs regarded the situation as 'disturbing'. Maloney reported continuing delays in the processing of POWs and in repatriating men still in Poland. Great hope was placed in a proposed 'direct approach' to Stalin by Roosevelt, but in the meantime Maloney was instructed to keep the pressure on the Soviets: 'You might express to Molotoff [sic] our serious anxiety as to the effect on public opinion if it were established that there was any avoidable neglect by the various Soviet authorities in connection with Australian ex-prisoners.'[21]

Maloney did indeed try once again to speak with Molotov himself, but on this occasion was fobbed off to Andrei Vyshinski, the Soviet Deputy Commissar for Foreign Affairs. As Canberra had requested, he passed on the concerns about the fate of Australian ex-POWs, but in the meantime a quite specific POW-related matter had emerged which demanded some diplomatic attention. Three Australian ex-POWs had made their way to Odessa – they were privates A.M. MacCallum, W.V. Hawking and W.S. Grayston – accompanied by their Soviet wives! All three couples had married in Krakow the previous month. But the Soviet authorities would not permit the wives to sail with their men – they would need to return to their homes and lodge applications for release from citizenship. This, they were told, would take some time. Maloney emerged from his meeting with Vyshinski with the clear impression that this was an issue on which the Soviets would not budge.[22]

Whether the Soviets wanted to acknowledge their presence or not, the truth was that Australians were turning up in Odessa, where they were being concentrated and prepared for repatriation to the UK by ship. These were men who had made their way to the Crimea under widely varying circumstances, with or without Soviet help, but universally in a state of exhaustion. Typically they had not experienced the elation of a single moment of liberation; rather, having removed themselves from their labour detachments or marching columns, they instinctively headed towards Soviet lines, placing their fate in the hands of the Poles or Russians they encountered.

One man in this predicament was Charlie Parrott, who was in a sorry state even as his odyssey to Odessa commenced. Due to a work accident in a Silesian coalmine, he was on crutches as his forced march towards the west began on 20 January. He got through the first day, planting his crutches in the snow and urging his body forward. But in the middle of the first night out of camp he took refuge in a school building, knowing he could make it no further. It was there that the advancing Soviet forces came across him, but they left him there, not knowing how they would care for a cripple. Later that afternoon two Poles approached, recognising from his battledress that he was British, and found a stretcher to take him to the township of Beuthen (today in Polish Bytom), where they deposited him in a convent.[23]

Parrott's life was saved by Polish nuns, above all by a certain Sister Marcella, who possessed some medical knowledge and a visceral contempt for the godless Soviets. She called on the services of an aging German doctor, who performed an operation without anaesthetic on Parrott's leg, opening it up with a scalpel to drain off the septic muck that had built up inside it. The doctor then applied a course of injections which finally healed the leg and enabled him to move on to Krakow under Soviet orders, accompanied by two South Africans. Others, too, received the succour of the nuns, and not just other POWs. Parrott recalled the arrival in the convent of girls of just twelve years of age, blood running down the insides of their legs, the victims of rape by Soviet soldiers.[24]

It was the Soviets once more who gathered Parrott together with other POWs and sent them on to Odessa. Fortunately through this trial Parrott had the services of a Polish woman who acted as interpreter. He had noticed that it was not helpful to announce to the Soviets that he was Australian, because he risked being held for an Austrian, so the Polish interpreter presented him as English, only to have one Soviet officer respond with an angry 'Pig Englander'.

Parrott's journey from Krakow to Odessa was not his first by cattle wagon, but it lasted the longest. By his reckoning it was all of 17 days, and it was every bit as uncomfortable as the journeys

LIBERATION

he had made under German supervision. The shortage of food was just as acute as on the trains that had brought them north from Salonika four years earlier. Luckily for Parrott, Ukrainian peasants were permitted to approach the carriages at stops, eager to barter. For an item of clothing such as a shirt or pair of boots, the men could receive a wedge of bread or perhaps a hard-boiled egg. Temporary relief was afforded in Lemberg, where they were showered and deloused. It was a rare interlude of humane treatment.

Finally the train arrived at Odessa, where a British colonel inspected them, incredulous at the shortage of clothing. Ahead of Parrott was an Australian to whom the colonel said, 'Good gracious, sir, is that all the clothes you've got?', to which the Australian replied, 'Yes, sir, and if I was on this bloody train tomorrow I wouldn't have these.' A converted school provided temporary lodgings. Out of boredom Parrott volunteered to sort clothing, then found himself promoted to sergeant and in command of ten men detailed to help him. Red Cross clothing was again reaching them, having followed them all the way to the shores of the Black Sea. For some it was superfluous, or at least they had other priorities. For those who found a way out of their makeshift prison, a pullover was worth a night with a woman in Odessa.

It was a British ship they boarded in Odessa. On the wharf were Russian policewomen with fixed bayonets and sub-machine guns, prepared for the preposterous possibility that an Australian or British soldier might prefer to stay there. For Parrott the mere thought that the POWs might wish to spend any further time in Soviet captivity was 'hysterically funny'.[25]

Barney Roberts was another who organised his own liberation by the Soviets. He was on a rural work detachment in eastern Austria and was well aware that the Red Army was getting ever closer – he could hear the fighting in the nearby Vorau valley. He and two mates working with him in the forest contemplated the delicate and dangerous moment of presenting themselves to a new set of captors. Allies though the Soviets were, they could be forgiven for being permanently trigger-happy as they occupied the Reich. With the Soviets camped nearby one evening, Roberts drew the shortest of three straws and, walking towards the Red Army encampment, hoped that calling out 'Comradski' would settle the soldiers' nerves. Seconds later a torch was shone in his face, implicitly demanding that his first attempt at communication be followed by a combination of utterances and pantomime with which he might identify himself. The one word which was understood was 'America', so in the raw moment of liberation he and his two friends were 'Americanski airmen'.[26]

Passed from one group of soldiers to the next, they had to account for their presence in the forests of Austria numerous times until their identities as POWs were acknowledged and recorded by a commanding officer. To support his case, Roberts was able to brandish a pullover with a 'Made in Australia' label. Their status established, the officer released his captives with the instruction that they might go where they wished. Yet he happily met Roberts' request that he write out a chit to identify them when, almost inevitably, they encountered further troops. Issued on 17 April 1945 on the side of a road at a place called Kleinschlag, it saved Roberts and his companions much effort, possibly saved their lives, and entitled them to free rides in whichever direction they chose.[27]

Eventually they made their way to Budapest, where in the railway yards they noticed British prisoners of war sitting in the doorways of box wagons. They had come from Stalag XVII A at Krems, many via a Viennese hospital. Their train was heading to Odessa, an opportunity Roberts thought too good to pass up. Through Timisoara, Bucharest and Focsani, then down through Bessarabia, the train finally made its way to Odessa, where the journey ended. At their destination the men bathed in the warm waters of the Black Sea, and then, on 3 May 1945, four years and four days since his capture in Greece, Roberts embarked for Naples and its repatriation camp on the Norwegian freighter *Bergenfjord*.[28]

Altogether some 150 Australians[29] made their way to freedom via Odessa, across the Black Sea and down through the Dardanelles, at which point some might have been pondering the fate of an earlier generation. By the middle of April, the first of them were back in Australia. They were forbidden from talking to the press, but they were able to let the authorities know how the Soviets had treated them, and by and large they seem to have had few complaints. They told of how they had avoided the forced marches by hiding from the Germans, before taking up contact with the Red Army and moving to Odessa. The circumstances in which they were held might have been primitive, but they were no worse than those with which the Soviet soldiers themselves had to contend. On reaching Odessa they were given better quarters and better treatment, allegedly because of reports of the favourable treatment of Soviets liberated on the Western Front. As for the delicate issue of working for the Soviets, the men confirmed that this had been required, but they brushed it aside as a bone of contention – a 'no work no food' policy was being applied, after all, throughout Soviet occupied territory.[30]

When Allied ground forces from East and West famously met up at Torgau on the Elbe on Anzac Day 1945, tensions were eased, at least for the time being. The fate of the Reich was sealed; with every day men of all Allied armies were being liberated. Moreover, the use of Odessa as a transit camp was now redundant. British and American soldiers liberated by the Red Army could now be sent west along a land route, as could Soviets towards the east. At least in theory.

Many ex-POWs lacked the patience to stay put while the authorities organised formal exchanges. Despite the obvious dangers involved in a country still very much at war, many took their fate into their own hands, seeking to flee the Soviet zone, crossing front lines and running the gauntlet of a scared or even hostile population to seek the haven of British or American forces. In some cases the Soviets were happy for them to go – with a war still to be won, unless the ex-POWs could offer some useful service then they were little more than extra, unwelcome mouths to feed. Yet even with the elation of liberation and impending victory, high politics continued to raise its ugly head.

This was evident in the case of the large Soviet-liberated camps still holding substantial populations of British and American POWs. Stalag III A Luckenwalde, located just south of Berlin, was one of them. So many POWs had been marched west to Luckenwalde, including airmen from Stalag Luft III, that by April it was brimming. In other circumstances Luckenwalde would have been nothing more than a halfway house, but with Allied forces approaching from east and west, there was nowhere else to go.

Much to the disappointment of the British POWs, it was the Soviets who got to Luckenwalde first. Had the Senior British Officer in the camp, Wing Commander R.C.M. Collard, had his way, then all of those under his command would have broken out beforehand to strike towards American lines. The window of opportunity slammed shut before any action could be taken. The Germans left the camp on 21 April; by 22 April the Red Army was at the gates. An armoured column entered the camp to the loud cheers of the inmates, its tanks effortlessly demolishing the barbed wire fences which had held so many for so long. Yet for the Australians and many others inside, it was a moment of intense ambivalence, signalling both liberation and an agonising thwarting of the boundless relief which should have marked that moment. The Soviets were not prepared to let the British and Americans go, at least not yet. They happily allowed Soviet POWs to leave the camp, but not the rest, not until certain matters pending were resolved elsewhere.[31]

The exquisite frustration of the situation was not lost on the Australian airman Wilf Hodgson, who had been evacuated to Luckenwalde from Stalag Luft III. The initial joy was followed by the sobering realisation that all was not over. As the first wave of Soviets passed, the POWs were left to fend for themselves; foraging parties had to be organised to requisition food supplies and livestock in the surrounding area. But in the chaos of the last days of the war, there were competing claims for precious foodstuffs as soldiers, civilians, refugees and POWs crisscrossed the countryside, desperate to avoid the ironic fate of a cruel death on the very eve of peace.[32] Within a week Soviet staff had taken up residence in the camp, though much of the internal administration remained in the hands of British and American POWs. Food supplies and standards of sanitation became desperate, despite the best efforts of the forage parties.[33]

Finally on 3 May an American convoy of ambulances arrived and took away, with the approval of the Soviets, all seriously ill American and six of the ill British POWs. Three days later an American prisoner of war contact officer from SHAEF arrived with a convoy of lorries to remove the remaining British and American POWs. The Soviets would have none of it, claiming they had not received orders to allow an evacuation. Undeterred, the Americans attempted to stage the evacuation anyway, but as they loaded the lorries the Soviets began to fire over their heads. Some POWs had been loaded and could still make good their evacuation in this way; the Americans, the Australian airman Wes Betts believed, 'looked after us like their own'.[34] But most of the men were still stuck in the camp, their morale, as Wing Commander Collard noted, 'naturally deplorable'.[35]

On 7 May, the German surrender just a day away, another American officer turned up with yet another convoy of trucks. The officer was persuaded to initiate negotiations with the Soviets to avoid a repeat of the events four days earlier. This time the Americans were told that the Soviets would be in possession of repatriation orders the following day, so they agreed to return then, only to find the Soviets still unprepared to part with men who now had effectively become their POWs. As the haggling continued, the Americans began loading their trucks and staged a partial evacuation without Soviet agreement. When the Soviets became aware that the men were being whisked away, they intervened to insist that the remaining lorries depart empty. It was clear to Collard that the Soviets were prepared to use arms to prevent further departures.[36]

Not until 19 May, with the war over more than a week, did the Soviets give word that the remaining British and American POWs would be sent west across the Elbe the following day. True to their word this time, they delivered the men to American forces, who took them to Halle and from there flew them to the UK. Understandably, the frustrations of the previous weeks had left a sour taste in the mouths of these men, even if Collard acknowledged that the Soviets' flaws did not necessarily stem from ill-will. Those, like himself, who came in contact with them 'took a friendly though somewhat exasperated view of them', while those who merely suffered their recalcitrance from a distance 'probably gained the impression that they were aggressive, incompetent and uncultured'.[37]

The other major camp with a sizeable population to be liberated by the Red Army was Stalag IV B Mühlberg in Saxony. It, too, had a mixture of soldiers and airmen among its swollen ranks. By the time they had the dubious pleasure of being liberated by Soviet forces on 23 April, the camp was in a truly wretched state. A report filed by the Protecting Power in February had lamented the decline in standards since the previous visit. Conditions in the barracks, the inspectors chided, 'are now even more appalling. Window panes broken and barracks soaking. Since the arrival of American POWs there is serious overcrowding with approximately 1200 POWs per barracks [. . .] These conditions are causing an increase in cases of dysentery, diphtheria and respiratory problems.'[38]

As the Eastern Front approached, the Germans laid a couple of enticing options before their prisoners. They could either join their guards in heading west across the Elbe, away from the Soviets, or they could stay behind and fend for themselves in the camp. Some of the prisoners, including Poles, took the first option, but Ron Zwar stayed put to witness the arrival of Cossacks on horseback, galloping across the Elbe plain in pursuit of retreating Germans. Zwar was among those evacuated to a camp at Riesa, 25 kilometres to the south, where he was held for some weeks. Far from imposing their authority on the camp, the Soviets allowed the POWs to forage for their own food – indeed, they had no option but to feed themselves. Zwar found them every bit as trigger happy as the Germans had been – he was shot at not once but twice. It was with great relief then that he, too, was transferred to American care in Halle.[39]

Zwar's fellow South Australian Jim Reeves was also based at Mühlberg, but as a soldier he was at a work detachment near the Czech border when the end of hostilities neared. With the Red Army approaching, the guards marched him and his fellow POWs over the border heading south-west, until one morning they woke up to find that the guards had deserted their post. Their freedom had arrived as they slept, and it presented a new set of problems. Continuing their trek westwards, they came across a company of Red Army soldiers, whose commanding officer invited them to stay with them. He added ominously, however, that he would be obliged to take them back to Russia. It was a prospect which appeared to suit neither party. The Soviets' first priority on that evening was to seek the comfort of the bottle. As they slept, Reeves and his companions stole their vehicle, putting as much distance between themselves and the Soviets as they could before ditching the truck and heading further west on foot.

The last stage of Reeves' bid for freedom was negotiated on a bicycle, acquired with sufficient money gained by gambling to satisfy the civilian owner. In the company of just one other Australian at this time, Reeves and his companion passed uneventfully through a desultory German defence line. In truth its soldiers might well have preferred the ignominy of surrender to two Australian ex-POWs on bicycles than a further encounter with the wrath of the Red Army. But Reeves and his friend were delighted to leave both 'Jerry' and 'Ivan' behind as they entered the mobile, welcoming and implausibly well-stocked world of the American Third Army.[40]

For others, too, the contact with the Soviets was mercifully brief. Phil Loffman was one of those who had arrived in Germany via a sojourn in Italy. He worked at the Sudetenländische Treibstoffwerke, a massive fuel plant producing petrol from coal, until it had to be evacuated in May 1945 as the Red Army approached. He, a Briton called Sailor and a mass of civilian labourers set off to the south-west in the hope of an uneventful crossing of American lines. But it was Soviet forces in the form of a roadblock that they encountered at Kasterec nad Ohr. In a moment of high suspense, Loffman had to employ his skills of persuasion to convince his Soviet interlocutors that he and his British companion were Allies. Persuaded and mollified, the Soviets allowed the ragtag crew to commandeer a German horse and cart with which to continue their journey westwards; it was an outcome which suited both parties. Within a short distance they were able to swap the horse and cart for a German utility vehicle to continue across no-man's land. It was a place laden with mortal dangers, resembling, as Loffman puts it, 'the eye of the cyclone – deserted, quiet, tense, uneasy'. Near Carlsbad they finally reached American lines, and with them the comfort that liberation would take the form of a plane ride to Brussels and then England rather than a journey east into the unfamiliar world of a Soviet Union ravaged by war.[41]

Kevin McAuliffe's contact with the Red Army was longer but had the same outcome. He was working on a farm near Spittal in Austria when he slipped away on 1 April. With another Australian, Richard Head, he managed to survive for some five weeks outside captivity until Soviet forces arrived. When approached these Soviets, too, were understandably apprehensive, but both sides had sufficient knowledge of French to be persuaded to trust each other. Indeed, the two Australians spent a couple of weeks with the Soviet platoon, whose brief was to collect motor vehicles of all kinds and send them to the Soviet Union. As they did so, they moved westwards across Austria, running at times into small pockets of German resistance, until they reached a river near Linz. On the other side of it were Americans, who agreed to take over the care of the two Australians. The Americans, too, found some use for them, posting them to one of their own platoons before evacuating them to Britain.[42]

As they hurried east through southern Germany and Austria, eager to nip in the bud any prospect that German forces might assemble in an Alpine redoubt, American forces picked up countless POW stragglers. They were expecting them and, with the kind of logistics of which the Red Army could only dream, were better equipped to look after them. SHAEF had set up a department labelled PWX to deal with them, and all of the Allied powers, including Australia, had liaison officers attached to PWX.[43] The bulk of the work of those officers was not devoted to the stragglers but to the men in the camps, now being liberated one by one. There were 16 Australian officers who had the job of combing those liberated camps, looking for Australians, or at least reliable word on where they might be, and then arranging transport to the UK.[44]

It was the Americans who liberated the bloated monster that Stalag VII A at Bavarian Moosburg had become. It was a *Stalag* with which Australians had a long association dating back to 1941, when many had been taken there directly from Salonika. But in 1945 the great majority of its miserable denizens had been evacuated there from the east, and after reaching Moosburg there was nowhere else to go.

There were even airmen among them, including Noel Collins, who along with thousands of others impatiently awaited the Americans' arrival. He had been evacuated from Nuremberg to Moosburg, surviving raids by American fighter aircraft along the way, and finding a hideously overfilled camp when he reached Moosburg on Hitler's last birthday, 20 April 1945. The arrival of American ground forces was just a question of time. Early one morning he awoke to find that there was not a German in sight – all of the personnel had left the camp. Then a rumbling noise became audible, until American tanks came into view, bursting over a hill and setting a course for the camp. Pausing only to blast a die-hard machine-gun nest, the tanks drove straight through the gates, knocking down the barbed wire separating the compounds. In their trail of destruction walked an American general toting pearl-handled pistols, announcing his pleasure at liberating the captives and reassuring them they would be home soon. In his footsteps, about an hour later, a mobile bakery arrived distributing fresh white bread, tacitly proclaiming the arrival of a new order.[45]

John Mathews, also an airman, remained alive to witness the arrival of the Americans, but it had been a close thing. Suffering from chronic dysentery, he found two items in the Red Cross parcels invaluable, if not life-saving. Each parcel had a piece of hard cheddar cheese and a cake of unsweetened dark chocolate. His mate fed him these two items, both known as 'bung holes', for three days on end as he sat on the toilet, until the dysentery mercifully abated. Then it was a matter of passing the time through a period of acute privation – among other things by pulling apart and reknitting a woollen scarf perhaps twenty times – until the Americans arrived.[46]

Inside the camp he and others heard enough of hostilities to know of the Americans' proximity, then word went around that the prisoners should stay in their barracks, ensure they had sufficient food, and not expose themselves to any danger of being caught up in the fighting. Suddenly it was apparent that the guards had disappeared, and then the American tanks made short work of the barbed wire fences. The Americans sought to impress on the men the need to stay put, but the starving Soviets ignored them and made their way immediately to the nearby village, scouting for food. They soon returned with slaughtered animals. On the second day of freedom, Mathews too ventured outside the camp and into the village, where he talked with the locals, who were deeply depressed but making an effort to be pleasant now that the tables had turned. It was a strange place, Mathews noted, devoid of males between the ages of about fifteen and fifty.[47]

Ray Corbett, one of the Australian soldiers liberated in Moosburg, had marched there all the way from Blechhammer in Silesia and been placed in an NCO compound. He, too, recalls the arrival of the Americans and the scattering of the Germans into the distance across the surrounding fields. After the hardship of the last months of the war, and especially of the march, his mood was not of elation and exuberance; rather, he felt like a 'stunned mullet'. Nor did he detect elation on the faces of the Americans. Quite the opposite; in his recollection they were white with anger. Nearby Dachau had just been liberated; by this point at the latest the American forces had a clear idea of what they were dealing with.[48]

The main British NCOs' camp at Hohenfels in Bavaria was also liberated by Americans. Keith Hooper was among the 'Hohenfellows' determined to stay in the camp as the Americans approached it. He was among seven Australians who secreted themselves in cellars, keen to avoid the perils of a forced march on the open road. Others were under the barracks or even in the latrines. The discomforts of hiding were balanced by the sounds of artillery

LIBERATION

getting closer day by day. Eventually he and a mate called Frank escaped from the camp, by now guarded in a cursory fashion, and headed off to meet American lines. The greatest highlight was not the initial moment of contact but shortly thereafter at the airport in Erlangen. He not only saw Marlene Dietrich as she stepped, clad in an American uniform, from a DC3, but he managed to kiss her. She was, he recalled, shorter than expected.[49]

Back at Hohenfels the eventual arrival of the Americans was heralded by wing-dipping Thunderbolts. On 22 April ground forces followed to claim the camp, now emptied of its guards, triggering huge relief and a lively barter with the civilians in the local village. For a time after liberation some of the men even lived in the village, hosted by families who had calculated that a last-minute display of compassion towards their new masters would hold them in good stead in the longer term.[50]

Laurie West was among those who had been force-marched out of Hohenfels before the Americans arrived. Conditions in the camp had reached desperation point. To heat the barracks, every second slat from the bunks and every second beam from the ceilings had been burnt, and in some cases even walls had been removed and fed into the little stove as it strained to keep winter at bay. There was no other fuel available. To take their minds off the cold, during the day the men would stare at the massive formations of American aircraft blacking out the sky. The knowledge that Patton's ground forces would surely follow helped keep their spirits high. But then most of the men were marched towards Regensburg, stopping in provisional accommodation along the way and trying to keep clear of strafing American fighters. White Angels – lorries bearing Red Cross parcels – brought some temporary relief, but more than in the past few years the men relied on their own resourcefulness, and their scrounging instincts, to survive. Eventually a single reconnaissance aircraft foretold the appearance of a sprinkle of American soldiers, which in turn became a mass as Patton's 80th Division materialised in their midst and declared their captivity over. Most of the Americans pressed on to the east, but one of the American sergeants paused to express his pleasure. For him the liberation of these men – the first POWs they had come across – was the greatest day of the war; it had made the landing at Omaha Beach and the fighting since then worthwhile.[51]

British forces, too, played the role of liberators, both in the deep south of the Reich and in the north. And like the other Allies, they liberated men already on the run, those in columns trudging through the German countryside, as well as those confined to camps. With the capitulation of German forces in Italy in early May, British forces were free to spill over the Alps and into Austria, where there were still good numbers of Australians, especially at Stalag XVIII A Wolfsberg. There had been some evacuations to Markt Pongau in April, but as the last month of the war began most waited impatiently in the *Stalag* for their liberators to appear. On 8 May five British soldiers parachuted into a nearby field, and Camp Commandant Steiner, proper to the last, handed command to the Senior British Medical Officer and the various Men of Confidence, including the Australian Ernest Stevenson. On that joyful day a kind of multinational conference was staged on the camp parade ground, the *Appellplatz*, and then the POWs formally relieved their erstwhile guards of their weapons and took control of the armoury, the post office and the local railway station.[52]

Other parts of Austria witnessed similar scenes. The very next day, 9 May, units of the British 8th Army arrived at Stalag XVIII A/Z Spittal, formally taking over a camp that in effect was already in the hands of its prisoners. The Americans, too, got in on the act of liberating Spittal; later that day they conducted a bombing raid on the camp, its payload comprising several hundred kilograms of food supplies, cigarettes and sweets. So intense was the raid that, as the YMCA delegate who happened to be in the camp noted, roofs, walls and windows were destroyed – and happily no lives lost. The rejoicing, he wrote, was 'indescribable'.[53]

Doug Nix, too, was in southern Austria as British forces approached from the south, but he was not in a camp. Like the POWs, the locals, too, were relieved to learn that it was a British and not a Soviet front which was destined to envelop their district. For them it had no longer been a case of winning or losing the war, but of just who would claim the spoils of victory first. They went so far as to cheer the British presence. Nix and others commandeered a car and made to the British lines, encountering a forward party in a tank. Behind that first line there were British field security authorities who could use his knowledge of the area and his German language skills. For a time Nix acted as a kind of interpreter and intermediary, tracking down and questioning Austrian collaborators. After about a month he was instructed to report to an authority in Klagenfurt. From there he was transferred by plane to the UK via Naples.[54]

In north-western Germany it was British forces which liberated men who were still in their marching columns, having spent the last weeks of the war shunted from one overcrowded camp to the next. Paul Brickhill was among the airmen marched from Sagan in January and then from the naval camp at Westertimke in April. From there the column had headed north; even the guards may not have known what their destination might be. One day a couple of tanks approached Brickhill's column; at first it was unclear if they were German or British. The tension was broken when two 'Tommies' emerged from the hatch of the leading tank, the first of them proclaiming in a thick cockney accent the liberation of the bedraggled masses gathered before him.[55]

Westertimke, which Brickhill had been forced to leave, was liberated by British forces on 28 April. By that time the population of naval personnel in the Marlag and merchant seamen in the Milag had swollen to include soldiers and airmen. Not far away across the plain, the camps at Fallingbostel, both Stalag XI B and Stalag 357, had been freed on 16 April. There to witness the event was the Australian war correspondent Chester Wilmot. Wilmot had observed the battlefield heroics of Australian forces in the Western Desert, when they had cut physically imposing figures. Four years of captivity in the Reich had changed all that: 'I saw them in hospital – drawn, haggard, starved – starved beyond description – limbs like matchsticks, bodies shrunken till their bones stood out like knuckles.'[56]

Not all made it to the end. Caught cruelly short was Sydneysider

Lawrence Saywell, a veteran of Crete. In early January he and a New Zealander, Sydney 'Mac' Kerkham, escaped from a detachment at Pardubice and found refuge in Czech territory near the village of Zderaz. An image in the Australian War Memorial shows Saywell during his period in hiding from the Germans. He and Kerkham remained there until the first week of May 1945, when they made their way to Miretin. There they became embroiled in a confrontation between retreating German forces and a Czech–Soviet partisan group which had taken German officers hostage in a school. Saywell intervened, offering his services to break the standoff, but then was shot by a German soldier.[57] It was 8 May, the very last day of the war in Europe. Saywell was the 242nd and last of the Australian POWs to die in Europe.[58]

The living were shepherded to collecting points in Halle, Brussels and Rheims, from where they would be flown to the UK in American Dakotas or RAF Lancasters; a minority were sent south of the Alps to Naples or Bari to commence their journeys home by ship. Physically the men had been removed from the Reich, yet mentally it was apparent that part of them was still there, as one of the Lancaster pilots, Peter Johnson, observed: 'They were tired and still numb from their freedom. Many were emaciated from lack of proper food. It was queer that not one of those that I brought back said "Thank you" to the crew.'[59]

The airman Ron Mackenzie has fond memories of his English 'homecoming' after four years in captivity. He and others wept openly so as nearly to drown the aircraft. They flew over 'grey and dirty and lovely London' before landing to be greeted by WAAFs, who insisted on carrying the men's bags. To his surprise, Mackenzie soon found that he, too, was being carried down the ladder by the women; now he laughed quite madly while they cried because he was almost not there at all, so much weight had he lost in the preceding weeks. The next steps were simple enough: 'Deloused. Waited. Met several blokes, drank tea and ate a very little – still ill – then by truck to London.'[60]

The Australians were then taken to the south coast of England. For the Australian soldiers a reception centre was established in

Gowrie House in Eastbourne. Billets and messes were set up in large residential buildings in the town; the men could renew acquaintances and swap stories as they waited for news of berths on ships heading to Australia.

For the airmen being flown from the Continent, the coast of England was no novelty, but it was a no less welcome sight for that. For them this was more of a homecoming than it was for the soldiers, for most of whom England was a foreign country. But the airmen knew something of England, had acquaintances or perhaps even girlfriends there. For some 900 of them an ex-POWs' reception centre was set up in Brighton's Metropole Hotel, also on the Sussex coast. Staffed with welfare, rehabilitation and education officers, Brighton, like Eastbourne to its east, was a crucial step in the preparation for life after captivity and war.[61] Ron Mackenzie and others were 'fed like princes and lived like lords'.[62]

For most of the men who had freshly emerged from POW camps, even the most benign institutions, as Eastbourne and Brighton were, could not hold them long. Providing they passed their medical tests and completed debriefings, they collected pay, a leave pass and a ticket entitling them to free travel throughout the UK, and they set off to see the country, perhaps to visit relatives close or far, and to savour liberty at long last.[63]

Freedom meant the chance to spend time with the locals, not least with women. The company of women was a huge fillip after up to four years behind barbed wire. British women had found young men to be in short supply for some years, and in 1945 they confronted the stark reality of another demographic imbalance caused by war. There was much that spoke in favour of liaisons being formed in those postwar weeks and months in Britain; in many cases they turned into years and decades on the other side of the world. By the time the Parrott boys, Charlie and Mark, both of them former POWs, were ready to return to Australia, they had married sisters. On his wedding day Charlie weighed all of 45 kilograms.[64]

Through May, June and July thousands of Australian ex-POWs were given berths to the other side of the world.[65] Typically they were taken by rail to Liverpool, from where they sailed via the Panama Canal and New Zealand to Australia – an Australia that was still at war.

Aftermath

The library in Colditz Castle contained a book by the Australian author Ernestine Hill titled *My Love Must Wait*.[1] It was Hill's only fictional work, based closely on the life of Matthew Flinders. Shortly before leaving on his great voyage to circumnavigate Australia, Flinders had married his sweetheart, Ann Chappell. The Royal Navy insisted Ann could not possibly accompany her husband on his voyage. She stayed behind, writing letters to Matthew on the other side of the globe, expressing her love and her desire that he would return home soon. Alas, in sailing home in a leaking boat, Flinders was forced to call at the French island of Mauritius, or Île de France. Unbeknown to him, France and England were again at war. He was duly detained, effectively a prisoner of war. Not until 1810 did he make landfall in England to be reunited with Ann, from whom he had been separated for some nine years. By this time his health was irretrievably compromised, and Flinders died a slow and painful death in 1814.

Published in Sydney in 1941, *My Love Must Wait* was a resounding success. English and American editions soon followed. Clearly Hill had struck a nerve among a readership for whom the ache of extended absence had become so widely shared. The imprisonment of Australians, whether by Germans, Italians or Japanese, was a burden not only for the POWs themselves but for their friends and loved ones a world away.

Not much could be done to ease the load of those whose love had to wait. Like Matthew and Ann, the POWs and their families could write, but there were limits to what could be said. Parcels, too, might be sent, but they might take a long time to reach their addressee, if they reached him at all. While the Red Cross did what it could to keep the minds and bodies of POWs in good order, it tried to salve the pain of the relatives back home as well. From May 1942 it issued a monthly newsletter, *The Prisoner of War*, and sent it free of charge to all registered next of kin.[2] With its staged photographs and carefully worded reports, it was not necessarily a reliable guide to what the POWs were experiencing, but for all its confected rosiness its offerings were at least better than total ignorance.

The men who finally came back in the second half of 1945 were no longer the lads who had departed years earlier. Even in the best of times, those years of their lives would have changed them. But these men had lived through the worst of times; physically and mentally they had been exposed to challenges quite alien to the worlds of their loved ones back home. The world to which they now returned would take some getting used to. When the POWs arrived from Europe through the middle months of 1945, it was to an Australia still at war. The formal Japanese surrender would not be signed until September. The men arrived to find an austere and still anxious homeland. Some learned of the passing of a parent or a sibling; those with children of their own discovered how much they had grown up during the years of their absence. With the relief of survival and return recorded, the men and their families had to renegotiate their relationships, even to try to get to know each other afresh.

Physically the former POWs appeared well enough, especially when compared, as they inevitably were, with the men returning from Japanese captivity through September and October. But that appearance deceived. Their time in Eastbourne, Brighton and on the ships sailing halfway round the world had restored flesh to their bones, but secretly they carried wounds and illnesses that would plague them for what remained of their lives.

Numbers by themselves tell a story. More than 22,000 Australians had become POWs of the Japanese, and of them over 8000 had perished in captivity. By contrast 8592 Australians became POWs in Europe, of whom all but 242 experienced liberation.[3] On figures alone, the POWs in Japanese hands had it worse – much worse. And yet behind those stark statistics a study carried out in the 1980s among some 2000 ex-POWs, from both European and Japanese captivity, revealed some remarkable similarities and surprises. In both groups, just over a quarter still suffered from hypertension needing treatment, while a similar number suffered from chronic indigestion. Even four decades after the war 14.5 per cent of the POWs from Europe still had chronic diarrhoea. The greatest cause of complaint in both groups was impotence, reaching one-third among the POWs from Japan and about one-sixth in the POWs from Europe.

Hard work, poor nutrition and the shortage of adequate medication and treatment caused other ongoing problems, ranging from heart disease to skin problems and chronic bronchitis – pneumonia had been a major cause of death in the camps and work detachments. The habit of smoking to relieve both boredom and hunger not only caused damage during captivity – which was longer for most of the POWs in Europe than those in Japanese captivity – but typically continued into postwar civilian life with predictably deleterious consequences.

The physical health of those who were liberated was assessed easily enough; the impact on their mental health was a thornier issue. The results of tests were disturbing. In both groups there were very high levels of men who suffered from anxiety – nearly half of the 'Japanese' and 37 per cent of the 'Europeans'. Interestingly, a diagnosis of stress was made in relation to a higher proportion of the latter – about 31 per cent, compared with 28 per cent of the prisoners of the Japanese. In the diagnosis of nervous dyspepsia, too, the 'Europeans' had the dubious distinction of recording higher levels – 26 per cent compared to 25 per cent. In both groups it was noted that many had difficulties concentrating for any length of time, many suffered nightmares and were unable to sleep without the aid of a sedative, and their marriages ended in an above average number of divorces.[4] In short, as the study put it with pithy directness, psychologically 'all POW took an enormous battering'.[5]

Given the experiences they had endured, none of this could be surprising; indeed, it was predicted that mental health problems would emerge with return to civilian life. They might stem from acute trauma, but they might equally have their origins in profound, prolonged and demoralising boredom – a danger recognised as early as in a 1944 psychological report. Over years of camp captivity, the report's author P.H. Norman observed, 'the prisoner is relieved from the struggle of life; he no longer has to work for his living, shoulder responsibility, or worry financially. Nothing that he does within the camp can relieve any threatening situation at home, and therefore his occupations lose their significance as acts of vital importance and become merely a pastime to amuse himself and defeat his own boredom.' In short, the prisoner finds great difficulty in attributing a greater meaning to his activity, a difficulty which might well accompany him into his post-captivity years. On returning home, Norman warned, the former prisoner might be inclined to suffer 'restlessness, irritability, disrespect for discipline and authority, irresponsibility and even dishonesty. Other symptoms that occur are the fear of enclosed spaces, cynicism, embarrassment in society, rebellious views against any code which tends to restrict the repatriated man's activities, and a tendency to quick and violent temper.' Under these circumstances it was vital that men showing such symptoms 'shall not be regarded as abnormal', because in reality he was 'a normal person attempting to bridge a gap in his life'.[6]

Help, then, in adjusting to post-captivity existence was of the greatest importance. The ex-POW, Norman warned, was 'temporarily without the sheet anchor of his daily routine, he has laid aside his habits of recreational relaxation and he has lost the art of working for his living'. It was reasonable, then, to suppose 'that at this point a little help from someone who understands the position may be of great assistance'.[7] The British War Office's POW Directorate agreed that something had to be done to help these men, advising accordingly that all POWs who had spent more than four years in captivity, and most who had spent more than three – these categories covered most of the Australians – would need 'mental rehabilitation'. Even a fifth of those who had endured fewer than three years would need psychiatric help.[8]

It was in the reception centres in England that the first steps to adjusting to life outside captivity would be taken. Great effort was made to render the transition to life outside the barbed wire as smooth as possible, because the men, the experts concurred, would not tolerate even minor annoyances well. 'Physical disabilities, psychological disturbances as a result of their confinement, harsh treatment and isolation in camps, all help to make the ex POW an individual to whom special treatment must be offered.'[9]

Back in Australia, alas, there was precious little help available. Authorities were dimly aware of a phenomenon among veterans of the Great War to which the hopelessly fuzzy label 'shell shock' had been attached, but they had little sense of how it might be treated. An effective treatment of trauma, whether experienced before or during captivity, was at best a pipe-dream in a time when the term 'post traumatic stress disorder' was still to be coined. No formal mechanisms were put in place to allow the ex-POWs to work though their experiences and adjust to a frightening new world not confined by barbed-wire fences and regulated by an iron routine.

Not only were there no formal structures to guide men through readjustment, commonly the stories they wished to tell went unheard even by those closest to them. As long as the war still raged in the Pacific, there was little incentive to listen to – or indeed to tell – tales of years spent in captivity on the other side of the world. Hal Finkelstein, a medical orderly repatriated before the end of the war, observed the slide into silence when he was back in Perth. At first he would talk about what he had been through, albeit leaving out the grimmer parts. But then things changed: 'Strangely enough, about a year or so later when I met the girl I got married to, in her home, nobody ever said a word about the war and I felt a little bit slighted that they weren't even interested in where I'd been and what had happened. I never said anything, and years and years later their sister told me they were forbidden to.'[10] The men retreated into reticence. If there were few willing listeners, except perhaps the small circles of their fellow sufferers who knew exactly what they had been through, then it was best to keep their stories to themselves. After all, if a taciturn resilience had guided them through the hard years of the Depression and the bleaker years of captivity, then it would serve through the aftermath of war as well.

Amid the silent world of a retreat into their memories, many struggled to attribute redemptive qualities to their captivity. The most sanguine among them reasoned that the war had given them a breadth of knowledge which they could not have acquired in Australia. Reg Worthington acknowledged his war had given him 'an awful lot of experience, a lot of understanding of human nature'. Four years of living in often crowded circumstances among men suffering many forms of hardship, mental and physical, taught him tolerance and patience. 'That's one thing in the army, in the prison camp, you need is patience. Time drags very slowly at times.'[11] Charlie Parrott, too, was able to find the positive in his experiences: 'We weren't war mongers, we wanted adventure. Although I did four years in a prisoner of war camp it was a great adventure. I saw a lot of the world I'd never ever have seen if I hadn't.'[12]

Hal Finkelstein sagely balanced the good with the bad. Captivity in Germany had deprived him of the rich times he might have experienced as a young man still growing up in Australia. On the other hand, his years as a POW had brought experiences of a kind 'that you wouldn't get in three lifetimes. I never regretted going to the war and I don't regret any of the experiences that I had because they enriched my life incredibly.' His time in captivity, he says, 'taught me how to live with people, be more tolerant and it made me appreciate a lot of things about the community that we lived in'.[13] In a similar vein the airman Calton Younger conceded that he had learned much from his time as a POW and did not regret those years. Yet, he lamented, 'it was a very long time before I conquered a restless preoccupation with the past'.[14]

Doug Nix was among the many who suffered various health consequences from his POW years, including recurring nervous reactions. Eventually he too was classified 'TPI' – Totally and Permanently Incapacitated. Yet he wonders nonetheless whether the prolonged hardship might have toughened him up, conferring a level of endurance he would not otherwise have had.[15] Mentally, too, that piece of his past is always with him. All the experiences and exposure to human beings it provided made him into a much more careful observer of human behaviour than he would otherwise have been.[16]

Others, however, could draw only an unremittingly bleak assessment of the years behind barbed wire. They saw them as lost years, as time stolen by malevolent forces beyond their control; there was no adequate recompense then, nor could there ever be. The postwar world was one of a silence filled with suffering and anger, not redemption. Captivity had cost them opportunities to prove their valour on the field of battle, to make their way up through the ranks, to do their bit to bring the Reich to its knees. For these men the war had been 'a waste of time'.[17] Years that might have been spent in the bosom of family and community had been irretrievably lost. Moreover, they found it hard not to dwell on a litany of physical problems they could trace to their time in Germany, to injuries incurred at work, illnesses contracted in captivity that they could never completely shake.

It was the legacy of mental anguish, however, its causes and its cures so elusive, that caused the greatest difficulties for the men and their families. Many noted a tormenting restiveness, an inability to settle down. Patrick Toovey was one of them; his health was poor and he could not settle into a new career. Eventually he was diagnosed with 'war neurosis' and given shock treatment. He retired at 49 and, like many former POWs, became a member of the TPI Association and the Ex-POW Association. There was some comfort, at least, in seeking the company of those who had gone through similar misfortune.

Ernest Brough recognised a kind of wildness within himself, a legacy of living on his instincts for so long. It was no easy matter to tame it, and in the worst of the postwar years there were days when 'you would only have to look at me the wrong way back then and I'd have a go at you'. He eventually entered a rehabilitation program, but he knew full well in himself that it would take 'a long, long time yet to work the war out of my system'.[18] The depths of despair led him, like countless others, to contemplate suicide: 'One shot would fix everything, I thought.' He was one of the lucky ones who did not go so far.[19]

Some turned to drink. Bill Cousins recalls a phase after the war when he would take a 'bomb' at night in the hope of a sleep without dreams – or nightmares.[20] The airman Alex Jenkins, a veteran of the vicious raid on Dresden, recalls experiencing nightmares even decades after the war. In his sleep he would inadvertently kick his wife black and blue until she would wake him as he screamed or was bathed in a cold sweat. For him and many others who knew what it was to be – and to have been – a 'kriegie', pubs were a place where they could share their memories in the hope of coming to terms with them.[21]

For Laurie West the physical legacy of protracted imprisonment was long evident but eventually overcome as his body, after many months of freedom, returned to the weight of the 21-year-old who had enlisted many years earlier. Alas, the mental legacy was more enduring, and he himself was aware that worlds of maturity distinguished him from other young men who had not known war or captivity. His character had acquired a seriousness quite alien to men not much younger than himself. Moreover, many years of taking orders from others, of living within the tight, unbudging parameters of the POW, with neither the freedom nor the need to make many decisions of his own, had lent his character a passive edge. He observed a diffidence, a lack of assertiveness in his behaviour which accompanied him through the postwar years, even as he worked to build a new life.[22]

As for Wal Steilberg, the escape artist who had spent some six horrifying months in the Small Fortress at Terezín, he was one of those who for decades tended to suffer in silence. Yet if his mental anguish was hidden, the physical signs of an ongoing torment were there – ulcers, hypertension, and ultimately heart attacks. There were gaps in his experience which his memory at first could not fill. Over time he managed to slot more pieces into place, only to be reminded of some of the terrors he had witnessed. And then, he found, he was condemned to the new trauma of memories he could neither eject nor share: 'It's taken my whole life to get rid of the smell of that place. I try to forget it but, you know, it's impossible. If you weren't there, you just couldn't believe it, you just can't grasp what went on in that place. That's why I never talked about it.'[23]

In Europe, too, there were consequences. Hitler, the man ultimately responsible in the command structures of the Reich for the treatment of POWs, pre-empted any postwar reckoning, taking his own life in the garden of the Reich Chancellery, already a ruin, days before war's end. His record on POW matters alone would have guaranteed his execution had he ever faced justice, but of course his prosecutors would have had an abundance of indictments from which to choose.

The same might be said of those at the next level down in the Reich military hierarchy. Wilhelm Keitel, Hermann Göring and Alfred Jodl faced the International Military Tribunal in Nuremberg shortly after the war. The indictment for war crimes listed a number of instances of alleged breaches of international law, among them the murder of POWs.[24] Their roles in the cold-blooded murder of the 50 airmen who escaped from Stalag Luft III in March 1944 figured prominently in the charges against them, even if they had the death of countless others, overwhelmingly Soviets, on their conscience. In international law as it was practised at Nuremberg, the Geneva Convention meant something. As the hangman's noose was slipped around his neck, Keitel might well have wondered why Hitler had agreed to the Reich's ratification of Geneva in 1934. Alfred Jodl, who as Chief of Wehrmacht Operations also bore some responsibility for POW affairs, trod the same path to the gallows. As for Göring, unrepentant to the end, he took the coward's exit with the aid of a cyanide phial smuggled into his Nuremberg cell.

Heinrich Himmler, who took over responsibility for POWs from October 1944, ultimately betrayed his Führer; in an act of delusion, he sent out peace feelers, imagining that the Allies might deal with him of all people as the representative of the Reich. Dismissed of all posts and apprised of his moral standing in the eyes of the Allies, he sought to make himself scarce, was captured but took poison before he could be interrogated. His SS underling Ernst Kaltenbrunner in effect stood in for the dead Himmler at Nuremberg, where he shared the fate of Keitel and Jodl.

Himmler's right-hand man, Gottlob Berger, was luckier – much luckier, especially given his record of uncompromising devotion to his various SS offices before taking on the running of POW affairs. Berger's twelfth-hour theatrics performed before Colditz's *Prominente* was in all likelihood a calculated pitch to the postwar order, and it worked. Berger was, of course, put on trial after the war. Those who sat in judgment grappled with the ambivalence of his actions over many years, from his untiring devotion to the SS, his vicious suppression of Slovak resistance, to his deliberate contradiction of Hitler's wishes in aiding the Red Cross to supply food to POWs and in guiding the *Prominente* to safety. In the end he bore the distinction of being the only SS general tried at Nuremberg who, on appeal, was pronounced innocent.[25] A later appearance before an American military tribunal established that he had been guilty of war crimes, including atrocities against civilians. This time he was sentenced to 25 years in prison, but that was reduced to ten, and by 1951 he was a free man.

The hand of justice reached down to the lower levels of the perpetrator hierarchy as well, at least for a time. In the immediate aftermath of war, authorities scurried to collect evidence against all who might have been responsible for the death or maltreatment of POWs, including Australian POWs. The so-called Dulag Luft trial was held in Wuppertal in late 1945; in the dock were those Germans held responsible for the maltreatment of airmen in the transit camp. Interrogation was itself no crime in international law, but the forced extraction of information was. It was established that the Germans had indeed used the overheating of cells and threats of delivery into the hands of the Gestapo to achieve their ends. Of the five accused, three were found guilty.[26]

Treachery, too, did not go unpunished. Jacques Desoubrie, the French double-agent who betrayed many of the airmen sent to Buchenwald, was put on trial by a French court after the war, found guilty of treason and executed.[27] The English traitor and progenitor of the British Free Corps, John Amery, met a similar fate. His trial was like that of Lord Haw-Haw, quick and crowned with a judgment of guilty followed with almost indecent haste by the carrying out of the death sentence. In Amery's case the swiftness was especially controversial amid some suspicion that his loyalty to Franco in the Spanish Civil War had extended to the taking of Spanish citizenship.[28]

As in the major trial at Nuremberg, a special place in these postwar investigations and trials was reserved for those who had blood on their hands after the murder of the 50 airmen. Anthony Eden, after all, had sworn that the culprits would be brought to 'exemplary justice'.[29] To this end the Royal Air Force assembled its own Special Investigation Branch. Under the dedicated leadership of Francis McKenna, it left no stone unturned in tracking down those responsible for the murders. Their investigations completed, two trials were held in Hamburg in 1947 and 1948, 60 were charged with war crimes, leading ultimately to the execution by hanging of 13 of the perpetrators and to prison sentences for 17 others. One of the executed was Johannes Post, tracked down by McKenna's men in Minden. Without the merest hint of contrition, Post confessed that by following the orders of the Danzig Gestapo Chief Dr Günther Venediger, he had murdered James Catanach and others. Asked whether he wanted to enter any plea in mitigation, Post refused. Along with 12 others he was hanged in Hameln jail on 27 February 1948.[30]

Higher forces, perhaps, had already intervened in the judgments of two of the murderers of the Australians. Lux was killed in fighting around Breslau as the end of the war approached. Wilhelm

Scharpwinkel appears to have fallen into Soviet hands, where he could expect no favours. It is likely that he perished in Soviet captivity in October 1947.[31]

By the middle of 1948, the Cold War having warmed up, the British government was losing its taste for bringing German war criminals to account. 'Exemplary justice', it seems, had a use-by date determined by high politics.[32] Founded in May 1949, the Federal Republic of Germany became an ally in the Cold War, while the new face of totalitarianism was the Soviet Union, the state whose POWs had suffered most numerously and most severely in German captivity.

In all likelihood the last of the Reich's perpetrators of crimes against POWs to face justice was Anton Malloth, one of the guards at Terezín's Small Fortress, who earned the epithet 'schöner Toni' – 'handsome Tony'. It was not ironic – in the war he had been a dapper young man whose care devoted to his own experience contrasted strikingly with the vicious disregard he showed for the well-being of others. Malloth, who hailed from Austrian Innsbruck, had evaded the grasp of the Red Army in 1945 but was later snaffled in Austria. Czech authorities sought his extradition, and as they waited sentenced him to death in absentia. Rather than meeting their neighbour's request, the Austrians released Malloth, who promptly vanished into Italy. When in the 1970s there was revived interest in Terezín, West German justice began to show an interest in him, but the trail went cold. A German journalist by the name of Peter Finkelgruen, who thought Malloth to be his grandfather's murderer, continued to follow the scent, finding Malloth by now living near Munich and drawing on help provided to his ilk by Heinrich Himmler's daughter. It was only the appearance of a fresh witness, however, that brought Malloth, by now 89 years of age and in a wheelchair, before a court.[33] In June 2001 he was sentenced to life imprisonment.[34]

In Australia, the ex-POWs struggled for a different kind of justice. POWs of the Germans and Japanese alike pushed a case which was known as the 'Claim for Special Allowance to Ex-Prisoners of War 1939–1945'. To many it was simply the 'three shillings a day' case. When they were released from captivity, the men were able to receive their back pay, and for most there was a lot of it. What they were not granted, however, was the subsistence allowance to which soldiers living away from their base, and therefore needing to feed themselves, were entitled. This allowance amounted to three shillings a day. To receive that amount after the war, calculated over the period of their captivity, would have compensated them for time and money spent supporting themselves – and thereby saving the government money.

It was an idea first raised by the Ex-Prisoners of War Association in 1946, when the Chifley Labor government was in power. The government saw things differently.[35] It would be impossible to calculate the extent of disadvantage, and in any case the appropriate source of compensation and reparations was the detaining power. In the 1949 election campaign the Menzies Liberals made a 'three shillings a day' pitch to the POWs and their families. In power, however, they tied compensation to gaining reparations from the former detaining powers and in any case disowned the view that 'subsistence pay' was a right to which all former POWs were entitled.[36]

If there was recognition for those who returned from Europe, then it was at best in popular culture, and it was of the most ambivalent kind. Representations of POW experiences in film and on television were based on actual events, but in the most tenuous ways. Focusing on tales of escape and depicting an enemy that was either gormlessly naive or wickedly debonair, they had little to do with the everyday lives of the vast majority of POWs. When former POWs sought to tell their side of the story, then it was typically the officers' tales of spending their days outwitting Jerry which found publishers and readerships.

The lives of the many fell quietly into oblivion. If Australians had any inkling at all that there were ANZACs in the Second World War, then few wished to acknowledge that they had been captured in poorly conceived and dismally executed campaigns. Stories of subjection to wretched conditions in captivity before and during transport to the Reich, of mundane lives comprising back-breaking work and unrelieved boredom, fell largely on deaf ears. The tortures of the long marches and persistent anxieties as to their fate in the early months of 1945, followed by the assaults on their physical and mental health stretching long beyond the war, similarly went unheeded. If these men were to be accorded a place in the Anzac pantheon at all, then it was a quiet and dimly lit corner.

Decades after the war had ended, there were some rumblings of change. The Anzac myth had been built around the figure of the warrior hero, an imposing physical figure of resolute mind, who had triumphed in combat. By the end of the century the myth had broadened to encompass other qualities too, qualities which might manifest themselves beyond the field of battle as well as on it. Stoic resilience in the face of lasting hardship was one of them, mental agility in dealing with the unforeseen another. Above all, perhaps, there emerged an understanding of mateship which embraced not just altruism under fire but compassionate action outside of battle as well. The face and voice of this version of the Anzac legend was the former army surgeon 'Weary Dunlop', veteran of the campaigns in North Africa and Greece, but famous, and ultimately lionised, for his selfless devotion to the POWs of the Japanese.

It was a sign of these changing values that in 2001 the federal government granted ex-POWs a one-off grant in belated recognition of their suffering in the war and beyond it. But it was a grant made only to those who had been in Japanese captivity. The 'Europeans', from 1945 in the long shadow of their 'Japanese' mates, were explicitly denied this recognition. Apparently they had not suffered enough. Calling once more on their fighting powers, they fought for recognition, and, eventually, they won.

Today there are just a few hundred of these men alive. They have lived rich lives beyond the war; their time in captivity alone does not define who they are. But it shaped them, and it shaped those around them. To know what they have been through helps us to understand them, and ourselves.

Glossary

AIF	Australian Imperial Force
AA	Auswärtiges Amt (German Foreign Office)
AWA	Allgemeines Wehrmachtsamt (General Military Forces Office)
AWM	Australian War Memorial
AWStW	Auswertestelle West (the Luftwaffe's Intelligence Evaluation Centre at Oberursel)
BAMA	Bundesarchiv-Militärarchiv Freiburg im Breisgau (Federal Military Archives)
BFC	British Free Corps
Campo PG	*Campo Prigionieri di Guerra* (Italian prisoner of war camp)
CMF	Citizens Military Force
Dulag	*Durchgangslager* (transit camp)
EATS	Empire Air Training Scheme
Ferret	German guard checking for untoward behaviour
Gestapo	*Geheime Staatspolizei* (Secret State Police)
Heilag	*Heimkehrerlager* (camp for POWs to be repatriated)

GLOSSARY

ICRC	International Committee of the Red Cross
Ilag	*Internierungslager* (civilian internment camp)
IMI	Italian Military Internee
IWM	Imperial War Museum
Kriegie	Slang for *Kriegsgefangener* (prisoner of war)
LMF	Lacking Moral Fibre
Luftwaffe	German Air Force
NAA	National Archives of Australia
NCO	Non-commissioned officer
NSDAP	Nationalsozialistische Deutsche Arbeiterpartei (Nazi Party)
Oflag	*Offizierslager* (officers' camp)
OKH	Oberkommando des Heeres (High Command of the German Army)
OKH/Gen.Qu./Abt.K.V.	Abteilung Kriegsverwaltung des Generalquartiermeisters des Heeres (Department for POW Administration of the Army's General Quartermaster)
OKL	Oberkommando der Luftwaffe (Supreme Command of the Luftwaffe)
OKW	Oberkommando der Wehrmacht (High Command of the German Armed Forces)
PA-AA	Politisches Archiv des Auswärtigen Amtes (Political Archive of the German Foreign Office)
Penguin	POW carrying bags in trouser legs to dispose of tunnel dirt
RAAF	Royal Australian Air Force
RAF	Royal Air Force (UK)
RAN	Royal Australian Navy
RN	Royal Navy (UK)
RSHA	Reichssicherheitshauptamt (Reich Main Security Office)

GLOSSARY

SBO	Senior British Officer
SD	Sicherheitsdienst (German Security Service, part of the RSHA)
SHAEF	Supreme Headquarters of the Allied Expeditionary Force
SOE	Special Operations Executive (UK)
SS	*Schutzstaffel* (protective squadron – initially a squad of guards for Hitler but grew to embrace multiple functions)
Stalag	*Stamm-Mannschaftslager* (camp for other ranks)
Stooge	POW placed at key point to observe guards
TPI	Totally and Permanently Incapacitated
TNA	The National Archives (Kew)
USAAF	United States Army Air Force
Vertrauensmann	Man of Confidence
Wehrmacht	German Armed Forces
WASt	Wehrmachtauskunftstelle (Wehmacht Information Office)
YMCA	Young Men's Christian Association

Placenames

The text generally observes the spellings of locations as used during the Second World War. There were and indeed still are alternative transcriptions of Greek and Cretan placenames – these are listed below. When parts of Eastern Europe fell under German control, German placenames were adopted and are commonly used in historical literature. The column on the right records the names adopted since the end of the war.

Auschwitz	Oświęcim
Bankau	Bąków
Beuthen	Bytom
Blechhammer	Blachownia Śląska
Breslau	Wrocław
Brüx	Most
Canea	Khania/Chania
Krakow	Krakau, Kraków
Danzig	Gdansk
Drau	Drava
Georgioupolis	Georgoupoli
Graudenz	Grudziądz

PLACENAMES

Gross-Tychow	Tychowo
Heraklion	Heraklio, Iraklion
Heydekrug	Šilutė
Kiefheide	Podborsko
Laibach	Ljubljana
Lamsdorf	Łambinowice
Lemberg	Lvov, Lviv, Lwów
Marburg	Maribor
Mogadiscio	Mogadishu, Muqdisho
Nafplion	Nauplio, Navplio
Ottmachau	Otmuchów
Pankratz	Pankrác
Reichenberg	Liberec
Retimo	Rethymnon, Rethymno
Sagan	Żagan
Salonika	Salonica, Thessaloniki
Schubin	Szubin
Semic	Semich
Sphakia	Sfakia, Sphakion/Hora Sphakion
Suda Bay	Souda Bay
Teschen	Cieszyn
Theresienstadt	Terezín
Thorn	Toruń
Tost	Toszek

Notes

In citing works in the notes, short titles have generally been used. Works frequently cited have been identified by the following abbreviations:

AAWFA	The Australians at War Film Archive
ACIRC	Archives du Comité international de la Croix-Rouge (Archives of the Committee of the Red Cross, ICRC, Geneva)
AWM	Australian War Memorial
BArch	Bundesarchiv Berlin-Lichterfelde (Federal Archives, Berlin)
BA-MA	Bundesarchiv-Militärarchiv Freiburg im Breisgau (Federal Military Archives, Freiburg)
Buchenwald-Arch	Gedenkstätte Buchenwald Archiv (Buchenwald Memorial Archive, Germany)
HL	Hadtörténeti Levétár (War History Archives, Budapest)
PA-AA	Politisches Archiv des Auswärtigen Amtes (Political Archive of the Foreign Office, Berlin)
NAA	National Archives of Australia
TNA	The National Archives, Kew, UK
YMCAA	YMCA Archives, Geneva

NOTES

INTRODUCTION

1. Winston S. Churchill, *My Early Life*, p. 256.
2. I Samuel XV 3, cited in Vasilis Vourkoutiotis, *Prisoners of War and the German High Command*, p. 11.
3. Deuteronomy 20: 16–18, cited in Vourkoutiotis, p. 11.
4. Gaius Stern, 'Roman World', in Jonathan F. Vance (ed.), *Encyclopedia of Prisoners of War and Internment*, p. 254.
5. Vourkoutiotis, p. 17.
6. Montesquieu, *De l'ésprit des lois*, Paris: Librairies Barnier Frères, n.d., pp. 127–9, cited in Vourkoutiotis, p. 17.
7. Jean Jacques Rousseau, trans. Christopher Betts, *The Social Contract*, p. 52.
8. Patrick M. O'Neil, 'Hague Conventions of 1899 and 1907', in Jonathan F. Vance (ed.), p. 125.
9. Vourkoutiotis, p. 24.
10. Peter Stanley, 'Introduction', in Richard Reid et al., *Stolen Years*, p. 4.
11. The story has of course been told in film, but see also Nick Bleszynski, *Shoot Straight, You Bastards!*, 2002.
12. Reid et al., p. 11.
13. ibid., p. 10.
14. Günter Bischof, Stefan Karner and Barbara Stelz-Marx, 'Einleitung': in Günter Bischof, Stefan Karner and Barbara Stelz-Marx (eds), *Kriegsefangene des Zweiten Weltkrieges*, p. 9: K.W. Böhme, *Zur Geschichte der deutschen Kriegsgefangenen des Zweiten Weltkrieges*, p. x.
15. Reid et al., p. 28.

PART 1: CAPTURE

Chapter 1: To War

1. Quoted in Paul Hasluck, *The Government and the People*, p. 152.
2. Joan Beaumont, 'Australia's War: Europe and the Middle East', in Joan Beaumont (ed.), *Australia's War 1939–1945*, p. 5.
3. Jeffrey Grey, *A Military History of Australia*, p. 148.
4. Chester Wilmot, *Tobruk 1941*, p. 61.
5. Ray J. Corbett, interview with the author, 9 January 2010.

Chapter 2: From the Skies

1. Gavin Long, *The Six Years War*, p. 26.
2. Patrick Bishop, *Bomber Boys*, p. 44.
3. Ross A. Pearson, *Australians at War in the Air 1939–1945*, Volume 2, p. 33.
4. Pearson, p. 42.

NOTES

5. Long, p. 392.
6. Bishop, p. 231.
7. ibid., pp. 226, 230.
8. James Hampton, *Selected for Aircrew*, p. 343.
9. Long, p. 393.
10. Jack Champ and Colin Burgess, *The Diggers of Colditz*, p. 131.
11. Frank Johnson (ed.), *R.A.A.F. Over Europe*, pp. 10–11. After his escape in 1942 Fowler was awarded the MC and promoted. He was later posted to an experimental station, where he was killed on duty.
12. Geoff Cornish, (film archive interview AAWFA). See also Helen Hayes, *Beyond the Great Escape. Geoff Cornish: The One Who Got Away*, Elanora, Qld: Possum Publishing, 2004, pp. 58–61.
13. Paul Brickhill and Conrad Norton, *Escape to Danger*, p. 197.
14. Brickhill and Norton, pp. 211–12.
15. Bruce Loane's story is told in Ross A. Pearson, *Australians at War in the Air*, Volume 1, pp. 65–6, 110–12.
16. Oliver Clutton-Brock, *Footprints on the Sands of Time*, p. 196.
17. Gordon Stooke, *Flak and Barbed Wire*, p. 94.
18. Pearson, Volume 1, p. 62.
19. Bert Stobart, AAWFA interview.
20. Peter Giles, interview with the author, 18 October 2007.
21. Alex Jenkins, AAWFA interview.
22. John Ulm, AAWFA interview.

Chapter 3: From the Seas

1. Artillery report of *Kormoran* in encounter with *Mareeba* is contained in Commissioner Terence R.H. Cole's report 'The Loss of HMAS Sydney II', Vol. 1, Canberra: Department of Defence, July 1990, p. 164, viewed 30 May 2009, www.defence.gov.au/sydneyii/FinalReport/volume%201.htm.
2. James Taylor, *Prisoner of the* Kormoran, pp. 18ff.
3. Edward J. Sweeney, *A Merchant Seaman's Survival*, pp. 66–73.
4. ibid., pp. 78–85.
5. 'The Rangitane Story', viewed 4 September 2009, www.thebells.btinternet.co.uk/rangitane/story.htm.
6. Karl August Muggenthaler, *German Raiders of World War II*, p. 80.
7. 'Rangitane's Crew and Passenger List', viewed 4 September 2009, www.thebells.btinter net.co.uk/rangitane/crew.htm.
8. W. Wynne Mason, *Prisoners of War*, p. 36.
9. Letitia White, AAWFA interview.
10. ibid.

NOTES

11 Vic Marks, *Autobiography & Prisoner of War Experience*, pp. 29–45.
12 Wynne Mason, pp. 36–7.
13 John Moremon, 'Australian Prisoners of War: Selected Biographies', in Richard Reid et al., *Stolen Years*, p. 36.
14 A. Denholm, 'I Was a Prisoner'.
15 Muggenthaler, pp. 50, 129.
16 ibid., p. 52.
17 Denholm, p. 28.
18 ibid., pp. 30–1.
19 Gabe Thomas, *MILAG*, p. 1.
20 Report of the Directorate of Prisoners of War and Internees at Army Headquarters Melbourne 1939–1951, viewed 18 September 2010, www.army.gov.au/AHU/POWs_and_Internees.asp.

Chapter 4: Desert War

1 Craig Stockings, *Bardia*, pp. 2, 403.
2 Bernd Stegemann, 'The Italo-German Conduct of the War in the Mediterranean and North Africa', p. 658.
3 A.E. Field, 'Prisoners of the Germans and Italians', p. 755.
4 Stegemann, p. 678.
5 'Western Desert Campaign', in I.C.B. Dear and M.R.D. Foot (eds), *Oxford Companion to the Second World War*, p. 1269.
6 AWM54 779/1/22: Reports and Statements by Major R.J. Binns 2/8 Field Ambulance and Capt. E.W. Levinger RMO 2/3 Anti-Tank Regiment AIF on Gruppignano POW Camp Italy, 1943.
7 Edwin N. Broomhead, *Barbed Wired in the Sunset*, p. 14.
8 ibid., p. 19.
9 ibid., p. 22.
10 Allan S. Walker, *Australia in the War of 1939–1945*, pp. 184, 400.
11 Field, p. 755.
12 W.E.H. Cousins, *A Lot of Fun in My Life!*, pp. 99–101.
13 Richard Reid, *Victory in Europe 1939–1945*, p. 21.
14 Ray Jones, interview with the author, 3 December 2009.
15 Peter Stanley, Remembering 1942: Ruin Ridge, 26–27 July 1942, viewed 28 October 2009, www.awm.gov.au/atwar/remembering1942/alamein/transcript.asp; Field, p. 755.
16 Phil Loffman, interview with the author, 26 February 2009.
17 Patrick Toovey, AAWFA interview.
18 Jim Paterson, *Partisans, Peasants and POWs*, p. 27.

NOTES

19 Lawrence Calder, AAWFA interview.
20 Paterson, p. 45.
21 Ted Faulkes, 'Becoming a POW', in Bill Rudd et al., 'AIF in Switzerland', p. 5.
22 Paterson, p. 28.
23 Faulkes, p. 5.
24 Ernest Brough, *Dangerous Days*, pp. 121–7.
25 Hugh Clarke, Colin Burgess and Russell Braddon, *Prisoners of War*, p. 32.

Chapter 5: Greece

1 Gerhard Weinberg, *A World at Arms*, p. 208.
2 Ciano, *Diary*, 12 October 1940, p. 300, cited in Weinberg, p. 209.
3 Weinberg, p. 212.
4 Graham Freudenberg, *Churchill and Australia*, p. 249.
5 Joan Beaumont (ed.), *Australia's War 1939–1945*, p. 13.
6 ibid.
7 Maria Hill, *Diggers and Greeks*, pp. 52–3.
8 Robert Menzies, *Afternoon Light*, p. 71.
9 Freudenberg, p. 255.
10 Charles Messenger, *The Second World War in the West*, p. 88.
11 Detlef Vogel, 'German Intervention in the Balkans', p. 487.
12 Detlef Vogel, 'Das Eingreifen Deutschlands auf dem Balkan', in Gerhard Schreiber, Bernd Stegemann and Detlef Vogel, *Das Deutsche Reich und der Zweite Weltkrieg. Band 3. Der Mittelmeerraum und Südosteuropa*, p. 462.
13 Reginald Worthington, AAWFA interview.
14 Vogel, 'German Intervention in the Balkans', p. 511.
15 Hill, p. 176.
16 Vogel, 'Das Eingreifen', pp. 473–4.
17 George A. Morley, *Escape from Stalag XVIII A*, pp. 8–9.
18 Frank Cox, interview with the author, 17 July 2008.
19 Transcript of an interview with Alf Stone by Judy Lindsay, Zwar collection, p. 8.
20 Barney Roberts, *A Kind of Cattle*, pp. 21–3.
21 Vogel, 'Das Eingreifen', p. 474.
22 John Crooks, *My Little War*, pp. 34–41.
23 ibid., pp. 42–4.

NOTES

24 Doug Nix, interview with the author, 25 July 2009.
25 Ralph Churches, unpublished memoirs, pp. 12–15.
26 Charles Granquist, *A Long Way Home*, p. 72.
27 Hill, p. 311.

Chapter 6: Crete

1 Antony Beevor, *Crete: The Battle and the Resistance*, p. 73.
2 Detlef Vogel, 'German Intervention in the Balkans', p. 530.
3 Documents on German Foreign Policy Series D, Volume XII, No 403, cited in Beevor, p. 74.
4 ibid.
5 Vogel, p. 537.
6 Beevor, p. 79.
7 Cited in John Laffin, *ANZACs at War*, p. 118.
8 Laffin, p. 119.
9 Callum Macdonald, *The Lost Battle*, p. 169.
10 Ray Corbett, interview with the author, 9 January 2010.
11 Macdonald, p. 170.
12 Beevor, p. 108.
13 AWM PR 82/816: Diaries and Autobiography of Maj. Gen. Ian Campbell CO 2/1st Bn, AIF. Diary of I.R. Campbell, p. 109.
14 Terry Fairbairn, AAWFA interview.
15 Vogel, p. 547.
16 Peter Thompson, *ANZAC Fury*, pp. 376–8.
17 Campbell, pp. 112–13.
18 E.C. Givney (ed.), *The First at War*, pp. 204–5.
19 *Gebirgsjäger auf Kreta*, translated by Australian POW B. McGeoch, cited in Gavin Long, *Greece, Crete and Syria*, p. 277.
20 Thompson, p. 404.
21 Vogel, p. 551.
22 Cited in Sean Damer and Ian Frazer, *On the Run*, p. 19.
23 Keith Hooper, interview with the author, 19 January 2008.
24 Corbett, interview with the author, 9 January 2010.
25 Laurie West, interview with the author, 18 July 2008.
26 Charlie Parrott, AAWFA interview.
27 Charles Jager, *Escape from Crete*, p. 28.
28 Jager, p. 30.
29 Leslie Le Souef, *To War Without a Gun*, p. 19.

NOTES

30 ibid., p. 152.
31 Arthur Leggett, *Don't Cry For Me*, pp. 158–9.
32 ibid., p. 160.
33 Hal Finkelstein, In and Out of Barbed Wire, p. 25.
34 Damer and Frazer, p. 73.
35 NAA AWM54, 781/6/6: File containing material for use by official historians.
36 Thompson, p. 413.
37 ibid., pp. 394–5.
38 Damer and Frazer, pp. 197–8.
39 Margaret Barter, *Far Above Battle*, p. 121.
40 Hugh Clarke, Colin Burgess, Russell Braddon, *Prisoners of War*, p. 34.
41 Vogel, p. 552.
42 PA-AA, R 40/924: Englische Kriegsgefangene in Deutschland. Arbeitseinsatz und Entlohnung. Memorandum Konzept Ref. VLR Dr Sethe, 20.10.1942.

Chapter 7: Syria

1 Joan Beaumont (ed.), *Australia's War 1939–45*, p. 16.
2 Gavin Long, *The Six Years War*, p. 87.
3 Beaumont, p. 16.
4 John Bellair, *From Snow to Jungle*, p. 49.
5 Walter Irvine Summons, *Twice Their Prisoner*, p. 18.
6 Summons, p. 20.
7 Long, pp. 92–3.
8 Summons, pp. 33–8.
9 ibid., pp. 45–51.
10 ibid.

Chapter 8: Into the Reich

1 Mark Mazower, *Dark Continent*, pp. 146–7.
2 James Taylor, *Prisoner of the 'Kormoran'*, pp. 155–65.
3 Gabe Thomas, *MILAG*, pp. 55–6.
4 W. Wynne Mason, *Prisoners of War*, pp. 35–6.
5 ibid., p. 37.
6 BA-MA RH/20/12/208: Gefangenenaussagen von 9 gefangenen Australiern am 14.4.41.

NOTES

7. A.E. Field, 'Prisoners of the Germans and Italians' in Barton Maughan, *Tobruk and El Alamein*, p. 773.
8. Yoav Gelber, 'Palestinian POWs in German Captivity', p. 8.
9. NAA A816, 54/301/172: Australian and British Prisoners of War Interned in Germany, Italy, and France – Reports on Camps. P. 116. Red Cross Report 'Camp de Prisonniers de Guerre de Corinthe', Visited 12 to 18 May 1941.
10. BA-MA RH/20/12/208: Aktennotiz. Über Besichtigung der Gef. Sammelstelle Korinth und Besuch bei der Feldkdtr. 569 am 17.5.1941.
11. John Crooks, *My Little War*, p. 43.
12. Ralph Churches, unpublished memoirs, pp. 16–18.
13. ibid., p. 21.
14. Reg Worthington, AAWFA interview.
15. Mason, p. 37.
16. Allan S. Walker, *Australia in the War of 1939–1945*, pp. 405–6.
17. Gelber, p. 13.
18. Mason, p. 65.
19. Charles Jager, *Escape from Crete*, p. 199.
20. ibid., p. 203.
21. Sean Damer and Ian Frazer, *On the Run*, p. 51.
22. Charles Robinson, *Journey to Captivity*, p. 75.
23. Laurie West, interview with the author, 18 July 2008.
24. Roy E.L. East, 'POW Experiences', Zwar collection.
25. Charlie Parrott, *An Aussie Nobody*, p. 50.
26. Walker, p. 416.
27. Arthur Leggett, 'Incidence of ill-treatment whilst being held as a Prisoner-of-War in Germany from 1941 until 1945', unpublished manuscript, Zwar collection, p. 1.
28. ibid., p. 1.
29. Lindsay P. Lawrence, Blessed Be the Olive Trees, p. 74.
30. Laurie West, interview with the author, 18 July 2008.
31. Mason, p. 78.
32. Walker, p. 409.
33. Parrott, p. 53.
34. Frank Atkins, 'A Brief Stay in Salonika POW Camp Late 1941', Zwar collection.
35. Alexander McClelland, *The Answer – Justice*, p. 72.
36. Philip Arthur Brown, statutory declaration, 6 September 2001, Zwar collection.

NOTES

37 Albert Gibb, 'The War Years 1939', Zwar collection, p. 5.
38 Hal Finkelstein, In and Out of Barbed Wire, pp. 35–6.
39 Leggett.
40 Lawrence, pp. 80–1.
41 ibid., p. 82.
42 Mark Mazower, *Salonica, City of Ghosts*, pp. 396–411.
43 Churches, p. 27.
44 Field, p. 785.
45 Jack Wooding, letter to Arthur Leggett, 3 September 2001, Zwar collection.
46 Ray J. Corbett, *Behind German Wire*, p. 53.
47 Leslie Le Soeuf, *To War Without a Gun*, pp. 174–7.
48 These are the camps identified in a report to the Prime Minister's Department from the High Commissioner in London, 18 June 1943. NAA A 816, 67/301/16: Australian prisoners of war in Germany and Italy – reports on camps – File III, p. 29.
49 Richard Reid, 'In Captivity: Australian Prisoners of War in the Twentieth Century', in Richard Reid et al., *Stolen Years*, p. 14.
50 James W. Reeves, *One Man's War*, pp. 44–51, 127–32.
51 Ernest Brough, *Dangerous Days*, pp. 131–3.
52 AWM54 779/1/22: Reports and Statements by Major R.J. Binns 2/8 Field Ambulance and Capt. E.W. Levinger RMO 2/3 Anti-Tank Regiment AIF on Gruppignano POW Camp Italy. 1943.
53 Walker, p. 403.
54 ibid., p. 404.
55 Lawrence Calder, AAWFA interview.
56 W.E.H. (Bill) Cousins, *A Lot of Fun in My Life!*, pp. 119–20. The Australian World War II Nominal Roll lists Edward William Symons WX1982 as a POW who died 20 May 1943.
57 Field, p. 766.
58 Peter Thompson, *ANZAC Fury*, p. 423.
59 Cyril George Jenkins, *POW Number 226002 – And That Is Now My Identity*, original diaries written during the Second World War, Ringwood, Hampshire: 1999, p. 97, cited in Achim Kilian, *Mühlberg 1939–1948*, p. 132.
60 Rüdiger Overmans, 'Die Kriegsgefangenenpolitik des Deutschen Reiches 1939 bis 1945'.
61 Gerhard Weinberg, *A World at Arms*, p. 486.
62 'Complete Nominal Roll Swiss 'Free Men', compiled by Bill Rudd, viewed 10 October 2009, www.aifpow.com.

NOTES

63   Bill Bunbury, *Rabbits and Spaghetti*, p. 75.
64   Department of Veterans' Affairs, 'Private James McCracken', viewed 10 October 2009, www.awm.gov.au/exhibitions/stolenyears/ww2/italy/story3.asp.
65   Ray Jones, interview with the author, 3 December 2009.
66   Gordon Stooke, *Flak and Barbed Wire*, pp. 83–6.
67   Wilf Hodgson, *Bombs and Barbed Wire*, p. 62.
68   AWM MSS 1566: Henry John Bastian. Memoirs of Henry John Bastian 24.12.17 to 25.7.89, compiled by son Raymond Henry Bastian.

PART 2: CAPTIVITY

Chapter 9: Hitler's Behemoth

1   Ian Kershaw, *Hitler 1936–1945*, p. 52.
2   Jürgen Förster, *Die Wehrmacht im NS-Staat*, p. 46.
3   Kershaw, p. 58.
4   Rüdiger Overmans, 'German Prisoner of War Policy in World War II', p. 172.
5   Overmans, p. 171.
6   Rüdiger Overmans, 'Die Kriegsgefangenenpolitik des Deutschen Reiches 1939 bis 1945', p. 785.
7   Overmans, 'German Prisoner of War Policy', p. 171.
8   S.P. MacKenzie, 'The Treatment of Prisoners of War in World War II', pp. 487–8.
9   Overmans, 'German Prisoner of War Policy', p. 176; MacKenzie, p. 492.
10   TNA WO32/10719: Australia to Dominions Office No. 456, 11 October 1942. See also Waters, 'Australia, the British Empire and the Second World War', pp. 93–107.
11   Overmans, 'German Prisoner of War Policy', p. 176. See also S.P. MacKenzie, 'The Shackling Crisis: Krieger in Ketten, Eine Fallstudie über die Dynamik der Kriegsgefangenenpolitik', in Rüdiger Overmans (ed.), *In der Hand des Feindes*, pp. 45–68; Jonathan F. Vance, 'Men in Manacles', pp. 483–504.
12   Jonathan Vance, 'Shackling Incident', in Jonathan F. Vance (ed.), *Encyclopedia of Prisoners of War and Internment*, p. 270.
13   MacKenzie, 'The Treatment of Prisoners of War', p. 492.
14   NAA AWM54 779/4/21: Reports by International Red Cross and Protecting Powers on Conditions existing in Prisoners of War Camps in Germany and Italy: Red Cross Report on Oflag VII B Eichstätt 2 Nov. 1942.

NOTES

15 Lindsay P. Lawrence, *Blessed Be the Olive Trees*, p. 104.
16 Keith Hooper, personal communication, 10 May 2007.
17 David Rolf, *Prisoners of the Reich*, p. 104.
18 NAA AWM54 779/4/21: Red Cross report on Oflag VII B Eichstätt 29.1.1945.
19 Kershaw, p. 357.
20 Willi Dressen, 'Kommissarbefehl', in Wolfgang Benz et al. (eds), *Enzyklopädie des Nationalsozialismus*, pp. 547–8.
21 Martyn Housden, *Hitler: Study of a Revolutionary*, p. 132.
22 Dressen, pp. 547–8.
23 Cited in Vasilis Vourkoutiotis, 'Commando Order', in Vance (ed.), *Encyclopedia of Prisoners of War and Internment*, p. 62.
24 Vourkoutiotis, p. 62.
25 Volker Riess, 'Kommandobefehl', in Wolfgang Benz et al., p. 547.
26 Overmans, 'Die Kriegsgefangenenpolitik', p. 853.
27 ibid.
28 Stefan Geck, *Das Deutsche Kriegsgefangenenwesen 1939–1945*, Masters thesis, University of Mainz, 1998, p. 16.
29 ibid., p. 17.
30 ibid., p. 20.
31 ibid., p. 20; Overmans, 'Die Kriegsgefangenenpolitik', pp. 852–3.
32 Geck, p. 17.
33 ibid., pp. 24–5.
34 ibid., p. 25.
35 Overmans, 'Die Kriegsgefangenenpolitik', p. 741.
36 David Foy, *For You the War is Over*, p. 19.
37 Edith Petschnigg, *Von der Front aufs Feld*, p. 52.
38 Geck, p. 93.
39 PA-AA R 41/021: Kriegsgefangene in Deutschland 1941–1944.
40 Foy, p. 24.
41 Cited in Foy, p. 22.

Chapter 10: The World of the Camps

1 Stefan Geck, *Das deutsche Kriegsgefangenenwesen 1939–1945*, p. 35.
2 Hubert Speckner, *Kriegsgefangene in der 'Ostmark' 1939–1945*, p. 13.
3 BA-MA MSG 1/2012: Zusammenstellung der Kriegsgefangenen im OKW-Bereich, einschl. Luftw. und Marine. Stand 1.8.1944.
4 Geck, p. 38.

NOTES

5 Speckner, p. 91.
6 Rüdiger Overmans, 'Die Kriegsgefangenenpolitik des Deutschen Reiches 1939 bis 1945', p. 740.
7 Speckner, p. 238.
8 ibid., p. 441.
9 Edith Petschnigg, *Von der Front aufs Feld*, p. 43
10 Speckner, p. 419.
11 NAA A816 67/301/16: Australian Prisoners of War in Germany and Italy – Reports on Camps – File III, p. 410.
12 PA-AA R/40/972B: Red Cross Report on Stalag XVIII D, 21 July 1941.
13 TNA FO916/240: Red Cross Report on Stalag XVIII B, 23.10.1941.
14 Allan Slocombe, communication with Edith Petschnigg 11 March 2002, in Petschnigg, p. 44.
15 TNA WO 224/46: Red Cross Reports on Camps. Report on SVIII D 16.9.1942.
16 Speckner, p. 419.
17 Harry Giesen, *Seventh Time Lucky*, p. 11.
18 TNA WO 224.45A: Red Cross Reports Stalag XVIII A. Report from visit 24 October 1941.
19 PA-AA R/40/972B: Red Cross Report on Stalag XVIII A, 22 July 1941.
20 NAA A816, 54/301/172: Australian and British Prisoners of War Interned in Germany, Italy, and France – Reports on Camps, p. 47.
21 Petschnigg, p. 40.
22 PRO WO 224/45: ICRC report 28.10.1944.
23 Ray Norman, communication with Edith Petschnigg 10 February 2002, in Petschnigg, p. 43.
24 Giesen, pp. 12–13.
25 A.E. Field, 'Prisoners of the Germans and Italians', p. 782.
26 TNA FO 916/1147: Reports on German Camps. ICRC Report on Stalag XVIII A, visited 5–13 December 1941.
27 Digitised record viewed 20 May 2009, www.awm.gov.au/cms_images/AWM192/00203/002030864.pdf.
28 David Foy, *For You the War is Over*, p. 66.
29 NAA AWM54 779/4/21: Reports by International Red Cross and Protecting Powers on Conditions Existing in Prisoners of War Camps in Germany and Italy; Roland Zimmer, 'Stalag VII A: A History 1939–1945', viewed 25 May 2009, www.moosburg.org/info/stalag/st95eng.html.
30 Lindsay P. Lawrence, Blessed Be the Olive Trees, p. 86.
31 NAA AWM54 779/4/21: Reports by International Red Cross and Protecting Powers on Conditions Existing in Prisoners of War Camps in

NOTES

Germany and Italy. Cable from PM's Department Canberra to High Commissioner's Office London 29.4.1942.

32 TNA FO 916/243: ICRC Reports. Report on VII A, visited 25.11.1941 by Dr Exchaquet.
33 NAA AWM54 779/4/21: Reports by International Red Cross and Protecting Powers on Conditions Existing in Prisoners of War Camps in Germany and Italy. Extract from Cable 4245 dated 11 May 1942 from High Commissioner's Office London.
34 NAA AWM54 779/4/21: Reports by International Red Cross and Protecting Powers on Conditions Existing in Prisoners of War Camps in Germany and Italy. Extract from Cable 10547 dated 14 November 1942 from High Commissioner's Office London.
35 Geck, p. 45.
36 'Stalag VIII B (344) Lamsdorf', viewed 28 May 2009, www.cmjw.pl/www/index_gb.php?id=stalag_8b.
37 'Stalag 318/VIII F (344) Lamsdorf', viewed 28 May 2009, www.cmjw.pl/www/index_gb.php?id=stalag_318.
38 AICRC, CSC Reports on Stalag 344 Lamsdorf. Report of 30.10.1943.
39 AICRC, CSC Reports on Stalag VIII B Lamsdorf. Report of 5.9.1942.
40 'Prisoners of War', New Zealand Electronic Text Centre, at www.nzetc.org/tm/scholarly/tei-WH2Pris-_N95868.html, p. 369.
41 NAA A816/1 54/301/191: British and Australian Prisoners of War in Germany and Italy – Reports on Camps, File 2.
42 Geck, p. 38.
43 AWM PR 82/816. Diaries and Autobiography of Maj. Gen. Ian Campbell C.O. 2/1st Bn, AIF.
44 David Rolf, *Prisoners of the Reich*, p. 35.
45 NAA A816 67/301/16: Australian Prisoners of War in Germany and Italy – Reports on Camps, File III, p. 413: International Red Cross Report, Oflag V B, visited 19 July 1941.
46 NAA A816 67/301/16: Australian Prisoners of War in Germany and Italy – Reports on Camps, File III, p. 367.
47 ICRC report cited in Field, p. 791.
48 Field, p. 793.
49 NAA AWM54 781/6/6: Material for official war history. 'Australian POW in Europe. Numbers in Enemy PW Camps.'
50 W.P. Skene, quoted in Field, p. 797.
51 W. Wynne Mason, *Prisoners of War*, p. 37.
52 NAA A816 67/301/16: Australian Prisoners of War in Germany and Italy – Reports on Camps – File III, p. 243.
53 R. Mercer, 'Marlag und Milag Nord', in E.G.C. Beckwith (ed.), *Selections from the Quill*, p. 203.

NOTES

54 Rolf, p. 111.
55 ibid., p. 112.
56 Quoted in Rolf, p. 114.
57 'Cotton, Frederick Sidney (1894–1969)', ADB online, www.adbonline.anu.edu.au/biogs/A130563b.htm; For Cotton's full story see: Jeff Watson, *Sidney Cotton*.
58 H. Satow and M. J. See, *The Work of the Prisoners of War Department During the Second World War*, p. 93.
59 Mason, p. 38.
60 ibid., p. xxiv.
61 PA-AA R 41/401: Australische Kriegsgefangene.
62 PA-AA R 41/487: Zivilgefangene – Auskunft. Australien.
63 PA-AA R 41/401: Hester Burden to AA 27.7.1940.
64 PA-AA R 41/401: Australische Zivilgefangene in Deutschland.
65 Satow, p. 95.
66 NAA A816/1.54/301/191: British and Australian Prisoners of War in Germany and Italy – Reports on Camps, File 2.
67 NAA A816 544/301/172: Australian and British Prisoners of War Interned in Germany, Italy, and France – Reports on Camps. Report on Inspection of Civilian Internment Camp at Tost, Silesia, p. 219.
68 Satow and See, pp. 95–6.
69 NAA A816 67/301/16: Australian Prisoners of War in Germany and Italy – Reports on Camps – File III, p. 82.
70 Satow and See, pp. 97–8.
71 ibid., pp. 98–9.
72 NAA A816 67/301/16: Australian Prisoners of War in Germany and Italy – Reports on Camps – File III, p. 77.
73 ibid., p. 118.

Chapter 11: Göring's Empire

1 Stefan Geck, *Dulag Luft/Auswertestelle West*, p. 1; Raymond Toliver, *The Interrogator*, p. 16.
2 Geck, p. 30.
3 TNA WO32/18490: Reports on Dulag Luft, cited in Geck, p. 64.
4 Geck, p. 82.
5 Toliver, p. 17.
6 David Foy, *For You the War is Over*, p. 53.
7 Geck, pp. 161, 167.
8 Ron Zwar, AAWFA interview.

NOTES

9 Geck, p. 170.
10 Toliver, p. 16; Geck, p. 176; Foy, p. 58.
11 Foy, p. 59.
12 Geck, p. 287.
13 Toliver, passim.
14 Geck, pp. 217–18.
15 ibid., p. 253.
16 Toliver, p. 17.
17 Geck, p. 301.
18 Calton Younger, *No Flight from the Cage*, p. 15.
19 Delmar T. Spivey, *POW Odyssey*, p. 17.
20 Geck, p. 302.
21 Foy, p. 54.
22 Geck, p. 303.
23 ibid., p. 314.
24 ibid., p. 306.
25 ibid., p. 307.
26 Geoff Taylor, *A Piece of Cake*, p. 82.
27 BA-MA, RL 2 II/986: Gefangenenvernehmung und Beuteauswertung, pp. 40ff, in Geck, p. 321.
28 TNA WO 309/136: A.D.I (k) Report No. 328/1945, cited in Geck, p. 311.
29 Geck, p. 319.
30 Cited in Eric Cuddon (ed.), *Trial of Erich Killinger, Heinz Junge, Otto Boehringer, Heinrich Eberhardt, Gustav Bauer-Schlichtegroll (The Dulag Luft Trial)*, p. 173.
31 Geck, p. 312.
32 TNA WO 309/136: A.D.I. (k) Report No. 328/1945, AWSW, 14 June 1945, p. 14, nr. 135, in Geck, p. 327.
33 Geck, p. 320.
34 ibid., p. 515.
35 ibid., p. 332.
36 TNA WO 309/136: A.D.I. (k) Report No. 328/1945, p. 13, cited in Geck, p. 107.
37 Geck, p. 333.
38 ibid., p. 335.
39 See especially Cuddon (ed.), passim; Geck, p. 11.
40 Geck, p. 477.

NOTES

41 TNA WO 208/4642, UK-G/B 63, United Nations War Crimes Commission reference 171/UK/G/48, 741596 Victor Albert Bain, Warrant Officer, Pilot RAF, p. 2, cited in Geck, p. 489.
42 Jack Liley, *Jack's War*, pp. 124–5.
43 AWM MSS 1566: Henry John Bastian. Memoirs of Henry John Bastian 24.12.17 to 25.7.89, compiled by son Raymond Henry Bastian, p. 106.
44 John Matthews, AAWFA interview.
45 Bastian, p. 109.
46 PA-AA R 40/972A: Kriegsgefangene in Deutschland – Allgemein. Red Cross Report on Stalag Luft I, 2.7.1941.
47 Foy, p. 69.
48 ibid., p. 70.
49 ibid., p. 70.
50 David Rolf, *Prisoners of the Reich*, p. 39.
51 Taylor, pp. 104–5.
52 ibid., p. 107.
53 ibid., pp. 114–15.
54 J.E. Holliday (ed.), *Stories of the RAAF POWs of Lamsdorf Including Chronicles of Their 500 Mile Trek*, p. 2.
55 NAA AWM54 779/3/126: Statements by Royal Australian Air Force Personnel from Prisoners of War Camps in Germany and Italy. Part I of II parts. Report by Squadron Leader R. Sherman 4 July 1945.
56 Raymond Ryan in Imelda Ryan (ed.), *POWs Fraternal*, p. 86.
57 NAA AWM54 779/3/126: Statements by Royal Australian Air Force Personnel from Prisoners of War Camps in Germany and Italy. Part I of II parts. Report by Squadron Leader R. Sherman 4 July 1945.

Chapter 12: Comrades Unarmed

1 Edith Petschnigg, *Von der Front aufs Feld*, p. 14.
2 Rüdiger Overmans, 'Die Kriegsgefangenenpolitik des Deutschen Reiches', p. 787.
3 ibid., p. 790.
4 Petschnigg, p. 34.
5 ibid., p. 35.
6 Calton Younger, *No Flight from the Cage*, p. 95.
7 PA-AA R 40/954: Englische Kriegsgefangene in Deutschland – Lager 1941–1942. OKW Abt. Kriegsgefangenenwesen to AA 25.7.1941.
8 BArchiv R 58/187: SD-Berichte zu Inlandsfragen, 12 August 1943. Britische Kriegsgefangene im Reich im Urteil der deutschen Bevoelkerung.
9 Laurie West, interview with the author, 18 July 2008.

NOTES

10 Achim Kilian, *Mühlberg 1939–1948*, p. 149.
11 'Das Kriegsgefangenenwesen der Wehrmacht', viewed 15 January 2010, www.lexikon-der-wehrmacht.de/Gliederungen/Kriegsgefangenenlager/Kriegsgefangenenwesen.
12 Doug Nix, interview with the author, 25 July 2009.
13 Christopher Burney, *Solitary Confinement*, p. 205.
14 Petschnigg, p. 27.
15 ibid., p. 27.
16 ibid., pp. 27–8.
17 Overmans, p. 837.
18 Overmans reports that the number of Soviet POWs is put between 5.35 and 5.75 million, Overmans, p. 820.
19 Overmans, p. 800.
20 ibid., p. 800.
21 ibid., p. 801.
22 Christian Streit, 'Sowjetische Kriegsgefangene – Massendeportationen – Zwangsarbeiter', in Wolfgang Michalka (ed.), *Der Zweite Weltkrieg*, p. 747.
23 Zygmunt Klukowski, *Diary from the Years of Occupation, 1939–1944*, p. 173.
24 Mark Mazower, *Dark Continent: Europe's Twentieth Century*, p. 168.
25 Overmans, 'Die Kriegsgefangenenpolitik', p. 810.
26 Albert Gibb, 'The War Years 1939–1945', Zwar collection.
27 Frank Cox, manuscript recollections, Zwar collection.
28 Doug Nix, interview with the author, 25 July 2009.
29 Arthur Henry Buxton, unpublished recollections, Zwar collection.
30 Lawrence Calder, AAWFA interview.
31 Bert Stobart, AAWFA interview.
32 Rüdiger Overmans, 'German Prisoner of War Policy in World War II', p. 178; Overmans, 'Die Kriegsgefangenenpolitik', pp. 743–55, 870–1.
33 Overmans, 'Die Kriegsgefangenenpolitik', p. 766.
34 ibid., pp. 779–85.
35 Yoav Gelber, 'Palestinian POWs in German Captivity'.
36 Interrogation of S. Secher and E. Asir, 18 June 1941. Central Zionist Archives S-25/9263, cited in Gelber, p. 3.
37 Y. Ben-Aharon, 'Be Shevi ha-Nazim', in Z. Shefer (ed.), *Sefer ha-Hitnadvut*, Jerusalem: 1949, p. 650, cited in Gelber, p. 4.
38 Gelber, pp. 15–16.
39 NAA AWM54 779/4/21: Reports by International Red Cross and Protecting Powers on Conditions existing in Prisoners of War Camps in Germany and Italy. Report on Stalag XVIII A visit by Red Cross 24.10.1942.

NOTES

40 TNA WO 224/46: Red Cross Reports on Camps. Report on XVIII D Marburg visited 21.7.1941.
41 TNA FO 916/1150: Reports on German Camps. Report on Work Detachments Dependent on Stalag VIII B Teschen 2.3.1945.
42 S. Slodash, *Be-Kavley ha-Shevi*, Tel Aviv: n.p. 1946, p. 177, cited in Gelber, p. 23.
43 Gelber, p. 37.
44 TNA FO 916/567: Welfare of Jewish Prisoners of War in Germany: General Observations. Letter War Office to Sir Harold Satow of Prisoners of War Department 18.2.1943.
45 TNA FO 916/567: Letter Satow to War Office 4.3.43.
46 TNA FO 916/567: His Majesty's Minister at Berne to Principal Secretary of State for Foreign Affairs 22.4.1943.
47 TNA WO 224/223: General Conditions in POW Camps. May 1943–October 1945. Note from Federal Political Department Berne to British Foreign Office 14.5.1943.
48 The list 'Australian Jewish Prisoners of War WWII' was kindly made available to me by Shannon Maguire of the Sydney Jewish Museum. A number of these were held in Japanese captivity.
49 For the full story of Cullen's life see Kevin Baker, *Paul Cullen, Citizen and Soldier*.
50 ibid., pp. 73–95.
51 ibid., 2005, pp. 17–23. I am indebted also to Shannon Maguire at the Sydney Jewish Museum for information on Paul Cullen.
52 Baker, p. 97.
53 See Wolfe Greenstein, World War II Nominal Roll, viewed 30 April 2008, www.ww2roll.gov.au/script/veteran.asp?serviceID=A&VeteranID=138325.
54 Keith Hooper, interview with the author, 19 January 2008.
55 Hal Finkelstein, In and Out of Barbed Wire, p. 80.
56 ibid., p. 4.
57 'Captain Reginald Walter (Reg) Saunders, MBE', www.awm.gov.au/people/302.asp.
58 Lawrence Calder, AAWFA interview.
59 Robert H. Hall, *The Black Diggers*, p. 61.
60 NAA B883 WX7218: Jim Brennan service record.
61 McClelland uses the spelling Gursdorf. More likely the correct spelling is Gersdorf. There is a town of Gersdorf in Czechoslovakia, but there is a good possibility that the location was Neu Gersdorf (today Nowy Gieraltow) in Lower Silesia, adjacent to the Czech border.
62 Alexander McClelland, *The Answer – Justice*, p. 85.

NOTES

Chapter 13: Kriegie Life

1. Winston S. Churchill, *My Early Life*, p. 256.
2. Hubert Speckner, Kriegsgefangene in der 'Ostmark' 1939–1945, p. 102.
3. David Rolf, *Prisoners of the Reich*, pp. 32–3.
4. Speckner, p. 102.
5. Doug Nix, interview with the author, 25 July 2009.
6. Edith Petschnigg, *Von der Front aufs Feld*, p. 164.
7. Younger, p. 21.
8. Petschnigg, p. 165.
9. Lindsay P. Lawrence, Blessed Be the Olive Trees, p. 86.
10. TNA WO 224/46: Red Cross Reports Stalag XVIII B 1941 July–1942 November. Report on visit 16.9.1942.
11. Ron Zwar, 'Compo. Claim Details POW. Experiences and Treatment', Zwar collection.
12. Gordon Stooke, *Flak and Barbed Wire*, p. 86.
13. Earle M. Nelson, *If Winter Comes*, p. 54.
14. PA-AA R 41/063: Englische Kriegsgefangene in Deutschland. Verpflegung einschliesslich Genussmittel 1941–1944.
15. Rolf, p. 53.
16. Hal Finkelstein, In and Out of Barbed Wire, p. 14.
17. Rüdiger Overmans, 'Die Kriegsgefangenenpolitik des Deutschen Reiches 1939 bis 1945', p. 787.
18. PA-AA R 41/063: Englische Kriegsgefangene in Deutschland.
19. 'Claim for Special Allowance to Ex-Prisoners of War 1939–1945', Zwar collection, p. 25.
20. Charlie Parrott, AAWFA interview.
21. Charlie Parrott, *An Aussie Nobody*, p. x.
22. Ray Corbett, *Behind German Wire*, p. 122.
23. Younger, p. 26.
24. Frank Cox, interview with the author, 17 July 2008.
25. Thomas Fielder, *I Flew I Fell I Survived*, pp. 175–6.
26. ibid., p. 176.
27. BA-MA MSG/194/58: YMCA Report on Stalag VIII B 8–10 September 1942.
28. Jack Liley, *Jack's War*, pp. 146–7.
29. Ron Mackenzie, *An Ordinary War 1940–1945*, p. 56.
30. Younger, p. 26.
31. ibid.

NOTES

32. ibid., p. 44.
33. ibid., p. 19.
34. ibid., p. 44.
35. ibid.
36. ibid., p. 166.
37. NAA AWM54, 779/4/21: Reports by International Red Cross and Protecting Powers on Conditions Existing in Prisoner of War Camps in Germany and Italy. P.H. Norman, 'The Prisoner of War Mentality: Its Effect after Repatriation'.
38. Petschnigg, p. 222.
39. ibid., p. 223.
40. Boberach, *Meldungen aus dem Reich*, Vol. 12, p. 5610. In Petschnigg, p. 225.
41. P.W. Luckett, cited in Petschnigg, p. 232.
42. Interview with Maria Burton, in Petschnigg, p. 226.
43. Younger, p. 106.
44. Mackenzie, p. 63.
45. Basil Brudenell-Woods, *Four Packs to Freedom*, p. 24.
46. Laurie West, interview with the author, 18 July 2008.
47. YMCAA, World War II Work – Germany. SS1 – T.11. Vol. 4. Report on visit to VIII B 31 August to 1 September 1943.
48. Ray Corbett, interview with the author, 9 January 2010.
49. TNA WO 224.55A: Red Cross Reports Stalag 383 1943 Jan.–1945 Mar. 'Education in Stalag 383'.
50. ibid.
51. Colin Burgess, Hugh Clarke and Russell Braddon, *Prisoners of War*, p. 25.
52. Mackenzie, p. 65.
53. PA-AA R40/919: Wissenschaftliche Fortbildung der Kriegs- und Zivilgefangenen – England. OKW an Auswärtiges Amt betr. Lesestoff für britische Kriegsgefangene 7.11.1941.
54. PA-AA R 40/943: Englische Kriegsgefangene in Deutschland – Freizeitgestaltung (Sport, Unterhaltung, Bücher). Kriegsgefangenenwesen an AA 5.3.1942.
55. Mackenzie, p. 61.
56. Rolf, p. 85.
57. ibid., p. 87.
58. ibid., p. 86.
59. Ron Zwar, interview with the author, 7 May 2010.
60. Petschnigg, p. 170.
61. ibid., p. 171.

NOTES

62 Mackenzie, p. 63.
63 PA-AA R 40/943: Reichsministerium Volksaufklärung und Propaganda an AA, 13.10.44.
64 Stooke, p. 104.
65 Doug Nix, interview with the author, 25 July 2009.
66 John Mathews, AAWFA interview.
67 BA-MA MSG/194/58: YMCA report on camps in Germany.
68 BA-MA RW 6/v. 272, cited in Geck, 'Das deutsche Kriegsgefangenenwesen 1939–1945, p. 98.
69 Based on Eric Williams' book, *The Wooden Horse*.
70 Arthur H. (Dick) Bird, *Farewell Milag*, pp. 96–7.
71 Vic Marks, *Autobiography & Prisoner of War Experience*.
72 Warwick Franks, 'Cricket in Stalag 344', p. 84.
73 ibid.
74 ibid., p. 86.
75 ibid., pp. 86–7.
76 Frank Johnson, *RAAF over Europe*, pp. 184–5.
77 Corbett, *Behind German Wire*, p. 81.
78 Speckner, p. 108.
79 Maurice Gaul, 'Footy Behind the Wire', p. 10.
80 ibid., pp. 10–11.
81 Laurie West, interview with the author, 18 July 2008.
82 YMCAA: World War II Work – Germany. SSI – T.11. File 1–11. Vol. 4, General Report on Stalag VIIIA, 30.6.1944.
83 Franks, p. 89.
84 Charles Raymond Willoughby, *I Was There*, pp. 62–3.
85 Franks, pp. 82–3.

Chapter 14: Working for the Führer

1 Mark Mazower, *Dark Continent*, pp. 154–5.
2 David Rolf, *Prisoners of the Reich*, p. 62.
3 Frank Cox, interview with the author, 17 July 2008.
4 Leslie Le Souef, *To War without a Gun*, p. 274.
5 Gerald H. Davis, 'Prisoners of War in Twentieth-century War Economies', p. 623.
6 OKW order, 15 June 1942, cited in Edith Petschnigg, *Von der Front aufs Feld*, p. 63.
7 Petschnigg, pp. 64–5.

NOTES

8. BA-MA RH53-17/195, Kommandeur des Kriegsgefangenenwesen im Wehrkreis, Vienna, 2 July 1942.
9. Rolf, p. 65.
10. Gavan Daws, *Prisoners of the Japanese*, p. 223.
11. BArch R 58/178: Meldungen aus dem Reich, Nr. 340, p. 13.
12. BArch R 58/187: SD-Berichte zu Inlandsfragen, 'Britische Kriegsgefangene im Reich im Urteil der deutschen Bevölkerung', p. 79.
13. BArch R 58/187: SD-Berichte zu Inlandsfragen, 'Britische Kriegsgefangene im Reich im Urteil der deutschen Bevölkerung', p. 79.
14. BArch R 58/187 f. 81: SD-Berichte zu Inlandsfragen. 'Britische Kriegsgefangene im Reich im Urteil der deutschen Bevölkerung', 12 August 1943.
15. BA-MA XLAK, 11652: Order of the 40th Corps Headquarters on the subject of collecting and guarding booty and the concentration of captives, 1 May 1941, cited in Yoav Gelber, 'Palestinian Captives in German Captivity', p. 7.
16. Gelber, p. 8.
17. Reginald Worthington, AAWFA interview.
18. Arthur Jilbert Marshall, The Trials and Tribulations of POW Life, diary manuscript, Zwar collection.
19. Roy Douglas Heron, statutory declaration, 19 July 2001, Zwar collection.
20. Charlie Parrott, AAWFA interview; Charlie Parrott, *An Aussie Nobody*, p. 50.
21. Charles Jager, *Escape from Crete*, p. 308.
22. Roy E.L. East, 'POW Experiences', Zwar collection.
23. L.J. Lind, *Escape from Crete*, p. 44.
24. A.E. Field, 'Prisoners of the Germans and Italians', p. 761.
25. 'SX8622 Milbank J. 2/8th Field Ambulance', Zwar collection.
26. Edwin N. Broomhead, *Barbed Wire in the Sunset*, pp. 56–7.
27. ibid., p. 56.
28. W.E.H. (Bill) Cousins, *A Lot of Fun in My Life!*, pp. 110–11.
29. Ray Jones, interview with the author, 3 December 2009.
30. Davis, p. 628.
31. NAA AWM MSS 1586: James Wright, The Lantern of Hope, manuscript, 1991.
32. Worthington, AAWFA interview.
33. Jack Wooding, letter to Arthur Leggett, 3 September 2001, Zwar collection.
34. Laurie West, interview with the author, 18 July 2008.

NOTES

35 Peter M. Barrett, letter to Ron Zwar, 26 August 2001, Zwar collection.
36 TNA WO 309/1863: War Crimes. Ill-Treatment of Sapper Leonard – AIF. Stanley Leonard, statutory declaration, 11 February 1946.
37 'Claim for Special Allowance to Ex-Prisoners of War 1939–1945', Zwar collection, pp. 11–12. According to the WWII Nominal Roll, Victor Clive Makepeace died as a POW on 17 February 1942.
38 Petschnigg, p. 53.
39 Doug Nix, interview with the author, 25 July 2009.
40 Patrick Toovey, AAWFA interview.
41 TNA WO 224/45: Report of ICRC visit to Stalag XVIII A Wolfsberg, 28 October 1944.
42 Petschnigg, p. 71.
43 Lyle Cullinger, letter, 23 August 2001, Zwar collection.
44 John Williamson, statutory declaration, 19 September 2001, Zwar collection.
45 Lindsay Lawrence, Blessed Be the Olive Trees, p. 88.
46 TNA WO 224/24: Stalag VII A. 1941 Oct.–1945 Apr. Red Cross Report on Labour Detachment 2780. Stalag VII A. Visited 7.3.42.
47 Rolf, p. 64.
48 The list was compiled by Bill France, who was attached to the administration office at Görlitz in 1944. In Phillip Loffman (ed.), POW, p. 5.
49 Ray J. Corbett, *Behind German Wire*, p. 52.
50 George W. Blanch, statutory declaration, Rutherford, 25 August 2001, in Zwar collection.
51 John Williamson, statutory declaration, 19 December 2001, Zwar collection.
52 Primo Levi, *If This Is a Man* and *The Truce*, London: Abacus, 1996, p. 105.
53 The three Australians listed were John Potts, Thomas Warren and Kelvin Cornell. The document from the State Museum of Auschwitz-Birkenau confirming arrival of POW Work Detachment E 738 at Trzebinia is dated 25 February 1944 and was kindly made available by Dr Piotr Setkiewicz, Head of Archives, State Museum of Auschwitz-Birkenau.
54 Rolf, pp. 67–8.
55 ibid., p. 68.
56 Corbett, p. 69.
57 Ray Corbett, interview with the author, 9 January 2011.
58 Phillip Loffman, statutory declaration, 11 March 2002, Zwar collection.
59 Sean Longden, *Hitler's British Slaves*, p. 65.
60 Arthur Leslie Leggett, statutory declaration, Bassendean, 16 August 2001, Zwar collection.

NOTES

61 Norman Tuckwell, unpublished statement, Zwar collection.
62 East.
63 Parrott, *An Aussie Nobody*, p. 73.
64 ibid.
65 TNA FO 916/519: 'Conditions of labour in prisoner of war camps 1943'.
66 PA-AA R 40/721: Schweizerische Gesandschaft, Abteilung Schutzmachtangelegenheiten an Auswärtiges Amt, 30 January 1945.
67 TNA FO 916/519: 'Conditions of labour in prisoner of war camps 1943.'
68 Hubert Speckner, Kriegsgefangene in der 'Ostmark' 1939–1945, p. 214.
69 PA-AA R 40/924: Englische Kriegsgefangene in Deutschland. Arbeitseinsatz und Entlohnung. Memorandum, Auswärtiges Amt an Schweizerische Gesandschaft, Abteilung Schutzmachtangelegenheiten, 30 September 1944.

Chapter 15: Crime and Punishment

1 Reg Worthington, AAWFA interview.
2 ibid.
3 BA-MA RH/49/37: Merkblatt für die Truppe. 10 Gebote für die Behandlung von Kriegsgefangenen, undated.
4 Charlie Parrott, AAWFA interview.
5 Lindsay P. Lawrence, Blessed Be the Olive Trees, p. 86.
6 Hubert Speckner, Kriegsgefangene in der 'Ostmark' 1939–1945, p. 202.
7 David Rolf, *Prisoners of the Reich*, p. 105.
8 BA-MA RH/49/38: Anweisung für Führer und Wachmannschaften von Kriegsgefangenen-Arbeitskommandos, 1 May 1944.
9 TNA WO 208/3244: Report by Air Force Prisoners of War in Germany, p. 35.
10 Ray J. Corbett, *Behind German Wire*, p. 82.
11 BArch R 58/187 f. 16: Meldungen aus dem Reich Nr. 340. 3.12.1942.
12 Younger, p. 108.
13 Doug Nix, interview with the author, 25 July 2009.
14 Speckner, p. 172.
15 Geoff Taylor, *A Piece of Cake*, p. 183.
16 TNA FO 916/520: Conditions of Labour in Prisoners of War Camps 1943. 'The Foreign Worker in Germany: 18 Supplement 1.5.43'.
17 TNA WO 224/45: Stalag XVIII A. Report of Red Cross visit 5–13 December 1944.
18 Corbett, p. 60.
19 Parrott, AAWFA interview.

NOTES

20 Lawrence Calder, AAWFA interview.
21 Doug Nix, interview with the author, 25 July 2009.
22 S. Slodash, *Be-Kavley ha-Shevi*, Tel Aviv: n.p. 1946, p. 177, cited in Yoav Gelber, 'Palestinian POWs in German Captivity', p. 23.
23 Ron Mackenzie, *An Ordinary War 1940–1945*, p. 65.
24 Charlie Parrott, *An Aussie Nobody*, p. 59.
25 Edwin N. Broomhead, *Barbed Wired in the Sunset*, p. 64.
26 Doug Nix, interview with the author, 25 July 2009.
27 Judy Lindsay, transcript of an interview with Alf Stone, Zwar collection.
28 Stefan Geck, 'Das deutsche Kriegsgefangenenwesen 1939–1945', p. 70.
29 PA-AA R 40/850A: Strafverfahren gegen Kriegsgefangene in Deutschland.
30 TNA WO 224/45: Stalag XVIII A. Report of visit 22 April 1944.
31 Charles Granquist, *A Long Way Home*, pp. 142–59.
32 Charles Worthington, AAWFA interview.
33 Doug Nix, interview with the author, 25 July 2009.
34 Leslie 'Aussie' Osborn, As I Saw It, p. 54, Zwar collection.
35 Lyle Cullinger, letter to Ron Zwar, 23 August 2001, Zwar collection.
36 ibid.
37 BArch NS 19/1963: Himmler an den Beauftragten für den Vierjahresplan and den Generalbevollmächtigten für den Arbeitseinsatz, 17 December 1943.
38 David Foy, *For You the War is Over*, p. 68.
39 ibid.
40 Champ and Burgess, *The Diggers of Colditz*, p. 191; Henry Chancellor, *Colditz*, p. xiii. Chancellor argues for over 310 escape attempts, 32 of which were successful, 15 from within the castle walls.
41 TNA FO 916/16: Reports on German POW Camps. American Report on IV C (Colditz) October 1941.
42 Chancellor, p. 77.
43 Rolf, p. 150.
44 TNA WO 224/69: Red Cross Reports on Oflag IV C – Colditz. 1941 May–1945 April. Report of visit 7 October 1944.
45 Champ and Burgess, p. 8.
46 ibid., p. 114.
47 ibid., pp. 147–52.
48 ibid., p. 163.
49 Colin Burgess (ed.), *Freedom or Death*, pp. 41–3.
50 ibid., pp. 48–50.

NOTES

51 TNA AIR 2/5754: Report by F/Lt. H.N. Fowler on his escape from German Prisoner of War Camp OFLAG IVC.
52 Champ and Burgess, pp. 135–7.
53 ibid., p. 170.
54 ibid., pp. 175–8.
55 Howard Satow and M. J. See, *The Work of the Prisoners of War Department during the Second World War*, p. 45.
56 PA-AA R 40/858: Strafverfahren gegen englische Kriegsgefangene in Deutschland.
57 PA-AA R 40/858: OKW an das Auswärtige Amt, 31 December 1942.
58 Satow and See, p. 46.
59 PA-AA R 40/856, R 40/857: Strafverfahren gegen englische Kriegsgefangene in Deutschland.
60 PA-AA R 40/858: Strafverfahren gegen Kriegsgefangene in Deutschland.
61 Ian Ramsay, *P.O.W.*, pp. 104–17.
62 Ramsay, p. 12.
63 PA-AA R 40/858: Strafverfahren gegen Kriegsgefangene in Deutschland.
64 Ramsay, p. 127.
65 TNA WO 311/160: Murder of Pte. W. Trainor. AIF at Torgau Military Prison 1942. Affidavit by Ian Ramsay.
66 ibid.

Part 3: Into the Abyss

Chapter 16: Total War

1 Cited in Richard J. Evans, *The Third Reich at War*, p. 424.
2 Olaf Groehler, *Bombenkrieg gegen Deutschland*, p. 343.
3 Ralf Blank, 'Kriegsalltag und Luftkrieg an der "Heimatfront"', in Jörg Echternkamp (ed.), *Das Deutsche Reich und der Zweite Weltkrieg. Bd. 9. Die deutsche Kriegsgesellschaft 1939 bis 1945*, p. 448.
4 BArch NS 19/344: Himmler an alle Hauptant chefs, 10 August 1943.
5 Stefan Geck, *Dulag Luft/Auswertestelle West*, p. 454.
6 Geck, p. 451.
7 ibid.
8 International Military Tribunal, Vol. XXVI, 731-PS (RF-1407), pp. 275ff; cited in Geck, p. 457.
9 Blank, p. 450, uses the figure of 350; Rüdger Overmans, 'Die Kriegsgefangenenpolitik des Deutschen Reiches 1939 bis 1945', p. 865, suggests 30.
10 John Mathews, AAWFA interview.

NOTES

11 Overmans, p. 858.
12 ibid., p. 860.
13 ibid., p. 861.
14 BArch R58/397: Geheime Staatspolizei – Staatspolizeistelle Köln. Aussendienststelle Aachen. Rundbrief an alle Staatspolizeileitstellen betr. 'Massnahmen gegen wiederergriffene flüchtige kriegsgefangene Offiziere mit Ausnahme britischer und amerikanischer Kriegsgefangener', 4 March 1944.
15 Jorg Bottger, 'Bullet Decree', in Jonathan F. Vance (ed.), *Encyclopedia of Prisoners of War and Internment*, pp. 35–6. See also S.P. MacKenzie, 'The Treatment of Prisoners of War in World War II', p. 499.
16 BArch R58/397: 'Massnahmen gegen weiderergriffene flüchtige kriegsgefangene Offiziere', 4 March 1944.

Chapter 17: The Great Escape

1 Paul Brickhill and Conrad Norton, *Escape to Danger*, pp. 243–53.
2 Alan Burgess, *The Longest Tunnel*, pp. 36–7.
3 Brickhill and Norton, pp. 271–2.
4 Burgess, p. 111.
5 Hugh Clarke, Colin Burgess and Russell Braddon, *Prisoners of War*, pp. 44–5.
6 ibid., p. 45.
7 ibid.
8 Allen Andrews, *Exemplary Justice*, pp. 43–4.
9 ibid., pp. 44–5.
10 NAA AWM 54 779/3/126: Part 1. Report by P. Kingsford-Smith.
11 NAA AWM54 779/1/22: Reports and statements by Major R.J. Binns 2/8 Field Ambulance and Capt. E.W. Levinger RMO 2/3 Anti-Tank Regiment AIF on Gruppignano POW Camp Italy. 1943.
12 NAA A705 163/64/183: Williams, John Edwin Ashley.
13 Andrews, p. 210.
14 This information is according to Royle's POW identity card – Personalkarte – held in the National Archives of Australia. NAA AA1969 100/543 Box 1.
15 Brickhill and Norton, pp. 313–15.
16 Burgess, p. 231.
17 Brickhill and Norton, pp. 318–21.
18 ibid., pp. 323–4.
19 NAA A1608/1 AT 20/1/1: Summary of Proceedings of Court of Enquiry Held to Investigate the Shooting of Air Force Personnel at Stalag Luft III, p. 2.

NOTES

20 Burgess, p. 159.
21 Brickhill and Norton, pp. 328–34.
22 Burgess, p. 156.
23 ibid., pp. 156, 270–3.
24 Andrews, p. 10.
25 ibid., p. 178.
26 Burgess, p. 270; Rob Davis, 'The Great Escape: The Real Escape', viewed 10 October 2010, www.historyinfilm.com/escape/real8.htm.
27 Burgess, p. 158; Davis, 'The Great Escape: The Real Escape'.
28 Andrews, p. 186.
29 Rob Davis and F. Fedorowicz, 'Stalag Luft 3: The Great Escape', viewed 10 October 2010, http://luft3.webpark.pl.
30 BA-MA Pers 6/2056: Personalakte Westhoff, Adolf.
31 BA-MA MSG 1/2014: Aussage Adolf Westhoff, 9. Oktober 1946, betr. Erschiessung der 50 britischen Fliegeroffiziere aus dem Stalag Luft III Sagan.
32 BA-MA MSG 1/2014: Aussage Westhoff, 9. Oktober 1946.
33 BA-MA MSG 1/2014: Aussage Westhoff, 9. Oktober 1946.
34 BA-MA Pers 6/2056: Personalakte Westhoff, Adolf.
35 BA-MA MSG 1/2014: Vorgänge bei der Flucht und Erschiessung der 51 britischen Fliegeroffiziere aus dem Luftstalag III Sagan.
36 NAA A1608/1 AT 20/1/1: Summary of Proceedings of Court of Enquiry Held to Investigate the Shooting of Air Force Personnel at Stalag Luft III, p. 2.
37 NAA A1608/1 AT 20/1/1: Summary of Proceedings, p. 3.
38 Arieh J. Kochavi, *Confronting Captivity*, p. 175.
39 NAA AA1969 100/543 Box 1: Royle's POW identity card.
40 Kochavi, p. 175.
41 ibid., p. 177.
42 ibid.
43 David Foy, *For You the War is Over*, pp. 32–3.
44 Kochavi, p. 178.
45 ibid., p. 177.
46 The Right Honourable Anthony Eden to the House of Commons on 23 June 1944, in Andrews, pp. 212–13.

Chapter 18: Sojourn in Buchenwald

1 Charlie Parrott, *An Aussie Nobody*, p. 59.
2 Colin Burgess, *Destination Buchenwald*, p. xx.
3 Ray Perry, 'Flight to Betrayal', in Arthur G. Kinnis and Stanley Booker, *168 Jump into Hell*, p. 59.

NOTES

4 Perry, p. 60.
5 ibid., p. 61.
6 ibid., p. 63.
7 ibid.
8 Oliver Clutton-Brock, *Footprints on the Sands of Time*, p. 195.
9 Burgess, pp. 51–6; Clutton-Brock, p. 196.
10 Buchenwald-Arch 55-101/6: Untersuchungsliste Lagerarzt.
11 Kurt Mellach and Paul Springer, 'The Tent Camp', in David A. Hackett (ed. and trans.), *The Buchenwald Report*, p. 277.
12 Buchenwald-Arch 55-101/6: Untersuchungsliste Lagerarzt.
13 Perry, p. 64.
14 Karl Feurer, 'Mass Murder of Russian Prisoners of War', in Hackett, p. 236.
15 National Mahn- und Gedenkstätte Buchenwald (ed.), *Buchenwald*, pp. 350–1; Harry Stein (trans. Judith Rosenthal), *Buchenwald Concentration Camp 1937–1945*, p. 171.
16 Christopher Burney, *Solitary Confinement and The Dungeon Democracy*.
17 National Mahn- und Gedenkstätte Buchenwald, pp. 344–7.
18 Interpretation Reports. A.2613. Attack on Weimar (Buchenwald) on 24 August 1944, in Kinnis and Booker, p. 239.
19 National Mahn- und Gedenkstätte Buchenwald, p. 349.
20 Daniel G. Dancocks, *In Enemy Hands*, p. 183.
21 Hackett, pp. 253–4.
22 Buchenwald-Arch NARA: Veränderungsmeldung K.L. Buchenwald 19. Oktober 1944. Washington RG 242 Film 9.
23 Jim 'Paladin' Fore and Larry Jacks, *Tragedy and Triumph*, p. 121.
24 Burgess, p. 138.
25 Kinnis and Booker, pp. 64, 238.

Chapter 19: Himmler Steps In

1 TNA FO 916/871: Ill treatment of Prisoners of War in Germany (Article 46 of Prisoners of War Convention) 1944. War Office to the Prisoners of War Department, Devonshire House, Piccadilly,14 August 1944.
2 NA WO 32/15543: SHAEF Board of Enquiry Report on Treatment of American and British POW. Exhibit H.
3 Stefan Geck, Das deutsche Kriegsgefangenenwesen 1939–1945, p. 28.
4 ibid., p. 30.
5 ibid., p. 29.

6 'Das Kriegsgefangenenwesen der Wehrmacht', viewed 15 January 2010, http://lexikon-der-wehrmacht.de/Gliederungen/Kriegsgefangenenlager/Kriegsgefangenenwesen.

7 BA-MA MSG/1 2012: Adolf Westhoff, Aufgabe und Arbeitsweise des Chefs bzw. Inspekteurs des KGW im OKW und Anlagen, p. 2.

8 Geck, p. 23.

9 S.P. MacKenzie, 'The Treatment of Prisoners of War in World War II', p. 495.

10 Rüdiger Overmans, 'Die Kriegsgefangenenpolitik des Deutschen Reiches 1939 bis 1945', p. 730.

11 ibid., p. 797.

12 International Military Tribunal, *Trial of the German Major War Criminals*, Nuremberg: HMSO, 1946–49, Vol. 16, pp. 48–9, cited in MacKenzie, p. 496.

13 Overmans, p. 865.

14 BA-MA Pers 6/2056: Personalakte Westhoff, Adolf; BA-MA MSG 1/2014: Personalakte Adolf Westhoff Aussage Westhoff Oberursel 9. Oktober 1946.

15 BA–MA MSG 1/2012: Adolf Westhoff, Aufgabe und Arbeitsweise des Chefs bzw. Inspekteurs des KGW im OKW und Anlagen, p. 2.

16 Geck, p. 23.

17 BArch SSO/058, SS-Führerpersonalakten. Gottlob Berger.

18 See also Mark M. Boatner, *Biographical Dictionary of World War II*, p. 35.

19 Overmans, p. 862.

20 ibid., p. 849.

21 Geck, p. 34.

22 TNA WO 208/4440: Gottlob Berger. CSDIC (UK) GG Report.

23 Henry Chancellor, *Colditz: The Definitive History*, pp. 352–61.

24 ibid., p. 363.

25 ibid., pp. 363–4.

26 ibid., pp. 365–6.

27 Leslie Le Souef, *To War without a Gun*, pp. 333–4.

Chapter 20: The Small Fortress

1 Bill Rudd, 'ANZAC POW Free Men in Europe, Part Five', viewed 10 December 2010, www.aifpow.com/part_5-free_men-elsewhere-in-europe/chapter_7-germany_and_austria.

2 'Theresienstadt 1941–1945 – Ein Nachschlagewerk. Die Kleine Festung – Gefängnis der Gestapo', viewed 12 December 2010, www.ghetto-theresienstadt.info/terezingefaeng nis.htm.

NOTES

3 ibid.
4 Paul Rea, *Voices from the Fortress*, p. 19.
5 A list compiled by the Concentration Camps Committee in the Department of Veterans' Affairs contains the names of 17 Australians who claimed they had been in Terezín. Of these, six (Frederick Lawrence, Alexander McClelland, Denis McMahon, Jack Porteous, Walter Riley, Walter Steilberg) received payments. List kindly provided by Keith Hooper.
A list provided by Voytech Blodig from the Terezín Memorial contains the name Cecil Froom. See Jim Saleam, 'The Historian as Detective Versus the Journalist as Investigator: Were Australian, British and New Zealand Prisoners of War Massacred at Theresienstadt Concentration Camp in 1945?' 2 October 2004 at //home.alphalink.com.au/~radnat/terezin.html. This is almost certainly Cecil Froome, a butcher from Uralla in NSW who served in the 2/1st Field Ambulance and was captured in Greece.
His service record shows him at Lamsdorf on 2 March 1945 and reported as recovered in Europe by 16 May.
6 Rea, p. 36.
7 ibid., p. 37.
8 Douglas Collins, *POW*, p. 164.
9 HL HM Ált. 21. oszt. 21 tétel 481. 169. 2–3: Angol hadifoglyok elfogása ügyében jelent, 1 June 1943; HL HM Ált. 21. oszt. 21 tétel 481. 169. 4–5: Ferguson Malcon és 2 társa angol hadifoglyok kikérdezé, 7 June 1943. Record provided courtesy Laszlo Ritter.
10 NAA AWM54 781/6/6: Prisoner of War Statements – Europe. NX1164 Sapper Walter Henry Chrestense Steilberg. Award of the British Empire Medal. Citation.
11 Rea, p. 100.
12 ibid., p. 101.
13 ibid., p. 107.
14 Citing the testimony of a British survivor Rea suggests about 180 English-speaking prisoners were released on 4 April 1944, Rea, pp. 26, 257. Jim Saleam, citing correspondence with the official historian of the Terezín Memorial, Voytech Blodig, suggests a figure of 63, including four Australians, but not including US-Americans. Blodig's list contains the name Cecil Froome but not Riley and McClelland, Saleam, p. 19.
15 Rea, p. 145.
16 ibid., p. 159.
17 ibid., pp. 160–2.
18 ibid., p. 194.
19 Alexander McClelland, *The Answer – Justice*, p. 124.
20 ibid., p. 125.
21 ibid., pp. 124–5.

NOTES

22 TNA WO 311/199 20447, cited in Rea p. 257.
23 Rea, pp. 194–5, 238.
24 'Theresienstadt 1941–1945 – Ein Nachschlagewerk. Die Kleine Festung – Gefängnis der Gestapo'.
25 TNA FO 916/1166: Ill-treatment of Prisoners of War in German Hands 1945; TNA WO 311/199: Theresienstadt Concentration Camp Germany: Ill-treatment of British POWs. See also Rea pp. 202–53; Saleam, passim.
26 Rea, pp. 182–3.
27 McClelland, p. 128.

Chapter 21: Holidaying for Hitler

1 Conversation between Ray Corbett and the author, 20 March 2010.
2 Ray Corbett, interview with the author, 9 January 2010.
3 ibid.
4 Alexander McClelland, *The Answer – Justice*, p. 103.
5 Barney Roberts, *A Kind of Cattle*, pp. 115–16.
6 The Australian Nominal Roll contains the name of the POW Rex Dakers, a chaplain from Scotsdale in Tasmania, viewed 10 November 2010, www.ww2roll.gov.au/script/veteran.asp?serviceID=A&VeteranID=416896.
7 Charlotte Higgins, 'Elisabeth Schwarzkopf dies at 90', *Guardian*, 4 August 2006.
8 Roberts, p. 118.
9 Vanessa Allen, 'Revealed: British opera singer turned spy who performed for Hitler with secret documents hidden in her underwear', *Daily Mail*, 10 September 2010, www.dailymail.co.uk/news/article-1310484/Margery-Booth-British-opera-singer-turned-spy-performed-Hitler.html.
10 Roberts, p. 120.
11 ibid., pp. 118–20.
12 ibid., pp. 121–2.
13 ibid., p. 122.
14 Karl Heinz Pfeffer, *Die bürgerliche Gesellschaft in Australien*.
15 'Karl Heinz Pfeffer', Wikipedia, viewed 11 March 2010, http://de.wikipedia.org/wiki/Karl_Heinz_Pfeffer.
16 Roberts, pp. 128–9.
17 James W. Reeves, *One Man's War*, p. 100.
18 ibid., p. 103.
19 ibid., p. 101.
20 S.P. MacKenzie, *The Colditz Myth*, pp. 300–1.
21 ibid., pp. 301–2.
22 Carolle J. Carter, *The Shamrock and the Swastika*, pp. 19–20.

NOTES

23 ibid., pp. 124–5; David Rolf, *Prisoners of the Reich*, pp. 118–19.
24 This was the assumption made by MI5 officer Lieutenant Colonel V.H. Seymer in his report from 27 March 1945 on the Holiday Camps. Report viewed 20 March 2010, www.stephen-stratford.co.uk/mi5_and_bfc.htm.
25 Hans Werner Neulen, *An deutscher Seite. Internationale Freiwillige von Wehrmacht und Waffen-SS*, p. 135.
26 Terry Fairbairn, 'The Irish Brigade and Camp, Plus Other Matters', in E.C. Givney (ed.), *The First at War*, p. 524. See also Terry Fairbairn, AAWFA interview.
27 Fairbairn, AAWFA interview.
28 Fairbairn, 'The Irish Brigade', p. 525.
29 Laurie West, interview with the author, 18 July 2008.
30 BA-MA RH/53/17/183: Wehrkreis XVII. OKW Kriegsgef. Allg. (1a) an alle Wehrkreiskommandos, 22.1.1942.
31 BA-MA MSG/1 201L: Die propagandistische Einwirkung auf die während des zweiten Weltkrieges in deutscher Hand befindlichen Kgf. p. 8.
32 PA-AA R 27/835: Handakten Ritter OKW 04.03.1944–08.12.1944. April 1944. Schmidt, Aufzeichnung über Gliederung und Tätigkeit der Kriegs-gefangenenorganisation des Auswärtigen Amtes.
33 ibid.
34 Auswärtiges Amt (ed.), *Biographisches Handbuch des deutschen Auswärtigen Dienstes 1871–1945. Bd. 2 G-K*, Paderborn: Auswärtiges Amt, 2005, pp. 296–7.
35 Information via correspondence courtesy Herbert Karbach, PA-AA, 30 November 2010.
36 TNA WO 224/93: Memorandum on possible Political Aspects of the so-called 'Holiday Camps'.
37 PA-AA R 27/835: Handakten Ritter OKW 04.03.1944–08.12.1944. April 1944. Aufzeichnung über Gliederung und Tätigkeit der Kriegsgefangenenorganisation des Auswärtigen Amtes.
38 TNA WO 224 55B: Officers Recreation Camp Steinburg Bavaria. Stalag 383/Z. Memorandum by Repatriated Officer Captain Montgomery Belgion on Political Aspects of So-Called Holiday Camps.
39 BArch NS/2162: Chef Kriegsgefangenenwesen an den Reichsführer-SS. Betr. Sonderlager für britische Kriegsgefangene, 4 November 1944.
40 Oliver Clutton-Brock, *Footprints on the Sands of Time*, p. 191.
41 BArch NS/2162: Betr. Sonderlager für britische Kriegsgefangene.
42 TNA WO 224/84: Report on Steinburg holiday camp by Albert Kadler dated 25 June 1944.
43 ibid.
44 Clutton-Brock, p. 193.

NOTES

45 Rolf, p. 120.
46 Cited in S.P. MacKenzie, *The Colditz Myth*, p. 251.
47 PA-AA R 27/835: Handakten Ritter. Aufzeichnung.
48 ibid.
49 Report to Reich Foreign Minister by Baron von Steengracht, cited in Hans Werner Neulen, *An deutscher Seite*, p. 129.
50 Neulen, pp. 130–1.
51 The interpretation of the Third Reich which stresses the multitude of competing agencies and individuals, and the dynamics resulting from that competition, is commonly referred to as 'structuralist' or 'functionalist'. The label 'polycratic' stems from one of the proponents of that interpretation, Martin Broszat. See Broszat, *The Hitler State*.
52 PA-AA R 27/835: Handakten Ritter. Aufzeichnung.
53 ibid.
54 ibid.
55 BArchiv NS 19/3097: Leiter der Volksdeutschen Mittelstelle (SS-Obergruppenführer Lorenz) an den Reichsführer-SS, 14 June 1942, p. 2.
56 BArchiv NS 19/594: Richtlinien für eine Sonderbehandlung deutschstämmiger Kriegsgefangener aus Übersee.
57 BArchiv NS 19/3097: Reichsführer-SS an Lorenz, 29 June 1942.
58 BArchiv NS 19/3097: Reichsführer-SS an SS-Obersturmbannführer Wagner im Auswärtigen Amt, 5 October 1943.
59 BArchiv NS 19/3097: Reichsführer-SS an den Chef der Sicherheitspolizei und des SD, Chef des Hauptamtes Volksdeutsche Mittelstelle, Chef des SS-Hauptamtes, 30 January 1944.
60 BArch NS 19/2162: Stroop, Höhere SS-U. Pol. Führer Rhein/Westmark an Himmler, 14 October 1944.
61 'Jürgen Stroop', Wikipedia, viewed 10 March 2010, http://en.wikipedia.org/wiki/J%C3%BCrgen_Stroop.
62 BArch NS 19/2162: Himmler an Berger, 14 October 1944.
63 BArch NS 19/2162: Betr. Sonderlager für britische Kriegsgefangene.
64 BArch NS 19/2162: SS-Obergruppenführer Berger, Chef des Kriegsgefangenenwesens an Himmler, 4 November 1944.
65 BArch NS 19/2162: Auswärtiges Amt an Brandt, Persönlicher Stab RFSS, 5 December 1944.
66 ibid.
67 BArch NS 19/2162: SS Standartenführer R. Brandt, Personalstab RFSS an Standartenführer Wagner, Auswärtiges Amt, 8 December 1944.
68 TNA WO 224 55B: Officers Recreation Camp Steinburg Bavaria. Stalag 383/Z. Federal Political Department, Foreign Interests Division (Switzerland) to British Minister Berne, 3 January 1945.

NOTES

69 TNA AIR 40/280: cited in Clutton-Brock, p. 192.
70 MacKenzie, p. 252.
71 John Brown, *In Durance Vile*, passim.
72 ibid., pp. 11–53.
73 ibid., p. 73.
74 NAA B883 NX34657: Holroyd Ralph, p. 8.
75 Allen.
76 A. Weale, *Renegades*, Chapter 7.
77 Adrian Weale, *Patriot Traitors*, pp. 174–5.
78 Brown, p. 148.
79 Diary of G.F.W. Wilson, 14 May 1944, Imperial War Museum, cited in MacKenzie, p. 304.
80 NAA A471/1: Court Martial of Private Albert James Stokes, 17 August 1945, cited in Robert Loeffel, 'Treasonous Conduct', p. 22.
81 NAA A471/1: Courtmartial of Private Albert James Stokes. Statement by Private Robert Chipchase, cited in Loeffel, p. 22.
82 Loeffel, p. 22.
83 Lieutenant Colonel V.H. Seymer, Report on Holiday Camps, 27.3.1945, viewed 20 March 2010, www.stephen-stratford.co.uk/mi5_and_bfc.htm.
84 Loeffel, p. 21.
85 Gabe Thomas, *MILAG*, p. 260.
86 ibid.
87 Loeffel, p. 23.
88 ibid.
89 Thomas, p. 260.

Part 4: Freedom

Chapter 22: Escape

1 TNA WO 208/3242: Historical Record of MI9. Specimen Lecture for Army Units on Conduct if Cut Off from Unit, or Captured by Enemy.
2 BA-MA RH49/112: Schulung in Verhinderung von Fluchten, p. 8, cited in Stefan Geck, 'Das deutsche Kriegsgefangenenwesen 1939–1945', p. 86.
3 Charles Granquist, *A Long Way Home*, p. 159.
4 Jim Paterson, *Partisans, Peasants and POWs*, p. 62.
5 ibid., pp. 62–3.
6 Hugh Clarke, Colin Burgess, Russell Braddon, *Prisoners of War*, p. 40.
7 NAA AWM54 781/6/6: File containing material for use by official historian.
8 'Franz von Werra', Wikipedia, viewed 11 October 2010, http://en.wikipedia.org/wiki/Franiz_von_Werra.

NOTES

9   NAA AWM54 781/6/6: Material for use by official historian.
10 ibid.
11 Geck, p. 75.
12 NAA AWM54 781/6/6: Material for use by official historian.
13 Ron Zwar, interview with the author, 7 May 2010.
14 TNA WO 208/3242: Historical Record of MI9.
15 ibid.
16 Graham Pitchfork, *Shot Down and on the Run*, p. 27.
17 Charles Jager, *Escape from Crete*, p. 203.
18 ibid., pp. 224–9.
19 Arthur Henry Buxton, Brief Outline of Time Spent as POW, manuscript, Zwar collection, p. 15.
20 AWM PRO1535: Papers of P.J. Cusack, Wallet 1.
21 Keith Hooper, interview with the author, 19 January 2008.
22 Frank Atkins, Salonika, Greece, to Lamsdorf, Germany: Memories of a Sojourn in a Cattle Truck, unpublished manuscript, Zwar collection.
23 Lindsay P. Lawrence, Blessed Be the Olive Trees, p. 83
24 Unpublished statement by Norman Tuckwell, Zwar collection.
25 Doug Nix, interview with the author, 25 July 2009.
26 NAA AWM54 781/6/6: Material for use by official war historian. Citation for Francis Alfred Barrett.
27 Edward J. Sweeney, *A Merchant Seaman's Survival*, pp. 133–247.
28 Bill Rudd, 'ANZAC POW Free Men in Europe, Part 4', viewed 30 July 2009, www.aifpow.com.
29 Jack Champ and Colin Burgess, *The Diggers of Colditz*, pp. 47–8.
30 ibid., pp. 49–51.
31 ibid., pp. 52–3.
32 ibid., p. 53.
33 ibid., pp. 36–8.
34 ibid., p. 58.
35 ibid., pp. 64–8.
36 ibid., pp. 69–71.
37 ibid., p. 72.
38 Oliver Clutton-Brock, *Footprints on the Sands of Time*, pp. 467–9.
39 Clarke, Burgess and Braddon, p. 47.
40 Edith Petschnigg, *Von der Front aufs Feld*, p. 92.
41 Ray Jones, interview with the author, 3 December 2009.
42 ibid.

NOTES

43   Philip Loffman (ed.), *POW*, pp. 57–8.
44   Fred Vardy, '1200 Mile Trek South to Allied Lines September 43–May 44', in Loffman (ed.), pp. 41–2.
45   James W. Reeves, *One Man's War*, pp. 87–92.
46   Loffman (ed.), pp. 45, 139–40, 150.
47   ibid., p. 178.
48   NAA AWM54 781/6/6: Material for use by official war historian.
49   Lawrence Calder, AAWFA interview.
50   Hubert Speckner, Kriegsgefangene in der 'Ostmark' 1939–1945, p. 168.
51   Ralph Churches, *A Hundred Miles as the Crow Flies*, p. 9.
52   ibid., pp. 22–45.
53   ibid., pp. 52–63.
54   ibid., pp. 65–89.
55   ibid., pp. 91–140.
56   ibid., p. 158.
57   Paterson, pp. 70–91.
58   ibid., pp. 92–3.
59   ibid., pp. 112–57.
60   NAA AWM54 781/6/6: Material for use by official war historian.
61   Bill Bunbury, *Rabbits and Spaghetti*, pp. 100–3.
62   ibid., p. 103.
63   ibid., pp. 126–7.
64   ibid., p. 157.
65   AWM PR 03098: Papers of Lt. J.D. Peck.
66   Bunbury, p. 166.
67   ibid., p. 170.
68   ibid., p. 180.

Chapter 23: Exchanges and Repatriation

1   Richard Reid, *Stolen Years*, p. 16.
2   Jonathan F. Vance (ed.), *Encyclopedia of Prisoners of War and Internment*, p. 226.
3   David Miller, *Mercy Ships*, p. 13.
4   PA-AA R 40/774: Kriegsgefangenen-Austausch mit England.
5   Miller, p. 14; PA-AA R 40/775: Kriegsgefangenen-Austausch mit England 1941–1945.
6   David Rolf, *Prisoners of the Reich*, p. 131.
7   Rüdiger Overmans, 'Die Kriegsgefangenenpolitik des Deutschen Reiches 1939 bis 1945', p. 791.

NOTES

8   A.E. Field, 'Prisoners of the Germans and Italians', p. 772.
9   Field, p. 772.
10 George Worledge, AAWFA interview.
11 Miller, pp. 17–18.
12 Hal Finkelstein, In and Out of Barbed Wire, p. 68.
13 F.G. Atkins, 'POW Exchanges – 2/11th Personnel', in K.T. Johnson, *The 2/11th (City of Perth) Australian Infantry Battalion*, p. 179.
14 Charles Robinson, *Journey to Captivity*, p. 168.
15 ibid., p. 169.
16 Miller, p. 19; Field, p. 805.
17 PA-AA R 40/796: Austausch schwerverwundeter und kranker Kriegsgefangener zwischen Deutschland und England. Bericht über die Repatriierungsaktion 26.5.1944.
18 Field, p. 807.
19 Frank Cox, interview with the author, 17 July 2008.
20 NAA A1066/4, IC45/6/2/14: Prisoners of War – Australian. Australian Prisoners of War in Europe. Fifth Exchange of Sick and Wounded with Germany.
21 Atkins, p. 178.

Chapter 24: On the Move

1   Daniel G. Dancocks, *In Enemy Hands*, p. 172.
2   AWM MSS 1566: Henry John Bastian. Memoirs of Henry John Bastian 24.12.17 to 25.7.89, compiled by son Raymond Henry Bastian, pp. 138–9.
3   ibid.
4   NAA AWM54, 779/3/126: Statements by Royal Australian Air Force Personnel from Prisoners of War Camps in Germany and Italy. Part I of II parts. Report by W/O T.A. Roberts.
5   Jack Liley, *Jack's War*, p. 156.
6   AWM MSS 1566: Henry John Bastian, p. 145.
7   ibid., p. 147.
8   ibid., p. 148.
9   Arieh J. Kochavi, *Confronting Captivity*, p. 203.
10 BA-MA RH/3 378: Abteilung Kriegsverw. (QU 4). Vortragsnotiz für Herrn Generalquartiermeister.
11 Kochavi, p. 203.
12 Ron Mackenzie, *An Ordinary War 1940–1945*, p. 85.
13 Allan Campbell, letter to Ron Zwar, 30 May 2001, Zwar collection.
14 Hugh Clarke, Colin Burgess and Russell Braddon, *Prisoners of War*, pp. 50–1.

NOTES

15 Kochavi, p. 205.
16 David Rolf, *Prisoners of the Reich*, pp. 167–8.
17 Paul Brickhill and Conrad Norton, *Escape to Danger*, pp. 340–1.
18 Wilf Hodgson, *Bombs and Barbed Wire*, p. 82.
19 J.E. Holliday (ed.), *Stories of the RAAF POWs of Lamsdorf Including Chronicles of Their 500 Mile Trek*, p. 194.
20 Reg Centillon, diary extract, in Holliday (ed.), p. 281.
21 Rolf, pp. 155–6.
22 Centillon, p. 286.
23 Doug Butterworth, in Holliday (ed.), p. 255.
24 ibid., p. 25.
25 Rolf, p. 155.
26 Ray Corbett, *Behind German Wire*, p. 168.
27 ibid., p. 170.
28 Arthur Leggett, Incidence of ill-treatment whilst being held as a Prisoner-of-War in Germany from 1941 until 1945, unpublished manuscript, Zwar collection.
29 ibid.
30 Mackenzie, p. 98.
31 Leggett.
32 G.C. Anderson, 'The Long March. Domrova, Poland to Regensburg, Bavaria', in K.T. Johnson (ed.), *The 2/11th (City of Perth) Infantry Battalion*, p. 169.
33 Letter from Bill Bosse to Mrs Williams 5 September 1945, in Glenn Matthews (ed.), *In the Pink*, p. 87.
34 TNA AIR 40/2361: Camp Conditons and Treatment of Prisoners.
35 TNA FO 916/1152: ICRC Reports on German camps. Report on Oflag VII B Eichstätt, 8 February 1945.
36 TNA WO 224/55A: Stalag 383 1943 Jan. – 1945 Mar. Report of Stalag 383 Hohenfels, 14 March 1945.
37 Rolf, p. 169.
38 NAA A816/1, 67/301/134: Prisoners of War. Prisoners of War Camp etc. in Germany and Occupied Europe. File 5. Cablegram Australian Legation Moscow to Department of External Affairs, Canberra, 20 April 1945.
39 ibid.
40 NAA A1066 IC45/6/2/16: Prisoner of War – Australia. Australian Prisoners of War in Europe. German proposal for non-removal of POWs. Cablegram High Commissioner's Office London to Department of External Affairs, received 25 April 1945.
41 Kochavi, p. 220.
42 Allan S. Walker, *Australia in the War of 1939–1945*, p. 486.

NOTES

Chapter 25: Liberation

1. As reported by Viscount Cranborne in a cablegram to the Commonwealth Government 1 February 1945, in W.J. Hudson and Wendy Way (eds), *Documents on Australian Foreign Policy 1937–1949*, p. 35.
2. Harold Satow and M.J. See, *The Work of the Prisoners of War Department During the Second World War*, p. 67.
3. ibid., p. 36.
4. ibid., p. 37.
5. ibid., p. 36.
6. Commonwealth Government to Cranborne, Canberra, 5 February 1945, in Hudson and Way (eds), p. 39.
7. Cranborne to Commonwealth Government, London, 5 February 1945, in Hudson and Way (eds), p. 40.
8. Commonwealth Government to Cranborne, Canberra, 7 February 1945, in Hudson and Way (eds), p. 41.
9. Commonwealth Government to Cranborne, Canberra, 9 February 1945, in Hudson and Way (eds), p. 42.
10. Commonwealth Government to Cranborne, Canberra, 9 February 1945, in Hudson and Way (eds), p. 43.
11. Cranborne to Curtin, London, 9 February 1945, in Hudson and Way (eds), pp. 44–5.
12. J.J. Maloney was Australia's Minister to Moscow from 1943 to 1946. He wrote an account of his experiences there after the war under the title *Inside Red Russia*.
13. Herbert Evatt to J.J. Maloney, Canberra, 9 February 1945, in Hudson and Way (eds), p. 43.
14. NAA A1066 IC45/6/2/1 PART 1: Prisoners of War – Australian. Australian Prisoners of War in Europe. Treatment of Prisoners of War Liberated by USSR. Cablegram Secretary of State for Dominoin Affairs London to Prime Minister's Department, Canberra, 13 Feb. 1945.
15. The point is made in a Cablegram, Maloney to Department of External Affairs, Moscow, 1 March 1945, in Hudson and Way (eds), p. 79.
16. NAA A1066 IC45/6/2/1 PART 1: Cablegram Australian Legation Moscow to Department of External Affairs, Canberra, 3 April 1946.
17. Maloney to Department of External Affairs, Moscow, 12 February 1945, in Hudson and Way (eds), pp. 48–9.
18. NAA A1066 IC45/6/2/1 PART 1: Cablegram Australian Legation Moscow to Department of External Affairs, Canberra, 30 March 1945.
19. TNA FO 934/5/55 (1): Enclosure, letter from Lawford to Dixon, 20 July 1945, in Rohan Butler, M.E. Pelly and H.J. Yasamee (eds), *Documents on British Policy Overseas*, pp. 804–5.

NOTES

20 Maloney to Department of External Affairs, Moscow, 1 March 1945, in Hudson and Way (eds), p. 79.
21 Department of External Affairs to Maloney, Canberra, 22 March 1945, in Hudson and Way (eds), pp. 92–3.
22 Maloney to Department of External Affairs, Moscow, 25 March 1945, in Hudson and Way (eds), pp. 94–5.
23 Charlie Parrott, AAWFA interview.
24 ibid.
25 Charlie Parrott, *An Aussie Nobody*, p. 84.
26 Barney Roberts, *A Kind of Cattle*, pp. 167–8.
27 ibid., pp. 170–1.
28 ibid., pp. 175–6.
29 Hugh Clarke, Colin Burgess and Russell Braddon, *Prisoners of War*, p. 53.
30 NAA A1066 IC45/6/2/1 Part 1: Confidential information for censors by Chief Publicity Censor, 17 April 1945.
31 TNA WO 224/6: Conditions in Camps Stalag III A. Report by Wing Commander R.C.M. Collard on Stalag 3A Luckenwalde Germany 12.4.1945 to 20.5.1945.
32 Wilf Hodgson, *Bombs and Barbed Wire*, p. 83.
33 TNA WO 224/6: Report by Wing Commander R.C.M. Collard on Stalag 3A Luckenwalde.
34 Wesley Betts, statutory declaration, 23 January 2002, Zwar collection.
35 TNA WO 224/6: Report by Wing Commander R.C.M. Collard on Stalag 3A Luckenwalde.
36 ibid.
37 ibid.
38 TNA WO 208/3242: Swiss Protecting Power Report to Foreign Office, London, 5 February 1945.
39 Ron Zwar, 'Compo. Claim Details POW. Experiences and Treatment', Zwar collection; Ron Zwar, interview with the author, 7 May 2010.
40 James W. Reeves, *One Man's War*, pp. 107–12.
41 Philip Loffman (ed.), *POW*, p. 100.
42 ibid., p. 102.
43 NAA AWM54 779/4/21: Reports by International Red Cross and Protecting Powers on Conditions existing in Prisoners of War Camps in Germany and Italy. Report, 'Repatriation of Australian Prisoners of War in Europe'.
44 NAA AWM54 779/4/21: Report, 'Repatriation of Australian Prisoners of War in Europe'.
45 Noel Collins, *I Flew Tigers to Bombers*, pp. 173–4.
46 John Mathews, AAWFA interview.

NOTES

47 ibid.
48 Roy Corbett, interview with the author, 9 January 2010.
49 Keith Hooper, interview with the author, 19 January 2008.
50 Keith Hooper, 'Hiding and Hoping', in M.N. McKibbin et al., *Barbed Wire: Memories of Stalag 383*.
51 Laurie West, interview with the author, 18 July 2008.
52 'History of Stalag XVIII A', viewed 10 July 2009, www.stalag18a.org.uk/frameset.html.
53 YMCAA: Henry Soderberg, Report of Work among Prisoners of War in Germany During the Months of April and May 1945, 20 June 1945, World War Work II – Germany. SSI – T.11. File 1 – 11. Vol. 7.
54 Doug Nix, interview with the author, 25 July 2009.
55 Paul Brickhill and Conrad Norton, *Escape to Danger*, p. 341.
56 David Rolf, *Prisoners of the Reich*, p. 183.
57 Czech Meritorious Cross: Private L.P. Saywell, Australian Army Service Corps, 17 Infantry Brigade, 6 Division, viewed 10 December 2010, http://cas.awm.gov.au/item/OL00552.001.
58 Peter Thompson, *ANZAC Fury*, p. 431; statistics from AWM Encyclopaedia, viewed 10 December 2010, www.awm.gov.au/encyclopedia/pow/ww2/index.asp. Material made available to the official war historian broke the casualties down as follows: died of wounds while POW – 56; killed and presumed dead while POW – 91; died of sickness, disease and injury while POW – 95; see also AWM54 781/6/6: Material for official war history.
59 Peter Johnson, *The Withered Garland*, p. 260.
60 Ron Mackenzie, *An Ordinary War 1940–1945*, p. 104.
61 NAA AWM 845/2/7: The Scheme for Repatriation of RAAF Prisoners of War ex Germany. 'Special Administrative Section No. 11 PDRC'.
62 Mackenzie, p. 105.
63 NAA AWM 845/2/7: 'Special Administrative Section No. 11 PDRC'.
64 Parrott, AAWFA interview.
65 Clarke, Burgess and Braddon, p. 53.

Aftermath

1 Mentioned by Jack Champ and Colin Burgess in *The Diggers of Colditz*, p. 159.
2 David Rolf, *Prisoners of the Reich*, p. 85.
3 'Australian prisoners of war: Second World War – prisoners in Europe', viewed 20 December 2010, www.awm.gov.au/encyclopedia/pow/ww2.

NOTES

4   I.L. Duncan et al., 'Morbidity of Prisoners of War', n.p.: POW Association of Australia, 1985, pamphlet in Zwar collection.
5   ibid., p. 6.
6   NAA AWM54 779/4/21: Reports by International Red Cross and Protecting Powers on Conditions Existing in Prisoner of War Camps in Germany and Italy. P.H. Norman, 'The Prisoner of War Mentality. Its Effect after Repatriation'.
7   ibid.
8   Rolf, p. 175.
9   NAA AWM 845/2/7: The Scheme for Repatriation of RAAF Prisoners of War ex Germany. 'Special Administrative Section No. 11 PDRC', p. 2.
10 Hal Finkelstein, In and Out of Barbed Wire, pp. 75–6.
11 Reg Worthington, AAWFA interview.
12 Charlie Parrott, AAWFA interview.
13 Finkelstein, p. 82.
14 Calton Younger, *No Flight from the Cage*, p. 256.
15 Doug Nix, interview with the author, 25 July 2009.
16 ibid.
17 Alf Stone, interview by Judy Lindsay, Zwar collection.
18 Ernest Brough, *Dangerous Days*, pp. 290–1.
19 ibid., p. 310.
20 W.E.H. (Bill) Cousins, *A Lot of Fun in My Life!* p. 184.
21 Alex Jenkins, AAWFA interview.
22 Laurie West, interview with the author, 18 July 2008.
23 Cited in Paul Rea, *Voices from the Fortress*, p. 242.
24 *The Trial of German Major War Criminals*, p. 26.
25 Hubert Speckner, Kriegsgefangene in der 'Ostmark' 1939–1945, p. 224.
26 Eric Cuddon (ed.), *The Trial of Erich Killinger, Heinz Junge, Otto Boehringer, Heinrich Eberhardt, Gustav Bauer-Schlichtegroll (The Dulag Luft Trial)*, passim.
27 Oliver Clutton-Brock, *Footprints on the Sands of Time*, p. 196.
28 Hans Werner Neulen, *An deutscher Seite*, p. 132.
29 The Right Honourable Antony Eden to the House of Commons, 23 June 1944, cited in Allen Andrews, *Exemplary Justice*, pp. 212–13.
30 Andrews, p. 199.
31 ibid., p. 217.
32 ibid., p. 7; Priscilla Dale Jones, 'Nazi Atrocities Against Allied Airmen', pp. 543–65.

NOTES

33 Thomas Karny, 'Rechenschaft statt Rache'.
34 'Theresienstadt 1941–1945 – Ein Nachschlagewerk. Die Kleine Festung – Gefängnis der Gestapo', viewed 20 January 2011, www.ghetto-theresienstadt.info/terezingefaeng nis.htm.
35 Hank Nelson, *Prisoners of War*, p. 211.
36 Stephen Garton, *The Cost of War*, p. 222.

Bibliography

PRIMARY SOURCES

Archives du Comité international de la Croix-Rouge (Archives of the International Committee of the Red Cross, ICRC, Geneva) (ACICR)

Items from the following series:

C SC Service des camps

Australian War Memorial (AWM)

PERSONAL PAPERS AND MANUSCRIPT MATERIAL

AWM MSS 1551 Flight Lieutenant. R.A. Bethell

AWM MSS 1566 Henry John Bastian

AWM MSS 1600 Victor Hillas

AWM MSS 1675 Beecroft, James M

AWM PR 01451 Papers of Farrell, George

AWM PR 01535 Papers of P.J. Cusack

AWM PR 03000 Papers of Playfair, Alfred (Flight Lieutenant) 1910–1983

AWM PR 03098 Papers of Lieutenant J.D. Peck

AWM PR 03211 Papers of Flight Lieutenant Peter Kingsford-Smith

AWM PR 82/816 Diaries and Autobiography of Major General Ian Campbell CO 2/1st Battalion, AIF

BIBLIOGRAPHY

NATIONAL ARCHIVES OF AUSTRALIA (NAA) MATERIAL HELD IN AWM

Items from the following series:
AWM54 Written Records, 1939–1945 War
AWM63 2nd AIF Headquarters (Middle East), registry records

Bundesarchiv Berlin-Lichterfelde (Federal Archives, Berlin) (BArch)

Items from the following series:
NS 6 Partei-Kanzlei der NSDAP
NS 19 Persönlicher Stab Reichsführer SS
R 43 Reichskanzlei
R 58 Reichssicherheitshauptamt
R 901 Auswärtiges Amt
R 1501 Reichsministerium des Innern

Bundesarchiv-Militärarchiv Freiburg im Breisgau (Federal Military Archives, Freiburg) (BA-MA)

MSG (Militärgeschichtliche/Sachthematische Sammlung) 1 Chef bzw. Inspekteur des Kriegsgefangenenwesens im OKW
MSG 194 Evangelisches Hilfswerk e.V.
Pers 6/2056 Personalakte Adolf Westhoff
RH 20-12 Kreta
RH 49 Wehrkreiskommandos
RH 53 3 Wehrkreiskommando III (Berlin)
RH 53 8 Werhkreiskommando VIII (Breslau)
RH 53 17 Wehrkreiskommando XVII (Salzburg)
RH 53 18 Wehrkreiskommando XVIII (Graz)
RL 23 Bautruppen, Landesschütze und KGL der Luftwaffe
RW 2 Chef des Oberkommandos der Wehrmacht Wehrmachtrechtsabteilung. Völkerrechtsverletzungen Kreta
RW 60 Wehrmachtgerichte

Gedenkstätte Buchenwald Archiv (Buchenwald Memorial Archive, Germany) (Buchenwald-Arch)

Following files held in the Buchenwald Archive:
Buchenwald-Arch 55-101/6 Untersuchungsliste Lagerarzt
NARA (National Archives and Record Administration) Washington RG 242 Film 9, 33
Thüringisches Staatsarchiv Weimar NS 4 Bu Häftlingsnummernkartei

BIBLIOGRAPHY

Hadtörténeti Levétár (War History Archives, Budapest) (HL)

Angol hadifoglyok elfogása ügyében jelent, 1 June 1943. HL HM Ált. 21. oszt. 21 tétel 481. 169. 2-3

Ferguson Malcon és 2 társa angol hadifoglyok kikérdezé, 7 June 1943. HL HM Ált. 21. oszt. 21 tétel 481. 169. 4-5

The National Archives, Kew, UK (TNA) (formerly Public Record Office)

Items from the following series:

AIR MINISTRY

AIR 2 Air Ministry, Registered Files
AIR 14 Bomber Command
AIR 20 Unregistered Papers
AIR 40 Directorate of Intelligence and Other Intelligence Papers

CABINET RECORDS

CAB 122 British Joint Staff Mission: Washington Office Files

COLONIAL OFFICE

CO 980 Prisoners of War and Civilian Internees Department

MINISTRY OF DEFENCE

DEFE 2 Combined Operations Headquarters and Ministry of Defence Records

FOREIGN OFFICE

FO 916 War of 1939 to 1945: Consular (War) Department: Prisoners of War and Internees

HOME OFFICE

HO 215/122 Camps – Conditions

WAR OFFICE

WO 32 Registered Files: General Series
WO 163 War Office Council and Army Council Records. Imperial Prisoners of War Committee
WO 208 Directorate of Military Intelligence
WO 219 War of 1939 to 1945, Military Headquarters Papers: SHAEF
WO 224 War of 1939 to 1945: Enemy Prisoner of War Camps: Reports of the International Red Cross and Protecting Powers

BIBLIOGRAPHY

WO 309 War of 1939 to 1945: HQ BAOR: War Crimes Group (NEW): Files

WO 311 War of 1939 to 1945: Military Deputy, Judge Advocate General: War Crimes Files

WO 344 Directorate of Military Intelligence: Liberated Prisoners of War Interrogation Questionnaires

National Archives of Australia (NAA)

Items from the following series:

A433 Department of the Interior. Correspondence files, Class 2 (Restricted Immigration)

A705 Department of Air, Central Office. Correspondence files, multiple number (Melbourne) series

A816 Department of Defence. Correspondence files, multiple number (Melbourne) series

A1066 Department of External Affairs. Correspondence files, multiple number series

A2217 Overseas Headquarters RAAF United Kingdom. Correspondence files

A2908 Australian High Commission, United Kingdom. Correspondence files

A5954 Department of Defence. The Shedden Collection

A9300 Department of Air. RAAF Officers Personnel files

B883 2 Echelon Army Headquarters. Second AIF Personnel Dossiers 1939–1947

B3856 2 Echelon Army Headquarters. Correspondence files

M1416 Personal papers of P.M. Curtin

MP 385/6 Security classified (confidential) correspondence

MP 385/7 Command Headquarters, Southern Command [I], Australian Military Forces. Correspondence files

MP 508/1 Army Headquarters, Department of Defence. General Correspondence files

MP 385/6 Security classified (confidential) correspondence

MP 729/6 Department of the Army, Central Office. Secret correspondence files

Politisches Archiv des Auswärtigen Amtes Berlin (Political Archive of the Foreign Office, Berlin) (PA-AA)

Items from the following series:

R 40/704 to R 41/124 Rechtsabteilung Kriegsrecht

R 27/834 Handakten Ritter

R 27/835 Handakten Ritter OKW 04.03.1944–08.12.1944

R 60/655 A. Abt. Inf. Kriegsgefangene 1939–1943

BIBLIOGRAPHY

YMCA Archives, Geneva (YMCAA)

World Alliance of YMCAs – Archives. World War II Work – Germany. SS1 – T.11

Zwar collection

Various documents – correspondence, statutory declarations, first-hand accounts, newspapers clippings etc. – offered in support of claim for compensation. Held by Ron Zwar, Adelaide.

Unpublished manuscripts

Allan, Ron, The Prisoner of War Experiences of Ron Allan and F.O. (Olly) Booth

Churches, Ralph, Retreat and Capture

Dodd, Keith, Diary of Keith Dodd. Transcription, State Library of South Australia PRG 244/3. www.slsa.sa.gov.au/saatwar/collection/transcripts/noimage.htm

Finkelstein, Hal, In and Out of Barbed Wire: My Story as a Prisoner of War. Transcribed from a recording by Hal Finkelstein with Bob Huston for Army Museum of WA, 21 November 1988

——, An Oral History of World War II. Transcribed from a recording by Hal Finkelstein with Bob Huston for Army Museum of WA, 21 November 1988

Lawrence, Lindsay P., Blessed Be the Olive Trees

Ottaway, Jim, Doug Nix – POW (Europe), 2007

Randolph, E., An Unexpected Odyssey

Interviews

INTERVIEWS CONDUCTED BY PETER MONTEATH

Ron Allan (26 February 2009); Ralph Churches (various 2008, 2010); Ray J. Corbett (9 January 2010); Frank Cox (17 July 2008); Peter Giles (18 October 2007); Keith Hooper (19 January 2008); Ray Jones (3 December 2009); Arthur Leggett (August 2007); Phil Loffman (26 February 2009); Doug Nix (25 July 2009); Laurie West (18 July 2008); Ron Zwar (various 2008–2010)

INTERVIEWS IN THE AUSTRALIANS AT WAR FILM ARCHIVE (AAWFA)

Transcripts of interviews with: Rex Austin, Lawrence Calder, Geoff Cornish, Ken Drew, Eric Edwards, Terry Fairbairn, Douglas Hutchinson, Alexander Jenkins, John Mathews, Charles Parrott, Albert Stobart, Patrick Toovey, John Ulm, Letitia White, George Worledge, Reginald Worthington, Ronald Zwar

BIBLIOGRAPHY

INTERVIEWS IN THE IMPERIAL WAR MUSEUM (IWM)

Kerr, Alexander McBride 24826/12; Royle, Paul 26605/6; Younger, Calton 23329/27

Published primary sources

'Agreement relating to Prisoners of War and Civilians Liberated by Forces operating under Soviet Command and Forces operating under British Command. Crimea, 11 February 1945', Australian Treaty Series 1945 No. 3, www.austlii.edu.au/au/other/dfat/treaties/1945/3.html

Ahronson, Ellis, *I Was Hitler's Reluctant Guest*, Ourimbah, NSW: Bookbound, 2001

Barnett, Alex, *Hitler's Digger Slaves: Caught in the Web of Axis Labour Camps*, Loftus, NSW: Australian Military History Publications, 2001

Beckwith, E.J.C. (ed.), *Selections from the Quill: A Collection of Prose, Verse and Sketches by Officers Prisoners of War in Germany, 1940–1945*, London: Country Life, 1947

Bird, Arthur H., *Farewell Milag*, St Leonards-on-Sea: Literatours, 1995

Brickhill, Paul, *The Great Escape*, New York: Norton, 1950

Broomhead, Edwin N., *Barbed Wired in the Sunset*, Melbourne: The Book Depot, 1944

Brough, Ernest, *Dangerous Days: A Digger's Great Escape*, Sydney: Harper Collins, 2009

Brown, John, *In Durance Vile*, London: Hale, 1981

Brudenell-Woods, Basil, *Four Packs to Freedom*, East Roseville, NSW: Kangaroo Press, 1998

Buckland, John, *Adriatic Adventure*, Melbourne: Robertson & Mullens, 1945

Burgess, Colin (ed.), *Freedom or Death: Australia's Greatest Escape Stories from Two World Wars*, St Leonards, NSW: Allen and Unwin, 1994

Burney, Christopher, *Solitary Confinement and The Dungeon Democracy*, London: Macmillan, 1984

Butler, Rohan, M.E. Pelly and J.J. Yasamee (eds), *Documents on British Policy Overseas*, Vol. 1, London: HMSO, 1984

Caulfield, Michael (ed.), *Voices of War: Stories from the Australians at War Film Archive*, Sydney: Hodder, 2006

—— (ed.), *War Behind the Wire: Australian Prisoners of War*, Sydney: Hachette, 2008

Churches, Ralph, *A Hundred Miles As the Crow Flies*, Adelaide: self-published, 1996

Churchill, Winston S., *My Early Life: A Roving Commission*, London: Odhams Press, 1947

Coates, Ted, *Lone Evader: The Escape from France of RAAF Sergeant, Pilot Ted Coates, 1942–1943*, Loftus, NSW: Australian Military History Publications, 1995

BIBLIOGRAPHY

Collins, Douglas, *POW*, London: Robert Hale, 1968

Collins, Noel, *I Flew Tigers to Bombers*, Bunbury, WA: Milligan House, 1999

'Convention Relative to the Treatment of Prisoners of War. Geneva, 27 July 1939' (Geneva Convention), viewed 30 June 2008, www.icrc.org/ihl.nsf/FULL/305?OpenDocument

Corbett, Ray, *Behind German Wire: Autobiography of an Australian Prisoner of War 1941–1945*, Clayfield, QLD: Broadwater Publishers, n.d.

Cousins, W.E.H. (Bill), *A Lot of Fun in My Life! Memories of W.E.H. (Bill) Cousins*, St Lucia, QLD: POD Centre, 2002

Crooks, John, *My Little War*, Mansfield: self-published, 2006

Denholm, A., 'I Was a Prisoner', *Life Australia*, 1 August 1941, pp. 24–31

Documents on German Foreign Policy. Series D. London: HMSO, 1983

Fielder, Thomas L., *I Flew, I Fell, I Survived: The Story of an Australian Aircrew Prisoner of War*, Kilsyth, VIC: T. Fielder, 1999

Fore, Jim 'Paladin' and Larry Jacks, *Tragedy and Triumph: A Pilot's Life Through War and Peace*, Colorado Springs, Colorado: Skyward Press, 1996

Gammon, Victor F., *Not All Glory! True Accounts of RAF Airmen Taken Prisoner in Europe, 1939–1945*, London: Arms & Armour, 1996

——, *No Time for Fear: True Accounts of RAF Airmen Taken Prisoner in Europe, 1939–1945*, London: Arms and Armour, 1998

Giesen, Harry, *Seventh Time Lucky: A True Story of Escapes from German Captivity; A Private Soldier's Exploits in Love and War*, Waverley, VIC: Sid Harta, 2008

Granquist, Charles, *A Long Way Home: One POW's Story of Escape and Evasion during World War II*, Newport, NSW: Big Sky, 2010

Gullett, Henry (Joe), *Not as a Duty Only: An Infantryman's War*, Melbourne: Melbourne University Press, 1976

Hallihan, Frank, *In the Hands of the Enemy: A Record of the Experiences of Frank Hallihan, 21st Battalion, in German Prison Camps*, Ballarat: Baxter and Stubbs, n.d.

Hayes, Helen, *Beyond the Great Escape: Geoff Cornish, the One Who Got Away*, Elanora, QLD: Possum Publishing, 2004

Hodgson, Wilf, *Bombs and Barbed Wire*, Attadale, WA: self-published, 2000

Holliday, J.E. (ed.), *Stories of the RAAF POWs of Lamsdorf Including Chronicle of Their 500 Mile Trek*, Holland Park, QLD: RAAF POWs Association, 1992

Hooper, Keith, 'Fear of Friendly Bombing', *Wartime* 28, November 2004, pp. 64–5

Hudson, W.J. and Wendy Way (eds), *Documents on Australian Foreign Policy 1937–1949*, Vol. VIII, Canberra: Australian Government Publishing Service, 1989

I Was in Prison, Geneva: World Alliance of the YMCA, 1945

Jager, Charles, *Escape from Crete*, Sydney: Floradale, 2004

BIBLIOGRAPHY

Johnson, Peter, *The Withered Garland: Doubts and Reflections of a Bomber*, London: New European Publications, 1996

Leggett, Arthur, *Don't Cry For Me: An Autobiography*, Perth: Linellen Press, 2006

Le Souef, Leslie, *To War without a Gun*, Perth: Artlook, 1980

Liley, Jack, *Jack's War*, Melbourne: Michael J. Liley, 2001

Lind, L.J., *Escape from Crete*, Sydney: Australian Publishing Co., n.d.

Lind, Lew, *Flowers of Rethymion: Escape from Crete*, Kenthurst, NSW: Kangaroo Press, 1991

Loffman, Philip (ed.), *POW: 2/28th Australian Infantry Battalion Including the Antitankers Who Fought with Them; Prisoners of War Captured During Actions at Defence of Tobruk, Ruin Ridge, El Alamein*, Perth: self-published, 1995

Mackenzie, Ron, *An Ordinary War 1940–1945*, Wangaratta: Shoestring Press, 1995

Maloney, J.J., *Inside Red Russia*, Sydney: Angus and Robertson, 1948

Manning, David, *One Sailor's War: An Oral History*, Ballarat: Goodenia Rise Publishers, 1999

Marks, Vic, *Autobiography & Prisoner of War Experience*, Adelaide: Barr Smith Library, 2001

Matthews, Glenn (ed.), *In the Pink: The Letters of William Johnson Williams: Prisoner of War – Europe WWII*, n.p.: self-published, 2006

McClelland, Alexander C., *The Answer – Justice: An Australian Prisoner of War and Witness in The Small Fortress Terezin Concentration Camp in 1945*, Toronto, NSW, 1998

McDougall, Susan, *Five Years under the Führer: The Life Story of Bruce Ross*, Bassendean, WA: Access Press, 2006

McKibbin, Marcus, Willie Kemp, Wick Pollock and Keith Hooper, *Barbed Wire: Memories of Stalag 383*, London: Staples, 1947

Menzies, Robert, *Afternoon Light: Some Memories of Men and Events*, Melbourne: Cassell, 1967

Moll, Martin (ed.), *'Führer-Erlasse' 1939–1945*, Stuttgart: Franz Steiner, 1997

Morley, George A., *Escape from Stalag XVIIIA*, Cranbourne: Meni Publishing, 2007

Nelson, Earle M., *If Winter Comes*, Lovely Banks, VIC: self-published, 1989

Parrott, Charlie, *An Aussie Nobody: The Story of an Ordinary Man in Extraordinary Circumstances*, Darwin: self-published, 1997

Paterson, Jim, *Partisans, Peasants and POWs: A Soldier's Story of Escape World War II*, Perth: self-published, 2008

Prisoners of War: British Army 1939–1945: Alphabetical Nominal Registers (including Rank, POW Number, Regiment or Corps and Camp Location Details) Listing Over 107,000 British Army Prisoners of War of All Ranks Held in Germany and German Occupied Territories. Vol. II covers Armies

BIBLIOGRAPHY

and Other Land Forces of the British Empire, Vol. III covers Naval and Air Forces of Great Britain and the Empire, Polstead: J. B. Hayward in association with the Imperial War Museum, Department of Printed Books, 1990

Probert, Sherriff, *Prisoner of Two Wars: An Australian Soldier's Story*, Kent Town, SA: Wakefield, 2001

Ramsay, Ian, *P.O.W.: A Digger in Hitler's Prison Camps 1941–45*, South Melbourne: Macmillan, 1985

Reeves, James W., *One Man's War: A True Story. Memoirs of James W. Reeves*, West Lakes, SA: Seaview Press, 2007

Reid, Miles, *Last on the List*, London: Leo Cooper, 1974

'Report of the Directorate of Prisoners of War and Internees at Army Headquarters Melbourne 1939–1951', viewed 18 September 2010, www.army.gov.au/AHU/POWs_and_Internees.asp

Report of the International Committee of the Red Cross on Its Activities During the Second World War, Geneva: ICRC, 1948

Responsibilities of a Prisoner of War, 3rd edition, London: Air Publication 1548, April 1944

Roberts, Barney, *A Kind of Cattle*, Sydney: Collins, 1987

Robinson, Charles, *Journey to Captivity*, Canberra: Australian War Memorial, 1991

Romilly, Giles and Michael Alexander, *The Privileged Nightmare*, London: Weidenfeld and Nicolson, 1954

Rudd, Bill et al., *AIF in Switzerland: A Compendium*, Melbourne: self-published, 2002

Rushton, Colin, *Spectator in Hell: A British Soldier's Story of Imprisonment in Auschwitz*, Chichester: Summersdale, 2007

Ryan, Imelda (ed.), *POWs Fraternal*, Perth: Hawthorn Press, 1990

Sabey, Ian, *Noel Nocturne and Other POW Poems*, Adelaide: The Hassell Press, 1944

——, *Stalag Scrapbook*, Melbourne: F.W. Chesire, 1947

Someday: A Book for Those Who Serve, Sydney: Snelling Printing Works, 1942

Spivey, Delmar T., *POW Odyssey: Recollections of Center Compound, Stalag Luft III and the Secret Mission in World War II*, Attleboro, Massachusetts: Colonial Lithograph, 1984

Stooke, Gordon, *Flak and Barbed Wire: 'In the Wake of Wuppertal'*, Loftus, NSW: Australian Military History Publications, 1997

Strong, Tracy (ed.), *We Prisoners of War*, New York: Associated Press, 1941

Stuckey, John Eric Frederick, *Sometimes Free: My Escapes from German POW Camps*, Ashhurst, NZ: self-published, 1977

Summons, Walter Irvine, *Twice Their Prisoner*, Melbourne: Oxford University Press, 1946

Sweeney, Edward J., *A Merchant Seaman's Survival: An Autobiography*, Margate, Kent: Edward Sweeney, 1999

BIBLIOGRAPHY

Taylor, Geoff, *A Piece of Cake*, London: Peter Davies, 1956

Taylor, James, *Prisoner of the 'Kormoran': W.A. Jones' Amazing Experiences on the German Raider 'Kormoran' and as a Prisoner of War in Germany*, Sydney: Australasian Publishing, 1944

Thomas, Walter Babington, *Dare To Be Free*, London: Allan Wingate, 1955

Trial of the Major War Criminals: Proceedings of the International Tribunal Sitting at Nuremberg, Germany, London: HMSO, 1946

Vuillet, André, *Journey Among Captives: A Record of YMCA Service Among Prisoners, Internees and Displaced Persons during World War II*, n.p.: YMCA, 1946

Walley, Brian (ed.), *Silk and Barbed Wire*, Perth: RAF Ex-Prisoners of War Association (Australian Division), 2000

Watt, Donald, *Stoker*, Sydney: Simon and Schuster, 1995

Willoughby, Charles Raymond, *I Was There: The War Experience of Charles Raymond Willoughby*, ed. Elaine Thompson, Brewarrina, NSW: Brewarrina and District Historical Society, 1994

Younger, Calton, *No Flight from the Cage*, new edition, London: W.H. Allen, 1981

SECONDARY SOURCES

Adam-Smith, Patsy, *Prisoners of War: From Gallipoli to Korea*, Ringwood, VIC: Viking, 1992

American Ex-Prisoners of War, Inc. National Medical Research Committee, *The European Story*, Packet No. 8. Sann Sommers, Marshfield, Wisconsin, 1980

Andrews, Allen, *Exemplary Justice*, London: Harrap, 1976

Baker, Kevin, *Paul Cullen, Citizen and Soldier: The Life and Times of Major General Paul Cullen AC, CBE, DSO and Bar, ED, FCA*, Dural, NSW: Rosenberg, 2005

Barber, Noel, *Prisoner of War: The Story of British Prisoners of War Held by the Enemy*, London: Harrap, 1944

Bard, Mitchell G., *Forgotten Victims: The Abandonment of Americans in Hitler's Camps*, Boulder: Westview Press, 1994

Barrett, Craig, ' "Matters Still Outstanding": Australian ex-POWs of the Japanese and claims for reparations', in Martin Crotty and Marina Larsson (eds), *ANZAC Legacies: Australians and the Aftermath of War*, Melbourne: Australian Scholarly Publishing, 2010, pp. 187–210

Barter, Margaret, *Far Above Battle: The Experience and Memory of Australian Soldiers in War 1939–1945*, St Leonards, NSW: Allen & Unwin, 1994

Bauer, Herbert, *Stalag III A: Das ehemalige Kriegsgefangenenlager des Zweiten Weltkrieges bei Luckenwalde*, Luckenwelde: n.p., 1996

Baybutt, Ron, *Camera in Colditz*, London: Hodder and Stoughton, 1982

Beaumont, Joan, 'POWs in Australian National Memory', in Bob Moore and Barbara Hately-Broad (eds), *Prisoners of War, Prisoners of Peace: Captivity,*

Homecoming and Memory in World War II, Oxford, New York: Berg, 2005, pp. 185–94

——, 'Prisoners of War', in Peter Dennis, Jeffrey Grey, Ewan Morris and Robin Prior (eds), *Oxford Companion to Australian Military History*, Melbourne: OUP, 1995, pp. 472–81

——, 'Protecting Prisoners of War, 1939–1945', in Bob Moore and Kent Fedorowich, K. (eds), *Prisoners of War and Their Capture in World War II*, Oxford: Berg, 1996, pp. 277–97

——, 'Rank, Privilege and Prisoners of War', *War and Society*, 1, 1, 1983, pp. 67–94

—— (ed.), *Australia's War 1939–1945*, Sydney: Allen & Unwin, 1988

Beevor, Antony, *Crete: The Battle and the Resistance*, London: John Murray, 1991

Bell, Trevor, 'RMS Rangitane', viewed 4 September 2009, www.thebells.btinternet.co.uk/rangitane/story.htm

Bellair, John, *From Snow to Jungle: A History of the 2/3rd Australian Machine Gun Battalion*, Sydney: Allen & Unwin, 1987

Beltrone, Art and Lee, *A Wartime Log: A Remembrance from Home Through the American YMCA*, Charlotteville, Virginia: Howell Press, 1994

Benz, Wolfgang et al. (eds), *Enzyklopädie des Nationalsozialismus*, Stuttgart: dtv, 2007

Bird, Tom, *American POWs of World War II: Forgotten Men Tell Their Stories*, Westport: Praeger, 1992

Bischof, Günter, Stefan Karner and Barbara Stelz-Marx (eds), *Kriegsgefangene des Zweiten Weltkrieges: Gefangennahme – Lagerleben – Rückkehr*, Vienna and Munich: Oldenbourg, 2005

Bishop, Patrick, *Bomber Boys: Fighting Back 1940–1945*, London: Harper, 2007

Blank, Ralf, 'Kriegsalltag und Luftkrieg an der "Heimatfront"', in Militärgeschichtliches Forschungsamt (ed.), *Das Deutsche Reich und der Zweite Weltkrieg*, Bd. 9, *Die deutsche Kriegsgesellschaft 1939 bis 1945*, Munich: Deutsche Verlagsanstalt, 2004

Bleszynski, Nick, *Shoot Straight, You Bastards! The Truth Behind the Killing of Breaker Morant*, Milson's Point, NSW: Random House, 2002

Boatner, Mark M., *Biographical Dictionary of World War II*, Novato, California: Presidio, 1996

Böhme, K.W., *Zur Geschichte der deutschen Kriegsgefangenen des Zweiten Weltkrieges*, Bielefeld: Gieseking, 1974

Bolger, William, *The Fiery Phoenix: The Story of the 2/7 Australian Infantry Battalion 1939–1946*, Melbourne: 2/7 Battalion Association, 2000

Borgsen, Werner and Klaus Volland, *Stalag X B Sandbostel: zur Geschichte eines Kriegsgefangenen- und KS-Auffanglagers in Norddeutschland 1943–1945*, Bremen: Temmen, 1991

BIBLIOGRAPHY

Brickhill, Paul, *Escape or Die: Authentic Stories of the RAF Escaping Society*, London: Pan Books, 1954

—— and Conrad Norton, *Escape to Danger*, London: Faber and Faber, 1956

Broszat, Martin, *The Hitler State*, London: Longman, 1981

Buchenwald: Mahnung und Verpflichtung; Dokumente und Berichte, ed. Nationale Mahn- und Gedenkstätte Buchenwald, 4th edition, Berlin: VEB Deutscher Verlag der Wissenschaften, 1983

Bunbury, Bill, *Rabbits and Spaghetti: Captives and Comrades, Australians, Italians and the War 1939–1945*, Fremantle, WA: Fremantle Arts Centre Press, 1995

Burgess, Alan, *The Longest Tunnel: The True Story of the Great Escape*, London: Bloomsbury, 1990

Burgess, Colin, *'Bush' Parker: An Australian Battle of Britain Pilot in Colditz*, Loftus, NSW: Australian Military History Publications, 2007

——, *Destination Buchenwald*, Sydney: Kangaroo Press, 1995

—— (ed.), *Freedom or Death: Australia's Greatest Escape Stories from Two World Wars*, St Leonards, NSW: Allen and Unwin, 1994

—— and Hugh Clarke, *Barbed Wire and Bamboo: Australian POWs in Europe, North Africa, Singapore, Thailand and Japan*, Sydney: Allen and Unwin, 1992

Carell, Paul and Guenter Baeddeker, *Die Gefangenen: Leben und Überleben deutscher Soldaten hinter Stacheldraht*, Frankfurt: Ullstein, 1986

Carroll, Tim, *Great Escapers: The Full Story of the Second World War's Most Remarkable Mass Escape*, Prahran, VIC: Hardie Grant, 2004

Carter, Carolle J., *The Shamrock and the Swastika: German Espionage in Ireland in World War II*, Palo Alto, California: Pacific Books, 1977

Caulfield, Michael, *War Behind the Wire: Australian Prisoners of War*, Sydney: Hachette, 2010

Cawthorne, Nigel, *The Iron Cage*, London: Fourth Estate, 1993

Champ, Jack and Colin Burgess, *The Diggers of Colditz*, revised edition, Kenthurst, NSW: Kangaroo Press, 1997

Chancellor, Henry, *Colditz: The Definitive History*, London: Hodder and Stoughton, 2001

Chorley, W.R., *Royal Air Force Bomber Command Losses of the Second World War*, Vol. 2, *Aircraft and Crew Losses 1941*, Midland: Hinckley, 1993

Clarke, Hugh, Colin Burgess and Russell Braddon, *Prisoners of War*, Sydney: Time-Life and John Ferguson, 1988

Clutton-Brock, Oliver, *Footprints on the Sands of Time: RAF Bomber Command Prisoners of War in Germany, 1939–1945*, London: Grub Street, 2003

Cohen, Roger, *Soldiers and Slaves: American POWs Trapped by the Nazis' Final Gamble*, New York: Alfred A. Knopf, 2005

Coward, Roger, *Sailors in Cages*, London: Macdonald, 1967

BIBLIOGRAPHY

Crawley, Aidan, *Escape from Germany: The Methods of Escape Used by RAF Airmen During the Second World War*, London: HMSO, 1985

Cruickshank, Charles, *Greece, 1940–1941*, London: David-Poynter, 1975

Cuddon, Eric (ed.), *Trial of Erich Killinger, Heinz Junge, Otto Boehringer, Heinrich Eberhardt, Gustav Bauer-Schlichtegroll (The Dulag Luft Trial)*, London: William Hodge, 1952

Damer, Sean and Ian Frazer, *On the Run: Anzac Escape and Evasion in Enemy-Occupied Crete*, Auckland: Penguin, 2006

Damousi, Joy and Marilyn Lake (eds), *Gender and War: Australians at War in the Twentieth Century*, Melbourne: Cambridge University Press, 1995

Dancocks, Daniel G., *In Enemy Hands: Canadian Prisoners of War, 1939–1945*, Edmonton: Hurtig, 1983

Davis, Gerald H., 'Prisoners of War in Twentieth-Century War Economies', *Journal of Contemporary History* 12, 1977, pp. 623–34

Daws, Gavan, *Prisoners of the Japanese: POWs of World War II in the Pacific – The Powerful Untold Story*, New York: W. Morrow, 1994

Dear, I.C.B. and M.R.D. Foot (eds), *Oxford Companion to the Second World War*, Oxford: Oxford University Press, 1995

Dennis, Peter et al., *The Oxford Companion to Australian Military History*, 2nd edition, Melbourne: Oxford University Press, 2008

Drooz, Daniel B., *American Prisoners of War in German Death, Concentration, and Slave Labor Camps: Germany's Lethal Policy in the Second World War*, New York: Edwin Mellen, 2003

Durand, Arthur, *Stalag Luft III: The Secret Story*, Baton Rouge: Louisiana University Press, 1988

Eberlein, Michael, Roland Müller, Michael Schöngarth and Thomas Werther, *Militärjustiz im Nationalsozialismus: Das Marburger Militärgericht*, Marburg: Geschichtswerkstatt Marburg, 1994

Echternkamp, Jörg (ed.), *Das Deutsche Reich und der Zweite Weltkrieg*, Bd. 9, *Die deutsche Kriegsgesellschaft 1939 bis 1945*, Munich: Deutsche Verlags-Anstalt, 2005

Engelbert, Otto, *Kriegsgefangenschaft: Berichte über das Leben in Kriegsgefangenenlagern der Alliierten*, Munich: Oldenbourg, 1991

Evans, Richard J., *The Third Reich at War: How the Nazis Led Germany from Conquest to Disaster*, London: Penguin, 2008

Ewer, Peter, *Forgotten ANZACs: The Campaign in Greece, 1941*, Carlton, VIC: Scribe, 2008

Favez, Jean-Claude, *The Red Cross and the Holocaust*, Cambridge: Cambridge University Press, 1999

Field, A.E., 'Prisoners of the Germans and Italians', in Barton Maughan, *Tobruk and El Alamein*, Canberra: Australian War Memorial, 1966, pp. 755–822

Firkins, Peter, *Australians in Nine Wars: Waikato to Long Tan*, Adelaide: Rigby, 1971

BIBLIOGRAPHY

Förster, Jürgen, *Die Wehrmacht im NS-Staat: Eine strukturgeschichtliche Analyse*, Munich: R. Oldenbourg, 2007

Forwick, Helmuth, 'Zur Behandlung alliierter Kriegsgefangener im Zweiten Weltkrieg: Anweisung des Oberkommandos der Wehrmacht über Besuche ausländischer Kommissionen in Kriegsgefangenenlagern', *Militärgeschichtliche Mitteilungen*, 1, 2, 1967, pp. 119–34

Foy, David, *For You the War Is Over: American Prisoners of War in Nazi Germany*, New York: Stein and Day, 1984

Franks, Warwick, 'Cricket in Stalag 344: Sport in German Prisoner-of-War Camps During World War II', *Sporting Traditions* 11, 2, November 1994, pp. 81–90

Freudenberg, Graham, *Churchill and Australia*, Sydney: Pan Macmillan, 2008

Frey, Hans K, *Die disziplinarische und gerichtliche Bestrafung von Kriegsgefangenen: Die Anwendung des Kriegsgefangenenabkommens von 1929 auf die angelsächsischen und deutschen Kriegsgefangenen während des Zweiten Weltkriegs*, Vienna: Springer-Verlag, 1948

Garrett, Richard, *P.O.W.*, London: David and Charles, 1981

Garton, Stephen, *The Cost of War: Australians Return*, Melbourne: Oxford University Press, 1996

Gaul, Maurice, 'Footy Behind the Wire', *AFL Record*, 25–27 April 2003, pp. 9–12

Geck, Stefan, *Das deutsche Kriegsgefangenenwesen 1939–1945*, Masters thesis, University of Mainz, 1998

——, *Dulag Luft/Auswertestelle West: Vernehmungslager der Luftwaffe für Westalliierte Kriegsgefangene im Zweiten Weltkrieg*, Frankfurt: Peter Lang, 2008

Gelber, Yoav, 'Palestinian POWs in German Captivity', *Yad Vashem Studies* 14, 1981, viewed 30 June 2009, www.yadvashem.org/odot_pdf/Microsoft%20Word%20-%206565.pdf

Gill, G. Hermon, *Royal Australian Navy 1939–1942: Australia in the War of 1939–1945*, Series 2, No. 1, Canberra: Australian War Memorial, 1957

Gillison, D., *Royal Australian Air Force, 1939–1942*, Canberra: Australian War Memorial, 1962

Givney, E.C. (ed.), *The First at War: The Story of the 2/1st Infantry Battalion 1939–1945, the City of Sydney Regiment*, Earlwood, NSW: Association of First Infantry Battalions Editorial Committee, 1987

Goodhart, David, *The History of the 2/7th Australian Field Regiment*, Adelaide: Rigby, 1952

Grey, Jeffrey, *A Military History of Australia*, Cambridge: Cambridge University Press, 1999

Groehler, Olaf, *Bombenkrieg gegen Deutschland*, Berlin: Akademie, 1990

Hackett, David A. (ed. and transl.), *The Buchenwald Report*, Boulder: Westview Press, 1995

BIBLIOGRAPHY

Hall, Robert, *The Black Diggers: Aboriginal and Torres Strait Islanders in the Second World War*, North Sydney: Allen & Unwin, 1989

Hampton, James, *Selected for Aircrew*, London: Air Research Publications, 1974

Hasluck, Paul, *The Government and the People, 1939–1941*, Canberra: Australian War Memorial, 1952

Hass, Gerhard et al., *Deutschland im Zweiten Weltkrieg*, Bd. 1, *Vorbereitung, Entfesselung und Verlauf des Krieges bis zum 22. Juni 1941*, Cologne: Pahl-Rugenstein, 1974

Hay, David, *Nothing Over Us: The Story of the 2/6th Australian Infantry Battalion*, Canberra: Australian War Memorial, 1984

Herington, John, *Air War against Germany and Italy 1939–1943*, Canberra: Australian War Memorial, 1954

Hill, Maria, *Diggers and Greeks: The Australian Campaigns in Greece and Crete*, Sydney: University of New South Wales Press, 2010

Hoff, Gordon, *The Rise, Fall and Regeneration of the 2/7th Australian Field Ambulance*, Adelaide: Peacock, 1995

Housden, Martyn, *Hitler: Study of a Revolutionary*, London and New York: Routledge, 2000

Jochmann, Werner (ed.), *Adolf Hitler: Monologe im Führer-Hauptquartier 1941–1944; Die Aufzeichnungen Heinrich Heims*, Hamburg: Albrecht Knaus, 1980

Johnson, Frank (ed.), *R.A.A.F. Over Europe*, London: Eyre and Spottiswoode, 1946

Johnson, K.T., *The 2/11 (City of Perth) Australian Infantry Battalion, 1939–1945*, Swanbourne, WA: John Burridge Military Antiques, 2000

Jones, Priscilla Dale, 'Nazi Atrocities Against Allied Airmen: Stalag Luft III and the End of British War Crimes Trials', *Historical Journal* 41, 2, June 1998, pp. 543–65

Karny, Thomas, 'Rechenschaft statt Rache: Nach 56 Jahren steht der SS-Mann Anton Malloth vor Gericht', *Wiener Zeitung*, 25 May 2001

Kershaw, Ian, *Hitler: 1936–1945, Nemesis*, London: Penguin, 2000

Kilian, Achim, *Mühlberg, 1939–1948: Ein Gefangenenlager mitten in Deutschland*, Cologne: Böhlau, 2001

Kinnis, Arthur G. and Stanley Booker, *168 Jump Into Hell: A True Story of Betrayed Allied Airmen*, Victoria, British Columbia: Arthur G. Kinnis, 1999

Klee, Ernst, *Das Personenlexikon zum Dritten Reich: Wer war was vor und nach 1945*, Frankfurt a.M.: Fischer, 2005

Klukowski, Zygmunt, *Diary from the Years of Occupation, 1939–1944*, Urbana: University of Illinois Press, 1993

Kochavi, Arieh J., *Confronting Captivity: Britain and the United States and their POWs in Nazi Germany*, Chapel Hill: University of North Carolina Press, 2005

BIBLIOGRAPHY

Konzentrationslager Buchenwald 1937–1945: Begleitband zur ständigen historischen Ausstellung, Göttingen: Verlag Wallstein, 1999

Kübler, Robert (ed.), *Chef Kgw: Das Kriegsgefangenenwesen unter Gottlob Berger; Nachlass*, Lindhorst: Askania, 1984

Kwiet, Konrad, 'Anzac and Auschwitz: The Unbelievable Story of Donald Watt', Internet Journal – *Antisemitism and Holocaust: From Prejudice to Genocide*, viewed 6 June 2005, www.tu-berlin.de/-sfa/journal/kkwiet002.htm

Laffin, John, *ANZACs at War: The Story of Australian and New Zealand Battles*, London: Abelard-Schuman, 1965

Lauerwald, Hannelore, *In Fremdem Land: Kriegsgefangene im STALAG VIII A Görlitz; Tatsachen, Briefe, Dokumente*, Görlitz: Viadukt, 1996

Loeffel, Robert, 'Treasonous Conduct: Assessing the Wartime Activities, Post-War Trials and Tribulations of Australian Collaborators in the Second World War', *Australian Journal of Politics and History*, 55, 1, 2009, pp. 17–31

Loffman, Phil, *POW: 2/28th Australian Infantry Battalion*, Perth: self-published, 1999

Long, Gavin, *Australia in the War of 1939–1945*, Vol. 1, *To Benghazi*, Canberra: Australian War Memorial, 1952

——, *Australia in the War of 1939–1945*, Vol. II, *Greece, Crete and Syria*, Canberra: Australian War Memorial, 1953

——, *Australia in the War of 1939–1945*, Vol. VII, *The Final Campaigns*, Canberra: Australian War Memorial, 1963

——, *The Six Years War*, Canberra: Australian War Memorial, 1973

Longden, Sean, *Hitler's British Slaves: British and Commonwealth POWs in German Industry 1939–1945*, Adlestrop: Arris, 2005

Macdonald, Callum, *The Lost Battle: Crete 1941*, London: Macmillan, 1993

MacKenzie, S.P., *The Colditz Myth: The Real Story of POW Life in Nazi Germany*, Oxford: Oxford University Press, 2004

——, 'Prisoners of War and Civilian Internees: The European and Mediterranean Theatres', in Lloyd E. Lee (ed.), *World War II in Europe, Africa, and the Americas, with General Sources: A Hand Book of Literature and Research*, Westport: Greenwood, 1996, pp. 302–12

——, 'The Shackling Crisis: A Case Study in the Dynamics of Prisoners-of-War Diplomacy in the Second World War', *International History Review*, 17, 1, February 1995, pp. 79–98

——, 'The Treatment of Prisoners of War in World War II', *Journal of Modern History* 66, 3, 1994, pp. 487–520

Macksey, Kenneth, *Godwin's Saga: A Commando Epic*, London: Brassey's, 1987

Mai, Uwe, *Kriegsgefangene in Brandenburg: Stalag III A in Luckenwalde 1939–1945*, Berlin: Metropol, 1999

Marshall, A. J. (ed.), *Nulli Secundus Log: The 2/2 Australian Infantry Battalion AIF*, Sydney: Consolidated Press, 1946

BIBLIOGRAPHY

Masel, Philip, *The Second 28th: The Story of a Famous Battalion of the Ninth Australian Division*, Perth: 2/28th Battalion and 24 Anti-Tank Company Association, 2000

Mason, W. Wynne, *Prisoners of War: Official History of New Zealand in the Second World War*, Wellington: History Branch, Department of Internal Affairs, Oxford University Press, 1954

Mattiello, G. and W. Vogt, *Deutsche Kriegsgefangenen- und Internierteneinrichtungen 1939–1945: Handbuch und Katalog. Lagergeschichte und Lagerzensurstempel*, Vol. 1, *Stammlager (Stalag)*; Vol. 2: *Oflag, BAB, Dulag usw.*, Koblenz: self-published, 1986, 1987

Maughan, Barton, *Tobruk and El Alamein*, Canberra: Australian War Memorial, 1966

Mazower, Mark, *Dark Continent: Europe's Twentieth Century*, New York: Vintage, 2000

——, *Salonica City of Ghosts: Christians, Muslims and Jews, 1430–1950*, New York: Alfred J. Knopf, 2005

McClelland, James, *Special File: Australians Executed by the Enemy, 1939–1945*, Silverdale, NSW: James McClelland Research, 1987

McKernan, Michael, *The War Never Ends: The Pain of Separation and Return*, St Lucia, QLD: University of Queensland Press, 2001

Messenger, Charles, *The Second World War in the West*, London: Cassell, 2001

Michalka, Wolfgang (ed.), *Der Zweite Weltkrieg: Analysen, Grundzüge, Forschungsbilanz*, Munich: Piper, 1989

Miller, David, *Mercy Ships: The Untold Story of Prisoner-of-War Exchanges in World War II*, London: Continuum, 2008

Mommsen, Hans, 'Der Arbeitseinsatz sowjetischer Kriegsgefangener 1941–1945', in Haus der Geschichte der Bundesrepublik (ed.), *Kriegsgefangene: Sowjetische Kriegsgefangene in Deutschland; Deutsche Kriegsgefangene in der Sowjetunion*, Düsseldorf: Droste, 1995, pp. 135–40

Monteath, Peter, 'Australian POW in German Captivity in the Second World War', *Australian Journal of Politics and History*, 54, 3, 2008, pp. 421–33

Moore, Bob and Kent Fedorowich (eds), *Prisoners of War and Their Capture in World War II*, Oxford: Berg, 1996

Moore, Bob and Barbara Hately-Broad (eds), *Prisoners of War, Prisoners of Peace: Captivity, Homecoming and Memory in World War II*, Oxford: Berg, 2005

Moorehead, Alan, *The Desert War: The North Africa Campaign, 1940–1943*, London: Sphere, 1968

Muggenthaler, Karl August, *German Raiders of World War II*, London: Pan, 1980

Muir, Kirsty, 'Public Peace, Private Wars: The Psychological Effects of War on Australian Veterans', *War & Society* 26, 1, May 2007, pp. 61–78

Neave, Denny and Craig Smith, *Aussie Soldier: Prisoners of War*, Wavell Heights, QLD: Big Sky, 2009

BIBLIOGRAPHY

Nelson, Hank, *Prisoners of War: Australians under Nippon*, Crows Nest, NSW: ABC, 1990

Neulen, Hans Werner, *An deutscher Seite: Internationale Freiwillige von Wehrmacht und Waffen-SS*, Munich: Universitas, 1985

Nichol, John and Tony Rennell, *The Last Escape: The Untold Story of Allied Prisoners of War in Germany, 1944–1945*, London: Penguin Books, 2002

Nowak, Edmund, *Schatten von Lambinowice: Versuch einer Rekonstruktion der Geschichte des Arbeitslagers in Lambinowice in den Jahren 1945–1946*, Opole: Muzeum Slaska Opolskiego, 1994

Osterloh, Jörg, *Ein ganz normales Lager: Das Kriegsgefangenen-Mannschaftsstammlager 304 (IV H) in Zeithain bei Riesa/Sa. 1941–1945*, Leipzig: Kiepenheuer, 1997

Otto, Reinhard, and Rolf Keller, 'Das Massensterben der sowjetischen Kriegsgefangenen und die Wehrmachtbürokratie: Unterlagen zur Registrierung der sowjetischen Kriegsgefangenen 1941–1945 in deutschen und russischen Institutionen; Ein Forschungsbericht', *Militärgeschichtliche Mitteilungen* 57, (1998,) pp. 149–80

Overmans, Rüdiger, 'Die Kriegsgefangenenpolitik des Deutschen Reiches 1939 bis 1945', in Jörg Echternkamp (ed.), *Das Deutsche Reich und der Zweite Weltkrieg*, Bd. 9, *Die Deutsche Kriegsgesellschaft 1939 bis 1945*, Munich: Deutsche Verlags-Anstalt, 2005, pp. 729–875

—— (ed.), *In der Hand des Feindes: Kriegsgefangenschaft von der Antike bis zum Zweiten Weltkrieg*, Cologne: Böhlau, 1999

——, 'German Prisoner of War Policy in World War II', in Bernard Mees and Samuel P. Koehne (eds), *Terror, War, Tradition: Studies in European History*, Adelaide: Australian Humanities Press, 2007, pp. 171–80

Palazzo, Albert, *Battle of Crete*, 2nd edition, Canberra: Army History Unit, 2007

Patrick, Donald L. and Peter J.D. Heaf, *Long-term Effects of War-Related Deprivation on Health: A Report on the Evidence*, Haverhill, Suffolk: Panda Press, 1981

Pearson, Ross A., *Australians at War in the Air*, 2 vols, Kenthurst, NSW: Kangaroo Press, 1995

Petschnigg, Edith, *Von der Front aufs Feld: Britische Kriegsgefangene in der Steiermark 1941–1945*, Graz: Selbstverlag des Vereins zur Förderung der Forschung von Folgen nach Konflikten und Kriegen, 2003

Pfeffer, Karl Heinz, *Die bürgerliche Gesellschaft in Australien*, Berlin: Junker und Dünnhaupt, 1936

Pitchfork, Graham, *Shot Down and on the Run: The RAF and Commonwealth Aircrews Who Got Home from Behind Enemy Lines, 1940–1945*, Kew: National Archives, 2003

Popiolek, Stefan, *Museum des Martyriums der Kriegsgefangenen in Lambinowice*, n.p.: Museum of Martyrology, n.d.

Psychoundakis, George, *The Cretan Runner: His Story of the German Occupation*, London: John Murray, 1955

BIBLIOGRAPHY

Rea, Paul, *Voices from the Fortress: The Extraordinary Stories of Australia's Forgotten Prisoners of War*, Sydney: ABC Books, 2007

Reid, Pat and Maurice Michael, *Prisoner of War: The Inside Story of the POW from the Ancient World to Colditz and After*, New York: Beaufort, 1986

Reid, Richard, *In Captivity: Australian Prisoners of War in the 20th Century*, Canberra: Department of Veterans' Affairs, 1999

——, *Victory in Europe 1939–1945: Australians at War in the Middle East, North Africa and Europe*, Canberra: Department of Veterans' Affairs, 2005

—— et al., *Stolen Years: Australian Prisoners of War*, Canberra: Department of Veterans' Affairs and Australian War Memorial, 2002

Rolf, David, *Prisoners of the Reich: Germany's Captives, 1939–1945*, London: Leo Cooper, 1988

Rollings, Charles, *Prisoners of War: Voices of Captivity during the Second World War*, London: Ebury, 2007

Rousseau, Jean Jacques, trans. Christopher Betts, *The Social Contract*, Book 1, Chapter IV, Oxford: Oxford University Press, 1994

Rudd, Bill et al., *AIF in Switzerland: A Compendium*, Melbourne: self-published, 2002

Saleam, Jim, 'The Historian as Detective Versus the Journalist as Investigator: Were Australian, British and New Zealand Prisoners of War Massacred at Theresienstadt Concentration Camp in 1945?', 2 October 2004, http://home.alphalink.com.au/~radnat/terezin.html

Satow, Harold, and M.J. See, *The Work of the Prisoners of War Department During the Second World War*, London: Foreign Office, 1950

Saylor, Thomas, *Long Hard Road: American POWs During World War II*, St Paul, Minnesota: Minnesota Historical Society Press, 2007

Schönborn, Siegfried, *Kriegsgefangene und Fremdarbeiter in unserer Heimat 1939–1945*, Freigericht: Naumann, 1990

Schreiber, Gerhard, *Die italienischen Militärinternierten im deutschen Machtbereich 1943 bis 1945*, Munich: Oldenbourg, 1990

Schreiber, Gerhard, Bernd Stegemann and Detlef Vogel, *Das Deutsche Reich und der Zweite Weltkrieg*, Bd. 3, *Der Mittelmeerraum und Südosteuropa*, Stuttgart: Deutsche Verlagsanstalt, 1984

Seth, Ronald, *Jackals of the Reich: the Story of the British Free Corps*, London: New English Library, 1972

Smith, Neil C., *Australians Captured by the Raider Wolf*, Gardenvale, VIC: Mostly Unsung Military History Research and Publications, 2006

Sobocinska, Agnieszka, 'Prisoners of Opinion: Australians in Asian Captivity, 1942–2005', *Australian Studies* 1, 1, 2009, pp. 1–28

Speckner, Hubert, Kriegsgefangene in der 'Ostmark' 1939–1945: Zur Geschichte der Mannschaftsstammlager und Offizierslager in den Wehrkreisen XVII und XVIII, doctoral dissertation, University of Vienna, 1999

Stadt Moosburg a. d Isar (ed.), *Stalag VII A: 1939–1945; Moosburg a.d. Isar*, Moosburg: Stadt Moosburg a.d.Isar, 1982

BIBLIOGRAPHY

Stegemann, Bernd, 'The Italo-German Conduct of the War in the Mediterranean and North Africa', in Research Institute for Military History (ed.), *Germany and the Second World War*, Vol. III, *The Mediterranean, South-east Europe, and North Africa, 1939–1941*, Oxford: Clarendon Press, 1995

Stein, Harry, transl. Judith Rosenthal, *Buchenwald Concentration Camp 1937–1945: A Guide to the Permanent Historical Exhibition*, Göttingen: Wallstein Verlag, 2004

Stelzl-Marx, Barbara, *Zwischen Fiktion und Zeitzeugenschaft: Amerikanische und sowjetische Kriegsgefangene im Stalag XVII B Krems-Gneixendorf*, Tübingen: Günter Narr Verlag, 2000

Stockings, Craig, *Bardia: Myth, Reality and the Heirs of Anzac*, Sydney: University of New South Wales Press, 2009

Stopsack, Hans-Hermann and Eberhard Thomas (eds), *Stalag VI A, Kriegsgefangenenlager 1939–1945: Eine Dokumentation*, Hemer: Stadt Hemer, 1993

Streit, Christian, 'Sowjetische Kriegsgefangene – Massendeportationen – Zwangsarbeiter', in Wolfgang Michalka (ed.), *Der Zweite Weltkrieg: Analysen, Grundzüge, Forschungsbilanz*, Munich: Piper, 1989, pp. 747–60

Strong, Tracy, 'Service with Prisoners of War', in Clarence Prouty Shedd et al., *History of the World's Alliance of Young Men's Christian Associations*, London: SPCK, 1955, pp. 545–88

Thomas, Gabe, *MILAG: Captives of the Kriegsmarine: Merchant Navy Prisoners of War in Germany 1939–1945*, Glamorgan: Milag Prisoner of War Association, 1995

Thompson, Peter, *ANZAC Fury: The Bloody Battle of Crete 1941*, North Sydney: William Heinemann, 2010

Toliver, Raymond F., *The Interrogator: The Story of Hans-Joachim Scharff, Master Interrogator of the Luftwaffe*, Fallbrook, California: AERO Publishers, 1978

Tracey, Michael P., *Australian Prisoners of War*, Canberra: Department of Defence, 1999

Tzobanakis, Stella, *Creforce: The Anzacs and the Battle of Crete*, Fitzroy, VIC: Black Dog, 2010

Ueberschär-von Livonius, Ute, 'Sagan 1944', in Gerd R. Ueberschär (ed.), *Orte des Grauens: Verbrechen im Zweiten Weltkrieg*, Darmstadt: Primus, 2003, pp. 217–23

Urban, Thomas, *Zwangsarbeit im Tagebau: Der Einsatz von Kriegsgefangenen und auslaendischen Zivilarbeitern im mitteldeutschen Braunkohlenbergbau 1939 bis 1945*, Essen: Klartext, 2006

Uren, M., *A Thousand Men at War: The Story of the 2/16th Battalion, AIF*, Melbourne: Heinemann, 1959

Vance, Jonathan F., 'Men in Manacles: The Shackling of Prisoners of War, 1942–1943', *Journal of Military History*, 59, 3, July 1995, pp. 483–504

———, 'The War Behind the Wire: The Battle of Escape from a German Prison Camp', *Journal of Contemporary History*, 28, 4, October 1993, pp. 675–93

——— (ed.), *Encyclopedia of Prisoners of War and Internment*, Santa Barbara, California: ABC-Clio, 2000

Vogel, Detlef, 'German Intervention in the Balkans', in Research Institute for Military History (ed.), *Germany and the Second World War*, Vol. III, *The Mediterranean, South-East Europe, and North Africa, 1939–1941*, Oxford: Clarendon Press, 1995

Vourkoutiotis, Vasilis, *Prisoners of War and the German High Command: The British and American Experience*, London: Palgrave Macmillan, 2003

Vuillet, Andre, *Journey Among Captives: A Record of YMCA Service Among Prisoners, Internees and Displaced Persons During World War II*, n.p.: n.d. (circa 1946)

———, *The YMCA and Prisoners of War: War Prisoners Aid YMCA During World War II*, International Committee of the YMCA, 1946

Walker, Allan S., *Australia in the War of 1939–1945: Middle East and Far East (Medical)*, Canberra: Australian War Memorial, 1953

Waters, Christopher, 'Australia, the British Empire and the Second World War', *War and Society*, 19, 1, May 2001, pp. 93–107

Watson, Jeff, *Sidney Cotton: The Last Plane Out of Berlin*, Sydney: Hodder Headline, 2004

Watt, Molly, *The Stunned and the Stymied: The POW Experience in the History of the 2/11th Battalion, 1939–1945*, Perth: Westralian Publishers, 1997

Weale, Adrian, *Renegades: Hitler's Englishmen*, London: Weidenfeld and Nicolson, 1995

———, *The SS: A New History*, London: Little, Brown, 2010

Weinberg, Gerhard, *A World at Arms: A Global History of World War II*, Oxford: Oxford University Press, 1994

Whitlock, Flint, *Given Up for Dead! American GIs in the Nazi Concentration Camp at Berga*, Cambridge, Massachusetts: Westview, 2005

Williams, Eric, *The Wooden Horse*, London: Collins, 1949

Wilmot, Chester, *Tobruk 1941: Capture – Siege – Relief*, Sydney: Angus and Robertson, 1944

Winton, Andrew S., *Open Road to Faraway: Escapes from Nazi POW Camps 1941–1945*, Dunfermline: Cualann Press, 2001

Xylander, Marlen von, *Die deutsche Besatzungsherrschaft auf Kreta 1941–1945*, Freiburg: Rombach, 1989

Filmography

Wear Death Wears a Smile, Frank Heimans and Paul Rea, Cinetel Productions, 1985

The Great Escape: The Reckoning, Steve Westh, Electric Films, 2009

BIBLIOGRAPHY

Select Websites

AIF POW Free Men in Europe: www.aifpow.com

Australian Dictionary of Biography online: www.adb.online.anu.edu.au

Australian War Memorial: www.awm.gov.au

Australians at War Film Archive: www.australiansatwarfilmarchive.gov.au

Centralnym Muzeum Jeńców Wojennych w Łambinowicach (Central War Museum Łambinowice): www.cmjw.pl

Davis, Rob, 'Stalag Luft 3: The Great Escape', http://luft3.webpark.pl/

Museum of Allied Prisoners of War Martyrdom: http://www.muzeum.zagan.pl/index.php?id=0&lng=eng

National Archives of Australia: www.naa.gov.au

Oflag IV C Colditz: www.colditz-4c.com

Prisoner of War: http://www.pegasusarchive.org/pow/frames.htm

Prisoner of War: www.prisonerofwar.org.uk

RAF Ex-POWs: www.rafinfo.org.uk/rafexpow

Stalag Luft III and the Great Escape: www.u.zagan.pl/luft3/reprisal.hm

Stalag VII A Moosburg: www.moosburg.org/info/stalag

Stalag XVIII A Wolfsberg: www.stalag18a.org.uk

The Great Escape: The Real Escape: www.historyinfilm.com/escape/real8.htm

Theresienstadt 1941–1945 – Ein Nachschlagewerk. Die Kleine Festung – Gefängnis der Gestapo: (Theresienstadt 1941–1945 – A reference work. The Small Fortress – Gestapo prison), www.ghetto-theresienstadt.info/terezingefaengnis.htm

Wadley, Patricia, 'Even One Is Too Many: An Examination of the Soviet Refusal to Repatriate Liberated American World War II Prisoners of War': www.aiipowmia.com/research/wadley.html

World War II Nominal Roll: www.ww2roll.gov.au

Acknowledgements

This book had a long gestation; it was made possible through the generous efforts of many people in many places – in Australia, Great Britain, Germany, Switzerland, Poland and Hungary. Historians stand on the shoulders of fellow historians and of the librarians and archivists who advise them. For their information and advice, served in large portions and small, I extend my warm thanks to Jürgen Förster, Rüdiger Overmans, Fabrizio Bensi, Claude-Alain Danthe, Eric Carpenter, Sita Austin, Shannon Maguire, Paul Rea, Jo Jarrah, Guy Olding, Fania Khan, Lee Kersten, Laszlo Ritter, Jonas Eberhardt, Sabine Schafferdt, Sabine Stein, Wolfgang Benz, Konrad Kwiet, Daniel Boćkowski, Janette Condon, Jim Ottaway, Robert Loeffel, Barbara Schätz, Albert Knoll, Johannes Eberhardt, Agnieska Klys, Johannes Ibel, Wolfgang Röll, Stefan Geck, Thomas Zarwel, Herbert Karbach, Michael David, Peter Stanley, Piotr Setkiewicz, Wolfgang Oleschinski and Krzysztof Lada. Michael Caulfield kindly secured permission for me to use material from the Australians at War Film Archive, an invaluable resource for historians and others. In helping me to assemble and to create some sense of order from a vast array of material I received unstinting support from my research assistants, Michael Foster, Jim Anderson

ACKNOWLEDGEMENTS

and Evan Smith. All of them, I think, can rightly view this book as a product of their labours. Whatever flaws the book may contain are by no means attributable to them.

Without financial support even the most avid intentions would have come to little. Fortunately I was able to gain assistance from the Department of Defence's Army History Unit, from the Alexander von Humboldt Foundation, and from Flinders University. I owe a debt of gratitude to all of them.

For their role in converting an idea into a manuscript and then a book let me thank my agent Margaret Gee as well as Tom Gilliatt and Catherine Day at Pan Macmillan. My former colleague Brian Dickey, too, was a helpful, patient and insightful reader of my manuscript. The judicious guidance of all of the above got me over the finishing line in time.

Last, but by no means least, I must thank the former POWs who helped me. Many gave their time to allow me to interview them, and for this I thank Arthur Leggett, Peter Giles, Ray Corbett, Lawrie West, Frank Cox, Ray Jones, Ron Zwar, Keith Hooper, Ron Allan, Phil Loffman, Doug Nix. Others, among them Bill Rudd, Ralph Churches, Hal Finkelstein, Ray Middleton and John Crook, provided invaluable assistance by correspondence and telephone. The most persistent of my correspondents was Keith Hooper, who not only had a crystal clear recollection of his time in Hohenfels but also had a great breadth of knowledge of the war which had done so much to change his life. He was a steadfast source of knowledge, encouragement and friendship. Sadly he died in early 2009, before I could show him the fruits of my labours. I dedicate the book to the memory of Keith Hooper and of those like him.

Index

Aboriginal POWs 193–5
Absalom, Roger 118
Abwehr, the 137, 294
Admiral Scheer 43, 341
AE2 7
Afrika Korps 49, 51, 52, 53
AIF *see* Australian Imperial Force (2nd AIF)
aircraft
  Blenheim 281
  Dakotas 414
  Dorniers 26
  Halifax 28, 281, 293
  Hampden 27, 281
  Hurricanes 120
  Lancasters 24, 27, 32, 34, 272, 378, 414
  Messerschmitts 27
  Stukas 66, 79
  Thunderbolts 411
  Typhoons 384
airmen 22–37, 270–1, 303
  betrayal of 294
  Buchenwald, at 292–8, 427

  escape from Stalag Luft III 276–89
  escape, training for 348–9
  interrogations 162, 164–73, 427
  lynching 270–2
  shoot on capture order 303
  Terrorflieger (terror flyers) 270–1
  Total War declaration 269–72, 348
Aitken, Captain A.H. 260
Albania 59, 60, 61, 113, 117
Alexandria 74, 83
Aliakmon Line 65, 66
Alken 30
Allied commando forces 272
Alsace 187
Amery, John 332, 427
Anderson, George 389
Annerer, Maria 208
Aquileia 373
Arab Legion 325–6
Arab POWs 188–9
Arcadia 107
Athens 67, 68, 70, 96, 120
Atkins, Frank 108, 351, 374
Atlantis 43, 44

INDEX

Atock, Ken 'Bluey' 105
Auschwitz II-Birkenau 111, 237, 310, 384, 389
  Monowitz industrial plant 237–8, 459
Australian Citizens Military Force (CMF) 15–16, 20
Australian Imperial Force (2nd AIF)
  see also Royal Australian Air Force (RAAF); Royal Australian Navy (RAN)
  enlistment 15, 18, 20–1
  2/5th Australian General Hospital 104
  2/1 Battalion 78, 80, 192, 194
  2/4 Battalion 73, 83
  2/6 Battalion 86, 180, 353, 355
  2/7 Battalion 78, 82, 89, 234
  2/8 Battalion 82
  2/11 Battalion 78, 80, 88, 180, 194
  2/17 Battalion 78, 85
  2/24 Battalion 51, 228
  2/28 Battalion 54–5, 194
  2/32 Battalion 340
  2/48 Battalion 53
  16th Brigade 69
  18th Brigade 51
  6th Division *see* 6th Division
  7th Division 18, 49, 53, 53, 94
  9th Division 18, 49, 51, 53
  2/7 Field Ambulance 87
  2/8 Field Ambulance 49, 227
  2/3 Field Regiment 89
  2/3 Light Anti-Aircraft Regiment 83
  2/2 Machine Gun Battalion 327
  2/3 Machine Gun Battalion 95
  2/2 Pioneer Battalion 95
Australian POWs 8–9, 180–1
  AFL in camps 218–19
  after-effects 419–22
  airmen *see* airmen
  Boer War 7
  concentration camps 309–17, 467
    see also concentration camps
  deaths 8, 414, 478
  escape to Switzerland 118, 153, 194, 259, 352–3, 357–8, 361, 367–8
  execution *see* executions/murders
  government disagreement with Soviet proposal 395–8
  Great War 7–8
  losses at sea 114
  mental health 419–21, 423–5
  Monowitz industrial plant 237–8, 459
  nationality status 177
  postwar 417–25, 428–9
  work performance 224
Australian United Steam Navigation Company 39
Austria 111, 113, 141, 145, 147, 149, 159, 207–8, 218, 229, 232–3, 274, 307, 312, 321, 352, 360, 390–1, 402, 408, 412, 413
Auswärtiges Amt (AA) (German Foreign Office) 136, 328, 329
  Prisoner of War Organisation 328, 333
  propaganda work 328–9, 332–7
Ayers, Sir Henry 26

Baden Württemberg 111
Bader, Douglas 370
Badoglio, Marshal Pietro 116
Bain, Victor 170
Bari 114
Barker, Ronald David 340–2
Barnes, Crofton 'Teddy' 72, 352
Barrett, Francis 352
Barrett, Peter 232
Bastian, Henry 120, 171, 173–4, 378, 380
Battle of Alama el Halfa 52
Battle of Bardia 47
Battle of Berlin 32
Battle of Britain 26, 162
Battle of Cannae 2–3
Battle of El Alamein 23, 52–4, 57, 120, 171, 194

INDEX

Battle of France 26
Battle of Tempe Gorge 191
Battle of the Ruhr 28
Bauer-Schlichtegroll, Lieutenant 167–8
Bavaria 129, 142, 145, 149, 152, 153, 154, 194, 222, 229, 231, 232, 234, 251, 254, 291, 313, 355, 360, 382, 386, 387, 388, 389, 390, 409, 410
Baxter, Rex 355–6
Beck, L.C. 298
Beecroft, James 385
Beeston, Doris 41
Belgium 19, 23, 98, 125–6, 182
Belgrade 64, 120, 352
Benghazi 52, 56, 57, 58, 113, 114, 194, 228
Benghazi Handicap 49, 50, 51
Benns, Andy 353–4
Berchtesgaden 36, 280, 286
Bergenfjord 402
Berger, SS General Gottlob 134, 304–8, 335–6, 426
Bergsland, Peter 285
Berlin 32, 319, 320–1, 323, 324
Betts, Wes 405
Bewährungslager (punishment camp) 194, 252–3
Binns, Major Raymond Thomas 49–50
Bird, Arthur 'Dicky' 217
Blackforce 97
Blain, Harold 359
Blamey, General Thomas 63
Blanch, George 236
Blechhammer work camp 202, 208, 210, 238, 247, 318–19, 320, 337, 338, 387, 410
Blitzkrieg 19, 66, 185
Boer War 1, 7, 196
Bohemia-Moravia, Protectorate of 98
Booth, Margery 322, 338, 339
Bormann, Martin 139

Bose, Subhas Chandra 325
Bosse, Bill 389
Brallos Pass 66, 73, 104
Bremen 100, 155, 356
Brennan, Jim 194, 359–60
Brickhill, Paul 278, 413
Bridgehead Prison 263
Brindisi 56
Britain 13, 23
  Anglo–German relations on POW matters 178
  Dominions and defence 14
British Advocate 341
British 8th Army 54
British Empire Medal 312, 364
British Expeditionary Force 19
British 14th Brigade 77
British Free Corps (BFC) 320, 326, 332, 337, 338–41
British POWs 179–80
  escape statistics 347
  German military courts 261–2
  work performance 223–5
British 7th Armoured Division 46
British Special Operations Executive (SOE) 90, 296
British War Office
  Prisoners of War Department 190, 300
Brooke, Rupert 62
Broomhead, Edwin 50, 227–8
Brough, Ernest 57–8, 114–15, 424
Brown, John 'Busty' 319, 322, 335, 337–9
Brown, Philip 109
Brown, William 151
Bruce, Stanley 17, 242
Brudenell-Woods, Basil 209
Brüx 239, 284
Buchenwald 291–8
  Polizeihäftlinge (police prisoners) 292
  Soviet POWs 295–6
Budapest 402
Bulgaria 61, 65, 98, 361

INDEX

Burden, Hester 158
Burnett, Captain J. 38
Burney, Christopher 296
Burton, Arthur 350
Burton, Harry 208
Bush Veldt Carbineers 7
Butterworth, Doug 386
Buxton, Arthur 186
Byron, Lord 62

Cairo 52, 53, 63, 67, 78, 82
Calcaterra, Vittorio 115
Calder, Lawrence (Jack) 56, 115, 186, 194, 250, 361
camp commandants 115, 141–2, 148, 149, 162, 244
Campbell, Allen 383–4
Campbell, Lieutenant Colonel Ian 78, 80–1, 83–4, 152
Campo PG (Prigioneri di Guerra) 57 114
camps 140–60 *see also* conditions in camps
  absence of women, effect 206–7
  alcohol 202
  Armee-Kriegsgefangenen-sammelstellen (AGSST) 141
  athletics 219
  books 212
  branch of armed forces and 140–1
  bribes 246–7
  camaraderie 205–6
  cards 214
  commanders *see* camp commandants
  communities within 202–5
  concentration *see* concentration camps
  cricket 216–18
  designation 142
  disciplinary treatment 252–3
  Durchgangslager (transit camp) *see* Dulag Luft; *Dulags*
  educational opportunities 210–12

entertainment 209–20
evacuations due to advancing Red Army 377–92
Ferienlager (holiday camp) 319–42
'ferrets' 277, 432
films 214
football 218–19
formalities 196–7
gambling 214
geographical divisions 141
Geschlechtsverkehr-Verbrechen (sex crimes) 206–7
Heimkehrerlager (repatriation preparation) 142–3 *see also* repatriation
homosexuality 208–9
international inspection 144
Internierungslager (civilian internee camp) *see* Ilags
isolation cells 248
Lagergeld 213, 214, 224
letters and postcards 213–14
liberation by Americans 410–12
liberation by British forces 412–13
liberation by Red Army 404–5
magazines 212
Man of Confidence (*Vertrauensmann*) 143, 148, 151, 210, 253, 362
Marlag (*Marine-Lager*) 155 *see also* Westertimke naval prison camp
Milag (*Marine-Internierten-Lager*) 155 *see also* Westertimke naval prison camp
military districts (*Wehrkreise*) 141–2, 145
military ranks and 140, 142
misdemeanours 248
offences 261–3
official newspaper (*The Camp*) 212, 329
Offizierslager (Officers' Camp) *see* Oflags

INDEX

Personalkarte 196–7
punishments 248–50, 252–5, 261–4
radios 213
reception 141
satellite (*Zweiglager*) 142, 152
self-rule 143
sex crimes (*Geschlechtsverkehr-Verbrechen*) 206–7
sports 215–20
Stamm-Mannschaftslager see Stalags
Straflager 252–4
survival in 202–4
theatrical productions 209
tobacco 199–200
transit (Durchgangslager/Dulag) see Dulag Luft; *Dulags*
Vertrauensmann (Man of Confidence) 143, 148, 151, 210, 253, 362
Wehrkreise (military districts) 141–2, 145
Zweiglager (satellite camps) 142, 152
Canea 78, 79, 82
Capua 114
Carmody, Flight Lieutenant Keith 218
Carter, Mrs Anne 157
Casement, Roger 326
Catanach, Squadron Leader James 281, 284–5
Centillon, Reg 386
Chamberlain, Neville 14
Champ, Jack 355–6
Chappell, Ann 417
Chiavari 114
Chipchase, Robert 340, 341
Chisholm, Keith 356
Churches, Ralph 72–3, 103, 111, 362–4, 365
Churchill, Winston 1, 62–4, 78, 128–9, 196, 285, 394, 396
Ciano, Count 60

Clarke, Michael 89–90
Clarke, Nobby 95
Clifton, Brigadier George 331
Cochrane, Captain 108
Cohen, George Judah 192
Colditz (Oflag IV C) 255–60, 286, 338, 354, 417, 461
Collard, Wing Commander R.C.M. 404, 405
Collins, Douglas 312
Collins, Noel 409
Cologne 27
Comet escape line 294
Commissaire Ramel 44
Concentration Camp Committee 309–10
concentration camps 291–8, 309–10
    Auschwitz II-Birkenau 111, 237, 310, 310, 384, 389
    Buchenwald 291–8
    Dachau 291, 310, 410
    Mauthausen 274, 310
    Sachsenhausen 286, 291
    Terezín 310–17, 360, 424, 428
conditions in camps 3–4, 56
    bedbugs 108
    clothing 146, 147, 198–9
    end of war 383–6
    food 105, 107–8, 199–201, 404–5
    latrines 106, 109, 115, 147
    lice 56–7, 72, 103, 106, 108–9, 315, 382
    rats 109, 153
    shelter 105, 147, 197–8
    space 147
    transport 109–10
    work detachments *see* work detachments
Conklin, Norm 119
Convention of Geneva *see also* Geneva Convention, the 'For the Amelioration of the Condition of Sick and Wounded Armies in the Field' 5

INDEX

Corbett, Ray 21, 79, 85–6, 109, 112, 202, 208, 210, 218, 219, 236, 238–9, 247, 318–20, 387, 410
Corinth Canal 69, 70, 102
Corinth POW camp 70, 71, 102–3, 225–6
Cornell, Kelvin 238, 459
Cornish, Geoff 27
Cotton, Sidney 156
Cousins, Bill 51–2, 115–16, 228, 424
Cox, Frank 69, 185, 203, 222, 375–6
Cranborne, Viscount 395–6
Craven, Clarrie 119
Crawford, Doug 355–6
Crete 19, 72, 75–92, 99, 191, 192, 198, 223, 349, 361, 414
   Allied troops 78
   Australian evaders 90, 347
   Australian losses/POWs 91
   defence 80–2
   Eagle of the Paratroopers 226
   evacuation 82–3
   Galatas camp 104–5, 133, 226, 349–50, 366
   German losses 91
   German plan 76–9
   POW camps 104–6
   POWs 83–9
   strategic importance 75
Croatia 98
Crooks, John 71, 102–3
Crouch, Frank 95
Cullen, Herb 311, 314
Cullen, Paul Alfred 191–2
Cullinger, Lyle 234, 254
Curtin, John 396
Cusack, Percy 350
Cyrenaica 48–9
Czechoslovakia 360

Dachau 291, 310, 410
Dakers, Captain Rex 322, 468

Damascus 96
Davis, Harry 194
de Gaulle, Charles 93–4, 96
de Montesquieu, Baron 4
de Zitter, Prosper 31, 294
Dekanazov, Vladimir 398
Denholm, A. 43–4
Denmark 160
Dentz, Commissioner Henri 94, 96
Depression, the 14, 120
Derbyshire, Max 350
Derna 49, 50, 227
Desoubrie, Jacques 294–5, 427
Detmers, Captain Theodor 38
Dhurringile 127
Dieburg 113
Dieppe 128, 131, 272
Dietrich, Marlene 411
Distinguished Conduct Medals 339, 352
Djenné 373
Dodge, Major Johnnie 285
Donaldson, Don 257
Dortmund 34
Dresden 34, 303, 324, 341, 424
Duderstadt 386
Dulag Luft 119, 120, 133, 161–4, 175, 257, 294 *see also* Oberursel
   isolation rooms 165
   postwar trial 426
Dulags (transit camps) 133–4
   Salonika (Dulag 183) 101–2, 103–4, 106–7, 110–11, 113, 133, 142, 153
Dunkirk 19, 112, 119, 337
Dunlop, Edward 'Weary' 57, 430
Dunne, Noel 366
Durchgangslager (transit camps) *see* Dulag Luft; *Dulags*
Durmitor 44

Eagle of the Paratroopers 226
Earl of Hopetoun 256
East, Roy 226, 240
Eben Emael 76

INDEX

Eden, Anthony 288, 289, 393, 397, 427
Edwards, Pat 30
Egypt 18, 52, 53, 82, 130
Eichmann, Adolf 111
Eichstätt camp *see Oflags*
El Daba 56
Elphinstone, Lord 308
Empire Air Training Scheme (EATS) 17–18, 22, 29
England Committee 329
'Enigma' machines 77
Ermland 43
Ersatzheer (the Replacement Army) 145, 299–300, 305, 336
escapes 5, 174, 216, 248, 252, 258–60, 273, 345–68
  airmen, training for 348–9
  Colditz, from 257–60, 461
  dangers 347–8, 367–8
  death zones 300–1
  help from locals 348
  home runs 255, 258–60, 276, 285, 347, 355, 356–7, 358–9, 361
  Kugel-Erlass (the Bullet Decree) 274–5
  motivation 345–7
  'penguins' 277
  Reich's Office of Criminal Police C2K Bureau 274
  Stalag Luft III, from 276–89, 347
  train-jumping 351–3
  Warburg Wire Job 354–6
Evatt, Herbert 397
exchanges 3, 369–76
  sick and wounded 371–3
executions/murders 2, 3, 116, 190, 274, 368
  escapes, for 105, 280, 283–9, 359–60
  postwar trial 427–8
  Soviet POWs 295–6
Ex-POW Association 423, 429

Fairbairn, Terry 81, 129, 327
Fairclough, Mervyn 292
Faulkes, Ted 56
Feldpost 12545 227, 251
Feldscher, Dr 307
Ferienlager (holiday camp) 319–42
  officers, for 330–1
  propaganda purpose 319–20, 325–8, 331
Ferrero, G.S. 'Pat' 217
Fielder, Thomas 203–4
Finkelgruen, Peter 428
Finkelstein, Hal 88, 109, 193, 200, 373–4, 421, 422
Finland 98
Fladungen 231
Flinders, Matthew 417
Fore, Jim 297–8
Fort St Catherine 97
Fort Zinna 263, 264
4th Indian Division 46
Fowler, Flight Lieutenant Hedley Nevile 'Bill' 26, 255, 258–60, 356, 439
France 19, 23, 94, 98, 117, 160
  Resistance movement 93, 293
  Vichy France 93, 95, 98, 187–8
Frankfurt 30, 34, 112, 119, 163–4, 294
Free India Legion 325
Freiburg 6
French POWs 181
Fresnes 31, 119, 292, 293
Freyberg, General Bernhard 77–8, 80, 82
Fromm, Friedrich 299
Froome, Cecil 467
Fry, Arthur 262
Fullarton, Jack 358
Fury, Roy 149

Galatas camp 104–5, 349–50
Gallipoli 62, 67
Geheime Staatspolizei (Secret State Police) *see* Gestapo

INDEX

General Anderson 376
Geneva Convention, the 6, 9, 99, 125, 127, 128, 130, 132, 134, 135, 141, 143–4, 151, 154, 157, 160, 165–6, 177, 183, 223, 231, 234, 242, 252, 261, 262, 272, 289, 302, 304, 348, 369, 371
Genshagen holiday camp 319–25, 330, 334, 335, 337, 340
Georgioupolis 78, 366
Gephard, Stabsfeldwebel 258
German armed forces
  VIII Air Corps 76
  XI Air Corps 76
  5th Armoured Division 68
  9th Armoured Division 64
  XXX Corps 64
  XXXX Divisions 64
  XVIII Mountain Corps 64
German Foreign Office (Auswärtiges Amt) 328, 329
  Prisoner of War Organisation 328, 333
  propaganda work 328–9, 332–7
German military courts 261–4
Germany 13–14, 19, 23
  Allied bombing raids 270
  Anglo-German relations on POW matters 178
  creation of Third Reich 123–4
  desert campaign 47–51
  Foreign Office 136
  Greater German Reich 98–100
  labour demands of war 221–2
  Military Districts 141–2, 145
  Ministry of Labour 137–8
  miscegenation fears 206
  moving POWs from Red Army path 377–92, 302, 390–1
  Oberkommando des Heeres (OKH) (Army High Command) 133, 302
  Plenipotentiary for Labour 138
  POW policy and administration 124–5, 127–8, 130, 132–9, 149, 157, 273–4, 290–1, 299–306, 333–6
  recruitment of Allied POWs 326–7, 331–2, 338–41
  Total War declaration 269–70, 348
  transfer of POWs into Reich 98–120
Gersdorf 194–5, 454
Gestapo (*Geheime Staatspolizei* – Secret State Police) 31, 119, 137, 169–70, 273, 292, 294, 310
Gibb, Albert 109, 185
Giesen, Harry 147, 148
Gilbert, Captain G. 49
Giles, Peter 32–4, 378, 380, 382–3
Gillon, Phillipa 108
Giralt, Léonarda Maria Louisa 31
Goebbels, Joseph 138, 269–70, 271, 303, 328, 329, 332–3
Goethe Oak 291
Gomm, Angelina 157
Goodwin, Captain Jim 363
Göring, Hermann 76, 120, 135–6, 140, 158, 161–76, 229, 239, 276, 280, 283, 377, 425–6
Gradisca 375
Graf, Alma 157
Granquist, Charles 73, 253, 346, 365
Graudenz military prison 263–4
Gravina 114
Grayston, W.S. 399
Graziani, Marshal Rudolfo 46
Great Escape, The 276
Great War, the 6, 7, 18, 19, 20, 124–6, 162
Greece 19, 59–74, 98, 99, 113, 117, 126, 191, 198, 362
  ANZAC forces 66–7
  Australian losses/POW numbers 73–4
  Australian role 63–4
  deployment of POW labour 225
  evacuation of Allied forces 67–73
  German strategy 64–6

512

INDEX

Green, Captain Julius 338
Green, Thomas 'Tommy' Harold (Negus) 194
Greenstein, Wolfe 192–3
Greer, Jimmy 108
Grey-Smith, Flight Lieutenant Guy E. 26
Gripsholm 375
Grotius, Hugo
  De Jure Belli ac Pacis 4
Gruppignano 114, 115, 366
Güssefeld, Lieutenant 155–6
Gwilliam, James 292

Hague Conventions 5–6, 183, 184
  loopholes 6
  'With Respect to the Laws and Customs of War on Land' 5
Haig, Captain 256
Hake, Albert 278, 281, 283, 285, 289
Halder, General 48
Hallstadt 231
Hamburg 27, 29
Handcock, Peter J. 7
Hannibal 3
Harris, Air Chief Marshal Arthur 27
Harvey, William 359
Hawking, W.V. 399
Hayes, Norman 'Nobby' 45
Head, Richard 408
Heilag (*Heimkehrerlager* – repatriates' camp) Annaburg 287
Heimpel, Major 338
Helfgott, Hermann 188
Hemmens, Philip 298
Heraklion 78, 79, 81, 82, 83
Herman, Joe 28
Heron, Roy 226
Hesse, Dr Fritz 329
Heydrich, Reinhard 360
Hiddlestone, Frank 204
Hill, Ernestine
  My Love Must Wait 417–18

Himmler, Heinrich 99, 135, 137, 169, 229, 270–1, 273, 274–5, 279–80, 286, 289, 290, 296, 305, 339, 426, 428
  influence in POW matters 273–4, 290–1, 299–302, 304, 333–6
historical views of POWs 1–3
Hitler, Adolf 3, 6, 13, 19, 47, 52, 59–61, 73, 75–6, 92, 98–9, 117, 123–5, 128–9, 184, 207, 271, 272, 279, 296, 301, 306, 381, 425
  attempted assassination of 290, 299–300
  Commando Order 131–2, 272–3
  Commissar Order 130–1, 184, 187
  declaration of Operational Zones 117
  Führer principle 135
  Great War, effect on POW policy 124–7
  Nazi ideology 130, 132
  power and popularity 124
  reciprocity principle 124–5, 127–8, 130, 149, 157, 304
  rise to power 123–4
  views on POWs 124–5, 303–4, 332–3
Hitler Youth 379
Hoare, Sir Samuel 374
Hodgson, Wilf 119, 384, 404
'holiday' camps (*Ferienlager*) 319–42
Holland 19, 23, 98, 182
Holroyd, Lieutenant Ralph 338
Hooper, Keith 85, 129, 192–3, 212, 351, 410
human shields 6, 163, 303
Humphreys, Edgar 'Hunk' 281, 283
Hundred Years War (1337–1453) 3
Hungary 61, 98, 360

INDEX

Ilags (Internierungslager) 143, 156–7
  Biberach 159–60
  Laufen (Ilag VII H) 159
  Spittal (Ilag XVIII) 159
  Tost 159
  Wülzburg (Ilag XIII A) 156–7, 159
illnesses
  beriberi 90, 108, 115, 387
  dysentery 57, 72, 85, 105–6, 107, 110, 115, 147, 199, 382, 386, 409
  malaria 108, 115, 147
  typhus 186, 315, 316
Imperial 82
Indian Ocean 100
Indian POWs 178–9
Inspekteur Kriegsgefangenenwesen (Inspector of POW Affairs) 135, 302–3
Insterburg 378
Intelligence Assessment Centre 161
International Committee of the Red Cross (ICRC) 129, 143, 146, 148, 182, 200, 241, 252, 370, 392 *see also* Red Cross
International Conference of Red Cross Societies 157
international POW law 5
internees 156–9 *see also* Ilags
  Germans 371
  women 157–9
Internierungslager (civilian internment camp) *see* Ilags
interrogations 162, 164–73, 427
  Red Cross forms, use of 165–6, 168, 171
Irish Brigade 326–7
Italienische Militärinternierte (Italian military internees) 117, 183
Italy 19, 23, 114, 116, 126, 269
  anti-semitism 117
  Fascist Grand Council 116
  Italian POWs 47

Mediterranean strategy 59–60
  partisans 118
  POW camps 116–17, 228
  10th Army 47

Jager, Charles 86–7, 226, 349–50
Japan 9, 14, 16, 53
Java 97
Jean II, King (France) 3
Jenkins, Alex 34–5, 424
Jewish POWs 187–93
Jöckel, Commandant Heinrich 311
Jodl, Alfred 425
Johnson, Peter 414
Johnston, Eric 292
Jones, Ray 53–4, 118, 228, 357–8
Jones, W.A. 'Syd' 39–40, 100
Joyce, William 326, 338

Kalamata 69, 70–2, 102, 188, 225
Kaltenbrunner, Ernst 280, 307, 426
Kassel 29, 152
Keays, Tom 95
Keitel, Field Marshal Wilhelm 132–3, 280, 286–7, 330, 336, 425
Kelly, Ted 202
Kerkham, Sydney 'Mac' 414
Kidston, Jack 66
Kiefheide 379
Kierath, Flight Lieutenant Reginald V. 'Rusty' 281, 283–4
Killinger, Erich 162
Kinder, James 84–5
King's African Rifles 44
Kingsford-Smith, Flight Lieutenant Peter 280
Kinka Maru 39
Komet 41, 43
Komitades 87
Kommandeur der Kriegsgefangenen see camp commanders
Kommissarbefehl (Commissar Order) 130, 184, 187
Könisburg 378

514

INDEX

Kormoran, HSK 16, 38–9, 40, 100
Krakow 240, 389, 400
Kreuzberg 159
Kriegsmarine 17, 40, 73, 141, 161, 379–80
  POWs 155–6
Kugel-Erlass (the Bullet Decree) 274–5
Kulmerland 41

Lacey, Merchant Seaman Charles 43
Lacking Moral Fibre (LMF) 35
Lamason, Philip 292
Lang, David 361
Lark, Charles 'Chick' 28
Lawrence, Frederick 311, 467
Lawrence, Lindsay 107, 110, 198, 234–5, 244, 351
Laws, Les 362
Le Soeuf, Lieutenant Colonel Leslie 87–8, 113, 160, 223, 308, 350
Leggett, Arthur 88, 106, 110, 240, 387–9
Leigh, Thomas B. 281, 285
Leonard, Stanley 232
Levi, Primo 237
liberation 493–416
  reception centres 414–15, 421
Liddel, Clive 359
Liebenau 159
Light, Kevin 292
Liley, Jack 170–1, 204, 379–80
Lind, Lew 227
Livy 3
Loane, Bruce 30
Lockie, Bert 358
Loffman, Phil 54–5, 239, 407–8
Lord Haw Haw (William Joyce) 326, 338, 427
Lübeck 152, 257, 353, 355, 381, 383
Luckett, Don 207–8
Luftwaffe 64, 66, 70, 119, 140, 161–2, 169–70, 272, 279, 290
  see also German armed forces

Oberkommando der Luftwaffe (OKL) (Supreme Command of the Luftwaffe) 173
Lux (Gestapo officer) 284, 285, 427

McAuliffe, Kevin 408
MacCallum, A.M. 399
McCarter, Major Lew 54
McClelland, Alex 108, 194, 311, 315–17, 320–1, 467
McColm, Malcom 257
McCracken, James 118
Mackenzie, RAAF Wireless Air Gunner Ron 204, 209, 211, 212, 213, 251, 383, 388, 414–15
McMahon, Denis 467
McSweyn, Allan 356–7, 365
McTigue, John 232–3
Maginot Line 19
Makepeace, V.C. 233
Malbork Commonwealth War Cemetery 265
Malcolm, Thomas 292, 298
Maleme 78, 79, 80, 81–2, 88, 120, 226, 227
Malloth, Anton 428
Maloney, J.J. 397, 398, 399, 476
Mareeba, SS 39, 100
Marks, Vic 43, 217
Marlag-Milag Nord *see* Westertimke naval prison camp
Marshall, Arthur 226
Massey, Group Captain Herbert 283, 287, 289
Mathews, John 171–3, 214, 271–2, 409–10
Mauthausen concentration camp 274, 310
Megara 70
Menzies, Robert Gordon 14, 63–4
merchant seamen 43–4
Merdjayoun 95
Metaxas Line 65, 66
Milbank, John 227
military intelligence 77
  German 137
  Ultra decrypts 77, 78, 80, 81

INDEX

military prisons 262–3
Militia (Australian Citizens Military Force) 15–16, 20
Mills, Keith 292
Mills, Robert 292, 295
Ministry of Popular Enlightenment and Propaganda (Reichsministerium für Volksaufklärung und Propaganda) 138, 214, 332
MI9 90, 116, 338, 348
Molotov, Vyacheslav 398, 399
Mondschein, Jerzy 283
Moore, Newt 358
Morant, Harry 'Breaker' 7
Morley, George 68–9
Morshead, Lieutenant General Leslie 52–3
Moscow
British Military Mission 397
Müller, Heinrich 280
Muller, Jens 285
Munich 111, 234, 361
Murchison 127
murders *see* executions/murders
Mussolini, Benito 19, 48, 59–60, 99, 113, 116

Nafplion 71
Nantes 119
Naples 114
Navarino 114
Naville, Gabriel 287–8, 289
Nebe, Criminal Police Chief Arthur 280
Nelson, Earle 200
Netherlands 99
Neumann, Franz 136
New Zealand Division 64
New Zealand POWs 181
Nicholls, John 'Ticker' 359
Night of the Long Knives 123, 305
Nino Bixio 114
9th Division *see* Australian Imperial Force (2nd AIF)

9th Durham Light Infantry 331
Nix, Doug 71–2, 181, 185, 197, 214, 233, 250, 251, 253–4, 352, 412–13, 423
Norman, P.H. 420
Norman, Ray 148
North Africa 19–21, 23, 46–58, 62, 98, 113, 171, 198, 227
  Australian casualties/POW numbers 58
  transfer of POWs 50–1, 55–6, 113
Norton, Clifford 288
Norway 98, 132, 182
Notou 40

Oberkommando der Wehrmacht (OKW) (High Command of the German Armed Forces) 133, 135, 140, 155, 173, 175, 179, 189, 211, 223–4, 245, 305, 318, 328, 371
  Allgemeines Wehrmachsamt (AWA) (General Military Forces Office) 133–4, 302
  propaganda work 328, 332–7
Oberkommando des Heeres (OKH) 133, 302
Oberursel 119, 161–73, 258, 294
  see also Dulag Luft
  Auswertestelle West (Intelligence Assessment Centre) 161–3, 169
  Beute-und Nachrichtenauswertung (Captured Materials Evaluation Section) 164
  isolation rooms 165
Odessa 398, 399–403
officer POWs 6, 8
Oflags 143, 147, 151–2
  Biberach (Oflag V B) 112, 152, 153, 159, 355
  Colditz (Oflag IV C) 255–60, 461
  Edelbach (Oflag XVII) 218
  Eichstätt (Oflag VII B) 129, 130, 153, 355, 390
  Laufen (Oflag VII C) 152

516

INDEX

Lübeck (Oflag X C) 112, 152, 153
Osnabrück-Eversheide (Oflag VI C) 188
Prenzlau (Oflag II A) 258
Spangenberg (Oflag IX A) 152, 153, 217, 356
Teillager/Zweiglager (annex) 152
Warburg (Oflag VI B) 152, 153, 353–4
Weinsberg (Oflag V A) 153
Operation *Barbarossa* 52, 76, 92, 94, 96, 130, 131, 182, 184–5, 221, 305
Operation *Demon* 67
Operation *Lustre* 64
Operation *Marita* 64, 65
Operation *Merkur* 76, 91
Operation *Seelöwe* (Sea-Lion) 27, 119
Oranje 374
Orion 40–3, 83, 352
Osborn, Leslie 'Aussie' 254
Ottoman Turkey 7–8

Pacific Ocean 100
Padulla 114
Palestine 53, 57, 94, 95, 350
Palestinian POWs 189
Pankrác Gestapo prison 312, 314, 315
Papagos, General 67
Paris 19
Parker, Vincent 'Bush' 257
Parrott, Charlie 86, 106, 108, 201, 226, 240, 244, 250, 251, 291, 400–1, 415, 422
Parrott, Mark 415
Parsons, Jack 223
Paterson, Jim 55, 56, 346, 362, 364–5
Paulus, General Friedrich 269
Pearson, Flying Officer 218
Peck, John 366–8
Perry, Flight Sergeant Raymond 292, 293
Perth, HMAS 45

Pétain, Marshal Philippe 93
Pfeffer, Professor Karl Heinz 323
Phillips, Mark 192–3
Pinguin 43
Piraeus 64
Playoust, Captain Roger 257
Pohe, John (Porokoru Patapu) 285
Poitiers 119
Poland 13, 19, 23, 99, 182–3
Porpoise 114
Porteous, Jack 467
Portland, MS 262
Post, Johannes 284–5
Potts, John 238, 459
POW Standstill Agreement 391–2
POWs 1–9
  airmen 161–76
  Australian *see* Australian POWs
  bombing raids 163–4, 239, 297
  Britain and Dominions, from 178–9
  chaplains 204
  commandos 131–2
  execution 118, 132 *see also* executions/murders
  German escapes 347
  German, transferred to Australia 127
  guards 244–8
  guilt and shame 55–6, 73, 86, 346
  human shields 6, 163, 303
  interrogation *see* interrogations
  Italian 117
  'kriegie' life 196–220
  liberation 493–416
  maltreatment 115–16, 126, 130, 232–3, 313–17, 378–80, 426–7
  medical staff 160
  mental health 203, 419–21
  military ranks and 140, 142, 154
  nationalities 177–9
  official sanctions 243
  Prominente 256, 306–8, 426
  reciprocity principle 124–5, 127–8, 130, 149, 157, 304

INDEX

POWs cont'd
  sea voyages 114
  segregation 190
  shackling 128–30
  Soviet 126–7, 130–1
  theft 248–9
  transfer to Reich 98–120
  work detachments *see* work detachments
  wounded 50, 52
Price, Fred 358
Prinz zu Hohenlöhe, Rittmeister 238
Prisoners of War Information Bureau (Australia) 134
Protecting Power 135, 136, 143, 147, 150, 159, 160, 163, 165, 178, 182, 190, 241–2, 255, 261, 283, 287, 288, 302, 307, 371, 392, 406
  role 144

Qattara Depression 52
Quinn, Frank 352

Ramsay, Ian 263–4
Rangitane, RMS 40, 42
Rats of Tobruk 51
Rawson, Johnny 260, 353–4
Recknagel, Lieutenant Otto-Walter 166
Red Cross 4, 108, 115, 129, 135, 149, 151, 153, 165, 174, 189–90, 199, 215, 234, 235, 253, 390
  see also International Committee of the Red Cross (ICRC)
  parcels 112, 160, 200–2, 214, 246, 297, 306, 353, 387, 390, 409, 411
  Prisoner of War 418
Reed, William 356
Reeves, Jim 114, 324, 359, 406–7
Regensburg 41
Reggio Calabria 114
Reichernärungsministerium (Reich Food Ministry) 138

Reichssicherheitshauptamt (RSHA) (Reich Main Security Office) 137, 273, 307
Sicherheitsdienst (SD) (German Security Service) 132, 169, 275
Reinecke, General Hermann 134
  Abteilung Wehrmachtverluste und Kriegsfegangenwesen) (Department of Wehrmacht Casualties and POW affairs) 134
repatriation 369–76
  Heimkehrerlager (repatriation preparation) 142–3
  medical grounds 369–70
  Mixed Medical Commission 369–70, 371, 372, 376
  'Protected Personnel' 369, 370–1
  Soviet delays 398–9
Retimo 78, 79, 80, 81, 82, 83, 84, 88, 152, 194, 314, 315
Riley, Wal 311, 314–15, 467
Roberts, Barney 70, 321–4, 401–2
Roberts, Thomas 379
Robinson, Charles 105, 374–5
Roettig, Major General Otto 135
Rojko, Stefan 312–13
Romania 60
Romilly, Giles 256, 307
Rommel, Lieutenant General Erwin 48–9, 51, 52, 58, 62, 130
Rousseau, Jean-Jacques 4
Royal Air Force (RAF) 66
  Bomber Command 23–5, 27
  Coastal Command 17, 23, 25
  Fighter Command 23, 25
  gunners 24
  33 Squadron 120
  53 Squadron 281
  61 Squadron 29
  72 Squadron 281
  76 Squadron 281
  145 Squadron 36
  214 Squadron 272
Royal Australian Air Force (RAAF) 17–18, 22–37

INDEX

450 Squadron 281
454 Squadron 23
460 Squadron 30, 32, 34, 36, 119
463 Squadron 32
466 Squadron 30, 293
life expectancy 25
Middle East operations 25
POWs 25–6, 119–20
Royal Australian Army Medical Corps 108, 181, 223
Royal Australian Navy (RAN) 16–17 *see also* seamen
Royal Navy (RN) 14, 44, 67, 71, 79, 82, 84, 87, 155, 262, 417
Royle, Paul Gordon 281–2, 283, 285
Ruin Ridge 54–5, 57
Ryan, Raymond 176

Sachsenhausen concentration camp 286, 291
Sagan (Stalag Luft III) 26, 174, 200, 204, 205, 209, 210, 215, 216, 218, 220, 275, 356, 404, 413
  evacuation 384
  Great Escape 174, 276–89
  Organisation X 277
St Médard en Jalles 100, 352
Salonika 65, 68, 69, 94, 96, 114, 145, 147, 152, 185, 226, 229, 232, 234, 235, 236, 240, 314, 327, 350–1
  deaths in POW camp 108
  German occupation 101–2
  POW transit camp (Dulag 183) 101–2, 103–4, 106–7, 110–11, 113, 133, 142, 153
Sandover, Ray 84, 88, 89
Sanyet el Miteiriya 54
Sark 128, 131
Sauckel, Fritz 138, 229
Saunders, Reg 89, 193
Saxony-Anhalt 381
Saywell, Lawrence 414
Scharff, Hanns Joachim 164

Scharpwinkel (Gestapo officer) 285, 428
Schutzstaffel (SS) (Protective Squadron) 137, 187, 229, 273, 291, 296–7, 301, 302, 303, 305, 307–8, 316, 333–5, 368, 426
  death squads 131
  Einsatzgruppen (special action groups) 131
  Einsatzkommandos (special action commandos) 131
  SS *Leibstandarte* Adolf Hitler 64, 66
Scipio Africanus 3
Scott, Norm 90
seamen 38–45
Sebastiano Venier 114
Second World War 13–21
  Australia and 14–15
  bombing raids 270
  D-Day landings 377
  Total War declaration by Germany 269–70, 348
Serbia 98, 182
Servigliano 114
7th Division *see* Australian Imperial Force (2nd AIF)
Shackling Crisis 128–30, 131, 176, 178, 272, 373
SHAEF (the Supreme Headquarters of the Allied Expeditionary Forces) 394, 405, 408
  PWX 408
Shelswell, Ernie 104
Sherman, Raphael 176
Shove, Syd 358
Sicily 116
Sidi Barrani 46–7
Sidney-Smith, Lorna 158–60
Singapore 16
6th Division 16, 20, 63–5, 87, 94
  Libyan campaign 46–7
  24th Anti-Tank Company 49
Skines camp 226, 349
Slovakia 98

INDEX

Snedden, Alan 217
Soderberg, Henry 337
SOE (British Special Operations Executive) 90, 296
soldiers, status of 4
  officer POWs 6, 8
  sick and wounded 5, 50
  working for enemy 8
Somaliland 44
Sonderlager (special camps) 334
South Australian Mounted Rifles 7
Soviet POWs 126–7, 130–1
  Buchenwald 295–6
  German treatment of 126–7, 130–1, 183–7
Soviet Union 11, 60, 61, 76, 428
  Buchenwald 295–6
  draft reciprocal agreement for treatment of POWs 394–7
  German treatment of POWs 126–7, 130–1, 183–7
  liberation of Allied prisoners 393
  offensive 1945 381
  Operation *Barbarossa see* Operation *Barbarossa*
  POW Information Bureau 184
  relationship with Western allies 393–4
Speer, Albert 229
Sphakia 84–6, 104, 192, 226, 366
Spitfires 36, 281
Spreewald 100
Spriggs, Tom 90
SS (*Schutzstaffel*) 137, 187, 229, 273, 291, 296–7, 301, 302, 303, 305, 307–8, 316, 333–5, 368, 426
  death squads 131
  Einsatzgruppen (special action groups) 131
  Einsatzkommandos (special action commandos) 131
  SS *Leibstandarte* Adolf Hitler 64, 66
Stalags Luft 173
  Bankau (Stalag Luft VII) 174

  Barth (Stalag Luft I) 173–4, 204, 211, 258, 381
  Gross Tychow (Stalag Luft IV) 174, 380–3
  Heydekrug (Stalag Luft VI) 174, 204, 217, 247, 377–8, 382, 383
  Sagan (Stalag Luft III) *see* Sagan (Stalag Luft III)
  work detachments 222–3
Stalags (*Stamm-Mannschaftslager* – camp for other ranks) 144–51
  administration 144
  compounds 144
  Dieburg (Stalag IX B) 113
  Fallingbostel (Stalag XI B and 357) 130, 382–4, 388, 413
  Front-Stamm-Mannschaftslager 133, 141, 221
  Görlitz (Stalag VIII A) 117, 150, 235, 282, 283, 285, 385–6
  guards (*Landesschutzbataillonen*) 144–5, 244–8
  Hammelburg (Stalag XIII C) 112, 151, 194, 231, 384
  Himmler and 274
  Hohenfels (Stalag 383) 154, 180, 209, 210–12, 217, 222, 232, 327, 390, 410
  Krems (Stalag XVII A) 402
  Lamsdorf (Stalag VIII B) 112, 117, 129, 142, 150–1, 176, 189, 201, 204, 209–10, 217, 219, 223, 237, 240, 312, 314, 356, 374, 385
  Landesschutzbataillonen (guards) 144–5, 244–8
  Luckenwalde (Stalag Luft VII) 384–5, 404
  Marburg (Stalag XVIII D) 111, 145–6, 186, 189, 199, 230, 362, 363
  Markt Pongau (Stalag XVIII C) 233, 253, 307, 391, 412
  Moosburg (Stalag VII A) 111, 117, 149–50, 174, 194, 198,

INDEX

234–5, 240, 244, 361, 384, 386, 389, 390, 409, 410
Mühlberg (Stalag IV B) 175–6, 186, 203, 223, 248, 260, 406
Nuremberg (Stalag XIII D) 384, 386, 409
Sandbostel (Stalag X B) 100, 155
Spittal (Stalag XVIII B/Z) 117, 146, 203, 222, 376, 408, 412
Teschen (Stalag VIII B) 190, 385
Thorn (Stalag XX A) 154, 264, 339, 378, 383
Wolfsberg (Stalag XVIII A) 111, 147–9, 150, 181, 185, 189, 197, 214, 215, 219, 230, 233–4, 249, 251, 252, 254, 263, 264, 340, 362, 391, 412
Ziegenhain 385–6
Stalin, Jacob 184
Stalin, Joseph 3, 96, 183–4, 394, 399
Stalingrad 269
Stamatios G. Embirikos 39
Stamm-Mannschaftslager (camp for other ranks) *see Stalags Luft*; *Stalags*
Steilberg, Wal 311–13, 316, 365, 424, 467
Steinburg officers' holiday camp 330–1, 334, 335, 337
Steiner, Captain 148, 412
Steiner, General Felix 341
Stevenson, Warrant Officer Ernest Ferdinand 148–9, 412
Steward, James Edward 262
Stobart, Bert 32, 186
Stokes, Albert James 340, 341
Stone, Alf 69–70, 251–2
Stooke, Gordon 30–1, 119, 199
Storch, Albin 311
Storm Troopers 123
Straflager (punishment camp) 194, 252–3
Stroop, Jürgen 334–5
Student, General Kurt 76, 78, 80, 83

Suda Bay 78, 79, 81, 82, 88, 106, 107, 114, 226
Sudetenändische Treibstoffwerke (Sudetenland Fuel Works) 239, 407
Suez Canal 47, 51, 52, 53
Sulmona 114
Summons, Wally 95–7
Sweden 257, 258
Sweeney, Edward 40–1, 43, 352
Switzerland 118, 153, 163, 191, 307, 357–8, 360, 361, 367, 370
Sydney 38–9
Symons, Edward William 'Socks' 115–16
Syria 53, 54, 57, 93–7
  Australian role 93, 94–5

T. Manlius Torquatus 3
Tamaki, Tami 315
Tatura 158
Taylor, Geoff 166, 175, 248–9
Teddy, M/T 43
Terezín concentration camp 310–17, 360, 424, 428, 467
Thälmann, Ernst 296–7
Thebes 68
Theresienstadt concentration camp *see* Terezín concentration camp
Thermopylae Line 66, 67–8
Thompson, D.H. 308
Thor 45
Tobruk 49, 50–2, 53, 57, 58, 373
Toch, Henry 356
Toovey, Patrick 54–5, 57, 233, 423
Torbay, HMS 89
Torgau 262–3, 403
TPI Association 423
Trainor, Bill 264–5
transit camps (*Durchgangslager*) *see Dulags*; Dulag Luft
Treaty of Westphalia 4
Treblinka 310
Triadic 43
Triona 41–2

INDEX

Tripoli 57, 58, 113, 228
Tuckwell, Norm 240, 351
Tunisia 116
Turakina 40
Turturano 114

Udine 114
Ukraine 99
Ulm, Charles 36
Ulm, John 36–7

van der Stok, Bram 285
van Doorninck, Lieutenant Commander Damiaen 259
Varallo 118
Vardy, Fred 358
Vasey, Brigadier George 78–9
Vercelli labour camp 116, 228, 357–9, 366
Vichy France 93, 95, 98, 187–8
Vivash, John 'Irish' 28
Völkischer Beobachter 139
Voltaire 45
von Blomberg, Field Marshal Werner 124
von der Schulenburg, Brigadier 135
von Graevenitz, Brigadier Hans 134, 286–7
von Hindenburg, President Paul 123
von Lindeiner-Wildau, Colonel Friedrich-Wilhelm 279
von Müller, Kommandant 173–4
von Ribbentrop, Joachim 136, 330
von Stauffenberg, Claus Graf Schenck 290, 296, 299
von Trott zu Solz, Adam 330
von Werra, Baron Franz Xaver 347
Vyshinski, Andrei 399

Wadi El Fetei 49
Walker, Lieutenant Stewart 331
war, conduct of 1–4
Warren, Thomas 238, 459
Wavell, General Sir Archibald 46, 63, 67, 78

Wehrmacht 124, 131, 132, 136, 145, 187, 197, 272, 273–4, 300, 302, 304 *see also* German armed forces
Wehrmachtauskunftstelle für Kriegsverluste und Kriegsgefangene (Wehrmacht Information Bureau for War Casualties and Prisoners of War) (WASt) 134
West, Laurie 86, 107, 180, 209, 211, 231, 327, 411, 424
Western Desert 53
Westertimke naval prison camp 45, 101, 155–6, 161, 216, 331, 341, 384, 413
Westhoff, Colonel Adolf 134, 286–7, 290, 302–3, 304, 336–7
Weston, Major General E.C. 87
Wetzlar 164
Whellum, Les 292
White, Maureen 41–3
Whyte, Major 181
Wildermuth, Mr 157
Williams, Bill 389
Williams, John E.A. 'Willy' 281, 283–4
Williams, Lieutenant Kenneth 271
Williamson, John 234, 236–7
Williamson, N.G. 357
Willoughby, Charles 219–20
Wilmot, Chester 21, 413
Wilson, Captain D.E.L. 281
Wilson, Sir Henry Maitland 'Jumbo' 63, 67
Wise, Walter 311, 313–14
Wodehouse, P.G. 159
Wolfe, Ernie 359
Wood, Lionel Herbert Battinson 340, 341
Wooding, Jack 231
work detachments 116, 150, 154, 190, 207–8, 221–42, 249
  agricultural labour (*Landwirtschaft*) 228–33

522

INDEX

airmen 222–3
Arbeitsamt 230
Arbeitskommando 229
burying German dead 226
escape possibilities 357–60
German need for labour 221–2
Gewerbewirtschaft (industrial labour) 229, 233–9
Italy, in 228–9
Landwirtschaft (agricultural labour) 228–33
NCOs 222–4, 232
officers 222
pay 224
Red Army approach and 386–9
sabotage 251–2
shirking 249–50
Silesian coalmines 239–42, 250, 254
war-related employment 226–8
Worledge, George 373

Worthington, Reg 66, 104, 225–6, 230–1, 244, 253, 422
Wuppertal 30, 426

Yalta Conference 394, 397–8
Young Men's Christian Association (YMCA) 144, 209, 211, 215, 219, 337
Younger, Calton 165, 179, 198, 202–3, 205–6, 208–9, 247, 422–3
Yugoslavia 61, 64, 65, 101, 117, 118, 126, 360, 361–5
  partisans 362–5
  Tito's Liberation Army 364–5

Zama 3
Ziegfeld, Arnold Hillen 329, 335
Zwar, Ron 29, 32, 163, 168, 199, 213, 348, 406